UNIVERSITY CASEBOOK SERIES®

CASES AND MATERIALS

# THE PRACTICE AND POLICY OF ENVIRONMENTAL LAW

**FOURTH EDITION**

J.B. RUHL
David Daniels Allen Distinguished Chair in Law
Vanderbilt University Law School

JOHN COPELAND NAGLE
John N. Matthews Professor of Law
University of Notre Dame

JAMES SALZMAN
Donald Bren Distinguished Professor of Environmental Law
School of Law
University of California, Los Angeles
Bren School of Environmental Science and Management
University of California, Santa Barbara

ALEXANDRA B. KLASS
Distinguished McKnight University Professor
University of Minnesota Law School

444 Cedar Street, Suite 700
St. Paul, MN 55101
1-877-888-1330

Printed in the United States of America

**ISBN:** 978-1-63460-811-4

To Lisa
JBR

To Lisa
JCN

To Jamie and Ben, as they depart college
JES

To Steve
ABK

# PREFACE TO THE FOURTH EDITION

It has been 40 years since the wave of federal statutory initiatives of the early 1970s ushered in the modern era of environmental law. Seen then as a specialized "niche" area of practice and policy, environmental law has since matured into a broad and complex body of law which, like tax law, touches many aspects of business and social relations. Today, virtually all law firms of any substantial size have practitioners, if not departments of practitioners, devoted to their clients' environmental law needs. Many federal, state, and regional agencies and local governments also have substantial numbers of environmental attorneys to help navigate or enforce the maze of regulations. Every law school in the nation offers at least the survey course in environmental law, and many offer numerous upper level courses in the field. In short, environmental law is no longer an unusual or fringe subject—it has become a mainstream field of legal practice and policy resting on a complex array of statutes, regulations, and cases.

We have tried in this book to make environmental law come alive, to demonstrate for the student what environmental law is about and then place that subject matter in practice settings to show the range of what environmental lawyers actually experience. In teaching the environmental survey course, all four of us felt that our students could analyze well the policy aspects of environmental law, but were more guarded about their understanding of what practicing environmental law really feels like. We believe this focus of the book—making practice settings and practice problems a prominent feature for instructors and students—significantly distinguishes it from the many other commendable casebooks available on the topic of environmental law. Indeed, we would not have bothered to add to the array of environmental law casebooks if we did not believe ours would offer an alternative that is different in a meaningful and useful way.

Environmental law is an exciting field, and many are drawn to the dynamic subject matter—the world around us—and its rich interdisciplinary confluence of politics, economics, science, and philosophy. The design and implementation of environmental law can make a substantial difference in the quality of life for present and future generations, and each practitioner has a realistic expectation of being able to participate in that effect. Because of its important mission, moreover, environmental law reaches across many fields of social and economic life, allowing its practitioners to interact with other professionals and to work in a variety of settings. And because the environment changes so, too, does environmental law, making its practice anything but static and monotonous. In short, practicing environmental law can be stimulating and personally rewarding.

Alas, there is another side to all of these positive qualities. As a body of law drawing from so many disciplines, environmental law can appear to have no central foundation or theme. As a body of law that so profoundly affects the quality of life today and into the future, tremendous pressure often is placed on the institutions and practitioners of environmental law. As a body of law that touches so many different walks of life, environmental law can appear fragmented and overly detailed. And as a body of law in constant flux, environmental law can appear to have no deliberate direction. In short, practicing environmental law can, on occasion, be frustrating and even personally draining. Nonetheless, we believe it is one of the most exciting and important areas of practice in the entire legal field.

Our experience includes over 35 years of combined environmental law practice, in both government, corporate, and private firm settings, and a combined 75 years of full-time law school teaching. Reflecting our practice backgrounds, this text has been specifically designed to match the modern realities of environmental law. We begin with an introductory chapter, designed to provide the student's first exposure to environmental law though the experience of environmental lawyers. Using a series of case studies, this introduction emphasizes the importance of thinking about environmental law in three dimensions: (1) the basic approaches employed by environmental law; (2) the diversity of practice settings in which environmental law arises as a driving factor; and (3) the breadth of policy issues facing the future of environmental law.

Following the introductory chapter, in Part I of the book we build a conceptual foundation in the substantive law for the student with a survey of six approaches to environmental law: (1) conservation of environmental amenities; (2) regulating environmental harms; (3) remedying environmental harms; (4) planning and information programs; (5) public lands management; and (6) climate change regulation. Rather than attempt to canvass every environmental law, we use one or two exemplary statutes for each theme in the typology and cover related statutes and materials in sufficient detail to further illustrate the relevant approach. Deeper instruction in other statutes and legal institutions comes in subsequent parts of the book in connection with development of the practice and policy themes rather than as discrete divisions of study.

Part II is the most innovative facet of the text, using practice settings as a way of giving life to the substantive content of environmental law. Put simply, Part II focuses on what environmental lawyers actually do. This section uses examples and problems to illustrate five key practice contexts: (1) administrative rulemaking and permitting; (2) compliance counseling; (3) enforcement; (4) private litigation; and (5) business and real estate transactions. Attention to practice settings at this breadth and level of detail is unprecedented among environmental law casebooks, and we believe it will make our text particularly useful to instructors wishing to impart some appreciation of practice challenges and to students eager to get a taste of what environmental practitioners experience.

As has been true since our first edition, environmental law has continued to evolve since the publication of the third edition of this text almost four years ago. Unlike our prior editions, however, this fourth edition introduces no significant structural changes to the organization of the text. We believe we found the ideal balance and order of topics in the third edition and have stayed the course!

This edition thus is primarily an update covering significant new statutes, rules, cases, and other materials. Although events involving the Clean Air Act and regulation of greenhouse gas emissions have been the most dynamic in that regard (see chapters 3 and 8), every chapter of the text required attention to the ongoing development of the field.

We have also steadfastly maintained what we believe distinguishes this text from others in the field of environmental law—substantial coverage of practice contexts, with chapters on administrative rulemaking and permitting, compliance counseling, enforcement, private litigation, and business transactions. As in prior editions, practice-oriented problems also appear in the chapters covering substantive topics of environmental law including endangered species, air pollution controls, water pollution controls and wetlands conservation, hazardous waste regulation and remediation, planning and information programs, public lands management, and climate change and renewable energy. We are hopeful that our combination of substantive overview chapters with those covering the practical dimensions of environmental law provides instructors and students fertile ground for exploring the rich context of environmental law.

As always, we are grateful to those who supported our work to keep the text up to date and relevant, including our respective institutions, Vanderbilt, Notre Dame, the University of California, and Minnesota, our research assistants, the team at Foundation Press, and our families and friends. We are delighted to hear from instructors and students about the book—please feel free to contact any of us at jb.ruhl@vanderbilt.edu, nagle.8@nd.edu, salzman@ucsb.edu, and aklass@umn.edu.

JBR
JCN
JES
ABK

August 2016

# ACKNOWLEDGMENTS

Richard Epstein, *Environmental Law 101* (Oct. 27, 1998 speech at the Hoover Institution). Reprinted with permission.

Eileen Gauna et al., *Environmental Justice* (Center for Progressive Regulation White Paper, March 2005) at 4–5. Reprinted by permission.

Dennis Hirsch, *Lean and Green? Environmental Law and Policy and the Flexible Production Economy*, 79 INDIANA L.J. 611 (2004).

Bradley C. Karkkainen, *Information as Environmental Regulation: TRI and Performance Benchmarking, Precursor to a New Paradigm?*, 89 GEO.L.J. 257, 289–338 (2001). Reprinted by permission.

Richard J. Lazarus, *The Reality of Environmental Law in the Prosecution of Environmental Crimes: A Reply to the Department of Justice*, 83 GEO.L.J. 2539 (1995). Reprinted by permission.

James R. May, *Now More Than Ever: Trends In Environmental Citizen Suits At 30*, 10 WID. L. SYMP. J. 1–5 (2003). Reprinted by permission.

Joel A. Mintz, *Civil Enforcement*, in MICHAEL GERRARD, ED., PRACTICAL GUIDE TO ENVIRONMENTAL LAW 12–65 TO 12–94 (2004). Reprinted by permission.

Christopher R. Kelley and James A. Lodoen, *Federal Farm Program Conservation Initiatives: Past, Present, and Future*, NATURAL RESOURCES & ENV'T, Winter 1995, at 17. Reprinted with permission.

Douglas A. Kysar, *Preferences For Processes: The Process/Product Distinction and the Regulation of Consumer Choice*, 118 HARV. L. REV. 525, 553–572 (2004). Reprinted by permission.

Melody Kapilialoha MacKenzie, Susan K. Serrano, and Koalani Laura Kaulukukui, *Environmental Justice for Indigenous Hawaiians: Reclaiming Land and Resources*, NATURAL RESOURCES & ENVIRONMENT, Winter 2007, at 37. Reprinted with permission.

J.B. Ruhl, *Ecosystem Services and the Common Law of the "Fragile Land System,"* 20 NATURAL RESOURCES & ENVIRONMENT 3 (Fall 2005). Reprinted with permission.

J.B. Ruhl, *The Disconnect Between Environmental Assessment and Adaptive Management*, 36 TRENDS 1 (July–Aug. 2005). Reprinted with permission.

J.B. Ruhl, *The Pardy-Ruhl Dialogue on Ecosystem Management, Part IV: Narrowing and Sharpening the Questions*, 24 PACE ENVTL. L. REV. 25 (2007). Reprinted with permission.

J.B. Ruhl, James Salzman, and Kai-Sheng Song, *Regulatory Traffic Jams*, 2 WYOMING L. REV. 253, 256–265 (2002). Reprinted by permission.

James Salzman, *Valuing Ecosystem Services*, 24 ECOLOGY L.Q. 887 (1997). Reprinted with permission.

Lois J. Schiffer and James Simon, *The Reality of Prosecuting Environmental Criminals: A Response to Professor Lazarus*, 83 GEO. L.J. 2531 (1995). Reprinted by permission.

Sara Beth Watson and Kristina M. Woods, *Environmental Issues in Transactions: Old Swamps ad New Bridges,* 15 NATURAL RESOURCES & ENV'T 75 (2000). Reprinted with permission.

# SUMMARY OF CONTENTS

# TABLE OF CONTENTS

# TABLE OF CASES

The principal cases are in bold type.

UNIVERSITY CASEBOOK SERIES®

CASES AND MATERIALS

# THE PRACTICE AND POLICY OF ENVIRONMENTAL LAW

FOURTH EDITION

# INTRODUCTION TO ENVIRONMENTAL PRACTICE AND POLICY

## CHAPTER 1

# AN INTRODUCTION TO ENVIRONMENTAL LAW IN PRACTICE

**CHAPTER OUTLINE**

I. Environmental Protection in Context—The View from the Trenches

II. The Drivers of Environmental Conflicts

- A. Scientific Uncertainty
- B. Market Failures
  1. Public Goods
  2. The Tragedy of the Commons
  3. Collective Action and Free Riders
  4. Externalities
- C. Mismatched Scales
- D. Conflicting Values
- E. Environmental Justice

III. Tools for Environmental Protection—"The Five P's"

- A. Prescriptive Regulation
- B. Property Rights
- C. Penalties
- D. Payments
- E. Persuasion

IV. What Do Environmental Lawyers Do?

- A. An Evolving Field of Law
- B. An Evolving Practice of Law

## I. ENVIRONMENTAL PROTECTION IN CONTEXT—THE VIEW FROM THE TRENCHES

The leading compilations of federal environmental statutes contain nearly 2,000 pages of law. Within those pages one encounters the Clean Air Act, the Clean Water Act, the Endangered Species Act, the National Environmental Policy Act, the Noise Control Act, and the Pollution Prevention Act, to name just a few. The enforcement of these statutes, in turn, is variously assigned to the Environmental Protection Agency, the Fish and Wildlife Service, the Forest Service, the Bureau of Land Management, and the Army Corps of Engineers, with other agencies playing important roles as well. And those are just the federal laws and federal agencies. In most instances states have a parallel statute administered by one or more state agencies. Dozens of states also expressly incorporate environmental protection into their constitutions. For example, the "right to a clean and healthful environment" is the first of the "inalienable rights" that Montana itemizes in its constitution. MONT. CONST. Art. II, § 3. Moreover, there are many instances in which the law beyond "environmental law" addresses environmental concerns. Local zoning ordinances account for environmental concerns when deciding whether to permit a proposed use of the land. State and federal tax laws can reward or punish designated activities depending upon how they affect the environment.

These environmental laws affect lots of people. A list of just a few of the parties involved in recent environmental litigation includes the AFL-CIO, City of Albuquerque, American Society for the Prevention of Cruelty to Animals, Association of Irritated Residents (AIR), Biodiversity Legal Foundation, Black Hills Regional Rail Shippers Association, California Air Resources Board, Chesapeake Bay Foundation, Desert Fishes Council, E.I. Dupont De Nemours & Co., Federal Aviation Administration, Fruit of the Loom Inc., Montana Farm Bureau, National Association of Home Builders, New Mexico Council of Churches, New Jersey Institute of Technology, State of New York, Pierre Chamber of Commerce, Rio Grande silvery minnow, Shell Oil Company, South Dakota Wheat Growers Association, Tennessee Valley Authority, Zoological Society of San Diego, and innumerable government officials and private individuals. Of course, the reported cases represent just a tiny fraction of the instances in which industry, developers, individuals, environmental groups, and others were affected by the provisions of environmental law.

Then there are the lawyers. More than 10,000 attorneys are members of the ABA's Section on Environment, Energy, and Resources. Again, that figure neglects the many attorneys who occasionally encounter an environmental issue in the course of corporate transactions, litigation, land development, and many more unexpected contexts.

This collection of laws, affected parties, and lawyers can produce a nearly infinite combination of legal questions involving the protection of the natural environment. We will encounter many, though assuredly not all, of the most interesting and important laws and legal issues in the course of this book. Before we begin that survey, though, we will begin with two case studies that illustrate the tasks confronting environmental law, and how that affects the institutions, regulated parties, and lawyers that make environmental law work. Environmental law is often described as covering two broad areas—pollution and natural resources. The first case is short and focuses on pollution, setting out the challenges of pollution associated with energy development in the Susquehanna River watershed in Maryland, Pennsylvania, and New York. The second case addresses natural resources through a conflict on the other side of the country, exploring the difficult balance between urban development and conservation of the endangered Delhi Sands Flower-Loving Fly.

## Fracking Along the Susquehanna River

Hydraulic fracturing—or "fracking"—is a process for collecting oil and natural gas that cannot be obtained through traditional drilling technologies. Fracking involves drilling deep into the earth to a strata of shale rock, then drilling horizontally from that point into the shale. The fracturing occurs when explosive charges are dropped down the bore hole and into the horizontal opening, where their explosion causes fissures in the rock. Next, millions of gallons of highly pressurized water, sand, and chemicals are pumped into the hole to expand the fissures and hold them open. Natural gas or oil flows upward to the surface, along with the wastewater.

Fracking has been around since 1947, but it became common only during the past decade. The portion of U.S. natural gas production that came from shale jumped from 1.6% in 2000 to 23.1% in 2010. *See* NATHAN RICHARDSON ET AL., THE STATE OF STATE SHALE GAS REGULATION (June 2013), available at http://www.rff.org/RFF/Documents/RFF-Rpt-StateofStateRegs_Report.pdf. The increase in fracking has resulted in a significant decline in U.S. oil imports that is expected to continue for decades, along with the United States transitioning from a net importer of natural gas as recently 2013, to a net exporter of natural gas by 2017. *See* U.S. Energy Info. Admin., Executive Summary, Annual Energy Outlook 2015, Apr. 14, 2015. But all of that fracking has produced as much concern as it has applause. Fracking has been associated with water pollution, dwindling water supplies, interference with wildlife habitat, and even earthquakes. Many of these effects are contested as scientific studies seek to ascertain the true consequences of fracking, for good or ill. Fracking also promises the continued use of oil and natural gas at a time when climate change activists are striving to discontinue the use of fossil fuels.

Fracking prompted American Rivers to list the Susquehanna River as the nation's most endangered river in 2011. American Rivers is a non-profit organization—founded in 1973 and boasting 65,000 members—that is dedicated to "standing up for healthy rivers so our communities can thrive." Each year, American Rivers announces its list of the most endangered rivers in the United States. Those rivers are threatened by a variety of events, such as industrial pollution, the unintentional runoff of toxic chemicals, the construction or operation of dams, and excessive withdrawals for irrigation. The Susquehanna River, which topped the list in 2011, flows 444 miles from New York to Pennsylvania to Maryland into the Chesapeake Bay. American Rivers explained its selection in the following document.

#1 SUSQUEHANNA RIVER

NEW YORK, PENNSYLVANIA, MARYLAND

THREAT: NATURAL GAS EXTRACTION

AT RISK: CLEAN DRINKING WATER

SUMMARY

One of the longest rivers in America, the Susquehanna River provides over half of the freshwater to the Chesapeake Bay and drinking water to six million people. Unfortunately, the river is threatened by natural gas development, which requires millions of gallons of water per well, produces dangerous toxic waste, and threatens clean water and the river's health. Unless Pennsylvania, New York, and the Susquehanna River Basin Commission announce a complete moratorium on water withdrawals and hydraulic fracturing until the issuance and enforcement of comprehensive, highly protective regulations for natural gas development, public health and drinking water will be at risk.

THE RIVER

The Susquehanna River drains 27,500 square miles, and provides drinking water to six million people. Long regarded as one of the best smallmouth bass fisheries in the country, the Susquehanna is believed to be one of the most ancient rivers on earth. The Susquehanna's many tributaries have been home to native brook trout populations since the last Ice Age, and scores of communities and businesses depend on the river for drinking water, commerce, hydropower generation, and recreational boating.

THE THREAT

The Susquehanna River and its tributaries flow over the Marcellus Shale region, a rock formation underlying much of New York and Pennsylvania, containing vast reserves of natural gas. The rush to develop this abundant resource has come fast and furious, without consideration of the potential cumulative impacts to clean water, rivers, and human health.

The seriousness of the threat to the entire Susquehanna watershed cannot be overstated. Industry estimates indicate the potential for 400,000 wells across the Marcellus Shale—a number that would require, conservatively, 1.5 times the annual flow of the Susquehanna River to sustain. As part of the hydraulic fracturing (or "fracking") process to extract natural gas, massive amounts of water are withdrawn from rivers and streams. Many of the streams being used for Marcellus Shale water withdrawals provide critical habitat for trout—a concern, especially during summer months when stream flows are already low. The water is then mixed with sand and toxic chemicals and pumped underground to fracture the shale under extreme pressure. A portion of that highly toxic, highly saline, and potentially radioactive wastewater will return to the surface, and requires specialized treatment, but at this time, only a limited number of wastewater treatment facilities have the capacity to handle it. Already, spills from trucks hauling wastewater, leaks from lined fluid holding pits, and cracked well casings have contaminated private water wells. The potential for future environmental and public health catastrophes along the Susquehanna will only increase when considering the number of new wells projected, and the amount of toxic wastewater produced.

WHAT MUST BE DONE

While Pennsylvania and New York have been working to improve clean water safeguards for natural gas development, they fall short of adequately protecting the water supply for millions of Americans. It is the responsibility of these states, along with the Susquehanna River Basin Commission (SRBC), to analyze all of the potential cumulative impacts that could result from natural gas extraction, and ensure proper regulations are in place and capable of being enforced before development is allowed to continue.

Pennsylvania, New York, and the SRBC must issue a complete moratorium on all water withdrawals for natural gas extraction and the use of hydraulic fracturing until regulations are implemented and enforced that will protect the health of the river and the people who use it.

Likewise, the U.S. Congress must take responsibility for the health of citizens across the nation and remove all exemptions from federal environmental legislation for oil and gas development. This industry must be subject to the same safeguards and oversight as other industries. Removing these exemptions and requiring full disclosure of the chemicals used in hydraulic fracturing would be a major step towards protecting the health of Americans across the country for generations to come.

---

## Development and the Delhi Sands Flower-Loving Fly

Our second problem takes us across the country to the Delhi sand dunes (also known as the Colton Dunes), the only inland sand dune system in the Los Angeles basin. The Delhi sand dunes were created long ago when the Santa Ana winds picked up sand from several creeks and deposited it over about 35,000 acres of land located about sixty miles east of the Pacific Ocean in southern California. At first glance, the dunes are inhabited only by blowing sand and scattered shrubs. But contrary to the popular image of deserts as barren of wildlife, desert ecosystems are in fact teeming with birds, insects, reptiles, mammals and plants. The Delhi Sands are a good example of what one finds in a coastal sage scrub ecosystem. Birds such as Western meadowlarks and burrowing owls frequent the area. The San Diego horned lizard and the legless lizard live in the dunes, as do insects such as the Delhi sands metalmark butterfly and the Delhi sands Jerusalem cricket. The onset of night entices the Los Angeles pocket mouse, the San Bernardino kangaroo rat and other small mammals to survey the land. Primrose, goldfields and other wildflowers flourish after the winter rains, replaced later in the year by the wild buckwheat and the colorful butterflies that the plant attracts. The yellow flowers of telegraph weeds appear in the summer.

Increasingly, though, the Delhi Sands are home to many people, too. The area had long been inhabited by many different Native American peoples, including the Serrano, the Cahuilla, the Chemehuevi and the Mojave. Spanish and Mormon missionaries traveled across the land during the eighteenth and early nineteenth centuries, and the first European settlements in what is now western San Bernardino and Riverside Counties began after California became a state in 1850 and after the railroad reached the area in the early 1870s. The city of Colton, for example, was first settled in 1874 and named after a Civil War general who also served as the vice president of the Southern Pacific Railroad. The settlers immediately began planting citrus orchards despite concerns that the land was inadequate for farming. The citrus thrived in the warm climate once irrigated water was delivered from the nearby Santa Ana River, and much of the land was cultivated for grapes, oranges and other fruits by the late 1800s. Dairies, residential homes, and commercial and industrial development were the next to appear on the scene.

The results of the human settlements have not been especially attractive. The California Portland Cement Company mined Slover Mountain for over 100 years, leaving a pile of granite and no dunes in its wake. Similar enterprises have taken the sand for road fill and other purposes. Junk yards and petroleum tank farms abound. The Southern Pacific Railroad and Interstate 10 bisect the area. A landfill, a sewage treatment facility and many illegally dumped cars are also nearby. Off-road vehicle enthusiasts alter the terrain of the little bit of the dunes that remains.

The human population of the dunes is as diverse as the wildlife population. Nearly sixty percent of the residents of Colton, for example, are of Hispanic origin. Another fifteen percent of Colton's residents are African-Americans, Asians, or Native Americans. The city's median family income is only slightly above $30,000, making it one of the poorest cities in California. The closure of many military bases and the loss of defense jobs in San Bernardino County caused the region to suffer a significant economic recession beginning in the 1980s. The economic plight of the area was illustrated by the creation of the Agua Mansa Enterprise Zone, which was established by San Bernardino and Riverside Counties and the cities of Colton, Rialto, and Riverside in an effort to lure economic development to a 10,000 acre site in the region. The 1986 environmental study preceding the creation of the enterprise zone assured that there were no rare or endangered species living on the affected land.

The growth in the human population has produced a corresponding shrinkage of the original Delhi sands. Most of the original dunes were destroyed by the onset of agricultural uses at the end of the nineteenth century. Over the next one hundred years, commercial, industrial, and residential development eliminated much of the remaining dunes. A shopping center replaced seventy acres of dunes in the early 1990s, and a county park split another segment of the dunes in 1998. Only about forty square miles of dunes—or about two percent of the original sands—exist in several patches stretching between the cities of Colton and Mira Loma.

As the Delhi sands have disappeared, so has the native wildlife. Pringle's monardella, a wildflower that once grew only in the Delhi sands, has already gone extinct. The number of meadowlarks and burrowing owls has diminished as their habitats have been converted into human uses, though both birds have displayed a surprising resiliency in the presence of bulldozers and landfills and the like. And the area is the still the only place on earth where the Delhi Sands Flower-Loving Fly clings to life.

The Fly—known to entomologists as *Rhaphiomidas terminatus abdominalis*—is colored orangish and brown, with dark brown oval spots on its abdomen and emerald green eyes. It is one inch long, much larger than a common house fly. Beyond that, entomologists do not know a whole lot about the Fly. They think that the Fly undergoes a metamorphosis from egg to larva to pupa to adult fly over a three-year period. Once it emerges from the sand at the end of the three years, an individual Fly lives for about a week in August and September. As its name suggests, the Fly loves flowers. It hovers like a hummingbird as it removes nectar from the native buckwheat flowers with its long tubular proboscis, thus serving as an essential pollinator. There is no indication, though, that the Fly provides any nutritional, medicinal or other tangible benefit to people. The first Fly was collected in 1888, but it was not until a century later that the Fly was identified as a separate subspecies. The Fly probably lived throughout the full historic extent of the Delhi Sands, but today it survives in just five locations within an eight mile radius along the border of San Bernardino and Riverside Counties. No one knows for sure how many Flies are alive today, though estimates run from a couple hundred to less than a thousand. What everyone agrees upon, though, is that the number of Flies is shrinking and that the species may soon become extinct.

The Fly faces a variety of threats to its survival. Birds, reptiles, dragonflies, and the Argentine ant—an insect that is not native to the area—sometimes attack and kill a larval or adult Fly. Pesticides used for agricultural purposes eliminate the native vegetation upon which the Fly relies for its survival. Native plants have been smothered by local dairies that have dumped tons of cow manure on sections of the dunes—often without the landowner's permission—thus providing nutrient-rich soil for exotic plants. Mustard, cheeseweed, the Russian thistle, and other plants that are new to the area affect the soil in a way that is harmful to the Fly. The native vegetation is trampled by off-road vehicle riders and removed for fire control efforts. The Fly lives best in those few areas that have yet to be disturbed by human activities. Also, the fact that so few populations of the Fly still exist makes the entire species vulnerable to catastrophic events such as fires and droughts. The small, scattered populations reduce the genetic variability of the Fly—and thus, its ability to respond to environmental stresses—as well.

Mostly, though, the Fly is on the brink of extinction because the Delhi sands are disappearing in the wake of human development. An estimated 98% of the Fly's original habitat has been destroyed. By 1993, the Delhi sands that remained were threatened by a host of residential, commercial and industrial development projects. The most notable development to threaten the Fly was a hospital. Plans to replace San Bernardino's aging County Medical Center began in the late 1970s. County officials designed a large regional medical center that could resist earthquakes and satisfy the demands of federal health officials. The site of the hospital was a vacant piece of land just north of I-10 in Colton. By September 1993, the county was finally ready to break ground for its new Arrowhead Regional Medical Center.

Meanwhile, the Fly had attracted the attention of Greg Balmer, a graduate student in entomology at the University of California at Riverside. Balmer viewed the Fly as "spectacular," yet he quickly became concerned about its plight. The rapid residential, commercial and industrial development of the region posed a grave threat to the survival of the dunes, and thus to the survival of the Fly. So Balmer did what any smart entomologist would do: he filed a petition with the United States

Fish & Wildlife Service (FWS) to list the Fly as "endangered" under the Endangered Species Act of 1973.

Congress had enacted the ESA in 1973 during the heyday of federal environmental legislation. The proponents of the law evoked images of bald eagles, grizzly bears, alligators and other national symbols that were on the brink of disappearing from this land. Almost immediately, though, the ESA was deployed to protect much less popular creatures. The listing of the snail darter as endangered just months after the ESA became law resulted in the Supreme Court's decision in Tennessee Valley Authority v. Hill, 437 U.S. 153 (1978) (reprinted in Chapter 2), confirming that the multi-million dollar Tellico Dam project could not be completed because of the threat that the dam posed to the snail darter's survival. In more recent years, the law's application to the northern spotted owl became a focal point for broader debates between the timber industry and environmentalists in the Pacific Northwest.

Balmer had asked the FWS to list the Fly on an emergency basis because of the urgency of the development pressures on all of the Fly's remaining habitat. The agency did not act until September 1993, when it agreed to add the Fly to the permanent list of endangered species. That also happened to be the day before construction was to begin on San Bernardino County's new hospital project smack in the middle of some of the Fly's prime habitat. At the first meeting between local officials and the FWS, a FWS employee surveyed the scene and suggested that nearby I-10—the major east-west highway between the San Bernardino Valley and Los Angeles—would have to be closed two months each year when the Fly was above ground.

Local officials were stuck. They protested to Congress. And they tried to cut a deal with the FWS. At first, the parties agreed that the hospital could be built if it was moved three hundred feet to the north and if the county established a refuge for the Fly. The "refuge" was vacant land adjacent to the hospital that was bordered by orange plastic fencing. Happily, the Fly loved the fencing. Then the county realized that they would need to build a new electrical substation to power the hospital; that resulted in seven more acres for the refuge. But when the county sought permission to reconfigure the roads in the area surrounding the hospital, the FWS balked. The county sued, joined by local developers, claiming that the ESA could not be constitutionally applied to regulate construction projects involving a species like the Fly that lived in only one state and that neither moved within nor affected interstate commerce itself. The district court held that such an application of the ESA was constitutional, as did a divided D.C. Circuit, and any hope for a constitutional exit disappeared in June 1998 when the Supreme Court denied certiorari. *See* National Ass'n of Home Builders v. Babbitt, 949 F. Supp. 1 (D.D.C. 1996), *aff'd*, 130 F.3d 1041 (D.C. Cir. 1997), *cert. denied*, 524 U.S. 937 (1998).

The Fly, thanks to the ESA, now occupied a position of great strength in future discussions about the development of the region. A host of developments were challenged because of their possible impact on the Fly and its remaining habitat. The projects included:

- A 2.8 million square foot Wal-Mart distribution facility to be built in the dunes near Colton.
- A 27-hole golf course and accompanying 202-home development slated for Fontana, which a city official defended because the sighting of a couple of Flies there over a two-year period is "just not enough science to put people's land at risk."
- A truck stop and industrial center to be built by Kaiser Ventures, which estimated that the project could create 5,300 jobs and add $75 million per year to the San Bernardino County economy.
- A cement plant and a facility that produces sidewalk pavers in Rialto that was blocked by a federal court when the FWS claimed that the plant would wipe out a major portion of the Fly's habitat, but which the FWS approved in 1999 when the company agreed to set aside 30.5 acres of land for Fly habitat.
- A large project that would include new homes, theaters, and restaurants in Fontana.
- The proposal of Viny Industries, a paper products company, to create 400 jobs by building on sixty acres of land in Colton.
- A $110 million plant to make fiberboard from recycled waste wood which opened in the Agua Mansa Industrial Center in May 1999 only after the industrial center contributed $450,000 to purchase other habitat for the Fly.
- In August 2002, a single Fly was discovered on a parcel of land where the city of Colton had hoped to build a small-scale replica of an historic major-league sports complex. The project immediately stalled. The city finally abandoned it in 2006, complaining that the FWS "took a project and doubled it in price and shrunk it down over a fly."

The hospital itself finally opened in March 1999 after the county set aside a total of twelve acres of land for a Fly refuge. The county estimated that moving the site of the hospital, establishing the Fly preserves, and otherwise accommodating the Fly cost the county nearly $3,000,000.

The Fly also interfered with environmental cleanup activities in the area. When petroleum leaking from a nearby tank farm contaminated the groundwater, the presence of the Fly underground so complicated any remediation work that the tank farm owner planned to wait for the plume of contamination to migrate past the Fly's habitat. Additionally, the vacant, sandy land favored by the Fly was an attractive spot for the illegal dumping of trash, including abandoned appliances, used diapers, and yard debris. Local officials wanted to remove that trash, but the FWS insisted that the trash must be picked up by hand instead of by the ordinary heavy machinery that could disturb the Fly larvae buried in the sand. To prevent additional trash from being dumped in the area, Riverside and Colton enacted ordinances authorizing the forfeiture of any vehicle used to transport trash that is dumped in the sands. Other local towns are considering similar ordinances, in part because of concerns that they will become havens from trash dumpers who fear the more stringent sanctions imposed in neighboring communities.

In early 1999, Fontana officials warned that the Fly could cause the city to default on $42 million in municipal bonds. The city had issued the bonds in 1991 to build streets, sewers, lighting, and other improvements on vacant land adjacent to a small shopping center. The possibility that the Fly lived on the land prevented the expected commercial development of the land, and when the landowner stopped paying taxes on the land, the city began to use its reserve funds to pay the bondholders. The Fly did facilitate one source of new employment: developers hired consultants to determine the extent of the presence of the Fly in the area. It was only when the landowner paid its taxes after one such survey failed to find any Flies on the property that Fontana barely avoided defaulting on the bonds in October 1999.

The Fly continued to block the proposed road construction projects that resulted in the commerce clause litigation. Colton officials and the FWS had not reached an agreement that would permit the realignment of roads near the new hospital despite meetings held throughout 1999. Similarly, when Riverside County asked the FWS for permission to build new ramps for I-15 in Mira Loma, the federal agency responded that the county would need to establish a 200-acre preserve for the Fly. The agency reasoned that although the ramps would only displace a little more than eight acres of Fly habitat, the effect on the Fly of the accompanying development and increased traffic justified a larger reserve. The purchase of that much land would cost the county as much as $32 million in an area where land sells for up to $160,000 an acre, which would make the Fly reserve more expensive than the highway ramps themselves. More generally, when officials representing Colton, Fontana, Rialto, and other local cities met with the FWS in July 1999 to propose setting aside 850 acres of land for Fly habitat in exchange for permission to develop throughout the area, they were told that FWS biologists were seeking 2,100 acres that could cost $220 million to purchase. Much of that land—including a former dairy in Ontario—would have to be rehabilitated in order to serve as viable habitat for the Fly.

The Fly was vilified. Fontana Mayor David Eshleman complained that the Fly "is costing the Inland Empire thousands of jobs and millions of dollars. I think we should issue fly swatters to everyone." Colton's city manager estimated the stalled development, uncollected tax revenue, and lost jobs attributable to the Fly totaled $661 million. Local residents were quick to offer their own reactions to the predicament: one man claimed that the Fly "larva is the same I've seen in tequila bottles being imported here from Mexico," and a woman worried that children and schools were "an endangered species that gets no help." Julie Biggs, the Colton city attorney, characterized the Fly's habitat as "a bunch of dirt and weeds." Jerry Eaves, the chairman of the San Bernardino County Board of Supervisors, stated that "the Endangered Species Act was intended to save eagles and bears. Personally, I don't think we should be spending this money to save cockroaches, snails and flies." Advocates for reform of the ESA seized on the controversy as an example of the kinds of problems that the law created, with the "people vs. flies" argument being voiced frequently.

The Fly has been featured on network television news shows, leading newspapers across the country, *National Geographic*, and other national media. CBS described it as "superfly, with the power to stop bulldozers." The *Los Angeles Times* reported that the Fly could become "the snail darter of the 1990s." Many portrayals of the Fly have been unsympathetic. The *Washington Post* described the Fly as "a creature that spends most of its life underground, living as a fat, clumsy, enigmatic maggot." The *Washington Times* editorialized that "one could build the flies their own mansion in Beverly Hills . . . fill it up from top to bottom with leftover potato salad and other fly delicacies, and it would still be cheaper than the royal estate Fish & Wildlife has in mind for them."

By contrast, UCLA professor Rudy Mattoni described the Fly as "a national treasure in the middle of junkyards. . . . It's a fly you can love. It's beautiful." A FWS official told CNN that the Fly "isn't as charismatic as a panda bear or a sea otter, but that doesn't make it any less important." Another FWS official insisted that "the value of the fly to mankind is a very difficult thing to judge. It's much more of a moral issue. Do we have the right to destroy another creature when we, in our day-to-day activities, have the ability not to destroy a creature?" The statement of county supervisor Jerry Eaves that the ESA was not intended to save flies provoked a letter to the editor of the *Los Angeles Times* complaining that "developers and their minions in public office will go to any length to satisfy their corporate greed." Environmentalists also emphasized the importance of the dune ecosystem rather than the Fly. Greg Balmer, the entomologist who proposed the Fly's listing under the ESA, explained that the Fly "is an umbrella species in that preserving its habitat preserves for posterity the entire community with which it lives." A FWS biologist reminded that "every ecosystem has its intrinsic value, and maybe we can't quite put a dollar value on it. But every time one disappears, it's an indication that something else is wrong." Dan Silver, the head of the Endangered Habitats League, asserted that the ESA "is saving Riverside County from itself, its own short-sightedness. It is forcing people to take a longer view."

Having lost in the courts, the local communities turned to Congress. They paid $48,000 for a Washington lobbyist to persuade Congress to remove the Fly from the list of protected species. Democratic state representative Joe Baca introduced a resolution in the California legislature calling for lifting the ESA's protection of the Fly; the voters rewarded him by electing him to Congress in 1999. Republican Senate candidate Matt Fong was not so fortunate in 1998: he campaigned against the Fly's impact on development in the region, but he lost to incumbent Senator Barbara Boxer, a supporter of the ESA. The lobbying effort continued in 2002 when Colton Mayor Deirdre Bennett wielded a giant flyswatter while speaking at the press conference denouncing the Fly and its protectors. "To us and the majority of Americans with any common sense at all," protested Mayor Bennett, flies "are pests, nothing more, nothing less—pests we have historically grown up swatting." The protected status of the Fly survived all of these efforts.

Another strategy involved crafting a habitat conservation plan (HCP) that would set aside some land for habitat for the Fly and other wildlife while allowing other land—including wildlife habitat—to be developed (learn more about HCPs in Chapter 2). Eleven local cities joined San Bernardino County in planning a HCP that would encompass over 300,000 acres of land comprised of eight different kinds of ecosystems and containing the Fly and other rare species such as the San Bernardino kangaroo rat and the Santa Ana River wooly-star. Several years of negotiations failed to produce an agreeable plan. Indeed, Colton and other nearby cities and counties temporarily withdrew from their negotiations with the FWS in the summer of 2002, claiming that the anticipated $3 million cost of setting aside 33 acres as habitat for the Fly amounted to "legalized extortion." A FWS spokesperson responded that the agency has worked with cities all across the country "in partnership to develop a plan that makes biological sense and balance the conservation needs of the species and opportunity for economic development." The federal Department of the Interior provided local communities with nearly three million dollars in grants in 2003 for the purchase of some of the Fly's habitat and for the continued preparation of the HCP.

Meanwhile, both economic development and protection of the Fly proceeded on a piecemeal basis. The typical approach involved a landowner agreeing to set aside some of its property to serve as habitat for the Fly in exchange for FWS permission to build on another part of its property. In other instances a developer simply paid for the purchase of other land that could be used by the Fly. For example, in August 2000 the developer of a warehouse project agreed to pay $82,500 so that a community group could purchase habitat for the Fly. But neither side was really satisfied by such arrangements: environmentalists worried that the haphazard patches of protected land would not sustain a healthy population of the Fly, while developers watched as their proposed building sites remained vacant as the economic boom of the 1990s ended.

In June 2005, the FWS reached an agreement with Vulcan Materials Company, an Alabama rock and asphalt business that acquired land in Colton as a result of corporate mergers. According to the agreement, 150 acres of land owned by Vulcan will be permanently preserved as part of a new conservation bank containing habitat for the Fly. Greg Balmer described the land as the largest undeveloped parcel remaining of the Colton Dunes ecosystem. The conservation bank will be expanded as other businesses donate land that can serve as habitat for the Fly in order to receive development credits from the FWS. The first sale from the conservation bank occurred in January 2006, when a commercial developer paid $300,000 for two credits, thus preserving two acres of habitat in order to obtain FWS approval to develop five acres of degraded habitat elsewhere in the area. Such conservation banks have become common throughout the nation, but this was the first such bank designed to protect a rare insect.

But even that device frustrated the city officials in Colton. In January 2006, the city council worried about the amount of lands set aside "by open space conservation agreements, easements, and other contractual mechanisms by their owners to insure that these properties will never be used for anything except open space conservation and Delhi Fly Habitat, despite the properties' current land use and zoning designations which may allow for some reasonable development." Accordingly, the city council passed an emergency ordinance requiring the rezoning of any protected land as "Open Space" and the receipt of a conditional use permit before any land within the city may be encumbered with an easement or other device to protect the Fly. At the same time, Mayor Bennett again asked the FWS to delist the Fly, claiming that (1) there is already sufficient habitat to protect the Fly; (2) the FWS had improperly acted as if critical habitat had been designated for the Fly without going through the formal designation process; (3) the recovery plan for the Fly is ambiguous and not achievable; and perhaps most strikingly, (4) the Fly is in fact an invasive species that is not native to the area, and actually threatens the native species there.

So government officials, developers, environmentalists, and other interested parties still debate the needs of the Fly, the dunes, and the people who live there. The FWS continues to meet with local county and city officials in an effort to resolve both specific proposed projects and the broader issues raised by the Fly. Scientists are trying to breed the Fly in captivity, though they have not succeeded yet. Private efforts to help the Fly have begun, such as the work of volunteers and local students to restore a four-acre right-of-way owned by Southern California Edison. Nonetheless, scientists and federal officials still fear that the Fly will go extinct early this century despite all of the efforts to save it.

---

## QUESTIONS AND DISCUSSION

**1.** What is the role of environmental law in the Susquehanna River and Delhi Sands Flower-Loving Fly disputes? What laws do you expect have played a role in those controversies so far?

**2.** What is the role of lawyers in resolving these problems? More specifically, as an attorney, what advice would you offer to American Rivers? The states of Maryland, New York, and Pennsylvania? People who own land along the Susquehanna River? An environmental group that wants to protect the Delhi Sands and the Fly? A commercial landowner in Colton? The United States Fish & Wildlife Service?

Or assume that you are the land use attorney for the City of Colton, and that you have been asked to report on how to protect the Delhi Sands Flower-Loving Fly while still accounting for human needs in the economically depressed city. What would you recommend?

**3.** The story of the Susquehanna River and the saga of the Delhi Sands Flower-Loving Fly raise innumerable questions about the nature of environmental policy, whether expressed directly or indirectly through the law. How would you answer the following questions:

- What are the appropriate uses of the Susquehanna River? Who should make that decision? Who should decide whether, where, and under what conditions, fracking should be permitted?
- Why should we preserve the Delhi Sands? Why should we preserve the Fly?
- What cost should we be willing to pay to protect the Susquehanna River? To save the Fly? Who should pay those costs?
- Are some rivers or species more worth saving than others? Who should make that decision?
- What role should private efforts play in protecting the Susquehanna River and preserving the Fly? What role should the law play?
- Is the condition of the Susquehanna River and the survival of the Fly best addressed by common law, local ordinances, state statutes, federal law, or international law—or some combination of those sources of law?

**4.** September 23, 2003 marked the tenth anniversary of the listing of the Fly. The Riverside *Press Enterprise* noted the event by condemning the "[m]illions spent, millions lost in 10 years to accommodate a rare fly that has bedeviled developers and government officials from Colton to Mira Loma." Ten years passed without the problem being solved. What report would you expect to read on the 35th anniversary of the listing of the Fly in 2018?

American Rivers ranked the Susquehanna River as the nation's most endangered river in 2007, as well as in 2011. The two primary threats in 2007 were a proposed inflatable dam project and runoff from old abandoned coal mines. The dam project was scuttled and some progress was made on cleaning the mines, but then fracking emerged as a new threat. Then, in 2016, the Susquehanna River ranked third on the list of most endangered rivers. This time the threat is presented by the Conowingo Dam, which has trapped nearly a century's worth of pollutants since it was built in 1928. The dam is up for relicensing by the Federal Energy Regulatory Commission, which could allow Maryland to impose its state water pollution standards to address the problem. *See* https://www.americanrivers.org/endangered-rivers/2016-susquehanna/.

What do you expect American Rivers to say about the condition of the Susquehanna River in the organization's future reports?

**5.** Since fracking is occurring nationwide with major impacts on interstate commerce, you might think that this would be an important area for federal regulation. Surprisingly, though, the federal government plays only a small role supervising fracking on private lands. The reason lies in politics.

In 2005, an amendment to the Energy Policy Act exempted fluids used for the fracking extraction process from regulation under the Underground Injection Control program of the Safe Drinking Water Act. This was subsequently known as "The Halliburton Loophole," in recognition of the role played by then-Vice President Dick Cheney, former CEO of Halliburton, in forcing the amendment through.

Given the widespread public concern that has developed over fracking and its impacts on water quality, why do you think Congress has not repealed the Halliburton Amendment?

In the absence of congressional action, in 2016, EPA moved forward using its Clean Air Act authority, enacting the first set of regulations governing methane emissions from new oil and gas fracking wells on private lands and began the process of promulgating similar regulations governing existing oil and gas fracking wells on private lands. These regulations are discussed in Chapter 3.

**6.** In the absence of congressional and EPA action to regulate fracking operations, cities, counties, and other local governmental entities have attempted to fill the gap through their zoning authority. In particular, cities in Texas, Colorado, and Pennsylvania have enacted extensive regulations governing the time of fracking operations, truck traffic, noise impacts, groundwater management, and well locations. Some have banned fracking entirely.

These local actions have prompted several state legislatures to preempt (or displace) local authority in order to ensure that oil and gas operators have a single, uniform set of laws to follow without additional local imitations. State supreme courts in Colorado, and Ohio have upheld state laws preempting local fracking regulation while courts in New York and Pennsylvania have sided with local governments. *See, e.g.*, City of Longmont v. Colo. Oil and Gas Ass'n, 369 P.3d 573 (Colo. 2016); State ex rel. Morrison v. Beck Energy Corp., 37 N.E.3d 128 (Ohio 2015); Wallach v. Town of Dryden, 16 N.E.3d 1188 (N.Y. 2014); Robinson Twp. v. Commonwealth of Pennsylvania, 83 A.3d 901 (Pa. 2013).

Throughout much of this textbook, we discuss the tensions that inevitably arise between the federal government and state governments over which level should have primacy over a host of environmental regulatory issues. As shown by the example of fracking regulation, similar tensions arise between state and local governments.

Which do you think is more important—that oil and gas operators have a uniform set of guidelines to follow for their operations within a state or that local governments are able to protect their citizens from what they regard as the adverse impacts from this type of industrial activity? At which level of government is there more concern over industry capture of the regulatory process?

**7.** We do not know how the stories of the Susquehanna River and the Delhi Sands will end. Given the complex decisions that need to be made in these two cases, perhaps that should not be surprising. In the meantime, American Rivers provides periodic updates about each of its listed rivers on its website, and the Susquehanna River Basin Commission (SRBC) provides current information about the river at http://www.srbc.net/. The best sources of new information about the controversy surrounding the Delhi Sands Flower-Loving Fly are the reports of the *Press-Enterprise* (the Riverside newspaper which is available on LEXIS and at its website at http://www.pe.com/). For additional material on the Fly's happenings, *see, e.g.*, Determination of Endangered Status for the Delhi Sands Flower-loving Fly, 58 Fed. Reg. 49881 (1993); U.S. FISH AND WILDLIFE SERVICE, PACIFIC REGION, FINAL RECOVERY PLAN FOR THE DELHI SANDS FLOWER-LOVING FLY (1997); National Ass'n of Home Builders v. Babbitt, 130 F.3d 1041 (D.C. Cir. 1997), *cert. denied*, 524 U.S. 937 (1998); Kenneth J. Kingsley, *Behavior of the Delhi Sands Flower-Loving Fly (Diptera: Mydidae), A Little-Known Endangered Species*, 89 ANNALS OF THE ENTOMOLOGICAL SOC'Y OF AMERICA 883 (1996). Both the Susquehanna River and the Delhi Sands are discussed in greater detail in JOHN COPELAND NAGLE, LAW'S ENVIRONMENT: HOW THE LAW SHAPES THE PLACES WE LIVE (2010).

## II. THE DRIVERS OF ENVIRONMENTAL CONFLICTS

Environmental law covers a vast breadth, and the Susquehanna River and Fly case studies address the two major fields within its coverage—pollution control and natural resource conservation. While the basic aspects of pollution control—ensuring clean air and clean water or remediating contaminated soil—might on their face seem to present fundamentally different challenges than those present in natural resource conservation—whether protecting endangered species or managing national forests—these two seemingly disparate fields share many important similarities. The actors, the location, and the nature of the concerns raised in pollution and natural resource conflicts may well be different in the particulars, but the *underlying* causes of the environmental problems can often be understood best as simple variants on common themes.

This section briefly introduces some basic themes that run throughout environmental law and policy—the themes of scientific uncertainty, market failure, mismatched scale, conflicting values, and environmental justice. It is no exaggeration to say that these resonate throughout the entire field of environmental law and policy, irrespective of the particular issue. Understanding their implications is a critical first step in understanding the practical challenges of resolving environmental conflicts. To put the point more starkly, environmental law conflicts are usually about much more than the law. Particular regulations or statutes may frame the specific contours of the problem, but the cause of the conflict runs far deeper. Only by understanding these drivers can one hope to find truly sustainable solutions.

## A. SCIENTIFIC UNCERTAINTY

In many respects scientific uncertainty is *the* defining feature of environmental policy. Most environmental problems involve complex technical and economic issues. But lawmakers rarely have anything approaching perfect knowledge when asked to make specific decisions. Certainty may come too late, if ever, to design optimal legal and policy responses.

In the context of the Susquehanna River, for example, what are the likely effects of increased fracking on water quality? What are the likely impacts on drinking water quality? More specifically, what are the impacts of these potential actions *on the margins*? Environmental decisions are incremental. Should we allow one more fracking operation, or increase wastewater discharges by another 5%? We may be able to predict with reasonable certainty that a massive increase in discharges will cause particular harms, but the science is often too complicated to make such statements on the margins, where the real decisions often must be taken.

Troubling levels of uncertainty are present when conserving natural resources, as well. How much land needs to be set aside to provide adequate habitat for the endangered Fly population. Will an acre provide sufficient habitat for its survival? Does habitat set aside need to be connected by corridors so different Fly populations can interbreed? If so, how big should these corridors be? The simple fact is that we do not know enough about the Fly's life history or recent population declines to answer these management questions with certainty, yet actions need to be taken today or risk extinction of the species in the future, perhaps the near future.

In fact, uncertainties over the magnitude of environmental problems, their causes, and future impacts bedevil law and policy. What we would like to know as policy makers rarely approaches our actual knowledge. But if we do not understand well the current situation, then how can we predict the future impacts of our laws and policies? Does prudence dictate waiting until we have better information or taking early action in the face of potentially serious threats?

The obvious response to such arguments is that waiting for more scientific certainty, if it ever comes, imposes costs of its own. In the face of a credible and significant threat, the argument goes, we must act today so as to avoid the present and future harms (which may well be greater) imposed by delay. To employ a nautical metaphor, we should be bailing water out of our sinking ship as fast as possible, not standing on the deck studying the angle and rate of descent.

The exact same dynamic is at work in the examples of Susquehanna River pollution and the Fly. Delay while we study the threats to the river may result in an increase in fish kills and other environmental harms that could have been prevented. Delay in the case of the Fly may lead to greater understanding, but of a now-extinct species. Yet, as the voices of caution warn, overreaction imposes its own real costs in the form of higher prices, foregone development, and scarce public monies that could have been better spent elsewhere. In these and countless other examples, there are good reasons to wait and reduce the uncertainty, and good reasons to avoid potential future costs by acting now. Thus perhaps the first question of environmental law and policy is how to act in the face of uncertainty.

There are two basic strategies to address this intractable problem. The first is to develop better information. As we shall see later in the book, many environmental statutes require generation of considerable information to provide a surer basis on which to create policy. A second strategy is known as the *precautionary principle*. Influential in the field of international environmental law, in its simplest form the principle counsels caution in the face of significant but uncertain threats. It's hard to argue against such an obvious rule of conduct but people differ significantly over how the principle should be applied in practice. In its most extreme form, the principle would forbid any activity that potentially could produce significant harms, regardless of the likelihood that these harms may occur. The problem, though, is that such a view counsels inaction in the face of uncertainty, no matter what the cost. The strategy, moreover, is paralyzing in the context of risk-risk choices, where every alternative poses significant risks and one must choose among them. Such risk-risk choices arise commonly in the environmental field, such as deciding whether to build a nuclear power plant or a coal-fired plant. Each option poses environmental concerns and potential harms.

In the international context, the precautionary principle generally has been viewed as shifting the burden of proof from those who would prevent an offending activity to those who wish to commence or continue the activity. This shift in burden could shorten the time period between when a threat to the environment is recognized and a legal response is developed. In the Fly example, the developer would shoulder the burden of proving that the loss of habitat will not threaten the survival of the Fly. Fracking operators would bear the responsibility of justifying that increased withdrawals and effluent levels pose no significant ecological or health risks to the Susquehanna River.

This shift in burden changes the tenor and nature of the debate over *how well understood* the problem must be before taking action. But it does not shed light on an equally important question—*how serious* the problem must be before taking action (i.e., which risks are worth addressing), much less the appropriate action to take. As we shall see below, these are fundamentally political, not scientific, questions, and they pose additional levels of uncertainty.

## B. MARKET FAILURES

Misaligned incentives underlie most environmental conflicts. While protecting the environment often provides a net benefit to society, the economic interests of individual parties involved often can encourage harmful activities. Thus a basic challenge to an environmental lawyer lies in understanding the reward structures of the parties and then changing incentives so that environmental protection reinforces rather than collides with the parties' self-interest. In the following examples, consider how costs and benefits are allocated.

Consider the case of hog farming in a watershed. A company may choose voluntarily to treat its manure, but it may end up raising its operating costs and losing market share if its competitors in other parts of the state, much less in other states, do not reduce their effluent as well. A downstream neighbor of a hog farm may be having constant stomach upsets because of effluent, but the bother isn't worth the cost of bringing a lawsuit. All of her neighbors have stomach aches, too, but they can't seem to get together to negotiate with or sue the hog farm.

On its face, one might think that the market would automatically promote environmental protection. The most basic principle of economics, after all, is supply and demand. As the supply of a valuable good becomes scarce, its price rises. Since clean air and water are clearly valuable, one would expect that as they become scarcer their price should also rise, making it more expensive to pollute. Yet this clearly does not happen in real life. The market has somehow failed, as it does when the hog farm refuses to reduce its effluent and the neighbors can't agree to sue. To correct these market failures and craft an effective legal response, we first need to understand the distortions at play.

### 1. PUBLIC GOODS

Try to buy some clean air. Sure, you can buy real estate in the wilds of Alaska where the air is clean, but you own the land there, not the air. In fact, your neighbor can breathe it right after it blows through. It turns out that many environmental amenities, such as clean air and scenic vistas, are *public goods*. Their benefits can be shared by everyone, but owned by no one. No one owns the air. No one can sell it or prevent others from using it.

The same is true for *ecosystem services*. Largely taken for granted, healthy ecosystems provide a variety of critical services. Created by the interactions of living organisms with their environment, these ecosystem services provide both the conditions and processes that sustain human life—purifying air and water, detoxifying and decomposing waste, renewing soil fertility, regulating climate, mitigating droughts and floods, controlling pests, and pollinating plants. Not surprisingly, recent research has demonstrated the extremely high costs to replace many of these services if they were to fail. Looking at just one ecosystem service that soil provides, the provision of nitrogen to plants, serves as an example. Nitrogen is supplied to plants through both nitrogen-fixing organisms and recycling of nutrients in the soil. If nitrogen were provided by commercial fertilizer rather than natural processes, the lowest cost estimate for crops in the U.S. would be $45 billion; the figure for all land plants would be $320 billion.

The value of $320 billion is estimated by calculating replacement costs—what we'd have to pay to replace the ecosystem service of nitrogen fixing by other means. But what are these natural goods and services *really* worth? Perhaps surprisingly, in the eyes of the market they are not worth anything. We have no shortage of markets for ecosystem goods (such as clean water and apples), but the services underpinning these goods (such as water purification and pollination) are free. Make no mistake, these environmental amenities are valuable—just ask yourself how much it's worth to you to breathe unpolluted air—but they have no *market value*. There is no market to exchange public goods such as ecosystem services and, as a result, they have no price. This explains the riddle of why pollution does not become expensive as clean air is "used up." Because there's no market for clean air or climate stability, there are no direct price mechanisms to signal the scarcity or degradation of these public goods until they fail. Hence, despite their obvious importance to our well-being, ecosystem services largely have been ignored in environmental law and policy. Partly as a result, ecosystems are degraded.

### 2. THE TRAGEDY OF THE COMMONS

Imagine you are a shepherd who grazes twenty sheep on a village common. Along with your pan pipes and bag lunch, you herd your flock to the common every day. So long as the number of sheep on the common remains small, the grass remains plentiful and the sheep contentedly munch away. Assume, though, that shepherds from over the mountain have heard of the wonderful grass in the common and bring their flocks. With each hour these sheep graze, there is less grass available for future grazing. In fact, you soon realize that this increased level of grazing will nibble the grass down to the roots, with the result of not enough forage in the future for anyone's flock, including your own. Yet you and the other shepherds will likely continue to allow your sheep to overgraze. Why?

The answer lies in the economic incentives. The more the sheep graze the fatter and more valuable they will be when they come to market. You could stop your flock's grazing, of course, to try and preserve the pasture for other days; but there is no guarantee your fellow shepherds will be similarly conscientious. In that case, you're a chump, sacrificing your own interests for no benefit. As a result, you may well encourage your sheep to graze as much as possible, and your neighbors will do the same. "Might as well get the grass in my sheep's tummies before it disappears in others'," you think. The result is individually rational in the short term—if the resource will be depleted, you might as well ensure you get your fair share—but collectively disastrous in the long term. It would be far better for each shepherd to restrain her flock's grazing, but seeking to maximize immediate economic gain ensures long term economic—and environmental—collapse.

This same phenomenon, known as *the tragedy of the commons*, can be identified in many open access resources, as farmers race to pump water from an underground aquifer, fishing boats with ever larger nets chase fewer and fewer fish, and wildcat drillers race to pump out oil as fast as they can. In each case, individually rational behavior is collectively disastrous. Individuals' personal incentives work *against* the best long-term solution.

### 3. COLLECTIVE ACTION AND FREE RIDERS

So what is to be done? Perhaps you could negotiate with all the shepherds and collectively agree to graze less. This may work when there are a handful of shepherds who all come from the same village. But it becomes increasingly difficult to reach agreement as the number of shepherds increases (and more difficult still if they come from different places without shared cultural norms and informal means of enforcement). This obstacle is known as a *collective action problem* and is due to the increased transaction costs in negotiating solutions as the number of parties increases. At a certain point, it's simply too expensive and difficult to reach consensus agreement. To see this in action, try to decide on which movie to see or settle a restaurant check with more than four friends.

Perhaps, as a last resort, in frustration at the inability to agree on a common solution, some of you decide to stop grazing your flock so that the grass on the common can grow back. Noble intent, no doubt, but there is a risk that other shepherds will take advantage of your generosity and keep their sheep on the common. More food for their flocks, they may smirk. These shepherds benefiting from your sacrifice are known as *free riders*. A similar phenomenon might occur even if all the shepherds agreed to graze less. New shepherds might come in and start grazing all the time, free-riding off of your sacrifice. Thus any solution to commons problems must overcome both the high transaction costs in reaching agreement among many parties (collective action) and counterproductive behavior by parties outside the agreement (free riders).

### 4. EXTERNALITIES

Assume you have sold your sheep, moved on from the now trampled and scraggly common, and own a chemical factory. When you balance your firm's financial books, you notice something odd. In figuring out your bottom line, you subtract your costs to operate (such as labor, materials, utilities, and so on) from the revenue you earn from selling your chemicals. But the pollution from your smokestacks does not reduce your bottom line. Make no mistake; your factory *is* causing real costs in the form of acid rain, smog, and reduced air visibility. But, as described above, because clean air is a public good you do not have to pay as you "use up" the clean air. It acts as a sink for your pollution at no cost. As a result, in seeking to maximize short-term economic gain, you do not consider the cost of your pollution. You can "overuse" the air and continue polluting. The costs from damage to forests, increased respiratory ailments, and reduced pleasure in clear vistas from your pollution are very real, but they are *external* to the costs you currently pay to operate. These costs are borne by the public and known as *externalities*.

If, on the other hand, your factory has to pay for the external harm it causes, then it will reduce its pollution. The process for forcing the factory to recognize environmental and social costs is known as *internalizing externalities* and reflects a basic lesson of economics—when we have to pay for something, we use less of it than if it is free. By internalizing externalities, we correct the market failure by charging for environmental harms and providing more accurate price signals to buyers.

This works both ways. Assume that you own a wetland beside your factory. The wetland provides a nursery for young fish to spend their first few months in relative safety before entering the adjacent river. The outdoors enthusiasts who fish along the river and the sporting good stores who sell fishing tackle all benefit from the services your wetland provides, but they don't pay you for them. While your factory's pollution generates *negative externalities*, your wetland provides *positive externalities*. Just as the fact that you don't have to pay for the costs caused by your pollution removes any incentive to reduce pollution so, too, does the fact that you are not paid for the benefits provided by the wetland remove any incentive to conserve rather than pave it over for a parking lot.

If all negative externalities were internalized—if all costs imposed on the environment were borne by the polluting party—then environmentally harmful products and processes would be relatively more costly and the market would reinforce environmental protection. Equally, if positive externalities were internalized—if benefits generated by ecosystem services such as flood control and water purification were paid for by the recipients—then habitat conservation would be truly valued in the marketplace. A central problem, of course, is "getting the prices right." Even if we had the authority to charge a factory for the damage its pollution caused, how much would that be? As with clean air, there are no markets for environmental harms, either; thus their costs must be estimated. But even rough estimates would be an improvement over the current situation where negative externalities are costless to polluters and positive externalities are not rewarded. One of the key goals of environmental law is to bring environmental externalities into the marketplace.

## C. MISMATCHED SCALES

Natural boundaries rarely track political boundaries. The communities downstream of the hog farms along the Susquehanna River suffer the impacts of pollution, yet have no political control over local land management decisions upstream. At a larger scale, a map of the western United States shows states and counties with straight lines and right angles. Map the region's watersheds, ecosystems, or forests, however, and nary a straight line will appear. Ecological concerns were, not surprisingly, far from the politicians' and surveyors' minds when these political jurisdictions were created, but the mismatch of natural and political scales poses difficult challenges for environmental management. Air pollution, water pollution, and wildlife certainly pay no heed to local, state or national borders, with the result that often the generator of the pollution is politically distinct from those harmed.

Acid rain was hard to control in the 1970s and 1980s because of political jurisdictions. The costs of reducing emissions downwind were borne by those who received no benefit and, similarly, those benefiting from reduced pollution upwind did not have to pay for it. Midwestern power plants were far removed from the polluted lakes and forests of the Northeast and Canada. New York, Vermont, and certainly Canadian voters couldn't vote in Ohio or Pennsylvania. Thus those with the greatest cause for concern did not live in the areas where their concerns could be most effectively expressed. Similar problems of scale are evident in wildlife protection, where draining or filling prairie potholes in the Great Plains, for example, may benefit the local farmers but imperils migratory birds from Mexico to Canada. Pumping carbon dioxide in the air may not seem significant to someone driving an SUV in Montana, but to an islander on a low-lying Pacific atoll the prospects of sea-level rise are a good deal more unsettling.

As a result of these *geographical spillovers* across jurisdictions, transboundary environmental problems often pose the challenges of collective action (the high transaction costs to bring differing parties together), equity (ensuring that the parties enjoying the benefits of environmental protection also bear a share of the costs), and enforcement (monitoring compliance at a distance from the source of authority). This is as true with national laws as with international ones.

Mismatched political and natural boundaries also pose challenges of management authority. This is often expressed as a problem of federalism. Who should control pollution and natural resource management: local or national authorities? Locals are closer to the problems, often understand them better, and have to live with the consequences of the environmental policy. At the same time, if the problem is one of transboundary pollution, the locals don't live with the consequences of their pollution. Those downstream do.

With natural resources, locals may well feel an entitlement. The inhabitants of Colton are furious over the loss of potential local development because some bureaucrats from Washington say they have to protect the Fly, even if the Fly lives on private land. Does the biodiversity represented by the Fly "belong" to the nation as a whole? If so, then perhaps it should be managed at the national level. But is it just or wise to effectively overrule local decisions about land uses, when it is the locals who must bear the opportunity costs from Fly conservation?

In another variant of this problem, scales can be mismatched as markets encompass multiple political jurisdictions. Imagine, for example, that in order to attract business Arkansas decides to lower its standards for water pollution from hog farms. This not only poses a transboundary concern for the border states of Louisiana and Alabama; it also pressures states with similar industries, such as North Carolina, to lower their standards as well in order to prevent industry relocation. The dynamic of local jurisdictions competing with one another by lowering environmental standards to attract industry is known as the *race-to-the-bottom*. Realize, as well, that concerns over the race-to-the-bottom can not only pressure jurisdictions to lower their standards but can also chill efforts in states seeking to strengthen standards (because industry will threaten to relocate if their costs of regulatory compliance are increased). If this is the case, then nationwide standards seem necessary. The same phenomenon can also occur in the international context, as nations compete with one another for business investment.

The fact that companies choose their locations based in part on costs of doing business is indisputable. There is a strong debate, however, over the extent to which a race-to-the-bottom really occurs in the environmental field. For one thing, states can compete on many grounds, perhaps lowering tax rates or workplace safety requirements to attract business. Hence it's not a given that they would reduce environmental standards to attract industry. Indeed, because environmental quality is an important amenity, there's an argument that local jurisdictions are more likely to engage in a "race-to-the-top," competing for industry by offering *higher* environmental quality. The data on international industry relocation suggest that stringency of environmental regulation is less important to companies than proximity to markets, labor costs, raw material costs, political stability, etc. And this makes sense, since environmental costs are usually a small percentage of total business costs. In those industries where environmental costs are relatively high, though, such as in the chemicals sector, there is evidence that companies have relocated with environmental compliance costs in mind. Perhaps more important, though, is the fact that many regulators believe the race-to-the-bottom occurs, whether that is borne out in fact or not, and act accordingly.

Problems of scale occur in time as well as in space. Decisions must be made today that may prevent harm ten or twenty years from now or, indeed, in generations not yet born. Ozone depletion and climate change are two examples. CFCs (which are the major cause of stratospheric ozone depletion) and greenhouse gases we emit today will cause impacts over the next 50 years or longer. The same distributional asymmetry is at play here as with physical scale. The costs of refraining from an action fall on us today, while the benefits are enjoyed (most likely by others) far later. Yet these future beneficiaries can't express their preferences in today's voting booth or courtroom. Indeed, the temporal scale of many environmental problems makes it difficult even to hold current elected officials accountable, since many of their actions will not cause harms until they are no longer in office. Supporting overfishing today may keep a local politician in office, for example, while the stark impacts may not be evident until years later when the stock has collapsed. As a result, many environmental advocates claim to be acting on behalf of the interests of future generations, but deciding what the proper sacrifice today should be for future benefits that may or may not be appreciated is easier said than done.

## D. CONFLICTING VALUES

Why should we care about protecting the Fly or the fish and freshwater ecosystems along the Susquehanna River? "Because it's important to do so" may be a heartfelt answer, but the fact is that not everyone attributes the same importance to environmental protection or nature conservation. In a democracy, that can (and does) make environmental management a tricky business. Consider, for example, the conflict in Colton. On the one side are those, supported by the Endangered Species Act, who argue that conserving the remnant populations of the Fly is important enough to slow, or even halt, commercial development. And Mayor Deirdre Bennett's fly swatter pretty well sums up the contrasting perspective on the value of the Fly.

A vast subject in itself, environmental ethics encompasses our relationship with the environment. While seemingly secondary to the hard nuts and bolts of environmental law and policy, "soft" values often in competition with one another lie at the core of many environmental conflicts, and understanding the nature of the values conflict is essential to crafting durable solutions.

At one end of the spectrum lies the ethic of biocentrism. The term "deep ecology," for example, is based on the premise of a kinship with nature. Consider, for example, the core principles set out below.

> 1. The well-being and flourishing of human and nonhuman life on Earth have value in themselves. These values are independent of the usefulness of the nonhuman world for human purposes.
>
> 2. Richness and diversity of life forms contribute to the realization of these values and are also values in themselves.
>
> 3. Humans have no right to reduce this richness and diversity except to satisfy *vital* needs.
>
> 4. The flourishing of human life and cultures is compatible with a substantial decrease of the human population. The flourishing of nonhuman life requires such a decrease.
>
> 5. Present human interference with the nonhuman world is excessive, and the situation is rapidly worsening.
>
> 6. Policies must therefore be changed. These policies affect basic economic, technological, and ideological structures. The resulting state of affairs will be deeply different from the present.

BILL DEVALL & GEORGE SESSIONS, DEEP ECOLOGY: LIVING AS IF NATURE MATTERED ix, 65–70 (1985).

Certain animal rights advocates would likewise argue that non-humans have basic rights that must be respected.

At the other extreme lies the anthropocentric, human-based perspective. From this perspective, the most important measure of something's value is its value to us. Utilitarianism is perhaps the most widely accepted argument for anthropocentrism. As John Stuart Mill famously described, utilitarianism seeks to provide the greatest good to the greatest number of people. While some may find it odd to think of utilitarianism as an ethical viewpoint, it is a rights-based view of the world insofar as decisions ought to be made on the basis of social welfare (as measured for humans). In a classic defense of utilitarianism as the proper guiding ethic for environmental policy, William Baxter described a report that the use of DDT was harming penguin populations. Even if that were true, however, he denied that we must therefore stop using DDT:

> My criteria are oriented to people, not penguins. Damage to penguins, or sugar pines, or geological marvels is, without more, simply irrelevant. One must go further, by my criteria, and say: Penguins are important because people enjoy seeing them walk about rocks; and furthermore, the well-being of people would be less impaired by halting use of DDT than by giving up penguins. In short, my observations about environmental problems will be people-oriented, as are my criteria. I have no interest in preserving penguins for their own sake.
>
> It may be said by way of objection to the position, that it is very selfish of people to act as if each person represented one unit of importance and nothing else was of any importance. It is undeniably selfish. Nevertheless I think it is the only tenable starting place for analysis for several reasons. First, no other position corresponds to the way most people really think and act—i.e., corresponds to reality. . . . I do not know how we could administer any other system. . . . Penguins cannot vote now and are unlikely subjects for the franchise—pine trees more unlikely still. Again each individual is free to cast his or her vote so as to benefit sugar pines if that is his inclination. But many of the more extreme assertions one hears from some conservationists amounts to tacit assertions that they are specially appointed representatives of sugar pines, and hence that their preferences should be weighted more heavily than the preferences of other humans who do not enjoy equal rapport with "nature." * * *
>
> I reject the proposition that we *ought* to respect "the balance of nature" or to "preserve the environment" unless the reason for doing so, express or implied, is the benefit of man.
>
> I reject the idea that there is a "right" or "morally correct" state of nature to which we should return. The word "nature" has no normative connotations. Was it "right" or "wrong" for the earth's crust to heave in contortion and create mountains and seas? Was it "right" for the first amphibian to crawl up out of the primordial ooze? . . . No answers can be given to these questions because they are meaningless questions.
>
> All this may seem obvious to the point of being tedious, but much of the present controversy over environment and pollution rests on tacit normative assumptions about just such nonnormative phenomena: that it is "wrong" to impair penguins with DDT, but not to slaughter cattle for prime rib roasts. . . . Every man is entitled to his own preferred definition of Walden Pond, but there is no definition that has any moral superiority over another, except by reference to the selfish needs of the human race.

WILLIAM BAXTER, PEOPLE OR PENGUINS: THE CASE FOR OPTIMAL POLLUTION 4–9, 12 (1974).

Somewhere between the nature-based ethic of biocentrism and the human-based ethic of anthropocentrism lies what has probably become the most influential ethic in the American environmental movement—the Land Ethic. Its champion, Aldo Leopold, was a pioneer in the field of resource management. In addition to his efforts in the U.S. Forest Service to preserve wild tracts of land, Leopold helped found the Wilderness Society in 1935. In his collection of essays, published posthumously in *A Sand County Almanac*, Leopold traced the development of ethics, arguing that subsequent generations had progressively expanded the community of rights-holders. In the time of ancient Greece, girls suspected of misbehavior were hanged. "This hanging involved no question of propriety. The girls were property. The disposal of property was then, as now, a matter of expediency, not of right and wrong." ALDO LEOPOLD, A SAND COUNTY ALMANAC—AND SKETCHES HERE AND THERE 201 (1949). Over time, ethics established rules over the relations between the individual and society, yet "[t]here is as yet no ethic dealing with man's relation to land and to the animals and plants which grow upon it." *Id.* at 203. In his Land Ethic, Leopold proposed:

> The "key-log" which must be moved to release the evolutionary process for an ethic is simply this: quit thinking about decent land-use as solely an economic problem. Examine each question in terms of what is ethically and esthetically right, as well as what is economically expedient. A thing is right when it tends to preserve the integrity, stability, and beauty of the biotic community. It is wrong when it tends otherwise.

*Id.* at 224–225.

Even if we could reached society-wide agreement regarding environmental values (which of course, we cannot), we would also need to address the conflicting values regarding governance and law. These conflicts seemed to be absent when an overwhelming bipartisan congressional majority enacted the landmark federal environmental laws of the late 1960s and early 1970s. Throughout 1970, President Nixon and Senator Edmund Muskie (the presumptive Democratic presidential candidate in 1972) tried to one-up each other by proposing more and more stringent versions of what became the Clean Air Act. But the honeymoon ended quickly. Congress has not enacted any sweeping new framework environmental laws since a lame-duck session rushed to enact hazardous waste legislation (CERCLA, which we study in Chapter 5) after the November 1980 elections. Congress has amended the original statutes on a number of occasions, perhaps most notably the 1990 amendments to the Clean Air Act, but even substantial statutory amendments have become less common in recent years. The House of Representatives narrowly approved the 1,428-page American Clean Energy and Security

Act in 2009, but the Senate failed to follow suit and such federal climate change legislation appears unlikely within the foreseeable future.

The current period of congressional dormancy is not the result of widespread satisfaction with our current environmental statutes. To the contrary, most experts, policymakers, and activists have numerous ideas about how each statute could be improved. Those ideas, however, are often diametrically opposed. Many environmentalists want to further empower administrative experts to employ scientific expertise to impose legally binding regulations needed to save the natural environment. Their opponents see agencies such as the Environmental Protection Agency as an out-of-control, unaccountable bureaucracy intent on reshaping American society regardless of the economic and other costs. Shared environmental values, in other words, are not enough if there is not an agreement on how to achieve those values.

## E. ENVIRONMENTAL JUSTICE

A final driver of environmental conflicts arises from inequity. The burdens of environmental harms and regulations are not allocated equally among individuals and groups within our society. Indeed our environmental laws historically have ignored distributive issues. During the heady days of the 1970s when most of our framework statutes were passed, supporters of strong environmental laws emphasized environmental rights, while those more sympathetic to economic concerns argued for greater consideration of costs; virtually no one asked how environmental harms or regulatory costs were distributed.

This began to change in 1978 when Governor James Hunt of North Carolina proposed disposing of soil tainted with polychlorinated biphenyls (PCBs) in a new waste dump to be opened in Warren County, a poor region in the northeastern part of the state with a population that was sixty-four percent African American and Native American. Joined by national civil rights leaders, local residents blocked the entrance to the dump site for over two weeks, arguing that the county had been chosen for the site because it was a minority community with little political power. Although the campaign ultimately failed to keep the PCB-laced soils from the site, it attracted national attention to the issue of environmental justice and forced the governor to support state legislation prohibiting additional landfills in Warren County.

Warren County was not an anomaly. Study after study has since demonstrated that low-income communities and communities of color bear the greatest burdens of environmental harms. Studies have shown strong correlation between race and exposure to air pollution, race and lead poisoning, race and pesticides, race and exposure to occupational hazards, and other environmental harms. Similar correlations have been established for low income communities, as well. Consider the following summary of information taken from EPA sources:

*Lead.* Almost two-thirds of American housing units were built before 1970. Although the use of lead paint for houses was banned in the 1970s, older homes often contain paint with high concentrations of lead. Additional sources of lead in the home are: drinking water extracting lead from lead pipes and fixtures, lead in dust (usually from paint), and contaminated soils carried in from outside. The primary pathway for exposure is from ingestion of paint chips and dust containing lead. There is a particularly high concentration of lead problems in low-income and culturally diverse populations, who live in the inner city where the public housing units were built before 1970.

*Waste Sites.* Low income, and quite often culturally diverse populations, are more likely than other groups to live near landfills, incinerators, and hazardous waste treatment facilities.

*Air Pollution.* In 1990, 437 of the 3,109 counties and independent cities in the U.S. failed to meet at least one of EPA's ambient air quality standards. Many Americans live in these communities: 57 percent of all whites, 65 percent of African Americans, and 80 percent of Hispanics.

*Pesticides.* Approximately 90 percent of the 2 million hired farm workers in the United States are people of color, including Chicanos, Puerto Ricans, Caribbean blacks, and African Americans. Through direct exposure to pesticides, farm workers and their families may face serious health risks. It has been estimated that as many as 313,000 farm workers in the U.S. may suffer from pesticide-related illnesses each year.

*Wastewater: City Sewers.* Modern sewage systems were developed to carry sewage and storm water separately to prevent overflow problems that are common in older, urban areas. Many inner cities still have sewer systems that are not designed to handle storm overflow. As a result, raw sewage may be carried into local rivers and streams during storms, creating a health hazard.

*Wastewater: Agricultural Runoff.* More recently, streams and rivers in rural areas with concentrations of commercial truck farms and animal feedlots have suffered mysterious lesions in fish and algae blooms resulting in fish kills. High levels of phosphorus support algae growth, which blocks re-aeration, reducing the level of oxygen needed to support aquatic life. It is suspected that the increased use of commercial fertilizers and concentrations of animal wastes contribute to the degradation of receiving streams and rivers in rural areas, with communities that are often low income and culturally diverse.

Environmental justice focuses both on the distribution of environmental burdens and policies (*substantive* environmental justice) and on the process by which environmental decisions are made in the United States (*procedural* environmental justice). In the view of most advocates of environmental justice, local communities should have a significant, if not controlling voice in decisions and activities that impact their residents' lives. Decision-making processes in turn should be open to interested parties, which should also include access to the scientific studies and other information underpinning the policy proposals. Environmental justice advocates thus push for decisions to be made at the local level through democratic processes. This runs counter to the modern emphasis in American environmental policy on *federal* decision-making by *expert* agencies. Environmental justice advocates also have had concerns about traditional environmental groups, which tend to have few minority employees and accomplish much of their work in the courts and the halls of Congress rather than in local communities, though this has been changing in recent years.

Establishing the fact of a strong correlation between environmental burdens and both the poor and people of color made clear that something needed to be done. The problem, however, lies in what to do. Put another way, unless we understand the *drivers* of environmental injustice, then it is not at all clear how to remedy them. If the siting of hazardous waste facilities in poor communities of color is driven by racism, for example, the policy response may involve litigation under civil rights laws. Indeed, many residents of minority communities believe that racism is at work and have fought efforts to locate facilities in their communities, labeling such efforts *environmental racism*. If, by contrast, this correlation is driven primarily by the real estate market, the opportunity for government intervention is much smaller. A number of regional studies have suggested that housing dynamics are instead at fault: after a facility is located in a community, those who can relocate to other neighborhoods move out of the area and housing prices fall, making the community more attractive to minorities and poorer individuals who previously could not afford to live there. Vicki Been & Francis Gupta, *Coming to the Nuisance or Going to the Barrios? A Longitudinal Analysis of Environmental Justice Claims*, 24 ECOLOGY L.Q. 1 (1997). To the degree that more systemic problems such as housing underlie the greater exposure of minorities and the poor to industrial and waste facilities, changes in environmental policies by themselves will unfortunately not eliminate distributional inequities. Other studies have found a close correlation between the siting of undesirable land uses and a community's voting rate, with less politically active communities suffering greater environmental justice problems. James T. Hamilton, *Testing for Environmental Racism: Prejudice, Profits, Political Power?,* 14 J. OF POLICY ANALYSIS AND MANAGEMENT 107, 127 (1995). Thus many recent studies have sought to understand better the nature of the correlation between demographics and environmental justice.

Regardless of whether the governmental agencies that oversee the siting and permitting of such facilities intentionally discriminate, minority communities frequently have less political power and may be at a number of procedural disadvantages. Local residents may find it difficult to attend relevant hearings, which may be held in state or county capitals hundreds of miles away from the affected community; the siting agency might not publish notices and other materials in Spanish and other locally spoken languages or provide interpreters for hearings; and few minority communities have the resources to hire scientists and other experts needed to rebut the claims of the facility owners.

In response to such concerns, the federal government has taken a number of steps to improve environmental equity. In 1994, President Bill Clinton issued Executive Order 12898, still in effect, that requires all federal agencies to incorporate environmental justice into their decision making "by identifying and addressing, as appropriate, disproportionately high and adverse human health or environmental effects." Some governmental agencies also have adopted their own policies designed to reduce the chances that their decisions will impact minority communities on a disproportionate basis. In licensing nuclear facilities, for example, the Nuclear Regulatory Commission engages in an environmental equity analysis designed to identify and avoid both intentional discrimination and disproportionate burdens. In 1997, the Commission rejected an application to build a uranium enrichment plant in the African American community of Homer, Louisiana, because the Commission's staff had not adequately examined whether racial discrimination had played a role in the site selection process. *See* In the Matter of Louisiana Energy Services, L.P., Decision of the Nuclear Regulatory Commission Atomic Safety and Licensing Board, May 1, 1997.

Community members seeking to keep environmentally hazardous facilities out of their neighborhoods increasingly have tried to use Title VI of the Civil Rights Act of 1964 to address issues of environmental racism. Title VI prohibits any program or activity that receives federal funds from discriminating on the basis of race, color, or national origin; most state and local environmental programs receive some federal funding and thus are subject to Title VI. Although a plaintiff who sues in court under Title VI must prove intentional discrimination, federal agencies may adopt a lower burden of proof for administrative proceedings.

EPA prohibits disproportionate impacts, whether or not caused by intentional discrimination, in programs receiving EPA funding. In 2000, faced by an increasing number of Title VI complaints, EPA issued a Draft Revised Guidance for investigating administrative complaints alleging violations of Title VI. The interim guidance proved controversial with state and local governments and EPA has yet to adopt a final guidance document.

Discriminatory siting decisions may not be the only or even the principal reason why environmentally dangerous facilities end up located disproportionately in minority communities. Although virtually all studies agree that minority and poor communities host a disproportionate share of industrial and waste facilities, they disagree as to why.

Although environmental justice discussions have focused on the siting of industrial and waste facilities, environmental justice also provides a framework for addressing environmental policy more broadly. Many advocates of environmental justice, for example, observe that the government provides for strong protection of environmental amenities such as biodiversity that have little immediate importance to the urban and rural poor while taking a more relaxed stance on issues such as pesticide exposure that are of immediate importance to these populations. The Endangered Species Act thus does not consider cost in protecting endangered species, but the Federal Insecticide, Fungicide, and Rodenticide Act permits cost to be considered in deciding whether to allow pesticides to be used in the United States.

Environmental justice advocates also suggest that the government should consider distributional impacts in choosing and designing its regulatory tools. As discussed in Chapter 3, for example, the government has adopted tradable emission credits under the Clean Air Act. Under the trading program, a factory that finds it relatively inexpensive to reduce its air emissions can reduce its emission by more than the regulations require and then sell its "excess credits" to a factory that finds it more expensive to reduce emissions; the second factory can then use the credits to help meet its regulatory requirements. Emissions trading can achieve the same overall emission reduction at a lower cost and is thus economically efficient. But if the trading system is not carefully designed and implemented, factories in poorer areas of a region might become net purchasers of the pollution credits—resulting in more pollution in the poorer areas, so-called "hotspots," at the same time as the air becomes cleaner in other areas.

---

## QUESTIONS AND DISCUSSION

**1.** Using the case of climate change, give examples of how the following drivers play out in the climate setting:

- Uncertainty over impacts (biophysical and economic, current and future)
- Uncertainty over policies (current and future)
- The market failure of public goods
- The market failure of externalities
- The market failure of collective action and free riders

- Problems of physical and political scale
- Conflicting values

Explain the types of obstacles these drivers present to reducing greenhouse gas emissions.

**2.** Uncertainty can cut both ways—acting today to address an uncertain future harm may be an overreaction, causing immediate economic and social harm; yet not acting in the face of an uncertain future harm may prove an under-reaction, causing economic and social harm at a later date. Discuss the issue of nuclear power in terms of uncertainty and policy choices. Does the uncertain, though potentially massive, harm from climate change suggest we should move with all deliberate speed to shift toward non-carbon energy sources, including nuclear power? Or does the potential harm from the operation of nuclear power plants and dangers from transport and disposal of hazardous waste caution against its use? How should policy makers balance these competing sources of uncertainty?

**3.** For each school of environmental ethics described above, in whom (or what) do the rights inhere?

- In inanimate objects (e.g., rocks or a river)?
- In living things (e.g., a newt or whale)?
- In living communities (e.g., a particular forest)?
- In people living today in America?
- In future generations of people?

**4.** How would the major schools of thought described above (i.e., deep ecology, the land ethic, utilitarianism, etc.) analyze the decisions:

- To kill a few individual members of the Delhi Sands Flower-Loving Fly to build a new hospital;
- To kill half the population of the Fly to build a new hospital;
- To kill the only known population of the Fly to build a new hospital.

Assume that the Fly has been studied and has no clear commercial value. Assume the hospital will provide jobs and health care to an economically depressed community. Would the answers differ if the species were a cuddly panda instead of the Fly?

**5.** How does the vantage of environmental justice affect your consideration of the following conflicts?

- A Native American tribe has long suffered from high unemployment and poverty on its reservation. The Waste Company, Inc., approaches the tribal leadership and offers to open a hazardous waste disposal site on the reservation. The facility will produce significant income and employment for the tribe. Despite strong opposition from many tribal members, the tribal leadership decides to build the waste site on the reservation close to its border. A small farming town just outside the reservation objects to the environmental risks posed by the hazardous waste site.

- Cars that sit idling in traffic produce significant pollution. Every morning, traffic piles up for miles trying to get on the bridges leading from the mainland into Bay City. To reduce both congestion and pollution, Bay City proposes charging significantly higher tolls for use of the bridges during the peak commuter hours of the morning and late afternoon. The higher tolls will pose a problem for the working poor, who will not be able to afford the higher tolls and do not have jobs with flexible working hours.

## III. TOOLS FOR ENVIRONMENTAL PROTECTION—"THE FIVE P'S"

While values, market failures, scientific uncertainty and the other themes discussed in this chapter drive environmental conflicts, policies still need to be implemented. The rubber meets the road in determining which type of instrument to use in the regulatory toolkit. To explore the possibilities, let's return to the classic environmental problem described above—the tragedy of the commons. Recall that you have a herd of sheep that grazes on the public common. The common, though, is an open access resource (the defining problem for many natural resource issues). This means that anyone can graze as many sheep as she likes. So long as the resource is under little pressure (i.e., few sheep are grazing) there is no need for government intervention because there is no problem of scarcity. Once significant competing uses of a resource develop, however, then the need for state action arises. In the context of the commons, once more and more people graze more and more sheep, the commons is in danger of becoming overgrazed and denuded. So we need to do something, but how should we best head off the tragedy currently in the making? What is the appropriate mix of property and regulation? It is useful to think of the range of policy instruments as "The Five P's"—Prescriptive regulation, Property rights, Penalties, Payments, and Persuasion.

### A. PRESCRIPTIVE REGULATION

In relying on prescriptive regulation, the government mandates behavior—thou shalt do this, thou shalt not do that. This strategy explicitly directs behavior of regulated parties and is the most common policy approach in environmental law. In the case of the commons, for example, the government might decide to limit access. The most obvious measure would be to restrict the number of sheep that may graze, perhaps allowing no more than 250 sheep per month. The government may further determine that certain commons areas must be set aside for re-vegetation and allow no grazing at all.

Such prescriptive regulation, also referred to as "command-and-control" regulation, can be very effective but there is considerable debate over its efficiency. The underlying assumption, of course, is that the agency, staffed with experts, knows best. For the agency to make wise decisions, though, it must have access to accurate information and not be subject to capture by special interest groups or to other public choice pressures. It needs monitoring capabilities to check for compliance and credible sanctioning authority to ensure rules will be followed. In practice, none of these preconditions are guaranteed. And even if they are, satisfying these requirements suggests that administrative costs could be significant.

## B. PROPERTY RIGHTS

A classic solution to the tragedy of the commons is reliance on private property rights. Assume the state carves up the common into square parcels of land and grants fee simple title to the current shepherds using the common, including you. Are you still as eager to overgraze as before? All of a sudden, your previous incentive to use up the resource as fast as possible (before everyone else did) is no longer relevant. Instead, your interests are probably best served by carefully tending your part of the common so it remains fertile long into the future—so it is sustainably managed. In a variant of the privatization approach, assume the entire commons now belongs to you. What would you do? You may well charge other shepherds to use the commons, or even let them on for free, but you would only do so to the extent that the resource base remains intact and productive—i.e., so long as the commons are not overgrazed. The property rights approach is based on the common sense intuition that people take better care of their own property. In financial terms, people will safeguard their assets over the longer term to maximize long term profits.

Implicit in a property rights approach is the importance of technology. To enforce your rights, you need both to know whether someone is making unauthorized use of your resource (an issue of monitoring capacity) as well as to have the ability to exclude others' use. It was only with the invention of barbed wire that settlers in the American west could effectively exclude cattle from grazing on their lands (i.e., could privatize the commons). Prior to this technology, there was no affordable way to keep cattle from grazing wherever they wanted. In a more modern context, decoders have allowed satellite television channels to privatize the airwave commons. Unless satellite channel providers could exclude other's use of their signal by scrambling it and then selling decoders, there would be no way for them to sell their product (since people would use it for free).

Despite the increasing interest and application of property rights approaches to environmental protection, there are some significant obstacles. The first is that many environmental resources are not easily amenable to commodification. Consider endangered species, for example. One might privatize their habitat, but what if the species is mobile?

There may be normative concerns, as well, that are raised by proposals for privatization of national parks or other environmental amenities in the public domain. If the Disney Corporation owned Yellowstone, for example, would you would feel the same way about your visit even if the experience were identical in every other way to that of the current national park?

Practically, there are difficult allocation issues for the initial privatization of environmental resources. Using the commons as an example, assume that the government has decided to divide up the land into 50 separate parcels. Whom should be given title? Should the land be auctioned to the highest bidder? This might ensure the most efficient use of the resource, but it would likely favor wealthier newcomers and corporate interests over traditional, small-scale users. Giving more deference to communities, perhaps the allocation should be based on historic use or current levels of consumption. This approach might seem more equitable, though realize that it freezes out newcomers who might use the land more efficiently or even set it aside for conservation. And if these lands belong to the nation, where's the fairness in effectively shutting out outsiders? Any allocation mechanism will tend to favor some groups at the expense of others.

Nor, finally, is it clear that privatization will lead to the most socially most beneficial use of the land. It is easy to imagine, for example, the problem of holding out. Perhaps the new owners of the commons wish to use it for mini-golf while the sheep starve. This may be economically efficient if it accurately reflects the land's most valuable use (as measured by willingness to pay). If the government wishes to ensure the important public goals of a secure food supply or supporting family farms, they will need to step in. Property rights advocates would approve of this course of action, so long as the government paid the property holders. But, one might ask, if the most valuable use, as demonstrated by the market, is for the commons to be used for mini-golf, why should government intervene at all?

Market-based thinking can lead to alternative ways of regulating property rights, however, as so-called "environmental markets" have been growing in popularity and represent a hybrid of private property and prescriptive regulation. To date, for example, emissions trading programs have reduced emissions of a wide range of pollutants, managed fisheries and lobster harvests, and channeled habitat development. The basis for trading environmental commodities is a regulatory proscription of behavior followed by regulatory permission of the behavior under controlled conditions.

In establishing an environmental market, the government first creates a new form of property—legal entitlements to emit pollutants, catch fish, develop habitat—then bans an activity absent these entitlements, and finally imposes a set of rules governing their exchange—i.e., creates a market. All trading programs therefore take place within carefully constructed markets. Absent legal restrictions on pollutant emissions, fish landings, or wetlands development, and the creation of alienable entitlements to these activities, few if any trades would take place.

To make this more concrete, imagine how a trading program would work with grazing on the commons. Government policy makers decide that the commons can sustain no more than 400 sheep grazing per year. It therefore creates 400 permits. Each permit entitles the holder to graze one sheep for the calendar year. Unless the shepherd has a separate permit for each sheep grazing on the commons, he is breaking the law. The government then allocates the permits in some fashion and lets trading commence. In theory, those for whom grazing is most valuable will buy the permits, ensuring that the commons are dedicated to the most valuable use.

One downside of trading is similar to that for private property rights approaches—the difficulty of initial allocation of permits in an equitable fashion. Moreover, constructing smoothly functioning markets is not simple. There must be a refined currency of trade, one that is fungible and reflects the desired environmental quality. There must also be a sufficient and well-defined marketplace and community of market participants. Thus, for example, it would be a stretch to consider allowing coastal developers in Florida to "trade" wetland values they eliminate for increasing endangered species habitat in Oregon. But where the environmental good (or bad, so to speak) can be captured in a measurable unit (whether that be kilos of fish or tons of sulfur dioxide) and market service areas and participants are well-defined, trading programs have had demonstrable success in a variety of contexts, increasing the efficiency and flexibility of prescriptive instruments.

## C. PENALTIES

Another strategy of environmental protection relies explicitly on economic incentives and disincentives. Using the commons example again, these may take the form of an entrance fee to graze on the commons. One might levy a tax, perhaps on the number of sheep or time spent grazing. Such market instruments are attractive because they lead to self-regulation of use. If the fees and taxes are set correctly, this instrument quite literally internalizes externalities and provides a direct incentive to modify behavior, aligning environmental and economic interests. People will find cheaper ways to conserve those scarce resources and less of the resource will be used over time.

Setting the correct level of the tax, though, can be difficult. After all, what managers care about is the overall effect of many polluting sources or resource users. What level should the individual tax or fee be set at to reach the desired aggregate resource extraction or pollution level? More practically, there is strong public and political opposition to significant taxes. In most cases, even when environmental taxes have been set, they've been intended more for revenue-raising than serious behavior modification.

## D. PAYMENTS

Another market approach with broad use is public subsidy. Rather than financially penalizing undesirable behavior, one rewards the desired behavior. In the context of the tragedy of the commons, the government can pay shepherds not to graze their sheep. In contrast to such "environmental subsidies," however, many (in fact, most) subsidies actively promote degradation of environmental amenities. Suppose, for example, you graze your sheep on public lands. The government charges you less than the private lessee across the fence pays to graze her sheep. It sends you a check when you are unable to sell your lambs or their wool at a statutory target price. And it sells you water at a below-market price which you use to grow alfalfa to feed your sheep in the winter when the grazing land is covered with snow. If the subsidies are reduced, you may decide to stop grazing altogether, reduce the number of sheep you run, or perhaps find a more efficient way to graze, all of which will benefit an overgrazed range. Subjecting you to the discipline of the market can turn out to be good for the environment, but eliminating subsidies won't always produce environmental gains. Suppose that you stop grazing and the pasture is replaced with tract homes?

## E. PERSUASION

Where regulatory or property approaches are politically infeasible, a "softer" approach may be found in laws requiring information production and dissemination. The theory behind such approaches is that forcing a regulated party or government agencies, themselves, to gather information and make it public, or at least to consider information, will change the party's behavior. In the context of the commons, the government might require shepherds to record and publish the number of sheep that graze or the amount of time they graze, subjecting them to peer pressure from the community. They may try to educate the shepherds with brochures or presentations on the causes and dangers of overgrazing. It may be more effective, though, to bypass the regulated party entirely and go directly to the consumer. For example, in the early 1990s, labeling cans of tuna "dolphin friendly" rapidly changed the fishing practices of tuna fleets in the Southern Pacific, from purse seine netting that killed tens of thousands of dolphins annually to much less harmful techniques. California passed a law requiring all 2009 model cars for sale to display a global warming score, on a scale of one to 10, based on how vehicles in the same model year compare to one another for emissions and fuel efficiency. New York adopted a similar measure for 2010. California's data is posted on the web at the state's DriveClean website, www.driveclean.ca.gov/index.php.

Similar (often nongovernmental) eco-labeling initiatives certify and label sustainably harvested timber, coffee, etc. The theory behind such programs is to provide green consumers reliable information on which to base their purchases and favor environmentally friendlier products in the marketplace. Government can also support pilot programs or demonstration projects to show industries or farmers the benefits of alternative approaches to production or farming.

In general, information approaches are used when there is either inadequate political support to impose regulatory instruments or such instruments are ill-suited to the problem. In a number of cases, particularly in the case of pollution, requirements to collect and disseminate information on regulated parties' behavior have led to concrete changes even in the absence of overt prescriptive regulation. *See* Eric Orts, *Reflexive Environmental Law*, 89 NW. U.L. REV. 1227 (1995).

## QUESTIONS AND DISCUSSION

**1.** Apply the Five P's to the problem of reducing greenhouse gas emissions. Once you have come up with examples of policy instruments, assess the following:

- Which instrument do you think will be most effective?
- Which most efficient?
- And which most equitable?

**2.** The Five P's lists only government policy instruments. Nongovernmental P's might include Protest by concerned individuals or Private companies adopting their own corporate environmental policies. Can you think of other nongovernmental strategies (even if they don't start with a P . . .)?

**3.** While trading programs can reduce compliance costs by allowing regulated parties to pay for the least-cost solutions, they can also cause harmful side effects. In particular, the problem of "hotspots" can occur when pollutants are concentrated in a particular area (e.g., because the polluting factories are buying pollution credits from somewhere else). Hotspots often are located in or near poor communities of color, raising environmental justice concerns. Can you think of a way to design an air pollution trading program that avoids the danger of hotspots?

**4.** Given that public subsidies often result in environmentally-damaging resource allocation, a number of environmental groups have joined forces with taxpayers' groups and fiscal conservatives to lobby against particular congressional subsidies. The *Green Scissors Report*, for example, published annually by Friends of the Earth, the U.S. Public Interest Research Group, and Taxpayers for Common Sense, identifies environmentally wasteful programs. Operating for close to two decades, the Green Scissors Campaign claims to have "successfully cut or eliminated more than 20 environmentally wasteful programs, saving taxpayers more than $26 billion." Their most recent report can be found at http://www.greenscissors.com. This strategy, however, can act as a double-edged sword. Should the campaign be concerned over subsidies for renewable energy research and national park visitors? Is it possible, or fair, to pick and choose among subsidies or are subsidies simply the oil that makes the wheels of politics run?

**5.** The Political Economy Research Center (better known as PERC), is one of the leading think tanks for free market environmentalism. Their approach to resource management is based on four tenets:

- Private property rights encourage stewardship of resources.
- Government subsidies often degrade the environment.
- Market incentives spur individuals to conserve resources and protect environmental quality.
- Polluters should be liable for the harm they cause others.

None of these contentions are exceptional, so why is PERC so controversial? Primarily because their policy prescriptions often call for much stronger reliance on markets, property rights and the common law than the current emphasis on prescriptive regulation. In advocating repeal of the Endangered Species Act, for example, former PERC Executive Director Terry Anderson has argued that

> This Act creates perverse incentives by penalizing people who oversee resources. I'd start by scrapping the approach that's there and implementing new ones. First, by encouraging private environmental groups to contract with land owners, and second, by using financial resources (from user fees on public land, for example) to compensate land owners for preservation procedures.

http://www.perc.org/articles/article435.php.

Does PERC's approach adequately account for the transaction costs incurred by those with diffuse interests? Consider for example, what it will take for multiple private environmental groups to marshal their resources to compete with a single landowner for the purchase of an old growth forest that provides critical habitat for an endangered species. While PERC's views have surely been controversial, it has succeeded in pushing the envelope of policy tools. PERC's website has a number of "success stories" it argues should serve as models for resource management. *See* http://www.perc.org/psolutions.php. For further reading on free market environmentalism, *see* TERRY L. ANDERSON & DONALD R. LEAL, FREE MARKET ENVIRONMENTALISM (2nd ed. 2001). For the views of the other influential free market environmentalist think tank, see the Foundation for Research on Economics and the Environment's website, at www.free-eco.org.

## IV. WHAT DO ENVIRONMENTAL LAWYERS DO?

What is an *environmental* lawyer, and what do they do? To answer this requires some appreciation of the field of environmental law and the different settings within which it is practiced. Indeed, the remainder of this text is devoted to answering this question. The chapters in Part I explore the depth and breadth of substantive environmental law and Part II places the substance in different practice contexts.

## A. AN EVOLVING FIELD OF LAW

The substantive scope of environmental law has evolved substantially since its emergence in the 1970s and is continuing to change rapidly. Of course, it is to some degree arbitrary to draw lines between what is and is not *environmental* law. Many fields of law have a profound influence on the environment. Land use law, for example, necessarily must consider environmental impacts of land use decisions. But that is not the primary focus of land use lawyers; rather, they are concerned with how particular land uses are approved or disapproved by government authorities, and the environment is just one consideration among many (others would include traffic, schools, aesthetics, demographics, fiscal burden, and so on). Likewise, environmental law at its broadest ought to include substantive laws the primary objective of which is managing the relation of humans to the physical environment.

Of course, there are many such laws, and we don't intend to list them all here. Rather, it is instructive to see how lawyers who hold themselves out as environmental lawyers have described their field. As mentioned above, for example, the American Bar Association has a section devoted to environmental law, and the related fields of energy law and natural resources law, known as the Section on Environment, Energy, and Resources (SEER), which in turn has committees devoted to different topics. The history of that section tells a lot about the evolution of environmental law as a field.

To begin with, SEER is the current denomination of the ABA section that originally went by the Section of Natural Resources Law (SNRL). For decades SNRL was focused primarily on the law of natural resource extractive industries, such as mining, water uses, oil and natural gas, and forestry. Indeed, even as of 1987 SNRL had only four committees in the section's "environmental group" (see Table 1). By 1997, SNRL had been renamed the Section on Natural Resources, Energy, and Environmental Law (SONREEL), and the number of committees had more than doubled. By 2007 SONREEL had become SEER, with "environment" getting top billing, and the number of committees under the environmental banner was close to 20.

**Table 1: ABA SEER Environmental Committees 1987–2007**

| 1987 | 1997 | 2007 |
|---|---|---|
| Air Quality | Air Quality | Air Quality |
| Environmental Quality | Environmental Quality | — |
| Solid and Hazardous Waste | Solid and Hazardous Waste | Waste Management |
| Toxic and Environmental Torts Litigation | Environmental Litigation | Environmental Litigation and Toxic Torts |
| Water Quality | Water Quality and Wetlands | Water Quality and Wetlands |
| | **New Committees** | |
| | Agricultural Management | Agricultural Management |
| | Brownfields | Environmental Transactions and Brownfields |
| | Endangered Species | Endangered Species |
| | Environmental Crimes and Enforcement | Environmental Crimes and Enforcement |
| | International Environmental Law | International Environmental Law |
| | State and Regional Environmental Cooperation | State and Regional Environmental Cooperation |
| | | **New Committees** |
| | | Environmental Disclosure |
| | | Environmental Justice |
| | | Pesticides, Chemical Regulation, and Right to Know |
| | | Site Remediation |
| | | Superfund and Natural Resources Damages Litigation |
| | | Sustainable Development, Ecosystems, and Climate Change |
| | | Environmental Impact Assessment |
| | | Environmental Values and Ethics |
| | | Innovation, Management Systems and Trading |

Notice also how the committees proliferated over time. In the days of SNRL, they were the obvious choices: air, water, waste, litigation, and the catch-all "environmental quality." Air, water, waste, and litigation had staying power, but by 2007 SEER had unpacked environmental quality into over a dozen subfields, every one of which, we are pleased to say, is covered in substantial detail in this text. Moreover, many of the committees that have traditionally been housed in the section's "resource group" have come to look increasingly like environmental law topics. For example, SEER includes in that category committees on forest resources, marine resources, Native American resources, public land resources, and water resources. The SEER committee structure has been relatively stable since 2007, with a few committees consolidated or eliminated and one, Smart Growth and Green Buildings, added. What would you predict the next new big issue in environmental law to be, and what would you name SEER's new committee charged to follow it?

Of course, few environmental issues involve all or even most of the different topics covered in that list, but most do involve more than one. Consider the Delhi Fly case study from Part I of this chapter. Clearly, it was first and foremost about the Endangered Species Act, the domain of SEER's Endangered Species Committee. But it raised questions that also would have fallen in the zone of interest of other committees SEER had in place in 2007:

- The Agriculture Management Committee would have an interest in how the agricultural land uses affected the Fly and were regulated under the ESA. (See Chapter 2)
- The Environmental Transactions and Brownfields Committee would have an interest in the effect of Fly habitat on transactions involving the transfer of land and facilities in the area of the Fly's range. (See Chapter 13)
- The Environmental Disclosure Committee would have an interest in how landowners and companies operating in the Fly's range disclose the presence of Fly habitat. (See Chapter 10)
- The Environmental Justice Committee would have an interest in the impact of ESA regulation on communities of color and low income. (See Chapter 1)
- The Sustainable Development, Ecosystems, and Climate Change Committee would have an interest in exploring how the Fly's habitat is being managed in a way that will adapt to climate change. (See Chapter 8)
- The Environmental Impact Assessment Committee would have an interest in how the presence or absence of Fly habitat in the region is reflected and evaluated in environmental impact assessments public and private entities prepare in connection with land use and environmental permits. (See Chapter 6)
- The Environmental Values and Ethics Committee would be interested in the ethical dimensions of protecting the Fly. (See Chapter 2)

- The Innovation, Management Systems and Trading Committee would be interested in exploring mechanisms to make protecting the Fly more efficient and effective, such as a habitat conservation bank. (See Chapter 2)

Suffice it to say, in other words, that environmental law has evolved considerably since its "air, water, waste, litigation" days. It is a broad field reaching far and wide into the social and economic life of Americans. And it changes rapidly, not only as we learn more about the environment, but also as the nature of human impacts on the environment change and as norms toward the environment change. Needless to say, this makes the practice of environmental law challenging, but by the same token this makes it stimulating and rewarding.

## B. AN EVOLVING PRACTICE OF LAW

SEER's evolution of substantive topics also traces an evolution of the practice of environmental law. In the "air, water, waste, litigation" days of environmental law, practitioners generally focused on rules, permits, and litigation in those narrow fields. Today, however, environmental practitioners necessarily must follow where the substantive law leads them, and that has become quite a diverse array of practice settings. Whereas it may have been possible in the early 1970s for one lawyer to grasp a wide reach of the field at the time—to be an "air, water, waste" lawyer—today that kind of Renaissance practitioner would likely commit malpractice in no time. It is simply not possible to practice competently in all of the substantive fields mentioned above. Most environmental lawyers today specialize, and private and public interest law firms as well as government agencies employ numerous specialists in practice groups to be able to offer "full service" environmental representation to their clients.

Consider the possibilities once again in the context of the Fly case study from Part I of this chapter. Which environmental lawyers doing what kind of practice might have become involved? Tracking the chapters in Part II of this text, the answer is, quite a few:

- *Rulemaking and Permits*. The listing of the Fly was a rulemaking event carried out by the U.S. Fish and Wildlife Service (FWS) pursuant to Section 4 of the Endangered Species Act. Lawyers for FWS review listing rules to ensure compliance with the standards of the ESA, and lawyers for potentially regulated parties, which could include state and local governments and private landowners, routinely do as well. So do lawyers for non-governmental organizations that represent environmental advocacy groups and trade and industry groups. (See Chapter 9)
- *Compliance Counseling*. Landowners and businesses in the area where the Fly is found face regulation under the "take

prohibition" of Section 9 of the ESA (see Chapter 2), which as the case study reveals can impose significant constraints on land development and business operations. Lawyers for these regulated entities may be asked to assist in evaluating the legal consequences and compliance strategies associated with the ESA. (See Chapter 10)

- *Enforcement*. The ESA contains a "citizen suit" provision allowing any citizen to bring an enforcement action against alleged violators of the ESA, including those who violate the take prohibition of Section 9 by modifying Fly habitat in such a way as to injure a Fly. Also, Section 7 of the ESA requires all federal agencies to "consult" with FWS regarding whether proposed funding and permit actions could jeopardize the Fly as a species. Lawyers for citizen groups and for their targeted defendants, public and private, would advise their respective clients about the litigation risks, procedures, and strategies associated with such suits. (See Chapter 11)
- *Private Litigation*. The impact of the Fly listing on the local economy and social context could lead to numerous private disputes. What if, for example, a landowner who knew that the Fly listing was imminent and that his or her parcel had Fly habitat on it sold the land to someone else without revealing those facts, or even while disclaiming the presence of Fly habitat? A contract fraud action might follow. (See Chapter 12)
- *Business Transactions*. Many businesses and land parcels affected by the Fly nonetheless are likely to forge ahead with plans to sell facilities and parcels. Lawyers for buyers and seller thus may be asked to advise about how to identify the risks associated with Fly habitat and reflect those risks in the business transaction negotiations. (See Chapter 13)

Like any complex legal matter, moreover, the mix of lawyers in the Fly events changed over time. As the case study discusses, in the early stages of the matter lawyers for FWS and the County negotiated a set of measures the hospital would take to avoid causing injury to the Fly. This set of lawyers consisted primarily of ESA permitting experts, the goal being to avoid the need for a permit by avoiding injury to the Fly. Later, however, litigation ensued over the need for a permit, and litigation expertise entered the arena. And as the regulatory effects of the Fly spread over time throughout the region, likely more and more of the kinds of environmental law practice settings mentioned above came into play.

For today's students of environmental law—the readers of our text—there is good news in the rapid evolution of environmental law substance and practice: even the most seasoned practitioner cannot remain an expert in the law or practice for very long without a constant effort to keep pace with the changes, meaning that new entrants to the field can relatively quickly "catch up." Like the Red Queen from *Alice in Wonderland*, all environmental lawyers must run just to stay in place! The remaining chapters of this text, we hope, will give you a head start.

# PART 1

# APPROACHES TO ENVIRONMENTAL LAW

# CHAPTER 2

# PROTECTING ENDANGERED SPECIES

**CHAPTER OUTLINE**

I. Identifying Which Species to Protect
   - A. Eligibility for Listing
   - B. Determining Whether a Species Is Endangered or Threatened

II. Federal Government Responsibilities Under the Endangered Species Act
   - A. Listing Agency Responsibilities Under the ESA
     1. Critical Habitat
     2. Recovery Plans
   - B. Responsibilities of All Federal Agencies Under the ESA
     1. The Consultation Duty
     2. The Jeopardy Prohibition

III. Private Party Responsibilities Under the Endangered Species Act
   - A. The Scope of the "Take" Prohibition
   - B. Constitutional Objections to the "Take" Prohibition
     1. Congressional Power to Protect Endangered Species
     2. Duties to Compensate Property Owners Affected by Endangered Species Regulations
   - C. Incidental Take Permits and Habitat Conservation Plans

---

There is much about our natural environment that we want to conserve. Americans have long been fascinated by the natural wonders of this country, ranging from Niagara Falls to the geysers of Yellowstone to the vast wilderness of Alaska. The landscape paintings of the Hudson River School artists in the nineteenth century captured the public imagination. Forests, waters, and animals were viewed as seemingly inexhaustible resources. By the twentieth century, though, we began to realize that many of these features of the environment were disappearing in the face of expanding development. Thus began a body of laws specifically designed to conserve certain features of the environment. National parks were first (as we will describe in Part II of Chapter 6), and other public lands were set aside in categories such as national forests and wilderness areas.

Congress enacted the Endangered Species Act in 1973 to avert the extinction of numerous familiar species of wildlife. Since then, scientists, policymakers, and lawyers have devoted increased attention to biological diversity—or biodiversity—in wetlands and forests, deserts and mountains, rivers and oceans, and every other kind of ecosystem. We will consider the ESA in detail, and then provide a brief overview of the law of ecosystem management, to introduce you to the ways in which the law works to conserve our favored parts of the environment.

The Endangered Species Act (ESA) is the most revered and reviled of federal environmental laws. Its champions praise it for saving the bald eagle from extinction, for blocking many misconceived development projects, and for providing a tool to protect ecosystems ranging from the southern California coast to the majestic forests of the Pacific northwest. Its detractors accuse it of sacrificing timber jobs for obscure owls, nearly completed dams for tiny fish, and small farmers for unknown rodents. The basis for these claims lies in the unparalleled stringency of the ESA's provisions. Most other environmental statutes contain numerous opportunities for environmental interests to be balanced against other human needs. The ESA, by contrast, has long been viewed as requiring efforts "to halt and reverse the trend toward species extinction, *whatever the cost*." Tennessee Valley Authority v. Hill, 437 U.S. 153, 184 (1978) (emphasis added). There are some who question whether the ESA is really so intransigent, *see* Oliver A. Houck, *The Endangered Species Act and Its Implementation by the U.S. Departments of Interior and Commerce*, 64 U. COLO. L. REV. 277, 292 (1993) (asserting that the actual implementation of the ESA is much more relaxed), but the fact that environmentalists turn to the ESA to save whole ecosystems when other laws fail suggests that the common impression of the ESA's potential power is well founded.

During the early 1990s, environmentalists pressed to expand the coverage of the ESA to include whole ecosystems that were imperiled by human developments or other causes. Conversely, the ESA was blamed for causing economic dislocation throughout the Pacific northwest as a result of the listing of the northern spotted owl. The most sustained effort to reform—or gut, depending on your perspective—the ESA occurred in 1994. Speaker of the House Newt Gingrich established an ESA task force that held hearings across the country in areas that had chafed under the restrictions of the law. Landowners and developers told horror stories of widows losing their life's savings when the presence of an endangered songbird prevented them from building on their land and of farmers facing federal prosecutions for attempting to prevent fires in a manner that harmed endangered kangaroo rats. Several bills were introduced to amend the ESA by requiring more rigorous scientific evidence before a species could be listed, helping private landowners who confront a listed species on their property, and speeding recovery efforts so that a species could be delisted. The bills stalled in the face of a certain presidential veto and pressure from environmentalists, religious leaders, moderate politicians, and others who were intent on saving rare wildlife.[1] Despite renewed efforts in recent years, it appears unlikely that any significant changes to the ESA are forthcoming. Meanwhile, the ESA must now encounter the problem of global climate change, as we explain in Chapter 8.

As amended, the ESA has ten sections. The statute's principal provisions are as follows:

§ 2 Congressional findings and purposes of the law

§ 3 definitions of key statutory terms

§ 4 procedures for listing a species as "endangered" or "threatened"

§ 5 authority to purchase land to conserve wildlife and plants, not just listed species

§ 6 means of encouraging federal cooperation with state preservation efforts

§ 7 duties imposed on federal agencies to conserve listed species and not to jeopardize the continued existence of a species or its critical habitat

§ 8 means of encouraging cooperation with the efforts of foreign governments to preserve listed species

§ 9 prohibition on killing, harming, smuggling, or any other "taking" of any endangered species

§ 10 permits and exceptions from the prohibitions in Section 9

§ 11 enforcement mechanisms and penalties for violating the law

§ 18 Secretary of the Interior's duty to provide an annual report to Congress on the cost of measures to preserve each listed species

The ESA charges the Secretary of the Interior with the primary responsibility for implementing the act with respect to most kinds of species. The Secretary, in turn, has delegated that authority to the United States Fish & Wildlife Service (FWS), an agency within the Department of the Interior. An exception to that structure exists for marine species, which are under the jurisdiction of the Secretary of Commerce, who has delegated that statutory authority to the National Marine Fisheries Service (NMFS), which is also known as NOAA-Fisheries. Thus, the FWS and the NMFS are the federal agencies with the most responsibility for enforcing the ESA, though the law also calls upon all federal agencies to support that effort.

---

[1] For an account describing perhaps the unlikeliest foe of the proposed changes tc the ESA, *see* Michael J. Bean, *The Gingrich That Saved the ESA*, ENVTL. FORUM, at 26–32 (1999).

There are, of course, many extremely helpful sources of information about the ESA. The provisions of the law are detailed in MICHAEL J. BEAN & MELANIE J. ROWLAND, THE EVOLUTION OF NATIONAL WILDLIFE LAW 198–276 (3d ed. 1997); RICHARD LITTELL, ENDANGERED SPECIES AND OTHER PROTECTED SPECIES: FEDERAL LAW AND REGULATION (1992); and STANFORD ENVIRONMENTAL LAW SOCIETY, THE ENDANGERED SPECIES ACT (2001). Current information about the law, lists of protected species, and succinct explanations of the ESA's provisions are available at the FWS's web site at http://www.fws.gov/endangered. REBUILDING THE ARK: NEW PERSPECTIVES ON ENDANGERED SPECIES REFORM (Jonathan Adler ed., 2011); and THE ENDANGERED SPECIES ACT AT THIRTY (Dale D. Goble, J. Michael Scott & Frank W. Davis eds. 2006), provide insightful collections of essays on the working of the law and possible reforms. For more popular accounts of the ESA and its implementation, see JOE ROMAN, LISTED: DISPATCHES FROM AMERICA'S ENDANGERED SPECIES ACT (2011); CHARLES C. MANN & MARK L. PLUMMER, NOAH'S CHOICE: THE FUTURE OF ENDANGERED SPECIES (1995).

## I. IDENTIFYING WHICH SPECIES TO PROTECT

The title of the ESA provides an accurate description of the scope of the law. The law only applies to a species that is "endangered" or "threatened." The ESA offers no help to deer and cardinals and dolphins because they are not endangered or threatened with extinction, so a landowner can "take" a deer without threat of federal sanction. More importantly, the ESA protects only those species that have been formally listed as endangered or threatened. The ESA operates to protect species only once they are formally listed, no matter how endangered they may be in fact.

The ESA's other limitation is that it applies to species, not to individual animals or entire ecosystems. The demise of a popular animal such as Ling-Ling, the panda who lived in Washington's National Zoo, can be cause for sadness, but the ESA's sole concern is about the survival of the panda as a species. The only exceptions to the focus on a whole species involve the ESA's protection of "subspecies" and of separate populations of a species. Similarly, while increased understanding of the importance of ecosystems has prompted numerous calls for an endangered ecosystems act, no such statute has yet emerged from Congress.

The ESA protects nearly every kind of species that biologists recognize. Section 3(16) indicates that the Act applies to "fish or wildlife or plants." "Fish or wildlife," in turn, "means any member of the animal kingdom, including without limitation any mammal, fish, bird . . . amphibian, reptile, mollusk, crustacean, arthropod or other invertebrate." ESA § 3(8). And "[t]he term plant means any member of the plant kingdom." ESA § 14. The only exception to the universal coverage of the ESA concerns "a species of the Class Insecta determined by the Secretary to constitute a pest whose protection under the provisions of this chapter would present an overwhelming and overriding risk to man." ESA § 3(6); 50 C.F.R. § 424.02(k).

The ESA contains two procedures for the consideration of whether a species should be listed. The FWS or the NMFS can initiate the process itself based on information collected by agency scientists, as the FWS did for the Illinois cave amphipod and many other species. Alternately, any interested person may petition the appropriate agency to list a species, as illustrated by the thirty environmental groups that petitioned the FWS to list the northern spotted owl in 1987. The same substantive standards apply to the agency's subsequent determination of whether the species is endangered, threatened, or neither.

In 1982, Congress amended Section 4 to establish a specific schedule for the evaluation of petitions to list a species. To the maximum extent practical, the agency must determine whether the petition presents substantial evidence that listing is warranted within 90 days after the petition is filed. The agency then has 12 months to decide whether listing is warranted, unwarranted, or warranted but precluded by higher agency priorities. Once the agency proposes to list the species, it must reach a final decision within 12 months (with a possible six month extension). During that time, the public has 60 days after the proposal to submit comments on the proposed listing, and a public hearing will be held if requested within 45 days of the proposal. At the end of the 12 months, the agency will either list the species or decide to withdraw the proposal to list the species.

Judicial review of any final decision regarding a species is available to any party who can establish standing to sue. Judicial review is also available if the agency fails to make a decision within the statutory period. The courts have generally been sympathetic to the FWS when it fails to act within the statutory deadlines, but they have ordered the agency to comply nonetheless. *See, e.g.*, Biodiversity Legal Foundation v. Badgley, 1999 WL 1042567 (D.Or. 1999) (establishing a tight compliance schedule for findings that were over three years overdue); Biodiversity Legal Foundation v. Babbitt, 63 F. Supp. 2d 31 (D.D.C. 1999) (ordering the FWS to act on a 1997 petition to list the Baird's sparrow). Conversely, the courts have been unwilling to void a decision to list a species when the FWS acted beyond the statutory period. *See* Idaho Farm Bureau Fed'n v. Babbitt, 58 F.3d 1392 (9th Cir. 1995); Endangered Species Comm. of the Bldg. Ind. Ass'n of Southern Cal. v. Babbitt, 852 F. Supp. 32 (D.D.C. 1994).

The ESA's listing procedure has been criticized in recent years both by landowners and developers who believe that many species are listed without adequate scientific studies, and by environmentalists who complain that the federal government has moved much too slowly to add disappearing species to the list. The controversy about the listing process even resulted in a temporary moratorium on the listing of any new species during most of 1995 and the beginning of 1996. The moratorium was supposed to have enabled Congress to address the problems with the listing process, but the absence of a sufficient consensus about which changes were appropriate has left the listing process unchanged since the last congressional amendments to Section 4 in 1982. Congress has not amended the statute, and the Bush Administration has been criticized for listing fewer species and for manipulating the scientific criteria for determining whether or not a species should be listed.

Conservation groups, individuals, and others take advantage of the petition process. In recent years, the Center for Biological Diversity (CBD) has embraced the ESA's listing petitions with special zeal. The CBD and WildEarth Guardians have introduced a new innovation to the listing process by petitioning to list hundreds of species at a time. See CBD, Petition to List 404 Aquatic, Riparian and Wetland Species From The Southeastern United States as Threatened or Endangered Under the Endangered Species Act (Apr. 20, 2010); A Petition to List 206 Critically Imperiled or Imperiled Species in the Mountain-Prairie Region of the United States as Threatened or Endangered Under the Endangered Species Act, 16 U.S.C. §§ 1531 et seq. (July 24, 2007); A Petition to List All Critically Imperiled or Imperiled Species in the Southwest United States as Threatened or Endangered Under the Endangered Species Act, 16 U.S.C. §§ 1531 et seq. (June 18, 2007). The FWS has embraced the listing of multiple species at the same time when those species are part of the same ecosystem. The agency defended that approach when it listed 45 plants, two birds, and one picture-wing fly species that live on the Hawaiian island of Kauai:

> On the island of Kauai, as on most of the Hawaiian Islands, native species that occur in the same habitat types (ecosystems) depend on many of the same biological features and on the successful functioning of that ecosystem to survive. We have therefore organized the species addressed in this final rule by common ecosystem. Although the listing determination for each species is analyzed separately, we have organized the specific analysis for each species within the context of the broader ecosystem in which it occurs to avoid redundancy. In addition, native species that share ecosystems often face a suite of common threat factors that require similar management actions to reduce or eliminate those threats. Effective management of these threat factors often requires implementation of conservation actions at the ecosystem scale to enhance or restore critical ecological processes and provide for long-term viability of those species in their native environment. Thus, by taking this approach, we hope to not only organize this final rule effectively, but also to more effectively focus conservation management efforts on the common threats that occur across these ecosystems, restore ecosystem function for the recovery of

each species, and provide conservation benefits for associated native species, thereby potentially precluding the need to list other species under the Act that occur in these shared ecosystems.

Determination of Endangered Status for 48 Species on Kauai and Designation of Critical Habitat, 75 Fed. Reg. 18960, 18961 (2010).

As of July 2016, a total of 2,270 species are listed under the ESA. There are 1,816 endangered species and 474 threatened species. The list of endangered or threatened species includes 901 flowering plants, 387 mammals, 336 birds, 184 fish, 137 reptiles, 90 clams, 79 insects, 51 snails, 44 amphibians, 31 ferns and allies, 27 crustaceans, 22 corals, 12 arachnids, six conifers and cycads, and two lichens. 1,321 of those species live in the United States; the balance live in other countries throughout the world. Within the United States, Hawaii has the most species with 434, followed by California (305) Alabama (127), Florida (124), and Tennessee (93). Only nine listed species each are found in North Dakota and Rhode Island. (For the latest totals, *see* the FWS web site at http://ecos.fws.gov/tess_public/reports/box-score-report).

## A. ELIGIBILITY FOR LISTING

### Northwest Ecosystem Alliance v. United States Fish and Wildlife Service

United States Court of Appeals for the Ninth Circuit, 2007.
475 F.3d 1136.

■ GOODWIN, CIRCUIT JUDGE:

. . . The definition of the term "species" is at the heart of the instant appeal. The ESA defines "species" to include "any subspecies of fish or wildlife or plants, and any *distinct population segment* of any species of vertebrate fish or wildlife which interbreeds when mature." 16 U.S.C. § 1532(16) (emphasis added). Thus, a population of wildlife that does not constitute a taxonomic species may nevertheless qualify for listing as a [distinct population segment (DPS)]. The statute does not expressly define the term "distinct population segment." The [United States Fish and] Service and the National Marine Fisheries Service ("NMFS") have jointly adopted a policy statement to guide their evaluation of whether a population group should be treated as a DPS. Policy Regarding the Recognition of Distinct Vertebrate Population Segments Under the Endangered Species Act, 61 Fed. Reg. 4722 (Feb. 7, 1996) ("DPS Policy"). The DPS Policy sets forth two factors for consideration: the "[d]iscreteness of the population segment in relation to the remainder of the species to which it belongs," and the "significance of the population segment to the species to which it belongs." Discreteness is satisfied if a population segment is "separated from other populations of the same taxon [here meaning species] as a consequence of physical, physiological, ecological, or behavioral factors," or if a population's boundaries are marked by international borders. Significance, in turn, is analyzed under four nonexclusive factors: (1) whether the population persists in a unique or unusual ecological setting; (2) whether the loss of the population would cause a "significant gap" in the taxon's range; (3) whether the population is the only surviving natural occurrence of a taxon; and (4) whether the population's genetic characteristics are "markedly" different from the rest of the taxon. A population qualifies as a DPS if it is both discrete and significant. If a population is deemed to be a DPS, the inquiry then proceeds to whether it is endangered or threatened.

B. *Western Gray Squirrels in Washington*

*Sciurus griseus*, a subspecies of the western gray squirrel, is the largest native tree squirrel in the Pacific Northwest. Status Review and 12-Month Finding for a Petition To List the Washington Population of the Western Gray Squirrel, 68 Fed. Reg. 34,628, 34,629 (June 10, 2003) ("Final Finding"). Members of the subspecies are "silvery-gray with dark flanks and creamy white underneath." They live in trees, rarely venture into open spaces, and subsist principally on acorn and nuts. Historically, the western gray squirrel was widespread throughout Washington, Oregon, California, and western Nevada. Today, the western gray squirrel is fairly common in California, where it is a regulated game species, with an estimated population of eighteen million. In Oregon, the subspecies is not rare and is legally hunted, but its distribution appears to be much reduced from historical levels. In Nevada, the western gray squirrel is rare and has been classified as a "protected species" under state law.

In Washington, the western gray squirrel once ranged from the Puget Sound to the Columbia River, and from the Cascade Mountains to Lake Chelan. The population has long been separated from the rest of the subspecies by the Columbia River. During the last century, its distribution has been reduced to three geographically isolated populations: the Puget Trough population, the North Cascades population, and the South Cascades population.

The Puget Trough population, which is found near the Puget Sound, lives in a transitional ecological setting. The population's habitat of Oregon white oak woodlands is nestled between upland Douglas-fir forests and prairies. The habitat is wetter, flatter, and contains fewer mast-producing trees than the rest of the subspecies' range. Consequently, the Puget Trough population is more dependent on the Oregon white oak for sustenance than populations in ecologically more diverse habitats. "Although the western squirrel was once common on the partially wooded prairies adjacent to the Puget Sound, the surviving Puget Trough population is now centered on Fort Lewis," a military reservation. "During intensive surveys in 1998 and 1999, only 6 western grey squirrels . . . were detected in over 4,000 hours of survey effort."

Some researchers have concluded that the Puget Trough population is "at a high risk of extirpation."

The North Cascades population is found in Chelan and Okanogan Counties. Unlike the Puget Trough, the North Cascades habitat lacks oaks, the main source of winter foods for the western gray squirrel in most of its range. Instead, the North Cascades population subsists on seeds and nuts produced by pine trees, big leaf maples, and English walnut trees. A survey in 2000 detected only three remnants out of the eighty-nine nests recorded in a 1996 survey, and found eighteen previously unreported nests. The reduced number of nests suggests a corresponding population decline.

The South Cascades population, which constitutes the largest remaining population of western gray squirrels in Washington, is found in Skamania, Klickitat, and Yakima counties. One study has found western gray squirrels in Klickitat to have substantially larger body measurements than elsewhere in the subspecies' range. The study also concluded that the Klickitat population have substantially larger home range sizes and more nests per squirrel than elsewhere. Surveys in 2000 and 2001 produced population density estimates of 0.08–0.13 squirrel per hectare in the Klickitat Wildlife Area, as compared with 1.37 per hectare in Lake County, California, or with 2.47 per hectare in Yosemite Valley in California.

[In 2001, the Northwest Ecosystem Alliance, Center for Biological Diversity, and Tahoma Audubon Society (collectively, the "Alliance") petitioned the FWS for an emergency listing of the Washington population of the western grey squirrel as endangered or threatened. "An early draft decision prepared by the Service's staff scientists recommended listing the Washington population as an endangered DPS. However, the Service ultimately denied the petition in a June 2003 decision published in the Federal Register. Final Finding, 68 Fed. Reg. at 34,628. The Service determined that the Washington population was not significant, under the DPS Policy, to the taxon to which it belonged." The Alliance then sought judicial review, and the district court granted summary judgment for the FWS. On appeal, the Ninth Circuit held that the DPS Policy was a reasonable interpretation of the ESA entitled to judicial deference, so it proceeded to consider whether the FWS properly applied that policy to the petition to list the squirrel.]

C. *Whether the Service's Denial of the Petition Was Arbitrary and Capricious*

Applying the DPS Policy, the Service found that western gray squirrels in Washington constitute a discrete population, but are not significant to the taxon. It therefore denied the petition. The Alliance vigorously challenges the Service's determination on the "significance" prong.

We note that the Service's internal draft finding of May 16, 2003 recommended granting the petitioned action. The Alliance complains that the Service's final finding reached the opposite conclusion without citing any new data. However, the Service may change its mind after internal deliberation. The only question before us is whether the Service, in reaching its ultimate finding, "considered the relevant factors and articulated a rational connection between the facts found and the choices made."

The DPS Policy sets forth the following four factors to be used to determine a population's significance to its taxon:

> 1. Persistence of the discrete population segment in an ecological setting unusual or unique for the taxon,
>
> 2. Evidence that loss of the discrete population segment would result in a significant gap in the range of a taxon,
>
> 3. Evidence that the discrete population represents the only surviving natural occurrence of a taxon that may be more abundant elsewhere as an introduced population outside its historic range, or
>
> 4. Evidence that the discrete population segment differs markedly from other populations of the species in its genetic characteristics.

61 Fed. Reg. at 4725. The Service found that the first, second, and fourth factors warranted analysis and that none of those factors established the Washington gray squirrels' significance to their taxon. The Alliance argues that the Service's findings on those factors were arbitrary and capricious, and not supported by the scientific evidence in the record.

1. *Ecological Setting*

First, the Alliance challenges the Service's finding that the North Cascades and the Puget Trough do not constitute unusual or unique ecological settings for the taxon. The North Cascades habitat is notable for its lack of oak trees, which are the main source of winter foods in most of the sub-species' range. Gray squirrels in the North Cascades, as noted, subsist primarily on the seeds of pine trees. The Alliance believes that the lack of oak trees compels the finding that the North Cascades habitat is a unique ecological setting. However, the Service offered reasonable grounds for its contrary conclusion. While recognizing that oak trees are absent from the North Cascades, the Service emphasized that "throughout their range, western gray squirrels consume a variety of types of tree seeds, including many conifer species." In other words, the North Cascades habitat is not unique, because the squirrels there consume conifer tree seeds just as they do in a variety of habitats. That reasoning is not arbitrary or capricious.

The Alliance also attacks the Service's finding on the Puget Trough habitat. Unlike the North Cascades, the Puget Trough is notable for its concentration of oak trees, which makes the Puget Trough's vegetation more homogenous than elsewhere in the subspecies' range. In contrast, "[e]lsewhere in the subspecies' range, Oregon white oaks occur in communities having a wider range of mast-producing tree species, including a variety of oak and pine species." While recognizing the concentration of oak in the Puget Trough habitat, the Service concluded that the difference between the Puget Trough and other habitats "are not so great" as to constitute a "unique or unusual ecological setting for the western gray squirrel." Although the Service could have explained its reasoning in more detail, it is clear in context that the Service had in mind the widespread persistence of the Oregon white oak throughout the subspecies' range. Because it is undisputed that Oregon white oaks are not unique to the Puget Trough habitat, the Service's conclusion was not arbitrary or capricious.

2. *Significant Gap in the Range*

The Alliance also disputes the Service's finding that a hypothetical loss of the entire Washington population would not cause a significant gap in the range of the taxon. For purposes of the "gap in the range" analysis, the term "significant" has "its 'commonly understood meaning,' which is 'important.' "

The Service's discussion of this factor is not a paragon of clarity. Nonetheless, the Service's reasoning can be discerned with careful reading. At the outset, the Service noted that Washington gray squirrels constitute an isolated, peripheral population at the northern portion of the subspecies' range. As a general matter, peripheral populations often face ecological circumstances not found elsewhere in the taxon's range, and may consequently develop distinctive morphological, behavioral, or genetic characteristics through adaptation to local conditions. The Service then considered whether the Washington population had developed such distinctive qualities.

First, the Service considered evidence suggesting that Washington gray squirrels may be more shy and secretive—as they are rarely seen and often flee from human observers—than their counterparts in Oregon and California. The Service found the evidence to be indeterminate. The Service noted that the evidence was anecdotal, and that there are no comparative studies on elusive behavior across the range of the species. The Service also cited evidence that secretive behavior was not unique to Washington squirrels, because similar behavior had also been observed among Oregon squirrels. The Service further stated that even if such behavior does indeed characterize Washington squirrels, there was no evidence that it was caused by adaptation to a peripheral habitat. In the Service's view, behavioral differences, if any, could simply be attributable to the larger populations south of the Columbia River and their adaptability and proximity to urban areas.

The Service next considered evidence on morphology and home range size. A study of gray squirrels in Klickitat County, part of the

South Cascades population, found them to be significantly larger in body dimension than elsewhere in the subspecies' range. The same study also found that the gray squirrels in Klickitat County had substantially larger home range size when compared with elsewhere in the subspecies' range. The Service, however, declined to credit the results of the study. The Service noted that the study was based on a small sample size—which the record showed to be fewer than fifty squirrels—in a small area of Klickitat county. The Service further theorized that variations in measurement methods, rather than actual differences, might account for the observed results in home range size. Even if the results were accurate, the Service could discern no basis for attributing them to the peripheral location of Washington gray squirrels.

The Service ultimately determined that, while a hypothetical loss of the Washington population would "represent a serious reduction in the species['] range," it would not be of biological and ecological significance to the taxon as a whole. Put differently, the Service believed that any gap caused by the loss of the Washington population would not be significant because the population lacks biologically distinctive traits.

The Alliance complains that the Service dismissed evidence purely on the basis of scientific uncertainty. The ESA instructs the Service to make its determinations "solely on the basis of the best scientific and commercial data available," 16 U.S.C. § 1533(b)(1)(A), and the Service may not ignore evidence simply because it falls short of absolute scientific certainty. *See* Defenders of Wildlife v. Babbitt, 958 F. Supp. 670, 679–80 (D.D.C. 1997) (Service applied wrong legal standard in dismissing scientific evidence because it was not "conclusive"); Center for Biological Diversity v. Lohn, 296 F. Supp. 2d 1223, 1236–40 (W. D. Wash. 2003) (NMFS was capricious and arbitrary in relying on outdated taxonomic classifications which the best available science showed to be incorrect). We are unpersuaded that the Service was justified in rejecting the secretive behavior evidence and Klickitat County study solely because they were anecdotal. Of course a rigorous, large-scale study of Washington gray squirrels' behavior and morphology would be preferable, but in the absence of such a study, credible anecdotal evidence represents the "best scientific . . . data *available*" and cannot be ignored. Nevertheless, we hold that the Service did not arbitrarily and capriciously fail to find a significant gap on the basis of such data. Similarly shy and secretive behavior has been documented among Oregon squirrels, and the Klickitat County study was limited geographically to a subset of one of the three Washington habitats of the gray squirrel. While crediting the anecdotal evidence, the Service could have concluded that the extirpation of squirrels whose behavior is not unique and whose larger size is known to exist only in a single county would not create a significant gap in the taxon.

The Alliance further challenges the Service's determination that a "serious reduction" in the subspecies' range does not amount to a "significant gap" due to the absence of biologically distinctive traits in the Washington population. The Alliance analogizes the "significant gap" factor in the DPS Policy to 16 U.S.C. § 1532(6), which defines an "endangered species" as a species that is "in danger of extinction throughout all or a significant portion of its range." We have recognized that a species can be considered extinct throughout a significant portion of its range "if there are major geographical areas in which it is no longer viable but once was." Defenders of Wildlife v. Norton, 258 F.3d 1136, 1145 (9th Cir. 2001). It does not follow that a serious reduction in the western gray squirrel's geographic range similarly suffices to satisfy the "significant gap" factor. Unlike § 1532(6), the "significance" inquiry under the DPS Policy is not limited to geographic factors. On its face, the DPS Policy considers ecological, historical, and genetic factors in addition to geography. Nothing in the DPS Policy or in the ESA limits the Service's significant gap inquiry to geographic factors.

The Alliance counters that previous administrative applications of the DPS Policy have found "significant gaps" in the range of taxa solely on account of geographic factors. The Alliance asserts that the Service's current refusal to do the same for Washington gray squirrels is arbitrary and capricious. The Alliance cites four prior administrative decisions. Three actually considered biological factors as part of their "significant gap" analyses.[11] Only one of the four relied solely on geography to find that the population's extirpation would cause a significant gap.[12] In practice, the Service has regarded the "significant gap" inquiry as a flexible one, and has considered various non-geographic factors on different occasions. Here, the Service has articulated a reasonable basis—the Washington population's lack of biologically and ecologically distinguishing features—for its conclusion that the loss of the population would not cause a significant gap. We cannot say that the Service's analysis, which is in fact substantially more detailed than those cited by the Alliance, is an arbitrary and capricious departure from prior practice.

---

[11] *See* Final Endangered Status for a Distinct Population Segment of Smalltooth Sawfish (Pristis pectinata) in the United States, 68 Fed. Reg. 15,674, 15,675–76 (Apr. 1, 2003) (finding that loss of U.S. smalltooth sawfish population would create a significant gap partly because the population "comprises an important component of the sawfishes' remaining global biological diversity"); Final Rule to List the Columbia Basin Distinct Population Segment of the Pygmy Rabbit (Brachylagus idahoensis) as Endangered, 68 Fed. Reg. 10,388, 10,397–98 (Mar. 5, 2003) (finding that loss of Columbia Basin pygmy rabbits would constitute a significant gap partly because the population is experiencing increased "directional selection" and "exhibiting genetic consequences of long-term isolation"); Final Endangered Status for a Distinct Population Segment of Anadromous Atlantic Salmon (Salmo salar) in the Gulf of Maine, 65 Fed. Reg. 69,459, 69,460 (Nov. 17, 2000) (finding that loss of the Gulf of Maine population of Atlantic salmon would "negatively affect the genetic resources of Atlantic salmon as a whole because it would contribute to further range reduction").

[12] Determination of Threatened Status for the Northern Population of the Copperbelly Water Snake, 62 Fed. Reg. 4183, 4184 (January 29, 1997) ("The loss of the peripheral, isolated, northern population [of copperbelly water snakes] is considered as significant as characterized under policy, as it would result in a significant reduction in the range of the taxon.").

3. *Marked Genetic Differences*

The third factor the Service considered was whether the Washington population's genetic characteristics differ "markedly" from the remainder of the subspecies' range. "Under the DPS Policy, 'markedly' is given its common meaning, which in this context is 'appreciably.' " The parties do not dispute that some genetic differences exist between Washington gray squirrels and the rest of the taxon in Oregon and California. The question is whether their genetic profiles differ "markedly."

The Service based its decision on a peer-reviewed study of genetic differences among gray squirrel populations in Washington, Oregon, and California. The study was carried out by Kenneth I. Warheit, a senior research scientist with the Washington Department of Fish and Wildlife. Dr. Warheit conducted microsatellite DNA analysis on samples from 3 California gray squirrels, 24 Oregon squirrels, and 101 Washington squirrels. He analyzed the samples' alleles, which are series of two or more different genes that occupy the same position on a chromosome. He found that each population in California and Oregon showed at least three "private alleles" that are present only in that population. In contrast, no Washington population had private alleles. In other words, "all alleles present in each of the Washington population are also present in at least one of the Oregon or California populations." At the same time, he found reduced genetic diversity in the Washington populations compared with Oregon and California, and "considerably more genetic differentiation between Washington and Oregon or California[ ] than there is between Oregon and California populations." He then conducted mitochondrial control region sequence analysis on a subset of 67 squirrels. He determined that no haplotype—which is the set of one allele of each gene, and which comprises the genetic constitution of an individual or taxon—was shared across the Columbia river. Mitochondrial DNA analysis also demonstrated that the Washington population had substantially less genetic diversity. Dr. Warheit found only 3 haplotypes from 40 Washington squirrels, compared with 14 haplotypes from 27 California and Oregon squirrels.

After reviewing Dr. Warheit's study, the Service concluded that "[w]hile there is clearly some genetic information that shows that the Washington populations are different from other populations . . . at this time we do not believe them to be markedly so." The Service explained that evidence of genetic differentiation is "counterbalanced" by the fact that the Washington population has no private alleles, "that some haplotypes in Washington are more closely related to haplotypes in Oregon than other haplotypes in Washington," and "the fact that the Washington populations . . . show reduced genetic diversity." The Service further explained that the results of the study may have been confounded by "the effects of small population size and the consequent inbreeding and genetic drift" in Washington. The Service also noted that the study used a small sample size for the California population.

The Alliance contends that the presence of unique haplotypes in the Washington population is sufficient to establish marked genetic differentiation, notwithstanding the fact that the population has no private alleles. However, we must defer to the agency's interpretation of complex scientific data. We decline the Alliance's invitation to impose our own view on whether alleles or haplotypes constitute the best markers of genetic differentiation.

Next, the Alliance maintains that reduced genetic diversity in Washington is itself evidence of the population's genetic distinctiveness. Nothing in the DPS Policy or in the ESA compels the Service to focus on relative genetic diversity, rather than on the presence or absence of unique alleles, as the best indicators of genetic differentiation. As an internal Service memorandum explained, because "there was no evidence from the analysis that [Washington] populations possessed unique microsatellite alleles . . . most of the differentiation [between Washington and the rest of the range] comes from reduced numbers of alleles" in Washington. Whether the Service was correct to focus on the alleles is beside the point; interpretation of complex genetic data falls within the domain of the Service's scientific discretion, to which we must defer so long as the Service has articulated a rational basis for its conclusion.

Lastly, the Alliance argues that whether some haplotypes in Washington are closer to haplotypes in Oregon than to others in Washington is irrelevant for the question of overall genetic differences between Washington and Oregon. This argument ignores the inference that if all of the Washington haplotypes were closer to each other than to haplotypes in California and Oregon, the overall genetic profile of the Washington population would be more distinct.

Because the Service has articulated reasoned connections between the record and its conclusion, its genetic analysis was not arbitrary or capricious.

---

## QUESTIONS AND DISCUSSION

**1.** Why would the law allow a truly distinct population segment of the western gray squirrel species to be listed as endangered even if there are still many western gray squirrels living elsewhere? Michael Bean and Melanie Rowland offered one answer when they stated that "[a]voiding local extirpation of a species is desirable not only because a series of local extirpations frequently leads to endangerment of the species as a whole, but also because of the ecological, recreational, aesthetic, and other values populations provide in their localities." Bean & Rowland, *supra*, at 200. By contrast, when federal officials threatened to remove a beaver that had been eating the cherry trees surrounding Washington's Tidal Basin, Idaho's Representative Helen Chenoweth mockingly suggested that "[t]his distinct population segment of the Rodentia family must be saved." 145 CONG. REC. H1840 (daily ed. Apr. 12, 1999).

Two attorneys have argued that "[d]espite the warnings of potential abuse and the congressional mandate that the 'distinct population segment' concept be used sparingly, federal agencies have nonetheless used the DPS concept to substantially increase [Evolutionary Significant Units] ESU listings," especially among the salmon species in the Pacific northwest. Leslie Marshall Lewallen & Russell C. Brooks, Alsea Valley Alliance v. Evans *and the Meaning of "Species" Under the Endangered Species Act: A Return to Congressional Intent*, 25 ENVTL. L. 731, 742 (2002). The courts are beginning to have more occasions to review the listing of a distinct population segment of a species. For example, the Ninth Circuit reversed such a listing in National Association of Home Builders v. Norton, 340 F.3d 835 (9th Cir. 2003). There the FWS listed the tiny population of ferruginous pygmy-owls that lives in Arizona as distinct from the somewhat more abundant population that lives in Mexico. The court deferred to the agency's judgment that the different conservation status of the owls in Arizona and Mexico justified the identification of the populations as "discrete." But the court further held that the agency failed to explain why the discrete Arizona population was "significant," as required by the FWS's policy governing distinct population segments. In particular, the court concluded that "the Listing Rule does not contain evidence of genetic variability between the Arizona and northwestern Mexico pygmy-owls," *id.* at 847, and it held that the FWS failed to "find significance to the taxon as a whole, not just to the United States." *Id.* at 852.

**2.** How do we even know that western gray squirrel is a "species?" The ESA does not provide much help in determining what constitutes a "species." The standard scientific taxonomy dates from eighteenth century Swedish botanist Carl Linnaeus, who developed a hierarchy that now progresses from kingdom to phylum to class to order to family to genus to species. The western gray squirrel, for example, is a member of the animal kingdom, the mammal class, the Rodentia order, the Sciuridae family, the Sciurus genus, and the griseus species—with the latter two designations comprising the Latin name of the species, *Pseudemys alabamensis*. What that neat formula omits is any indication of what features support the characterization of the Western gray squirrel as a distinct species from any other type of squirrel. The prevailing explanation adheres to the definition of a species offered by Harvard evolutionary biologist Ernst Mayr: "A species is a reproductive community of populations, reproductively isolated from other populations, that occupies a specific niche in nature." ERNST MAYR, THE GROWTH OF BIOLOGICAL THOUGHT 273 (1982). But that approach still leaves ample room for debate about the nature of a "community of populations," the meaning of reproductive isolation, and the scope of the relevant niche in nature. As Professor Kevin Hill has written, "Ambiguity is inherent in the taxonomic classification of endangered species." Kevin D. Hill, *What Do We Mean By Species?*, 20 B.C. ENVTL. AFF. L. REV. 239, 257 (1993). Even accounting for that ambiguity, Hill faults "the drafters of the ESA and frequently the Fish and Wildlife Service" because they "seem to have a very simplistic view of what constitutes a species. Quite often, under the Act, species are treated as discrete entities under a traditional typological approach emphasizing physical characteristics. Thus, a species is defined if it has a particular kind of shape, size, color, or other attribute. The purpose of many endangered species programs was to preserve this particular snapshot of present day characteristics, ignoring the changes caused by evolutionary adaptation." *Id.* at 253.

Courts have been reluctant to overturn the FWS's decisions concerning a species. "Two fish, or not two fish? That is the question" considered by the Eleventh Circuit in Alabama-Tombigbee Rivers Coalition v. Kempthorne, 477 F.3d 1250 (11th Cir. 2007). Besides paraphrasing Shakespeare, the court quoted popular author Bill Bryson, who wrote that taxonomy "is described sometimes as a science and sometimes as an art, but really it's a battleground." *Id.* at 1250 (quoting BILL BRYSON, A SHORT HISTORY OF NEARLY EVERYTHING 437 (2003)). In the case itself, the Court deferred to the FWS's decision that the Alabama sturgeon is a distinct species from the shovelnose sturgeon. "Given the nature of taxonomy," the court explained, "it would be surprising if there were not some disagreement about the proper classification of the Alabama sturgeon, but disagreement in the field does not preclude agency decision making." *Id.* at 1260. The Eleventh Circuit reached a similar conclusion in United States v. Guthrie, 50 F.3d 936 (11th Cir. 1995), which upheld the treatment of the Alabama red-bellied turtle as a separate species "despite the absence of total agreement within the scientific community." *Id.* at 946.

**3.** Why should we try to save the squirrel from extinction? More practically, what can the government do to halt the tide toward its extinction? If it were feasible to eliminate the threats, should we do so regardless of cost? If not, how much is too much to spend?

**4.** The ESA defines "species" to include "any subspecies of fish or wildlife or plants." 16 U.S.C. § 1532(16). "Subspecies" is undefined in the statute and imprecisely defined elsewhere. *See, e.g.*, EDWARD O. WILSON, THE DIVERSITY OF LIFE 406 (1992) (definition of a "subspecies" is "[s]ubdivision of a species. Usually defined narrowly as a geographical race: a population or series of populations occupying a discrete range and differing genetically from other geographical races of the same species."). The protection of subspecies has potentially sweeping consequences. The Delhi Sands Flower-Loving Fly is a subspecies; so is the northern spotted owl whose listing resulted in tremendous controversies in the Pacific northwest.

Why protect subspecies? That question elicited contrasting responses during the 1995 congressional hearings on the ESA. Opponents of the listing of subspecies argued that they need not be protected unless their survival was essential to the survival of the species as a whole. At a minimum, they argued, "[t]he sub-species or sub-sub-species of kangaroo rat should not receive the same treatment as the California condor." *Endangered Species Act—Vancouver, Washington: Hearing Before the Task Force on Endangered Species of the House Resources Comm.*, 104th Cong., 1st Sess. 65 (1995) (testimony of Barbara Tilly, Chairman, Chelan County Public Utility District Board of Commissioners). Secretary of the Interior Bruce Babbitt answered that "[s]hould a subspecies begin to decline, this may be a warning that the species as a whole may be in danger," and that an early response to that trend can improve the likelihood and decrease the cost of protection efforts. He added that the existence of genetically distinct subspecies "improve the ability of the species as a whole to survive." *Endangered Species Act: Washington, DC—Part III: Hearing Before the Task Force on Endangered Species of the House Resources Comm.*, 104th Cong., 1st Sess. 261–62 (1995).

**5.** The Ninth Circuit accepted the FWS's interpretation of the scientific evidence regarding the western gray squirrels. The ESA, in turn, provides that science should be the determinative factor in deciding whether to list a species as endangered or threatened. *See* ESA § 4(b)(1)(A) (stating that the Secretary of the Interior's decision whether to list a species must be made "solely on the basis of the best scientific and commercial data available at the time the decision is made"). The problem posed in this circumstance—and in many others—is how to respond to scientific uncertainty regarding the status of a species. The scientific credibility of ESA listing decisions has been buffeted from all sides.

On the one hand, note that the FWS rejected the advice of its staff scientists, who would have listed the Washington population of western gray squirrels as an endangered DPS. In recent years, the FWS has faced relentless criticism for allegedly allowing political concerns to influence scientific judgments. According to one report prepared by the Center for Biological Diversity, "political appointees in the Department of Interior . . . have slowed decision-making with multiple reviews and edits and bullied agency scientists to reverse their conclusions." Noah Greenwald, Politicizing Extinction: The Bush Administration's Dangerous Approach to Endangered Wildlife 7 (2007) (report from the Center for Biological Diversity). The report accused Department officials of reversing or otherwise interfering with the recommendations of FWS biologists involving the Gunnison sage grouse and "greater sage grouse, Mexican garter snake, marbled murrelet, delta smelt, wolverine, trumpeter swan, Gunnison's prairie dog, white-tailed prairie dog, and roundtail chub." *Id.* The senior Interior Department official overseeing the implementation of the ESA resigned in the face of allegations that she had manipulated the scientific studies of FWS biologists in order to prevent new species from being listed.

On the other hand, the opponents of ESA listings complain that species are listed without scientific justification. The ESA does not require the government or the party requesting the listing of a species to conduct any research concerning the status of a species. Instead, the listing decision must be made with whatever scientific information is available. The quality of the scientific evidence supporting ESA listing decisions has been controversial in recent years. For example, a proposal to list four California plants provoked objections that the scientific data supporting the listing "was either inaccurate, insufficient, inconsistent, erroneous, unsubstantiated, unverified, unjustified, based only on biased opinions in favor of listing the species, not peer-reviewed," collected only during drought years when the plants would not be present, and collected by illegal trespassing. *See* Determination of Threatened Status for Four Plants from the Foothills of the Sierra Nevada Mountains in California, 63 Fed. Reg. 49022, 49025 (1998). The FWS has responded that the statute "does not require us to possess detailed or extensive information about the general biology of a species or to make an actual determination of the causes for the species' status to make a listing determination." Final Rule to List the Flatwoods Salamander as a Threatened Species, 64 Fed. Reg. 15691, 15695 (1999).

The courts have rejected all attempts to require additional scientific research prior to the determination of whether a species should be listed. In an effort to dispel the concerns about the adequacy of the scientific evidence used to list species, the FWS and the NMFS have adopted a scientific peer review policy that promises to "[s]olicit the expert opinions of three appropriate and independent specialists regarding pertinent scientific or commercial data and assumptions relating to the taxonomy, population models, and supportive biological and ecological information for species under consideration for listing." Notice of Interagency Cooperative Policy for Peer Review in Endangered Species Act Activities, 59 Fed. Reg. 34270 (1994). Nonetheless, some members of Congress continue to insist that the listing process must be informed by better science.

## B. DETERMINING WHETHER A SPECIES IS ENDANGERED OR THREATENED

### Tucson Herpetological Society v. Salazar

United States Court of Appeals for the Ninth Circuit, 2009.
566 F.3d 870.

■ TASHIMA, CIRCUIT JUDGE:

Conservation organizations and individual biologists (collectively "Plaintiffs") contend that the Secretary of the Interior's (the "Secretary") decision to withdraw a rule proposing that the flat-tailed horned lizard (the "lizard") be listed as a threatened species is contrary to the requirements of the Endangered Species Act ("ESA" or the "Act"), 16 U.S.C. § 1531 *et seq.*, and the Administrative Procedure Act ("APA"), 5 U.S.C. § 706. They appeal from the district court's order granting summary judgment in favor of the Secretary. . . .

#### STATUTORY BACKGROUND

The ESA provides "a means whereby the ecosystems upon which endangered species and threatened species depend may be conserved." 16 U.S.C. § 1531(b). In service of this goal, the Act directs the Secretary to maintain a list of threatened and endangered species, and defines the phrase "endangered species" as "any species which is in danger of extinction throughout all or a significant portion of its range." *Id.* § 1532(6). A threatened species is one "which is likely to become an endangered species within the foreseeable future throughout all or a significant portion of its range." *Id.* § 1532(20). "The term 'species' includes any subspecies of fish or wildlife or plants, and any distinct population segment of any species of vertebrate fish or wildlife which interbreeds when mature." *Id.* § 1532(16). The Secretary has delegated his authority to administer the ESA to the Fish and Wildlife Service ("FWS"). 50 C.F.R. § 402.01(b).

The ESA requires the Secretary to consider five factors when determining whether a species is threatened or endangered: (1) the present or threatened destruction, modification, or curtailment of the species' range; (2) overutilization for commercial, recreational, scientific, or educational purposes; (3) disease or predation; (4) the inadequacy of existing regulatory mechanisms; and (5) other natural or man-made factors affecting the species' continued existence. 16 U.S.C. § 1533(a)(1); 50 C.F.R. § 424.11(c). The Secretary must reach a listing determination "solely on the basis of the best scientific and commercial data available to him." 16 U.S.C. § 1533(b)(1)(A).

## FACTUAL AND PROCEDURAL BACKGROUND

The lizard at issue in this case is "a small, cryptically colored iguanid . . . that is restricted to flats and valleys of the western Sonoran desert." 58 Fed. Reg. 62,624, 62,625 (Nov. 29, 1993). Its natural habitat stretches across parts of southern California, southwestern Arizona, and northern Mexico. In California, the lizard can be found in the Coachella Valley, the west side of the Salton Sea and Imperial Valley, and the east side of the Imperial Valley. In Arizona, the lizard can be found in the Yuma Desert south of the Gila River and west of the Gila and Butler Mountains. 68 Fed. Reg. 331, 332 (Jan. 3, 2003). Very little is known about the lizard's range in Mexico, but it has been observed south of the California border in Baja California, south of Arizona from the international border to the Pinacate Region, and around Puerto Penasco and Bahia de San Jorge, Sonora.

*A flat horned lizard*

FWS estimates that man-made factors are responsible for the destruction of 1,103,201 acres of the lizard's estimated 4,875,624-acre historic range. 71 Fed. Reg. 36,745, 36,749–51 (Jun. 28, 2006). Agricultural and urban development have resulted in fragmentation of the lizard's remaining habitat. 68 Fed. Reg. at 332. Fragmentation creates isolated subpopulations that, because of their reduced size, have an increased probability of extinction. 58 Fed. Reg. 62,624, 62,626–27 (Nov. 29, 1993). Remaining lizard habitat in the United States can be divided into four distinct geographical sections: the Coachella Valley, west side of the Imperial Valley/Salton Sea, and east side of the Imperial Valley in California, and the Yuma Valley in Arizona. 68 Fed. Reg. at 332. . . .

The Secretary first proposed listing the lizard as threatened in 1993, citing documented and anticipated population declines. *See* 58 Fed. Reg. at 62,624. The proposed listing identified urban expansion, off-highway vehicle ("OHV") use, energy development, and military activities as the primary threats to the lizard's remaining habitat, and concluded that three of the five statutory listing criteria had been satisfied. *Id.* at 62,625–28.

Upon proposing a species for listing, the ESA requires the Secretary to make a final determination (or formally extend the time for making a final decision) on whether to list within twelve months. *See* 16 U.S.C. § 1533(b)(6)(A). That time period lapsed without the Secretary issuing a final decision, and Defenders of Wildlife, along with several of the plaintiffs in this action, sued the Secretary to compel a determination on whether or not to list the lizard. In response to a court order requiring a final decision within sixty days, the Secretary issued a rule withdrawing the 1993 proposed listing (the "1997 withdrawal"). 62 Fed. Reg. 37,852 (July 15, 1997).

The 1997 withdrawal relied, in part, on the adoption of the Flat-Tailed Horned Lizard Conservation Agreement (the "Conservation Agreement"). *Id.* at 37,853–55. In 1997, seven state and federal agencies jointly entered into the Conservation Agreement, and agreed to implement a management strategy to address threats to the lizard's remaining habitat on public lands. *Id.* The parties to the Conservation Agreement agreed to take steps aimed at "reducing threats to the species, stabilizing the species' populations, and maintaining its ecosystem." In addition to reliance on the Conservation Agreement, the 1997 withdrawal concluded that population trend data did not conclusively demonstrate significant declines, and that many of the threats cited in the 1993 proposed listing had either been reduced or eliminated. *See id.* at 37,859–60. The Secretary also found that known threats to lizard habitat on private lands did not warrant listing, because adequate habitat existed on public lands to ensure the species' continued viability. *See id.* at 37,860.

[Defenders sought judicial review of 1997 withdrawal. The district court granted summary judgment for the Secretary, but the Ninth Circuit reversed because the Secretary had failed to consider whether the lost and threatened portions of the lizard's range amounted to a "significant portion" of the species' overall range. Defenders of Wildlife v. Norton, 258 F.3d 1136, 1138–40, 1145 (9th Cir. 2001). On remand, FWS again issued a rule withdrawing the proposed listing (the "2003 withdrawal"), but the district court held that the agency failed to comply with the Ninth Circuit's decision in *Defenders* because it "assumed without explanation that large swaths of lost habitat were of no significance at all." Finally, in 2006, after another round of public comment, the Secretary again issued a rule withdrawing the proposed listing (the "2006 withdrawal"), explaining that the lizard's lost range was not "significant" within the meaning of the ESA. 71 Fed. Reg. 36,745 (June 28, 2006). The district court granted summary judgment in favor of the Secretary's 2006 decision, and Plaintiffs appealed.]

## DISCUSSION

### I. *The Lizard's Lost Historical Range*

#### A. The Secretary's Compliance with *Defenders*

. . . The Secretary was directed first to quantify the lizard's historical range in order to establish a "temporal baseline," and then to determine whether the lost habitat, measured against that baseline, amounts to a "significant portion" of the species' overall range.

. . . In the 2006 withdrawal, the Secretary offered a set of reasons for discounting the significance of the lizard's lost historical range (approximately 23% of the species' baseline range). He explained that: (1) lizard populations persist across most of the species' current range despite habitat loss and fragmentation; (2) much of the lizard's lost habitat was converted to agricultural, commercial, and residential development long ago; (3) the lost portions of the lizard's range do not carry any special biological or genetic importance for the species as a whole; and (4) lost historical habitat represents a relatively small portion of the lizard's baseline range. *See* 71 Fed. Reg. at 36,751.

Plaintiffs are correct that the Secretary's stated reasons all rely, to varying degrees, on the premise that lizard populations persist throughout most of the species' remaining range. For example, the 2006 withdrawal states that lost portions of the lizard's range are not necessary for the preservation of gene flow because the isolated lizard populations outside of the Coachella Valley "are large enough to be self-sustaining." 71 Fed. Reg. at 36,748. Elsewhere, the Secretary finds that the habitat lost early in the 20th Century (the majority of the lizard's overall lost range) is not significant because the species' "continued persistence over a span of nearly 100 years is a strong indication that the species will continue to persist into the foreseeable future despite the loss of historical habitat." *Id.* at 36,751.

It is insufficient . . . to point to one area or class of areas where lizard populations persist to support a finding that threats to the species elsewhere are not significant; the ESA requires a more thorough explanation. Plaintiffs argue that this is precisely what the Secretary has done here.

The Secretary's explanations, however, exhibit more nuance than Plaintiffs acknowledge. Although he places considerable weight on the lizard's persistence throughout most of its remaining range, reliance on persistence is not *per se* inconsistent with *Defenders*. The 2006 withdrawal analyzes the lizard's lost habitat in a site-specific manner, and cites lizard persistence to corroborate its conclusion that the lost portions of the lizard's range do not provide any unique or critical function for the well-being of the species. Moreover, the Secretary offers two supplemental reasons that do not depend on persistence alone. He cites to a study of migration between isolated lizard populations and reasonably concludes that the lizard's lost range does not represent a critical pathway for maintenance of genetic diversity. 71 Fed. Reg. at 36,750. He also notes that most of the lizard's lost range was converted to agricultural or commercial uses decades ago, is generally not recoverable, and is thus of limited significance to the lizard's long-term survival. *Id.* at 36,751. Taking these reasons together, and according the Secretary due interpretive deference, we conclude that his understanding of the phrase "significant portion of its range" does not run afoul of *Defenders*.

B. Is the Lizard Persisting Throughout Most of its Range?

The next question is whether the administrative record supports the Secretary's finding that lizard populations outside of the Coachella Valley are persisting. An action will be deemed arbitrary and capricious where the agency offers an explanation for an action "that runs counter to the evidence before the agency, or is so implausible that it could not be ascribed to a difference in view or the product of agency expertise." Motor Vehicle Mfrs. Ass'n v. State Farm Mut. Auto. Ins. Co., 463 U.S. 29, 43 (1983). "While our deference to the agency is significant, we may not defer to an agency decision that 'is without substantial basis in fact.'" Sierra Club v. U.S. EPA, 346 F.3d 955, 961 (9th Cir. 2003) (quoting Federal Power Comm'n v. Florida Power & Light Co., 404 U.S. 453, 463 (1972)).

The Secretary argues that FWS relied on population studies to conclude that the lizard "is persisting in the vast majority of its range." Yet, in the 2003 withdrawal, the Secretary reported that "[i]nformation concerning population dynamics of flat-tailed horned lizard populations is limited and inconclusive." 68 Fed. Reg. at 332; *see also* Teresa Woods & Steve Morey, *Uncertainty and the Endangered Species Act*, 83 IND. L.J. 529, 531–32 (2008) (explaining the difficulty in carrying out population studies from which inferences about extinction risk can be made, given budgetary constraints and short regulatory and court-ordered time frames for decision-making). Apparently, the Secretary infers from the uncertainty in the population studies that lizard populations "remain[ ] viable throughout most of [the lizard's] current extant range." 71 Fed. Reg. at 36,751. This conclusion is conceptually distinct from and relied on different evidence than the Secretary's determination that the species does not face significant *threats* in most of its current range. The latter conclusion is premised on an estimate of existing and potential threats to lizard *habitat*, existing management plans that mitigate those threats, and a variety of other risk assessment factors. The persistence finding, however, relies solely on the conclusion that lizard populations are in fact viable and stable throughout most of the species' current range. It is this conclusion that ultimately requires reversal.

If the science on population size and trends is underdeveloped and unclear, the Secretary cannot reasonably infer that the absence of evidence of population decline equates to evidence of persistence. The absence of conclusive evidence of persistence, standing alone, without persuasive evidence of widespread decline, may not be enough to establish that the Secretary *must* list the lizard as threatened or endangered. *See* Cook Inlet Beluga Whale v. Daley, 156 F. Supp. 2d 16, 21–22 (D.D.C. 2001) (holding that the ESA does not require listing "simply because the agency is unable to rule out factors that could contribute to a population decline"); *cf.* Balt. Gas & Elec. Co. v. Natural Res. Def. Council, Inc., 462 U.S. 87, 103 (1983) (holding that when examining decisions made under conditions of scientific uncertainty "a reviewing court must generally be at its most deferential"). But this is a different case. The Secretary affirmatively relies on ambiguous studies as evidence of persistence (*i.e.*, stable and viable populations), and in turn argues that this "evidence" of persistence satisfies *Defenders'* mandate and proves that the lizard's lost range is insignificant for purposes of the ESA. This conclusion is unreasonable. The studies do not lead to the conclusion that the lizard persists in a substantial portion of its range, and therefore cannot support the Secretary's conclusion.

Both parties acknowledge that the formerly common "scat count" method of estimating lizard population size has been discredited; thus, that nearly all of the existing data on lizard populations (including FWS' 1998 Population Viability Assessment—which itself concluded that population trends could not be reliably determined) must be set aside as unhelpful. Results from studies utilizing an allegedly more accurate "capture-mark-recapture" methodology are just now emerging. 68 Fed. Reg. at 333. In the 2006 withdrawal, the Secretary cites one such study for the proposition that, between 2003 and 2005, in two discrete sections of the lizard's current range (both within designated lizard MAs), there is no evidence of a "large decline in population" for the areas for which the researchers had more than one year of data. 71 Fed. Reg. at 36,751. This single attenuated finding represents the extent of the agency's evidentiary support for its sweeping conclusion that viable lizard populations persist throughout most of the species' current range.

Contrary to the lesson the Secretary draws from the study (*i.e.*, that lizard populations in the study areas show no sign of decline), the author's primary conclusion is that the study's population estimates can serve as a "baseline for future monitoring." Further, the study's author warns that the population estimates it reports "should be viewed with caution as they were based on sparse data." We thus conclude that the administrative record does not support the Secretary's determination that lizard populations persist throughout most of the species' current range. . . .

II. *Threats to the Lizard's Current Range*

The 2003 withdrawal reports that the Coachella Valley in California is the only segment of the lizard's current range where the species is in immediate jeopardy. *See* 68 Fed. Reg. at 345. The Secretary concluded that the likely extinction of the Coachella Valley lizard population is not significant because of the population's relatively small size (approximately sixteen thousand acres, or, one percent if the lizard's remaining range, 68 Fed. Reg. at 334), isolation from other remaining lizard populations, and lack of importance for maintenance of genetic diversity. *See id.* at 348. In essence, the Secretary determined that the Coachella Valley is home to a very small (in comparison with the three other segments of the lizard's remaining domestic range) non-unique lizard population. As such, the demise of the Coachella Valley population would not be significant within the meaning of the ESA. This is a reasonable approach to assessing the significance of threatened range, and one that complies with *Defenders*. *See* 258 F.3d at 1145 (requiring only that the Secretary "explain [his] conclusion that the area in which [the lizard] can no longer live is not a 'significant portion of its range' ").

Plaintiffs also challenge the Secretary's assessment of threats to the lizard's remaining habitat outside of the Coachella Valley.

First, they object to the Secretary's assertion that the Conservation Agreement and management strategy have diminished threats to the lizard's remaining habitat on public lands, and emphasize the management strategy's slow and still incomplete implementation. The Secretary acknowledges that the Conservation Agreement has not yet been fully implemented, but points to specific conservation benefits that the agreement has achieved since it came into being in 1997. *See* 68 Fed. Reg. at 347 (noting that pesticide use and OHV racing have been limited in the lizard MAs). Moreover, the 2003 withdrawal states that its assessment of threats to the species' current range is not "dependent on full implementation" of the Conservation Agreement's management strategy. *Id.* Kevin Young, one of the four independent biologists that reviewed FWS' assessment of the lizard's viability, offers support for the Secretary's position. He opined that the Conservation Agreement's protective measures alone were "adequate" to protect the species' remaining domestic range (outside of the Coachella Valley). We conclude that the limited benefits that the 2003 withdrawal points to are supported by the record, and the Secretary did not err in taking the Conservation Agreement into account.

Next, Plaintiffs argue that OHV use in the lizard's current range presents a much greater threat to the species than the Secretary acknowledges. Plaintiffs' argument, however, relies on inferences from indeterminate scientific evidence. Plaintiffs *have* shown that OHV use is on the rise throughout the lizard's remaining range. The available studies analyzing OHV-related impacts on the lizard, however, do not conclusively show that OHV use amounts to a significant threat to the species' viability. Both Plaintiffs and the Secretary point to scientific studies supporting their respective views on the effects of OHVs, but the merits of the conflicting studies is not a proper subject for this court to resolve.

Finally, Plaintiffs challenge the Secretary's treatment of scattered threats posed by energy and mineral development projects, increased Border Patrol activity, and the possible construction of large-scale infrastructure projects in the lizard's current range. Plaintiffs' arguments follow the same course as their attack on the agency's analysis of OHV use. In short, they have not presented conclusive evidence to rebut the Secretary's determination that such threats, either alone or in concert, are not likely to cause the "destruction, modification, or curtailment of [the species'] habitat or range." 16 U.S.C. § 1533(a)(1)(A).

## CONCLUSION

For the reasons set forth above, we reverse and remand the judgment of the district court with instructions that the matter be further remanded to the Secretary so that the Secretary can again consider whether to withdraw the proposed listing of the lizard.

■ NOONAN, CIRCUIT JUDGE, concurring and dissenting:

This case began in 1993 when the Secretary of the Interior first proposed listing the species. After careful and conscientious consideration by this court, it is now in 2009 remanded to continue to be litigated for an indefinite time. The pattern of the litigation is scarcely unfamiliar in environmental cases. Congress has enacted law designed to conserve species of wildlife threatened with extinction. 16 U.S.C. § 1531 et seq. A federal agency has been entrusted with enforcement. Using its expertise, the agency has determined what protection should be afforded a particular species. Its determination has been challenged by a private nonprofit organizations concerned with the existence of the species. The district court has heard the resulting litigation more than once, and this court has heard it more than once. The various decisionmakers and participants—the agency, the nonprofits, the district court, and the court of appeals—are not motivated by private passion or grudge, but seek to see the fair application of broad legislation to highly particularized and often elusive data. The legal system does not confide the definitive judgment to the agency entrusted with enforcement of the law but subjects that judgment first to the challenges of the nongovernmental organizations and then to the supervision of judges who are not expert in the scientific matters at stake and not familiar with the species whose survival is at stake.

As if this interplay of governmental and private groups did not create room for tension, misunderstandings, and passionate disagreement, the problems in this case have been exacerbated by the simple absence of information. How many flat-tailed horned lizards are there?

No one knows the answer to that question. Nor does anyone know how many lizards disappeared when portions of their range disappeared. It is supposed that a diminution in range correlates with a diminution in lizards. This hypothesis is plausible. It has not been shown to be probable. Yet the case turns on what measures are necessary to keep this unknown population in existence. The court concludes that the Secretary erred in finding that the lizard has not lost a significant portions of its range. The old method of counting lizards is out. A new method has not been tried very much. It's anybody's guess whether the lizards are multiplying or declining. In a guessing contest one might defer to the government umpire. The court, however, finds the Secretary's conclusion impacted by over-reliance on fragmenting evidence of the lizard's persistence; so the court decides to give the Secretary another crack at the problem.

If the Secretary does not know what the lizard population was to begin with, or what it was in 1993, or what it is now in May 2009, how will he know if it is increasing, staying the same, or declining?

A style of judging, familiar to readers of the old English reports, characterizes the judge as *dubitante*. That is probably the most accurate term for me, which leads me to concur in the majority opinion insofar as it rejects the contentions of the Tucson Herpetological Society and to dissent from the remand whose command to the Secretary of the Interior is, Guess again.

---

## QUESTIONS AND DISCUSSION

**1.** Why did the FWS conclude that the lizard satisfied the ESA's five criteria for judging whether a species is endangered? What threats does the lizard face? Why aren't the existing laws sufficient to protect it? Should it matter whether the lizard was always rare, or whether it only recently become endangered? And how should we respond to the point made by Judge Noonan that we don't know how many flat-tailed horned lizards there are? *Cf.* Kalyani Robbins, *Strength in Numbers: Setting Quantitative Criteria for Listing Species Under the Endangered Species Act*, 27 UCLA J. ENVTL. L. & POL'Y 1 (2009) (proposing the use of numerical measurements of individual populations or percentage of population decline to judge whether a species is endangered).

**2.** A species is endangered if it "is in danger of extinction," whereas a species is threatened if it "is likely be become an endangered species in the foreseeable future." ESA § 3(6), 3(20). Congress included the "threatened" category "not only as a means of giving some protection to species before they become endangered, but also as a means of gradually reducing the level of protection for previously endangered species that had been successfully 'restored' to the point at which the strong protective measures for that category were no longer necessary." Bean & Rowland, *supra*, at 201. There are only a few practical consequences between the two categories. The restrictions on "taking" a species automatically apply to endangered species, but their application to threatened species is within the discretion of the FWS. Most of the time the agency simply extends the takings prohibitions to threatened species, but in an increasing number of controversial cases the agency has developed somewhat less stringent prohibitions for threatened species. Another difference between endangered and threatened species lies in the greater penalties that the ESA imposes on those who violate the law with respect to an endangered species.

**3.** The protections of the ESA do not attach until a species is formally listed as endangered or threatened. Some individuals have sought to avoid the ESA's regulations by destroying a species or its habitat before the species is listed. *See* Dean Lueck & Jeffrey A. Michael, *Preemptive Habitat Destruction Under the Endangered Species Act*, 46 J. LAW & ECON. 27 (2003). The law seeks to prevent such actions through Section 4(b)(7), which allows the FWS to immediately list any fish, wildlife or plant species for 240 days when there is an "emergency posing a significant risk to the well-being of" the species. These emergencies have included unauthorized county road construction that threatened the survival of the bull trout in Nevada's Jarbridge River, rapid development amidst the breeding sites of the California tiger salamander, and hungry mountain lions feeding on the California bighorn sheep in the Sierra Nevada mountains. The leading case involving an emergency listing—*City of Las Vegas v. Lujan*, 891 F.2d 927 (D.C. Cir. 1989)—upheld the FWS's protection of the Mojave Desert population of the desert tortoise pursuant to a more deferential standard of judicial review appropriate given the exigencies of the situation. The FWS must then decide whether to list a species on a permanent basis by the end of the 240 days following an emergency listing.

**4.** Listing is not supposed to be forever. The goal of the ESA is to help a species recover so that it is no longer in danger of extinction and no longer in need of the law's protections. Toward that end, the FWS can delist a species when it is no longer endangered or threatened according to the same five criteria set forth in Section 4(a)(1) that are used to determine whether a species should be listed in the first place. Ideally, a species will be removed from the list when it has recovered. A species may also be delisted when new scientific information indicates that it is more abundant than previously realized or that it is not really a distinct species at all. Less happily, a species can be delisted if it is extinct. As of July 2016, 63 species have been delisted:

34 had recovered, 19 were delisted because of new information or taxonomical changes, and ten were believed to have become extinct. The list of delisted species is available at http://ecos.fws.gov/tess_public/Delisting Reportdo.

---

## PROBLEM EXERCISE:
### LISTING THE COW KNOB SALAMANDER

In 2012, the Center for Biological Diversity (CBD) and several renowned scientists petitioned the FWS to list 53 amphibians and reptiles as endangered or threatened species under the ESA. One of those species is the Cow Knob salamander. The Secretary of the Interior—your boss—has asked you to prepare a memorandum responding to the petition, which states as follows:

NATURAL HISTORY, BIOLOGY, AND STATUS

Range: [T]his species has a narrow range in the Shenandoah, North, and Great North mountains, in George Washington National Forest, Virginia (Augusta, Rockingham, and Shenandoah Counties) and West Virginia from 735–1,200m above sea level (but mainly from 900–1,200m above sea level). Graham examined Nathaniel Mountain, West Virginia, which revealed new records on Elliot Knob, extending the known range several miles south.

Habitat:

This species occurs in ridge and valley areas in mixed deciduous forest interspersed with Virginia pine and hemlock and numerous rock outcrops. It is found in old-growth forests with many downed logs and in areas with an abundance of surface rocks, including talus, especially on north-facing slopes. During the day, it is found under rocks and logs or in burrows.

Biology:

Cow Knob salamanders are opportunistic carnivores on and above the forest floor during wet conditions. Most active foraging apparently occurs at night, and individuals have been observed to climb on tree trunks and rocks at night. Adults and juveniles prey on a wide variety of invertebrates, including ants, collembolans, beetles, dipterans, coleopterans, orthopterans, insect larvae, millipedes, centipedes, spiders, and mite. The size of the prey item is positively correlated with the size of the salamander. . . .

Population Status:

Federal protection for the Cow Knob salamander is needed because its populations are declining and its occupied range is shrinking, mostly due to habitat loss across its narrow range.

According to NatureServe, deforestation has likely reduced distribution and abundance compared to historical levels.

THREATS

Habitat alteration and destruction: A principal threat to this species has been deforestation through logging because it prefers oldgrowth forests with many downed logs. As such, forest management practices such as short rotation forestry are a threat to the species. Firewood collection is also a potential threat. Mortality can be minimized if logging occurs outside the seasonal activity period but any intensive logging is detrimental.

It is also threatened by defoliation by gypsy moths (Lymantria dispar).

Spraying pesticides to control gypsy moths might also impact the salamanders but the effect is unknown.

Overutilization: There is a Candidate Conservation Agreement between the U.S. Forest Service (USFS) and the U.S. Fish and Wildlife Service (USFWS) that prohibits the collection of the Cow Knob salamander on the national forest. Nevertheless, overcollection of individuals is a potential threat.

Inadequacy of existing regulatory mechanisms: The George Washington National Forest includes the Cow Knob salamander as a Management Indicator Species in the draft forest plan. As such, 47,000 acres are managed for the salamander with a forest plan species diversity objective to "[m]aintain a stable and/or increasing population trend for the Cow Knob salamander over the planning period through protection and maintenance of the Cow Knob Salamander Habitat Conservation Area.").

While this objective provides important benefits for the salamander, it only applies to those populations within the management area of the George Washington National Forest.

In addition, a formal Conservation Agreement exists, via a Memorandum of Understanding between the George Washington National Forest and the U.S. Fish and Wildlife Service, which affords the habitat of this species on public lands some protection from logging and other potentially damaging operations. But this agreement is only voluntary and cannot ensure that its limited habitat will be adequately protected.

Timber management with cutting, temporary road-building, and oil and gas leasing with Controlled Surface Occupancy is planned within the salamander's range. The Forest Service also continues to run off-highway vehicle routes through the salamanders' home territory.

Because the rarity of this species was realized after some preliminary studies, the Cow Knob salamander was recognized as a species of special concern by the Virginia Department of Game and

Inland Fisheries and by the West Virginia Division of Natural Resources. But such designation provides no habitat protection, which is needed to ensure species viability.

Other factors: Cow Knob salamanders are also likely threatened by the loss of hemlock trees by the introduced hemlock woolly adelgid (Adelges tsugae).

---

## II. FEDERAL GOVERNMENT RESPONSIBILITIES UNDER THE ENDANGERED SPECIES ACT

Once a species has been listed as endangered or threatened, the substantive obligations of the ESA come into play. The substantive commands of the ESA for the federal government can be divided into two groups. The first set of commands applies to the agency that is responsible for the species once it is listed. This is usually the FWS, though the NMFS is the responsible agency for marine mammals and fish listed under the ESA. The second set of commands applies to *all* federal agencies. Those commands are often difficult to enforce because they require an agency to protect biodiversity even when such protection conflicts with the agency's primary statutory responsibility to, for example, promote military readiness or respond to natural disasters.

### A. LISTING AGENCY RESPONSIBILITIES UNDER THE ESA

#### 1. CRITICAL HABITAT

One of the congressional purposes in enacting the ESA was "to provide a means whereby the ecosystems upon which endangered species and threatened species depend may be conserved." ESA § 2(b), 16 U.S.C. § 1531(b). How can that goal be accomplished? Most of the substantive provisions of the ESA focus on the species itself, rather than the habitat of a species. There are only a few provisions that specifically aim to protect habitat. Section 5 of the ESA authorizes the government to purchase land that serves as the habitat of an endangered or threatened species. Section 9 of the ESA has been interpreted to prohibit certain private or governmental actions that adversely affect the habitat of a species. *See* Babbitt v. Sweet Home Chapter of Communities for a Great Oregon, 515 U.S. 687 (1995). And Section 4 authorizes the designation of the "critical habitat" of a species.

The ESA defines "critical habitat" as "the specific areas within the geographical area occupied by the species, at the time it is listed on which are found those physical and biological features (I) essential to the conservation of the species and (II) which may require special management considerations or protections." ESA § 3(5)(i); *see also* ESA § 3(5)(ii) (adding that critical habitat can also include areas outside the current range of a listed species if the Secretary determines that "such areas are essential for the conservation of the species"). If critical habitat is designated, the only regulatory consequence is that ESA Section 7 requires all federal agencies to insure that none of their actions "result in the destruction or adverse modification" of the designated critical habitat of a species. The most famous example of that prohibition is *Tennessee Valley Authority v. Hill*, 437 U.S. 153 (1978), which blocked the completion of the Tellico Dam because the resulting impoundment would have destroyed the endangered snail darter's critical habitat. The designation of critical habitat itself has no effect on the activities of private parties or state governments unless they are seeking federal funding or a federal permit that triggers the Section 7 scrutiny. Moreover, the prohibition on federal actions that destroy or modify critical habitat usually overlaps the restrictions imposed by Section 9's ban on the "take" of a protected species. Yet the official designation of critical habitat has been controversial. Why?

## Markle Interests v. United States Fish & Wildlife Service

United States Court of Appeals for the Fifth Circuit, 2016.
2016 U.S. App. LEXIS 12066.

■ STEPHEN A. HIGGINSON, CIRCUIT JUDGE:

This appeal requires us to consider the United States Fish and Wildlife Service's inclusion of private land in a critical-habitat designation under the Endangered Species Act. Misconceptions exist about how critical-habitat designations impact private property. Critical-habitat designations do not transform private land into wildlife refuges. A designation does not authorize the government or the public to access private lands. Following designation, the Fish and Wildlife Service cannot force private landowners to introduce endangered species onto their land or to make modifications to their land. In short, a critical-habitat designation alone does not require private landowners to participate in the conservation of an endangered species. In a thorough opinion, District Judge Martin L. C. Feldman held that the Fish and Wildlife Service properly applied the Endangered Species Act to private land in St. Tammany Parish, Louisiana. As we discuss below, we AFFIRM Judge Feldman's judgment upholding this critical-habitat designation.

### FACTS AND PROCEEDINGS

This case is about a frog-the Rana sevosa-commonly known as the dusky gopher frog. These frogs spend most of their lives underground in open-canopied pine forests. They migrate to isolated, ephemeral ponds to breed. Ephemeral ponds are only seasonally flooded, leaving them to dry out cyclically and making it impossible for predatory fish to survive. After the frogs are finished breeding, they return to their underground habitats, followed by their offspring. When the dusky gopher frog was listed as an endangered species, there were only about 100 adult frogs known to exist in the wild. Although, historically, the frog was found in parts of Louisiana, Mississippi, and Alabama, today, the frog exists only in Mississippi. The primary threat to the frog is habitat degradation.

In 2010, under the Endangered Species Act ("ESA"), the United States Fish and Wildlife Service ("the Service") published a proposed rule to designate 1,957 acres in Mississippi as "critical habitat" for the dusky gopher frog. In response to concerns raised during the peer-review process about the sufficiency of this original proposal, the Service's final designation of critical habitat expanded the area to 6,477 acres in four counties in Mississippi and one parish in Louisiana. The designated area in Louisiana ("Unit 1") consists of 1,544 acres in St. Tammany Parish. Although the dusky gopher frog has not occupied Unit 1 for decades, the land contains historic breeding sites and five closely clustered ephemeral ponds. The final critical-habitat designation was the culmination of two proposed rules, economic analysis, two rounds of notice and comment, a scientific peer-review process including responses from six experts, and a public hearing.

Together, Plaintiffs-Appellants Markle Interests, L.L.C., P&F Lumber Company 2000, L.L.C., PF Monroe Properties, L.L.C., and Weyerhaeuser Company (collectively, "the Landowners") own all of Unit 1. Weyerhaeuser Company holds a long-term timber lease on all of the land that does not expire until 2043. The Landowners intend to use the land for residential and commercial development and timber operations. Through consolidated suits, all of the Landowners filed actions for declaratory judgment and injunctive relief against the Service, its director, the Department of the Interior, and the Secretary of the Interior. The Landowners challenged only the Service's designation of Unit 1 as critical habitat, not the designation of land in Mississippi.

The district court allowed the Center for Biological Diversity and the Gulf Restoration Network (collectively, "the Intervenors") to intervene as defendants in support of the Service's final designation. All parties filed cross-motions for summary judgment. Although Judge Feldman granted summary judgment in favor of the Landowners on the issue of standing, he granted summary judgment in favor of the Service on the merits. See Markle Interests, LLC v. U.S. Fish & Wildlife Serv., 40 F. Supp. 3d 744, 748, 769 (E.D. La. 2014). The Landowners timely appealed.

STANDARD OF REVIEW

We review a district court's grant of summary judgment de novo. Our review of the Service's administration of the ESA is governed by the Administrative Procedure Act ("APA"). When reviewing agency action under the APA, this court must "set aside agency action, findings, and conclusions found to be-(A) arbitrary, capricious, an abuse of discretion, or otherwise not in accordance with law; (B) contrary to constitutional right, power, privilege, or immunity; [or] (C) in excess of statutory jurisdiction, authority, or limitations." Review under the arbitrary-and-capricious standard is "extremely limited and highly deferential," and "there is a presumption that the agency's decision is valid," The plaintiff has the burden of overcoming the presumption of validity.

Under the arbitrary-and-capricious standard, we will not vacate an agency's decision unless it has relied on factors which Congress had not intended it to consider, entirely failed to consider an important aspect of the problem, offered an explanation for its decision that runs counter to the evidence before the agency, or is so implausible that it could not be ascribed to a difference in view or the product of agency expertise. We must be mindful not to substitute our judgment for the agency's. That said, we must still ensure that "[the] agency examine[d] the relevant data and articulate[d] a satisfactory explanation for its action." Id. (internal quotation marks omitted). "We will uphold an agency's action if its reasons and policy choices satisfy minimum standards of rationality."

DISCUSSION

The Landowners raise three challenges to the Service's designation of Unit 1 as critical habitat for the dusky gopher frog. They argue that the designation (1) violates the ESA and the APA, (2) exceeds the Service's constitutional authority under the Commerce Clause, U.S. Const. art. I, § 8, cl. 3, and (3) violates the National Environmental Policy Act ("NEPA"), 42 U.S.C. § 4321 et seq. As we discuss below, each of their arguments fails.

I. Endangered Species Act

Congress enacted the ESA "to provide a means whereby the ecosystems upon which endangered species . . . depend may be conserved" and "to provide a program for the conservation of such endangered species." The ESA broadly defines "conservation." It includes "the use of all methods and procedures which are necessary to bring any endangered species . . . to the point at which the measures provided [by the ESA] are no longer necessary." In other words, "the objective of the ESA is to enable [endangered] species not merely to survive, but to recover from their endangered or threatened status."

To achieve this objective, the ESA requires the Service to first identify and list endangered and threatened species. Listing a species as endangered or threatened then triggers the Service's statutory duty to designate critical habitat "to the maximum extent prudent and determinable." "Critical habitat designation primarily benefits listed species through the ESA's [Section 7] consultation mechanism." Under this section, once habitat is designated as critical, federal agencies are prohibited from authorizing, funding, or carrying out any action that is likely to result in "the destruction or adverse modification" of that critical habitat without receiving a special exemption. To satisfy the requirements of Section 7, federal agencies must consult with the Service before taking any action that might negatively affect critical habitat. Only federal agencies—not private parties—must engage in this Section

7 consultation process. Thus, as Judge Feldman explained, "absent a federal nexus, [the Service] cannot compel a private landowner to make changes to restore his designated property into optimal habitat.". . . .

The ESA expressly envisions two types of critical habitat: areas occupied by the endangered species at the time it is listed as endangered and areas not occupied by the species at the time of listing. To designate an occupied area as critical habitat, the Service must demonstrate that the area contains "those physical or biological features . . . essential to the conservation of the species." To designate unoccupied areas, the Service must determine that the designated areas are "essential for the conservation of the species." As Judge Feldman noted below, "Congress did not define 'essential' but, rather, delegated to the Secretary the authority to make that determination." Thus, when the Service promulgates, in a formal rule, a determination that an unoccupied area is "essential for the conservation" of an endangered species, Chevron deference is appropriate.

In addition, under the regulations in place at the time of the critical-habitat designation at issue here, before the Service could designate unoccupied land as critical habitat, it first had to make a finding that "a designation limited to [a species'] present range would be inadequate to ensure the conservation of the species." Unit 1 is unoccupied. [The Service determined that] "Unit 1 is essential to the conservation of the dusky gopher frog because it provides: (1) Breeding habitat for the dusky gopher frog in a landscape where the rarity of that habitat is a primary threat to the species; (2) a framework of breeding ponds that supports metapopulation structure important to the long-term survival of the dusky gopher frog; and (3) geographic distance from extant dusky gopher frog populations, which likely provides protection from environmental stochasticity."

. . . On appeal, the Landowners do not dispute the scientific or factual support for the Service's determination that Unit 1 is essential. Instead, they argue that the Service "exceeded its statutory authority" under the ESA and acted arbitrarily and capriciously when it designated Unit 1 as critical habitat because Unit 1 is not currently habitable, nor "currently supporting the conservation of the species in any way," nor reasonably likely to support the conservation of the species in the "foreseeable future." They contend that such land cannot rationally be called "essential for the conservation of the species," because if it can be, then the Service would have "nearly limitless authority to burden private lands with a critical habitat designation."

As Judge Feldman noted, Congress has not defined the word "essential" in the ESA. Hence the Service has the authority to interpret the term. The ESA leaves to the Secretary the task of defining 'prudent' and 'determinable.'" To issue a formal rule designating critical habitat for the frog, the Service necessarily had to interpret and apply the applicable ESA provisions, including the word "essential." The Service issued the designation as a formal agency rule after two rounds of notice and comment. Thus, the Service's interpretation of the term "essential" is entitled to Chevron deference.

When, as here, "an agency's decision qualifies for Chevron deference, we will accept the agency's reasonable construction of an ambiguous statute that the agency is charged with administering." The question presented, then, is whether the Landowners have demonstrated that the Service interpreted the ESA unreasonably when it deemed Unit 1 "essential" for the conservation of the dusky gopher frog. Although the Landowners acknowledge that "the Service undoubtedly has some discretion in interpreting the statutory language of the ESA," they contend that the Service "does not have the authority to apply the term 'essential' in a way that is contrary to its plain meaning." The Landowners do not explain what they think the "plain meaning" of essential is, however, save to argue, circularly, that we must "insist[ ]" that " 'essential' must truly mean essential.

We consider first their argument that it is an unreasonable interpretation of the ESA to describe Unit 1 as essential for the conservation of the dusky gopher frog when Unit 1 is not currently habitable by the frog. The statute does not support this argument. There is no habitability requirement in the text of the ESA or the implementing regulations. The statute requires the Service to designate "essential" areas, without further defining "essential" to mean "habitable." The Landowners' proposed extra-textual limit on the designation of unoccupied land-habitability-effectively conflates the standard for designating unoccupied land with the standard for designating occupied land. As Judge Feldman insightfully observed, "[their position] is . . . contrary to the ESA; [the Landowners] equate what Congress plainly differentiates: the ESA defines two distinct types of critical habitat, occupied and unoccupied; only occupied habitat must contain all of the relevant [physical or biological features]." Thus, the plain text of the ESA does not require Unit 1 to be habitable. "[R]ather," as Judge Feldman elaborated, "[the Service] is tasked with designating as critical unoccupied habitat so long as it determines it is 'essential for the conservation of the species' and 'only when a designation limited to its present range would be inadequate to ensure the conservation of the species.'" Here, the Service provided scientific data to support its finding that Unit 1 is essential, and as Judge Feldman held, "[the Landowners] have not demonstrated that [the Service's] findings are implausible." Thus, the Landowners have not shown that the Service employed an unreasonable interpretation of the ESA when it found that the currently uninhabitable Unit 1 was essential for the conservation of the dusky gopher frog and designated the land as critical habitat.

We consider next the argument that it is an unreasonable interpretation of the ESA to describe Unit 1 as essential for the conservation of the dusky gopher frog when Unit 1 "is not currently supporting the conservation of the species in any way and the Service has no reasonable basis to believe that it will do so at any point in the foreseeable future." Like their proposed habitability requirement, the Landowners' proposed temporal requirement—considering whether the frog can live on the land "currently" or in the "foreseeable future"—also lacks legal support and is undermined by the ESA's text. The ESA's critical-habitat provisions do not require the Service to know when a protected species will be conserved as a result of the designation. The Service is required to designate unoccupied areas as critical habitat if these areas are "essential for the conservation of the species." The statute defines "conservation" as "the use of all methods and procedures which are necessary to bring any endangered species . . . to the point at which the measures provided . . . are no longer necessary." Neither of these provisions sets a deadline for achieving this ultimate conservation goal. And the Landowners do not explain why it is impossible to make an essentiality determination without determining when (or whether) the conservation goal will be achieved. As Judge Feldman concluded, "[the Service's] failure (as yet) to identify how or when a viable population of dusky gopher frogs will be achieved, as indifferent and overreaching by the government as it appears, does not serve to invalidate its finding that Unit 1 was part of the minimum required habitat for the frog's conservation." We also note that, in contrast to the habitat-designation provision at issue here, the ESA's recovery-plan provisions do require the Service to estimate when a species will be conserved. Congress's inclusion of a conservation-timeline requirement for recovery plans, but omission of it for critical-habitat designations, further underscores the weakness of the Landowners' argument.

Moreover, we observe that the Landowners' proposed temporal requirement could effectively exclude all private land not currently occupied by the species from critical-habitat designations. By the Landowners' logic, private landowners could trump the Service's scientific determination that unoccupied habitat is essential for the conservation of a species so long as they declare that they are not currently willing to modify habitat to make it habitable and that they will not be willing to make modifications in the foreseeable future. Their logic would also seem to allow landowners whose land is immediately habitable to block a critical-habitat designation merely by declaring that they will not-now or ever-permit the reintroduction of the species to their land. The Landowners' focus on private-party cooperation as part of the definition of "essential" finds no support in the text of the ESA. Nothing in the ESA requires that private landowners be willing to participate in species conservation. 17 Summing up the Landowners' arguments on this point, Judge Feldman observed that the Landowners "effectively ask the Court to endorse-contrary to the express terms and scope of the statute-a private landowner exemption from unoccupied critical-habitat designations. This, the Third Branch, is the wrong audience for addressing this matter of policy." We agree. Thus, the Landowners have not shown that the Service employed an unreasonable interpretation of the ESA when it found that Unit 1 was essential for the conservation of the dusky gopher frog without first establishing that Unit 1 currently supports, or in the "foreseeable future" will support, the conservation of the dusky gopher frog.

We next consider the argument that that the Service has interpreted the word "essential" unreasonably because its interpretation fails to place "meaningful limits" on the Service's power under the ESA. Thus, we consider whether, in designating Unit 1, the Service abided the meaningful limits that the ESA and the agency's implementing regulations set on the Service's authority to designate unoccupied areas as critical habitat. Under the regulations in effect at the time that Unit 1 was designated, the Service had to find that the species's occupied habitat was inadequate before it could even consider designating unoccupied habitat as critical. In part, this preliminary determination provided a limit to the term "essential" as it relates to unoccupied areas. Unoccupied areas could be essential only if occupied areas were found to be inadequate for conserving the species. Here, the Service made that threshold inadequacy determination-a determination that the Landowners do not challenge.

Next, under the ESA itself, the Service can designate unoccupied land only if it is "essential for the conservation of the species." "Conservation" is defined as "the use of all methods and procedures which are necessary to bring any endangered species . . . to the point at which the measures provided . . . are no longer necessary." In light of this definition, we find implausible the Landowners' parade of horribles in which they suggest that, if the Service can designate an area like Unit 1 as critical habitat, it could designate "much of the land in the United States" as well. They contend that "[b]ecause any land may conceivably be turned into suitable habitat with enough time, effort, and resources, th[e] [Service's] interpretation gives the Service nearly limitless authority to burden private lands with a critical habitat designation." But we find it hard to see how the Service would be able to satisfactorily explain why randomly chosen land-whether an empty field or, as the Landowners suggest, land covered in "buildings" and "pavement"-would be any more "necessary" to a given species' recovery than any other arbitrarily chosen empty field or paved lot. Here, the Service confirmed through peer review and two rounds of notice and comment a scientific consensus as to the presence and rarity of a critical (and difficult to reproduce) feature—the ephemeral ponds—which justified its finding that Unit 1 was essential for the conservation of the dusky gopher frog. . . .

In sum, the designation of Unit 1 as critical habitat was not arbitrary and capricious nor based upon an unreasonable interpretation of the ESA. The Service reasonably determined (1) that designating occupied habitat alone would be inadequate to ensure the conservation of the dusky gopher frog and (2) that Unit 1 is essential for the conservation of the frog. We thus agree with Judge Feldman: "the law authorizes such action and . . . the government has acted within the law."

[The court also held that the Service's designation of critical habitat for the dusky gopher frog satisfied the commerce clause and that the Service did not violate NEPA by failing to prepare an environmental impact statement before designating Unit 1 as critical habitat.]

■ PRISCILLA R. OWEN, CIRCUIT JUDGE, dissenting:

There is a gap in the reasoning of the majority opinion that cannot be bridged. The area at issue is not presently "essential for the conservation of the [endangered] species" because it plays no part in the conservation of that species. Its biological and physical characteristics will not support a dusky gopher frog population. There is no evidence of a reasonable probability (or any probability for that matter) that it will become "essential" to the conservation of the species because there is no evidence that the substantial alterations and maintenance necessary to transform the area into habitat suitable for the endangered species will, or are likely to, occur. Land that is not "essential" for conservation does not meet the statutory criteria for "critical habitat."

The majority opinion interprets the Endangered Species Act to allow the Government to impose restrictions on private land use even though the land: is not occupied by the endangered species and has not been for more than fifty years; is not near areas inhabited by the species; cannot sustain the species without substantial alterations and future annual maintenance, neither of which the Government has the authority to effectuate, as it concedes; and does not play any supporting role in the existence of current habitat for the species. If the Endangered Species Act permitted the actions taken by the Government in this case, then vast portions of the United States could be designated as "critical habitat" because it is theoretically possible, even if not probable, that land could be modified to sustain the introduction or reintroduction of an endangered species.

The majority opinion upholds the governmental action here on nothing more than the Government's hope or speculation that the landowners and lessors of the 1,544 acres at issue will pay for removal of the currently existing pine trees used in commercial timber operations and replace them with another tree variety suitable for dusky gopher frog habitat, and perform other modifications as well as future annual maintenance, that might then support the species if, with the landowners' cooperation, it is reintroduced to the area. The language of the Endangered Species Act does not permit such an expansive interpretation and consequent overreach by the Government.

Undoubtedly, the ephemeral ponds on the property at issue are somewhat rare. But it is undisputed that the ponds cannot themselves sustain a dusky gopher frog population. It is only with significant transformation and then, annual maintenance, each dependent on the assent and financial contribution of private landowners, that the area, including the ponds, might play a role in conservation. The Endangered Species Act does not permit the Government to designate an area as "critical habitat," and therefore use that designation as leverage against the landowners, based on one feature of an area when that one feature cannot support the existence of the species and significant alterations to the area as a whole would be required.

The majority opinion's holding is unprecedented and sweeping. . . .

---

## QUESTIONS AND DISCUSSION

**1.** The designation of critical habitat is supposed to occur at the same time that the listing agency determines that a species is endangered or threatened. The court in the gnatcatcher case expected that the agency would decline to designate critical habitat only in "rare" circumstances. In fact, it is more common for the agency *not* to designate the critical habitat of a species. As of June 2016, critical habitat had been designated for 757 species.

**2.** If "a critical-habitat designation alone does not require private landowners to participate in the conservation of an endangered species," as the court emphasized, then why did the landowners object to the designation?

**3.** An area can be excluded from the designated critical habitat if the benefits of exclusion outweigh the benefits of inclusion, unless the failure to designate the area as critical habitat will result in the extinction of the species. In conducting that balance, the ESA directs the listing agency to consider "the economic impact, and any other relevant impact, of specifying any particular area as critical habitat." 16 U.S.C. § 1533(b)(2). And how should one calculate the economic impact attributable to the designation of critical habitat? The FWS has insisted that any economic impact of the listing of the species should not count toward the determination of the economic impact of designating critical habitat. Thus, for example, any economic losses that landowners suffer because the listing of the frog them from developing their property would not be relevant in calculating the economic impact of designating that land as the frog's critical habitat. That baseline approach greatly reduced the likelihood that the costs of designating critical habitat would outweigh the benefits. But in New Mexico Cattle Growers Association v. FWS, 248 F.3d 1277 (10th Cir. 2001), the court held that the statutory language of the ESA requires FWS to consider "all of the economic impact of the [critical habitat designation], regardless of whether those impacts are caused co-extensively by any other agency action (such as listing) and even if those impacts would remain in the absence of the" designation. Applying that approach, what would the FWS need to investigate to decide whether the economic impacts of designating certain land as the critical habitat of the frog outweigh the benefits?

**4.** The landowners also brought a constitutional challenge to the designation of their property as the critical habitat for the frog. Specifically, they argued that their use of Unit 1 would not affect interstate commerce, and was thus beyond the scope of congressional power under the commerce clause. The court held that the constitutional objection was foreclosed by the Fifth Circuit's prior decision in GDF Realty Invs., Ltd. v. Norton, 326 F.3d 622, 633 (5th Cir. 2003), which rejected a similar commerce clause argument against the listing of six species of subterranean invertebrates found only within two counties in Texas. We review the constitutional questions in greater detail below in section B(1) of this chapter.

**5.** "Although the Service listed the dusky gopher frog as endangered in 2001," the Fifth Circuit explained, "it declined to designate critical habitat at that time because of budget limitations." It took a lawsuit filed by the Center for Biological Diversity to produce a settlement agreement which culminated in the deadlines for the Service to designate critical habitat for the frog. Similarly, when sued for not designating critical habitat for 245 listed Hawaiian plants, the agency responded that "if the FWS must complete prudency determinations for all 245 plants by 2000, it will need to suspend all other listing activity" in that region. Conservation Council for Hawai'i v. Babbitt, 24 F. Supp. 2d 1074, 1078 (D. Hawai'i 1998). The environmental plaintiffs pointed out, though, that the agency had received all of the funds that it had requested from Congress. The court fashioned a compromise that required the agency to publish proposed rules regarding the designation of critical habitat for 100 of the plants by November 30, 2000, with the remaining plants to be addressed by April 30, 2002. Also, the court deferred to the agency's decision to consider plants in the same Hawaiian ecosystem first, rather than accepting the environmentalists's suggestion to first consider those plants most directly affected by federal actions. Additional examples of how courts have responded to the FWS's resource limitations with respect to designating critical habitat include Forest Guardians v. Babbitt, 164 F.3d 1261 (10th Cir. 1998) (holding that the Secretary of the Interior failed to perform his statutory duty to designate the critical habitat of the Rio Grande silvery minnow, and that claims of impossibility because of resource limitations were premature); Center for Biological Diversity v. FWS, 350 F. Supp. 2d 23 (D.D.C. 2004) (advising that "[t]he Court cannot meaningfully assess whether the agency has efficiently used the resources available to it simply by taking the agency at its word"); and Biodiversity Legal Foundation v. Norton, 285 F. Supp. 2d 1 (D.D.C. 2003) (giving the agency sixty days to adopt a schedule for designating critical habitat for the Cape Sable seaside sparrow, one of the most endangered birds in the United States).

The FWS insists that its limited resources should not be devoted to critical habitat designations. "Imagine an emergency room where lawsuits force the doctors to treat sprained ankles while patients with heart attacks expire in the waiting room and you've got a good picture of our endangered species program right now," explained Assistant Secretary of the Interior for Fish and Wildlife and Parks Craig Manson in May 2003. In an accompanying statement addressing a series of questions and answers concerning critical habitat, FWS explained that "the average cost of designating critical habitat for a species is approximately $400,000," or twice the cost of listing a new species. The agency also offered this question and answer:

> **Why hasn't the Interior Department asked for enough funds from Congress to do all the designations?**
>
> The President's FY 2004 budget request for listing totals nearly $12.3 million, an amount that, if approved by Congress, is almost double the $6.2 million appropriated in FY 2000 and a 35 percent increase over FY 2003. However, no matter how much funding was provided, it would take many years to complete this process. The real question is whether the benefits of critical habitat warrant the large expenditures that would be required were it to be designated for all listed species.

What is the answer to the latter question? John Kostyack of the National Wildlife Federation testified before Congress in April 2003 that "the ESA's requirement to designate and protect a listed species' critical habitat is among the most important of the ESA's habitat protection provisions" for three reasons: (1) the identification of which habitat is critical for the survival of a species "helps educate people about the natural world they inhabit, and more importantly, helps to ensure that key habitats are not destroyed out of sheer ignorance;" (2) critical habitat includes "all habitats needed for recovery," not just the areas currently inhabited by a species; and (3) critical habitat designation triggers the Section 7 prohibition on federal agency actions that are likely to result in the "destruction or adverse modification" of critical habitat. Does that answer the "real question" posed by the FWS? And is that really the *real* question?

**6.** The ESA requires the designation of critical habitat "to the maximum extent prudent and determinable." ESA § 4(a)(3). There have not been many instances when the listed agency has refused to designate critical habitat because it was indeterminable. Critical habitat is not determinable if there is inadequate information about biological needs of the species or the impacts of a designation. 50 C.F.R § 424.12(a)(2). Yet the courts have been wary of the instances in which the FWS has claimed that critical habitat is not determinable. *See* Northern Spotted Owl v. Lujan, 758 F. Supp. 621 (W.D. Wash. 1991) (holding that the failure to provide any reason for concluding that the critical habitat of the northern spotted owl was not determinable was arbitrary and capricious); Colorado Wildlife Federation v. FWS, 36 E.R.C. (BNA) 1409 (D. Colo. 1992) (holding that the agency's fear of designating too large an area as critical habitat because of the inadequacy of current information violated the statutory directive to make the determination based on whatever information was presently available).

The most common reason the FWS has given for deciding not to designate critical habitat is that such a designation is not "prudent." But the Ninth Circuit's decision has rejected the agency's broad understanding of when a critical habitat designation is not prudent is already producing different results. In Natural Resources Defense Council v. U.S. Department of the Interior, 113 F.3d 1121 (9th Cir. 1997), the court overturned the FWS's refusal to designate more land as critical habitat for the coastal California gnatcatcher. The FWS erred in two ways, according to the court. First, the agency failed to weigh the benefits of designation against its risks (such as encouraging landowners to destroy, rather than protect, gnatcatcher sites). Second, the agency wrongly asked whether critical habitat would benefit most of the gnatcatchers, instead of asking whether critical habitat would benefit the species as a whole. On remand, the FWS designated over 500,000 acres in five southern California counties as the critical habitat of the California gnatcatcher. Final Determination of Critical Habitat for the Coastal California Gnatcatcher, 65 Fed. Reg. 63680 (2000). The Ninth Circuit's decision also prompted the FWS to reverse its original determination and conclude that it would be prudent to designate critical habitat for ten newly listed plants on Maui, Molokai, Lanai and Kahoolawe. *See* Final Endangered Status for 10 Plant Taxa from Maui Nui, HA, 64 Fed. Reg. 48307, 48319 (1999).

**7.** Plants are not as broadly protected as animals from take under section 9 of the ESA. *See* 16 U.S.C. § 1538(a)(2)(B) (prohibiting removal or destruction on federal lands or in violation of certain state laws). They nevertheless pose a particular problem for the designation of critical habitat. Rare plants are attractive to collectors, and plants are stationary, so identifying where rare plants can be found is often counterproductive. For example, when declining to designate critical habitat for the San Diego thornmint and three other southern Californian plants, the Fish and Wildlife Service explained:

> Landowners may mistakenly believe that critical habitat designation will be an obstacle to development and impose restrictions on their use of their property. Unfortunately, inaccurate and misleading statements reported through widely popular medium available worldwide, are the types of misinformation that can and have led private landowners to believe that critical habitat designations prohibit them from making use of their private land when, in fact, they face potential constraints only if they need a Federal permit or receive Federal funding to conduct specific activities on their lands. . . . A designation of critical habitat on private lands could actually encourage habitat destruction by private landowners to rid themselves of the perceived endangered species problem. Listed plants have limited protection under the Act, particularly on private lands. . . . Thus, a private landowner concerned about perceived land management conflicts resulting from a critical habitat designation covering his property would likely face no legal consequences if the landowner removed the listed species or destroyed its habitat. For example, in the spring of 1998, a Los Angeles area developer buried one of the only three populations of the endangered *Astragalus brautonii* in defiance of efforts under the [California Environmental Quality Act] to negotiate mitigation for the species. The designation of critical habitat involves the publication of habitat descriptions and mapped locations of the species in the Federal Register, increasing

the likelihood of potential search and removal activities at specific sites.

Determination of Endangered or Threatened Status for Four Plants from Southwestern California and Baja California, Mexico, 63 Fed. Reg. 54938, 54951–52 (1998). Are these explanations for resisting the designation of the critical habitat of endangered plants persuasive?

**8.** Congress amended the critical habitat provisions of the ESA in the 2004 Defense Department appropriations bill, which allows the FWS to decline to include military lands in critical habitat designations if the harm to national security outweighs the conservation benefit, or if the Interior Department determines that approved resource management plans will adequately protect the species. Pursuant to that provision, the FWS excluded thousands of acres from the critical habitat of the Riverside fairy shrimp and the arroyo toad, and it declined to designate any critical habitat for the Lane Mountain milk-vetch. *See* Endangered and Threatened Wildlife and Plants; Designation of Critical Habitat for the Riverside Fairy Shrimp, Part II, 70 Fed. Reg. 19154 (2005); Endangered and Threatened Wildlife and Plants; Final Designation of Critical Habitat for the Arroyo Toad (Bufo californicus), Part II, 70 Fed. Reg. 19562 (2005); Endangered and Threatened Wildlife and Plants; Designation of Critical Habitat for Astragalus jaegerianus (Lane Mountain milk-vetch), Part V, 70 Fed. Reg. 18220 (2005).

---

## 2. RECOVERY PLANS

Section 4 of the ESA directs the Secretary of the Interior to "develop and implement [recovery plans] for the conservation and survival of endangered and threatened species . . . unless he finds that such a plan will not promote the conservation of the species." ESA § 4(f), 16 U.S.C. § 1533(f). The FWS does not develop a recovery plan for a species if (1) the species is thought to be extinct, (2) state management plans serve as an adequate substitute, or (3) ecosystem initiatives addressing the recovery of multiple species exist. The law further describes how to establish priorities among species for recovery plans and what must be included in a recovery plan. To the maximum extent practicable, priority is to be given to listed species "that are most likely to benefit from such plans, particularly those species that are, or may be, in conflict with construction or other development projects or other forms of economic activity." ESA § 4(f)(1)(A), 16 U.S.C. § 1533(f)(1)(A). Taxonomic classification is not to be considered in establishing such priorities. The contents of a recovery plan—again, to the maximum extent practicable—must include (1) "a description of such site-specific management actions as may be necessary to achieve the plan's goal for the conservation and survival of the species," (2) "objective, measurable criteria which, when met, would result in a determination . . . that the species be removed from the list" of endangered or threatened species; and (3) "estimates of the time required and cost to carry out those measures needed to achieve the plan's goal and to achieve intermediate steps toward that goal." ESA § 4(f)(1)(B), 16 U.S.C. § 1533(f)(1)(B). Public comments on a proposed recovery plan must be considered, and the Secretary must report to Congress every two years regarding the status of efforts to develop recovery plans and the status of species for which plans have been developed. ESA § 4(f)(1)(C), (D), 16 U.S.C. § 1533(f)(1)(C), (D).

Recovery plans were in place for 1,158 species as of July 2016. Some kinds of species—such as snails, clams, and ferns and other plants—are much more likely to have a recovery plan than other kinds of species, such as mammals. *See* John Copeland Nagle, *Playing Noah*, 82 MINN. L. REV. 1171, 1200 n.114 (1998) (indicating that recovery plans existed for 80% of arachnids, 78% of snails, 71% of ferns and certain other plants, 69% of clams, 62% of fishes, 58% of flowering plants, 57% of insects, 44% of amphibians, 33% of crustaceans, 27% of reptiles, 26% of birds, 25% of conifers, and 12% of mammals as of July 1991). Why are endangered and threatened snails so likely to have a recovery plan, but listed mammals are not?

Judicial review of the content and implementation of recovery plans has been deferential to the agency. One notable exception is The Fund for Animals v. Babbitt, 903 F. Supp. 96 (D.D.C. 1995), where the court rejected many objections to the recovery plan for the grizzly bear, but the court ordered the agency to reconsider the plan because it failed to adequately address some of the threats to the grizzlies and because it failed to justify a population target that was lower than what the environmentalists sought. More typical is Morrill v. Lujan, 802 F. Supp. 424, 433 (S.D. Ala. 1992), where the court stated that the contents of a recovery plan are discretionary, and therefore refused to order the Fish and Wildlife Service to block the construction of a lounge in an area occupied by the endangered Perdido Key beach mouse. Should the courts take a more active role in managing the recovery process?

Almost by definition, a species that has become endangered no longer lives in many areas where it once could be found. Efforts to save the species often seek to reintroduce it to areas from which it has disappeared, or even to areas where it never lived but which offer suitable habitat. The list of species that have been reintroduced into former or new habitat since the enactment of the ESA includes California condors, grizzly bears, black-footed ferrets, peregrine falcons, and many others. Many other recovery plans list reintroduction as a possible step toward the preservation of a species. But a 1994 study of 145 reintroduction efforts involving 115 species concluded that only sixteen had produced populations that were sustaining themselves in the wild, and that only half of those species had been endangered. *See* Mark Derr, *As Rescue Plan for Threatened Species, Breeding Programs Falter*, N.Y. TIMES, Jan. 19, 1999, at F1. The reintroduction of the red wolf into the Great Smoky Mountains National Park was abandoned in 1998 when government officials removed the remaining wolves because the wolves could not find enough prey to survive. Reintroduction efforts fact other criticisms as well. They are costly: reintroduction of the condor, wolf and black-footed ferret alone have cost a total of more than $50 million. They are dependent upon adequate habitat, and so face the same challenges as existing populations of wild species in the face of human development. And they can be controversial among local residents, as best illustrated by the reaction of local residents to the reintroduction of wolves in Yellowstone National Park, in southern Arizona and New Mexico, and in North Carolina.

Numerous proposals have been offered for reforming the ESA's recovery planning process, though none have become law. In 1988, though, Congress amended the ESA to require the FWS to report biannually on how much money is spent on the conservation of each listed species. See ESA § 18, 16 U.S.C. § 1548. The chinook salmon placed first in the fiscal year 2011 expenditure report, with $80,004,247 spent on its recovery. Fish species—mostly salmon and trout—rounded out the top nine with expenditures ranging from $30 million to $55 million each. The most spent on a non-fish species was the nearly $27 million for the red-cockaded woodpecker. At the other extreme, only $100 each was spent on a Californian daisy and on four mussels in Tennessee; the report did not explain what $100 could buy for each species. *See* U.S. Fish & Wildlife Service, Federal and State Endangered and Threatened Species Expenditures: Fiscal Year 2011 (2011).

---

## B. RESPONSIBILITIES OF ALL FEDERAL AGENCIES UNDER THE ESA

Congress has charged the FWS (and in some circumstances, the NMFS) with the responsibility for taking the lead on federal efforts to protect species listed as endangered or threatened under the ESA. While the FWS leads, other federal agencies are supposed to follow. The ESA requires all federal agencies to consider the effects of their activities on listed species. That means that a Federal Highway Administration interstate project, an Air Force missile range, and a Corps of Engineers river dredging project must all account for any listed species that they might affect. In particular, the ESA imposes an affirmative duty and a negative duty on federal agencies.

The affirmative duty directs all agencies to conserve listed species. Specifically, ESA Section 7(a)(1) provides that the Secretary of the Interior "shall review other programs administered by him and utilize such programs in furtherance of the purposes of this chapter. All other Federal agencies shall, in consultation with and with the assistance of the Secretary, utilize their authorities in furtherance of the purposes of this chapter by carrying out programs for the conservation of endangered species and threatened species." Most courts have interpreted the conservation duty narrowly. *See, e.g.*, Pyramid Lake Paiute Tribe of

Indians v. United States Department of the Navy, 898 F.2d 1410 (9th Cir. 1990) (holding that the Navy did not violate Section 7(a)(1) when it took water from the Truckee River to suppress dust that interfered with flight training despite the possible adverse effect on endangered fish living in Pyramid Lake resulting from the reduction in the lake's water level); Strahan v. Linnon, 966 F. Supp. 111 (D. Mass. 1997) (rejecting the claim that the Coast Guard violated Section 7(a)(1) by refusing to impose speed limits and other constraints on vessels operating in waters containing the Northern Right whale and other endangered marine species); Center for Marine Conservation v. Brown, 917 F. Supp. 1128, 1149–50 (S.D. Tex. 1996) (concluding that the federal agencies responsible for regulating fishery resources did not violate Section 7(a)(1) when they refused to take additional steps to protect endangered sea turtles from commercial shrimping operations); *but see* Sierra Club v. Glickman, 156 F.3d 606 (5th Cir. 1998) (holding that the Department of Agriculture may have failed to comply with Section 7(a)(1) when it declined to take actions necessary to prevent the contamination of the Edwards Aquifer in central Texas); Florida Key Deer v. Stickney, 864 F. Supp. 1222 (S.D. Fla. 1994) (finding that FEMA violated Section 7(a)(1) when it failed to undertake *any* actions to protect the endangered Florida Key deer). Most recently, the Eleventh Circuit ruled that FEMA failed to comply with Section 7(a)(1) in its implementation of the National Flood Insurance Act, which environmentalists blame for encouraging developing in the coastal habitat of listed species. The court had

> no trouble concluding that FEMA's program to conserve amounts to the total inaction that other courts have condemned. Through the program, FEMA has offered incentives for communities to develop conservation plans for approximately nine years, and yet FEMA has cited no record evidence that even a single community has developed or adopted such a plan in response. The program has had no effect whatsoever despite its long tenure, and it is therefore not a program to conserve.

Florida Key Deer v. Paulison, 522 F.3d 1133, 1141 (11th Cir. 2008).

The negative duty stated in Section 7(a)(2) prohibits federal agencies from jeopardizing the continued existence of a listed species or adversely affecting the designated critical habitat of a species. (Federal agencies must also comply with the ESA Section 9's prohibition against taking a listed species, but that provision is discussed later in this chapter because it applies to governmental and private parties alike). The jeopardy prohibition has received much more attention than the conservation duty to date, but there are indications that the conservation duty could begin to become a more prominent feature of the act.

1. THE CONSULTATION DUTY

## Karuk Tribe of California v. United States Forest Service

United States Court of Appeals for the Ninth Circuit, 2012.
681 F.3d 1006, *cert. denied*, 133 S. Ct. 1579 (2013).

■ W. FLETCHER, CIRCUIT JUDGE:

We consider whether the U.S. Forest Service must consult with appropriate federal wildlife agencies under *Section 7* of the Endangered Species Act ("ESA") before allowing mining activities to proceed under a Notice of Intent ("NOI") in critical habitat of a listed species. The ESA requires consultation with the Fish and Wildlife Service or the NOAA Fisheries Service for any "agency action" that "may affect" a listed species or its critical habitat. 16 U.S.C. § 1536(a)(2); 50 C.F.R. § 402.14(a). There are two substantive questions before us.

The first is whether the Forest Service's approval of four NOIs to conduct mining in the Klamath National Forest is "agency action" within the meaning of *Section 7*. Under our established case law, there is "agency action" whenever an agency makes an affirmative, discretionary decision about whether, or under what conditions, to allow private activity to proceed. The record in this case shows that Forest Service District Rangers made affirmative, discretionary decisions about whether, and under what conditions, to allow mining to proceed under the NOIs.

The second is whether the approved mining activities "may affect" a listed species or its critical habitat. Forest Service regulations require a NOI for all proposed mining activities that "might cause" disturbance of surface resources, which include fisheries and wildlife habitat. 36 C.F.R. §§ 228.4(a), 228.8(e). In this case, the Forest Service approved mining activities in and along the Klamath River, which is critical habitat for threatened coho salmon. The record shows that the mining activities approved under NOIs satisfy the "may affect" standard.

We therefore hold that the Forest Service violated the ESA by not consulting with the appropriate wildlife agencies before approving NOIs to conduct mining activities in coho salmon critical habitat within the Klamath National Forest.

I. Background

The Karuk Tribe has inhabited what is now northern California since time immemorial. The Klamath River originates in southeastern Oregon, runs through northern California, and empties into the Pacific Ocean about forty miles south of the California-Oregon border. In northern California, the Klamath River passes through the Six Rivers and Klamath National Forests. The Klamath River system is home to several species of fish, including coho salmon. Coho salmon in the

Klamath River system were listed as "threatened" under the ESA in 1997. The Klamath River system and adjacent streamside riparian zones were designated as critical habitat for coho salmon in 1999. The Karuk Tribe depends on coho salmon in the Klamath River system for cultural, religious, and subsistence uses.

The rivers and streams of the Klamath River system also contain gold. Commercial gold mining in and around the rivers and streams of California was halted long ago due, in part, to extreme environmental harm caused by large-scale placer mining. *See generally* People v. Gold Run Ditch & Mining Co., 4 P. 1152 (Cal. 1884) (affirming injunction against hydraulic gold mining because of impacts on downstream rivers); GREEN VERSUS GOLD: SOURCES IN CALIFORNIA'S ENVIRONMENTAL HISTORY 101–40 (Carolyn Merchant ed., 1998) (describing environmental impacts of the California Gold Rush). However, small-scale recreational mining has continued. Some recreational miners "pan" for gold by hand, examining one pan of sand and gravel at a time. Some conduct "motorized sluicing" by pumping water onto streambanks to process excavated rocks, gravel, and sand in a sluice box. As the material flows through the box, a small amount of the heavier material, including gold, is slowed by "riffles" and is then captured in the bottom of the box. The remaining material runs through the box and is deposited in a tailings pile. Finally, some recreational miners conduct mechanical "suction dredging" within the streams themselves. These miners use gasoline-powered engines to suck streambed material up through flexible intake hoses that are typically four or five inches in diameter. The streambed material is deposited into a floating sluice box, and the excess is discharged in a tailings pile in or beside the stream. Dredging depths are usually about five feet, but can be as great as twelve feet.

The Karuk Tribe contends that these mining activities adversely affect fish, including coho salmon, in the Klamath River system. The Tribe challenges the Forest Service's approval of four NOIs to conduct mining activities in coho salmon critical habitat in the Klamath National Forest, without first consulting with federal wildlife agencies pursuant to *Section 7 of the ESA*.

A. Mining Regulations

Under the General Mining Law of 1872, a private citizen may enter public lands for the purpose of prospecting and mining. 30 U.S.C. § 22. The Organic Administration Act of 1897 extended the Mining Law to the National Forest system but authorized the Secretary of Agriculture to regulate mining activities in the National Forests to protect the forest lands from destruction and depredation. 16 U.S.C. §§ 482, 551. The Act specified that prospectors and miners entering federal forest lands "must comply with the rules and regulations covering such national forests." *Id.* § 478. We have repeatedly upheld the Forest Service's authority to impose reasonable environmental regulations on mining activities in

National Forests, so long as they do not prohibit or impermissibly encroach on legitimate mining uses.

In 1974, the Forest Service promulgated regulations to minimize the adverse environmental impacts of mining activities in *National Forests.* The regulations establish three different categories of mining, based on whether the proposed activities "will not cause," "might cause," or "will likely cause" significant disturbance of surface resources, which include fisheries and wildlife habitat. The first category, *de minimis* mining activities that "will not cause" significant disturbance of surface resources, may proceed without notifying the Forest Service or obtaining the agency's approval or authorization. The third category, mining activities that "will likely cause" significant disturbance of surface resources, may not proceed until the Forest Service approves a Plan of Operations ("Plan") submitted by the miner. A Plan requires relatively detailed information, including "the approximate location and size of areas where surface resources will be disturbed" and "measures to be taken to meet the requirements for environmental protection." Within 30 days of receiving a Plan, or 90 days if necessary, the Forest Service must approve the proposed Plan or notify the miner of any additional environmental conditions necessary to meet the purpose of the regulations.

At issue in this appeal is the middle category of mining activities: those that "might cause" disturbance of surface resources. Forest Service mining regulations require that any person proposing such activities must submit a Notice of Intent to operate, or NOI, to the appropriate District Ranger. A NOI is less detailed than a Plan. It need only contain information "sufficient to identify the area involved, the nature of the proposed operations, the route of access to the area of operations and the method of transport." Within 15 days of receiving a NOI, the District Ranger must notify the miner whether a Plan is required. . . .

B. 2004 Mining Season

Before the start of the 2004 mining season, representatives of the Karuk Tribe expressed concern to the Forest Service about the effects of suction dredge mining on fisheries in the Klamath River system. The District Ranger for the Happy Camp District of the Klamath National Forest, Alan Vandiver, responded by organizing meetings that included Tribal leaders, miners, and district officials. Vandiver also consulted with Forest Service biologists Bill Bemis and Jon Grunbaum. . . . [Eventually, Vandiver approved a number of NOIs, and the tribe sued the Forest Service for allegedly violating the ESA, the National Environmental Policy Act, and the National Forest Management Act. The district court rejected the tribe's claims, and a Ninth Circuit panel affirmed that decision 2–1. The Ninth Circuit then agreed to rehear the case en banc.]

Consultation Under the Endangered Species Act

We have described *Section 7* as the "heart of the ESA." W. Watersheds Project v. Kraayenbrink, 632 F.3d 472, 495 (9th Cir. 2011). *Section 7* requires federal agencies to ensure that none of their activities, including the granting of licenses and permits, will jeopardize the continued existence of listed species or adversely modify a species' critical habitat.

*Section 7* imposes on all agencies a duty to consult with either the Fish and Wildlife Service or the NOAA Fisheries Service before engaging in any discretionary action that may affect a listed species or critical habitat. Turtle Island Restoration Network v. Nat'l Marine Fisheries Serv., 340 F.3d 969, 974 (9th Cir. 2003). The purpose of consultation is to obtain the expert opinion of wildlife agencies to determine whether the action is likely to jeopardize a listed species or adversely modify its critical habitat and, if so, to identify reasonable and prudent alternatives that will avoid the action's unfavorable impacts. *Id.* The consultation requirement reflects "a conscious decision by Congress to give endangered species priority over the 'primary missions' of federal agencies." Tenn. Valley Auth. v. Hill, 437 U.S. 153, 185 (1978).

*Section 7(a)(2) of the ESA* provides:

> Each Federal agency shall, in consultation with and with the assistance of the Secretary, insure that any action authorized, funded, or carried out by such agency (hereinafter in this section referred to as an "*agency action*") is not likely to jeopardize the continued existence of any endangered species or threatened species or result in the destruction or adverse modification of [critical] habitat of such species. . . .

*16 U.S.C. § 1536(a)(2)* (emphasis added).

Regulations implementing *Section 7* provide:

> Each Federal agency shall review its actions at the earliest possible time to determine whether any action *may affect* listed species or critical habitat. If such a determination is made, formal consultation is required. . . .

*50 C.F.R. § 402.14(a)* (emphasis added).

We discuss the "agency action" and "may affect" requirements in turn.

1. Agency Action

*Section 7 of the ESA* defines agency action as "any action authorized, funded, or carried out by [a federal] agency." The ESA implementing regulations provide:

> Action means all activities or programs of any kind authorized, funded, or carried out, in whole or in part, by Federal agencies in the United States or upon the high seas.

> Examples include, but are not limited to: (a) actions intended to conserve listed species or their habitat; (b) the promulgation of regulations; (c) the granting of licenses, contracts, leases, easements, rights-of-way, permits, or grants-in-aid; or (d) actions directly or indirectly causing modifications to the land, water, or air.

50 C.F.R. § 402.02. There is "little doubt" that Congress intended agency action to have a broad definition in the ESA, and we have followed the Supreme Court's lead by interpreting its plain meaning "in conformance with Congress's clear intent." Pac. Rivers Council v. Thomas, 30 F.3d 1050, 1054–55 (9th Cir. 1994) (citing *Tenn. Valley Auth.,* 437 U.S. at 173).

The ESA implementing regulations limit Section 7's application to " 'actions in which there is discretionary Federal involvement or control.' " Nat'l Ass'n of Home Builders v. Defenders of Wildlife, 551 U.S. 644, 666 (2007) (quoting 50 C.F.R. § 402.03). The Supreme Court explained that this limitation harmonizes the ESA consultation requirement with other statutory mandates that leave an agency no discretion to consider the protection of listed species. *Home Builders*, 551 U.S. at 665–66.

Our "agency action" inquiry is two-fold. First, we ask whether a federal agency affirmatively authorized, funded, or carried out the underlying activity. Second, we determine whether the agency had some discretion to influence or change the activity for the benefit of a protected species.

a. Affirmative Authorization

We have repeatedly held that the ESA's use of the term "agency action" is to be construed broadly. Examples of agency actions triggering Section 7 consultation include the renewal of existing water contracts, Natural Res. Def. Council v. Houston, 146 F.3d 1118, 1125 (9th Cir. 1998), the creation of interim management strategies, Lane Cnty. Audubon Soc'y v. Jamison, 958 F.2d 290, 293–94 (9th Cir. 1992), and the ongoing construction and operation of a federal dam, *Tenn. Valley Auth.,* 437 U.S. at 173–74. We have also required consultation for federal agencies' authorization of private activities, such as the approval and registration of pesticides, Wash. Toxics Coal. v. Envtl. Prot. Agency, 413 F.3d 1024, 1031–33 (9th Cir. 2005), and the issuance of permits allowing fishing on the high seas, *Turtle Island,* 340 F.3d at 974.

An agency must consult under *Section 7* only when it makes an "affirmative" act or authorization. Where private activity is proceeding pursuant to a vested right or to a previously issued license, an agency has no duty to consult under *Section 7* if it takes no further affirmative action regarding the activity. Similarly, where no federal authorization is required for private-party activities, an agency's informal proffer of advice to the private party is not "agency action" requiring consultation.

Here, the Forest Service's mining regulations and actions demonstrate that the agency affirmatively authorized private mining activities when it approved the four challenged NOIs. By regulation, the Forest Service must authorize mining activities before they may proceed under a NOI. The regulations require that a miner submit a NOI for *proposed* mining activities. By contrast, a miner conducting *de minimis* mining activities, such as gold panning or mineral sampling, may proceed without submitting anything to, or receiving anything from, the Forest Service. When a miner submits a NOI, the regulations also require that the Forest Service inform the miner within 15 days whether the mining may proceed under the NOI or whether he must prepare a Plan of Operations instead. In other words, when a miner proposes to conduct mining operations under a NOI, the Forest Service either affirmatively authorizes the mining under the NOI or rejects the NOI and requires a Plan instead. . . .

The Forest Service and the Miners contend that the underlying mining activities are authorized by the General Mining Law, rather than by the agency's approval of the NOIs. But private activities can and do have more than one source of authority, and more than one source of restrictions on that authority. *See* 50 C.F.R. § 402.02 (agency "action" under the ESA includes all private activities authorized "in part" by a federal agency). The Mining Law and the Organic Act give miners "a statutory right, not mere privilege," to enter the National Forests for mining purposes, but Congress has subjected that right to environmental regulation. The Forest Service concedes that its approval of a Plan of Operations "authorizes" mining activities and constitutes an "agency action" under the ESA, even though the Mining Law presumably "authorized" those activities as well. The same logic extends to the agency's approval of a NOI.

The Forest Service contends that approval of a NOI is merely a decision not to regulate the proposed mining activities. But the test under the ESA is whether the agency *authorizes*, funds, or carries out the activity, at least in part. 50 C.F.R. § 402.02 (emphasis added). As shown above, the Forest Service authorizes mining activities when it approves a NOI and affirmatively decides to allow the mining to proceed. Moreover, the record in this case demonstrates that the Forest Service controls mining activities through the NOI process, whether or not such control qualifies a NOI as a "regulatory instrument." As discussed below, the Forest Service formulated precise criteria for the protection of coho salmon, communicated those criteria to prospective miners, and approved the miners' activities under a NOI only if they strictly conformed their mining to the specified criteria. The Forest Service also monitored the miners' compliance with those criteria. . . .

In sum, the Forest Service's approval of the four challenged NOIs constituted agency action under *Section 7 of the ESA*.

b. Discretionary Involvement or Control

The ESA implementing regulations provide that *Section 7* applies only to actions "in which there is discretionary Federal involvement or control." 50 C.F.R. § 402.03. There is no duty to consult for actions "that an agency is *required* by statute to undertake once certain specified triggering events have occurred." *Home Builders,* 551 U.S. at 669 (emphasis in original); *id. at 672–73* (no duty to consult where Clean Water Act required Environmental Protection Agency ("EPA") to transfer regulatory authority to a state upon satisfaction of nine specified criteria). However, to avoid the consultation obligation, an agency's competing statutory mandate must require that it perform specific nondiscretionary acts rather than achieve broad goals. An agency "cannot escape its obligation to comply with the ESA merely because it is bound to comply with another statute that has consistent, complementary objectives." The competing statutory objective need only leave the agency "some discretion."

To trigger the ESA consultation requirement, the discretionary control retained by the federal agency also must have the capacity to inure to the benefit of a protected species. The relevant question is whether the agency *could* influence a private activity to benefit a listed species, not whether it *must* do so.

Here, the Forest Service's mining regulations and actions demonstrate that the decision whether to approve a NOI is a discretionary determination through which the agency can influence private mining activities to benefit listed species. . . . The agency's exercise of discretion under the mining regulations also may influence the mining activities to protect a listed species. The overriding purpose of the regulations is "to minimize [the] adverse environmental impacts" of mining activities on federal forest lands. The touchstone of the agency's discretionary determination is the likelihood that mining activities will cause significant disturbance of surface resources, which include fisheries and wildlife habitat. Thus, the Forest Service can exercise its discretion to benefit a listed species by approving or disapproving NOIs based on whether the proposed mining activities satisfy particular habitat protection criteria. The agency can reject a NOI and require that the prospective miner instead submit a Plan of Operations, under which the Forest Service can impose additional habitat protection conditions.

The record in this case reveals at least three ways in which the Forest Service exercised discretion when deciding whether, and under what conditions, to approve NOIs for mining activities in the Klamath and Six Rivers National Forests.

First, the Forest Service exercised discretion by formulating criteria for the protection of coho salmon habitat. . . . Second, the Forest Service exercised discretion by refusing to approve a detailed NOI submitted by the New 49'ers for mining activities in the Orleans District of the Six Rivers National Forest. . . . Third, the Forest Service exercised discretion when it applied different criteria for the protection of fisheries habitat in different districts of the Klamath National Forest.

Under our established case law, there is "agency action" sufficient to trigger the ESA consultation duty whenever an agency makes an affirmative, discretionary decision about whether, or under what conditions, to allow private activity to proceed. As to all four NOIs challenged in this appeal, the Forest Service made an affirmative, discretionary decision whether to allow private mining activities to proceed under specified habitat protection criteria. Accordingly, we hold that the Forest Service's approval of the NOIs constituted discretionary agency action within the meaning of *Section 7 of the ESA*.

2. May Affect Listed Species or Critical Habitat

An agency has a duty to consult under *Section 7 of the ESA* for any discretionary agency action that "may affect" a listed species or designated critical habitat. An agency may avoid the consultation requirement only if it determines that its action will have "no effect" on a listed species or critical habitat. Once an agency has determined that its action "may affect" a listed species or critical habitat, the agency must consult, either formally or informally, with the appropriate expert wildlife agency. If the wildlife agency determines during informal consultation that the proposed action is "not likely to adversely affect any listed species or critical habitat," formal consultation is not required and the process ends. Thus, actions that have any chance of affecting listed species or critical habitat—even if it is later determined that the actions are "not likely" to do so—require at least some consultation under the ESA.

We have previously explained that "may affect" is a "relatively low" threshold for triggering consultation. Cal. ex rel. Lockyer v. U.S. Dep't of Agric., 575 F.3d 999, 1018 (9th Cir. 2009). " '*Any possible effect*, whether beneficial, benign, adverse or of an undetermined character,' " triggers the requirement. *Id.* at 1018–19 (quoting 51 Fed. Reg. 19,926, 19,949 (June 3, 1986)) (emphasis in *Lockyer*). The Secretaries of Commerce and the Interior have explained that "[t]he threshold for formal consultation must be set sufficiently low to allow Federal agencies to satisfy their duty to 'insure' " that their actions do not jeopardize listed species or adversely modify critical habitat. 51 Fed. Reg. at 19,949.

Whether the mining activities approved by the Forest Service in this case "may affect" critical habitat of a listed species can almost be resolved as a textual matter. By definition, mining activities that require a NOI "might cause" disturbance of surface resources. "Surface resources" include underwater fisheries habitat. The Forest Service approved NOIs to conduct mining activities in and along the Klamath River system, which is designated critical habitat for listed coho salmon. If the phrase "might cause" disturbance of fisheries habitat is given an ordinary meaning, it follows almost automatically that mining pursuant to the approved NOIs "may affect" critical habitat of the coho salmon. Indeed, the Forest Service does not dispute that the mining activities in the Klamath River system "may affect" the listed coho salmon and its critical habitat.

The Miners, however, contend that the record is "devoid of any evidence" that the mining activities may affect coho salmon. The Miners make two arguments in support of their contention. . . . First, the Miners argue that there is no evidence "that even a single member of any listed species would be 'taken' by reason" of the mining activities approved in the NOIs. "Take" has a particular definition under the ESA. 16 U.S.C. § 1532(19) ("The term 'take' means to harass, harm, pursue, hunt, shoot, wound, kill, trap, capture, or collect, or to attempt to engage in any such conduct."); *see also* 50 C.F.R. § 17.3 (further defining "harm" and "harass"). Whether mining activities effectuate a "taking" under *Section 9 of the ESA* is a distinct inquiry from whether they "may affect" a species or its critical habitat under *Section 7*. The Miners also fault the Tribe for failing to identify "so much as a single endangered fish or fish egg ever injured by this [mining] activity." But where, as here, a plaintiff alleges a procedural violation under *Section 7 of the ESA*, as opposed to a substantive violation under *Section 9*, the plaintiff need not prove that a listed species has in fact been injured. The plaintiff need only show, as the Tribe has done here, that the challenged action "may affect" a listed species or its critical habitat.

Second, the Miners argue that Vandiver's consultation with Forest Service biologists, and the resulting habitat protection criteria, "assured" that there would be "no impact whatsoever on listed species." This argument cuts against, rather than in favor of, the Miners. The fact that District Ranger Vandiver formulated criteria to mitigate effects of suction dredging on coho salmon habitat does not mean that the "may affect" standard was not met. Indeed, that Vandiver consulted with Forest Service biologists in an attempt to reduce a possible adverse impact on coho salmon and their habitat suggests exactly the opposite. . . .

We conclude that the mining activities approved by the Forest Service in this case "may affect" the listed coho salmon and its critical habitat. Indeed, as a textual matter, mining activities in designated critical habitat that require approval under a NOI likely satisfy the low threshold triggering the duty to consult under the ESA.

3. Burden on the Forest Service

The burden imposed by the consultation requirement need not be great. Consultation under the ESA may be formal or informal. Formal consultation requires preparation of a biological opinion detailing how the agency action affects listed species or their critical habitat, but informal consultation need be nothing more than discussions and correspondence with the appropriate wildlife agency. If the wildlife agency agrees during informal consultation that the agency action "is not likely to adversely affect listed species or critical habitat," formal consultation is not required and the process ends. Thus, whereas approval of a Plan of Operations—for mining activities that "will likely cause significant disturbance of surface resources"—may often require formal consultation and preparation of a biological opinion, informal consultation may often suffice for approval of a NOI. . . .

■ M. SMITH, CIRCUIT JUDGE, with whom KOZINSKI, CHIEF JUDGE, joins, and with whom IKUTA and MURGUIA, CIRCUIT JUDGES, join as to Parts I through VI, dissenting:

. . . Until today, it was well-established that a regulatory agency's " 'inaction' is not 'action' " that triggers the Endangered Species Act's (ESA) arduous interagency consultation process. W. Watersheds Project v. Matejko, 468 F.3d 1099, 1108 (9th Cir. 2006). Yet the majority now flouts this crystal-clear and common sense precedent, and for the first time holds that an agency's decision *not to act* forces it into a bureaucratic morass. . . .

The majority asserts that the Forest Service's *decision* not to require a Plan of Action for the mining activities described in a Notice of Intent constitutes an *implicit authorization* of those mining activities, therefore equating the Forest Service's "decision" with an agency "authorization" under the ESA.

The Forest Service never contemplated such a result. The Forest Service's explanation of its mining regulations establishes that a Notice of Intent is used as an information-gathering tool, not an application for a mining permit. Consistent with the Forest Service's interpretations, the Ranger's response to a Notice of Intent is analogous to the Notice of Intent itself, and provides merely notice of the agency's review decision. It is not a permit, and does not impose regulations on private conduct as does a Plan of Operations. The Forest Service interprets the Notice of Intent as . . . "a *simple notification procedure*" that would

> "assist prospectors in determining whether their operations would or would not require the filing of an operating plan. Needless uncertainties and expense in time and money in filing unnecessary operating plans could be avoided thereby. . . . [The 1974 notice-and-comment rulemaking] record makes it clear that *a notice of intent to operate was not intended to be a regulatory instrument; it simply was meant to be a notice* given to the Forest Service by an operator which describes the operator's plan to conduct operations on [National Forest Service] lands. Further, this record demonstrates that the intended trigger for a notice of intent to operate is reasonable uncertainty on the part of the operator as to the significance of the potential effects of the proposed operations. In such a circumstance, *the early alert provided by a notice of intent to operate* would advance the interests of both the Forest Service and the operator by *facilitating resolution of the question*, "Is

submission and approval of a plan of operations required before the operator can commence proposed operations?"

[Clarification as to When a Notice of Intent To Operate and/or Plan of Operation Is Needed for Locatable Mineral Operations on National Forest System Lands, 70 Fed. Reg. 32,713, at 32,728 (June 6, 2005) (emphasis added)].

Under the Forest Service's regulations, a Notice of Intent is exactly what its name implies: a *notice* from the miner, not a *permit* or *license* issued by the agency. It is merely a precautionary agency notification procedure, which is at most a preliminary step prior to agency action being taken.

**Precedent distinguishing "action" from "inaction"**

Our precedent establishes that there is a significant difference between a *decision not to act* and an *affirmative authorization*. These cases distinguish between "agency action" and "agency inaction," and illustrate the meaning of the operative regulation's reference to "licenses," "permits," and the like. 50 C.F.R. § 402.02 (2004). In the pertinent cases involving "agency action," the agency takes an *affirmative step* that allows private conduct to take place; without the agency's affirmative action (such as issuing a permit, license, or contract), the private conduct could not occur.[5] In the pertinent cases involving agency *inaction*, private conduct may take place until the agency takes affirmative steps to intervene. The relevant case law requires us to identify the default position: if the agency does nothing, can the private activity take place? If the activity can proceed regardless of whether the agency takes any actions, then the activity does not involve the agency's "granting of licenses, contracts, leases, easements, rights-of-way, permits, or grants-in-aid" as required for "agency action" under the regulations. *Id.* . . .

**VII. Brave New World**

*Abandon all hope, ye who enter here.*

— Dante Alighieri, THE DIVINE COMEDY, Inferno Canto III

I cannot conclude my dissent without considering the impact of the majority's decision in this case, and others like it, which, in my view, flout our precedents and undermine the rule of law. In doing so, I intend no personal disrespect or offense to any of my colleagues. My intent is solely to illuminate the downside of our actions in such environmental cases.

By rendering the Forest Service impotent to meaningfully address low impact mining, the majority effectively shuts down the entire suction dredge mining industry in the states within our jurisdiction. The informal Notice of Intent process allows projects to proceed within a few weeks. In contrast, ESA interagency consultation requires a formal biological assessment and conferences, and can delay projects for months or years. Although the ESA generally requires agencies to complete consultations within ninety days, 16 U.S.C. § 1536(b), the agencies frequently miss their deadlines due to personnel shortages. One study found that nearly 40 percent of U.S. Fish and Wildlife Service ESA consultations were untimely, with some taking two or three years. Government Accountability Office, *More Federal Management Attention is Needed to Improve the Consultation Process*, March 2004. Moreover, formal consultation comes at great costs to the private applicants, often requiring them to hire outside experts because the agency is backlogged. Most miners affected by this decision will have neither the resources nor the patience to pursue a consultation with the EPA; they will simply give up, and curse the Ninth Circuit.

As a result, a number of people will lose their jobs and the businesses that have invested in the equipment used in the relevant mining activities will lose much of their value. In 2008, California issued about 3,500 permits for such mining, and 18 percent of those miners received "a significant portion of income" from the dredging. *See* Justin Scheck, *California Sifts Gold Claims*, THE WALL STREET JOURNAL, April 29, 2012. The gold mining operation in this case, the New 49ers, organizes recreational weekend gold-mining excursions. The majority's opinion effectively forces these people to await the lengthy and costly ESA consultation process if they wish to pursue their mining activities, or simply ignore the process, at their peril. . . .

No legislature or regulatory agency would enact sweeping rules that create such economic chaos, shutter entire industries, and cause thousands of people to lose their jobs. That is because the legislative and executive branches are directly accountable to the people through elections, and its members know they would be removed swiftly from office were they to enact such rules. In contrast, in order to preserve the vitally important principle of judicial independence, we are not politically accountable. However, because of our lack of public accountability, our job is constitutionally confined to *interpreting* laws, not *creating* them out of whole cloth. Unfortunately, I believe the record is clear that our court has strayed with lamentable frequency from its constitutionally limited role . . . when it comes to construing environmental law. When we do so, I fear that we undermine public support for the independence of the judiciary, and cause many to despair of the promise of the rule of law.

I respectfully dissent. . . .

## NOTES & QUESTIONS

**1.** Why does Judge Fletcher think that the Forest Service needs to consult with the FWS regarding possible impacts on endangered species whenever the Forest Service issues a NOI? Why does Judge Smith think that consultation is unnecessary at that time? What decisions could the Forest Service make regarding mining in national forests that would not require consultation according to Judge Fletcher? What decisions could the Forest

Service make that would require consultation according to Judge Smith? What, after all, is the purpose of section 7's consultation requirement?

**2.** Suppose that a federal highway project is proposed for Las Vegas, the fastest growing city in the United States. Scores of other commercial, residential, and road projects are under consideration, about to begin construction, or already being built. Some of these projects are supported or authorized by federal agencies; others are state, local or private projects with no federal nexus. The area is also home to the endangered desert tortoise and a number of other listed species and species under consideration for listing. In determining the effect of the federal highway project, must the cumulative impact of all of the other projects be considered, or only some of them? Must the impact on species that are not listed be considered?

**3.** What happens if the federal agency action changes or additional information is learned about a species—or a new species is listed—after the consultation is completed? The FWS regulations provide that an agency must reopen consultation when (1) the amount or extent of a taking specified in an incidental take statement is exceeded, (2) new information reveals effects of the action that may affect listed species or critical habitat in a manner or to an extent not previously considered, (3) the identified action is subsequently modified in a manner that causes an effect to the listed species or critical habitat that was not considered in the biological opinion, or (4) a new species is listed or critical habitat designated that may be affected by the identified action. 50 C.F.R. § 402.16. The application of the regulations is illustrated by Sierra Club v. Marsh, 816 F.2d 1376 (9th Cir. 1987), where the Army Corps of Engineers agreed as a result of a consultation with the FWS to purchase 200 acres of land to protect two endangered birds that could be affected by a Corps highway and flood control project. When the land proved to be difficult to obtain, the Corps continued work on the project but refused to reinitiate consultation with the FWS. The court held that the Corps could not proceed with the project until it further consulted with the FWS or it acquired the land because of the "institutionalized caution mandated by section 7 of the ESA."

**4.** Judge Smith, joined by Chief Judge Kozinski, claims that the majority's interpretation of the ESA is ill-founded because "[n]o legislature or regulatory agency would enact sweeping rules that create such economic chaos, shutter entire industries, and cause thousands of people to lose their jobs." Can you think of any examples of a legislature or regulatory agency enacting such rules? If such rules are to be enacted, who should enact them?

**5.** Judge Smith also claims that the Ninth Circuit's entire ESA jurisprudence—indeed, its whole environmental jurisprudence—is flawed. He is not the only one to make that argument, which has inspired repeated attempts to divide the Ninth Circuit in a way that separates presumably pro-environmental Californians from those in other western states who are more skeptical of federal environmental regulation. None of those efforts have come close to succeeding. But unlike the Ninth Circuit, the Supreme Court has been seemingly hostile to the broad application of the ESA, *see* J.B. Ruhl, *The Endangered Species Act's Fall from Grace in the Supreme Court*, 36

HARV. ENVTL. L. REV. 487 (2012)—with the dramatic exception of the following case.

---

## 2. THE JEOPARDY PROHIBITION

### Tennessee Valley Authority v. Hill

Supreme Court of the United States, 1978.
437 U.S. 153.

■ MR. CHIEF JUSTICE BURGER delivered the opinion of the Court.

The questions presented in this case are (a) whether the Endangered Species Act of 1973 requires a court to enjoin the operation of a virtually completed federal dam—which had been authorized prior to 1973—when, pursuant to authority vested in him by Congress, the Secretary of the Interior has determined that operation of the dam would eradicate an endangered species; and (b) whether continued congressional appropriations for the dam after 1973 constituted an implied repeal of the Endangered Species Act, at least as to the particular dam.

I

The Little Tennessee River originates in the mountains of northern Georgia and flows through the national forest lands of North Carolina into Tennessee, where it converges with the Big Tennessee River near Knoxville. The lower 33 miles of the Little Tennessee takes the river's clear, free-flowing waters through an area of great natural beauty. Among other environmental amenities, this stretch of river is said to contain abundant trout. Considerable historical importance attaches to the areas immediately adjacent to this portion of the Little Tennessee's banks. To the south of the river's edge lies Fort Loudon, established in 1756 as England's southwestern outpost in the French and Indian War. Nearby are also the ancient sites of several native American villages, the archeological stores of which are to a large extent unexplored. These include the Cherokee towns of Echota and Tennase, the former being the sacred capital of the Cherokee Nation as early as the 16th century and the latter providing the linguistic basis from which the State of Tennessee derives its name.

In this area of the Little Tennessee River the Tennessee Valley Authority, a wholly owned public corporation of the United States, began constructing the Tellico Dam and Reservoir Project in 1967, shortly after Congress appropriated initial funds for its development. Tellico is a multipurpose regional development project designed principally to stimulate shoreline development, generate sufficient electric current to heat 20,000 homes, and provide flatwater recreation and flood control, as well as improve economic conditions in "an area characterized by underutilization of human resources and outmigration of young people." Of particular relevance to this case is one aspect of the project, a dam which TVA determined to place on the Little Tennessee, a short distance from where the river's waters meet with the Big Tennessee. When fully operational, the dam would impound water covering some 16,500 acres—much of which represents valuable and productive farmland—thereby converting the river's shallow, fast-flowing waters into a deep reservoir over 30 miles in length.

The Tellico Dam has never opened, however, despite the fact that construction has been virtually completed and the dam is essentially ready for operation. Although Congress has appropriated monies for Tellico every year since 1967, progress was delayed, and ultimately stopped, by a tangle of lawsuits and administrative proceedings. After unsuccessfully urging TVA to consider alternatives to damming the Little Tennessee, local citizens and national conservation groups brought suit in the District Court, claiming that the project did not conform to the requirements of the National Environmental Policy Act of 1969 (NEPA). After finding TVA to be in violation of NEPA, the District Court enjoined the dam's completion pending the filing of an appropriate environmental impact statement. The injunction remained in effect until late 1973, when the District Court concluded that TVA's final environmental impact statement for Tellico was in compliance with the law.

A few months prior to the District Court's decision dissolving the NEPA injunction, a discovery was made in the waters of the Little Tennessee which would profoundly affect the Tellico Project. Exploring the area around Coytee Springs, which is about seven miles from the mouth of the river, a University of Tennessee ichthyologist, Dr. David A. Etnier, found a previously unknown species of perch, the snail darter, or Percina (Imostoma) tanasi. This three-inch, tannish-colored fish, whose numbers are estimated to be in the range of 10,000 to 15,000, would soon engage the attention of environmentalists, the TVA, the Department of the Interior, the Congress of the United States, and ultimately the federal courts, as a new and additional basis to halt construction of the dam.

Until recently the finding of a new species of animal life would hardly generate a cause celebre. This is particularly so in the case of darters, of which there are approximately 130 known species, 8 to 10 of these having been identified only in the last five years.[7] The moving force behind the snail darter's sudden fame came some four months after its discovery, when the Congress passed the Endangered Species Act of 1973 (Act). This legislation, among other things, authorizes the Secretary of the Interior to declare species of animal life "endangered" and to identify the "critical habitat" of these creatures. When a species or its habitat is

[7] In Tennessee alone there are 85 to 90 species of darters, of which upward to 45 live in the Tennessee River system. New species of darters are being constantly discovered and classified—at the rate of about one per year. This is a difficult task for even trained ichthyologists since species of darters are often hard to differentiate from one another.

so listed, the following portion of the Act—relevant here—becomes effective:

> "The Secretary [of the Interior] shall review other programs administered by him and utilize such programs in furtherance of the purposes of this chapter. All other Federal departments and agencies shall, in consultation with and with the assistance of the Secretary, utilize their authorities in furtherance of the purposes of this chapter by carrying out programs for the conservation of endangered species and threatened species listed pursuant to Section 1533 of this title and *by taking such action necessary to insure that actions authorized, funded, or carried out by them do not jeopardize the continued existence of such endangered species and threatened species or result in the destruction or modification of habitat of such species* which is determined by the Secretary, after consultation as appropriate with the affected States, to be critical." 16 U.S.C. § 1536 (1976 ed.) (emphasis added).

In January 1975, the respondents in this case and others petitioned the Secretary of the Interior to list the snail darter as an endangered species. After receiving comments from various interested parties, including TVA and the State of Tennessee, the Secretary formally listed the snail darter as an endangered species on October 8, 1975. In so acting, it was noted that "the snail darter is a living entity which is genetically distinct and reproductively isolated from other fishes." More important for the purposes of this case, the Secretary determined that the snail darter apparently lives only in that portion of the Little Tennessee River which would be completely inundated by the reservoir created as a consequence of the Tellico Dam's completion.[12] The Secretary went on to explain the significance of the dam to the habitat of the snail darter:

> "[The] snail darter occurs only in the swifter portions of shoals over clean gravel substrate in cool, low-turbidity water. Food of the snail darter is almost exclusively snails which require a clean gravel substrate for their survival. *The proposed impoundment of water behind the proposed Tellico Dam would result in total destruction of the snail darter's habitat.*" (emphasis added).

Subsequent to this determination, the Secretary declared the area of the Little Tennessee which would be affected by the Tellico Dam to be the "critical habitat" of the snail darter. [TVA tried to find an alternative

---

[12] Searches by TVA in more than 60 watercourses have failed to find other populations of snail darters. The Secretary has noted that "more than 1,000 collections in recent years and additional earlier collections from central and east Tennessee have not revealed the presence of the snail darter outside the Little Tennessee River." It is estimated, however, that the snail darter's range once extended throughout the upper main Tennessee River and the lower portions of its major tributaries above Chattanooga—all of which are now the sites of dam impoundments.

river to which it could relocate the snail darters, but those efforts failed. TVA continued to seek congressional funding for the dam, which Congress and President Carter approved in a December 1975 appropriations bill containing funds for the continued construction of the dam. In February 1976, a University of Tennessee law student named Hiram Hill sued TVA to enjoin the completion of the dam based on Section 7 of the ESA. The district court refused to issue an injunction, but the Sixth Circuit reversed and ordered a permanent injunction against the construction of the Tellico Dam. TVA officials testified before congressional committees at several times during the course of the litigation, and each time the committee stated its understanding that the dam should be completed notwithstanding the ESA.]

II

We begin with the premise that operation of the Tellico Dam will either eradicate the known population of snail darters or destroy their critical habitat. Petitioner does not now seriously dispute this fact. In any event, under § 4(a)(1) of the Act, the Secretary of the Interior is vested with exclusive authority to determine whether a species such as the snail darter is "endangered" or "threatened" and to ascertain the factors which have led to such a precarious existence. By § 4(d) Congress has authorized—indeed commanded—the Secretary to "issue such regulations as he deems necessary and advisable to provide for the conservation of such species." As we have seen, the Secretary promulgated regulations which declared the snail darter an endangered species whose critical habitat would be destroyed by creation of the Tellico Reservoir. Doubtless petitioner would prefer not to have these regulations on the books, but there is no suggestion that the Secretary exceeded his authority or abused his discretion in issuing the regulations. Indeed, no judicial review of the Secretary's determinations has ever been sought and hence the validity of his actions are not open to review in this Court.

(A)

It may seem curious to some that the survival of a relatively small number of three-inch fish among all the countless millions of species extant would require the permanent halting of a virtually completed dam for which Congress has expended more than $100 million. The paradox is not minimized by the fact that Congress continued to appropriate large sums of public money for the project, even after congressional Appropriations Committees were apprised of its apparent impact upon the survival of the snail darter. We conclude, however, that the explicit provisions of the Endangered Species Act require precisely that result.

One would be hard pressed to find a statutory provision whose terms were any plainer than those in § 7 of the Endangered Species Act. Its very words affirmatively command all federal agencies "to *insure* that actions *authorized, funded, or carried out* by them do not *jeopardize* the continued existence" of an endangered species or "*result* in the destruction or modification of habitat of such species. . . ." 16 U.S.C. § 1536 (1976 ed.). (Emphasis added.) This language admits of no exception. Nonetheless, petitioner urges, as do the dissenters, that the Act cannot reasonably be interpreted as applying to a federal project which was well under way when Congress passed the Endangered Species Act of 1973. To sustain that position, however, we would be forced to ignore the ordinary meaning of plain language. It has not been shown, for example, how TVA can close the gates of the Tellico Dam without "carrying out" an action that has been "authorized" and "funded" by a federal agency. Nor can we understand how such action will "*insure*" that the snail darter's habitat is not disrupted. Accepting the Secretary's determinations, as we must, it is clear that TVA's proposed operation of the dam will have precisely the opposite effect, namely the eradication of an endangered species.

Concededly, this view of the Act will produce results requiring the sacrifice of the anticipated benefits of the project and of many millions of dollars in public funds. But examination of the language, history, and structure of the legislation under review here indicates beyond doubt that Congress intended endangered species to be afforded the highest of priorities. . . .

The legislative proceedings in 1973 are, in fact, replete with expressions of concern over the risk that might lie in the loss of any endangered species. . . . Congress was concerned about the unknown uses that endangered species might have and about the unforeseeable place such creatures may have in the chain of life on this planet.

In shaping legislation to deal with the problem thus presented, Congress started from the finding that "[the] two major causes of extinction are hunting and destruction of natural habitat." Of these twin threats, Congress was informed that the greatest was destruction of natural habitats. Witnesses recommended, among other things, that Congress require all land-managing agencies "to avoid damaging critical habitat for endangered species and to take positive steps to improve such habitat." Virtually every bill introduced in Congress during the 1973 session responded to this concern by incorporating language similar, if not identical, to that found in the present § 7 of the Act. These provisions were designed, in the words of an administration witness, "for the first time [to] *prohibit* [a] federal agency from taking action which does jeopardize the status of endangered species," furthermore, the proposed bills would "[direct] all . . . Federal agencies to utilize their authorities for carrying out programs for the protection of endangered animals." (Emphasis added.)

As it was finally passed, the Endangered Species Act of 1973 represented the most comprehensive legislation for the preservation of endangered species ever enacted by any nation. Its stated purposes were "to provide a means whereby the ecosystems upon which endangered species and threatened species depend may be conserved," and "to provide a program for the conservation of such . . . species. . . ." In furtherance of these goals, Congress expressly stated in § 2(c) that "all Federal departments and agencies *shall* seek *to conserve endangered species* and threatened species. . . ." (Emphasis added.) Lest there be any ambiguity as to the meaning of this statutory directive, the Act specifically defined "conserve" as meaning "to use and the use of *all methods and procedures which are necessary* to bring *any endangered species* or threatened species to the point at which the measures provided pursuant to this chapter are no longer necessary." (Emphasis added.) Aside from § 7, other provisions indicated the seriousness with which Congress viewed this issue: Virtually all dealings with endangered species, including taking, possession, transportation, and sale, were prohibited, except in extremely narrow circumstances. The Secretary was also given extensive power to develop regulations and programs for the preservation of endangered and threatened species. Citizen involvement was encouraged by the Act, with provisions allowing interested persons to petition the Secretary to list a species as endangered or threatened, and bring civil suits in United States district courts to force compliance with any provision of the Act.

Section 7 of the Act, which of course is relied upon by respondents in this case, provides a particularly good gauge of congressional intent. As we have seen, this provision had its genesis in the Endangered Species Act of 1966, but that legislation qualified the obligation of federal agencies by stating that they should seek to preserve endangered species only "*insofar as is practicable and consistent with [their] primary purposes. . . .*" Likewise, every bill introduced in 1973 contained a qualification similar to that found in the earlier statutes. Exemplary of these was the administration bill, H.R. 4758, which in § 2(b) would direct federal agencies to use their authorities to further the ends of the Act "*insofar as is practicable and consistent with [their] primary purposes. . . .*" (Emphasis added.) Explaining the idea behind this language, an administration spokesman told Congress that it "would further signal to all . . . agencies of the Government that this is the *first priority, consistent with their primary objectives*." (Emphasis added.) This type of language did not go unnoticed by those advocating strong endangered species legislation. A representative of the Sierra Club, for example, attacked the use of the phrase "consistent with the primary purpose" in proposed H.R. 4758, cautioning that the qualification "could be construed to be a declaration of congressional policy that other agency purposes are necessarily more important than protection of endangered species and would always prevail if conflict were to occur."

What is very significant in this sequence is that the final version of the 1973 Act carefully omitted all of the reservations described above. . . . It is against this legislative background that we must measure TVA's claim that the Act was not intended to stop operation of a project which, like Tellico Dam, was near completion when an endangered species was discovered in its path. While there is no discussion in the legislative history of precisely this problem, the totality of congressional action makes it abundantly clear that the result we reach today is wholly in accord with both the words of the statute and the intent of Congress. The plain intent of Congress in enacting this statute was to halt and reverse the trend toward species extinction, whatever the cost. This is reflected not only in the stated policies of the Act, but in literally every section of the statute. All persons, including federal agencies, are specifically instructed not to "take" endangered species, meaning that no one is "to harass, harm, pursue, hunt, shoot, wound, kill, trap, capture, or collect" such life forms. Agencies in particular are directed by §§ 2(c) and 3(2) of the Act to "use . . . *all methods* and procedures which are necessary" to preserve endangered species. (emphasis added). In addition, the legislative history undergirding § 7 reveals an explicit congressional decision to require agencies to afford first priority to the declared national policy of saving endangered species. The pointed omission of the type of qualifying language previously included in endangered species legislation reveals a conscious decision by Congress to give endangered species priority over the "primary missions" of federal agencies.

It is not for us to speculate, much less act, on whether Congress would have altered its stance had the specific events of this case been anticipated. In any event, we discern no hint in the deliberations of Congress relating to the 1973 Act that would compel a different result than we reach here. Indeed, the repeated expressions of congressional concern over what it saw as the potentially enormous danger presented by the eradication of any endangered species suggest how the balance would have been struck had the issue been presented to Congress in 1973.

Furthermore, it is clear Congress foresaw that § 7 would, on occasion, require agencies to alter ongoing projects in order to fulfill the goals of the Act. Congressman Dingell's discussion of Air Force practice bombing, for instance, obviously pinpoints a particular activity—intimately related to the national defense—which a major federal department would be obliged to alter in deference to the strictures of § 7. . . . One might dispute the applicability of these examples to the Tellico Dam by saying that in this case the burden on the public through the loss of millions of unrecoverable dollars would greatly outweigh the loss of the snail darter. But neither the Endangered Species Act nor Art. III of the Constitution provides federal courts with authority to make such fine utilitarian calculations. On the contrary, the plain language of the Act, buttressed by its legislative history, shows clearly that Congress viewed the value of endangered species as "incalculable." Quite obviously, it would be difficult for a court to balance the loss of a sum certain—even $100 million—against a congressionally declared "incalculable" value, even assuming we had the power to engage in such a weighing process, which we emphatically do not. . . .

Notwithstanding Congress' expression of intent in 1973, we are urged to find that the continuing appropriations for Tellico Dam constitute an implied repeal of the 1973 Act, at least insofar as it applies to the Tellico Project. In support of this view, TVA points to the statements found in various House and Senate Appropriations Committees' Reports; as described in Part I, *supra*, those Reports generally reflected the attitude of the *Committees* either that the Act did not apply to Tellico or that the dam should be completed regardless of the provisions of the Act. Since we are unwilling to assume that these latter Committee statements constituted advice to ignore the provisions of a duly enacted law, we assume that these Committees believed that the Act simply was not applicable in this situation. But even under this interpretation of the Committees' actions, we are unable to conclude that the Act has been in any respect amended or repealed. There is nothing in the appropriations measures, as passed, which states that the Tellico Project was to be completed irrespective of the requirements of the Endangered Species Act. These appropriations, in fact, represented relatively minor components of the lump-sum amounts for the entire TVA budget. To find a repeal of the Endangered Species Act under these circumstances would surely do violence to the " 'cardinal rule . . . that repeals by implication are not favored.' . . . The doctrine disfavoring repeals by implication "applies with full vigor when . . . the subsequent legislation is an appropriations measure." . . . Perhaps mindful of the fact that it is "swimming upstream" against a strong current of well-established precedent, TVA argues for an exception to the rule against implied repealers in a circumstance where, as here, Appropriations Committees have expressly stated their "understanding" that the earlier legislation would not prohibit the proposed expenditure. We cannot accept such a proposition. Expressions of committees dealing with requests for appropriations cannot be equated with statutes enacted by Congress, particularly not in the circumstances presented by this case. First, the Appropriations Committees had no jurisdiction over the subject of endangered species, much less did they conduct the type of extensive hearings which preceded passage of the earlier Endangered Species Acts, especially the 1973 Act. . . . Second, there is no indication that Congress as a whole was aware of TVA's position, although the Appropriations Committees apparently agreed with petitioner's views.

(B)

Having determined that there is an irreconcilable conflict between operation of the Tellico Dam and the explicit provisions of § 7 of the Endangered Species Act, we must now consider what remedy, if any, is appropriate. It is correct, of course, that a federal judge sitting as a chancellor is not mechanically obligated to grant an injunction for every violation of law. . . . As a general matter it may be said that "[since] all or almost all equitable remedies are discretionary, the balancing of equities and hardships is appropriate in almost any case as a guide to the chancellor's discretion." . . . But these principles take a court only so far. Our system of government is, after all, a tripartite one, with each branch having certain defined functions delegated to it by the Constitution. While "[it] is emphatically the province and duty of the judicial department to say what the law is," Marbury v. Madison, 1 Cranch 137, 177 (1803), it is equally—and emphatically—the exclusive province of the Congress not only to formulate legislative policies and mandate programs and projects, but also to establish their relative priority for the Nation. Once Congress, exercising its delegated powers, has decided the order of priorities in a given area, it is for the Executive to administer the laws and for the courts to enforce them when enforcement is sought. Here we are urged to view the Endangered Species Act "reasonably," and hence shape a remedy "that accords with some modicum of common sense and the public weal." But is that our function? We have no expert knowledge on the subject of endangered species, much less do we have a mandate from the people to strike a balance of equities on the side of the Tellico Dam. Congress has spoken in the plainest of words, making it abundantly clear that the balance has been struck in favor of affording endangered species the highest of priorities, thereby adopting a policy which it described as "institutionalized caution." Our individual appraisal of the wisdom or unwisdom of a particular course consciously selected by the Congress is to be put aside in the process of interpreting a statute. Once the meaning of an enactment is discerned and its constitutionality determined, the judicial process comes to an end. We do not sit as a committee of review, nor are we vested with the power of veto. The lines ascribed to Sir Thomas More by Robert Bolt are not without relevance here:

> "The law, Roper, the law. I know what's legal, not what's right. And I'll stick to what's legal. . . . I'm not God. The currents and eddies of right and wrong, which you find such plain-sailing, I can't navigate, I'm no voyager. But in the thickets of the law, oh there I'm a forester. . . . What would you do? Cut a great road through the law to get after the Devil? . . . And when the last law was down, and the Devil turned round on you—where would you hide, Roper, the laws all being flat? . . . This country's planted thick with laws from coast to coast—Man's laws, not God's—and if you cut them down . . . d'you really think you could stand upright in the winds that would bellow then? . . . Yes, I'd give the Devil benefit of law, for my own safety's sake." R. Bolt, A Man for All Seasons, Act I, p. 147 (Three Plays, Heinemann ed. 1967).

We agree with the Court of Appeals that in our constitutional system the commitment to the separation of powers is too fundamental for us to pre-empt congressional action by judicially decreeing what accords with "common sense and the public weal." Our Constitution vests such responsibilities in the political branches.

■ MR. JUSTICE POWELL, with whom MR. JUSTICE BLACKMUN joins, dissenting.

The Court today holds that § 7 of the Endangered Species Act requires a federal court, for the purpose of protecting an endangered species or its habitat, to enjoin permanently the operation of any federal project, whether completed or substantially completed. This decision casts a long shadow over the operation of even the most important projects, serving vital needs of society and national defense, whenever it is determined that continued operation would threaten extinction of an endangered species or its habitat. This result is said to be required by the "plain intent of Congress" as well as by the language of the statute.

In my view § 7 cannot reasonably be interpreted as applying to a project that is completed or substantially completed when its threat to an endangered species is discovered. Nor can I believe that Congress could have intended this Act to produce the "absurd result"—in the words of the District Court—of this case. If it were clear from the language of the Act and its legislative history that Congress intended to authorize this result, this Court would be compelled to enforce it. It is not our province to rectify policy or political judgments by the Legislative Branch, however egregiously they may disserve the public interest. But where the statutory language and legislative history, as in this case, need not be construed to reach such a result, I view it as the duty of this Court to adopt a permissible construction that accords with some modicum of common sense and the public weal.

. . . I have little doubt that Congress will amend the Endangered Species Act to prevent the grave consequences made possible by today's decision. Few, if any, Members of that body will wish to defend an interpretation of the Act that requires the waste of at least $53 million, and denies the people of the Tennessee Valley area the benefits of the reservoir that Congress intended to confer. There will be little sentiment to leave this dam standing before an empty reservoir, serving no purpose other than a conversation piece for incredulous tourists.

But more far reaching than the adverse effect on the people of this economically depressed area is the continuing threat to the operation of every federal project, no matter how important to the Nation. If Congress acts expeditiously, as may be anticipated, the Court's decision probably will have no lasting adverse consequences. But I had not thought it to be the province of this Court to force Congress into otherwise unnecessary action by interpreting a statute to produce a result no one intended.

[JUSTICE REHNQUIST dissented because he concluded that the district court's refusal to issue an injunction was not an abuse of discretion]

---

## QUESTIONS AND DISCUSSION

**1.** In 1979, six years after voting for the ESA, Tennessee Senator Howard Baker described the snail darter as "the bold perverter of the Endangered Species Act." 125 CONG. REC. 23867 (1979). Was he right?

**2.** If the TVA had succeeded in its efforts to relocate the snail darter to any river, would that have been an acceptable solution?

**3.** What would happen if the snail darter was discovered just *after* the dam was completed, but before the darter's habitat was destroyed? Would TVA have to tear down the dam? The ESA has never been applied to require the destruction or removal of an existing structure. But some environmentalists have been pressing to remove some of the dams on the Columbia River system in the Pacific Northwest in order to protect several endangered species of salmon. *See* Michael C. Blumm et al., *Saving Snake River Water and Salmon Simultaneously: The Biological, Economic, and Legal Case for Breaching the Lower Snake River Dams, Lowering the John Day Reservoir, and Restoring Natural River Flows*, 28 ENVTL. L. 997 (1998).

**4.** Perhaps the most dramatic recent jeopardy finding occurred in April 2001 when the FWS and NMFS advised the federal Bureau of Reclamation that its annual operating plan for the Klamath Reclamation Project would jeopardize the continued existence of the endangered Lost River sucker, the shortnose sucker, and the Southern Oregon/Northern California Coast coho salmon. Congress authorized the irrigation project as part of its effort to encourage the settlement of previously arid parts of Oregon. By 2001, though, farmers relying upon irrigation water competed with the suckers and salmon living in the Klamath River, bald eagles preying upon waterfowl in the Lower Klamath National Wildlife Refuge, and members of the Klamath and Yurok Tribes who revered the suckers and who possessed treaty rights to the rivers. Then a drought was predicted for 2001. An ESA Section 7 consultation between FWS, NMFS, and the Bureau of Reclamation resulted in a biological opinion that the Bureau's plans to provide irrigation water from the project would jeopardize the suckers and the salmon, so the Bureau issued a revised plan that denied water to most of the farmers who had historically relied upon it. The farmers and their irrigation district then sought an injunction against that revised plan for the Klamath Reclamation Project. The district court denied the injunction because the balance of hardships did not tip sufficiently in favor of the plaintiffs: while there was "no question that farmers who rely upon irrigation water and their communities will suffer severe economic hardship" from the plan, the court cited *TVA v. Hill* as evidence that "[t]hreats to the continued existence of endangered and threatened species constitute ultimate harm." Kandra v. United States, 145 F. Supp. 2d 1192, 1200–01 (D. Or. 2001).

The jeopardy finding and the court's refusal to enjoin the revised plan triggered civil unrest in Oregon throughout the summer of 2001. Farmers watched as their crops died during the record drought. In early July, "100 to 150 people formed a human chain and shielded men who cut off the headgate's lock using a diamond-bladed chainsaw and a cutting torch, sending water from the Upper Klamath Lake into the canal." *Farmers Force*

*Open Canal in Fight with U.S. Over Water*, N.Y. TIMES, July 6, 2001, at A10. The irrigation canal's headgates were opened three more times in a symbolic protest against the lack of irrigation water. The protestors withdrew after the September 11 terrorists attacks, but controversy gained a racial edge when three men were arrested in December for driving through the town of Chiloquin, Oregon while firing shotguns and deriding Native Americans as "sucker lovers." And then the premise for the dispute was called into question when the National Academy of Sciences reported in February 2002 that the provision of water to the endangered suckers and salmon instead of the farmers did not yield any appreciable benefit to the fish. *See* National Academy of Sciences, Scientific Evaluation of the Biological Opinions on Endangered and Threatened Fishes in the Klamath River Basin: Interim Report (2002).

Looking back on the dispute concerning the Klamath River, Holly Doremus and Dan Tarlock identify "the root cause" as "too many demands competing for too little water." They conclude that "[s]cience alone cannot determine how water should be allocated among those competing demands. It is a mistake to demand that scientists identify the magic point at which agricultural water withdrawals can be precisely balanced with environmental protection. . . . Instead, policymakers should understand that they are dealing with a clash of cultures, and must make value choices. Society must choose between farming and fish, or find a way to accommodate both." Holly Doremus & A. Dan Tarlock, *Fish, Farms, and the Clash of Cultures in the Klamath Basin*, 30 ECOLOGY L.Q. 279, 349 (2003). Marcilynn Burke offers another perspective on the dispute, arguing that the political rhetoric accompanying the Klamath controversy "lures its audience into a world where costs eclipse benefits, conjecture prevails over sound science, and species protection abrogates private property rights." Marcilynn A. Burke, *Klamath Farmers and Cappuccino Cowboys: The Rhetoric of the Endangered Species Act and Why It (Still) Matters*, 14 DUKE ENVTL. L. & POL'Y F. 441, 520 (2004). Nor are such disputes between endangered fish (and other species) and competing users of water limited to the Pacific Northwest. Similar controversies arose in 2003 involving the Missouri and Rio Grande Rivers. *See* Rio Grande Silvery Minnow v. Keys, 333 F.3d 1109 (10th Cir. 2003) (holding that the Bureau of Reclamation has the discretion to reduce the delivery of water for irrigation in order to satisfy Section 7 of the ESA); American Rivers v. United States Army Corps of Engineers, 271 F. Supp. 2d 230 (D.D.C. 2003) (enjoining the Corps from managing its operations along the Missouri River in a way that would jeopardize the least tern, piping plover, and pallid sturgeon); Sandra B. Zellmer, *A New Corps of Discovery for Missouri River Management*, 83 NEB. L. REV. 305 (2004).

**5.** Professor Oliver Houck counters that the vast majority of Section 7 consultations result in no jeopardy findings. His 1993 study determined that fewer than .02% of all consultations have resulted in the termination of the project in question. "No major public activity, nor any major federally-permitted activity was blocked" in any of the 99 FWS jeopardy opinions issued between 1987 and 1992 that Houck examined. Indeed, he argues that FWS has wrongly avoided the invocation of the jeopardy provision by narrowly viewing the agency action at issue, by failing to apply the section to federal projects overseas, by conflating jeopardy and critical habitat, and by improperly declining to list species in the first place. *See* Oliver A. Houck, *The Endangered Species Act and Its Implementation By the U.S. Departments of Interior and Commerce*, 64 U. COLO. L. REV. 277, 317–26 (1993). Daniel Rohlf reached a similar conclusion when he asserted that "the concept of jeopardy often amounts to little more than a vague threat employed by FWS and NMFS to negotiate relatively minor modifications to federal and non-federal actions." Daniel J. Rohlf, *Jeopardy Under the Endangered Species Act: Playing a Game Protected Species Can't Win*, 41 WASHBURN L. REV. 114, 115 (2001).

**6.** The Supreme Court's decision in *TVA v. Hill* was not the end of the fight between the Tellico Dam and the snail darter. Later in 1978, Congress responded by adding a provision to the ESA that established an Endangered Species Committee empowered to waive the jeopardy prohibition in appropriate circumstances. This committee—commonly known as the "God Squad" because of its power to determine the fate of a species on the brink of extinction—is comprised of seven federal officials and one individual selected by the President from each of the states involved. The exemption process may be triggered by a request from the federal agency proposing the action, the governor of the state in which the action will occur, and a private applicant for federal permit or license that results in a jeopardy finding. The committee is empowered to waive the prohibitions of Section 7 (and also Section 9, whose provisions are discussed later in Chapter 5) only if at least five of its members determine that (1) there are no reasonable and prudent alternatives to the federal agency action, (2) the benefits of the agency action clearly outweigh alternatives that would protect the species, (3) the agency action is of national or regional significance, and (4) no irreversible or irretrievable commitment of resources are made prior to the committee's ruling. *See* ESA § 7(e).

Not surprisingly, the God Squad made its debut when TVA requested a waiver for the Tellico Dam. More surprisingly, in January 1979 the committee unanimously rejected the request. As Secretary of the Interior Cecil Andrus stated, "Frankly, I hate to see the snail darter get the credit for stopping a project that was ill-conceived and uneconomical in the first place."

The subtle approach having failed, congressional supporters of the Tellico Dam responded by adding a provision to the 1980 Interior appropriations bill that exempted the dam from *all* federal laws. The House approved the bill without debate, but it passed the Senate by a narrow 48–44 margin. President Carter opposed the exemption for the dam, but he signed the bill anyway because of the other things that it contained.

The fight against the dam had one last gasp. The congressional waiver protected the dam from any federal statutory requirements, but it did not—and probably could not—bar constitutional objections to the dam. A group of Native Americans claimed that the dam would result in flooding of their sacred sites and would thus violate their first amendment right to the free exercise of their religion. The courts said no. *See* Sequoyah v. Tennessee

Valley Auth., 480 F. Supp. 608 (E.D. Tenn. 1979), *cert. denied*, 449 U.S. 953 (1980).

Finally, on November 29, 1979, the Tellico Dam was completed and the Little Tennessee River was impounded. Again, the consequences were not at all expected. The economic development forecast by the supporters of the dam never quite materialized. An early proposal would have located a hazardous waste facility near the newly created reservoir, but instead a retirement community known as Tellico Village developed at the site. On the other hand, the snail darter did not become extinct, either. Nearly one year after the dam was completed, the same scientist who had discovered the snail darter on the Little Tennessee River in 1973 found other populations of snail darters in four other rivers in Tennessee whose conditions were not supposed to have been acceptable for the fish. Apparently the snail darters did not know that, though, and they survive in such abundance that the species was downlisted from endangered to threatened in 1984.

The saga of the snail darter and the Tellico Dam is told in ZYGMUNT J.B. PLATER, THE SNAIL DARTER AND THE DAM: HOW PORK-BARREL POLITICS ENDANGERED A LITTLE FISH AND KILLED A RIVER (2013); CHARLES C. MANN & MARK L. PLUMMER, NOAH'S CHOICE: THE FUTURE OF ENDANGERED SPECIES 147–175 (1995); WILLIAM B. WHEELER & MICHAEL J. MCDONALD, TVA AND THE TELLICO DAM, 1936–1979 (1986).

**7.** Congress designed the Endangered Species Committee with the snail darter in mind, but the committee remains a permanent fixture in the ESA. It has been employed infrequently. Only a handful of applications have been made to invoke the committee to waive a jeopardy finding, and only twice has the committee agreed to do so. The first instance occurred in 1979, when the committee approved a settlement that allowed the operation of Nebraska's Greyrocks Dam and Reservoir consistent with the needs of the endangered whooping crane. The committee granted its second waiver in 1992 when it exempted 13 out of a requested 44 proposed Oregon timber sales despite the presence of the northern spotted owl, but a court decision questioning the committee's procedures and the advent of the Clinton Administration resulted in the timber sales never actually occurring. The exemption process has not been invoked since then, though there has been speculation that the listing of several species of salmon in the Pacific Northwest could trigger a request for an exemption if a federal water project is found to jeopardize the salmon. Most recently, the irrigation districts denied water pursuant to the jeopardy finding described above in note 2 sought to obtain an exemption in the summer of 2001, but Interior Secretary Gale Norton concluded that the districts were not among the parties empowered by the statute to invoke the exemption process.

---

## III. PRIVATE PARTY RESPONSIBILITIES UNDER THE ENDANGERED SPECIES ACT

Despite all of the land that it owns and all of its responsibilities, the efforts of the federal government alone cannot save most endangered species. Half of the species listed under the ESA have at least 80% of their habitat on private lands, and many of the threats to particular species are attributable to the actions of state and local governments and private individuals.

Habitat destruction presents the greatest threat to the survival of species in the United States and throughout the world. The drafters of the ESA recognized as much when they stated that the purpose of the law is "to provide a means whereby the ecosystems upon which endangered species and threatened species depend may be conserved." ESA § 2(b). Yet the ESA does not contain a provision that protects all of the habitats of all listed species from destruction or other harms. Instead, the ESA addresses habitat destruction through several different kinds of provisions. Section 4 authorizes the FWS to designate the critical habitat of a species. Section 5 directs appropriate federal agencies to acquire land used as habitat by listed species.

The ESA addresses the conduct of all public and private parties in Section 9. That provision makes it illegal to "import," "export," "possess," "transport," or "take" a listed species of fish or wildlife, just to list a few of the verbs contained in the law. 16 U.S.C. § 1538(a)(1) (Section 9 provides a different and less comprehensive set of protections to endangered plants). In other words, the ESA prohibits the smuggling of a listed fish or wildlife species—dead or alive—into the United States, and it prohibits poaching or killing of such a species. Section 9 may also encompass a variety of other indirect actions that can harm a species. The contested cases have featured disoriented baby sea turtles attracted to beachfront lights, grizzly bears feasting on grain spilled on railroad tracks as another train looms, and the fear that bald eagles would be poisoned by lead shot used to kill deer. Federal, state and local governments often find themselves accused of injuring listed species by failing to take actions necessary to protect them from a variety of threats.

But Section 9 applies to other conduct, too. "Take" is defined to include "to harass, harm, pursue, hunt, shoot, wound, kill, trap, capture, or collect, or to attempt to engage in any such conduct." ESA § 3(18). Those terms, in turn, open the possibility that the unintentional destruction of the habitat of a listed species runs afoul of the law. The extension of the ESA to private developers and landowners whose actions adversely impact the habitat of a species has resulted in most of the controversy surrounding the law in recent years. Private landowners object that while the discovery of gold or oil makes a property owner rich, the discovery of a rare animal or bird on one's property threatens bankruptcy if that blocks the landowner from using the property. Yet the preservation of habitat is essential for the survival of biodiversity, especially given that habitat destruction is the primary cause of the decline of most endangered species. The same actions that environmentalists view as critical for the survival of a species are often denounced as overzealous government interference with private landowners. The provisions of the ESA itself are at issue in this debate, which shows no signs of ending any time soon.

## A. THE SCOPE OF THE "TAKE" PROHIBITION

### Babbitt v. Sweet Home Chapter of Communities for a Great Oregon

Supreme Court of the United States, 1995.
515 U.S. 687.

■ JUSTICE STEVENS delivered the opinion of the Court.

The Endangered Species Act of 1973 (ESA or Act), contains a variety of protections designed to save from extinction species that the Secretary of the Interior designates as endangered or threatened. Section 9 of the Act makes it unlawful for any person to "take" any endangered or threatened species. The Secretary has promulgated a regulation that defines the statute's prohibition on takings to include "significant habitat modification or degradation where it actually kills or injures wildlife." This case presents the question whether the Secretary exceeded his authority under the Act by promulgating that regulation.

I

Section 9(a)(1) of the Endangered Species Act provides the following protection for endangered species:

> Except as provided in Sections 1535(g)(2) and 1539 of this title, with respect to any endangered species of fish or wildlife listed pursuant to Section 1533 of this title it is unlawful for any

> person subject to the jurisdiction of the United States to . . . (B) take any such species within the United States or the territorial sea of the United States[.]

Section 3(19) of the Act defines the statutory term "take": "The term 'take' means to harass, harm, pursue, hunt, shoot, wound, kill, trap, capture, or collect, or to attempt to engage in any such conduct." The Act does not further define the terms it uses to define "take." The Interior Department regulations that implement the statute, however, define the statutory term "harm": "Harm in the definition of 'take' in the Act means an act which actually kills or injures wildlife. Such act may include significant habitat modification or degradation where it actually kills or injures wildlife by significantly impairing essential behavioral patterns, including breeding, feeding, or sheltering." This regulation has been in place since 1975.

A limitation on the § 9 "take" prohibition appears in § 10(a)(1)(B) of the Act, which Congress added by amendment in 1982. That section authorizes the Secretary to grant a permit for any taking otherwise prohibited by § 9(a)(1)(B) "if such taking is incidental to, and not the purpose of, the carrying out of an otherwise lawful activity."

. . . Respondents in this action are small landowners, logging companies, and families dependent on the forest products industries in the Pacific Northwest and in the Southeast, and organizations that represent their interests. They brought this declaratory judgment action against petitioners, the Secretary of the Interior and the Director of the Fish and Wildlife Service, in the United States District Court for the District of Columbia to challenge the statutory validity of the Secretary's regulation defining "harm," particularly the inclusion of habitat modification and degradation in the definition. Respondents challenged the regulation on its face. Their complaint alleged that application of the "harm" regulation to the red-cockaded woodpecker, an endangered species, and the northern spotted owl, a threatened species, had injured them economically.

Respondents advanced three arguments to support their submission that Congress did not intend the word "take" in § 9 to include habitat modification, as the Secretary's "harm" regulation provides. First, they correctly noted that language in the Senate's original version of the ESA would have defined "take" to include "destruction, modification, or curtailment of [the] habitat or range" of fish or wildlife, but the Senate deleted that language from the bill before enacting it. Second, respondents argued that Congress intended the Act's express authorization for the Federal Government to buy private land in order to prevent habitat degradation in § 5 to be the exclusive check against habitat modification on private property. Third, because the Senate added the term "harm" to the definition of "take" in a floor amendment without debate, respondents argued that the court should not interpret the term so expansively as to include habitat modification.

[The District Court upheld the regulation. On appeal, the D.C. Circuit first upheld the regulation 2–1, but on rehearing the court struck down the regulation 2–1 after Judge Williams changed his mind.]

II

. . . The text of the Act provides three reasons for concluding that the Secretary's interpretation is reasonable. First, an ordinary understanding of the word "harm" supports it. The dictionary definition of the verb form of "harm" is "to cause hurt or damage to: injure." In the context of the ESA, that definition naturally encompasses habitat modification that results in actual injury or death to members of an endangered or threatened species.

Respondents argue that the Secretary should have limited the purview of "harm" to direct applications of force against protected species, but the dictionary definition does not include the word "directly" or suggest in any way that only direct or willful action that leads to injury constitutes "harm." Moreover, unless the statutory term "harm" encompasses indirect as well as direct injuries, the word has no meaning that does not duplicate the meaning of other words that § 3 uses to define "take." A reluctance to treat statutory terms as surplusage supports the reasonableness of the Secretary's interpretation.

Second, the broad purpose of the ESA supports the Secretary's decision to extend protection against activities that cause the precise harms Congress enacted the statute to avoid. In *TVA v. Hill*, 437 U.S. 153 (1978), we described the Act as "the most comprehensive legislation for the preservation of endangered species ever enacted by any nation." Whereas predecessor statutes enacted in 1966 and 1969 had not contained any sweeping prohibition against the taking of endangered species except on federal lands, the 1973 Act applied to all land in the United States and to the Nation's territorial seas. As stated in § 2 of the Act, among its central purposes is "to provide a means whereby the ecosystems upon which endangered species and threatened species depend may be conserved. . . ."

Respondents advance strong arguments that activities that cause minimal or unforeseeable harm will not violate the Act as construed in the "harm" regulation. Respondents, however, present a facial challenge to the regulation. Thus, they ask us to invalidate the Secretary's understanding of "harm" in every circumstance, even when an actor knows that an activity, such as draining a pond, would actually result in the extinction of a listed species by destroying its habitat. Given Congress' clear expression of the ESA's broad purpose to protect endangered and threatened wildlife, the Secretary's definition of "harm" is reasonable.

Third, the fact that Congress in 1982 authorized the Secretary to issue permits for takings that § 9(a)(1)(B) would otherwise prohibit, "if such taking is incidental to, and not the purpose of, the carrying out of an otherwise lawful activity," strongly suggests that Congress understood § 9(a)(1)(B) to prohibit indirect as well as deliberate takings. The permit process requires the applicant to prepare a "conservation plan" that specifies how he intends to "minimize and mitigate" the "impact" of his activity on endangered and threatened species, making clear that Congress had in mind foreseeable rather than merely accidental effects on listed species. No one could seriously request an "incidental" take permit to avert § 9 liability for direct, deliberate action against a member of an endangered or threatened species, but respondents would read "harm" so narrowly that the permit procedure would have little more than that absurd purpose. "When Congress acts to amend a statute, we presume it intends its amendment to have real and substantial effect." Congress' addition of the § 10 permit provision supports the Secretary's conclusion that activities not intended to harm an endangered species, such as habitat modification, may constitute unlawful takings under the ESA unless the Secretary permits them. . . .

We need not decide whether the statutory definition of "take" compels the Secretary's interpretation of "harm," because our conclusions that Congress did not unambiguously manifest its intent to adopt respondents' view and that the Secretary's interpretation is reasonable suffice to decide this case. *See generally Chevron U.S.A. Inc. v. Natural Resources Defense Council, Inc.*, 467 U.S. 837 (1984). The latitude the ESA gives the Secretary in enforcing the statute, together with the degree of regulatory expertise necessary to its enforcement, establishes that we owe some degree of deference to the Secretary's reasonable interpretation. *See* Breyer, *Judicial Review of Questions of Law and Policy*, 38 Admin. L. Rev. 363, 373 (1986). . . .

In the elaboration and enforcement of the ESA, the Secretary and all persons who must comply with the law will confront difficult questions of proximity and degree; for, as all recognize, the Act encompasses a vast range of economic and social enterprises and endeavors. These questions must be addressed in the usual course of the law, through case-by-case resolution and adjudication.

■ JUSTICE O'CONNOR, concurring.

My agreement with the Court is founded on two understandings. First, the challenged regulation is limited to significant habitat modification that causes actual, as opposed to hypothetical or speculative, death or injury to identifiable protected animals. Second, even setting aside difficult questions of scienter, the regulation's application is limited by ordinary principles of proximate causation, which introduce notions of foreseeability. These limitations, in my view, call into question *Palila v. Hawaii Dept. of Land and Natural Resources*, 852 F.2d 1106 (CA9 1988) (*Palila II*), and with it, many of the applications derided by the dissent. Because there is no need to strike a regulation on a facial challenge out of concern that it is susceptible of erroneous application, however, and because there are many habitat-related circumstances in which the regulation might validly apply, I join the opinion of the Court. . . .

■ JUSTICE SCALIA, with whom THE CHIEF JUSTICE and JUSTICE THOMAS join, dissenting.

I think it unmistakably clear that the legislation at issue here (1) forbade the hunting and killing of endangered animals, and (2) provided federal lands and federal funds for the acquisition of private lands, to preserve the habitat of endangered animals. The Court's holding that the hunting and killing prohibition incidentally preserves habitat on private lands imposes unfairness to the point of financial ruin—not just upon the rich, but upon the simplest farmer who finds his land conscripted to national zoological use. I respectfully dissent.

---

## QUESTIONS AND DISCUSSION

**1.** So who is right? Does one "take" an endangered species when one adversely affects its habitat? Did the Congress that enacted the ESA in 1973 intend for Section 9 to apply to habitat modification? Or did that Congress plan to protect habitat through other provisions in the act? Does the addition of Section 10's incidental take provision in 1982 suggest that "take" must be read to include habitat modification?

**2.** Justice O'Connor's concurrence indicates that she questions the application of the take prohibition in *Palila II*. The palila is a six-inch bird that lives in mamane and naio forests on the slopes of Mauna Key on the island of Hawaii. That area is also home to the Mauna Kea Game Management Area, where the state introduced wild goats and sheep to facilitate game hunting, an otherwise rare commodity in Hawaii. The goats and the sheep were eating the seedlings, leaves, stems, and sprouts of the mamane and naio trees on which the palila depended for its survival. In *Palila I*, the courts held that the state's act of permitting the goats and the sheep to live in the area constituted a take of the palila. Palila v. Hawaii Dep't of Land & Natural Resources, 471 F. Supp. 985 (D. Haw. 1979), *aff'd*, 639 F.2d 495 (9th Cir. 1981). *Palila II* reached a similar conclusion regarding the state's introduction of mouflon sheep into the same area, sheep that were prized by hunters but which fed on the mamane trees. Palila v. Hawaii Dep't of Land & Natural Resources, 649 F. Supp. 1070 (D. Haw. 1986), *aff'd*, 852 F.2d 1106 (9th Cir. 1988). The fact that the goats and sheep were destroying the habitat on which the palila depended led the courts to find a take in both cases, even though there was no evidence of an actual injury to any individual palila and even though the numbers of palilas had not dropped. Subsequently, the state's resulting "[u]ngulate eradication efforts have become so successful that hunters frequently cannot find any sheep to shoot" in the game area. Palila v. Hawaii Dep't of Land & Natural Resources, 73 F. Supp. 2d 1181, 1184 (D. Haw. 1999). A group of frustrated hunters then moved to dissolve the court's orders, but the court held that the balance of the equities favored the species because "mouflon sheep can always be reintroduced on Mauna Kea," whereas "[p]alila once extinct are gone forever." *Id.* at 1187.

**3.** Which of the following activities constitute a prohibited "take" of an endangered species?

a. A train spilled grain alongside the railroad tracks, thus attracting hungry grizzly bears to the area. Environmentalist claim that both the failure to remove the grain and the railroad's ongoing operations constitute a take. National Wildlife Fed'n v. Burlington N. R.R., 23 F.3d 1508 (9th Cir. 1994).

b. A Tucson school district wants to build a new high school on part of a 73 acre site. A pygmy-owl has been seen on the north part of the property, outside the area where the school will be built but near the construction activities and where the student parking lot will be located. Defenders of Wildlife; Southwest Center for Biological Diversity v. Bernal, 204 F.3d 920 (9th Cir. 2000).

c. An irrigation district pumps water from the Sacramento River. Salmon are killed when they crash into a fish screen that was installed by the state wildlife agency, but the district claims that it has not committed a prohibited take because it did not install the fish screen that is killing the fish. United States v. Glenn-Colusa Irrigation Dist., 788 F. Supp. 1126 (E.D. Cal. 1992).

d. Dewitt DeWeese wants to build a lounge on ten acres of his land on Perdido Key north of Florida's Highway 182. The critical habitat of the Perdido Key Beach mouse occupies 88 acres south of the highway. A biologist contends that the lounge would result in three different prohibited takes of the mouse because (1) construction activities might actually kill or injure some mice, even though no mouse has been seen on DeWeese's property; (2) the project will degrade the habitat of the mouse; or (3) the lounge will attract cats that will prey upon the mouse. Morrill v. Lujan, 802 F. Supp. 424 (S.D. Ala. 1992).

e. A timber company wants to clear cut 93 acres of its old growth forest land. A pair of spotted owls forages on the land, but also on similar forest on neighboring property as well. United States v. West Coast Forest Resources Ltd. Partnership, 2000 WL 298707 (D. Or. 2000).

**4.** The FWS has tried to respond to the uncertainty that continues to surround the precise scope of the ESA's take prohibition in the aftermath of *Sweet Home.* Whenever it lists a new species, the agency specifies which activities would constitute a take and which would not. For example, when it listed two snails in Alabama as endangered, the FWS advised that it would not view the following activities as a prohibited take: existing permitted discharges into the snail's habitat; typical agricultural and silvicultural practices carried out in compliance with existing state and federal regulations and best management practices; development and construction activities designed and implemented according to state and local water quality regulations; existing recreational activities such as swimming, wading, canoeing, and fishing; and the use of pesticides and herbicides in accordance with the label restrictions within the species' watersheds. But the agency warned that other activities could result in a take, including unauthorized collection or capture of the snails; dredging, channelization, the withdrawal of water, and other unauthorized destruction or alteration of the habitat of the snails; the violation of any discharge or water withdrawal permit; and illegal discharge or dumping of toxic chemicals or other pollutants into waters supporting the snails. Endangered Status for the Armored Snail and Slender Campeloma, 65 Fed. Reg. 10033, 10038 (2000). Is that guidance consistent with *Sweet Home*? Is it likely to be helpful to local residents and landowners? Note that the agency's advice is nonbinding, but the agency promises to answer questions about the application of the take prohibition to particular activities.

**5.** Colorado Representative Dan Schaeffer has objected to what he views as the litigious radical wing of the environmental movement because of its willingness to employ the ESA's take prohibition to block certain activities. He offered two examples: "In Massachusetts, environmentalists sued the state for merely licensing fishermen who used certain kinds of lobster traps because the traps actually worked. In Florida, one radical environmental group sued in the name of the Loggerhead Turtles because they believed aggressive local actions to curb beach-front lighting were not aggressive enough." 144 Cong. Rec. E2362 (daily ed. Dec. 21, 1998). Both of the cases mentioned by Representative Schaeffer involve the application of the ESA's take prohibition to the government's failure to regulate private conduct that harms an endangered species. In Strahan v. Coxe, 127 F.3d 155 (1st Cir. 1997), the First Circuit held that the Massachusetts state agency responsible for regulating fishing violated the ESA's take prohibition when it issued permits to fishermen whose nets entangled endangered Northern Right whales. Similarly, in Loggerhead Turtle v. County Council of Volusia County, Florida, 148 F.3d 1231 (11th Cir. 1998), *cert. denied*, 526 U.S. 1081 (1999), the court held that the defenders of the turtle made a sufficient causal showing to establish standing to contend the county violated the take prohibition when it failed regulate lighting in homes and businesses along the beach because the lights confuses newly-hatched sea turtles and make them more susceptible to predators and less likely to reach the safety of the water. On remand, however, the district court held that the county's new lighting regulations did not constitute a take because they were designed to help the turtle, and because the county could not be held liable for the unwillingness of private individuals to abide by the regulations. Loggerhead Turtle v. County Council of Volusia County, Fla., 92 F. Supp. 2d 1296 (M.D. Fla. 2000). Another example (not mentioned by Representative Schaeffer) occurred in *Defenders of Wildlife v. Administrator, Environmental Protection Agency*, 882 F.2d 1294 (8th Cir. 1989), where the court held that EPA's licensing of pesticides that were ultimately ingested by black-footed ferrets constituted a prohibited take. Remember, too, that Hawaii violated the take prohibition when it managed state lands for hunting sheep and goats that injured the habitat of the palila.

Do such "vicarious take" cases satisfy the understanding of the take prohibition articulated in *Sweet Home*? Should state or local officials be held liable for failing to regulate conduct that harms a species?

---

## B. CONSTITUTIONAL OBJECTIONS TO THE "TAKE" PROHIBITION

### 1. CONGRESSIONAL POWER TO PROTECT ENDANGERED SPECIES

### Rancho Viejo, LLC v. Norton

United States Court of Appeals for the District of Columbia Circuit, 2003.
323 F.3d 1062.

■ GARLAND, CIRCUIT JUDGE:

Rancho Viejo is a real estate development company that wishes to construct a 202-acre housing development in San Diego County, California. The United States Fish and Wildlife Service determined that Rancho Viejo's construction plan was likely to jeopardize the continued existence of the arroyo southwestern toad, which the Secretary of the Interior has listed as an endangered species since 1994. Rather than accept an alternative plan proposed by the Service, Rancho Viejo filed suit challenging the application of the Endangered Species Act, 16 U.S.C. §§ 1531 *et seq.*, to its project as an unconstitutional exercise of federal authority under the Commerce Clause. The district court dismissed the suit. We conclude that this case is governed by our prior decision in *National Association of Home Builders v. Babbitt*, 327 U.S. App. D.C. 248, 130 F.3d 1041 (D.C. Cir. 1997), and therefore affirm. . . .

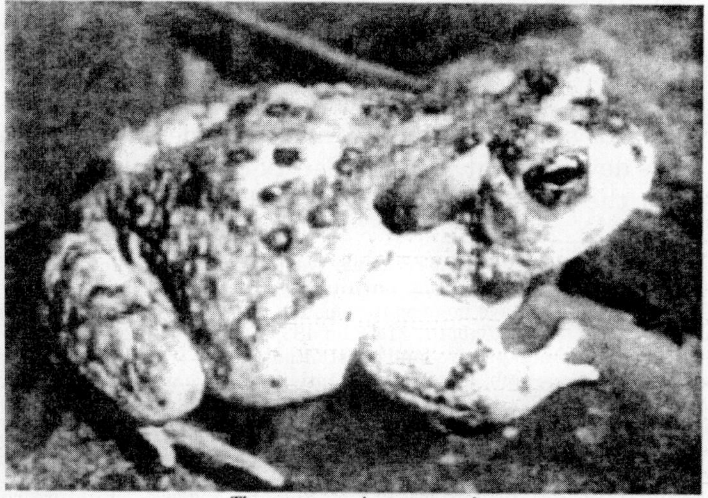

*The arroyo southwestern toad*

In *NAHB*, this circuit applied [United States v. Lopez, 514 U.S. 549 (1995)], in a case challenging the application of the ESA to a construction project in an area that contained the habitat of the Delhi Sands Flower-Loving Fly. . . . A majority of the *NAHB* court held that the take provision of ESA § 9, and its application to the facts of that case, constituted a valid exercise of Congress' commerce power. 130 F.3d at 1042, 1057 (Wald, J.); *id.* at 1057 (Henderson, J., concurring). The court found that application of the ESA fell within the third *Lopez* category, concluding that the regulated activity "substantially affects" interstate commerce. In so holding, the majority agreed upon two rationales: (1) "the loss of biodiversity itself has a substantial effect on our ecosystem and likewise on interstate commerce"; and (2) "the Department's protection of the flies regulates and substantially affects commercial development activity which is plainly interstate." *Id.* at 1058 (Henderson, J., concurring); *see id.* at 1046 n.3, 1056 (Wald, J.). Examining those two rationales within the context of *Lopez*, the *NAHB* court concluded that application of the ESA to the county's proposed construction project was constitutional. *Id.* at 1042, 1057 (Wald, J.); *id.* at 1057 (Henderson, J., concurring). Because the second *NAHB* rationale readily resolves this case, it is the focus of the balance of our discussion.[2] . . . .

The fourth *Lopez* factor is whether the relationship between the regulated activity and interstate commerce is too attenuated to be regarded as substantial. Although Rancho Viejo avers that the effect on interstate commerce of preserving endangered species is too tenuous to satisfy this test, it does not argue that the effect of commercial construction projects is similarly attenuated. Because the rationale upon which we rely focuses on the activity that the federal government seeks to regulate in this case (the construction of Rancho Viejo's housing development), and because we are required to accord congressional legislation a "presumption of constitutionality," [United States v. *Morrison*, 529 U.S. 598, 607 (2000)], plaintiff's failure to demonstrate (or even to argue) that its project and those like it are without substantial interstate effect is fatal to its cause.

This conclusion is not diminished by the fact that the arroyo toad, like the Flower-Loving Fly, does not travel outside of California, or that Rancho Viejo's development, like the San Bernardino hospital, is located wholly within the state. *See NAHB*, 130 F.3d at 1043–44 (Wald, J.)

---

[2] In focusing on the second *NAHB* rationale, we do not mean to discredit the first. Nor do we mean to discredit rationales that other circuits have relied upon in upholding endangered species legislation. We simply have no need to consider those other rationales to dispose of the case before us. *See, e.g., Gibbs v. Babbitt*, 214 F.3d 483, 497 (4th Cir. 2000) ("The protection of the red wolf on both federal and private land substantially affects interstate commerce through tourism, trade, scientific research, and other potential economic activities."); *United States v. Bramble*, 103 F.3d 1475, 1477, 1481 (9th Cir. 1996) (upholding the Bald and Golden Eagle Protection Act's prohibition on the possession of eagle feathers, *see* 16 U.S.C. § 668(a), because "extinction of the eagle would substantially affect interstate commerce by foreclosing any possibility of several types of commercial activity," including "future commerce in eagles," "future interstate travel for the purpose of . . . studying eagles," "or future commerce in beneficial products derived . . . from analysis of their genetic material").

(noting that the fly has an eight-mile radius, limited to California alone). As Judge Henderson said in *NAHB*, the regulation of commercial land development, quite "apart from the characteristics or range of the specific endangered species involved, has a plain and substantial effect on interstate commerce." *Id.* at 1059. There, "the regulation related to both the proposed redesigned traffic intersection and the hospital it [was] intended to serve, each of which had an obvious connection with interstate commerce." *Id.* (Henderson, J., concurring); *accord id.* at 1048, 1056 (Wald, J.). Here, Rancho Viejo's 202-acre project, located near a major interstate highway, is likewise one that "is presumably being constructed using materials and people from outside the state and which will attract" construction workers and purchasers "from both inside and outside the state." *Id.* at 1048 (Wald, J.).[7] . . . .

Rancho Viejo does not seriously dispute that *NAHB* is indistinguishable from this case. Rather, plaintiff argues that, as a result of subsequent Supreme Court decisions in *United States v. Morrison*, 529 U.S. 598 (2000), and *Solid Waste Agency v. United States Army Corps of Eng'rs ("SWANCC")*, 531 U.S. 159 (2001), *NAHB* is no longer "good law.". . . . Rancho Viejo contends that *Morrison* stands for the proposition that whether the regulated activity is economic is not simply a factor in the analysis, but instead is outcome determinative: that noneconomic activity, whatever its *effect* on interstate commerce, cannot be regulated under the Commerce Clause. Although plaintiff acknowledges that *Morrison* expressly "declined to 'adopt a categorical rule against aggregating the effects of any noneconomic activity' because a categorical rule was unnecessary to the outcome of that case," it argues that the Court "came pretty close" to adopting such a rule. Because the arroyo toad is not itself "the subject of commercial activity," Rancho Viejo argues that regulation of the toad fails *Morrison*'s (and *Lopez*'s) first factor.

But how close the Court came to embracing plaintiff's view is irrelevant to the disposition of this appeal, because the ESA *regulates takings, not toads*. *Morrison* instructs that "the proper inquiry" is whether the challenge is to "a *regulation of activity* that substantially affects interstate commerce." 529 U.S. at 609 (emphasis added). Similarly, *SWANCC* declares that what is required is an evaluation of "*the precise object or activity* that, in the aggregate, substantially affects interstate commerce." 531 U.S. at 173 (emphasis added). When, as directed, we turn our attention to the precise activity that is regulated in this case, there is no question but that it is economic in nature.

That regulated activity is Rancho Viejo's planned commercial development, not the arroyo toad that it threatens. The ESA does not purport to tell toads what they may or may not do. Rather, Section 9

[7] Application of the ESA to habitat degradation has a further impact on interstate commerce by removing the incentives for states "to adopt lower standards of endangered species protection in order to attract development," thereby preventing a destructive "race to the bottom." *NAHB*, 130 F.3d at 1054–56 (Wald, J.).

limits the taking of listed species, and its prohibitions and corresponding penalties apply to the persons who do the taking, not to the species that are taken. *See* 16 U.S.C. § 1538(a)(1), (a)(1)(B) (making it "unlawful *for any person . . . to take* any such species") (emphasis added); *id.* § 1540 (providing civil and criminal penalties for "any person who knowingly violates" the ESA). In this case, the prohibited taking is accomplished by commercial construction, and the unlawful taker is Rancho Viejo. . . .

Finally, Rancho Viejo draws our attention to *Morrison*'s declaration that "the Constitution requires a distinction between what is truly national and what is truly local." 529 U.S. at 617–18. Plaintiff argues that the ESA represents an unlawful assertion of congressional power over local land use decisions, which it describes as an area of traditional state regulation. The ESA, however, does not constitute a general regulation of land use. Far from encroaching upon territory that has traditionally been the domain of state and local government, the ESA represents a national response to a specific problem of "truly national" concern.

In making these points, we can do little to improve upon the Fourth Circuit's opinion in *Gibbs*, which upheld, as a valid exercise of federal power under the Commerce Clause, an FWS regulation that limited the taking of red wolves. 214 F.3d at 487. As Chief Judge Wilkinson explained, regulation of the taking of endangered species "does not involve an 'area of traditional state concern,' one to which 'States lay claim by right of history and expertise.' " *Id.* at 499 (quoting *Lopez*, 514 U.S. at 580, 583 (Kennedy, J., concurring)). Rather, as the Supreme Court acknowledged in *Minnesota v. Mille Lacs Band of Chippewa Indians*, "although States have important interests in regulating wildlife and natural resources within their borders, this authority is shared with the Federal Government when the Federal Government exercises one of its enumerated constitutional powers." 526 U.S. 172, 204 (1999). Moreover, while "states and localities possess broad regulatory and zoning authority over land within their jurisdictions, . . . it is well established . . . that Congress can regulate even private land use for environmental and wildlife conservation." *Gibbs*, 214 F.3d at 500. Tracing a hundred-year history of congressional involvement in natural resource conservation, Chief Judge Wilkinson concluded that "it is clear from our laws and precedent that federal regulation of endangered wildlife does not trench impermissibly upon state powers." *Id.* at 500–01.

The Fourth Circuit also recognized the national scope of the problem posed by species conservation. Citing the ESA's legislative history, the court noted Congress' concern that " 'protection of endangered species is not a matter that can be handled in the absence of coherent national and international policies: the results of a series of unconnected and disorganized policies and programs by various states might well be confusion compounded.' " *Gibbs*, 214 F.3d at 502 (quoting H.R. REP. NO. 93–412, at 7 (1973)). As the *Gibbs* court explained: "States may decide to forego or limit conservation efforts in order to lower these costs, and other states may be forced to follow suit in order to compete." *Id.* at 501. Our court has recognized this problem as well. *See NAHB*, 130 F.3d at 1055 (Wald, J.) (noting that states may be "motivated to adopt lower standards of endangered species protection in order to attract development"). And the Supreme Court, as the Fourth Circuit observed, "has held that Congress may take cognizance of this dynamic and arrest the 'race to the bottom' in order to prevent interstate competition whose overall effect would damage the quality of the national environment." *Gibbs*, 214 F.3d at 501 (citing *Hodel v. Virginia Surface Mining & Reclamation Ass'n*, 452 U.S. 264 (1981)).

For these reasons, the protection of endangered species cannot fairly be described as a power "which the Founders denied the National Government and reposed in the States." *Morrison*, 529 U.S. at 618. Rather, "the preservation of endangered species is historically a federal function," *Gibbs*, 214 F.3d at 505, and invalidating this application of the ESA "would call into question the historic power of the federal government to preserve scarce resources in one locality for the future benefit of all Americans," *id.* at 492. We therefore agree with Chief Judge Wilkinson that to sustain challenges of this nature "would require courts to move abruptly from preserving traditional state roles to dismantling historic federal ones." *Id.* at 504. . . .

■ GINSBURG, CHIEF JUDGE, concurring: Although I do not disagree with anything in the opinion of the court, I write separately because I do not believe our opinion makes clear, as the Supreme Court requires, that there is a logical stopping point to our rationale for upholding the constitutionality of the exercise of the Congress's power under the Commerce Clause here challenged. . . . In this case I think it clear that our rationale for concluding the take of the arroyo toad affects interstate commerce does indeed have a logical stopping point, though it goes unremarked in the opinion of the court. Our rationale is that, with respect to a species that is not an article in interstate commerce and does not affect interstate commerce, a take can be regulated if—but only if—the take itself substantially affects interstate commerce. The large-scale residential development that is the take in this case clearly does affect interstate commerce. Just as important, however, the lone hiker in the woods, or the homeowner who moves dirt in order to landscape his property, though he takes the toad, does not affect interstate commerce. . . .

---

## QUESTIONS AND DISCUSSION

**1.** The D.C. Circuit voted 8–2 not to rehear the case en banc. In dissent, Judge—and now Chief Justice—Roberts observed that "[t]he panel's approach in this case leads to the result that regulating the taking of a hapless toad that, for reasons of its own, lives its entire life in California constitutes regulating 'Commerce . . . among the several states.' U.S. CONST. ART I, § 8, cl. 3." Rancho Viejo, LLC v. Norton, 334 F.3d 1158, 1160 (D.C. Cir. 2003) (Roberts, J., dissenting from denial of rehearing en banc). He insisted that the panel wrongly asked "whether the challenged *regulation* substantially affects interstate commerce, rather than whether the *activity* being regulated does so." *Id.* Judge Roberts believed that the proper query was whether "the incidental taking of arroyo toads can be said to be interstate commerce," *id.*, not whether the proposed development constituted interstate commerce. What is the difference? Which focus is correct? Earlier, in *NAHB*, the three judges reached different conclusions because they asked three different questions. Judge Wald asked whether there was a sufficient relationship between *endangered species* and interstate commerce. Judge Henderson asked whether there was a relationship between the *hospital* and interstate commerce. Judge Sentelle asked whether there was a relationship between the *fly* and interstate commerce. Who asked the right question? *See* John Copeland Nagle, *The Commerce Clause Meets the Delhi Sands Flower-Loving Fly*, 97 MICH. L. REV. 174 (1998).

**2.** The court emphasized that the housing development proposed by Rancho Viejo possessed numerous connections to interstate commerce. But the arroyo southwestern toad is also threatened by off-road vehicles (ORVs) that "cause extensive damage to the shallow pools in which arroyo toads breed," children that collect the toads while on camping trips, accidental road kill at nighttime, and "[l]ight and noise pollution from adjacent developments." Determination of Endangered Status for the Arroyo Southwestern Toad, 59 Fed. Reg. 64859, 64862–64 (1994). Could Congress regulate any or all of those activities?

**3.** Most courts to confront the constitutional question have agreed with the result in *Rancho Viejo*, albeit sometimes for different reasons. But one district court has held that federal regulation of Utah prairie dogs on non-federal land exceeds the scope of the ESA's authority under the Commerce Clause, because "although the Commerce Clause authorizes Congress to do many things, it does not authorize Congress to regulate takes of a purely intrastate species that has no substantial effect on interstate commerce." People for the Ethical Treatment of Property Owners v. FWS, 57 F. Supp. 3d 1337 (D. Utah 2014). The government has appealed that decision to the Tenth Circuit.

---

## 2. DUTIES TO COMPENSATE PROPERTY OWNERS AFFECTED BY ENDANGERED SPECIES REGULATIONS

### Good v. United States

United States Court of Appeals for the Federal Circuit, 1999.
189 F.3d 1355, *cert. denied*, 529 U.S. 1053 (2000).

■ EDWARD R. SMITH, SENIOR CIRCUIT JUDGE:

[In 1973, Lloyd A. Good, Jr. purchased Sugarloaf Shores, (which consists of thirty-two acres of wetlands and freshwater marsh) and eight acres of uplands on Lower Sugarloaf Key, Florida. The sales contract for the land stated that "[t]he Buyers recognize that certain of the lands covered by this contract may be below the mean high tide line and that as of today there are certain problems in connection with the obtaining of State and Federal permission for dredging and filling operations." In 1980, Good hired Keycology, Inc., a land planning and development firm, to obtain the federal, state, and county permits necessary to develop Sugarloaf Shores into a residential subdivision. In their contract, Good and Keycology acknowledged that "obtaining said permits is at best difficult and by no means assured." In March 1981, Good applied to the U.S. Army Corps of Engineers ("Corps") for a permit to fill 7.4 acres of salt marsh and excavate another 5.4 acres of salt marsh in order to create a 54-lot subdivision and a 48-slip marina. The Corps permit was required for dredging and filling navigable waters of the United States, including wetlands adjacent to navigable waters, under the Rivers and Harbors Act of 1899 and under § 404 of the Clean Water Act. In May 1983, Good obtained a permit that was good for five years.

Good was less successful in his efforts to get state and county approval for his plan. His struggles to satisfy state and local environmental regulations took so long that Good had to receive another, slightly revised permit from the Corps in 1988. By the end of 1989, Good had satisfied most of the county's requirements, but he was unable to receive the approval of the South Florida Water Management District (SFWMD) because of the impact of the proposed project on wetlands and on the habitat of the mud turtle and Lower Keys marsh rabbit, both of which were protected under Florida law. So in 1990 Good submitted a new plan to the Corps to build only sixteen homes, a canal, and a tennis court.

Meanwhile, the FWS had listed the Lower Keys marsh rabbit as an endangered species under the ESA. In the ensuing ESA Section 7 consultation with the Corps, the FWS concluded that the project proposed in Good's 1990 permit application would not jeopardize the continued existence of the marsh rabbit, though it nonetheless recommended denial of the permit based on the development's overall environmental impact. Next, the FWS listed another species—the silver rice rat—as endangered in April 1991. The consultation triggered by that listing resulted in a December 1991 biological opinion issued by the FWS that determined that both the 1988 and 1990 plans jeopardized the continued existence of both the Lower Keys marsh rabbit and the silver rice rat. FWS recommended that the Corps deny the 1990 application and modify the 1988 permit to include the "reasonable and prudent alternatives" of locating all homesites in upland areas and limiting water access to a single communal dock. The impact of project on the two endangered species caused the Corps to deny Good's 1990 permit application on March 17, 1994, and to notify Good that his 1988 permit had expired. Good then filed suit in the United States Court of Federal Claims alleging that the Corps' denial of his permit application constituted a taking of his property without just compensation in violation of the fifth amendment. The court rejected Good's claim, and he appealed.]

*The Lower Keys marsh Rabbit*

ANALYSIS

The Fifth Amendment to the United States Constitution provides that private property shall not "be taken for public use, without just compensation." U.S. Const. amend. V. The government can "take" private property by either physical invasion or regulatory imposition. *See, e.g.*, Loretto v. Teleprompter Manhattan CATV Corp., 458 U.S. 419 (1982); Lucas [v. South Carolina Coastal Council], 505 U.S. 1003 [(1992)]. Appellant in this case alleges a regulatory taking.

It has long been recognized that "while property may be regulated to a certain extent, if regulation goes too far it will be recognized as a taking." Pennsylvania Coal Co. v. Mahon, 260 U.S. 393, 415 (1922). The Supreme Court has set out "several factors that have particular significance" in determining whether a regulation effects a taking. Penn Central [Transp. Co. v. New York City], 438 U.S. [104], 124 [(1978)]. These factors are (1) the character of the government action, (2) the extent to which the regulation interferes with distinct, investment-backed expectations, and (3) the economic impact of the regulation. *See id. See also* Loveladies Harbor, Inc. v. United States, 28 F.3d 1171, 1179 (Fed. Cir. 1994); Florida Rock Inds., Inc. v. United States, 18 F.3d 1560, 1567 (Fed. Cir. 1994); Creppel v. United States, 41 F.3d 627, 632 (Fed. Cir. 1994). Because we find the expectations factor dispositive, we will not further discuss the character of the government action or the economic impact of the regulation.

REASONABLE, INVESTMENT-BACKED EXPECTATIONS

For any regulatory takings claim to succeed, the claimant must show that the government's regulatory restraint interfered with his investment-backed expectations in a manner that requires the government to compensate him. The requirement of investment-backed expectations "limits recovery to owners who can demonstrate that they bought their property in reliance on the non-existence of the challenged regulation." *Creppel*, 41 F.3d at 632. These expectations must be reasonable. *See* Ruckelshaus v. Monsanto Co., 467 U.S. 986, 1005–1006 (1984).

Reasonable, investment-backed expectations are an element of every regulatory takings case. *See Loveladies Harbor*, 28 F.3d at 1179. *See also id.* at 1177 ("In legal terms, the owner who bought with knowledge of the restraint could be said to have no reliance interest, or to have assumed the risk of any economic loss. In economic terms, it could be said that the market had already discounted for the risk, so that a purchaser could not show a loss in his investment attributable to it."); *Creppel,* 41 F.3d at 632 ("One who buys with knowledge of a restraint assumes the risk of economic loss.").

Good argues that the Supreme Court has eliminated the requirement for reasonable, investment-backed expectations, at least in cases where the challenged regulation eliminates virtually all of the economic value of the landowner's property. In support, Appellant cites *Lucas*, 505 U.S. at 1015, and argues that *Loveladies Harbor* should be reversed as contrary to *Lucas*.

However, we agree with the *Loveladies Harbor* court that the Supreme Court in *Lucas* did not mean to eliminate the requirement for reasonable, investment-backed expectations to establish a taking. It is true that the Court in *Lucas* set out what it called a "categorical" taking "where regulation denies all economically beneficial or productive use of land." 505 U.S. at 1015. The *Lucas* Court, however, clarified that by "categorical" it meant those "categories of regulatory action [that are] compensable without case-specific inquiry *into the public interest advanced in support of the restraint." Id.* (emphasis added). A *Lucas*-type taking, therefore, is categorical only in the sense that the courts do not balance the importance of the public interest advanced by the regulation against the regulation's imposition on private property rights. *See Loveladies Harbor*, 28 F.3d at 1179.

The *Lucas* Court did not hold that the denial of all economically beneficial or productive use of land eliminates the requirement that the landowner have reasonable, investment-backed expectations of developing his land. In *Lucas*, there was no question of whether the plaintiff had satisfied that criterion. *See* 505 U.S. at 1006–1007 ("In 1986, petitioner David H. Lucas paid $975,000 for two residential lots on the Isle of Palms in Charleston County, South Carolina, on which he intended to build single-family homes. In 1988, however, the South Carolina Legislature enacted the Beachfront Management Act, S.C. Code Ann. § 48–39–250 *et seq.* (Supp. 1990), which had the direct effect of barring petitioner from erecting any permanent habitable structures on his two parcels.").

In addition, it is common sense that "one who buys with knowledge of a restraint assumes the risk of economic loss. In such a case, the owner presumably paid a discounted price for the property. Compensating him for a 'taking' would confer a windfall." *Creppel,* 41 F.3d at 632 (citations omitted).

Appellant alternatively argues that he had reasonable, investment-backed expectations of building a residential subdivision on his property. Appellant reasons that the permit requirements of the Rivers and Harbors Act and the Clean Water Act are irrelevant to his reasonable expectations at the time he purchased the subject property, because he obtained the federal dredge-and-fill permits required by those acts three times, and was only denied a permit, based on the provisions of the Endangered Species Act ("ESA"), when two endangered species were found on his property. Therefore, since the ESA did not exist when he bought his land, he could not have expected to be denied a permit based on its provisions.

Appellant's position is not entirely unreasonable, but we must ultimately reject it. In view of the regulatory climate that existed when Appellant acquired the subject property, Appellant could not have had a reasonable expectation that he would obtain approval to fill ten acres of wetlands in order to develop the land.

In 1973, when Appellant purchased the subject land, federal law required that a permit be obtained from the Army Corps of Engineers in order to dredge or fill in wetlands adjacent to a navigable waterway. Even in 1973, the Corps had been considering environmental criteria in its permitting decisions for a number of years. *See* Deltona Corp. v. United States, 657 F.2d 1184, 1187 (Ct. Cl. 1981) ("On December 18, 1968, in response to a growing national concern for environmental values and related federal legislation, the Corps [announced that it] would consider the following additional factors in reviewing permit applications: fish and wildlife, conservation, pollution, aesthetics, ecology, and the general public interest."). *See also* 657 F.2d at 1190 ("Since the late 1960's the regulatory jurisdiction of the Army Corps of Engineers has substantially expanded pursuant to § 404 of the [Clean Water Act] and—under the spur of steadily evolving legislation—the Corps has greatly added to the substantive criteria governing the issuance of dredge and fill permits."). By 1973, the Corps had denied dredge-and-fill permits solely on environmental grounds. *See, e.g.*, Zabel v. Tabb, 430 F.2d 199 (5th Cir. 1970).

In addition to the federal regulations, development of the subject land required approval by both the state of Florida and Monroe County. . . .

At the time he bought the subject parcel, Appellant acknowledged both the necessity and the difficulty of obtaining regulatory approval. The sales contract specifically stated that "the Buyers recognize that . . . as of today there are certain problems in connection with the obtaining of State and Federal permission for dredging and filling operations." Appellant thus had both constructive and actual knowledge that either state or federal regulations could ultimately prevent him from building on the property. Despite his knowledge of the difficult regulatory path ahead, Appellant took no steps to obtain the required regulatory approval for seven years.

During this period, public concern about the environment resulted in numerous laws and regulations affecting land development. For example:

- In December 1973, the Endangered Species Act was enacted. 16 U.S.C. § 1531 *et seq.* (1994). The ESA prohibited federal actions that would be "likely to jeopardize the continued existence of any endangered species," 16 U.S.C. § 1536(a)(2), and made it unlawful to "take" (i.e., kill, harass, etc.) any endangered animal. *See* 16 U.S.C. §§ 1532(19), 1538(a)(1)(B).
- In 1975, the Corps of Engineers issued regulations broadening its interpretation of its § 404 authority to regulate dredging and filling in wetlands. *See* United States v. Riverside Bayview Homes, 474 U.S. 121, 123–124 (1985). In 1977, the Corps further broadened its definition of wetlands subject to § 404's permit requirements. *See id.*
- Also in 1977, Florida enacted its own Endangered and Threatened Species Act, Fla. Stat. Ann. § 372.072 (West 1997), further emphasizing the public concern for Florida's environment. In 1979, the Florida Keys Protection Act was enacted, designating the Keys an Area of Critical State Concern. Fla. Stat. Ann. § 380.0552 (West 1997).

Thus, rising environmental awareness translated into ever-tightening land use regulations. Surely Appellant was not oblivious to this trend.

The picture emerges, then, of Appellant in 1973 acknowledging the difficulty of obtaining approval for his project, then waiting seven years, watching as the applicable regulations got more stringent, before taking any steps to obtain the required approval. When in 1980 he finally retained a land development firm to seek the required permits, he acknowledged that "obtaining said permits is at best difficult and by no means assured."

While Appellant's prolonged inaction does not bar his takings claim, it reduces his ability to fairly claim surprise when his permit application was denied. Appellant was aware at the time of purchase of the need for regulatory approval to develop his land. He must also be presumed to have been aware of the greater general concern for environmental matters during the period of 1973 to 1980. As our predecessor court stated on similar facts: "When Deltona acquired the property in 1964, it knew that the development it contemplated could take place only if it obtained the necessary permits from the Corps of Engineers. Although at that time Deltona had every reason to believe that those permits would be forthcoming when it subsequently sought them, it also must have been aware that the standards and conditions governing the issuance of permits could change. Deltona had no assurance that the permits would issue, but only an expectation." *Deltona*, 657 F.2d at 1193.

Here, as in *Deltona*, Appellant "must have been aware that the standards and conditions governing the issuance of permits could change." *Id.* In light of the growing consciousness of and sensitivity toward environmental issues, Appellant must also have been aware that standards could change to his detriment, and that regulatory approval could become harder to get.

We therefore conclude that Appellant lacked a reasonable, investment-backed expectation that he would obtain the regulatory approval needed to develop the property at issue here. We have previously held that the government is entitled to summary judgment on a regulatory takings claim where the plaintiffs lacked reasonable, investment-backed expectations, even where the challenged government action "substantially reduced the value of plaintiffs' property." Avenal v. United States, 100 F.3d 933, 937 (Fed. Cir. 1996). Here, too, Appellant's lack of reasonable, investment-backed expectations defeats his takings claim as a matter of law. . . .

---

## QUESTIONS AND DISCUSSION

**1.** When did it become unreasonable for Lloyd Good to expect that he could develop his property in the manner that he had hoped? In 1973, when he bought it? Later that year, when Congress enacted the ESA? In 1979, when the state designated the entire Florida Keys an area of critical state concern? In 1980, when a contractor informed him of the environmental obstacles facing development? In 1990, when the FWS listed the Lower Keys marsh rabbit as endangered under the ESA? Or at some other time?

**2.** The takings clause has been the subject of intense judicial and scholarly debate in recent years. Governmental regulation of private property has resulted in countless claims that the government must compensate landowners for their inability to use their land as they would like. Few courts, however, have held that the ESA produced a taking for which the government must pay the property owner. *See* Casitas Municipal Water Dist. v. United States, 543 F.3d 1276 (Fed. Cir. 2008) (2–1 decision reversing summary judgment for the government on a takings claim involving the diversion of irrigation water to conserve the West Coast steelhead trout); Tulare Lake Basin Water Storage Dist. v. United States, 49 Fed. Cl. 313 (2001) (holding that water use restrictions imposed to protect the endangered delta smelt and winter-run chinook salmon worked a taking of the contractual water rights held by two county water districts). Why have the courts found so few takings?

**3.** *Seiber v. United States*, 364 F.3d 1356 (Fed. Cir. 2004), illustrates the denominator problem in takings law, which considers the proper comparison between the size of a property owner's land and the amount of land affected by government regulation. Marsha and Alvin Seiber wanted to cut the timber on 40 of their 200 acres in Linn County, Oregon. In July 2000, the FWS denied an ESA incidental take permit because the application did not adequately mitigate the impact on nearby threatened northern spotted owls. In June 2002, the FWS informed the Seibers that a permit was no longer necessary because "the area will no longer be likely to attract and maintain spotted owls." *Id.* at 1362. The Seibers alleged that the government had taken their property for two years. The Federal Circuit disagreed. With respect to the denominator problem, the court rejected the suggestion that each individual tree could serve as the appropriate denominator—a test that would require compensation whenever a property owner is prohibited from cutting down a single tree. The court also held that there had not been a temporary physical occupation for the denial of "the right to exclude others (i.e., the spotted owls)." *Id.* at 1366.

**4.** Property rights advocates have publicized a number of "horror stories" about individuals who suffered economic losses because of the ESA. One of the most sympathetic stories concerns Margaret Rector, who purchased land outside of Austin, Texas in 1973 as an investment for retirement. When she sought to realize her investment two decades later, she discovered that it was "virtually impossible to find a buyer for a tract of land that has been labeled habitat of the golden-cheeked warbler." Endangered Species Act Implementation: Hearing Before the House Committee on Resources, 104th Cong., 2d Sess. 14–15 (1996). She complained that "I'm 74 years old. I want the money so I can go to a nice rest home. . . . I think it is unfair for me to bear the burden when the bird belongs to everyone." Ralph Haurwitz, *Who Pays? Warbler Stokes Debate: Landowner Sees Retirement Money Fly Away* *on Endangered Songbird's Wings*, AUSTIN AMERICAN STATESMAN, Sept. 26, 1994, at A25. Many of the other so-called "horror stories," though, are questioned by supporters of the ESA. *See* Michael Allan Wolf, *Overtaking The Fifth Amendment: The Legislative Backlash Against Environmentalism*, 6 FORDHAM ENVTL. LAW J. 637 (1995).

Such stories have led to claims that fairness dictates that landowners be paid if the presence of an endangered species makes their land less valuable. Before the court decided against his claim, Lloyd Good testified before a congressional committee examining the impact of the ESA on private property rights. He complained that "the designation of this property as the habitat of these two species has in effect rendered it valueless. Real estate brokers won't touch it. Other developers won't touch it. Bankers won't even look at it. Mortgage brokers aren't interested. It's dead." Good concluded that "[t]he Endangered Species Act must, if it is going to continue, contain some provision for the protection of private property rights." *Endangered Species Act Implementation Hearing*, *supra*, at 16–17. Similarly, when Nebraska Senator Chuck Hagel introduced his proposed Private Property Fairness Act of 1999, he explained that "if the Government condemns part of a farm to build a highway, it has to pay the farmer for the value of his land. But if the Government requires that same farmer [to] stop growing crops on that same land in order to protect endangered species or conserve wetlands, the farmer gets no compensation." 145 CONG. REC. S734 (daily ed. Jan. 20, 1999).

Likewise, Professor Barton Thompson argues that "both incentive and fairness considerations militate in favor of at least partial compensation to landowners injured by the imposition of Section 9's constraint on habitat modification." He explains:

> Absent any compensation under Section 9, some landowners will destroy the habitat value of their land in order to escape ESA regulation—unnecessarily wasting valuable societal resources to annihilate the very public good that the ESA seeks to preserve. Others will refrain from creating or improving habitat. So long as the listing of a species remains a prerequisite of Section 9 regulation, a no compensation rule will also encourage property owners to oppose new listings of endangered species, undermining all recovery efforts for those species. A no compensation rule biases those species-recovery efforts that do occur toward property-focused efforts and, because property owners vary among themselves in the political power they enjoy, distorts which property is used for habitat preservation and which landowners bear the burden of preservation. Finally, a no compensation rule is inequitable. The ESA's impact on particular parcels of land depends not on the behavior of the landowner or even on his ability to finance public services, but on the happenstance of where the remaining habitat of an endangered species is.

Barton H. Thompson, Jr., *The Endangered Species Act: A Case Study in Takings & Incentives*, 49 STAN. L. REV. 305, 375 (1997).

Are Good, Professor Thompson, and Senator Hagel right? Should landowners be entitled to compensation if the presence of an endangered species limits their ability to use their land? Is Good deserving of compensation? Is Rector? If so, who should pay them?

**5.** The inability to persuade the courts to extend the fifth amendment's takings clause to force the government to compensate private landowners constrained by wildlife regulations led property rights advocates to propose legislative solutions. A bill considered by Congress in 1995 would have required federal agencies to compensate any private property owner whose land suffers at least a twenty percent reduction of value as a result of restrictions on the use of the property to protect endangered species. The agencies, moreover, would have to pay for such compensation out of their own budgets. Compensation would *not* be required if a landowner's activities are proscribed by state law, constitute a nuisance, or are prohibited by a local zoning ordinance, or if the federal agency is acting to prevent public health or safety hazards, to prevent damage to other property, or pursuant to navigational servitudes. *See* Private Property Protection Act of 1995, H.R. 925, 104th Cong., 1st Sess. (1995); *see also* H.R. Rep. No. 46, 104th Cong., 1st Sess. (1995) (outlining the arguments of supporters and opponents of the bill).

Dean William Treanor has advocated narrowly focused takings legislation that seeks to compensate those most harshly affected by government regulation. He proposes to compensate landowners when "unanticipated regulations destroy a significant portion of the total assets of a property owner." William Michael Treanor, *The Armstrong Principle, the Narratives of Takings, and Compensation Statutes*, 38 WM. & MARY. L. REV. 1151, 1155 (1997). The three qualifications insure that someone who was aware of applicable government regulation or who is a repeat player who loses on one investment but gains on others need not be compensated. Compensation is provided, though, to the small landowners who could lose their life's savings, the individuals most deserving of compensation and those whose predicament has informed much of the current debate. How is that test different from the constitutional formula announced in *Lucas*? From H.R. 925? Would Good receive compensation under the bill or under Professor Treanor's proposal? Would Rector?

**6.** Are there other ways to encourage private landowners to manage their land in a way to protects biodiversity besides the ESA's prohibition on adversely affecting the habitat of a species? Section 9 operates as a stick to force landowners not to harm an endangered species. Conversely, there is a broad consensus that the law should offer landowners and others affected by the ESA a carrot as well. Congress has considered several proposed bills that would provide a tax incentive to private landowners who act to protect endangered species. The Endangered Species Recovery Act of 2007, introduced by Idaho Senator Mike Crapo, would provide a tax credit to individuals who enter into agreements to protect the habitats of endangered and threatened species. *See* S. 700, 110th Cong., 1st Sess. (2007). The National Wildlife Federation has proposed that several tax and financial incentives be extended to landowners and that technical and financial assistance be offered to small private landowners, states, tribes, and local communities. *See* National Wildlife Federation, *Support Landowner Incentives to Promote Endangered Species Conservation*, http://www.nwf.org/endangered/hcp/lndinc.html. What other incentives should be offered to private landowners and others so that they will act to protect endangered species? *See generally* John F. Turner & Jason C. Rylander, *The Private Lands Challenge: Integrating Biodiversity Conservation and Private Property*, in PRIVATE PROPERTY AND THE ENDANGERED SPECIES ACT: SAVING HABITATS, PROTECTING HOMES 116–23 (Jason F. Shogren ed. 1998) (describing possible incentive programs).

---

## C. INCIDENTAL TAKE PERMITS AND HABITAT CONSERVATION PLANS

In 1982, Congress added section 10(a)(1)(B) to the ESA, which authorizes the FWS to permit an "incidental take" of a listed species. An incidental take is an action that constitutes a "take" within ESA Section 9, but the take is "incidental to, and not the purpose of, the carrying out of an otherwise lawful activity." To apply for such a permit, the applicant first must submit a comprehensive conservation plan, which has come to be known as a "habitat conservation plan" or HCP. To issue the permit, the Service must scrutinize the plan and find, after affording opportunity for public comment, that: (1) the proposed taking of an endangered species will be "incidental" to an otherwise lawful activity; (2) the permit applicant will minimize and mitigate the impacts of the taking "to the maximum extent practicable"; (3) the applicant has insured adequate funding for its conservation plan; and (4) the taking will not appreciably reduce the likelihood of the survival of the species. Michael Bean and Melanie Rowland assert that "this provision likely increased the Secretary's leverage over activities that incidentally take endangered species because it substituted a flexible regulatory authority for a threat of prosecution that few found credible." Bean & Rowland, *supra*, at 234.

*Friends of Endangered Species, Inc. v. Jantzen*, 760 F.2d 976 (9th Cir. 1985), upheld the first incidental take permit (ITP) issued by the FWS. In *Jantzen*, a developer sought to build a large residential and commercial project on San Bruno Mountain near land that is also home to the endangered Mission Blue butterfly. The developer worked with local environmentalists and government officials to prepare the first habitat conservation plan (HCP), which committed the developer to preserving 81% of its land as wildlife habitat and to pay $60,000 annually to finance a habitat conservation program. The upshot of the HCP was that some of the butterfly's habitat is protected while the developers are permitted to build amidst other parts of butterfly habitat. Why would the government agree to that deal? Why would the developer? Note that since the HCP went into effect, 800 housing units have been built on the San Bruno Mountain, while developers and homeowners have paid $70,000 annually to remove non-native plants, replant native species, and monitor the activities of the butterflies. A 1999 study concluded that "[a]t best, the HCP has been a wash. The development has not drastically decreased the population of endangered species on the mountain, but the restoration projects have not dramatically raised the numbers either." Marcus E. Walton, *San Bruno Ecology Faces Threat of Urban Sprawl*, SAN JOSE MERCURY NEWS, June 16, 1999. Most recently, the FWS and the nearby City of Brisbane agreed to spend a total of over one million dollars to purchase a part of the mountain that provides ten percent of the habitat of the callippe silverspot butterfly.

Despite the enactment of Section 10(a)(1)(B), only three HCPs were adopted between 1982 and 1989. Then the number of HCPs boomed. By September 1995, over 100 HCPs had been approved and about 200 were in various stages of development. By 2009, 849 HCPs were in effect and 168 have already expired. The most prominent efforts to develop HCPs that cover entire regions exist in southern California and around Austin, Texas. Over 20 million acres are now covered by HCPs. The increased scope of HCPs also extends to the number of species. For example, two of the California plans protect 63 and 47 species, respectively. Collectively, the existing HCPs protect more than 200 endangered or threatened species. Additionally, many plans apply to species that have not yet been listed under the ESA.

The development of a HCP may include reliance upon conservation banking. "A conservation bank is like a biological bank account," explains the FWS, in which lands that are managed for endangered or otherwise rare species may be sold "to developers or others who need to compensate for the environmental impacts of their projects." FWS, Conservation Banking: Incentives for Stewardship (July 2005), *available at* http://www.fws.gov/endangered/landowner/banking.7.05.pdf. For example, recall the new conservation bank that has been established for the preservation of the Delhi Sands Flower-Loving Fly, as discussed in Chapter 1.

During the Clinton Administration, Interior Secretary Bruce Babbitt trumpeted the development of HCPs as evidence of the success of the ESA. When he signed the Karner blue butterfly HCP, he described it as "the first comprehensive statewide Habitat Conservation Plan and the most inclusive agreement of its kind in the country. . . . It is an excellent example of how the flexibility of the Endangered Species Act can promote regional habitat conservation planning by states and local governments and is a model for what other states and their partners might consider." More generally, Babbitt described HCPs as "one of the vanguards in a Quiet Revolution in American conservation," adding that "I know these plans work. Businesses know they work. Individual citizens know they work." U.S. Fish & Wildlife Service, *Habitat Conservation Plans: The Quiet Revolution* 5 (1998), *available at* http://endangered.fws.gov/hcp/Quiet/03–09.pdf.

Environmentalists are more skeptical. They complain that HCPs are being developed without adequate scientific guidance. They further charge that the FWS is abandoning the safeguards that are supposed to characterize HCPs in its rush to approve more plans. Many of the recent HCPs, they say, are inadequately funded and monitored. They conclude that many HCPs are "habitat giveaways" that cater to the interests of developers rather than furthering the purposes of the ESA. *See, e.g.*, Patrick Parenteau, *Rearranging The Deck Chairs: Endangered Species Act Reforms in an Era Of Mass Extinction*, 22 WM. & MARY ENVTL. L. & POL'Y REV. 227; John Kostyack, *"Surprise!"*, 15 ENVTL. FORUM 19 (1998).

Some environmental organizations have cautiously approved of HCPs, but only provided that steps are taken to make the plans more protective of the species they are designed to preserve. The National Wildlife Federation (NWF) advocates the inclusion of five additional safeguards in the HCP process: (1) clarify that HCPs must be consistent with an overall recovery strategy before approving them, (2) allow greater participation by concerned citizens and independent scientists, (3) encourage conservation strategies that prevent the need to list species, (4) provide regulatory assurances only when a credible adaptive management strategy is in place, and (5) ensure that HCPs are adequately funded to ensure that they are an effective strategy for conserving biodiversity. National Wildlife Federation, *Habitat Conservation Plans: Safeguards Are Needed to Ensure that the Endangered Species Act's Recovery Goal is Not Undermined*, http://www.nwf.org/endangered/hcp/hcpsaf.html. What objections might landowners raise to any of those recommendations? What other actions would improve the HCP process?

Initially, the courts tended to defer to the FWS's application of the standards for granting an incidental take permit pursuant to a HCP. For example, in *Center for Biological Diversity v. FWS*, 202 F. Supp. 2d 594 (W.D. Tex. 2002), the court produced a lengthy opinion expressing significant concerns about the wisdom of a proposed shopping development near San Antonio, but the court concluded that the FWS had not acted arbitrarily or capriciously in determining that the developer satisfied the statutory requirements for an incidental take permit. A district court did invalidate the Natomas Basin HCP designed to protect habitat and facilitate development around Sacramento, *see* National Wildlife Fed'n v. Babbitt, 128 F. Supp. 2d 1274 (E.D. Cal. 2000), but the court later approved a revised HCP that remedied the earlier problems. *See* National Wildlife Fed'n v. Norton, 2005 WL 2175874 (E.D. Cal. 2005). Recently, though, a federal district court struck down the ITP for 85 species that was at the heart of San Diego's habitat conservation planning. *See* Southwest Center for Biological Diversity v. Bartel, 457 F. Supp. 2d 1070 (S.D. Cal. 2006). The court concluded "that the ITP would permit monumental destruction" of the species because the "malleable" conservation standard in the plan "virtually guarantees development and the ersatz mitigation measures run counter to the realistic needs of these dwindling vernal pool species and may hasten their extinction." *Id.* at 1073. And in Arizona Cattle Growers' Association v. FWS, 273 F.3d 1229 (9th Cir. 2001), the court held that the FWS could not issue an incidental take permit that imposed conditions on federal grazing permits where there was no evidence that the grazing would result in a take of an endangered species in the first place.

The attractiveness of HCPs to private landowners further increased as a result of the "No Surprises" rule adopted by the FWS, the NMFS, and NOAA. *See* Habitat Conservation Plan Assurances ("No Surprises") Rule, 63 Fed. Reg. 8859 (1998). According to that rule, "[o]nce an HCP permit has been issued and its terms and conditions are being fully complied with, the permittee may remain secure regarding the agreed upon cost of conservation and mitigation. If the status of a species addressed under an HCP unexpectedly worsens because of unforeseen circumstances, the primary obligation for implementing additional conservation measures would be the responsibility of the Federal government, other government agencies, or other non-Federal landowners who have not yet developed an HCP." *Id.* at 8867. Many environmentalists object to the "No Surprises" rule, arguing that the dynamic nature of ecosystems makes it impossible to predict the needs of a species or the pressures on a species that will occur in future years.

The "No Surprises" Rule is only one example of recent efforts to reduce the regulatory impact of the ESA on private parties. The FWS has adopted several regulatory reforms designed to encourage private landowners to protect biodiversity. A safe harbor agreement lifts the restrictions of the ESA from a private landowner whose voluntary habitat creation, restoration or improvement attracts a new species to the land. "For example," under the Safe Harbor Agreement that FWS drafted for the Karner blue butterfly in September 2005, "if two Karner blue butterfly family groups are present when the baseline is established and the population grows by three family groups over the next decade, the landowner is responsible only for the two family groups, not five, should he or she change land management goals." News Release, FWS, Public Input Sought on Plan to Conserve Endangered Butterfly in Northern Indiana (Sept. 22, 2005). Another regulatory device known as a candidate conservation agreement offers a similar promise of reduced ESA regulation to a landowner who takes agreed upon steps to conserve the habitat of a species that has not yet been listed under the ESA. For a discussion of each mechanism, *see* Darcy H. Kishida, Note, *Safe Harbor Agreements Under the Endangered Species Act: Are They Right for Hawai'i?*, 23 HAWAI'I L. REV. 507 (2001); Francesca Ortiz, *Candidate Conservation Agreements as a Devolutionary Response to Extinction*, 33 GA. L. REV. 413 (1999); J.B. Ruhl, *The Endangered Species Act and Private Property: A Matter of Timing and Location*, 8 CORNELL J.L. & PUB. POL'Y 37 (1998).

---

## PROBLEM EXERCISE

The Everglades of southern Florida are home to a number of endangered species. Two of the most endangered are the Everglade snail kite and the Cape Sable seaside sparrow. The population of the kite dropped to less than 100 birds before the bird was listed endangered under the predecessor of the Endangered Species Act (ESA) in 1967. There are now nearly 1,000 kites and 3,000 sparrows, but both species are still listed as endangered under the ESA. The fate of both species depends upon the human management of water in the Everglades and southern Florida.

Historically, a natural "sheet of water" flowed south through the Everglades with periodic cycles of flooding and drought. The swamps of southern Florida, however, were perceived as obstacles to human progress. Accordingly, efforts began in the nineteenth century to "reclaim" the land and make it habitable for human settlement. Those efforts culminated in the Central and Southern Florida Project, an extensive collection of canals, levees, water control structures, and pumping stations stretched across 4,660,000 hectares from Orlando to the southern tip of Florida. This system has disrupted the natural volume, timing, and flow of surface and ground water throughout the Everglades. The water reaching the Everglades is polluted by runoff from nearby agricultural and urban activities, and parts of the Everglades that used to be swampy are now nearly dry. At the same time, the failure to operate the system would quickly result in the flooding of the heavily populated areas of Miami and south Florida. The operation of the Central and Southern Florida Project is managed by federal and state officials who seek to accommodate the competing needs of the state's agricultural and mining industries, the millions of people who are moving to Florida, and the area's native wildlife.

The Everglade snail kite is a raptor that lives in lowland freshwater marshes from Florida to South America. In the United States, the kite lives in the watersheds of the Everglades, where the kite feeds almost exclusively on apple snails. The kite favors freshwater marshes and the shallow vegetated edges of lakes (both natural and man-made) where apple snails can be found. The kite avoids dense vegetation because they require foraging areas that are relatively clear and open in order to visually search for apple snails. The kite hunts apple snails either by flying less than ten meters above the water, or by swooping down from a perch. The kite catches snails with its talons, never actually plunging into the water. Historically, the kite lived throughout much of Florida, but today they are restricted to the central and southern portions of the state. The watersheds that host the kite have experienced, and continue to experience, pervasive degradation resulting from urban development and agricultural activities. The kite struggles during years of drought or low water in southern Florida, with its nests become more vulnerable to predators and as the population of apple snails drops as well. "Nearly continuous flooding of wetland for > 1 year is needed to sustain apple snail populations." The kite was listed as endangered by the United States Fish & Wildlife Service (FWS) "because of the very small population and increasingly limited amount of fresh marsh with sufficient water to ensure an adequate supply of snails on which it depends for food." The FWS designated critical habitat for the kite in 1977. Today "[t]he principal threat to the snail kite is the loss or degradation of wetlands in central and South Florida."

The Cape Sable seaside sparrow is a medium-sized sparrow—about 13 centimeters long—that lives in freshwater marshes in southern Florida. The sparrow had been the last new bird species identified in the United States, only to lose that status when it was reclassified as a one of eight subspecies of seaside sparrows. The sparrow was first found in the early 1930s on Cape Sable, the southernmost point of Florida which is now part of the Everglades National Park. But a 1935 hurricane flooded Cape Sable and replaced the area's freshwater plants with vegetation that is tolerant of salt water. Ironically, the Cape Sable seaside sparrow no longer lives on Cape Sable. Instead, the sparrow now survives in several parts of the freshwater marshes of Everglades National Park, where the sparrow had never lived until the changes in the hydrology of southern Florida wrought by hurricanes and human engineering.

The Cape Sable seaside sparrow is sedentary, secretive, and non-migratory. It prefers mixed marl prairie communities, which are grassy areas supported by a thin layer of soil atop limestone bedrock. Those prairie communities should be dry during the breeding season from February through early August, or at least have surface water levels of less than 10 centimeters in order to support the right kind of vegetation for the sparrow. The prairie communities are susceptible to periodic fires, which prevent the growth of hardwood trees and the accretion of dead plant material, both of which would decrease the suitability of habitat for the sparrow. The sparrow tends to avoid areas with dense or woody vegetation. The sparrow eats a variety of insects that it finds on low vegetation or along the ground. An individual sparrow lives two or three years, thus preventing the species from surviving extended poor conditions.

The FWS designated critical habitat for the Cape Sable sparrow in 1977. By the 1990's, the designated areas failed to account for the actual populations of the sparrow, and it included land that had been converted to agriculture or otherwise abandoned by the sparrow. Thus, in October 2006, the FWS proposed to designate 71,000 additional acres in Everglades National Park as critical habitat for the sparrow. The newly designated land would include both areas that now host sparrows and unoccupied areas containing suitable potential habitat for the sparrow.

Here is how one recent news report described the problem: "Deciding how deep water flows should be could determine what species will thrive in a region once dominated by the kite but now critical habitat for the sparrow, begging the question whether two federally protected species with vastly different habitat needs can survive in the same habitat." How would you solve this problem? What actions should be taken to facilitate the survival and recovery of both the Everglade snail kite and the Cape Sable seaside sparrow, while complying the requirements of the law?

# CHAPTER 3

# THE CLEAN AIR ACT

## CHAPTER OUTLINE



---

The primary task of environmental law is to protect the environment—and the people and other living things in that environment—from various harms. The air, water, and land all suffer from pollution sometimes caused by natural events, but far more often resulting from human activities. That pollution threatens human health, disrupts natural ecosystems, interferes with our use of the environment, is unsightly, and is simply objectionable to increasing numbers of people. Traditionally, the common law provided a limited number of remedies for the victims of pollution. During the past half century, though, the common law framework has been superseded by an exhaustive body of regulations designed to prevent pollution and the harms that it causes. It would be impossible to learn all of those regulations in one course; indeed, it is challenging to understand fully any single regulatory scheme. The following three chapters provide examples of how environmental law has attempted to respond to the problem of pollution of air, water, and land.

The air that surrounds us is polluted by toxic chemicals, fine particulates, and unsightly smoke emitted by factories, power plants, cars, barbeques, lawnmowers, forest fires, volcanoes, and many other culprits. Factory smokestacks discharge clouds of smoke that obscure the view of natural landscapes. Thousands of cars emit fumes that cause respiratory difficulties for the elderly and for children. Power plants discharge sulfur dioxide that can fall to the earth as acid rain that injures plants and wildlife hundreds of miles away. Indoor air pollution results from individuals smoking cigarettes in an office. There are, in short, countless ways in which individuals and businesses release substances into the air that cause a variety of harms to other people and to the natural environment itself.

The attention paid to air pollution during the past fifty years has made great strides in alleviating the problem. Cleaner fuels, dispersed industries, and political pressure have yielded substantial improvements in air quality. Lead concentrations in the air experienced an especially dramatic decline once lead was removed from gasoline in the 1970s. Nonetheless, many places continue to suffer from unhealthy or unsightly skies. Mexico City, Bangkok, Cairo, and Delhi are among the cities experiencing rapid economic development without a concomitant effort to protect the air. In 2013, air pollution levels in China's capital of Beijing soared, making it impossible even to see buildings across the street and creating a major public health crisis. *See, e.g.,* Edward Wong, *2 Major Air Pollutants Increase in Beijing*, N.Y. TIMES, April 4, 2013.

Air pollution has been reduced dramatically in the United States since the congressional enactment of the Clean Air Act (CAA) in 1970, with further reductions in the past decade. Even so, the American Lung Association (ALA) identifies the following problems associated with air pollution:

- More than half of the U.S. population lives in counties that have unhealthful levels of either ozone or particle pollution.
- More than half of the U.S. population lives in areas with unhealthful levels of ozone.
- Almost 15 percent of people in the United States live in an area with unhealthful short-term particle pollution.
- Nearly one in five people in the United States lives in an area with unhealthful year-round pollution.
- About 22.8 million Americans—over 7 percent of the population—live in counties with unhealthy levels of all three: ozone and short term and year-round particle pollution.

AMERICAN LUNG ASSOCIATION, STATE OF THE AIR 8 (2016). The ALA also cites the CAA as the reason why "since 1970, the air has gotten cleaner while the population, the economy, energy use and miles driven increased greatly." *Id.* at 4. To help understand why the CAA is so central to this progress, we will provide some background on the CAA, then explore its provisions and implementation in detail.

# I. AIR POLLUTION REGULATION BEFORE 1970

Air pollution is not a new phenomenon. J.R. McNeill reports that "[u]rban smoke darkened marble in ancient cities, annoyed classical writers such as the Roman poet Horace, and provoked a spate of laws among the ancient Jews." J.R. MCNEILL, SOMETHING NEW UNDER THE SUN 55 (2000). The skies above London were smoky as early at the thirteenth century, and resembled "hell upon earth" by the seventeenth century. *Id.* at 57. Chinese cities experienced notable air pollution during the Song dynasty (960–1279 A.D.), especially from unchecked emissions from copper smelters. The Industrial Revolution of the nineteenth century spread air pollution throughout Europe and the United States due to dramatic increases in the burning of coal and other fossil fuels. Then air pollution grew much worse during the twentieth century. Dense smoke was blamed for traffic accidents, blackened buildings, and dirty laundry in numerous cities early in the twentieth century. More ominously, dozens of people died and thousands became ill during severe episodes of air pollution in Glasgow in 1909, Belgium in 1930, England in 1931, Donora, Pennsylvania in 1948, and London again in 1952. These fatal events remained relatively uncommon, but air pollution caused many more deaths in places where it persisted for longer periods of time. In the United States, the steel industry of Pittsburgh and the cars of Los Angeles earned both cities reputations for especially polluted air. Nuisance law served as the common law's response to air pollution. Indeed, several of the twentieth century's most famous nuisance cases involved air pollution. Two early twentieth century cases involved the air pollution emitted by a copper smelter in Ducktown, Tennessee near the Georgia and North Carolina borders.

## Madison v. Ducktown Sulphur Copper & Iron Co.

Tennessee Supreme Court, 1904.
83 S.W. 658.

■ NEIL, J.

These three cases were instituted separately in the court below, but tried together here. They embrace, in the main, the same facts and the same questions of law, and will be disposed of in a single opinion. The bills are all based on the ground of nuisance, in that the two companies, in the operation of their plants at and near Ducktown, in Polk county, in the course of reducing copper ore, cause large volumes of smoke to issue from their roast piles, which smoke descends upon the surrounding lands, and injures trees and crops, and renders the homes of complainants less comfortable and their lands less profitable than before. The purpose of all the bills is to enjoin the further operation of these plants;. . . .

The following general facts are applicable to all of the cases: Prior to 1870 one Rhat began the operation of a copper mine at Ducktown, and worked it for several years. Subsequently it was owned by the Union Consolidated Mining Company, Mr. Rhat's successor. These operations were continued until the year 1879, and were then suspended until 1891. During the latter year the Ducktown Sulphur, Copper & Iron Company commenced operating the properties formerly owned and operated by the Union Consolidated Mining Company, and has continued to operate them ever since. The Pittsburg & Tennessee Copper Company began operations at Ducktown about the year 1881, and continued until about 1899, when it sold out to the defendant Tennessee Copper Company. The latter began its operations in 1900, and commenced roasting ores in May, 1901. It has continued its works ever since. Ducktown is in a basin of the mountains of Polk county, in this state, not far from the state line of the states of Georgia and North Carolina. This basin is six or eight miles wide. The complainants are the owners of small farms situated in the mountains around Ducktown.

The method used by the defendants in reducing their copper ores is to place the green ore, broken up, on layers of wood, making large open-air piles, called "roast piles," and these roast piles are ignited for the purpose of expelling from the ore certain foreign matters called "sulphurets." In burning, these roast piles emit large volumes of smoke. This smoke, rising in the air, is carried off by air currents around and over adjoining land. . . .

[The complainants'] lands are all thin mountain lands, of little agricultural value. The general effect produced by the smoke upon the possessions and families of the complainants is as follows, viz.: Their timber and crop interests have been badly injured, and they have been annoyed and discommoded by the smoke so that the complainants are prevented from using and enjoying their farms and homes as they did prior to the inauguration of these enterprises. The smoke makes it impossible for the owners of farms within the area of the smoke zone to subsist their families thereon with the degree of comfort they enjoyed before. They cannot raise and harvest their customary crops, and their timber is largely destroyed. There is a finding that the Ducktown Sulphur, Copper & Iron Company acquired its plant in 1891, and that it has spent several hundred thousand dollars since that time in improving and enlarging the plant.

The Court of Chancery Appeals finds that the defendants are conducting and have been conducting their business in a lawful way, without any purpose or desire to injure any of the complainants; that they have been and are pursuing the only known method by which these plants can be operated and their business successfully carried on; that the open-air roast heap is the only method known to the business or to science by means of which copper ore of the character mined by the defendants can be reduced; that the defendants have made every effort to get rid of the smoke and noxious vapors, one of the defendants having spent $200,000 in experiments to this end, but without result. It is to be inferred from the description of the locality that there is no place more remote to which the operations referred to could be transferred.

It is found, in substance, that, if the injunctive relief sought be granted, the defendants will be compelled to stop operations, and their property will become practically worthless, the immense business conducted by them will cease, and they will be compelled to withdraw from the state. It is a necessary deduction from the foregoing that a great and increasing industry in the state will be destroyed, and all of the valuable copper properties of the state become worthless.

The following facts were also found, viz.: That the total tax aggregate of Polk County for the year 1903 was $2,585,931.43, of which total the assessments of the defendants amounted to $1,279,533. It is also found that prior to the operations of these companies there lived in the district where these works are located only 200 people, whereas there are now living in this district, almost wholly dependent upon these copper industries, about 12,000 people. It is also found that one of the defendants, the Tennessee Copper Company, employs upon its pay roll 1,300 men, and that the average pay roll is about $40,000 per month, nearly all of which employees have been drawn from the population of Polk and neighboring counties.

It is quite apparent that the two companies pay out annually vast sums of money, which are necessarily of great benefit to the people of the county, and that they are conducting and maintaining an industry upon which a laboring population of from ten to twelve thousand people are practically dependent; and it is found, in substance, by the Court of Chancery Appeals, that, if these industries be suppressed, these thousands of people will have to wander forth to other localities to find shelter and work.

While there can be no doubt that the facts stated make out a case of nuisance, for which the complainants in actions at law would be entitled to recover damages . . . if the injury can be adequately compensated at law by a judgment for damages, equity will not interfere. . . . The question now to be considered is, what is the proper exercise of discretion, under the facts appearing in the present case? Shall the complainants be granted, in the way of damages, the full measure of relief to which their injuries entitle them, or shall we go further, and grant their request to blot out two great mining and manufacturing enterprises, destroy half of the taxable values of a county, and drive more than 10,000 people from their homes? We think there can be no doubt as to what the true answer to this question should be.

In order to protect by injunction several small tracts of land, aggregating in value less than $1,000, we are asked to destroy other property worth nearly $2,000,000, and wreck two great mining and manufacturing enterprises, that are engaged in work of very great importance, not only to their owners, but to the state, and to the whole country as well, to depopulate a large town, and deprive thousands of working people of their homes and livelihood, and scatter them broadcast. The result would be practically a confiscation of the property of the defendants for the benefit of the complainants—an appropriation without compensation. The defendants cannot reduce their ores in a manner different from that they are now employing, and there is no more remote place to which they can remove. The decree asked for would deprive them of all of their rights. We appreciate the argument based on the fact that the homes of the complainants who live on the small tracts of land referred to are not so comfortable and useful to their owners as they were before they were affected by the smoke complained of, and we are deeply sensible of the truth of the proposition that no man is entitled to any more rights than another on the ground that he has or owns more property than that other. But in a case of conflicting rights, where neither party can enjoy his own without in some measure restricting the liberty of the other in the use of property, the law must make the best arrangement it can between the contending parties, with a view to preserving to each one the largest measure of liberty possible under the circumstances. We see no escape from the conclusion in the present case that the only proper decree is to allow the complainants a reference for the ascertainment of damages, and that the injunction must be denied to them. . . .

---

## Georgia v. Tennessee Copper Co.

Supreme Court of the United States, 1907.
206 U.S. 230.

■ MR. JUSTICE HOLMES delivered the opinion of the court:

This is a bill in equity filed in this court by the state of Georgia, in pursuance of a resolution of the legislature and by direction of the governor of the state, to enjoin the defendant copper companies from discharging noxious gas from their works in Tennessee over the plaintiff's territory. It alleges that, in consequence of such discharge, a wholesale destruction of forests, orchards, and crops is going on, and other injuries are done and threatened in five counties of the state. It alleges also a vain application to the state of Tennessee for relief. A preliminary injunction was denied; but, as there was ground to fear that great and irreparable damage might be done, an early day was fixed for the final hearing, and the parties were given leave, if so minded, to try the case on affidavits. . . .

The case has been argued largely as if it were one between two private parties; but it is not. The very elements that would be relied upon in a suit between fellow-citizens as a ground for equitable relief are wanting here. The state owns very little of the territory alleged to be affected, and the damage to it capable of estimate in money, possibly, at least, is small. This is a suit by a state for an injury to it in its capacity of quasi-sovereign. In that capacity the state has an interest independent of and behind the titles of its citizens, in all the earth and air within its domain. It has the last word as to whether its mountains shall be stripped of their forests and its inhabitants shall breathe pure air. It might have to pay individuals before it could utter that word, but with it remains the final power. The alleged damage to the state as a private owner is merely a makeweight, and we may lay on one side the dispute as to whether the destruction of forests has led to the gullying of its roads.

The caution with which demands of this sort, on the part of a state, for relief from injuries analogous to torts, must be examined, is dwelt upon in Missouri v. Illinois, 200 U.S. 496, 520, 521. But it is plain that some such demands must be recognized, if the grounds alleged are proved. When the states by their union made the forcible abatement of outside nuisances impossible to each, they did not thereby agree to submit to whatever might be done. They did not renounce the possibility of making reasonable demands on the ground of their still remaining quasi-sovereign interests; and the alternative to force is a suit in this court. Missouri v. Illinois, 180 U.S. 208, 241.

Some peculiarities necessarily mark a suit of this kind. If the state has a case at all, it is somewhat more certainly entitled to specific relief than a private party might be. It is not lightly to be required to give up quasi-sovereign rights for pay; and, apart from the difficulty of valuing such rights in money, if that be its choice it may insist that an infraction of them shall be stopped. The states, by entering the Union, did not sink to the position of private owners, subject to one system of private law. This court has not quite the same freedom to balance the harm that will be done by an injunction against that of which the plaintiff complains, that it would have in deciding between two subjects of a single political power. Without excluding the considerations that equity always takes into account, we cannot give the weight that was given them in argument to a comparison between the damage threatened to the plaintiff and the calamity of a possible stop to the defendants' business, the question of health, the character of the forests as a first or second growth, the commercial possibility or impossibility of reducing the fumes to sulphuric acid, the special adaptation of the business to the place.

It is a fair and reasonable demand on the part of a sovereign that the air over its territory should not be polluted on a great scale by sulphurous acid gas, that the forests on its mountains, be they better or worse, and whatever domestic destruction they have suffered, should not be further destroyed or threatened by the act of persons beyond its control, that the crops and orchards on its hills should not be endangered from the same source. If any such demand is to be enforced this must be notwithstanding the hesitation that we might feel if the suit were between private parties, and the doubt whether, for the injuries which they might be suffering to their property, they should not be left to an action at law.

The proof requires but a few words. It is not denied that the defendants generate in their works near the Georgia line large quantities of sulphur dioxide which becomes sulphurous acid by its mixture with the air. It hardly is denied, and cannot be denied with success, that this gas often is carried by the wind great distances and over great tracts of Georgia land. On the evidence the pollution of the air and the magnitude of that pollution are not open to dispute. Without any attempt to go into details immaterial to the suit, it is proper to add that we are satisfied, by a preponderance of evidence, that the sulphurous fumes cause and threaten damage on so considerable a scale to the forests and vegetable life, if not to health, within the plaintiff state, as to make out a case within the requirements of Missouri v. Illinois, 200 U.S. 496. Whether Georgia, by insisting upon this claim, is doing more harm than good to her own citizens, is for her to determine. The possible disaster to those outside the state must be accepted as a consequence of her standing upon her extreme rights.

It is argued that the state has been guilty of laches. We deem it unnecessary to consider how far such a defense would be available in a suit of this sort, since, in our opinion, due diligence has been shown. The conditions have been different until recent years. After the evil had grown greater in 1904 the state brought a bill in this court. The defendants, however, already were abandoning the old method of roasting ore in open heaps and it was hoped that the change would stop the trouble. They were ready to agree not to return to that method, and, upon such an agreement being made, the bill was dismissed without prejudice. But the plaintiff now finds, or thinks that it finds, that the tall chimneys in present use cause the poisonous gases to be carried to greater distances than ever before, and that the evil has not been helped.

If the state of Georgia adheres to its determination, there is no alternative to issuing an injunction, after allowing a reasonable time to the defendants to complete the structures that they now are building, and the efforts that they are making to stop the fumes.

Injunction to issue.

---

## QUESTIONS AND DISCUSSION

**1.** Why did the courts reach different results in the two cases? How would you explain the importance that local economics played in the decision?

Following the Supreme Court's decision, one company agreed to settle and set up a fund to compensate those injured and to restrict operations during summer months, but the other company refused to settle and was enjoined from emitting more than specified amounts of pollution. The company then developed new pollution control technology that is still a model of pollution abatement.

**2.** The next famous air pollution nuisance case occurred in 1970 at the height of the effort to enact more sweeping environmental statutes. In Boomer v. Atlantic Cement Co., 257 N.E.2d 870 (N.Y. 1970), Atlantic Cement operated a large cement plant near Albany that employed over 300 people and was worth over $45 million. The plant contained state-of-the-art pollution control technology, but eight neighboring landowners sued because they were injured by dirt, smoke, and vibrations from the plant. The New York Court of Appeals agreed that the plant was a nuisance, but it struggled with the appropriate remedy. Indeed, the court was concerned that air pollution was too big a problem for the court to try to solve by itself. So the court issued an injunction against the operation of the plant, but agreed to lift the injunction provided that the plant paid for the permanent damages suffered by the plaintiffs. The court thought this approach did justice between the parties, while creating an incentive to conduct research to avoid pollution. Judge Jasen, however, dissented because he believed that the court's solution wrongly allowed the plant to continue to pollute the air. He would have enjoined the operation of the plant unless it abated the nuisance within 18 months.

**3.** In the early 2000s, states, local governments, and individuals began to invoke the nuisance doctrine to compel automobile companies and utilities to limit emissions of pollutants, including $CO_2$ emissions that lead to climate change. These cases resulted in some early successes at the lower court levels, most notably in a 2009 decision by the Court of Appeals for the Second Circuit finding that states, cities, and land trusts had standing to sue major power plants for harm associated with greenhouse gas (GHG) emissions on federal public nuisance grounds and that the political question doctrine did not bar the claims. *See* Connecticut v. American Electric Power Company, 582 F.3d 309 (2d Cir. 2009), *rev'd and remanded*, 131 S. Ct. 2527 (2011). *See also* Cooper v. Tennessee Valley Authority, 593 F. Supp. 2d 812 (W.D.N.C. 2009) (ordering TVA to install additional pollution control technology on certain TVA plants in Tennessee on grounds that emissions from the plants were causing a nuisance in North Carolina), *rev'd and remanded* 615 F.3d 291 (4th Cir. 2010); Comer v. Murphy Oil, USA, 585 F.3d 855 (5th Cir. 2009) (finding plaintiffs suing oil companies for contributing to climate change and, consequently, the severity of Hurricane Katrina, had standing to assert claims for property damage based on nuisance, trespass, and other common law theories and that the political question doctrine did not bar the claims) (opinion withdrawn).

Upon later review, however, higher courts overturned most of these decisions, limiting significantly the ability of plaintiffs to seek both injunctive relief and damages associated with GHG emissions under federal and state common law nuisance theories. *See* American Electric Power Company v. Connecticut, 131 S. Ct. 2527 (2011) (holding that the CAA and EPA actions it authorizes displace any federal common law right to seek abatement of $CO_2$ emissions from fossil-fuel fired power plants, but remanding the plaintiffs' state law nuisance claims for further consideration by the lower court); Cooper v. Tennessee Valley Authority, 615 F.3d 291 (4th Cir. 2010) (holding that lower court injunction requiring pollution control equipment on power plants to control GHG emissions "would encourage courts to use vague public nuisance standards to scuttle the nation's carefully created system for accommodating the need for energy production and the need for clean air" and would result in "a balkanization of clean air regulations and a confused patchwork of standards, to the detriment of industry and the environment alike."); Comer v. Murphy Oil USA, 607 F.3d 1049 (5th Cir. 2010) (granting *en banc* review of the 5th Circuit panel decision, which had held the plaintiffs had standing to bring nuisance claims for damages associated with Hurricane Katrina, and then, after vacating the panel decision as a result of the grant of *en banc* review, determined that only 8 of the 16 judges in the circuit did not have a conflict of interest in hearing the case and, now having no quorum, determined the only course was to reinstate the district court decision dismissing the claims for lack of standing).

In addition to the limits these appellate courts have placed on common law nuisance claims, other courts have found at the outset that such suits are barred by the political question doctrine or standing limitations. *See* California v. General Motors Corporation, 2007 WL 2726871 (N.D Cal. 2007) (dismissing nuisance claim against auto companies on political question grounds); Native Village of Kivalina v. ExxonMobil Corp., 663 F. Supp. 2d 863 (N.D. Cal. 2009) (dismissing federal public nuisance claim by native village in Alaska against oil companies for their contribution to climate change and the erosion and destruction of plaintiffs' land on standing and political question grounds), *aff'd*, 696 F.3d 849 (9th Cir. 2012) (affirming dismissal on grounds that, applying *American Elec. Power v. Connecticut*, the CAA and EPA regulatory actions displace the plaintiffs' common law nuisance claims). One of the fundamental problems with using nuisance doctrine as opposed to nationwide regulation to address air pollution is that such claims require an individualized, fact-intensive balancing of benefits, burdens, and equitable factors to reach a result, and that result applies only to the parties to the litigation. On the other hand, nuisance doctrine and the common law generally continue to remain potentially valuable as a supplement to federal (as well as state and local) regulation of air pollution, particularly in cases where existing regulation does not squarely apply to the activity in question.

**4.** The common law of nuisance was not the only means of limiting air pollution prior to the 1970s. Many states and local governments enacted and enforced regulations to limit air pollution from factories, ships, and other industrial operations. In 1960, in Huron Portland Cement Co. v. City of Detroit, 362 U.S. 440 (1960), the U.S. Supreme Court upheld the validity of the City of Detroit's smoke abatement code as it applied to ships operating in interstate commerce. Two of the ships in question emitted black smoke when docked in Detroit for loading and unloading. The Court held that the ordinance could be constitutionally applied to the ships and cited to Congressional legislation recognizing that "the problem of air pollution is peculiarly a matter of state and local concern." Why do the Court and Congress believe that air pollution is "peculiarly a matter of state and local concern"? Do you agree?

5. Scott Dewey draws several conclusions from his study of the history of the air pollution regulation before 1970. He sees the victory of economic concerns over efforts to reduce air pollution—in other words, the treatment of pollution as an externality by those whose activities produce pollution—as "[p]erhaps the most fundamental theme in the history of air pollution control and general environmental policy." SCOTT HAMILTON DEWEY, DON'T BREATHE THE AIR: AIR POLLUTION AND U.S. ENVIRONMENTAL POLITICS, 1945–1970 (2000). He also cites "the tendency to study air pollution to death while letting business proceed as usual." *Id.* at 30. Other lessons are more surprising. Dewey challenges the myths that the public did not care about air pollution before World War II, that the actions of corporations rather than ordinary citizens were responsible for air pollution, that air pollution used to be viewed as an aesthetic problem rather than public health problem, and that technology could not control air pollution before World War II. *Id.* at 7–10. How do these lessons compare to the issue decided by the Court in *Madison v. Ducktown Sulfur* and *Georgia v. Tennessee Copper*?

## II. OVERVIEW OF THE CLEAN AIR ACT

The CAA stands out amidst our many environmental laws. A massive law, the CAA was also historic. Unlike earlier laws passed by Congress, the CAA boasted *uniform, national standards* covering a wide range of pollutants and sources. Passed just one year after we put a man on the Moon, the CAA reflected both the technological optimism of the times and the frustration with poor air quality in our cities.

With the passage of the CAA it was assumed that our nation's clean air problems would be largely solved within the decade. Over three decades and hundreds of billions of dollars later, however, the CAA presents a curious contradiction. With few exceptions, the concentrations of major air pollutants have dropped despite greatly increased economic activity. Overall, the air we breathe is cleaner than in 1970. Yet many of our largest cities still fail to meet the clean air requirements of the CAA. How have we done so poorly by doing so well?

A review of the CAA provides a fascinating study of tense federalism, strategic choice of regulatory targets, and cutting-edge environmental policy instruments. From a regulator's perspective, the air pollution problem is made difficult because air pollutants arise from different sources. Vehicle emissions are responsible for all the CO and about half of NOx and VOCs. Power plants are major emitters of $SO_2$ and NOx. Incinerators, power plants, and industrial facilities are major sources of hazardous air pollutants but, perhaps surprisingly, so are small sources and motor vehicles. Moreover, these pollutants mix in the atmosphere, moving with the winds subject to local topography and climate but paying no heed to state and county lines.

If one thinks back to 1970, then, the architects of the CAA faced a formidable challenge. In place of the available common law nuisance actions, which necessarily provided only retrospective remedies and required proof of causation and harm, in place of a patchwork of state laws with poor effectiveness, the drafters of the CAA needed to create an overarching national law for an entire class of pollutants from disparate sources. Indeed, this would be the *first* truly national pollution law. Congress needed to decide not only how clean we want our air to be, but how much are we willing to pay for clean air and who should pay for it. To clarify this challenge, consider how the law needed to address the policy questions posed by *what, how much, where,* and *how* to regulate. As you proceed through this chapter consider how Congress has attempted to address each of these policy questions.

In part because the CAA was the first modern pollution law and in part because air pollution is such an important problem, the CAA has provided fertile ground for a whole range of policy approaches. Given the many different sources of air pollutants, which mix of regulatory tools will work best? Should mobile sources (e.g., cars and trucks) be regulated differently than stationary sources such as incinerators and power plants? Should new sources be treated differently than sources in operation when the law was passed? Since air pollution pays no heed to state lines, uniform national standards for air pollutants would seem to make a lot of sense, but is treating every location in the country the same economically efficient? In political terms, what role do such national standards leave for the states?

The CAA passed in 1970 (actually amending an earlier CAA from 1963) and, with its subsequent amendments in 1977 and in 1990, had to address all of these challenges, and more. As a result, it is a massive piece of legislation. In fact, some professors spend almost their entire survey course covering *only* the CAA! Much of the CAA can be understood as the product of what might be called "cooperative federalism," as a dynamic balance between federal standard setting and state implementation. *See* John P. Dwyer, *The Practice of Federalism Under the Clean Air Act*, 54 MD. L. REV. 1183 (1995). Once you understand which areas were reserved purely for federal regulation, the act starts to make more sense.

As enacted in 1970, and as amended in 1977 and 1990, the CAA is divided into the following six titles:

- Title I: Programs and Activities—This title contains the principal sections of the CAA. They require EPA to identify "air pollutants," provide for the establishment of the National Ambient Air Quality Standards (NAAQS), and direct each state to produce a state implementation plan (SIP) to achieve each of the NAAQS. Title I sets new source performance standards for stationary sources of air pollution (NSPS) as well as standards for hazardous air pollutants (HAPs). It also specifies the consequences of the failure to attain the NAAQS (nonattainment areas), and it requires the prevention of significant deterioration (PSD) of air quality in areas where the NAAQS are already satisfied (attainment areas). *See* CAA §§ 101–193, 42 U.S.C. §§ 7401–7515.

- Title II: Emission Standards for Moving Sources—This title covers the regulation of air pollution emitted from cars and other vehicles (usually called mobile sources) by targeting the permissible emissions from vehicles and the types of fuels that they use, while encouraging alternatives to traditional vehicles and fuels. *See* CAA §§ 202–259, 42 U.S.C. §§ 7521–7590.
- Title III: General Provisions—The enforcement provisions appear in this title, including the citizen suit provision empowering any affected party to sue to enforce the law and the provisions governing judicial review of EPA decisions implementing the CAA. *See* CAA §§ 301–328, 42 U.S.C. §§ 7601–7628.
- Title IV–A: Acid Deposition—Congress added this title in 1990 to create a market-based approach to controlling emissions from large electric utility plants. *See* CAA Sections 401–416, 42 U.S.C. §§ 7651–7651(*o*).
- Title V: Permits—Congress added this provision in 1990, too, which establishes the first direct permit requirements for air pollution sources in the CAA (as opposed to state plans to implement the CAA). *See* CAA §§ 501–507, 42 U.S.C. §§ 7661–7661f.
- Title VI: Stratospheric Ozone Protection—This provision requires the phaseout of the production, use, and consumption of certain substances that contribute to depletion of the earth's stratospheric ozone layer. *See* CAA §§ 601–618, 42 U.S.C. §§ 7671–7671q.

We will examine many (though not all) of these provisions in the following pages. EPA's summary of the CAA is contained in THE PLAIN ENGLISH GUIDE TO THE CLEAN AIR ACT and EPA's website contains abundant information about the CAA and its implementation at https://www.epa.gov/regulatory-information-topic/regulatory-information-topic-air. For other overviews of the law, see THE CLEAN AIR ACT HANDBOOK (Julie R. Domike & Alec C. Zacaroli eds. 3d ed. 2011); MARK S. SQUILLACE & DAVID R. WOOLEY, AIR POLLUTION (3d ed. 1999); WILLIAM H. RODGERS, JR., ENVIRONMENTAL LAW 123–245 (2d ed. 1994). For a view of how the 1970 CAA evolved from earlier federal air pollution legislation, see Christopher D. Ahlers, *Origins of the Clean Air Act: A New Interpretation*, 45 ENVTL. L. 47 (2015).

The follow paragraphs provide a roadmap to the primary CAA programs within the Titles described above. Each program is discussed in greater detail in the remainder of this chapter.

National Ambient Air Quality Standards (NAAQS) (§§ 108–09): Upon its inception, the primary focus of the CAA was to ensure clean and healthy air throughout the nation, with the primary method of achieving these ends being the issuance of national standards for certain "criteria pollutants." Section 108 (42 U.S.C. § 7408) of the CAA requires EPA to identify those pollutants which are suitable for a national standard, and section 109 (42 U.S.C. § 7409) requires EPA to issue those standards in the form of National Ambient Air Quality Standards. NAAQS are divided into two categories, primary and secondary, with primary NAAQS being set at a level which is "requisite to protect the public health" while allowing for an "adequate margin of safety." 42 U.S.C. § 7409(b)(1). Secondary NAAQS are to be set at a level which "is requisite to protect the public welfare from any known or anticipated adverse effects associated with the presence of such air pollutant in the ambient air." 42 U.S.C. § 7409(b)(2). Thus far, NAAQS have been established for the following criteria pollutants: nitrogen dioxide ($NO_x$); Carbon Monoxide (CO); lead (Pb); particulate matter (which is divided into two subcategories based on size of the particles); sulfur dioxide ($SO_2$); and ozone ($O_3$). 40 C.F.R. Part 50.

State Implementation Plans (SIPs) (§§ 107 and 110): After EPA establishes a NAAQS for a certain criteria pollutant, the CAA requires each individual state to respond with an implementation plan that it creates detailing the steps it will take in order to bring polluted areas into attainment. Specifically, each plan submitted to EPA for review must provide for the "implementation, maintenance, and enforcement" of the NAAQS within each air quality control region in the state. 42 U.S.C. § 7410(a). This is the section of the CAA which is most often referred to as representing a system of "cooperative federalism," as the federal government sets the standard that must be met yet allows for the states in their individual capacities to allocate the burden of the necessary pollution reductions among their citizens. However, if the state submits an incomplete SIP or fails to submit a SIP entirely, EPA is required to establish a Federal Implementation Plan (FIP) within two years for that particular state. 42 U.S.C. § 7610(c).

New Source Review (NSR): Construction of a new source of air pollution or modification of an existing source may trigger preconstruction review and permitting. The nature of that permitting is based on whether the source is located in an area that attains the NAAQs (attainment area) or an area that has failed to attain the NAAQs (nonattainment area). Sources located in attainment areas are subject to the Prevention of

Significant Deterioration (PSD) permit program while sources in nonattainment areas are subject to the nonattainment permit program. The NSR requirements apply to "major" stationary sources. For the PSD program, a "major source" is one that has the potential to emit at least 250 tons per year (tpy) of a regulated pollutant or at least 100 tpy of a regulated pollutant if the source is within one of 28 listed source categories. The nonattainment program defines a "major" source as one with the potential to emit at least 10 to 100 tpy of the nonattainment pollutant, depending on the pollutant and the seriousness of the nonattainment problem in that area.

Prevention of Significant Deterioration Program (PSD) (CAA §§ 160–169B): The PSD program attempts to preserve existing good air quality as well as ensure that areas in attainment of the NAAQS remain in attainment. 42 U.S.C. §§ 7470–7492. New emission sources and modifications of existing sources subject to the PSD program are required by the CAA to implement the Best Available Control Technology (BACT) which is set according to the most effective technology already in use in the marketplace. 42 U.S.C. § 7475(a)(4) (BACT provisions).

Nonattainment Program (CAA §§ 171–189): New major stationary sources or major modifications of existing sources in nonattainment areas must receive a state nonattainment permit prior to construction. State permit programs must include a requirement that major new or modified sources achieve the Lowest Achievable Emission Rate (LAER) defined as "the most stringent emission limitation" contained in any SIP or that is "achieved in practice" by the same or a similar source category, whichever is more stringent. In order to ensure progress toward the NAAQS, the state permit program must require that the proposed new or modified source offset increased emissions of the nonattainment pollutant by obtaining emissions reductions from nearby facilities at a greater than one-to-one ratio.

New Source Performance Standards (NSPS) (CAA §§ 111): New stationary sources (such as power plants, refineries, and other categories of industrial activities) are required to meet New Source Performance Standards (NSPS) established by EPA. 42 U.S.C. § 7411. EPA also establishes performance standards for new and existing sources under the New Source Review (NSR) program. 42 U.S.C. § 7475 (PSD permits); 42 U.S.C. § 7503 (nonattainment permits).

Mobile Sources (CAA §§ 202–259): The 1970 amendments to the CAA established what were at the time the first comprehensive regulatory scheme for mobile emission sources, principally automobiles and trucks, however also including other vehicles such as trains and airplanes. The regulations preempt all states except California from adopting standards that differ from the federal standards, unless they adopt the standards set by California, which must still apply for a waiver from EPA before it is allowed to implement stricter standards. 42 U.S.C. § 7543. California is granted special status in regulating mobile sources because its regulation of mobile source emissions predated that of the federal government and also because of the unique pollution challenges California has historically faced from automobiles.

Acid Rain Emission Trading (CAA §§ 401–416): One of the most pioneering provisions included in the 1990 amendments to the CAA was the establishment of the marketable emission permits trading scheme for $SO_2$ and NOx, which were identified as the cause of acid rain. 42 U.S.C. § 7651. By establishing a nationwide cap on $SO_2$ and $NO_x$ emissions from fossil-fuel-powered utilities, and creating tradable emission permits which equated to the set cap, regulators were able to reduce overall emissions while allowing the market to determine who bore the brunt of the costs. The program has achieved considerable success in reducing the overall emission levels for $SO_2$ and $NO_x$, and was the model for the many of the cap and trade frameworks that have been proposed to address rising $CO_2$ emissions that lead to climate change.

## III. NATIONAL AMBIENT AIR QUALITY STANDARDS (NAAQS)

The keystone of the CAA is its treatment of the most common pollutants of concern in the outside air, and most of the CAA's provisions are driven by its regulation of these so-called "criteria pollutants." Defined as numerous or diverse sources that can endanger public health or welfare, criteria pollutants include many of the pollutants mentioned above—$O_3$, $NO_x$, CO, fine particles, $SO_2$—as well as lead. The CAA requires that these pollutants not exceed uniform levels at *any* outside point to which the public has access. Thus the standards don't apply indoors or on private land.

The sources of these pollutants and the harms that they cause are illustrated in the following table:

| Pollutant | Description | Sources | Harms |
|---|---|---|---|
| Carbon monoxide (CO) | Odorless, colorless gas formed when carbon in fuel is not burned completely | Vehicle emissions<br>Industrial processes<br>Wildfires | Cardiovascular disease<br>Reduced oxygen intake<br>Impaired vision |
| Lead (Pb) | Naturally occurring metal that used to be added to gasoline | Industrial processes<br>Waste disposal<br>Vehicle emissions | Organ damage<br>Neurological impairments<br>High blood pressure |
| Nitrogen dioxide ($NO_2$) | Highly reactive gas formed when fuel is burned at high temperatures | Vehicle emissions<br>Electric power plants<br>Residential heaters | Respiratory illnesses<br>Acid rain<br>Impaired visibility |
| Ozone ($O_3$) | Smog formed from the combination of volatile organic compounds (VOCs) and nitrogen oxides ($NO_x$) | Vehicle emissions<br>Industrial sources<br>Consumer products | Respiratory illnesses<br>Reduced plant growth |
| Particulates | Dust, soot, and smoke formed from chemical reactions or burning fuels | Vehicle emissions<br>Electric power plants<br>Industrial facilities<br>Windblown roads | Respiratory illnesses<br>Impaired visibility<br>Property damage |
| Sulfur dioxide ($SO_2$) | Gas formed when fuel containing sulfur is burned, and that dissolves easily in water | Industrial facilities<br>Electric power plants | Respiratory illnesses<br>Acid rain<br>Impaired visibility |

Notably, emissions of each of these pollutants have dropped significantly since 1980:

**Percent Change in Emissions**

| | 1980 vs 2014 | 1990 vs 2014 | 2000 vs 2014 |
|---|---|---|---|
| Carbon Monoxide (CO) | -69 | -62 | -46 |
| Lead (Pb) | -99 | -80 | -50 |
| Nitrogen Oxides ($NO_x$) | -55 | -51 | -45 |
| Volatile Organic Compounds (VOC) | -53 | -38 | -16 |
| Direct $PM_{10}$ | -58 | -19 | -16 |
| Direct $PM_{2.5}$ | --- | -25 | -33 |
| Sulfur Dioxide ($SO_2$) | -81 | -79 | -70 |

Notes:

1. --- Trend data not available
2. Direct $PM_{10}$ emissions for 1980 are based on data since 1985
3. Negative numbers indicate reductions in emissions
4. Percent change in emissions based on thousand tons units

U.S. EPA, Air Quality Trends, at http://www.epa.gov/airtrends/aqtrends.html.

These national ambient air quality standards (NAAQS) are set for each criteria pollutant at a level that must "protect the public health" with an "adequate margin of safety." But what constitutes an adequate margin of safety and *whose* health is the public health? These questions were addressed in Lead Industries Association v. EPA, 647 F.2d 1130 (D.C. Cir. 1980). Here, in setting the NAAQS for lead, EPA chose a very vulnerable population—inner-city children. The court upheld this choice and allowed the agency to err on the side of caution in determining an adequate margin of safety. NAAQS levels must be based solely on health considerations and the agency may not consider economic or technical feasibility (though it is interesting to note that EPA refused to choose the *most* vulnerable population—those inner-city children who had high blood-lead levels from other sources, such as paint.).

There are actually two types of NAAQS. "Primary standards," described above, protect human health while secondary standards protect the public welfare, broadly defined to include effects on animals, wildlife, water and visibility. EPA is required to review these NAAQS and make appropriate revisions at least every five years. In practice, however, EPA has been very reticent to do so because of the tremendous political and economic costs involved. Notably, there have been only seven NAAQS established. As a result, environmental groups have had to sue EPA on a number of occasions to initiate reviews and, even when the reviews have been initiated, EPA has often chosen to retain the current standards.

The uniform application of NAAQS and EPA's inability to consider their costs and benefits have been criticized by some as inefficient. The health impacts of dirty air clearly vary from place to place, as do the costs of control. Just think of setting the NAAQS for lead emissions based on the target population of inner-city children. By setting a uniform national standard to protect the most vulnerable population (and assuming the standard is accurately set), this will necessarily lead to "overprotection" of people in much of the country. Indeed, it does seem odd to mandate the same level of pollutants in an inner city as in a sparsely inhabited valley (unless, perhaps, that valley happens to be the Grand Canyon). Given this seeming inefficiency, why would Congress choose a uniform approach over air quality standards that vary from region to region?

The NAAQS approach provides a classic example of inflexible but easily-administered standards. Such "one-size-fits-all" standards make it easier for an agency to establish, monitor and enforce than the more flexible and tailored local standards that vary from place to place. Local standards are also, one would expect, more susceptible to local political pressure than national standards and some areas would certainly resent having lower air quality standards than others.

From a health perspective, given our uncertainties in epidemiology and growing understanding of the health effects of air pollutants, a standard that seemed overprotective a decade ago may not seem so today. Moreover, despite the prohibition of cost consideration, given the nature of the political process perhaps it is unrealistic to assume that the costs of compliance and its effect on jobs and local economies would not enter into the NAAQS standard setting, even if only indirectly and unofficially.

Another major reason for the NAAQS approach is that it stifles potential interstate competition for industry. A driving force behind the CAA was the historic failure of state programs to control air quality and the consequent fear that, absent national standards, states might be willing to sacrifice air quality for economic growth. In other words, because there existed no national clean air requirements prior to the CAA, each state was free to set standards as it wished. This made it potentially easy for states to become "pollution havens," offering lax environmental standards in exchange for an influx of new industries and jobs. This could encourage an environmental "race-to-the-bottom," much as Delaware has led the race to create a corporate-friendly state, sacrificing air quality for economic growth or, worse for industry, the potential of a "race-to-the-top." There has been a vigorous debate over whether environmental races to the bottom actually occur, but national standards in the context of air emissions made the point moot.

## A. ESTABLISHING NAAQS

The following excerpt from an early NAAQS case, *Natural Resources Defense Council v. Train*, provides a concise summary of the process under which NAAQS are set:

> The 1970 Clean Air Act Amendments provide two different approaches for controlling pollutants in the air. One approach, incorporated in §§ 108–110, provides for the publication of a list of pollutants adverse to public health or welfare, derived from "numerous or diverse" sources, the promulgation of national ambient air quality standards for listed pollutants, and subsequent implementation of these standards by the states. . . .
>
> The relevant section of § 108 reads as follows:
>
> (a)(1) For the purpose of establishing national primary and secondary ambient air quality standards, the Administrator shall within 30 days after December 31, 1970, publish, and shall from time to time thereafter revise, a list which includes each air pollutant—
>
> (A) which in his judgment has an adverse effect on public health or welfare;
>
> (B) the presence of which in the ambient air results from numerous or diverse mobile or stationary sources; and
>
> (C) for which air quality criteria had not been issued before December 31, 1970, but for which he plans to issue air quality criteria under this section.
>
> Once a pollutant has been listed under § 108(a)(1), §§ 109 and 110 of the Act are automatically invoked. These sections require that for any pollutant for which air quality criteria are issued under § 108(a)(1)(C) after the date of enactment of the Clean Air Amendments of 1970, the Administrator must simultaneously issue air quality standards. Within nine months of the promulgation of such standards, states are required to submit implementation plans to the Administrator. § 110(a)(1). The Administrator must approve or disapprove a state plan within four months. § 110(a)(2). If a state fails to submit an acceptable plan, the Administrator is required to prepare and publish such a plan himself. § 110(c). State implementation plans must provide for the attainment of primary ambient air quality standards no later than three years from the date of approval of a plan. § 110(a)(2)(A)(i). Extension of the three-year period for attaining the primary standard may be granted by the Administrator only in very limited circumstances, and in no case for more than two years. § 110(e).

Natural Resources Defense Council v. Train, 545 F.2d 320 (2d Cir. 1976).

Thus, once the EPA Administrator determines a pollutant should be added to the NAAQS list because it meets the criteria in CAA Section 108, the Administration must then promulgate standards for the pollutant and states must meet those standards in their SIPs.

## QUESTIONS AND DISCUSSION

**1.** Section 302(g) of the CAA defines "air pollutant" as "any air pollutant agent or combination of such agents, including any physical, chemical, radioactive (including source material, special nuclear material, and byproduct material) substance or matter which is emitted into or otherwise enters the ambient air." 42 U.S.C. § 760(g). So what is an air pollutant? And why have NAAQS been established for so few of them? The Senate Report cited by the Court twice lists "odors" as pollutants of concern. Should NAAQS be established for odors? How would EPA determine the acceptable standards for unwanted smells?

**2.** In 2007, the Supreme Court addressed the contested question of whether carbon dioxide ($CO_2$)—a key cause of global warming—constitutes a "pollutant" for purposes of the CAA. In 2002, EPA rejected a petition filed by a group of states, cities, and environmental organizations claiming that the CAA obligated the agency to regulate $CO_2$ emissions as a pollutant under Section 202(a) of the CAA (which governs the regulation of pollutants from new motor vehicles). In Massachusetts v. EPA, 549 U.S. 497 (2007), a 5–4 Court overturned EPA's decision. Justice Stevens explained:

> The Clean Air Act's sweeping definition of "air pollutant" includes "*any* air pollution agent or combination of such agents, including any physical, chemical . . . substance or matter which is emitted into or otherwise enters the ambient air. . . ." § 7602(g) (emphasis added). On its face, the definition embraces all airborne compounds of whatever stripe, and underscores that intent through the repeated use of the word "any." Carbon dioxide, methane, nitrous oxide, and hydrofluorocarbons are without a doubt "physical [and] chemical . . . substances which [are] emitted into . . . the ambient air." The statute is unambiguous.

*Id.* at 1460. The Court went on to hold that as a result of its finding that $CO_2$ and other GHGs were air pollutants under the CAA, the EPA was required to determine under Section 202(a) whether or not emissions of such GHGs from new motor vehicles cause or contribute to air pollution which may be reasonably be anticipated to endanger public health or welfare, or whether the science is too uncertain to make a reasoned decision. In dissent, Justice Scalia agreed that $CO_2$ was a covered substance within the CAA's definition, but he added that "[i]n order to be an 'air pollutant' under the Act's definition, the 'substance or matter [being] emitted into . . . the ambient air' must also meet the *first* half of the definition—namely, it must be an 'air pollution agent or combination of such agents.' The Court simply pretends this half of the definition does not exist." *Id.* at 1476 (Scalia, J., dissenting). Justice Scalia would have deferred to EPA's determination that GHGs are not "agents" of "air pollution."

EPA's initial response to the Court's decision was to do nothing, leading several states and environmental groups to notify EPA of their intent to sue the agency for failing to regulate GHG emissions from ships, aircrafts, and off-road vehicles. In April 2009, after a change in Presidential Administrations, however, the EPA Administrator proposed to find that six GHGs, including $CO_2$, from new motor vehicles, "cause or contribute" to air pollution that "may reasonably be anticipated to endanger public health or welfare." After public comment, in December 2009, EPA finalized its "endangerment finding" which consequently required EPA to regulate $CO_2$ and other GHG emissions at least under Section 202(a) of the CAA relating to new motor vehicles (as opposed to also regulating such emissions from stationary sources). *See* U.S. EPA, Endangerment and Cause or Contribute Findings for Greenhouse Gases under Section 202(a) of the Clean Air Act, at http://www.epa.gov/climatechange/endangerment/.

EPA found that the current and projected concentrations of the six key well-mixed GHGs—carbon dioxide ($CO_2$), methane (CH4), nitrous oxide (N2O), hydrofluorocarbons (HFCs), perfluorocarbons (PFCs), and sulfur hexafluoride (SF6)—in the atmosphere threaten the public health and welfare of current and future generations, and that the combined emissions of these GHGs from motor vehicles contribute to the GHG pollution which threatens public health and welfare. *Id.* Does this finding now require EPA to set NAAQS for $CO_2$ and other GHGs? Recall that CAA Section 108 requires EPA to establish NAAQS when the agency determines that emissions of an air pollutant "cause or contribute to air pollution which may reasonably be anticipated to endanger public health or welfare" and where "the presence of [such pollutant] in the ambient air results from numerous or diverse mobile or stationary sources." 42 U.S.C. § 7408(a)(1). EPA's regulations of GHGs subsequent to its endangerment finding is discussed later in this chapter and in Chapter 8. Scholars continue to debate whether the CAA is really the appropriate tool to use in regulating $CO_2$ and other GHG emissions as opposed to more tailored legislation on climate change.

**3.** The CAA contains a separate regulatory scheme for so-called "hazardous air pollutants" or HAPs. *See* 42 U.S.C. § 7412. These are pollutants that can be extremely harmful even when released into the air in very small doses. The 4,000 people who died when an American pesticide manufacturing in Bhopal, India released methyl isocyanate into the air in 1984 demonstrate the immediate and deadly effects of exposure to toxic materials in the air. The 189 HAPs include such substances as asbestos, benzene, hydrochloric acid, and vinyl chloride. But the history of the CAA's regulation of HAPs has not been nearly as successful as the six criteria pollutants. *See* John P. Dwyer, *The Pathology of Symbolic Legislation*, 17 ECOLOGY L.Q. 233, 258 (1990). EPA struggled to identify the relevant pollutants and how to control them until Congress took matters into its own hands in 1990, expressly listing the 189 HAPs and directing EPA to promulgate the maximum achievable control technology (MACT) for regulating them. *See* 42 U.S.C. § 7412(b)(1).

**4.** In 2012, EPA promulgated the Mercury and Air Toxics Standards (MATS) for power plants, also known as the "Utility MACT," which required coal-fired power plants to achieve a 91 percent reduction from uncontrolled emissions of mercury, nine other toxic metals, and three acid gases, all of which Congress listed as HAPs in the 1990 CAA Amendments. 77 Fed. Reg. 9304 (Feb. 16, 2012) (codified at 40 C.F.R. §§ 60, 63). According to EPA, over 50% of existing coal-fired units could meet the standard with existing pollution control equipment while the rest would be required to install new equipment at an annual cost of $9.6 billion. EPA estimated that the annual benefits of the rule would be between $37 billion and $90 billion and would avoid up to 11,000 premature deaths annually. Industry challenged the MATS rule and, although it was initially upheld by the D.C. Circuit, the U.S. Supreme Court reversed in a 5–4 decision. Michigan v. EPA, 135 S. Ct. 2699 (2015). The Court held that 42 U.S.C. § 7412(n), which directs EPA to determine whether regulation of electric utility steam generating units is "appropriate and necessary," required EPA to consider costs in its determination of whether to regulate such units in the first place, not only in its determination of what level of stringency to set the regulatory standard. On remand, the D.C. Circuit allowed the rule to remain in effect while EPA conducted the required cost-benefit analysis, which it completed in 2016. For more information on the rule and the costs and benefits associated with it, see JAMES E. MCCARTHY, CONGRESSIONAL RESEARCH SERVICE, CLEAN AIR ISSUES IN THE 114TH CONGRESS: AN OVERVIEW 8–9 (Jan. 21, 2016); U.S. EPA, Final Mercury and Air Toxics Standards for Power Plants, www.epa.gov/mats. For analysis of the case and the role of cost-benefit analysis, see Daniel A. Farber, *Taking Costs Into Account: Mapping the Boundaries of Judicial and Agency Discretion*, 40 HARV. ENVTL. L. REV. 87 (2016).

---

## B. REVISING NAAQS

Section 109(d) of the CAA requires EPA to review and revise as appropriate its air quality criteria and the related NAAQS at five-year intervals. The basic idea behind such a review process is to slowly ratchet down the emission levels allowed under the NAAQS as scientific control methods improve over time. The review process has seen mixed results. Multiple lawsuits have been brought in attempts to force EPA to complete reviews for certain pollutants, such as Environmental Defense Fund v. Thomas, 870 F.2d 892 (2d Cir. 1989), in which several environmental groups along with six states brought suit against EPA based on EPA's failure to revise the NAAQS for $SO_2$. EPA has also been hesitant to revise NAAQS because of the significant administrative burden, the numerous lawsuits that follow each revision, the political backlash from both sides, as well as the fact that each time EPA revises a NAAQS, each state must amend its SIP which is then subject to lengthy EPA review.

The case below illustrates the nature of the disputes that arise over NAAQS. In the 1990s, EPA reviewed both the ozone and particulate matter (PM) NAAQS in existence at that time. In 1997, EPA reduced the ozone standard and, while keeping the PM standard in place, it added a new standard for fine particles of 2.5 microns or less. *See* 60 Fed. Reg. 38,652, 38,762 (July 18, 1997) (PM standards) (codified at 40 C.F.R. § 50.7); 60 Fed. Reg. 38856 (July 18, 1997) (codified at 40 C.F.R. §§ 50.9, 50.10) (ozone standards). These new standards were challenged by numerous parties and the case ultimately made its way to the Supreme Court which issued the following decision.

## Whitman v. American Trucking Associations, Inc.

Supreme Court of the United States, 2001.
531 U.S. 457.

■ JUSTICE SCALIA delivered the opinion of the Court.

. . . Section 109(a) of the CAA requires the Administrator of the EPA to promulgate NAAQS for each air pollutant for which air quality criteria have been issued under § 108, 42 U.S.C. § 7408. Once a NAAQS has been promulgated, the Administrator must review the standard (and the criteria on which it is based) "at five-year intervals" and make "such revisions . . . as may be appropriate." CAA § 109(d)(1), 42 U.S.C. § 7409(d)(1). These cases arose when, on July 18, 1997, the Administrator revised the NAAQS for particulate matter (PM) and ozone. *See* NAAQS for Particulate Matter, 62 Fed. Reg. 38652 (codified in 40 C.F.R. § 50.7 (1999)); NAAQS for Ozone, *id.* at 38856 (codified in 40 C.F.R. §§ 50.9, 50.10 (1999)). American Trucking Associations, Inc., and its co-respondents in No. 99–1257—which include, in addition to other private companies, the States of Michigan, Ohio, and West Virginia—challenged the new standards in the Court of Appeals for the District of Columbia Circuit, pursuant to 42 U.S.C. § 7607(b)(1). . . . The District of Columbia Circuit . . . unanimously rejected respondents' argument that the court should depart from the rule of Lead Industries Assn., Inc. v. EPA, 647 F.2d 1130, 1148 (D.C. Cir. 1980), that the EPA may not consider the cost of implementing a NAAQS in setting the initial standard.

II

In *Lead Industries Assn., Inc. v. EPA, supra*, at 1148, the District of Columbia Circuit held that "economic considerations [may] play no part in the promulgation of ambient air quality standards under Section 109" of the CAA. In the present cases, the court adhered to that holding, as it had done on many other occasions. Respondents argue that these decisions are incorrect. We disagree. . . .

Section 109(b)(1) instructs the EPA to set primary ambient air quality standards "the attainment and maintenance of which . . . are requisite to protect the public health" with "an adequate margin of safety." 42 U.S.C. § 7409(b)(1). Were it not for the hundreds of pages of briefing respondents have submitted on the issue, one would have thought it fairly clear that this text does not permit the EPA to consider costs in setting the standards. The language, as one scholar has noted, "is absolute." D. Currie, Air Pollution: Federal Law and Analysis 4–15 (1981). The EPA, "based on" the information about health effects contained in the technical "criteria" documents compiled under § 108(a)(2), 42 U.S.C. § 7408(a)(2), is to identify the maximum airborne concentration of a pollutant that the public health can tolerate, decrease the concentration to provide an "adequate" margin of safety, and set the standard at that level. Nowhere are the costs of achieving such a standard made part of that initial calculation.

Against this most natural of readings, respondents make a lengthy, spirited, but ultimately unsuccessful attack. They begin with the object of § 109(b)(1)'s focus, the "public health." When the term first appeared in federal clean air legislation—in the Act of July 14, 1955 (1955 Act), 69 Stat. 322, which expressed "recognition of the dangers to the public health" from air pollution—its ordinary meaning was "the health of the community." Webster's New International Dictionary 2005 (2d ed. 1950). Respondents argue, however, that § 109(b)(1), as added by the Clean Air Amendments of 1970 (1970 Act), 84 Stat. 1676, meant to use the term's secondary meaning: "the ways and means of conserving the health of the members of a community, as by preventive medicine, organized care of the sick, etc." *Ibid.* Words that can have more than one meaning are given content, however, by their surroundings, and in the context of § 109(b)(1) this second definition makes no sense. Congress could not have meant to instruct the Administrator to set NAAQS at a level "requisite to protect" "the art and science dealing with the protection and improvement of community health." Webster's Third New International Dictionary 1836 (1981). We therefore revert to the primary definition of the term: the health of the public.

Even so, respondents argue, many more factors than air pollution affect public health. In particular, the economic cost of implementing a very stringent standard might produce health losses sufficient to offset the health gains achieved in cleaning the air—for example, by closing down whole industries and thereby impoverishing the workers and consumers dependent upon those industries. That is unquestionably true, and Congress was unquestionably aware of it. Thus, Congress had commissioned in the Air Quality Act of 1967 (1967 Act) "a detailed estimate of the cost of carrying out the provisions of this Act; a comprehensive study of the cost of program implementation by affected units of government; and a comprehensive study of the economic impact of air quality standards on the Nation's industries, communities, and other contributing sources of pollution." § 2, 81 Stat. 505. The 1970 Congress, armed with the results of this study, *see* The Cost of Clean Air, S. Doc. No. 91–40 (1969) (publishing the results of the study), not only anticipated that compliance costs could injure the public health, but provided for that precise exigency. Section 110(f)(1) of the CAA permitted the Administrator to waive the compliance deadline for stationary sources if, *inter alia,* sufficient control measures were simply unavailable and "the continued operation of such sources is *essential . . . to the public health* or welfare." 84 Stat. 1683 (emphasis added). Other provisions explicitly permitted or required economic costs to be taken into account in implementing the air quality standards. Section 111(b)(1)(B), for example, commanded the Administrator to set "standards of performance" for certain new sources of emissions that as specified in § 111(a)(1) were to "reflect the degree of emission limitation achievable through the application of the best system of emission reduction which (taking into account the cost of achieving such reduction) the Administrator determines has been adequately demonstrated." Section 202(a)(2) prescribed that emissions standards for automobiles could take effect only "after such period as the Administrator finds necessary to permit the development and application of the requisite technology, giving appropriate consideration to the cost of compliance within such period." 84 Stat. 1690. *See also* § 202(b)(5)(C) (similar limitation for interim standards); § 211(c)(2) (similar limitation for fuel additives); § 231(b) (similar limitation for implementation of aircraft emission standards). Subsequent amendments to the CAA have added many more provisions directing, in explicit language, that the Administrator consider costs in performing various duties. *See, e.g.*, 42 U.S.C. § 7545(k)(1) (reformulate gasoline to "require the greatest reduction in emissions . . . taking into consideration the cost of achieving such emissions reductions"); § 7547(a)(3) (emission reduction for nonroad vehicles to be set "giving appropriate consideration to the cost" of the standards). We have therefore refused to find implicit in ambiguous sections of the CAA an authorization to consider costs that has elsewhere, and so often, been expressly granted. *See* Union Elec. Co. v. EPA, 427 U.S. 246, 257 (1976). *Cf.* General Motors Corp. v. United States, 496 U.S. 530, 538, 541 (1990) (refusing to infer in certain provisions of the CAA deadlines and enforcement limitations that had been expressly imposed elsewhere).

Accordingly, to prevail in their present challenge, respondents must show a textual commitment of authority to the EPA to consider costs in setting NAAQS under § 109(b)(1). And because § 109(b)(1) and the NAAQS for which it provides are the engine that drives nearly all of Title I of the CAA, 42 U.S.C. §§ 7401–7515, that textual commitment must be a clear one. Congress, we have held, does not alter the fundamental details of a regulatory scheme in vague terms or ancillary provisions—it does not, one might say, hide elephants in mouseholes. Respondents' textual arguments ultimately founder upon this principle.

Their first claim is that § 109(b)(1)'s terms "adequate margin" and "requisite" leave room to pad health effects with cost concerns. Just as we found it "highly unlikely that Congress would leave the determination of whether an industry will be entirely, or even substantially, rate-regulated to agency discretion—and even more unlikely that it would achieve that through such a subtle device as permission to 'modify' rate-filing requirements," so also we find it implausible that Congress would give to the EPA through these modest words the power to determine whether implementation costs should moderate national air quality standards.

The same defect inheres in respondents' next two arguments: that while the Administrator's judgment about what is requisite to protect the public health must be "based on [the] criteria" documents developed under § 108(a)(2), see § 109(b)(1), it need not be based *solely* on those criteria; and that those criteria themselves, while they must include "effects on public health or welfare which may be expected from the presence of such pollutant in the ambient air," are not necessarily *limited* to those effects. Even if we were to concede those premises, we still would not conclude that one of the unenumerated factors that the agency can consider in developing and applying the criteria is cost of implementation. That factor is *both* so indirectly related to public health *and* so full of potential for canceling the conclusions drawn from direct health effects that it would surely have been expressly mentioned in §§ 108 and 109 had Congress meant it to be considered. Yet while those provisions describe in detail how the health effects of pollutants in the ambient air are to be calculated and given effect, *see* § 108(a)(2), they say not a word about costs.

Respondents point, finally, to a number of provisions in the CAA that *do* require attainment cost data to be generated. Section 108(b)(1), for example, instructs the Administrator to "issue to the States," simultaneously with the criteria documents, "information on air pollution control techniques, which information shall include data relating to the cost of installation and operation." 42 U.S.C. § 7408(b)(*l*). And § 109(d)(2)(C)(iv) requires the Clean Air Scientific Advisory Committee to "advise the Administrator of any adverse public health, welfare, social, economic, or energy effects which may result from various strategies for attainment and maintenance" of NAAQS. 42 U.S.C. § 7409(d)(2)(C)(iv). Respondents argue that these provisions make no sense unless costs are to be considered in setting the NAAQS. That is not so. These provisions enable the Administrator to assist the States in carrying out their statutory role as primary *implementers* of the NAAQS. It is to the States that the Act assigns initial and primary responsibility for deciding what emissions reductions will be required from which sources. *See* 42 U.S.C. §§ 7407(a), 7410 (giving States the duty of developing implementation plans). It would be impossible to perform that task intelligently without considering which abatement technologies are most efficient, and most economically feasible—which is why we have said that "the most important forum for consideration of claims of economic and technological infeasibility is before the state agency formulating the implementation plan." Thus, federal clean air legislation has, from the very beginning, directed federal agencies to develop and transmit implementation data, including cost data, to the States. *See*

1955 Act, § 2(b), 69 Stat. 322; Clean Air Act of 1963, amending §§ 3(a), (b) of the CAA, 77 Stat. 394; 1967 Act, §§ 103(a)–(d), 104, 107(c), 81 Stat. 486–488. That Congress chose to carry forward this research program to assist States in choosing the means through which they would implement the standards is perfectly sensible, and has no bearing upon whether cost considerations are to be taken into account in formulating the standards. . . .

---

## QUESTIONS AND DISCUSSION

**1.** In *Lead Industries*, Chief Judge J. Skelly Wright concluded for the D.C. Circuit that the rule against "consider[ing] economic and technological feasibility in setting air quality standards . . . was the result of a deliberate decision by Congress to subordinate such concerns to the achievement of health goals." 647 F.2d at 1149. Why would Congress dictate that approach? Should the health effects of air pollution be eliminated "whatever the cost?" *Cf.* Tennessee Valley Authority v. Hill, 437 U.S. 153, 184 (1978) (interpreting the Endangered Species Act). Is there any role for balancing the costs and benefits of air pollution regulations? Why should costs be taken into account in the initial determination of whether to regulate HAPs from power plants (at least according to *Michigan v. EPA*, discussed earlier) but not be taken into account in setting NAAQS?

**2.** *Whitman* is perhaps most famous for its rejection of a constitutional nondelegation challenge. According to the nondelegation doctrine, Congress may not delegate legislative powers to administrative agencies, and an implicit delegation occurs if the powers exercised by such agencies are not sufficiently constrained. The D.C. Circuit held that the CAA § 109(b)(1) violated the nondelegation doctrine by granting power to EPA without providing an "intelligible principle" to guide the agency's exercise of authority. American Trucking Assn's, Inc. v. EPA, 175 F.3d 1027, 1034 (D.C. Cir. 1999). The Supreme Court disagreed. It explained that when Congress confers decisionmaking authority upon agencies, "*Congress* must lay down by legislative act an intelligible principle to which the person or body authorized to [act] is directed to conform." *Whitman*, 531 U.S. at 472 (citations omitted). Applying that test, the Court concluded that section 109(b)(1) "fits comfortably within the scope of discretion permitted by our precedent." *Id.* at 475–76.

**3.** The periodic revision of NAAQS has not been a smooth process. The *Whitman* case was a challenge to the 1997 NAAQS for particulate matter. A few years after *Whitman*, in 2006, EPA enacted a new, more restrictive NAAQS for particulates and two lawsuits were filed: one claimed that EPA should have lowered the standard even further, while another claimed that the standard should not have been lowered at all. These cases were consolidated and the Court of Appeals for the D.C. Circuit held in 2009 that the EPA had failed to adequately explain why its NAAQS for particulate matter would provide an adequate margin of safety against morbidity in children and other vulnerable subpopulations. *See* American Farm Bureau

Federation v. EPA, 559 F.3d 512 (D.C. Cir. 2009). In 2012, EPA proposed and adopted revisions to the particulate NAAQS, lowering the annual $PM_{2.5}$ NAAQS to 12 micrograms per cubic meter, from 15. The daily $PM_{2.5}$ NAAQS remained at 35 micrograms per cubic meter (which had been significantly lowered from 65 micrograms per cubic meter in 2006). EPA retained the existing NAAQS for $PM_{10}$. *See* 78 Fed. Reg. 3086 (Jan. 15, 2013); EPA, Regulatory Actions, Particulate Matter, https://www3.epa.gov/pm/actions.html.

---

The following case provides another illustration of the back and forth between the EPA, regulated parties, and the courts over the periodic revision of NAAQS, this time in the context of the $SO_2$ NAAQS.

## National Environmental Development Association's Clean Air Project v. EPA

United States Court of Appeals for the District of Columbia Circuit, 2012.
686 F.3d 803.

▪ SENTELLE, CHIEF JUDGE:

Several states and state regulatory agencies, together with corporations and industrial associations, petition for review of the Environmental Protection Agency's rule entitled "Primary National Ambient Air Quality Standard for Sulfur Dioxide," and of the subsequent denial of petitions for reconsideration of the standard. Petitioners contend . . . that the agency arbitrarily set the maximum sulfur dioxide ($SO_2$) concentration at a level lower than statutorily authorized. For the reasons discussed more fully below, we conclude that . . . EPA did not act arbitrarily in setting the level of $SO_2$ emissions and therefore deny that portion of the petitions for review.

The Clean Air Act (CAA) in §§ 108 and 109 requires EPA to establish, review, and revise air quality criteria and standards, allowing an "adequate margin of safety." 42 U.S.C. §§ 7408, 7409. The 1970 amendments to the Act required the Administrator to publish a list of air pollutants it intended to regulate under the Act, including all those pollutants the Administrator found reasonably could be anticipated to endanger public health. 42 U.S.C. § 7408(a)(1). For each listed pollutant, the Administrator had to issue air quality criteria that "accurately reflect[ed] the latest scientific knowledge useful in indicating the kind and extent of all identifiable effects on public health or welfare which may be expected from the presence of such pollutant in the ambient air, in varying quantities," including the effects of a pollutant when it combines with other factors such as atmospheric conditions or other pollutants. 42 U.S.C. § 7408(a)(2).

The CAA required the Administrator to promulgate a primary and secondary National Ambient Air Quality Standard (NAAQS) for each listed pollutant by 1971 and to review and revise those standards as appropriate every five years. 42 U.S.C. § 7409(a), (d)(1). The Act requires that the primary standards "be ambient air quality standards the attainment and maintenance of which in the judgment of the Administrator, based on such criteria and allowing an adequate margin of safety, are requisite to protect the public health." 42 U.S.C. § 7409(b)(1).

The Act vests each State with "the primary responsibility for assuring air quality within the entire geographic area comprising such State. . . ." 42 U.S.C. § 7407(a). After EPA promulgates a new final standard, the Act gives States a chance to recommend whether areas within their boundaries should be designated as "nonattainment," "attainment," or "unclassifiable," and the Agency makes the final designation. 42 U.S.C. § 7407(d). States then must submit State Implementation Plans (SIPs), which, after receiving EPA approval, impose federally enforceable controls on air pollution sources so States can attain and maintain the NAAQS. 42 U.S.C. §§ 7410, 7502, 7514–7514a.

Sulfur dioxide, a "highly reactive colorless gas," derives mostly from fossil fuel combustion. It smells like rotting eggs and, at elevated concentrations in the air, can cause acid rain. Its presence in the ambient air can cause adverse health effects, particularly in asthmatics. *See* Am. Lung Ass'n v. EPA, 134 F.3d 388, 389 (D.C. Cir. 1998).

On April 30, 1971, EPA promulgated the first primary NAAQS for SO2 concentrations in the ambient air. The standard set a 24-hour concentration limit of 140 parts per billion (ppb) $SO_2$, and an annual average limit of 30 ppb. Over the next three decades, EPA reviewed the standard, but did not revise it.

In 1988, EPA declined to revise the NAAQS, but requested comment on a proposal to add a new 1-hour primary standard of 400 ppb to protect against five- to ten-minute bursts of $SO_2$ concentrations. In response to those comments and other developments, in 1994, EPA offered several more options for comment, including the addition of a five-minute standard of 600 ppb. After concluding its review of these proposals and comments in 1996, EPA announced it would not revise the NAAQS. In its review, it found that under the current standards at that time, thousands of asthmatics could be exposed to enough short-term bursts of $SO_2$ that their lung function could be impaired. EPA concluded, however, that such effects "do not pose a broad public health problem when viewed from a national perspective" and did not warrant revisions to the $SO_2$ NAAQS.

The American Lung Association and the Environmental Defense Fund challenged before this Court the Administrator's decision not to implement a five-minute standard. We found that EPA had failed to explain adequately how it reached its decision not to revise the NAAQS, given that the Administrator had found that short-term exposures to bursts of $SO_2$ could significantly affect the lung function of thousands of asthmatics. Am. Lung Ass'n, 134 F.3d at 392–93 (D.C. Cir. 1998). Accordingly, we remanded the decision to EPA.

In response, EPA initiated the review of the $SO_2$ NAAQS that eventually led to this proceeding. Based on that review, EPA proposed a rule to revise the primary $SO_2$ standard. EPA proposed, inter alia, to revoke the current 24-hour and annual standards and to establish a standard to target short-term bursts of $SO_2$ exposure—specifically, a 99th percentile 1-hour daily maximum standard level set somewhere between 100 ppb and 50 ppb. EPA also proposed to amend ambient air monitoring, reporting, and network design requirements. The proposal focused on increasing and updating the monitoring network to support the proposed 1-hour standard.

After receiving comments on its rule proposal, EPA issued a final rule addressing the primary $SO_2$ standard. Petitioners challenge two parts of the final rulemaking, which we describe here—the level at which EPA set the standard and a portion of its statements regarding the implementation plan for the standard.

EPA mandated that States must meet a new 1-hour $SO_2$ standard using a 99th percentile form, set at 75 ppb maximum SO2 concentration. The goal of the new standard is to prevent asthmatics from being exposed to short-term, five- to ten-minute bursts of $SO_2$, which EPA found could cause lung function decrements in asthmatics.

EPA explained that it conducted substantial amounts of new research to determine the appropriate level for the 1-hour $SO_2$ NAAQS. In 2008, EPA staff prepared an Integrated Science Assessment (ISA), which summarized the latest scientific knowledge regarding effects of exposure to $SO_2$. In 2009, EPA staff prepared a Risk and Exposure Assessment (REA) to quantify the public health effects of exposure to $SO_2$ in the ambient air. The ISA and REA focused on two types of studies—controlled human exposure clinical studies and epidemiologic studies. The controlled human exposure studies examined the effects of varying levels of $SO_2$ on unmedicated asthmatics performing exercises. The studies did not test subjects with severe asthma because of ethical concerns. The epidemiologic studies considered whether a statistical association exists between levels of $SO_2$ in the ambient air and the occurrence of events such as hospital admissions and emergency room visits for respiratory ailments. The ISA and REA also reviewed animal studies.

The epidemiologic studies showed that in geographic areas meeting the previous 24-hour and annual concentration limits, there were positive associations between ambient air concentrations of $SO_2$ and respiratory symptoms in children, emergency department visits, and hospitalizations for respiratory conditions.

Clinical studies showed that mild and moderate asthmatics exposed to $SO_2$ concentrations as low as 200 to 300 ppb for five to ten minutes experienced moderate or greater decrements in lung function. As $SO_2$ exposure increased, both the severity of the decrements and the number of asthmatics affected increased. At 400 ppb and greater, the effects often were statistically significant at the group mean level and were accompanied by respiratory symptoms. In the REA, EPA deter-mined that a 1-hour NAAQS set at 50 to 100 ppb could limit exposures of exercising asthmatic children to five-minute peak $SO_2$ levels greater than or equal to 400 ppb. A 1-hour 150 ppb standard could limit their exposure to five-minute 400 ppb concentrations, but would provide "appreciably less" protection to five-minute exposures of 200 ppb concentrations.

The EPA Administrator determined that the studies showed that the NAAQS should protect asthmatics from 200 ppb short-term bursts of $SO_2$. She concluded that a 1-hour standard level set at 75 ppb would accomplish this goal and provide an adequate margin of safety. . . .

Several states and environmental regulatory bodies of states charged with implementing the $SO_2$ standards, along with several companies and coalitions that represent industries that emit $SO_2$ as a byproduct of their industrial activities, petition for review of the EPA's rulemaking.

Under the Clean Air Act, the EPA Administrator must set NAAQS at a level "requisite to protect the public health," "allowing an adequate margin of safety." 42 U.S.C. § 7409(b)(1). This Court has recognized that Congress defined public health broadly, requiring NAAQS to "protect not only average healthy individuals, but also 'sensitive citizens,'" such as children or people afflicted with asthma, emphysema, or other conditions causing sensitivity to air pollution. The Supreme Court has held that NAAQS are set at the "requisite" level if they are set at a level "not lower or higher than is necessary" to protect public health. Whitman v. Am. Trucking Ass'ns, 531 U.S. 457, 475–76 (2001).

Petitioners first argue that the Administrator's decision to adopt a 75 ppb standard was arbitrary and capricious because EPA misinterpreted the controlled human exposure clinical studies. Specifically, they criticize how EPA applied guidelines published by the American Thoracic Society (ATS) regarding what constitutes an adverse effect of air pollution.

The ATS guidelines recommend that reversible loss of lung function in individuals in combination with respiratory symptoms should be considered adverse. The guidelines also recommend that an increased risk to a population caused by a pollutant, even if the risk to a single individual is not increased, should be considered an adverse effect because individuals within that group would have diminished reserve function and would be at an increased risk if affected by another agent.

Petitioners argue that EPA concedes that the clinical studies only have shown that five-minute exposures to $SO_2$ produce adverse effects at 400 ppb and above. Thus, Petitioners reason, EPA has not shown that five-minute exposures to $SO_2$ levels below 400 ppb cause adverse effects in individuals. Regarding the population-level standard, petitioners claim first that EPA failed to find a causal relationship between five-minute exposures to $SO_2$ at levels below 400 ppb and the decrements in lung function and, second, that EPA extrapolated individual data from the clinical studies to represent the effect of $SO_2$ on a population level.

EPA, however, was not bound to set the $SO_2$ standard according to the ATS guidelines. The guidelines merely provided one reference point to help EPA and the public understand what should be considered an adverse effect of $SO_2$ on human health.

On the other hand, the EPA Administrator is bound by statute to promulgate NAAQS that are "requisite to protect the public health" "allowing an adequate margin of safety." 42 U.S.C. § 7409(b)(1). It could not then exceed EPA's authority to choose a level below that which produced adverse effects in the clinical studies in order to set a standard that allows an adequate margin of safety. Further, the clinical studies did not test severe asthmatics or very young children. EPA concluded that it was reasonable to assume that those vulnerable populations would suffer more serious health effects than mild and moderate asthmatics. We cannot say it was unreasonable for EPA to consider these vulnerable populations in setting the standard.

Further, in issuing the final rule, EPA considered more than the ATS adversity standards. EPA explains it considered the advice and recommendations it received from Clean Air Scientific Advisory Committee, an independent scientific review committee, and the conclusions drawn from previous NAAQS reviews. EPA also considered epidemiologic studies, which we discuss in greater detail below, to inform its view of the population-level risk. . . .

Based on its review of all of those studies, EPA found a "causal relationship between respiratory morbidity and short-term (5-minutes to 24-hours) exposure to $SO_2$." A "causal relationship" finding is the strongest finding the ISA can make. *Id.* EPA concluded that the collected evidence showed that five- to ten-minute exposures to $SO_2$ concentrations at least as low as 200 ppb can result in adverse health effects in five to thirty percent of the exercising asthmatics tested in the controlled human exposure studies, and that a 75 ppb 1-hour limit would "substantially limit asthmatics' exposure" to such concentrations, allowing a reasonable margin for safety.

Based on the record discussed above, we cannot conclude that the choice EPA made to give especial weight to the three studies conducted in the United States that accounted for the effects of $SO_2$ concentrations using multi-pollutant regression models was arbitrary or capricious. . . .

Finally, Petitioners argue that the new $SO_2$ standard is arbitrary and capricious because EPA ignored its own finding that the new standard would create few new health benefits compared to current air quality standards and other CAA provisions that would prevent air quality from deteriorating to the level of the existing NAAQS. Petitioners explain that the CAA only gives EPA authority to revise NAAQS "as appropriate" and reason that it is inappropriate for EPA to revise the standards when current air quality does not warrant a revision to protect public health.

Nothing in the CAA requires EPA to give the current air quality such a controlling role in setting NAAQS. And as Petitioners themselves note, the CAA gives EPA significant discretion to decide whether to revise NAAQS. Further, in the final rule, EPA cites evidence that current levels of $SO_2$ in the ambient air, even when the air quality meets the current $SO_2$ NAAQS, still cause respiratory effects in some areas. In short, EPA had discretion to revise the NAAQS and Petitioners' argument is unavailing.

## QUESTIONS AND DISCUSSION

**1.** How important should current air quality influence setting a NAAQS? Did Congress give too much deference to EPA in setting NAAQS or, in the alternative, are the burdens on EPA too great? What are the pros and cons of greater or less deference when it comes to rulemaking? To legal challenges to that rulemaking?

**2.** A recent illustration of the controversy surrounding the revision of NAAQS is the effort by the Obama administration to revise the ozone NAAQS. In 2003, health and environmental plaintiffs sued the EPA because it had been more than five years since the agency had reviewed the current ozone standard. EPA negotiated a consent decree with the plaintiffs, which ultimately led to EPA adopting in 2008 an ozone primary (health-based) NAAQS and secondary (public welfare-based) NAAQS of 75 ppb over an 8-hour period (the prior standard was 80 ppb). Various parties immediately challenged the new ozone NAAQS in the D.C. Circuit Court of Appeals as both too lax and too stringent. Before briefing in the case, however, the incoming Obama administration agreed with the parties and the court to stay the case while it reviewed the 2008 standard.

In January 2010, EPA published a proposal to lower the ozone NAAQS to a level between 60 and 70 ppb. Over the next year, the administration was subject to constant pressure from industry groups and members of Congress to delay tightening the standard beyond the 2008 levels, citing costs to the economy as a result of the recession and the fact that a 60 ppb standard would put 85 percent of U.S. counties in nonattainment for ozone. Health and environmental groups, on the other hand, disputed the economic costs of the lowered standard and argued that the savings in direct and indirect health care-related costs would more than offset implementation costs, and, moreover, the CAA does not allow EPA to consider costs when setting NAAQS (*see Whitman v. American Trucking* above). Ultimately, in September 2011, President Obama announced he was requesting EPA Administrator Lisa Jackson to withdraw the proposed ozone standard and that the standard would be reviewed again in 2013.

At that point, the D.C. Circuit set a briefing schedule for the case challenging the 2008 ozone NAAQS. In July 2013, the court upheld EPA's decision to set the primary ozone NAAQS at 75 ppb but reversed and remanded EPA's decision to set the secondary NAAQS at the same level, citing inadequate evidence to support the standard and remanding to EPA for further explanation or reconsideration. In the interim, however, the court left the secondary ozone NAAQS in place rather than vacating the rule entirely. *See* Mississippi v. EPA, 723 F.3d 246 (D.C. Cir. 2013). In 2015, EPA completed its evaluation and set both the primary and secondary ozone standard at 70 ppb. *See* 80 Fed. Reg. 65,292 (Oct. 26, 2015); U.S. EPA, 2015 Revision to 2008 Ozone National Ambient Air Quality Standards (NAAQS) Supporting Documents, https://www.epa.gov/ozone-pollution/2015-revision-2008-ozone-national-ambient-air-quality-standards-naaqs-supporting.

---

# IV. STATE IMPLEMENTATION PLANS (SIPS)

## A. OVERVIEW

In practice, the inflexible and uniform approach of the NAAQS has been tempered in implementation. EPA sets ambient air quality standards nationwide, and each state then has the responsibility (and discretion) of setting emission standards that will result in attainment and maintenance of those standards. Each state is required to submit a State Implementation Plan (SIP) that demonstrates how the NAAQS will be achieved by the deadline dates established in the statute. In principle, the SIP should satisfy the NAAQS while taking into account local conditions, thus allowing a degree of flexible, site-specific standards. In fact, the opportunity for local adaptation is even greater because there are roughly 250 areas in which NAAQS are measured, known as air quality control regions. In simple terms, a state creating a SIP must first inventory the current emissions from sources, choose control strategies for reductions, and then demonstrate through computer modeling that the SIP will satisfy the NAAQS levels.

On its face, this is a broad grant of authority, giving the states a great deal of freedom to allocate emissions. In practice, however, the exceptions in the CAA serve to take back to the federal government much of what it had seemed to give away. The New Source Performance Standards, described later, establish federal standards for new sources and major modifications of existing sources. And even existing sources that do not increase emissions must employ federally-mandated "reasonably achievable control technologies" if located in areas that fail to meet the NAAQS.

What's left, then, for the states to plan? Primarily tightening the standards on existing sources. Importantly, EPA may only consider the overall question of whether the SIP will satisfy the NAAQS. Thus, *how* the SIP satisfies the NAAQS, whether by forcing certain companies to go bankrupt or greatly increasing the emissions for others, may not be considered so long as other parts of the CAA are not violated. With few exceptions, EPA can only look at the overall question of whether the NAAQS will be met, not every permit the state issues. Thus states have great discretion to achieve their NAAQS through regulating existing sources. And the differences from state to state can be striking. According to their SIPs, a coal plant in Ohio can emit 20 times more $SO_2$ than similarly sized plant in Connecticut.

If EPA believes the SIP will not achieve the NAAQS, EPA may start a process that effectively supplants the SIP and requires the state to comply with the EPA's Federal Implementation Plan (FIP). A FIP was developed for Los Angeles in the 1970s but was extremely controversial, as any proposed curbs on land use or driving naturally would be. Indeed, in 1977, in Section 110(a)(5)(A)(i), Congress took away EPA's authority to require states include in their SIPs programs for "indirect sources" of air pollution such as roads, highways, parking lots, and buildings, which may attract mobile sources (i.e., vehicles). Later, in 1990, Congress added Section 131, stating that nothing in the CAA constitutes an infringement of state or local land use control or transfers authority over such land use to the federal government.

## B. EPA REVIEW AND APPROVAL OF SIPs

Section 110(a)(1) of the CAA requires each state to prepare "a plan which provides for implementation, maintenance, and enforcement of each [NAAQS] in each air quality control region (or portion thereof) within such state." 42 U.S.C. § 7410(a)(1). These state implementation plans (SIPs) are at the heart of the CAA's effort to regulate air pollution. Section 110 identifies the necessary provisions of a SIP, including "enforceable emissions limitations and other control measures, means, or techniques (including economic incentives such as fees, marketable permits, and auctions of emissions rights), as well as schedules and timetables for compliance, as may be necessary and appropriate to meet the [NAAQS]." *Id.* § 7410(a)(2)(A). In other words, the CAA gives each state substantial discretion in deciding how best to achieve the NAAQS for each pollutant within the state.

A SIP becomes effective only after it has been approved by EPA. EPA may approve a SIP in whole or in part, or it may grant conditional approval to a SIP, or it may disapprove the SIP. As noted above, a state that fails to prepare an approved SIP may be subjected to a federal implementation plan (FIP) prepared by EPA, which of course no state wants to experience because the state would lose control over its desired mix of air pollution control strategies. Once a SIP is approved by EPA, it is subject to judicial review. But businesses or other parties whose activities are regulated by a SIP may not challenge the SIP itself once the 60-day statutory period for appealing a SIP has passed. *See* CAA § 307(b)(1), 42 U.S.C. § 7607(b)(1).

The following case illustrates the complexity of the SIP process, the relationship between EPA and the states in meeting NAAQS, and the difficulty of addressing the impact of emissions from upwind states on the NAAQS compliance status of other states.

## Environmental Protection Agency v. EME Homer City Generation

Supreme Court of the United States, 2014.
134 S. Ct. 1584.

■ JUSTICE GINSBURG delivered the opinion of the Court.

These cases concern the efforts of Congress and the Environmental Protection Agency to cope with a complex problem: air pollution emitted in one State, but causing harm in other States. Left unregulated, the emitting or upwind State reaps the benefits of the economic activity causing the pollution without bearing all the costs. Conversely, downwind States to which the pollution travels are unable to achieve clean air because of the influx of out-of-state pollution they lack authority to control. To tackle the problem, Congress included a Good Neighbor Provision in the Clean Air Act (Act or CAA). That provision, in its current phrasing, instructs States to prohibit in-state sources "from emitting any air pollutant in amounts which will . . . contribute significantly" to downwind States' "nonattainment . . . , or interfere with maintenance," of any EPA-promulgated national air quality standard. 42 U.S.C. § 7410(a)(2)(D)(i).

Interpreting the Good Neighbor Provision, EPA adopted the Cross-State Air Pollution Rule (commonly and hereinafter called the Transport Rule). The rule calls for consideration of costs, among other factors, when determining the emission reductions an upwind State must make to improve air quality in polluted downwind areas. The Court of Appeals for the D.C. Circuit vacated the rule in its entirety. It held, 2 to 1, that the Good Neighbor Provision requires EPA to consider only each upwind State's physically proportionate responsibility for each downwind State's air quality problem. That reading is demanded, according to the D.C. Circuit, so that no State will be required to decrease its emissions by more than its ratable share of downwind-state pollution.

. . . Satisfied that the Good Neighbor Provision does not command the Court of Appeals' cost-blind construction, and that EPA reasonably interpreted the provision, we reverse the D.C. Circuit's judgment.

Air pollution is transient, heedless of state boundaries. Pollutants generated by upwind sources are often transported by air currents, sometimes over hundreds of miles, to downwind States. As the pollution travels out of state, upwind States are relieved of the associated costs. Those costs are borne instead by the downwind States, whose ability to achieve and maintain satisfactory air quality is hampered by the steady stream of infiltrating pollution.

For several reasons, curtailing interstate air pollution poses a complex challenge for environmental regulators. First, identifying the upwind origin of downwind air pollution is no easy endeavor. Most upwind States propel pollutants to more than one downwind State, many downwind States receive pollution from multiple upwind States, and some States qualify as both upwind and downwind. The overlapping and interwoven linkages between upwind and downwind States with which EPA had to contend number in the thousands.

Further complicating the problem, pollutants do not emerge from the smokestacks of an upwind State and uniformly migrate downwind. Some pollutants stay within upwind States' borders, the wind carries others to downwind States, and some subset of that group drifts to States without air quality problems. "The wind bloweth where it listeth, and thou hearest the sound thereof, but canst not tell whence it cometh, and whither it goeth." The Holy Bible, John 3:8 (King James Version). In crafting a solution to the problem of interstate air pollution, regulators must account for the vagaries of the wind.

Finally, upwind pollutants that find their way downwind are not left unaltered by the journey. Rather, as the gases emitted by upwind polluters are carried downwind, they are transformed, through various chemical processes, into altogether different pollutants. The offending gases at issue in these cases—nitrogen oxide ($NO_X$) and sulfur dioxide ($SO_2$)—often develop into ozone and fine particulate matter ($PM_{2.5}$) by the time they reach the atmospheres of downwind States. Downwind air quality must therefore be measured for ozone and $PM_{2.5}$ concentrations. EPA's chore is to quantify the amount of upwind gases ($NO_X$ and $SO_2$) that must be reduced to enable downwind States to keep their levels of ozone and $PM_{2.5}$ in check.

Over the past 50 years, Congress has addressed interstate air pollution several times and with increasing rigor. . . . In 1970, Congress made this instruction more concrete, introducing features still key to the Act. For the first time, Congress directed EPA to establish national ambient air quality standards (NAAQS) for pollutants at levels that will protect public health. See 42 U.S.C. §§ 7408, 7409. Once EPA settles on a NAAQS, the Act requires the Agency to designate "nonattainment" areas, *i.e.,* locations where the concentration of a regulated pollutant exceeds the NAAQS. § 7407(d).

The Act then shifts the burden to States to propose plans adequate for compliance with the NAAQS. Each State must submit a State Implementation Plan, or SIP, to EPA within three years of any new or revised NAAQS. § 7410(a)(1). If EPA determines that a State has failed to submit an adequate SIP, either in whole or in part, the Act requires the Agency to promulgate a Federal Implementation Plan, or FIP, within two years of EPA's determination, "unless the State corrects the deficiency" before a FIP is issued. § 7410(c)(1).

The Act lists the matters a SIP must cover. Among SIP components, the 1970 version of the Act required SIPs to include "adequate provisions for intergovernmental cooperation" concerning interstate air pollution. § 110(a)(2)(E), 42 U.S.C. § 1857c–5(a)(2)(E). This statutory requirement, with its text altered over time, has come to be called the Good Neighbor Provision. . . .

Congress most recently amended the Good Neighbor Provision in 1990. The statute, in its current form, requires SIPs to "contain adequate provisions . . . prohibiting . . . any source or other type of emissions activity within the State from emitting any air pollutant in amounts which will . . . contribute significantly to nonattainment in, or interfere with maintenance by, any other State with respect to any . . . [NAAQS]." 42 U.S.C. § 7410(a)(2)(D)(i). The controversy before us centers on EPA's most recent attempt to construe this provision.

Under the Transport Rule, EPA employed a "two-step approach" to determine when upwind States "contribute[d] significantly to nonattainment," and therefore in "amounts" that had to be eliminated. At step one, called the "screening" analysis, the Agency excluded as *de minimis* any upwind State that contributed less than one percent of the three NAAQS to any downwind State "receptor," a location at which EPA measures air quality. If all of an upwind State's contributions fell below the one-percent threshold, that State would be considered not to have "contribute[d] significantly" to the nonattainment of any downwind State States in that category were screened out and exempted from regulation under the rule.

The remaining States were subjected to a second inquiry, which EPA called the "control" analysis. At this stage, the Agency sought to generate a cost-effective allocation of emission reductions among those upwind States "screened in" at step one.

The control analysis proceeded this way. EPA first calculated, for each upwind State, the quantity of emissions the State could eliminate at each of several cost thresholds. Cost for these purposes is measured as cost per ton of emissions prevented, for instance, by installing scrubbers on powerplant smokestacks. EPA estimated, for example, the amount each upwind State's NOx emissions would fall if all pollution sources within each State employed every control measure available at a cost of $500 per ton or less. The Agency then repeated that analysis at ascending cost thresholds.

Armed with this information, EPA conducted complex modeling to establish the combined effect the upwind reductions projected at each cost threshold would have on air quality in downwind States. The Agency then identified "significant cost threshold[s]," points in its model where a "noticeable change occurred in downwind air quality, such as . . . where large upwind emission reductions become available because a certain type of emissions control strategy becomes cost-effective." For example, reductions of NOx sufficient to resolve or significantly curb downwind air quality problems could be achieved, EPA determined, at a cost threshold of $500 per ton (applied uniformly to all regulated upwind States). "Moving beyond the $500 cost threshold," EPA concluded, "would result in only minimal additional . . . reductions [in emissions]."

Finally, EPA translated the cost thresholds it had selected into amounts of emissions upwind States would be required to eliminate. For each regulated upwind State, EPA created an annual emissions "budget." These budgets represented the quantity of pollution an upwind State would produce in a given year if its in-state sources implemented all pollution controls available at the chosen cost thresholds. If EPA's projected improvements to downwind air quality were to be realized, an upwind State's emissions could not exceed the level this budget allocated to it, subject to certain adjustments not relevant here.

Taken together, the screening and control inquiries defined EPA's understanding of which upwind emissions were within the Good Neighbor Provision's ambit. In short, under the Transport Rule, an upwind State "contribute[d] significantly" to downwind nonattainment to the extent its exported pollution both (1) produced one percent or more of a NAAQS in at least one downwind State (step one) and (2) could be eliminated cost-effectively, as determined by EPA (step two). Upwind States would be obliged to eliminate all and only emissions meeting both of these criteria. For each State regulated by the Transport Rule, EPA contemporaneously promulgated a FIP allocating that State's emission budget among its in-state sources. For each of these States, EPA had determined that the State had failed to submit a SIP adequate for compliance with the Good Neighbor Provision. These determinations regarding SIPs became final after 60 days, and many went unchallenged. EPA views the SIP determinations as having triggered its statutory obligation to promulgate a FIP within two years, see § 7410(c), a view contested by respondents.

A group of state and local governments (State respondents), joined by industry and labor groups (Industry respondents), petitioned for review of the Transport Rule in the U.S. Court of Appeals for the D.C. Circuit. Over the dissent of Judge Rogers, the Court of Appeals vacated the rule in its entirety.

EPA's actions, the appeals court held, exceeded the Agency's statutory authority in two respects. By promulgating FIPs before giving States a meaningful opportunity to adopt their own implementation plans, EPA had, in the court's view, upset the CAA's division of responsibility between the States and the Federal Government. . . .

The D.C. Circuit also held that the Agency's two-part interpretation of the Good Neighbor Provision ignored three "red lines . . . cabin[ing the] EPA's authority. First, the D.C. Circuit interpreted the Good Neighbor Provision to require upwind States to reduce emissions in "a manner proportional to their contributio[n]" to pollution in downwind States. The Transport Rule, however, treated all regulated upwind States alike, regardless of their relative contribution to the overall problem. It required all upwind States "screened in" at step one to reduce emissions in accord with the uniform cost thresholds set during the step two control analysis. Imposing these uniform cost thresholds, the Court of Appeals observed, could force some upwind States to reduce emissions by more than their "fair share."

We granted certiorari to decide whether the D.C. Circuit had accurately construed the limits the CAA places on EPA's authority. . . .

Once EPA has calculated emission budgets, the D.C. Circuit held, the Agency must give upwind States the opportunity to propose SIPs allocating those budgets among in-state sources before issuing a FIP. . . .

[W]e hold that the text of the statute supports EPA's position. As earlier noted, the CAA sets a series of precise deadlines to which the States and EPA must adhere. Once EPA issues any new or revised NAAQS, a State has three years to adopt a SIP adequate for compliance with the Act's requirements. See 42 U.S.C. § 7410(a)(1). Among those requirements is the Act's mandate that SIPs "shall" include provisions sufficient to satisfy the Good Neighbor Provision. § 7410(a)(2).

If EPA determines a SIP to be inadequate, the Agency's mandate to replace it with a FIP is no less absolute:

> "[EPA] shall promulgate a [FIP] at any time within 2 years after the [Agency]
>
> "(A) finds that a State has failed to make a required submission or finds that the plan or plan revision submitted by the State does not satisfy the minimum [relevant] criteria . . . , or
>
> "(B) disapproves a [SIP] in whole or in part,
>
> "unless the State corrects the deficiency, and [EPA] approves the plan or plan revision, before the [Agency] promulgates such [FIP]."

§ 7410(c)(1).

In other words, once EPA has found a SIP inadequate, the Agency has a statutory duty to issue a FIP "at any time" within two years (unless the State first "corrects the deficiency," which no one contends occurred here).

The D.C. Circuit also held that the Transport Rule's two-step interpretation of the Good Neighbor Provision conflicts with the Act . . .

We routinely accord dispositive effect to an agency's reasonable interpretation of ambiguous statutory language. *Chevron U.S.A. Inc. v. Natural Resources Defense Council, Inc.,* 467 U.S. 837 (1984), . . .

We conclude that the Good Neighbor Provision delegates authority to EPA at least as certainly as the CAA provisions involved in *Chevron.* The statute requires States to eliminate those "amounts" of pollution that "contribute significantly to *nonattainment*" in downwind States. 42

U.S.C. § 7410(a)(2)(D)(i) (emphasis added). Thus, EPA's task is to reduce upwind pollution, but only in "amounts" that push a downwind State's pollution concentrations above the relevant NAAQS. As noted earlier, however, the nonattainment of downwind States results from the collective and interwoven contributions of multiple upwind States. The statute therefore calls upon the Agency to address a thorny causation problem: How should EPA allocate among multiple contributing upwind States responsibility for a downwind State's excess pollution?

A simplified example illustrates the puzzle EPA faced. Suppose the Agency sets a NAAQS, with respect to a particular pollutant, at 100 parts per billion (ppb), and that the level of the pollutant in the atmosphere of downwind State A is 130 ppb. Suppose further that EPA has determined that each of three upwind States—X, Y, and Z—contributes the equivalent of 30 ppb of the relevant pollutant to State A's airspace. The Good Neighbor Provision, as just observed, prohibits only upwind emissions that contribute significantly to downwind *nonattainment*. EPA's authority under the provision is therefore limited to eliminating a *total* of 30 ppb, *i.e.,* the overage caused by the collective contribution of States X, Y, and Z.

How is EPA to divide responsibility among the three States? Should the Agency allocate reductions proportionally (10 ppb each), on a per capita basis, on the basis of the cost of abatement, or by some other metric? The Good Neighbor Provision does not answer that question for EPA. Under *Chevron,* we read Congress' silence as a delegation of authority to EPA to select from among reasonable options. See *United States v. Mead Corp.,* 533 U.S. 218, 229 (2001).

Yet the Court of Appeals believed that the Act speaks clearly, requiring EPA to allocate responsibility for reducing emissions in "a manner proportional to" each State's "contributio[n]" to the problem Nothing in the text of the Good Neighbor Provision propels EPA down this path. . . .

To illustrate, consider a variation on the example set out above. Imagine that States X and Y now contribute air pollution to State A in a ratio of one to five, *i.e.,* State Y contributes five times the amount of pollution to State A than does State X. If State A were the only downwind State to which the two upwind States contributed, the D.C. Circuit's proportionality requirement would be easy to meet: EPA could require State Y to reduce its emissions by five times the amount demanded of State X.

The realities of interstate air pollution, however, are not so simple. Most upwind States contribute pollution to multiple downwind States in varying amounts. Suppose then that States X and Y also contribute pollutants to a second downwind State (State B), this time in a ratio of seven to one. Though State Y contributed a relatively larger share of pollution to State A, with respect to State B, State X is the greater offender. Following the proportionality approach with respect to State B would demand that State X reduce its emissions by seven times as much as State Y. Recall, however, that State Y, as just hypothesized, had to effect five times as large a reduction with respect to State A. The Court of Appeals' proportionality edict with respect to *both* State A and State B appears to work neither mathematically nor in practical application. Proportionality as to one downwind State will not achieve proportionality as to others. Quite the opposite. And where, as is generally true, upwind States contribute pollution to more than two downwind receptors, proportionality becomes all the more elusive. . . .

Persuaded that the Good Neighbor Provision does not dictate the particular allocation of emissions among contributing States advanced by the D.C. Circuit, we must next decide whether the allocation method chosen by EPA is a "permissible construction of the statute." As EPA interprets the statute, upwind emissions rank as "amounts [that] . . . contribute significantly to nonattainment" if they (1) constitute one percent or more of a relevant NAAQS in a nonattaining downwind State and (2) can be eliminated under the cost threshold set by the Agency. In other words, to identify which emissions were to be eliminated, EPA considered both the magnitude of upwind States' contributions and the cost associated with eliminating them.

The Industry respondents argue that, however EPA ultimately divides responsibility among upwind States, the final calculation cannot rely on costs. The Good Neighbor Provision, respondents and the dissent emphasize, "requires each State to prohibit only those *'amounts'* of air pollution emitted within the State that 'contribute significantly' to another State's nonattainment." The cost of preventing emissions, they urge, is wholly unrelated to the actual "amoun[t]" of air pollution an upwind State contributes. Because the Transport Rule considers costs, respondents argue, "States that contribute identical 'amounts' . . . may be deemed [by EPA] to have [made] substantially *different*" contributions.

But, as just explained, the Agency cannot avoid the task of choosing which among equal "amounts" to eliminate. The Agency has chosen, sensibly in our view, to reduce the amount easier, *i.e.,* less costly, to eradicate, and nothing in the text of the Good Neighbor Provision precludes that choice. . . .

Using costs in the Transport Rule calculus, we agree with EPA, also makes good sense. Eliminating those amounts that can cost-effectively be reduced is an efficient and equitable solution to the allocation problem the Good Neighbor Provision requires the Agency to address. Efficient because EPA can achieve the levels of attainment, *i.e.,* of emission reductions, the proportional approach aims to achieve, but at a much lower overall cost. Equitable because, by imposing uniform cost thresholds on regulated States, EPA's rule subjects to stricter regulation those States that have done relatively less in the past to control their pollution. Upwind States that have not yet implemented pollution controls of the same stringency as their neighbors will be stopped from free riding on their neighbors' efforts to reduce pollution. They will have to bring down their emissions by installing devices of the kind in which neighboring States have already invested.

Suppose, for example, that the industries of upwind State A have expended considerable resources installing modern pollution-control devices on their plants. Factories in upwind State B, by contrast, continue to run old, dirty plants. Yet, perhaps because State A is more populous and therefore generates a larger sum of pollution overall, the two States' emissions have equal effects on downwind attainment. If State A and State B are required to eliminate emissions proportionally (*i.e.,* equally), sources in State A will be compelled to spend far more per ton of reductions because they have already utilized lower cost pollution controls. State A's sources will also have to achieve greater reductions than would have been required had they not made the cost-effective reductions in the first place. State A, in other words, will be tolled for having done more to reduce pollution in the past. EPA's cost-based allocation avoids these anomalies.

The D.C. Circuit stated two further objections to EPA's cost-based method of defining an upwind State's contribution. Once a State was screened in at step one of EPA's analysis, its emission budget was calculated solely with reference to the uniform cost thresholds the Agency selected at step two. The Transport Rule thus left open the possibility that a State might be compelled to reduce emissions beyond the point at which every affected downwind State is in attainment, a phenomenon the Court of Appeals termed "over-control. Second, EPA's focus on costs did not foreclose, as the D.C. Circuit accurately observed, the possibility that an upwind State would be required to reduce its emissions by so much that the State no longer contributed one percent or more of a relevant NAAQS to any downwind State. This would place the State below the mark EPA had set, during the screening phase, as the initial threshold of "significan[ce]."

We agree with the Court of Appeals to this extent: EPA cannot require a State to reduce its output of pollution by more than is necessary to achieve attainment in every downwind State or at odds with the one-percent threshold the Agency has set. If EPA requires an upwind State to reduce emissions by more than the amount necessary to achieve attainment in *every* downwind State to which it is linked, the Agency will have overstepped its authority, under the Good Neighbor Provision, to eliminate those "amounts [that] contribute . . . to nonattainment." Nor can EPA demand reductions that would drive an upwind State's contribution to every downwind State to which it is linked below one percent of the relevant NAAQS. Doing so would be counter to step one of the Agency's interpretation of the Good Neighbor Provision.

Neither possibility, however, justifies wholesale invalidation of the Transport Rule. First, instances of "over-control" in particular downwind locations, the D.C. Circuit acknowledged, may be incidental to reductions necessary to ensure attainment elsewhere. Because individual upwind States often "contribute significantly" to nonattainment in multiple downwind locations, the emissions reduction required to bring one linked downwind State into attainment may well be large enough to push other linked downwind States over the attainment line. As the Good Neighbor Provision seeks attainment in *every* downwind State, however, exceeding attainment in one State cannot rank as "over-control" unless unnecessary to achieving attainment in *any* downwind State. Only reductions unnecessary to downwind attainment *anywhere* fall outside the Agency's statutory authority.

Second, while EPA has a statutory duty to avoid over-control, the Agency also has a statutory obligation to avoid "under-control," *i.e.,* to maximize achievement of attainment downwind. For reasons earlier explained, a degree of imprecision is inevitable in tackling the problem of interstate air pollution. Slight changes in wind patterns or energy consumption, for example, may vary downwind air quality in ways EPA might not have anticipated. The Good Neighbor Provision requires EPA to seek downwind attainment of NAAQS notwithstanding the uncertainties. Hence, some amount of over-control, *i.e.,* emission budgets that turn out to be more demanding than necessary, would not be surprising. Required to balance the possibilities of under-control and over-control, EPA must have leeway in fulfilling its statutory mandate. . . .

If any upwind State concludes it has been forced to regulate emissions below the one-percent threshold or beyond the point necessary to bring all downwind States into attainment, that State may bring a particularized, as-applied challenge to the Transport Rule, along with any other as-applied challenges it may have. Satisfied that EPA's cost-based methodology, on its face, is not "arbitrary, capricious, or manifestly contrary to the statute," we uphold the Transport Rule. The possibility that the rule, in uncommon particular applications, might exceed EPA's statutory authority does not warrant judicial condemnation of the rule in its entirety.

In sum, we hold that the CAA does not command that States be given a second opportunity to file a SIP after EPA has quantified the State's interstate pollution obligations. We further conclude that the Good Neighbor Provision does not require EPA to disregard costs and consider exclusively each upwind State's physically proportionate responsibility for each downwind air quality problem. EPA's cost-effective allocation of emission reductions among upwind States, we hold, is a permissible, workable, and equitable interpretation of the Good Neighbor Provision. . . .

---

## QUESTIONS AND DISCUSSION

**1.** The Transport Rule (also known as the Cross State Air Pollution Rule or "CSAPR") covers fossil-fuel power plant units in 28 eastern states and the District Columbia. It was intended to build on the acid rain cap-and-trade program discussed later in this chapter. Some states fall under the caps for both annual emissions of $SO_2$ and NOx and ozone season NOx while others are controlled for only ozone season NOx and yet others are controlled for only annual $SO_2$ and NOx emissions. Both caps were tightened in 2015 with even more stringent caps to be in place in 2017. EPA's Regulatory Impact Analysis found that the rule's benefits exceeded its costs by 50–1, and resulted in a reduction of up to 34,000 premature deaths annually. *See* JAMES E. MCCARTHY, CONGRESSIONAL RESEARCH SERVICE, CLEAN AIR ISSUES IN THE 114TH CONGRESS: AN OVERVIEW 7–8 (Jan. 21, 2016); U.S. EPA, Cross-State Air Pollution Rule (CSAPR), https://www3.epa.gov/crossstaterule/basic.html. For an analysis of the *EME Homer City Generation* case, see Ann E. Carlson & Megan M. Herzog, *Text in Context: The Fate of Emergent Climate Regulation after* UARG *and* EME Homer, 39 HARV. ENVTL. L. REV. 23 (2015).

**2.** Each state has only one SIP, but that SIP and its subsequent revisions often contain different provisions for each air quality control region (AQCR) within the state. Generally, a state must first determine the existing level of air pollution and how that compares to the applicable NAAQS. Next a state will decide how to limit or reduce pollution as necessary to achieve the NAAQS. A state needs to consider the many sources of pollution (such as industrial facilities, motor vehicles, and power plants), the types of regulatory responses (such as strict emissions standards, permit requirements, economic incentives, and voluntary programs), and the appropriate means of enforcing the resulting rules. Modeling plays a critical role in this process, with sophisticated computer programs attempting to predict how certain actions will affect future air quality. Each state crafts its SIP differently, and each SIP evolves to reflect changes in scientific understanding, technological advances, and public policy preferences.

This is the place in the book where you could expect to read an actual SIP in order to illustrate what such plans contain and how they operate. Be thankful that we have not included a SIP here. A SIP is not a single document which we could readily excerpt for your reading pleasure. Rather, a SIP is a collection of state statutes, regulations, orders, planning documents, computer simulations, and specific plans addressing particular pollutants in particular locations within a state. You can find each state's SIP on the EPA website by visiting the appropriate EPA region and then looking for documents related to air pollution. For example, the Texas Commission on Environmental Quality's website provides a 25-page history of the state's SIP along with a 67-slide PowerPoint show describing the state's SIP current process. Or consider Georgia. Its SIP contains separate documents governing ozone in Atlanta and lead in Muscogee County, along with over sixty different emissions standards for such sources as incinerators, sulfuric acid plants, consumer and commercial products, and dry cleaners. The technical detail is illustrated by the emission standard for particulate emissions from cotton gins, which governs permissible emissions according to the equation $E = 7B^{0.5}$, where E is the allowable emission rate in pounds per hour, and B is the number of 500 pound finished bales of cotton per hour. Applying that formula, the Georgia SIP states that 26.19 pounds of particulates per hour may be emitted from a cotton gin that processes 14 bales per hour. *See* GA. RULES AND REGS pt. 391–3–1–.02(q) (2005). We could provide more examples—lots of them, in fact—but we think you get the idea.

**3.** Several experts question the efficacy of the SIP process. Professor Arnold Reitze noted that "approximately 133 million people in 2001 lived in counties that violated one or more NAAQS." Arnold W. Reitze, Jr., *Air Quality Protection Using State Implementation Plans: Thirty-Seven Years of Increasing Complexity*, 15 VILL. ENVTL. L.J. 209, 358 (2004). Reitze identified the following twelve "reasons for the failure of many SIPs to meet the NAAQS": (1) continuing population and consumption increases; (2) unwillingness to bear all of the costs of implementing the CAA; (3) larger vehicles that are driven more miles; (4) sprawling land development; (5) incorrect air quality models; (6) the persistence of older sources of pollution; (7) expensive and unpopular control measures; (8) increased gasoline volatility; (9) inadequate enforcement; (10) ozone transport from upwind states; (11) lack of accountability; (12) EPA's unwillingness to sanction states; and (13) EPA's failure to pressure states to meet the ozone NAAQS. *Id.* at 359–65. Reitze concludes that "[t]he SIP program may have largely outlived its usefulness," and that "SIPs will continue to become both more complex and irrelevant." *Id.* at 365. He expects that "federally mandated measures will be the major cause of the additional emissions reductions that are needed if progress is to be made." *Id.* at 366. Might this be one of the reasons why EPA took the approach it did with the Transport Rule?

## C. NONATTAINMENT OF NAAQS AND THE SIP PROCESS

Generally, an air quality region must attain the NAAQS "as expeditiously as practicable, but no later than 5 years from the date the area was designated as nonattainment." 42 U.S.C. § 7502(a)(2)(A). EPA may extend that period for up to ten years and a state can request two additional one-year extensions 42 U.S.C. § 7502(a)(2)(C). The 1990 amendments customized those deadlines for attaining the ozone NAAQS, giving marginal nonattainment areas three years and extreme nonattainment areas twenty years to achieve the ozone NAAQS. *See* 42 U.S.C. § 7511. The CAA also provides for graduated attainment dates for areas that have not attained the particulate NAAQS, again depending upon the severity of the area's pollution. *See* 42 U.S.C. § 7513. In Association of Irritated Residents v. EPA, 423 F.3d 989 (9th Cir. 2005), a group of local residents challenged the EPA's approval of an extended particulate attainment deadline for the San Joaquin Valley, but the court held that the existence of specific particulate attainment deadlines did not deny EPA its general power to extend nonattainment deadlines.

Congress neglected to say in the original 1970 version of the CAA what should happen if an area failed to attain the NAAQS established for a pollutant. EPA's initial response once it realized that the SIPs would not necessarily achieve the NAAQS was to develop an offset policy, whereby new sources emitting additional pollutants were required to reduce similar pollutants from existing sources. Congress began to address the nonattainment problem in the 1977 CAA amendments, and then it added a number of new nonattainment provisions in the 1990 amendments. Under the 1990 amendments, states must require "reasonably available control technology" (RACT) on existing stationary sources in nonattainment areas whereas new "major" stationary sources in nonattainment areas must install emissions control technology that meets a "lowest achievable emissions reduction" (LAER) standard for that source. The definition of major source varies by region and the threshold is lower or higher based on the severity of the air quality problem in the area. *See* 42 U.S.C. § 7501–7515 (nonattainment program). These standards are more stringent than those imposed on new and existing stationary sources in attainment areas.

In order to provide cost effective methods for emitters to reduce their overall emission levels EPA allows for the use of two similar strategies, the first being an "offset" approach and the second being a "bubble" approach. Under the offset approach, a limit is set for the total emissions allowed by a particular source. This limit will usually be less than the source is currently emitting, and in order to comply with the limit one of the available reduction strategies is to purchase the right to emit further emissions. Such purchases can be made either from another source who is able to cost-effectively reduce its emissions below the established level, or from certified projects which reduce overall emissions of specific pollutants. The latter of these two approaches is what is generally referred to as an offset. Thus, by paying someone else to reduce its emissions, the source providing the money obtains the rights to those emissions, and is able to continue emitting above their established level.

Under the bubble approach EPA allows emission sources to treat multiple emission sources all located within one facility as within a single "bubble." Emitters are allowed to increase emissions from one source within the bubble, so long as they ensure there are equivalent reductions from another source within the same bubble. This allows emitters to seek out cost-effective reduction strategies within their existing facilities, rather than implement more costly reductions in order to meet regulatory standards. EPA's decision to allow regulated facilities to treat multiple emission sources under one "bubble" was the subject of the Supreme Court's landmark decision in Chevron U.S.A. v. NRDC, 467 U.S. 837 (1984), which set forth what is now known as the "*Chevron* doctrine" for judicial review of an agency's construction of a statute under which it has delegated authority. The bubble approach to emissions is similar to a cap-and-trade system, which sets an overall emission level for a given pollutant, grants emission permits which equal out to that set level, and allows emitters of that pollutant to trade permits among themselves so as to effectively allocate costs.

The 1990 CAA amendments also created a new approach to the nonattainment of ozone, carbon monoxide, and particulates. The ozone nonattainment provisions are particularly instructive. There are five types of nonattainment—marginal, moderate, serious, severe, and extreme—with additional SIP requirements imposed as the nonattainment gets worse. The possible requirements include an inventory of emissions sources, increased emissions offsets, transportation and fuel restrictions, and the application of a "lowest achievable emissions reduction" (LAER) for new sources of pollution. The areas that have been redesignated from nonattainment to attainment for ozone since 1990 must implement a maintenance plan for ten years in order to ensure that the ozone NAAQS will remain satisfied.

The CAA specifies the procedures through which the EPA may redesignate an area from nonattainment to attainment. The process begins when the governor of a state submits a request for redesignation. 42 U.S.C. § 7407(d)(3)(D), giving the EPA administrator 18 months to approve or deny the request for redesignation. The EPA Administrator may not redesignate an area from nonattainment to attainment unless all of the following factors are met: (1) the Administrator determines that the area has attained the NAAQS; (2) the Administrator has fully approved the applicable implementation plan for the area; (3) the Administrator determines that the improvement in air quality is due to permanent and enforceable reductions in emissions resulting from implementation of the applicable implementation plan and applicable Federal air pollutant control regulations and other permanent and enforceable reductions; (4) the Administrator has fully approved a maintenance plan for the area; and (5) the State containing such area has met all requirements applicable to the area under section 7410(k) (establishing requirements for state submissions and EPA review process). *See* 42 U.S.C. § 7407(d)(3)(E).

The CAA authorizes a number of possible sanctions upon states that fail to achieve the NAAQS in a timely fashion. The loss of federal highway funds and the imposition of a 2:1 offset ratio for new sources of pollution are the most stringent sanctions available to EPA. *See* 42 U.S.C. § 7509(b). But EPA has been extremely reluctant to sanction any states, especially through a politically charged cutoff of federal highway funds. What else should be done to encourage states to attain the NAAQS?

In a 1997 case, Southwestern Pennsylvania Growth Alliance v. Browner, 121 F.3d 106 (3rd Cir. 1997), the Court of Appeals for the Third Circuit upheld EPA's decision to deny Pennsylvania's request that EPA redesignate the Pittsburgh-Beaver Valley nonattainment area to attainment status for ozone. The court found that even though the nonattainment status threatened serious economic harm for the area and the nonattainment may have been in part due to upwind sources outside the area, the data demonstrated that the area did not maintain the NAAQS for ozone (violating the first of the Section 407(d)(3)(E) factors) and the EPA Administrator was correct to refuse to redesignate the area. Pittsburgh is hardly the only city to fail to attain the NAAQS prescribed by the CAA. As of 2016, there were 216 counties (or parts of counties) in 24 states and the District of Columbia in nonattainment for ozone. *See* https://www3.epa.gov/airquality/greenbook/hnsum.html.

## V. REGULATING AND PERMITTING NEW AND MODIFIED SOURCES OF AIR POLLUTION

The NAAQS regulate the air we breathe. By contrast, the rest of the CAA regulates emissions from smokestacks and vehicles as an indirect means of influencing the quality of the ambient air. Presumably the tighter the standards of emissions, the better the quality of the air we breathe. The following sections discuss the primary means by which the CAA controls emissions from new or modified specific sources, namely (1) technology-based standards for specific industrial facilities or equipment, such as boilers, power plants, cement plants, oil refineries, etc. which are known as New Source Performance Standards (NSPS) and (2) permitting and performance standards for new "major" sources and "major modifications" to existing sources in both attainment and nonattainment areas, known as New Source Review (NSR). Both programs are discussed below.

### A. NEW SOURCE PERFORMANCE STANDARDS

As we have seen, the SIP process allows states to impose restrictions on emissions from stationary sources such as incinerators, power plants, and industrial sites. Section 111 of the CAA, however, shields many of these sources from state control by requiring EPA to set emission standards (or "standards of performance") of harmful pollutants for new or modified stationary sources. These New Source Performance Standards (NSPS) have now been determined for over 70 categories of facilities and apply to "major sources" or major modifications (i.e., changes that result in increased emissions of *xx* tons annually). These emission limits or "standards of performance" (the term used in Section 111) are technology-based, and are the "best system of emission reduction which (taking into account the cost of achieving such reduction and any nonair quality health and environmental impact and energy requirements) the Administrator determines has been adequately demonstrated." 72 U.S.C. 7411(a) (defining "standard of performance"). This "best system of emission reduction" (often referred to as "BSER") indirectly ensures costs will be taken into account, since presumably exorbitant control technologies wouldn't be commercially feasible. Section 111(b) applies to new sources and Section 111(d) applies to existing sources.

By its very name, the NSPS provision assumes that new and existing stationary sources should be treated differently. But why, given that both cause pollution? One might argue that it promotes technological development, creating a market by forcing new sources to employ the best available technologies commercially available. But this would apply equally well if older facilities were also covered. Part of the reason was clearly political: sources that would be new after passage of the Clean Air Act would not be able to organize and lobby against the Act's provisions, whereas existing sources were already organized and active. By limiting federal performance standards to new sources, the CAA carved out an important exemption for classes of facilities that were already operating at the time of the Act's passage. These "grandfathered" plants do not have to meet the NSPS requirements unless they undertake major modifications, as defined in the Act. For utilities, grandfathering has allowed older power plants to emit 4 to 10 times more $SO_2$ and $NO_x$ per megawatt-hour than new sources. In this way, the CAA shifted the bulk of pollution control costs from existing businesses onto market entrants.

To be fair, this grandfather exemption seemed only fair at the time, given the high costs of retrofitting existing plants. And it would not be of long term importance, it was assumed, since the grandfathered plants would shut down over time to make way for more modern, efficient, and cleaner facilities. At least that was the plan. Consider, though, whether grandfathering can create an incentive to keep older facilities operating as long as possible. What would you do if you owned a major facility that was grandfathered and wanted to increase its capacity? Might you try to use regular maintenance and repairs as an opportunity to gradually rebuild the plant, classifying these as minor improvements rather than major modifications? As shown in the *Environmental Defense v. Duke Energy Corporation* case discussed in the notes in the next section below, the EPA alleged that this is exactly what a number of utilities had done over the last 30 years, violating the spirit and intent of the CAA.

Even if one chooses to regulate new and existing plants differently, why reserve the regulation of major new sources to the federal government rather than to the states through the SIP process? This certainly would give the states more flexibility in achieving the NAAQS. In pure cost terms, national NSPS standards make sense because it is much more efficient for the EPA than for 50 separate states to obtain knowledge of the technical capability of industries to control pollutants. One might imagine, as well, that powerful local industries would have more influence at the state level to lobby for lax standards than at the national level (though this is debatable). Perhaps most important, setting national standards for new sources and major modified sources stifles potential interstate competition for industry. It would seem odd, indeed, to battle the dangers of a race-to-the-bottom by mandating a uniform, national strategy of NAAQS while, at the same time, allowing states eager for economic growth to entice major new facilities with the lure of lax emissions standards.

Ever since the Supreme Court's decision in *Massachusetts v. EPA*, there has been pressure on EPA from states and environmental groups to regulate GHG emissions through NSPS. This is because the electricity generator sector is the single largest source of U.S. GHG emissions, at over 30% of total U.S. GHG emissions. In 2015, EPA finalized the standards of performance to reduce carbon emissions from new fossil-fuel fired power plants under Section 111(b). Applying the BSER (defined above), the NSPS rule for new fossil-fuel plants sets one standard for new natural gas-fired power plants and another standard for coal-fired power plants. New natural gas-fired power plants can emit no more than 1,000 pounds (lbs) of $CO_2$/megawatt-hour (MWh) of electricity produced, which is achievable with the latest combined cycle technology. New coal-fired power plants can emit no more than 1,400 lbs $CO_2$/MWh, which, as a practical matter, requires the use of carbon capture and storage (CCS) technology. *See* 80 Fed. Reg. 64510 (Oct. 23, 2015) (codified at 40 C.F.R. § 60, subpart TTTT).

On the same day it issued the final NSPS for new fossil-fuel fired power plants under Section 111(b), EPA exercised its authority under Section 111(d) to impose standards for GHG emissions from existing fossil-fuel fired power plants. This rule is known as the Clean Power Plan (CPP) and is one of the most significant EPA initiatives in decades, as it has the potential to completely transform the electric utility industry. The limits, which EPA established as the BSER, are 1,305 pounds of $CO_2$ per MWh of electricity generated by existing coal-fired power plants, and 771 pounds of $CO_2$ per MWh of electricity generated by natural gas-fired plants. 80 Fed. Reg. 64662, 64667 (Oct. 23, 2015).

EPA then set carbon limit "goals" for each state based on the BSER limits set out above, the number of fossil-fuel fired plants in each state, and the amount of electricity the plants generate annually. Each state must then write a compliance plan to accomplish its individual state goal by either requiring that each individual plant meet the CPP limit or, in the alternative, by using a menu of strategies to reduce overall emissions, including through emissions trading between sources within the state or with sources in other states. EPA also discussed three "building blocks" states may rely upon to meet their CPP goals, including (1) greater coal plant efficiency; (2) transition away from coal to natural gas; (3) transition from coal to renewable energy resources. States can also rely more heavily on nuclear power and energy efficiency to reduce emissions from existing sources of GHGs. The CPP does not apply in those states that are not connected to the U.S electric grid (Hawaii and Alaska, Guam, Puerto Rico) and those states that do not have any GHG-emitting power plants (Vermont and Washington, D.C.).

Not surprisingly, industry groups, the coal industry, and numerous states immediately challenged the CPP (even before EPA finalized the rule) and, in February 2016, the U.S. Supreme Court stayed the enforcement of the rule while the cases challenging the CPP in the D.C. Circuit were pending. Twenty-eight states have challenged the CPP while eighteen states and numerous cities have intervened on behalf of EPA. Some states are continuing to prepare their compliance plans despite the stay. The CPP and its implications for GHG reductions and global climate change are discussed in more detail in Chapter 8.

In another major initiative under the NSPS program, EPA has begun to regulate GHG emissions from the oil and gas industry, specifically from hydraulic fracturing operations which have resulted in major increases in U.S. oil and gas production since 2007 and thus an increase in emissions from VOCs and methane (a powerful GHG) from that industry sector. In 2016, EPA issued a final rule under Section 111(b) setting emission standards for methane and VOCs for new hydraulically fractured oil and gas wells. *See* U.S. EPA, Oil and Natural Gas Sector: Emission Standards for New and Modified Sources, 81 Fed. Reg. 35824 (June 3, 2016) (to be codified at 40 C.F.R. § 60); U.S. EPA, Oil and Natural Gas Air Pollution Standards, Regulatory Actions, https://www3.epa.gov/airquality/oilandgas/actions.html. Also in 2016, EPA issued a draft information request to the oil and gas industry to begin the process of regulating VOCs, methane, and other pollutants from existing oil and gas operations. *See* https://www3.epa.gov/airquality/oilandgas/methane.html. Not surprisingly, the oil and gas industry is strongly opposed to these rules, which will undoubtedly be subject to legal challenges.

## B. NEW SOURCE REVIEW

All new or modified sources within the more than 70 covered industrial source categories are subject to the federal, technology-based NSPS standards discussed above. In addition, however, construction of a new source of air pollution or modification of an existing source of air pollution may also trigger preconstruction review and permitting, known as New Source Review (NSR). The nature of the preconstruction review depends on whether the source is in an attainment area (in which case it is subject to the PSD permit program) or is in a nonattainment area (in which case it is subject to the nonattainment permit program). The NSR program is the means by which the CAA attempts to maintain air quality in PSD areas and improve air quality in nonattainment areas.

The NSR requirements apply only to "major" stationary sources and "major modifications" to existing sources. For the PSD permit program, a "major source" is one that has the potential to emit at least 250 tons per year (tpy) of a regulated pollutant or at least 100 tpy of a regulated pollutant if the source is within one of 28 listed source categories. The nonattainment permit program defines a "major" source as one with the potential to emit at least 10 to 100 tpy of the nonattainment pollutant, depending on the pollutant and the seriousness of the nonattainment problem in that area. Sources subject to the PSD permit program are required by the CAA to implement the Best Available Control Technology (BACT), which is set according to the most effective technology already in use in the market place. 42 U.S.C. § 7475(a)(4) (BACT provisions). Sources subject to the nonattainment permit program must achieve the Lowest Achievable Emission Rate (LAER) defined as "the most stringent emission limitation" contained in any SIP or that is "achieved in practice" by the same or a similar source category, whichever is more stringent. For a general overview of the NSR Program, which, remember, includes both the PSD program and the nonattainment review program, visit EPA's website at https://www.epa.gov/nsr/nonattainment-nsr-basic-information.

The PSD program itself is quite complex. In simple terms, it divides the country into three classes with varying degrees of restriction. Class I areas include areas subject to special protection such as national parks and wilderness areas, while Class II and III areas cover the rest of the country. The class category determines the amount of development allowed through so-called "growth increments." These increments place an upper limit on the increase in ambient concentration of pollutants in the area. The growth increment for particulates, for example, in Class I areas is 5 micrograms/cubic meter while in Class II areas it is 19 micrograms/cubic meter. In other words, Class II areas can accept almost four times more increased emissions than Class I areas. When a new source or major modification seeks a permit to pollute, the source must calculate by modeling whether the increased pollution will violate the growth increment. Both non-attainment and attainment areas are pollutant-specific. An area can be non-attainment area for ozone but attainment for particulates.

At first glance, the PSD program is puzzling. Presumably there are no health issues involved because the NAAQS are met. The public health is already protected with an adequate margin of safety. According to the CAA, the air is already "clean." One possible explanation is the importance of preserving clean air in undeveloped regions and national parks. Another possible explanation is political—it restrains the flight of industry from dirty to clean areas and ensures nonattainment regions remain competitive by making it costly to move into attainment areas.

The next case explores the problem of what happens when GHG emissions are included in the pollutants regulated under the CAA. Recall from earlier in this chapter that EPA's "endangerment finding" with regard to GHGs in 2009 triggered stationary source permitting for GHGs. Do the same minimum thresholds triggering PSD review apply? How much flexibility does the EPA have to "tailor" the PSD rules to address the unique challenges of regulating GHG emissions?

## Utility Air Regulatory Group v. Environmental Protection Agency, et al.

Supreme Court of the United States, 2014.
134 S. Ct. 2427.

Justice SCALIA announced the judgment of the Court and delivered the opinion of the Court with respect to Parts I and II.

Acting pursuant to the Clean Air Act, the Environmental Protection Agency recently set standards for emissions of "greenhouse gases" (substances it believes contribute to "global climate change") from new motor vehicles. We must decide whether it was permissible for EPA to determine that its motor-vehicle greenhouse-gas regulations automatically triggered permitting requirements under the Act for stationary sources that emit greenhouse gases.

The Clean Air Act regulates pollution-generating emissions from both stationary sources, such as factories and powerplants, and moving sources, such as cars, trucks, and aircraft. This litigation concerns permitting obligations imposed on stationary sources under Titles I and V of the Act. . . .

[Under the PSD program] [i]t is unlawful to construct or modify a "major emitting facility" in "any area to which [the PSD program] applies" without first obtaining a permit. §§ 7475(a)(1), 7479(2)(C). To qualify for a permit, the facility must not cause or contribute to the violation of any applicable air-quality standard, § 7475(a)(3), and it must comply with emissions limitations that reflect the "best available control technology" (or BACT) for "each pollutant subject to regulation under" the Act. § 7475(a)(4). The Act defines a "major emitting facility" as any stationary source with the potential to emit 250 tons per year of "any air pollutant" (or 100 tons per year for certain types of sources). § 7479(1). It defines "modification" as a physical or operational change that causes the facility to emit more of "any air pollutant." § 7411(a)(4).

In addition to the PSD permitting requirements for construction and modification, Title V of the Act makes it unlawful to *operate* any "major source," wherever located, without a comprehensive operating permit. § 7661a(a). Unlike the PSD program, Title V generally does not impose any substantive pollution-control requirements. Instead, it is designed to facilitate compliance and enforcement by consolidating into a single document all of a facility's obligations under the Act. The permit must include all "emissions limitations and standards" that apply to the source, as well as associated inspection, monitoring, and reporting requirements. § 7661c(a)–(c). Title V defines a "major source" by reference to the Act-wide definition of "major stationary source," which in turn means any stationary source with the potential to emit 100 tons per year of "any air pollutant." §§ 7661(2)(B), 7602(j).

[After EPA's endangerment finding for GHGs, it] issued its "final decision" regarding the prospect that motor-vehicle greenhouse-gas standards would trigger stationary-source permitting requirements. 75 Fed. Reg. 17004 (2010) (hereinafter Triggering Rule). EPA announced that beginning on the effective date of its greenhouse-gas standards for motor vehicles, stationary sources would be subject to the PSD program and Title V on the basis of their potential to emit greenhouse gases. As expected, EPA in short order promulgated greenhouse-gas emission standards for passenger cars, light-duty trucks, and medium-duty passenger vehicles to take effect on January 2, 2011. 75 Fed. Reg. 25324 (hereinafter Tailpipe Rule).

EPA then announced steps it was taking to "tailor" the PSD program and Title V to greenhouse gases. 75 Fed. Reg. 31514 (hereinafter Tailoring Rule). Those steps were necessary, it said, because the PSD program and Title V were designed to regulate "a relatively small number of large industrial sources," and requiring permits for all sources with greenhouse-gas emissions above the statutory thresholds would radically expand those programs, making them both unadministrable and "unrecognizable to the Congress that designed" them. EPA nonetheless rejected calls to exclude greenhouse gases entirely from those programs, asserting that the Act is not "ambiguous with respect to the need to cover [greenhouse-gas] sources under either the PSD or title V program." Instead, EPA adopted a "phase-in approach" that it said would "appl[y] PSD and title V at threshold levels that are as close to the statutory levels as possible, and do so as quickly as possible, at least to a certain point."

[EPA's phase-in approach would apply the PSD and Title V permit programs first to sources that emit GHGs in the range of 75,000 to 100,000 tons per year, with potential expansion to sources emitting lower amounts of GHG at later dates]

This litigation presents two distinct challenges to EPA's stance on greenhouse-gas permitting for stationary sources. First, we must decide whether EPA permissibly determined that a source may be subject to the PSD and Title V permitting requirements on the sole basis of the source's potential to emit greenhouse gases. Second, we must decide whether EPA permissibly determined that a source already subject to the PSD program because of its emission of conventional pollutants (an "anyway" source) may be required to limit its greenhouse-gas emissions by employing the "best available control technology" for greenhouse gases. The Solicitor General joins issue on both points but evidently regards the second as more important; he informs us that "anyway" sources account for roughly 83% of American stationary-source greenhouse-gas emissions, compared to just 3% for the additional, non-"anyway" sources EPA sought to regulate at Steps 2 and 3 of the Tailoring Rule.

We review EPA's interpretations of the Clean Air Act using the standard set forth in *Chevron U.S.A. Inc. v. Natural Resources Defense Council, Inc.*, 467 U.S. 837, 842–843 (1984).... The question for a reviewing court is whether in doing so the agency has acted reasonably and thus has "stayed within the bounds of its statutory authority."

We first decide whether EPA permissibly interpreted the statute to provide that a source may be required to obtain a PSD or Title V permit on the sole basis of its potential greenhouse-gas emissions.

EPA thought its conclusion that a source's greenhouse-gas emissions may necessitate a PSD or Title V permit followed from the Act's unambiguous language. The Court of Appeals agreed and held that the statute "compelled" EPA's interpretation. We disagree. The statute compelled EPA's greenhouse-gas-inclusive interpretation with respect to neither the PSD program nor Title V.

The Act-wide definition says that an air pollutant is "any air pollution agent or combination of such agents, including any physical, chemical, biological, [or] radioactive . . . substance or matter which is emitted into or otherwise enters the ambient air." § 7602(g). In *Massachusetts,* the Court held that the Act-wide definition includes greenhouse gases because it is all-encompassing; it "embraces all airborne compounds of whatever stripe." But where the term "air pollutant" appears in the Act's operative provisions, EPA has routinely given it a narrower, context-appropriate meaning.

That is certainly true of the provisions that require PSD and Title V permitting for major emitters of "any air pollutant." Since 1978, EPA's regulations have interpreted "air pollutant" in the PSD permitting trigger as limited to *regulated* air pollutants—a class much narrower than *Massachusetts*' "all airborne compounds of whatever stripe," 549 U.S., at 529. And since 1993 EPA has informally taken the same position with regard to the Title V permitting trigger, a position the Agency ultimately incorporated into some of the regulations at issue here. Those interpretations were appropriate: It is plain as day that the Act does not envision an elaborate, burdensome permitting process for major emitters of steam, oxygen, or other harmless airborne substances. It takes some cheek for EPA to insist that it cannot possibly give "air pollutant" a reasonable, context-appropriate meaning in the PSD and Title V contexts when it has been doing precisely that for decades.

Nor are those the only places in the Act where EPA has inferred from statutory context that a generic reference to air pollutants does not encompass every substance falling within the Act-wide definition. Other examples abound . . .

[Other examples provided by the Court omitted]

Although these limitations are nowhere to be found in the Act-wide definition, in each instance EPA has concluded—as it has in the PSD and Title V context—that the statute is not using "air pollutant" in *Massachusetts*' broad sense to mean any airborne substance whatsoever.

*Massachusetts* did not invalidate all these longstanding constructions. That case did not hold that EPA must always regulate greenhouse gases as an "air pollutant" everywhere that term appears in the statute, but only that EPA must "ground its reasons for action *or inaction* in the statute," 549 U.S., at 535 (emphasis added), rather than on "reasoning divorced from the statutory text," *id.,* at 532. . . .

In sum, there is no insuperable textual barrier to EPA's interpreting "any air pollutant" in the permitting triggers of PSD and Title V to encompass only pollutants emitted in quantities that enable them to be sensibly regulated at the statutory thresholds, and to exclude those atypical pollutants that, like greenhouse gases, are emitted in such vast quantities that their inclusion would radically transform those programs and render them unworkable as written.

Having determined that EPA was mistaken in thinking the Act *compelled* a greenhouse-gas-inclusive interpretation of the PSD and Title V triggers, we next consider the Agency's alternative position that its interpretation was justified as an exercise of its "discretion" to adopt "a reasonable construction of the statute." We conclude that EPA's interpretation is not permissible.

Even under *Chevron*'s deferential framework, agencies must operate "within the bounds of reasonable interpretation." And reasonable statutory interpretation must account for both "the specific context in which . . . language is used" and "the broader context of the statute as a whole." . . .

EPA itself has repeatedly acknowledged that applying the PSD and Title V permitting requirements to greenhouse gases would be inconsistent with—in fact, would overthrow—the Act's structure and design. In the Tailoring Rule, EPA described the calamitous consequences of interpreting the Act in that way. Under the PSD program, annual permit applications would jump from about 800 to nearly 82,000; annual administrative costs would swell from $12 million to over $1.5 billion; and decade-long delays in issuing permits would become common, causing construction projects to grind to a halt nationwide. The picture under Title V was equally bleak: The number of sources required to have permits would jump from fewer than 15,000 to about 6.1 million; annual administrative costs would balloon from $62 million to $21 billion; and collectively the newly covered sources would face permitting costs of $147 billion. Moreover, "the great majority of additional sources brought into the PSD and title V programs would be small sources that Congress did not expect would need to undergo permitting." EPA stated that these results would be so "contrary to congressional intent," and would so "severely undermine what Congress sought to accomplish," that they necessitated as much as a 1,000-fold increase in the permitting thresholds set forth in the statute.

Like EPA, we think it beyond reasonable debate that requiring permits for sources based solely on their emission of greenhouse gases at the 100- and 250-tons-per-year levels set forth in the statute would be "incompatible" with "the substance of Congress' regulatory scheme." . . .

We conclude that EPA's rewriting of the statutory thresholds was impermissible and therefore could not validate the Agency's interpretation of the triggering provisions. An agency has no power to "tailor" legislation to bureaucratic policy goals by rewriting unambiguous statutory terms.... It is hard to imagine a statutory term less ambiguous than the precise numerical thresholds at which the Act requires PSD and Title V permitting. When EPA replaced those numbers with others of its own choosing, it went well beyond the "bounds of its statutory authority." . . .

In the Tailoring Rule, EPA asserts newfound authority to regulate millions of small sources—including retail stores, offices, apartment buildings, shopping centers, schools, and churches—and to decide, on an ongoing basis and without regard for the thresholds prescribed by Congress, how many of those sources to regulate. We are not willing to stand on the dock and wave goodbye as EPA embarks on this multiyear voyage of discovery . . .

For the reasons we have given, EPA overstepped its statutory authority when it decided that a source could become subject to PSD or Title V permitting by reason of its greenhouse-gas emissions. But what about "anyway" sources, those that would need permits based on their emissions of more conventional pollutants (such as particulate matter)? We now consider whether EPA reasonably interpreted the Act to require those sources to comply with "best available control technology" emission standards for greenhouse gases.

. . . To obtain a PSD permit, a source must be "subject to the best available control technology" for "each pollutant subject to regulation under [the Act]" that it emits. § 7475(a)(4). The Act defines BACT as "an emission limitation based on the maximum degree of reduction of each pollutant subject to regulation" that is "achievable . . . through application of production processes and available methods, systems, and techniques, including fuel cleaning, clean fuels, or treatment or innovative fuel combustion techniques." § 7479(3). BACT is determined "on a case-by-case basis, taking into account energy, environmental, and economic impacts and other costs." *Ibid.*

Some petitioners urge us to hold that EPA may never require BACT for greenhouse gases—even when a source must undergo PSD review based on its emissions of conventional pollutants—because BACT is fundamentally unsuited to greenhouse-gas regulation. BACT, they say, has traditionally been about end-of-stack controls "such as catalytic converters or particle collectors"; but applying it to greenhouse gases will make it more about regulating energy use, which will enable regulators to control "every aspect of a facility's operation and design," right down to the "light bulbs in the factory cafeteria."

The question before us is whether EPA's decision to require BACT for greenhouse gases emitted by sources otherwise subject to PSD review is, as a general matter, a permissible interpretation of the statute under *Chevron*. We conclude that it is.

The text of the BACT provision is far less open-ended than the text of the PSD and Title V permitting triggers. It states that BACT is required "for each pollutant subject to regulation under this chapter" (*i.e.,* the entire Act), § 7475(a)(4), a phrase that—as the D.C. Circuit wrote 35 years ago—"would not seem readily susceptible [of] misinterpretation." *Alabama Power Co. v. Costle,* 636 F.2d 323, 404 (1979). Whereas the dubious breadth of "any air pollutant" in the permitting triggers suggests a role for agency judgment in identifying the subset of pollutants covered by the particular regulatory program at issue, the more specific phrasing of the BACT provision suggests that the necessary judgment has already been made by Congress. The wider statutory context likewise does not suggest that the BACT provision can bear a narrowing construction: There is no indication that the Act elsewhere uses, or that EPA has interpreted, "each pollutant subject to regulation under this chapter" to mean anything other than what it says.

Even if the text were not clear, applying BACT to greenhouse gases is not so disastrously unworkable, and need not result in such a dramatic expansion of agency authority, as to convince us that EPA's interpretation is unreasonable. We are not talking about extending EPA jurisdiction over millions of previously unregulated entities, but about moderately increasing the demands EPA (or a state permitting authority) can make of entities already subject to its regulation. And it is not yet clear that EPA's demands will be of a significantly different character from those traditionally associated with PSD review. In short, the record before us does not establish that the BACT provision as written is incapable of being sensibly applied to greenhouse gases.

To sum up: We hold that EPA exceeded its statutory authority when it interpreted the Clean Air Act to require PSD and Title V permitting for stationary sources based on their greenhouse-gas emissions. Specifically, the Agency may not treat greenhouse gases as a pollutant for purposes of defining a "major emitting facility" (or a "modification" thereof) in the PSD context or a "major source" in the Title V context. To the extent its regulations purport to do so, they are invalid. EPA may, however, continue to treat greenhouse gases as a "pollutant subject to regulation under this chapter" for purposes of requiring BACT for "anyway" sources. The judgment of the Court of Appeals is affirmed in part and reversed in part.

[partial dissent of Justice Breyer, joined by Justices Ginsburg, Sotomayor, and Kagan omitted]

---

## QUESTIONS AND DISCUSSION

**1.** To what extent does the Court's decision in *Utility Air Regulatory Group* limit EPA's authority to control GHGs from stationary sources? To what extent does it allow regulation? As a result of the decision, EPA issued guidance with regards to permits issued under the now-invalid Tailoring Rule and how it intended to treat "anyway sources" (described in the decision as those sources subject to PSD permitting for pollutants other than GHGs) and "non-anyway sources." *See* U.S. EPA, Clean Air Permitting for Greenhouse Gases, https://www.epa.gov/nsr/clean-air-act-permitting-greenhouse-gases. For further discussion on the Tailoring Rule and the Utility Air Regulatory Group case, see Jody Freeman & David B. Spence, *Old Statutes, New Problems*, 163 U. PA. L. REV. 1 (2014); Carlson & Herzog, *supra*.

**2.** In the 1990s and early 2000s, many of the major disputes between EPA and industry regarding NSR and PSD permitting were over what constituted a "major modification" of an existing source subject to NSR and what was "routine maintenance, repair, and replacement," which under EPA regulations did not trigger NSR. *See* 40 C.F.R. § 52.21(b)(2). This issue is significant because, for regulated parties, the NSR process can be very expensive and time-consuming and can limit the ability to make capital improvements. In 1999, EPA filed lawsuits against seven electric utilities and 51 power plants alleging the defendants had made non-routine physical changes that resulted in increased emissions without going through the NSR process. Near the end of the Clinton Administration, several defendants reached settlements with EPA and agreed to significant emission reductions at several facilities. Other defendants continued to litigate, and the Supreme Court ultimately addressed the question in Environmental Defense v. Duke Energy, 549 U.S. 561 (2007). In that case, the Supreme Court held that EPA could impose NSR so long as the modification triggered an increase in the annual emissions rate even if the modification did not trigger an increase in the hourly emissions rate. Notably, there was no dispute in *Duke Energy* that the modifications to the facility would leave the hourly emissions rate the same but would increase the annual emissions rate by allowing the plants to operate for longer hours, causing the total annual emissions to increase.

In 2002 and 2003 (after the EPA lawsuits were filed but prior to the *Duke Energy* decision in 2007), EPA enacted changes to the NSR rules to provide more flexibility for regulated parties. These rules resulted in fewer unit changes triggering NSR and expanded several regulatory exemptions. EPA also adopted a bright-line rule for when a project constituted routine maintenance, repair, and replacement for purposes of avoiding NSR. Under the new rule, a capital project was exempt if the project replaces existing equipment with identical equipment or equipment that serves the same purpose, the project costs do not exceed 20% of the current replacement value of the entire unit, and the project does not alter the basic design of the unit or cause it to exceed any applicable emissions limitations for that unit. In 2006, the D.C. Circuit vacated the rule, finding the exception was contrary to the plain language of the CAA. New York v. EPA, 443 F.3d 880 (D.C. Cir. 2006), *cert. denied*, 550 U.S. 928 (2007). As is evident from the NSR rules and the litigation with the utilities, there are significant incentives for regulated parties to continue to repair and modify old facilities rather than construct new ones. What are the rationales for providing laxer standards for repairs for older facilities than for new facilities? Are these rationales consistent with the goals of the CAA?

**3.** The purpose of the PSD program is to keep clean air unpolluted. But why? Suppose that we decided that additional pollution was acceptable, presumably because it will not jeopardize the health standards incorporated in the NAAQS. Where should the extra pollution be located? Should we be more concerned about preserving pristine air in areas far from large human populations, or about reducing the level of pollution experienced by those who live near large metropolitan areas?

## VI. TITLE V OPERATING PERMITS

In 1990, Congress amended the Clean Air Act to add Title V to assist in compliance and enforcement of air pollution controls. *See* 42 U.S.C. § 7661. Under Title V, a "major source" of air pollution is required to obtain an operating permit, which establishes the CAA requirements for, among other things, emission limitations relevant to the particular polluting source. A "major source" means any stationary source or group of sources in a contiguous area that emits or has the potential to emit, considering controls; (1) 100 tons per year or more of any air pollutant; (2) 10 tons per year or more of any hazardous air pollutant; or (3) 25 tons per year or more of any combination of hazardous air pollutants. *See* 42 U.S.C. §§ 7602(j), 7412, 7661. The intent of Title V is to consolidate into a single document (the operating permit) all of the clean air requirements applicable to a particular source of air pollution. The Title V permit program generally does not impose new substantive air quality control requirements but instead enables the source, states, EPA and the public to understand better the requirements to which the source is subject, and whether the source is meeting those requirements. *See* Operating Permit Program, 57 Fed. Reg. 32,250, 32,251 (July 21, 1992) (codified at 40 C.F.R. § 70). Title V authorizes each state to design its own stationary source permitting program and to submit that program to the EPA for approval. 42 U.S.C. § 7661a.

The Senate Committee that considered the 1990 CAA amendments endorsed the creation of a permit requirement:

> The Clean Air Act currently contains no explicit Federal requirement for sources of air pollution to obtain an operating permit. This is a serious gap in the current Act. Operating permits are needed to (1) better enforce the requirements of the law by applying them more clearly to individual sources and allowing better tracking of compliance, and (2) provide an expedited process for implementing new control requirements.

S. REP. NO. 101–228, 101st Cong., 1st Sess. 346 (1989). The committee added:

> Another benefit of the permit program . . . is the simplification and expediting of procedures for modifying a source's pollution control obligations. In general, under the current Act, for sources subject to a SIP, the vast majority of changes in the source's pollution control obligations, no matter how minor, must be developed by the State and then approved or disapproved by EPA through informal, notice-and-comment rulemaking. This "double-key" system has long been recognized as being laborious and resource-intensive, and has led to unacceptably long delays in EPA action on even relatively minor SIP revisions. Typically, EPA has taken 12–14 months to act on a SIP revision, and in some cases, EPA has taken much longer. The new permit program should eliminate this problem for source-specific SIP revisions by placing a strict time limit on EPA review. After the State revises the permit, EPA will have only 90 days to review it; if EPA takes no action, the revised permit will automatically become effective.

*Id.* at 348. The committee explained that "[t]he operating permit program contained in this Act is based on the essential features of the Clean Water Act's permit program, which has successfully imposed pollution controls on large numbers of sources in a readily enforceable and administratively flexible manner." *Id.* at 346. We describe the CWA's permit program in chapter 4.

The CAA allows EPA to object to permits issued by a state. New York Public Interest Research Group, Inc. v. Johnson, 427 F.3d 172 (2d Cir. 2005), raised the issue of whether EPA was *required* to object to such a permit. NYPIRG objected to permits that the New York State Department of Environmental Conservation (DEC) had issued to two of the largest coal-fired electric power plants in the state. NYPIRG alleged that the permits violated the CAA by not including PSD limits, a compliance schedule, and certain reporting requirements. DEC and EPA disagreed, insisting that such matters should be addressed through administrative discretion. The court agreed with NYPIRG that "EPA should not have issued an operating permit without a compliance schedule" because the plants already were not in compliance with the PSD requirements. The court also observed that while permit violations must be "promptly" reported, 42 U.S.C. § 7661b(b)(2), EPA exceeded its discretion by reading "promptly" to mean "quarterly for opacity violations and every six months for all other emission deviations." *NYPIRG*, 427 F.3d at 185.

## VII. ALTERNATIVE REGULATORY APPROACHES

Most of the CAA's provisions impose requirements on states and other government officials who are then expected to regulate air pollution. The CAA also contains several other provisions that rely upon a different regulatory model that often directly affects private businesses and other organizations. We will consider two of those provisions in this last section of the chapter: the regulation of air pollution from motor vehicles and the acid rain emissions trading scheme.

## A. MOTOR VEHICLES

Automobile manufacturers continued to deny any relationship to the air pollution in Los Angeles as late as the 1960s. As Scott Dewey explains, the notion that cars were the primary cause of smog "came as a surprise and was long resisted by industrialists and individual citizens alike." In 1953, "[a] Ford Motor Company representative insisted that auto exhausts 'dissipated in the atmosphere quickly and do not present an air pollution problem.'" In 1965, the automobile industry "still claimed that there was insufficient evidence that cars were a problem anywhere else [besides southern California] to justify introducing nationwide controls." Such uncertainty extended beyond the polluting industry. Medical researchers participating in a 1966 conference "complained of the general lack of knowledge regarding contaminated air's health effects, the difficulty of differentiating the effects of smog from those of all the other health-impairing practices of modern humans, such as smoking, and the near impossibility of finding non-exposed people to serve as control groups in experiments." SCOTT HAMILTON DEWEY, DON'T BREATHE THE AIR: AIR POLLUTION AND U.S. ENVIRONMENTAL POLITICS, 1945–1970 46, 49, 75, 92, 179, 185–87, 198, 203–08, 212–19 (2000).

Cars emit pollutants into the air in three ways: evaporation of fuel, refueling losses, and exhaust emissions. While the first two sources of emissions are significant, they pale in comparison to the pollutants emitted from a car's exhaust. Most of these pollutants result from the incomplete burning of the car's fuel. Gasoline is a mixture of hydrocarbons that contain hydrogen and carbon atoms. Perfect combustion would change the gasoline and air into $CO_2$, water, and the nitrogen that was already in the air. A more typical engine combustion produces some unburned hydrocarbons, $NO_x$, CO, and water. Motor vehicles are responsible for up to half of the VOCs and NOx that form smog, produce more than half of air toxics, and produce up to 90 percent of the CO in urban air.

The CAA regulates mobile sources by requiring limits on tailpipe emissions (thus regulating the auto industry) and by regulating fuel content. Section 202(a) requires EPA to enact regulations setting emission standards applicable to the emission of any air pollutant from classes of new motor vehicles which in EPA's judgment cause or contribute to air pollution which may reasonably be anticipated to endanger public health or welfare (the provision at issue in *Massachusetts v. EPA*). EPA has enacted different standards for different classes of vehicles, including passenger vehicles, light duty trucks, heavy duty vehicles, and motorcycles. *See* 40 C.F.R. part 86.

Under Section 211(c), EPA is authorized to restrict or prohibit the use of any fuel additive that "causes, or contributes, to air pollution which may reasonably be anticipated to endanger public health or welfare." EPA has used this authority to restrict the lead content of gasoline and, under additional provisions added as part of the 1990 Amendments to the CAA, EPA has administered an oxygenated gasoline program in CO nonattainment areas which requires gasoline in those areas to contain a minimum oxygen content to ensure more complete combustion and reduce CO emissions. Ethanol and MTBE are additives used to achieve the required oxygen content, although leaking MTBE from storage tanks has resulted in significant groundwater contamination in many areas.

Under Section 209, Congress has preempted (i.e., prohibited) states from setting motor vehicle emission standards that are more stringent than those set by the federal government. There is a special exception, however, for California, which is allowed to petition EPA for a preemption waiver to adopt its own, stricter standards. Once a waiver is granted, California can apply its standard to all vehicles sold in California and other states can choose to adopt the California standards. Thus, there is always the potential for two sets of vehicle emissions standards nationwide—the federal standard and the California standard. California was granted this special preemption waiver based on its history of regulating auto emissions (which predates federal regulation) and its unique problems with auto pollution, particularly in the Los Angeles area. As a result of federal regulation as well as improved technology, pollution from cars has decreased significantly in the last 30 years, even though vehicle miles traveled have increased significantly.

Using its authority to innovate in the area of motor vehicle emissions, California has for decades adopted aggressive, technology-forcing emission standards for motor vehicles that have served as a model for other states and, ultimately, EPA. As of 2016, California regulations require that 4.5% of an auto manufacturer's model year 2018 cars delivered for sale in California to be Zero Emissions Vehicles (ZEVs), with that percentage increasing each year up to 22% by 2025. ZEVs are battery-electric vehicles such as the Nissan Leaf and the Tesla or hydrogen fuel cell vehicles. 13 CCR § 1962.2. California also worked with EPA and NHTSA to develop the 2012 federal rule to reduce overall vehicle fleet emissions described in more detail below. Other states have followed California's lead and have created a variety of incentives and mandates for ZEVs. *See Federal Tax Credits for All-Electric and Plug-in Hybrid Vehicles*, U.S. Dept. of Energy, https://www.fueleconomy.gov/feg/taxevb.shtml. For more details on California's ZEV program, see California Air Resources Board, Zero Emission Vehicle Program, at http://www.arb.ca.gov/msprog/zevprog/zevprog.htm.

Perhaps the most familiar air pollution regulation associated with cars does not appear in the CAA. The Corporate Average Fuel Economy

(CAFE) standards require each auto manufacturer to satisfy a fleet-wide fuel efficiency standard. The result for air pollution, of course, is that fewer pollutants are emitted when less gasoline is burned. Congress established the CAFE standards in 1975 as part of the Energy Policy Conservation Act. The standards are implemented by the National Highway Traffic Safety Administration (NHTSA) within the United States Department of Transportation. Between 1990 and 2009 when (as explained later in this section) the Obama Administration instituted major changes in this area, the CAFE standard for passenger cars remained at 27.5 miles per gallon (mpg), though there were numerous calls to increase that amount, both to reduce air pollution and to conserve oil resources. *See, e.g.*, 153 CONG. REC. S168–70 (daily ed. Jan. 4, 2007) (statement of Sen. Stevens) (proposing to increase the CAFE standards for passenger cars to 40 mpg). Until 2011, most SUVs and pickup trucks were exempt from the CAFE standards. Manufacturers pay a civil penalty if their fleet of cars fails to achieve the required CAFE standard. Surprisingly, European manufacturers have over $500 million in civil penalties since 1983, while neither American nor Asian manufacturers have ever paid a civil penalty for violating the CAFE standards. A more detailed overview of the CAFE standards appears at the NHTSA website at http://www.nhtsa.gov/cars/rules/CAFE/overview.htm.

The case below explores the relationship between NHTSA's authority to set CAFE standards, EPA's authority to set air pollution emission standards for automobiles under the CAA, and California's authority to enact its own technology-forcing standards under Section 209 of the CAA.

## Central Valley Chrysler-Jeep, Inc. v. Goldstene

United States District Court for the Eastern District of California, 2007.
529 F. Supp. 2d 1151.

■ ISHII, DISTRICT JUDGE.

. . .

### FACTUAL BACKGROUND AND UNDISPUTED MATERIAL FACTS

#### I. California Regulatory Background

In 2002, the California Legislature enacted Assembly Bill 1493 ("AB 1493"), codified at California Health and Safety Code, section 43018.5. Section 43018.5(a) required CARB to "develop and adopt regulations that achieve the maximum feasible and cost-effective reduction of greenhouse gas emissions from motor vehicles" not later than January 1, 2005. The regulations directed by AB 1493 are to be applied to motor vehicles beginning with the 2009 model year. AB 1493 required CARB to develop its regulations taking into account the technical feasibility of implementing the regulations within the time frames provided and to take into account "environmental, economic, social, and technological factors." The regulations to be set by CARB were also to be "[e]conomical to an owner or operator of a vehicle, taking into account the full life-cycle costs of the vehicle." Cal. Health & Safety Code, § 43018.5(i)(2).

In 2004, CARB completed the development of regulations to reduce greenhouse gas emissions and ultimately adopted those regulations in its resolution 04–28 (hereinafter the "AB 1493 Regulations"). The AB 1493 Regulations provide that carbon dioxide emissions for passenger cars and light duty trucks less than 3750 pounds be less than 323 grams per mile starting with the 2009 model year, and decrease to 205 grams per mile of carbon dioxide in the 2016 vehicle year and beyond. The corresponding values for emissions of carbon dioxide in grams per mile for light duty trucks over 3751 pounds and medium duty passenger vehicles is 439 grams per mile in 2009, and 332 grams per mile in 2016 and beyond. The AB 1493 Regulations address four greenhouse gases: carbon dioxide, methane, nitrous oxide and hydrofluorocarbons. Although the emissions standards are expressed in grams of carbon dioxide per mile, the AB 1493 Regulations provide formulae for the conversion of other greenhouse gas pollutants to their carbon dioxide equivalents. The AB 1493 Regulations detail the method for computation of fleet average carbon dioxide emissions for the vehicle fleets being regulated.

## II. Federal Regulatory Background

The United States Environmental Protection Agency ("EPA") is empowered through the Clean Air Act to promulgate regulations necessary to prevent deterioration of air quality. 42 U.S.C., § 7601(a). Section 202(a)(1) of the Clean Air Act, codified at 42 U.S.C. § 7521(a)(1), empowers EPA to prescribe by regulation " 'standards applicable to the emission of any air pollutant from any class or classes of new motor vehicles or new motor vehicle engines, which in [the EPA Administrator's] judgment cause, or contribute to, air pollution which may reasonably be anticipated to endanger public health or welfare . . . ' " Massachusetts [v. EPA], 127 S. Ct. at 1447.

Generally, the Clean Air Act expressly preempts state regulation of motor vehicle emissions. 42 U.S.C. § 7543(a). However, section 209 of the Clean Air Act, codified at 42 U.S.C. § 7543(b)(1) (hereinafter "section 209") provides that "any state which has adopted standards (other than crankcase emission standards) for the control of emissions from new motor vehicles or new motor vehicle engines prior to March 30, 1966," may be granted a waiver to impose standards more stringent than those imposed by the Clean Air Act, if specified criteria are met. California is the only state to have regulated new motor vehicle emissions prior to March 30, 1966, and so is the only state that may apply to EPA for a grant of waiver of preemption. Although other states may not request waivers for standards they develop, other states may, pursuant to 42 U.S.C. § 7507, adopt standards that are promulgated by California and for which a waiver of preemption is granted by EPA pursuant to section 209. Compliance with any California standards that are granted waiver of preemption under section 209 is deemed compliance with corresponding standards promulgated by EPA pursuant to 42 U.S.C., section 7543(b)(3), which provides:

> In the case of any new motor vehicle or new motor vehicle engine to which State standards apply pursuant to a waiver granted under paragraph (1), compliance with such State standards shall be treated as compliance with applicable Federal Standards for purposes of this subchapter.

The Energy Policy and Conservation Act ("EPCA") directs the Secretary of the Department of Transportation ("DOT") to improve the efficiency of motor vehicles by establishing federal fuel economy standards for new vehicles on a fleet-wide basis. 49 U.S.C. §§ 32902(a), 32902(c). The Secretary of the Department of Transportation has delegated the authority under EPCA to determine the maximum feasible mileage standard to the National Highway Traffic Safety Administration. ("NHTSA"). 49 C.F.R. § 1.50(f). In determining the maximum feasible average fuel economy, NHTSA must consider: "technological feasibility, economic practicability the effect of other Federal motor vehicle standards on fuel economy and the need of the nation to conserve energy." 49 U.S.C., § 32902(f); see Green Mountain, 508 F. Supp. 2d at 305–307; Doc.#533 at 12–14.

EPCA contains an express preemption provision as follows:

> When an average fuel economy standard prescribed under this chapter is in effect, a State or a political subdivision of a State may not adopt or enforce a law or regulation related to fuel economy standards or average fuel economy standards for automobiles covered by an average fuel economy standard under this chapter.

49 U.S.C. § 32919. Unlike the Clean Air Act, EPCA provides no waiver mechanism for its preemptive effect that would allow California or any other state to adopt a regulation relating to fuel economy standards. . . .

## MOTIONS FOR SUMMARY JUDGMENT/SUMMARY ADJUDICATION ON PLAINTIFFS' CLAIM OF EPCA PREEMPTION

### III. Preemption, Preclusion, and EPCA

"The Supremacy Clause of Article VI of the United States Constitution grants Congress the power to preempt state or local law." Where the interrelationship of two federal laws is at issue, preemption doctrine per se does not apply. Rather, the issue becomes whether one federal law has preclusive effect on the applicability of the other.

A major contention underpinning AIAM's motion for summary judgment is the legal proposition that California's AB 1493 Regulations, when and if they are granted a waiver of preemption under section 209 of the Clean Air Act, are and remain state regulations and therefore subject to preemption. Defendants take the opposite position and ask the court to reconsider its order holding that a state law that is granted waiver of preemption under the Clean Air Act does not become "federalized" and therefore immune from preemption. . . .

This court concludes that a more productive approach is to first analyze the interplay between the regulatory function of the Clean Air Act and EPCA's mileage-setting authority. Specifically, the court's analysis begins by asking if EPA may promulgate emission control regulations that have an effect on fuel economy. If so, the next question is whether any new EPA-promulgated regulations that would have the incidental effect of requiring greater fuel efficiency than is required under existing regulations set by NHTSA under the CAFE program are precluded by EPCA. Finally, the court will ask if there is any basis for treating a state regulation that has been granted waiver under section 209 any differently than a regulation that has been promulgated by EPA.

**A. EPA's Authority to Promulgate Emission Control Regulations Having an Effect on Fuel Economy**

Pertinent to the issues raised by Plaintiffs' claim of preemption under EPCA, the Supreme Court, in its discussion of potential conflict between EPCA and EPA's authority to regulate carbon dioxide, held:

> EPA finally argues that it cannot regulate carbon dioxide emissions from motor vehicles because doing so would require it to tighten mileage standards, a job (according to EPA) that Congress has assigned to DOT. *See* 68 Fed. Reg. 52929. But that DOT sets mileage standards in no way licenses EPA to shirk its environmental responsibilities. EPA has been charged with protecting the public's "health" and "welfare," 42 U.S.C. § 7521(a)(1), a statutory obligation wholly independent of DOT's mandate to promote energy efficiency. *See* Energy Policy and Conservation Act § 2(5), 89 Stat. 874, 42 U.S.C. § 6201(5). The two obligations may overlap, but there is no reason to think the two agencies cannot both administer their obligations and yet avoid inconsistency.
>
> "While the Congresses that drafted § 202(a)(1) might not have appreciated the possibility that burning fossil fuels could lead to global warming, they did understand that without regulatory flexibility, changing circumstances and scientific developments would soon render the Clean Air Act obsolete." (internal quotation marks omitted). Because greenhouse gases fit well within the Clean Air Act's capacious definition of "air pollutant," we hold that EPA has the statutory authority to regulate the emission of such gasses from new motor vehicles.

*Massachusetts*, 127 S. Ct. 1438, 1461–1462.

. . . The above-quoted portion of *Massachusetts* indicates that the threshold inquiry should not be aimed at the likelihood the California standards would interfere with EPCA's regulatory scheme; rather, the threshold inquiry is to examine the scope of EPCA's ability to preclude regulations that are aimed at the prevention of damage to public health or welfare from greenhouse gas emissions where those regulations may impact mileage standards.

Two elements of the previously quoted portion of the *Massachusetts* decision indicate clearly that Congress empowered EPA to enact controls on greenhouse gasses notwithstanding that such regulation might require increased fuel efficiency. First, the Supreme Court noted that EPA is specifically tasked with protection of the public health and welfare under the Clean Air Act, and that DOT, under EPCA, is not. In its discussion on plaintiffs' standing in *Massachusetts*, the Supreme Court acknowledged that carbon dioxide emissions from human activities constitute a causal connection with global warming and that the widely recognized consequences of global climate change constitute an increasingly severe threat to human health and welfare. *See Massachusetts*, 127 S. Ct. at 1455–56.

This appreciation of the scope and extent of the threat posed by global climate change on human health and welfare forms the relevant backdrop to the Supreme Court's holding in the first paragraph quoted above that EPA's duty to regulate greenhouse gas emissions that it finds threaten health and welfare are independent of the effect such regulation may have on fuel efficiency. It also forms the relevant backdrop for the Supreme Court's opinion in the second paragraph that the regulatory authority of EPA was created broadly by Congress to enable EPA to respond to threats that were not adequately known or envisioned at the time section 202(a)(1) of the Clean Air Act was drafted. The Supreme Court's strong statement of EPA's authority to regulate carbon dioxide emissions informs this court's conclusion that Congress intended EPA to be able to promulgate emissions control regulations for the protection of public health and welfare notwithstanding the potential effect of those regulations on average fleet fuel economy standards determined under EPCA.

### B. Non-Preclusion of EPA's Regulations by EPCA

As previously noted, in questions of both preemption of state law and preclusion of federal statutory remedies by other federal statutes, the touchstone is congressional intent. "To determine the congressional intent [. . .], [the court] look[s] to the language, structure, subject matter, context and history-factors that typically help courts determine a statute's objectives and thereby illuminate its text."

As the Supreme Court's decision in *Massachusetts* makes clear, the EPA's congressionally established purpose is to protect the public's health and welfare, 42 U.S.C. § 7521(a)(1), a task EPA can and must undertake independent of NHTSA's duty to set mileage standards. *Massachusetts*, 127 S. Ct. at 1462. While the *Massachusetts* Court recognized that the "obligations of the two agencies may overlap," it opined that "there is no reason to think the two agencies cannot both administer their obligations and yet avoid inconsistency." *Id.* What remains unaddressed is the mechanism by which the two agencies should resolve inconsistencies between the two regulatory regimes. Put more directly, the question to be answered is what happens when EPA, independently fulfilling its duty to regulate emissions that threaten the public's health and welfare, imposes a regulatory structure that would result in fuel efficiency standards that are more stringent than the currently-operative CAFE standards? . . .

EPCA's language requires NHTSA to give consideration to "other motor vehicle standards of the Government," including, explicitly, regulations promulgated by EPA. 49 U.S.C. § 32902(f). There is no corresponding statutory duty by EPA to give consideration to EPCA's regulatory scheme. This asymmetrical allocation by Congress of the duty to consider other governmental regulations indicates that Congress intended that DOT, through NHTSA, is to have the burden to conform its CAFE program under EPCA to EPA's determination of what level of regulation is necessary to secure public health and welfare. . . .

This conclusion is supported by noting how the factors EPA must consider to discharge its duty to formulate regulations necessary to protect public health and welfare overlap with the factors NHTSA is required to consider in formulating the highest possible fuel efficiency standards. In formulating emissions regulations, EPA is obliged to give consideration to factors including the level of emissions reductions achievable through available technology, cost, and energy and safety factors associated with the application of the emission-reduction technology. 42 U.S.C. § 7521(a)(3)(A). NHTSA, as previously mentioned, must consider technological feasibility, economic practicability, and the need of the nation to conserve energy, in addition to the effect of other government regulations. Thus, EPA is required to give consideration to the same factors NHTSA must consider in formulating its fuel efficiency standards while NHTSA is not directly empowered to consider EPA's goal to protect public health and welfare. . . .

When the overlap in the factors NHTSA and EPA must consider in formulating their respective regulations is viewed in light of the Supreme Court's observation in *Massachusetts*, reflecting Congress' concern that changing circumstances and scientific developments related to global warming not be allowed to prevent EPA from acting, the congressional purpose behind EPCA's "shall consider" language becomes apparent. While Congress did not empower NHTSA to consider the impact of mileage standards on public health and welfare, Congress did empower NHTSA to consider the impact of "other motor vehicle standards of the Government" on mileage standards. Thus, Congress enabled NHTSA to conform the mileage standards it sets through the EPCA process to the pollution reduction requirements that are determined by EPA to be necessary for the protection of public health and welfare.

Current events illustrate the point. Ongoing scientific research into the area of climate science has produced a continuous stream of analytical documents that, over recent time, point with increasing alarm to the rapidity of evolution of measurable changes in climate instability and evince a growing consensus that human-caused greenhouse gas emissions must be curtailed more rather than less and sooner rather than later. It is not important to this discussion that there may be disagreements as to the accuracy of any particular assessment. Rather, what is important is the very present possibility that EPA, in discharging its duty to protect public health and welfare, may determine that it is compelled by the weight of scientific evidence to implement regulations substantially limiting greenhouse gas emissions in order to secure the protection of public health and welfare. It is further possible that the regulations EPA deems necessary conflict with existing standards set by NHTSA under EPCA. The Supreme Court's decision in *Massachusetts* makes it clear that, while Congress could not have foreseen the evolution of climate change science that would bring EPA's mandate to protect health and welfare into conflict with NHTSA's goals in setting mileage standards, Congress intended that under such circumstances, EPA would not be prevented from necessary action. *See Massachusetts*, 127 S. Ct. at 1462 (holding that Congress did not intend to allow changes in scientific developments to render the Clean Air Act obsolete).

As the Supreme Court's decision in *Massachusetts* explicitly stated, there is no necessary conflict between the Clean Air Act's purpose to protect health and welfare and EPCA's purpose to establish maximum feasible fuel efficiency standards. While some level of conflict may arise in a situation where EPA is compelled to act on the basis of current climate science to achieve deep reductions in greenhouse gas emissions, EPCA empowers NHTSA to import EPA's determination of the necessity of the regulation through EPCA's "shall consider" provision and conform its mileage standards to what EPA determines is necessary for the protection of health and welfare. Given the level of impairment of human health and welfare that current climate science indicates may occur if human-generated greenhouse gas emissions continue unabated, it would be the very definition of folly if EPA were precluded from action simply because the level of decrease in greenhouse gas output is incompatible with existing mileage standards under EPCA.

Simply put, the court concludes that where EPA, consistent with its obligation to protect public health and welfare, determines that regulation of pollutants under the Clean Air Act is necessary and where such regulation conflicts with average mileage standards established pursuant to EPCA, EPA is not precluded from promulgating such regulation. The court further concludes the agency designated by EPCA to formulate average mileage standards is obliged to consider such regulations pursuant to 49 U.S.C. § 32902(f) and is further obliged to harmonize average fuel efficiency standards under EPCA with the standards promulgated by EPA. . . .

### C. The Status of State Regulations Granted Waiver by EPA

. . . Having now determined that EPA may promulgate regulations that are in conflict with fuel efficiency standards, the court re-posits the question to ask whether a state regulation that is granted waiver of preemption under the Clean Air Act should stand in any different stead with respect to inconsistencies or conflicts it may have with EPCA-established fuel efficiency standards.

Section 209 of the Clean Air Act imposes three conditions on state regulations that are submitted to EPA for waiver of preemption (other than the requirement that they be proposed by California). First, the proposed regulations must "be, in the aggregate, at least as protective of the public health and welfare as applicable Federal standards." 42 U.S.C. § 7543(b)(1). Second, EPA must determine the state regulations are necessary to "to meet compelling and extraordinary conditions," and that the regulations were not promulgated in an arbitrary and capricious fashion. *Id.* Finally, the proposed regulations must be consistent with section 7521(a), which requires that air pollution standards be formulated in consideration of technological feasibility, the time necessary to apply the requisite technology, the cost of compliance, and energy and safety factors associated the application of the technology. 42 U.S.C. §§ 7543(b)(1)(c) and 7521(a)(2) and (3).

If EPA concludes that California's regulations meet these three requirements, EPA is obliged to grant the waiver application. Although regulations proposed by California pursuant to section 209 must broadly advance EPA's primary purpose to protect public health and welfare, and must be at least as stringent as the corresponding EPA regulations in the aggregate, the proposed California regulations need not establish perfect compliance with all provisions of the Clean Air Act. Id. In creating the waiver provisions of section 209, Congress determined that California should have the " 'broadest possible discretion in selecting the best means to protect the health of its citizens.' [Citation.]" *Id.* " 'In short, Congress consciously chose to permit California to blaze its own trail with a minimum of federal oversight.' [Citation.]" *Id.* (quoting Ford Motor Co. v. EPA, 606 F.2d 1293, 1297 (D.C. Cir. 1979)). . . .

Defendants contend, and Plaintiffs and AIAM do not directly dispute that a California regulation that has been granted waiver of preemption under section 209 of the Clean Air Act is an "other motor vehicle standard[ ] of the Government" that must be considered by NHTSA in the formulation of average fleet mileage standards under EPCA. . . . AIAM contends that the extent of consideration of the California regulation is confined to a determination that the regulation has a de minimis effect on fuel efficiency. AIAM contends that if NHTSA's consideration of the California regulation indicates an effect of fuel efficiency that is anything more than de minimis, then the California regulation is preempted.

The most thorough and persuasive analysis of the issue so far as the court has found was offered as part of the decision in *Green Mountain* wherein that court rejected plaintiffs' claim of EPCA preemption. The *Green Mountain* court observed:

> Section 502(d) of EPCA as originally enacted provided that any manufacturer could apply to the Secretary of Transportation for modification of an average fuel economy standard for model years 1978 through 1980 if it could show the likely existence of a "Federal standards fuel economy reduction," defined to include EPA-approved California emissions standards that reduce fuel economy. § 502(d)(1–3); *see also* S. Rep. No. 94–516 at 156 (1975), 1975 U.S.C.C.A.N. 1956, 1997. Thus, in 1975 when EPCA was passed, Congress unequivocally stated that federal standards included EPA-approved California emissions standards. § 502(d)(3)(D)(i). In 1994, when EPCA was recodified, all reference to the modification process applicable for model years 1978 through 1980, including the categories of federal standards, was omitted as executed. However the 1994 recodification was intended to "revise[ ], codif[y], and enact [ ]" the law "without substantive change." Pub.L. No. 103–272, 108 Stat. 745 745 (1994); *see also* H.R. Rep. No. 103–180, at 1 (1994), reprinted in 1994 U.S.C.C.A.N. 818, 818; S. Rep. No. 103–265, at 1 (1994). If the recodification worked no substantive change in the law, then the term "other motor vehicle standards of the Government" continues to include both emission standards issued by EPA and emission standards for which EPA has issued a waiver under section 209(b) of the [Clean Air Act], as it did when enacted in 1975. NHTSA has consistently treated EPA-approved California emissions standards as "other motor vehicle standards of the government," which it must take into consideration when setting maximum feasible average fuel economy under § 32902.

*Green Mountain*, 508 F. Supp. 2d at 345. Based on this analysis from the *Green Mountain* court and on the foregoing discussion, the court concludes there is nothing in statute or in case law to support the proposition that a regulation promulgated by California and granted waiver of preemption under section 209 is anything other than a "law of the Government" whose effect on fuel economy must be considered by NHTSA in setting fuel economy standards.

In sum, when a California regulation is granted waiver of preemption pursuant to section 209 of the Clean Air Act, the California regulation assumes three attributes. First, the California regulation becomes available for adoption by any other state, subject only to the identicality and leadtime requirements. Second, compliance with the

California regulation or standard is deemed "compliance with applicable Federal standards for purposes of [Subchapter II–Emissions Standards for Moving Sources]." 42 U.S.C. § 7543(b)(3). Third, as discussed in *Green Mountain*, the California regulation or standard becomes an "other motor vehicle standard[ ] of the government" that affects fuel economy and that the Secretary of Transportation must consider in formulating maximum feasible average fuel economy standards under EPCA. 49 U.S.C. § 32902(f). *Green Mountain*, 508 F. Supp. 2d at 347.

The court can discern no legal basis for the proposition that an EPA-promulgated regulation or standard functions any differently than a California-promulgated and EPA-approved standard or regulation. Either EPA-promulgated regulations or California-promulgated regulations that are approved by EPA may be implemented to achieve compliance by any state, and both must be considered by NHTSA in formulating average fuel economy standards. In either case, where there is conflict between new EPA-promulgated or California-promulgated regulations that are EPA approved and existing EPCA fuel economy standards, DOT is empowered through EPCA to take the new regulations into consideration when revising its CAFE standards.

The court concludes that, just as the *Massachusetts* Court held EPA's duty to regulate greenhouse gas emissions under the Clean Air Act overlaps but does not conflict with DOT's duty to set fuel efficiency standards under EPCA, so too California's effort to regulate greenhouse gas emissions through the waiver of preemption provisions of the Clean Air Act overlaps, but does not conflict with DOT's activities under EPCA. . . .

[The court proceeded to find that, assuming that EPA granted a preemption waiver for the California regulations under the CAA, EPCA did not expressly or impliedly preempt or those regulations and that the regulations were not subject to foreign policy preemption]

---

## QUESTIONS AND DISCUSSION

**1.** Why should California be given so much authority in setting auto emission standards in our federalist system of government? Shouldn't all the states be equal in this regard? What are the pros and cons of California having this authority both with regard to California itself and the country as a whole?

**2.** Just months after this decision EPA denied California's petition for a preemption waiver under Section 209 of the CAA. 73 Fed. Reg. 12,156 (March 6, 2008). In its denial, EPA acknowledged that climate change would have substantial effects on California, but found that those effects were not sufficiently different from conditions in the nation as a whole to justify separate standards. California challenged the waiver denial in federal court but soon after, EPA, now under the Obama Administration, agreed to reconsider the denial, and then granted the waiver on June 30, 2009. At that time, thirteen states and the District of Columbia had adopted the California standards and other states had indicated that they would do the same.

Also in 2009, the Obama Administration began to take significant action with regard to federal vehicle efficiency standards. Two years earlier, in the Energy Independence and Security Act of 2007 (EISA), Congress had required the National Highway Traffic Safety Administration (NHTSA) to increase combined passenger car and light truck fuel economy standards to at least 35 miles per gallon (mpg) by 2020, up from roughly 26.6 mpg in 2007. But in April 2010, after reaching agreement between the auto manufacturers, California, federal agencies, and other interested parties, EPA and NHTSA promulgated a joint rulemaking to establish the first national GHG emission standards for new passenger cars, light-duty trucks, and medium-duty passenger vehicle and establish new CAFE standards for vehicle model years 2012–2016. The rule requires these vehicles to meet an estimated combined average emissions level of 250 grams of $CO_2$ per mile in model year 2016, equivalent to 35.5 mpg if the automotive industry were to meet this $CO_2$ level exclusively through fuel economy improvements. The result of this rule was that vehicles were required to meet the CAFE standards Congress mandated in EISA four years earlier than Congress required. These new standards brought the federal standards in line with the California standards, and resulted in significantly increased fuel economy and GHG emission reductions on a faster timetable.

Then, in August 2012, the parties reached agreement on another joint EPA and NHTSA rule for even more stringent standards for vehicle model years 2017–2025. The final standards are projected to result in an average industry fleet-wide level of 163 grams/mile of $CO_2$ in model year 2025, which is equivalent to 54.5 mpg if achieved exclusively through fuel economy improvements. For more information on the joint rulemaking as well as the proposed fuel savings and $CO_2$ emissions reductions associated with the new rules, see EPA, Transportation and Climate, Regulations and Standards, at http://www.epa.gov/otaq/climate/regs-light-duty.htm#new1. EPA and NHTSA have also issued GHG emission and fuel efficiency standards for medium- and heavy-duty engines and vehicles. *See* www.epa.gov/otaq/climate/regs-heavy-duty.htm.

---

## B. ACID RAIN EMISSIONS TRADING

Acid rain refers to precipitation that contains sulfuric or nitric acid. Typically, acid rain results from the emission of $SO_2$ and NOx from electrical power plants that burn lots of coal, especially Eastern and Midwestern coal with a high sulfur content. Once those pollutants are emitted into the air, they can be carried for hundreds or even thousands of miles until they mix with the moisture and fall back to the earth as acid rain. In the United States, that often means that power plants in the

Midwest are responsible for acid rain along the east coast. Acid rain changes the chemical composition of lakes and rivers, often to the detriment of the wildlife there, and it can harm forests as well. The injuries to humans that are attributable to acid rain include respiratory problems and property damage.

In order to address this problem, in 1990 Congress enacted Title IV of the CAA and created the first, large-scale tradable emissions approach to air pollution. Under Title IV, Congress enacted a nationwide cap on $SO_2$ emissions from fossil-fuel powered utilities and created tradable allowances to emit $SO_2$. Each unit allowance permits the emission of one ton of $SO_2$ during or after the calendar year it is issued. Congress limited the total number of allowances to utilities based on past fuel consumption (creating a cap on total emissions) and then reduced that cap in 2000. Once the allowances were issued, they were freely tradable. EPA also auctions some allowances each year through the Chicago Board of Trade. Title IV provided that by the year 2000, $SO_2$ emissions from power plants had to be reduced by 10 million per year from 1980 levels and also required reductions of NOx emissions by approximately 2 million tons per year below 1980 levels. The statute provided for "bonus" allowances available at various points in time for actions such as installing scrubbers to reduce regulated emissions and to reward utilities that invest in "clean coal" technology and renewable energy.

Experts have concluded that the Title IV program has reduced emissions from 1990 levels faster and at a lower cost than anticipated. By 2005, $SO_2$ emissions from regulated power plants had fallen 35%. EPA studies have calculated hundreds of billions of dollars in cost savings from the program, based mainly on the reduction in premature deaths and reduced cases of chronic disease associated with acid rain. EPA publishes yearly progress report on the Title IV program. Both the progress reports and basic information on the program are found at https://www.epa.gov/airmarkets.

When Congress enacted Title IV, the assumption was that most utilities would install scrubbers to obtain the required emission reductions. Instead, however, most utilities switched to low-sulfur coal or blended fuels, creating a significant, negative economic impact in states that historically were large producers of high-sulfur coal. This impact resulted in some states turning to legislation to protect their market in this area, which then led to cases like the following:

## Alliance for Clean Coal v. Bayh

United States Court of Appeals for the Seventh Circuit 1995.
72 F.3d 556.

■ CUMMINGS, CIRCUIT JUDGE:

Because of the sulfur contained in the coal they burn, coal-fired generating plants are a principal source of atmospheric sulfur dioxide emissions. The sulfur content of coal burned by utilities depends upon the geological origin of the coal: whereas coal mined in the western United States has the lowest sulfur content, almost all of the coal mined in the "Illinois Basin," including most of Illinois and parts of Indiana and western Kentucky, has a relatively high sulfur content.

Congressional enactment of the Clean Air Act Amendments of 1970 required newly constructed generating units to use systems of emissions control approved by the Environmental Protection Agency ("EPA"). The EPA initially provided two methods for controlling sulphur dioxide emissions: (1) the use of low-sulfur coal; and (2) the installation of a device to scrub high-sulfur coal emissions before they reach the atmosphere. Because scrubbing was costlier than using low-sulfur western coal, states producing high-sulfur coal suffered competitively.

In 1990 the Clean Air Act was amended again to require drastic reductions in industrial sulfur dioxide emissions by the year 2000. 42 U.S.C. §§ 7401–7671q. The 1990 Act implemented an innovative market-driven approach to emissions regulation, allowing for the free transfer of emissions "allowances." The Act is aimed at reducing emissions efficiently and allows utilities to meet the standards in the cheapest manner possible. To comply with the new emissions limitations, utilities now have a choice of the following strategies: (1) installing pollution control devices; (2) using low-sulfur coal; (3) purchasing allowances to emit sulfur dioxide; (4) switching to another fuel; (5) closing down certain units; (6) offsetting emissions at one plant by over-complying at another; or (7) adopting some combination. According to Alliance, because of the high costs associated with installing pollution devices, the 1990 amendments should result in a decline in demand for the Illinois Basin's high-sulfur coal.

High-sulfur coal-mining states like Indiana considered legislation responsive to the foregoing federal acts. Thus in 1991 Indiana adopted its ECPA. IC §§ 8–1–27–1 to 8–1–27–23. This statute permits electric utilities to avail themselves of early prudency review by submitting plans for complying with the federal legislation to the Commission. In order to approve a utility's plan, the Commission must find that the plan (A) meets the Clean Air Act Amendments of 1990; (B) constitutes a reasonable and least cost strategy over the life of the investment consistent with providing reliable, efficient, and economical electrical service; (C) is in the public interest; and (D) either:

> (i) provides for continued or increased use of Indiana coal in the coal-consuming electric generating units owned or operated by the public utility and affected by the Clean Air Act Amendments of 1990; or (ii) if the plan does not provide for continued or increased use of Indiana coal, such nonprovision is justified by economic considerations including the effects in the regions of Indiana in which the mining of coal provides

employment and in the service territory of the public utility. IC § 8–1–27–8(1).

A plan that has a negative impact on Indiana coal is subject to continuing annual surveillance. . . . In the court below Alliance moved for summary judgment on the ground that the ECPA unjustifiably discriminated against interstate commerce. The district court concluded that the ECPA was intended to promote high-sulfur coal at the expense of western coal and unconstitutionally burdens interstate commerce.

The threshold inquiry we must make in deciding whether the ECPA violates the Commerce Clause is whether it "is basically a protectionist measure, or if it can fairly be viewed as a law directed to legitimate local concerns with effects upon interstate commerce that are only incidental." Oregon Waste Systems, Inc. v. Dept. of Environmental Quality, 511 U.S. 93 (1994).

As the district judge recognized, the outcome of this case is controlled by Alliance for Clean Coal v. Miller, 44 F.3d 591 (7th Cir. 1995). There we invalidated the Illinois Coal Act, also enacted on the heels of the Clean Air Act Amendments of 1990, on the ground that it was repugnant to the Commerce Clause of the United States Constitution. The Illinois Coal Act provided that in preparing and approving compliance plans, the Illinois Commerce Commission and utilities were required to "take into account . . . the need to maintain and preserve as a valuable State resource the mining of coal in Illinois." The Act also encouraged implementing scrubbers to allow the continued use of high-sulfur coal by guaranteeing utilities the ability to recover the installation costs of scrubbers by including such costs in their rate base. We stated "[t]he Illinois Coal Act is a none-too-subtle attempt to prevent Illinois electric utilities from switching to low-sulphur western coal as a Clean Air Act compliance option." Therefore, we concluded that the Act was "repugnant to the Commerce Clause and the principle of a unitary national economy which that clause was intended to establish."

The ECPA contains provisions that are virtually identical to the sections of the Illinois Coal Act discussed above. First, in determining whether to approve a plan that includes a compliance option calling for a decrease in the use of Indiana coal, the ECPA requires the Commission to take into account "the effects in the regions of Indiana in which the mining of coal provides employment and in the service territory of the public utility." IC § 8–1–27–8(1). The ECPA also provides incentives for utilities to install scrubbers to continue to use high-sulfur fuel by guaranteeing a recoupment of the implementation costs. IC § 8–1–27–12 & 19.

We agree with the district court that, just as in *Miller*, the ECPA discriminates against interstate commerce based solely upon geographic origin, and thus violates the Commerce Clause. The clear intent of the statute is to benefit Indiana coal at the expense of western coal. The fact that the ECPA does not explicitly forbid the use of out-of-state coal or require the use of Indiana coal, but "merely encourages" utilities to use high-sulfur coal by providing economic incentives does not make the ECPA any less discriminatory.

Because the ECPA discriminates against interstate commerce, the burden lies with the defendants to prove that this discrimination is justified by a legitimate and compelling governmental interest. Defendants provide the following justification. They argue that a viable competitive Midwest high-sulfur coal market is a major component of low-cost electrical service by Indiana utilities and that the ECPA seeks only to ensure that market. However, ensuring such a regional market is not a proper justification for discriminating against interstate commerce.

While we do not doubt that a healthy Indiana mining industry and a fully employed workforce may aid Indiana in achieving a low cost electrical service, that is not a legitimate justification for discrimination against interstate commerce. Protection of local, or even regional, industry is simply not a legislative action that is consistent with the Commerce Clause.

---

## QUESTIONS AND DISCUSSION

**1.** The acid rain trading program established in Title IV of the 1990 CAA amendments represents a unique approach to addressing air pollution. An electric power plant must have one allowance for each ton of $SO_2$ that it wants to emit, so the plant must either buy additional allowances or reduce its $SO_2$ emissions if its existing operations would emit too much $SO_2$. How should a plant choose between changing its operations or buying more allowances? And how does this approach reduce acid rain?

**2.** How should the law attempt to address the inevitable market changes that will result from preferring the natural resources or industry from one region over another? Here, Title IV created a new, significant market for low-sulfur, western coal at the expense of high-sulfur Midwestern coal. This resulted in major changes in local and regional employment opportunities (or lack thereof) and revenues. Should Congress create funding to soften the impact of such economic effects by creating a national source of revenue through industry or other taxes or rebates?

**3.** Notably, in the early 2010s, the market for cheaper, high-sulfur coal from the Midwest improved, at least for a time. In 2012, Illinois exported 13 million tons of coal, up from 2.5 million in 2010 and 5.5 million tons in 2011, making the state the fifth-biggest coal producing state in 2012. While some of this coal made its way to 18 different countries, most notably China and other Asian countries where demand for coal is high, demand in the U.S. was also strong, even as U.S. coal production dropped 11 percent overall as a result of utilities switching to cheaper natural gas made available as a result of new drilling technologies such as hydraulic fracturing. One of the reasons cited for the increase in use of high-sulfur coal is the fact that coal-fired power plants have increasingly added more efficient pollution control technologies to comply with ever-increasing CAA regulations, allowing utilities to use Midwest coal and remain in compliance with emissions regulations. *See* Associated Press, *Illinois Coal Industry Enjoyed Record Exports in 2012*, DAILY HERALD, May 1, 2013. Since 2012, however, as a result of cheaper natural gas and increasingly stringent CAA regulations on coal-fired power plants, electric utilities' use of coal to produce electricity has dropped precipitously across the country. In 2015, coal accounted for only 34% of U.S. electricity generation—its lowest share since recordkeeping began—as compared with 50% of total U.S. electricity generation as recently as 2005. *See Coal, Gas, Nuclear, Hydro? How Your State Generates Power*, NAT'L PUBLIC RADIO (Sept. 10, 2015); Seth Feaser, *IEEFA Data Bite: Wind on the Rise, Coal on the Wane*, INSTITUTE FOR ENERGY ECONOMICS AND FINANCIAL ANALYSIS, May 12, 2016.

**4.** The 2009 acid rain allowance auction resulted in the sale of 125,000 allowances in the spot auction and another 125,000 allowances sold in the seven-year advance auction. The average price on the spot auction was $69.74, with a high price of $500. The average price on the seven-year advance auction was $6.65, with a high price of $200. By contrast, in 2013, the average and high prices in the spot auction were $0.28 and $5.00, respectively and the average and high prices in the seven-year advance auction were $0.04 and $5.00, respectively. Why the significant drop in allowance prices?

According to one expert, when the Obama Administration proposed the Transport Rule, also known as the Cross-State Air Pollution Rule or "CSAPR" (discussed earlier in this chapter) it negatively impacted the $SO_2$ market. This is because the Transport Rule, in addition to its caps on $SO_2$, significantly limited interstate $SO_2$ trades (and allowed only intrastate trades), thus acting as "the death-knell for the $SO_2$ allowance trading program, though the program remains nominally in place, since it dramatically reduced the scope for cost-effective interstate trades." *See* Richard Schmalensee & Robert N. Stavins, *The $SO_2$ Allowance Trading System: The Ironic History of a Grand Policy Experiment*, 27 J. OF ECON. PERSPECTIVES 103 (2013). There are also good arguments that reduced natural gas prices and improved emissions control technologies imposed on utilities by other CAA regulations such as MATS, among other factors, had an equally significant impact on trading and the drop in allowance prices.

**5.** In 2009, JP Morgan bought 124,984 of the 125,000 allowances on the seven-year market for a total price of nearly $1 million. Why would such financial services businesses be interested in buying so many allowances? Note that the same year, University of Tampa Environmental Coalition and the Bates College Environmental Economics class each bought one allowance on the spot auction, for $500 and $73.01, respectively. In prior years, the environmental law societies at the Maryland, Iowa, Creighton, and California Western law schools each bought one allowance for prices ranging from $247.10 to $950. Why would those organizations want to buy the right to emit one ton of $SO_2$ into the air?

**6.** The acid rain emissions trading program is generally regarded as a success, but it has generated some criticism. Congress picked the initial targeted ten million ton reduction in the emission of sulfur dioxide without much scientific deliberation, *see* Lisa Heinzerling, *Selling Pollution, Forcing Democracy*, 14 STAN. ENVTL. L.J. 300, 323–24 (1995); and there was little effort "to allocate emissions between upwind states and downwind states in an optimal way." Richard Revesz, *Federalism and Interstate Environmental Externalities*, 155 U. PA. L. REV. 2341, 2361 (1996). New York tried to prohibit companies within the state from selling their allowances to upwind states, but the state law was held preempted by Title IV of the CAA. *See* Clean Air Markets Group v. Pataki, 338 F.3d 82 (2d Cir. 2003). More generally, emissions trading programs have been attacked for creating "hot spots" where many polluting facilities choose to locate, for endorsing a "right to pollute" that compromises the social norm against pollution. How would you address those criticisms?

**7.** While the U.S. has never signed onto the Kyoto Protocol's efforts to control global warming, legislation introduced in both houses of Congress in 2009 would have created a mandatory GHG cap-and-trade system affecting entities within many different sectors of the economy, ranging from agriculture to energy providers. The House bill, known as the Waxman-Markey bill, would have created a new Title VII to the Clean Air Act, establishing a GHG cap-and-trade system with reduction goals of 20 percent below 2005 levels by 2020, and 83 percent below 2005 levels by 2050. The bill would have allowed covered entities to increase their emissions above their allowances by purchasing offsets and limited the total amount of offsets allowed at two billion tons per year. The bill was silent on one of the most contentious issues, however, regarding whether allowances would be auctioned or granted to the covered entities. The Senate bill, known as the Boxer-Kerry bill, created a similar structure as the Waxman-Markey bill although the bills differed in that Waxman-Markey prevented EPA from regulating greenhouse gases under the CAA for a period of years, while Boxer-Kerry contained no such provision. As discussed in more detail in chapter 8, the Senate bill was never passed and there remains no comprehensive federal GHG emission reduction program in the United States. Instead, there are the EPA limits on vehicle emissions as well as the proposed limits on a narrow range of stationary sources discussed earlier in this chapter.

**8.** Besides the recent efforts in Congress to create a cap-and-trade system for GHGs, the acid rain trading program has not been widely imitated. Is there anything about acid rain that could explain why emissions trading in that context has been more successful? Is there anything about other kinds of air pollution that makes emissions trading more difficult?

---

## CHAPTER 4

# PROTECTING WATER RESOURCES

**CHAPTER OUTLINE**



## I. REGULATION OF POINT AND NONPOINT SOURCE WATER POLLUTION

The law of water pollution regulation is an incredible patchwork of federal, state, and local initiatives. The major force in that body of law and the major focus in this Chapter is the Federal Water Pollution Control Act, also known by the name of its 1972 amendatory legislation, the Clean Water Act.

### A. HISTORY AND DEVELOPMENT OF WATER POLLUTION LAW

The original demand for water pollution control arose in response to the recognition of the transportation of disease and germs through our nation's waterways caused by the discharge of raw sewage, usually consisting of human waste, into many drinking water sources.

Nonetheless, one of the first pieces of federal water pollution legislation, the Rivers and Harbors Act of 1899, which prohibited unpermitted discharges of pollutants into navigable waterways, was not intended to improve health conditions but to ensure effective transportation of economic goods. Thus, such health problems continued to accelerate through the middle of the 20th century, reaching their peak just after World War II as industrial wastes were increasingly added to our waterways.

Congress then responded with the Water Quality Act of 1948, which provided funding for state water pollution control programs, and the Federal Water Pollution Control Act of 1956, which provided federal aid for the construction of municipal wastewater treatment plants. Congress further strengthened water pollution controls with the Water Quality Act of 1965, which required states to adopt water quality standards for interstate waters which were subject to federal approval. However, state adoption of such standards was still slow, and by 1972 only approximately one-third of the states had adopted anything.

In response, federal lawmakers and others began searching for an effective method to improve water quality and reduce pollutant discharges. One unique solution was by a Wisconsin Congressman who discovered a *qui tam* provision within the Rivers and Harbors Act and began bringing suit against dischargers within his state. *Qui tam* provisions allow citizens who bring suit to receive up to half of the penalties imposed, and in this case the Congressman returned those funds to Wisconsin's Department of Natural Resources to be used for further water quality improvement efforts. Such a strategy was adopted by environmentally minded U.S. Attorneys across the country throughout the late 1960s. These actions helped spur a demand for the development of more effective national water pollution legislation.

In 1972, Congress passed the Federal Water Pollution Control Act, which, after subsequent major amendments, would become known as the Clean Water Act (CWA). Designed "to restore and maintain the chemical, physical, and biological integrity of the Nation's waters," the CWA remains the preeminent federal statute regulating water pollution. For an excellent history of the social, economic, and legal events leading up to the passage of the FWPCA, see William L. Andreen, *The Evolution of Water Pollution Control in the United States—State, Local, and Federal Efforts*, 1789–1972: Part I, 22 STANFORD ENVTL. L. J. 145 (2003), and *Part II*, 22 STANFORD ENVTL. L. J. 215 (2003). For a retrospect of the CWA's lasting success as well as some of its current limitations, see William L. Andreen, *Success and Backlash: the Remarkable (Continuing) Story of the Clean Water Act*, 4 GEO. WASH. J. OF ENERGY & ENVTL. L. 25 (Winter 2013).

## B. CLEAN WATER ACT OVERVIEW

The CWA is a lengthy and involved statute. To aid in understanding such a comprehensive piece of legislation, the following is a brief outline of its major provisions. The operation and implementation of these provisions will be discussed in further detail in the sections that follow.

§ 101 *Goals.* Declares the national goals of the CWA to create fishable/swimmable waters by 1983 and the elimination of pollutant discharges into navigable waters by 1985. While neither of these deadlines were met, these goals continue to be the thrust of the CWA. 33 U.S.C. § 1251.

§ 301 *Discharge Prohibition and Effluent Limitations.* Prohibits "the discharge of any pollutant by any person" except as in compliance with law. "The discharge of any pollutant" is defined in § 502 as the addition of any pollutant to navigable waters from any point source or to the waters of the ocean or contiguous zone from any source other than a vessel. This section also imposes effluent limitations on discharges of pollutants which vary depending on the nature of the pollutant discharged and the type of water body into which the pollutant is discharged. 33 U.S.C. § 1311.

§ 302 *Water Quality Related to Effluent Limitations.* Authorizes the establishment of more stringent effluent limitations for any discharge of pollutants from a point source or group of point sources that would otherwise interfere with the attainment or maintenance of the water quality in a specific portion of the navigable waters. 33 U.S.C. § 1312.

§ 303 *State Water Quality Standards & Total Maximum Daily Loads (TMDLs).* Requires states to establish water quality criteria and water quality standards, subject to EPA approval, which identify waters where water quality standards may not be met, or are not being met, and to establish TMDLs for specific pollutants for those waters. These standards are to be reviewed every three years. If EPA does not approve the standard, EPA shall set its own standard for the water body. 33 U.S.C. § 1313.

§ 304 *Federal Water Quality Guidelines and Criteria.* Requires EPA to establish water quality criteria for effluent limitations, pretreatment programs, and provides for administration of the NPDES permit program. 33 U.S.C. § 1314.

§ 306 *New Source Performance Standards.* Requires EPA to establish national standards for new sources of pollutant discharges which reflect the best demonstrated control technology. 33 U.S.C. § 1316.

§ 307 *Toxic and Pretreatment Effluent Standards.* Requires dischargers of toxic pollutants to meet established effluent limits reflecting the best economically available control technologies and directs

EPA to establish pretreatment standards to prevent discharges from interfering with POTWs. 33 U.S.C. § 1317.

§ 309 *Enforcement.* Authorizes compliance orders, civil actions, criminal penalties, and administrative penalties as enforcement options for violations of the CWA. 33 U.S.C. § 1319.

§ 319 *Nonpoint Source Management Provisions.* Requires states and tribes to identify water bodies that cannot meet water quality standards due to discharges from nonpoint sources and to identify the responsible sources and create a plan to control such sources. 33 U.S.C. § 1329.

§ 401 *State Water Quality Certification.* Requires applicants for federal licenses and permits to obtain certification from the state within which the discharge will occur that it will not interfere with the state's efforts in achieving water quality standards. 33 U.S.C. § 1341.

§ 402 *NPDES Permit Program.* Establishes the National Pollutant Discharge Elimination System permit program, which may be administered by the states or tribes through delegation from EPA. This is known by many as the centerpiece of the CWA, and was specifically designed to address many of the weaknesses of earlier water pollution legislation. 33 U.S.C. § 1342.

§ 404 *Permits for Dredged or Fill Materials.* Requires permits to be obtained through the U.S. Army Corps of Engineers for the disposal of dredged or fill material into navigable waters unless it occurs as part of "normal" farming operations or as part of the maintenance of dams or other water control structures. 33 U.S.C. § 1344.

§ 505 *Citizen Suits.* Creates standing for citizens to bring suit against anyone who violates an effluent standard or order and also against EPA for failure to perform any nondiscretionary duty. 33 U.S.C. § 1365.

## C. REGULATED POINT SOURCE DISCHARGES

Section 301 of the CWA prohibits "the discharge of any pollutant by any person" unless done in compliance with a provision of the Act authorizing such activities. 33 U.S.C. § 1311(a). One such provision establishes the National Pollutant Discharge Elimination System, or NPDES, permit program. *Id.* § 1342. Generally speaking, the NPDES program requires dischargers to obtain permits that place limits on the type and quantity of pollutants that can be released into the nation's waters. The CWA provides that states may obtain authorization from EPA to administer part or all of the NPDES program within the state. If EPA approves a state's NPDES program, then NPDES permits are issued by the state, not EPA. As of 2015, EPA has authorized 46 states to administer part or all of the NPDES program. EPA continues to monitor each state's program and citizens may petition EPA to withdraw the state's authority on grounds that the state is not meeting the requirements of the CWA. For more information, see EPA, NDPES State Program Information, at https://www.epa.gov/npdes/npdes-state-program-information.

The CWA defines the phrase "discharge of a pollutant"—which requires a NPDES permit—to mean "any addition of any pollutant to navigable waters from any point source." *Id.* § 1362(12). A "point source," in turn, is defined as "any discernible, confined and discrete conveyance," such as a pipe, ditch, channel, or tunnel, "from which pollutants are or may be discharged." *Id.* § 1362(14). The courts and EPA have provided some illumination on how all these terms fit together.

## Friends of the Everglades v. South Florida Water Management District

United States Court of Appeals for the Eleventh Circuit, 2009.
570 F.3d 1210.

■ CARNES, CIRCUIT JUDGE:

This appeal turns on whether the transfer of a pollutant from one navigable body of water to another is a "discharge of a pollutant" within the meaning of the Clean Water Act, 33 U.S.C. § 1362(12). If it is, a National Pollution Discharge Elimination System permit is required. 33 U.S.C. §§ 1311(a), 1342(a). The Act defines "discharge of a pollutant," but the meaning of that definition is itself disputed. During the course of this litigation, the Environmental Protection Agency adopted a regulation addressing this specific matter. The issue we face . . . is whether we owe that EPA regulation deference under Chevron, U.S.A., Inc. v. Natural Res. Defense Council, Inc., 467 U.S. 837 (1984).

The unique geography of South Florida is once again before us. Lake Okeechobee is part of that geography. Historically, the lake had an ill-defined southern shoreline because during rainy seasons it overflowed, spilling a wide, shallow sheet of water overland to the Florida Bay. "But progress came and took its toll, and in the name of flood control, they made their plans and they drained the land."[1]

In the 1930s the Herbert Hoover Dike was built along the southern shore of Lake Okeechobee. It was intended to control flooding but failed during the hurricanes of 1947 and 1948. Congress then authorized the Central and Southern Florida Flood Project; as part of it the Army Corps of Engineers expanded the Hoover Dike and built pump stations including S-2, S-3, and S-4. Under the modern version of that project, nearly all water flow in South Florida is controlled by a complex system of gates, dikes, canals, and pump stations.

The area south of Lake Okeechobee's shoreline was designated the Everglades Agricultural Area. The Corps dug canals there to collect rainwater and runoff from the sugar cane fields and the surrounding

---

[1] John Anderson, Seminole Wind, on Seminole Wind (BMG Records 1992).

industrial and residential areas. Not surprisingly, those canals contain a loathsome concoction of chemical contaminants including nitrogen, phosphorous, and un-ionized ammonia. The water in the canals is full of suspended and dissolved solids and has a low oxygen content.

Those polluted canals connect to Lake Okeechobee, which is now virtually surrounded by the Hoover Dike. The S-2, S-3, and S-4 pump stations are built into the dike and pump water from the lower levels in the canals outside the dike into the higher lake water. They do that by spewing water through the dike and into "rim canals" open to the lake. This process moves the water containing Agricultural Area contaminants uphill into Lake Okeechobee, a distance of some sixty feet. The pumps do not add anything to the canal water; they simply move it through pipes. At full capacity, the pumps within the S-2, S-3, and S-4 stations can each move 900 cubic feet of water per second—more than 400,000 gallons per minute. The South Florida Water Management District operates the pumping stations.

Two organizations, the Friends of the Everglades and the Fishermen Against the Destruction of the Environment, filed this lawsuit against the Water District in 2002. The plaintiffs (whom we will call collectively the Friends of the Everglades) sought an injunction to force the Water District to get a permit under the Clean Water Act's National Pollution Discharge Elimination System (NPDES) program before pumping the polluted canal water into the lake. The court allowed a number of interveners to enter the lawsuit. Asserting that the pollution of Lake Okeechobee threatens its way of life, the Miccosukee Tribe joined on the plaintiffs' side. The United States, "on behalf of" the EPA and the Corps, joined on the defense side, as did the U.S. Sugar Corporation.

. . . [W]e turn now to whether the S-2, S-3, and S-4 pumps require NPDES permits. The Clean Water Act bans the "discharge of any pollutant" without a permit. 33 U.S.C. §§ 1311, 1342(a)(1). "Discharge" is defined as "any addition of any pollutant to navigable waters from any point source." 33 U.S.C. § 1362(12).

It is undisputed that the agricultural and industrial runoff in the canals contains "pollutants," that Lake Okeechobee and the canals are "navigable waters," and that these three pump stations are "point sources" even though they add nothing to the water as they move it along. *See* S. Fla. Water Mgmt. Dist. v. Miccosukee Tribe, 541 U.S. 95, 102, 105 (2004). The question is whether moving an existing pollutant from one navigable water body to another is an "addition . . . to navigable waters" of that pollutant.[4] The district court decided that it is, but that decision

[4] The permitting requirement does not apply unless the bodies of water are meaningfully distinct. Miccosukee, 541 U.S. at 112, The district court concluded that Lake Okeechobee and the agricultural canals are meaningfully distinct based on ten fact findings that it detailed at considerable length. . . . Given the fact findings the district court made, we are satisfied that the agricultural canals and Lake Okeechobee are meaningfully distinct water bodies.

came before the EPA adopted its regulation. Our review is de novo. United States v. DBB, Inc., 180 F.3d 1277, 1281 (11th Cir. 1999).

The Water District's central argument is based on the "unitary waters" theory. That theory is derived from the dictionary definition of the word "addition," which is not defined in the Act. *See generally* S.D. Warren Co. v. Me. Bd. of Envtl. Prot., 547 U.S. 370, 376 (2006) (stating that an undefined statutory term is to be read "in accordance with its ordinary or natural meaning" (quotation omitted)). The dictionary definition of "addition" is "to join, annex, or unite" so as to increase the overall number or amount of something. Webster's Third New International Dictionary 24 (1993).

The unitary waters theory holds that it is not an "addition . . . to navigable waters" to move existing pollutants from one navigable water to another. An addition occurs, under this theory, only when pollutants first enter navigable waters from a point source, not when they are moved between navigable waters. The metaphor the Supreme Court has adopted to explain the unitary waters theory is: "If one takes a ladle of soup from a pot, lifts it above the pot, and pours it back into the pot, one has not 'added' soup or anything else to the pot." *Miccosukee*, 541 U.S. at 110 (alteration and quotation marks omitted). Under that metaphor the navigable waters of the United States are not a multitude of different pots, but one pot. Ladling pollution from one navigable water to another does not add anything to the pot. So no NPDES permit is required to do that.

The unitary waters theory has a low batting average. In fact, it has struck out in every court of appeals where it has come up to the plate. *See, e.g.,* Catskill Mountains Ch. of Trout Unlimited, Inc. v. City of New York *(Catskills I)*, 273 F.3d 481, 491 (2d Cir. 2001) ("[T]he transfer of water containing pollutants from one body of water to another, distinct body of water is plainly an addition and thus a 'discharge' that demands an NPDES permit."); Catskill Mountains Ch. of Trout Unlimited, Inc. v. City of New York (*Catskills II*), 451 F.3d 77, 83 (2d Cir. 2006) (concluding that "[t]he City also reasserts the unitary-water theory of navigable waters. Our rejection of this theory in *Catskills I*, however, is . . . not undermined" by *Miccosukee*, 541 U.S. 95); Dague v. City of Burlington, 935 F.2d 1343, 1354–55 (2d Cir. 1991) (rejecting the idea that pollutants are "added" only on first entry into any navigable water); Dubois v. U.S. Dep't of Agric., 102 F.3d 1273, 1296 (1st Cir. 1996) ("[T]here is no basis in law or fact for the district court's 'singular entity' [unitary waters] theory."); N. Plains Res. Council v. Fidelity Exploration and Dev., 325 F.3d 1155, 1163 (9th Cir. 2003). Even the Supreme Court has called a strike or two on the theory, stating in *Miccosukee* that "several NPDES provisions might be read to suggest a view contrary to the unitary waters approach." 541 U.S. at 107. The Court has not, however, called the theory out yet.

We have no controlling circuit precedent on the unitary waters theory. We did at one time decide to reject it, but that decision was vacated. . . .

In *Miccosukee*, we addressed whether the law required an NPDES permit before polluted water could be moved through the S-9 pump from some particular Everglades canals into a water conservation area. 280 F.3d at 1367. In a footnote, we declined to adopt the unitary waters theory. *Id.* at 1368 n. 5 ("We reject the Water District's argument that no addition of pollutants can occur unless pollutants are added from the outside world insofar as the Water District contends the outside world cannot include another body of navigable waters."). Instead we said that "the receiving body of water is the relevant body of navigable water" and that "the relevant inquiry is whether—but for the point source—the pollutants would have been added to the receiving body of water." *Id.* at 1368. For that proposition we cited *Catskills I*, a Second Circuit decision rejecting the unitary waters theory. Because the polluted canal water would not have flowed into the conservation area but for S-9's pumping, we concluded that S-9 was adding pollutants to a meaningfully distinct water body, so an NPDES permit was required. *Id.* at 1368–69. The Supreme Court vacated our decision and remanded for further factfindings, however, because the existing record did not convince it that the canals and the water conservation area were meaningfully distinct water bodies. *Miccosukee*, 541 U.S. at 112. The Court also stated that the Water District's unitary waters argument was to be available on remand. *Id.* at 112.

In sum, all of the existing precedent and the statements in our own vacated decision are against the unitary waters theory. That precedent and those statements take the view that the transfer of pollutants from one meaningfully distinct navigable body of water to another is an "addition . . . to navigable waters" for Clean Water Act permitting purposes. If nothing had changed, we might make it unanimous. But there has been a change. An important one. Under its regulatory authority, the EPA has recently issued a regulation adopting a final rule specifically addressing this very question. Because that regulation was not available at the time of the earlier decisions, they are not precedent against it. We are the first court to address the "addition . . . to navigable waters" issue in light of the regulation—to decide whether the regulation is due *Chevron* deference.

The EPA's new regulation, which became final on June 13, 2008, explains that it was adopted to:

> clarify that water transfers are not subject to regulation under the National Pollution Discharge Elimination System (NPDES) permitting program. This rule defines water transfers as an activity that conveys or connects waters of the United States without subjecting the transferred water to intervening industrial, municipal, or commercial use.

NPDES Water Transfers Rule, 73 Fed. Reg. 33,697–708 (June 13, 2008) (codified at 40 C.F.R. § 122.3(i)). Everyone agrees that the EPA's regulation is entitled to *Chevron* deference if it is a reasonable construction of an ambiguous statute. Under Smiley v. Citibank, 517 U.S. 735, 740–41 (1996), and United States v. Morton, 467 U.S. 822, 835 n.21 (1984), it does not matter that the regulation was proposed and issued well after the beginning of this lawsuit. Neither does it matter if it was done in response to this or similar lawsuits. *See* Barnhart v. Walton, 535 U.S. 212, 221 (2002). Nor does it matter whether the new regulation is a dramatic shift in EPA policy. Natl. Cable & Telecomm. Assoc. v. Brand X Internet Servs., 545 U.S. 967, 981 (2005) ("Agency inconsistency is not a basis for declining to analyze the agency's interpretation under the *Chevron* framework.").

All that matters is whether the regulation is a reasonable construction of an ambiguous statute. *Chevron*, 467 U.S. at 842–43 ("If the intent of Congress is clear, that is the end of the matter; for the court, as well as the agency, must give effect to the unambiguously expressed intent of Congress."). . . .

The Friends of the Everglades' position is that the EPA's regulation does not warrant *Chevron* deference because the meaning of the "addition . . . to navigable waters" language is clear and its lack of ambiguity forecloses the unitary waters theory. *Cf., e.g.,* Ala. Power Co. v. U.S. Dep't of Energy, 307 F.3d 1300, 1312 (11th Cir. 2002) (finding that, because "using traditional tools of statutory construction," the Nuclear Waste Policy Act provision in question was clear, no level of deference applied to the agency's contrary interpretation); *Brand X*, 545 U.S. at 982–83 ("Only a judicial precedent holding that the statute unambiguously forecloses the agency's interpretation, and therefore contains no gap for the agency to fill, displaces a conflicting agency construction."). The defendants have two alternative positions. Their bolder position is that the EPA's regulation mirrors the unambiguous meaning of the statute. Their more modest one is that even if the statute is ambiguous, the regulation is one reasonable interpretation of it. The true conflict, and most of our discussion, centers on whether there is ambiguity. . . .

None of the decisions the parties have thrown our way helps either side much. The Water District's decisions found ambiguity in the relevant provision of the Clean Water Act as it applied to dams involving the same bodies of water, not to pumps transferring pollutants between meaningfully distinct bodies of water. The Friends of the Everglades' decisions, though involving the same factual context, decided only how best to construe the statutory language—not whether that language is ambiguous and could reasonably be construed another way. We turn to that issue now.

The Clean Water Act outlaws "the discharge of any pollutant" subject to several exceptions, one of which is where an NPDES permit is obtained. 33 U.S.C. §§ 1311, 1342(a)(1). "Discharge" includes "any addition of any pollutant to navigable waters from any point source." 33 U.S.C. § 1362(12). "Navigable waters," in turn, is defined as "the waters of the United States." 33 U.S.C. § 1362(7). The Supreme Court has recently instructed that the term "discharge of pollutants" and its definition is "of particular significance" within a "complicated statute." *S.D. Warren Co.*, 547 U.S. at 380.

The question is whether "addition . . . to navigable waters"—meaning addition to "the waters of the United States"—refers to waters in the individual sense or as one unitary whole. Under the Water District's unitary waters theory, "to navigable waters" means to all navigable waters as a singular whole. As a result, pollutants can be added to navigable waters only once, and pollutants that are already in navigable waters are not added to navigable waters again when moved between water bodies. Conversely, the Friends of the Everglades' position is that "to navigable waters" refers to each individual water body. As a result, the statute means "any addition of any pollutant to any navigable waters," even though those are not the words the statute uses. Under the Friends of the Everglades' reading, pollutants existing in one navigable water, like the agricultural canals, are "added . . . to navigable waters" when they are transferred into another navigable water, like Lake Okeechobee.

The common meaning of the term "waters" is not helpful. In ordinary usage "waters" can collectively refer to several different bodies of water such as "the waters of the Gulf coast," or can refer to any one body of water such as "the waters of Mobile Bay." An "addition . . . to navigable waters" could encompass any addition to a single body of navigable water regardless of source (like water pumped from one navigable body of water to another), or it could mean only an addition to the total navigable waters from outside of them (like a factory pumping pollutants into a navigable stream). Because the statutory language could be used either way, we turn next to its immediate context.

The context in which language is used is important. . . . The Water District argues that the context of 33 U.S.C. § 1362(12) demonstrates that Congress intentionally selected each word in the definition of "discharge" to deliver a specific meaning. It asserts that the Friends of the Everglades' reading of the statute would require us to add words to the law, which is impermissible.

"Discharge" is defined in the Act as "[a]ny addition of any pollutant to navigable waters from any point source." 33 U.S.C. § 1362(12). According to the Water District, the conspicuous absence of "any" before "navigable waters" in § 1362(12) supports the unitary waters theory because it implies that Congress was not talking about any navigable water, but about all navigable waters as a whole. The Friends of the Everglades' reading effectively asks us to add a fourth "any" to the statute so that it would read: "Any addition of any pollutant to any navigable waters from any point source." But we are not allowed to add or subtract words from a statute; we cannot rewrite it. . . . Besides, if the meaning of language is plain, no alteration should be necessary to clarify it. The addition or subtraction of words indicates that the unaltered language is not plain.

There is also the fact that Congress knows how to use the term "any navigable water[s]" when it wants to protect individual water bodies instead of navigable waters as a collective whole. Within the Clean Water Act itself, Congress authorized the EPA to investigate "the pollution of any navigable waters," 33 U.S.C. § 1254(a)(3), and referred to the EPA's dissemination of information about changes in the flow "of any navigable waters." 33 U.S.C. § 1314(f)(2)(F). Other water protection statutes also use the term "any navigable water[s]." *See, e.g.*, 33 U.S.C. § 407 ("It shall not be lawful to throw, discharge, or deposit . . . any refuse matter . . . into any navigable water of the United States. . . ."); 33 U.S.C. § 419 ("The Secretary of the Army is authorized . . . to govern the transportation and dumping into any navigable water, or waters adjacent thereto, of dredgings, earth, garbage, and other refuse materials. . . ."); 33 U.S.C. § 512 ("No bridge shall at any time unreasonably obstruct the free navigation of any navigable waters of the United States."). The common use by Congress of "any navigable water" or "any navigable waters" when it intends to protect each individual water body supports the conclusion that the use of the unmodified term "navigable waters" in § 1362(12) (or the use in its definition, "the waters of the United States," at § 1362(7)) means the waters collectively. *See* Delgado v. U.S. Att'y Gen., 487 F.3d 855, 862 (11th Cir. 2007). . . .

Congress common-interp. = waters collectively

The result so far is that we are not persuaded that the meaning of the statutory provision at issue, read either in isolation or in conjunction with similar provisions, is plain one way or the other. The statutory context indicates that sometimes the term "navigable waters" was used in one sense and sometimes in the other sense. . . .

No one disputes that the NPDES program is restricted to point sources. Non-point source pollution, chiefly runoff, is widely recognized as a serious water quality problem, but the NPDES program does not even address it. *See generally Rapanos*, 547 U.S. at 777 (Kennedy, J., concurring) (observing that agricultural runoff from farms along the Mississippi River creates an annual hypoxic "dead zone" in the Gulf of Mexico that is nearly the size of New Jersey); Or. Natural Desert Ass'n v. U.S. Forest Serv., 550 F.3d 778, 780 (9th Cir. 2008) (stating that the "disparate treatment of discharges from point sources and nonpoint sources is an organizational paradigm of the [Clean Water] Act"). Not only are ordinary non-point sources outside the NPDES program, but Congress even created a special exception to the definition of "point source" to exclude agricultural storm water discharges and return flows from irrigation, despite their known, substantially harmful impact on water quality. 33 U.S.C. § 1362(14).

NPDES is ONLY point source

The point is that it may seem inconsistent with the lofty goals of the Clean Water Act to leave out of the permitting process the transfer of pollutants from one navigable body of water to another, but it is no more so than to leave out all non-point sources, allowing agricultural run-offs to create a huge "dead zone" in the Gulf of Mexico. Yet we know the Act does that. What this illustrates is that even when the preamble to legislation speaks single-mindedly and espouses lofty goals, the legislative process serves as a melting pot of competing interests and a face-off of battling factions. What emerges from the conflict to become the enactment is often less pure than the preamble promises. The provisions of legislation reflect compromises cobbled together by competing political forces, and compromise is the enemy of single-mindedness. It is not difficult to believe that the legislative process resulted in a Clean Water Act that leaves more than one gap in the permitting requirements it enacts. Wyeth v. Levine, 555 U.S. 555 (2009) (Thomas, J., concurring) ("Legislators may compromise on a statute that does not fully address a perceived mischief, accepting half a loaf to facilitate a law's enactment." (quotation omitted)); Bd. of Governors v. Dimension Fin. Corp., 474 U.S. 361, 373–74 (1986) ("Application of 'broad purposes' of legislation at the expense of specific provisions ignores the complexity of the problems Congress is called upon to address and the dynamics of legislative action. . . . [T]he final language of the legislation may reflect hard-fought compromises.").

. . . There are two reasonable ways to read the § 1361(12) language "any addition of any pollutant to navigable waters from any point source." One is that it means "any addition . . . to [any] navigable waters;" the other is that it means "any addition . . . to navigable waters [as a whole]." As we have held before, "the existence of two reasonable, competing interpretations is the very definition of ambiguity." United States v. Acosta, 363 F.3d 1141, 1155 (11th Cir. 2004) (quotation marks omitted).

Having concluded that the statutory language is ambiguous, our final issue is whether the EPA's regulation, which accepts the unitary waters theory that transferring pollutants between navigable waters is not an "addition . . . to navigable waters," is a permissible construction of that language. *Chevron*, 467 U.S. at 843. In making that determination, we "need not conclude that the agency construction was . . . the reading the court would have reached if the question initially had arisen in a judicial proceeding." *Id.* at 837, 843 n.11; *see also id.* at 844 ("[A] court may not substitute its own construction of a statutory provision for a reasonable interpretation made by the administrator of an agency."). Because the EPA's construction is one of the two readings we have found is reasonable, we cannot say that it is "arbitrary, capricious, or manifestly contrary to the statute." *Id.* at 844.

Sometimes it is helpful to strip a legal question of the contentious policy interests attached to it and think about it in the abstract using a hypothetical. Consider the issue this way: Two buckets sit side by side, one with four marbles in it and the other with none. There is a rule prohibiting "any addition of any marbles to buckets by any person." A person comes along, picks up two marbles from the first bucket, and drops them into the second bucket. Has the marble-mover "add[ed] any marbles to buckets"? On one hand, as the Friends of the Everglades might argue, there are now two marbles in a bucket where there were none before, so an addition of marbles has occurred. On the other hand, as the Water District might argue and as the EPA would decide, there were four marbles in buckets before, and there are still four marbles in buckets, so no addition of marbles has occurred. Whatever position we might take if we had to pick one side or the other we cannot say that either side is unreasonable.

Like the marbles rule, the Clean Water Act's language about "any addition of any pollutant to navigable waters from any point source," 33 U.S.C. § 1362(12), is ambiguous. The EPA's regulation adopting the unitary waters theory is a reasonable, and therefore permissible, construction of the language. Unless and until the EPA rescinds or Congress overrides the regulation, we must give effect to it.

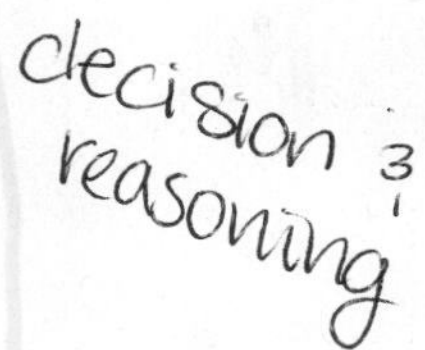


In the defendants' appeal, we REVERSE the district court's judgment that the operation of the S-2, S-3, and S-4 pumps without NPDES permits violates the Clean Water Act. We DISMISS AS MOOT the plaintiffs' cross-appeal from the dismissal of the Water District on Eleventh Amendment grounds.

---

## QUESTIONS AND DISCUSSION

**1.** From the perspective of advancing water resource management goals, does the "unitary waters" argument make any sense? Why would Congress require a permit to discharge pollutants from a point source into one discrete waterbody, but not to transfer the polluted water from that waterbody to another? Notably, not all courts have agreed with the Eleventh Circuit's analysis with regard to the reasonableness of the Water Transfer Rule. As of 2016, its validity remains in question after the Eleventh Circuit later found it did not have subject matter jurisdiction over the challenge, and a federal district court in New York invalidated the rule as arbitrary and capricious. *See* Catskill Mountains Chapter of Trout Unlimited, Inc. v. EPA, 8 F. Supp. 3d 500, 567 (S.D.N.Y. 2014); Friends of the Everglades v. EPA, 699 F.3d 1280 (11th Cir. 2012) (finding that original jurisdiction to review rule was in the district court and not in the circuit courts). *See also* Chris Reagen, *The Water Transfers Rule: How an EPA Rule Threatens to Undermine the Clean Water Act*, 83 U. COLO. L. REV. 307 (2011).

**2.** Although the setting of the Everglades may suggest that this is an exotic and unique case, as shown in the other cases the Eleventh Circuit cites, the transfer of water from one water body to another is fairly common in many parts of the country, particularly in the West, as a water supply management technique.

**3.** Can you think of examples other than the one in this case where water is transferred within and between navigable waters as part of industrial or agricultural activities?

**4.** What about stormwater discharges from roads, buildings, or other surfaces that contain pollutants? Are those point sources under the CWA? In 33 U.S.C. § 1342(p), Congress exempted certain discharges of stormwater runoff because of the difficulty of managing such discharges. Specifically, that provision exempts from NDPES permitting "discharges composed entirely of stormwater," § 1342(p)(1), but directs EPA to require permits for stormwater discharges "associated with industrial activity." § 1342(p)(2)(B). Congress also directed EPA to develop separate discharge regulations for municipal storm sewer systems (called MS4s) and EPA has done so, with different phases of regulations for different size cities. *See* CLAUDIA COPELAND, CONGRESSIONAL RESEARCH SERVICE, STORMWATER PERMITS: STATUS OF EPA'S REGULATORY PROGRAM (July 12, 2012); 80 Fed. Reg. 34,403 (June 16, 2015) (EPA regulation creating new NDPES multi-sector general permit (MSGP) for various stormwater discharges from industrial facilities).

In 2013, the U.S. Supreme Court considered whether stormwater discharges from logging roads were stormwater discharges "associated with industrial activities" requiring a NPDES permit. Just prior to oral argument, EPA issued a rule stating that the stormwater discharges from logging roads were not associated with "industrial activities" because such activities within the logging context are limited to more direct logging operations such rock crushing, gravel washing, log sorting, and log storage facilities. In its decision, the Court reversed a Ninth Circuit decision finding the stormwater discharges from logging roads required NPDES permits and held instead that the activities at issue were not point sources and did not require a NPDES permit. *See* Decker v. Northwest Environmental Defense Center, 133 S. Ct. 1326 (2013). *See also* 77 Fed. Reg. 72,970 (Dec. 7, 2012) (amending various provisions of 40 C.F.R. pt. 122 to state that a NPDES permit is not required for stormwater discharges from logging roads).

**5.** According to research by Eric Biber and J.B. Ruhl, "roughly 6800 major pollution sources and 44,000 nonmajor sources are required to hold a specific NPDES permit, and over 133,000 nonmajor sources are authorized by a general NPDES permit." Eric Biber & J.B. Ruhl, *The Permit Power Revisited: The Theory and Practice of Regulatory Permits in the Administrative State*, 64 DUKE L.J. 133, 150 (2014).

---

The CWA contains several different performance standards to guide EPA regulations covering different classes and categories of both dischargers and pollutants. For instance, existing discharges were to employ "best practicable" control technology (BPT) by 1977 and "best available" technology (BAT) by 1983. New dischargers were required to meet BAT requirements. Congress later extended the BAT deadline for toxic pollutants to 1984 and created a new, more relaxed, standard for conventional pollutants known as "best conventional" technology (BCT) to be implemented by 1984. Of course, Congress later extended these deadlines again as it took EPA far longer than expected to establish the relevant effluent limitations. The following case explores the various CWA technology-based standards, particularly as applied to "bypasses," or diversions of waste streams from effluent treatment facilities.

## Natural Resources Defense Council, Inc. v. U.S. EPA

United States Court of Appeals for the D.C. Circuit, 1987.
822 F.2d 104.

■ STARR, CIRCUIT JUDGE:

The objective of the Clean Water Act is to "restore and maintain the chemical, physical, and biological integrity of the Nation's waters." 33 U.S.C. § 1251 (1982). Under the Act, the discharge of any pollutant into the navigable waters of the United States is unlawful. *Id.* § 1311(a). This basic rule admits of a critical exception—the discharge of pollutants is permitted if the source obtains and complies with a permit that limits the amounts and kinds of pollutants which can lawfully be discharged. Thus, the cornerstone of the Clean Water Act's pollution control scheme is the National Pollution Discharge Elimination System (NPDES) permit program, established under the Federal Water Pollution Control Act Amendments of 1972. *See* 33 U.S.C. § 1342 (1982).

This opinion addresses the various challenges mounted by the Industry petitioners, on the one hand, and NRDC, on the other, to regulations which (1) define "new source"; (2) grant a ten-year grace period to new sources from more stringent technology-based standards of performance; (3) require permit applicants to identify all toxic pollutants used or manufactured in the industrial process; and (4) prohibit "bypasses," that is, diversions of waste streams from effluent treatment facilities. . . .

The fundamental premise of the Clean Water Act is that "the discharge of any pollutant by any person shall be unlawful" except as otherwise permitted under the Act. 33 U.S.C. § 1311(a) (1982). A "discharge of a pollutant" is defined, in pertinent part, as "any addition of any pollutant to [the waters of the United States] from any point source." *Id.* § 1362(12)(A). The term "pollutant" is broadly defined to include, among other things, solid waste; industrial, municipal, and agricultural waste; sewage sludge; biological or radioactive materials; wrecked or discarded equipment; heat; rock; sand; and cellar dirt. *Id.* § 1362(6). A "point source" is "any discernible, confined and discrete conveyance." *Id.* § 1362(14).

Thus, the Act allows the discharge of pollutants from a point source only in compliance with limitations established in the Act. The Act imposes effluent limitations[4] through two programs. The first applies water-quality based standards. *Id.* § 1313. It imposes on a point source effluent limitations that are based on the amounts and kinds of pollutants in the water in which the point source discharges. *Id.* § 1312(a). The second applies technology-based standards. It imposes on a point source effluent limitations based on how much of a reduction technology can achieve. *Id.* §§ 1311(b), (e), 1314(b).

To describe briefly the second approach, technology-based effluent limitations, as their name suggests, derive from standards formulated with reference to pollution control technology. *See id.* § 1314(b). The standard applicable in a particular case depends on the kind of pollutant—toxic, conventional, or non-conventional—and on whether the point source is a new or existing source. Under section 301, existing sources must achieve effluent limits on nonconventional pollutants that reflect the reduction in effluents that can be achieved through "the application of the best available technology economically achievable." *Id.* § 1311(b)(2)(A). This is known as the "BAT" standard. New sources, on the other hand, are subject to stricter effluent limitations with respect to nonconventional pollutants. Section 306 prescribes new source performance standards (NSPS) that must reflect the "best available demonstrated control technology." *Id.* § 1316(a)(1). This more stringent standard for new sources is known as the "BACT" standard. Toxic pollutants, whether from new or existing sources, are subject to effluent limitations based on application of the BAT standard. *Id.* § 1317(a)(2). Finally, by 1984 new and existing sources were to achieve effluent reductions in "conventional" pollutants that reflect the application of the "best conventional pollutant control technology," known as a "BCT" standard. *Id.* §§ 1311(b)(2)(E), 1314(a)(4), (b)(4)(B).

In addition to technology-based standards, Section 302 of the Act provides for water-quality related effluent limitations. These limitations supplement technology-based standards and protect specific bodies of water. *Id.* § 1312. Whenever a technology-based effluent limitation is insufficient to make a particular body of water fit for the uses for which it is needed, the EPA is to devise a water-quality based limitation that will be sufficient to the task. *Id.* § 1312(a).

These national standards establish a nationwide floor for the achievement of pollution control. At the same time, the Act contemplates the delegation of permit-writing and enforcement authority (as well as some standard-setting authority) to the several States. To date, thirty-seven States have assumed responsibility for issuing NPDES permits.[2]

---

[4] Effluent limitations consist of restrictions on quantities, rates, or concentrations of pollutants and compliance schedules for the achievement of such restrictions. *See id.* § 1362(11).

[2] [As of 2010, 46 out of 50 states had delegated NDPES authority. The only states that do not have delegated authority are Idaho, Massachusetts, New Hampshire, and New Mexico.—Eds.]

Both national and state effluent standards are enforced through the NPDES permit program. The NPDES permits thus "transform generally applicable effluent limitations and other standards . . . into the obligations (including a timetable for compliance) of the individual discharger." EPA v. California ex rel. State Water Resources Control Board, 426 U.S. 200, 205 (1976). All dischargers are required to obtain a permit, which is issued after public notice and an opportunity for public hearing. 33 U.S.C. § 1342(a)(1), (b)(3).

Permits are issued only so long as the point source meets all applicable effluent limitations. *Id.* § 1342(a)(1). If no national standards have been promulgated for a particular category of point sources, the permit writer is authorized to use, on a case-by-case basis, "best professional judgment" to impose "such conditions as the permit writer determines are necessary to carry out the provisions of [the Clean Water Act.]" *Id.* Thus, compliance with a permit is generally deemed to constitute compliance with the Act's requirements. *Id.* § 1342(k).

The effluent limitations set forth in an NPDES permit are ordinarily drafted in terms of limitations on the amount, rate, or concentration of a specific pollutant. Permits may also include limitations on key generic parameters, such as pH or biochemical oxygen demand (BOD). Permits generally include other provisions, such as monitoring and reporting requirements, compliance schedules, and management practices. *See id.* §§ 1314, 1318, 1342(a)(2). . . .

In the 1984 final regulations, EPA chose to retain its regulation prohibiting bypasses, which are defined as "the intentional diversion of waste streams from any portion of a treatment facility." 40 C.F.R. § 122.41(m)(1)(i) (1985). Bypasses which do not cause effluent limits to be exceeded are permissible in order to perform "essential maintenance to assure efficient operation." *Id.* § 122.41(m)(2). The regulation also permits bypasses which may cause effluent limitations to be exceeded if such bypasses are "unavoidable to prevent loss of life, personal injury, or severe property damage." *Id.* § 122.41(m)(4). The regulation thus ensures that treatment systems chosen by the permittee are operated as anticipated by the permit writer, that is, as they are designed to be operated and in accordance with the conditions set forth in the permit.

Industry attacks the bypass regulation as "arbitrary and unwarranted" on two principal grounds, namely, that the bypass prohibition is (1) unauthorized by the Clean Water Act, and (2) inconsistent with the policies underlying the Act. We conclude, however, that EPA enjoyed authority to adopt such a regulation; that the regulation directly promotes the goals of the Act; that it is fully consistent with the technology-forcing framework of the Act; and that the rule is reasonable.

To return for a moment to basic principles, the Clean Water Act is, as we have seen, quite broad in its sweep. EPA is not limited by statute to the task of establishing effluent standards and issuing permits, but is empowered by section 501(a) of the Act to prescribe regulations necessary to carry out its functions under the Act. 33 U.S.C. § 1361(a). It is also clear that permissible conditions set forth in NPDES permits are not limited to establishing limits on effluent discharge. To the contrary, Congress has seen fit to empower EPA to prescribe as wide a range of permit conditions as the agency deems appropriate in order to assure compliance with applicable effluent limits. 33 U.S.C. § 1342(a)(2); *see also id.* § 1314(e). Keeping in mind that, under *Chevron*, the court must defer to the agency's construction as long as it is a reasonable interpretation of the statute, *Chevron*, 467 U.S. at 843–45, a permit condition prohibiting bypass seems to us to fall within the agency's broad statutory authority.

Faced with the breadth of the statutory language, Industry mounts its principal challenge—that the regulation is contrary to one element of legislative intent informing the Clean Water Act, namely to avoid dictating specific treatment technologies, thus encouraging experimentation with alternative means of pollution reduction. Statements in the legislative history indicate that this goal would be attained through imposition of end-of-the-pipe discharge limitations rather than a national prescription of a specific, uniform "best technology." This is a policy, we hasten to note, articulated in the legislative history, although not in the Act itself. *See* S. Rep. No. 414, 92d Cong., 1st Sess. 59 (1971), *reprinted in* 1972 Legislative History at 1477; H.R. Rep. No. 911, 92d Cong., 2d Sess. 107 (1972), *reprinted in* 1972 Legislative History at 794.

The pedigree of the policy itself aside, Industry concedes that the bypass regulation does not, in fact, dictate that a specific treatment technology be employed; instead, the regulation requires that a system be operated as designed and according to the conditions of the NPDES permit. Industry argues, however, that requiring the treatment system chosen by the discharger to be operated without bypass, even where the effluent limitations are not exceeded, is barred under a faithful discernment of Congress' intent.

We do not agree. First, this argument requires the assumption that "on-off" regulation constitutes a choice of treatment technologies. Since that sort of option does nothing to further the goal of exploring diverse treatment technologies, we are unpersuaded that the "on-off" decision is the sort of technological choice Congress intended to leave entirely to the discharger.

Second, Industry ignores other, highly pertinent policies repeatedly expressed in the statute itself and which are furthered by this regulation. The first principle of the statute is, as we have seen, that it is unlawful to pollute at all. The Clean Water Act does not permit pollution whenever that activity might be deemed reasonable or necessary; rather, the statute provides that pollution is permitted only when discharged under the conditions or limitations of a permit. 33 U.S.C. § 1311(a); NRDC v.

Costle, 568 F.2d 1369, 1374–77 (D.C. Cir. 1977). The foremost national goal enunciated by Congress is the complete elimination of the discharge of pollutants. 33 U.S.C. § 1251(a)(1). This ambitious objective is underscored by the statutory instruction that "new source performance standards" not only reflect the best technology but also include, "where practicable, a standard permitting no discharge of pollutants." *Id.* § 1316(a)(1) (emphasis added). In view of the far-reaching goals of the Act, compliance with an effluent standard cannot fairly be viewed as the ultimate object of the statute. In the context of a statute which seeks the elimination of pollution, it is difficult to believe that Congress intended that dischargers be entitled to shut off their treatment facilities and "coast" simply because they were momentarily not in danger of violating effluent limitations.

Third, Industry's argument, if accepted, would undermine the statutory framework of technology-based standards. As we have seen, the regulatory scheme is structured around a series of increasingly stringent technology-based standards (beginning with the implementation of the best "practicable" technology (BPT), *id.* § 1311(b)(1), and progressing toward implementation of pollution controls to the full extent of the best technology which would become available (BAT), *id.* § 1311(b)(2). New sources would, again, be subject to the most stringent technology-based standards of all, namely "new source performance standards."[18] *Id.* § 1316(b)(1)(B). In setting new source standards, EPA is statutorily required to give serious consideration to a standard permitting no discharge of pollutants. *Id.* § 1316(a)(1). Thus, the most salient characteristic of this statutory scheme, articulated time and again by its architects and embedded in the statutory language, is that it is technology-forcing. See S. Rep. No. 414, 92d Cong., 1st Sess. 42 (1971), reprinted in 1972 Legislative History at 1460; 117 Cong. Rec. 38,808 (1971) (Sen. Montoya), reprinted in 1972 Legislative History at 1278; 118 Cong. Rec. 33,693, 33,696 (1972) (Sen. Muskie), reprinted in 1972 Legislative History at 163, 170; Tanners' Council, Inc. v. Train, 540 F.2d 1188, 1195 (4th Cir. 1976). The essential purpose of this series of progressively more demanding technology-based standards was not only to stimulate but to press development of new, more efficient and effective technologies. This policy is expressed as a statutory mandate, not simply as a goal. The bypass prohibition comports with this goal, because it requires that the applicable treatment technology, implemented for the purpose of achieving pollution reduction equivalent to the "best technology," be operated as designed. Considering the nature of the statutory scheme, which pushes all dischargers to achieve ever-increasing efficiencies and improvements in pollution control, it is difficult to find a Congressional intent that dischargers who are achieving their current target levels of pollution control be at liberty to

[18] Such sources must implement the "best available demonstrated control technology," which presumably would include more effective alternatives than those available to existing sources.

shut down temporarily for no reason other than the belief that they will not be in technical violation of their permit. Such bypasses appear, rather, at odds with the statutory scheme. . . .

Industry next argues that the regulation is a de facto effluent limitation for pollutants which the agency has chosen not to regulate specifically through a section 304 effluent limitation. This argument is prompted by EPA's explanation of the bypass regulation as a means of minimizing the discharge of indirectly regulated pollutants. Industry's argument suggests that the agency's decision not to regulate a pollutant with an effluent guideline works a waiver of its power to regulate that pollutant. EPA replies, with persuasive force, that it frequently does not impose specific effluent guidelines for certain pollutants, especially in regulating toxics, but instead treats other "regulated" pollutants as "indicators" of the probable level of the unregulated pollutants because the model treatment technology (the basis for effluent guidelines) removes both. *See* 49 Fed. Reg. at 38,000 38,036–37. The agency admits that it cannot be absolutely certain that the "unregulated" pollutants are indeed being removed in all cases, for a discharger may utilize a dissimilar technology; the regulation, however, is defended as a workable and efficient (for both agency and permittee) means of regulating the numerous pollutants which do not have individual effluent limitations.

Industry's argument in this respect fails for the reason that the de facto limitations which Industry has identified are due to EPA's practice of indirect regulation of pollutants, not to the bypass regulation. Industry does not challenge the practice of indirectly regulating pollutants without promulgation of specific effluent limits under section 304. This is unsurprising, for this practice has been upheld in several instances. *See, e.g.,* Reynolds Metals Co. v. EPA, 760 F.2d 549 (4th Cir. 1985) (total toxic organics (TTO) not regulated with BAT standard because TTO is controlled through regulation of oil and grease; copper, lead, zinc, and manganese not regulated with BAT standards because they are removed by model technology if operated efficiently enough to remove other pollution parameters).

Since the bypass regulation is not a de facto effluent limitation, Industry's related argument—that the record shows the costs of regulation to outweigh its benefits—begins from a mistaken premise. The Clean Water Act requires EPA to undertake a cost-benefit calculus in establishing effluent limitations. *See, e.g.*, 33 U.S.C. § 1314(b)(1)(B); 118 Cong. Rec. 33,696 (1972), *reprinted in* 1972 Legislative History at 169–70. Neither the statute nor the legislative history, however, imposes such a requirement when EPA issues regulations under its broad authority to implement the Act. *See* 33 U.S.C. § 1361(a). Indeed, the bypass regulation is not easily susceptible to cost-benefit analysis. As noted above, the agency admits that it is difficult to measure the reduction of pollutants that are indirectly regulated under this regulation. Thus, the costs and benefits of the regulation will vary, depending, among other things, on how it applies to a particular operation. Until it is so applied, the specific facts necessary to conduct a cost-benefit analysis are missing. In short, Industry's argument about cost-benefit analysis has no basis in law or logic.

We are mindful that Congress did not specifically address the question whether bypasses may be permitted. But, as *Chevron* teaches, in the face of Congressional silence, we cannot merely substitute our judgment for that of the agency. Our role is more limited, and that is to determine whether EPA's decision to prohibit bypasses reflects an acceptable interpretation of the Clean Water Act. *See, e.g.,* Young v. Community Nutrition Institute, 476 U.S. 974 (1986). The agency's adoption of a bypass regulation which incorporates two broad and sensible exceptions (bypasses which do not cause effluent limits to be exceeded for purposes of essential maintenance and bypasses which may cause effluent limits to be exceeded in order to avoid personal injury or severe property damage) is, in our view, reasonable and therefore lawful.

---

### QUESTIONS AND DISCUSSION

**1.** Note that the court holds that EPA can, but does not have to use cost-benefit analysis in establishing CW implementing regulations. As you proceed through the remainder of the textbook consider how Congress has allowed (and not allowed) cost-benefit analysis in setting standards for pollution prevention in a variety of areas. When should Congress allow for cost-benefit analysis and when should it prohibit it? Is it Congress that should make the decision in the first instance or, in is it best for EPA to have the discretion to use or not use cost-benefit analysis in light of changing technology and changing environmental protection needs?

**2.** The EPA regulation at issue in the case, 40 C.F.R. § 122.41(m), currently prohibit bypasses except if such bypasses are "unavoidable to prevent loss of life, personal injury, or severe property damage" and there are no "feasible alternatives" to the bypass, such as "the use of auxiliary treatment facilities, retention of untreated wastes, or maintenance during normal periods of equipment downtime." In a 1999 decision, the U.S. District Court for the Northern District of Ohio held that any bypass which occurs because of inadequate plant capacity is unauthorized to the extent there are "feasible alternatives" which include the construction or installation of additional treatment capacity. United States v. City of Toledo, 63 F. Supp. 2d 834 (N.D. Ohio 1999).

---

## D. THE NONPOINT SOURCE POLLUTION PROBLEM

As shown earlier, under the CWA, a point source is a discharge of regulated pollutants from "any discernable, confined and discrete conveyance, including but not limited to any pipe, ditch, channel, tunnel, conduit, well, discrete fissure, container, rolling stock, concentrated animal feeding operation, or vessel or other floating craft, from which pollutants are or may be discharged." 33 U.S.C. § 1362(14). As all-encompassing as this definition seems, it misses a huge component of water pollution sources. First, by exclusion, any regulated pollutant not so discharged is a so-called nonpoint source of pollution. This includes, significantly, overland runoff from rain and snowmelt that is not collected in storm sewers. As EPA explains in *What Is Nonpoint Source Pollution?*, http://water.epa.gov/polwaste/nps/whatis.cfm:

> Unlike pollution from industrial and sewage treatment plants, nonpoint source (NPS) pollution comes from many diffuse sources. NPS pollution is caused by rainfall or snowmelt moving over and through the ground. As the runoff moves, it picks up and carries away natural and human-made pollutants, finally depositing them into lakes, rivers, wetlands, coastal waters, and even our underground sources of drinking water. These pollutants include:
>
> - Excess fertilizers, herbicides, and insecticides from agricultural lands and residential areas;
> - Oil, grease, and toxic chemicals from urban runoff and energy production;
> - Sediment from improperly managed construction sites, crop and forest lands, and eroding streambanks;
> - Salt from irrigation practices and acid drainage from abandoned mines;
> - Bacteria and nutrients from livestock, pet wastes, and faulty septic systems;
> - Atmospheric deposition and hydromodification.

Second, by definition, most agricultural pollution, including irrigation return flows carried, believe it or not, *in ditches and pipes*, is not point source pollution. *See* 33 U.S.C. § 1362(14). Therein lies the problem: EPA has identified agricultural pollution as the leading cause of impairment to our nation's rivers, lakes, and wetlands, and not far behind in all of those cases is urban runoff. In other words, today's leading causes of impairment to freshwater resources are the two significant sources of water pollution that are *not* regulated as point sources under the CWA.

So how has federal law managed these nonpoint sources? Not very well. Efforts to address nonpoint source water pollution in the CWA and other statutes have been feeble, unfocused, and underfunded. Section 208 of the CWA requires states to develop areawide waste treatment management plans that include a process for identifying nonpoint sources and establishing feasible control measures. *See* 33 U.S.C. § 1288(a). With high expectations for this program, Congress used it as the rationale for moving irrigation return flows from the point source side of the CWA to the nonpoint source side of the CWA. *See* S. Rep. No. 370, at 35 (1977), *reprinted in* 1977 U.S.C.C.A.N. 4326, 4360 ("All such sources, regardless of the manner in which the flow was applied to the agricultural lands, and regardless of the discrete nature of the entry point, are more appropriately treated under the requirements of Section 208"). Similarly, in the 1987 amendments, Congress added Section 319 to the statute to require states to prepare "state assessment reports" that identify waters that cannot reasonably be expected to meet water quality standards because of nonpoint source pollution. 33 U.S.C. § 1329(a). States must prepare "state management programs" prescribing the "best management practices" to control sources of nonpoint pollution. When EPA approves a state's assessment reports and the management plans, the state is eligible for financial assistance to implement its programs. In April 2013, EPA published a new set of guidelines for nonpoint source program grants to states under CWA Section 319. *See* http://water.epa.gov/polwaste/nps/cwact.cfm. These revised guidelines provide updated program direction, an increased emphasis on watershed project implementation in watersheds with impaired waters, and increased accountability measures.

In the absence of any concrete, enforceable federal blueprint for addressing nonpoint source pollution, the efficacy of the Section 208 and Section 319 programs depended largely on state initiative to develop new approaches. It is little surprise, then, that neither Section 208 nor Section 319 has achieved meaningful results. An EPA Federal Advisory Committee summed up the weakness of the Section 208 and 319 programs by explaining that "EPA had no 'hammer' provision for states not adopting programs and no ability to establish a program if a State chose not to." EPA TMDL Federal Advisory Committee, Discussion Paper, Nonpoint Source-Only Waters 5 (1997).

Congress thus took a more aggressive step in Section 6217 of the Coastal Zone Act Reauthorization Amendments of 1990. Pub. L. No. 101–508, Title VI, § 6217 (1990). This legislation amended the Coastal Zone Management Act (CZMA) to add a requirement that any state with a federally approved coastal zone management program must develop a Coastal Nonpoint Pollution Program subject to federal review and approval. States must identify land uses leading to nonpoint pollution and develop measures to apply "best available nonpoint pollution control practices, technologies, processes, siting criteria, operating methods, or other alternatives." 16 U.S.C. § 1455b(g)(5). When EPA and the National Oceanic and Atmospheric Administration approve a state's Coastal Nonpoint Pollution Program, the federal government agrees not to fund, authorize, or carry out projects inconsistent with the state's plan. *Id.* 1455b(k). For coastal states, this requirement can serve as an impetus for more aggressive regulation of nonpoint source pollution generally, though funding assistance from the federal government is woefully short of the expected cost of Coastal Nonpoint Pollution Program plan preparation and implementation for the states.

By the mid-1990s, therefore, it had become clear that the primary objective of environmental policy for freshwater resources had to be getting a handle on nonpoint source water pollution, but that significant obstacles would need to be overcome, not the least of which is the gaping hole in the CWA. Congress remained essentially inert on such matters through the 1990s. Thus, on October 18, 1997, during the Clean Water Act's 25th Anniversary celebration, then Vice President Gore requested that the Secretary of Agriculture and the EPA Administrator, in consultation with affected federal agencies, devise an action plan to address enhanced protection from public health threats posed by water pollution; more effective control of polluted runoff; and promotion of water quality protection on a watershed basis. The result, the *Clean Water Action Plan: Restoring and Protecting America's Waters* (CWAP), outlined an ambitious agenda for coordinating existing federal water conservation authorities. A principal focus of this component of the CWAP agenda was bringing nonpoint source pollution more fully within the federal water policy umbrella, but its scope also extended to wetland conservation policy and the broader ambition of developing a watershed-based framework for resource management.

Subsequent administrations also have announced comprehensive water quality plans: The Bush Administration in 2003 unveiled the *500-Day Water Quality Plan: Twice as Clean by 2015*, and the Obama Administration in 2011 announced the *Clean Water Framework*. To implement such plans, EPA develops a Strategic Plan by which it is able to set goals and monitor progress towards improved water quality throughout the nation. Specifically, the plan is intended to provide quantifiable estimates of how EPA's planned actions will improve human and environmental health standards. In order to comply with the Government Performance and Results Act of 1993 (Pub. L. 103–62, Aug. 3, 1993, 107 Stat. 285, codified in various sections), EPA is required to update this Strategic Plan every three years. Currently, EPA is operating under the 2014–2018 Strategic Plan, which with regard to water, directs EPA to continue effective implementation of core national water programs, help sustain and secure the networks of pipes and treatment facilities that constitute the nation's water infrastructure, and apply a watershed approach to restoring polluted waters across the country. The plan also highlights two agency priority goals with regard to water: (1) improving public health protection for persons served by small drinking water systems (which account for more than 97% of public water systems) and strengthen the technical, managerial, and financial capacity of those systems; and (2) enhancing state nonpoint source programs to address the nation's largest source of water pollution. In recent years, the EPA has also issued a National Water Program Guidance on an annual basis to explain how EPA will work with states, tribes, and territories to improve the nation's waters and implement provisions of the Strategic Plan. See https://www.epa.gov/water-planning-evaluation/national-water-program-guidance.

---

## QUESTIONS AND DISCUSSION

**1.** Knowing what we now know about their impact on water quality, why hasn't Congress regulated nonpoint sources more aggressively? One factor is that they are fundamentally different from point sources in terms of amenability to regulation. Point sources such as chemical plants and wastewater treatment facilities generally are highly regulated enterprises. They discharge water pollutants in discrete, easily monitored locations and events. The discharge is usually a byproduct or waste of a technological process that can be altered with technological solutions. Regulation of point sources, in other words, is primarily a technology issue, not a land use issue. Most categories of nonpoint sources, by contrast, are diffuse and diverse land uses. Take farms for example. There are about two million farms in the United States today, using over 900 million acres for crop and livestock production. Differences in weather, soil, and other local factors lead to tremendous diversity of farming practices around the nation. While modern farming is more technologically intensive than in the past, it is still primarily a local land use practice, and the federal government has traditionally been reluctant to regulate local land uses directly. Still, given how significant the nonpoint source pollution problem is, does it surprise you that Congress has responded how it has? For a discussion of the challenges of addressing water pollution from agricultural operations under the Clean Water Act, see Jan G. Laitos & Heidi Ruckriegle, *The Clean Water Act and the Challenges of Agricultural Pollution*, 37 VT. L. REV. 1033 (2013).

**2.** In addition to the several programs initiated under the CWA specifically to address nonpoint source pollution, over 30 other federal programs deal with nonpoint source pollution in some way or another. Many of these programs provide funding assistance and incentives to states or private actors to improve nonpoint source pollution management-for example, to improve farm runoff control practices. Some of the programs address actions on federal lands, where the solution is more amenable to direct regulation of private actors or altering federal agency action. Overall, the federal government spends over $3 billion per year implementing this array of programs, with EPA, USDA, and the Department of the Interior as the lead agencies. For an overview of the programs, see U.S. GENERAL ACCOUNTING OFFICE, FEDERAL ROLE IN ADDRESSING—AND CONTRIBUTING TO—NONPOINT SOURCE POLLUTION, GAO/RCED–99–45 (Feb. 1999).

**3.** Perhaps it is understandable that Congress has not tried to undertake comprehensive nation-wide regulation of nonpoint sources such as farms. Have the states closed that gap? Generally, no. Most states follow the federal lead and focus regulatory clout almost entirely on point sources. Some states have authorities in place that could, arguably, be used to regulate nonpoint sources, but have not used them in any concerted effort to do so. And the few states that have ventured into more aggressive regulation of nonpoint sources generally leave the worst offender—farms—relatively untouched. *See* ENVIRONMENTAL LAW INSTITUTE, ENFORCEABLE STATE MECHANISMS FOR THE CONTROL OF NONPOINT SOURCE WATER POLLUTION (1997); ENVIRONMENTAL LAW INSTITUTE, ALMANAC OF ENFORCEABLE STATE LAWS TO CONTROL NONPOINT SOURCE WATER POLLUTION (1998); James M. McElfish, *State Enforcement Authorities for Polluted Runoff*, 28 ENVTL. L. REP. (ELI) 10,181 (1998). Several states, however, have received federal approval of a Nonpoint Source Pollution Control Program under Section 6217 of the Coastal Zone Management Act. In July 2000, California became the first state to receive such approval. Its 400-page, state-wide plan addresses nonpoint source pollution from agriculture, forestry, urban areas, marinas, and other sources over a 15-year planning horizon. It contemplates an initial period of voluntary improvement by each source category followed by aggressive regulation and enforcement if improvements are not brought about voluntarily. California also plans to use state implementation of a controversial federal program—the total maximum daily load program—as the cornerstone of nonpoint source management, including agricultural nonpoint source pollution (the so-called TMDL program is the subject of the materials in a later section of this chapter). It may be, therefore, that states will use the opportunity of compiling their coastal nonpoint source plans to reverse the trend of general neglect of nonpoint source pollution.

**4.** One type of agriculture pollution Congress has regulated as a point source since the enactment of the CWA is Concentrated Animal Feeding Operations (CAFOs), although only those over a certain size. *See* 40 C.F.R. 122.23(c) (setting forth minimum size thresholds). A 2003 EPA rule revised existing effluent limits for CAFOs and required all CAFOs to apply for a NPDES permit if there was a potential to discharge to navigable waters (even if there was no actual discharge), expanding the number of covered operations from 12,800 to 15,500. At the time, EPA acknowledged that permitting and enforcement of CAFOs had been inadequate and that only 4,000 CAFOs actually had permits. A number of groups challenged the 2003 rule and, in a 2008 decision, the U.S. Court of Appeals for the Second Circuit upheld EPA's authority to regulate through the permits the discharge of manure, litter, or process wastewater that a CAFO applies to a land application area for fertilizer and also upheld the EPA's decision not to regulate precipitation-related discharges, known as "agricultural stormwater discharges." However, it found that EPA could not require CAFOs to apply for permits based solely on a potential to discharge. Instead, the CWA only requires permits for actual discharges. Waterkeeper Alliance, et al., v. EPA, 399 F.3d 486 (2d Cir. 2005). This led EPA to enact a new CAFO rule in 2008, which was also subject to legal challenge. In 2011, the Fifth Circuit upheld parts of the 2008 rule and invalidated others. *See* National Pork Producers Council v. EPA, 635 F.3d 738 (5th Cir. 2011). For a discussion of the CAFO rules and the impact of the litigation, see CLAUDIA COPELAND, CONGRESSIONAL RESEARCH SERVICE, ANIMAL WASTE AND WATER QUALITY: EPA'S RESPONSE TO THE *WATERKEEPER ALLIANCE* COURT DECISION ON REGULATION OF CAFOS (Nov. 8, 2011); MEGAN STUBBS, CONGRESSIONAL

RESEARCH SERVICE, ENVIRONMENTAL REGULATION AND AGRICULTURE 15–18 (June 16, 2014).

**5.** Groundwater is very much a factor in the surface water hydrological system and ecology. Yet, even more so than for nonpoint source pollution, the CWA leaves management and regulation of groundwater pollution to the states. Some courts have held that the regulatory arm of the CWA—the NPDES permit program—covers discharges of pollutants to groundwater that is hydrologically connected to jurisdictional surface waters. *See, e.g.*, Idaho Rural Council v. Bosma, 143 F. Supp. 2d 1169 (D. Idaho 2001); Sierra Club v. Colorado Refining Co., 838 F. Supp. 1428 (D. Colo. 1993). Most courts, however, have held that the statute does not reach that far, *see, e.g.*, Village of Oconomowoc Lake v. Dayton Hudson Corp., 24 F.3d 962 (7th Cir. 1994); Exxon Corp. v. Train, 554 F.2d 1310 (5th Cir. 1977), and no court has applied the CWA to isolated groundwater. *See generally* Anna Makowski, *Beneath the Surface of the Clean Water Act: Exploring the Depth of the Act's Jurisdictional Scope of Groundwater Pollution*, 91 Or. L. Rev. 495 (2012); Jason R. Jones, *The Clean Water Act: Groundwater Regulation and the National Pollutant Discharge Elimination System*, 8 DICKINSON J. ENVTL. LAW & POLICY 93 (1999).

Some states, however, regulate to protect both groundwater quality and quantity more comprehensively. In the central Texas "Hill Country" around San Antonio and Austin, for example, the Edwards Aquifer is a highly productive karst (limestone) aquifer providing a bountiful and valuable source of high-quality water for residential and industrial purposes. It is the principal water supply for San Antonio and a major source of agricultural irrigation water in counties farther west. Through natural spring openings, the aquifer also supplies water to many surface streams and rivers that are home to a host of endangered aquatic species. Given the importance of this resource to the state, in 1993, the Texas Legislature enacted the Edwards Aquifer Authority Act, delegating to the Edwards Aquifer Authority, a state agency, the power to regulate development over the aquifer's recharge zone to preserve the resource and prevent intrusion of pollutants and contaminants. *See* 30 Tex. Admin. Code ch. 213. But the ability of the commission to adequately regulate the aquifer has been called into question in recent years as a result of Texas court decisions holding first, that landowners have property interests in the groundwater under their land and, second, that regulatory limits on groundwater use result in a regulatory "taking" of private property requiring the state to pay "just compensation." *See* Edwards Aquifer Authority v. Day, 369 S.W.3d 814, 843 (Tex. 2012) (holding landowners have property rights to groundwater beneath their property); Edwards Aquifer Authority v. Bragg, 421 S.W.3d 118 (Tex. Ct. App. 2013) (holding a farmer was entitled to damages arising from the state's denial of and limits in permits for groundwater extraction). Based on these decisions, in 2016, a Texas jury awarded a pecan farmer over $2.5 million in damages associated with the state's denial of groundwater extraction permits.

California has also enacted legislation protecting groundwater resources as a result of increasing droughts in the western United States, which has placed significant stress on that resource. In 2014, the California legislature enacted the Sustainable Groundwater Management Act of 2014, which "requires the formation of local groundwater sustainability agencies (GSAs) that must assess conditions in their local water basins and adopt locally-based management plans." *See* Association of California Water Agencies, http://www.acwa.com/content/groundwater/groundwater-sustainability. The law provides GSAs with authority to require groundwater well registration, manage and measure groundwater extraction, require reports and assess fees, and request revisions of basin boundaries. *See* Fact Sheet, Sustainable Groundwater Management Act of 2014, http://www.acwa.com/sites/default/files/post/groundwater/2014/04/2014-groundwater-fact-sheet.pdf. The law also provides a role for state intervention to protect groundwater resources if local efforts fall short.

**6.** One major use of groundwater resources is the bottling of water for consumption in individual serving sizes. For instance, in 2012, overall consumption of bottled water jumped by 6.2 percent from the prior year to 9.67 billion gallons, while sales increased by 6.7 percent, totaling $11.8 billion. This translates to every American consumer drinking an average of 30.8 gallons of bottled water in 2012, up 5.3 percent from the prior year. For several years, bottled water has been the fastest growing segment of the beverage industry. Reasons usually cited for this trend are the population's increased awareness of the positive health effects of water ingestion coupled with the convenience and perceived superior purity and taste of bottled water compared to tap water.

Americans, of course, did not discover bottled water, so while our trend seems significant to us, which it is, on a global scale it is overshadowed. Indeed, the worldwide market for bottled water is over $100 billion annually and rates of consumption are rising more rapidly in the Pacific Rim and Asian nations than in North America and Western Europe. The price of bottled water, about one dollar per 12 oz. bottle, is 500–1000 times the price of tap water in most markets. By contrast, production costs of the water in bottled water are under a dime per gallon. The significant production costs of bottled water are the bottles, bottling, transportation, and marketing. At the same time, however, over 1 billion people worldwide have no access to safe drinking water and millions of people die each year from diseases brought on by unsanitary water. *See generally* JAMES SALZMAN, DRINKING WATER: A HISTORY (2012).

Following on the heels of this trend has been an increasing concern by many observers that bottling of water presents serious adverse environmental effects. Chief among these are the demand bottling of water places on local water supply resources, the resources consumed and pollution generated in the production of plastic bottles and shipping of the bottled water, and the waste management problems of discarded plastic bottles. There have also been public health concerns expressed regarding the possible uneven quality of bottled water. Consider these statistics:

- Over 75% of bottled water sold in the U.S. finds a protected spring or well as its source. The rest is bottled from purified tap water.

- Most large bottlers have many sources (e.g., Nestle/Perrier collects water from over 75 springs in the U.S.), and thus most bottled water is consumed within markets that are relatively local to the source. Worldwide, 75% of bottled water is consumed in the same region it is produced.
- Nevertheless, transportation of bottled water does contribute to pollution emissions, and must be accounted for to make an accurate assessment of the overall balance of effects.
- Polyethylene terephthalate (PET) is the plastic of choice for the bottles. Producing a kilo of PET consumes petroleum products and, ironically in the case of PET for water bottles, requires 17.5 gallons of water. The production process results in emissions of sulfur oxides, hydrocarbons, carbon monoxide, nitrogen oxide, and carbon dioxide.
- Over 1.5 million tons of PET are used each year to contain bottled water.
- Estimates are that as much as 90 percent of used water bottles were discarded rather than recycled, albeit in many cases perhaps after some level of reuse (filling from taps or filtered taps). PET is essentially non-biodegradable.
- Compared to glass and aluminum, however, PET provides a superior bottle container in terms of weight, breakage, production emissions, reuse rate, recycling rate, and solid waste disposal rate.

Bottled water thus presents a mixed bag: it is a healthy trend, but it uses ecologically sensitive resources; overall its production and consumption in plastic containers are sources of environmental degradation, but in some categories are less so than for other beverages and container types. For more on the topic, see Tara Boldt-Van Rooy, *"Bottling Up" Our Natural Resources: The Fight over Bottled Water Extraction in the United States*, 18 J. LAND USE & ENVTL. L. 267 (2003).

## E. WATER QUALITY STANDARDS AND TOTAL MAXIMUM DAILY LOAD (TMDL) PROGRAMS

Although the main focus of the CWA is on technology-based effluent limits, it also requires states to set Water Quality Standards (WQS) for their waters and to identify waters that do not meet those standards. It requires that NPDES permits include effluent limitations sufficient to achieve WQSs, allows states to veto federal activities that would interfere with achieving WQS, and requires that states develop Total Maximum Daily Loads (TMDLs) for impaired waterbodies to bring them into compliance with the WQS.

Under Section 303 of the CWA, states must identify the designated uses of each water body in the state (e.g., recreational purposes, propagation of fish and wildlife, public water supplies) and then create "water quality criteria" designed to protect the designated use. Water quality criteria quantitatively describe the physical, chemical, and biological characteristics of waters necessary to support the designated uses. State water criteria generally are based on federal water quality criteria EPA promulgates under Section 304(a) for more than 150 pollutants. The federal criteria are not enforceable standards but are instead guidance states can use to determine appropriate numerical criteria for water bodies in the state. In 2015, EPA issued a rule designed to update the existing WQS regulation "to provide a better-defined pathway for states and authorized tribes to improve water quality and protect high quality waters." *See* 80 Fed. Reg. 51,020 (Aug. 21, 2015) (amending various provisions of 40 C.F.R. pt. 131).

The combination of designated uses and water quality criteria result in WQSs, which are limits on the ambient concentration of pollutants in particular classes of waters. For example, a standard may state that the level of arsenic in a stream used to support certain fish cannot exceed 0.2 milligrams per liter. States must review their WQSs every three years and must submit the standards to EPA for review, modification, and approval. States have been slow to enact WQSs and often have adopted "narrative" standards that do not create numerical limits on the ambient concentrations of pollutants. Without numerical limits, of course, it is difficult to use WQSs to impose additional limitations on pollutant discharges to water bodies.

Section 303(d) of the CWA requires each state to identify and establish a priority ranking for water bodies for which effluent limitations are insufficient to attain and maintain applicable WQSs. For those "impaired waters," states must establish and submit to EPA for approval the total maximum daily load (TMDL) for those pollutants identified by EPA as suitable for TMDL calculation. If a state fails to submit the necessary TMDLs, EPA must establish a list of impaired water bodies and TMDLs for the state. A TMDL sets the total amount of a particular pollutant that a segment of water may receive from point sources, nonpoint sources, and background sources without exceeding applicable water quality criteria, allocates allowable pollutant loads among the sources contributing the pollutant to that water body, and provides the basis for attaining or maintaining the WQS.

States have been very slow to submit lists of impaired waters to EPA and even slower in developing TMDLs. The task is huge. EPA data shows that there are over 42,000 impaired waters in the United States, many of which are impaired for multiple pollutants. Since 1995, EPA has approved over 70,000 TMDLs. For a list of TMDLs, an inventory of impaired waters by state, and the causes of impairments, see U.S. EPA, National Summary of Impaired Waters and TMDL Information, https://iaspub.epa.gov/waters10/attains_nation_cy.control?p_report_type=T. The difficulty in developing TMDLs is caused by a lack of necessary data, technological support, and cost. A 1996 EPA study found the costs of preparing a TMDL can reach $1 million and those costs today are significantly more. The slow progress of TMDLs is also a function of the fact that EPA essentially ignored the TMDL program for decades, focusing instead on developing technology-based effluent standards. Numerous citizen lawsuits beginning in the 1990s resulted in EPA coming under court order to establish TMDLs in more than 20 states and EPA overhauling its TMDL regulatory program. These regulatory changes have met with significant resistance, particularly regulations expressly applying the TMDL rules to water bodies impaired solely by nonpoint sources of pollution and EPA action creating its own list of impaired waters for states that refused to list waters as impaired if the pollutants were exclusively from nonpoint sources.

Despite these problems, the TMDL program is a significant bridge between the NPDES Program and the WQS Program. In essence, the TMDL program answers the question of what happens when a particular WQS for a waterbody is not met even though all the NPDES-regulated discharges into the waterbody are complying with the most stringent technology-based limits applicable to the relevant industries. Because NPDES limits are based on end-of-the-pipe effluent concentrations, and WQSs are based on ambient conditions in the entire waterbody, no obvious connection exists by which to adjust the NPDES discharges. The TMDL program is designed to produce that connection, albeit in ways that are far less than obvious. The following materials provide additional detail on the WQS and TMDL programs and demonstrate how even they may be ineffective in the long run for dealing with nonpoint source pollution.

## Pronsolino v. Nastri

United States Court of Appeals for the Ninth Circuit, 2002.
291 F.3d 1123.

■ BERZON, CIRCUIT JUDGE.

. . .

Section 303(d)(1)(A) requires each state to identify as "areas with insufficient controls" "those waters within its boundaries for which the effluent limitations required by Section [301(b)(1)(A)] and Section [301(b)(1)(B)] of this title are not stringent enough to implement any water quality standard applicable to such waters." Id. The CWA defines "effluent limitations" as restrictions on pollutants "discharged from point sources." CWA § 502(11), 33 U.S.C. § 1362(11). Section 301(b)(1)(A) mandates application of the "best practicable control technology" effluent limitations for most point source discharges, while § 301(b)(1)(B) mandates application of effluent limitations adopted specifically for secondary treatment at publicly owned treatment works. § 301(b)(1), 33 U.S.C. § 1311(b)(1).

For waters identified pursuant to § 303(d)(1)(A)(the § 303(d)(1) list), the states must establish the "total maximum daily load" ("TMDL") for pollutants identified by the EPA as suitable for TMDL calculation. § 303(d)(1)(C). "A TMDL defines the specified maximum amount of a pollutant which can be discharged or 'loaded' into the waters at issue from all combined sources." Dioxin/Organochlorine Center v. Clarke, 57 F.3d 1517, 1520 (9th Cir. 1995). The TMDL "shall be established at a level necessary to implement the applicable water quality standards. . . ." § 303(d)(1)(C).

Section 303(d)(2), in turn, requires each state to submit its § 303(d)(1) list and TMDLs to the EPA for its approval or disapproval. If the EPA approves the list and TMDLs, the state must incorporate the list and TMDLs into its continuing planning process, the requirements for which are set forth in § 303(e). § 303(d)(2). If the EPA disapproves either the § 303(d)(1) list or any TMDLs, the EPA must itself put together the missing document or documents. Id. The state then incorporates any EPA-set list or TMDL into the states continuing planning process. *Id.*

. . .

The final pertinent Section of § 303, § 303(e), requiring each state to have a continuing planning process, gives some operational force to the prior information-gathering provisions. The EPA may approve a state's continuing planning process only if it "will result in plans for all navigable waters within such State" that include, inter alia, effluent limitations, TMDLs, areawide waste management plans for nonpoint sources of pollution, and plans for "adequate implementation, including schedules of compliance, for revised or new water quality standards." § 303(e)(3).

The upshot of this intricate scheme is that the CWA leaves to the states the responsibility of developing plans to achieve water quality standards if the statutorily-mandated point source controls will not alone suffice, while providing federal funding to aid in the implementation of the state plans. See *Dombeck*, 172 F.3d at 1097; § 303(e); see also § 319(h), 33 U.S.C. § 1329(h) (providing for grants to states to combat nonpoint source pollution). TMDLs are primarily informational tools that allow the states to proceed from the identification of waters requiring additional planning to the required plans. See Alaska Center for the Environment v. Browner, 20 F.3d 981, 984–85 (9th Cir. 1994). As such, TMDLs serve as a link in an implementation chain that includes federally-regulated point source controls, state or local plans for point and nonpoint source pollution reduction, and assessment of the impact of such measures on water quality, all to the end of attaining water quality goals for the nation's waters.

II. Factual and Procedural Background

In 1992, California submitted to the EPA a list of waters pursuant to § 303(d)(1)(A). Pursuant to § 303(d)(2), the EPA disapproved

California's 1992 list because it omitted seventeen water segments that did not meet the water quality standards set by California for those segments. Sixteen of the seventeen water segments, including the Garcia River, were impaired only by nonpoint sources of pollution. After California rejected an opportunity to amend its § 303(d)(1) list to include the seventeen sub-standard segments, the EPA, again acting pursuant to § 303(d)(2), established a new § 303(d)(1) list for California, including those segments on it. California retained the seventeen segments on its 1994, 1996, and 1998 § 303(d)(1) lists.

California did not, however, establish TMDLs for the segments added by the EPA. Environmental and fishermen's groups sued the EPA in 1995 to require the EPA to establish TMDLs for the seventeen segments, and in a March 1997 consent decree the EPA agreed to do so [and established a TMDL for the Garcia River].

The Garcia River TMDL for sediment is 552 tons per square mile per year, a sixty percent reduction from historical loadings. The TMDL allocates portions of the total yearly load among the following categories of nonpoint source pollution: a) "mass wasting" associated with roads; b) "mass wasting" associated with timber-harvesting; c) erosion related to road surfaces; and d) erosion related to road and skid trail crossings.

In 1960, appellants Betty and Guido Pronsolino purchased approximately 800 acres of heavily logged timber land in the Garcia River watershed. In 1998, after re-growth of the forest, the Pronsolinos applied for a harvesting permit from the California Department of Forestry ("Forestry").

In order to comply with the Garcia River TMDL, Forestry and/or the state's Regional Water Quality Control Board required, among other things, that the Pronsolinos' harvesting provide for mitigation of 90% of controllable road-related sediment run-off and contain prohibitions on removing certain trees and on harvesting from mid-October until May 1. The Pronsolino's forester estimates that a large tree restriction will cost the Pronsolinos $750,000.

Larry Mailliard, a member of the Mendocino County Farm Bureau, submitted a draft harvesting permit on February 4, 1998, for a portion of his property in the Garcia River watershed. Forestry granted a final version of the permit after incorporation of a 60.3% reduction of sediment loading, a requirement included to comply with the Garcia River TMDL. Mr. Mailliard's forester estimates that the additional restrictions imposed to comply with the Garcia River TMDL will cost Mr. Mailliard $10,602,000.

Bill Barr, another member of the Mendocino County Farm Bureau, also applied for a harvesting permit in 1998 for his property located within the Garcia River watershed. Forestry granted the permit after incorporation of restrictions similar to those included in the Pronsolino's permit. A forester states that these additional restrictions, included to comply with the TMDL, will cost Mr. Barr at least $962,000. . . .

III. Analysis

Section 303(d)(1)(A) requires listing and calculation of TMDLs for "those waters within [the states] boundaries for which the effluent limitations required by Section [301(b)(1)(A)] and Section [301(b)(1)(B)] of this title are not stringent enough to implement any water quality standard applicable to such waters." § 303(d) (emphasis added). The precise statutory question before us is whether, as the Pronsolinos maintain, the term "not stringent enough to implement . . . water quality standard[s]" as used in § 303(d)(1)(A) must be interpreted to mean both that application of effluent limitations will not achieve water quality standards and that the waters at issue are subject to effluent limitations. As only waters with point source pollution are subject to effluent limitations, such an interpretation would exclude from the § 303(d) listing and TMDL requirements waters impaired only by nonpoint sources of pollution.

The EPA, as noted, interprets "not stringent enough to implement . . . water quality standard[s]" to mean "not adequate" or "not sufficient . . . to implement any water quality standard," and does not read the statute as implicitly containing a limitation to waters initially covered by effluent limitations. According to the EPA, if the use of effluent limitations will not implement applicable water quality standards, the water falls within § 303(d)(1)(A) regardless of whether it is point or nonpoint sources, or a combination of the two, that continue to pollute the water.

Whether or not the appellants' suggested interpretation is entirely implausible, it is at least considerably weaker than the EPA's competing construction. The Pronsolinos' version necessarily relies upon: (1) understanding "stringent enough" to mean "strict enough" rather than "thorough going enough" or "adequate" or "sufficient"; (2) reading the phrase "not stringent enough" in isolation, rather than with reference to the stated goal of implementing "any water quality standard applicable to such waters." Where the answer to the question "not stringent enough for what?" is "to implement any [applicable] water quality standard," the meaning of "stringent" should be determined by looking forward to the broad goal to be attained, not backwards at the inadequate effluent limitations. One might comment, for example, about a teacher that her standards requiring good spelling were not stringent enough to assure good writing, as her students still used bad grammar and poor logic. Based on the language of the contested phrase alone, then, the more sensible conclusion is that the § 303(d)(1) list must contain any waters for which the particular effluent limitations will not be adequate to attain the statute's water quality goals. . . .

There is one final aspect of the Act's structure that bears consideration because it supports the EPA's interpretation of § 303(d):

The list required by § 303(d)(1)(A) requires that waters be listed if they are impaired by a combination of point sources and nonpoint sources; the language admits of no other reading. Section 303(d)(1)(C), in turn, directs that TMDLs shall be established at a level necessary to implement the applicable water quality standards. . . . Id. (emphasis added). So, at least in blended waters, TMDLs must be calculated with regard to nonpoint sources of pollution; otherwise, it would be impossible "to implement the applicable water quality standards," which do not differentiate sources of pollution. This court has so recognized. *Browner*, 20 F.3d at 985 ("Congress and the EPA have already determined that establishing TMDLs is an effective tool for achieving water quality standards in waters impacted by non-point source pollution.").

Nothing in the statutory structure—or purpose—suggests that Congress meant to distinguish, as to § 303(d)(1) lists and TMDLs, between waters with one insignificant point source and substantial nonpoint source pollution and waters with only nonpoint source pollution. Such a distinction would, for no apparent reason, require the states or the EPA to monitor waters to determine whether a point source had been added or removed, and to adjust the § 303(d)(1) list and establish TMDLs accordingly. There is no statutory basis for concluding that Congress intended such an irrational regime.

Looking at the statute as a whole, we conclude that the EPA's interpretation of § 303(d) is not only entirely reasonable but considerably more convincing than the one offered by the plaintiffs in this case.

The Pronsolinos finally contend that, by establishing TMDLs for waters impaired only by nonpoint source pollution, the EPA has upset the balance of federal-state control established in the CWA by intruding into the state's traditional control over land use. *See* Solid Waste Agency of Northern Cook County v. United States Army Corps of Eng'rs, 531 U.S. 159, 172–73 (2001). That is not the case.

The Garcia River TMDL identifies the maximum load of pollutants that can enter the Garcia River from certain broad categories of nonpoint sources if the river is to attain water quality standards. It does not specify the load of pollutants that may be received from particular parcels of land or describe what measures the state should take to implement the TMDL. Instead, the TMDL expressly recognizes that "implementation and monitoring" "are state responsibilities" and notes that, for this reason, the EPA did not include implementation or monitoring plans within the TMDL.

Moreover, § 303(e) requires—separately from the § 303(d)(1) listing and TMDL requirements—that each state include in its continuing planning process "adequate implementation, including schedules of compliance, for revised or new water quality standards" "for all navigable waters within such State." § 303(e)(3). The Garcia River TMDL thus serves as an informational tool for the creation of the state's implementation plan, independently—and explicitly—required by Congress.

California chose both if and how it would implement the Garcia River TMDL. States must implement TMDLs only to the extent that they seek to avoid losing federal grant money; there is no pertinent statutory provision otherwise requiring implementation of § 303 plans or providing for their enforcement. *See* CWA § 309, 33 U.S.C. § 1319; CWA § 505, 33 U.S.C. 1365.

---

## Friends of Pinto Creek v. EPA

United States Court of Appeals for the Ninth Circuit, 2007.
504 F.3d 1007.

■ HUG, CIRCUIT JUDGE:

In this case, we determine whether the Environmental Protection Agency ("EPA") properly issued a National Pollution Discharge Elimination System ("NPDES") permit under the Clean Water Act to Carlota Copper Company ("Carlota"). The permit allows mining-related discharges of copper into Arizona's Pinto Creek, a waterbody already in excess of water quality standards for copper. Based upon provisions of the Clean Water Act, the implementing regulations, and their applicability to the factual scenario of this case, we vacate the permit and remand.

I. FACTUAL BACKGROUND

Pinto Creek is a desert river located near Miami, Arizona, approximately 60 miles east of Phoenix. It has been listed by the American Rivers Organization as one of the country's most endangered rivers due to threats from proposed mining operations. Pinto Creek and its riparian environs are home to a variety of fish, birds, and other wildlife, some of which are specially protected. Due to excessive copper contamination from historical mining activities in the region, Pinto Creek is included on Arizona's list of impaired waters under § 303(d) of the Clean Water Act, 33 U.S.C. § 1313(d), as a water quality limited stream due to non-attainment of water quality standards for dissolved copper.

Carlota proposed to construct and operate an open-pit copper mine and processing facility approximately six miles west of Miami, Arizona, covering over 3000 acres while extracting about 100 million tons of ore. Part of the operation plan includes constructing diversion channels for Pinto Creek to route the stream around the mine, as well as groundwater cut-off walls to block the flow of groundwater into the mine. . . . The EPA ultimately issued [a] permit, and the Environmental Appeals Board ("Appeals Board"), the internal appellate board of the EPA, denied review.

II. ISSUES

Whether the issuance of the permit to discharge a pollutant, dissolved copper, into Pinto Creek, which already exceeded the amount of dissolved copper allowed under the Section 303(d) Water Quality Standard, is in violation of the Clean Water Act and the applicable regulations. . . .

IV. ANALYSIS

It is important to consider the objectives and purpose of the 1972 revisions of the Clean Water Act, which are presently applicable to the considerations involved here. 33 U.S.C. § 1251 (1987) provides: The objective of this chapter is to restore and maintain the chemical, physical, and biological integrity of the nation's waters. In order to achieve this objective it is hereby declared that, consistent with the provisions of this chapter-(1) it is the national goal that the discharge of pollutants into the navigable waters be eliminated by 1985. . . . (3) it is the national policy that the discharge of toxic pollutants in toxic amounts be prohibited. Under the 1972 revisions of the Clean Water Act, there is direct federal regulation of the discharge of pollutants from point sources. Pronsolino v. Nastri, 291 F.3d 1123, 1126 (9th Cir. 2002). "[P]oint sources of pollution are those [where the pollutant flows] from a discrete conveyance, such as a pipe or tunnel. Nonpoint sources of pollution are non-discrete sources" and are the responsibility of the states, with certain federal oversight. *Id.* at 1125–27. An example of a non-discrete source is runoff from a farmland or timber harvesting. Our Pronsolino opinion provides a detailed description of the operation of the Clean Water Act. We here summarize the provisions pertinent to this case.

Under § 303 of the Clean Water Act, 33 U.S.C. § 1313, the states are required to set water quality standards for all waters within their boundaries, regardless of the sources of the pollution entering the waters. Pursuant to § 303(d)(1), 33 U.S.C. § 1313(d)(1), each state is required to identify those waters that do not meet the water quality standard which is frequently called the "§ 303(d)(1) list." For impaired waters identified in the § 303(d)(1) list, the states must establish a TMDL for pollutants identified by the EPA. A TMDL specifies the maximum amount of pollutant that can be discharged or loaded into the waters from all combined sources, so as to comply with the water quality standards.

Each state is required to submit its § 303(d)(1) list and its TMDL to the EPA for its approval or disapproval. If the EPA disapproves either of those documents, the EPA is responsible for preparing that document. The state then incorporates its § 303(d)(1) list and its TMDL or the EPA's approved document into its continuing planning process as required by § 303(e), 33 U.S.C. § 1313(e). In this case, the state had prepared the § 303(d)(1) list, but it had not prepared a TMDL. Therefore, in response to the Petitioners' objection, the EPA prepared the TMDL utilized in its awarding of the permit.

The Petitioners contend that as a "new discharger" Carlota's discharge of dissolved copper into a waterway that is already impaired by an excess of the copper pollutant violates the intent and purpose of the Clean Water Act. Under the NPDES permitting program, 40 C.F.R. § 122.4(i) addresses the situation where a new source seeks to permit a discharge of pollutants into a stream already exceeding its water quality standards for that pollutant. Section 122.4 states in relevant part:

> No permit may be issued: . . .
>
> (i) To a new source or a new discharger if the discharge from its construction or operation will cause or contribute to the violation of water quality standards. The owner or operator of a new source or new discharger proposing to discharge into a water segment which does not meet applicable water quality standards or is not expected to meet those standards . . . and for which the State or interstate agency has performed a pollutants load allocation for the pollutant to be discharged, must demonstrate, before the close of the public comment period, that:
>
> (1) There are sufficient remaining pollutant load allocations to allow for the discharge; and
>
> (2) The existing dischargers into that segment are subject to compliance schedules designed to bring the segment into compliance with applicable water quality standards.

40 C.F.R. § 122.4 (2000).

The plain language of the first sentence of the regulation is very clear that no permit may be issued to a new discharger if the discharge will contribute to the violation of water quality standards. This corresponds to the stated objectives of the Clean Water Act "to restore and maintain the chemical, physical, and biological integrity of the nation's waters." 33 U.S.C. § 1251(a) (1987). And that "it is the national policy that the discharge of toxic pollutants in toxic amounts be prohibited." 33 U.S.C. § 1251(a)(3) (1987).

The EPA contends that the partial remediation of the discharge from the Gibson Mine will offset the pollution. However, there is nothing in the Clean Water Act or the regulation that provides an exception for an offset when the waters remain impaired and the new source is discharging pollution into that impaired water. The regulation does provide for an exception where a TMDL has been performed and the owner or operator demonstrates that before the close of the comment period two conditions are met, which will assure that the impaired waters will be brought into compliance with the applicable water quality standards. The plain language of this exception to the prohibited discharge by a new source provides that the exception does not apply unless the new source can demonstrate that, under the TMDL, the plan is designed to bring the waters into compliance with applicable water quality standards.

The EPA argues that under the requirements of clause (1), there are sufficient remaining load allocations to allow for the discharge because the TMDL provides a method by which the allocations could be established to allow for the discharge. There is no contention, however, that these load allocations represent the amount of pollution that is currently discharged from the point sources and nonpoint sources, and there is no indication of any plan that will effectuate these load allocations so as to bring Pinto Creek within the water quality standards. The TMDL merely provides for the manner in which Pinto Creek could meet the water quality standards if all of the load allocations in the TMDL were met, not that there are sufficient remaining pollutant load allocations under existing circumstances.

With regard to the requirements of clause (2), the EPA argues that the requirement of "compliance schedules" pertains only to point sources for which there is a permit. This does not correspond to the plain language of clause (2), which provides "the existing discharges into that segment [of Pinto Creek] are subject to compliance schedules designed to bring the segment into compliance with applicable water quality standards." 40 C.F.R. § 122.4(i)(2) (2000).

We examine that language utilizing the definitions provided in the regulation. The term "discharge" is defined to mean "the discharge of a pollutant." 40 C.F.R. § 122.2 (2000). The term "discharge of a pollutant," is defined as any addition of any "pollutant" or combination of pollutants to "waters of the United States" from "any point source." Id. at § 122.2(a) (emphasis added). Thus, under the plain language of the regulation, compliance schedules are not confined only to "permitted" point source discharges, but are applicable to "any" point source.

The EPA contends that this would amount to a complete ban of the discharge of pollution to impaired waters. This is based on its misreading of the plain language of the regulation to state that the remediation has to be completed before Carlota's discharge. The plain language of clause (2) of the regulation, instead, provides that existing discharges into that segment (of the waters) are "subject to compliance schedules designed to bring the segment into compliance with applicable water quality standards." 40 C.F.R. § 122.4(i)(2) (2000) (emphasis added). This is not a complete ban but a requirement of schedules to meet the objective of the Clean Water Act.

Here the existing discharges from point sources are not subject to compliance schedules designed to bring Pinto Creek into compliance with water quality standards. Thus, Carlota has not demonstrated that clause (2) of 40 C.F.R. § 122.4(i) has been met. This is the regulation upon which Carlota and the EPA rely for issuance of the permit. . . .

In Carlota's case, there are no plans or compliance schedules to bring the Pinto Creek segment "into compliance with applicable water quality standards," as required by § 122.4(i)(2), which Carlota and the EPA both acknowledge is the applicable section with which Carlota must comply. The error of both the EPA and Carlota is that the objective of that section is not simply to show a lessening of pollution, but to show how the water quality standard will be met if Carlota is allowed to discharge pollutants into the impaired waters. . . .

The EPA contends that it cannot be judicially compelled to act against point sources that are illegally discharging into Pinto Creek. The EPA notes that while it has the authority to act against violators, its decision to do so in ordering its priorities is a matter that is typically committed to its absolute discretion, citing Sierra Club v. Whitman, 268 F.3d 898, 903 (9th Cir. 2001) and Heckler v. Chaney, 470 U.S. 821, 831–32 (1985).

In Carlota's case, there is nothing in § 122.4(i) that compels the EPA to act against point sources that are violating the Clean Water Act by their discharges into Pinto Creek or requiring judicial review of the EPA's ordering of priorities in any failure to act. The requirement of § 122.4(i)(2) is simply a condition that must be met before a permit can be issued to a new discharger into impaired waters. There is no compulsion on the EPA to act against point source violators, as in *Sierra Club* or *Heckler*. The EPA remains free to establish its priorities; it just cannot issue a permit to a new discharger until it has complied with § 122.4(i)(2).

In this case, the Petitioners do not argue for an absolute ban on discharges into a waterway that is in violation of the water quality standards. Rather, the Petitioners point to the § 122.4(i) exception by which a new discharger can comply with the Clean Water Act requirements. Those requirements simply were not met. . . .

---

## QUESTIONS AND DISCUSSION

1. The TMDL process, in essence, is the following:
   - States identify specific waters where problems exist or are expected as a result of point *and/or nonpoint* sources.
   - States allocate pollutant loadings among point *and nonpoint* sources contributing to the impairment, and EPA approves State actions or acts in lieu of the State if necessary.
   - Point *and nonpoint* sources then reduce pollutants to achieve the pollutant loadings established by the TMDL through a wide variety of Federal, State, Tribal, and local authorities, programs, and initiatives.

As it relates to point source pollution, *Pinto Creek* illustrates that the TMDL program can serve as a major hurdle to new discharges of pollutants into impaired waters. However, not all courts are in agreement with *Pinto Creek* that offsets of existing sources of pollutants are insufficient to allow new discharges of pollutants if the waterbody remains impaired. Courts in Maryland and Minnesota have held, contrary to *Pinto Creek*, that regulatory authorities may permit new sources of discharges to impaired waters if they offset existing sources of pollution. *See* Assateague Coastkeeper v. Maryland Dept. of Envt., 28 A.3d 178 (Md. Ct. App. 2011) (holding that "MDE's construction of 40 C.F.R. § 122.4(i), as allowing the consideration of pollution offsets in determining whether a discharge "causes or contributes" to a violation of water quality standards, is reasonable."); In re Cities of Annandale and Maple Lake NPDES/SDS Permit Issuance for the Discharge of Treated Wastewater, 731 N.W.2d 502 (Minn. 2007) (same). For a general discussion of issues associated with the TMDL program with regard to new point sources and nonpoint sources, see CLAUDIA COPELAND, CONGRESSIONAL RESEARCH SERVICE, CLEAN WATER ACT AND POLLUTANT TOTAL MAXIMUM DAILY LOADS (TMDLS) (Jan. 17, 2014).

As it relates to nonpoint source pollution, application of the TMDL program is more complicated, and breaks down into three discrete questions. First, can impairment resulting entirely or mostly from nonpoint sources be considered when deciding whether a water body must be listed as impaired for purposes of Section 303? Second, if a water body impaired in part by nonpoint sources can be listed, can a TMDL waste load allocation be made that includes nonpoint sources contributing to impairment of the water body? Finally, if a TMDL waste load allocation can be made to nonpoint sources, how can it be enforced against them?

In *Pronsolino*, the court of appeals provided what was seen by many as a victory on the first two issues for advocates of using the TMDL program as the hook for controlling nonpoint source pollution. Plaintiffs in that case argued that EPA lacked authority to require TMDLs for waters of the Garcia River in Northern California impaired solely by nonpoint sources of pollution due to sediment from soil erosion caused by timber harvesting along the river's banks. The court disagreed, ruling that EPA has authority to require states to list waters receiving only nonpoint source pollutants on a state's Section 303(d) list and subsequently to prepare TMDLs for the listed waters.

**2.** But what about the third question—enforcement of the TMDL against nonpoint sources? Here *Pronsolino* has been less helpful to those who would use the TMDL program as the basis of nonpoint source regulation. The court observed that EPA could not regulate land use because that matter was reserved for the states. The court further concluded that, although Section 303(e) of the CWA requires states to include TMDLs such as the Garcia River sediment TMDL in their continuing planning processes, California is free to decide whether to implement the TMDL by regulating nonpoint sources such as farms and timber operations through its land use practices, and is free to risk possible loss of federal environmental grant funds if it decides not to implement the TMDL. So where does that leave matters? Do you think most states will accept the invitation to regulate nonpoint sources? Or will they bite the bullet, leave their nonpoint sources alone, and forego federal monies? Will it depend on who the nonpoint sources are? And, if the states do refuse to go after the nonpoint sources, what happens to the TMDL?

**3.** In an effort to entice states into including nonpoint sources in their TMDL implementation programs, EPA ingeniously (some have said deviously) unveiled a plan to take advantage of the point source side of the TMDL program as leverage for the nonpoint source side. Point sources, of course, have long been subject to direct, technology-based regulation under the CWA NPDES permitting program. Nonpoint sources have not. It is reasonable to assume, therefore, that the marginal cost of satisfying TMDL waste load allocations—i.e., the cost of reducing a unit of pollutant load—will be more for point sources than it will for nonpoint sources. Hence, as an alternative to direct regulation of nonpoint sources, EPA suggested that states could allow NPDES dischargers to pay for nonpoint source dischargers' reductions in discharge loads and thereby avoid additional load restrictions in their NPDES permits. *See* Revisions to the Water Quality Planning and Management Regulation and Revisions to the National Pollutant Discharge Elimination System Program in Support of Revisions to the Water Quality Planning and Management Regulation, 65 Fed. Reg. 43,586 (July 13, 2000) (amending various provisions of 40 C.F.R. pts. 9, 122, 123, 124, 130). Provided the state can demonstrate with reasonable assurance that the nonpoint source load reduction measures will actually lead to load reductions, such trading can take advantage of the disparity in marginal cost of load unit of reduction—i.e., point sources could actually save money by paying for nonpoint source reductions. Of course, this plan won't work for waters impaired entirely by nonpoint sources, such as those involved in *Pronsolino*.

**4.** There is far from universal agreement, however, that EPA has the authority the *Pronsolino* court believed it does. The history of EPA's efforts to establish its position in this regard is a story in bizarre politics, though one many would regard as politics as usual. In 1999, EPA published proposed revisions to its TMDL regulations that would have brought the program squarely in line with *Pronsolino* and the strategy for nonpoint sources the court endorsed. *See* 64 Fed. Reg. 46,057 (1999); 64 Fed. Reg. 46,011 (1999); *see generally* Lisa E. Roberts, *Is the Gun Loaded This Time? EPA's Proposed Revisions to the Total Maximum Daily Load Program*, 6 ENVTL. LAWYER 635 (2000). These proposals immediately attracted controversy. EPA received over 34,000 comments on the proposed rules. Farming groups initiated litigation challenging EPA's authority to implement the TMDL program so as to assign allocations to nonpoint sources. The National Governors Association immediately sought federal legislation to add funding and flexibility to the TMDL program. Some members of Congress also questioned EPA's authority in this regard and took measures to block implementation of the final rules. Indeed, prior to EPA's promulgation of the final rules, Congress adopted a rider to the Military Construction/Supplemental Appropriations bill (the bill dealt with funding of U.S. Forces in Kosovo and of Columbian anti-drug efforts) that prevented EPA not only from enforcing new TMDL rules before fiscal year 2002, but also from even finishing its work on the proposed rules and adopting them as final. In a political gambit to thwart Congress, EPA adopted the final rules in 2000 (cited above), which retained most of the relevant structure of the proposed rules, before President Clinton signed the appropriations bill restricting the agency from doing so. In other words, the rules went on the books, but were "not effective until 30 days after the date that Congress allows EPA to implement this regulation." 65 Fed. Reg. at 53,586.

**5.** Soon after that, of course, a new administration took command of EPA. In July 2001, one year after the final rules were "adopted," the Bush administration announced that it would further delay implementation of the rules so that it could reconsider them in light of concerns raised by stakeholders, with spring 2002 as a projected target date for proposing any changes to the rules. *See* 66 Fed. Reg. 41,817 (Aug. 9, 2001). In the summer of 2001, EPA began developing a new concept it called the "TMDL/Watershed" rule, and later that year conducted five public "listening sessions" around the country to receive input on the basic approach of linking TMDLs to a broader watershed-based implementation program that would use watershed assessment scales, rely heavily on state implementation plans, and promote pollutant trading between emission sources. In June 2002 EPA announced that it was drafting the new rule and would propose it by the end of that year. That didn't happen, but a draft rule was "leaked" in April 2003 and in March 2003 EPA did take the step of formally withdrawing the 2000 TMDL rule. *See* 68 Fed. Reg. 13,608 (Mar. 19, 2003). As of this writing EPA has not proposed any form of the so-called TMDL/Watershed rule. In other words, as of 2016, the TMDL regulations that apply are those adopted in 1985 and amended in 1992. *See* 40 C.F.R. Part 130; 68 Fed. Reg. 13,608 (Mar. 19, 2003).

**6.** Assuming the TMDL rules that are eventually put into effect retain the basic features EPA adopted in July 1999, and do apply to nonpoint sources at least as far as *Pronsolino* says they do, to what extent can the TMDL program become a useful tool in the watershed management effort? The events leading up to *Pronsolino* suggest that states will be reluctant to take on regulation of agricultural interests; costs of TMDL calculation, not to mention implementation, are staggering; local land use decisions are highly complex and must be coordinated with state TMDL decisions; and so on. Some concerns with the TMDL program are physical: TMDLs may be very difficult to accomplish in small watersheds; TMDLs are too narrow in focus, failing to take into account habitat quality and water quantity issues; and nonpoint source pollution often is caused in part by physical environment conditions beyond the control of regulators or dischargers. *See generally* Jory Ruggiero, *Toward a Law of the Land: The Clean Water Act as a Mandate for the Implementation of an Ecosystem Approach to Land Management*, 20 PUBLIC LAND AND RESOURCES L.J. 31 (1999). For a contrary view based on the experience of TMDL implementation in Texas, see Margaret Hoffman, *Integrating TMDLs into Watershed-Based Water Quality Management*, 31 ST. BAR OF TEXAS ENVTL. L.J. 193 (2001). Were the EPA under the Clinton administration, as well as the environmental advocates that sued the agency into action, asking too much of the TMDL program?

**7.** Although EPA has not issued any new regulations for the TMDL program, it has issued a series of guidance documents setting forth a revised framework for implementing the program. The first of these was issued in 2013 and entitled *A Long Term Vision for Assessment, Restoration, and Protection Under the Clean Water Act Section 303(d) Program*. The EPA issued a further guidance memorandum in 2015 entitled *Information Concerning 2016 Clean Water Act Sections 303(d), 305(b), and 314 Integrated Reporting and Listing Decisions* (Aug. 13, 2015). The 2015 memorandum directs states to set long-term prioritization goals out to 2022, establish priority rankings, consider alternative restoration approaches where appropriate, and implement EPA's Water Quality Framework to integrate EPA's data and information systems. These documents also build on earlier guidance documents which had moved the TMDL program implementation decidedly towards a watershed-based focus and, in some cases, a multi-jurisdictional approach when a watershed spans multiple states. As a result of this guidance, many states have developed multi-state TMDLs for particular pollutants (e.g., mercury, dissolved oxygen) and statewide TMDLs for a single pollutant (e.g., mercury, chloride, bacteria).

**8.** The most prominent and largest multi-jurisdictional TMDL is for the Chesapeake Bay spanning New York, Pennsylvania, Maryland, Delaware, Virginia, West Virginia, and District of Columbia. As a result of litigation by environmental groups over the failure of the states to protect the Bay, EPA issued a TMDL covering the region in 2010. The Third Circuit upheld the TMDL in 2015 in the face of industry challenge contending that the TMDL was beyond EPA's authority under the CWA and improperly allowed EPA to directly regulate farming practices, industrial activities, and land use, thus invading the province of the states. *See* American Farm Bureau Fed. v. EPA, 792 F.3d 281 (3rd Cir. 2015), *cert. denied*, 136 S. Ct. 1246 (2016).

**9.** Another action Congress took after EPA proposed its TMDL rule in 2000 was to commission the National Research Council (an arm of the National Academy of Sciences) to evaluate the scientific basis of the rule and the TMDL program in general. The Council's report concluded, among other things, that the TMDL program narrowly focuses on pollutant loads, whereas habitat degradation and stream channel modifications should play a key role in any water quality restoration program. Also, consistent with much of the literature on ecosystem management, the Council recommended that the TMDL program employ adaptive management techniques so that TMDLs can evolve as better data are collected and assessed. *See* NATIONAL ACADEMY OF SCIENCES/NATIONAL RESEARCH COUNCIL, ASSESSING THE TMDL APPROACH TO WATER QUALITY MANAGEMENT (2001).

**10.** The *Pronsolino* court noted that, because EPA has no authority to regulate nonpoint sources directly, the only leverage EPA really has over states that refuse to regulate nonpoint sources is withdrawing federal environmental grant funds. As the court explained, while this is not federal regulation, the withdrawal effects may be too severe for states that have become dependent on the federal dollars to help run state environmental programs. They may knuckle under, as the court put it, and apply the federal program uncritically and contrary to other legitimate state policy objectives.

Indeed, as explained in a 2013 guidance statement, EPA has hinged funding under Section 319 of the CWA (discussed above) on the states taking a watershed-based approach to bringing nonpoint sources into the TMDL fold. Specifically, states may use specified federal funds to develop nonpoint source TMDLs and watershed-based plans to implement nonpoint source TMDLs. These watershed-based plans must include at least the following elements listed below along with other elements relating to technical and financial assistance, educational outreach, schedules, interim milestones, benchmarking, and monitoring:

> a. An identification of the causes and sources or groups of similar sources that will need to be controlled to achieve the load reductions estimated in this watershed-based plan (and to achieve any other watershed goals identified in the watershed-based plan), as discussed in item (b) immediately below. Sources that need to be controlled should be identified at the significant subcategory level with estimates of the extent to which they are present in the watershed (e.g., X numbers of dairy cattle feedlots needing upgrading, including a rough estimate of the number of cattle per facility; Y acres of row crops needing improved nutrient management or sediment control; or Z linear miles of eroded streambank needing remediation).
>
> b. An estimate of the load reductions expected for the management measures described under paragraph (c) below (recognizing the natural variability and the difficulty in precisely predicting the performance of management measures over time). Estimates should be provided at the same level as in item (a) above (e.g., the total load reduction expected for dairy cattle feedlots; row crops; or eroded streambanks).
>
> c. A description of the NPS management measures that will need to be implemented to achieve the load reductions estimated under paragraph (b) above (as well as to achieve other watershed goals identified in this watershed-based plan), and an identification (using a map or a description) of the critical areas in which those measures will be needed to implement the plan. . . .

U.S. EPA, Nonpoint Source Program and Grants Guidelines for States and Territories (April 12, 2013).

**11.** The costs associated with TMDL compliance for individual landowners can be significant—in the *Pronsolino* case, some owners of timber land within the watershed would incur nearly a million dollars in costs associated with reducing sediment runoff and limiting removal of trees during certain times of the year. Why is it so expensive to reduce pollutant loads from such lands? Is it that forestry and other land management practices were so bad, or is it simply that controlling nonpoint source pollution is so difficult? If it will cost landowners tens of millions of dollars to comply with TMDLs in a single, small watershed, imagine the total national price tag for controlling nonpoint source pollution! Is it worth it? Should the cost be borne entirely by the private landowners?

**12.** Because the TMDL program depends on the WQS program as the driver of impairment determinations and then, for waters that are impaired, the TMDL load allocation process, the rise of the TMDL program has focused greater attention on the WQS program. One of the most controversial WQS issues in this regard has been the EPA's efforts to require states to establish quantitative numeric standards for nutrients, primarily nitrogen and phosphorus. The vast majority of states have established what are known as narrative standards for nutrients in waterbodies—qualitative descriptions of water quality such as Florida's declaration that "in no case shall nutrient concentrations of body of water be altered so as to cause an imbalance in natural populations of flora or fauna." By comparison, numeric standards stated in measurable parts per million or billion are more definitive and thus more amenable to impairment determinations and TMDL load allocations and enforcement. For many waterbodies, however, the primary source of nutrient pollution is nonpoint source flows from agriculture, which means any effort to move in the direction of numeric standards and TMDL program enforcement is in for a battle. Nowhere has this been more the case than for Florida, where EPA and the state engaged in contentious litigation and negotiations over EPA's court-ordered demand that the state adopt numeric nutrient standards. *See* Florida Wildlife Federation v. Jackson, 2009 WL 5217062 (N.D. Fla. Dec. 30, 2009). EPA finalized regulations for the state in 2010. *See* 75 Fed. Reg. 75,762 (Dec. 6, 2010) (amending various provisions of 40 C.F.R. pt. 131). Florida has since adopted standards meeting EPA's approval, which are available at https://www.epa.gov/wqs-tech/water-quality-standards-regulations-florida.

**13.** For more on the history of the TMDL program, particularly as it relates to nonpoint sources, see OLIVER A. HOUCK, THE CLEAN WATER ACT TMDL PROGRAM: LAW, POLICY, AND IMPLEMENTATION (Envtl. L. Inst. 1999); Linda A. Malone, *The Myths and Truths That Ended the 2000 TMDL Program*, 20 PACE ENVTL. L. REV. 63 (2002); Robert W. Adler, *Controlling Nonpoint Source Pollution: Is Help on the Way (From the Courts or EPA?)*, 31 ENVTL. L. REP. (ELI) 10270 (2001); Sarah Birkeland, *EPA's TMDL Program*, 28 ECOLOGY L.Q. 297 (2001); James Boyd, *The New Face of the Clean Water Act: A Critical Review of EPA's New TMDL Rules*, 11 DUKE ENVTL. L. & POL'Y F. 39 (2000); CLAUDIA COPELAND, CONGRESSIONAL RESEARCH SERVICE, CLEAN WATER ACT AND POLLUTANT TOTAL MAXIMUM DAILY LOADS (TMDLS) (Jan. 17, 2014).

**14.** Section 401 of the Clean Water Act requires state approval of any activity which may result in any discharge into navigable waters. 33 U.S.C. § 1331. The purpose of this so-called "401 certification" process is to ensure federal agencies do not carry out or authorize activities that will impede the states in achieving their water quality standards. The scope of the requirement is quite broad. For example, the Supreme Court ruled that the Federal Energy Regulatory Commission must obtain 401 certification for renewal of hydropower dam licenses, on the ground that the passage of water from the reservoir, through the dam, and then into the stream is a discharge within the meaning of Section 401. *See* S.D. Warren Co. v. Maine Board of Environmental Protection, 547 U.S. 370 (2006). On the other hand, the Ninth

Circuit held in 2008 that the 401 certification process does not apply to discharges from non-point sources of pollution, thus finding that the U.S. Forest Service could issue grazing permits to a cattle company without obtaining a state 401 certification. *See* Oregon Natural Desert Ass'n v. United States Forest Service, 550 F.3d 778 (9th Cir. 2008).

## F. THE SAFE DRINKING WATER ACT (SDWA)

Americans today enjoy the safest drinking water in human history, with more people having access to safe drinking water than ever before. Just a century ago, it was not uncommon for Americans to die of waterborne diseases. The famed aviator brother, Wilbur Wright, died of Typhoid. Such an event today is rare. The fact that we take clean tap water for granted is due primarily to the Safe Drinking Water Act (SDWA), the law safeguarding the water we drink. Passed in 1974, the SDWA regulates public water systems with at least 15 service connections or serving at least 25 people for at least 60 days a year. Together, this includes over 150,000 public water systems but excludes most private wells (which serve tens of millions of Americans). 42 U.S.C. §§ 300f–300j–26. *See generally,* JAMES SALZMAN, DRINKING WATER: A HISTORY (2012).

The key section of the law regulates contaminant levels in drinking water and works in three steps. The first is to decide "what's in and what's out"—which contaminants the law will regulate and which will remain outside legal control. EPA is supposed to assess the risk posed by contaminants and their likelihood to occur in public drinking water systems. For those posing the greatest risks, the agency sets maximum contaminant level goals (MCLGs)—the highest concentration of the contaminant in water that allows an adequate margin of safety. For many contaminants, such as microbes and carcinogens, this number is zero.

It may not be practical to eliminate these contaminants, though, so in the second step EPA then sets a maximum contaminant level (MCL). This is the practical standard, and it is as close to the MCLG as feasible, given technology and cost limitations. In the third step, the agency carries out a risk assessment and considers the costs to achieve the mandated reduction. The final level can then be modified to a level that "maximizes health risk reduction benefits at a cost that is justified by the benefits."

This final standard not only sets the maximum contaminant level but also includes testing requirements for water systems to ensure the standards are achieved. Put simply, if the presence of a regulated contaminant in a drinking water sample does not exceed the MCLs, then drinking water from our tap is legally determined to be safe. Water utilities must notify customers within 24 hours of any violations with potential health consequences.

In practice, the SDWA is implemented by state and local authorities that have applied to EPA for "primacy" to carry out the SDWA's requirements in their jurisdictions (except for Wyoming and Washington, DC). This poses particular challenges because 90% of the public water systems are small, serving fewer than 10,000 people. The capacity of these systems to monitor and treat water effectively varies enormously and EPA must bear in mind that treatment technologies appropriate for major cities' water treatment plants may be unaffordable for smaller systems and communities.

EPA is supposed to periodically reevaluate the stringency of the standards, revising them in light of new data and considering new contaminant candidates to add. Since its passage, the SDWA has regulated over ninety contaminants. That sounds impressive until one realizes that more than sixty thousand chemicals are used within the United States, and the number is growing. Moreover, many of the standards for chemicals that are listed have not been revised since the 1980s or 1970s, when the law was first passed. Given this track record, it seems unlikely that the law will address the new generation of water pollutants—such as endocrine disruptors and pharmaceuticals—anytime soon.

The SDWA has two other features worth noting. In the 1996 amendments, Congress directed EPA to protect source waters. Rather than only treating water at the plant, the idea was to prevent contamination in the first place by addressing land use practices that contaminate waters before they ever reached the plant. Water utilities are given primary responsibility for addressing threats to source waters but have few tools at their disposal beyond creating an inventory of potential threats (known as a source water assessment) and sharing this information. These limits of the SDWA are most evident with nonpoint source pollution such as fertilizer and pesticide runoff from farms. Water utilities rarely have land use control authority and the source of the pollutants may well lie outside the municipal boundaries.

Two drinking water crises in 2014 provided good examples of these shortcomings. In Charleston, West Virginia, a chemical tank farm sitting above a bluff of the Elk River leaked a compound used to clean coal just one mile above the intake for the region's water treatment plant. Residents could not use any tap water for more than a week. Later that year, Toledo, Ohio, told its citizens not to use the tap water because of a huge algal bloom in Lake Erie that was producing toxins in the water. In neither case did the water utility have any control over the source of the problem—industrial site management in Charleston and agricultural nonpoint source pollution around Toledo.

The SDWA also seeks to protect groundwater through its underground injection control (UIC) program. The UIC provisions regulate injection wells to ensure that fluids are not discharged into an underground source of drinking water. The reasons for such protection seem obvious, which explains why there has been such controversy over the "Halliburton Loophole" in Section 322 the Energy Policy Act of 2005, Pub. L. 109–58. This provision specifically excludes fracking activities from UIC coverage. States can regulate the discharge of fracking fluids into aquifers, but EPA has no authority to do so under the SDWA.

## QUESTIONS AND DISCUSSION

**1.** While the vast majority of American tap water is safe to drink, it contains more than just $H_2O$. We all ingest pharmaceutical products when we drink water. A 1999 study by the U.S. Geological Survey identified eighty-two contaminants, many of them pharmaceuticals and personal care products, in 80% of the streams they sampled in thirty states. A 2006 Geological Survey study of private wells was similarly eye opening. In a widely publicized study, the Associated Press documented the presence of fifty-six pharmaceuticals or their by-products in treated drinking water, including in the water of metropolitan areas supplying more than forty million people across the nation. But how do the drugs get in the water? *See* Jeff Donn, Martha Mendoza, & Justin Pritchard, *Pharmaceuticals Lurking in U.S. Drinking Water*, MSNBC.COM., Mar. 10, 2008.

The dominant contributor seems to be us. Despite warnings against the practice, many people flush unused drugs down the toilet. We contribute unintentionally, as well. When we take a pill, our bodies metabolize some of the active ingredients but not all. The remainder are excreted and flushed down our toilets, making their way through sewers and treatment plants into the environment and, eventually, drinking water sources. Most treatment plants are not designed to remove drug residues, and few actually test for their presence. Nor is this only a concern in highly populated areas. Drugs given to cattle make their way into water tables in agricultural areas.

There are no regulations requiring testing for the presence of pharmaceuticals in drinking water or limiting their concentration (and realize that these are present in bottled water, as well). The Associated Press study contacted sixty-two major drinking water providers. Twenty-eight of those—just under half—tested for drugs in water. Those not testing included facilities serving some of our nation's largest cities—New York, Houston, Chicago, and Phoenix.

Should we be concerned? Scientists tell us that the concentrations are extremely low—sometimes in parts per billion or even parts per trillion. This is far, far below the level of a prescribed medical dose. The EPA refers to these chemicals and others as "emergent contaminants." The risk may be real, but it is largely unknown. Christian Daughton, one of EPA's leading authorities on the topic, explains the safety dilemma well: "Scientists have only recently become able to detect contaminants at the extremely low levels at which drugs appear in water supplies—typically, around one part per trillion. You're at the outer envelope of toxicology. Historically we've worried about substances like pesticides that are present in much higher concentrations. It's also very hard to study effects at that level because the doses are so small, and the effects are subtle and delayed." *Ibid.*

What do you think should be done about the presence of emerging contaminants in our drinking water? We can upgrade our treatment plants to filter these out, but at great expense and beyond the capacity of many small systems.

**2.** Enforcement remains a major challenge for the SDWA. An investigative study by the *New York Times* in 2009 reported that more than 20% of the water treatment systems across the country had violated key provisions of the SDWA over the past few years. Yet only a handful of these systems, a mere 6%, had been fined or punished by state or federal officials. Charles Duhigg, *Millions in U.S. Drink Dirty Water, Records Show*, N.Y. TIMES, Dec. 8, 2009. Part of this meager enforcement record was due to inadequate funding, but part was institutional. Most water treatment systems are operated by local governments, and the lion's share of violations occur in the smaller systems—those serving fewer than twenty thousand residents. This should not be surprising, since it is at these smallest systems where resources for testing and maintenance are smallest, as well. As Professor David Uhlmann, former chief of the Environmental Crimes Section at the Department of Justice, explained, it is difficult for one arm of government to sue the other: "There is significant reluctance within the EPA and Justice Department to bring actions against municipalities, because there's a view that they are often cash-strapped, and fines would ultimately be paid by local taxpayers." *Ibid.*

**3.** Drinking water became a national concern in 2015 as events in Flint, Michigan, unfolded. For decades, the city of Flint had received its water from the Detroit Water Department. To save money, an Emergency Manager supervising the affairs of the cash-strapped city decided to shift over to water from nearby Lake Huron, but there was a two-year gap while the new pipeline was completed. In the meantime, the city reactivated its local treatment plant and took water directly from the Flint River, just as it had done prior to using Detroit's water.

From the outset, residents complained that the Flint water was colored and smelly. Despite positive tests for coliforms and some boil water advisories, government officials insisted the water was safe to drink. To ensure greater disinfection, the water utility increased the chlorine in the water. Soon after, a number of tests found highly elevated lead levels in some homes. An EPA scientist investigating the water samples wrote a memo expressing concern that the Flint treatment plant had not added an anti-corrosion treatment to the water that would have counteracted the natural acidity of the river (in addition to the chlorination treatments). If the treatment was not added, then the acidic water would cause lead to leach from pipes into the water.

And why might there be lead pipes in the water system? A city ordinance from 1897 had actually required the installation of lead service lines and there were over 15,000 in the city connecting private homes with the city water mains. Dismissing concerns over lead contamination, the spokesperson for the state Department of Environmental Quality denounced the EPA scientist as "a rogue employee," stating there was no problem with lead in the water. Arthur Delaney, *EPA Official Says "False Allegations"*

*Forced Her Resignation Over Flint Water Crisis,* HUFFINGTON POST, March 15, 2016.

Alerted by a Flint pediatrician who was seeing elevated lead levels in her patients' blood, Marc Edwards, a chemist at Virginia Tech University who had helped expose lead contamination in Washington, D.C.'s water a decade earlier sent his team to Flint to collect water samples. He found sample after sample of lead levels far above the SDWA thresholds. At this point, the story became a major news item across the nation. In short order, the county issued Do Not Drink health advisories, Flint reconnected to Detroit's water system, and a series of public hearings took place. This story is still playing out, with criminal indictments underway against officials who allegedly misreported and altered test results.

There are three key lessons to take from this saga. The first is governmental ethics and attitude. The SDWA has redundancy built into its structure. When states are given primacy, local water utilities implement the law but they are overseen by state officials who, in turn, are overseen by EPA. There was any number of red flags that should have triggered more careful oversight but, each time, officials were more concerned with perception than public health. The EPA scientist who first raised concerns was personally denounced by the state agency for releasing his memo. Why didn't the agency focus, instead, on the possibility that he was correct about Flint's potential failure to add corrosion controls?

The second lesson concerns environmental justice. Flint is a poor city largely populated by African Americans. The driving force to change water supplies was budget cutting. It seems unlikely that a wealthy white community would have faced the same difficulty in persuading the authorities to take a closer look at problems with the water supply.

The third lesson concerns drinking water more generally. The average citizen is in no position to assess the safety of her drinking water. A store-bought water filter would not have removed the lead in Flint's water. Residents who cannot afford bottled water have no choice but to trust that water utilities and agency officials are doing their jobs correctly. When this trust is misplaced, as happened in Flint at every level of governance—from local to state to federal—the trust that underlies environmental protection more generally breaks down. Re-establishing this level of confidence—feeling assured that the water you drink from the tap really is safe—will take time and renewed oversight and transparency to ensure its credibility.

## II. WETLANDS PROTECTION

Only one other environmental statute comes as close as the Endangered Species Act does to establishing federal regulatory power over local land uses—Section 404 of the Clean Water Act, which regulates "the discharge of dredged or fill material into the navigable waters." While that might not immediately strike you as the foundation for a land use control statute, section 404 has evolved into the nation's primary authority for protecting *wetlands*.

Wetlands can be broadly divided into two categories: coastal wetlands and inland wetlands. Coastal wetlands are mostly marshes and swamps that are flooded by the tides. Non-tidal inland wetlands include wetlands along rivers and lakes, as well as isolated wetlands that are not directly connected to a major body of water but which are nonetheless valuable ecological resources. An important example of the latter variety is the "prairie pothole," which provides habitat for about half of the U.S. waterfowl population.

Among the most biologically productive of land types, wetlands cover approximately 4 to 6 percent of the Earth's land surface. Their high productivity results from the essential characteristic of a wetland: an area that is flooded part of the time but not all of the time. This flooding ensures that the wetlands have ample supplies of water and minerals. In addition to their high biological productivity, wetlands are important habitat for birds, fish, and other species. Wetlands are also important cleansing mechanisms for preventing pollutants from farms and other land uses from running off and degrading water quality in rivers, lakes, and streams.

Several federal studies document the massive loss of wetland resources our nation has witnessed over the past 200 years. *See* U.S. FISH AND WILDLIFE SERVICE, STATUS AND TRENDS OF WETLANDS IN THE COTERMINOUS UNITED STATES 2004 TO 2009 (2011); U.S. FISH AND WILDLIFE SERVICE, STATUS AND TRENDS OF WETLANDS IN THE COTERMINOUS UNITED STATES 1998 TO 2004 (2006); U.S. FISH AND WILDLIFE SERVICE, STATUS AND TRENDS OF WETLANDS IN THE COTERMINOUS UNITED STATES 1986 TO 1997 (2000); USDA, NATURAL RESOURCES CONSERVATION SERVICE, NATIONAL RESOURCES INVENTORY (2000); Lori A. Sutter, et al., *Science and Policy of U.S Wetlands*, 29 TUL. ENVTL. L.J. 31 (2015). At the time of European settlement, the area that is today the coterminous United States had approximately 221 million acres of wetlands. The most recent assessment of wetland status estimates there are just over 110 million acres of wetlands in the coterminous United States, the vast majority of which are freshwater wetlands. Six states have lost over 85 percent of their wetlands, and 22 have lost more than 50 percent. None of the lower 48 states has lost less than 20 percent of its original wetlands. Florida has lost the most acres of wetlands—9.3 million acres—though it also is the state with the most remaining acres of wetlands, other than Alaska. Alaska adds 170 million acres of wetlands to the total, only a small fraction of which have been lost in the last 200 years.

Although the rate of gains from reestablishment of wetlands increased by 17 percent from 2004 to 2009 compared to 1998 to 2004, the wetland loss rate increased 140 percent during the same period. As a consequence, national wetland losses have outpaced gains. *See* U.S. FISH AND WILDLIFE SERVICE (2011), *supra*. Even earlier reports suggesting the tide has turned on wetland losses, with an estimated net gain of over

190,000 acres since 1998, were controversial. These numbers included artificial freshwater ponds such as farm stock ponds, golf course ponds, and urban stormwater control ponds, which as a category increased by 700,000 acres since 1998. If those artificial wetlands are not counted, then a net loss of wetlands since 1998 would be the result. For more information on wetland status in the united States, see http://water.epa.gov/type/wetlands/vital_status.cfm.

Most of the nation's history of wetland losses is attributable to drainage of wetlands for conversion to agriculture, a practice that began in earnest with the earliest European settlers and was the official federal and state policy throughout most of the 1800s. Wetlands were considered undesirable, swampy, mosquito-infested wastelands that truly were wasted if not converted to some better use, usually agriculture but increasingly for urban development. This attitude prevailed well into the 1900s. Consider Gene Zion's 1957 children's book, *Dear Garbage Man*, which tells the supposedly happy story of how garbage should be used:

> That night as the city slept, the tugboats chugged and whistled softly as they pulled the barges down the river. The trash and ashes they carried would be used to fill in swampland. Then parks and playgrounds would be built there.

And many such parks and playgrounds were built. But as the ecological value of wetlands was increasingly understood and appreciated, protection of wetlands became a major public policy objective by the mid-1970s. That trend, plus the gradual decline in conversion of land to agricultural uses significantly dampened the rate of wetland losses. During the 1990s, we lost on average only about 58,500 acres annually to a combination of urban development (30%), agriculture (26%), forestry (23%), and rural development (21%), which was a dramatic reduction from the previous decade.

A threshold question inevitably confronted when designing wetland conservation policy is where exactly are these wetlands, and which of them are subject to federal, state, or local regulatory authority? That question has befuddled federal policy for decades. Section 404 of the Clean Water Act establishes the primary federal program for answering those questions of boundary and application. Section 404 is jointly administered by the U.S. Army Corps of Engineers (Corps), with primary responsibility for implementing a permitting program regulating discharges of "fill" material into waters of the United States, including wetlands, and by the Environmental Protection Agency (EPA), which has authority to define environmental guidelines the Corps must follow. The materials in this section explain how these two agencies have dealt with the problem of defining which wetland areas are subject to federal jurisdiction, which activities constitute regulated fill of those jurisdictional wetlands, and on what terms a regulated activity can receive a permit to authorize the fill.

## A. JURISDICTIONAL WETLANDS: *RIVERSIDE BAYVIEW HOMES*, *SWANCC*, AND *RAPANOS*

The term "wetland" implies the existence of "dryland" and thus a geographic limit to the ecosystem unit identified for management under Section 404 of the CWA. Identifying where wet ends and dry begins under Section 404, however, has not been as simple as it may seem. Indeed, wetness is not the exclusively dispositive factor. Questions of federalism and statutory construction have thrust legal issues to the forefront of what otherwise might be thought of as a straightforward bio-physical question.

The relevant provisions of the Clean Water Act originated in the Federal Water Pollution Control Act Amendments of 1972, 86 Stat. 816, and have remained essentially unchanged since that time. Under Sections 301 and 502 of the Act, 33 U.S.C. §§ 1311 and 1362, any discharge of dredged or fill materials into "navigable waters"—defined as the "waters of the United States"—is forbidden unless authorized by a permit issued by the Corps pursuant to Section 404, 33 U.S.C. § 1344. After initially construing the Act to cover only waters navigable in fact, in 1975 the Corps issued interim final regulations redefining "the waters of the United States" to include not only actually navigable waters but also tributaries of such waters, interstate waters and their tributaries, and nonnavigable intrastate waters whose use or misuse could affect interstate commerce. *See* 40 Fed. Reg. 31,320 (1975) (amending various provisions of 29 C.F.R. pt. 209). The Corps also construed the Act to cover all "freshwater wetlands" that were adjacent to other covered waters. A "freshwater wetland" was defined as an area that is "periodically inundated" and is "normally characterized by the prevalence of vegetation that requires saturated soil conditions for growth and reproduction." 33 CFR § 209.120(d)(2)(h) (1976). In 1977, the Corps refined its definition of wetlands by eliminating the reference to periodic inundation and making other minor changes. The 1977 definition read as follows:

> The term "wetlands" means those areas that are inundated or saturated by surface or ground water at a frequency and duration sufficient to support, and that under normal circumstances do support, a prevalence of vegetation typically adapted for life in saturated soil conditions. Wetlands generally include swamps, marshes, bogs and similar areas. 33 CFR § 323.2(c) (1978).

In 1982, the 1977 regulations were replaced by substantively identical regulations that remain in force today. *See* 33 C.F.R. § 328.2(c)(4).

In 1985, the Supreme Court addressed whether the provision extending jurisdiction to "adjacent" wetlands was consistent with the scope of federal jurisdiction established under the Clean Water Act. *See*

United States v. Riverside Bayview Homes, Inc., 474 U.S. 121 (1985). The Court held that it was:

> The regulation extends the Corps' authority under § 404 to all wetlands adjacent to navigable or interstate waters and their tributaries. Wetlands, in turn, are defined as lands that are "inundated or saturated by surface or ground water at a frequency and duration sufficient to support, and that under normal circumstances do support, a prevalence of vegetation typically adapted for life in saturated soil conditions." 33 CFR § 323.2(c) (1985). The plain language of the regulation refutes the Court of Appeals' conclusion that inundation or "frequent flooding" by the adjacent body of water is a sine qua non of a wetland under the regulation. Indeed, the regulation could hardly state more clearly that saturation by either surface or ground water is sufficient to bring an area within the category of wetlands, provided that the saturation is sufficient to and does support wetland vegetation. . . .
>
> We cannot say that the Corps' conclusion that adjacent wetlands are inseparably bound up with the "waters" of the United States—based as it is on the Corps' and EPA's technical expertise—is unreasonable. In view of the breadth of federal regulatory authority contemplated by the Act itself and the inherent difficulties of defining precise bounds to regulable waters, the Corps' ecological judgment about the relationship between waters and their adjacent wetlands provides an adequate basis for a legal judgment that adjacent wetlands may be defined as waters under the Act.

Relative calm remained until Solid Waste Agency of Northern Cook County v. United States Army Corps of Engineers, 531 U.S. 159 (2001) (*SWANCC*). In that case the Court addressed whether the Corps could apply Section 404 to "isolated" wetlands—wetlands neither adjacent to nor hydrologically connected to navigable waters but that serve as a habitat for migratory birds (the "migratory bird rule"). At issue was whether a proper reading of CWA supported the migratory bird rule, and, if so, whether the existence of migratory birds was sufficient to give Congress the authority to regulate such intrastate, isolated wetlands under the Commerce Clause in the first place. The Court addressed the statutory issue (whether the CWA supported the migratory bird rule) but not the constitutional issue. Over a blistering dissent, the majority held these wetlands were beyond what Congress intended to be within the scope of Section 404:

> This is not the first time we have been called upon to evaluate the meaning of § 404(a). In United States v. Riverside Bayview Homes, Inc., 474 U.S. 121 (1985), we held that the Corps had § 404(a) jurisdiction over wetlands that actually abutted on a navigable waterway. In so doing, we noted that the term

"navigable" is of "limited import" and that Congress evidenced its intent to "regulate at least some waters that would not be deemed 'navigable' under the classical understanding of that term." *Id.*, at 133. But our holding was based in large measure upon Congress' unequivocal acquiescence to, and approval of, the Corps' regulations interpreting the CWA to cover wetlands adjacent to navigable waters. *See id.*, at 135–139. We found that Congress' concern for the protection of water quality and aquatic ecosystems indicated its intent to regulate wetlands "inseparably bound up with the 'waters' of the United States." *Id.,* at 134.

It was the significant nexus between the wetlands and "navigable waters" that informed our reading of the CWA in *Riverside Bayview Homes*. Indeed, we did not "express any opinion" on the "question of the authority of the Corps to regulate discharges of fill material into wetlands that are not adjacent to bodies of open water. . . ." *Id.*, at 131–132, n.8. In order to rule for respondents here, we would have to hold that the jurisdiction of the Corps extends to ponds that are not adjacent to open water. But we conclude that the text of the statute will not allow this.

We . . . decline respondents' invitation to take what they see as the next ineluctable step after *Riverside Bayview Homes*: holding that isolated ponds, some only seasonal, wholly located within two Illinois counties, fall under § 404(a)'s definition of "navigable waters" because they serve as habitat for migratory birds. As counsel for respondents conceded at oral argument, such a ruling would assume that "the use of the word navigable in the statute . . . does not have any independent significance." We cannot agree that Congress' separate definitional use of the phrase "waters of the United States" constitutes a basis for reading the term "navigable waters" out of the statute. We said in *Riverside Bayview Homes* that the word "navigable" in the statute was of "limited effect" and went on to hold that § 404(a) extended to nonnavigable wetlands adjacent to open waters. But it is one thing to give a word limited effect and quite another to give it no effect whatever. The term "navigable" has at least the import of showing us what Congress had in mind as its authority for enacting the CWA: its traditional jurisdiction over waters that were or had been navigable in fact or which could reasonably be so made.

The lower federal courts were quick to apply *SWANCC* in a variety of circumstances with the effect of cutting off federal jurisdiction over isolated waters. *See, e.g.*, Rice v. Harken Exploration Co., 250 F.3d 264 (5th Cir. 2001) (construing *SWANCC* to mean that the CWA applies only to a "body of water that is actually navigable or is adjacent to an open body of navigable water"); U.S. v. Newdunn, 195 F. Supp. 2d 751 (E.D. Va. 2002) (Corps had no jurisdiction over 38 acres of wetlands in the absence of proof of connection to navigable waters); U.S. v. Rapanos, 190 F. Supp. 2d 1011 (E.D. Mich. 2002) (dismissing criminal prosecution for unauthorized filling of wetlands because Corps did not prove area was navigable or an adjacent water). Over time, however, lower court opinions after *SWANCC* scattered around the apparently fine lines dividing jurisdictional and non-jurisdictional waters with no apparent resolution. The Fifth Circuit's *Harken* decision and later decision in In re Needham, 354 F.3d 340 (5th Cir. 2003), represented the broadest construction of *SWANCC*, with the Fourth and Ninth Circuits interpreting *SWANCC* more narrowly. *See* United States v. Deaton, 332 F.3d 698 (4th Cir. 2003); Treacy v. Newdunn Associates, 344 F.3d 407 (4th Cir. 2003); Headwaters Inc. v. Talent Irrigation District, 243 F.3d 526 (9th Cir. 2001). *See also* Stan Millan, *Clean Water Act Waters Have a Beginning, But Do They Have an End?*, 35 ENV'T REP. (BNA) 964 (2004); Joan Mulhern and Michael Lozeau, *Federal Agencies: In Brief, Follow Your Own Counsel*, NATIONAL WETLANDS NEWSLETTER, July–Aug. 2003, at 9; Mark A Ryan, *CWA Jurisdiction Four Years After* SWANCC, NATURAL RESOURCES & ENV'T, Fall 2005, at 63.

As these cases piled up in the lower federal courts, EPA and the Corps wrestled with how to interpret *SWANCC*. On January 10, 2003, EPA and the Corps issued a guidance document taking a fairly broad view of the holding in *SWANCC*, leading to a narrow view of federal power to regulate wetlands. The guidance instructed Corps regional offices that "field staff should not assert CWA jurisdiction over isolated waters that are both intrastate and non-navigable," where the sole basis available for asserting CWA jurisdiction rests on any of the factors listed in the "Migratory Bird Rule." The guidance also outlined the uncertainty ostensibly left by *SWANCC* and its lower court progeny over questions such as whether the other interstate commerce criteria in the Corps' regulations (e.g., use of waters by interstate travelers) would justify assertion of jurisdiction over intrastate, non-navigable waters, and whether *SWANCC* affects jurisdiction over tributaries that are neither navigable nor immediately adjacent to navigable waters. To resolve some of those posited ambiguities, the agencies also jointly issued an Advance Notice of Proposed Rulemaking to "further the public interest by clarifying what waters are subject to CWA jurisdiction." 68 Fed. Reg. 1991 (Jan. 15, 2003) (attaching the guidance document as Appendix A). Almost one year and 135,000 public comments later, however, the agencies decided in December 2003 to rescind the notice, but to keep the guidance in place. Most of the comments were form cards or short e-mails urging the agencies not to codify the broad reading of *SWANCC* suggested in the guidance document. The belief that the agencies might do just that was confirmed when, a few weeks before the rescission announcement, a draft rule "leaked" to the *Los Angeles Times* revealed that the agencies were planning to propose a rule that would resolve the ambiguous cases by erring on the side of limiting federal jurisdiction. For some accounts of this continuing saga, see Robert R.M. Verchick, *Toward Normative Rules for Agency Interpretation: Defining Jurisdiction Under the Clean Water Act*, 55 ALA. L. REV. 845 (2004); Sheila Deely & Mark Latham, *The Federal Wetlands Program: A Regulatory Program Run Amuck*, 34 ENV'T REP. (BNA) 966 (2003); *The Public Speaks Out: Comments from the Federal Docket*, NATIONAL WETLANDS NEWSLETTER, July–Aug. 2003, at 13. An instructive study also can be found in GENERAL ACCOUNTING OFFICE, WATERS AND WETLANDS: CORPS OF ENGINEERS NEEDS TO EVALUATE ITS DISTRICT PRACTICES IN DETERMINING JURISDICTION (2004), which not surprisingly found that more consistency and greater transparency is needed throughout the Corps in the determination of when to assert jurisdiction.

Then along came Rapanos v. United States, 547 U.S. 715 (2006), which resolved two consolidated cases from the Sixth Circuit. In one case, the United States brought an enforcement action alleging that property owners and their affiliated businesses deposited fill materials into wetlands without a permit, in violation of the CWA. In the other, property owners were denied a permit to deposit fill material in a wetland approximately one mile from a lake and, after exhausting their administrative appeals, they filed suit. The wetland areas in both cases thus were neither obviously isolated from, nor obviously adjacent to, navigable waters. In both cases, the district court found that there was federal regulatory jurisdiction over the sites in question, and the Sixth Circuit affirmed. The Supreme Court consolidated the cases and granted certiorari to decide whether the wetlands were "waters of the United States" under the CWA, and, if so, whether it is within Congress's authority under the Commerce Clause to regulate such intrastate, isolated wetlands. Like in *SWANCC*, the Court in *Rapanos* did not reach the constitutional question but instead based its decision solely on an interpretation of the CWA. However, as the following post-*Rapanos* decision from the Sixth Circuit explains, the Court's 4–1–4 decision did little to clarify the law in this area.

## United States v. Cundiff

United States Court of Appeals for the Sixth Circuit, 2009.
555 F.3d 200.

■ MARTIN, JR., CIRCUIT JUDGE.

After eight years of failed negotiations and ignored orders, the United States sued George Rudy Cundiff (who goes by Rudy) and his son, Christopher Seth Cundiff (who goes by Seth), seeking injunctive relief and civil penalties against them for discharging "pollutants" into "waters of the United States" without a permit in violation of the Clean Water Act. 33 U.S.C. § 1362. The district court granted summary judgment for the government, imposed injunctive relief in the form of a restoration plan for the Cundiffs' wetlands, and imposed a civil penalty of $225,000.

All but $25,000 of that penalty was suspended, however, provided that the Cundiffs implemented the restoration plan. The district court also dismissed the Cundiffs' array of statutory, common law, and constitutional counterclaims. While the original appeal in this case was pending, the Supreme Court issued its splintered ruling in Rapanos v. United States, 547 U.S. 715 (2006), which defined the Act's jurisdiction over "waters of the United States." In light of *Rapanos*, we returned the case to the district court to reconsider whether jurisdiction was proper over the Cundiffs' wetlands. The district court determined that it was because the Cundiffs' wetlands were in fact waters of the United States, and the Cundiffs appealed. We affirm the district court on all grounds.

I.

Defendants Rudy and Seth Cundiff own two adjacent tracts of land in Muhlenberg County, Kentucky. Their properties together sit next to Pond and Caney Creeks, which are tributaries of the Green River. The Green River, in turn, flows into the Ohio River. In 1990, Rudy Cundiff bought the southern tract, which contains roughly eighty-five acres of wetlands and an upland area where his house sits. When Rudy bought it, portions of the wetlands contained exceptionally acidic orangish to reddish colored water that had drained out of an abandoned coal mine located on a neighbor's nearby property. As a result, locals referred to the Cundiffs' property as a putrid eyesore, and this stagnant, discolored water caused the wetlands to become a festering mosquito haven—though the Cundiffs knew all this when they bought it.[1] Shortly after his purchase, Cundiff began excavating drainage ditches and clearing trees to make the wetlands suitable for farming.

In October 1991, federal officials from the Army Corps of Engineers and state officials from the Kentucky Division of Water observed ditches, artificially filled wetlands, and mechanically cleared land on the wetlands. The Corps suspected possible Clean Water Act violations. Rudy had failed to obtain a section 404 permit as required for such dredging and filling activities, . . . Consequently, the Corps sent him a cease-and-desist letter "specifically prohibiting any further activity involving the placement of excavated or fill material into these jurisdictional wetlands" without a federal permit.

Federal and state officials then began meeting with Cundiff in 1992, though they reached no agreement. Instead, he insisted on converting the wetlands into farmland and continued to drain and clear the property. The Corps referred the matter to the Environmental Protection Agency. Over the next several years, Cundiff continued his draining and

[1] Singer-songwriter John Prine has colorfully recounted Muhlenberg County's sordid ecological history: And daddy won't you take me back to Muhlenberg County / Down by the Green River where Paradise lay / Well, I'm sorry my son, but you're too late in asking / Mister Peabody's coal train has hauled it away. . . . / Then the coal company came with the world's largest shovel / And they tortured the timber and stripped all the land / Well, they dug for their coal 'til the land was forsaken / Then they wrote it all down as the progress of man. . . . John Prine, Paradise, on John Prine (Atlantic Records 1971).

ditch digging activities, simply ignoring whatever government directives came his way. In 1997 he planted wheat on the southern tract, and government officials observed downed trees in that area. The EPA issued an Order of Compliance informing him that he had violated the Clean Water Act by depositing fill material into waters of the United States without authorization, and it directed him to "immediately cease participating in or causing any additional discharges" of pollutants.

In 1998 Rudy's son, Seth, purchased a tract of land located north of Rudy's which contains roughly 103 acres of wetlands. (Seth leases this property back to Rudy for the exact amount of the mortgage payment.) Rudy quickly began excavating and clearing that property as well, activity of which Seth was aware. In October 1998, officials from the EPA informed Rudy Cundiff that he needed a permit for this work too. Rudy—somewhat surprisingly—said that, though he knew he needed a permit, he thought the Corps would never grant him one so he planned on digging his ditches anyway. He eventually completed a two-hundred foot ditch through the wetlands that extended all the way to Caney Creek, . . . In 1999, Kentucky officials told Cundiff that he was destroying wetlands without a permit in violation of state law (he ignored this too), and the EPA issued additional Orders of Compliance to both Rudy and Seth Cundiff requiring them to cease their excavation activities and to restore the unauthorized ditches by refilling them. The Cundiffs responded to these orders as they had to the others. . . .

III.

Congress enacted the Clean Water Act in 1972 "to restore and maintain the chemical, physical, and biological integrity of the Nation's waters." 33 U.S.C. § 1251(a). Section 301(a) of the Act prohibits "the discharge of any pollutant by any person" except in compliance with the Act. 33 U.S.C. § 1311(a). "[D]ischarge of any pollutant" is broadly defined to mean "any addition of any pollutant to navigable waters from any point source." 33 U.S.C. § 1362(12)(A). In turn, "pollutant" is defined to include not only traditional contaminants, but also solids such as "dredged spoil, . . . rock, sand [and] cellar dirt." 33 U.S.C. § 1362(6). The Act defines "navigable waters" to mean "the waters of the United States, including the territorial seas." 33 U.S.C. § 1362(7).

The Act also sets up two permit schemes. Section 404(a) authorizes the Secretary of the Army (through the United States Army Corps of Engineers), or a state with an approved program, to issue permits "for the discharge of dredged or fill material into the navigable waters at specified disposal sites." 33 U.S.C. § 1344(a). Section 402 authorizes the Environmental Protection Agency (or a state with an approved program) to issue a National Pollutant Discharge Elimination System (NPDES) permit for the discharge of pollutants other than dredged or fill material. 33 U.S.C. § 1342. The Corps and the EPA share responsibility for implementing and enforcing Section 404. *See, e.g.,* 33 U.S.C. § 1344(b)–(c).

Although at one time the term "navigable waters" included only waters that were navigable in fact, The Daniel Ball, 77 U.S. (10 Wall.) 557, 563, 19 L.Ed. 999 (1870), "navigable waters" is a defined term in the Act that expressly includes all "waters of the United States." 33 U.S.C. § 1362(7). The Supreme Court has repeatedly recognized that, with this definition, Congress "evidently intended to repudiate limits that had been placed on federal regulation by earlier water pollution control statutes and to exercise its powers under the Commerce Clause to regulate at least some waters that would not be deemed 'navigable' under the classical understanding of that term." United States v. Riverside Bayview Homes, Inc., 474 U.S. 121, 133 (1985). As a result, the Corps and EPA have put out substantively equivalent regulatory definitions of "waters of the United States," compare 33 C.F.R. § 328.3(a), with 40 C.F.R. § 230.3(s), that define it to encompass not only traditional navigable waters of the kind susceptible to use in interstate commerce, but also tributaries of traditional navigable waters and wetlands adjacent to covered waters. *See* 33 C.F.R. § 328.3(a)(1), 328(3)(a)(5), 328(a)(7).

A. Are the Wetlands "Waters of the United States"?

1. *Rapanos*

*Rapanos* involved two consolidated cases in which the Act had been applied to actual or proposed discharges of pollutants into wetlands adjacent to nonnavigable tributaries of traditional navigable waters. 547 U.S. at 729–30. Although there was no single majority opinion, all the Justices agreed that the statutory phrase "waters of the United States" encompasses some waters not navigable in the traditional sense. *See id.* at 731 (Scalia, J., plurality opinion); *id.* at 767–68 (Kennedy, J., concurring in the judgment); *id.* at 793 (Stevens, J., dissenting). The four-Justice plurality interpreted the Act to cover "relatively permanent, standing, or continuously flowing bodies of water," 547 U.S. at 739, that are connected to traditional navigable waters, *id.* at 742, as well as wetlands with a continuous surface connection to such water bodies. *Id.* at 732 n.5 (observing that the Act's reference to "relatively permanent" waters "d[id] not necessarily exclude streams, rivers, or lakes that might dry up in extraordinary circumstances, such as drought," or "seasonal rivers, which contain continuous flow during some months of the year but no flow during dry months").

Justice Kennedy, writing only for himself, interpreted the term to cover wetlands that "possess a 'significant nexus' to waters that are or were navigable in fact or that could reasonably be so made." *Id.* at 759, 126 S. Ct. 2208 (KENNEDY, J., concurring in the judgment) (quoting Solid Waste Agency v. United States Army Corps. of Eng'rs., 531 U.S. 159 (2001)). He explained:

> [W]etlands possess the requisite nexus, and thus come within the statutory phrase "navigable waters," if the wetlands, either alone or in combination with similarly situated lands in the

> region, significantly affect the chemical, physical, and biological integrity of other covered waters more readily understood as "navigable." When, in contrast, wetlands' effects on water quality are speculative or insubstantial, they fall outside the zone fairly encompassed by the statutory term "navigable waters."

*Id.* at 780. And Justice Kennedy, relying on *Riverside Bayview,* concluded that the Corps' assertion of jurisdiction over "wetlands adjacent to navigable-in-fact waters" may be met "by showing adjacency alone." *Id.* On the other hand, where the wetlands are adjacent to nonnavigable tributaries, "[a]bsent more specific regulations," Justice Kennedy would require the government to "establish a significant nexus on a case-by-case basis." *Id.* He therefore concurred in the judgment vacating the lower court's decision and voted to remand the case for more fact-finding on whether the government could prove the existence of a significant nexus between the wetlands and nearby navigable-in-fact waters.

The dissenters, with Justice Stevens writing, would have upheld the determination that the wetlands at issue were "waters of the United States" as a reasonable agency interpretation of the Act under Chevron U.S.A. Inc. v. Natural Resources Defense Council, Inc., 467 U.S. 837 (1984). In the dissenters' view, any "significant nexus" requirement—insofar as the Act contained one—would be "categorically satisfied as to wetlands adjacent to navigable waters or their tributaries." *Rapanos,* 547 U.S. at 807–08.

Parsing any one of *Rapanos*'s lengthy and technical statutory exegeses is taxing, but the real difficulty comes in determining which—if any—of the three main opinions lower courts should look to for guidance. As the Chief Justice observed: "It is unfortunate that no opinion commands a majority of the Court on precisely how to read Congress' limits on the reach of the Clean Water Act. Lower courts and regulated entities will now have to feel their way on a case-by-case basis." *Id.* at 758 (Roberts, C.J., concurring) (citing Grutter v. Bollinger, 539 U.S. 306, 325 (2003), and Marks v. United States, 430 U.S. 188 (1977)). The dissent, for its part, offered its view of what lower courts should do:

> In these cases, however, while both the plurality and Justice Kennedy agree that there must be a remand for further proceedings, their respective opinions define different tests to be applied on remand. Given that all four Justices who have joined this opinion would uphold the Corps' jurisdiction in both of these cases-and in all other cases in which either the plurality's or Justice Kennedy's test is satisfied-on remand each of the judgments should be reinstated if either of those tests is met.

*Rapanos,* 547 U.S. at 810 (emphasis added). Fortunately, as the following section explains, jurisdiction is proper here under each of the primary *Rapanos* opinions and therefore we do not have to decide here, once and for all, which test controls in all future cases.

2. *Marks*-meets-*Rapanos*

In *Marks v. United States*, the Supreme Court instructed that "[w]hen a fragmented Court decides a case and no single rationale explaining the result enjoys the assent of five Justices, the holding of the Court may be viewed as that position taken by those Members who concurred in the judgments on the narrowest grounds." 430 U.S. at 193 (quoting Gregg v. Georgia, 428 U.S. 153, 169 n.15 (1976) (opinion of Stewart, Powell, and Stevens, JJ.)). But all is not always so rosy. The Supreme Court has oft-noted Marks' limitations, stating that it is "more easily stated than applied to the various opinions supporting the result," *Grutter,* 539 U.S. at 325, and that "[i]t does not seem useful to pursue the *Marks* inquiry to the utmost logical possibility when it has so obviously baffled and divided the lower courts that have considered it," Nichols v. United States, 511 U.S. 738, 745 (1994) (quotations omitted).

In its short life, *Rapanos* has indeed satisfied any "bafflement" requirement. The first court to decide what opinion was controlling decided to ignore all of them and instead opted for earlier circuit precedent which it felt was clearer and more readily applied. United States v. Chevron Pipe Line Co., 437 F. Supp. 2d 605, 613 (N.D. Tex. 2006). The Courts of Appeals have not fared much better. The Ninth Circuit has stated that Justice Kennedy's test applies in most instances, Northern California River Watch v. City of Healdsburg, 496 F.3d 993, 1000 (9th Cir. 2007), while the Eleventh Circuit has held that the Act's coverage may be established only under his test. United States v. Robison, 505 F.3d 1208, 1219–22 (11th Cir. 2007). By contrast, the First and the Seventh Circuits, though differing somewhat in their analyses, have followed Justice Stevens' advice and held that the Act confers jurisdiction whenever either Justice Kennedy's or the plurality's test is met. United States v. Johnson, 467 F.3d 56, 60–66 (1st Cir. 2006); United States v. Gerke Excavating, Inc., 464 F.3d 723, 725 (7th Cir. 2006). This is the approach the district court here followed, largely in reliance on the First Circuit's thoughtful reasoning.

Taken literally, *Marks* instructs lower courts to choose the "narrowest" concurring opinion and to ignore dissents. *Marks,* 430 U.S. at 193. But what does "narrowest" mean? Marks considered an earlier Supreme Court obscenity decision, A Book Named "John Cleland's Memoirs of a Woman of Pleasure" v. Attorney General of Massachusetts, 383 U.S. 413 (1966), where the Court split on whether a particular work was protected by the First Amendment. In *Marks,* the Court determined that the *Memoirs* plurality's standard controlled because, while two Justices would have held that the First Amendment applies equally to all materials . . . the plurality would have afforded protection only to non-obscene materials, *id.* at 419–20, and therefore that concurring opinion was doctrinally the "narrowest."

The so-called *Marks* rule in fact derived from the Court's earlier opinion in Gregg v. Georgia, 428 U.S. 153 (1976). *Gregg* had interpreted

Furman v. Georgia, 408 U.S. 238 (1972), in which a majority found that Georgia's death penalty scheme was unconstitutional. Two Justices believed that the death penalty was per se unconstitutional, while three others merely stated that it was unconstitutional as then administered in Georgia. So the *Gregg* Court stated that "[s]ince five Justices wrote separately in support of the judgments in *Furman,* the holding of the Court may be viewed as that position taken by those Members who concurred in the judgments on the narrowest grounds. . . ." 428 U.S. at 169 n.15.

As these cases indicate—and contrary to assertions by the Cundiffs and their amici—Marks does not imply that the "narrowest" *Rapanos* opinion is whichever one restricts jurisdiction the most. But it also makes little sense for the "narrowest" opinion to be the one that restricts jurisdiction the least, as the government's amici allege; the ability to glean what substantive value judgments are buried within concurring, plurality, and single-Justice opinions would require something like divination to be performed accurately. Instead, "narrowest" opinion refers to the one which relies on the "least" doctrinally "far-reaching-common ground" among the Justices in the majority: it is the concurring opinion that offers the least change to the law. *See* Johnson v. Board of Regents of the Univ. of Ga., 263 F.3d 1234, 1247 (11th Cir. 2001); *Johnson*, 467 F.3d at 63. In both *Memoirs* and *Furman* the controlling opinion was less doctrinally sweeping. The *Memoirs* controlling opinion did not agree that obscenity laws per se violated the Constitution, and the *Furman* controlling opinion did not agree that the death penalty was per se unconstitutional.

Yet problems await. For cases like *Furman* and *Memoirs, Marks*' application is straightforward. But when "one opinion supporting the judgment does not fit entirely within a broader circle drawn by the others, *Marks* is problematic." King v. Palmer, 950 F.2d 771, 782 (D.C. Cir. 1991) (en banc). Specifically, "*Marks* is workable—one opinion can be meaningfully regarded as 'narrower' than another—only when one opinion is a logical subset of other, broader opinions." *Id.* at 781. Where no standard put forth in a concurring opinion is a logical subset of another concurring opinion (or opinions) that, together, would equal five votes, *Marks* breaks down.

Enter *Rapanos.* Although "in most cases in which [Justice Kennedy] concludes that there is no federal authority he will command five votes (himself plus the four Justices in the *Rapanos* plurality)," in other cases Justice Kennedy "would vote against federal authority only to be outvoted 8-to-1 (the four dissenting Justices plus the members of the *Rapanos* plurality) because there was a slight surface hydrological connection." *Gerke,* 464 F.3d at 725. Indeed, there is quite little common ground between Justice Kennedy's and the plurality's conceptions of jurisdiction under the Act, and both flatly reject the other's view. *See Rapanos,* 547 U.S. at 756 (Scalia, J., plurality opinion) ("[Justice

Kennedy's] test simply rewrites the statute."); *id.* at 778, (Kennedy, J., concurring) ("[T]he plurality reads nonexistent requirements into the Act.").

Thus, because *Rapanos* is not easily reconciled with *Marks,* the question becomes what to do. Fortunately, we need not reconcile *Rapanos* with *Marks.* Here, jurisdiction is proper under both Justice Kennedy's and the plurality's tests (and thus also the dissent's). Recently, this Court addressed an analogous situation:

3. Jurisdiction is proper under both tests

Justice Kennedy's test. Under this test, the Clean Water Act applies to wetlands that "possess a significant nexus to waters that are or were navigable in fact or that could reasonably be so made." *Rapanos,* 547 U.S. at 758. This nexus exists "if the wetlands, either alone or in combination with similarly situated lands in the region, significantly affect the chemical, physical, and biological integrity of other covered waters more readily understood as navigable." *Id.* at 755. By contrast, "[w]hen . . . wetlands' effects on water quality are speculative or insubstantial, they fall outside the zone fairly encompassed by the statutory terms 'navigable waters.' " *Id.* This standard must be met on a case-by-case basis. *Id.*

The district court found that the Cundiffs' wetlands have a significant nexus with the navigable-in-fact Green River, via Pond and Caney Creeks, which are tributaries of that river. The court credited the government's expert who testified that the wetlands perform significant ecological functions in relation to the Green River and the two creeks, including: temporary and long-term water storage, filtering of the acid runoff and sediment from the nearby mine, and providing an important habitat for plants and wildlife. And the court found that the Cundiffs' alterations-unauthorized ditch digging, the mechanical clearing of land, and the dredging of material and using it as filler-have undermined the wetlands' ability to store water which, in turn, has affected the frequency and extent of flooding, and increased the flood peaks in the Green River. Thus, it has "impact[ed] navigation, crop production in bottomlands, downstream bank erosion, and sedimentation." The district court further credited another government expert's testimony who stated that Rudy Cundiff's ditch digging had created channels so that the acid mine runoff would largely bypass his wetlands and instead flow more directly into Pond and Caney Creek and thus the Green River. It found that these channels cause "direct and significant impacts to navigation (via sediment accumulation in the Green River) and to aquatic food webs . . . that are not adapted to thrive in acid waters and/or sediment-choked environments." The record supports this conclusion and the district court found that the government's witnesses were credible, and so we cannot say that its conclusion was clearly erroneous.[4]

---

[4] For instance, if one dropped a poison into the Cundiffs' wetlands, the record indicates that it would find its way to the two creeks and the Green River, therefore indicating a

The Cundiffs do not really dispute these findings. Instead, they assert that a "significant nexus" may only be proved by "laboratory analysis" of soil samples, water samples, or through other tests. Though no doubt a district court could find such evidence persuasive, the Cundiffs point to nothing—no expert opinion, no research report or article, and nothing in any of the various Rapanos opinions—to indicate that this is the sole method by which a significant nexus may be proved such that the district court's finding was inherently improper. So the district court properly concluded that the government passed Justice Kennedy's test.

The Plurality's test. Under this standard, the government must make two showings to establish jurisdiction: "First, that the adjacent channel contains a 'wate[r] of the United States,' (i.e., a relatively permanent body of water connected to traditional interstate navigable waters); and second, that the wetland has a continuous surface connection with that water, making it difficult to determine where the 'water' ends and the 'wetland' begins." *Rapanos,* 547 U.S. at 742.

The first question is whether the adjacent property contains a "water of the United States." The district court held that jurisdiction was proper under the plurality's standard because the South Channel (located on the northern tract of the wetlands), and Pond and Caney Creeks were all "relatively permanent bodies of water connected to a traditional interstate navigable water, the Green River." Regarding the South Channel, the district court found that the water flows through the channel into Pond Creek for all but a few weeks a year, the two creeks are open waterbodies with significant flowing water, and that both flow into the Green River. (Pond Creek itself is navigable in part.) So the first prong of the plurality's test is met.

The second question is whether the wetlands possess a "continuous surface connection" with the Green River and its tributaries. The Cundiffs argue that, because the wetlands are at a different elevation level than the two creeks and it is not readily apparent that water perpetually flows between them, there is no continuous surface connection. The district court, observing that *Riverside Bayview* stated that it is often ambiguous where the transition between water and dry land exactly exists, 474 U.S. at 132, 135 n. 9, disagreed and held that a continuous surface connection existed. Specifically, the Court observed that the inquiry was whether it was ambiguous where land stopped and water began, because otherwise the plurality's recognition of these gradual transitions would be "completely eviscerat[ed]."

We agree; the Cundiffs' argument proves too much. Although the term "continuous surface connection" clearly requires surface flow, it does not mean that only perpetually flowing creeks satisfy the plurality's

---

significant chemical, physical, or biological connection between the wetlands and the nearby navigable-in-fact waters.

test. Indeed, the *Rapanos* plurality, in tipping its hat to *Riverside Bayview,* fashioned its test to determine when wetlands were "waters of the United States," and therefore implicitly recognized that wetlands are neither navigable-in-fact nor even literally bodies of water. Instead, wetlands are merely "inundated or saturated" soil that can "support . . . under normal circumstances . . . a prevalence of vegetation typically adapted for life in saturated soil conditions." 33 C.F.R. § 328.3(b). In other words, the plurality's test requires a topical flow of water between a navigable-in-fact waterway or its tributary with a wetland, and that connection requires some kind of dampness such that polluting a wetland would have a proportionate effect on the traditional waterway. If the Cundiffs' restrictive version of the plurality's test was accurate, then the plurality could have saved itself time and effort by saying that wetlands could never be "waters of the United States" and overruled *Riverside Bayview*'s holding to the contrary. It did not do that; instead, the plurality went through a lengthy analysis and therefore the standard is broader than the Cundiffs assert.

Further undermining their argument is the fact that the district court took note of the South Channel, which provides a largely uninterrupted permanent surface water flow between the wetlands and traditional waterways. The district court also found that the existence of additional (and substantial) surface connections between the wetlands and permanent water bodies "during storm events, bank full periods, and/or ordinary high flows" provides additional evidence of a continuous surface connection. Finally, Cundiff personally went a long way towards creating a continuous surface connection when he dug or excavated ditches to enhance the acid mine drainage into the creeks and away from his wetlands; in determining whether the Act confers jurisdiction, it does not make a difference whether the channel by which water flows from a wetland to a navigable-in-fact waterway or its tributary was manmade or formed naturally. Thus, we affirm the district court's determination that the Act confers jurisdiction over the Cundiffs' wetlands because both tests are met.

## QUESTIONS AND DISCUSSION

**1.** Before going to the legal merits of *Rapanos* and its aftermath, it is important to consider what was put at stake ecologically and administratively. Ecologically, EPA estimated during the litigation that if the petitioners' position—the position adopted in Justice Scalia's plurality opinion—were to prevail, roughly 30 percent of all streams and associated wetlands in the United States outside of Alaska, about 20 million acres in all, would have been pushed outside of Section 404 jurisdiction. While this figure was debated, it was clear to all interests that *Rapanos*, depending on how it was implemented, could significantly shrink what the federal government previously asserted to be under Section 404. Moreover, as an administrative matter Justice Kennedy's highly fact-intensive "significant nexus" test suggested that the Corps would face daunting resource demands in order to prove the existence of such conditions. Indeed, litigation initiated not long after *Rapanos* led ultimately to the Fourth Circuit kicking back a Corps permit denial to the agency on the ground that it had not adequately established the factual presence of a significant nexus. *See* Precon Development Corp. v. U.S. Army Corps of Engineers, 633 F.3d 278 (4th Cir. 2011). Beyond Section 404, moreover, *Rapanos* threw into doubt how to implement other programs under the statute, such as the TMDL program, that use the term "waters of the United States" to define the scope of federal jurisdiction. *See* Symposium, Rapanos v. United States, 22 NATURAL RESOURCES & ENV'T (Summer 2007). Hence, determining which test to apply and how to apply it presented substantial consequences.

**2.** Given the potential impact of *Rapanos* in these two respects, legal eyes quickly turned to the interpretation of the odd 4–1–4 opinion and resolution of the multitude of questions it praises. Congress has produced no solutions as of this writing. Surprised? Most courts have adopted the view that the Corps may assert jurisdiction so long as either the plurality's test or Justice Kennedy's test is satisfied. *See* Richard E. Glaze, Jr., Rapanos *Guidance III: Waters Revisited*, 42 ENVTL. L. REP. 10118 (2012) (providing a survey of the cases). But that does not answer *how* to apply the tests. It took the Corps and EPA until June 5, 2007, a year after the Court's decision, to develop guidance for agency determinations of jurisdictional wetlands consistent with *Rapanos*. *See* Clean Water Act Jurisdiction Following the U.S. Supreme Court's Decision in Rapanos v. United States and Carabell v. United States, 72 Fed. Reg. 31,824 (June 8, 2007). The guidance essentially adopted Justice Kennedy's case-by-case "significant nexus" approach, but in so doing it was not clear how much clarification the guidance delivered. In 2008, the agencies provided some limited revisions and clarifications to the 2007 guidance. *See* Clean Water Act Jurisdiction Following the U.S. Supreme Court's Decision in Rapanos v. United States and Carabell v. United States (Dec. 2, 2008), http://water.epa.gov/lawsregs/guidance/wetlands/CWAwaters.cfm.

**3.** A few years later, under the Obama Administration, the agencies took another stab at draft guidance in 2011, this time adopting the "either/or" approach the courts have gravitated around but, say many landowner interests, implementing the "significant nexus" test so as to extend jurisdiction far more broadly than did the 2007 guidance. *See* Draft Guidance on Identifying Waters Protected by the Clean Water Act, 76 Fed. Reg. 24479 (May 2, 2011). Then, in 2015, the EPA and the Corps published a final rule addressing the definition of "waters of the United States." *See* Clean Water Rule: Water of the United States, 40 Fed. Reg. 37,054 (June 29, 2015) (to be codified at 33 C.F.R. pt. 328). The "WOTUS" rule, as it is called, covers (1) traditional navigable waters; (2) interstate waters; (3) the territorial seas; (4) impoundments of waters otherwise defined as "waters of the United States"; (5) tributaries of traditional navigable waters, interstate waters, and the territorial seas; (6) adjacent waters to those described in (1)–(5); and (7) waters with a "significant nexus" to traditional navigable waters, interstate waters, and territorial seas on a case by case basis. The rule also specifically excludes from "waters of the United States" (and thus CWA jurisdiction) artificially irrigated areas, farm and stock watering ponds and irrigation ponds, groundwater, ditches with ephemeral or intermittent flow (i.e., only when it rains), along with a restatement of exclusions that existed under current law or practice (i.e., prior converted cropland). With regard to "adjacent" waters, the rule created a subset of adjacent waters known as "neighboring" waters, and set bright line distance limits in making adjacency determinations. One of the EPA's Fact Sheets issued with the rule contains a chart explaining waters that are included and are not included in CWA jurisdiction. *See* U.S. EPA, Fact Sheet, Clean Water Rule, https://www.epa.gov/sites/production/files/2015-05/documents/fact_sheet_summary_final_1.pdf. Thus, as compared to the 2011 guidance, the rule reduces the number of case by case evaluations of individual waters in favor of more bright line inclusions and exclusions.

Not surprisingly, the rule was subject to immediate legal challenge by agricultural groups, developers, states, and local governments on grounds that the rule improperly expanded federal jurisdiction, did not follow Justice Kennedy's "substantial nexus" test in *Rapanos*, and was not adopted through proper administrative proceedings. As of this writing, lawsuits are pending in numerous federal district and appellate courts. In late 2015, the Sixth Circuit placed a nationwide stay on the rule pending a determination on jurisdiction (there is uncertainty over whether jurisdiction is properly vested in the district courts or appellate courts). Also in 2015, a district court in North Dakota stayed the rule in 15 states, holding jurisdiction was in the district courts, and that the plaintiffs were likely to succeed on the merits of their claim that the rule exceeded the agencies' jurisdiction under the CWA. *See* North Dakota v. EPA, 127 F. Supp. 2d 1027 (D.N.D. 2015). Congress has also attempted to override the WOTUS rule. In 2015, the Congress enacted a joint resolution for "congressional disapproval" of the WOTUS rule but President Obama vetoed the legislation in January 2016. *See* Veto Message from the President—S.J. 22 (Jan. 19, 2016), https://www.whitehouse.gov/the-press-office/2016/01/19/president-obama-vetoes-sj-22.

For a thorough discussion of *Rapanos*, subsequent cases, and agency action following *Rapanos*, see ROBERT MELTZ & CLAUDIA COPELAND, CONGRESSIONAL RESEARCH SERVICE, THE WETLANDS COVERAGE OF THE CLEAN WATER ACT (CWA): *RAPANOS* AND BEYOND (Jan. 29, 2013). For a detailed discussion of the WOTUS rule and the subsequent litigation and Congressional action, see CLAUDIA COPELAND, CONGRESSIONAL RESEARCH SERVICE, EPA AND THE ARMY CORPS' RULE TO DEFINE "WATERS OF THE UNITED STATES" (Jan. 4, 2016); CLAUDIA COPELAND, CONGRESSIONAL RESEARCH SERVICE, EPA AND THE ARMY CORPS' "WATERS OF THE UNITED STATES" RULE: CONGRESSIONAL RESPONSE AND OPTIONS (Jan. 20, 2016). While these lawsuits are pending, how would you advise the agencies to implement *Rapanos*? What measures would you advise landowners to take to ensure development of property on which intermittent streams and washes are located does not violate section 404?

**4.** When can a landowner challenge a jurisdictional wetland determination? In 2012, the U.S. Supreme Court held that a landowner facing a compliance order may seek declaratory and injunctive relief in federal court and need not wait until an enforcement action is brought. *See* Sackett v. EPA, 132 S. Ct. 1367 (2012). But is a wetland jurisdictional determination equivalent to a compliance order? In *Hawkes Co. v. U.S. Army Corps of Engineers*, the Corps moved to dismiss a lawsuit by a landowner challenging a jurisdictional determination over a wetland area in northwestern Minnesota where the landowner wished to engage in peat mining. The Corps argued that a jurisdictional determination was not subject to judicial review because the plaintiff had neither completed the CWA permitting process nor attempted to mine in violation of the jurisdictional determination and thus the decision was not a "final agency action" subject to judicial review under the Administrative Procedure Act. The Supreme Court disagreed and held that the jurisdictional determination itself constituted a final agency action subject to immediate challenge in court. *Hawkes Co. v. U.S. Army Corps of Engineers*, 136 S. Ct. 1807 (2016). What are the implications of the two Supreme Court decisions for EPA and the Corps? For landowners?

**5.** In *Riverside Bayview* the Court gave short shrift to the "spurious" argument that the requirement that a developer seek a Corps permit under CWA Section 404 before filling jurisdictional wetlands constitutes a taking of property. The landowner in that situation seeks a judicial remedy before exhausting available administrative remedies—the permit procedure—and thus, under settled doctrine, has no ripe takings case to present to a court. *See* Williamson County Regional Planning Commission v. Hamilton Bank, 473 U.S. 172 (1985). But what about the case where a permit has been sought and denied? Is that a so-called regulatory taking of property? There have been more such takings challenges lodged against Section 404 wetlands permit decisions than have been brought against any other federal environmental program. Early in the program's history those challenges failed routinely. *See* Deltona Corp. v. United States, 657 F.2d 1184 (Ct. Cl. 1981); Jentgen v. United States, 657 F.2d 1210 (Ct. Cl. 1981). In the late 1980s, however, courts began issuing more landowner-friendly rulings, albeit based on rather extreme circumstances. *See* Florida Rock Industries v. United States, 791 F.2d 893 (Fed. Cir. 1986); Loveladies Harbor, Inc. v. United States, 15 Cl. Ct. 381 (1988). Takings litigation under Section 404 then gained steam after the Supreme Court's decision in Lucas v. South Carolina Coastal Council, 505 U.S. 1003 (1992), ruling that newly-enacted land use regulations that both deprive the landowner of all economic value of the land and go beyond codifying pre-existing common law nuisance restrictions constitute takings per se—i.e., without regard to a balancing of public and private interests. Since then, takings challenges under Section 404 have mounted, though still with mixed results. *See* Good v. United States, 189 F.3d 1355 (Fed. Cir. 1999) (no taking); Palm Beach Isles Associates v. United States, 231 F.3d 1354 (Fed. Cir. 2000) (taking found). For a thorough discussion of the background of the regulatory takings issue in the wetlands regulation context, see Robert Meltz, *Wetlands Regulation and the Law of Regulatory Takings*, 30 ENVTL. L. REP. 10468 (2000); Robert Meltz, *Wetland Regulation and the Law of Property Rights "Takings,"* NATIONAL WETLANDS NEWSLETTER, May–June 2001, at 1.

**6.** As controversial as was the statutory interpretation the majority reached in *SWANCC*, most Court-watchers agreed that an equally important aspect of the case was the majority's constitutionally-based concern that the regulation of isolated wetlands would result in a "significant impingement of the States' traditional and primary power over land and water use." The majority did not go so far as to base its decision on the constitutional footing, but did warn that

> Permitting respondents to claim federal jurisdiction over ponds and mudflats falling within the "Migratory Bird Rule" would result in a significant impingement of the States' traditional and primary power over land and water use. *See, e.g.,* Hess v. Port Authority Trans-Hudson Corporation, 513 U.S. 30, 44 (1994) ("[R]egulation of land use [is] a function traditionally performed by local governments"). Rather than expressing a desire to readjust the federal-state balance in this manner, Congress chose to "recognize, preserve, and protect the primary responsibilities and rights of States . . . to plan the development and use . . . of land and water resources. . . ." 33 U.S.C. § 1251(b). We thus read the statute as written to avoid the significant constitutional and federalism questions raised by respondents' interpretation, and therefore reject the request for administrative deference.

The Court's *dicta* in *SWANCC* appears to have endorsed the view that there is, indeed, a limit to how far Congress can regulate to protect wetlands, and that isolated wetlands are too far afield. *See* Jonathan Adler, *The Ducks Stop Here? The Environmental Challenge to Federalism*, 9 SUPREME COURT ECONOMIC REV. 205 (2001). But how far do you think the Court believes this concern reaches? For more on this topic in the Endangered Species Act setting, see Chapter 2.

**7.** There are a number of federal programs relating to wetlands protection that will withstand any future Commerce Clause scrutiny of Section 404 because they are non-regulatory in scope and based on a source of federal authority other than the power to regulate interstate commerce, such as the spending power. For example, the so-called Swampbuster Program withdraws agricultural subsidies from farmers that plant commodity crops (corn, wheat, soybeans, etc.) on lands converted from wetlands lands after 1985. 16 U.S.C. § 3821. The subsidy restriction does not apply to normal farming operations in wetlands, such as rice production, or to draining for non-crop uses such as cranberry farming or raising poultry. Because it involves withdrawal of subsidies to induce compliance with its goals, rather than regulation, the dicta in *SWANCC* regarding the limits of Congress's Commerce Clause authority should pose no threat to Swampbuster. *See* United States v. Dierckman, 201 F.3d 915 (7th Cir. 2000) (finding Swampbuster is based on Congress's spending power, not its interstate commerce power). Several other nationwide agriculture programs, including the Agriculture Conservation Easement Program and the Conservation Reserve Program, are geared specifically to provide subsidies to qualifying farmers who retire wetlands from agricultural uses, and thus should also withstand scrutiny under the evolving Commerce Clause jurisprudence.

While these programs have their own inherent limits, they have proven valuable for wetland conservation policy and are always at the forefront of Congress' Farm Bill deliberations. *See* Roger L. Pederson, *Farms and Wetlands Benefit from Farm Bill Conservation Measures*, NATIONAL WETLANDS NEWSLETTER, Sept.–Oct. 2001, at 9. Other wetland programs depend for their authority on the power of the federal government to regulate itself. For example, the Fish and Wildlife Coordination Act requires that federal agencies, when considering whether to construct or finance water resources development projects, give equal consideration to wildlife conservation, including wetlands habitat impacts, as they give to other purposes of proposed projects. 16 U.S.C. § 661.

8. An implicit message of *SWANCC*, of course, is that states are free to regulate isolated wetlands, to fill in whatever gap in coverage the opinion opened. Many observers quickly reacted to *SWANCC*, however, assumed political and economic constraints would prevent states from taking such action, and thus derided the decision as exposing isolated wetlands to rampant destruction. *See, e.g.*, Jon Kusler, *The SWANCC Decision and the States—Fill in the Gaps or Declare Open Season?*, NATIONAL WETLANDS NEWSLETTER, Mar.–Apr. 2001, at 9. The concern that *SWANCC* opened a gap in states without their own wetlands protection programs seemed well founded when, not long after the opinion, anecdotal reports from around the nation suggested that land developers were moving to fill wetlands. *See* Traci Wilson, *Developers Rush to Build In Wetlands After Ruling*, USA TODAY, Dec. 6, 2002, at 15A. But in fact, many states responded to *SWANCC* by enacting or recommending the enactment of relatively aggressive regulatory programs to protect isolated wetlands now beyond the reach of the federal government. *See* Michael Gerhardt, *The Curious Flight of the Migratory Bird Rule*, 31 ENVTL. L. REP. (ELI) 10079 (2001); *New and Revised State Wetland Regulations Take Effect Across the County*, NATIONAL WETLANDS NEWSLETTER Sept.–Oct. 2001, at 18. Hence the concern that states would not fill the gap seems mostly unfounded, though one can always debate whether they have gone far enough fast enough. For a series of articles presenting positive reviews of state and local efforts in Wisconsin, Illinois, Virginia, and Indiana, see Symposium, *SWANCC and the States*, NATIONAL WETLANDS NEWSLETTER, July–Aug. 2002, at 1. For gloomier assessments of state and local progress, see Turner Odell, *On Soggy Ground—State Protection for Isolated Wetlands*, NATIONAL WETLANDS NEWSLETTER, Sept.–Oct. 2003, at 7; Bowden Quinn, *Indiana's New Wetland Legislation: Threat to Isolated Wetlands . . .* , NATIONAL WETLANDS NEWSLETTER, May–June 2004, at 1. *See also* John D. Ostergren, Note, SWANCC *in Duck Country: Will Court-Ordered Devolution Fill the Prairie Potholes?*, 22 STAN. ENVTL. L. REV. 381 (June 2003) (arguing that state regulation may not protect the environmentally-significant wetlands in the prairie pothole region of western Minnesota and the Dakotas after *SWANCC* but that existing federal farm programs—particularly Swampbuster—will continue to provide the first line of defense for these wetlands). You can find descriptions of all the state wetlands regulation programs that "fill the gap" through the Association of State Wetland Managers, www.aswm.org.

---

## B. REGULATED DISCHARGES

*Riverside Bayview Homes*, *SWANCC*, and *Rapanos* involve the question of the *geographic* boundary of federal regulatory jurisdiction over wetlands. Another boundary is erected by the definition of *activities* subject to that jurisdiction. Even where an area indisputably is a surface water or an adjacent wetland subject to federal control, the activity taking place within the wetlands must fit the parameters of Section 404 for the regulatory program to attach. This activity-based limit on the Section 404 program has also proved significant and controversial. For example, in 1997 the D.C. Circuit held that mechanized drainage, excavation, and channelization of wetlands is not subject to Section 404 merely because of the "incidental fallback" of dirt and debris from the machine parts. *See* National Mining Association v. Army Corps of Engineers, 145 F.3d 1399 (D.C. Cir. 1998). The Corps had previously taken the position, in the so-called "Tulloch Rule" (named after one of the parties in the cases leading to its development), that incidental fallback does trigger Section 404 and that, since it is virtually impossible to conduct mechanized activities in wetlands without some incidental fallback, such activities necessarily require permits. 58 Fed. Reg. 45,008 (Aug. 25, 1993). After the D.C. Circuit opinion in *National Mining Association*, the Corps revised its rules to impose only a rebuttable presumption that such activities require permits. The presumption is removed if "project-specific evidence shows that the activity results in only incidental fallback." 66 Fed. Reg. 4550, 4575 (Jan. 17, 2001); 33 C.F.R. § 323.2 (2008); 40 C.F.R. § 232.2 (2015). New litigation ensued over that interpretation, which resulted in the following decision:

### National Association of Home Builders v. U.S. Army Corps of Engineers

United States District Court for the District of Columbia, 2007.
2007 WL 259944.

■ JAMES ROBERTSON, DISTRICT JUDGE.

Plaintiffs challenge a regulation jointly issued by the Army Corps of Engineers and the Environmental Protection Agency that governs when the use of mechanized earth-moving equipment results in the discharge of dredged or fill material and is thus subject to a permitting regime administered by the Corps. Plaintiffs contend that the agencies have exceeded their authority under the Clean Water Act, the Administrative Procedure Act, and the Tenth Amendment. In an earlier order, I dismissed these claims as unripe. 311 F. Supp. 2d 91 (2004). That decision was reversed . . . and the case was remanded for determination of the parties' cross-motions for summary judgment. . . .

Section 301 of the Clean Water Act (CWA) prohibits the "discharge of any pollutant" unless pursuant to a permit. 33 U.S.C. § 1311(a). The statute defines a "discharge" as the "addition of any pollutant to navigable waters from any point source." *Id.* § 1362(12). Under Section 404(a) of the CWA, the Corps is authorized to issue permits for the discharge of "dredged or fill material" into the waters of the United States. *Id.* § 1344(a). The Corps, in turn, requires such permits. 33 C.F.R. § 323.3(a).

This suit is the most recent manifestation of a longstanding legal dispute about just what constitutes the discharge of dredged material. Between 1986 and 1993, the Corps defined the discharge of dredged material as "any addition of dredged material into the waters of the United States" while expressly excluding "*de minimis*, incidental soil movement occurring during normal dredging operations." Final Rule for Regulatory Programs of the Corps of Engineers, 51 Fed. Reg. 41,206, 41,232 (Nov. 13, 1986) (to be codified at 33 C.F.R. § 323.2(d)). In 1993, however, the Corps issued a new rule that eliminated the *de minimis* exception. This rule, promulgated as part of a settlement agreement in *California Wildlife Federation v. Tulloch*, Civ. No. C90–713–CIV–5–BO (E.D.N.C. 1996), became known as the "Tulloch Rule" or "*Tulloch I.*" It defined the discharge of dredged material as "any addition of dredged material into, including redeposit of dredged material within, the waters of the United States." Clean Water Act Regulatory Programs, 58 Fed. Reg. 45,008, 45,035 (Aug. 25, 1993)(to be codified at 33 C.F.R. § 323.2(d)(1) and 40 C.F.R. § 232.2(1))(emphasis added).

Industry trade associations challenged the expanded definition. The district court invalidated the regulation. *American Mining Cong. v. United States Army Corps of Engineers*, 951 F. Supp. 267 (D.D.C. 1997) (Harris, J.). The Court of Appeals affirmed, *National Mining Association v. United States Army Corps of Engineers*, 145 F.3d 1399 (D.C. Cir. 1998), agreeing with plaintiffs and the district court that "the straightforward statutory term 'addition' cannot reasonably be said to encompass the situation in which material is removed from the waters of the United States and a small portion of it happens to fall back." *Id.* at 1404. Because incidental fallback represents a "net withdrawal, not an addition, of material," *id.*, the Court held, it is not a discharge and cannot be regulated. The Court of Appeals was careful, however, to make clear that it was not prohibiting the regulation of any redeposit, but only incidental fallback:

> [W]e do not hold that the Corps may not legally regulate some forms of redeposit under its § 404 permitting authority. We hold only that by asserting jurisdiction over "any redeposit," including incidental fallback, the Tulloch Rule outruns the Corps's statutory authority. Since the [CWA] sets out no bright line between incidental fallback on the one hand and regulable redeposits on the other, a reasoned attempt by the agencies to

> draw such a line would merit considerable deference. But the Tulloch Rule makes no effort to draw such a line, and indeed its overriding purpose appears to be to expand the Corps's permitting authority to encompass incidental fallback and, as a result, a wide range of activities that cannot remotely be said to "add" anything.

*Id.* at 1405.

In 2000, the Corps and EPA proposed a new rule, which would have amended the definition by adding the following language:

> A discharge of dredged material shall be presumed to result from mechanized landclearing, ditching, channelization, in-stream mining, or other mechanized excavation activity in waters of the United States. This presumption is rebutted if the party proposing such an activity demonstrates that only incidental fallback will result from its activity.

Further Revisions to the Clean Water Act Regulatory Definition of "Discharge of Dredged Material," 65 Fed. Reg. 50,108, 50,117 (Aug. 16, 2000) (to be codified at 33 C.F.R. § 323.2(d)(2) and 40 C.F.R. § 232.2(1)). After receiving comments, in January 2001 the Corps and EPA issued their final rule, commonly known as *Tulloch II.* It states:

> The Corps and EPA regard the use of mechanized earth-moving equipment to conduct landclearing, ditching, channelization, in-stream mining or other earth-moving activity in the waters of the United States as resulting in a discharge of dredged material unless project-specific evidence shows that the activity results in only incidental fallback. This paragraph does not and is not intended to shift any burden in any administrative or judicial proceeding under the CWA.

66 Fed. Reg. 4550, 4575 (codified at 33 C.F.R. § 323.2(d)(2)(i) and 40 C.F.R. § 232.2(2)(i)). In addition, the agencies added a provision defining incidental fallback:

> Incidental fallback is the redeposit of small volumes of dredged material that is incidental to excavation activity in waters of the United States when such material falls back to substantially the same place as the initial removal. Examples of incidental fallback include soil that is disturbed when dirt is shoveled and the back-spill that comes off a bucket when such small volume of soil or dirt falls into substantially the same place from which it was initially removed.

*Id.* (codified at 33 C.F.R. § 323.2(d)(2)(ii) and 40 C.F.R. § 232.2(2)(ii)).

On February 6, 2001, plaintiffs filed this suit, challenging both provisions. My view, that the case was not fit for review, because "both the court and the agencies would benefit from letting the questions presented here 'arise in some more concrete and final form,'" 311 F.

Supp. 2d at 97–98 (quoting *State Farm Mut. Auto Ins. Co. v. Dole*, 802 F.2d 474, 479 (D.C. Cir. 1986)), was rejected, a panel of the Court of Appeals having concluded that "the legality *vel non* of the two challenged features will not change from case to case or become clearer in a concrete setting." . . .

Following the Court of Appeals' ruling on *Tulloch I*, Judge Harris warned the agencies against "parsing the language of [prior] decisions . . . to render a narrow definition of incidental fallback that is inconsistent with an objective and good faith reading of those decisions." *American Mining Cong. v. Army Corps of Eng.*, 120 F. Supp. 2d 23, 31 (D.D.C. 2000) (Harris, J.). Yet by defining incidental fallback partly in terms of volume, the EPA and the Corps appear to have done exactly what they were warned not to do.

Although the decisions of this court and the Court of Appeals have described incidental fallback in terms of volume, neither court has gone so far as to require that the volume of fallback be small. Conceivably, the operator of a shovel removing 500 tons of dirt could accidentally drop all 500 tons back to the earth without redepositing anything. In determining whether fallback is incidental—i.e., not an addition within the meaning of the Clean Water Act—the volume of material being handled is irrelevant. The difference between incidental fallback and redeposit is better understood in terms of two other factors: (1) the time the material is held before being dropped to earth and (2) the distance between the place where the material is collected and the place where it is dropped. In striking down *Tulloch I* because of its failure to exclude activities resulting only in incidental fallback, Judge Silberman stated:

> [T]he word addition carries both a temporal and geographic ambiguity. If the material that would otherwise fall back were moved some distance away and then dropped, it very well might constitute an "addition." Or if it were held from some time and then dropped back in the same spot, it might also constitute an "addition."

145 F.3d at 1410 (SILBERMAN, J., concurring). Although *Tulloch II* addresses the "geographic ambiguity" raised by Judge Silberman—material must fall back to "substantially the same place as the initial removal"—it makes no reference to the amount of time that the material is held before it is dropped. For that reason, and because it improperly includes a volume requirement, the rule must be rewritten.

As the Corps rewrites its definition of incidental fallback, it should also reconsider its statement that it "regards" the use of mechanized earth-moving equipment as resulting in a discharge of dredged material unless project-specific evidence shows otherwise. That statement, followed by the coy explanation that it "is not intended to shift any burden," 66 Fed. Reg. at 4575, essentially reflects a degree of official recalcitrance that is unworthy of the Corps.

The Court of Appeals, in striking down *Tulloch I*, recognized the difficult task of distinguishing incidental fallback, which cannot be regulated under the Clean Water Act, from other redeposits, which can. Because the Act sets out "no bright line" separating one from the other, the court suggested that "a reasoned attempt by the agencies to draw such a line would merit considerable deference." The agencies, however, have made no such attempt. Although the agencies contend that a bright-line rule would not be "feasible or defensible," the Court of Appeals has made clear, and the government has acknowledged, that not all uses of mechanized earth-moving equipment may be regulated. The agencies cannot require "project-specific evidence" from projects over which they have no regulatory authority.

Because the *Tulloch II* rule violates the Clean Water Act, it is invalid. Therefore, plaintiffs' motion for summary judgment will be granted, and the Corps and EPA will be enjoined from enforcing and applying the rule. An appropriate order accompanies this memorandum.

———

## QUESTIONS AND DISCUSSION

**1.** The *Home Builders* court lays out two parameters the Corps must use to develop a bright line test—distance between place of removal and place of redeposit and holding time—and one parameter that is off limits—volume. How would you go about advising the Corps to develop such a regulation? Should the rule state a specific distance and time?

**2.** The court also chided the Corps for its "coy" move of establishing a rebuttable presumption that all use of mechanized earth-moving equipment results in a discharge of dredged material unless project-specific evidence shows otherwise. When bright jurisdictional lines do not exist in statutes and regulations, or even when they do, if they are not easy to verify in the field, who should bear the burden of proving whether jurisdiction attaches to a particular place and activity? Under the Endangered Species Act, for example, the government bears the burden of proving habitat is occupied by a protected species and that an activity in that habitat has caused actual death or injury to the species. *See* Babbitt v. Sweet Home Chapter of Communities for a Great Oregon, 515 U.S. 687 (1995); Arizona Cattle Growers' Association v. United States Fish and Wildlife Service, 273 F.3d 1229 (9th Cir. 2001); Defenders of Wildlife v. Bernal, 204 F.3d 920 (9th Cir. 2000).

**3.** Why is the Corps trying to regulate as closely as possible to "incidental fallback" as the courts will let it? Consider what will happen if the Corps drafts a rule consistent with the *Home Builders* court's guidelines: volume of earth removed does not matter. Conducted properly, "mechanized earth moving" thus can escape regulation under Section 404 while accomplishing what a landowner engaging in the practice is hoping for—opening channels to drain the wetland and convert the entire area to non-jurisdictional upland. Once a wetland, not always a wetland.

**4.** A similar and equally controversial activity with unclear jurisdictional implications was "deep ripping," which is a form of "plowing" using extremely long plow prongs to open wetlands up to drainage. But the Ninth Circuit ruled that Section 404 covers this practice, *see* Borden Ranch Partnership v. U.S. Army Corps of Engineers, 261 F.3d 810 (9th Cir. 2001), and the Supreme Court, in a split 4–4 *per curiam* decision, upheld the Ninth Circuit's opinion. *See* Borden Ranch Partnership v. U.S. Army Corps of Engineers, 537 U.S. 99 (2002). What is the difference between "mechanized earth moving" and "deep ripping" in terms of whether either results in "fill" of a wetland area?

---

## C. PERMITTING AND MITIGATION

*Riverside Bayview*, *SWANCC*, and *Rapanos* define where Section 404 applies, and cases like *Home Builders* and *Borden Ranch* grapple with the meaning of discharge and fill. When actions in areas clearly within the federal side of the jurisdictional line clearly meet the action-based parameters of Section 404—i.e., result in a nonexempt discharge of fill material into wetlands—they trigger the procedures and standards of the Section 404 permitting program. The following subsections discuss the permitting process itself and the wetland mitigation requirements that accompany it.

### 1. THE PERMITTING PROCESS

Although the Corps of Engineers is the lead federal agency for these purposes, several other federal agencies are involved in the Section 404 process:

**Corps of Engineers**: makes site-specific wetland delineations; promulgates nationwide and regional general permits; makes decisions on individual permits; takes enforcement actions; promulgates regulations to implement these programs.

**EPA**: issues standards under CWA Section 404(b)(1) governing the environmental criteria for location of fill locations; can veto Corps permits based on environmental criteria.

**U.S. Fish and Wildlife Service**: reviews and comments on Corps permit applications pursuant to the Fish and Wildlife Coordination Act, 16 U.S.C. §§ 661–666c; may elevate disputes with the local Corps offices over permit issuance decisions to Corps Headquarters.

**National Oceanic and Atmospheric Administration**: reviews and comments on Corps permit applications and may also elevate local permit decisions.

The CWA provides several exemptions from permit requirements for activities in areas that otherwise might fit the parameters. For example, routine, ongoing farming operations are exempt from permitting, as are many maintenance activities for dikes, berms, dams, and bridges. *See* 33 U.S.C. § 1344(f)(1); 33 C.F.R. § 323.4. These exemptions do not allow new farming or construction in wetlands, however.

Activities requiring permits might qualify for one of the Corps' Nationwide Permits. These are so-called general permits, or permits by rule, that apply to specified low-impact activities with little or no application and review process. *See* 33 U.S.C. § 1344(c); 33 C.F.R. pt. 330. The Army Corps must find that activities covered by such permits generally will have minimal adverse impacts, separately and cumulatively. Some of the general permits require pre-discharge notifications to allow the Corps, on a case-by-case basis, to review impacts and deny the benefit of the general permit. The Corps may issue general permits on a regional and local basis as well.

Activities not qualifying for exemption or a general permit must undergo the Corps individual permit review process. *See* 33 C.F.R. pt. 325. An important facet of this program are the EPA's guidelines, issued pursuant to CWA Section 404(b)(1), governing where the Corps may specify sites for disposal of fill material. *See* 33 U.S.C. § 1344(b)(1). The criteria, which are binding on the Corps, include such factors as the effects on wildlife, on ecosystem diversity, productivity and stability, and on shorelines and beaches. *See* 40 C.F.R. pt. 230. EPA has used the guidelines to impose an "alternatives" analysis on Corps decisions, under which disposals in wetlands that are not associated with "water-dependent" activities are presumed to have financially practicable alternatives that are less environmentally damaging. *Id.* § 230.10(a).

For proposed disposals that meet EPA's environmental criteria and alternatives test, the Corps conducts a "public interest" analysis involving a wide variety of factors covering economic, environmental, and social interests. *See* 33 C.F.R. pt. 320. The Corps also submits the application to review by several other federal agencies through interagency consultation required under CWA Section 404(q), though recommendations derived from this process do not bind the Corps. Even the states get involved, as the Corps must obtain the state's certification that issuance of the permit will not cause a violation of state water quality standards developed pursuant to the CWA. *See* 33 U.S.C. § 1341(c). Lastly, although it has been used infrequently, EPA may veto Corps issuance of a permit if EPA concludes it would have "unacceptable adverse effect on . . . shellfish beds and fishery areas . . . wildlife, or recreational areas." 33 U.S.C. § 1344(c). Examples of the Corps' general permit and individual permit process are provided in Chapter 9 in the section on permitting. For a more detailed discussion of the Corps permitting process under Section 404 as well as regional variations in permitting approaches, see Dave Owen, *Regional Federal Administration*, 63 UCLA L. REV. 58 (2016) (using Corps permitting under Section 404 of the CWA as a case study of geographic decentralization within the federal government).

The following case explains the basic parameters of the Section 404 permitting process and the difficulties that arise when two agencies—here EPA and the Corps—have overlapping authority.

## Coeur Alaska, Inc. v. Southeast Alaska Conservation Council

United States Supreme Court 2009.
557 U.S. 261.

■ JUSTICE KENNEDY delivered the opinion of the Court.

These cases require us to address two questions under the Clean Water Act (CWA or Act). The first is whether the Act gives authority to the United States Army Corps of Engineers, or instead to the Environmental Protection Agency (EPA), to issue a permit for the discharge of mining waste, called slurry. The Corps of Engineers has issued a permit to petitioner Coeur Alaska, Inc. (Coeur Alaska), for a discharge of slurry into a lake in Southeast Alaska. The second question is whether, when the Corps issued that permit, the agency acted in accordance with law. We conclude that the Corps was the appropriate agency to issue the permit and that the permit is lawful.

With regard to the first question, § 404(a) of the CWA grants the Corps the power to "issue permits . . . for the discharge of . . . fill material." 86 Stat. 884; 33 U.S.C. § 1344(a). But the EPA also has authority to issue permits for the discharge of pollutants. Section 402 of the Act grants the EPA authority to "issue a permit for the discharge of any pollutant" "[e]xcept as provided in" § 404. 33 U.S.C. § 1342(a). We conclude that because the slurry Coeur Alaska wishes to discharge is defined by regulation as "fill material," 40 CFR § 232.2 (2008), Coeur Alaska properly obtained its permit from the Corps of Engineers, under § 404, rather than from the EPA, under § 402.

The second question is whether the Corps permit is lawful. Three environmental groups, respondents here, sued the Corps under the Administrative Procedure Act, arguing that the issuance of the permit by the Corps was "not in accordance with law." 5 U.S.C. § 706(2)(A). The environmental groups are Southeast Alaska Conservation Council, Sierra Club, and Lynn Canal Conservation (collectively, SEACC). The State of Alaska and Coeur Alaska are petitioners here.

SEACC argues that the permit from the Corps is unlawful because the discharge of slurry would violate an EPA regulation promulgated under § 306(b) of the CWA, 33 U.S.C. § 1316(b). The EPA regulation, which is called a "new source performance standard," forbids mines like Coeur Alaska's from discharging "process wastewater" into the navigable waters. 40 CFR § 440.104(b)(1). Coeur Alaska, the State of Alaska, and the federal agencies maintain that the Corps permit is lawful nonetheless because the EPA's performance standard does not apply to discharges of fill material.

Reversing the judgment of the District Court, the Court of Appeals held that the EPA's performance standard applies to this discharge so that the permit from the Corps is unlawful.

Petitioner Coeur Alaska plans to reopen the Kensington Gold Mine, located some 45 miles north of Juneau, Alaska. The mine has been closed since 1928, but Coeur Alaska seeks to make it profitable once more by using a technique known as "froth flotation." Coeur Alaska will churn the mine's crushed rock in tanks of frothing water. Chemicals in the water will cause gold-bearing minerals to float to the surface, where they will be skimmed off.

At issue is Coeur Alaska's plan to dispose of the mixture of crushed rock and water left behind in the tanks. This mixture is called slurry. Some 30 percent of the slurry's volume is crushed rock, resembling wet sand, which is called tailings. The rest is water.

The standard way to dispose of slurry is to pump it into a tailings pond. The slurry separates in the pond. Solid tailings sink to the bottom, and water on the surface returns to the mine to be used again.

Rather than build a tailings pond, Coeur Alaska proposes to use Lower Slate Lake, located some three miles from the mine in the Tongass National Forest. This lake is small—800 feet at its widest crossing, 2,000 feet at its longest, and 23 acres in area. Though small, the lake is 51 feet deep at its maximum. The parties agree the lake is a navigable water of the United States and so is subject to the CWA. They also agree there can be no discharge into the lake except as the CWA and any lawful permit allow.

Over the life of the mine, Coeur Alaska intends to put 4.5 million tons of tailings in the lake. This will raise the lakebed 50 feet—to what is now the lake's surface—and will increase the lake's area from 23 to about 60 acres. To contain this wider, shallower body of water, Coeur Alaska will dam the lake's downstream shore. The transformed lake will be isolated from other surface water. Creeks and stormwater runoff will detour around it. Ultimately, lakewater will be cleaned by purification systems and will flow from the lake to a stream and thence onward.

Numerous state and federal agencies reviewed and approved Coeur Alaska's plans. At issue here are actions by two of those agencies: the Corps of Engineers and the EPA.

The CWA classifies crushed rock as a "pollutant." 33 U.S.C. § 1362(6). On the one hand, the Act forbids Coeur Alaska's discharge of crushed rock "[e]xcept as in compliance" with the Act. CWA § 301(a), 33 U.S.C. § 1311(a). Section 404(a) of the CWA, on the other hand, empowers the Corps to authorize the discharge of "dredged or fill material." 33 U.S.C. § 1344(a). The Corps and the EPA have together defined "fill material" to mean any "material [that] has the effect of . . . [c]hanging the bottom elevation" of water. 40 CFR § 232.2. The agencies have further defined the "discharge of fill material" to include "placement of . . . slurry, or tailings or similar mining-related materials." *Ibid.*

In these cases the Corps and the EPA agree that the slurry meets their regulatory definition of "fill material." On that premise the Corps evaluated the mine's plan for a § 404 permit. After considering the environmental factors required by § 404(b), the Corp issued Coeur Alaska a permit to pump the slurry into Lower Slate Lake.

In granting the permit the Corps followed the steps set forth by § 404. Section 404(b) requires the Corps to consider the environmental consequences of every discharge it allows. 33 U.S.C. § 1344(b). The Corps must apply guidelines written by the EPA pursuant to § 404(b). *See ibid.*; 40 CFR pt. 230 (EPA guidelines). Applying those guidelines here, the Corps determined that Coeur Alaska's plan to use Lower Slate Lake as a tailings pond was the "least environmentally damaging practicable" way to dispose of the tailings. To conduct that analysis, the Corps compared the plan to the proposed alternatives.

The Corps determined that the environmental damage caused by placing slurry in the lake will be temporary. And during that temporary disruption, Coeur Alaska will divert waters around the lake through pipelines built for this purpose. Coeur Alaska will also treat water flowing from the lake into downstream waters, pursuant to strict EPA criteria. Though the slurry will at first destroy the lake's small population of common fish, that population may later be replaced. After mining operations are completed, Coeur Alaska will help "recla[im]" the lake by "[c]apping" the tailings with about 4 inches of "native material." The Corps concluded that

> [t]he reclamation of the lake will result in more emergent wetlands/vegetated shallows with moderate values for fish habitat, nutrient recycling, carbon/detrital export and sediment/toxicant retention, and high values for wildlife habitat.

If the tailings did not go into the lake, they would be placed on nearby wetlands. The resulting pile would rise twice as high as the Pentagon and cover three times as many acres. If it were chosen, that alternative would destroy dozens of acres of wetlands—a permanent loss. On the premise that when the mining ends the lake will be at least as environmentally hospitable, if not more so, than now, the Corps concluded that placing the tailings in the lake will cause less damage to the environment than storing them above ground: The reclaimed lake will be "more valuable to the aquatic ecosystem than a permanently filled wetland . . . that has lost all aquatic functions and values."

The EPA had the statutory authority to veto the Corps permit, and prohibit the discharge, if it found the plan to have "an unacceptable adverse effect on municipal water supplies, shellfish beds and fishery areas . . . , wildlife, or recreational areas." CWA § 404(c), 33 U.S.C.

§ 1344(c). After considering the Corps findings, the EPA did not veto the Corps permit, even though, in its view, placing the tailings in the lake was not the "environmentally preferable" means of disposing of them. By declining to exercise its veto, the EPA in effect deferred to the judgment of the Corps on this point.

The EPA's involvement extended beyond the agency's veto consideration. The EPA also issued a permit of its own—not for the discharge from the mine into the lake but for the discharge from the lake into a downstream creek. Section 402 grants the EPA authority to "issue a permit for the discharge of any pollutant," "[e]xcept as provided in [CWA § 404]." 33 U.S.C. § 1342(a). The EPA's § 402 permit authorizes Coeur Alaska to discharge water from Lower Slate Lake into the downstream creek, subject to strict water-quality limits that Coeur Alaska must regularly monitor.

The EPA's authority to regulate this discharge comes from a regulation, termed a "new source performance standard," that it has promulgated under authority granted to it by § 306(b) of the CWA. Section 306(b) gives the EPA authority to regulate the amount of pollutants that certain categories of new sources may discharge into the navigable waters of the United States. 33 U.S.C. § 1316(b). Pursuant to this authority, the EPA in 1982 promulgated a new source performance standard restricting discharges from new froth-flotation gold mines like Coeur Alaska's. The standard is stringent: It allows "no discharge of process wastewater" from these mines. 40 CFR § 440.104(b)(1).

Applying that standard to the discharge of water from Lower Slate Lake into the downstream creek, the EPA's § 402 permit sets strict limits on the amount of pollutants the water may contain. The permit requires Coeur Alaska to treat the water using "reverse osmosis" to remove aluminum, suspended solids, and other pollutants. Coeur Alaska must monitor the water flowing from the lake to be sure that the pollutants are kept to low, specified minimums.

SEACC brought suit against the Corps of Engineers and various of its officials in the United States District Court for the District of Alaska. The Corps permit was not in accordance with law, SEACC argued, for two reasons. First, in SEACC's view, the permit was issued by the wrong agency—Coeur Alaska ought to have sought a § 402 permit from the EPA, just as the company did for the discharge of water from the lake into the downstream creek. Second, SEACC contended that regardless of which agency issued the permit, the discharge itself is unlawful because it will violate the EPA new source performance standard for froth-flotation gold mines. (This is the same performance standard described above, which the EPA has already applied to the discharge of water from the lake into the downstream creek.) SEACC argued that this performance standard also applies to the discharge of slurry into the lake. It contended further that the performance standard is a binding implementation of § 306. Section 306(e) of the CWA makes it "unlawful" for Coeur Alaska to "operate" the mine "in violation of" the EPA's performance standard. 33 U.S.C. § 1316(e). . . .

Coeur Alaska and the State of Alaska intervened as defendants. Both sides moved for summary judgment. The District Court granted summary judgment in favor of the defendants.

The Court of Appeals for the Ninth Circuit reversed and ordered the District Court to vacate the Corps of Engineers' permit. Southeast Alaska Conservation Council v. United States Army Corps of Engs., 486 F.3d 638, 654–655 (2007). The court acknowledged that Coeur Alaska's slurry "facially meets the Corps' current regulatory definition of 'fill material,' " *id.*, at 644, because it would have the effect of raising the lake's bottom elevation. But the court also noted that the EPA's new source performance standard "prohibits discharges from froth-flotation mills." *Ibid.* The Court of Appeals concluded that "[b]oth of the regulations appear to apply in this case, yet they are at odds." Ibid. To resolve the conflict, the court turned to what it viewed as "the plain language of the Clean Water Act." *Ibid.* The court held that the EPA's new source performance standard "applies to discharges from the froth-flotation mill at Coeur Alaska's Kensington Gold Mine into Lower Slate Lake." *Ibid.*

In addition to the text of the CWA, the Court of Appeals also relied on the agencies' statements made when promulgating their current and prior definitions of "fill material." These statements, in the Court of Appeals' view, demonstrated the agencies' intent that the EPA's new source performance standard govern discharges like Coeur Alaska's. *Id.*, at 648–654.

The Court of Appeals concluded that Coeur Alaska required a § 402 permit for its slurry discharge, that the Corps lacked authority to issue such a permit under § 404, and that the proposed discharge was unlawful because it would violate the EPA new source performance standard and § 306(e).

The decision of the Court of Appeals in effect reallocated the division of responsibility that the Corps and the EPA had been following. We now hold that the decision of the Court of Appeals was incorrect.

The question of which agency has authority to consider whether to permit the slurry discharge is our beginning inquiry. We consider first the authority of the EPA and second the authority of the Corps. Our conclusion is that under the CWA the Corps had authority to determine whether Coeur Alaska was entitled to the permit governing this discharge.

Section 402 gives the EPA authority to issue "permit[s] for the discharge of any pollutant," with one important exception: The EPA may not issue permits for fill material that fall under the Corps' § 404 permitting authority. Section 402(a) states:

> Except as provided in . . . [CWA § 404, 33 U.S.C. § 1344], the Administrator may . . . issue a permit for the discharge of any

> pollutant, . . . notwithstanding [CWA § 301(a), 33 U.S.C. § 1311(a)], upon condition that such discharge will meet either (A) all applicable requirements under [CWA § 301, 33 U.S.C. § 1311(a); CWA § 302, 33 U.S.C. § 1312; CWA § 306, 33 U.S.C. § 1316; CWA § 307, 33 U.S.C. § 1317; CWA § 308, 33 U.S.C. § 1318; CWA § 403, 33 U.S.C. § 1343], or (B) prior to the taking of necessary implementing actions relating to all such requirements, such conditions as the Administrator determines are necessary to carry out the provisions of this chapter." 33 U.S.C. § 1342(a)(1) (emphasis added).

Section 402 thus forbids the EPA from exercising permitting authority that is "provided [to the Corps] in" § 404.

This is not to say the EPA has no role with respect to the environmental consequences of fill. The EPA's function is different, in regulating fill, from its function in regulating other pollutants, but the agency does exercise some authority. Section 404 assigns the EPA two tasks in regard to fill material. First, the EPA must write guidelines for the Corps to follow in determining whether to permit a discharge of fill material. CWA § 404(b); 33 U.S.C. § 1344(b). Second, the Act gives the EPA authority to "prohibit" any decision by the Corps to issue a permit for a particular disposal site. CWA § 404(c); 33 U.S.C. § 1344(c). We, and the parties, refer to this as the EPA's power to veto a permit.

The Act is best understood to provide that if the Corps has authority to issue a permit for a discharge under § 404, then the EPA lacks authority to do so under § 402.

Even if there were ambiguity on this point, the EPA's own regulations would resolve it. Those regulations provide that "[d]ischarges of dredged or fill material into waters of the United States which are regulated under section 404 of CWA" "do not require [§ 402] permits" from the EPA. 40 CFR § 122.3. . . .

The question whether the EPA is the proper agency to regulate the slurry discharge thus depends on whether the Corps of Engineers has authority to do so. If the Corps has authority to issue a permit, then the EPA may not do so. We turn to the Corps' authority under § 404.

Section 404(a) gives the Corps power to "issue permits . . . for the discharge of dredged or fill material." 33 U.S.C. § 1344(a). As all parties concede, the slurry meets the definition of fill material agreed upon by the agencies in a joint regulation promulgated in 2002. That regulation defines "fill material" to mean any "material [that] has the effect of . . . [c]hanging the bottom elevation" of water—a definition that includes "slurry, or tailings or similar mining-related materials." 40 CFR § 232.2. . . .

Rather than challenge the agencies' decision to define the slurry as fill, SEACC instead contends that § 404 contains an implicit exception. According to SEACC, § 404 does not authorize the Corps to permit a discharge of fill material if that material is subject to an EPA new source performance standard.

But § 404's text does not limit its grant of power in this way. Instead, § 404 refers to all "fill material" without qualification. Nor do the EPA regulations support SEACC's reading of § 404. The EPA has enacted guidelines, pursuant to § 404(b), to guide the Corps permitting decision. 40 CFR pt. 230. Those guidelines do not strip the Corps of power to issue permits for fill in cases where the fill is also subject to an EPA new source performance standard.

SEACC's reading of § 404 would create numerous difficulties for the regulated industry. As the regulatory regime stands now, a discharger must ask a simple question—is the substance to be discharged fill material or not? The fill regulation, 40 CFR § 232.2, offers a clear answer to that question; and under the agencies' view, that answer decides the matter—if the discharge is fill, the discharger must seek a § 404 permit from the Corps; if not, only then must the discharger consider whether any EPA performance standard applies, so that the discharger requires a § 402 permit from the EPA.

Under SEACC's interpretation, however, the discharger would face a more difficult problem. The discharger would have to ask—is the fill material also subject to one of the many hundreds of EPA performance standards, so that the permit must come from the EPA, not the Corps? The statute gives no indication that Congress intended to burden industry with that confusing division of permit authority.

The regulatory scheme discloses a defined, and workable, line for determining whether the Corps or the EPA has the permit authority. Under this framework, the Corps of Engineers, and not the EPA, has authority to permit Coeur Alaska's discharge of the slurry. . . .

The judgment of the Court of Appeals is reversed, and these cases are remanded for further proceedings consistent with this opinion.

## QUESTIONS AND DISCUSSION

**1.** So long as one federal agency (the Corps) is regulating the discharge at issue, why was it so important to the environmental group challenging the permit to have another federal agency (EPA) to regulate the discharge? Even if the two agencies have different views on certain permitting matters, isn't that solved by the CWA giving EPA veto authority over Corps permits? Why didn't the EPA exercise its veto authority in this case? What are the benefits of and drawbacks to granting both agencies overlapping authority for wetlands permitting?

**2.** As noted in the text prior to *Coeur Alaska*, and in the case itself, EPA may veto the Corps issuance of a permit if EPA concludes it would have an "unacceptable adverse effect on . . . shellfish beds and fishery areas . . . wildlife, or recreational areas." 33 U.S.C. § 1344(c). One recent case involving EPA veto of a Corps permit involves the controversial practice of "mountaintop mining" where mining companies remove the top of a mountain in order to recover the coal seams contained within it. The practice is widespread in six Appalachian states (Kentucky, West Virginia, Virginia, Tennessee, Pennsylvania, and Ohio). It creates large quantities of excess dirt or "spoil" which is generally disposed of in valley fills on the sides of the former mountain, burying streams that flow through the valley, thus requiring a wetland permit. In 2011, the EPA retroactively vetoed a permit the Corps had issued to the Spruce I mine in West Virginia in 2007, which would have been one of the largest surface mining operations in Appalachia. The waste from the mine would bury over seven miles of streams, impact 2,278 acres of forestland, and degrade water quality in streams adjacent to the mine. Although EPA had expressed concerns about the discharge prior to the 2007 issuance of the permit, at that time, it had declined to exercise its veto authority but later did so in 2011.

The mine owner, Mingo Logan Coal Company, challenged EPA's action in federal court. EPA argued that the after-the-fact veto under CWA Section 404(c), even though it was unusual, was justified because of the unacceptable environmental impacts of the mine operation and that it was currently reviewing other permits issued for mountaintop mining in the area. In 2012, the U.S. District Court for the District of Columbia held the CWA does not authorize EPA to invalidate permits that have already been issued by the Corps under Section 404. Instead, EPA only has authority to veto pending Corps permits, not permits that have already been issued. *See* Mingo Logan Coal Co. v. EPA, 850 F. Supp. 2d 133 (D.D.C. 2012).

In 2013, however, the U.S. Court of Appeals for the D.C. Circuit reversed, holding that the plain language in Section 404(c) grants EPA authority to veto a Corps wetlands permit even after the permit has been issued. According to the Court, "[s]ubsection 404(c) authorizes the [EPA] Administrator, after consultation with the Corps, to veto the Corps's disposal site specification—that is, the Administrator 'is authorized to prohibit the specification (including the withdrawal of specification) of any defined area as a disposal site, and . . . to deny or restrict the use of any defined area for specification (including the withdrawal of specification) as a disposal site'—'whenever he determines' the discharge will have an 'unacceptable adverse effect' on identified environmental resources. *Id.* § 1344(c)." *See* Mingo Logan Coal Co. v. EPA, 714 F.3d 608 (D.C. Cir. 2013). Is a retroactive veto fair to the permittee? Why might EPA have declined to veto the permit back in 2007 and then changed its mind in 2011?

### 2. WETLAND MITIGATION

One additional facet of the Section 404 program that should be covered here is the concept of "mitigation." The premise of any permit program, of course, is that *some* of the regulated activity will be allowed. But under what conditions, and at what cost to the both the regulated entity and the affected ecosystem? The Corps and EPA have grappled with these questions for many years under the Section 404 program. The 404(b)(1) guidelines at 40 C.F.R. pt. 230 provide extensive descriptions of wetlands values that the Corps should consider in assessing potential mitigation requirements. The two agencies also adopted the *Mitigation Guidance* policy in 1990 to clarify the role of wetlands mitigation under the 404(b)(1) guidelines. The *Mitigation Guidance* divides mitigation into three phases—avoidance, minimization, and compensatory mitigation—and required that those phases be conducted sequentially. Thus, the Corps "first makes a determination that potential impacts have been avoided to the maximum extent practicable . . . ;" if there are any "remaining unavoidable impacts," the Corps is to mitigate them "to the extent appropriate and practicable by requiring steps to [2] minimize impacts, and . . . [3] compensate for aquatic resource values." Mitigation banking is an option only if the third phase, compensatory mitigation, is reached.

According to the *Mitigation Guidance*, "mitigation should provide, at a minimum, one for one functional replacement (i.e., no net loss of values), with an adequate margin of safety." The *Mitigation Guidance* paid homage to the idea of "functions and values" in numerous instances. It committed the agencies to "strive to achieve a goal of no overall net loss of [wetlands] values and function" and purports to base "[t]he determination of what level of mitigation constitutes 'appropriate' mitigation . . . solely on the values and functions of the aquatic resource that will be impacted." The *Mitigation Guidance* attempts at quantitative valuation repeatedly focused on wetlands values and function, but it never defined these essential terms.

Notwithstanding its official status as the least-favored alternative in the agencies' sequencing pecking order, compensatory mitigation began to be used frequently in the 404 program. Over time, moreover, the Corps and EPA started shifting compensatory activities increasingly from on-site to off-site mitigation, thus opening the door to the wetlands "mitigation banking" technique. This approach, its proponents argued, would prove advantageous both in terms of economic efficiency and ecological integrity, aggregating small wetlands threatened by development into larger restored wetlands in a different location. It is defined generally as "a system in which the creation, enhancement, restoration, or preservation of wetlands is recognized by a regulatory agency as generating compensation credits allowing the future development of other wetland sites." In its most basic form, wetlands mitigation banking allows a developer to protect wetlands at one site in advance of development and then draw down the resulting bank of mitigation "credits" as development is implemented and wetlands at another site are filled. Indeed, the concept has progressed beyond this personal bank model. Today, large commercial and public wetlands banks, not tied to a particular development, sell mitigation piecemeal to third-party developers in need of compensatory mitigation.

In 1995, five United States agencies published the *Mitigation Banking Guidance* in order to detail the use and operation of mitigation banks. The document's introduction declared that the "objective of a mitigation bank is to provide for *the replacement of the chemical, physical, and biological functions of wetlands and other aquatic resources which are lost* as a result of authorized impacts." This perspective was later broadened to acknowledge that "[t]he overall goal of a mitigation bank is to provide *economically efficient and flexible mitigation opportunities*, while fully compensating for wetland and other aquatic resource losses in a manner that contributes to the long-term ecological functioning of the watershed within which the bank is to be located." The *Mitigation Banking Guidance* thus qualified the goal of replacing ecological functioning by acknowledging economic realities.

In June 2001, the National Research Council, an arm of the National Academy of Sciences, concluded that compensatory wetlands mitigation was an abject failure. *See* NATIONAL ACADEMY OF SCIENCES/NATIONAL RESEARCH COUNCIL, COMPENSATING FOR WETLAND LOSSES UNDER THE CLEAN WATER ACT (June 2001). For one thing, the Corps was doing a poor job, according to the report, accounting for the acre-for-acre trades, meaning even on an acre-counting basis the program is losing "value." But more problematic was that acres of "enhanced" or "recreated" wetlands generally are not as functionally valuable as the acres that are lost to development. Fungibility, in other words, was not being met either on an acre basis or on a functions basis. *See also* R. Eugene Turner et al., *Count It by Acre or Function—Mitigation Adds Up to Net Loss of Wetlands*, NATIONAL WETLANDS NEWSLETTER, Nov.-Dec. 2001, at 5; CHESAPEAKE BAY FOUNDATION, MARYLAND NONTIDAL WETLAND MITIGATION: A PROGRESS REPORT (1997). After publication of the NRC report, the Corps of Engineers issued a defense of its program in the form of a guidance document, *see* U.S. Army Corps of Engineers, Regulatory Guidance Letter No. 01–1 (Oct. 31, 2001), which numerous environmental advocacy organizations immediately condemned as "arrogant" and evidence of an "anything goes approach," and which even some congressional and Bush Administration interests found alarmingly premature given the Corps' lack of coordination with EPA. *See* National Wildlife Federation et al., Press Release, Conservation Community Outraged by Army Corps of Engineers' Reversal on Wetlands Policy (Nov. 6, 2001); *EPA, NMFS Slam Corps RGL on Wetlands Mitigation*, ENDANGERED SPECIES AND WETLANDS REPORT, Mar. 2002, at 13; *Corps Releases Mitigation Guidance*, NATIONAL WETLANDS NEWSLETTER, Nov.–Dec. 2001, at 21; *Army Corps Urged by House Chairman to Withdraw Guidance, Seek EPA Comment*, 32 ENV'T REP. (BNA) 2404 (2001).

The Corps soon began to change its tune. In December 2002, the Bush Administration issued the *National Wetlands Mitigation Action Plan* (Dec. 24, 2002) and a *Regulatory Guidance Letter on Compensatory Mitigation* (Dec. 27, 2002). The *Action Plan* listed action items that agencies will undertake to improve the effectiveness of the process of restoring wetlands affected by actions regulated under federal water quality laws. Prominent action items included integrating compensatory mitigation into a watershed context and clarifying performance standards for mitigation projects. The *Regulatory Guidance Letter* emphasized monitoring, long-term management, financial aid, and a focus on functional quality to promote the success of restored compensatory wetland mitigation projects. The two initiatives immediately attracted supporters and critics. *Compare* John Goodin et al., *Mitigation Guidance and Action Plan Make Improvements, Outline Future*, NATIONAL WETLANDS NEWSLETTER, Mar.–Apr. 2003, at 3 (lauding the initiatives) *with* Julie Sibbing, *Mitigation Guidance or Mitigation Myth*, NATIONAL WETLANDS NEWSLETTER, Jan.–Feb. 2003, at 9 (criticizing the initiatives).

Even mitigation banking itself has come under fire. One early study of wetland banking in Florida found that wetland banking trades, even within the same watershed, have produced "a transfer of wetlands from highly urbanized, high-population density areas to more rural low-population areas." *See* Dennis M. King & Luke W. Herbert, *The Fungibility of Wetlands*, NATIONAL WETLANDS NEWSLETTER, Sept.–Oct. 1997, at 10–11. In similar research two of your authors conducted, findings were that wetland mitigation bank sites are on average well over 15 miles from the associated development projects that purchase credits, and that population densities are on average about 10 times higher around the development projects compared to the area around the banks. *See* J.B. Ruhl & James Salzman, *The Effects of Wetlands Mitigation Banking On People*, NATIONAL WETLANDS NEWSLETTER, Mar.–Apr. 2006, at 1. And other studies question the merits of the assumption that trading many small isolated wetlands for a large, contiguous wetland necessarily improves the ecological value of the wetlands. Many species actually are adapted to using complexes of many small, detached wetlands given greater variability of conditions, insurance against total loss in natural disasters, and source-sink population dynamics that may not operate in a contiguous wetland of equal total size. *See* Raymond D. Semlitsch, *Size Does Matter: The Value of Small Isolated Wetlands*, NATIONAL WETLANDS NEWSLETTER, Jan.–Feb. 2000, at 5. So, moving wetlands around, even if total acreage and functions are held constant, may prove detrimental to some human populations as well as to some plant and wildlife species. For other articles that discuss the various studies and technical reports on wetlands mitigation and concludes that the federal compensatory mitigation process is not fulfilling its goals see Rebecca L. Kihslinger, *Success of Wetland Mitigation Projects*, 30 NAT'L WETLANDS NEWSLETTER 14 (2008); R. Kyle Alagood, *The Mythology of Mitigation Banking*, 46 Envtl. L. Rep. News & Analysis 10200 (2016).

In 2005, the Corps and EPA began an initiative to consolidate the various rules and polices governing mitigation decisions. Ultimately, in April 2008, the Corps and EPA issued new regulations regarding wetland mitigation. The regulations, which establish a "watershed approach" for mitigation projects, address situations where loss cannot be avoided or minimized and thus compensation is required. The regulations create a hierarchy of approaches, with mitigation banks ranked highest, followed by "in-lieu" fees which are paid to nonprofit organizations, and permittee-conducted site mitigation being ranked lowest. 73 Fed. Reg. 19,594 (April 10, 2008) (codified at 33 C.F.R. §§ 332.1 to 332.8 (Corps regulations); 40 C.F.R. §§ 230.91 to 230.98 (EPA regulations)). The rule also focuses on the need to place a high priority on compensatory mitigation compliance and provides principles for establishing ecological performance standards and criteria to ensure success of mitigation projects and to "take into account regional variations in aquatic resource characteristics, functions, and services." 73 Fed. Reg. at 19,601 (April 10, 2008).

---

## QUESTIONS AND DISCUSSION

**1.** Only recently have reliable data become available for determining the share of wetlands mitigation attributable to mitigation banks. Both the Corps and the Environmental Law Institute have found that banking accounts for over 30 percent of all mitigation under Section 404. *See* JESSICA WILKINSON AND JARED THOMPSON, 2005 STATUS REPORT ON COMPENSATORY MITIGATION IN THE UNITED STATES (Environmental Law Institute 2006); U.S. ARMY CORPS OF ENGINEERS, DRAFT ENVIRONMENTAL ASSESSMENT FOR PROPOSED COMPENSATORY MITIGATION REGULATION (Mar. 13, 2006).

**2.** The 2008 wetland mitigation rules summarized above mention "services," thus marking the first time the agencies have expressly incorporated the idea of ecosystem services into the mitigation calculus. Recent studies illustrate that wetlands provide significant service values in more than the obvious way of flood control. For example, in warmer agricultural regions one of the major risks of crop freeze comes from the heat-radiation effect—heat radiating away from the ground on dry winter nights rapidly lowers soil temperatures and freezes the moist root zone. Wetlands impede this effect by moisturizing the atmosphere, which can then better trap heat, and because the water in saturated soil retains heat better than dry soil. Based on an intense heat-radiation freeze event in 1993 that cost South Florida vegetable and sugar cane growers $300 million in lost crops, researchers at the U.S. Geological Survey developed models to contrast the heat-radiation effects that would be expected to occur with and without wetlands present in the region under similar circumstances. They found that most of the region would have stayed in the mid to upper 30s, avoiding a freeze, and other areas would have experienced a freeze of substantially shorter duration and thus less crop damage. *See* Curtis Marshall et al., *Crop Freezes and Land Use Change in Florida*, 426 NATURE 29 (2003). *See also* J.B. Ruhl et al., *Implementing the New Ecosystem Services Mandate of the Section 404 Compensatory Mitigation Program: A Catalyst for Advancing Science and Policy,* 38 STETSON L. REV. 251 (2009).

**3.** Mitigation banking appears in some cases to work as planned in terms of producing viable wetland resources. For example, the Little Pine Island Mitigation Bank in Florida is an ecological success story by any standard, ecological or economic. This highly productive 4,700-acre mangrove wetland was drained in the 1960s when "mosquito ditches" were installed. The aquatic habitat dried out and yielded to invasive upland species, and by the 1990s a 1600-acre area had become an exotic forest. The area today is state owned, but a $12 million restoration effort is being privately financed, the motivation being to sell wetland mitigation credits. The private mitigation banker, Mariner Properties, removed the exotic hardwood species and reconstructed the original hydrology, which after only seven years has restored 65 percent of the original wetland functions. The sale of mitigation credits will supply a permanent maintenance endowment and devote seven percent of bank revenues to a state fund to be used to secure additional wetland resources. Credits cost about $25,000 per credit in 1996, and have risen to over $53,000 per credit. Mariner Properties expects the bank to be "sold out" by 2020. *See* http://www.littlepineisland.com/mitigation.html. The cost of wetland banking credits varies significantly by region, based on the availability and price of land suitable for bank development and the cost to create an acre of wetland compensation within a given region. For a schedule of fees for 2015 for wetland banking credits in Minnesota see http://www.bwsr.state.mn.us/wetlands/wetlandbanking/fee_and_sales_data/Wetland_Bank_Fee_Schedule.pdf.

**4.** For a good discussion of the history of mitigation banking and the current economic options the expanding market for mitigation credits has created, see Fred Bosselman, *Swamp Swaps: The Second Nature of Wetlands*, 39 ENVTL. L. 577 (2009). For EPA's general overview of the Mitigation Banking program visit the EPA's website at https://www.epa.gov/cwa-404/compensatory-mitigation. For comprehensive overviews of wetland values and valuation methods, see James Boyd & Lisa Wainger, *Measuring Ecosystem Service Benefits for Wetland Mitigation*, NATIONAL WETLANDS NEWSLETTER, Nov.–Dec. 2002, at 1; Charles Andrew Cole and James G. Kooser, *HGM: Hidden, Gone, Missing?*, NATIONAL WETLANDS NEWSLETTER, Mar.–Apr. 2002, at 1; PAUL F. SCODARI, MEASURING THE BENEFITS OF FEDERAL WETLAND PROGRAMS (Envtl. L. Inst. 1997); Special Issue, *The Values of Wetlands; Landscape and Institutional Perspectives*, 35 ECOLOGICAL ECONOMICS 1 (2000). For a thorough description of the history and operation of wetlands mitigation banking programs, see ENVIRONMENTAL LAW INSTITUTE, BANKS AND FEES: THE STATUS OF OFF-SITE WETLAND MITIGATION IN THE UNITED STATES (2002); ENVIRONMENTAL LAW INST., WETLAND MITIGATION BANKING (1993); Royal C. Gardner, *Banking on Entrepreneurs: Wetlands, Mitigation Banking, and Takings*, 81 IOWA L. REV. 527 (1996).

**5.** If wetlands can be valued with sufficient accuracy to support mitigation banking, why bother with banking at all? Couldn't we simply allow the person proposing to fill the wetlands to provide *monetary* compensatory mitigation? For descriptions and criticisms of such programs, known as "in-lieu" or "fee" mitigation, see U.S. GENERAL ACCOUNTING OFFICE, GAO–01–325, WETLANDS PROTECTION: ASSESSMENTS NEEDED TO DETERMINE EFFECTIVENESS OF IN-LIEU-FEE MITIGATION (2001); Royal C. Gardner,

*Money for Nothing? The Rise of Wetland Fee Mitigation*, 19 VA. ENVTL. L.J. 1 (2000).

## III. THE PUBLIC TRUST DOCTRINE

Most of the environmental conservation materials covered in this text are based in federal, state, or local legislative initiatives. Does the common law have any role to play in environmental conservation? Generally, the answer has been no. Although the rare case has used doctrines of nuisance law to address broad environmental injuries, *see, e.g.*, Georgia v. Tennessee Copper Co., 240 U.S. 650 (1916) (using common law public nuisance law to address air pollution); Reserve Mining Co. v. EPA, 514 F.2d 492 (8th Cir. 1975) (using common law nuisance to address water pollution), these are, for the most part, limited applications of common law doctrine to extreme cases of pollution. To be sure, nuisance law and other common law doctrines remain in active use to challenge land uses causing pollution, but nothing approaching a judicial doctrine of water pollution regulation or wetlands protection has emerged from the common law.

One common law principle that many scholars have argued could defy this trend is known as the Public Trust Doctrine. The name is impressive, suggesting great possibilities. Indeed, in his landmark 1970 article, inspiring many since then to envision a Public Trust Doctrine motivating broad goals of natural resources conservation, Professor Joseph Sax outlined an ambitious agenda for just those purposes. *See* Joseph L. Sax, *The Public Trust Doctrine In Natural Resource Law: Effective Judicial Intervention*, 68 MICH. L. REV. 471 (1970). Sax argued that "[o]f all the concepts known to American law, only the public trust doctrine seems to have the breadth and substantive content which might make it useful as a tool of general application for citizens seeking to develop a comprehensive legal approach to resource management problems." *Id.* at 474. Over thirty-five years and hundreds of law review articles later, however, this vision remains largely unfulfilled hope. Why?

The Public Trust Doctrine is often described as tracing its roots to the Institutes of Justinian in Roman Law, which declared that there are three things common to all people: (1) air; (2) running water; and (3) the sea and its shores. Along with the Romans, this principle invaded what later became England and eventually became part of its common law, which the states imported with minor variations after the American Revolution. While the British version held that tidelands were held by the King for the benefit of all English subjects, the American version replaced the crown with the states, and the courts became the doctrine's chief enforcer.

The scope of the trust imposed by the Public Trust Doctrine can be thought of in several dimensions. First, it has a geographic reach that must be defined. In the American version, this has generally meant all lands subject to the ebb and flow of the tide, and all waters navigable in fact, such as rivers, lakes, ponds, and streams. Next, the uses that the trust protects and prohibits must be defined. In American jurisprudence, fishing, commerce, and navigation are core protected uses, with other uses such as boating, swimming, anchoring, and general recreation being recognized as well in most states. Uses inconsistent with those protected values may be prohibited—that is, even if the state wishes to facilitate such incompatible uses, it may be restrained from doing so. Finally, the Public Trust Doctrine carries with it restrictions on the alienation of public trust lands to private interests when to do so would undermine the protected public uses. Clearly, these are dimensions in which regulatory law operates as well, so the thought of linking the Public Trust Doctrine with environmental protection is by no means far-fetched.

A series of nineteenth century U.S. Supreme Court cases, focused principally on the scope of property rights associated with statehood, breathed apparent life into these parameters of the Public Trust Doctrine. First, in Martin v. Waddell's Lessee, 41 U.S. (16 Pet.) 367 (1842), the Court applied the doctrine in a case involving resolution of title to tidelands and tidal rivers. Next, in The Daniel Ball, 77 U.S. (10 Wall.) 557 (1870), the Court held that "[t]hose rivers must be regarded as public navigable rivers in law which are navigable in fact." But, as Professor Sax described it, the lodestar case of the Public Trust Doctrine, at least for purposes of thinking about it as a tool of resource conservation, came in the Court's 1892 opinion in Illinois Central Railroad Co. v. Illinois, 146 U.S. 387 (1892). The Court held that Illinois could not sell fee interests in the land under Chicago Harbor to private developers because

> the State holds the title to the lands under the navigable waters. . . . It is a title held in trust for the people of the State that they can enjoy the navigation of the waters, carry on commerce over them, and have liberty of fishing therein freed from the obstruction or interference of private parties.

*Id.* at 452. Almost 100 years later, the Court reiterated the principle using similar terms in Phillips Petroleum Co. v. Mississippi, 484 U.S. 469, 476 (1988) ("our cases firmly establish that the States, upon entering the Union, were given ownership over all the lands beneath the waters subject to the tides' influence"). Yet, that about sums up the Public Trust Doctrine as far as the U.S. Supreme Court is concerned—the states may not alienate fee title in tidelands, shores, and other public trust lands in violation of the Public Trust Doctrine. Suffice it to say that the Court has not championed Professor Sax's vision of doing more with the doctrine, limiting its jurisprudence largely to questions of who owns what, and much less so to the federalism question of what a state may do with public trust lands acquired as a matter of statehood.

The *Phillips Petroleum* decision did make clear, however, that "[i]t has been long established that the individual states have the authority to define the limits of the lands held in public trust." *Id.* at 475. As it is fundamentally a state law doctrine, therefore, many state courts have opined on the scope of the Public Trust Doctrine as well, some with a vigor not found in the U.S. Supreme Court jurisprudence. Perhaps the most famous of those opinions, known as the *Mono Lake* case, follows.

---

## National Audubon Society v. Superior Court of Alpine County

Supreme Court of California, 1983.
33 Cal.3d 419, 658 P.2d 709, 189 Cal.Rptr. 346.

■ BROUSSARD, JUSTICE.

Mono Lake, the second largest lake in California, sits at the base of the Sierra Nevada escarpment near the eastern entrance to Yosemite National Park. The lake is saline; it contains no fish but supports a large population of brine shrimp which feed vast numbers of nesting and migratory birds. Islands in the lake protect a large breeding colony of California gulls, and the lake itself serves as a haven on the migration route for thousands of Northern Phalarope, Wilson's Phalarope, and Eared Greve. Towers and spires of tufa on the north and south shores are matters of geological interest and a tourist attraction.

Although Mono Lake receives some water from rain and snow on the lake surface, historically most of its supply came from snowmelt in the Sierra Nevada. Five freshwater streams—Mill, Lee Vining, Walker, Parker and Rush Creeks—arise near the crest of the range and carry the annual runoff to the west shore of the lake. In 1940, however, the Division of Water Resources, the predecessor to the present California Water Resources Board, granted the Department of Water and Power of the City of Los Angeles (hereafter DWP) a permit to appropriate virtually the entire flow of four of the five streams flowing into the lake. DWP promptly constructed facilities to divert about half the flow of these streams into DWP's Owens Valley aqueduct. In 1970 DWP completed a second diversion tunnel, and since that time has taken virtually the entire flow of these streams.

As a result of these diversions, the level of the lake has dropped; the surface area has diminished by one-third; one of the two principal islands in the lake has become a peninsula, exposing the gull rookery there to coyotes and other predators and causing the gulls to abandon the former island. The ultimate effect of continued diversions is a matter of intense dispute, but there seems little doubt that both the scenic beauty and the ecological values of Mono Lake are imperiled.

This case brings together for the first time two systems of legal thought: the appropriative water rights system which since the days of the gold rush has dominated California water law, and the public trust doctrine which, after evolving as a shield for the protection of tidelands, now extends its protective scope to navigable lakes. Ever since we first recognized that the public trust protects environmental and recreational values (*Marks v. Whitney* (1971) 6 Cal.3d 251, 98 Cal.Rptr. 790, 491 P.2d 374), the two systems of legal thought have been on a collision course. (Johnson, *Public Trust Protection for Stream Flows and Lake Levels* (1980) 14 U.C. Davis L.Rev. 233.) They meet in a unique and dramatic setting which highlights the clash of values. Mono Lake is a scenic and ecological treasure of national significance, imperiled by continued diversions of water; yet, the need of Los Angeles for water is apparent, its reliance on rights granted by the board evident, the cost of curtailing diversions substantial.

Attempting to integrate the teachings and values of both the public trust and the appropriative water rights system, we have arrived at certain conclusions which we briefly summarize here. In our opinion, the core of the public trust doctrine is the state's authority as sovereign to exercise a continuous supervision and control over the navigable waters of the state and the lands underlying those waters. This authority applies to the waters tributary to Mono Lake and bars DWP or any other party from claiming a vested right to divert waters once it becomes clear that such diversions harm the interests protected by the public trust. The corollary rule which evolved in tideland and lakeshore cases barring conveyance of rights free of the trust except to serve trust purposes cannot, however, apply without modification to flowing waters. The prosperity and habitability of much of this state requires the diversion of great quantities of water from its streams for purposes unconnected to any navigation, commerce, fishing, recreation, or ecological use relating to the source stream. The state must have the power to grant nonvested usufructuary rights to appropriate water even if diversions harm public trust uses. Approval of such diversion without considering public trust values, however, may result in needless destruction of those values. Accordingly, we believe that before state courts and agencies approve water diversions they should consider the effect of such diversions upon interests protected by the public trust, and attempt, so far as feasible, to avoid or minimize any harm to those interests.

The water rights enjoyed by DWP were granted, the diversion was commenced, and has continued to the present without any consideration of the impact upon the public trust. An objective study and reconsideration of the water rights in the Mono Basin is long overdue. The water law of California-which we conceive to be an integration including both the public trust doctrine and the board-administered appropriative rights system-permits such a reconsideration; the values underlying that integration require it.

[The court reviewed the history of the state's water rights system and the public trust doctrine]

[T]he public trust doctrine and the appropriative water rights system . . . developed independently of each other. Each developed comprehensive rules and principles which, if applied to the full extent of their scope, would occupy the field of allocation of stream waters to the exclusion of any competing system of legal thought. Plaintiffs, for example, argues that the public trust is antecedent to and thus limits all appropriative water rights, an argument which implies that most appropriative water rights in California were acquired and are presently being used unlawfully. Defendant DWP, on the other hand, argues that the public trust doctrine as to stream waters has been "subsumed" into the appropriative water rights system and, absorbed by that body of law, quietly disappeared; according to DWP, the recipient of a board license enjoys a vested right in perpetuity to take water without concern for the consequences to the trust.

We are unable to accept either position. In our opinion, both the public trust doctrine and the water rights system embody important precepts which make the law more responsive to the diverse needs and interests involved in the planning and allocation of water resources. To embrace one system of thought and reject the other would lead to an unbalanced structure, one which would either decry as a breach of trust appropriations essential to the economic development of this state, or deny any duty to protect or even consider the values promoted by the public trust. Therefore, seeking an accommodation which will make use of the pertinent principles of both the public trust doctrine and the appropriative water rights system, and drawing upon the history of the public trust and the water rights system, the body of judicial precedent, and the views of expert commentators, we reach the following conclusions:

a. The state as sovereign retains continuing supervisory control over its navigable waters and the lands beneath those waters. This principle, fundamental to the concept of the public trust, applies to rights in flowing waters as well as to rights in tidelands and lakeshores; it prevents any party from acquiring a vested right to appropriate water in a manner harmful to the interests protected by the public trust.

b. As a matter of current and historical necessity, the Legislature, acting directly or through an authorized agency such as the Water Board, has the power to grant usufructuary licenses that will permit an appropriator to take water from flowing streams and use that water in a distant part of the state, even though this taking does not promote, and may unavoidably harm, the trust uses at the source stream. The population and economy of this state depend upon the appropriation of vast quantities of water for uses unrelated to in-stream trust values. California's Constitution, its statutes, decisions, and commentators all emphasize the need to make efficient use of California's limited water resources: all recognize, at least implicitly, that efficient use requires diverting water from in-stream uses. Now that the economy and population centers of this state have developed in reliance upon appropriated water, it would be disingenuous to hold that such appropriations are and have always been improper to the extent that they harm public trust uses, and can be justified only upon theories of reliance or estoppel.

c. The state has an affirmative duty to take the public trust into account in the planning and allocation of water resources, and to protect public trust uses whenever feasible. Just as the history of this state shows that appropriation may be necessary for efficient use of water despite unavoidable harm to public trust values, it demonstrates that an appropriative water rights system administered without consideration of the public trust may cause unnecessary and unjustified harm to trust interests. As a matter of practical necessity the state may have to approve appropriations despite foreseeable harm to public trust uses. In so doing, however, the state must bear in mind its duty as trustee to consider the effect of the taking on the public trust and to preserve, so far as consistent with the public interest, the uses protected by the trust.

Once the state has approved an appropriation, the public trust imposes a duty of continuing supervision over the taking and use of the appropriated water. In exercising its sovereign power to allocate water resources in the public interest, the state is not confined by past allocation decisions which may be incorrect in light of current knowledge or inconsistent with current needs.

The state accordingly has the power to reconsider allocation decisions even though those decisions were made after due consideration of their effect on the public trust. The case for reconsidering a particular decision, however, is even stronger when that decision failed to weigh and consider public trust uses. In the case before us, the salient fact is that no responsible body has ever determined the impact of diverting the entire flow of the Mono Lake tributaries into the Los Angeles Acqueduct. This is not a case in which the Legislature, the Water Board, or any judicial body has determined that the needs of Los Angeles outweigh the needs of the Mono Basin, that the benefit gained is worth the price. Neither has any responsible body determined whether some lesser taking would better balance the diverse interests. Instead, DWP acquired rights to the entire flow in 1940 from a water board which believed it lacked both the power and the duty to protect the Mono Lake environment, and continues to exercise those rights in apparent disregard for the resulting damage to the scenery, ecology, and human uses of Mono Lake.

It is clear that some responsible body ought to reconsider the allocation of the waters of the Mono Basin. No vested rights bar such reconsideration. We recognize the substantial concerns voiced by Los Angeles-the city's need for water, its reliance upon the 1940 board decision, the cost both in terms of money and environmental impact of obtaining water elsewhere. Such concerns must enter into any allocation decision. We hold only that they do not preclude a reconsideration and reallocation which also takes into account the impact of water diversion on the Mono Lake environment.

This opinion is but one step in the eventual resolution of the Mono Lake controversy. We do not dictate any particular allocation of water. Our objective is to resolve a legal conundrum in which two competing systems of thought-the public trust doctrine and the appropriative water rights system-existed independently of each other, espousing principles which seemingly suggested opposite results. We hope by integrating these two doctrines to clear away the legal barriers which have so far prevented either the Water Board or the courts from taking a new and objective look at the water resources of the Mono Basin. The human and environmental uses of Mono Lake-uses protected by the public trust doctrine-deserve to be taken into account. Such uses should not be destroyed because the state mistakenly thought itself powerless to protect them.

Let a peremptory writ of mandate issue commanding the Superior Court of Alpine County to vacate its judgment in this action and to enter a new judgment consistent with the views stated in this opinion.

---

## QUESTIONS AND DISCUSSION

**1.** The *Mono Lake* court emphasized that it did not dictate any particular allocation of water from Mono Lake to take into account the Public Trust Doctrine. Nor did the court mandate which institution should make that allocation, by when, under what specific criteria, or how. So, what did the *Mono Lake* court actually decide? Does the court's hesitance to go further suggest anything to you about the role the Public Trust Doctrine can play in environmental law and policy?

**2.** As *Mono Lake* is an example, the Public Trust Doctrine overall has had its chief impact as an arbiter of state property rights. It has by no means been transformed into a judicial natural resources management or pollution control program in any state. But *Mono Lake* illustrates that the doctrine is not without some role to play. Another noted case in this regard is from Wisconsin, in which the court found that the doctrine required that undisturbed wetland areas be limited to uses consistent with natural conditions. *See* Just v. Marinette County, 201 N.W.2d 761 (Wis. 1972). Several more recent cases are variations on that theme. *See e.g.*, Selkirk-Priest Basin Association v. Idaho ex rel. Andrus, 899 P.2d 949 (Idaho 1995) (doctrine allows environmental group standing to challenge timber sales on ground that sedimentation could injure fish spawning grounds); Vander Bloemen v. Wisconsin Department of Natural Resources, 551 N.W.2d 869 (Wis.App. 1996) (doctrine extends to protection of lakeside ecology). For a thorough discussion of these and other state law cases on the application of the Public Trust Doctrine in ecosystem protection contexts, see Arnold L. Lum, *How Goes the Public Trust Doctrine: Is the Common Law Shaping Environmental Policy?*, 18 NATURAL RESOURCES & ENV'T 73 (Fall 2003). Lum covers state cases extending the trust duties to public natural resources other than navigable waters, such as groundwater, parks, and extending the trust uses to recreational and ecological uses. On the other hand, he notes that not all state cases result in expansion of the doctrine's scope, e.g., Rettkowski v. Department of Ecology, 858 P.2d 232 (Wash. 1993) (does not apply to groundwater), and that few state courts have endorsed breach of trust claims against state agencies. Lum concludes that the force of the Public Trust Doctrine in environmental law is "growing," though by how much and how fast he does not estimate. By and large, however, the state courts have declined to mobilize Professor Sax's vision of the Public Trust Doctrine as a means of effective and broad judicial intervention in environmental policy.

**3.** Ironically, what has given the Public Trust Doctrine a bit of a boost recently is the aftermath of developments in the U.S. Supreme Court's takings jurisprudence. Several courts have found that the restrictions associated with the Public Trust Doctrine are part of the background principles of state property law for purposes of evaluating regulatory takings claims as outlined in Lucas v. South Carolina Coastal Council, 505 U.S. 1003 (1992). In McQueen v. South Carolina Coastal Council, 580 S.E.2d 116 (S.C. 2003), the South Carolina Supreme Court found no regulatory taking occurred when the state denied McQueen a permit to install bulkheads and fill in the tidelands situated behind it for purposes of developing residential housing units. The tideland area had been above the high water mark within the lots when purchased in the 1960s, but through McQueen's neglect of the property the shoreline eroded and much of the property became "critical area saltwater wetlands," which the state regulates closely. McQueen alleged the state committed a regulatory taking of the property when it denied the development permit, but the court observed that the tideland area appeared on the property as a result of the forces of nature and McQueen's lack of vigilance, and hence "the tidelands included on the McQueen's lots are public trust property subject to control of the state." As a result, "McQueen's ownership rights do not include the right to backfill or place bulkheads on public trust land and the state need not compensate him for the denial of the permits to do what he cannot otherwise do."

Similarly, the Ninth Circuit held that the State of Washington has always incorporated the Public Trust Doctrine in its property law and thus the restrictions associated with it run with the title to land. The City of Seattle's denial of a permit to develop shoreline property on Elliott Bay did not take the landowner's property, therefore, because the Public Trust Doctrine already attached to the property and would have restricted the state from approving the permits. *See* Esplanade Properties, LLC v. City of Seattle, 307 F.3d 978 (9th Cir. 2002). Yet, as much as these cases remind us that the Public Trust Doctrine inheres in the title to private property, they address only what the state may accomplish through public legislation—they do not give affirmative force to the doctrine itself as an instrument of ecosystem management.

**4.** By contrast to the experience in the courts, since Professor Sax's seminal work many environmental law scholars have charted and claimed all sorts of environmental protection goals for the Public Trust Doctrine. Of course, doing so requires that one or more of the doctrine's parameters be expanded beyond present judicial interpretations. So, for example, courts could extend the geographic scope to encompass regulation of private lands adjacent to public trust lands, or they could add other resources to the protected lands. The doctrine might even be transformed from its current status as a restriction on state power to alienate public trust lands or to allow incompatible uses, to one imposing an affirmative *duty* of environmental protection and resources management. For examples of these and other academically posited stretchings of the doctrine, see JACK H. ARCHER ET AL., THE PUBLIC TRUST DOCTRINE AND THE MANAGEMENT OF AMERICA'S COASTS (1994); Jack H. Archer & Terrance W. Stone, *The Interaction of the Public Trust and the "Takings" Doctrines: Protecting Wetlands and Critical Coastal Areas*, 20 VERMONT L. REV. 81 (1995); Robin Kundis Craig, *Mobil Oil Exploration, Environmental Protection, and Contract Repudiation: It's Time to Recognize the Public Trust in the Outer Continental Shelf*, 30 ENVTL. L. REP. (Envtl. L. Inst.) 11104 (2000); Ralph W. Johnson and William C. Galloway, *Can the Public Trust Doctrine Prevent Extinctions?*, in BIODIVERSITY AND THE LAW 157 (William J. Snape III ed., 1996).

What explains the chasm between the judicial and the academic visions of the Public Trust Doctrine? What keeps academics coming back to the Public Trust Doctrine, asking ever more of it, but keeps judges from taking it that far? One rather obvious possibility is that, not long after Professor Sax suggested how its latent power could be tapped, the legislative revolution of the 1970s unfolded to bring one after the other of comprehensive environmental laws into being. In short, who needs the Public Trust Doctrine? By comparison to the targeted legislative agenda that brought on line the Clean Water Act and other environmental and resources laws spawned in that era and which remain the workhorses of today, the Public Trust Doctrine seems, like many common law doctrines, hopelessly open-ended, amorphous, and unwieldy. Perhaps, in addition to seeing no critical need to go down the road Sax mapped, courts see trouble ahead were they tempted to start the journey.

**5.** Indeed, in counter to the Saxian vision, Professor Richard Lazarus has argued that the Public Trust Doctrine, if shaped as Sax wanted, could actually be antithetical to proactive and innovative environmental and resource management. *See* Richard J. Lazarus, *Changing Conceptions of Property and Sovereignty in Natural Resources: Questioning the Public Trust Doctrine*, 71 IOWA L. REV. 631 (1986). For one thing, he argued, it places too much reliance on a judiciary that is not always in tune with what the academic vision of the Public Trust Doctrine appears to want have happen. The growth of the police power state, its authorities grown and channeled since World War II into a huge administrative law apparatus, seem a far better prospect for carrying out an environmentalist agenda. And at its core the Public Trust Doctrine is about property rights in the form of public rights to *use* the environment of public trust lands. Like any trust, the purpose of the public trust lands is not merely to preserve their corpus, but to put them to public benefit. The administrative law version of environmental law is potentially more flexible—its course charted by congressional will and agency policy.

**6.** Striking more of a middle ground between Sax and Lazarus, while resisting the urge to expand the traditional scope of the doctrine, two of your authors have argued that the traditional Public Trust Doctrine, given its utilitarian values, could be used to protect the trust resources that provide ecosystem services of economic value to human populations, such as storm surge mitigation, groundwater recharge, and flood control. *See* J.B. Ruhl & James Salzman, *Ecosystem Services and the Public Trust Doctrine: Working Change from Within*, 15 SOUTHEASTERN ENVIRONMENTAL L.J. 223 (2006). As such nonmarket values of the environment become more evident, can the Public Trust Doctrine step in to give them the same protected status as fishing, boating, and other traditional protected uses? What would be the implications?

**7.** The Supreme Court has made clear that the "the public trust doctrine remains a matter of state law . . . [and] the contours of that public trust do not depend upon the Constitution." PPL Montana, LLC v. Montana, 132 S. Ct. 1215 (2012). But is there a *federal* version of a trust that mirrors the Public Trust Doctrine? If so, it amounts to little, according to Professor Eric Pearson. He observes that federal courts have virtually never applied any form of public trust duties to federal government use and regulation of public lands and resources. *See* Eric Pearson, *The Public Trust Doctrine in Federal Law*, 24 J. LAND, RESOURCES & ENVTL. LAW 173 (2004). As he points out, the seminal case describing the federal government's public trust duties, Light v. United States, 220 U.S. 523 (1911), ruled that "it is not for the courts to say how that trust shall be administered. That is for Congress to determine. The courts cannot compel it to set aside lands for settlement; or to suffer them to be used for agricultural purposes; nor interfere when, in the exercise of its discretion, Congress establishes a forest reserve for what it decides to be national and public purposes." *Id.* at 537. As Professor Pearson observes, therefore, "the public trust doctrine in state law empowers the judicial branch to overturn substantive choices made by political branches of government. The public trust doctrine in federal law works to the opposite end. In federal law, the doctrine empowers the political branches of government to implement substantive choices despite objections in the judicial branch. Night, meet day." Pearson, *supra* at 176–77. What could be the justification for this legal dichotomy?

**8.** Many states have embodied variations of the Public Trust Doctrine in their constitutions, in some cases using language going well beyond the traditional scope of the common law doctrine. A notable example is Article I, Section 27 of the Pennsylvania Constitution, which the state's electorate adopted in 1971 by an overwhelming margin. Known as the Environmental Rights Amendment, Article I, Section 27 provides:

> The people have a right to clean air, pure water, and to the preservation of the natural, scenic, historic and esthetic values of the environment. Pennsylvania's public natural resources are the common property of all the people, including generations yet to come. As trustee of these resources, the Commonwealth shall conserve and maintain them for the benefit of all the people.

In *Robinson Township v. Commonwealth of Pennsylvania*, 623 Pa. 564 (Pa. 2013), a majority of the Pennsylvania Supreme Court held unconstitutional major parts of Pennsylvania's "Act 13," a 2012 oil and gas law the state General Assembly adopted in response to controversy over development of natural gas from the Marcellus Shale formation through hydrofracturing technology, more commonly known as "fracking." Act 13 delegated permitting authority over oil and gas operations, including fracking, to the state Department of Environmental Protection, but went further to declare that state environmental laws "occupy the entire field" of oil and gas regulation, "to the exclusion of all local ordinances." The legislation stated that it "preempts and supersedes the local regulation of oil and gas operations" and required "all local ordinances regulating oil and gas operations" to "allow for the reasonable development of oil and gas resources."

In a lengthy opinion, a plurality of the court struck down these provisions as beyond the state General Assembly's power (a concurring opinion, needed to form the majority, found the provisions violated the substantive due process rights of private landowners). The plurality opinion began by describing the scope of the constitutional provision broadly:

> The second right reserved by Section 27 is the common ownership of the people, including future generations, of Pennsylvania's public natural resources. On its terms, the second clause of Section 27 applies to a narrower category of "public" natural resources than the first clause of the provision. The drafters, however, left unqualified the phrase public natural resources, suggesting that the term fairly implicates relatively broad aspects of the environment, and is amenable to change over time to conform, for example, with the development of related legal and societal concerns. At present, the concept of public natural resources includes not only state-owned lands, waterways, and mineral reserves, but also resources that implicate the public interest, such as ambient air, surface and ground water, wild flora, and fauna (including fish) that are outside the scope of purely private property.

The plurality explained that "the third clause of Section 27 establishes the Commonwealth's duties with respect to Pennsylvania's commonly-owned public natural resources, which are both negative (*i.e.*, prohibitory) and affirmative (*i.e.*, implicating enactment of legislation and regulations)." It was of particular importance to the plurality that the provision designates "the Commonwealth," not the General Assembly, as trustee. The distinction proved to be dispositive:

> We have explained that, as a result, all existing branches and levels of government derive constitutional duties and obligations with respect to the people. The municipalities affected by Act 13 all existed before that Act was adopted; and most if not all had land use measures in place. Those ordinances necessarily addressed the environment, and created reasonable expectations in the resident citizenry. To put it succinctly, our citizens buying homes and

raising families in areas zoned residential had a reasonable expectation concerning the environment in which they were living, often for years or even decades. Act 13 fundamentally disrupted those expectations, and ordered local government to take measures to effect the new uses, irrespective of local concerns. The constitutional command respecting the environment necessarily restrains legislative power with respect to political subdivisions that have acted upon their Article I, Section 27 responsibilities: the General Assembly can neither offer political subdivisions purported relief from obligations under the Environmental Rights Amendment, nor can it remove necessary and reasonable authority from local governments to carry out these constitutional duties. Indeed, if the General Assembly had subsumed local government entirely by Act 13—it did not, instead it required local government essentially to be complicit in accommodating a new environmental regime irrespective of the character of the locale—the General Assembly could not eliminate the commands of Article I, Section 27. Rather, the General Assembly would simply have shifted the constitutional obligations onto itself. And those obligations include the duty to "conserve and maintain" the public natural resources, including clean air and pure water, "for the benefit of all the people." The Commonwealth, by the General Assembly, declares in [Act 13] that environmental obligations related to the oil and gas industries are of statewide concern and, on that basis, the Commonwealth purports to preempt the regulatory field to the exclusion of all local environmental legislation that might be perceived as affecting oil and gas operations. Act 13 thus commands municipalities to ignore their obligations under Article I, Section 27 and further directs municipalities to take affirmative actions to undo existing protections of the environment in their localities. The police power, broad as it may be, does not encompass such authority to so fundamentally disrupt these expectations respecting the environment. Accordingly, we are constrained to hold that, in enacting this provision of Act 13, the General Assembly transgressed its delegated police powers which, while broad and flexible, are nevertheless limited by constitutional commands, including the Environmental Rights Amendment.

Predictably, after the decision many local jurisdictions in Pennsylvania adopted or enforced existing restrictions on fracking, leading to litigation by the oil and gas industry challenging the ordinances on a variety of grounds. For example, one court struck down a local ordinance completely banning fracking as beyond local authority. *Pa. General Energy Company, LLC v. Grant Twp.,* 2015 U.S. Dist. LEXIS 139921 (W.D. Pa. 2015). Some commentators, however, have pointed to *Robinson Township* as potentially sparking a new wave of judicial action on the Public Trust Doctrine and constitutional environmentalism:

*Robinson Township* is a potentially important corrective to judicial under-engagement of environmental constitutionalism. Within

> Pennsylvania, the case forces lawyers and decision makers to closely examine the text of Article I, Section 27 and treat it as constitutional law. It is particularly noteworthy that the decision was issued in the context of a significant social, economic, and environmental controversy—Marcellus Shale development. The plurality opinion is also a powerful vindication of constitutional environmentalism and may represent a significant step forward for American constitutional environmental rights in particular. The case may have far-reaching implications in other states and countries. The Pennsylvania Supreme Court attended to almost every significant issue that courts around the world are reckoning with, including standing, self-execution, interpretation of constitutional provisions, the public trust doctrine, and enforcement of constitutional environmental provisions. And it has done so in a way that takes seriously the environmental interests of the general public and of future generations. It is likely that other courts within and outside Pennsylvania will take notice, even though these views did not command a majority of the Pennsylvania court.

John Dernbach et al., Robinson Township v. Commonwealth of Pennsylvania: *Examination and Implications*, 67 RUTGERS U. L. REV. 1195–96 (2015). Do you agree?

**9.** Climate change has renewed interest in the Public Trust Doctrine. For example, both proponents and opponents of renewable energy projects have looked to the public trust doctrine to advance their goals. Proponents of large-scale renewable energy projects point to the environmental and climate change benefits associated with renewable energy development and argue that the use of public lands and large tracts of private lands to facilitate such projects are both in the public interest and consistent with the public trust doctrine. At the same time, parties opposed to particular renewable energy projects have argued that the land-intensive nature of these projects as well as their potential adverse impacts on endangered species, open space, aesthetic values, and pristine landscapes will result in a violation of the public trust doctrine. *See* Alexandra Klass, *Renewable Energy and the Public Trust Doctrine*, 45 U.C. DAVIS L. REV. 1021 (2012).

**10.** More broadly, Our Children's Trust, an Oregon-based nonprofit, made headlines in 2011 when it began filing lawsuits on behalf of children against states and several federal agencies alleging that these governmental entities have violated the common law Public Trust Doctrine by failing to limit greenhouse gas emissions that contribute to climate change. The claims seek judicial declaration that states and the federal government have a fiduciary duty to future generations with regard to an "atmospheric trust" and that states and the federal government must take immediate action to protect and preserve that trust. Courts in several states, including Colorado, Oregon, Arizona, Washington, Arkansas, and Minnesota dismissed the cases early on, finding no basis for an "atmospheric trust" under state common law. Also, consistent with Professor Pearson's assessment of the limited scope of a federal public trust doctrine discussed above, the D.C. Circuit rejected the petitioners' claims against EPA on the ground that the Public Trust Doctrine is exclusively a matter of state law with no application to the federal government. *See* Alec L. v. Jackson, 561 Fed. Appx. 7 (D.C. Cir. 2014).

The petitioners made initial headway in some states by withstanding motions to dismiss, but their claims ultimately failed on procedural or substantive grounds in subsequent rulings. *See, e.g.*, Sanders-Reed v. Martinez, 350 P.3d 1221 (N.M. Ct. App. 2015); TCEQ v. Bonser-Lain, 438 S.W. 2d 887 (Tx. Ct. App. 2014); Butler v. Brewer, 2013 WL 1091209 (Ariz. Ct. App. 2013). In some opinions, however, courts have suggested in dicta that there may be a basis for extending the state's Public Trust Doctrine to the atmosphere, though declining to rule that this would impose affirmative regulatory duties on the state government to regulate greenhouse gas emissions. *See* Kanuk v. Alaska, 335 P.3d 1088 (Alaska 2014). Appeals are pending in several states and litigation is still in early stages in others, with updates available at http://ourchildrenstrust.org/US/LawsuitStates. The theory of the atmospheric trust has been forged primarily my law professor Mary Wood. *See* MARY WOOD, NATURE'S TRUST: ENVIRONMENTAL LAW FOR A NEW ECOLOGICAL AGE (2013). For more on the Public Trust Doctrine and climate change, see Chapter 8.

**11.** For thorough reviews of the Public Trust Doctrine in each of the states, including an assessment of its "ecological" focus, see Robin Kundis Craig, *A Comparative Guide to the Western States' Public Trust Doctrine: Public Values, Private Rights, and the Evolution Toward an Ecological Public Trust*, 37 ECOLOGY LAW QUARTERLY 53 (2010); Robin Kundis Craig, *A Comparative Guide to the Eastern Public Trust Doctrine: Classifications of States, Property Rights, and State Summaries*, 16 PENN STATE ENVIRONMENTAL LAW REVIEW 1 (2007). For a discussion of how state courts have integrated state constitutional and statutory water resource protection provisions into their analysis of the public trust doctrine, see Alexandra B. Klass, *Modern Public Trust Principles: Recognizing Rights and Integrating Standards*, 82 NOTRE DAME L. REV. 699 (2006). For a critique of legal scholars' quest for extending the Public Trust Doctrine, see Hope M. Babcock, *What Can Be Done, If Anything, About the Dangerous Penchant of Public Trust Scholars to Overextend Joseph Sax's Original Conception: Have We Produced a Bridge Too Far?,* 23 N.Y.U. ENVTL. L.J. 390–433 (2015).

## NOTE ON WATER RIGHTS

*Mono Lake* is at bottom a water rights case, as the central holding is that "[t]he state has an affirmative duty to take the public trust into account, in the planning and allocation of water resources, and to protect public trust uses whenever feasible." Environmental policy over water turns on two core interrelated issues—quality and quantity. Over time, increasing regulatory efforts to address water quality and quantity have run head on into what in many parts of the nation is dearer than diamonds—water rights. Congress understood the potential for this collision at the dawn of the environmental legislation movement in the early 1970s. For example, one policy of the Endangered Species Act is "that Federal agencies shall cooperate with State and local agencies to resolve water resource issues in concert with conservation of endangered species." 16 U.S.C. § 1531(c)(2). Alas, that has been easier said than done. The law of water rights and water allocation has become nothing short of ground zero in the controversy over how far environmental policy will go in controlling resource uses that are vital to economic development, making it critical for environmental law practitioners to have some familiarity with the law of water rights.

Generally speaking, freshwater is far scarcer in supply west of the nation's 100th meridian, which has led to the development of two different, but equally rich, bodies of water law. Water in its natural watercourses is in all the states managed by the states as a public resource, but rights to *use* of the water can be privately held. In the final analysis, use is really what matters, and the states have developed highly articulated legal regimes for distributing that right.

In the East, where water is generally more plentiful, surface water has traditionally been allocated under the common law "riparian rights" system, under which water is treated essentially as common property of all owners of land underlying or bordering the water body, known as riparian lands. Under strict riparian rules, only riparian land may use the water, and the water may be used only on and for the riparian landowners, though for obvious reasons (e.g., public water supplies) many states have altered that rule to allow specified offsite uses. Also, although the amount of water that may be used was in early versions of the system limited such that the landowner had to leave the "natural flow" of the watercourse unimpaired, conventional riparian rights systems are based on a "reasonable use" standard that allows some reduction in natural flow so long as other riparian owners are not harmed. What constitutes a reasonable use depends on a variety of factors such as the purpose of the use, suitability of the use to the watercourse, its economic and social values, and the extent of harm to others. To summarize, several general characteristics define the classic riparian rights system:

1. riparian rights are of equal priority;

2. the right is not quantified, but rather extends to the amount of water which can be reasonably and beneficially used on the riparian parcel;

3. riparian rights are correlative, so that during times of water shortage, the riparian proprietors share the shortage;

4. water may be used only upon that portion of the riparian parcel which is within the watershed of the water source;

5. the riparian right does not extend to seasonal storage of water;

6. the riparian right is part of the riparian land and cannot be transferred for use on other lands;

7. a riparian right is not lost by non-use; and

8. the riparian rights remain with the land when riparian lands are sold, but parcels which are severed from the adjacent

water source lose their riparian rights unless the rights are reserved by deed.

The conventional riparian rights system, based as it is on the balancing test applied for reasonable use, can lead to significant uncertainty as to the quantity of water to which each riparian owner is entitled and how to resolve disputes between them. The on-site use requirement can also constrain economic development. In general, moreover, as a common ownership property system it leaves water flows generally unregulated and unplanned. Most of the eastern states, therefore, have moved to a permit allocation system which, while preferring riparian uses, focuses primarily on the purpose of the use and facilitates a more orderly monitoring and enforcement of approved uses. About half of the eastern states have adopted this system, often referred to as "regulated riparianism." *See* Joseph W. Dellapenna, *The Law of Water Allocation in the Southeastern States at the Opening of the Twenty-First Century*, 2 U. ARK. LITTLE ROCK L. REV. 9, 33 (2002).

As for groundwater, the eastern states follow several different doctrines. The so-called "rule of capture" or "absolute ownership" allows landowners to withdraw unlimited supplies of groundwater from beneath the surface regardless of the consequences for other landowners drawing from the same source. Some states temper this under the doctrine of "correlative rights," which allows use only in proportion to the relative size of the surface estate unless using more would not injure other users from the same source. And about a third of the eastern states have adopted a "reasonable use" rule that recognizes proper beneficial uses, such as domestic supply, irrigation, and mining, and allows withdrawal so long as no injury is caused to other beneficial uses relying on the same source. As has happened with surface water, however, most of the eastern states have adopted a more formal permitting system for groundwater uses that approves and monitors withdrawals. Agricultural uses, even in these permit states, are usually exempt or minimally covered.

Although water in the east was a plentiful resource well into the twentieth century, a growing population has demanded ever more supply, agriculture in the east has increased the use of irrigation as insurance against drought, and environmental concerns have made water quantity an important factor in the management of water quality and wildlife habitat. *See* Richard F. Ricci et al., *Battles Over Eastern Water*, NATURAL RESOURCES & ENV'T, Summer 2006, at 38; Steven T. Miano and Michael E. Crane, *Eastern Water Law: Historical Perspectives and Emerging Trends*, NATURAL RESOURCES & ENV'T, Fall 2003, at 14. Hence, no longer is it the case that "water is for fightin' " only in the West.

In the West, where water supply has always been scarce and unreliable, allocation of surface and groundwater supplies generally follows an "appropriative rights" system that implements a rule of "first in time, first in right." Four core principles guide this system:

1. water in its natural course is the property of the public and is not subject to private ownership;

2. a vested right to use the water may be acquired by appropriation and application to a beneficial use;

3. the person first in time is first in right; and

4. beneficial use is the basis, measure, and limit of the right.

What matters under this approach, in other words, is appropriation of water to a beneficial use, which defines a user's allocation from the particular stream. The time of appropriation is of the utmost importance, with the "senior" appropriators who put water in a stream to use earlier than "junior" users having a priority when water supplies are short. In dry periods, therefore, the senior user takes as much as his or her allocation allows, the next most senior user comes next, and so on until the supply is exhausted, meaning some junior users may have no water at all.

Although it makes water rights more predictable than does the riparian system (which is why the western states abandoned riparianism early in their settlement), there are flaws in the appropriative rights system as well. For example, senior uses may not be the most economically useful or efficient, but will nonetheless trump socially superior junior uses in dry periods. The risk associated with junior rights also can deter investment in watersheds that have unreliable supplies. New users may be able to purchase rights from senior users, but many states severely restrict inter-watershed transfers of water. Also, because senior users must maintain their beneficial use to keep their rights intact, the appropriative system does not reward water conservation. In many watersheds, moreover, the quantity of appropriated rights and the quantity of water supply were sometimes far from certain, a problem many states address through an "adjudication" process requiring users to prove their seniority and amount of beneficial use in a multi-party proceeding that results in each user's rights being established through an "adjudicated right."

The appropriative rights system has evolved with many different nuances among the western states. For example, some states prioritize beneficial uses, usually with domestic and agricultural uses receiving the highest priority. And some states—California and Texas are prominent examples—recognize limited riparian rights, creating a hybrid system. But one of the most controversial issues has been how to ensure that, for recreational and wildlife purposes, some minimum amount of water remains undiverted and not consumed, known as "instream flow." The catch has been that the conventional appropriation system requires a beneficial use *and* a diversion. Some state courts have recognized instream flow as a beneficial use not requiring a diversion. *See, e.g.*, Nevada v. Morros, 766 P.2d 263 (Nev. 1988). Most states, however, handle this through statutes allowing public agencies to "reserve" instream flow under prescribed conditions and procedures. Some states also are beginning to allow nongovernmental entities to lease instream flows. An excellent summary of state instream flow law is found at Jesse A. Boyd, *Hip Deep: A Survey of State Instream Flow Law from the Rocky Mountains to the Pacific Ocean*, 43 NATURAL RESOURCES J. 1151 (2003). For an in-depth look at Oregon's innovative approaches to instream flows, see Janet Neuman et al., *Sometimes a Great Notion, Oregon's*

*Instream Flow Experiments*, 36 ENVIRONMENTAL LAW 1125 (2006). The instream flow issue is likely to become more intense as climate change disrupts water systems, putting pressure on both water rights systems and pollution control programs at the same time. *See* William L. Andreen, *No Virtue Like Necessity: Dealing with Nonpoint Source Pollution and Environmental Flows in the Face of Climate Change*, 34 VA. ENVTL. L.J. 255 (2016).

Groundwater rights are even more varied among the western states, ranging from a pure "rule of capture," to a rule of "correlative rights" assigning rights in an aquifer relative to surface area of the land, to a rule of "reasonable use," to a system basically the same as the surface water appropriative rights approach. The bottom line in all cases, though, is that the various systems define water *rights*—real property rights that can transferred, sold, abandoned, and, importantly, which if taken by the government can give rise to a claim for just compensation.

There are two important additional layers to western water law. One, the doctrine of "reserved rights," results from the fact that the federal government owns so much land in the West. Under this doctrine, the federal government acts as a public trustee to ensure adequate water supplies for federal public land purposes. Whenever federal land is withdrawn from general public domain for a specific use, such as a national park or a Tribal reservation, water arising on or flowing across the land is reserved in sufficient quantity to accomplish in a reasonable manner the present *and future* purposes. As the Supreme Court explained in Winters v. United States, 207 U.S. 564 (1908), this reserved right vests at the time of the reservation of the lands, regardless of when the water is put to use, and is superior to all subsequent appropriated rights. This has caused significant disruption of "settled" water rights in states where Tribal reservations have in recent years sought to quantify their reserved rights long after numerous other users—junior to the federal reserved right—thought they had secured a water supply through their place in line.

The federal government also plays a leading role in the second wrinkle—the history of "reclamation" in the arid West. One of the major authorities of the Bureau of Reclamation (BOR), an agency of the Department of the Interior, has been to manage and allocate water for the promotion of agriculture and settlement in the western states. Starting with the Reclamation Act of 1902, 43 U.S.C. §§ 371 *et seq.*, the idea was to have the BOR reclaim arid lands in certain states through irrigation projects and then open those lands to entry by homesteaders. This required the federal agency to secure water rights under state law, and then to distribute irrigation water through contractual arrangements with irrigation districts and individual farmers. This project led over time to a convoluted, but deeply embedded, system of water distribution throughout many parts of the West, upon which vast investments of public and private capital have been based to this day.

This summary of water law scratches the surface of a complex field of law covered in far more detail in countless law books and articles. The law of water rights is taken as a given by courts and law practitioners around the nation, and considered sacrosanct by those who believe they hold precious water rights. Enter environmental law. Simply put, the demands of federal environmental laws such as the Endangered Species Act, Section 404 of the Clean Water Act, the Public Trust Doctrine, and of broader federal and state ecosystem management policies, include demands on water quantity. The substantive and procedural dictates of this growing body of law have rocked settled expectations about water use in many states, putting water rights under a microscope. The *Mono Lake* case is but one example. This trend has revealed in many ways that what was once thought of as a cohesive, self-contained system is in fact an amalgam of several different property regimes the workings of which may come unglued when confronted by a force as powerful as environmental law.

# CHAPTER 5

# REGULATING AND REMEDIATING HAZARDOUS SUBSTANCES AND WASTE

**CHAPTER OUTLINE**



---

## I. THE RESOURCE CONSERVATION AND RECOVERY ACT (RCRA)

Americans have a remarkable quality of life, enjoying a range of goods and services that kings and queens in past centuries could only have dreamt of. This material wealth comes at a cost, though, for it also generates a remarkable amount of waste. As with air and water pollutants, wastes come in all shapes and sizes. Some wastes are toxic and highly hazardous, and some can be treated to become non-hazardous or are easily assimilated by the environment. To get a sense of the enormous volumes involved in waste management, consider that in 2013, we generated the equivalent of 4.40 pounds of municipal solid waste daily for every American man, woman and child, for a total of 254 million tons, an almost 70% increase since 1960. This comprises a wide range of different waste streams—from household garbage (55–65% by weight of all waste) and industrial waste to construction and biomedical waste. *See* U.S. EPA, ADVANCING SUSTAINABLE MATERIALS MANAGEMENT: 2013 FACT SHEET (June 2015). Of all this household waste generated, only about 1% of it is considered hazardous to health. Most hazardous waste is generated by industrial facilities—over 18,000 large quantity hazardous waste generators produced nearly 35 million tons in 2013. *See* U.S. EPA, https://rcrainfo.epa.gov/rcrainfoweb/action/modules/br/trends.

Why is waste a problem? One concern has been the so-called "landfill crisis," the concern that we're running out of places to dispose of our waste. From 1988 to 1999, almost 70% of the nation's municipal landfills closed. While the closure of these sites has largely been in response to stricter regulations, the lack of *new* landfills is not due to lack of space. Rather, NIMBY pressures (Not In My Back Yard) from communities that do not want to live near a dump have resulted in a lack of landfill permits. Another concern is that waste means inefficiency. By throwing away or burning so much waste, we create the need to extract more virgin materials from the earth. The concerns here are both depletion of natural resources and harmful environmental impacts caused by extraction and synthesis of these materials that are then transformed into wastes. By reducing waste through better product and process design, increased re-use of materials, and greater recycling we can reduce life-cycle impacts.

The single biggest environmental problem posed by waste (and certainly the biggest public concern), though, is its health effects. Drinking water, for example, can be contaminated by waste "leachate." This is easy to understand if one thinks of a landfill as a giant "Mr. Coffee" filter. As water percolates through the landfill it becomes contaminated with hazardous constituents. This leachate then mixes with the groundwater and surface water that may be consumed by humans. Incinerators burning waste are a major source of dioxins, mercury and other hazardous air pollutants. While hard to believe, a study of the Chesapeake Bay found that up to 30 percent of the nitrogen in the Chesapeake Bay comes from atmospheric deposition. Incinerators are the primary source of mercury in the Bay, as well.

Prior to the 1970s there were poor and, in some cases, no requirements for waste disposal. The precursor to RCRA, the 1965 Solid Waste Disposal Act, merely encouraged states to develop waste management programs. The tougher Clean Air Act and Clean Water Act had required installation of pollution control devices on smokestacks and pipes throughout the nation, but where was the *waste* collected in the filters supposed to go? Many landfills were simply holes in the ground that were compacted by bulldozers until full, and then covered over by topsoil and turned into golf courses or commercial developments. Nor were there stringent recordkeeping requirements to identify where the waste had come from (a failure that would curse the Superfund program, described later in this chapter). Congress enacted The Resource Conservation and Recovery Act (RCRA) to fill this regulatory void.

RCRA is an amendment to the earlier Solid Waste Disposal Act and accomplishes four basic goals. It (1) creates definitions to determine the classes of wastes coming under its authority; (2) creates a tracking system for hazardous waste from its creation to its disposal (the first environmental law to take such a life-cycle approach); (3) establishes handling standards for the waste from its generation to its disposal; and (4) provides authority for mandatory cleanup of polluted treatment, storage and disposal sites.

The key provisions in RCRA deal with the disposal of solid waste (regulated in Subtitle D of the Act) and the treatment and disposal of hazardous waste (regulated in Subtitle C). Because it is much more expensive to dispose of hazardous waste, much of RCRA's legal history can be read as a "great escape" story of industry attempts to avoid having its waste considered hazardous waste and, once within the grips of Subtitle C's coverage, to avoid being classified as a treatment, storage or disposal (TSDF) facility. As with every other federal environmental law, it goes without saying, at the time of RCRA's passage Congress greatly underestimated the size and complexity of the problem.

For many students, studying RCRA quickly becomes a voyage into Alice's Wonderland, a statutory dreamscape where "solid" includes liquid and gas, where "hazardous" may not look hazardous, and where the King Midas fable is reversed with certain wastes turning everything they touch into even more waste. To understand RCRA, then, one must accept at the outset that it is internally consistent and relies on bright-line distinctions, but many of the critical terms have specific, often counterintuitive meanings within the statutory structure. To wind one's way through RCRA, two existential questions to keep in mind are "what is it?" and "who am I?"

## A. WHAT IS IT? THE DEFINITIONS OF SOLID AND HAZARDOUS WASTE

Because RCRA's requirements for handling solid hazardous waste are very expensive, companies want to avoid their waste being characterized as either solid or hazardous waste. Thus the first practical questions in any RCRA analysis are (1) is it "solid" waste, and (2) is it solid "hazardous" waste?

### 1. SOLID WASTE AND STRATEGIC BEHAVIOR

RCRA regulates only the disposal of "solid waste." If your waste is not considered solid waste under RCRA's regulatory definitions, you can laugh at the statute with impunity. The term "solid," however, is far broader than everyday usage, and covers virtually every form of matter except uncontained gases. This broad definition was necessary to prevent parties from converting their wastes to avoid coverage. Add enough water and mix, and most solid wastes become liquid.

The coverage of solid waste is not as extensive as the overbroad definition might suggest, though, because there are a number of important, gaping exemptions. Some wastes are exempted because they are regulated by other statutes. Thus RCRA does not cover sewage that passes through a public water treatment plant, wastewater discharges regulated by a Clean Water Act permit, mining wastes, or nuclear wastes, just to name some of the largest exceptions. A very large waste stream that may contain small amounts of hazardous materials—e.g., batteries and pesticides in household garbage—is exempted for practical reasons because of its sheer size. And other wastes, such as irrigation return flows, are exempted for political reasons because of the farm lobby's clout (note that Congress exempted these from the Clean Water Act's coverage, as well).

While a case can be made to justify every one of these exemptions, the net result encourages strategic behavior by the regulated community. The more onerous and expensive RCRA regulation of waste becomes, the stronger the incentive to fall out of its coverage entirely and into another statute. And rest assured that there are often significant differences over how statutes treat the same wastes. Some laws are far more rigorous than others, depending on the politics of the area and the time when the statutes were passed. The less demanding treatment of waste water under the Clean Water Act, for example, explains the large percentage of hazardous waste that is disposed of through either the public sewage system or direct emissions into a waterway.

While it may seem a stupid point to make, RCRA only covers solid wastes that are waste products. This seemingly redundant statement becomes important because waste can also resemble products and raw materials. Imagine, for example, that you run a farm and mix large vats of pesticides for application on crops. Under the Federal Insecticide, Fungicide, and Rodenticide Act (FIFRA), these pesticides can legally be sprayed onto fields, only to wash off into streams and drinking water supplies. But, under RCRA, the same pesticides that remain in the barrel cannot be disposed of on fields or in landfills without extensive and expensive pre-treatment. They are now RCRA hazardous waste.

Consider, too, the challenge posed by recycling. One of RCRA's goals was to encourage recycling. This not only reduces the amount of waste destined for disposal but the amount of raw materials needed for production, as well. Because recycling turns waste into a raw material for the manufacturing process, this avoids the environmental impacts from synthesis and production of virgin materials. Set against this, though, are the legislative goals of protecting the environment from hazardous substances and not interfering with the production process. While often held out as a wonderful and blessedly green activity, recycling can be a dirty business, creating significant wastes itself. In fact, a number of recycling sites later became Superfund sites. How, then, to create regulations that define solid waste in a manner that can be meaningfully applied and enforced, that encourage recycling, and that prevent sham recycling?

RCRA's definition of solid waste includes a number of waste streams, such as garbage, liquid material, solid material, "and other discarded material" resulting from certain activities. RCRA § 1004(27). In American Mining Congress v. EPA, 824 F.2d 1177 (D.C. Cir. 1987) (*AMC I*), the American Mining Congress argued that wastes produced in its manufacturing processes should not be considered solid waste if they would later be used again in the process—for the simple reason that they were not being "discarded." They were, instead, being recycled. To make this clearer, consider a process that turns squares into circles, and in so doing produces a by-product of triangles. If the triangles can be re-inserted back into the manufacturing process, are they discarded wastes (and therefore subject to RCRA) or raw materials?

The D.C. Circuit agreed, holding that waste should not be considered discarded if it would later be used in an ongoing manufacturing process. The court held that the materials had "not yet become part of waste problem; rather they are destined for beneficial reuse or recycling in a continuous process by the generating industry itself." The dissent took a more functional view. Promoting recycling is surely a goal of RCRA, but its overarching goal is environmental protection. Thus the main issue is whether the waste material creates the opportunity to cause environmental harm by spilling or leaking, even if it eventually will be recycled. If so, then EPA should be able to regulate it as a solid waste. After this decision, RCRA's definition of solid waste depended as much on the owner's plans for the materials as on the nature of the materials. Did the owner plan to sell the materials (in which case they are covered by RCRA) or re-use them in the process? As you might expect, this created an incentive for "sham recycling," stating you would re-use the materials in the manufacturing process but really just storing them indefinitely.

These problems were addressed in a subsequent case with the same parties, American Mining Congress v. EPA, 907 F.2d 1179 (D.C. Cir. 1990) (*AMC II*). Here, plaintiffs argued that sludge stored in a surface impoundment (a holding pond) should not be considered RCRA solid waste because it was being held for potential re-use (despite the fact that in the meantime the wastes might overflow or leak into other bodies of water). Cutting back on its earlier holding in *AMC I*, the court stated that the recycling exemption only applied to wastes that were safely stored for immediate re-use in an on-going process. Otherwise, the materials had become part of the waste disposal problem and must be regulated as solid waste. In practice, "immediate" has been interpreted to mean use within 90 days and "on-going process" to mean the same process.

As a result of these cases and subsequent decisions, the by-products of a production process destined for recycling are not considered solid wastes if stored safely and used within 90 days in the same process (a practice known as closed-loop recycling). If any of these conditions are not met, these materials are regulated as solid waste. A final example of how the same materials can receive different regulatory treatment may be found in American Petroleum Institute v. EPA, 906 F.2d 729 (D.C. Cir. 1990). Building off the logic of *AMC I* and *AMC II*, plaintiffs argued that the metal by-products of a manufacturing process should not be considered solid waste once they arrived at a reclamation facility for recycling. Further distancing itself from *AMC I*, however, the court declared that once waste arrives at a reclamation facility it remains solid waste because it has already become part of the waste disposal problem. In other words, the materials cannot shed their label of solid waste once they entered the reclamation facility gates, even though they clearly will be recycled. Unlike the children's game of Tag, RCRA doesn't provide a safe "base."

The following case further explores this issue.

## United States v. Interstate Lead Company, Inc.

United States Court of Appeals for the Eleventh Circuit, 1993.
996 F.2d 1126.

■ FAY, CIRCUIT JUDGE:

Over the years in the United States there has been a steady increase in the number of vehicle batteries which become useless and subject to disposal. In 1986 the number stood at approximately 70,000,000. Each spent battery is a potential pollutant of the environment and can have serious deleterious effects on people and animals living in the area where the battery may be discarded. Even a small number of batteries thrown into the woods, discarded along roadways or in government designated garbage areas represent a significant threat to the water we drink, the food we eat and under limited circumstances, the air we breathe. The source of this trouble in a battery is lead. . . . [Because lead is an expensive element, an industry has developed over the years] to reclaim the lead from spent batteries. . . . [In the mid-Seventies] there were approximately 50 secondary lead smelters in the United States reclaiming the lead from about 90% of all spent batteries. The smelters were themselves a major source of pollution; surface water run-off and process water discharged by the smelters created very real health-threatening problems; on-site and off-site storage or disposition of waste became an increasing risk to the quality of life; and even the air was dangerously polluted by emissions from the smelters. [In response to these problems] all levels of government began to amend existing laws and to enact new laws and regulations placing much greater controls over ownership and operation of such smelters. Compliance with these new environmental laws and regulations . . . placed such a financial burden on the operation of secondary lead smelters that about 60% of the smelters operating in 1976 were out of business by 1986, and the approximately 20 smelters remaining were reclaiming only about 70% . . . [of all discarded batteries.] Thus in 1986 only 55,000,000 of the available 70,000,000 batteries were reclaimed, leaving the 15,000,000 unreclaimed spent batteries to endanger the health of all persons near the site of their repose. The 55,000,000 reclaimed batteries produced about 60% of all lead used in the United States. . . . [This brief overview demonstrates the secondary lead smelting industry] is a most vital industry not only to our economy but also to [our] environment. . . . Without the industry, over 70,000,000 contaminated batteries would be scattered throughout our country annually. [Nevertheless, the heart of this industry centers around the handling of hazardous materials. Exempting the industry from regulation cannot be justified on the theory that its contribution to resolving our environmental problems outweighs the environmental harm caused by its operations.]

Against this industry backdrop the present case unfolds, spanning nearly a decade of interaction between the Environmental Protection Agency ("EPA"), the Alabama Department of Environmental Management ("ADEM") and Interstate Lead Company, Inc. ("ILCO"). The voluminous facts are very briefly set forth.

ILCO owned and operated a secondary lead smelting facility in Leeds, Alabama, from the 1960's until operations ceased in 1992. As such, it was one of the 20 smelters remaining in the country which reclaimed spent batteries. In 1986 ILCO reclaimed over 2,500,000 batteries, or about 5% of those reclaimed in the United States. Diego Maffei is the president and majority shareholder of ILCO.

ILCO purchased batteries from various suppliers and placed them in a reclamation process. Incoming batteries were cracked open and drained of sulfuric acid. The rubber or black plastic battery boxes were chipped and washed to remove lead particles. The lead battery components known as "plates and groups" were then removed from the broken batteries and run through ILCO's smelting process to produce lead ingots for sale. The operation produced several waste products which were the subject of litigation in the district court: waste acid, wastewater treatment sludge, broken battery casings or "chips," and emission control dust and blast slag from the smelting process. EPA asserted, and continues to argue on appeal, that the reclaimed lead plates and groups were also waste products. The defendants viewed the plates and groups as raw materials essential to the lead recovery industry.

EPA and ADEM initiated this case as an enforcement action against ILCO and its president, Diego Maffei, seeking an injunction to curtail ongoing violations of environmental laws and regulations at ILCO's plant in Leeds and seeking penalties for past violations. . . .

This appeal arises from a finding of liability against ILCO and Maffei under the CWA and the RCRA, and a judgment awarded to EPA for cleanup costs. . . .

The sole question of law raised by EPA on appeal is whether lead parts, which have been reclaimed from spent car and truck batteries for recycling purposes, are exempt from regulation under RCRA. The standard of review is de novo. Reviewing the interpretive decisions of an administrative agency is a two-step process: If Congress has clearly and directly spoken to the precise question at issue, effect must be given to the expressed intent of Congress. If the court finds the statute silent or ambiguous with respect to the specific issue, it must ask whether the agency's regulation is based on a "permissible" or "reasonable" construction of the statute. Chevron USA, Inc. v. National Resources Defense Council, 467 U.S. 837, 842–45 (1984). Considerable weight and deference are afforded an agency's interpretation of a statute entrusted to its administration.

Because Congress has not spoken to the precise question at issue, we must decide whether EPA has reasonably construed the RCRA to permit regulation of the recycling of hazardous materials. There is no question that the materials at issue are hazardous; the district court specifically found the plates and groups were "Extraction Procedure toxic" for lead and cadmium. If it is permissible for EPA to determine that "solid waste," as defined by Congress, includes materials that are recycled, then the lead plates and groups were "hazardous waste" and must be managed accordingly. We conclude that EPA's regulations are a reasonable exercise of its authority granted by Congress. For this reason and those to follow, we find the lead plates and groups that ILCO reclaims from spent batteries fall squarely within the law and regulations governing the storage, disposal and treatment of hazardous waste. . . .

Before a material can be designated and regulated as a "hazardous waste," it must first be determined to be a "solid waste." *See* 42 U.S.C. § 6903(5) (1988). Solid waste includes:

> any garbage, refuse, sludge from a waste treatment plant, water supply treatment plant, or air pollution control facility and other discarded material, including solid, liquid, semisolid, or contained gaseous material resulting from industrial, commercial, mining, and agricultural operations, and from community activities . . .

42 U.S.C. § 6903(27) (1988) (emphasis added). 42 U.S.C. § 6921 directs the Administrator of the EPA to identify those solid wastes which are "hazardous" and whose management should therefore be governed by RCRA. In particular, § 6921 requires the Administrator both to "promulgate criteria for identifying the characteristics of hazardous waste" and, using these criteria, to list "specific hazardous wastes."

Pursuant to its authority, EPA has promulgated regulations which specifically address discarded lead-acid batteries. Without clarifying the meaning of "discarded," Congress defined solid waste as "any discarded material" not otherwise exempted from regulation. EPA has filled the statutory gap by defining "discarded material" as any material which is abandoned, recycled, or inherently wastelike. 40 C.F.R. § 261.2(a)(2) (1992). "Recycled material" refers to, inter alia, spent material which has been reclaimed. 40 C.F.R. § 261.2(c)(3) (1992). A material is " 'reclaimed' if it is processed to recover a usable product, or if it is regenerated. Examples are recovery of lead values from spent batteries. . . ." 40 C.F.R. § 261.1(c)(4) (1992). "Reclaimed material" clearly includes lead values derived from the plates and groups at issue here. Furthermore, these battery components fall within the § 261.1(c)(4) definition of recycled material because ILCO runs the plates and groups through a smelting process to recover a usable product, lead, which is then cast into ingots and sold. Thus, having met the definition of "recycled," the lead components are discarded material as defined in 40 C.F.R. § 261.2(a)(2).

The regulations also specify those recycled materials which are solid wastes. They include "spent materials" that are recycled by "reclamation," or are "accumulated, stored, or treated before recycling" by reclamation. 40 C.F.R. § 261.2(c) (1992). A "spent material" is "any material that has been used and as a result of contamination can no longer serve the purpose for which it was produced without processing." 40 C.F.R. § 261.1(c)(1) (1992). Thus, the applicable regulations are unambiguous with respect to spent lead components used in a recycling process: spent materials "are solid wastes when reclaimed." 40 C.F.R. § 261.2(c)(3).

ILCO argues that it has never "discarded" the plates and groups and, therefore, the material it recycles is not "solid waste" as defined in RCRA § 6903(27). The lead plates and groups are, no doubt, valuable feedstock for a smelting process. Nevertheless, EPA, with congressional authority, promulgated regulations that classify these materials as "discarded solid waste." Somebody has discarded the battery in which these components are found. This fact does not change just because a reclaimer has purchased or finds value in the components.

The regulations reflect EPA's policy decision that spent batteries, including their lead components, became "part of the waste disposal problem," American Mining Congress v. EPA, 824 F.2d at 1186 (D.C. Cir. 1987) (*AMC I*), when the original consumer discarded the battery. It is unnecessary to read into the word "discarded" a congressional intent that the waste in question must finally and forever be discarded, as ILCO seems to argue. It is perfectly reasonable for EPA to assume Congress meant "discarded once." Were we to rule otherwise, waste such as these batteries would arguably be exempt from regulation under RCRA merely because they are potentially recyclable. Previously discarded solid waste, although it may at some point be recycled, nonetheless remains solid waste. *See American Petroleum*, 906 F.2d at 741 (holding that "discarded" material sent by steel mills to a metal recovery facility remained a solid waste in the hands of the metal recoverer); and American Mining Congress v. EPA, 907 F.2d 1179, 1186–87 (D.C. Cir. 1990) (*AMC II*) (materials awaiting recycling may be classified as "discarded," whether the materials were discarded by one user and sent to another for recycling, or stored before recycling by the person who initially discarded them in land disposal units). *Compare AMC I*, 824 F.2d at 1187, n.14 (used oil collected and recycled by a reclaimer is "discarded" and subject to regulation) *with* 824 F.2d at 1184, 1190 ("materials retained [by the generating industry] for immediate reuse" or "passing in a continuous stream or flow from one production process to another" are not "discarded" within the meaning of RCRA). Therefore, we find these batteries and their contents are "discarded" within the everyday sense of the word. Their secondary character as recyclable material is irrelevant to that determination.

We have found nothing in the language of the statute, and ILCO has brought forth nothing from the legislative history to show that EPA's policy choice is not one Congress would have sanctioned. On the contrary, application of these regulations to spent batteries and parts generated by consumers comports with Congress' intent in RCRA to address the problems posed by hazardous waste. The House Committee explained:

> It is not only the waste by-products of the nation's manufacturing processes with which the committee is concerned: but also the products themselves once they have served their intended purposes and are no longer wanted by the consumer. For these reasons the term discarded materials is used to identify collectively those substances often referred to as industrial, municipal or post-consumer waste; refuse, trash, garbage and sludge.

H.R. REP. No. 1491, 94th Cong., 2d Sess. 2 (1976). We, therefore, will not disturb an agency's policy choice that is reasonably consistent with the purpose of the statute.

## QUESTIONS AND DISCUSSION

**1.** Taken together, *Interstate Lead Co.* and the other cases discussed in this section provide stark examples of the difficulties in drafting regulation. By-products processed on-site at a plant for re-use within 90 days are unregulated by RCRA, yet the identical treatment at an off-site reclamation facility is highly regulated. This different treatment of the same activities is perhaps an inevitable result of trying to develop regulations that encourage recycling while, at the same time, closing loopholes. Indeed, the greatest challenge in drafting regulations can lie in trying to fulfill the statute's intent while knowing full well that the regulated community will act strategically to take advantage of any possibility of favorable treatment. In this regard, it is instructive to note that EPA convened a task force in the early 1990s to create a better definition of "solid waste," one that promoted genuine rather than sham recycling. In its 1994 report, the task force proposed a comprehensive four-part classification for regulating different types of recycling. Due to its complexity, the proposal was never adopted. In fact, in 2003 the agency proposed revisions to just the secondary hazardous materials recycling provisions of the solid waste definition, three years later withdrew the proposal, and then in 2007 issued a new proposed rule with over 40 pages of explanatory materials on the subject. *See* 72 Fed. Reg. 14,172 (Mar. 26, 2007) (codified at 40 C.F.R. pts. 260, 261).

**2.** Then, in October 2008, EPA adopted new regulations amending the definition of solid waste to create two new exclusions from RCRA (the "2008 DWS Rule"). The first exclusion (the "generator controlled exclusion") excludes from the definition of solid waste hazardous secondary materials that are legitimately reclaimed under the control of the generator. *See* 40 C.F.R. § 261.4(a)(23). The second exclusion (the "transfer-based exclusion") excludes from the definition of solid waste materials transferred to a third party for recycling and reclamation. *See* 40 C.F.R. § 261.4(a)(24). The rule requires the generator to make various showings to establish that the materials are not part of a sham recycling operation. *See* 73 Fed. Reg. 64,668 (2008) (codified at 40 C.F.R. pts. 260, 261, and 270); U.S. EPA, REVISIONS TO THE DEFINITION OF SOLID WASTE FINAL RULE COMPILATIONS: THE LEGITIMATE RECYCLING STANDARD (JUNE 2010), at http://www.epa.gov/osw/hazard/dsw/downloads/legit-recycling.pdf.

**3.** In 2009, after environmental and public health concerns were raised about the 2008 DSW Rule, EPA began conducting an extensive environmental justice analysis that examined the location of recycling facilities and their impact on adjacent communities. In January 2015, EPA issued a final rule on RCRA's definition of "solid waste" (the "2015 DSW Rule"). *See* Definition of Solid Waste, 80 Fed. Reg. 1694 (Jan. 13, 2015) (to be codified at 40 C.F.R. pts. 260, 261). The Rule revised numerous recycling provisions under RCRA. Specifically, the 2015 DSW Rule retained the generator-owned exclusion; replaced the transfer-based exclusion with a new, verified recycler exclusion; codified new approaches for in-process recycling and commodity-grave recycled materials; and finalized a new, remanufacturing exclusion. *See* U.S. EPA, Fact Sheet and Overview of the 22015 Definition of Solid Waste Rule, https://www.epa.gov/hwgenerators/fact-sheet-and-overview-2015-definition-solid-waste-final-rule.

**4.** At the time *Interstate Lead Co.* was decided in 1993, what would have been the implication of the court's decision if ILCO wished to continue to operate? What about under the 2008 and 2015 regulations discussed in the prior notes?

## 2. SOLID HAZARDOUS WASTE AND CLOSING LOOPHOLES

For any regulatory scheme to work, the regulated business has to know clearly what is required of it and the regulator needs to know how to verify this. If a manufacturing site produces Dimethyl Terrible as a waste stream, what must be done to dispose of it legally? In RCRA, this basic issue of regulatory coverage has also proven challenging. Imagine, for a moment, that you were the EPA official in charge of identifying and defining the wastes that will be covered by RCRA. Intuitively, given the range of toxicity among various wastes it might seem most effective to distinguish among separate categories of waste, subjecting the most hazardous wastes to the most stringent controls. But this is easier said than done. Should the mere presence of a hazardous substance in a waste stream make the entire stream hazardous, or should there be some kind of assessment to determine the overall hazard it poses? Realize, as well, that there are tens of thousands of types of waste streams. Precision has a cost.

RCRA distinguishes between two broad categories of covered wastes. If a material is considered a solid waste, it is covered by Subtitle D. If it a solid waste *and* hazardous it falls under the much more onerous, and costly, coverage of Subtitle C. So the regulated community cares a great deal about the definition of "hazardous waste." In contrast to determining whether or not materials are "solid waste" under RCRA or fall under the various exemptions, however, defining a material as a solid "hazardous waste" is relatively straightforward.

RCRA identifies two categories of hazardous waste—"listed wastes" and "characteristic wastes." RCRA § 3001; 40 C.F.R. pt. 261. Listed wastes are, as the name suggests, substances that EPA has determined routinely contain hazardous constituents or exhibit hazardous qualities. These are listed in the Code of Federal Regulations. If a company produces a listed waste but believes that it should not be treated as hazardous waste, it may petition EPA to de-list the waste but this is an expensive and lengthy process.

It would be nice, of course, if EPA produced a comprehensive list of wastes but given the fact that over 50,000 chemicals are now used in commerce EPA is lucky to list even a fraction of the possible current wastes. Thus the second category identifies hazardous wastes by their characteristics. If a waste is not a listed waste but has the characteristics of being ignitable (i.e., products that are capable of causing fire during routine transportation, storage, or disposal), corrosive, reactive, or toxic (set at levels 100 times more protective than the Safe Drinking Water Act) then it is treated as a hazardous waste. While the burden of identifying listed wastes falls on EPA (since, after all, it creates the list), the burden of identifying characteristic wastes falls on the waste generators who must determine through standard tests whether their waste is ignitable, corrosive, reactive, or toxic. Hence the need for rigorous compliance monitoring by EPA.

Recall the previous discussion on how companies producing solid waste could avoid RCRA coverage if they satisfied the recycling exemption. Companies producing hazardous waste would clearly like to avoid Subtitle C coverage, as well. But how? As described above, they could petition for de-listing of specific waste but this is an expensive process. They could also try to modify their waste so that it no longer looked like a hazardous waste. What happens when waste is transformed, either through mixing with other wastes, dilution, or synthesis into another compound? Assume you're still working at EPA. Should you regulate it as a hazardous waste (once a waste, always a waste), or has it escaped the coverage of Subtitle C? With the thousands of sites using hazardous wastes in all kinds of processes, how can EPA ensure credible enforcement?

EPA treats listed and characteristic wastes differently. If characteristic wastes no longer exhibit their hazardous characteristics, they are treated simply as solid waste and fall out of Subtitle C's coverage. Listed wastes, though, are subject to two rules. The "mixture rule" states that any mixture of a listed waste with another solid waste is *still* considered a hazardous waste (with an exemption for municipal solid waste). The "derived from rule" requires that wastes derived from the treatment of a hazardous waste are also treated as hazardous wastes, including contaminated soil and water. As a consequence, EPA has created a perverse variation on King Midas' tragic gift. Whereas everything Midas touched turned to gold, everything hazardous listed waste touches turns to more listed waste. The related "contained-in" policy holds that contaminated media (generally soil) becomes a hazardous waste. This has important consequences for CERCLA (discussed later in this chapter), since contaminated soil at Superfund sites must often be treated as hazardous waste.

In combination with RCRA's broad exemptions, the mixture and derived from rules have created a bizarre situation. The rules require strict treatment of many wastes that are significantly less hazardous than wastes that are not covered *at all* because of the broad exemptions for wastewater discharges, mining wastes, etc. The increasingly quixotic dilemma of creating precise, clear and fair definitions of solid and hazardous waste remains unresolved after more than two decades, frustrated by strategic behavior by firms to avoid having their waste fall under these definitions.

Environmental law practitioners who deal on a regular basis with RCRA usually employ flow-charts to make sense of the foregoing. Indeed, even federal agencies find the definition confusing, prompting the Federal Facilities Environmental Stewardship and Compliance Assistance Center to develop the following guide for federal facilities:

## Hazardous Waste Identification Flowchart

http://www.fedcenter.gov/assistance/facilitytour/hazardous/whatis/flowchart/.

### Step 1

**Is Your Material a Solid Waste?** The first step is to determine if the material in question is classified as a solid waste. If the material is NOT a solid waste, it cannot be a hazardous waste.

- The statutory definition of a solid waste is completely irrespective of the physical form of the waste. A solid waste can be just as easily liquid or gas. A material is considered a solid waste if it:
    - Is a solid, semi-solid, liquid, or contained gaseous material which is discarded or has served its intended purpose?
    - Is abandoned?
    - Is being recycled by being placed on the ground (and that is not the normal use), burned for energy recovery, reclaimed, or accumulated more than one year.
    - Is inherently waste-like (e.g., dioxin wastes)?
- If the material in question meets any of the provisions above, you may have a solid waste. If you answered NO to all of the above provisions, you do not have a solid waste.

**Step 2**

**Is Your Solid Waste Excluded from Hazardous Waste Regulations?** After you have determined that you have a solid waste on hand, the next step is to determine if that solid waste is excluded from RCRA regulation.

- EPA grants specific exclusions from some hazardous waste regulations if certain conditions are met. Some materials are excluded from the definition of solid waste, while some solid wastes are excluded from the definition of hazardous waste. Knowing these exclusions can be helpful in waste management programs.
- Some materials that are excluded from the definition of solid waste (and therefore are NOT hazardous) include:
    - Domestic sewage
    - Industrial wastewater discharges
    - Radioactive waste
    - Spent wood preserving solutions that are reclaimed and reused in the wood preserving process
    - Processed scrap metal
    - Irrigation return flow
    - In situ mining waste
    - Secondary materials that are reclaimed and returned to the original process, if the reclamation and return process is totally enclosed.

These wastes are not hazardous because they are not considered solid waste.

- Some solid wastes are excluded from the definition of hazardous wastes:
  - Household waste (pesticides, cleaners)
  - Some agricultural wastes that are returned to the soils as fertilizers
  - Fossil fuel combustion wastes
  - Cement kiln dust (unless the facility burns hazardous waste as fuel)
  - Arsenically treated wood wastes generated from a person using wood for its intended purpose
  - Petroleum-contaminated media that is subject to the UST corrective action program
  - Used oil filters that have been hot drained
  - Used chlorofluorocarbon refrigerants that are being reclaimed for further use.

These solid wastes are excluded from the definition of hazardous waste by EPA.

- In addition, some recycled materials are not classified as solid waste. Materials are not solid wastes IF:
  - They are being used as substitutes for commercial products
  - Returned back to the original process without first being reclaimed or land disposed.

This exemption is not valid if the materials are burned for energy recovery or used to make a product that will be applied to the land.

- Samples collected for lab analysis are exempt from RCRA regulation until it is determined that they are to be disposed of.
- Used oil that exhibits hazardous characteristics can be excluded if recycled. It is regulated under Standards for the Management of Used Oil (40 CFR Part 279).
- Universal wastes (including batteries, pesticides, mercury-containing thermostats, switches, and thermometers, and electric lamps) may also qualify for reduced regulation.
- The list above is NOT comprehensive. If your waste is not on the list above, it may still be excluded from RCRA regulation. See 40 CFR 261.4 for a complete list of those wastes exempt from hazardous waste regulation. Furthermore, if your waste IS listed above, that does not mean you are automatically exempt. Each exemption above is conditional and facility managers should review

applicable Sections of 40 CFR 261 and contact their State's hazardous waste program for clarification on exemptions.

**Step 3**

**Is Your Solid Waste a Listed Waste?** Once you have determined that your solid waste is not excluded from RCRA requirements, the next step is to determine if the material is a listed waste.

- EPA lists hazardous wastes that fall into four categories:
  - **F-listed wastes:** The F list includes wastes from common industrial processes. Because they are not specific to one type of industry, they are called wastes from non-specific sources. This list includes for example many types of spent (or used) solvents. See 40 CFR 261.31 to see if your waste is F-listed.
  - **K-listed wastes:** The K list includes wastes from specific industrial processes, such as wood preservation, organic chemical production, and pesticide manufacturing. See 40 CFR 261.32 for the complete list of manufacturing process wastes to see if your facility might have a K-listed waste.
  - **P- and U-listed wastes:** These two lists designate certain commercial chemical products as hazardous when disposed of unused. These unused chemicals may become wastes in a number of ways. Some can be spilled while in use while others can be intentionally discarded if out of specification. For a waste to qualify as a P-or U-listed waste, it must meet all three of the following criteria:
    - The formulation must contain at least one chemical on the P or U list
    - The chemical in the waste must be unused
    - The chemical in the waste must be in the form of a CCP.*

    *A CCP is a chemical that is of technical (commercial) grade, 100% pure, and the only active ingredient in the formulation.

There are hundreds of P-and U-listed wastes. Facility managers should look in 40 CFR 261.33 to see if chemicals present on-site are hazardous if disposed of unused. Please note that the chemicals with the "P" code are acutely hazardous. Generators with acutely hazardous waste are subject to different accumulation limits for those wastes.

**Step 4**

**Is Your Solid Waste a Characteristic Waste?** If your waste is not listed in 40 CFR Part 261, it may still be a hazardous waste. The next step is to see if your waste is a characteristic hazardous waste.

- Solid wastes that are not directly listed in 40 CFR Part 261 may still be hazardous. EPA uses a classification system based on the four properties of solid wastes. **If a material exhibits at least one of these characteristics, it is classified as a hazardous waste.** The four properties are:
  - **IGNITABILITY**

    A substance is ignitable if it displays any of the following properties.
    - A liquid with a flashpoint of less than 60° C (140° F);
    - A non-liquid that is capable, under standard temperature and pressure, of causing fire through friction, absorption of moisture, or spontaneous chemical changes, and when ignited, burns so vigorously and persistently that it creates a hazard;
    - An ignitable compressed gas;
    - An oxidizer (such as a chlorate or peroxide).

    Details on the ignitability characteristic are included in 40 CFR 261.21.
  - **CORROSIVITY**

    A substance is corrosive if it displays any of the following properties:
    - An aqueous material with a pH less than or equal to 2 or greater than or equal to 12.5;
    - A liquid that corrodes steel at a rate of at least 0.25 inches per year at 55° C (130° F); **NOTE**: A waste that is not aqueous and contains no liquid falls outside the definition of EPA corrosivity.

    Details on the corrosivity characteristic are included in 40 CFR 261.22.
  - **REACTIVITY**

    A substance is reactive if it displays any of the following properties.
    - Normally unstable and readily undergoes violent change without detonating;
    - Reacts violently with water;

- Forms potentially explosive mixtures with water;
- A cyanide or sulfide bearing waste which can generate fumes in a quantity sufficient to present a danger to human health.
- Capable of detonation
- A forbidden explosive, or a Class A or Class B explosive, as defined in Department of Transportation regulations in 49 CFR Part 173.

Details on the reactivity characteristic are included in 40 CFR 261.23.

- **TOXICITY**

  A substance is toxic if it exceeds the concentrations for contaminants listed in the "**Maximum Concentration of Contaminants for the Toxicity Characteristic**" table, presented in 40 CFR 261.24. A specific test, the **Toxicity Characteristic Leaching Procedure (TCLP)** must be conducted to determine if the waste is classified as toxic. Details on the toxicity characteristic are included in 40 CFR 261.24.

- EPA designates specific, standardized test methods that are to be used when determining the characteristics of a waste. These techniques are listed in the above mentioned sections.

**Step 5**

**Is Your Solid Waste Subject to the Mixture Rule?** Even though your solid waste is not a listed or characteristic waste, it could become a hazardous waste if mixed with materials classified as hazardous. The next step is to determine if your waste is a mixture of a solid waste and a hazardous waste.

- The **Mixture Rule** states that mixtures of solid waste and listed hazardous waste must be regulated as hazardous waste. There are two ways to determine if a material is regulated under the mixture rule:
  - If the material is a mixture of a solid waste and a hazardous waste, and the mixture exhibits one or more of the characteristics of hazardous waste;
  - If the material is a mixture of a solid waste and a listed waste. The mixture rule is intended to discourage generators from mixing wastestreams. More information can be reviewed at 40 CFR 261.3(a)(iii) and (iv).

**Step 6**

**Is Your Solid Waste Subject to the Derived-From Rule?** Your material is not a listed or characteristic waste, nor is it classified as hazardous due to the mixture rule. Yet the material might still be a hazardous waste. Hazardous waste treatment, storage, and disposal processes often generate residues that may contain high concentrations of hazardous constituents. The derived-from rule governs the regulatory status of such waste residues.

- According to the Rule, any solid waste derived from the treatment, storage, or disposal of a hazardous waste is considered hazardous. Derived from wastes include sludges, spill residue, ash, emission control dust, and leachate. Some examples are drums that have been used for storage of a hazardous waste, or ash from the incineration of hazardous waste. This principle applies regardless of the actual risk to human or environmental health. More details about the "derived-from" rule and exemptions to the rule are included in 40 CFR Part 261.3 (c) and (d).

---

### QUESTIONS AND DISCUSSION

**1.** If you remain somewhat in the dark about the definition of solid and hazardous waste, you are in good company, as even EPA officials have conceded it is a challenging regulatory maze. *See* Randolph L. Hill, *An Overview of RCRA: The "Mind-Numbing" Provisions of the Most Complicated Environmental Statute*, 21 ENVTL. L. REP. 10254 (1991). As one EPA official stated with respect to the definition of hazardous waste, the regulations are "a regulatory cuckoo land of definition. . . . I believe we have five people in the agency who understand what 'hazardous waste' is." United States v. White, 766 F. Supp. 873, 882 (E.D. Wash. 1991) (quoting Don R. Clay, EPA Assistant Administrator for Office of Solid Waste and Emergency Response). Nevertheless, EPA has a webpage entitled "Learn the Basics of Hazardous Waste," which provides a summary of the basics set out in this section: https://www.epa.gov/hw/learn-basics-hazardous-waste.

**2.** For a discussion and evaluation of EPA's drafting of the solid waste/hazardous waste definition regulation during the 1990s, as well as the full set of original RCRA implementation rules, see MARC K. LANDY ET AL., THE ENVIRONMENTAL PROTECTION AGENCY: ASKING THE WRONG QUESTIONS—FROM NIXON TO CLINTON 89–132 (2d ed. 1994) (describing the process as a "self-perpetuating crisis").

---

## B. WHO AM I? GENERATORS, TRANSPORTERS, AND TSDFS

Just as RCRA divides the waste world into solid waste and solid hazardous waste (listed and characteristic) with very different requirements for each, RCRA divides the world of actors into three categories—generators, transporters, and "treatment, storage, and disposal facilities" (TSDFs). *See* RCRA §§ 3002 (generators); 3003 (transporters); 3004–3005 (TSDFs). While each class of actor faces differing responsibilities, all must comply with detailed tracking requirements. RCRA follows the disposal of waste by establishing a "cradle-to-grave" tracking scheme from the generators of waste to transporters through to disposal facilities. In principle, if we know where the waste is at all times and ensure that people handling the waste at each stage act responsibly, then no worries. To this end, when a generator produces a minimum amount of hazardous waste it must obtain an identification number for the waste from EPA and fill out a "manifest." This sheet accompanies the waste shipment to its final disposal and, at each stage it changes hands, the manifest stays with the shipment while a copy is sent back to the generator. When the TSDF finally receives the waste, it must inspect it to check that the contents match the manifest. This cradle-to-grave tracking ensures that the problem of unidentified wastes at contaminated sites, regulated by CERCLA and described later in this chapter, is not repeated.

In 2012, Congress enacted the Hazardous Waste Electronic Manifest Establishment Act which directed EPA to create and manage an "e-manifest" tracking system. Prior to the e-manifest law, actors subject to RCRA were required to maintain the manifests in accordance with federal law but were not required to submit them to EPA as a matter of course. The new law, which will be governed by EPA regulations issued in 2014, authorizes EPA to charge a fee to waste handlers using the manifest system in order to offset system development, operation, and maintenance costs. As of this writing, EPA is developing the e-manifest system and proposes to put it in operation in 2018. Once the system is operating, waste handlers will be able to submit manifests in paper form, in web based form, through a system to system application, and by mobile application, with different fees for different types of submissions (and with paper submissions paying the highest fees). For more information about the e-manifest law, the EPA regulations implementing the law, and for answers to frequently asked questions about the law, see U.S. EPA, Hazardous Waste Electronic Manifest System ("e-Manifest"), https://www.epa.gov/hwgenerators/hazardous-waste-electronic-manifest-system-e-manifest.

In addition to the manifest requirements, generators are subject to a variety of requirements. Generators must determine if their waste is a listed or characteristic hazardous waste. They must also ensure proper storage and labeling of wastes, keep records of waste generation and test results, and submit periodic reports. For small companies, these requirements can prove quite resource intensive. Indeed, RCRA was drafted primarily to regulate facilities routinely generating large amounts of the same small number of waste streams. In some relatively new sectors such as the biomedical industry, however, scores of different waste streams are infrequently produced. RCRA's requirements have come to be seen as so ill-fitting that the state of California created a special task force to reform its regulation of laboratory wastes. As the economy continues its trend toward custom manufacturing and biotech, the regulatory fit of RCRA will continue to be challenged.

Transporters face fewer requirements, but must comply with EPA and Department of Transportation requirements for the transportation of hazardous materials (identified as "hazmat" on highway signs), including proper packaging and labeling, reporting, record keeping and the manifest. These requirements take on added significance when one realizes that more than 3 billion tons of hazardous materials are transported each year, with over 800,000 shipments of these materials every day.

RCRA's requirements are *much* more onerous on TSDFs than on generators or transporters. Many Superfund sites were formerly TSDFs, and RCRA seeks to ensure not only clean operation but clean shut down at the end of the TSDF's life. To operate, a TSDF must obtain a permit from EPA or an authorized state agency. All facilities that currently or plan to treat, store, or dispose of hazardous wastes must obtain a RCRA permit. Also:

- New TSDFs must receive a permit before they even begin construction. They must prove that they can manage hazardous waste safely and responsibly. The permitting agency reviews the permit application and decides whether the facility is qualified to receive a RCRA permit. Once issued, a permit may last up to 10 years.
- Operating TSDFs with expiring permits must submit new permit applications six months before their existing permits run out.
- TSDFs operating under Interim Status must also apply for a permit. Congress granted interim status to facilities that already existed when RCRA was enacted. Interim status allows existing facilities to continue operating while their permit applications are being reviewed.

There are certain situations where a company is not required to obtain a RCRA a permit:

- Businesses that generate hazardous waste and transport it off site without storing it for long periods of time do not need a RCRA permit.
- Businesses that transport hazardous waste do not need a RCRA permit.
- Businesses that store hazardous waste for short periods of time without treating it do not need a permit.

The permit process often lasts from two to four years and the permit is effective for ten years. TSDFs must satisfy a range of operating requirements that include personnel training, record keeping, groundwater monitoring, security, and technical standards. The technical standards are rigorous and require, for example, that landfills have 2 or more impermeable liners and a leachate collection system. With the problem of contaminated sites in mind, TSDFs must also create comprehensive plans for closure. These address not only the closing of the facility but maintenance and monitoring the facility for a period of 30 years after closure. In addition, TSDFs must provide financial assurance (through insurance, bonds, or other means) that they will have enough money to pay for closure as well as consequent liability. While seemingly onerous, in light of the many TSDFs that shut down with no resources, leaving only contaminated land beneath them, these requirements are important in ensuring companies do not strategically plan bankruptcy.

Amendments to RCRA in 1984 by the Hazardous and Solid Waste Amendments (HSWA) provided another important tool to ensure that TSDFs did not become Superfund sites. EPA was given authority to require that TSDFs clean up present or past contamination on their sites if deemed necessary to protect human health or the environment. Known as "corrective actions," these clean-ups may be enforced through a civil action or by suspending operating permits, and represent a clear example of CERCLA and RCRA moving closer together. EPA authorizes states to implement the RCRA corrective action program through delegated authority. To date, 42 authorized states and one territory lead implementation at their corrective action facilities, with assistance from EPA grants. For a detailed discussion of the RCRA corrective action program and progress through 2012, see U.S. EPA, RCRA CORRECTIVE ACTION: CASE STUDIES REPORT (April 2013). The potential for conflict among federal and state enforcement authority under RCRA is discussed in *Harmon Industries, Inc. v. Browner*, 191 F.3d 894 (8th Cir. 1999), excerpted in Chapter 11.

In addition to government authority to compel cleanup of TSDFs, RCRA also provides the opportunity for private parties to sue under RCRA to compel remediation of hazardous waste. The RCRA citizen suit provision, 42 U.S.C. § 6972(a)(1)(B), provides a cause of action:

> against any person . . . including any past or present generator, past or present transporter, or past or present owner or operator of a treatment, storage, or disposal facility, who has contributed or who is contributing to the past or present handling, storage, treatment, transportation, or disposal of any solid or hazardous waste which may present an imminent and substantial endangerment to health or the environment.

42 U.S.C. § 6972(a)(1)(B). Courts interpreting this provision have focused on how certain the harm must be (in light of the word "may") and how significant and immediate the harm must be (in light of the words

"imminent and substantial endangerment"). *See* Meghrig v. KFC Western, Inc., 516 U.S. 479 (1996); Cordiano v. Metacon Gun Club, Inc., 575 F.3d 199 (2d Cir. 2009); Burlington Northern and Santa Fe Ry. Co. v. Grant, 505 F.3d 1013 (10th Cir. 2007); Dague v. City of Burlington, 935 F.2d 1343, 1355 (2d Cir. 1991), *judgment rev'd in part on other grounds*, 505 U.S. 557 (1992). As you will understand more fully after studying CERCLA later in this chapter, this citizen suit provision of RCRA is significant because it allows a potential means for private parties to compel owners and operators of hazardous waste facilities to remediate the property. By contrast, although CERCLA allows EPA to compel remediation of contaminated states, the only remedy available for private parties under CERCLA is to undertake the remediation themselves and then seek recovery of those costs from responsible parties. Moreover, RCRA covers certain wastes that are statutorily excluded under CERCLA, such as oil and gas related wastes. For a discussion of some of the overlapping provisions of RCRA and CERCLA, see Margot J. Pollans, *A "Blunt Withdrawal"? Bars on Citizen Suits for Toxic Site Cleanup*, 37 HARV. ENVTL. L. REV. 441 (2013).

---

## QUESTIONS AND DISCUSSION

**1.** The Hazardous and Solid Waste Amendments of 1984 (HSWA) also took aim at landfills. By the mid-1980s, Subtitle C's requirements for generators, transporters and TSDFs had clearly succeeded in at least one area—raising the cost of waste disposal. By making waste disposal more expensive, one would expect waste production to go down. And if waste was produced then EPA had clear preferences for its disposal. This was reflected in the so-called "waste hierarchy," the accepted rule of thumb in managing waste: first *reduce*, then *re-use*, then *recycle*, then *landfill*.

Raising the cost of waste disposal would certainly promote waste reduction, re-use and recycling, but how to minimize landfilling and the fear of groundwater contamination? HSWA greatly restricted the land disposal of wastes, requiring EPA to prohibit disposal of waste in landfills unless "there will be no migration of hazardous constituents" from the landfill. Congress did not ban the disposal of waste in landfills outright, however, for it created an exception for wastes that had been treated to "substantially diminish the toxicity of the waste" or the migration of hazardous constituents. This "land ban," then, effectively banned the disposal only of *untreated* hazardous wastes. Fearful of the Reagan administration delaying implementation, Congress included a unique "hammer" provision. It shifted the burden of delay from the agency or the public to industry by providing that if pretreatment regulations were not issued for a particular waste by a particular date, there would be no land-based disposal of that waste *at all*. Needless to say, spurred on by industry interests EPA moved on the issue quickly.

The interesting question Congress seemingly failed to answer, though, was how to determine the pre-treatment standards for hazardous waste. In implementing the requirement that there be "no migration of hazardous constituents" from landfills, should EPA emphasize the "no migration" text or the "hazardous constituents" language? If the key terms were "no migration," this effectively would ban the disposal of any hazardous waste in landfills since no one can guarantee there will be absolutely *no* migration. This would promote a technology-based approach, requiring extensive pre-treatment of wastes using the best technology or processes currently available. By contrast, if one focused on the "hazardous constituents" requirement, EPA would operate from the perspective of risk management, pre-treating the waste to the degree necessary to avoid unacceptable risk to the public and assuming some level of migration.

Put in simple terms, EPA was faced with two different approaches to protecting groundwater from landfilled waste. One approach would rely on pre-treatment based on best available technology—perhaps over-treating the waste to levels far below any health risk—the other would rely on comparative risk assessment—treating the waste to a level with acceptable risks to health. This choice of regulatory strategies poses unavoidable trade-offs—technology-based regulations that are inflexible but relatively easy to administer versus more complex but more flexible (and arguably economically efficient) risk-based standards. We saw this very same conflict between technology-based and risk-based standards in our discussion of NAAQS in the Clean Air Act and, in fact, it occurs throughout environmental law. At the end of the day, the "correct" implementation strategy depends on the regulator's priority, whether it be low cost of administration, impetus to force technological development, desire for potential over-treatment to reflect scientific uncertainty over health effects, or high cost of compliance to drive out marginal TSDFs and create barriers to entry for new participants. EPA's final decision to go with a technology-based standard was largely upheld in the case, Hazardous Waste Treatment Council v. EPA, 861 F.2d 270 (D.C. Cir. 1988).

**2.** Despite the importance of RCRA in regulating solid hazardous waste, the regulation of solid waste has largely remained the responsibility of state and local governments. And it's a *lot* of waste. In 2013, for example, municipal solid waste accounted for 254 million tons of waste. As might be expected, although exempted from Subtitle C, municipal waste still contains some hazardous waste (e.g., from batteries). Subtitle D of RCRA requires states to create plans that ensure responsible management of these wastes from collection to disposal. EPA has also created regulations for the design and operation of landfills, ensuring for example that landfills not discharge pollutants into surface waters or engage in open burning. In a clear example of cooperative federalism, these regulations set minimum standards, and states are free to regulate landfills more strictly as, indeed, Pennsylvania, New York and several other states have done. Subtitle C delegates permitting authorities to states, as well, so long as their programs are "equivalent" to and "consistent" with the federal program and provide for "adequate enforcement."

**3.** Despite its broad scope, it is important to note what RCRA does not cover. Consider the solid wastes involved in a typical manufacturing operation. The environmental impacts of the raw material inputs and product outputs are regulated, if at all, by other statutes. OSHA regulates occupational exposure to contaminants during the process. Otherwise, with rare exception Congress has intentionally left the manufacturing process issues alone. RCRA, then, only covers the waste stream, a narrow subset of total manufacturing operations. And not all wastes fall under RCRA. Congress intentionally chose not to regulate manufacturing processes, effectively treating the facility as a black box. Indeed, environmental law as a whole treats factories as giant black boxes, refusing to look at what happens inside. Our pollution statutes only kick in when the waste leaves the facility, whether as air and water pollution or as solid waste.

This "end-of-pipe" approach has certainly succeeded, given the improvements in air and water quality over the last three decades. But this approach also favors, indeed intentionally favors, a business-as-usual attitude known as "pollution control." In a pollution control strategy, the company collects the waste from its processes and then ships them off in compliance with RCRA. Waste disposal becomes a cost of doing business and the pollution control technologies—the filters, scrubbers and settling ponds—are nonproductive assets (insofar as they don't contribute to the bottom line). To be sure, RCRA has greatly increased the cost of waste disposal and this has provided an incentive for companies to reduce their waste generation. Importantly, because of the many exemptions, it has provided an even greater incentive to manage the waste so that it falls out of RCRA's coverage, either through the recycling exemption, discharge to sewers, or some other exempted route. As noted earlier, in 2013, Americans generated approximately 254 million tons of trash and recycled and composted over 87 million tons of this material (which would otherwise go to landfills and incinerators), equivalent to a 34.3% recycling rate. On average, we recycled and composted 1.51 pounds of our individual waste generation of 4.40 pounds per person per day. This compares favorably with a 15 percent recycling rate in 1990, but still results in a huge amount of waste disposal. *See* U.S. EPA, ADVANCING SUSTAINABLE MATERIALS MANAGEMENT: 2013 FACT SHEET (June 2015).

Instead of disposing of waste trapped at the end of the pipe, why not simply produce less waste in the first place? This strategy is known as "pollution prevention" (and known in Europe as "cleaner production"). Indeed, in many cases manufacturing waste is simply valuable raw material down the drain. Pollution prevention focuses on good housekeeping, waste audits, and closing production loops rather than more efficient technologies at the end of the pipe. Such strategies have allowed companies such as 3M, Dow, and Johnson Wax to reduce their waste by over 50%, saving money in the process both through less loss of raw materials and avoided costs of waste disposal. RCRA, though, does little directly to promote a pollution prevention approach. Beyond the recycling exemption, RCRA doesn't care how the waste gets produced. In fact, one might argue that, by failing to go to the heart of the production process, RCRA misses the most important waste disposal issue of all. Put simply, RCRA is limited in its ability to solve the hazardous waste problem by the fact that it only deals with a slice of the process. It can only encourage reduction or recycling by making disposal less attractive.

**4.** If investing in pollution prevention measures can save companies money, why don't more companies fully adopt this strategy? Part of the answer lies in the status quo businesses confront in managing pollution control, but sometimes there are sound financial reasons, as well. This can be understood through the investment measure known as ROCE. Assume, as an example, that your company's environmental manager has identified an investment that would alter a manufacturing process and save the company $20,000 annually because of reduced disposal fees and conserved raw material. Sounds like a no-brainer investment, right? The key question for a business, however, is not how much money this investment saves but, rather, how much more money the company could earn by spending the same amount of money somewhere else. If the money were invested in advertising or other process changes, for example, perhaps the bottom line would be improved by even more than $20,000 per year. This type of analysis focuses on the Return On Capital Employed (ROCE) and explains why pollution prevention investments can prove difficult. The environmental manager needs to demonstrate that the investment not only will save the company money, but will also save more money than a comparable investment. To facilitate such decisions, many companies have a minimum ROCE that investment proposals must satisfy (e.g., a 12% annual return) before they are seriously considered. How do you think companies should consider positive externalities created by their investments (e.g., more open space for the community, greater provision of ecosystem services, etc.) in their ROCE analysis?

**5.** Being dirty carries a real cost. Disposal fees for hazardous waste are as high in America as anywhere in the world. This is due in part to the many requirements RCRA imposes on waste disposal facilities and in part to the fact that demand exceeds supply. In recent years, commentators have decried the problem of a "landfill crisis." There surely is a problem, but it's not that we're running out of space for disposal facilities. Rather, the problem is that we can't open new ones as old disposal facilities shut down. Not surprisingly, no one wants to live near a waste disposal facility or accept other peoples' trash. One doesn't often see real estate ads boasting: "Beautiful house! Walking distance to playground, shops and dump!!" NIMBYism—effective local opposition to the permitting of waste facilities—has made it increasingly difficult to open new waste disposal sites and the shortage of disposal capacity has, in turn, driven up the cost of disposal.

As described above, while RCRA prescribes in detail how wastes should be tracked and treated, and how TSDFs and landfills should be operated, the law says nothing about *where* geographically the waste should go. Assume that you are a state that has some disposal capacity right now and want to preserve it. Can you refuse to accept waste from other states? This would certainly be a politically popular action, since voters clearly don't appreciate trucks filled with hazardous materials driving on their roads, much less leaving their wastes behind. On its face, this would seem fairly easy to do since the state interest in protecting the public health is clearly legitimate. Controlling the interstate flow of wastes, though, has proven very difficult in practice because of concerns over interstate commerce. The Supreme Court has directly addressed whether states can control the movement of wastes in a series of decisions popularly known as the "flow control cases."

The core decision underpinning the flow control cases, still good law today, is the 1978 case, Philadelphia v. New Jersey, 437 U.S. 617 (1978). The city of Philadelphia challenged a New Jersey law banning the disposal of out-of-state waste. The ban was not absolute, though. Out-of-state waste could still be shipped to New Jersey if the state EPA determined that the waste could be disposed without threat to the health and safety of New Jersey residents. The case, and those that followed, turned on whether the Court should characterize the movement of wastes as commerce and, if so, whether the New Jersey law had unduly interfered with its flow.

The Court concluded garbage is, in fact, commerce—there's plenty of money to be made in moving it around. On the critical issue of whether New Jersey interfered with the flow, the Court was unpersuaded by the state's insistence that the law was not motivated by protectionist concerns. While the Court acknowledged that New Jersey's interests were legitimate, its actions impermissibly distinguished waste solely on the bases of its geographic origin. One cannot look at hazardous waste and legitimately distinguish between garbage from Los Angeles, Chicago, or Newark. As the majority declared, "whatever New Jersey's ultimate purpose, it may not be accomplished by discriminating against articles of commerce coming from outside the State unless there is some reason, apart from their origin, to treat them differently. . . . What is crucial is the attempt by one State to isolate itself from a problem common to many by erecting a barrier against the movement of interstate trade." New Jersey, the Court concluded, was hoarding a valuable resource. It may find itself the unhappy recipient of other states' waste today, but in the future it may need to ship its wastes to Pennsylvania or New York. Unless the Court struck down the restriction, the majority reasoned, interstate commerce in waste would be blocked.

That's surely one way to view the issue, but consider the dissent by Justice Rehnquist. He characterized the situation not as hoarding an *economic good* for the greedy benefit of New Jersey residents (i.e., keeping its waste disposal capacity for itself) but, rather, in keeping out a *public health bad*. A line of Supreme Court quarantine cases has permitted states to ban the import of diseased animal carcasses, and is this really any different? Put another way, just because a state has to dispose of its own noxious articles, that doesn't mean they should have to accept noxious items from other states. Doing so would fail to protect the public health and welfare. Under this perspective, the Court should have treated the flow control law as environmental protection, not economic protectionism. Which perspective makes more sense to you? Now consider the following variations on the theme:

- State X bans the import of hazardous waste from states that did not have their own hazardous waste disposal facilities. *See* Chemical Waste Management v. Hunt, 504 U.S. 334 (1992).

- State Y passes a law that charges $25 per ton on all waste disposed in the state and an additional $72 per ton for out-of-state waste. It also caps the total waste disposed per year in any site. *See* Fort Gratiot Sanitary Landfill, Inc. v. Michigan Department of Natural Resources, 504 U.S. 353 (1992).
- State Z requires each county to adopt a twenty-year plan for disposal of its own wastes. No out-of-county waste can be accepted unless authorized by the plan. *See* Oregon Waste Systems, Inc. v. Department of Environmental Quality, 511 U.S. 93 (1994).
- County A enacts an ordinance requiring all local solid waste to be processed at a designated privately owned transfer station before leaving the municipality. *See* C & A Carbone, Inc. v. Clarkstown, 511 U.S. 383 (1994).
- County B enacts an ordinance requiring area waste to be taken to assigned county facilities only. Waste haulers that do not comply with these ordinances face fines, imprisonment, and revocation of their waste-hauling permits. The county facilities charge tipping fees—disposal charges—higher than those of private facilities in the region although they also provide additional recycling services as part of the fee. *See* United Haulers Ass'n v. Oneida-Herkimer Solid Waste Management Authority, 550 U.S. 330 (2007).

## II. THE COMPREHENSIVE ENVIRONMENTAL RESPONSE, COMPENSATION, AND LIABILITY ACT (CERCLA)

The presence of hazardous wastes in the environment evokes images of oozing barrels, multi-million dollar decontamination efforts, and Love Canal. During the 1890s, William T. Love hoped to bypass Niagara Falls and thus facilitate transportation and hydroelectricity in upstate New York. But the plan collapsed after Love dug about one mile of the canal, and by the 1940s the Hooker Chemical and Plastics Corporation used the ditch to bury over 20,000 tons of toxic waste. Hooker gave the property to the city in 1952, receiving only one dollar and a promise that the city would assume any liabilities associated with the site. The city built a school and a residential neighborhood there. Then, in 1978, an investigation into the unusual rate of illnesses experienced by people living in the area concluded that the toxic wastes were "a public health time bomb." The residents were relocated, and the problem of long-dormant hazardous wastes burst onto the national scene.

What to do about hazardous wastes remains a difficult scientific, policy and legal question. Scientists continue to learn about the effects of various toxic substances in the environment, both alone and in combination. Politicians struggle with choices about which kind of hazardous substances pose the greatest threats to human health and the environment, how to control those substances that are the most dangerous, and who should pay for any cleanup efforts for releases into the environment. The legal responses to hazardous wastes have evolved from traditional common law remedies to two sweeping federal statutes: the Resource Conservation and Recovery Act (RCRA), discussed earlier in this chapter and the Comprehensive Environmental Response, Compensation, and Liability Act (CERCLA), also known as the "Superfund" statute. The term "Superfund" comes from the Hazardous Substance Response Trust Fund created when CERCLA was enacted to fund EPA response actions at contaminated sites.

Many states have enacted their own "state superfund" laws modeled after CERCLA, some of which provide rights of recovery associated with the cleanup of hazardous waste and hazardous substances beyond those available under CERCLA. *See, e.g.,* ALASKA STAT. §§ 46.03.822, 46.03.824 (allowing recovery for personal injury and property damage in addition to cost recovery associated with the release of hazardous substances); Minn. Stat. §§ 115B.05; 115B.14 (allowing recovery for personal injury, lost profits, diminution in property, other damages, and attorneys' fees in addition to cost recovery associated with the release of hazardous substances); WASH. REV. CODE § 70.105D.080 (allowing recovery of expenses and reasonable attorneys' fees in connection with cost recovery actions).

With the possible exception of the Endangered Species Act, CERCLA is the most controversial environmental law, so we will study CERCLA in detail. We will begin with an examination of CERCLA's history and an overview of the law's provisions. Next we will consider the procedures CERCLA establishes for the cleanup of a contaminated site, and the enforcement mechanisms established by the law to achieve such cleanups. After that we will see how the parties who pay to clean up hazardous substances can recover their costs. We will examine the liability scheme embodied in CERCLA section 107, which identifies a broad range of parties who had any connection to a contaminated site, makes them liable for the costs of cleaning up the site, and provides a structure for allocating those costs among multiple liable parties.

## Remarks of President Carter on Signing Public Law 96–510, Dec. 11, 1980

16 Weekly Compilation of Presidential Documents, No. 50 (Dec. 11, 1980).

Almost 1½ years ago I sent to the Congress the original proposal for this landmark legislation, landmark in its scope and in its impact on preserving the environmental quality of our country. It was known as a superfund bill, which began a massive and a needed cleanup of hazardous wastes in our country, a problem that had been neglected for decades or even generations. It fills a major gap in the existing laws of our country and also will tend to focus the attention of the public on this very crucial problem that must be resolved. It provides adequate funding, coming primarily from industry, but also from government, and it establishes certain standards for liability if toxic chemicals are damaging to people or to property.

We responded directly and quickly to some of the highly publicized problems with toxic wastes that are just representative of many similar challenges and problems throughout the country. Love Canal and Valley of the Drums come to my memory right this moment. They are stark reminders of the neglect in our society to deal with a growing problem.

We've created in this country great prosperity and a leadership in the entire world with our chemical industry and with the energy industries, but we had neglected to pay part of the cost of that development. And now, of course, we must face that responsibility. The result here is a bill that substantially meets the criteria that I set out in the original proposal that I made to the Congress a year and a half ago. Most important, it enables the Government to recover from responsible parties the costs of their actions in the disposal of toxic wastes. While it does not deal with oil pollution in the way that I did propose, I understand that the Congress intends to act on a comprehensive oil pollution superfund similar to this in scope next year.

In my 4 years as President I think everyone who knows me understands that one of my greatest pleasures has been to strengthen the protection of our environment. Along with the Alaska lands bill and other major legislation, this superfund bill represents a fine achievement for the Congress and for my own administration and for the whole Nation.

I now take great pleasure in signing into law H.R. 7020, and I'm proud that the Congress and my administration have come together to produce this timely and urgently needed response.

---

## QUESTIONS AND DISCUSSION

**1.** The circumstances of CERCLA's enactment help to explain how the law works. Congress thought that it had solved the problem of hazardous wastes when it passed RCRA in 1976. Soon after RCRA's enactment, the public's consciousness was captured by the saga of hazardous wastes that had been disposed decades before. President Carter's signing statement cited two of the most infamous episodes: Love Canal and the Valley of the Drums, a five-acre site near Louisville where 17,000 fifty-five gallon drums of hazardous waste were leaking onto the ground and into a nearby river.

Congress considered several different bills addressing the problem of hazardous wastes and the "major gap" noted by President Carter. The House and the Senate approved quite different versions of a bill during the spring and summer of 1980. Then a majority of the American people voted on November 4, 1980 to replace Jimmy Carter with Ronald Reagan and to replace a Democratic majority in the Senate with a Republican one. The new

President and the new Senate did not take office, however, until January 20, 1981. The November election of Ronald Reagan and a Republican majority in the Senate created a new urgency for members of Congress and the Carter Administration who feared that all of their work would go for naught once the new Senate and President took office in January. So a bipartisan group of Senators acted immediately after the election to reach a compromise. The Senate passed their proposed bill on November 24, and it immediately warned the House that "the frailest, moment-to-moment coalition" that enabled CERCLA to prevail in the Senate "would now be impossible to pass the bill again, even unchanged." Fearful that no such law would be approved by President Reagan or a Republican Senate, the House quickly acquiesced on December 3rd, and when President Carter signed the bill, CERCLA became law on December 11, 1980. *See* 126 CONG. REC. 31,968–69 (1980) (statement of Rep. Florio) (indicating that "[t]he concern is whether we are going to have legislation or whether we [are] not going to have legislation"); *but see* John F. Barton, *Senate Tackles Superfund Bill*, U.P.I., Nov. 24, 1980 (reporting that members of the Reagan transition team—though not Reagan himself—had indicated that they wanted the legislation passed). For an excellent discussion of the history of CERCLA's enactment, *see* Frank P. Grad, *A Legislative History of the Comprehensive Environmental Response, Compensation and Liability ("Superfund") Act of 1980*, 8 COLUM. J. ENVTL. L. 1 (1982).

**2.** The hurry with which Congress and President Carter approved the law has been noted by numerous courts which have criticized CERCLA as poorly drafted. For example, note that CERCLA § 107(a)(1) imposes liability on "the owner *and* operator" of a facility, while CERCLA § 107(a)(2) imposes liability on "any person who . . . owned *or* operated" a facility when hazardous substances were disposed at the site. Most courts have held that both provisions apply to either the owner *or* the operator of a site, ignoring the difference between "and" and "or." In Redwing Carriers, Inc. v. Saraland Apartments, Ltd., 875 F. Supp. 1545 (S.D. Ala. 1995), *rev'd on other grounds*, 94 F.3d 1489 (11th Cir. 1996), however, the district court held that a party is liable under CERCLA § 107(a) only if it is both the current owner *and* the current operator of a facility. The court explained that the haste with which Congress passed CERCLA "does not justify judicial rewriting of a statute," and that it would not be absurd for Congress to impose liability on a party only if it is both the owner and operator of a facility. How should courts react to language in CERCLA that seems to be a mistake?

**3.** During the 1980s and 1990s, CERCLA was also criticized for its substantive implementation. President Clinton complained that "[f]or far too long, far too many Superfund dollars have been spent on lawyers and not nearly enough have been spent on clean-up." Message to the Congress on Environmental Policy, 31 WEEKLY COMP. PRES. DOC. 558 (1995). The chair of the House subcommittee responsible for CERCLA proclaimed that "Superfund has been enormously costly, grossly inefficient, patently unfair, and short on results." *Superfund Reauthorization (Part 2): Hearing Before the Subcomm. on Commerce, Trade, and Hazardous Materials of the House Commerce Comm.*, 104th Cong., 1st Sess. 135 (1995) (testimony of Rep.

Oxley). *See also* U.S. v. Ottati & Goss, Inc., 900 F.2d 429 (1st Cir. 1990) (opinion by then-Judge Breyer criticizing EPA for its actions during a long and drawn out cleanup, and asking, "[w]hy, for example, has this case taken ten years to litigate? The issues are complex, but not unfathomable. . . . Has the government itself caused a significant amount of contamination through negligent cleanup efforts? Has the government, in fact, spent enormous administrative (and judicial) resources in an effort to force improvement from "quite clean" . . . to "extremely clean," at three to four times the "quite clean" costs?"). Later in the 1990s, EPA Administrator Carol Browner acknowledged that "there is a need for major reform." *Superfund Reauthorization: Hearing Before the Subcomm. on Commerce, Trade, and Hazardous Materials of the House Commerce Comm.*, 104th Cong., 1st Sess. 2 (1995) [hereinafter *Superfund Reauthorization Hearing*]. Judge Posner ridiculed "Superfund Cloudcuckooland." G.J. Leasing Co., Inc. v. Union Elec. Co., 54 F.3d 379, 385 (7th Cir. 1995). Other courts described CERCLA as unfair, harsh, and inequitable. And the director of Illinois's environmental protection agency commented that "to say that the Superfund program is broken . . . falsely implies that the program worked at one time." *Superfund Reauthorization Hearing* at 89 (testimony of Mary A. Gade).

But such complaints have largely disappeared in recent years. Indeed, a review of the statute's history written by two practitioners on the occasion of CERCLA's twenty-fifth anniversary concluded that the law "can now be recognized as an arena in which EPA has achieved a high level of success." John Quarles & Michael W. Steinberg, *The Superfund Program at Its 25th Anniversary*, 36 E.L.R. NEWS & ANALYSIS 10364, 10365 (2006). The 35th Anniversary of the Superfund Program in 2016 also promoted a series of articles and blog posts reflecting on the significant changes the law has brought about in terms of protecting communities against hazardous substance contamination. *See* U.S. EPA, Superfund 35th Anniversary, at https://www.epa.gov/superfund/superfund-35th-anniversary. The law has achieved that success despite the inability of Congress to make any sweeping changes to the statute since 1986, when it approved the Superfund Amendments and Reauthorization Act (SARA). Numerous legislative reforms were proposed in Congress during the 1990s and 2000s, but the changes that took place were instead the result of administrative actions, the implementation of the law by the many parties and attorneys who were affected by it, and targeted Congressional action to eliminate or reduce liability for discrete parties (i.e., lenders and de micromis generators) seen as unduly burdened by CERCLA's liability scheme.

## A. THE CERCLA CLEANUP PROCESS

### 1. OVERVIEW OF CERCLA CLEANUPS

CERCLA contains countless details prescribing the identification, investigation, and cleanup of contaminated sites. Those details fit into a typical sequence that is well described in the following case.

## United States v. E.I. DuPont de Nemours and Company

United States District Court for the District of Delaware, 2004.
2004 WL 1812704.

■ ROBINSON, CHIEF JUDGE.

The DuPont-Newport Superfund Site consists of approximately 120 acres in New Castle County, Delaware near the interchange of I-95, I-495 and Delaware State Route 141 (the Site). The Site includes a paint pigment plant ("Newport facility"), a former chromium dioxide plant ("Holly Run facility"), and two unlined, industrial landfills (the "North landfill" and "South landfill"). The Site also includes wetlands adjacent to each landfill ("North wetlands" and "South wetlands"), a baseball field near the Newport Facility (the "Ballpark"), and a portion of the Christina River.

The Newport facility was originally owned by Herik J. Krebs and operated by Krebs Pigment & Chemical Company ("Krebs"). Between 1902 and 1929, Krebs used the Newport facility for the manufacture of lithopone, a white pigment used in paints comprised of barium sulphate and zinc sulfide. In 1929, DuPont purchase Krebs and its Newport facility, after which DuPont continued to use the facility for the manufacture of lithopone. In 1932, DuPont phased out the production of lithopone in favor of another white pigment, titanium dioxide.

During its history, DuPont used the Newport facility to manufacture other organic and inorganic pigments. In the 1940s, DuPont manufactured blue, green and yellow copper phthalocyanine pigments. In the 1950s, DuPont produced titanium metal. In the 1960s, it made nickel. In 1958, DuPont began producing quinarcidone pigment. Beginning in 1966, DuPont produced chromium dioxide, a coating for audio tapes, at the Newport facility.

In the late 1970s, the Holly Run facility was built at the Site to expand DuPont's production of chromium dioxide. DuPont later shifted its production of chromium dioxide to the Holly Run facility. In 1984, DuPont sold its Newport facility to Ciba. Since 1984, Ciba has continued to produce quinarcidone pigment at the Newport facility.

The North and South landfills have been owned and operated by DuPont or Krebs since 1902. During DuPont's operation of the Newport facility, both landfills were used to dispose of waste and/or off-grade product. From 1902 to 1974, the North landfill was used to dispose of wastes from manufacturing operations. From 1902 until 1953, the South landfill was used to dispose of large quantities of lithopone waste.

As a result of decades of industrial activity, the Site became heavily contaminated with various hazardous substances, including heavy metals such as arsenic, barium, cadmium, lead and zinc, as well as volatile organic compounds including tetrachloroethene and tricholoroethene.

Under CERCLA, the response to a release of hazardous substances is known as a "response action." Response actions are generally classified either as removal actions or remedial actions. Removal actions consist of a range of activities which include short-term actions necessary to stabilize or to clean up sites posing a threat to public health or the environment and includes certain planning actions such as remedial design. 42 U.S.C. § 9601(23). In contrast, a remedial action is more broadly comprised of response actions which are taken to implement long-term solutions to an environmental release and contamination and permanent abatement of such releases and contaminations. 42 U.S.C. § 9601(24).

The Superfund cleanup process is described in the National Contingency Plan which contains specific procedures that govern response actions at CERCLA sites. 40 C.F.R. Part 300. The first step in the Superfund cleanup process is site identification. At this stage, potential sites are brought to the attention of the Environmental Protection Agency ("EPA") through a variety of ways, including state referrals, citizen complaints and certain federal and state environmental reporting requirements. 40 C.F.R. § 300.405. A database of these sites that have been or will require agency evaluation is maintained by the EPA. 40 C.F.R. § 300.5

Following site identification, a Preliminary Assessment ("PA") and a Site Inspection ("SI") will be conducted to determine if a site poses a potential hazard and to screen sites that do not warrant further study. During the SI, data is gathered concerning potentially hazardous substances, potential exposure pathways, and human and environmental receptors. 40 C.F.R. §§ 300.420 and 300.5

Following the PA/SI, the data gathered from the site is used to generate a score for use in the Hazard Ranking System ("HRS"). The HRS is a screening mechanism to assist in evaluating a site's relative risk and determine its eligibility for placement on the National Priorities List ("NPL"). A site with a score of 28.50 or higher is eligible for placement on the NPL.

At any time during the Superfund cleanup process, a removal action may be implemented to stabilize or to clean up a site that poses a threat to human health or the environment. A removal action may consist of either short-term actions or various planning activities such as remedial design. 40 C.F.R. § 300.415.

At sites for which further study is required, a Remedial Investigation ("RI") and a Feasibility Study ("FS") will be performed. The purpose of a RI is to determine the nature and extent of contamination at a site and the associated health and environmental risks. A FS will use data obtained during the RI to develop and to evaluate options for remedial action. A FS may define the objectives of response action generally, develop remedial action alternatives, and undertake an initial screening and detailed analysis of those alternatives. 40 C.F.R. § 300.430.

Following completion of the RI/FS, the EPA will issue a proposed remedial action plan that identifies its preferred remedial alternative. The proposed plan includes information concerning the site and other remedial alternatives evaluated as part of the RI/FS. The proposed plan will also list opportunities for public input and requests comments from the public on each of the remedial alternatives. *Id.*

After receipt and consideration of all public comments, the EPA selects a remedial alternative for the site and issues a document called a Record of Decision ("ROD"). 42 U.S.C. §§ 9604(c)(4) and 9621(a). A ROD presents a comparative analysis of the options developed as part of the FS and identifies the selected remedy for the site. A ROD also will contain performance standards, which are measures that a selected remedy must attain to ensure it meets the objectives of protecting the public health and environment. 40 C.F.R. § 300.430(f)(4) and (5). A selected remedy is subject to modifications based upon developments in science, technology or site conditions. Depending on the degree of change, an Explanation of Significant Differences ("ESD") may be submitted to supplement the administrative record or an amendment may be made to the ROD. 40 C.F.R. § 300.430(f)(4) and (5).

After issuance of the ROD, a planning phase known as Remedial Design ("RD") begins. The RD involves technical analysis and procedures which result in a detailed set of plan specifications for implementation of the selected remedy. 40 C.F.R. § 300.435. A RD may be performed by either the EPA or a potentially responsible party ("PRP"). When RD is performed by a PRP, it is typically done under a consent decree or administrative order. At sites where the PRP conducts the RD, the EPA supervises to ensure that the PRP complies with CERCLA, the NCP, the ROD, the consent decree or administrative order, and any EPA-approved plans relating to the site.

The Site was identified as a potential threat to human health and the environment in the late 1970s and early 1980s. At that time, Dupont and the Delaware Department of Natural Resources and Environmental Control began sampling groundwater at the Site. The results indicated that the groundwater contained elevated levels of heavy metals and volatile organic compounds. In the mid 1980s, information was gathered by state and EPA officials to determine whether it should be placed on the NPL. In February 1990, the Site was placed on the NPL.

Pursuant to an Administrative Order on Consent ("AOC"), Dupont conducted an RI/FS which showed that soils, sediments, groundwater and plant tissue were extensively contaminated with numerous hazardous substances, including various heavy metals and volatile organic compounds. Results also demonstrated that elevated levels of contamination included at least one species of fish.

Using the results of the RI/FS, the EPA developed a proposed remedial action plan. The proposed plan and the RI/FS results were published on November 13, 1992. Following public comment on the proposed plan, the EPA issued a ROD containing its selected remedy on August 26, 1993. The selected remedy contained measures addressing the affected areas of the Site, including the Ballpark, North landfill, South landfill, South wetlands, Christina River, Newport facility, Holly Run facility and groundwater.

Following issuance of the ROD, the EPA sent special notice letters to DuPont and Ciba to initiate negotiations for the implementation of the ROD and demand payment for past and future response costs. When the parties were unable to reach agreement on implementation of the ROD, the EPA issued a unilateral administrative order to DuPont and Ciba, pursuant to § 106 of CERCLA, requiring them to implement the remedy described in the ROD.

DuPont and Ciba, consistent with the UAO, implemented the remedy in two stages, remedial design and remedial action. The EPA provided oversight of DuPont's and Ciba's activities in both stages. The supervision is contemplated by CERCLA and required by the NCP to insure compliance with CERCLA, the NCP, the ROD, the UAO and other EPA-approved plans applicable to the Site. Through the course of implementation, the EPA agreed to modify certain aspects of the ROD through ESDs.

---

## QUESTIONS AND DISCUSSION

**1.** The court's opinion provides an excellent summary of the steps in a typical CERCLA case. Two additional points help to explain the beginning and the end of the process. Initially, note that CERCLA does not contain a mechanism for inventorying old sites contaminated with hazardous substances that may need to be cleaned up. Instead, CERCLA § 103(a) requires the operator of a facility to notify the National Response Center of any release of hazardous substances above a specified amount. CERCLA § 104(e) authorizes EPA to enter facilities to obtain information about the release of hazardous substances. More generally, EPA's website observes that "[t]he release of hazardous substances may be discovered by various means, including: notifications by those that handled hazardous materials, investigations by state, tribal, or local governments, inventory efforts by government agencies, review of state and Federal records, formal citizen petitions, and informal community observation and notification." Obviously, this list depends upon the initiative of interested parties or the happenstance of a newly evident problem, which helps to explain why so many CERCLA cases involve hazardous substances that were disposed decades—or even centuries—ago. The end of the CERCLA process involves the litigation that is often necessary to determine who must pay for the cleanup costs. Application of CERCLA's expansive liability standards to potentially responsible parties (PRPs) is the most controversial aspect of the law and will be discussed in detail later in this chapter. Here, the district court's decision at the DuPont-Newport site held that the federal government could not recover its costs of supervising DuPont's cleanup, but the Third Circuit held that such costs could be recovered. *See* United States v. E.I. DuPont de Nemours & Co. Inc., 432 F.3d 161 (3d Cir. 2005) (en banc). Ultimately, the case settled with DuPont and Ciba agreeing to pay the federal government more than $1.6 million for cleanup costs, natural resource damages, and wetlands restoration projects.

**2.** Note that at least initially, EPA—not the states—directed most CERCLA cleanups. This difference in state involvement is striking compared to environmental statutes such as RCRA and the Clean Water Act, both of which give states broad powers to implement their provisions. CERCLA, by contrast, is more similar to the Endangered Species Act's emphasis on federal—not state—regulation. Why do you think Congress decided not to follow the traditional allocation of authority between federal and state government for CERCLA? Should states be given a greater role in determining how a particular site should be cleaned up? Or which parties to hold liable? In recent years, many sites that EPA has not chosen to remediate under its CERCLA authority have been remediated under the authority of state superfund laws enacted in the wake of CERCLA. According to two observers, "[w]ithout question, the states will play a much larger role than they have played in the past 25 years." John Quarles & Michael W. Steinberg, *The Superfund Program at Its 25th Anniversary*, 36 E.L.R. NEWS & ANALYSIS 10364, 10369 (2006). Moreover, a 2011 Southwestern Law Review symposium published several articles reflecting on CERCLA after 30 years, including a focus on the important role state law has played and will continue to play in the remediation of contaminated sites. *See* Alexandra B. Klass, *CERCLA, State Law, and Federalism in the 21st Century*, 41 SW. L. REV. 679 (2012). Why might EPA choose not to take action with regard to a large number of sites? Why might the emphasis have shifted from the federal government to the states so many years after CERCLA's enactment?

**3.** EPA's website lists the DuPont-Newport site as one of CERCLA's success stories. "The site cleanup is now complete, and it was finished ahead of schedule. More than 57,000 cubic yards of contaminated sediments were removed from the Christina River and the site's wetlands to protect aquatic life." *In Delaware, a Site Owner's Cooperation and a Cleanup that Exceeds Expectations*. The site now hosts a paint pigment manufacturer, a baseball field, and two wetlands areas.

---

## 2. THE NATIONAL PRIORITIES LIST (NPL)

The National Priorities List (NPL) is, as its name suggests, a list of the priority hazardous waste sites awaiting investigation and cleanup throughout the United States. As of May 2016, there were 1,328 sites (both private sites and federal facilities) on the list. Another 55 sites were proposed for listing as of that date, while 391 were once on the list but have since been deleted. *See* U.S. EPA, NPL Site Totals by Status and Milestone, at https://www.epa.gov/superfund/npl-site-totals-status-and-milestone. You can see where they are on EPA's map at https://www.epa.gov/superfund/search-superfund-sites-where-you-live.

Listing on the NPL does not necessarily mean that the site is among the most dangerous in the country. NPL listing is required, however, for EPA to use money from the Superfund to remediate or otherwise act with regard to a site. As noted later, NPL listing is NOT required for private parties to remediate a site and seek to recover those remediation costs from other responsible parties under CERCLA's cost recovery provisions. EPA says that "[t]he NPL primarily serves as an information and management tool." Specifically, "[t]he identification of a site for the NPL is intended primarily to guide EPA in:

- determining which sites warrant further investigation to assess the nature and extent of the human health and environmental risks associated with a site;
- identifying which CERCLA-financed remedial actions may be appropriate;
- notifying the public of sites EPA believes warrant further investigation; and
- serving notice to potentially responsible parties that EPA may initiate CERCLA-financed remedial action.

Inclusion of a site does not in itself reflect a judgment of the activities of its owner or operator, it does not require those persons to undertake any action, nor does it assign liability to any person."

## B & B Tritech, Inc. v. United States Environmental Protection Agency

United States Court of Appeals for the District of Columbia Circuit, 1992.
957 F.2d 882.

■ Before MIKVA, CHIEF JUDGE, EDWARDS and RUTH BADER GINSBURG, CIRCUIT JUDGES.

■ PER CURIAM:

Petitioners argue that the Environmental Protection Agency (the EPA or Agency) should not have listed the B & B Chemical Company site on the National Priorities List of hazardous waste releases. We deny the petition, but urge the Agency to promptly consider delisting the site.

The Comprehensive Environmental Response, Compensation, and Liability Act of 1980 ("CERCLA") requires the President to prepare a "national contingency plan for the removal of . . . hazardous substances," and therein to list "national priorities among the known releases or threatened releases throughout the United States." 42 U.S.C. § 9605(a) (1988). The EPA has been delegated responsibility for the National Priorities List ("NPL"), and periodically updates the list through informal rulemaking. The Hazard Ranking System ("HRS"), a mathematical model, is used to evaluate proposed NPL sites. Our prior decisions have fully described the NPL and the HRS. *See, e.g.,* Linemaster Switch Corp. v. EPA, 938 F.2d 1299 (D.C. Cir. 1991); City of Stoughton v. EPA, 858 F.2d 747 (D.C. Cir. 1988); Eagle-Picher Indus. v. EPA, 822 F.2d 132 (D.C. Cir. 1987) ("*Eagle-Picher III*"); Eagle-Picher Indus. v. EPA, 759 F.2d 922 (D.C. Cir. 1985) ("*Eagle-Picher II*"); Eagle-Picher Indus. v. EPA, 759 F.2d 905 (D.C. Cir. 1985) ("*Eagle-Picher I*").

Congress amended CERCLA in 1986. The Superfund Amendments and Reauthorization Act ("SARA") required a new HRS—one that would "assure, to the maximum extent feasible, that the . . . relative degree of risk to human health and the environment posed by sites and facilities [is accurately assessed]." 42 U.S.C. § 9605(c)(1) (1988). SARA set a 1988 deadline, which the EPA missed: the new model did not become effective until March, 1991. In *Linemaster Switch*, we held that the Agency could update the NPL with the original HRS, even though SARA's deadline had passed.

The B & B Chemical Company ("B & B") is a family-owned firm with a manufacturing facility in Hialeah, Florida. On June 24, 1988, the EPA proposed adding the Hialeah facility to the NPL. Groundwater sampling had revealed a plume of contamination underneath the site, in the shallow layer of the so-called Biscayne Aquifer. This plume apparently stemmed in part from "soakage pits" that B & B had once used for its waste water. The site received a proposed HRS score of 35.35 (the NPL threshold is 28.50), based solely on the risk that contamination would migrate through the ground water.

The Ground Water Migration Route score in the HRS is composed of two different factors: "Waste Characteristics" and "Targets." The Targets factor measures the risk that contamination will spread to a substantial population, and has two components: "Distance to Nearest Well/Population Served" and "Ground Water Use." The distance to nearest well "is measured from the hazardous substance . . . to the nearest well that draws water from the aquifer of concern." Population served "includes residents as well as others who would regularly use the water" from wells within three miles of the site, but those "who do not use water from the aquifer of concern are not to be counted." The HRS has formulas for quantifying and then combining these two components.

There are four public wellfields within three miles of the Hialeah site, and these connect to a regional distribution system serving some 750,000 people. However, the wellfields draw from deeper ground water, while the contamination underneath the site is largely confined to the shallow aquifer layer. Moreover, the regional water authority no longer uses the fields as a source of supply, and only pumps them for a short period each day, so as to keep the equipment operable. The EPA nonetheless counted the wellfields in B & B's Targets score: the B & B facility was scored as "serving" a population of 750,000, the "nearest well" was found to be within one mile of the site, and the Agency proposed a Distance to Nearest Well/Population Served score of 35 (out of 40).

B & B protested the proposed NPL listing, but the Agency refused to change its HRS score, and the Hialeah site was added to the NPL effective October 1, 1990. The company and its owners now petition for review.

Congress' goal in SARA was to assure that the HRS "accurately assesses relative risks to human health and the environment . . . within the context of the purpose for the National Priorities List; i.e., identifying for the States and the public those facilities and sites which appear to warrant remedial actions." H.R. CONF. REP. NO. 962, 99th Cong., 2d Sess. 199 (1986). The B & B site did not receive the benefit of SARA, but was scored under the original version of the HRS. This case shows why Congress required a new model.

Petitioners rightly argue that the EPA's calculation of the Distance to Nearest Well/Population Served subfactor was highly formulaic. The Agency made two crucial assumptions. First, the entire Biscayne Aquifer was treated as a single "aquifer of concern," and thus the shallow plume of contamination underneath the B & B site was presumed accessible to the nearby wellfields, despite the fact that these fields drew from the deep aquifer layer. The EPA's justification was that "traces" of contamination had been found in the deep layer, and that the boundary between the deep and shallow layers was sufficiently permeable for vertical migration. Second, the EPA found that 750,000 people were "using" the wellfields, despite the fact that the wellfields had been taken out of service and were only pumped intermittently to keep the equipment operable. The justification, here, was that a "limited amount of water from these wellfields enters the distribution system daily."

Despite our concern over the seemingly unfair effects of the overly formalistic approach followed by EPA in this case, we are constrained to deny the petition. Our case law endorses the "Hazard Ranking System's preference for using formulas," and emphasizes that "the NPL is simply a rough list of priorities, assembled quickly and inexpensively." Specifically, we have held that the EPA can treat two separate ground water routes as a single "aquifer of concern" if the two are connected. "[W]here a contaminated aquifer spreads water to an aquifer supplying a target population, contamination to the first is hazard to the second and the 'Agency reasonably treats them as a unit for purposes of the Hazard Ranking System.' The presence of trace contaminants in the deep aquifer layer, together with the direct evidence of vertical permeability, was sufficient to demonstrate a connection between the two layers of the Biscayne Aquifer." *See also Eagle-Picher III*, 822 F.2d at 150 (upholding NPL listing despite fact that "water naturally cleanses itself of contaminants as it moves [from the site] through geological formations to the wells from which the water is drawn").

We also have specifically permitted Agency imprecision in calculating the target population. In *Eagle-Picher I*, a general challenge to the HRS, we held that the EPA could "estimat[e] the population within a certain radius of the release [instead of] utiliz[ing] actual population figures." In *City of Stoughton*, we declared that the Agency need not divide the population into subgroups, even where subdivision would produce a more accurate score. Finally, in the recent *Linemaster Switch* case, we again allowed a challenged Targets score and emphasized that the EPA "properly . . . included within its calculation all people who draw water from wells located within three miles of the hazardous substances." Given these precedents, we are constrained to find that the EPA could count the four wellfields proximate to B & B: a population of 750,000 did indeed "use" the water from these fields, if this word is formulaically interpreted to cover minimally-used wells.

However, the Agency's decision remains a troubling one. The record does not disclose whether the B & B site poses any real risk to the public, because the EPA did not address that question. We do not know whether dangerous quantities of contaminants flow from the site to the wellfields, or from the fields into the regional distribution system. Agency counsel conceded at oral argument that the site would not be dangerous, indeed would not be listed, if the wellfields were only pumped once a year: that would be equivalent to zero pumping. But the Agency has not yet examined whether minimal daily pumping creates a significantly higher risk than zero pumping, given the "trace" wastes that B & B has contributed to the deep aquifer layer.

Despite the very real possibility that their facility does not endanger the population, petitioners must now bear the considerable costs that result from an NPL listing. Moreover, these costs might have been avoided if the Agency had more promptly complied with SARA. The ground water segment of the new HRS is quite sophisticated; inter alia, "[p]opulations served by wells whose water is blended with that from other drinking water sources are to be apportioned based on the well's relative contribution to the total blended system." In *Linemaster Switch*, where a listed site might have benefited from the new HRS, we acknowledged that the site would not need to be rescored. But we also emphasized that the "EPA has broad discretion in determining what remedial actions are warranted." Specifically, "[r]eleases may be deleted from or recategorized on the NPL where no further response is appropriate." We urge the EPA to move forward, quickly, to a remedial investigation to determine whether B & B poses any measurable or meaningful health risk; if not, the Agency should act with dispatch to delist the B & B site.[6]

---

[6] Furthermore, if the EPA finds that sites with no measurable or meaningful health risk continue to receive high HRS scores under the new model, it would seem prudent for the EPA to consider exempting such sites from the NPL.

The petition for review is denied. We uphold the EPA's decision to place the B & B facility on the National Priorities List.

---

## QUESTIONS AND DISCUSSION

**1.** Is the site at issue in *B & B Tritech* the kind of site that Congress had in mind when it created the NPL? Why did EPA place this site on the NPL? If the court believed that the site did not present any environmental threat, then why did the court uphold EPA's listing? How do you suppose that EPA learned about this site in the first place?

**2.** Sites may be scored under the Hazard Ranking System (HRS), which evaluates threat the human health and the environment posed by a site. It must "assure, to the maximum extent feasible, that the . . . relative degree of risk to human health and the environment posed by sites and facilities [is accurately assessed]." CERCLA § 105(c)(1). The toxicity of the hazardous substance, the size of the neighboring population, and the way in which the contamination can be spread are all factors under the HRS. Separate scores are calculated for the threat caused by the movement of contamination through groundwater, through surface water, and through the air. As in *B & B Tritech*, most of the highest scores are the result of groundwater contamination. Sites that are closer to heavily populated areas or to a particularly valuable environmental resource receive higher scores.

If a site's HRS score exceeds 28.5, EPA will publish a Federal Register notice proposing to list the site on the NPL. Interested parties—the owner of the site, local citizens, environmental groups, the State—can then submit public comments on the proposed listing. Based on those comments, EPA will decide whether to list the site. The owners of a site that is placed on the NPL can seek judicial review of the listing in the D.C. Circuit. Early cases always upheld EPA's listing, but as illustrated by *B & B Tritech*, some subsequent courts subjected EPA's listing decisions to more scrutiny. Even so, the D.C. Circuit still employs the deferential standard of judicial review articulated in *B & B Tritech*. *See, e.g.*, Honeywell Int'l, Inc. v. EPA, 372 F.3d 441 (D.C. Cir. 2004) (rejecting a challenge to the listing of an old industrial site along the Hudson River in New Jersey). In addition to listing sites based on their HRS scores, each state gets to choose one site in the State to put on the NPL automatically. That provision responded to the concerns of western states that their problems would be addressed, too. Few states have done this, but the threat of an automatic listing can be used as leverage to get a party to begin cleaning up a site.

**3.** Given the purposes of the NPL, why was B & B Tritech so upset that its property had been listed?

**4.** To fund EPA-led cleanups at non-federal NPL sites, EPA uses the Hazardous Substance Response Trust Fund, or "Superfund," from which EPA receives annual appropriations. At the time of CERCLA's enactment, the Superfund was financed primarily by taxes on crude oil and certain chemicals, as well as by an environmental tax on corporations based on their taxable income. However, the authority for these taxes expired in 1995 and has never been reinstated. At that time, the balance in the trust fund began to decline. Since 2001, appropriations from general revenues have been the primary source of funding for the trust fund, adding to funds recovered by the federal government in CERCLA cost recovery actions against responsible parties. At the end of fiscal year 2015, the trust fund had a balance of approximately $39 million. *See* U.S. EPA, FISCAL YEAR 2015 AGENCY FINANCIAL REPORT 58, 66 (Nov. 16, 2015). In general, Congressional funding for the Superfund program has declined each year since 2010 and was approximately $1 billion for FY 2015. *See* ROBERT ESWORTH & DAVID M. BEARDEN, ENVIRONMENTAL PROTECTION AGENCY (EPA): FY2016 APPROPRIATIONS 26–27 (Nov. 12, 2015). In addition to general revenues and the trust fund, EPA funds portions of the Superfund program through "special accounts" funded from PRP settlements amounting to approximately $1.7 billion in 2015, and a total of $6.3 billion between 1990 and 2015. *See* U.S. EPA, Superfund Special Accounts, at https://www.epa.gov/enforcement/superfund-special-accounts. What are some of the implications of a reduced Superfund for EPA with regard to remediation options? With regard to EPA negotiations with potentially responsible parties prior to the initiation of cleanup activities?

**5.** In recent years, EPA has created guidance for a "Superfund Alternative" (SA) approach by which EPA foregoes listing a site on the NPL so long as the potentially responsible party enters in a SA agreement with EPA. It is meant to save time and resources compared to NPL listing. The criteria for the SA approach include (1) site contamination is significant enough for NPL listing; (2) a long-term response action is anticipated at the site; and (3) there is a willing potentially responsible party who will negotiate and sign an agreement with EPA to investigate and/or remediate the site. The agreements are in the form of an administrative order on consent and a judicial consent decree for site cleanup. For information on the SA approach and the number of sites that have gone through the program, see http://www.epa.gov/compliance/resources/publications/cleanup/superfund/saa-baseline-rpt.pdf.

**6.** An early decision (and one that is reprinted later in this chapter) held that a site need not be on the NPL and a cleanup not be performed by EPA itself in order to for a state or private party to recover costs under the NCP. *See* New York v. Shore Realty Corp., 759 F.2d 1032 (2d Cir. 1985). Indeed, today a significant number of CERCLA response actions are undertaken by private parties at sites not on the NPL, followed by lawsuits to recover those costs from other responsible parties.

---

## B. WHICH CLEANUP COSTS MAY BE RECOVERED?

Congress designed CERCLA to shovel first, and sue later. CERCLA contains an extensive scheme governing the recovery of cleanup costs incurred by EPA, landowners, and others who have paid to address the presence of hazardous substances. That scheme provides strict rules regarding the kinds of costs that may be recovered, who may recover them, and who is liable for them. Pursuant to CERCLA Section 107(a), cleanup costs may be recovered only if (1) the property constitutes a "facility"; (2) there has been a "release" or "threatened release" of a hazardous substance; (3) the release has caused the plaintiff to incur "necessary costs of response" that are "consistent" with the National Contingency Plan (discussed below); and (4) the defendant fits within one of four categories of potentially responsible parties. In this section, we will consider the basics of the first three elements of CERCLA Section 107's cost recovery provisions governing the kinds of costs that may be recovered and who may recover them. We will turn to CERCLA's designation of the parties who are responsible for paying those costs in the next section.

CERCLA cleanups are expensive. Not surprisingly, those who pay such costs usually want someone else to reimburse them. Often that means an insurer. Almost as often that means pointing the finger at someone else allegedly responsible—or at least partially responsible—for paying the costs of cleaning up the contamination. But CERCLA prescribes very specific standards governing the recovery of cleanup costs. Response costs may be recovered only if they were incurred consistent with the National Contingency Plan (NCP)—or, in the case of EPA, if the agency's costs were "not inconsistent" with the (NCP). The NCP, promulgated as regulations by EPA (40 C.F.R. pt. 300), specifies the cleanup process that must be followed at a CERCLA site. The NCP derives from CERCLA § 105(a)'s command that EPA establish procedures for the cleanup of hazardous substances. Failure to follow the NCP will preclude a party from recovering their response costs from other responsible parties. But neither the NCP nor anything else in CERCLA contains the actual cleanup standards that must be met at a site. Instead, other federal laws provide the standards used in CERCLA cases. ARARs—applicable, relevant and appropriate requirements—establish the acceptable level of a particular pollutant as provided in RCRA, the Safe Drinking Water Act, the Clean Water Act, and other sources. States may impose their more stringent standards if they help to pay for the cleanup. *See* CERCLA § 121(d)(2)(C).

EPA's regulatory requirements for cleanups under the NCP also depend on whether EPA, a state or local government, or a private party is conducting a "removal" action or a "remedial action." Removal actions are time-sensitive responses to public health threats for which there is considerable leeway in structuring the cleanup. Superfund-financed removal actions generally are required to be terminated after $2 million has been obligated for the action or 12 months have elapsed from the date removal activities begin on-site. 40 C.F.R. § 300.415(b)(5). The EPA may exceed this cap, however, if it determines one of two exemptions applies: (i) There is an immediate risk to public health or welfare of the United States or the environment; continued response actions are immediately required to prevent, limit, or mitigate an emergency; and such assistance will not otherwise be provided on a timely basis; or (ii) Continued response action is otherwise appropriate and consistent with the remedial action to be taken. 40 C.F.R. § 300.415(b)(5); *see also* 42 U.S.C. § 9604(c)(1). By contrast, remedial actions are more permanent remedies to threats for which an urgent response is not warranted and thus there is no financial cap but there are more onerous requirements for notice, comment, and written report generation under the NCP. *See* 42 U.S.C. § 9601(23) (defining "removal"); 42 U.S.C. § 9601(24) (defining "remedial action"). *See also* United States v. W.R. Grace & Co., 429 F.3d 1224 (9th Cir. 2005) (discussing requirements for removal and remedial actions).

Litigation successfully challenging the consistency of various cleanups with the NCP includes Union Pacific R.R. Co. v. Reilly Industries, Inc., 215 F.3d 830 (8th Cir. 2000) (holding that a state environmental agency's role in a cleanup could not substitute for the NCP's public participation requirements); Public Service Co. of Colorado v. Gates Rubber Co., 175 F.3d 1177 (10th Cir. 1999) (agreeing that a state's role in a cleanup could not substitute for the NCP's public participation requirements); United States v. Broderick, 963 F. Supp. 951 (D. Colo. 1997) (holding that EPA violated the NCP by failing to reconsider its selected remedy once it became clear that the hazardous substances at issue were comprised of a much higher volume of solids than EPA originally anticipated). We will consider another such case here.

## Regional Airport Authority of Louisville and Jefferson County v. LFG, LLC

United States Court of Appeals for the Sixth Circuit, 2006.
460 F.3d 697.

■ SUHRHEINRICH, CIRCUIT JUDGE.

The Comprehensive Environmental Response, Compensation and Liability Act of 1980 (CERCLA), 42 U.S.C. §§ 9601–75, permits private party property owners to recover from prior private party property owners certain costs associated with the cleanup of contamination caused by the prior owners, where the cleanup costs were "necessary." "Necessary" costs means they were incurred in response to a threat to human health or the environment, *see* 42 U.S.C. § 9607(a)(4)(B), and "consistent" with the National Oil and Hazardous Substances Pollution Contingency Plan ("NCP"), *see* 42 U.S.C. § 9607(a). The NCP requires, among other things, completion of a remedial investigation ("RI"), feasibility study ("FS"), and a record of decision ("ROD"), along with an opportunity for public comment. *See* 40 C.F.R. pt. 300. In Kentucky, for any risk management-based alternatives for dealing with contamination (i.e., remediation that stops short of removing the contamination), the Kentucky Division of Waste Management ("the State") requires a baseline risk assessment ("BRA"). For soil remediation, the State must approve a soils management plan. Plaintiff-Appellant Regional Airport Authority of Louisville and Jefferson County ("the Authority") brought a CERCLA action against Defendants-Appellees LFG, LCC ("LFG") and Navistar International Transportation Corporation ("Navistar") (collectively, "Defendants") for costs the Authority allegedly incurred in the remediation of property previously owned by Defendants. The district court granted Defendants summary judgment on the CERCLA claims, holding that the remediation was unnecessary and that the Authority failed to comply with the NCP. The Authority now appeals from that judgment. . . .

In June 1988, the Authority commenced the Louisville Airport Improvement Program ("airport expansion"), whereby it intended to expand Standiford Field (also known as Louisville International Airport). In order to accomplish its objectives, the Authority needed to condemn hundreds of parcels of private property. Among those was a 130-acre parcel owned by LFG ("the Site") that had been put to heavy industrial use for nearly fifty years.[1] The plan was to build new runways on the Site. Defendants admit that they used hazardous materials on the Site throughout their occupancy of the Site, and the Authority knew the Site was contaminated at the time of condemnation.

The airport expansion involved the use of federal funds, which required the Authority to complete an environmental impact statement ("EIS"). The final EIS was prepared in 1990, three years before the Authority acquired the Site from Defendants and six years before it took possession in 1996. The EIS indicated that at least some remediation would be necessary, and that the cost to remediate the Site would account for $9.5 million of the estimated $17.5 million total cost of remediation for the airport expansion.

Following subsequent environmental investigation, the Authority contacted the State regarding the contamination. In 1994, the Authority retained Camp, Dresser & McKee, Inc. ("Camp Dresser") to investigate further the extent of the contamination and the need, if any, for remediation. In November 1996, Camp Dresser reported to the Authority the results of its investigation in its Data Summary Report. The Authority then relayed this report to the State a month later.

In January 1997, the Authority began the final demolition phase of the existing structures on the Site. In February, the State sent a letter to the Authority explaining that Camp Dresser had conducted sampling at the Site. The letter further explained that the Authority should begin to focus its efforts on determining appropriate remedial alternatives. Despite this, the Authority did not evaluate the risk or any potential remedial measures, nor did it seek to complete a BRA. In fact, one month later in a weekly status report, the Authority instructed the following:

---

1 Navistar owned the Site beginning in 1946. LFG bought the Site from Navistar in 1985.

> Major redirection has taken place on this job regarding the "model" that we are using for RI/FS. The NCP for the most part has been replaced with more of a no-nonsense approach to fulfilling Kentucky's requirements under their [sic] "mini-Superfund" program. Therefore, there are but three major deliverables on the horizon: 1) An RI/FS Work Plan (our "draft" to client on 3/13/97), 2) a "Soils Management Plan" (to be produced by others), and 3) an RI/FS Report, which will include preliminary design for groundwater remedy. A baseline risk assessment will not be completed.

In May 1997, shortly after the demolition was completed, the State conditionally approved the Authority's soil management plan.

Eventually, the Authority had Camp Dresser prepare an RI/FS to analyze the Authority's options for groundwater protection and to make specific recommendations. In September 1997, the Authority received the RI/FS. The Authority presented those reports to the State for approval in October. However, the Authority decided not to remove the contamination as recommended but instead pursued a risk management-based remedy. In the words of the runway project manager, the Authority "approved a substantial departure from the classic RI/FS model." The Site's west runway was completed and open for use in December 1997.

Following completion of the west runway, the Authority directed Camp Dresser to prepare a BRA. Camp Dresser delivered its findings in April 1998. The Authority submitted the BRA to the State later that month. In a letter dated almost a year after the runway was operational, the State notified the Authority that both the RI/FS and BRA had been approved. The letter also stated that the State "would support" any effort by the Authority to hold a formal public comment period, although the State noted that it might "not be worthwhile due to the fact that the work ha[d] already begun."

On February 24, 1999, the Authority published a notice in the Louisville Courier-Journal announcing a March 4 public meeting to discuss the remediation. A meeting was so held, but no one other than the Authority's lawyers attended.

The Authority never completed a ROD. In fact, the Authority decided sometime in late 2000 or 2001 that it would not file a ROD. Instead, in March 2002, the Authority filed with the State a Remedial Plan, which summarized the BRA, RI/FS, and soils management plan, and described the actions involved in preparing the Remedial Plan. The State approved the Remedial Plan in a letter dated May 24, 2002.

On May 15, 1998, after submitting the BRA to the State but before the State's response, the Authority filed the present action against Defendants to recover environmental response costs associated with the Site. . . . The district court granted summary judgment for Defendants on the Authority's CERCLA claims. The court reasoned that the Authority could not succeed at trial, because the evidence presented did not demonstrate that the costs incurred were "necessary," or that the Authority presented "appropriate remedial alternatives" in a timely manner. . . .

The first issue is whether the district court erred in granting summary judgment for Defendants on the Authority's CERCLA claims. . . . A prima facie case for CERCLA recovery under § 107(a) has four elements: (1) the property is a "facility"; (2) there has been a "release" or "threatened release" of a hazardous substance; (3) the release has caused the plaintiff to incur "necessary costs of response" that are "consistent" with the NCP; and (4) the defendant is in one of four categories of potentially responsible parties. Only the third element is at issue in this appeal. We analyze separately whether the response was "necessary" and whether it was "consistent" with the NCP.

As the language of the statute implies, whether the costs were "necessary" is a threshold issue for recovery under § 107(a). *See* 42 U.S.C. § 9607(a)(4)(B) (stating that a cause of action lies for "any other necessary costs of response incurred by any other person consistent with the [NCP]"); G.J. Leasing Co. v. Union Elec. Co. (*G.J. Leasing II*), 54 F.3d 379, 386 (7th Cir. 1995) ("The statutory limitation to 'necessary' costs of cleaning up is important. Without it there would be no check on the temptation to improve one's property and charge the expense of improvement to someone else."). Costs are "necessary" if incurred in response to a threat to human health or the environment. *See* 42 U.S.C. § 9607(a)(4) (liability attaches where "a release, or a threatened release . . . causes the incurrence of response costs"); Carson Harbor Vill., Ltd. v. Unocal Corp. (*Carson Harbor I*), 270 F.3d 863, 871 (9th Cir. 2001) (en banc) (noting that there is general agreement that "necessary" "requires that an actual and real threat to human health or the environment exist before initiating a response action"); Dedham Water Co. v. Cumberland Farms Dairy, Inc., 972 F.2d 453, 459–60 (1st Cir. 1992) (affirming denial of CERCLA recovery where plaintiff failed to establish that its costs were incurred in response to actual or threatened release); G.J. Leasing Co. v. Union Elec. Co. (*G.J. Leasing I*), 854 F. Supp. 539, 562 (S.D. Ill. 1994) ("For response costs to be 'necessary', [sic] plaintiffs must establish that an actual or real public health threat exists *prior to initiating a response action*."), *aff'd*, 54 F.3d 379 (7th Cir. 1995). Conversely, costs incurred at a time when the plaintiff was unaware of any threat to human health or the environment are not "necessary."

The Authority's response in this case was not "necessary." There is no evidence in the record demonstrating the need for a CERCLA-quality cleanup prior to constructing the runway. The first report, the soils management plan, was filed in May 1997—five months after demolition began. After requesting Camp Dresser to prepare an RI/FS and then passing it along to the State, the Authority nonetheless decided on its own to ignore the recommendations in the RI/FS and instead proceed with the construction as planned. After completion of the runway in December 1997, the Authority had Camp Dresser prepare a BRA. Camp Dresser did not provide the BRA to the Authority until April 1998. By the time the State approved the RI/FS and BRA in November 1998, the runway had been operational for almost a year. The timing of these events demonstrates that the cleanup costs could not have been incurred in response to a threat to human health or the environment, because the Authority did not have the relevant information at the time the costs were incurred.

The Authority responds that, at the very least, its 1990 EIS was a timely investigation into the need for remediation. Clearly, the EIS states that expanding the airport would require remediation at various locations, including the Site. However, the purpose behind the EIS, and hence its investigation, centered on the health and environmental effects of the airport expansion project as a whole, not around the health and environmental risks of the Site or any parcel as it then existed. The EIS addressed whether the airport should be expanded in the first place, without regard for any specific project that would be required as part of the expansion. For example, the EIS's proposed alternatives to airport expansion were to take no action, to develop a new site/new airport, to utilize alternative modes of transportation, or to increase service from other airports. The EIS does not say, and the Authority does not contend otherwise, that the Site as it existed in 1990 posed an environmental or public health risk.

Even absent the timing issues, neither the RI/FS nor the BRA shows that the response was "necessary." The RI/FS is irrelevant, since the Authority "approved a substantial departure" from it. The Authority cannot be heard now to say that the RI/FS is proof that the response costs were necessary. As for the BRA, the only potential threat identified was the presence of lead in the soil. To the extent that the BRA identified some risk of lead exposure to workers or on-site visitors, however, those conclusions were erroneous. First, the soils management plan (the only report approved prior to completion of the runway) had already stated that the lead concentrations at the Site were lower than what the federal Environmental Protection Agency ("EPA") has calculated to be acceptable risk levels for both residential and industrial use. Indeed, the mean total lead concentration in seven urban Louisville parks was nearly four times higher. Second, the BRA's author admitted that the lead calculations in the BRA were "not appropriate," and if she had to do it over again, she "would evaluate that in a different manner." Had the authority calculated the lead concentration levels under the EPA's CERCLA model, it would have found no unacceptable risk. Moreover, none of these reports indicated that the Site, as it sat when the Authority took control, needed remediation to protect the public health or the environment. They noted only potentially adverse impacts *of runway construction* on the Site.

Perhaps the most convincing evidence that the response costs were not "necessary" comes from the deposition testimony of Robert Brown, a representative of the Authority, that the areas not excavated as part of the runway construction were left untouched:

Q. Okay. With regard to the unexcavated areas of those three parcels, what did you do with that land?

A. Actually, in most cases, nothing.

Q. Okay. You just left it as-is?

A. Yes.

Q. Okay. If it was exposed soil, you left it as [sic] exposed; if it had asphalt on it, you left it with asphalt on it, right?

A. Yes.

Q. Okay. Or whatever the cover happened to be, right?

A. Right.

A Camp Dresser manager also testified that the Authority did not remediate the soil deeper than necessary to complete runway construction. Had remediation truly been necessary, the Authority presumably would have (and certainly should have) performed a cleanup of the entire area.

In any event, the soils management plan makes clear that any "concerns" would have been rectified through normal runway construction and a prohibition against the use of ground and surface waters. . . . In other words, the "response costs" and the runway construction costs were one and the same. Therefore, allowing the Authority to recoup its "response costs" would be tantamount to a reimbursement of its runway construction costs. "To require former occupants to assume liability for cleanup costs going beyond the level necessary to make the property safe for industrial use would be to provide an unwarranted windfall to the beneficiary of the cleanup." City of Detroit v. Simon, 247 F.3d 619, 630 (6th Cir. 2001). Likewise here, to require Defendants to assume liability for cleanup costs not in excess of normal construction or use costs would be to provide an unwarranted windfall to the Authority. . . .

This is not to say that parties are precluded from recovering all response costs incurred for self-serving motives. Parties often select a particular response based on commercial efficiency and convenience. To recover CERCLA damages in those cases, however, the parties must show that the threat to public health or the environment was the predicate for acting. Otherwise, businesses that happened to operate on contaminated property, yet took no additional measures in order to do so, would realize unearned fixed-cost advantages over their competitors. We do not believe that Congress, in enacting CERCLA, intended such a result. . . .

While a conclusion that response costs were not "necessary" alone defeats the Authority's CERCLA claims, we address the issue of whether the costs were "consistent" with the NCP in the alternative.

A contamination cleanup is consistent with the NCP "if, taken as a whole, it is in 'substantial compliance' with 40 C.F.R. § 300.700(c)(5)–(6), and results in a 'CERCLA-quality cleanup.'" Franklin County [Convention Facilities Auth. v. Am. Premier Underwriters, Inc., 240 F.3d 534, 543 (6th Cir. 2001)] (quoting 40 C.F.R. § 300.700(c)(3)(i)). An immaterial or insubstantial deviation, however, will not result in a cleanup that is "not consistent" with the NCP. 40 C.F.R. § 300.700(c)(4). The relevant provisions of the NCP for purposes of this appeal concern the RI/FS and selection of remedy, § 300.700(c)(5)(viii), and community relations and the opportunity for public comment, § 300.700(c)(6).

Section 300.700(c)(5)(viii) states that compliance with Section 300.430 is "potentially" required for a private CERCLA cause of action. Section 300.430(f)(1)(ii) states:

> The selection of a remedial action is a two-step process. . . . First, the lead agency [e.g., the State] . . . identifies a preferred alternative and presents it to the public in a proposed plan, for review and comment. Second, the lead agency shall review the public comments and consult with the state . . . in order to determine if the alternative remains the most appropriate remedial action for the site or site problem. The lead agency . . . makes the final remedy selection decision, which shall be documented in the ROD.

We believe that, under the facts of this case, compliance with Section 300.430 is required, but the Authority's response fails each provision. First, the State did not present the preferred alternative to the public in a proposed plan, because the Authority never provided the State with the proposed plan in the first place. The only opportunity for public comment on the chosen alternative occurred years after construction on the Site was completed. Second, the State had no public comments to consider. As a general proposition, recovery should not be precluded where the lead agency could not consider public comments because there simply were none to consult. It seems a different matter, however, where there are no public comments because the "proposal" was already completed by the time the public had an opportunity to comment on it. Finally, and most importantly, the State did not make the final remedy selection decision, and there was no ROD. The State could not have made the final remedy selection decision, as the Authority completed the remedy eleven months before the State even approved the RI/FS and BRA. Moreover, the unrefuted testimony from the Authority's environmental consultant was that the Authority had made an affirmative decision not to file a ROD. We conclude that the Authority failed to comply with this provision of the NCP.

Also, the Authority's preparation of the RI/FS fell short of substantial compliance with Section 300.430. The purpose of the RI is "to . . . develop[ ] and evaluat[e] effective remedial alternatives." 40 C.F.R. § 300.430(d)(1). The purpose of the FS is "to ensure that appropriate remedial alternatives are developed and evaluated such that relevant information concerning the remedial action options can be presented to a decision-maker and an appropriate remedy selected." 40 C.F.R. § 300.430(e)(1). Here again, neither of these purposes was fulfilled because the Authority had already implemented a remedy by the time the State approved the RI/FS. Finding this type of action to be in compliance with the NCP would reduce the NCP to a mere formality. Moreover, the meaninglessness of the Authority's RI/FS is further demonstrated by the Authority's approval of a "substantial departure" from the RI/FS shortly after it was submitted for approval.

Third, the Authority did not provide an opportunity for public comment on the planned remediation. *See* 40 C.F.R. § 300.700(c)(6) (stating that "[p]rivate parties undertaking response actions should provide an opportunity for public comment concerning the selection of the response action"). Where relevant, these "community relations" provisions require, inter alia, that a party solicit concerns from the public and prepare a formal community relations plan, § 300.430(c)(2)(i)–(ii), that the party make available for public comment a report describing the preferred remedy along with alternatives, § 300.430(f)(2)–(3), and that the ROD be made available for public inspection, § 300.430(f)(6)(ii).

Once again, the Authority did none of these. The Authority did not solicit concerns from the public, prepare a formal community relations plan, or make available for public comment a report describing the preferred remedy along with alternatives. However defined, any *meaningful* opportunity for public comment must occur before the final remedial action is chosen, let alone implemented. Thus, the public meeting held in March 1999—at least two years after the remedy was chosen and one year after it was completed-cannot satisfy the public comment requirement. And as already noted, the EIS did not address specific remediation plans or alternatives. Therefore, the public comment on the EIS in 1990 cannot satisfy the NCP. . . .

The Authority's alternative response to the district court's finding of non-compliance with the NCP is that the NCP is a loose guideline that is satisfied if the response "results in a CERCLA-quality cleanup." 40 C.F.R. § 300.700(c)(3)(i). The Authority concludes that, because its response (arguably) resulted in a CERCLA-quality cleanup, it satisfied the NCP. The problem with this argument is that recovery under § 107(a) requires *both* "substantial compliance" with the NCP *and* a "CERCLA-quality cleanup." *Franklin County,* 240 F.3d at 543. Thus, the fact that the Authority's response may have resulted in a CERCLA-quality cleanup alone is insufficient.

We recognize that "immaterial, insubstantial" deviations that do "not affect the overall quality of the cleanup" will not bar recovery. *Franklin County,* 240 F.3d at 545. But wholesale failure to comply with the NCP's remedy—selection process and community relations provisions-the very heart of the NCP—cannot reasonably be characterized as "immaterial" or "insubstantial."

---

## QUESTIONS AND DISCUSSION

**1.** Why did the court conclude that the airport authority's costs were not "necessary" within the meaning of CERCLA? And why did the court hold that those costs were not consistent with the NCP? What did the airport authority do wrong?

**2.** A neighborhood activist who objected to the airport's expansion characterized the authority's public participation process as "[d]o it, and do it as quick as you can." James Bruggers, *Airport Loses Cleanup Lawsuit,* THE COURIER-JOURNAL (Louisville, Ky.), Aug. 19, 2006, at 1B. The airport's expansion "made a major United Parcel Service hub possible, and is credited with producing hundreds of millions of dollars in economic benefits. But the project took three residential neighborhoods and several businesses." *Id.* One of those businesses—and the one from whom the airport authority was seeking to collect its costs was LFG, the Louisville Forge and Gear Works, which built engine crankshafts at the site from 1985 until the authority condemned the land a few years later. The company's owner then sold the business and bought a Louisville horse farm. *See* Patrick Howington, *Airport Expansion Dispute is Settled,* THE COURIER-JOURNAL (Louisville, Ky.), Dec. 21, 2006, at 1D.

**3.** The court implies that the airport authority acted "for self-serving motives." What were those motives? Why should they be relevant to whether the airport can be reimbursed for its expenses?

**4.** Why did Congress prescribe which kinds of cleanups are eligible for reimbursement under CERCLA? Why did the airport authority proceed with a cleanup that ignored those standards?

**5.** Only one of the four elements for recovery of cleanup costs under CERCLA was at issue in the case. The property easily satisfied the second element, which states that the property must be a facility. CERCLA § 101(9) defines "facility" to mean "(A) any building, structure, installation, equipment, pipe or pipeline (including any pipe into a sewer or publicly owned treatment works), well, pit, pond, lagoon, impoundment, ditch, landfill, storage container, motor vehicle, rolling stock, or aircraft, or (B) any site or area where a hazardous substance has been deposited, stored, disposed of, or placed, or otherwise come to be located; but does not include any consumer product in consumer use or any vessel." Basically, that means that a facility is any place that hazardous substances are located. There are, however, a few cases involving the definition of "facility." *See* Westfarm Associates Limited Partnership v. Washington Suburban Sanitary

Commission, 66 F.3d 669 (4th Cir. 1995) (rejecting argument that a sewer system was not a "facility"). The definition of "facility" in CERCLA Section 101(9) exempts "any consumer product in consumer use." Is a building containing asbestos a consumer product in consumer use? Is used transformer fluid that is sold to another party a consumer product in consumer use? Why would Congress exempt such products from coverage under the statute?

**6.** The third element of a CERCLA cost recovery action requires that there has been a "release" or "threatened release" of a hazardous substance. What evidence was there of a release or threatened release at the Louisville airport site? In *Shore Realty Corp.*, which follows below, the court held that "leaking tanks and pipelines, the continuing leaching and seepage from the earlier spills, and the leaking drums all constitute 'releases.' 42 U.S.C. § 9601(22). Moreover, the corroding and deteriorating tanks, Shore's lack of expertise in handling hazardous waste, and even the failure to license the facility, amount to a threat of release." 759 F.3d at 1045. Likewise, in A&W Smelter and Refiners, Inc. v. Clinton, 962 F. Supp. 1232 (N.D. Cal. 1997), the court held that a release or a threatened release occurred when a pile of mining wastes was left unsecured and uncovered at an abandoned mining site.

The release must be of a "hazardous substance." CERCLA's definition of "hazardous substance" is extremely broad, much broader than the definition of "hazardous waste" in RCRA. *See* CERCLA § 101(14) ("hazardous substance" includes any substance designated as hazardous under the Clean Air Act, Clean Water Act, RCRA, or any other substance EPA has designated as presenting "a substantial danger to the public health or welfare or the environment"). Furthermore, there is no minimum amount of hazardous substance that must be present at a site before CERCLA applies. For these reasons, there have been few disputes about whether hazardous substances are actually present at a site. The only significant exception to CERCLA's broad understanding of hazardous substance involves petroleum, which is exempted from coverage under the statute. *See* CERCLA § 101(14) (excluding "petroleum, including crude oil and any fraction thereof which is not otherwise specifically listed or designated as a hazardous substance"). The scope of CERCLA's petroleum exemption has been litigated in a number of cases. *See, e.g.,* Wilshire Westwood Assocs. v. Atlantic Richfield Corp., 881 F.2d 801 (9th Cir. 1989) (holding that refined gasoline is within the petroleum exclusion even though it contains lead, benzene and other additives that are considered hazardous).

**7.** The Louisville airport authority's failure to comply with the NCP made it unnecessary for the court to determine which of the authority's costs were reimbursable under CERCLA. That issue has arisen in a number of other cases, including United States v. E.I. Du Pont de Nemours & Co. Inc., 432 F.3d 161 (3d Cir. 2005) (en banc), which held that the federal government could recover its costs of supervising DuPont's cleanup of the DuPont Newport site discussed above. And in Key Tronic Corp. v. United States, 511 U.S. 809 (1994), the Supreme Court considered whether attorney's fees qualify as recoverable costs under CERCLA. During the 1970's, Key Tronic and other parties, including the United States Air Force, disposed of liquid chemicals at the Colbert Landfill in eastern Washington State. When EPA initiated a CERCLA action to remediate the site, Key Tronic entered into a partial settlement agreement pursuant to which the company contributed $4.2 million to a fund established by EPA for the cleanup. Key Tronic then sued the United States and other parties seeking to recover $1.2 million that it spent on attorney's fees for three types of legal services: (1) the identification of other potentially responsible parties (PRPs), including the Air Force, that were liable for the cleanup; (2) the preparation and negotiation of its agreement with the EPA; and (3) the prosecution of the case against the United States.

The Court first held that Key Tronic's action to recover cleanup costs was not a "response" within the meaning of CERCLA § 101(25), and therefore, the attorney's fees associated with that action were not "necessary costs of response" within CERCLA § 107(a)(4)(B). But the Court acknowledged that "some lawyers' work that is closely tied to the actual cleanup may constitute a necessary cost of response in and of itself under the terms of § 107(a)(4)(B)." Thus Key Tronic could recover money spent on identifying other potentially responsible parties because the work of identifying other parties could be performed by engineers, chemists, private investigators or other professionals who are not lawyers. In other words, litigation fees cannot be recovered by private parties, but money spent on lawyers for certain purposes such as identifying other responsible parties can be recovered. Justice Scalia, joined by Justices Blackmun and Thomas, would have held that private parties can recover *any* money spent on lawyers in the course of a CERCLA case, including the attorney's fees resulting from the litigation itself.

8. In addition to response costs, CERCLA imposes liability for another type of injury: damage to natural resources. Once a contaminated site has been cleaned up, CERCLA authorizes the restoration of fisheries, forests and other natural resources to their original position. Federal, state and tribal governments that serve as trustees of such natural resources are the only parties who can sue to collect the damages to natural resources. There is a different causation requirement for natural resource damages. CERCLA § 107(a)(4)(C) makes an owner liable for "damages for injury to, destruction of, or loss of natural resources, including the reasonable costs of assessing such injury, destruction, or loss resulting from such a release." One court has held that this provision requires that "the damage for which recovery is sought must still be causally linked to the act of the defendant." State of Idaho v. Bunker Hill Co., 635 F. Supp. 665, 674 (D. Idaho 1986). The First Circuit distinguished this case from actions to recover response costs, explaining that while the natural resources provision requires "a connection between the defendant and the damages to the natural resources," the general liability provision requires "a connection between the defendant and the response costs (and no mention is made of damages at all)." Dedham Water Co. v. Cumberland Farms Dairy, Inc., 889 F.2d 1146, 1154 (1st Cir. 1989).

There are also different ways of measuring natural resource damages. One measurement—the economic value of a fishery to those who use it, for instance—is relatively easy because it relies on traditional ideas of value for which the free market suggests a price. Such use values include both resource exploitation activities such as mining or fishing and less disruptive activities such as tourism. But natural resource damages also include "non-use" values—the value of simply knowing that a forest exists. While most would agree that people acknowledge such values, it is difficult to measure them. Indeed, one common form of measurement—called contingent valuation—surveys the general public to ask them how much they value a particular resource, or how much they would be willing to pay for it, but without qualifying the answers based on an individual's ability to pay. The huge numbers sometimes generated by contingent valuation surveys have caused the issue of natural resource damages to be among the most controversial topics within CERCLA.

**9.** CERCLA does not authorize anyone to recover for personal injuries arising from releases of hazardous substances, despite efforts by some members of Congress to include such a provision in 1980. As noted above, however, a few states have enacted superfund laws that allow for recovery for personal injuries in addition to more expansive property-related damage associated with the release of hazardous substances. *See, e.g.,* ALASKA STAT. §§ 46.03.822, 46.03.824 (allowing recovery for personal injury and property damage in addition to remediation costs associated with the release of hazardous substances); MINN. STAT. §§ 115B.05, 115B.14 (allowing recovery for personal injury, lost profits, diminution in property value, other damages, and attorneys' fees, in addition to remediation costs associated with the release of hazardous substances). State common law claims for nuisance, negligence, trespass, and strict liability are also available for recovery of personal injuries associated with the release of hazardous substances and wastes. Should CERCLA provide a remedy for these types of injuries? Finally, while CERCLA does not provide a vehicle for recovering for personal injuries, it does establish a program for medical monitoring of populations at significant risk of adverse health effects from exposure to hazardous substances. *See* 42 U.S.C. § 9604(i)(9); http://www.atsdr.cdc.gov/faq.html.

---

## PROBLEM EXERCISE

Between 2000 and 2010, JG-24, Inc. (JG-24) operated a fiberglass manufacturing facility in Vega Alta, Puerto Rico which utilized styrene, acetone, and other potentially harmful chemicals. In December 2010, EPA inspectors visited the Vega Alta site and described it as a "war zone," containing hundreds of deteriorating and leaking drums strewn throughout the site, evidence that waste materials had been burned or buried below ground, and high concentrations of airborne styrene and acetone vapors.

Following an April 2011 inspection, the EPA determined to undertake a removal action at the Vega Alta site, based on its express findings that (i) the metal drums continued to deteriorate and discharge hazardous substances; (ii) preliminary soil sample tests revealed high concentrations of those hazardous substances; (iii) this state of affairs created a fire risk, and because the site is situated on porous limestone atop a groundwater aquifer, it jeopardized local drinking water supplies; (iv) no other federal or state agency was equipped to undertake the cleanup; and (v) since the threatened release, migration, and fire were imminent, the removal action should be exempt from the normal $2 million cost cap.

In August 2012, the EPA filed a CERCLA action against JG-24 in federal district court. The EPA then obtained a court order for unimpeded access to the Vega Alta site, and during the period from October 2012 through August 2013, it removed from the site seven hundred cubic yards of soil contaminated with hazardous substances and two thousand five hundred leaking drums from its surface and subsurface. Subsequently, the EPA amended its complaint in the pending federal court action to seek recovery of its $4.1 removal costs at the Vega Alta site.

You have just been hired by JG-24 to represent it in all matters related to the Vega Alta site. How would you advise the company to respond to the pending CERCLA litigation?

## C. WHO PAYS FOR CERCLA CLEANUPS?

### 1. RESPONSIBLE PARTIES: OWNERS, OPERATORS, TRANSPORTERS, ARRANGERS, AND GENERATORS

Most CERCLA litigation involves who should have to pay for the costs of cleaning up hazardous substances at particular sites. Congress made a calculated decision not to rely upon traditional tort law rules for determining who is liable for the costs of cleaning up hazardous substances. Instead, CERCLA Section 107(a) identifies four categories of parties who are liable for those costs:

> (1) the owner and operator of a vessel or a facility,
>
> (2) any person who at the time of disposal of any hazardous substance owned or operated any facility at which such hazardous substances were disposed of,
>
> (3) any person who by contract, agreement, or otherwise arranged for disposal or treatment, or arranged with a transporter for transport for disposal or treatment, of hazardous substances owned or possessed by such person, by any other party or entity, at any facility or incineration vessel owned or operated by another party or entity and containing such hazardous substances, and
>
> (4) any person who accepts or accepted any hazardous substances for transport to disposal or treatment facilities, incineration vessels or sites selected by such person, from which there is a release, or a threatened release. . . .

These four categories of "potentially responsible parties" or "PRP" are often described as (1) current owners and operators, (2) past owners and operators, (3) generators (or arrangers), and (4) transporters. A party can quality under more than one category, but inclusion in only one category is sufficient for liability to attach under CERCLA. Given the stakes involved in many CERCLA cases, it is not surprising that parties continue to challenge their position within any of the four categories of responsible parties.

## New York v. Shore Realty Corp.

United States Court of Appeals for the Second Circuit, 1985.
759 F.2d 1032.

■ OAKES, CIRCUIT JUDGE:

This case involves several novel questions about the scope of the Comprehensive Environmental Response, Compensation, and Liability Act of 1980, 42 U.S.C. §§ 9601–9657 (1982) (CERCLA), and the interplay between that statute and New York public nuisance law. CERCLA—adopted in the waning hours of the Ninety-Sixth Congress, and signed by President Carter on December 11, 1980—was intended to provide means for cleaning up hazardous waste sites and spills, and may generally be known to the public as authorizing the so-called Superfund, the $1.6 billion Hazardous Substances Response Trust Fund, 42 U.S.C. §§ 9631–9633.

On February 29, 1984, the State of New York brought suit against Shore Realty Corp. ("Shore") and Donald LeoGrande, its officer and stockholder, to clean up a hazardous waste disposal site at One Shore Road, Glenwood Landing, New York, which Shore had acquired for land development purposes. At the time of the acquisition, LeoGrande knew that hazardous waste was stored on the site and that cleanup would be expensive, though neither Shore nor LeoGrande had participated in the generation or transportation of the nearly 700,000 gallons of hazardous waste now on the premises. [The district court] directed by permanent injunction that Shore and LeoGrande remove the hazardous waste stored on the property, subject to monitoring by the State, and held them liable for the State's "response costs," *see* 42 U.S.C. § 9607(a)(4)(A).

. . . LeoGrande incorporated Shore solely for the purpose of purchasing the Shore Road property. All corporate decisions and actions were made, directed, and controlled by him. By contract dated July 14, 1983, Shore agreed to purchase the 3.2 acre site, a small peninsula surrounded on three sides by the waters of Hempstead Harbor and Mott Cove, for condominium development. Five large tanks in a field in the center of the site hold most of some 700,000 gallons of hazardous chemicals located there, though there are six smaller tanks both above and below ground containing hazardous waste, as well as some empty tanks, on the property. The tanks are connected by pipe to a tank truck loading rack and dockage facilities for loading by barge. Four roll-on/roll-off containers and one tank truck trailer hold additional waste. And before June 15, 1984, one of the two dilapidated masonry warehouses on the site contained over 400 drums of chemicals and contaminated solids, many of which were corroded and leaking.

It is beyond dispute that the tanks and drums contain "hazardous substances" within the meaning of CERCLA. The substances involved—including benzene, dichlorobenzenes, ethyl benzene, tetrachloroethylene, trichloroethylene, 1,1,1-trichloroethene, chlordane, polychlorinated biphenyls (commonly known as PCBs), and bis (2-ethylhexyl) phthalate—are toxic, in some cases carcinogenic, and dangerous by way of contact, inhalation, or ingestion. These substances are present at the site in various combinations, some of which may cause the toxic effect to be synergistic.

The purchase agreement provided that it could be voided by Shore without penalty if after conducting an environmental study Shore had decided not to proceed. LeoGrande was fully aware that the tenants, Applied Environmental Services, Inc., and Hazardous Waste Disposal, Inc., were then operating—illegally, it may be noted—a hazardous waste storage facility on the site. Shore's environmental consultant, WTM Management Corporation ("WTM"), prepared a detailed report in July, 1983, incorporated in the record and relied on by the district court for its findings. The report concluded that over the past several decades "the facility ha[d] received little if any preventive maintenance, the tanks (above ground and below ground), pipeline, loading rack, fire extinguishing system, and warehouse have deteriorated." WTM found that there had been several spills of hazardous waste at the site, including at least one large spill in 1978. Though there had been some attempts at cleanup, the WTM testing revealed that hazardous substances, such as benzene, were still leaching into the groundwater and the waters of the bay immediately adjacent to the bulkhead abutting Hempstead Harbor. After a site visit on July 18, 1983, WTM reported firsthand on the sorry state of the facility, observing, among other things, "seepage from the bulkhead," "corrosion" on all the tanks, signs of possible leakage from some of the tanks, deterioration of the pipeline and loading rack, and fifty to one hundred fifty-five gallon drums containing contaminated earth in one of the warehouses. The report concluded that if the current tenants "close up the operation and leave the material at the site," the owners would be left with a "potential time bomb." WTM estimated that the cost of environmental cleanup and monitoring would range from $650,000 to over $1 million before development could begin. After receiving this report Shore sought a waiver from the State Department of Environmental Conservation ("DEC") of liability as landowners for the disposal of the hazardous waste stored at the site. Although the DEC denied the waiver, Shore took title on October 13,

1983, and obtained certain rights over against the tenants, whom it subsequently evicted on January 5, 1984.

Nevertheless, between October 13, 1983, and January 5, 1984, nearly 90,000 gallons of hazardous chemicals were added to the tanks. And during a state inspection on January 3, 1984, it became evident that the deteriorating and leaking drums of chemicals referred to above had also been brought onto the site. Needless to say, the tenants did not clean up the site before they left. Thus, conditions when Shore employees first entered the site were as bad as or worse than those described in the WTM report. As LeoGrande admitted by affidavit, "the various storage tanks, pipe lines and connections between these storage facilities were in a bad state of repair." While Shore claims to have made some improvements, such as sealing all the pipes and valves and continuing the cleanup of the damage from earlier spills, Shore did nothing about the hundreds of thousands of gallons of hazardous waste standing in deteriorating tanks. In addition, although a growing number of drums were leaking hazardous substances, Shore essentially ignored the problem until June, 1984.

On September 19, 1984, a DEC inspector observed one of the large tanks, which held over 300,000 gallons of hazardous materials, with rusting floor plates and tank walls, a pinhole leak, and a four-foot line of corrosion along one of the weld lines. On three other tanks, flakes of corroded metal "up to the size and thickness of a dime" were visible at the floorplate level. While defendants now claim that the large tank was not leaking, their denial is untimely; they did not formally dispute the fact before the district court rendered its October 15, 1984, order. Moreover, defendants' claim that the pinhole has been patched hardly makes the existence of the pinhole leak a triable issue of fact. In addition, defendants do not contest that Shore employees lack the knowledge to maintain safely the quantity of hazardous chemicals on the site. And, because LeoGrande has no intention of operating a hazardous waste storage facility, Shore has not and will not apply for a permit to do so. Nor do defendants contest that the State incurred certain costs in assessing the conditions at the site and supervising the removal of the drums of hazardous waste.

CERCLA's history reveals as much about the nature of the legislative process as about the nature of the legislation. In 1980, while the Senate considered one early version of CERCLA, the House considered and passed another. The version passed by both Houses, however, was an eleventh hour compromise put together primarily by Senate leaders and sponsors of the earlier Senate version. Unfortunately, we are without the benefit of committee reports concerning this compromise. Nevertheless, the evolution of the legislation provides useful guidance to Congress's intentions. The compromise contains many provisions closely resembling those from earlier versions of the legislation, and the House and Senate sponsors sought to articulate the differences between the compromise and earlier versions. One of the sponsors claimed that the version passed "embodie[d] those features of the Senate and House bills where there has been positive consensus" while "eliminat[ing] those provisions which were controversial." 126 CONG. REC. 30,932 (statement of Sen. Randolph).

As explained in F. ANDERSON, D. MANDELKER, & A. TARLOCK, ENVIRONMENTAL PROTECTION: LAW AND POLICY 568 (1984), CERCLA was designed "to bring order to the array of partly redundant, partly inadequate federal hazardous substances cleanup and compensation laws." It applies "primarily to the cleanup of leaking inactive or abandoned sites and to emergency responses to spills." And it distinguishes between two kinds of response: remedial actions—generally long-term or permanent containment or disposal programs—and removal efforts—typically short-term cleanup arrangements.

CERCLA authorizes the federal government to respond in several ways. EPA can use Superfund resources to clean up hazardous waste sites and spills. 42 U.S.C. § 9611. The National Contingency Plan ("NCP"), prepared by EPA pursuant to CERCLA, *id.* § 9605, governs cleanup efforts by "establish[ing] procedures and standards for responding to releases of hazardous substances." At the same time, EPA can sue for reimbursement of cleanup costs from any responsible parties it can locate, *id.* § 9607, allowing the federal government to respond immediately while later trying to shift financial responsibility to others. Thus, Superfund covers cleanup costs if the site has been abandoned, if the responsible parties elude detection, or if private resources are inadequate. In addition, CERCLA authorizes EPA to seek an injunction in federal district court to force a responsible party to clean up any site or spill that presents an imminent and substantial danger to public health or welfare or the environment. 42 U.S.C. § 9606(a). In sum, CERCLA is not a regulatory standard-setting statute such as the Clean Air Act. Id. §§ 7401–7642. Rather, the government generally undertakes pollution abatement, and polluters pay for such abatement through tax and reimbursement liability.

Congress clearly did not intend, however, to leave clean up under CERCLA solely in the hands of the federal government. A state or political subdivision may enter into a contract or cooperative agreement with EPA, whereby both may take action on a cost-sharing basis. 42 U.S.C. § 9604(c), (d). And states, like EPA, can sue responsible parties for remedial and removal costs if such efforts are "not inconsistent with" the NCP. *Id.* § 9607(a)(4)(A). While CERCLA expressly does not preempt state law, *id.* § 9614(a), it precludes "recovering compensation for the same removal costs or damages or claims" under both CERCLA and state or other federal laws, *id.* § 9614(b), and prohibits states from requiring contributions to any fund "the purpose of which is to pay compensation for claims . . . which may be compensated under" CERCLA, *id.* § 9614(c). Moreover, "any . . . person" who is acting consistently with the requirements of the NCP may recover "necessary costs of response." *Id.* § 9607(a)(4)(B). Finally, responsible parties are liable for "damages for injury to, destruction of, or loss of natural resources, including the reasonable costs of assessing such injury, destruction, or loss resulting from such a release." 42 U.S.C. § 9607(a)(4)(C).

Congress intended that responsible parties be held strictly liable, even though an explicit provision for strict liability was not included in the compromise. Section 9601(32) provides that "liability" under CERCLA "shall be construed to be the standard of liability" under Section 311 of the Clean Water Act, 33 U.S.C. § 1321, which courts have held to be strict liability, and which Congress understood to impose such liability. Moreover, the sponsors of the compromise expressly stated that Section 9607 provides for strict liability.[13] Strict liability under CERCLA, however, is not absolute; there are defenses for causation solely by an act of God, an act of war, or acts or omissions of a third party other than an employee or agent of the defendant or one whose act or omission occurs in connection with a contractual relationship with the defendant. 42 U.S.C. § 9607(b).

We hold that the district court properly awarded the State response costs under Section 9607(a)(4)(A). The State's costs in assessing the conditions of the site and supervising the removal of the drums of hazardous waste squarely fall within CERCLA's definition of response costs, even though the State is not undertaking to do the removal. *See id.* §§ 9601(23), (24), (25). Contrary to Shore's claims, the State's motion for summary judgment sought such costs, and Shore had ample opportunity for discovery. That a detailed accounting was submitted only at this court's request for supplemental findings is immaterial; Shore had an opportunity to contest the accounting but failed to make anything more than a perfunctory objection.

CERCLA holds liable four classes of persons: (1) the owner and operator of a vessel (otherwise subject to the jurisdiction of the United States) or a facility, (2) any person who at the time of disposal of any hazardous substance owned or operated any facility at which such hazardous substances were disposed of, (3) any person who by contract, agreement, or otherwise arranged for disposal or treatment, or arranged with a transporter for transport for disposal or treatment, of hazardous substances owned or possessed by such person, by any other party or entity, at any facility owned or operated by another party or entity and containing such hazardous substances, and (4) any person who accepts or accepted any hazardous substances for transport to disposal or treatment facilities or sites selected by such person. 42 U.S.C. § 9607(a).

---

[13] Both the earlier House and Senate versions contained language providing for strict, joint and several liability. As part of the compromise, the sponsors removed this language, inserted the reference to liability under the Clean Water Act and indicated that the joint and several liability question should be addressed by the courts and interpreted in light of the common law. Moreover, while we need not address the question, commentators have noted that joint and several liability is consistent with the contribution language of 42 U.S.C. § 9607(e)(2).

As noted above, Section 9607 makes these persons liable, if "there is a release, or a threatened release which causes the incurrence of response costs, of a hazardous substance" from the facility, for, among other things, "all costs of removal or remedial action incurred by the United States Government or a State not inconsistent with the national contingency plan."

Shore argues that it is not covered by Section 9607(a)(1) because it neither owned the site at the time of disposal nor caused the presence or the release of the hazardous waste at the facility. While Section 9607(a)(1) appears to cover Shore, Shore attempts to infuse ambiguity into the statutory scheme, claiming that Section 9607(a)(1) could not have been intended to include all owners, because the word "owned" in Section 9607(a)(2) would be unnecessary since an owner "at the time of disposal" would necessarily be included in Section 9607(a)(1). Shore claims that Congress intended that the scope of Section 9607(a)(1) be no greater than that of Section 9607(a)(2) and that both should be limited by the "at the time of disposal" language. By extension, Shore argues that both provisions should be interpreted as requiring a showing of causation. We agree with the State, however, that Section 9607(a)(1) unequivocally imposes strict liability on the current owner of a facility from which there is a release or threat of release, without regard to causation.

Shore's claims of ambiguity are illusory; Section 9607(a)'s structure is clear. Congress intended to cover different classes of persons differently. Section 9607(a)(1) applies to all current owners and operators, while Section 9607(a)(2) primarily covers prior owners and operators. Moreover, Section 9607(a)(2)'s scope is more limited than that of Section 9607(a)(1). Prior owners and operators are liable only if they owned or operated the facility "at the time of disposal of any hazardous substance"; this limitation does not apply to current owners, like Shore. . . .

Shore's causation argument is also at odds with the structure of the statute. Interpreting Section 9607(a)(1) as including a causation requirement makes superfluous the affirmative defenses provided in Section 9607(b), each of which carves out from liability an exception based on causation. Without a clear congressional command otherwise, we will not construe a statute in any way that makes some of its provisions surplusage. . . . Several other district courts explicitly have declined to read a causation requirement into Section 9607(a).

Our interpretation draws further support from the legislative history. Congress specifically rejected including a causation requirement in Section 9607(a). The early House version imposed liability only upon "any person who caused or contributed to the release or threatened release." The compromise version, to which the House later agreed, imposed liability on classes of persons without reference to whether they caused or contributed to the release or threat of release. Thus, the remarks of Representatives Stockman and Gore describing the House version containing the causation language, on which Shore relies, are inapposite.

Furthermore, as the State points out, accepting Shore's arguments would open a huge loophole in CERCLA's coverage. It is quite clear that if the current owner of a site could avoid liability merely by having purchased the site after chemical dumping had ceased, waste sites certainly would be sold, following the cessation of dumping, to new owners who could avoid the liability otherwise required by CERCLA. Congress had well in mind that persons who dump or store hazardous waste sometimes cannot be located or may be deceased or judgment-proof. We will not interpret Section 9607(a) in any way that apparently frustrates the statute's goals, in the absence of a specific congressional intention otherwise. . . .

Shore also claims that it can assert an affirmative defense under CERCLA, which provides a limited exception to liability for a release or threat of release caused solely by an act or omission of a third party other than an employee or agent of the defendant, or than one whose act or omission occurs in connection with a contractual relationship, existing directly or indirectly, with the defendant (except where the sole contractual arrangement arises from a published tariff and acceptance for carriage by a common carrier by rail), if the defendant establishes by a preponderance of the evidence that (a) he exercised due care with respect to the hazardous substance concerned, taking into consideration the characteristics of such hazardous substance, in light of all relevant facts and circumstances, and (b) he took precautions against foreseeable acts or omissions of any such third party and the consequences that could foreseeably result from such acts or omissions. 42 U.S.C. § 9607(b)(3). We disagree. Shore argues that it had nothing to do with the transportation of the hazardous substances and that it has exercised due care since taking control of the site. Who the "third part(ies)" Shore claims were responsible is difficult to fathom. It is doubtful that a prior owner could be such, especially the prior owner here, since the acts or omissions referred to in the statute are doubtless those occurring during the ownership or operation of the defendant. Similarly, many of the acts and omissions of the prior tenants/operators fall outside the scope of Section 9607(b)(3), because they occurred before Shore owned the property. In addition, we find that Shore cannot rely on the affirmative defense even with respect to the tenants' conduct during the period after Shore closed on the property and when Shore evicted the tenants. Shore was aware of the nature of the tenants' activities before the closing and could readily have foreseen that they would continue to dump hazardous waste at the site. In light of this knowledge, we cannot say that the releases and threats of release resulting of these activities were "caused solely" by the tenants or that Shore "took precautions against" these "foreseeable acts or omissions."

---

## QUESTIONS AND DISCUSSION

**1.** Is it fair to hold Shore Realty responsible for cleaning up contamination that it did not cause? Why would Congress have intended that result?

**2.** CERCLA does not specify the type of ownership interest that is necessary for a party to be deemed an "owner" for liability purposes. For an example of how a court addressed that issue, see Canadyne-Georgia Corp. v. NationsBank, N.A. (South), 183 F.3d 1269 (11th Cir. 1999), which reversed a lower court decision dismissing a CERCLA claim against a bank that held a general partnership interest in contaminated property. The district court had reasoned that the bank was not an "owner" because state law prohibited liability based on one's participation in a partnership. *See also* James Morrow, *Owning Up: Determining the Proper Test for Ownership Liability Under CERCLA*, 43 WASH. U. J.L. & POL'Y 333 (2014).

**3.** Past owners and operators are liable under CERCLA § 107(a)(2) only if they owned or operated the facility "at the time of the disposal." The courts are split on whether "passive disposals" qualify as disposals under CERCLA. Most circuits have held that past owners and operators are liable only if there was an affirmative act of disposal during their tenure at the site. *See, e.g.*, Carson Harbor Village, Ltd. v. Unocal Corp., 270 F.3d 863 (9th Cir. 2001) (en banc). Nurad, Inc. v. William E. Hooper & Sons Co., 966 F.2d 837 (4th Cir. 1992), is the leading case supporting liability for passive disposals. The parties held liable in *Nurad* included past owners of property who had no knowledge that underground storage tanks installed by the original owner sometime before 1935 had been leaking during the time of their ownership. What are the arguments *for* imposing liability for passive disposals? What do you think Congress intended?

**4.** The House's proposed bill imposed liability on persons who "caused or contributed to the release or threatened release" of hazardous substances. *See* H.R. 7020, 96th Cong., 2d Sess. § 3071(a)(D) (1980). As the committee report explained:

> The Committee intends that the usual common law principles of causation, including those of proximate causation, should govern the determination of whether a defendant "caused or contributed" to a release or threatened release. . . . Thus, for instance, the mere act of generation or transportation of hazardous waste, or the mere existence of a generator's or transporter's waste in a site with respect to which cleanup costs are incurred would not, in and of itself, result in liability under Section 3071. The Committee intends that for liability to attach under this section, the plaintiff must demonstrate a causal or contributory nexus between the acts of the defendant and the conditions which necessitated response action under Section 3041.

Similarly, then-Representative Gore repeatedly stressed that the bill required proof of causation. Who would pay to remediate the Shore Road property if Congress had enacted the House bill?

**5.** *Shore Realty* also held the defendants liable under the common law of public and private nuisance. The court cited the Restatement (Second) of Torts § 839 comment d (1979), which states that public nuisance "liability [of a possessor of land] is not based upon responsibility for the creation of the harmful condition, but upon the fact that he has exclusive control over the land and the things done upon it and should have the responsibility of taking reasonable measures to remedy conditions on it that are a source of harm to others." Thus:

> It is immaterial therefore that other parties placed the chemicals on this site; Shore purchased it with knowledge of its condition—indeed of the approximate cost of cleaning it up—and with an opportunity to clean up the site. LeoGrande knew that the hazardous waste was present without the consent of the State or its DEC, but failed to take reasonable steps to abate the condition. Moreover, Shore is liable for maintenance of a public nuisance irrespective of negligence or fault. Nor is there any requirement that the State prove actual, as opposed to threatened, harm from the nuisance in order to obtain abatement. . . .
>
> The district court could have also found that Shore is maintaining a public nuisance under two alternative theories. Shore's continuing violations of N.Y. Envtl. Conserv. Law § 27–0913(1) (not having a permit to store or dispose of hazardous waste), and of *id.* § 27–0914(1) (possessing hazardous waste without authorization), if not of *id.* § 27–0914(2) (disposing of hazardous waste without authorization), constitute a nuisance per se. And while we recognize that determining whether an activity is abnormally dangerous depends on the circumstances, a review of the undisputed facts under the guidelines stated in Doundoulakis v. Town of Hempstead, 368 N.E.2d 24, 27 (N.Y. 1977), convinces us that a New York court would find as a matter of law that Shore's maintenance of the site—for example, allowing corroding tanks to hold hundreds of thousands of gallons of hazardous waste—constitutes abnormally dangerous activity and thus constitutes a public nuisance. *See* Schenectady Chemicals, 103 A.D.2d at 37, 479 N.Y.S.2d at 1013; *see also* State v. Ventron Corp., 468 A.2d 150, 160 (N.J. 1983) (holding that "simply dumping [a hazardous substance] onto land or into water" is an abnormally dangerous activity).

759 F.2d at 1032. How does CERCLA liability differ from liability for a public or private nuisance?

**6.** The statutory defenses enumerated in CERCLA are notoriously difficult to prove. CERCLA § 107(b) enumerates three specific defenses which require a defendant to prove by a preponderance of the evidence that both the release and the consequent damages resulted from an act of God, an act of war, or an act of a third party completely unrelated to the defendant provided that the defendant exercised due care and took precautions against the release. As *Shore Realty* demonstrates, however, very few responsible parties have escaped liability by satisfying the requirements of the third party defense. The failure of the defendant to exercise due care is the most common reason why an attempt to assert the third party defense does not succeed.

The Act of God and the Act of War defenses are even more difficult to prove. In United States v. Alcan Aluminum Corp., 892 F. Supp. 648 (M.D. Pa. 1995), the court rejected a claim that "the torrential downpour of rain" resulting from a hurricane caused the release of hazardous substances. The court provided three reasons why the Act of God defense failed: the hurricane was not the *sole* cause of the release, the defendant failed to exercise due care because it disposed of hazardous wastes in a place where they could be easily swept away in a storm, and heavy rainfall is not sufficiently exceptional to qualify as an Act of God. Likewise, United States v. Shell, 294 F.3d 1045 (9th Cir. 2002), held that the federal government could not rely upon the act of war defense for contamination resulting from its World War II wartime contracts to purchase aviation fuel from the oil companies or its regulation of those companies' production of aviation fuel. By contrast, in 2014, the Second Circuit held that the Act of War defense prevented a real estate developer next door to the World Trade Center in New York from recovering the cost of removing pulverized dust from its property generated in the 9/11 attacks from the owners and operators of the World Trade Center. The court held that because the September 11 attack was an act of war, it was the "sole" cause of the release of hazardous substances and thus the costs were not recoverable under CERCLA. *See* In re September 11 Litigation, 751 F.3d 86 (2d Cir. 2014). For further reading on these cases and the Act of God and Act of War defenses under CERCLA, *see* Frank Leone & Mark A. Miller, *Acts of God, War, and Third Parties: The Previously Overlooked CERCLA Defenses*, 45 ENVTL. L. REP. NEWS & ANALYSIS 10129 (2015).

*Shore Realty* makes reference to the third-party defense designed to protect "innocent landowners" who purchased property without knowledge of the contamination and did not contribute to the contamination. Under Section 107(b)(3), it is a defense to CERCLA liability if the defendant establishes that the release of hazardous substances was caused by "an act or omission of a third party other than an employee or agent of the defendant or than one whose act or omission occurs in connection with a contractual relationship . . . with the defendant" and if the defendant establishes that he exercised due care with respect to the hazardous substances and took precautions against foreseeable acts or omissions of third parties. With the 1986 SARA amendments, Congress defined "contractual relationship" as used in Section 107(b)(3) to exclude parties that, at the time of purchase of the property did not know or have reason to know of hazardous substances on the property and, prior to the purchase of the property, carried out "all appropriate inquiries" into the previous ownership and uses of the facility in accordance with "generally accepted good commercial and customary standards and practices." CERCLA §§ 101(35)(A) & (B).

This provision was godsend to environmental consultants who were now retained as a matter of course by prospective purchasers of all types of property to investigate prior property uses and waste disposal practices to satisfy the statutory "all appropriate inquiries" (AAI) standard. In general, the innocent purchaser defense has been difficult to satisfy, with most courts finding the defense is not available to purchasers who knew about prior waste disposal practices on the property or who failed to adequately investigate waste disposal practices on the property prior to purchase. Such cases hold that the "contractual relationship" that destroys the third-party defense can be the contract for purchase and need not be related to hazardous substance release or disposal. *See, e.g.*, Hidden Lakes Dev. v. Allina Health System, 2004 WL 2203406 (D. Minn. 2004). The Second Circuit, by contrast, has held that the innocent landowner defense is available to all purchasers of property so long as there was no contractual relationship between the purchaser and the prior owner or other third party related to hazardous waste or that allowed the purchaser to exercise some control over the third party's activities. *See* New York v. Lashins Arcade Co., 91 F.3d 353 (2d Cir. 1996). In November 2005, EPA published a final rule establishing standards and practices to satisfy AAI under CERCLA Section §§ 101(35)(A) & (B) which are codified at 40 C.F.R. § 312. The rule requires that a prospective purchaser retain an "environmental professional" who will interview past and present owners, conduct other due diligence measures, and prepare a written report containing the findings of the investigation.

In 2002, Congress added a new category of "innocent owners" known as "bona fide prospective purchasers" (BFPPs) through the Small Business Liability Relief and Brownfields Revitalization Act of 2002. That Act added CERCLA Section 107(r)(1), which provides that a BFPP "whose potential liability for a release or threatened release is based solely on the purchaser's being considered to be an owner or operator of a facility shall not be liable as long as the [BFPP] does not impede the performance of a response action or natural resource restoration." CERCLA § 107(r)(1). A BFPP is defined in CERCLA as someone who acquires ownership of the property after January 11, 2002 and, among other things (1) who made all appropriate inquiry (AAI) into previous ownership and uses of the property (using the an EPA standard for AAI enacted in 2005 at 40 C.F.R. pt. 312); (2) where all disposal of hazardous substances occurred before the BFPP acquired the property; (3) who provided all legally required notices regarding the discovery or release of hazardous substances; (4) who exercises appropriate care regarding hazardous substances on the property to prevent continuing releases; (5) who provides full cooperation to persons conducting response actions on the property; and (6) is not otherwise liable under CERCLA or affiliated with any liable parties under CERCLA with regard to the property. CERCLA § 101(40). The 2002 Act also amended the definition of owner or operator to exclude persons who own property that has been contaminated only because of releases on contiguous property. CERCLA § 107(q). For a discussion of the BFPP defense and other CERCLA defenses, see Kenneth A. Hodson & Charles H. Oldham, *Defenses to Liability Under CERCLA*, 46 ARIZ. ST. L.J. 459 (2014); William R. Weissman & J. Michael Sowinski, Jr., *Revitalizing the Brownfields Revitalization and Environmental Restoration Act: Harmonizing the Liability Defense Language to Achieve Brownfield Restoration*, 33 VA. ENVTL. L.J. 257 (2015).

---

In addition to past and present owners of property, operators and transporters are regularly subject to CERCLA liability. Indeed, as the following case shows, parties often fit into more than one category of responsible party. But the statutory tests for each category are quite different from each other, and different from the common law's liability rules.

## American Cyanamid Company v. Capuano

United States Court of Appeals for the First Circuit, 2004.
381 F.3d 6.

■ TORRUELLA, CIRCUIT JUDGE.

In 1977, Warren Picillo, Sr. and his wife agreed to allow part of their pig farm in Coventry, Rhode Island (Picillo site) to be used as a disposal site for drummed and bulk waste. Later that year, after thousands of barrels of hazardous waste replaced what pigs at one time called home, a monstrous explosion ripped through the Picillo site. The towering flames, lasting several days, brought the waste site to the attention of the Rhode Island environmental authorities. Rhode Island investigators "discovered large trenches and pits filled with free-flowing, multi-colored, pungent liquid wastes." Violet v. Picillo, 648 F. Supp. 1283, 1286 (D.R.I. 1986). Recognizing the environmental disaster it had discovered, Rhode Island closed the pig farm and, with the federal government, began the cleanup process.

In a nutshell, this case involves an action under the Comprehensive Environmental Response, Compensation and Liability Act ("CERCLA") §§ 101–405, as amended by the Superfund Amendments and Reauthorization Act of 1986 ("SARA"), 42 U.S.C. §§ 9601–9675, brought by a company whose hazardous waste was deposited at the Picillo site against a group of people who were involved with the site.

. . . Defendants-appellants, Daniel Capuano, Jr.; Jack Capuano; United Sanitation, Inc.; A. Capuano Brothers, Inc.; and Capuano Enterprises, Inc. (hereinafter referred to as "the Capuanos"), were in the business of hauling hazardous waste. Jack Capuano was the president and sole shareholder of Sanitary Landfill, Inc., a landfill operation located in Cranston, Rhode Island. Jack Capuano and Daniel Capuano jointly owned United Sanitation, Inc., a waste hauling company. Jack Capuano was the president of United Sanitation and Daniel was the vice-president. In 1977, the Capuanos reached an agreement with Warren Picillo to dump hazardous waste on his pig farm.

In 1977, plaintiff-appellee, Rohm & Haas Company ("R & H") operated research facilities in Spring House and Bristol, Pennsylvania, which generated hazardous waste. Forty-nine of the 10,000 drums of waste at Picillo were generated by R & H. O'Neil v. Picillo, 682 F. Supp. 706, 709, 720 (D.R.I. 1988).

These drums ended up at the Picillo site in a round-about way. R & H's Spring House facility contracted with Jonas Waste Removal ("Jonas") to dispose of its waste. Jonas sent the waste to the Chemical Control Corporation, which later contracted with Chemical Waste Removal to dispose of the waste. Chemical Waste Removal disposed of the waste at the Picillo site. R & H's Bristol facility contracted with Scientific Chemical Processing ("SCP") to dispose of its waste. SCP later contracted with Daniel Capuano and United Sanitation to dispose of the waste at the Picillo site. . . .

In 1983, Rhode Island brought an enforcement action under CERCLA § 107 for cleanup costs at the Picillo site. This initial action was brought against 35 defendants "who were either owner/operators of the site, parties who allegedly transported waste there, parties alleged to have arranged for their waste to be transported to the site, and parties alleged to have produced waste deposited at the site." *O'Neil,* 682 F. Supp. at 709.

Rhode Island settled with twenty of the defendants, including the Capuanos. The Capuanos agreed to pay $500,000. Rhode Island went to trial against five of the remaining defendants, including R & H. After trial, the district court found R & H and two other companies jointly and severally liable for un-reimbursed past response costs of $991,937 and for "all future costs of removal or remedial action incurred by the state . . . including any costs associated with the removal of contaminated soil piles." *Id.* at 731. We affirmed the district court's holdings. O'Neil v. Picillo, 883 F.2d 176 (1st Cir. 1989).

The United States also sought reimbursement for its response costs associated with the soil cleanup at the Picillo site and settled with many parties, including the Capuanos. The Capuanos agreed to pay $1,500,000. The settling parties received contribution protection as part of the settlement agreement. *See* 42 U.S.C. § 9613(f)(2) ("A person who has resolved its liability to the United States or a State in an administrative or judicially approved settlement shall not be liable for claims for contribution regarding matters addressed in the settlement."). In 1989, the United States filed a cost recovery action under § 9607 against R & H and another company, American Cyanamid. *See* United States v. American Cyanamid Co., 794 F. Supp. 61 (D.R.I. 1990). The district court entered a judgment against them for $3,339,029 plus interest. United States v. American Cyanamid Co., 786 F. Supp. 152, 165 (D.R.I. 1992).

[The current litigation concerns the contaminated groundwater at the Picillo site. The United States settled with most of the responsible parties, including R & H, which paid $4,350,000 to compensate the United States for direct response costs related to groundwater cleanup, plus $110,000 towards oversight costs, and $69,000 towards natural resource damage. R & H then filed a contribution action against the Capuanos and 51 other potentially responsible parties seeking to recover the past and future costs that R & H incurred related to the groundwater cleanup. R & H filed the case in federal district court in New Jersey, but that court transferred the case to Rhode Island. After a trial there, the district court found the Capuanos liable to R & H for $2,651,838, plus $507,369 in prejudgment interest.]

The Capuanos appeal the district court's conclusion that the Capuanos transported hazardous waste to the Picillo site. CERCLA imposes transporter liability on "any person who accepts or accepted any hazardous substances for transport to disposal or treatment facilities, incineration vessels or sites selected by such person" from which there is a release of hazardous substances. 42 U.S.C. § 9607(a)(4). The district court concluded that United Sanitation and its officers, Jack and Daniel Capuano, were liable as transporters for 7.94% of the waste delivered to the Picillo site since Jack and Daniel selected the Picillo site and United Sanitation transported 960 55-gallon drums of hazardous waste to the site.

The Capuanos argue that the district court's finding was clearly erroneous because (1) United Sanitation did not transport hazardous waste; (2) United Sanitation and the Capuanos had no trucks capable of transporting hazardous waste; and (3) the only Capuano remotely identified with hazardous waste disposal was Anthony Capuano. After examining the record, we find that the district court's conclusion that the Capuanos were "transporters" was not clearly erroneous.

First, Picillo testified that "the Capuanos themselves brought their own waste down [to the Picillo site] on their own trucks" and that some of the barrels "came from Danny Capuano's place." Although this testimony supports the finding that the Capuanos physically transported some of the waste, we have interpreted CERCLA not to impose liability on a transporter who merely follows the directives of a generator. Rather, for CERCLA liability to attach, a transporter must "actively participate in the selection decision or have substantial input in that decision." In this case, the Capuanos had substantial input in the decision, often making the final determination whether to allow waste to be dumped at their own land fill or to send it on to the Picillo site. Further, the Capuanos arranged for employees of the Scientific Chemical Corporation to visit the Picillo site as a possible waste dumping location. After viewing the site, the visitors concluded "this would be an ideal spot."

Second, according to deposition and trial testimony, trucks carrying hazardous waste would arrive at the Capuanos place of business only to be redirected by the Capuanos, or their employee Louie Falcone, to the Picillo site. Indeed, since the Picillo site was difficult to find, the Capuanos would come to the Picillo site "in a pick-up truck in front of the big trucks and show them where the farm was and show them where the dump was, to dump" the hazardous waste. *See* 42 U.S.C. § 9601(26) (defining "transportation" as "the movement of a hazardous substance by any mode").

Third, when the drivers arrived at the Picillo site, they would give Picillo, Sr. a bill of lading. At the end of the week, Picillo, Sr. would take the bills of lading to the Capuanos to get paid. The record confirms that Mr. Picillo received United Sanitation checks signed by Jack Capuano and Dan Capuano. Although these payments do not, in and of themselves, prove that the Capuanos transported the waste, the payments do support the inference that the Capuanos were involved with the transportation of waste to the Picillo site.

The Capuanos appeal the district court's conclusion that the Capuanos were liable as operators of the Picillo site. CERCLA imposes liability on "the owner and operator of a vessel or a facility." 42 U.S.C. § 9607(a)(2). "The phrase 'owner and operator' is defined only by tautology . . . as 'any person owning or operating' a facility, § 9601(20)(A)(ii). . . ." United States v. Bestfoods, 524 U.S. 51, 56 (1998). The Supreme Court has clarified that, "under CERCLA, an operator is simply someone who directs the workings of, manages, or conducts the affairs of a facility." *Id.* at 66. More specifically, "an operator must manage, direct, or conduct operations specifically related to pollution, that is, operations having to do with the leakage or disposal of hazardous waste, or decisions about compliance with environmental regulations." *Id.* at 66–67.

The district court's conclusion that the Capuanos were operators of the site was not clearly erroneous. First, the Capuanos approached Warren Picillo with the idea of dumping on his pig farm. Once Warren agreed, he gave the Capuanos exclusive disposal rights at the site and the Capuanos hired a bulldozer to clear the trees and "dig a big, big hole." The Capuanos walked the operator of the bull-dozer to the site and "showed him what to do and how to do it." Such actions are consistent with those of an operator of a facility "who directs the workings of, manages, or conducts the affairs of a facility." *Id.* at 56 (1999).

Second, as discussed earlier, the Capuanos directed the hazardous waste to the Picillo site. If the drivers of the waste did not know how to reach the site, the Capuanos would drive them to the site so they could dump the waste. Further, the Capuanos managed and conducted the affairs of the Picillo site by organizing and implementing its payment structure. The waste generators paid the Capuanos to dispose of their waste and then the Capuanos would give Warren Picillo a share of the money. "Operator liability requires an ultimate finding of . . . involvement with operations having to do with the leakage or disposal of hazardous waste." United States v. Kayser-Roth Corp., 272 F.3d 89, 102 (1st Cir. 2001) (internal quotations and citation omitted). The fact that the Capuanos developed the idea for using the site, prepared the site for dumping, arranged for waste to be dumped at the site, showed transporters where to dump on the site, and collected payment and transmitted a share to Warren Picillo for dumping at the site demonstrates that the district court's conclusion that the Capuanos were liable as operators of the site was not clearly erroneous.

---

## QUESTIONS AND DISCUSSION

**1.** What does it mean to "operate" a facility? CERCLA's definition of "operator" is less than helpful: it simply describes an operator as "any person . . . operating a facility." 42 U.S.C. § 9601(20)(A). Is the authority to control operations sufficient? Is actual control of operations sufficient? What do you think Congress had in mind?

Operator liability often involves the details of corporate organization. The Supreme Court has held that a parent corporation can be an "operator" under CERCLA based on actions of a subsidiary corporation if the state common law rules for piercing the corporate veil are met or if the parent directly participated in the operation of the facility. United States v. Bestfoods, 524 U.S. 51 (1998). Likewise, a successor corporation—a corporation that acquires the assets of another corporation—can be an "operator" if (1) it agrees to assume liability, (2) the transaction amounts to a de facto merger, (3) the purchasing corporation continues to run the original corporation's business, or (4) the parties agreed to the transaction in a fraudulent attempt to avoid liability. *See* United States v. Mexico Feed & Seed Co., Inc., 980 F.2d 478 (8th Cir. 1992). Prior to *Bestfoods*, courts often imposed operator liability under CERCLA notwithstanding state corporate law principles in order to advance the principles of CERCLA and facilitate remediation of property. In *Bestfoods*, however, the Court stated that existing common law rules rather than CERCLA-specific rules should apply in these circumstances. As a result, courts generally no longer impose liability for parent corporations or successor corporations under CERCLA when that would go beyond general corporate law principles. *See* New York v. National Services Indus., 352 F.3d 682 (2d Cir. 2003) (holding that broader "substantial continuity" test for CERCLA liability could not be applied to successor corporation because that would impose liability beyond the common law rule under general corporate law principles).

Operator liability can also extend to individual corporate officials. Consider the court's discussion in *Shore Realty*:

> We hold LeoGrande liable as an "operator" under CERCLA, 42 U.S.C. § 9607, for the State's response costs. Under CERCLA "owner or operator" is defined to mean "any person owning or operating" an onshore facility, *id.* § 9601(20)(A), and "person" includes individuals as well as corporations, *id.* § 9601(21). More important, the definition of "owner or operator" excludes "a person, who, without participating in the management of a . . . facility, holds indicia of ownership primarily to protect his security interest in the facility." *Id.* § 9601(20)(A). The use of this exception implies that an owning stockholder who manages the corporation, such as LeoGrande, is liable under CERCLA as an "owner or operator."

> That conclusion is consistent with that of other courts that have addressed the issue. In any event, LeoGrande is in charge of the operation of the facility in question, and as such is an "operator" within the meaning of CERCLA. . . .

758 F.2d at 1052.

The scope of operator liability has reached banks, cities, individual corporate officials, insurance companies, and many others. One of the most controversial applications of operator liability occurred in United States v. Fleet Factors Corp., 901 F.2d 1550 (11th Cir. 1990), *cert. denied*, 498 U.S. 1046 (1991). CERCLA § 101(20)(A) excludes most lenders from the definition of "owner" and "operator," but it does not exclude lenders who participate in the management of a business. Thus court in *Fleet Factors* held that a lender who loaned money to a cloth printing business became an operator when the business went bankrupt and the lender foreclosed on its security interest in the business's equipment. That decision provoked a panic among banks and other lenders who feared that they could become liable for the environmentally destructive activities of their clients. Indeed, some banks feared that *Fleet Factors* created a "Catch-22" situation: banks needed to become involved in the management of failing companies in order to protect their loans, but such involvement could make them liable for environmental cleanup costs under CERCLA. In response, EPA promulgated a regulation limiting and clarifying the liability of lenders, but the D.C. Circuit overturned the regulation because EPA lacked the power to issue it. *See Kelley v. EPA*, 15 F.3d 1100 (D.C. Cir. 1994). Banks then turned to Congress to amend CERCLA to exempt them from liability, and Congress finally acted in 1996. The Asset Conservation, Lender Liability, and Deposit Insurance Protection Act exempts lenders from CERCLA liability in most instances unless they take an active role in the management of a contaminated facility. *See* 42 U.S.C. §§ 9601(20)(E) & (F).

**2.** The number of transporter cases is much smaller than the number of cases arising under the three other categories of responsible parties. Why?

A leading transporter case—Tippins Inc. v. USX Corp., 37 F.3d 87 (3d Cir. 1994), held that transporter liability attaches only if the transporter selected the site at which the hazardous substances were disposed. One writer endorsed the opposite result. *See* Alice Theresa Valder, Note, *The Erroneous Site Selection Requirement for Arranger and Transporter Liability Under CERCLA*, 91 COLUM. L. REV. 2074 (1991). What incentives would be created by imposing liability on transporters regardless of whether or not they selected the site at which the hazardous wastes are disposed?

---

As noted in the introduction to this section, in addition to owners, operators, and transporters of hazardous substances, CERCLA imposes liability upon "any person who by contract, agreement, or otherwise arranged for disposal or treatment, or arranged with a transporter for transport for disposal or treatment, of hazardous substances owned or possessed by such person, by any other party or entity, at any facility . . .

owned or operated by another party or entity and containing such hazardous substances." CERCLA § 107(a)(3). Liability under this subsection covers those parties who ship raw materials or chemicals to a facility for use in formulating or producing another chemical or product ("arranger liability") as well as those parties who generate hazardous substances at their own facility and then arrange for it to be transported to another facility for final disposal ("generator liability"). Until the Supreme Court decision reproduced below, the lower courts had generally decided arranger liability cases using two alternative tests, one imposing arranger liability if the party had the authority to control the handling and disposal of hazardous substances and the other imposing arranger liability only if the party had the obligation to exercise control rather than the authority to exercise control. *Compare* United States v. Aceto, 872 F.2d 1373 (8th Cir. 1989) (imposing arranger liability on pesticide manufacturer for cleanup costs of contamination at site of company that combined the products used in the pesticides) *with* General Electric Co. v. AAMCO Transmissions, Inc., 962 F.2d 281 (2d Cir. 1992) (refusing to impose arranger liability on oil companies for disposal of waste oil collected by the lessees of their service stations). Then in 2009, the Supreme Court weighed in on this issue.

## Burlington Northern & Santa Fe Railway Co. v. United States

Supreme Court of the United States, 2009.
556 U.S. 599.

■ JUSTICE STEVENS delivered the opinion of the Court.

In 1960, Brown & Bryant, Inc. (B & B), began operating an agricultural chemical distribution business, purchasing pesticides and other chemical products from suppliers such as Shell Oil Company (Shell). Using its own equipment, B & B applied its products to customers' farms. B & B opened its business on a 3.8 acre parcel of former farmland in Arvin, California, and in 1975, expanded operations onto an adjacent .9 acre parcel of land owned jointly by the Atchison, Topeka & Santa Fe Railway Company, and the Southern Pacific Transportation Company (now known respectively as the Burlington Northern and Santa Fe Railway Company and Union Pacific Railroad Company) (Railroads). Both parcels of the Arvin facility were graded toward a sump and drainage pond located on the southeast corner of the primary parcel. See Appendix, infra. Neither the sump nor the drainage pond was lined until 1979, allowing waste water and chemical runoff from the facility to seep into the ground water below.

During its years of operation, B & B stored and distributed various hazardous chemicals on its property. Among these were the herbicide dinoseb, sold by Dow Chemicals, and the pesticides D-D and Nemagon, both sold by Shell. Dinoseb was stored in 55-gallon drums and 5-gallon containers on a concrete slab outside B & B's warehouse. Nemagon was stored in 30-gallon drums and 5-gallon containers inside the warehouse. Originally, B & B purchased D-D in 55-gallon drums; beginning in the mid-1960's, however, Shell began requiring its distributors to maintain bulk storage facilities for D-D. From that time onward, B & B purchased D-D in bulk.

When B & B purchased D-D, Shell would arrange for delivery by common carrier, f.o.b. destination. When the product arrived, it was transferred from tanker trucks to a bulk storage tank located on B & B's primary parcel. From there, the chemical was transferred to bobtail trucks, nurse tanks, and pull rigs. During each of these transfers leaks and spills could-and often did-occur. Although the common carrier and B & B used buckets to catch spills from hoses and gaskets connecting the tanker trucks to its bulk storage tank, the buckets sometimes overflowed or were knocked over, causing D-D to spill onto the ground during the transfer process.

Aware that spills of D-D were commonplace among its distributors, in the late 1970's Shell took several steps to encourage the safe handling of its products. Shell provided distributors with detailed safety manuals and instituted a voluntary discount program for distributors that made improvements in their bulk handling and safety facilities. Later, Shell revised its program to require distributors to obtain an inspection by a qualified engineer and provide self-certification of compliance with applicable laws and regulations. B & B's Arvin facility was inspected twice, and in 1981, B & B certified to Shell that it had made a number of recommended improvements to its facilities.

Despite these improvements, B & B remained a "'[s]loppy' [o]perator." Over the course of B & B's 28 years of operation, delivery spills, equipment failures, and the rinsing of tanks and trucks allowed Nemagon, D-D and dinoseb to seep into the soil and upper levels of ground water of the Arvin facility. In 1983, the California Department of Toxic Substances Control (DTSC) began investigating B & B's violation of hazardous waste laws, and the United States Environmental Protection Agency (EPA) soon followed suit, discovering significant contamination of soil and ground water. Of particular concern was a plume of contaminated ground water located under the facility that threatened to leach into an adjacent supply of potential drinking water.

Although B & B undertook some efforts at remediation, by 1989 it had become insolvent and ceased all operations. That same year, the Arvin facility was added to the National Priority List, see 54 Fed.Reg. 41027, and subsequently, DTSC and EPA (Governments) exercised their authority under 42 U.S.C. § 9604 to undertake cleanup efforts at the site. By 1998, the Governments had spent more than $8 million responding to the site contamination; their costs have continued to accrue.

In 1991, EPA issued an administrative order to the Railroads directing them, as owners of a portion of the property on which the Arvin facility was located, to perform certain remedial tasks in connection with the site. The Railroads did so, incurring expenses of more than $3 million in the process. Seeking to recover at least a portion of their response costs, in 1992 the Railroads brought suit against B & B in the United States District Court for the Eastern District of California. In 1996, that lawsuit was consolidated with two recovery actions brought by DTSC and EPA against Shell and the Railroads.

The District Court conducted a 6-week bench trial in 1999 and four years later entered a judgment in favor of the Governments. In a lengthy order supported by 507 separate findings of fact and conclusions of law, the court held that both the Railroads and Shell were potentially responsible parties (PRPs) under CERCLA-the Railroads because they were owners of a portion of the facility, see 42 U.S.C. §§ 9607(a)(1)-(2), and Shell because it had "arranged for" the disposal of hazardous substances through its sale and delivery of D-D, see § 9607(a)(3). . . .

The Court of Appeals acknowledged that Shell did not qualify as a "traditional" arranger under § 9607(a)(3), insofar as it had not contracted with B & B to directly dispose of a hazardous waste product. 520 F.3d 918, 948 (C.A.9 2008). Nevertheless, the court stated that Shell could still be held liable under a " 'broader' category of arranger liability" if the "disposal of hazardous wastes [wa]s a foreseeable byproduct of, but not the purpose of, the transaction giving rise to" arranger liability. Relying on CERCLA's definition of "disposal," which covers acts such as "leaking" and "spilling," 42 U.S.C. § 6903(3), the Ninth Circuit concluded that an entity could arrange for "disposal" "even if it did not intend to dispose" of a hazardous substance. 520 F.3d, at 949.

Applying that theory of arranger liability to the District Court's findings of fact, the Ninth Circuit held that Shell arranged for the disposal of a hazardous substance through its sale and delivery of D-D:

> "Shell arranged for delivery of the substances to the site by its subcontractors; was aware of, and to some degree dictated, the transfer arrangements; knew that some leakage was likely in the transfer process; and provided advice and supervision concerning safe transfer and storage. Disposal of a hazardous substance was thus a necessary part of the sale and delivery process." *Id.*, at 950.

Under such circumstances, the court concluded, arranger liability was not precluded by the fact that the purpose of Shell's action had been to transport a useful and previously unused product to B & B for sale.

In these cases, it is undisputed that the Railroads qualify as PRPs under both §§ 9607(a)(1) and 9607(a)(2) because they owned the land leased by B & B at the time of the contamination and continue to own it now. The more difficult question is whether Shell also qualifies as a PRP under § 9607(a)(3) by virtue of the circumstances surrounding its sales to B & B.

To determine whether Shell may be held liable as an arranger, we begin with the language of the statute. As relevant here, § 9607(a)(3) applies to an entity that "arrange[s] for disposal . . . of hazardous substances." It is plain from the language of the statute that CERCLA liability would attach under § 9607(a)(3) if an entity were to enter into a transaction for the sole purpose of discarding a used and no longer useful hazardous substance. It is similarly clear that an entity could not be held liable as an arranger merely for selling a new and useful product if the purchaser of that product later, and unbeknownst to the seller, disposed of the product in a way that led to contamination. See Freeman v. Glaxo Wellcome, Inc., 189 F.3d 160, 164 (C.A.2 1999); Florida Power & Light Co. v. Allis Chalmers Corp., 893 F.2d 1313, 1318 (C.A.11 1990). Less clear is the liability attaching to the many permutations of "arrangements" that fall between these two extremes-cases in which the seller has some knowledge of the buyers' planned disposal or whose motives for the "sale" of a hazardous substance are less than clear. In such cases, courts have concluded that the determination whether an entity is an arranger requires a fact-intensive inquiry that looks beyond the parties' characterization of the transaction as a "disposal" or a "sale" and seeks to discern whether the arrangement was one Congress intended to fall within the scope of CERCLA's strict-liability provisions. *See* Freeman, 189 F.3d at 164; Pneumo Abex Corp. v. High Point, Thomasville & Denton R. Co., 142 F.3d 769, 775 (C.A.4 1998) ("'[T]here is no bright line between a sale and a disposal under CERCLA. A party's responsibility . . . must by necessity turn on a fact-specific inquiry into the nature of the transaction'" (quoting United States v. Petersen Sand & Gravel, 806 F. Supp. 1346, 1354 (N.D.Ill.1992))); *Florida Power & Light Co.*, 893 F.2d, at 1318.

Although we agree that the question whether § 9607(a)(3) liability attaches is fact intensive and case specific, such liability may not extend beyond the limits of the statute itself. Because CERCLA does not specifically define what it means to "arrang[e] for" disposal of a hazardous substance, we give the phrase its ordinary meaning. In common parlance, the word "arrange" implies action directed to a specific purpose. See Merriam-Webster's Collegiate Dictionary 64 (10th ed.1993) (defining "arrange" as "to make preparations for: plan[;] . . . to bring about an agreement or understanding concerning"). Consequently, under the plain language of the statute, an entity may qualify as an arranger under § 9607(a)(3) when it takes intentional steps to dispose of a hazardous substance.

The Governments do not deny that the statute requires an entity to "arrang[e] for" disposal; however, they interpret that phrase by reference to the statutory term "disposal," which the Act broadly defines as "the discharge, deposit, injection, dumping, spilling, leaking, or placing of any solid waste or hazardous waste into or on any land or water." 42 U.S.C. § 6903(3); see also § 9601(29) (adopting the definition of "disposal" contained in the Solid Waste Disposal Act). The Governments assert that by including unintentional acts such as "spilling" and "leaking" in the definition of disposal, Congress intended to impose liability on entities not only when they directly dispose of waste products but also when they engage in legitimate sales of hazardous substances knowing that some disposal may occur as a collateral consequence of the sale itself. Applying that reading of the statute, the Governments contend that Shell arranged for the disposal of D-D within the meaning of § 9607(a)(3) by shipping D-D to B & B under conditions it knew would result in the spilling of a portion of the hazardous substance by the purchaser or common carrier. See Brief for United States 24 ("Although the delivery of a useful product was the ultimate purpose of the arrangement, Shell's continued participation in the delivery, with knowledge that spills and leaks would result, was sufficient to establish Shell's intent to dispose of hazardous substances"). Because these spills resulted in wasted D-D, a result Shell anticipated, the Governments insist that Shell was properly found to have arranged for the disposal of D-D.

While it is true that in some instances an entity's knowledge that its product will be leaked, spilled, dumped, or otherwise discarded may provide evidence of the entity's intent to dispose of its hazardous wastes, knowledge alone is insufficient to prove that an entity "planned for" the disposal, particularly when the disposal occurs as a peripheral result of the legitimate sale of an unused, useful product. In order to qualify as an arranger, Shell must have entered into the sale of D-D with the intention that at least a portion of the product be disposed of during the transfer process by one or more of the methods described in § 6903(3). Here, the facts found by the District Court do not support such a conclusion.

Although the evidence adduced at trial showed that Shell was aware that minor, accidental spills occurred during the transfer of D-D from the common carrier to B & B's bulk storage tanks after the product had arrived at the Arvin facility and had come under B & B's stewardship, the evidence does not support an inference that Shell intended such spills to occur. To the contrary, the evidence revealed that Shell took numerous steps to encourage its distributors to reduce the likelihood of such spills, providing them with detailed safety manuals, requiring them to maintain adequate storage facilities, and providing discounts for those that took safety precautions. Although Shell's efforts were less than wholly successful, given these facts, Shell's mere knowledge that spills and leaks continued to occur is insufficient grounds for concluding that Shell "arranged for" the disposal of D-D within the meaning of § 9607(a)(3). Accordingly, we conclude that Shell was not liable as an arranger for the contamination that occurred at B & B's Arvin facility.

---

## QUESTIONS AND DISCUSSION

**1.** The *Burlington Northern* case involves the type of "arranger liability" that arises when one company ships raw products to another company for storage or use in connection with the creation of new products and releases of hazardous substances occur in the storage or formulation process. The other type of more obvious "arranger" subject to CERCLA liability is a generator of waste who then "arranges" for its final disposal. Generator liability had no counterpart in the common law when Congress enacted CERCLA in 1980. Since then, a few courts have imposed tort liability on generators of hazardous substances based on abnormally dangerous activities and nuisance theories. *See, e.g.*, Kenney v. Scientific, Inc., 497 A.2d 1310, 1320–21 (N.J. Super. 1985) (opining that "[a] company which creates the Frankenstein monster of abnormally dangerous waste should not expect to be relieved of accountability for the depredations of its creature merely because the company entrusts the monster's care to another"). Why would Congress impose liability on those who generate hazardous substances, and not just on those who dispose of hazardous substances?

**2.** Congress amended CERCLA in 1999 and 2002 to exempt certain generators of hazardous substances from arranger liability. CERCLA now contains exemptions for "de micromis" generators or transporters who contributed or transported less than 110 gallons of liquid material or 200 pounds of solid materials to a facility (CERCLA § 107(*o*)), for certain homeowners and small businesses that generate municipal solid waste (CERCLA § 107(p)), and for arrangers and transporters of recyclable materials (CERCLA § 127(b)).

**3.** Since the *Burlington Northern* decision, lower courts have had to grapple with which types of activities, relationships, and knowledge trigger arranger liability status. *See, e.g.,* U.S. v. General Elec. Co., 670 F.3d 377 (1st Cir. 2012) (General Electric was liable as an arranger for sending waste to a chemical scrapper who improperly disposed of the waste because General Electric considered the chemical to be a waste product rather than a useful product); Pakootas v. Teck Comico Metals, Ltd., 2012 WL 370105 (E.D. Wash., Feb. 3, 2012) (contract between mining company and State of Washington to mine ore on state lands that resulted in contamination did not make the state an arranger because no intent to dispose of hazardous substances); Vine St. LLC v. Borg Warner Corp., 776 F.3d 312 (5th Cir. 2015) (no arranger liability for company's sale of tetrachloroethene (PERC) to a dry cleaning business that used the PERC in its operations and also discharged PERC to the storm sewer resulting in contamination because the sale was of a useful, expensive product in a legitimate transaction with no evidence of intent to dispose of the PERC); Consolidated Coal Co. v. Georgia Power Co., 781 F.3d 129 (4th Cir. 2015) (electric utilities' sale of used transformers containing PCBs at auction that resulted in PCB spills by purchasing company did not constitute arranger liability no evidence to show the utilities auctioned the transformers intending to dispose of the PCBs); Nu West Mining v. U.S., 768 F. Supp. 2d 1082 (D. Idaho 2011) (federal government liable as an arranger due to management of mining leases on federally-owned land because government had authority to control or did control disposal of hazardous substances).

---

## 2. ALLOCATING LIABILITY AMONG RESPONSIBLE PARTIES

Multiple parties may qualify as responsible parties at any given CERCLA site. Indeed, some cases involve hundreds or even more than 1,000 potentially responsible parties. CERCLA liability has long been understood to be joint and several, so any one of those parties can be required to pay all of the cleanup costs at a site, or at least costs far out of proportion to the extent of the party's actual involvement in the contamination. That occurs more frequently than you might expect because of the many entities that become insolvent or disappear in the decades that can pass between the contamination of a site and the effort to clean it up. In many cases, though, there are a number of responsible parties who could pay for the cleanup costs, so CERCLA includes a procedure for determining how much each party should pay. The Supreme Court's 2009 *Burlington Northern* case reproduced above also addressed the issue of divisibility and allocation, as shown below.

### Burlington Northern and Santa Fe Railway Co. v. United States

Supreme Court of the United States, 2009.
556 U.S. 599.

[For a discussion of the facts of this case, see the earlier reproduction of this decision in this chapter]

We must [now] determine whether the Railroads were properly held jointly and severally liable for the full cost of the Governments' response efforts.

The seminal opinion on the subject of apportionment in CERCLA actions was written in 1983 by Chief Judge Carl Rubin of the United States District Court for the Southern District of Ohio. United States v. Chem-Dyne Corp., 572 F. Supp. 802. After reviewing CERCLA's history, Chief Judge Rubin concluded that although the Act imposed a "strict liability standard," it did not mandate "joint and several" liability in every case. Rather, Congress intended the scope of liability to "be determined from traditional and evolving principles of common law[.]" The Chem-Dyne approach has been fully embraced by the Courts of Appeals. See, e.g., In re Bell Petroleum Services, Inc., 3 F.3d 889, 901–902 (C.A.5 1993); United States v. Alcan Aluminum Corp., 964 F.2d 252, 268 (C.A.3 1992); O'Neil v. Picillo, 883 F.2d 176, 178 (C.A.1 1989); United States v. Monsanto Co., 858 F.2d 160, 171–173 (C.A.4 1988).

Following Chem-Dyne, the courts of appeals have acknowledged that "[t]he universal starting point for divisibility of harm analyses in

CERCLA cases" is § 433A of the Restatement (Second) of Torts. United States v. Hercules, Inc., 247 F.3d 706, 717 (C.A.8 2001); Chem-Nuclear Systems, Inc. v. Bush, 292 F.3d 254, 259 (C.A.D.C.2002); United States v. R.W. Meyer, Inc., 889 F.2d 1497, 1507 (C.A.6 1989). Under the Restatement,

> "when two or more persons acting independently caus[e] a distinct or single harm for which there is a reasonable basis for division according to the contribution of each, each is subject to liability only for the portion of the total harm that he has himself caused. Restatement (Second) of Torts, §§ 433A, 881 (1976); Prosser, Law of Torts, pp. 313–314 (4th ed.1971). . . . But where two or more persons cause a single and indivisible harm, each is subject to liability for the entire harm. Restatement (Second) of Torts, § 875; Prosser, at 315–316." Chem-Dyne Corp., 572 F. Supp., at 810.

In other words, apportionment is proper when "there is a reasonable basis for determining the contribution of each cause to a single harm." Restatement (Second) of Torts § 433A(1)(b), p. 434 (1963–1964).

Not all harms are capable of apportionment, however, and CERCLA defendants seeking to avoid joint and several liability bear the burden of proving that a reasonable basis for apportionment exists. See Chem-Dyne Corp., 572 F. Supp., at 810 (citing Restatement (Second) of Torts § 433B (1976)) (placing burden of proof on party seeking apportionment). When two or more causes produce a single, indivisible harm, "courts have refused to make an arbitrary apportionment for its own sake, and each of the causes is charged with responsibility for the entire harm." Restatement (Second) of Torts § 433A, Comment i, p. 440 (1963–1964).

Neither the parties nor the lower courts dispute the principles that govern apportionment in CERCLA cases, and both the District Court and Court of Appeals agreed that the harm created by the contamination of the Arvin site, although singular, was theoretically capable of apportionment. The question then is whether the record provided a reasonable basis for the District Court's conclusion that the Railroads were liable for only 9% of the harm caused by contamination at the Arvin facility.

The District Court criticized the Railroads for taking a " 'scorched earth,' all-or-nothing approach to liability," failing to acknowledge any responsibility for the release of hazardous substances that occurred on their parcel throughout the 13-year period of B & B's lease. According to the District Court, the Railroads' position on liability, combined with the Governments' refusal to acknowledge the potential divisibility of the harm, complicated the apportioning of liability. Yet despite the parties' failure to assist the court in linking the evidence supporting apportionment to the proper allocation of liability, the District Court ultimately concluded that this was "a classic 'divisible in terms of degree' case, both as to the time period in which defendants' conduct occurred, and ownership existed, and as to the estimated maximum contribution of each party's activities that released hazardous substances that caused Site contamination." Consequently, the District Court apportioned liability, assigning the Railroads 9% of the total remediation costs.

The District Court calculated the Railroads' liability based on three figures. First, the court noted that the Railroad parcel constituted only 19% of the surface area of the Arvin site. Second, the court observed that the Railroads had leased their parcel to B & B for 13 years, which was only 45% of the time B & B operated the Arvin facility. Finally, the court found that the volume of hazardous-substance-releasing activities on the B & B property was at least 10 times greater than the releases that occurred on the Railroad parcel, and it concluded that only spills of two chemicals, Nemagon and dinoseb (not D-D), substantially contributed to the contamination that had originated on the Railroad parcel and that those two chemicals had contributed to two-thirds of the overall site contamination requiring remediation. The court then multiplied .19 by .45 by .66 (two-thirds) and rounded up to determine that the Railroads were responsible for approximately 6% of the remediation costs. "Allowing for calculation errors up to 50%," the court concluded that the Railroads could be held responsible for 9% of the total CERCLA response cost for the Arvin site.

The Court of Appeals criticized the evidence on which the District Court's conclusions rested, finding a lack of sufficient data to establish the precise proportion of contamination that occurred on the relative portions of the Arvin facility and the rate of contamination in the years prior to B & B's addition of the Railroad parcel. The court noted that neither the duration of the lease nor the size of the leased area alone was a reliable measure of the harm caused by activities on the property owned by the Railroads, and-as the court's upward adjustment confirmed-the court had relied on estimates rather than specific and detailed records as a basis for its conclusions.

Despite these criticisms, we conclude that the facts contained in the record reasonably supported the apportionment of liability. The District Court's detailed findings make it abundantly clear that the primary pollution at the Arvin facility was contained in an unlined sump and an unlined pond in the southeastern portion of the facility most distant from the Railroads' parcel and that the spills of hazardous chemicals that occurred on the Railroad parcel contributed to no more than 10% of the total site contamination, some of which did not require remediation. With those background facts in mind, we are persuaded that it was reasonable for the court to use the size of the leased parcel and the duration of the lease as the starting point for its analysis. Although the Court of Appeals faulted the District Court for relying on the "simplest of considerations: percentages of land area, time of ownership, and types of hazardous products," these were the same factors the court had earlier acknowledged were relevant to the apportionment analysis. See id., at

936, n. 18 ("We of course agree with our sister circuits that, if adequate information is available, divisibility may be established by 'volumetric, chronological, or other types of evidence,' including appropriate geographic considerations" (citations omitted)).

The Court of Appeals also criticized the District Court's assumption that spills of Nemagon and dinoseb were responsible for only two-thirds of the chemical spills requiring remediation, observing that each PRP's share of the total harm was not necessarily equal to the quantity of pollutants that were deposited on its portion of the total facility. Although the evidence adduced by the parties did not allow the court to calculate precisely the amount of hazardous chemicals contributed by the Railroad parcel to the total site contamination or the exact percentage of harm caused by each chemical, the evidence did show that fewer spills occurred on the Railroad parcel and that of those spills that occurred, not all were carried across the Railroad parcel to the B & B sump and pond from which most of the contamination originated. The fact that no D-D spills on the Railroad parcel required remediation lends strength to the District Court's conclusion that the Railroad parcel contributed only Nemagon and dinoseb in quantities requiring remediation.

The District Court's conclusion that those two chemicals accounted for only two-thirds of the contamination requiring remediation finds less support in the record; however, any miscalculation on that point is harmless in light of the District Court's ultimate allocation of liability, which included a 50% margin of error equal to the 3% reduction in liability the District Court provided based on its assessment of the effect of the Nemagon and dinoseb spills. Had the District Court limited its apportionment calculations to the amount of time the Railroad parcel was in use and the percentage of the facility located on that parcel, it would have assigned the Railroads 9% of the response cost. By including a two-thirds reduction in liability for the Nemagon and dinoseb with a 50% "margin of error," the District Court reached the same result. Because the District Court's ultimate allocation of liability is supported by the evidence and comports with the apportionment principles outlined above, we reverse the Court of Appeals' conclusion that the Railroads are subject to joint and several liability for all response costs arising out of the contamination of the Arvin facility.

---

## QUESTIONS AND DISCUSSION

**1.** Prior to the Supreme Court's decision in *Burlington Northern*, it was very difficult for responsible parties to establish divisibility of harm and avoid joint and several liability. In these multi-party site cases, even when defendants argued that the harm caused was divisible, courts tended to accept EPA's (or other plaintiffs') arguments that the commingling of wastes rendered the harm indivisible. The significance of this issue for plaintiffs is that a finding of divisibility makes it much more difficult to recover all the response costs associated with a cleanup. In the absence of joint and several liability each responsible party is only responsible for the amount of harm the court allocates to it and the plaintiff (often the government), not the remaining defendants, will be responsible for any "orphan shares" associated with nonexistent or bankrupt responsible parties. As a policy matter, should the burden of "orphan shares" at a site be placed with the plaintiff or with the solvent defendants?

**2.** It is still too early to tell how much more receptive the lower courts will be to divisibility arguments as a result of *Burlington Northern* because, as the case itself illustrates, divisibility is such a fact-intensive inquiry. What is clear though, is that *Burlington Northern* provides defendants with more leverage to argue divisibility than prior to the case, even though there does not seem to be a groundswell of courts accepting divisibility arguments to date. *See, e.g.*, PCS Nitrogen, Inc. v. Ashley II of Charleston LLC, 714 F.3d 161 (4th Cir. 2013) (affirming district court's imposition of joint and several liability and finding no reasonable basis for apportioning harm despite defendant's presentation of evidence on divisibility based on volume of fill, years of operation, contaminant volume, and contaminated area); ITT Industries, Inc. v. Borgawarner, Inc., 700 F. Supp. 2d 848 (W.D. Mich. 2010) (court analyzed divisibility under *Burlington Northern* but found insufficient basis for divisibility); Board of County Commissioners of La Plata, Colorado v. Brown Retail Group, Inc., 768 F. Supp. 2d 1092 (D. Colo. 2011).

**3.** How should liability be allocated among a current owner and a generator? Between a transporter and a past operator? Between multiple parties in each category?

**4.** CERCLA § 113(f) authorizes a defendant who is found liable for response costs to seek contribution from other responsible parties. Section 113(f) provides that "[i]n resolving contribution claims, the court may allocate response costs among liable parties using such equitable factors as the court determines are appropriate." Thus, in cases where a court does impose joint and several liability, the issue then becomes how to apportion liability among those jointly and severally liable parties who will all have asserted claims against each other under Section 113(f). Many courts in these instances use what are known as the "Gore Factors" (because they were proposed by then-Representative Albert Gore as part of the SARA amendments) to apportion liability in an equitable fashion among the responsible parties before the court. The factors are (1) a responsible party's ability to demonstrate that its contribution to the harm at the site can be distinguished from other responsible parties; (2) the amount of hazardous waste attributable to the responsible party; (3) the toxicity of the waste; (4) the responsible party's involvement in the generation, transportation, treatment, storage, or disposal of the waste; (5) the degree of care the responsible party exercised with respect to the waste; and (6) the extent to which the responsible party cooperated with government officials in preventing further harm. In Control Data Corp. v. S.C.S.C. Corp., 53 F.3d 930 (8th Cir. 1995), the Eighth Circuit relied on the Gore factors to allocate response costs among several responsible parties, taking into account with regard to each party the volume of the waste contributed, the toxicity of the waste, and the party's response to learning of the existence of the waste and the need for remediation. In addition to the Gore factors, courts have considered the financial resources of the parties involved, the benefits the parties received from their activities, the knowledge of the parties of the contaminating activities, and other factors in deciding how to allocate liability. But sometimes a court will only consider one or two factors when allocating liability. In ASARCO, Inc. v. Mosher Steel of Kansas, Inc., 100 F.3d 792, 802–03 (10th Cir. 1996), the court upheld an allocation of liability that considered only the toxicity and volume of hazardous waste at a site. Why would a court focus on those two factors alone? The relationship between contribution actions under Section 113(f) and directly suing for response costs under Section 107 is discussed in more detail later in this chapter.

———

### 3. GOVERNMENT LIABILITY

## Cadillac Fairview/California, Inc. v. Dow Chemical Company

United States Court of Appeals for the Ninth Circuit, 2002.
299 F.3d 1019.

■ KLEINFELD, CIRCUIT JUDGE:

This is a CERCLA dispute about whether the federal government can make a company that discharged pollutants into the soil at the government's direction and under its control during World War II, in a war production plant, pay part of the cost of cleaning them up.

In 1942, the Japanese had conquered almost all of the world's major natural rubber-producing areas in Southeast Asia. The Germans had perfected a synthetic rubber substitute, Buna-S, which they were manufacturing as quickly as possible at several plants, including the I.G. Farben plant in Auschwitz that used Jewish slaves. American manufacture had been retarded by the Depression, which reduced demand for rubber, and by a cooperative research agreement Standard Oil had made with I.G. Farben in 1927, during the Weimar period. As a result of the rubber shortage, tires had to be strictly rationed in the United States to preserve rubber for such myriad military uses as truck and aircraft tires and tubes, tank treads, equipment hoses and belts, footwear, medical supplies, life rafts, flotation equipment, barrage balloons, waterproof equipment, landing boats, gas masks and wire insulation.

The war was not going well in 1942, until the Battle of Midway in June. Germany had conquered continental Europe, and Japan had conquered much of the Pacific. Japan invaded and occupied part of the United States, the Attu and Kiska islands in Alaska, from June of 1942 until the terrible Battle of Attu in May of 1943, which took a commitment of 100,000 men and cost 3,829 casualties just in the landing force. Then-Senator Truman chaired hearings on why our country was unprepared to meet its critical need for rubber. President Roosevelt established a committee of three, Bernard Baruch as chairman, along with the presidents of Harvard and M.I.T., to investigate and "recommend such action as will produce the rubber necessary for our total war effort." The Baruch Committee reported that 90% of our prewar sources of natural rubber had been lost to Japan, and we had no substantial synthetic rubber industry. "Of all critical and strategic materials, rubber is the one which presents the greatest threat to the safety of our nation and the success of the Allied cause. . . . If we fail to secure quickly a large new rubber supply our war effort and our domestic economy both will collapse." Baruch told industry representatives that the rubber program would be their job, and that "the bottleneck of the whole program would certainly be butadiene." Pursuant to this need for synthetic rubber, the government took steps to create, overnight, an industry to produce it. Acting through a series of agencies (referred to here as the "Rubber Reserve"), the government entered into agreements to finance and retain ownership of manufacturing facilities, which private companies would lease from the government and operate in exchange for management fees and royalties. The Rubber Reserve would pay all operating expenses. The companies would provide knowledge, management and use of their patents. The planning emphasized production of Buna-S synthetic rubber. Buna-S was made by attaching (or "polymerizing") molecules of butadiene (made from grain alcohol or petroleum) and styrene (made from ethylene and benzene). Dow Chemical was especially important to the war effort, as it was the only commercial producer of styrene, and therefore the only company able to provide practical experience with styrene production. . . .

This case arises out of a facility in Torrance, California, one of the most important synthetic rubber facilities at the time. Constructed in 1942, the 280-acre facility contained two rubber copolymerization plants (operated by Goodyear and the U.S. Rubber Co. (now Uniroyal), the "Rubber Companies"), a butadiene plant operated by Shell Oil, and a styrene plant operated by Dow Chemical.

In the terminology then used, the Torrance styrene plant was an "agent plant"—not a "contract plant." This meant that Dow agreed to operate the government-owned styrene plant as the "agent" of the United States and "at the expense and risk" of the United States. Dow built the facility, but the Rubber Reserve coordinated all phases of construction and made, approved, or ratified all significant operating decisions. The government owned the land; the government owned the plant; the government owned the raw materials; the government owned the byproducts and wastes; and the government owned the rubber. All activities at the site were subject to unrestricted control by the Rubber Reserve. Dow, as the company with the most expertise managing the facility, was required by its contract with the government to "carry out the orders, instructions, and specifications of Rubber Reserve." The government required monthly reports from Dow that included the volume of residues dumped. Under its contract with the government, Dow was entitled to reimbursement for the expense of waste disposal, so it had no financial incentive to use a cheap but dirty method rather than a clean but expensive method.

The production of rubber created toxic waste. Dow built evaporation ponds for aqueous wastes, such as aluminum chloride sludge, and dug pits for other wastes, such as sulfur and aluminum chloride tars. The government and Dow knew they were polluting the soil and, on account of runoff, the water, but the government made a policy decision not to divert scarce resources from the war effort to stop the pollution. As one government consultant reported:

> During this period, it was recognized that some raw and partially processed materials were lost into waste waters leaving the plants, and that some of these substances were causing a stream pollution problem. However, personnel could not be diverted from more pressing objectives to study the complex problems related to waste prevention or treatment—nor could construction materials be secured for such purposes.

Dow subsequently developed better ways to dispose of the waste and closed the disposal pits in 1947.

As part of the operating agreement entered into in 1942, the government signed a broad "hold harmless" agreement, protecting Dow Chemical from any liability to anyone for any damages to property:

> It is understood that in the performance of [these] contracts, [Dow] shall in no event be liable for, but shall be held harmless by [the United States] against, any damage to or loss or destruction of property (whether owned by [the United States] or others) or any injury to or death of persons, in any manner, arising out of or in connection with the work hereunder. . . .

After the war, in 1948, the operating agreement, with this broad hold harmless clause, was renewed. The Rubber Reserve interpreted this hold harmless agreement in its manual to indemnify Dow for any losses for which the United States would not reimburse Dow for the cost of insurance coverage. During the War, the Rubber Reserve paid a claim for deaths and illnesses of numerous cows from pollution from the plant, based on its interpretation of its obligation to pay pollution damages under its contract with Dow. The government participated in the decision about how to dispose of the sulfur tars, the byproduct of Buna-S production, and, with unrestricted control over what was done, decided that disposal in pits was the best way to do it. Government inspectors and consultants studied Dow's sulfur sludge pits at the Torrance plant and approved them.

Dow operated the facility until 1955, when the Rubber Reserve sold the Torrance facility to Shell Oil. Shell made synthetic rubber there until 1972, when it sold the site. Eventually ownership passed to a developer, Cadillac Fairview/California, Inc. Most of the plants were demolished, and the site is currently occupied by commercial and industrial facilities.

In 1980, 35 years after the war ended and eight years after rubber production ended, Congress enacted the Comprehensive Environmental Response, Compensation, and Liability Act (CERCLA). Under CERCLA, the Environmental Protection Agency (EPA) has broad authority to provide for remediation of sites contaminated by hazardous waste by conducting the cleanup itself or requiring liable parties to do so. Regardless of who performs the cleanup, financial liability lies with the parties responsible for the contamination. CERCLA allows any responsible party to seek contribution from other responsible parties and allows the district court to equitably apportion cleanup costs among liable parties.

In 1983, Cadillac Fairview/California, the developer that bought the site at issue here, sued Dow Chemical, the United States, Shell Oil, and several rubber companies for damages to cover the expenses of investigating the soil pollution, and for an injunction and declaratory judgment. The United States crossclaimed against Dow and the other companies. Dow counterclaimed for indemnity and contribution under CERCLA. The United States settled with the mesne owners after it sold the property and before Cadillac Fairview bought it.

This complex litigation has come before us twice before. We held, in 1988, that Cadillac Fairview did indeed state a claim upon which damages and injunctive relief could be granted, against an argument from the defendants that government action had to precede a private action, though we rejected the owner's claim to injunctive relief.[11]

In 1994, the litigation came before us again. Dow Chemical crossclaimed for contribution against the Rubber Companies that made the rubber at the site and pumped contaminated styrene to Dow for distilling to separate out the reusable chemicals from the waste that Dow dumped into the pits. The Rubber Companies had won summary judgment on the ground that they could not [be liable for having] "arranged for . . . treatment" under CERCLA,[12] because they neither owned nor controlled the contaminated styrene—the government did. We held that the statute provided for "arranger" liability independently of ownership and that we had upheld liability against an arranger that did not control the process leading to the pollution, so a trier of fact could conclude that the Rubber Companies were "arrangers," and remanded.

---

[11] Cadillac Fairview/Cal., Inc. v. Dow Chem. Co., 840 F.2d 691 (9th Cir. 1988).

[12] Cadillac Fairview/Cal., Inc. v. United States, 41 F.3d 562, 564 (9th Cir. 1994) (per curiam) (quoting 42 U.S.C. § 9607(a)(3)).

On remand, the district court granted partial summary judgment against Dow on the theory that it was an "operator" that could be liable for contribution under CERCLA. It then tried the issue of whether the United States, as well as the Rubber Companies, was also liable under CERCLA and how remedial costs should be allocated under Section 113(f) of CERCLA among Dow, the Rubber Companies, and the United States. The trial resulted in findings of fact and conclusions of law, and a judgment that the United States should bear 100% of the remediation expense.

The district court found that "the United States was informed and approved" of dumping the toxic tars into the pits and that its engineers "reviewed and approved" the dumping of the aqueous wastes into the sludge ponds, having been "fully informed during plant operations." The court found that because of the emergency conditions imposed by the War, the Rubber Reserve "made, approved or ratified all significant operating decisions." It obtained monthly reports on residues dumped, "directed and coordinated the operations of the plants," and "set policy on questions of trade waste disposal." Production (and consequent waste) was "in quantities directed by the Rubber Reserve." The Rubber Reserve in some respects (although not with regard to waste disposal) ordered changes in production techniques over Dow's recommendations to the contrary. The Executive Vice President of the Rubber Reserve had visited the Torrance plant and recommended disposing of wastes by getting them under the ground. "The United States was the ultimate authority over plant operations and was aware of, and acquiesced or actively participated in, the decisions concerning waste systems, including operation of the Pits and Ponds." Rubber Reserve officials had full and extensive knowledge of the waste pits and ponds, because they repeatedly inspected them and hired technical experts to advise the government on them. The waste disposal methods were "consistent with the state of knowledge and accepted industry practices of the time," and the only alternative at the time, burning the waste, was both impractical and more polluting. During and immediately after the War, when the pits were used for disposal, the government's contract with Dow prohibited Dow even from withdrawing from its arrangement with the government.

The district court held that the United States was liable for contribution as an owner, operator and arranger, and the Rubber Companies, Uniroyal and Goodyear, as arrangers. Although it did not enforce the government's hold harmless agreement as such, out of concern that under the Tucker Act only the Claims Court had jurisdiction to do so, it took the contract into account as an equitable factor under the CERCLA § 113 requirement that it "allocate response costs using such equitable factors as the court determines are appropriate." The court took into account that Dow and the Rubber Companies acted pursuant to agreements that made them "agents" of the United States acting at the "risk and account" of the Rubber Reserve. Their handling of the wastes as "agents" whose acts were subject to the control of and were ratified by the United States would, as a matter of agency law, also entitle them to indemnity.

The district court rejected the government's argument that it should consider the benefits to the Rubber Companies of their participation, because the evidence was weak and such benefits as they might have obtained were overwhelmed by the benefits to the United States. And it rejected the government's proposed conclusion suggesting an equal division of responsibility with Dow. The district court concluded that "equity requires that 100% of the recoverable remedial costs incurred or to be incurred with respect to the Del Amo Pit Site by the United States, Dow and the Rubber Companies should be paid by the United States."

The United States appeals this allocation.

Under Section 113 of CERCLA, the district court "may allocate response costs among liable parties using such equitable factors as the court determines are appropriate." Thus, CERCLA "gives district courts discretion to decide what factors ought to be considered, as well as the duty to allocate costs according to those factors. We reverse only for an abuse of the discretion to select factors, or for clear error in the allocation according to those factors." In this case, after close scrutiny of the record, we conclude that there was no such abuse of discretion or clear error, and we affirm.

The government's first argument is that because Dow actually dug the pits after deciding where to dig them, transported the waste to the pits, deposited the waste in the pits, and maintained security at the pits, all without any direct federal orders or supervision telling Dow to do so, it should have been held liable for at least some portion of the cleanup costs.

Of course the government is correct that Dow actually disposed of the waste and exercised some discretion in how it did so. Its management expertise was the reason why the government used Dow to operate the plant instead of operating it itself. But, as the district court found, the government owned the site, the pits, the plant, and all materials including the wastes, knew just what Dow was doing, had unfettered control over it, approved of it, had an agency relationship with Dow that would ordinarily require it to indemnify Dow for what it did, and had made an express written promise to hold Dow harmless for whatever it did. On these facts (and allocation cases generally turn on their facts), there was no inequity in allocating 100% of the costs to the government. Indeed, where the government promises to hold a firm harmless for what it did, and then seeks to impose harm on the firm, highly unusual facts would be required to justify what would ordinarily be a gross inequity. In another war pollution case, *United States v. Shell Oil Co.*, we affirmed a 100% allocation upon the United States for cleanup costs of wastes where private firms actually created the wastes and deposited them in the ground. To the extent that the case at bar is factually distinguishable, the distinctions make it an even more compelling one for such a 100% allocation.

The government next argues that the district court abused its discretion by deciding to give no weight to the benefits to Dow from its operation of the plant. The benefits to which the government points are reimbursement of expenses, management fees, and acquisition of knowledge and experience useful in subsequent endeavors, particularly Dow's post-war expansion into the plastics industry. Dow correctly points out that the evidence showed it shared its patents for amounts well below market rates, accepted a far below market management fee, and lost much of the benefit it might have realized when the government sold the plant to Shell Oil instead of Dow after the war. Reimbursement is, of course, no benefit at all, merely a squaring up. For example, it is not a benefit or additional compensation when the government reimburses the government's attorneys for their expense in traveling to court to argue this case.

The district court considered whether to weigh benefit to Dow as a factor and articulated a reasoned basis for disregarding it: "First, the evidence proffered by the United States to support this argument was in the main speculative, and, second, in the context of this case, the benefits to the United States clearly overwhelmed in magnitude those to Dow and the Rubber Companies." We could not substitute our judgment, even if it were different, because our review is limited to considering whether the district court abused its discretion, and in light of the reasons given, and the other reasons for the 100% allocation, it plainly did not.

The government argues that the district court clearly erred in finding the government control was as great as the findings of fact say. It characterizes its role as indirect, mostly involving setting production quotas and quality standards while letting Dow run the plant on a day to day basis, and it compares itself to a landlord whose tenant pollutes the leased property. We have carefully reviewed the record and cannot agree factually with that characterization. The government wanted Dow's management expertise as part of the deal, and it used it, but it retained full authority to control whatever it wished, and carefully and repeatedly reviewed how Dow disposed of the wastes with full authority to direct whatever different methods it might choose. In other matters, it did order Dow to deviate from the course of action Dow thought better, and Dow followed government orders. As for whatever details the government might not have known, that was only on account of its decision to use Dow's expertise and not spend government inspectors' and consultants' time finding out what Dow already knew. Dow's role was more nearly analogous to a soldier's than to a commercial tenant's.

We have carefully examined the record, and ascertained that the district court did not err in any of its factual findings regarding the government's knowledge and control.

Although the government had promised to hold Dow harmless, the government argues that its promise ought to have been disregarded by the district court in making the allocation. The hold harmless agreement said that Dow would

> in no event be liable for, but shall be held harmless by [the United States] against, any damage to or loss or destruction of property . . . or any injury to or death of persons, in any manner, arising out of or in connection with the work hereunder. . . .

. . . The government also argues that the indemnity agreement did not cover CERCLA costs, because, despite its broad language, the parties could not have contemplated that it would cover CERCLA costs, and the "damage to property" clause was not so broad as "any liability whatsoever" language would have been.

Because the district court did not grant judgment on a contract claim, we need not decide whether, had it done so, the contract would have embraced the damages for which it granted judgment. Obviously, the parties could not have contemplated, when they entered into the operating agreement, that decades later Congress would pass a law like CERCLA. Equally obviously, had CERCLA already been in effect, lawyers for such sophisticated corporations as those the government recruited for this war work would have recommended that their clients obtain language protecting them from CERCLA liability.

But none of this speculation matters, because the contract was considered as an equitable factor, and the sole basis for the judgment was allocation under Section 113(f) of CERCLA. There was no recovery on the contract, so its precise scope is immaterial. The district court did not abuse its discretion by considering the contract as evidence of the parties' mutual intent that the work done on the government's property, with government materials, producing rubber that the government at all times owned, and waste that at all times the government owned, which was disposed of in ways the government approved, subject to the unlimited control of the government and regular review and supervision of the government, as an agent for the government, be done entirely at the government's expense and risk.

The government's next argument is that the Rubber Reserve acted ultra vires, because under the Anti-Deficiency Act, it lacked authority to commit the government to holding Dow harmless. That statute prohibits government officials from obligating the government "on any contract 'for the payment of money' before an appropriation is made unless [the contract is] authorized by law." This argument is without force, because the agreement with Dow, including the hold harmless language, was authorized by law, namely the emergency powers Congress gave the President, and the regulations issued by the executive branch, for the prosecution of the war. The War Powers Act authorized the President to authorize agencies to make contracts "without regard to the provisions of law" such as the Anti-Deficiency Act, "whenever he deemed such action would facilitate the prosecution of the war." The president exercised this authority in an executive order particularly directed to the Rubber Reserve.

What's more, this is a red herring. Even if there were a serious question about whether the Rubber Reserve acted ultra vires in making the contract with Dow, it would make no difference, because in this case the contract was not enforced. It was merely considered as a factor in the equitable allocation of response costs.

This is a shocking case. The government is trying to take money from firms it conscripted for a critical part of a great war effort. The government's arguments are strikingly weak. The pollution occurred almost six decades ago. The polluting conduct was completely under the direction of the government, it was legal at the time, and the government promised to hold the polluters, who acted as government agents, harmless. The government decided at the time that polluting the land and water this way was preferable to diverting resources from the war effort to do anything about it. Now the government wants its servants to pay for what it told them to do and promised them they could do with no fear of liability.

This is the third World War II case of which we are aware, in the Circuit Courts, in which the government has lost its claim against its servants in the war effort. The Third Circuit said in *FMC Corp. v. U.S. Dep't of Commerce* that placing "a cost of war on the United States, and thus on society as a whole, [constitutes] a result which is neither untoward nor inconsistent with the policy underlying CERCLA." In *Shell*, we said that "the cleanup costs are properly seen as part of the war effort for which the American public as a whole should pay."

During oral argument we posed a hypothetical question to government counsel: Why wouldn't your argument require that the soldiers who fought the Japanese in the Aleutians be liable to pay part of the cleanup costs for the lead from their bullets that pollutes the ground on those islands? The government knew the question was coming, because the same hypothetical case was mentioned in the dissent in our 1998 decision. The government's response was that, "as a theoretical matter, they could be liable" for the lead pollution, but that the district court would not be likely to allocate costs to them because of the equities. Indeed not. Yet the government challenges such an allocation here and, evidently, would leave the soldiers to prosecutorial discretion. Reliance on prosecutorial discretion seems like an undue risk to those aged Aleutian campaign veterans and their widows and estates. It would be obscene to hold a soldier who fought to regain American soil in the Battle of Attu liable for polluting the ground with his lead bullets. That they would be liable "as a theoretical matter" shows that the government's theory is mistaken.

We have no difficulty affirming the district court's exercise of discretion not to impose liability in the too-analogous circumstances of this case. We would only have difficulty in a case that went the other way.

---

## QUESTIONS AND DISCUSSION

**1.** Do you agree with Judge Kleinfeld that this is "a shocking case?" What did the federal government do that made it liable for 100% of the cleanup costs? Why shouldn't Dow have to pay any cleanup costs?

**2.** What allocation of liability would be appropriate under the Gore factors?

**3.** How would you answer Judge Kleinfeld's hypothetical question regarding the bullets fired by soldiers during the Battle of Attu?

**4.** Some of the most contaminated hazardous wastes sites in the country are owned by the federal government itself. Of the over one hundred federal facilities on the NPL, a former nerve gas manufacturing facility outside Denver and former weapons plants in Washington and Colorado are among the most contaminated sites in the country. According to statistics cited by one writer, the federal government is twice as likely to violate pollution regulations than private companies, 63 percent of federal facilities have serious RCRA violations, and the cleanup of hazardous wastes at federal facilities will cost billions of dollars. *See* Daniel Horne, Note, F*ederal Facility Environmental Compliance After* United States Department of Energy v. Ohio, 65 U. COLO. L. REV. 631 (1996). *See also* Charles de Saillan, *The Use of Imminent Hazard Provisions of Environmental Laws to Compel Cleanup at Federal Facilities*, 27 STAN. ENVTL. L.J. 43 (2008). Indeed, during his 1988 presidential campaign, George H.W. Bush admitted that "some of the worst offenders [of federal environmental laws] are our own federal facilities." H.R. Rep. No. 111, 102d Cong., 2d Sess., 2–3 (1992), *reprinted in* 1992 U.S.C.C.A.N. 1287, 1288–89 (quoting Bush).

**5.** In 1986, Congress added Section 120 to CERCLA as part of the broader SARA changes to the statute. Section 120 governs the application of CERCLA to federal facilities. As of 2012, nearly 12% of the sites on the NPL are federal facilities, and about three-fourths of those are military facilities. *See* http://www.epa.gov/fedfac/documents/eoy_2012_npl_program_snapshot.htm. The range of contamination issues includes active military operations, bases that are slated to be closed and transferred to another federal agency or to private ownership, and unexploded ordnance. For an overview of these issues, see the Defense Environmental Restoration Program's website at http://aec.army.mil/usaec/cleanup/derp00.html.

**6.** Of course, the federal government is not the only governmental entity subject to CERCLA. Many cities have complained about the imposition of CERCLA liability for municipal landfills and sewage treatment plants. Efforts to amend CERCLA to largely exempt such facilities from liability have yet to succeed, though EPA has adopted an enforcement policy that minimizes the costs that the agency will seek to recover from municipal governments. *See* 62 Fed. Reg. 37,231 (1997). Other CERCLA defendants have objected to providing any special treatment to municipal governments.

State governments have been held liable under CERCLA as well, but the Supreme Court's decision in Seminole Tribe v. Florida, 517 U.S. 44 (1996), casts doubt on whether states can be sued under CERCLA in federal court. Indeed, states have escaped from CERCLA cases based on the eleventh amendment defense set forth in *Seminole Tribe. See* The Ninth Avenue Remedial Group v. Allis-Chalmers Corp., 962 F. Supp. 131 (N.D. Ind. 1997) (dismissing the State of Indiana from a case in which the state transportation department stored hazardous materials that leached into the groundwater).

**7.** There are several other ways in which a party may try to avoid paying the costs of a CERCLA cleanup. First, CERCLA § 107(e) provides that a party cannot avoid liability by entering into an indemnification agreement shifting liability to another party. While such agreements cannot eliminate a party's CERCLA liability, they can be enforced by a party to collect money spent on a cleanup from the party who agreed to pay those costs. Second, the courts are divided regarding the extent to which CERCLA liability can be discharged in a bankruptcy proceeding. Third, many parties try to invoke their insurance coverage, but the existence of "pollution exclusion" clauses in many older policies has resulted in a substantial amount of insurance litigation related to CERCLA in state courts.

---

## 4. SETTLEMENTS

### United States v. Southeastern Pennsylvania Transportation Authority

United States Court of Appeals for the Third Circuit, 2000.
235 F.3d 817.

■ GIBSON, CIRCUIT JUDGE:

American Premier Underwriters, Inc. appeals the entry of a consent decree that resolves the liability of Consolidated Rail Corporation (Conrail), National Railroad Passenger Corporation (Amtrak), and Southeastern Pennsylvania Transportation Authority (SEPTA) for environmental contamination at the Paoli Rail Yard Site[2] in Paoli, Pennsylvania. American Premier, a non-settling defendant, argues that the decree unfairly allocates responsibility for cleanup at the Site and that the contribution protection it provides to the settling parties is not permitted under the relevant statute. We affirm.

Operations that involved the service, repair, and storage of rail cars were conducted at Paoli Rail Yard from 1915 until the beginning of 1995. In the 1950s, electric rail cars that used dielectric fluid to cool their transformers were first stored and maintained at the yard. Dielectric

---

[2] The Site includes the 28-acre rail yard property and the surrounding 400-acre watershed.

fluid contains polychlorinated biphenyls (PCBs). PCBs, which pose substantial risks to human health and the environment, are released during the servicing of train transformers and volatilize if overheated during train operation. Operations at the yard allegedly caused PCB contamination throughout the rail yard property. The contamination eventually spread to other nearby properties through erosion.

From 1915 until 1976, American Premier and its predecessors owned and operated the rail yard. Pursuant to the Regional Rail Reorganization Act of 1973, American Premier conveyed the yard to Conrail on April 1, 1976. That same day, Conrail conveyed the yard to Amtrak. Amtrak still owns the property. Conrail operated the yard from April 1, 1976 until the end of 1982. SEPTA then took over the yard's operation, using it to maintain commuter trains from 1983 until January 1995, when it moved its maintenance operations to a different location. SEPT A gradually phased out the use of dielectric fluid that contained PCBs, ending its use in 1986.

In 1985, EPA representatives observed that access to the rail yard was unrestricted and that people walked through and children played in areas at and near the rail yard. They also saw signs of erosion indicating water runoff from the yard into nearby residential areas. Sampling revealed PCB contamination in the rail yard and residential soils and in the fish in nearby creeks.

The following year, the United States brought this action against SEPTA, Conrail, and Amtrak (collectively, the rail companies) pursuant to, inter alia, Sections 104, 106(a), and 107 of the Comprehensive Environmental Response, Compensation, and Liability Act (CERCLA), 42 U.S.C. §§ 9604, 9606(a), and 9607. The government sought injunctive relief and reimbursement of response costs in connection with the release of PCBs at the Site. The Commonwealth of Pennsylvania intervened as a plaintiff later that year.

In June 1986, the United States, Conrail, and SEPTA petitioned the district court that had overseen American Premier's bankruptcy reorganization to establish their right to proceed against American Premier. See In re Penn Cent. Transp. Co., 944 F.2d 164, 166 (3d Cir. 1991). American Premier's argument that the earlier reorganization discharged the CERCLA claims was ultimately unsuccessful. In 1992, the United States filed a separate action against American Premier, and the rail companies brought American Premier into this action as a third-party defendant. American Premier then sought a declaratory judgment that the government's claims were barred by a 1980 settlement agreement that resolved claims between American Premier and the United States arising from the valuation of American Premier's rail assets conveyed pursuant to the Regional Rail Reorganization Act. See Penn Cent. Corp. v. United States, 862 F. Supp. 437, 448–58 (Regional Rail Reorg. Ct. 1994). The court granted summary judgment to the government on this issue.

Since the government initiated this action, it has entered into five partial preliminary consent decrees with the rail companies under which they agreed to perform a variety of remedies at the Site. In 1986, SEPTA agreed to construct a combination fence that restricted access to the rail yard and limited further PCB migration into the area surrounding the yard. Later that year, all three rail companies agreed to conduct an engineering study addressing erosion and PCB migration from the rail yard and identifying possible remedies to limit the spread of PCBs. A dispute arose between the United States and the rail companies over the work necessary to implement the study, and EPA ended up constructing sedimentation basins and erosion control systems and removing and disposing of contaminated soil from several residential properties. Under the third partial preliminary consent decree, the rail companies conducted a remedial investigation to determine the extent of PCB contamination at the Site and a feasibility study of various remedial alternatives. As part of this decree, SEPTA entered into a stipulation that addressed worker protection at the rail yard and decontamination of the car shop, a building in which rail cars had been repaired since 1915. Under the fourth partial preliminary consent decree, the rail companies agreed to conduct a soil sampling program to determine the extent of PCB contamination in the residential areas and the surface water channels north of the rail yard. Finally, under the last partial decree, the rail companies excavated approximately 3500 cubic yards of contaminated soils from the residential area north of the yard. All told, the rail companies spent approximately $12 million on remedial action related to the Site before entering into the consent decree that is the subject of this appeal.

EPA placed the Paoli Rail Yard Site on the National Priorities List in 1990. In July 1992, EPA issued a Record of Decision that reviewed remedial alternatives and their projected costs and selected remedies for the Site. As modified, the Record of Decision requires: (1) excavation and on-site treatment of contaminated rail yard soils (estimated cost: $19,507,375), (2) groundwater treatment and fuel oil recovery (estimated cost: $1,131,120), (3) decontamination and demolition of rail yard buildings and structures (estimated cost: $1,471,905), (4) excavation of contaminated residential soils (estimated cost: $1,196,000), and (5) excavation of contaminated stream sediments (estimated cost: $5,701,720).

In 1995, EPA proposed a consent decree that would require all four defendants to clean up the rail yard by carrying out the first three remedies from the Record of Decision, while leaving American Premier responsible for cleaning up the watershed by carrying out the last two remedies.

In February 1996, American Premier offered to pay 20% of past and future remediation costs at the Site as part of a global settlement. American Premier told the rail companies not to view the proposal as a typical "opening bid," thus intimating that it would not be willing to increase its settlement offer. The rail companies responded that they were disappointed with the offer and that they believed that American Premier had "sorely misjudged" the probable outcome if the parties were to litigate. The United States was similarly unsatisfied with the offer.

On September 30, 1996, EPA issued a unilateral administrative order requiring American Premier to implement the remedies from the Record of Decision related to the watershed portion of the Site. Under this order, American Premier is responsible for the excavation of residential soils and stream sediments. Together, these remedies are estimated to cost $6,897,720.

On July 28, 1997, the United States filed a Praecipe to Lodge Consent Decree, with the proposed decree resolving the rail companies' liability to the United States and the Commonwealth for contamination at the Site. The consent decree contends "that the degree of involvement by American Premier . . . in the disposal of hazardous substances and the operation at the Site is at least equal to or maybe greater than the degree of involvement by all the Settling parties combined." It requires the rail companies to excavate and contain the rail yard soils, perform the groundwater treatment and fuel oil recovery, and decontaminate and demolish rail yard buildings and structures. Together, these remedies are estimated to cost $22,110,400. The decree also requires several payments by the rail companies: $500,000 to the EPA Hazardous Substance Superfund to reimburse past response costs, $100,000 to the Commonwealth to reimburse past response costs, and $850,000 for natural resource damages.

The decree gives contribution protection to the rail companies for the past, interim, and future response costs of the United States and the Commonwealth and for natural resource damages. It also gives them protection for all remedial actions they have performed or will perform at the Site, as well as for the work that American Premier is to perform under the administrative order. American Premier objected to the proposed settlement by submitting comments both to EPA and to the Commonwealth. On July 30, 1998, the United States moved for entry of the consent decree. American Premier opposed the motion. The district court granted the motion after finding the consent decree procedurally and substantively fair, reasonable, and consistent with CERCLA's goals. This appeal followed.

American Premier challenges the entry of the consent decree on two related grounds. First, it argues that CERCLA does not authorize the contribution protection provided to the rail companies by the decree. Second, it argues that the district court erred by approving the consent decree because the decree is substantively unfair.

We review a district court's decision to grant a motion for entry of a consent decree for abuse of discretion. *See, e.g.*, United States v. Cannons Eng'g Corp., 899 F.2d 79, 84 (1st Cir. 1990); United States v. Montrose

Chem. Corp., 50 F.3d 741, 746 (9th Cir. 1995). "We approach our task mindful that, on appeal, a district court's approval of a consent decree in CERCLA litigation is encased in a double layer of swaddling." Cannons, 899 F.2d at 84. The first layer is the deference the district court owes to EPA's expertise and to the law's policy of encouraging settlement; the second layer is the deference we owe to the district court's discretion. Thus, American Premier is faced with a "heavy burden" in its attempt to persuade us that the district court abused its discretion by approving the consent decree.

American Premier's argument that CERCLA does not authorize the type of contribution protection granted by the consent decree raises an issue of law, and we exercise plenary review of the district court's decision on this issue.

The district court held that the contribution protection provided by the consent decree is permissible under CERCLA. Under 42 U.S.C. § 9613(f)(2), "[a] person who has resolved its liability to the United States or a State in an administrative or judicially approved settlement shall not be liable for claims for contribution regarding matters addressed in the settlement."

Here, the consent decree defines "matters addressed" as

> all claims asserted by the United States and the Commonwealth in their respective complaints and all claims of the United States and the Commonwealth against the Settling Defendants for recovery of "Past Response Costs", "Interim Response Costs", "Future Response Costs," and "Natural Resource Damages" as those terms are defined in this Consent Decree, and all claims of the United States and the Commonwealth for all the costs of all past response actions performed by the Settling Defendants, the costs of, or performance of, the "Work" as that term is defined in this Consent Decree, and the cost or performance of all Work to implement that portion of the ROD [Record of Decision] which Settling Defendants are not being required to implement under this Consent Decree excluding those items covered under the reservation of rights and reopener provisions of Section XXII.

American Premier claims that CERCLA does not authorize the contribution protection provided by the decree. The problem, according to American Premier, is that the decree gives the rail companies contribution protection for the remedies that they will perform under the decree (which are matters addressed in the settlement) and for the remedies that American Premier will perform under the administrative order (which are not matters addressed in the settlement). In its view, this is a partial settlement, and the rail companies are only entitled to contribution protection for the remedies they are undertaking under the consent decree.

We reject American Premier's view. While legislative history indicates that "Congress contemplated that there would be partial settlements which would leave settling parties liable for matters not addressed in the agreement," United States v. Charter Int'l Oil Co., 83 F.3d 510, 515 (1st Cir. 1996), this is not a partial settlement. The Paoli Site does contain two distinct areas: the rail yard and the watershed. Under the settlement, the rail companies are responsible for cleaning up the rail yard. CERCLA does not require, however, that the matters addressed in the decree be limited to the rail yard.

The decree states that the United States and the rail companies "wish to finally conclude . . . all claims and causes of action set forth" in this litigation. This litigation relates to contamination of the entire Paoli Site. The rail companies agreed to take on the remedies necessary to clean up the rail yard in order to resolve their liability for contamination throughout the Site. Reading this settlement as a whole, it would be reasonable to conclude that the matters it addresses are matters related to the entire Site, even without an explicit definition of matters addressed. *See* John M. Hyson, *CERCLA Settlements, Contribution Protection and Fairness to Non-Settling Responsible Parties*, 10 Vill. Envtl. L.J. 277, 320 (1999) ("In light of Congress's intent to induce settlements, all settlements should be presumed to afford to the settlors protection against claims for contribution regarding an entire site, unless there is an explicit provision to the contrary."); *see also* Akzo Coatings, Inc. v. Aigner Corp., 30 F.3d 761, 771–74 (7th Cir. 1994) (Easterbrook, J., dissenting).

Furthermore, including a definition of matters addressed in the decree will foreclose future arguments over the scope of the contribution protection. The definition of matters addressed in this decree clarifies the extent of the contribution protection that the rail companies are receiving in exchange for their agreement to clean up the rail yard property, reimburse the United States and the Commonwealth for part of their response costs, and pay for a portion of natural resource damages. The district court did not err by holding the contribution protection provided by the decree permissible under CERCLA.

American Premier's second argument is that the district court should not have granted the motion to enter the consent decree because the decree is substantively unfair. A court should approve a proposed consent decree if it is fair, reasonable, and consistent with CERCLA's goals. See United States v. Cannons Eng'g Corp., 899 F.2d 79, 85 (1st Cir. 1990). The terms of a decree are substantively fair if they are based on comparative fault and if liability is apportioned according to rational estimates of the harm each party has caused.

According to American Premier, the court erred in three different ways: (1) by adopting a method of allocating responsibility based on years of ownership and operation, (2) by approving a decree that sets a minimum amount of liability for American Premier while setting a maximum amount of liability for the rail companies, prior to an allocation proceeding, and (3) by approving a decree that immunizes the rail companies from sharing liability for uncertain future costs.

As long as the measure of comparative fault on which the settlement terms are based is not "arbitrary, capricious, and devoid of a rational basis," the district court should uphold it. *Cannons*, 899 F.2d at 87. According to the decree, American Premier's responsibility for contamination at the Site is at least equal to and possibly greater than the responsibility of the rail companies combined. The district court accepted as fair the decree's apportionment of liability based on years of ownership of the Paoli Rail Yard and the likelihood of contamination during those years.

PCBs were used at the rail yard for at least twenty-five years while American Premier owned and operated the yard. Amtrak owned the yard for ten years while PCBs were used. During that ten-year period, first Conrail and then SEPTA operated the yard. Therefore, American Premier owned and operated the rail yard more than 70% of the time while PCBs were used.

American Premier argues that the district court "wholly disregarded" its settlement proposal, which was based on factors other than years of ownership, to assume 20% of the past and future costs of remediation at the Site. But the district court was not required to accept American Premier's methodology for apportioning liability. Once it found that the decree was based on a rational determination of comparative fault, its task was complete, whether or not it would have employed the same method of apportionment. The district court did not abuse its discretion by accepting years of ownership and operation as a plausible method on which to judge the fairness of the consent decree.

American Premier contends that the decree is unfair because it sets a minimum level of responsibility for American Premier by foreclosing it from receiving contribution from the rail companies for its costs, while setting a maximum level of responsibility for the rail companies by leaving them free to bring a contribution action against American Premier. This disparity does not establish that the decree is substantively unfair or that the district court abused its discretion by entering it.

Taking into account American Premier's share of Site remediation and assuming that it will have to reimburse the United States and the Commonwealth for the remainder of their past response costs and pay natural resource damages, American Premier will be responsible for costs that exceed $17 million. Eventually, the total amount expended on Site remediation and damages, including the $12 million already spent by the rail companies, will likely exceed $53 million. Because of the contribution protection provided to the rail companies, American Premier's minimum share of these costs is 33%. Its share may increase if the rail companies bring a successful contribution action against it.

American Premier's offer to assume responsibility for 20% of the costs was unacceptable to EPA and the rail companies, so they chose to settle without American Premier. The settlement reduces the rail companies' maximum share of liability from 100% to 67% in exchange for their agreement to clean up the rail yard and pay part of past response costs and natural resource damages:

> In most instances, settlement requires compromise. Thus, it makes sense for the government, when negotiating, to give a PRP [potentially responsible party] a discount on its maximum potential liability as an incentive to settle. Indeed, the statutory scheme contemplates that those who are slow to settle ought to bear the risk of paying more. . . .

United States v. DiBiase, 45 F.3d 541, 546 (1st Cir. 1995). The rail companies' share of liability may decrease if they bring a successful contribution action against American Premier.

We recently pointed out that the "intended effect" of protecting settling parties from contribution claims "is that 'non-settling defendants may bear disproportionate liability for their acts.' " United States v. Occidental Chem. Corp., 200 F.3d 143, 150 n.8 (3d Cir. 1999) (quoting B. F. Goodrich v. Betkoski, 99 F.3d 505, 527 (2d Cir. 1996)). In *Occidental Chemical*, EPA had already settled with one potentially responsible party when it issued an administrative order to Occidental, requiring it to participate in the cleanup. Occidental pointed out that, because the other party obtained contribution protection for matters addressed in the settlement, Occidental could end up paying more than its fair share. We responded, "While this is true, it is the result of a deliberate policy choice made by Congress in order to encourage settlements."

It is highly unlikely that this consent decree will result in a final allocation of responsibility for contamination at the Paoli Site. The rail companies will be able to bring a contribution action against American Premier and will be able to offer more specific evidence regarding the relative fault of the parties. The district court will then be able to determine whether American Premier is liable for a portion of the rail companies' costs. If the court chooses to do so, it will be able to take into account the costs incurred by American Premier which are not recoverable through contribution. *See* 42 U.S.C. § 9613(f)(1) (in a contribution action, "the court may allocate response costs among liable parties using such equitable factors as the court determines are appropriate").

This consent decree does set a floor for American Premier's liability while setting a ceiling for the rail companies' liability. That is part of the scheme enacted by Congress, and the district court did not abuse its discretion by rejecting the argument that this result made the decree unfair.

Finally, American Premier argues that the consent decree is unfair because it alone will be responsible for "highly speculative" future costs: those related to its share of Site remediation, natural resource damages, and future response costs of the United States and the Commonwealth. This, too, is an argument based on the contribution protection provided to the rail companies.

In every case where remedial measures have yet to be performed, the future costs are uncertain. But that uncertainty should not be used to hinder settlement. EPA used standard methodologies to estimate the costs of cleaning up the Site, and neither we nor the district court are in a position to second-guess these estimates. *See Cannons*, 899 F.2d at 90 ("If the figures relied upon derive in a sensible way from a plausible interpretation of the record, the court should normally defer to the agency's expertise."). The natural resource damages estimate was based on detailed assessments, and if these damages turn out to be "significantly greater" than the $5.3 million estimate, the consent decree does not prevent EPA from pursuing the rail companies for the excess. Finally, we doubt that the United States and the Commonwealth will incur much in the way of future response costs since the consent decree, along with the administrative order, will result in a complete remedy at the Paoli Rail Yard Site.

Whenever a non-settling party is barred from bringing a contribution action and work remains to be done, its future liability may exceed present estimates. The district court determined that this possibility did not render the consent decree unfair, and we see no abuse of discretion in that determination.

* * *

---

## QUESTIONS AND DISCUSSION

**1.** Do you think that the settlement in *SEPTA* was fair?

**2.** Most CERCLA cases settle. Why?

**3.** CERCLA § 122(g) authorizes de minimis settlements that involve a minor portion of the response costs at a facility. To be eligible for such a settlement, a party must have contributed a minimal amount of the total contamination at the facility or it must be a current owner who did not cause the contamination at the facility. EPA's de minimis settlement policy asks if a party acquired a site without reason to know of the contamination, if the party acquired the property involuntarily, and if the property was contaminated by third parties outside the chain of title. *See Superfund Program: De Minimis Landowner Settlements, Prospective Purchaser*, 54 Fed. Reg. 34,235 (1989). Small business groups, however, favor a more expansive de minimis exemption that would exempt parties that contributed less than one percent of the hazardous wastes found at a site.

The de minimis settlement provision has been criticized as doing little to encourage settlements with parties who had little role in causing the contamination at a site. As noted earlier, in 2002 Congress exempted "de micromis" generators and transporters from CERCLA liability entirely. *See* CERCLA § 107(*o*).

---

## PROBLEM EXERCISE

High in the mountains of central Idaho lies the Blackbird Mine, the only source of cobalt in the United States. Mineral deposits were first found in the area around 1893, and various small operators mined there for the next several decades.

In 1943, Howe Sound, a Maine corporation with extensive mining operations in North and South America, became interested in the area. As a result, an employee of Howe Sound began staking mining claims and acquiring options in the area. In addition, limited exploration activities took place. In 1944, Calera Mining Co., a wholly owned subsidiary of Howe Sound, took title to the property. Thereafter, further exploration occurred which culminated in full-scale cobalt production by 1951.

Calera sold all of the cobalt that it produced to the federal government. The beginning of World War II in Europe raised fears about the U.S. supply of cobalt, which was used a high-temperature alloy in jet engines. The United States Bureau of Mines (USBOM), an agency of the federal government, responded by encouraging private investors to mine cobalt. From 1951 to 1959, the USBOM paid a premium, above-market price for the cobalt that Calera produced from the Blackbird Mine. Even so, Calera never made much profit from the mine. By 1959, the USBOM decided to terminate its contract with Calera because the USBOM no longer needed more cobalt. After Calera unsuccessfully sought to persuade the USBOM to extend the contract, the company closed the Blackbird Mine.

The Hanna Mining Company acquired the Blackbird Mine in 1967. It never undertook any commercial mining there, though it did keep crews at the site. In 1980, Hanna formed a limited partnership with Noranda Exploration, Inc., and this partnership—known as Blackbird Mining Co.—acquired the mine and conducted limiting mining there from 1979 to 1982.

By the 1980s, the environmental effects of the earlier mining were becoming obvious. Open pit mining at the site left approximately 3.8 million tons of waste rock deposited in the headwaters of the Blackbird and Bucktail Creeks. Approximately one million tons of waste rock were removed during underground mining operations and deposited in the drainage of Blackbird, Meadow, and Bucktail Creeks. Until the 1950s, ore tailings were disposed of throughout the Blackbird Creek drainage system, including direct deposits into the creek. In 1950, a tailings dam was constructed to collect the tailings that washed downstream. The USBOM was not involved in any of these decisions, but it did issue a permit to allow the dam to be built and it proved technical advice regarding cobalt mining when asked by Calera.

Drainage from the mine and tailings contains significant concentrations of various forms of copper, cobalt and iron, and is very acidic. According to Idaho state biologists, drainage enters both ground and surface waters and has caused fish kills, reductions in or elimination of the spawning runs of anadromous fish, and other adverse effects on the aquatic life in streams receiving mine drainage. These and other impacts on the natural resources of the area commenced in the 1940s and persist today. Additionally, the dam built in 1950 now contains approximately two million tons of tailings, and it appears to be in danger of collapsing.

You are an attorney working for the Idaho Attorney General. Your primary objective is to resolve all of the environment problems identified above in the manner most favorable to Idaho. Your secondary objective is to reap the economic benefits that would come from reopening the mine. Identify the actions that the state could take pursuant to CERCLA to clean up and protect the environment surrounding the mine, indicate how the other affected parties will likely respond to such actions, and evaluate the likelihood that Idaho will succeed in such actions.

---

## D. PRIVATE COST RECOVERY AND CONTRIBUTION UNDER CERCLA

As detailed above, CERCLA establishes a statutory program for remediation of contaminated resources and provides the federal government authority to order potentially responsible parties (PRPs) to pay for remediation (section 106) or to conduct the remediation itself and seek recovery of its "response costs" (section 107(a)). Courts have agreed that CERCLA also creates a private right of action in section 107(a), which provides that PRPs shall be liable for "any other necessary costs of response incurred *by any other person*" that are consistent with the NCP. 42 U.S.C. § 9607(a)(4)(B) (emphasis added). It is important to keep in mind that while the EPA must first list a site on the NPL before conducting a remediation and seeking to recover response costs under section 107(a), that requirement does not apply to private parties who will be spending their own money rather than taxpayer money on the cleanup. Private parties (as well as state and local governments) can incur costs responding to a release of hazardous substances and then attempt to recover those costs from responsible parties so long as the costs are "necessary" and consistent with the NCP under section 107(a)(4)(B). As illustrated in the *Regional Airport Authority* case excerpted earlier in this chapter, NCP compliance is often difficult, and requires time, money, and attention to detail to meet the numerous requirements of the NCP regulations.

In addition, in amendments to the statute in 1986, Congress added a provision, in section 113(f), providing a right of contribution to recover an equitable share of costs a party has incurred either "during or following any civil action" or "in an administrative or judicially approved settlement" under CERCLA § 106 or § 107(a). The conditions required of the person incurring response costs to seek recovery under either avenue—direct cost recovery under section 107(a) or contribution under section 113(f)—have been the source of intense litigation throughout their histories.

## Cooper Industries, Inc. v. Aviall Services, Inc.

United States Supreme Court, 2004.
543 U.S. 157.

■ JUSTICE THOMAS delivered the opinion of the Court.

Section 113(f)(1) of the Comprehensive Environmental Response, Compensation, and Liability Act of 1980 (CERCLA) allows persons who have undertaken efforts to clean up properties contaminated by hazardous substances to seek contribution from other parties liable under CERCLA. Section 113(f)(1) specifies that a party may obtain contribution "during or following any civil action" under CERCLA § 106 or § 107(a). The issue we must decide is whether a private party who has not been sued under § 106 or § 107(a) may nevertheless obtain contribution under § 113(f)(1) from other liable parties. We hold that it may not.

Under CERCLA, 94 Stat. 2767, the Federal Government may clean up a contaminated area itself, see § 104, or it may compel responsible parties to perform the cleanup, see § 106(a). *See Key Tronic Corp. v. United States,* 511 U.S. 809, 814 (1994). In either case, the Government may recover its response costs under § 107, 42 U.S.C. § 9607 (2000 ed. and Supp. I), the "cost recovery" section of CERCLA. Section 107(a) lists four classes of potentially responsible persons (PRPs) and provides that they "shall be liable" for, among other things, "all costs of removal or remedial action incurred by the United States Government . . . not inconsistent with the national contingency plan." § 107(a)(4)(A). Section 107(a) further provides that PRPs shall be liable for "any other necessary costs of response incurred by any other person consistent with the national contingency plan." § 107(a)(4)(B).

After CERCLA's enactment in 1980, litigation arose over whether § 107, in addition to allowing the Government and certain private parties to recover costs from PRPs, also allowed a PRP that had incurred response costs to recover costs from other PRPs. More specifically, the question was whether a private party that had incurred response costs, but that had done so voluntarily and was not itself subject to suit, had a cause of action for cost recovery against other PRPs. Various courts held that § 107(a)(4)(B) and its predecessors authorized such a cause of action. *See, e.g., Wickland Oil Terminals v. Asarco, Inc.*, 792 F.2d 887, 890–892 (C.A.9 1986); *Walls v. Waste Resource Corp.*, 761 F.2d 311, 317–318 (C.A.6 1985); *Philadelphia v. Stepan Chemical Co.*, 544 F. Supp. 1135, 1140–1143 (E.D. Pa.1982).

After CERCLA's passage, litigation also ensued over the separate question whether a private entity that had been sued in a cost recovery action (by the Government or by another PRP) could obtain contribution from other PRPs. As originally enacted in 1980, CERCLA contained no provision expressly providing for a right of action for contribution. A number of District Courts nonetheless held that, although CERCLA did not mention the word "contribution," such a right arose either impliedly from provisions of the statute, or as a matter of federal common law. *See, e.g., United States v. New Castle County*, 642 F. Supp. 1258, 1263–1269 (D. Del.1986) (contribution right arises under federal common law); *Colorado v. ASARCO, Inc.*, 608 F. Supp. 1484, 1486–1493 (D. Colo.1985) (same); *Wehner v. Syntex Agribusiness, Inc.*, 616 F. Supp. 27, 31 (E.D. Mo.1985) (contribution right is implied from § 107(e)(2)). That conclusion was debatable in light of two decisions of this Court that refused to recognize implied or common-law rights to contribution in other federal statutes. See *Texas Industries, Inc. v. Radcliff Materials, Inc.*, 451 U.S. 630, 638–647 (1981) (refusing to recognize implied or common-law right to contribution in the Sherman Act or the Clayton Act); *Northwest Airlines, Inc. v. Transport Workers*, 451 U.S. 77, 90–99 (1981) (refusing to recognize implied or common-law right to contribution in the Equal Pay Act of 1963 or Title VII of the Civil Rights Act of 1964).

Congress subsequently amended CERCLA in the Superfund Amendments and Reauthorization Act of 1986 (SARA), 100 Stat. 1613, to provide an express cause of action for contribution, codified as CERCLA § 113(f)(1):

> "Any person may seek contribution from any other person who is liable or potentially liable under section 9607(a) of this title, during or following any civil action under section 9606 of this title or under section 9607(a) of this title. Such claims shall be brought in accordance with this section and the Federal Rules of Civil Procedure, and shall be governed by Federal law. In resolving contribution claims, the court may allocate response costs among liable parties using such equitable factors as the court determines are appropriate. Nothing in this subsection shall diminish the right of any person to bring an action for contribution in the absence of a civil action under section 9606 of this title or section 9607 of this title." *Id.*, at 1647, as codified in 42 U.S.C. § 9613(f)(1).

SARA also created a separate express right of contribution, § 113(f)(3)(B), for "[a] person who has resolved its liability to the United States or a State for some or all of a response action or for some or all of the costs of such action in an administrative or judicially approved settlement." In short, after SARA, CERCLA provided for a right to cost recovery in certain circumstances, § 107(a), and separate rights to contribution in other circumstances, §§ 113(f)(1), 113(f)(3)(B).

This case concerns four contaminated aircraft engine maintenance sites in Texas. Cooper Industries, Inc., owned and operated those sites until 1981, when it sold them to Aviall Services, Inc. Aviall operated the four sites for a number of years. Ultimately, Aviall discovered that both it and Cooper had contaminated the facilities when petroleum and other hazardous substances leaked into the ground and ground water through underground storage tanks and spills.

Aviall notified the Texas Natural Resource Conservation Commission (Commission) of the contamination. The Commission informed Aviall that it was violating state environmental laws, directed Aviall to clean up the site, and threatened to pursue an enforcement action if Aviall failed to undertake remediation. Neither the Commission nor the EPA, however, took judicial or administrative measures to compel cleanup.

Aviall cleaned up the properties under the State's supervision, beginning in 1984. Aviall sold the properties to a third party in 1995 and 1996, but remains contractually responsible for the cleanup. Aviall has incurred approximately $5 million in cleanup costs; the total costs may be even greater. In August 1997, Aviall filed this action against Cooper in the United States District Court for the Northern District of Texas, seeking to recover cleanup costs. The original complaint asserted a claim for cost recovery under CERCLA § 107(a), a separate claim for contribution under CERCLA § 113(f)(1), and state-law claims. Aviall later amended the complaint, combining its two CERCLA claims into a single, joint CERCLA claim. That claim alleged that, pursuant to § 113(f)(1), Aviall was entitled to seek contribution from Cooper, as a PRP under § 107(a), for response costs and other liability Aviall incurred in connection with the Texas facilities. Aviall continued to assert state-law claims as well.

Both parties moved for summary judgment, and the District Court granted Cooper's motion. The court held that Aviall, having abandoned its § 107 claim, sought contribution only under § 113(f)(1). The court held that § 113(f)(1) relief was unavailable to Aviall because it had not been sued under CERCLA § 106 or § 107. Having dismissed Aviall's federal claim, the court declined to exercise jurisdiction over the state-law claims.

A divided panel of the Court of Appeals for the Fifth Circuit affirmed. 263 F.3d 134 (2001). The majority, relying principally on the "during or following" language in the first sentence of § 113(f)(1), held that "a PRP seeking contribution from other PRPs under § 113(f)(1) must have a pending or adjudged § 106 administrative order or § 107(a) cost recovery action against it." *Id.,* at 145. The dissent reasoned that the final sentence of § 113(f)(1), the saving clause, clarified that the federal common-law right to contribution survived the enactment of § 113(f)(1), even absent a § 106 or § 107(a) civil action. *Id.,* at 148–150 (opinion of Wiener, J.).

On rehearing en banc, the Fifth Circuit reversed by a divided vote, holding that § 113(f)(1) allows a PRP to obtain contribution from other PRPs regardless of whether the PRP has been sued under § 106 or § 107. 312 F.3d 677 (2002). The court held that "[s]ection 113(f)(1) authorizes suits against PRPs in both its first and last sentence[,] which states without qualification that 'nothing' in the section shall 'diminish' any person's right to bring a contribution action in the absence of a section 106 or section 107(a) action." *Id.,* at 681. The court reasoned in part that "may" in § 113(f)(1) did not mean "may only." *Id.,* at 686–687. Three members of the en banc court dissented for essentially the reasons given by the panel majority. *Id.,* at 691–693 (opinion of Garza, J.).

Section 113(f)(1) does not authorize Aviall's suit. The first sentence, the enabling clause that establishes the right of contribution, provides: "Any person *may* seek contribution . . . *during or following* any civil action under section 9606 of this title or under section 9607(a) of this title," 42 U.S.C. § 9613(f)(1) (emphasis added). The natural meaning of this sentence is that contribution may only be sought subject to the specified conditions, namely, "during or following" a specified civil action.

Aviall answers that "may" should be read permissively, such that "during or following" a civil action is one, but not the exclusive, instance in which a person may seek contribution. We disagree. First, as just noted, the natural meaning of "may" in the context of the enabling clause is that it authorizes certain contribution actions—ones that satisfy the subsequent specified condition—and no others.

Second, and relatedly, if § 113(f)(1) were read to authorize contribution actions at any time, regardless of the existence of a § 106 or § 107(a) civil action, then Congress need not have included the explicit "during or following" condition. In other words, Aviall's reading would render part of the statute entirely superfluous, something we are loath to do. *See, e.g., Hibbs v. Winn,* 542 U.S. 88, 101 (2004). Likewise, if § 113(f)(1) authorizes contribution actions at any time, § 113(f)(3)(B), which permits contribution actions after settlement, is equally superfluous. There is no reason why Congress would bother to specify conditions under which a person may bring a contribution claim, and at the same time allow contribution actions absent those conditions.

The last sentence of § 113(f)(1), the saving clause, does not change our conclusion. That sentence provides: "Nothing in this subsection shall diminish the right of any person to bring an action for contribution in the absence of a civil action under section 9606 of this title or section 9607 of this title." 42 U.S.C. § 9613(f)(1). The sole function of the sentence is to clarify that § 113(f)(1) does nothing to "diminish" any cause(s) of action for contribution that may exist independently of § 113(f)(1). In other words, the sentence rebuts any presumption that the express right of contribution provided by the enabling clause is the exclusive cause of action for contribution available to a PRP. The sentence, however, does not itself establish a cause of action; nor does it expand § 113(f)(1) to authorize contribution actions not brought "during or following" a § 106 or § 107(a) civil action; nor does it specify what causes of action for contribution, if any, exist outside § 113(f)(1). Reading the saving clause to authorize § 113(f)(1) contribution actions not just "during or following" a civil action, but also before such an action, would again violate the settled rule that we must, if possible, construe a statute to give every word some operative effect. *See United States v. Nordic Village, Inc.*, 503 U.S. 30, 35–36 (1992).

Our conclusion follows not simply from § 113(f)(1) itself, but also from the whole of § 113. As noted above, § 113 provides two express avenues for contribution: § 113(f)(1) ("during or following" specified civil actions) and § 113(f)(3)(B) (after an administrative or judicially approved settlement that resolves liability to the United States or a State). Section 113(g)(3) then provides two corresponding 3-year limitations periods for contribution actions, one beginning at the date of judgment, § 113(g)(3)(A), and one beginning at the date of settlement, § 113(g)(3)(B). Notably absent from § 113(g)(3) is any provision for starting the limitations period if a judgment or settlement never occurs, as is the case with a purely voluntary cleanup. The lack of such a provision supports the conclusion that, to assert a contribution claim under § 113(f), a party must satisfy the conditions of either § 113(f)(1) or § 113(f)(3)(B).

Each side insists that the purpose of CERCLA bolsters its reading of § 113(f)(1). Given the clear meaning of the text, there is no need to resolve this dispute or to consult the purpose of CERCLA at all. As we have said: "[I]t is ultimately the provisions of our laws rather than the principal concerns of our legislators by which we are governed." *Oncale v. Sundowner Offshore Services, Inc.*, 523 U.S. 75, 79 (1998). Section 113(f)(1), 100 Stat. 1647, authorizes contribution claims only "during or following" a civil action under § 106 or § 107(a), and it is undisputed that Aviall has never been subject to such an action. Aviall therefore has no § 113(f)(1) claim.

Aviall and *amicus* Lockheed Martin contend that, in the alternative to an action for contribution under § 113(f)(1), Aviall may recover costs under § 107(a)(4)(B) even though it is a PRP. The dissent would have us so hold. We decline to address the issue. Neither the District Court, nor the Fifth Circuit panel, nor the Fifth Circuit sitting en banc considered Aviall's § 107 claim. In fact, as noted above, Aviall included separate § 107 and § 113 claims in its original complaint, but then asserted a "combined" § 107/§ 113 claim in its amended complaint. The District Court took this consolidated claim to mean that Aviall was relying on § 107 "not as an independent cause of action," but only "to the extent necessary to maintain a viable § 113(f)(1) contribution claim." Civ. Action No. 3:97–CV–1926–D (N.D. Tex., Jan. 13, 2000), App. to Pet. for Cert. 94a, n. 2. Consequently the court saw no need to address any freestanding § 107 claim. The Fifth Circuit panel likewise concluded that Aviall no longer advanced a stand-alone § 107 claim. 263 F.3d, at 137, n.2. The en banc court found it unnecessary to decide whether Aviall had waived the § 107 claim, because it held that Aviall could rely instead on § 113. 312 F.3d, at 685, n. 15. Thus, the court did not address the waiver issue, let alone the merits of the § 107 claim.

"We ordinarily do not decide in the first instance issues not decided below." *Adarand Constructors, Inc. v. Mineta,* 534 U.S. 103, 109 (2001) *(per curiam)* (internal quotation marks omitted). Although we have deviated from this rule in exceptional circumstances, *United States v. Mendenhall,* 446 U.S. 544, 551–552, n.5 (1980), the circumstances here cut *against* resolving the § 107 claim. Both the question whether Aviall has waived this claim and the underlying § 107 question (if it is not waived) may depend in part on the relationship between §§ 107 and 113. That relationship is a significant issue in its own right. It is also well beyond the scope of the briefing and, indeed, the question presented, which asks simply whether a private party "may bring an action seeking contribution pursuant to CERCLA Section 113(f)(1)." The § 107 claim and the preliminary waiver question merit full consideration by the courts below.

Furthermore, the parties cite numerous decisions of the Courts of Appeals as holding that a private party that is itself a PRP may not pursue a § 107(a) action against other PRPs for joint and several liability. *See, e.g., Bedford Affiliates v. Sills,* 156 F.3d 416, 423–424 (C.A.2 1998); *Centerior Serv. Co. v. Acme Scrap Iron & Metal Corp.,* 153 F.3d 344, 349–356 (C.A.6 1998); *Pneumo Abex Corp. v. High Point, T. & D.R. Co.,* 142 F.3d 769, 776 (C.A.4 1998); *Pinal Creek Group v. Newmont Mining Corp.,* 118 F.3d 1298, 1301–1306 (C.A.9 1997); *New Castle County v. Halliburton NUS Corp.,* 111 F.3d 1116, 1120–1124 (C.A.3 1997); *Redwing Carriers, Inc. v. Saraland Apartments,* 94 F.3d 1489, 1496, and n.7 (C.A.11 1996); *United States v. Colorado & E.R. Co.,* 50 F.3d 1530, 1534–1536 (C.A.10 1995); *United Technologies Corp. v. Browning-Ferris Industries,* 33 F.3d 96, 98–103 (C.A.1 1994). To hold here that Aviall may pursue a § 107 action, we would have to consider whether these decisions are correct, an issue that Aviall has flagged but not briefed. And we might have to consider other issues, also not briefed, such as whether Aviall, which seeks to recover the share of its cleanup costs fairly chargeable to Cooper, may pursue a § 107 cost recovery action for some form of liability other than joint and several. We think it more prudent to withhold judgment on these matters.

In addition to leaving open whether Aviall may seek cost recovery under § 107, we decline to decide whether Aviall has an implied right to contribution under § 107. Portions of the Fifth Circuit's opinion below might be taken to endorse the latter cause of action, 312 F.3d, at 687; others appear to reserve the question whether such a cause of action exists, *id.*, at 685, n. 15. To the extent that Aviall chooses to frame its § 107 claim on remand as an implied right of contribution (as opposed to a right of cost recovery), we note that this Court has visited the subject of implied rights of contribution before. *See Texas Industries,* 451 U.S., at 638–647; *Northwest Airlines,* 451 U.S., at 90–99. We also note that, in enacting § 113(f)(1), Congress explicitly recognized a particular set (claims "during or following" the specified civil actions) of the contribution rights previously implied by courts from provisions of CERCLA and the common law. *Cf. Transamerica Mortgage Advisors, Inc. v. Lewis,* 444 U.S. 11, 19 (1979). Nonetheless, we need not and do not decide today whether any judicially implied right of contribution survived the passage of SARA.

---

## QUESTIONS AND DISCUSSION

**1.** *Aviall* was decided on straightforward reasoning: "during or following a civil action" means what it says. But questions remained under section 113(f). For example, in many instances EPA enters into an "administrative order on consent" to resolve a PRPs liability rather than using a judicially approved consent decree. Do such administrative instruments qualify as "administratively or judicially approved settlement" under the separate contribution right provided in section 113(f)(3)(B)? Similar issues arise as to which state agency proceedings qualify response costs for contribution rights under CERCLA. For a background on the legal landscape prior to and after *Aviall*, and how *Aviall* left questions such as these unresolved, see Karl S. Bourdeau & Steven M. Jawetz, *25 Years of Superfund Liability: Progress Made, Progress Needed*, 37 ENV'T REP. 97 (2006); John M. Barkett, *Forward to the Past: The Aftermath of Aviall*, NATURAL RESOURCES & ENV'T, Winter 2006, at 27; Kathy Robb and Marian Waldman, *Supreme Court Limits Potentially Responsible Parties' Right to Bring Contribution Lawsuits Under CERCLA Section 113*, 36 ENV'T REP. 145 (2005); Alfred R. Light, *CERCLA's Snark: Contribution Protection, Review Preclusion, and the Government Defendant*, 19 TOXICS REP. 538 (2004).

**2.** Given that *Aviall* raised more questions than it answered, what advice would you provide a client facing potential CERCLA liability to enhance the prospects for recovering response costs from other PRPs? Bordeau and Jawetz, *supra*, suggest that possible options, depending on the jurisdiction and facts, include the following:

1. Pursue a section 107(a) cost recovery action by demonstrating "non-liability" under CERCLA;

2. Demonstrate that a section 113(f)(1) contribution claim is being brought during or following a civil action under sections 106 or 107(a) of CERCLA;

3. Demonstrate that a section 113(f)(3)(B) contribution claim is being brought by a party that has already "resolved" its liability to the United States or a state in an "administratively or judicially approved settlement;

4. Seek and obtain modifications to an existing settlement agreement so that it qualifies as a section 113(f)(3)(B) settlement;

5. Bring a cost recovery action under section 107(a);

6. Pursue a federal common law right of contribution;

7. Pursue contribution rights under state law; and

8. In a transactional context, seek contractual or insurance rights.

37 ENV'T REP. at 103. If that's the best set of options, how hopeful should your client be if it is a PRP that has voluntarily incurred response costs? What about if it is not a PRP but has voluntarily incurred response costs?

---

Although *Aviall* put the question to rest for purposes of section 113(f), an immediate question arose regarding the availability of recovery under § 107(a) for parties that voluntarily incur response costs. The majority in *Aviall* noted that numerous decisions of the Courts of Appeal hold that a private party that is itself a PRP may *never* pursue a § 107(a) action against other PRPs for joint and several liability or contribution. Once *Aviall* had held that such parties could not recover costs under § 113, PRPs had no incentive to undertake a cleanup without first being sued by a non-PRP under § 107. This, of course, would drastically reduce the number of voluntary cleanups by PRPs which, by this time, far exceeded the number of EPA and state-led cleanups. For a comprehensive review of *Aviall* and how courts in different circuits decided the interrelation of § 107(a) and 113(f), which shows they were all over the board on both of the questions arising under § 107(a), see Karl S. Bordeau & W. Parker Moore, *Options for Potentially Responsible Parties in the Wake of the Aviall Decision*, 38 ENV'T REP. 440 (2007). In the following case the Supreme Court resolved much of the confusion.

## United States v. Atlantic Research Corporation

United States Supreme Court, 2007.
551 U.S. 128.

■ JUSTICE THOMAS delivered the opinion of the Court.

Two provisions of the Comprehensive Environmental Response, Compensation, and Liability Act of 1980 (CERCLA)—§§ 107(a) and 113(f)—allow private parties to recover expenses associated with cleaning up contaminated sites. 42 U.S.C. §§ 9607(a), 9613(f). In this case, we must decide a question left open in Cooper Industries, Inc. v. Aviall Services, Inc., 543 U.S. 157 (2004): whether § 107(a) provides so-called potentially responsible parties (PRPs), 42 U.S.C. §§ 9607(a)(1)–(4), with a cause of action to recover costs from other PRPs. We hold that it does.

Courts have frequently grappled with whether and how PRPs may recoup CERCLA-related costs from other PRPs. The questions lie at the intersection of two statutory provisions—CERCLA §§ 107(a) and 113(f). Section 107(a) defines four categories of PRPs, 94 Stat. 2781, 42 U.S.C. §§ 9607(a)(1)–(4), and makes them liable for, among other things:

> "(A) all costs of removal or remedial action incurred by the United States Government or a State or an Indian tribe not inconsistent with the national contingency plan; [and]
>
> "(B) any other necessary costs of response incurred by any other person consistent with the national contingency plan." § 9607(a)(4)(A)–(B).

Enacted as part of the Superfund Amendments and Reauthorization Act of 1986 (SARA), 100 Stat. 1613, § 113(f) authorizes one PRP to sue another for contribution in certain circumstances. 42 U.S.C. § 9613(f).

Prior to the advent of § 113(f)'s express contribution right, some courts held that § 107(a)(4)(B) provided a cause of action for a private party to recover voluntarily incurred response costs and to seek contribution after having been sued. *See* Cooper Industries, *supra*, at 161–162 (collecting cases); Key Tronic Corp. v. United States, 511 U.S. 809, 816, n.7 (1994) same. After SARA's enactment, however, some Courts of Appeals believed it necessary to "direc[t] traffic between" § 107(a) and § 113(f). 459 F.3d 827, 832 (C.A.8 2006) (case below). As a result, many Courts of Appeals held that § 113(f) was the exclusive remedy for PRPs. *See Cooper Industries, supra,* at 169 (collecting cases). But as courts prevented PRPs from suing under § 107(a), they expanded § 113(f) to allow PRPs to seek "contribution" even in the absence of a suit under § 106 or § 107(a). Aviall Servs., Inc. v. Cooper Industries, Inc., 312 F.3d 677, 681 (C.A.5 2002) (en banc).

In Cooper Industries, we held that a private party could seek contribution from other liable parties only after having been sued under § 106 or § 107(a). 543 U.S., at 161. This narrower interpretation of § 113(f) caused several Courts of Appeals to reconsider whether PRPs have rights under § 107(a)(4)(B), an issue we declined to address in *Cooper Industries. Id.*, at 168. After revisiting the issue, some courts have permitted § 107(a) actions by PRPs. See Consolidated Edison Co. of N.Y. v. UGI Utilities, Inc., 423 F.3d 90 (C.A.2 2005); Metropolitan Water Reclamation Dist. of Greater Chicago v. North American Galvanizing & Coatings, Inc., 473 F.3d 824 (C.A.7 2007). However, at least one court continues to hold that § 113(f) provides the exclusive cause of action available to PRPs. E.I. DuPont de Nemours & Co. v. United States, 460 F.3d 515 (C.A.3 2006). Today, we resolve this issue.

In this case, respondent Atlantic Research leased property at the Shumaker Naval Ammunition Depot, a facility operated by the Department of Defense. At the site, Atlantic Research retrofitted rocket motors for petitioner United States. Using a high-pressure water spray, Atlantic Research removed pieces of propellant from the motors. It then burned the propellant pieces. Some of the resultant wastewater and burned fuel contaminated soil and groundwater at the site.

Atlantic Research cleaned the site at its own expense and then sought to recover some of its costs by suing the United States under both § 107(a) and § 113(f). After our decision in Cooper Industries foreclosed relief under § 113(f), Atlantic Research amended its complaint to seek relief under § 107(a) and federal common law. The United States moved to dismiss, arguing that § 107(a) does not allow PRPs (such as Atlantic Research) to recover costs. The District Court granted the motion to dismiss, relying on a case decided prior to our decision in Cooper Industries, Dico, Inc. v. Amoco Oil Co., 340 F.3d 525 (C.A.8 2003).

The Court of Appeals for the Eighth Circuit reversed. Recognizing that Cooper Industries undermined the reasoning of its prior precedent, 459 F.3d, at 830, n.4, the Court of Appeals joined the Second and Seventh Circuits in holding that § 113(f) does not provide "the exclusive route by which [PRPs] may recover cleanup costs." *Id.*, at 834 (citing *Consolidated Edison Co., supra*). The court reasoned that § 107(a)(4)(B) authorized suit by any person other than the persons permitted to sue under § 107(a)(4)(A). 459 F.3d, at 835. Accordingly, it held that § 107(a)(4)(B) provides a cause of action to Atlantic Research. To prevent perceived conflict between § 107(a)(4)(B) and § 113(f)(1), the Court of Appeals reasoned that PRPs that "have been subject to §§ 106 or 107 enforcement actions are still required to use § 113, thereby ensuring its continued vitality." *Id.*, at 836–837.

The parties' dispute centers on what "other person[s]" may sue under § 107(a)(4)(B). The Government argues that "any other person" refers to any person not identified as a PRP in §§ 107(a)(1)–(4). In other words, subparagraph (B) permits suit only by non-PRPs and thus bars Atlantic Research's claim. Atlantic Research counters that subparagraph (B) takes its cue from subparagraph (A), not the earlier paragraph (1)–(4). In accord with the Court of Appeals, Atlantic Research believes that subparagraph (B) provides a cause of action to anyone except the United States, a State, or an Indian tribe-the persons listed in subparagraph (A). We agree with Atlantic Research.

Statutes must "be read as a whole." King v. St. Vincent's Hospital, 502 U.S. 215, 221 (1991). Applying that maxim, the language of subparagraph (B) can be understood only with reference to subparagraph (A). The provisions are adjacent and have remarkably similar structures. Each concerns certain costs that have been incurred by certain entities and that bear a specified relationship to the national contingency plan. Bolstering the structural link, the text also denotes a relationship between the two provisions. By using the phrase "other necessary costs," subparagraph (B) refers to and differentiates the relevant costs from those listed in subparagraph (A).

In light of the relationship between the subparagraphs, it is natural to read the phrase "any other person" by referring to the immediately preceding subparagraph (A), which permits suit only by the United States, a State, or an Indian tribe. The phrase "any other person" therefore means any person other than those three. *See* 42 U.S.C. § 9601(21) (defining "person" to include the United States and the various States). Consequently, the plain language of subparagraph (B) authorizes cost-recovery actions by any private party, including PRPs. *See Key Tronic*, 511 U.S., at 818 (stating in dictum that § 107 "impliedly authorizes private parties to recover cleanup costs from other PRP[s]" (emphasis added)).

The Government's interpretation makes little textual sense. In subparagraph (B), the phrase "any other necessary costs" and the phrase "any other person" both refer to antecedents—"costs" and "person[s]"—located in some previous statutory provision. Although "any other necessary costs" clearly references the costs in subparagraph (A), the Government would inexplicably interpret "any other person" to refer not to the persons listed in subparagraph (A) but to the persons listed as PRPs in paragraphs (1)–(4). Nothing in the text of § 107(a)(4)(B) suggests an intent to refer to antecedents located in two different statutory provisions. Reading the statute in the manner suggested by the Government would destroy the symmetry of §§ 107(a)(4)(A) and (B) and render subparagraph (B) internally confusing.

Moreover, the statute defines PRPs so broadly as to sweep in virtually all persons likely to incur cleanup costs. Hence, if PRPs do not qualify as "any other person" for purposes of § 107(a)(4)(B), it is unclear what private party would. The Government posits that § 107(a)(4)(B) authorizes relief for "innocent" private parties—for instance, a landowner whose land has been contaminated by another. But even parties not responsible for contamination may fall within the broad definitions of PRPs in §§ 107(a)(1)–(4). *See* 42 U.S.C. § 9607(a)(1) (listing "the owner and operator of a . . . facility" as a PRP); *see also* United States v. Alcan Aluminum Corp., 315 F.3d 179, 184 (C.A.2 2003) ("CERCLA § 9607 is a strict liability statute"). The Government's reading of the text logically precludes all PRPs, innocent or not, from recovering cleanup costs. Accordingly, accepting the Government's interpretation would reduce the number of potential plaintiffs to almost zero, rendering § 107(a)(4)(B) a dead letter. *See* Louisville & Nashville R. Co. v. Mottley, 219 U.S. 467, 475 (1911) ("We must have regard to all the words used by Congress, and as far as possible give effect to them").

According to the Government, our interpretation suffers from the same infirmity because it causes the phrase "any other person" to duplicate work done by other text. In the Government's view, the phrase "any other necessary costs" "already precludes governmental entities from recovering under" § 107(a)(4)(B). Even assuming the Government is correct, it does not alter our conclusion. The phrase "any other person" performs a significant function simply by clarifying that subparagraph (B) excludes the persons enumerated in subparagraph (A). In any event, our hesitancy to construe statutes to render language superfluous does not require us to avoid surplusage at all costs. It is appropriate to tolerate a degree of surplusage rather than adopt a textually dubious construction that threatens to render the entire provision a nullity.

The Government also argues that our interpretation will create friction between § 107(a) and § 113(f), the very harm courts of appeals have previously tried to avoid. In particular, the Government maintains that our interpretation, by offering PRPs a choice between § 107(a) and § 113(f), effectively allows PRPs to circumvent § 113(f)'s shorter statute of limitations. *See* 42 U.S.C. §§ 9613(g)(2)–(3). Furthermore, the Government argues, PRPs will eschew equitable apportionment under § 113(f) in favor of joint and several liability under § 107(a). Finally, the Government contends that our interpretation eviscerates the settlement bar set forth in § 113(f)(2).

We have previously recognized that §§ 107(a) and 113(f) provide two "clearly distinct" remedies. *Cooper Industries*, 543 U.S., at 163, n.3. "CERCLA provide[s] for a right to cost recovery in certain circumstances, § 107(a), and separate rights to contribution in other circumstances, §§ 113(f)(1), 113(f)(3)(B)." *Id.*, at 163 (emphases added). The Government, however, uses the word "contribution" as if it were synonymous with any apportionment of expenses among PRPs; *see also, e.g.,* Pinal Creek Group v. Newmont Mining Corp., 118 F.3d 1298, 1301 (C.A.9 1997) ("Because all PRPs are liable under the statute, a claim by one PRP against another PRP necessarily is for contribution"). This imprecise usage confuses the complementary yet distinct nature of the rights established in §§ 107(a) and 113(f).

Section 113(f) explicitly grants PRPs a right to contribution. Contribution is defined as the "tortfeasor's right to collect from others responsible for the same tort after the tortfeasor has paid more than his or her proportionate share, the shares being determined as a percentage of fault." Black's Law Dictionary 353 (8th ed.1999). Nothing in § 113(f) suggests that Congress used the term "contribution" in anything other than this traditional sense. The statute authorizes a PRP to seek contribution "during or following" a suit under § 106 or § 107(a). 42 U.S.C. § 9613(f)(1). Thus, § 113(f)(1) permits suit before or after the establishment of common liability. In either case, a PRP's right to contribution under § 113(f)(1) is contingent upon an inequitable distribution of common liability among liable parties.

Accordingly, the remedies available in §§ 107(a) and 113(f) complement each other by providing causes of action "to persons in different procedural circumstances." *Consolidated Edison*, 423 F.3d at 99; *see also* E.I. DuPont de Nemours, 460 F.3d at 548 (Sloviter, J., dissenting). Section 113(f)(1) authorizes a contribution action to PRPs with common liability stemming from an action instituted under § 106 or § 107(a). And § 107(a) permits cost recovery (as distinct from contribution) by a private party that has itself incurred cleanup costs. Hence, a PRP that pays money to satisfy a settlement agreement or a court judgment may pursue § 113(f) contribution. But by reimbursing response costs paid by other parties, the PRP has not incurred its own costs of response and therefore cannot recover under § 107(a). As a result, though eligible to seek contribution under § 113(f)(1), the PRP cannot simultaneously seek to recover the same expenses under § 107(a). Thus, at least in the case of reimbursement, the PRP cannot choose the 6-year statute of limitations for cost-recovery actions over the shorter limitations period for § 113(f) contribution claims.

For similar reasons, a PRP could not avoid § 113(f)'s equitable distribution of reimbursement costs among PRPs by instead choosing to impose joint and several liability on another PRP in an action under § 107(a). The choice of remedies simply does not exist. In any event, a defendant PRP in such a § 107(a) suit could blunt any inequitable distribution of costs by filing a § 113(f) counterclaim. 459 F.3d at 835; *see also Consolidated Edison, supra*, at 100, n.9 (collecting cases). Resolution of a § 113(f) counter-claim would necessitate the equitable apportionment of costs among the liable parties, including the PRP that filed the § 107(a) action. 42 U.S.C. § 9613(f)(a) ("In resolving contribution claims, the court may allocate response costs among liable parties using such equitable factors as the court determines are appropriate").

Finally, permitting PRPs to seek recovery under § 107(a) will not eviscerate the settlement bar set forth in § 113(f)(2). That provision prohibits § 113(f) contribution claims against "[a] person who has resolved its liability to the United States or a State in an administrative or judicially approved settlement. . . ." 42 U.S.C. § 9613(f)(2). The settlement bar does not by its terms protect against cost-recovery liability under § 107(a). For several reasons, we doubt this supposed loophole would discourage settlement. First, as stated above, a defendant PRP may trigger equitable apportionment by filing a § 113(f) counterclaim. A district court applying traditional rules of equity would undoubtedly consider any prior settlement as part of the liability calculus. Cf. Restatement (Second) of Torts § 886A(2), p. 337 (1977) ("No tortfeasor can be required to make contribution beyond his own equitable share of the liability"). Second, the settlement bar continues to provide significant protection from contribution suits by PRPs that have inequitably reimbursed the costs incurred by another party. Third, settlement carries the inherent benefit of finally resolving liability as to the United States or a State.

Because the plain terms of § 107(a)(4)(B) allow a PRP to recover costs from other PRPs, the statute provides Atlantic Research with a cause of action. We therefore affirm the judgment of the Court of Appeals.

---

## QUESTIONS AND DISCUSSION

**1.** Is the private cause of action the Court finds arising under § 107 of CERCLA express or implied? The statute provides that persons identified as covered persons, known in practice as potentially responsible parties, are "liable for . . . any other necessary costs of response incurred by any other person." 42 U.S.C. § 9607(a)(4)(B). That establishes what PRPs are liable for, but does it establish to whom they are liable and that such persons have a cause of action? The Court said this passage by "its plain terms" provides a cause of action. Do you agree it is so plain, or is the cause of action better thought of as implied by the imposition of liability?

**2.** Regardless of the source of the cause of action, are you convinced by the Court's reasons for distinguishing between the direct cause of action under § 107 and the right of contribution provided under § 113? Note that the Court points to no legislative history supporting its distinction. Would it have made sense for Congress to limit the direct cause of action the same way it did the contribution claim—i.e., by allowing both only "during or following a civil action"? For a case that discusses the interplay between EPA consent orders and the CERCLA § 107 v. § 113 debate, see NCR Corp. v. George A. Whiting Paper Co., 768 F.3d 682 (7th Cir. 2014).

**3.** As the Supreme Court noted in *Atlantic Research*, CERCLA contains different statutes of limitations for different types of claims. A plaintiff may bring a § 107 cost recovery claim within three years from the completion of a removal action and six years from the completion of a remedial action. A plaintiff may bring a § 113 contribution claim within three years from the date of an administrative order or settlement with EPA. *See* 42 U.S.C. §§ 113(g)(2) and (3). But what if a plaintiff both enters into a settlement agreement with EPA and also completes a removal or remedial action and then seeks to recover costs? Which limitations period applies? In Hobart Corp. v. Waste Management of Ohio, Inc., 758 F.3d 757 (6th Cir. 2014), the plaintiff entered into a settlement agreement with EPA and then, after it completed a removal action pursuant to the settlement, sought reimbursement for those costs in a § 107 suit, alleging the limitations period did not begin run until completion of the removal action. The Sixth Circuit disagreed, holding that the limitations period began to run from the date of the settlement agreement, and thus the claim was time barred. *See also* ASARCO, LLC v. Celanese Chem. Co., 792 F.3d 1203 (9th Cir. 2015) (holding that private-party, judicially approved settlements trigger the statute of limitations and thus the plaintiff's contribution claim was time-barred).

**4.** In addition to its statutes of limitation for cost recovery and contribution claims, CERCLA also imposes a "discovery rule" on any state law claims for personal injury or property damage arising from hazardous substance contamination even though such damages are not recoverable under CERCLA itself. CERCLA refers to this discovery rule imposed on state law claims as the "federally required commencement date." *See* 42 U.S.C. § 9658. The effect of this CERCLA discovery rule is that any state law limitations period (whether two years, six years, or another designated time period) will not accrue until the plaintiff discovers or reasonably should have discovered his or her injury and that the harm was caused by the hazardous substance in question. Thus, if a state does not have its own discovery rule (as a matter of statute or common law), CERCLA imposes one for claims for personal injury or property damage associated with hazardous substance contamination. But does this provision apply equally to "statutes of repose"—which exist in some states to cut off the defendant's liability entirely after a particular date such as an expiration date on a drug or other product or after the last culpable act of the defendant? In 2014, the U.S. Supreme Court held that statutes of limitations are sufficiently different from statutes of repose that the discovery rule in 42 U.S.C. § 9658 applies solely to statutes of limitation and not to statutes of repose. CTS Corp v. Waldburger, 134 S. Ct. 2175 (2014). This decision barred a group of plaintiffs in North Carolina from recovering damages for personal injury and property damages associated with hazardous substance contamination at a former military base. The Court found that even if their claims would have been timely if a discovery rule applied, the state's statute of repose cutting off liability for the defendant after its last action at the site (i.e., when the defendant sold the site) was not subject to 42 U.S.C. § 9658. For a more detailed discussion of the *Waldburger* decision, see Alexandra B. Klass & Emma Fazio, *CERCLA, Federalism, and Common Law Claims, in* THE LAW AND POLICY OF ENVIRONMENTAL FEDERALISM: A COMPARATIVE ANALYSIS (Kalyani Robbins, ed., Edgar Elgar Publishing, 2015).

Is the Supreme Court's *Waldburger* decision fair to plaintiffs who may not even discover their injuries or the existence of hazardous substances until many years after the defendant's last action at the site? From another perspective, should Congress be able to interfere with state law in this way by imposing a discovery rule for causes of action based solely on state law? Because of the pure state law nature of these claims, does 42 U.S.C. § 9658 violate the Commerce Clause or the 10th Amendment to the U.S. Constitution? *See* Frier v. Westinghouse Elec. Corp., 303 F.3d 176 (2d Cir. 2012).

**5.** It is now quite common for property owners to voluntarily remediate contaminated sites for purposes of redevelopment even in the absence of an EPA action, which is why it was so important for the Supreme Court to resolve in *Atlantic Research* the CERCLA § 107 v. 113 problem created by *Aviall Services*. Without a CERCLA cost recovery remedy under either § 107 or 113, property owners have much less incentive to remediate contaminated property for redevelopment purposes. Redevelopment of such "brownfields" sites is critical not only because it facilitates necessary remediation of contaminated property but also because it allows residential, commercial, and industrial development to take place in existing urban and suburban areas rather than in uncontaminated "greenfields" areas, which exacerbates suburban sprawl. Many states and, now, EPA and Congress, have created mechanisms to provide owners, lenders, and prospective owners with a range statutory exemptions from liability (i.e., the CERCLA amendments to protect lenders and bona fide prospective purchasers from liability discussed above), or more informal "comfort letters" and memoranda of understanding issued by EPA or state agencies that allow some assurance that voluntarily remediating property contaminated by prior owners and operators will not result in CERCLA or state superfund liability. EPA and states also provide a range of grants and other funding mechanisms to encourage brownfields cleanups. For information on EPA programs and funding relating to brownfields development, see http://www.epa.gov/brownfields/.

---

# CHAPTER 6

# INFORMATION DISCLOSURE

CHAPTER OUTLINE



---

*Knowledge will forever govern ignorance, and a people who mean to be their own governors, must arm themselves with the power knowledge gives. A popular government without popular information or the means of acquiring it, is but a prologue to a farce or a tragedy or perhaps both.*

Letter from James Madison
to W.T. Barry (Aug. 4, 1822)

This chapter focuses on the "softest" of all policy instruments—Persuasion. Unlike the common approaches of prescriptive regulation, technology-forcing standards, market instruments, or focusing on conservation of endangered species, persuasion instruments mandate the generation of information about environmental harms, whether toxics released by a company, an individual's greenhouse gas emissions, or the impacts from a proposed government project. Knowledge is power, the saying goes, and these statutes are premised on the assumption that more information will lead to better decision making by government, companies, and individuals.

# I. THE NATIONAL ENVIRONMENTAL POLICY ACT

## A. INTRODUCTION

Signed into law by President Nixon on New Year's Day, 1970, the National Environmental Policy Act (NEPA) was the first major statute of the modern era of environmental law. A trail-blazer, NEPA relies solely on information generation and dissemination, forcing agencies to consider the environmental impacts of their proposed actions and the comparative impacts associated with reasonable alternatives to proposed actions. This approach reflects a New Deal faith in agency management—a belief that government will do the right thing if it has all of the relevant information before it. Without question, NEPA's influence has been far-reaching, with its progeny in the statute books of 19 states and over 130 of the world's nations as well as an international treaty.

Given its impact, NEPA is a remarkably short statute. Its operative provision, found at 42 U.S.C. § 4332, states that:

> All agencies of the Federal Government shall—
>
> * * *
>
> (C) include in every recommendation or report on proposals for legislation and other major Federal actions significantly affecting the quality of the human environment, a detailed statement by the responsible official on—
>
> (i) the environmental impact of the proposed action,
>
> (ii) any adverse environmental effects which cannot be avoided should the proposal be implemented,
>
> (iii) alternatives to the proposed action,
>
> (iv) the relationship between local short-term uses of man's environment and the maintenance and enhancement of long-term productivity, and
>
> (v) any irreversible and irretrievable commitments of resources which would be involved in the proposed action should it be implemented.

The chief tool for implementing NEPA is the "detailed statement" described above, known as an environmental impact statement (EIS). All federal agencies must create an EIS for "every recommendation or report on proposals for legislation and other major Federal actions significantly affecting the quality of the human environment." At first glance, this potentially takes in a *lot* of government activities, and preparing an EIS can be a considerable undertaking. Often the size of a phone book, the EIS analyzes the environmental impacts across a range of proposed actions. This analysis must consider both unavoidable adverse impacts and mitigation alternatives.

For example, concerns over the amount of traffic in Yosemite Valley led the National Park Service to propose and implement a decision to close parking lots in the Valley and create a shuttle bus service. Before undertaking this action, the Park Service prepared an EIS that considered not only the environmental impacts from this approach but also the impacts of different alternatives, ranging from doing nothing, consolidating parking in different areas of the Valley, to adding bicycle and pedestrian paths along some of the Valley's roads, charging tolls for using the road, or adding a light rail system. You can see the agency's record at http://www.nps.gov/yose/parkmgmt/upload/yvp.pdf.

An EIS may indicate a preferred alternative, but more often simply lays out the options for the decisionmaker. Above all, the key point is to ensure the decisions are informed.

NEPA also created the Council on Environmental Quality (CEQ), an office within the White House, to oversee the NEPA process and its implementation. The CEQ has promulgated detailed regulations to implement NEPA that are binding on all federal agencies and entitled to substantial deference by the courts. CEQ's website is at http://www.whitehouse.gov/ceq. *See generally* 40 C.F.R. Part 1500.

While only a few lines long, NEPA's requirements have generated thousands of lawsuits. It might seem strange that NEPA's seemingly innocuous requirement of preparing an EIS has led to more lawsuits than under any other environmental statute but, given NEPA's potential coverage, these numbers start to make sense. The regulations implementing NEPA have defined federal actions broadly to encompass wholly private actions that require a federal permit or some other form of federal approval before the action can proceed. 40 C.F.R. § 1508.18(b)(4). Thus development or use of federal lands or resources frequently requires a federal permit. A federal permit may even be required when development occurs wholly on private land. For example, a proposed mining operation on private lands that will damage or destroy wetlands may require a permit from the U.S. Army Corps of Engineers under Section 404 of the Clean Water Act. Likewise, a hydroelectric power project requires a license from the Federal Energy Regulatory Commission under the Federal Power Act, and a nuclear power plant requires a license from the Nuclear Regulatory Commission under the Atomic Energy Act.

Beyond its broad coverage, NEPA offers a range of benefits to litigants. As described above, the fundamental goal of NEPA is to *educate* agency decisionmakers, ideally by sensitizing them to environmental issues and helping the agencies find easy, inexpensive means of mitigating environmental impacts. From a *political* perspective, the EIS can be used to educate the public and provide information that can be used to fight the decision through the legislature or voting booth. As one court has explained, "The goal of NEPA is two-fold: (1) to ensure that the agency will have detailed information on significant environmental impacts when it makes decisions; and (2) to guarantee that this information will be available to a larger audience." Western Land Exchange Project v. BLM, 315 F. Supp. 2d 1068, 1086 (D. Nev. 2004). Implicit in these goals is that the EIS be understandable to the general public. From an *advocacy* perspective, the EIS provides information that can be used to fight the ultimate federal action in court, and such information from the agency is not easily dismissed. Finally, NEPA litigation can *delay* a project. The general remedy for a NEPA violation is a remand to the agency to stay its proposed project until it prepares and considers a satisfactory EIS. This allows time to organize opposition and, in some cases, make the project so costly that it expires on its own.

In sum, NEPA has provided plaintiffs with a powerful tool to stall or block agency action. In the context of natural resources management, for example, NEPA provided the essential legal basis for blocking the release of wilderness study areas, California v. Block, 690 F.2d 753 (9th Cir. 1982), for ensuring consideration of the environmental impacts of grazing at the local level, Natural Resources Defense Council v. Morton, 388 F. Supp. 829 (D.D.C. 1974), and for overturning timber sales, Save the Yaak Committee v. Block, 840 F.2d 714 (9th Cir. 1988).

While NEPA and its progeny offer important benefits, it must be kept in mind that information comes at a cost. NEPA can be used to increase the knowledge of agency decision making, but it can also be a powerful tool in NIMBY (Not In My Back Yard) battles where litigation by local opposition may delay and perhaps even kill a project that would benefit the public interest, such as a school, low-income housing, or a prison. A 2003 study found that on average an EIS took six years to complete for a cost ranging from $250,000 to $2,000,000. In an average year, agencies commence roughly 50,000 environmental assessments and 350 EIS. From 2001–2009, 126 NEPA cases were filed annually resulting in 24 injunctions or temporary restraining orders. GAO, NATIONAL ENVIRONMENTAL POLICY ACT: LITTLE INFORMATION EXISTS ON NEPA ANALYSES (APRIL 2014); Arnold W. Reitze, *The Role of NEPA in Fossil Fuel Resource Development and Use in the Western United States*, 39 B.C. ENVTL. AFF. L. REV. 283, 385 (2012).

There is an inevitable tension between the benefits of greater information and understanding, on the one hand, and the costs and time needed to gather, analyze and disseminate this information, on the other. Experience with NEPA has generated heated debate over whether, on balance, it improves agency actions or stymies them. Most everyone agrees in theory that more accurate information should improve decision making. The problem is that government resources are limited (as, of course, are private resources) and the time/money spent generating information means fewer resources and less time available to dedicate to other worthy needs. At what point does requiring more or better information become a counterproductive burden of "too much information"? And, in an age of heightened concerns over national security, at what point does public access to government information create risks of its own?

*Calvert Cliffs' Coordinating Committee v. U.S. Atomic Energy Commission*, 449 F.2d 1109 (D.C. Cir. 1971) was the first significant decision that interpreted NEPA and it provides a useful insight into agencies' lack of environmental concern at the time of NEPA's passage. In complying with NEPA for a nuclear plant licensing, the Atomic Energy Commission's proposed rules fully acknowledged that NEPA requires a "detailed statement" to be "prepared" and to "accompany" the licensing application for a nuclear plant. And, amazingly, this is exactly what would have happened. Under the agency's regulations implementing NEPA, the staff would prepare an environmental impact statement on the license application, and it would accompany the license throughout the process. But in a brilliant example of form over substance, *the statement need not be read or even considered by the licensing board.* It would simply go along for the ride. In his opinion, Judge Skelly Wright emphasized that the whole point of NEPA is to ensure that environmental considerations are taken into account by agency decision makers. Thus, to survive judicial review, "an agency must—to the *fullest* extent possible under its other statutory obligations—consider alternatives to its actions which would reduce environmental damage. . . . Such a full exercise of substantive discretion is required at every important, appropriate and nonduplicative stage of an agency's proceedings." *Id.* at 1128.

The implications of *Calvert Cliffs* were significant. NEPA required reviewing courts to examine the agency decisionmaking process and determine whether environmental concerns had been adequately considered. In decisions that followed, however, particularly *Strycker's Bay Neighborhood Council, Inc. v. Karlen,* 444 U.S. 223 (1980) and *Robertson v. Methow Valley Citizen's Council,* 490 U.S. 332 (1989), the Supreme Court made clear that NEPA is essentially a procedural statute. It does not require a particular substantive result. In *Robertson*, the Forest Service prepared an EIS that addressed, among other things, the impacts of a planned ski resort on the area's mule deer population. The plaintiffs had argued that the agency's mitigation plan was inadequate. In rejecting this argument, the Court stated:

> If the adverse environmental effects of the proposed action are adequately identified and evaluated, the agency is not constrained by NEPA from deciding that other values outweigh the environmental costs. In this case, for example, it would not have violated NEPA if the Forest Service, after complying with

> the Act's procedural prerequisites, had decided that the benefits to be derived from downhill skiing at Sandy Butte justified the issuance of a special use permit, notwithstanding the loss of 15 percent, 50 percent, or even 100 percent of the mule deer herd. Other statutes may impose substantive environmental obligations on federal agencies, but NEPA merely prohibits uninformed—rather than unwise—agency action.

*Id.* at 350–51.

Thus, so long as the agency has complied with the NEPA process and fully considered the EIS, NEPA does not require the agency to choose the environmentally preferable option. Of course, other statutes, such as the Endangered Species Act, might provide a basis for reviewing the substance of an agency's decision, and the NEPA document might provide a prospective litigant with information needed to support a challenge to the decision. Moreover, as the legal realists made clear over ninety years ago, the distinction between procedural and substantive review quickly breaks down. After all, how can the court take a hard look at whether the agency complied with NEPA's procedural requirements (i.e., whether it fully considered the relevant factors) unless the court assesses the agency's final decision (a substantive analysis)?

Because the CEQ does not have, nor does NEPA provide for, enforcement authority, NEPA enforcement has come primarily through legal actions filed under the Administrative Procedure Act. Plaintiffs bear the burden of proof in showing that an agency action has been "arbitrary and capricious, an abuse of discretion or otherwise not in accordance with the law." 5 U.S.C. § 706(2). EPA also provides oversight of agency compliance with NEPA. Section 309 of the Clean Air Act requires EPA to review and comment publicly on all EISs. 42 U.S.C. § 7609(a). In addition, EPA must refer any EIS decision to the CEQ that it believes is not satisfactory.

EIS preparation can be expensive and time-consuming, in no small part because CEQ regulations impose a range of requirements and agencies that fail to follow them offer an easy target for future litigants. In deciding whether to prepare an EIS on a proposed federal action, the CEQ rules require agencies first to consider whether the proposal is one that normally requires an EIS. If the agency does not have enough information to answer, it must prepare an Environmental Assessment (EA). An EA, which is intended to be a "concise public document" but can often be quite substantial, performs two important and distinct functions under NEPA. 40 C.F.R. § 1508.9. It provides the agency with sufficient information to decide whether a full EIS is warranted. It also allows the agency to analyze possible alternatives to the proposed action even where an EIS is not needed.

If the EA ultimately concludes that an EIS is unnecessary, sometimes because the agency commits to mitigating the significant adverse impacts, the agency will issue a FONSI (Finding of No

Significant Impact) and conclude that a full EIS is not needed. Indeed, this is the result in most cases, for agencies prepare EAs far more often that they do EISs. Whether or not an EIS is prepared, resource agencies often issue a "record of decision" (ROD) which memorializes the final decision reached by the agency, including any mitigation measures that the agency is committing to take. The ROD, including any decision not to prepare an EIS, can then be challenged in court.

When an agency prepares an EIS, a draft EIS is first distributed and made available for public comment for at least 45 days, and occasionally longer. The agency then prepares a final EIS and responds to categories of public comments. Once the EIS and ROD have been issued, there is a 30-day moratorium on agency action to afford opponents of the decision an opportunity to file legal challenges.

***The NEPA Decisionmaking Process***
*See* 40 C.F.R. § 1501.4

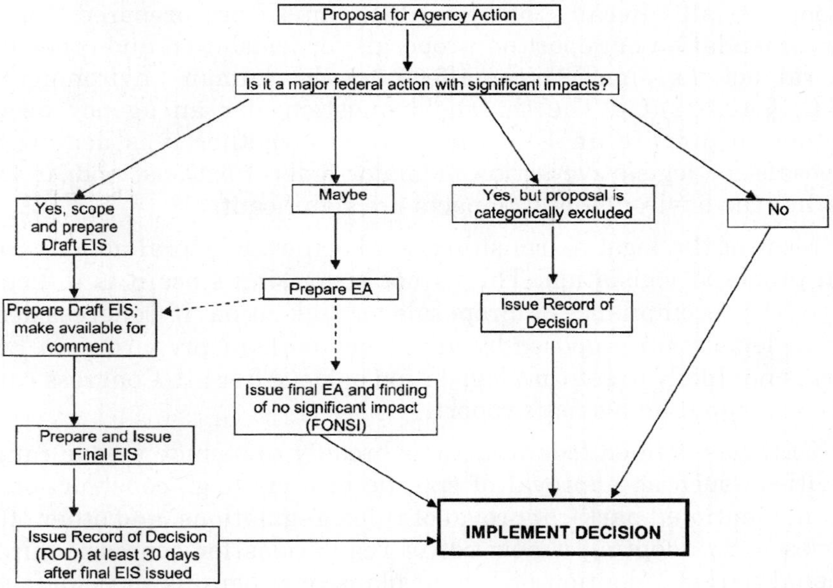

---

Despite the thousands of NEPA cases, they have generally raised the same two basic types of questions:

**(1)** ***Is an EIS required?***

This concerns whether there is a federal agency recommendation or report on proposals for legislation and other major federal action. Most attention has focused on major federal actions, but even if there is a major federal action, an EIS is only required if the action will significantly affect the quality of the human environment or if no relevant exceptions apply.

**(2)** ***Is the EIS adequate in terms of procedure and substance?***

This concerns whether the agency followed proper procedures in issuing the EIS and whether the EIS itself adequately considers the five factors detailed in Sections 4332(C)(i)–(v) set out at the beginning of this section.

The next two sections track these basic questions.

## B. IS AN EIS REQUIRED?

The logic behind preparation of an EIS is straightforward—a better informed agency will make better decisions. To conserve resources, time, and avoid hassle, though, it's equally obvious why, given the choice, some agencies would prefer not to prepare an EIS that questioned its proposed action, at all. Recall that an EIS must be prepared for any "recommendation or report on proposals for legislation and other major Federal actions significantly affecting" the human environment. 42 U.S.C. § 4332(2)(C). The threshold questions for an agency deciding whether to prepare an EIS, then, are (1) whether it is dealing with proposals for legislative action or major federal actions, and, if so, (2) whether the environmental impacts are significant.

Most of the legal skirmishing has been over federal actions rather than proposed legislation. This is not surprising since it is difficult to police NEPA compliance on proposals for legislation. If Congress decides to pass legislation proposed by an agency without preparing an EIS, a court is not likely to set that legislation aside. After all, Congress can act with or without an agency's report.

CEQ has defined federal actions broadly to include a wide range of activities—such as approval of specific projects (e.g., construction of a road in a national park), approval of rules, regulations, and other official policies (e.g., adopting a new set of regulations for concessionaires in national parks), adoption of formal plans or programs to guide agency decisions (e.g., a plan to permit local rangers greater discretion over their parks) and permitting or funding of private projects (e.g., approval of a river crossing for a power line). 40 C.F.R. § 1508.18. It even can include an agency's failure to act when such failure is reviewable under the APA. *Id., see also* 5 U.S.C. §§ 551(13), 706(1).

### 1. MAJOR ACTIONS

Deciding whether there is a federal action is a straightforward judgment in most instances, but it can become complicated when considering NEPA's qualifying adjectives—that the federal action be *major* and that it *significantly* affect the environment. For starters, it is often difficult for agencies to know the full impact of their actions before they are studied. Yet requiring an EIS as a matter of course for routine agency actions would risk trivializing NEPA (not to mention imposing a significant burden). A major federal action may have virtually no environmental impact (e.g., providing a congressman for the District of Columbia), yet one could also imagine relatively minor federal actions with significant environmental impacts.

Consider, for example, an application for a federal right-of-way so a private power line can cross a navigable waterway. The crossing of the waterway will, in itself, have little environmental impact. But construction of the private 67 mile power line will have significant impacts, and cannot be built unless it crosses the waterway. Winnebago Tribe of Nebraska v. Ray, 621 F.2d 269 (8th Cir. 1980). Minor federal actions that are associated with major private actions that might cause significant environmental consequences involve what are sometimes called the "small handle" problem. Do such cases require an EIS? Small handle cases go both ways, with some courts focusing on the impacts of the entire project made possible by federal activity (EIS required) and others just focusing on the discrete federal activity (no EIS). In the *Winnebago Tribe* case described above, for example, the court held that the agency issuing a permit for the 67-mile power line to cross a river need only consider the impact of the crossing and not the impact of the entire power line. In *Sierra Club v. Marsh*, by contrast, the First Circuit held that the Army Corps of Engineers had to prepare an EIS that considered the development and industrialization of an uninhabited island that might result from the Corps' issuance of permits for building a port and a causeway to the island. Sierra Club v. Marsh, 769 F.2d 868, 878 (1st Cir. 1985).

Agencies may also try to avoid NEPA's reach by dividing up or "segmenting" projects. At the extreme, for example, consider how the Forest Service might try to avoid preparing an EIS for its decision to build a 20-mile road in a National Forest. This 20-mile road certainly would seem to be a major federal action significantly affecting the environment. But what if, instead, the Forest Service transformed the project into twenty separate decisions to build one-mile roads? By segmenting, the agency can transform major projects into innocuous minor ones. In isolation, none of these one-mile roads will likely trigger the requirements for an EIS. In scrutinizing examples like this, therefore, courts have asked whether the separate segments have independent utility—whether they are "connected actions." If the road segment along mile 16 makes no sense without miles 17 and 15, then they must be considered together. *See e.g.*, Taxpayers Watchdog, Inc. v. Stanley, 819 F.2d 294 (D.C. Cir. 1987) (upholding an agency EIS that addressed only a small segment of a much larger proposed subway system for Los Angeles because the segment was found to have sufficient independent utility to stand on its own, and did not irretrievably commit the agency to any particular future course of action).

A related problem concerns attempts to analyze individually separate but related actions. Imagine, for example, that the Forest Service decides to build a small road into a heavily-timbered section of forest and does not prepare an EIS because the road will not, by itself, have significant impacts. Soon thereafter, the Forest Service approves timber sales now accessible by the road into the area but does not prepare an EIS because the timber harvest will not have significant effects. Should the road and timber sales have been addressed together in a single EIS? Consider this question as you read the following opinion, a classic NEPA case.

## Thomas v. Peterson

United States Court of Appeals for the Ninth Circuit, 1985.
753 F.2d 754.

■ SNEED, CIRCUIT JUDGE:

Plaintiffs sought to enjoin construction of a timber road in a former National Forest roadless area. The District Court granted summary judgment in favor of defendant R. Max Peterson, Chief of the Forest Service, and plaintiffs appealed. We affirm in part, reverse in part, and remand for further proceedings consistent with this opinion.

STATEMENT OF THE CASE

This is another environmental case pitting groups concerned with preserving a specific undeveloped area against an agency of the United States attempting to obey the commands given it by a Congress which is mindful of both environmentalists and those who seek to develop the nation's resources. Our task is to discern as best we can what Congress intended to be done under the facts before us.

Plaintiffs—landowners, ranchers, outfitters, miners, hunters, fishermen, recreational users, and conservation and recreation organizations—challenge actions of the United States Forest Service in planning and approving a timber road in the Jersey Jack area of the Nez Perce National Forest in Idaho. The area is adjacent to the Salmon River, a congressionally-designated Wild and Scenic River, and is bounded on the west by the designated Gospel Hump Wilderness and on the east by the River of No Return Wilderness. The area lies in a "recovery corridor" identified by the U.S. Fish & Wildlife Service for the Rocky Mountain Gray Wolf, an endangered species. * * *

After the passage of the Central Idaho Wilderness Act, the Forest Service, in keeping with its earlier expressed intention, proceeded to plan timber development in the Jersey Jack area. In November, 1980, the Forest Service solicited public comments and held a public hearing on a proposed gravel road that would provide access to timber to be sold. The Forest Service prepared an environmental assessment (EA) to determine whether an EIS would be required for the road. Based on the EA, the Forest Service concluded that no EIS was required, and issued a Finding of No Significant Impact (FONSI). The FONSI and the notice of the Forest Supervisor's decision to go ahead with the road were issued in a single document on February 9, 1981. The decision notice stated that "no known threatened or endangered plant or animal species have been found" within the area, but the EA contained no discussion of endangered species.

The EA for the road discussed only the environmental impacts of the road itself; it did not consider the impacts of the timber sales that the road was designed to facilitate. Subsequently, on November 23, 1981, and on June 30, 1982, the Forest Service issued EA's for, and approved, two of the timber sales. An EA for a third timber sale was also issued prior to the commencement of this action in district court. Each EA covered only the effects of a single timber sale; none discussed cumulative impacts of the sales or of the sales and the road. Each EA resulted in a FONSI, and therefore no environmental impact statements were prepared.

The plaintiffs appealed the Forest Supervisor's decision on the road to the Regional Forester, who affirmed the decision on May 26,1981. The Regional Forester's decision was then appealed to the Chief of the Forest Service, who affirmed the decision on November 24, 1981. The plaintiffs filed this action, challenging the Chief's decision, on June 30, 1982. * * *

After briefing and oral argument, the district court granted summary judgment for the Forest Service on all claims.

*The NEPA Claim*

The central question that plaintiffs' NEPA claim presents is whether the road and the timber sales are sufficiently related so as to require combined treatment in a single EIS that covers the cumulative effects of the road and the sales. If so, the Forest Service has proceeded improperly. An EIS must be prepared and considered by the Forest Service before the road can be approved. If not, the Forest Service may go ahead with the road, and later consider the environmental impacts of the timber sales.

Section 102(2)(C) of NEPA requires an EIS for "major Federal actions significantly affecting the quality of the human environment." While it is true that administrative agencies must be given considerable discretion in defining the scope of environmental impact statements, *see Kleppe v. Sierra Club,* 427 U.S. 390, 412–15 (1976), there are situations in which an agency is required to consider several related actions in a single EIS, *see id.* at 409–10. Not to require this would permit dividing a project into multiple "actions," each of which individually has an insignificant environmental impact, but which collectively have a substantial impact.

Since the Supreme Court decided the *Kleppe* case, the Council on Environmental Quality (CEQ) has issued regulations that define the circumstances under which multiple related actions must be covered by a single EIS. The regulations are made binding on federal administrative agencies by Executive Order. *See* Exec. Order No. 11991. The CEQ regulations and this court's precedents both require the Forest Service to prepare an EIS analyzing the combined environmental impacts of the road and the timber sales.

*CEQ Regulations*

*1. Connected Actions*

The CEQ regulations require "connected actions" to be considered together in a single EIS. *See* 40 C.F.R. § 1508.25(a)(1) (1984). "Connected actions" are defined, in a somewhat redundant fashion, as actions that:

> (i) Automatically trigger other action which may require environmental impact statements.
>
> (ii) Cannot or will not proceed unless other actions are taken previously or simultaneously.
>
> (iii) Are interdependent parts of a larger action and depend on the larger action for their justification.

The construction of the road and the sale of the timber in the Jersey Jack area meet the second and third, as well as perhaps the first, of these criteria. It is clear that the timber sales cannot proceed without the road, and the road would not be built but for the contemplated timber sales. This much is revealed by the Forest Service's characterization of the road as a "logging road," and by the first page of the environmental assessment for the road, which states that "[t]he need for a transportation route in the assessment area is to access the timber lands to be developed over the next twenty years." Moreover, the environmental assessment for the road rejected a "no action" alternative because that alternative would not provide the needed timber access. The Forest Service's cost-benefit analysis of the road considered the timber to be the benefit of the road, and while the Service has stated that the road will yield other benefits, it does not claim that such other benefits would justify the road in the absence of the timber sales. Finally, the close interdependence of the road and the timber sales is indicated by an August 1981 letter in the record from the Regional Forester to the Forest Supervisor. It states, "We understand that sales in the immediate future will be dependent on the early completion of portions of the Jersey Jack Road. It would be advisable to divide the road into segments and establish separate completion dates for those portions to be used for those sales."

We conclude, therefore, that the road construction and the contemplated timber sales are inextricably intertwined, and that they are "connected actions" within the meaning of the CEQ regulations.

*2. Cumulative Actions*

The CEQ regulations also require that "cumulative actions" be considered together in a single EIS. 40 C.F.R. § 1508.25(a)(2). "Cumulative actions" are defined as actions "which when viewed with other proposed actions have cumulatively significant impacts." Id. The record in this case contains considerable evidence to suggest that the road and the timber sales will have cumulatively significant impacts. The U.S. Fish & Wildlife Service, the Environmental Protection Agency, and the Idaho Department of Fish & Game have asserted that the road and the timber sales will have significant cumulative effects that should be considered in an EIS. The primary cumulative effects, according to these agencies, are the deposit of sediments in the Salmon River to the detriment of that river's population of salmon and steelhead trout and the destruction of critical habitat for the endangered Rocky Mountain Gray Wolf. These agencies have criticized the Forest Service for not producing an EIS that considers the cumulative impacts of the Jersey Jack road and the timber sales. For example, the Fish & Wildlife Service has written, "Separate documentation of related and cumulative potential impacts may be leading to aquatic habitat degradation unaccounted for in individual EA's (*i.e.,* undocumented cumulative effects). . . . Lack of an overall effort to document cumulative impacts could be having present and future detrimental effects on wolf recovery potential." These comments are sufficient to raise "substantial questions" as to whether the road and the timber sales will have significant cumulative environmental effects. Therefore, on this basis also, the Forest Service is required to prepare an EIS analyzing such effects.

*B. Ninth Circuit Precedents*

The conclusion that NEPA requires a single EIS that considers both road and sales is supported by our precedents. In *Trout Unlimited v. Morton,* 509 F.2d 1276 (9th Cir. 1974), we addressed the issue of when subsequent phases of development must be covered in an environmental impact statement on the first phase. We stated that an EIS must cover subsequent stages when "[t]he dependency is such that it would be irrational, or at least unwise, to undertake the first phase if subsequent phases were not also undertaken." Id. at 1285. The dependency of the road on the timber sales meets this standard; it would be irrational to build the road and then not sell the timber to which the road was built to provide access.

The same principle is embodied in standards that we have established for determining when a highway may be segmented for purposes of NEPA. In *Daly v. Volpe,* 514 F.2d 1106 (9th Cir. 1975), we held that the environmental impacts of a single highway segment may be evaluated separately from those of the rest of the highway only if the segment has "independent utility." 514 F.2d at 1110. In the light of *Trout Unlimited,* the phrase "independent utility" means utility such that the agency might reasonably consider constructing only the segment in question. The Forest Service has not alleged that the Jersey Jack road has sufficient utility independent from the timber sales to justify its construction. Severance of the road from the timber sales for purposes of NEPA, therefore, is not permissible.

---

## QUESTIONS AND DISCUSSION

**1.** At what point is the federal action in a project with significant environmental impact too small to be considered major? How would you rule on the following small-handle problem?

Just outside of Washington, D.C., the town of Rockville, Montgomery County, and the state of Maryland proposed a road project around Rockville, known as the "Rockville Circumferential Highway." How would you rule in the following case?

> All of the proposed road projects which would connect to form the alleged "Rockville Circumferential Highway," with one exception, are funded and have been planned by combinations of the City, County and State governments. No federal funds have been used in connection with any portion of Gude Drive, Ritchie Parkway or Research Boulevard and none have been requested. Furthermore, there have been no requests for federal approval of any crossings of the proposed roads over I-270.
>
> The one exception to the lack of federal involvement is a project referred to as the First Street Extension Project, which will extend First Street from Route 586 to Route 355, a distance of less than 0.2 miles. This project was originally designated to be constructed without federal funds but, in the mid-1970s, the City sought and received financial assistance from the Federal Highway Administration (FHA) so that the project will be funded primarily by the federal government. The first two stages of this project, construction of the railroad bridge and acquisition of the right-of-way, have been completed but the final stage, construction of the road itself, is still in the design stage.
>
> It is undisputed that no environmental impact statement has ever been prepared for any of the projects constituting the alleged "Rockville Circumferential Highway." No environmental impact statement was prepared for the federally funded First Street Extension project because of a determination by the FHA that the project was a "non-major action" for which no environmental impact statement was required. With respect to the other segments, financed entirely without federal funds, the State, County, and City officials have not considered the requirements of NEPA applicable and, therefore, have proceeded without any attempt to fulfill the mandates of the federal environmental statute.
>
> It is the lack of an environmental impact statement which forms the basis of the plaintiffs' asserted cause of action in this case. The plaintiffs contend that there is sufficient federal involvement to require an environmental impact statement with respect to the entire group of construction projects constituting the alleged "Rockville Circumferential Highway" and that no further action should be allowed with respect to such a system until an appropriate environmental impact statement has been prepared.

> Since the parties all agree that no environmental impact statement has ever been prepared for any portion of these projects, this case requires a determination of whether or not the provisions of NEPA require the preparation of such an environmental impact statement.

College Gardens Civic Association v. U.S. Department of Transportation, 522 F. Supp. 377 (D. Md. 1981). If an EIS is required, should it consider only the impacts of building the First Street extension, building the Rockville Circumferential Highway, or also examine the likely increase in development, traffic, other roads and population that will likely occur as a result of all the construction? *See* Western North Carolina Alliance v. North Carolina Dept. of Transportation, 312 F. Supp. 2d 765 (E.D.N.C. 2003).

**2.** Many small handle problems focus on permitting, but federal influence on a state or local project can occur through many forms. Consider a state project to eradicate Japanese beetles from state forests. The use of herbicides and other control measures will significantly affect the environment, but is it a major federal action if there is only partial federal funding in the form of a grant from the U.S. Department of Agriculture? What if federal officials from the Department of Agriculture work on the ground with state foresters? What if federal officials simply serve on the project's advisory board?

For this last example, at least, a court has held NEPA is not implicated. In *Almond Hill School v. United States Dept. of Agriculture*, 768 F.2d 1030, 1039 (9th Cir. 1985), the court declared:

> There are no clear standards for defining the point at which federal participation transforms a state or local project into major federal action. The matter is simply one of degree. . . . "Marginal" federal action will not render otherwise local action federal. "Where federal funding is not present, this court has generally been unwilling to impose the NEPA requirement." . . . The employment of federal officials in a state project, however, may be a factor in making the determination of whether the action is sufficiently federal to require an EIS when the officials are significantly involved in the state project.
>
> Here, no federal funds have been sought by the state or spent on the state's beetle eradication project. The appellants attempt to base their federal characterization of the project on the presence of three federal officials on the state's eight-member Japanese beetle advisory board. . . . [But the federal officials] did not possess the authority to implement those aspects of the eradication program challenged here. This is primarily a state project that is neither controlled nor funded by the federal government to any significant degree.

What test should the court use in determining whether indirect support should constitute a major federal action under NEPA?

**3.** The court states that the road and timber sale can be regarded both as connected and as cumulative actions. How would you describe the difference between these two doctrines? Do they require a different type of analysis?

**4.** As described in the Introduction, NEPA has inspired similar laws around the globe. The Convention on Environmental Impact Assessment in a Transboundary Context (Espoo Convention) was adopted in 1991 and sets out international guidelines for conducting environmental reviews when a project in one country has impacts in another country. The Convention requires that the country hosting a proposed activity "likely to cause a significant adverse transboundary impact":

- notify the affected country;
- provide "an opportunity to the public in the areas likely to be affected to participate in relevant environmental impact assessment procedures regarding proposed activities";
- undertake an environmental assessment "at the project level of the proposed activity"; and
- provide that the affected Party should "to the extent appropriate be given the opportunity to participate in this procedure."

---

## 2. SIGNIFICANTLY AFFECTING THE HUMAN ENVIRONMENT

In determining whether an action significantly affects the human environment (such as filling 30 acres of wetland), CEQ has directed agencies to consider the "context" and "intensity" of the proposed action. The rules for determining significance are, by necessity, far from bright line and ultimately require agencies to consider a range of factors in making a judgment call. As one court has described, " '[S]ignificant' is a 'chameleon-like' word that takes its functional meaning from its context." Louisiana Wildlife Fed'n v. York, 761 F.2d 1044, 1052 (5th Cir. 1985). CEQ regulations require agencies to assess a number of considerations when determining significance. For intensity, CEQ has proposed ten factors, including the degree to which the proposed action:

- is controversial or involves uncertain effects;
- is in geographical proximity to cultural resources or ecologically critical areas;
- has short or long term impacts;
- may adversely affect a threatened endangered species or its habitat;
- is likely to be highly controversial;
- affects public health or safety;
- may establish a precedent for future actions with significant effects;
- principle about a future consideration is primarily physical rather than social or economic.

40 C.F.R. § 1508.27.

Moreover, the impact must primarily be physical rather than social or economic. *Metropolitan Edison v. People Against Nuclear Energy*, 460 U.S. 766 (1983), for example, involved a decision to allow an energy company to restart a companion reactor at Three-Mile Island, after the other reactor had suffered a serious accident. The Nuclear Regulatory Commission performed an EIS that considered the effects of fog from cooling towers, the possibility of low-level radiation, or of another accident. Plaintiffs demanded, however, that the EIS also consider the psychological trauma to the community from restarting the reactor. The court rejected this claim, stating that even if psychological injuries are genuine, the risk of such injuries from restarting the reactor were too remote from the challenged action to be cognizable under NEPA. As Justice Brennan made clear in his concurring opinion, psychological injuries that arise from a "direct sensory impact of a change in the physical environment" remain cognizable under NEPA. But those psychological injuries that arise solely from a perception of risk associated with the agency's decision " 'lengthens the causal chain beyond' the reach of the statute." *Id.* at 779.

### 3. TIMING AND TIERING

To prove useful, an EIS must be considered before the agency decides on an action, early enough that it can meaningfully contribute to the decision making process. Otherwise it risks simply serving as a *post hoc* rationalization for a decision already taken. Equally, the agency must have something fairly concrete in mind, otherwise the scope of potential EISs might be too broad to be meaningful. The CEQ regulations address these concerns by requiring preparation of an EIS "as close as possible to the time the agency is developing a proposal. . . ." 40 C.F.R. § 1502.5. They further require the EIS to be prepared "early enough so that it can serve practically as an important contribution to the decisionmaking process. . . ." *Id.*

Challenging the timing of an EIS can be difficult for parties without insider's knowledge of the status of various initiatives under consideration. Indeed, decisionmaking within agencies is often an iterative process and, with memoranda and suggestions circulating back and forth, it may not even be clear to those inside the agency when a recommendation has crystallized into a proposal. Nonetheless, numerous judicial opinions have made clear that agencies may not make an "irreversible and irretrievable commitment" of federal resources before complying with NEPA.

One of the better known cases to address this issue is *Conner v. Burford*, 848 F.2d 1441 (9th Cir. 1988), *cert. denied*, 489 U.S. 1012 (1989). *Conner* involved numerous federal oil and gas leases in a national forest in Montana. The government had prepared an EA describing the effects of the leasing, but had failed to analyze the impacts of oil and gas development itself. On some of the leases the government had included "no surface occupancy" (NSO) stipulations, which precluded use of the surface unless and until the government lifted the stipulation. On other leases, however, no such stipulations were imposed. With these leases, the government had the right to impose reasonable regulations on mineral development, but could not wholly preclude a lessee from surface use. Citing with approval an earlier decision of the D.C. Circuit, the court held that "the sale of non-NSO leases entailed an irrevocable commitment of land to significant surface disturbing activities, including drilling and road building, and that such a commitment could not be made under NEPA without an EIS." *Id.* at 1449. *See also*, Sierra Club v. Peterson, 717 F.2d 1409 (D.C. Cir. 1983); Environmental Defense Fund v. Andrus, 596 F.2d 848 (9th Cir. 1979).

The *Thomas v. Peterson* case, excerpted above in the context of connected and cumulative actions, also rejected the Forest Service's arguments based on timing concerns, specifically *when* the cumulative effects must be considered. 753 F.2d 754 (9th Cir. 1985).

> The Forest Service argues that the cumulative environmental effects of the road and the timber sales will be adequately analyzed and considered in the EA's and/or EIS's that it will prepare on the individual timber sales. The EA or EIS on each action, it contends, will document the cumulative impacts of that action and all previous actions.
>
> We believe that consideration of cumulative impacts after the road has already been approved is insufficient to fulfill the mandate of NEPA. A central purpose of an EIS is to force the consideration of environmental impacts in the decisionmaking process. That purpose requires that the NEPA process be integrated with agency planning "at the earliest possible time," 40 C.F.R. § 1501.2, and the purpose cannot be fully served if consideration of the cumulative effects of successive, interdependent steps is delayed until the first step has already been taken.
>
> The location, the timing, or other aspects of the timber sales, or even the decision whether to sell any timber at all affects the location, routing, construction techniques, and other aspects of the road, or even the need for its construction. But the consideration of cumulative impacts will serve little purpose if the road has already been built. Building the road swings the balance decidedly in favor of timber sales even if such sales would have been disfavored had road and sales been considered together before the road was built. Only by selling timber can the bulk of the expense of building the road be recovered. Not to sell timber after building the road constitutes the "irrational" result that *Trout Unlimited's* standard is intended to avoid. Therefore, the cumulative environmental impacts of the road

and the timber sales must be assessed before the road is approved.

The Forest Service argues that the sales are too uncertain and too far in the future for their impacts to be analyzed along with that of the road. This comes close to saying that building the road now is itself irrational. We decline to accept that conclusion. Rather, we believe that if the sales are sufficiently certain to justify construction of the road, then they are sufficiently certain for their environmental impacts to be analyzed along with those of the road. Cf. City of Davis v. Coleman, 521 F.2d 661, 667–76 (9th Cir. 1975) (EIS for a road must analyze the impacts of industrial development that the road is designed to accommodate). Where agency actions are sufficiently related so as to be "connected" within the meaning of the CEQ regulations, the agency may not escape compliance with the regulations by proceeding with one action while characterizing the others as remote or speculative.

Moreover, the record contains substantial evidence that the timber sales were in fact at an advanced stage of planning by the time that the decision to build the road was made. The Forest Service issued EA's for, and approved, two of the timber sales nine and sixteen months after it issued the road EA, and it had issued an EA for a third sale by the time that this action was filed. In fact, one of the Forest Service's own affidavits shows that the Service was preparing the EA on at least one of the sales at the same time that it was preparing the EA on the road. The record plainly establishes that the Forest Service, in accordance with good administrative practices, was planning contemporaneously the timber sales and the building of the road. Either without the other was impractical. The Forest Service knew this and cannot insist otherwise to avoid compliance with NEPA.

We therefore reverse the district court on the NEPA issue and hold that, before deciding whether to approve the proposed road, the Forest Service is required to prepare and consider an environmental impact statement that analyzes the combined impacts of the road and the timber sales that the road is designed to facilitate.

Another way timing plays out is in the context of scope. For example, *Kleppe v. Sierra Club*, 427 U.S. 390 (1976), dealt with coal development policy on federal lands. It was clear to most observers during the Ford Administration in the mid-1970s that there was an ongoing plan to lease major areas in the northern Great Plains region to coal mining interests, but there had not yet been an official plan or announcement. When the Department of Interior prepared an EIS for its national coal leasing program and local plans for individual leases, the Sierra Club sued. The

Sierra Club claimed that Interior must conduct a regional EIS because the national EIS was too general to assess regional impacts and the project-specific EISs were too narrow. Impacts were greatest at the regional level and it was here that alternative approaches should be considered. The problem from Interior's perspective, though, was that there were many levels of decisionmaking at which one could reasonably prepare an EIS and it was unreasonable to demand an EIS at every stage.

The Supreme Court sided with Interior, stating that an EIS is required only where there is an actual report or recommendation on a proposal for major federal action. A comprehensive EIS is appropriate, the Court declared, when there are significant cumulative or synergistic environmental effects, but it is left to the discretion of the agency when this is the case. *Id.* at 409–410. In other words, the Court defers to agency discretion over the proper scale of analysis.

In practice, agencies have addressed this through the practice of "tiering," preparing successive EISs from broad scale to smaller. Thus an agency often prepares a "programmatic EIS" on the overall project, considering cumulative effects and overall alternatives, and then prepares site-specific supplemental EISs as they become appropriate. By tiering, an agency does not have to consider general effects each time it prepares an individual EIS, and does not need to be comprehensive in its programmatic EIS. The CEQ rules encourage agencies "to tier their environmental impact statements to eliminate repetitive discussions of the same issues and to focus on the actual issues ripe for decision at each level of environmental review." 40 C.F.R. § 1502.20; *see also,* 40 C.F.R. § 1508.28.

### 4. CATEGORICAL EXCLUSIONS

Of course, not all federal actions trigger NEPA. Some statutes, such as the Clean Air Act and parts of the Clean Water Act, specifically exempt agencies from EIS preparation. Other statutes have been interpreted to bypass NEPA because they are "functionally equivalent." As one court described in the context of hazardous waste and the Resource Conservation and Recovery Act (RCRA), for example, "If there were no RCRA, NEPA would seem to apply here. But RCRA is the later and more specific statute directly governing EPA's process for issuing permits to hazardous waste management facilities. As such, RCRA is an exception to NEPA and controls here." Alabama v. EPA, 911 F.2d 499, 504 (11th Cir. 1990). *See also* Alabamians for a Clean Env't v. Thomas, 26 ERC 2116 (N.D. Ala. 1987). Indeed, as a practical matter EPA is excused from complying with NEPA except for a small range of activities since the agency's basic purpose is environmental protection.

All agencies, whether environmental or not, can avoid NEPA compliance if the action is "categorically excluded"—that is, if categories of actions are specifically excluded in the agency's approved NEPA procedures. The CEQ rules define a "categorical exclusion" as "a category of actions which do not individually or cumulatively have a significant effect on the human environment and which have been found to have no such effect in procedures adopted by a Federal agency in implementation of [NEPA's] regulations . . ." 40 C.F.R. § 1508.4. For example, the Department of Agriculture's list of categorical exclusions covers "routine activities such as personnel, organizational changes, or similar administrative functions." 7 C.F.R. § 1508.4. Agencies must also provide for extraordinary circumstances in which a normally excluded action may warrant an EIS. 40 C.F.R. § 1508.7.

Categorical exclusions can provide an attractive means for an agency to avoid preparing an EIS and have generated a great deal of controversy. The most recent dispute concerning categorical exemptions arose in the aftermath of the Deepwater Horizon disaster in 2010, where a British Petroleum oil rig in the Gulf of Mexico caught on fire, killing eleven workers, blowing out its seabed drilling equipment, gushing oil into the Gulf for 87 days and ultimately releasing almost 5 million barrels of oil. As the excerpt below from the Presidential Commission examining the disaster concluded, the reliance on categorical exemptions was disturbing. This case provides a sobering view of what happens when NEPA compliance runs up against a mission-oriented agency and strong external pressure to speed up energy exploration activities.

## Deep Water: The Gulf Oil Disaster and the Future of Offshore Drilling

NATIONAL COMMISSION ON THE BP DEEPWATER HORIZON OIL SPILL AND OFFSHORE DRILLING 81–85 (2010).

In January 1981, the [Interior] Department promulgated final rules declaring that exploration plans in the central and western Gulf of Mexico were "categorically excluded" from NEPA review. At that same time, the Department also categorically excluded from NEPA review applications to drill wells (for exploration or subsequent development and production of oil and gas) "when said well and appropriate mitigation measures are described in an approved exploration plan, development plan, or production plan." In 1986, MMS [Minerals Management Service] scaled back the categorical exclusion to account for the possibility that NEPA review would be needed for these activities in certain narrowly defined "extraordinary circumstances." Extraordinary circumstances include those actions that have highly uncertain and potentially significant environmental effects or involve unique or unknown environmental risks.

But because MMS personnel were apparently reluctant to conclude that such extraordinary circumstances were present, the rule in practice in the Gulf of Mexico was the categorical exclusion—rather than the exception to that exclusion. MMS staff have reported that leasing coordinators and managers discouraged them from reaching conclusions about potential environmental impacts that would increase the burden on lessees, "thus causing unnecessary delays for operators." The Safety Oversight Board also noted that "[s]ome [MMS] environmental staff also reported that environmental assessments for smaller operators may be minimized if the [Regional Office of Field Operations] manager determines that implementing the recommendation may be too costly."

With regard to NEPA specifically, some MMS managers reportedly "changed or minimized the [MMS] scientists' potential environmental impact findings in [NEPA] documents to expedite plan approvals." According to several MMS environmental scientists, "their managers believed the result of NEPA evaluations should always be a 'green light' to proceed." In some cases, there may also have been built-in employee financial incentives that "distort[ed] balanced decision-making" to the extent that "[e]mployee performance plans and monetary awards [were] . . . based on meeting deadlines for leasing or development approvals."

Finally, just as a matter of sheer practicality, MMS personnel plainly lacked the substantial resources that would have been required to engage in meaningful NEPA review in light of the extraordinary expansion of leasing activity in the Gulf. There were literally hundreds of exploration, development, and production plans, as well as individual permit drilling applications to be processed. No President ever sought for MMS the level of resources that would have been required to prepare individual assessments concerning whether each of those activities required an environmental impact statement, let alone such a statement for those that did. Nor did Congress. It should be no surprise under such circumstances that a culture of complacency with regard to NEPA developed within MMS, notwithstanding the best intentions of many MMS environmental scientists. [Prior to the spill, MMS was routinely granting 250–400 categorical exemptions a year for projects in the Gulf.]

*The Macondo Well*

The gap between the protections promised by environmental statutes and regulations and actual practice is fully illustrated in the review and permitting of the Macondo well itself [the well site for Deepwater Horizon]. MMS engaged in no NEPA review of the well's permitting, and neither MMS nor other federal agencies gave significant attention to the environmental mandates of other federal laws.

MMS performed no meaningful NEPA review of the potentially significant adverse environmental consequences associated with its permitting for drilling of BP's exploratory Macondo well. MMS categorically excluded from environmental impact review BP's initial and revised exploration plans—even though the exploration plan could have qualified for an "extraordinary circumstances" exception to such exclusion, in light of the abundant deep-sea life in that geographic area and the biological and geological complexity of that same area. MMS similarly categorically excluded from any NEPA review the multiple applications for drilling permits and modification of drilling permits associated with the Macondo well. The justification for these exclusions was that MMS had already conducted NEPA reviews for both the Five-Year Program and the Lease Sale that applied to the Macondo well. The flaw in that agency logic is that both those prior NEPA reviews were conducted on a broad programmatic basis, covering huge expanses of leased areas of which the Macondo well was a relatively incidental part. Neither, moreover, included a "worst case analysis" because the President's Council on Environmental Quality had eliminated the requirement for such analysis under NEPA for all federal agencies in 1986. As a result, none of those prior programmatic reviews carefully considered site-specific factors relevant to the risks presented by the drilling of the Macondo well. * * *

[N]either BP, in crafting its Oil Spill Response Plan for the Gulf of Mexico applicable to the Macondo well, nor MMS in approving it, evidenced serious attention to detail. For instance, the BP plan identified three different worst-case scenarios that ranged from 28,033 to 250,000 barrels of oil discharge and used identical language to "analyze" the shoreline impacts under each scenario. To the same effect, half of the "Resource Identification" appendix (five pages) to the BP Oil Spill Response Plan was copied from material on NOAA websites, without any discernible effort to determine the applicability of that information to the Gulf of Mexico. As a result, the BP Oil Spill Response Plan described biological resources nonexistent in the Gulf—including sea lions, sea otters, and walruses.

---

## QUESTIONS AND DISCUSSION

**1.** The Presidential Commission report on the Deepwater Horizon states that BP's oil response plan discussed the potential impact on sea lions and walruses. Walruses likely have not been seen in the Gulf of Mexico since the last Ice Age. Why, then, do you think the BP plan addressed the impact of an oil spill on this marine mammal?

Perhaps more disturbing than BP discussing the impacts of Gulf oil spills on walruses is the fact that none of the government regulators spotted this. Given the clear intention of MMS management and most of its staff to facilitate drilling in the Gulf, do you think citizen suits could have played a meaningful role in ensuring greater compliance with NEPA?

**2.** As noted in the text, EPA actions are generally exempted from NEPA compliance because of the "functionally equivalent" doctrine. Given your understanding of NEPA's goals, does this broad exemption make sense? Wouldn't it be a good idea, for example, for the EPA to consider reasonable alternatives to proposed actions, such as permitting decisions, under both the Clean Air and Clean Water Acts? Why do you think the National Park Service has not been granted the same "functional equivalent exemption" as EPA?

**3.** When an agency chooses not to act, can such decisions become a major federal action that triggers an EIS? Consider, for example, the Alaska state program that allows state-licensed hunters to kill wolves that roam federal lands within the state's borders. The Secretary of the Interior has statutory authority to halt the hunting but is not required to take any action. Indeed, in this particular case the Secretary chooses not to act, thus allowing hunting to continue. An animal welfare group sues, alleging that NEPA applies and an EIS is required. How should the court rule? *See* Alaska v. Andrus, 591 F.2d 537 (9th Cir. 1979). Is the omission/commission distinction persuasive in this context?

**4.** One of the more controversial examples of a categorical exclusion has been a Forest Service exclusion for:

> Timber harvest which removes 250,000 board feet or less of merchantable wood products or salvage which removes 1,000,000 board feet or less of merchantable wood products; which requires one mile or less of low standard road construction, and assures regeneration of harvested or salvaged areas, where required.

Forest Service Manual, 1909.15, ch. 31.2.4; 57 Fed. Reg. 43209 (1992). In *Heartwood, Inc. v. United States Forest Service*, a federal district court struck down the timber sale categorical exclusion because the Forest Service had failed to explain its decision:

> The Court finds that the FS [Forest Service] did not provide any rationale for why this magnitude of timber sales would not have a significant effect on the environment. The Court cannot find and the defendants do not direct the Court to any evidence in the record to support the huge increase in the board feet limit from the prior 100,000 limit, except to refer to the FS' expertise and prior experience with timber sales having "these characteristics." 56 Fed. Reg. 19719. That is not sufficient. The FS does not identify nor detail the characteristics to which it refers (road construction length, size of salvage or live tree harvests, etc.) and provides absolutely no other rationale to the Court to explain how and why the agency arrived at these figures. In addition, the FS does not provide any documentation nor evidence regarding the details of these prior harvests nor the FS' analysis of their environmental effects upon which they based their opinion. . . . [T]he Court may not rely merely on the agency's expertise. To uphold the agency's decision, the Court must be convinced that the record contains adequate evidence supporting the agency's expert opinions and decisions, as well as evidence upon which the agency states it relied in making those decisions. When discussing an agency's fulfillment of its NEPA obligations, CEQ regulations state clearly that the record must contain the relevant environmental documents supporting the agency's decision. 73 F. Supp. 2d 962, 975–976 (S.D. Ill. 1999), *aff'd on other grounds*, 230 F.3d 947 (7th Cir. 2000).

In *Alaska Center for Environment v. U.S. Forest Service*, 189 F.3d 851 (9th Cir. 1999), an environmental group challenged the Forest Service's issuance of a one-year special use permit for helicopter-guided skiing and hiking tours in the Chugach National Forest in Alaska. The Forest Service argued that such permits fell within their categorical exclusion for "approval, modification, and continuation of minor, short-term (one-year or less) special uses of National Forest System lands," and that an example of such uses was "the intermittent use and occupancy by state-licensed outfitter or guide." *Id.* at 857. The environmental group contended that the categorical exclusion did not apply because motorized permits were beyond the intended scope of the exclusion and, in any case, this is a major federal action significantly affecting the environment and, therefore, inappropriate for an exclusion. How should the court decide this case?

**5.** Can significant impact include fear or anxiety over a proposed action? How far does the *Metropolitan Edison* ruling extend to other community-group challenges to land use decisions? Consider, for example, the NEPA challenge by local residents against the Department of Justice's decision to convert part of a local mental hospital campus into a federal prison hospital. The Olmsted Citizens group alleged that an EIS was necessary because the new use would "include the introduction of weapons and drugs into the area, an increase in crime, and a decrease or halt in neighborhood development." Olmsted Citizens for a Better Community v. United States, 793 F.2d 201, 205 (8th Cir. 1986). Recall that NEPA requires an EIS for significant impacts to the "human environment." Should an EIS be required? Should it matter whether these will be caused by physical or socioeconomic changes to the environment? Would your answer differ if the new hospital also were likely to increase traffic, the local population concentration, or water-supply problems?

**6.** CERN, a multinational research institution, built the world's largest particle accelerator. The U.S. government provided less than 10% of the accelerator's funding. While the particle accelerator is regarded as a safe piece of equipment, a small number of scientists argued that activating a particle accelerator this large could create a black hole that would swallow the Earth. These doom predictors had been denounced as "fringe scientists" and worse. Unperturbed, concerned parties filed suit in federal District Court alleging that an EIS was needed to evaluate the environmental impact of activating the particle accelerator. The court ruled against the plaintiffs. Since the US government provided less than 10% of the funding, this was not a "major federal action" and therefore was outside the scope of NEPA. *See* Sancho v. Department of Energy, 578 F. Supp. 2d 1258 (Hawaii 2008).

If a federally-funded activity, even if only partially funded, might result in the destruction of the planet shouldn't that qualify as a major federal action with significant impacts? If the federal government had provided more funding to CERN, should the court have ruled differently?

UPDATE: The particle accelerator has started operation and the Earth is still here.

---

### a. *Foreign Actions*

NEPA clearly applies to agency actions taken within the United States, but what about actions taken abroad? Court cases have turned on analysis of where the impacts are felt.

In perhaps the most creative of all NEPA challenges, the National Organization for the Reform of Marijuana Laws (NORML) alleged that a U.S.-supported narcotics program in Mexico that sprayed herbicide on marijuana and poppy plants would have significant health effects (by Americans smoking the herbicide-laden weed) in the United States and that an EIS must be prepared. The government agreed to conduct an EIS. National Organization for the Reform of Marijuana Laws v. United States Dep't of State, 452 F. Supp. 1226 (D.D.C. 1978). It seems clear that international actions that cause impacts in the United States remain subject to NEPA.

By contrast, in *Natural Resources Defense Council v. Nuclear Regulatory Commission*, the D.C. Circuit ruled that NEPA did not apply to the export of nuclear technology where the environmental impacts would occur exclusively in a foreign jurisdiction. 647 F.2d 1345 (D.C. Cir. 1981). The court stated: "the NEPA jurisprudence indicates that exclusively foreign impacts do not automatically invoke the statute's environmental obligations. I find only that NEPA does not apply to NRC nuclear export licensing decisions and not necessarily that the EIS requirement is inapplicable to some other kind of major federal action abroad." Id. at 1366.

Thus it remains unsettled what other kinds of foreign actions require an EIS. This is particularly so in the case of environmental impacts in the global commons (such as the high seas or Antarctica). In *Environmental Defense Fund v. Massey*, 986 F.2d 528 (D.C. Cir. 1993), the court held that NEPA applied to a proposal to build an incinerator on the global commons in Antarctica. Basing its decision both on Antarctica's unique status—a continent without sovereignty and over which the United States exercises great control—and the location of the government decision making process in the United States, the court held that NEPA applied. In other words, the court focused primarily on where the federal agency made the decision (the United States), not where the impacts of the decision occurred (Antarctica). This principle is known as the "headquarters theory." In its first extraterritorial NEPA case after *Massey*, however, the Federal District Court narrowed the potential scope of the *Massey* decision. In *NEPA Coalition of Japan v. Aspin*, 837 F. Supp. 466 (D.D.C. 1993), the court ruled that NEPA did not apply to the actions of the United States at certain military installations in Japan, accepting the government's argument that NEPA's requirements did not apply when treaty relations would clearly be affected.

## QUESTIONS AND DISCUSSION

**1.** Is the president subject to NEPA? You will recall that NEPA applies to "all agencies of the federal government." Does this include presidential actions? For example, after the U.S. had signed the North American Free Trade Agreement with Mexico but before it had been submitted to the Senate for ratification, environmental groups sued to force the Office of the United States Trade Representative to prepare an EIS for the treaty. To the collective gasp of the foreign policy community, the federal district court granted summary judgment and ordered USTR to prepare an EIS of NAFTA "forthwith." Public Citizen v. USTR, 822 F. Supp. 21, 31 (D.D.C. 1993). The D.C. Circuit reversed the lower court, however, holding that NEPA did not apply both because the president's signature of the trade agreement was not final agency action and because the president is not an agency. Public Citizen v. USTR, 5 F.3d 549, 553 (D.C. Cir. 1993), *cert. denied*, 510 U.S. 1041 (1994).

**2.** NEPA does not apply to actions in which an agency "lacks significant discretion," e.g., nondiscretionary statutory mandates that require a particular course of action. For example, a NEPA challenge was brought against Department of Transportation regulations allowing Mexican-based motor carriers to operate in the United States. Plaintiffs argued that the agency decision allowing Mexican trucks to operate across the border would increase air pollution and should be subject to an EIS. The Supreme Court held that NEPA did not apply because the president had lawfully ordered the Department of Transportation to allow Mexican trucks to cross the border and the agency had no authority to do otherwise. As the Court noted, "it would not, therefore, satisfy NEPA's 'rule of reason' to require an agency to prepare a full EIS due to the environmental impact of an action it could not refuse to perform." Department of Transportation v. Public Citizen, 541 U.S. 752 (2004); *see also* Citizens Against Rails-to-Trails v. Surface Transportation Board, 267 F.3d 1144 (D.C. Cir. 2001).

**3.** There are two important executive orders affecting environmental impact statements for foreign activities. President Carter's Executive Order 12114 (Jan. 1979) requires analysis of significant environmental impacts abroad from major federal actions. It covers impacts in the global commons (e.g., the oceans or Antarctica) and a range of actions that significantly affect the environment of a foreign nation. Several categories of actions are exempted from the Order, including actions taken by the president, actions taken when the national security or interest is involved, and votes and other actions in international conferences and organizations. Moreover, E.O. 12114 states that "nothing in this Order shall be construed to create a cause of action." Thus, as with all Executive Orders, noncompliance cannot be challenged in courts. What potentially environmentally damaging actions might fall under these exceptions?

Prior to the WTO Ministerial in Seattle, in November, 1999, President Clinton promulgated Executive Order 13141, requiring the Office of the United States Trade Representative (USTR) and CEQ to carry out environmental reviews of trade negotiations (including multilateral trade rounds, bilateral and plurilateral free trade agreements, and major new trade liberalization agreements in natural resource sectors). The goal is to inform negotiators of environmental opportunities and threats uncovered by increasing trade flows. While the focus of environmental reviews will be impacts in the United States, the Order provides for review of global and transboundary impacts where appropriate and prudent. The reviews to date may be viewed in the Environment section of the USTR website http://www.ustr.gov.

---

## 5. MITIGATION

Agencies can often use the EA process to reach a finding of no significant impact by including mitigation measures, known as a "mitigated FONSI." Consider, for example, the decision excerpted below. Plaintiffs charged that an EIS must be prepared for oil drilling by ASARCO in Forest Service lands near grizzly bear habitat. On its face, it certainly would appear that issuing a permit for this drilling would qualify as a major federal action significantly affecting the human environment, but the court found otherwise.

### Cabinet Mountains Wilderness v. Peterson

United States Court of Appeals for the D.C. Circuit, 1982.
685 F.2d 678, 681–684.

■ ROBB, CIRCUIT JUDGE.

This court has established four criteria for reviewing an agency's decision to forego preparation of an EIS: (1) whether the agency took a "hard look" at the problem; (2) whether the agency identified the relevant areas of environmental concern; (3) as to the problems studied and identified, whether the agency made a convincing case that the impact was insignificant; and (4) if there was impact of true significance, whether the agency convincingly established that changes in the project sufficiently reduced it to a minimum. *Maryland-National Capital Park and Planning Comm'n v. United States Postal Service*, 487 F.2d 1029, 1040 (1973). The fourth criterion permits consideration of any mitigation measures that the agency imposed on the proposal. As this court noted, "changes in the project are not legally adequate to avoid an impact statement unless they permit a determination that such impact as remains, after the change, is not 'significant.' " *Id.* Other courts have also permitted the effect of mitigation measures to be considered in determining whether preparation of an EIS is necessary. See, e.g., *Preservation Coalition, Inc. v. Pierce*, 667 F.2d 851, 860 (9th Cir. 1982); *City & County of San Francisco v. United States*, 615 F.2d 498, 501 (9th Cir. 1980); *Sierra Club v. Alexander*, 484 F. Supp. 455, 468 (N.D. N.Y.), *aff'd mem.*, 633 F.2d 206 (2d Cir. 1980). Logic also supports this result. NEPA's EIS requirement is governed by the rule of reason, *Committee for Auto Responsibility v. Solomon*, 195 U.S. App. D.C. at 421, 603 F.2d at 1003 (1979), and an EIS must be prepared only when significant environmental impacts will occur as a result of the proposed action. If, however, the proposal is modified prior to implementation by adding specific mitigation measures which completely compensate for any possible adverse environmental impacts stemming from the original proposal, the statutory threshold of significant environmental effects is not crossed and an EIS is not required. To require an EIS in such circumstances would trivialize NEPA and would "diminish its utility in providing useful environmental analysis for major federal actions that truly affect the environment." *Id.* * * *

Because the mitigation measures were properly taken into consideration by the agency, we have no difficulty in concluding that the Forest Service's decision that an EIS was unnecessary was not arbitrary or capricious. The record indicates that the Forest Service carefully considered the ASARCO proposal, was well informed on the problems presented, identified the relevant areas of environmental concern, and weighed the likely impacts.

When ASARCO submitted its four-year drilling proposal the agency prepared an environmental assessment, copies were circulated for comment, and public meetings were held. An extensive biological evaluation was conducted which concluded the proposed drilling could potentially affect the grizzly bears in two ways: habitat modification and increased human-bear interactions, including direct encounters and reductions in secure habitat due to human disturbances. The evaluation also pointed out that the cumulative effects of the proposal and other concurrent activities might be significantly greater than the effects of the drilling proposal considered by itself. *Id.* As to habitat modification, the evaluation concluded the adverse effect would be insignificant. *Id.* The total area involved in the drilling was estimated to be less than one-half acre and even this estimate was considered high because the drill sites could be reclaimed. The more serious threat was posed by the loss of secure habitat due to increased human activities in the area, particularly the disturbance of important denning and feeding sites. Timber sales and recreational activities were specifically referred to. *Id.* To reduce such potential adverse effects to a minimum, fourteen recommendations were made, including completion of project activities by October 31 of each year, restrictions of helicopter flights to specified corridors, measures to reduce helicopter noise, seasonal restrictions on the use of helicopters in particular areas, prohibition of project activities in the Copper Gulch area after July 31 in order to protect potentially important late summer and early fall food sources, daily restrictions on helicopter flights during important feeding periods, monitoring of the project by a biological technician, closure of various roads to protect the bears during feeding periods and to enhance their security, prohibiting the carrying of firearms by ASARCO personnel, prohibiting overnight camping by project personnel except in emergency situations, and daily removal of food wrappers, containers and excess food.

The Forest Service also initiated formal consultation with the FWS (U.S. Fish and Wildlife Service). In its biological opinion the FWS expressed concern over the cumulative effects of human activities in the area and agreed that displacement of the bears from secure habitats was the most serious impact of the proposal. Although the FWS concluded that the drilling program was likely to jeopardize the bears, it set forth a number of measures which were designed to avoid this result. To reduce adverse effects to a minimum the FWS stated that restrictions set forth in the biological evaluation prepared by the Forest Service must be strictly adhered to. Because the Chicago Peak area is a potentially important denning area, the FWS recommended that September 30, rather than October 31, should be the annual termination date for drilling activities. In assessing the cumulative effects of activities in the area, the FWS used a 10-mile travel radius for the bears to determine which other activities were relevant. This estimated travel radius was based on several expert studies of grizzly bears' home range. Using this method the FWS determined that certain timber sales and roads were relevant in addressing the problem of cumulative effects. Therefore, in addition to modifying ASARCO's period of operations, the FWS recommended rescheduling or eliminating certain timber sales and implementing specified road closures to provide a more secure habitat for the bears. According to the FWS, this course of action would "completely compensate in specific ways the cumulative adverse effects of the proposed project and other ongoing and proposed Forest Service activities" and would "avoid jeopardizing the continued existence of the grizzly bear." The Forest Service's final environmental assessment incorporated the recommendations made in the biological evaluation and biological opinion and expressly adopted the complete compensation plan devised by the FWS.

---

## QUESTIONS AND DISCUSSION

**1.** Assume, for argument's sake, that the Forest Service issues a permit to ASARCO but, bowing to political pressures in Washington, does not include any of the mitigation conditions it had pledged to carry out in its environmental assessment as permit conditions. Is the Forest Service bound by any mitigation pledges in its EA (or even in an EIS)? Are there any NEPA claims that can be filed at this point?

**2.** The CEQ rules define mitigation to include avoiding, minimizing, rectifying, reducing, or eliminating environmental impacts, or compensating for them by providing replacement or substitute resources. 40 C.F.R. § 1508.20. Mitigation is supposed to figure prominently in an environmental analysis. For example, the CEQ rules require agencies to describe appropriate mitigation measures for the proposed action and alternatives and for the environmental consequences that are expected from agency actions. 40 C.F.R. § 1502.16(e), (f), (g), and (h).

In 2011, CEQ issued a guidance document directed at FONSI's based on mitigation commitments. *See* CEQ, Appropriate Use of Mitigation and Monitoring and Clarifying the Appropriate Use of Mitigated Findings of No Significant Impact (Jan. 14, 2011). The guidance emphasizes that when agencies base their environmental analysis on a commitment to mitigate the environmental impacts of a proposed action, they should adhere to those commitments, monitor how they are implemented, and monitor the effectiveness of the mitigation. Specifically, the guidance affirms that agencies should:

- commit to mitigation in decision documents when they have based environmental analysis upon such mitigation (by including appropriate conditions on grants, permits, or other agency approvals, and making funding or approvals for implementing the proposed action contingent on implementation of the mitigation commitments);
- monitor the implementation and effectiveness of mitigation commitments;
- make information on mitigation monitoring available to the public, preferably through agency web sites; and
- remedy ineffective mitigation when the Federal action is not yet complete.

Does this guidance document create a cause of action under NEPA if an agency does not comply with its mitigation commitments?

**3.** NEPA does not require that agencies actually mitigate environmental harm, even if that mitigation can be accomplished at little or no additional cost. Robertson v. Methow Valley Citizens Council, 490 U.S. 332 (1989). By contrast, Canada has adopted an environmental assessment law that specifically mandates that government agencies implement appropriate mitigation measures when they approve actions that may adversely impact the environment. Canadian Environmental Assessment Act, ch. 37, § 37(2) (1992).

Even though NEPA does not mandate mitigation, agency action can almost always be challenged on the grounds that it is arbitrary and capricious and an agency that fails to take reasonable actions to mitigate environmental harm may be vulnerable on those grounds. Still, such questions are rarely black and white, and an agency that refuses to mitigate environmental harm may be able to justify its decision on the grounds of cost or inconvenience.

**4.** California's "mini-NEPA," known as the California Environmental Quality Act (CEQA), requires agencies to identify the significant environmental impacts from projects. It goes beyond this requirement shared by NEPA, however.

> Section 21081.6 of the Public Resources Code requires all state and local agencies to establish monitoring or reporting programs

> whenever approval of a project relies upon a mitigated negative declaration or an environmental impact report (EIR). The monitoring or reporting program must ensure implementation of the measures being imposed to mitigate or avoid the significant adverse environmental impacts identified in the mitigated negative declaration or EIR. * * *
>
> [W]henever a public agency either: (1) adopts a mitigated negative declaration, or (2) completes an EIR and makes a finding pursuant to Section 21081(a) of the Public Resources Code taking responsibility for mitigation identified in the EIR, the agency must adopt a program of monitoring or reporting which will ensure that mitigation measures are complied with during implementation of the project. When changes have been incorporated into the project at the request of an agency having jurisdiction by law over natural resources affected by the project, that agency, if so requested by the lead or responsible agency, must prepare and submit a proposed reporting or monitoring program for the changes. * * *
>
> Subdivision (b) of Section 21081.6 requires that mitigation measures be "fully enforceable through permit conditions, agreements, or other measures." Incorporating the mitigation measures into the conditions of approval applied to the project meets this requirement. Where the project consists of a general plan (or other type of policy plan), a regulation, or a public project, the mitigation measures can be incorporated into the policies of the plan, the regulations themselves, or the design of the project to meet the enforceability requirement.

Governor's Office of Planning and Research, *Tracking CEQA Mitigation Measures Under AB 3180,* 1996.

From a litigator's perspective, what types of cases can you likely bring under CEQA that you could not bring under NEPA?

**5.** What if the predictions of the EIS, upon completion, turn out to be inaccurate or ignored? Consider the plight of Ms. Noe. She owned a bookshop that apparently was rattled to the core by the nearby construction of Atlanta's metro system, MARTA. She sued for a temporary injunction, among other remedies, asserting "that the failure of MARTA and its builders to stay within the noise levels predicted by the environmental impact statement constituted a violation of that section of NEPA that requires the filing of such statements prior to beginning construction." Noe v. Metropolitan Atlanta Rapid Transit Authority, 644 F.2d 434, 435 (5th Cir. 1981). Both the district and circuit courts, however, refused to imply a private right of action for Noe to sue. As the circuit court explained,

> NEPA contains no . . . protections or prohibitions against conduct directed at private individuals. NEPA does not even require the protection of the environment. NEPA requires only that, prior to beginning construction of a project likely to affect the environment, an environmental impact statement be produced so that the individuals responsible for making the decision to go ahead with or

stop the project do so on a well-informed basis. In that sense, NEPA provides procedural rather than substantive protection.

*Id.* at 438.

---

## PROBLEM EXERCISE: DEVELOPING THE SQUAW VALLEY RESORT

Perini Land & Development Company, a private resort developer, has proposed to build a multi-million dollar, year-round resort in Squaw Valley, California. The resort will be built entirely on private land and, when completed, would include a major new ski area, a hotel, condominium, retail complex, and a new, 18-hole golf course. The Squaw Creek flows through the valley where much of the development will take place. Construction of the golf course will require Perini to fill eleven acres of wetlands adjacent to the creek. Perini has spent almost five years obtaining the necessary permits from the county board of supervisors, the regional water control board, the state water control board, and the U.S. Army Corps of Engineers (the Corps). Under Section 404 of the Clean Water Act, Perini needs a permit from the Corps in order to dredge and fill the wetlands (*see* the discussion of Section 404 in Part II of Chapter 4).

The Corps has granted a conditional 404 permit, allowing the wetlands to be developed but requiring Perini to mitigate by constructing 12.7 acres of new wetlands and restoring 117 acres of the meadow. The Corps has conducted an environmental assessment and determined that granting the 404 permit will not have a significant effect on the environment. Soon after the permit had been issued, the Corps was sued by a local resident who charged that the Corps improperly limited the scope of its analysis to the golf course rather than the entire resort complex and should prepare an EIS. The district court first issued a temporary restraining order preventing any development in the wetlands and soon after issued a preliminary injunction halting work on the entire resort. Perini has appealed. Assume you are the appellate judge's law clerk and have been asked to identify and assess the likely arguments raised by both sides. In drafting your response, consider the CEQ regulations described in *Thomas*, the determination of significance, and the following regulations adopted by the Corps in response to the CEQ rules:

> *b.* *Scope of Analysis*
>
> (1) In some situations, a permit applicant may propose to conduct a specific activity requiring a Department of the Army (DA) permit (*e.g.*, construction of a pier in a navigable water of the United States) which is merely one component of a larger project (*e.g.*, construction of an oil refinery on an upland area). The district engineer should establish the

scope of the NEPA document (*e.g.*, the EA or EIS) to address the impacts of the specific activity requiring a DA permit and those portions of the entire project over which the district engineer has sufficient control and responsibility to warrant Federal review.

(2) The district engineer is considered to have control and responsibility for portions of the project beyond the limits of Corps jurisdiction where the Federal involvement is sufficient to turn an essentially private action into a Federal action. These are cases where the environmental consequences of the larger project are essentially products of the Corps permit action.

Typical factors to be considered in determining whether sufficient "control and responsibility" exists include:

(i) Whether or not the regulated activity comprises "merely a link" in a corridor type project (*e.g.*, a transportation or utility transmission project).

(ii) Whether there are aspects of the upland facility in the immediate vicinity of the regulated activity which affect the location and configuration of the regulated activity.

(iii) The extent to which the entire project will be within Corps jurisdiction.

(iv) The extent of cumulative Federal control and responsibility.

33 C.F.R. Part 325, App. B, § 7.b.

---

## C. IS THE EIS ADEQUATE?

A standard EIS will include an explanation of the purpose and need for action, a full description of alternative actions, an assessment of the environmental impacts of these actions, and possible mitigation measures to reduce adverse impacts of the proposed actions. In taking a hard look at such an EIS, courts have focused on questions of alternatives, adequacy, uncertainty and new information. As we shall see, this has resulted in four related legal strategies to challenge the adequacy of an EIS—the EIS did not set forth responsible opposing views or alternatives, it was not compiled in objective good faith, it would not permit the decisionmaker to fully consider and balance the relevant factors, or the fact-finding did not have a substantial basis in fact.

### 1. SUFFICIENCY OF ANALYSIS

An agency must follow NEPA procedures, but the quality of an EIS analysis is subject to judicial review, as well. In practice, this means the agency has to address the issues seriously. In *Sierra Club v. U.S. Army*

*Corps of Engineers*, 701 F.2d 1011 (2d Cir. 1983), for example, the Corps prepared an EIS for filling part of the Hudson River to build a highway. The EIS described the area to be filled as a "biological wasteland," despite objections by EPA and the U.S. Fish & Wildlife Service. In requiring the Corps to prepare a supplemental EIS, the Second Circuit concluded that by ignoring the views of other expert agencies, by not adequately compiling relevant data and analyzing it reasonably, the Corps had reached a "baseless and erroneous factual conclusion" that "cannot be accepted as a 'reasoned' decision." Id. at 1034–35. In most cases though, wary of appearing to engage in substantive review, courts are reluctant to reverse agencies on this ground. Thus, in *Sierra Club v. Marita*, 46 F.3d 606 (7th Cir. 1995), plaintiffs sued the Forest Service, claiming that its EIS needed to employ an ecosystems approach based on advanced principles of conservation biology. Despite the testimony of thirteen distinguished scientists, the court rejected the plaintiff's argument. According to the Seventh Circuit, agencies must use "high quality" science and ensure the "scientific integrity" of their analysis. But the court will not mandate that they have to use any particular methodology.

As we have seen throughout the casebook, scientific uncertainty is an unavoidable aspect of environmental decision making. This arises in the context of NEPA when agencies must decide what to do if there is insufficient information to predict the impacts of particular options. Uncertainty is a common feature of environmental decision making, and even more so early in the process, when an EIS would be developed. When do agencies have to conduct more research? CEQ regulations state that if information essential to a reasoned choice among alternatives is not available and the cost of obtaining the information is not exorbitant, the agency must include the information in its analysis before making a decision. 40 C.F.R. § 1502.22(a). If, however, obtaining the relevant information is too difficult, expensive or time-consuming, the agency is obliged to include in the EIS, among other things, "a summary of existing credible scientific information" that is relevant to evaluating the "reasonably foreseeable significant adverse impacts" of the proposed action, and the agency's evaluation of such impacts "based upon theoretical approaches and research methods generally accepted in the scientific community." 40 C.F.R. § 1502.22(b). For purposes of this rule "reasonably foreseeable" is defined to include "impacts which have catastrophic consequences, even if their probability of occurrence is low . . ." In practice, this requires that agencies at least consider the tradeoffs between the costs of getting more information and the value of getting it. When possible, an agency should rely on credible scientific evidence and, if information is unavailable, admit that the effects are uncertain and unknown.

An important question that can arise in an extended EIS process is whether an agency must prepare a supplemental EIS when new information becomes available, perhaps significantly changing the range of impacts considered. Imagine, for example, that the area to be filled in the Hudson River really was a "biological wasteland." Soon after the filling of the river began, though, a local fisherman caught a fish listed under the ESA and it now appears that a population of the endangered fish lives nearby. Must the Corps stop construction and prepare a supplemental EIS?

The CEQ regulations address this problem by requiring supplementation of the EIS in two circumstances: (1) where the agency makes substantial changes in the proposed action that are relevant to environmental concerns, or (2) where there are significant new circumstances or information relevant to environmental concerns and bearing on the proposed action or its impacts. 40 C.F.R. § 1502.9(c)(1). In *Marsh v. Oregon Natural Resources Council*, 490 U.S. 360 (1989), the Supreme Court rejected a claim that the Army Corps of Engineers had violated NEPA when it failed to prepare a second supplemental EIS. In so doing, however, the Court made clear that agencies must consider new information even after a decision has already been made. As with other stages of the EIS process, this is subject to the rule of reason. Surely such a "post-decision" supplemental EIS is not necessary every time new information comes to light. Rather, an agency must look to the significance of the new information, its value to the decision making process, and how much of the federal action remains to be done.

## 2. ALTERNATIVES ANALYSIS

NEPA requires that the EIS contain a detailed statement on alternatives. According to CEQ, the alternative analysis is the "heart" of the EIS. "[I]t should present the environmental impacts of the proposal and the alternatives in comparative form, thus sharply defining the issues and providing a clear basis for choice among options by the decisionmaker and the public." 40 C.F.R. § 1502.14. Obviously, though, there is an endless number of potential alternatives an agency could consider. To address this, the CEQ regulations require agencies to consider only "reasonable alternatives," including the alternative of "no action." *Id.* But alternatives cannot be deemed unreasonable simply because they are outside the jurisdiction of the lead agency. Agencies must "[r]igorously explore and objectively evaluate all reasonable alternatives, and for alternatives that were eliminated from detailed study, briefly discuss the reasons for their having been eliminated." *Id.* at § 1502.14(a). The agency must also identify their "preferred alternative" if they have one. Mitigation measures for both the proposed action and alternatives must also be addressed in the EIS.

Courts have similarly required that agencies consider an array of alternatives that fairly represent the *range* of alternatives. In *California v. Block*, 690 F.2d 753 (9th Cir. 1982), for example, plaintiffs challenged the EIS informing the U.S. Forest Service's decision over which portions of a 62 million acre national forest should remain roadless and designated wilderness. There was no lack of interest on the part of the public, and the Service's draft EIS drew 264,000 public comments. In its final EIS, the Service considered eleven alternatives, ranging from the extremes of all wilderness to no wilderness. So far, so good. In between, however, none of the alternatives considered allocating more than 33 percent of the roadless area to wilderness. In holding that this was inadequate, the Ninth Circuit emphasized that an agency need not consider every alternative or alternatives that are unlikely to be implemented for legitimate reasons but, equally, it must not ignore important alternatives or bias its evaluation by arbitrarily narrowing the range of options considered. While NEPA remains a procedural statute, this type of analysis skates a very close line to substantive review.

Despite the importance of the alternatives analysis to NEPA compliance, agencies often struggle with this requirement since it can force them to consider options that they may not prefer and that may even be outside of their jurisdiction to implement. The following cases illustrate how agencies can narrow alternatives to favor their preferred course of action.

## Simmons v. U.S. Army Corps of Engineers

United States Court of Appeals for the 7th Circuit, 1997.
120 F.3d 664.

■ CUDAHY, CIRCUIT JUDGE.

Eight years have elapsed since the City of Marion, Illinois, first proposed building a new water reservoir in the southernmost tip of Illinois. In those eight years a tale has unfolded that is all too familiar. Lawsuits have stopped the project short; the case has visited the district court twice; and Marion still is no closer to a new water supply. As is routine in American administrative law, the litigation has little to do with what anybody really cares about. One side wants a dam built and a new lake created, and the other does not. Instead, the dispute, now in and out of federal court for five years, has centered on procedures—whether the U.S. Army Corps of Engineers fulfilled its procedural obligations under federal environmental law. All this is true. But the case provides a textbook vindication of the wisdom of Congress in insisting that agencies follow those procedures in the first place.

### I.

With passage of the National Environmental Policy Act, Congress established the nation's central and unique environmental policy for (self-)regulating the federal government. Although policymakers and courts have cooked up enough acronyms under NEPA for a feast of officialese, the thrust of NEPA is simply expressed. For all "major Federal actions significantly affecting the quality of the human environment," federal agencies must articulate why they have settled upon a particular plan and what environmental harms (or benefits) their choice entails.

NEPA mandates a searching inquiry into alternatives, but says nothing about which to choose. It binds federal officials to justify their plans in public, after a full airing of alternatives. It thus blends a faith in technocratic expertise with a trust in democracy. Officials must think through the consequences of—and alternatives to—their contemplated acts; and citizens get a chance to hear and consider the rationales the officials offer. But, if a federal agency has heard all the objections to a plan and considered all the sensible options before it, the agency has fulfilled its duty.

When a federal agency prepares an Environmental Impact Statement (EIS), it must consider "all reasonable alternatives" in depth. 40 C.F.R. § 1502.14. No decision is more important than delimiting what these "reasonable alternatives" are. That choice, and the ensuing analysis, forms "the heart of the environmental impact statement." To make that decision, the first thing an agency must define is the project's purpose. The broader the purpose, the wider the range of alternatives; and vice versa. The "purpose" of a project is a slippery concept, susceptible of no hard-and-fast definition. One obvious way for an agency to slip past the strictures of NEPA is to contrive a purpose so slender as to define competing "reasonable alternatives" out of consideration (and even out of existence). The federal courts cannot condone an agency's frustration of Congressional will. If the agency constricts the definition of the project's purpose and thereby excludes what truly are reasonable alternatives, the EIS cannot fulfill its role. Nor can the agency satisfy the Act. 42 U.S.C. § 4332(2)(E).

We are confronted here with an example of this defining-away of alternatives. In 1989, the City of Marion applied to the U.S. Army Corps of Engineers (the Corps) for permission to build a dam and reservoir, as required by § 404 of the Clean Water Act. The dam would block up Sugar Creek, a free-flowing stream in southern Illinois running seven miles southeast of Marion. Marion envisioned that the resulting Sugar Creek Lake would supply water not just to Marion, but to the Lake of Egypt Water District, which encompasses six counties and 15,000 rural customers. Sugar Creek Lake would drown a substantial area, with the usual environmental effects of drowning, including the transformation or obliteration of the riverine habitats of several species.

We discuss the details of the project's history below, but the case boils down to no more than those bare facts. From the beginning, Marion and the Corps have defined the project's purpose as supplying two users (Marion and the Water District) from a single source—namely, a new lake. Accordingly, when the Corps prepared an environmental impact statement, it confined the analysis to single-source alternatives. And therein lies the difficulty. At no time has the Corps studied whether this single-source idea is the best one—or even a good one. Marion and the

Lake of Egypt Water District share a common problem, a thirst for water. From this fact the Corps adduces the imperative for a common solution. We disagree. A single source may well be the best solution to the putative water shortages of Marion and the Lake of Egypt Water District. The Corps' error is in accepting this parameter as a given. To conclude that a common problem necessarily demands a common solution defies common sense. We conclude that the U.S. Army Corps of Engineers defined an impermissibly narrow purpose for the contemplated project. The Corps therefore failed to examine the full range of reasonable alternatives and vitiated the EIS. We reverse.

## II.

The City of Marion and the Lake of Egypt Water District both want more water. Since the 1920s, the City of Marion has drawn the bulk of its water from the man-made Marion City Lake. Marion's thirst for water has long since outstripped Marion City Lake's capacity of 1.1 million gallons per day, and Marion has had to go elsewhere for an additional 600,000 gallons per day. (The parties have not told us how or where.) Marion City Lake is a poor reservoir, to boot; its raw water requires costly chemical treatment to render it potable. Marion contends that a new reservoir—in particular, the proposed Sugar Creek Lake—would slake the City's thirst. The Lake of Egypt Water District, too, argues that it needs a new source of water. The Water District gets its water from the Lake of Egypt, another reservoir of marginal quality. The Water District turns out not to own the namesake lake, but instead must buy the water from an electric co-op, which does own the Lake of Egypt, and which limits diversion of the Lake's water.

Marion proposed to solve both problems in one stroke. A new reservoir was in order, and Marion thought a dam over Sugar Creek would work best. The dam would lie at the head of a valley about seven miles southeast of Marion. The new Sugar Creek Lake would be 2500 feet wide and 20,000 feet long, and would generate 8.9 million gallons per day of raw water. A 20-inch diameter pipeline would run the water to Marion. The Lake of Egypt Water District would then buy some of that water from Marion.

Then the federal government got involved. Sugar Creek falls under federal jurisdiction as one of the navigable waters of the United States. Section § 404 of the Clean Water Act, 33 U.S.C. § 1344, obliges anyone who would discharge "dredged or fill material into the navigable waters" to obtain a permit from the U.S. Army Corps of Engineers. A dam across Sugar Creek would require such a permit, *see* Van Abbema v. Fornell, 807 F.2d 633, 636 (7th Cir. 1986), and in 1989, Marion sought the Corps' approval. The need for Corps approval makes the proposed dam a kind of federal action, and thus NEPA was invoked.

In 1991 the Corps completed a preliminary study of the proposed dam, termed an "environmental assessment" in the argot of NEPA. If a federal project has no "significant impact" on the environment, there is no need to go forward with a much deeper study—the EIS (environmental impact statement). In its environmental assessment, the Corps concluded that the four-mile long, half-mile wide Sugar Creek Lake, which would flood a square mile-and-a-half of wetlands, woods, fields and farms and would block up "one of the last free-flowing streams in southern Illinois"—the Corps' own words—would have no "significant impact" on the environment. A group of plaintiffs (affected landowners plus the Sierra Club) filed suit in the Southern District of Illinois, claiming that the Corps' determination was arbitrary and capricious and that NEPA obliged the Corps to prepare an environmental impact statement. On this first round through the Southern District of Illinois, the case fell to Judge Foreman. He ruled for the plaintiffs. In his well-reasoned, graceful (and unfortunately unpublished) opinion, Judge Foreman found manifold flaws in the Corps' conclusion of no significant environmental impact. Hundreds and hundreds of acres would be flooded. The bald eagle and two federally protected bats (the Indian bat and the gray bat) would lose habitats. Two aquatic creatures in Sugar Creek, the least brook lamprey and the Indiana crayfish, would be "extirpated," in the Corps' ominous phrase. And every state and federal agency with environmental competence called at a minimum for the Corps to write up an environmental impact statement.

Not least among the flaws—and the most glaring in hindsight—was the Corps' failure to consider reasonable alternatives. Judge Foreman deemed the environmental assessment "incomplete and flawed," and found no hint "that the Corps gave independent thought to the feasibility of alternatives." To start, Judge Foreman faulted the Corps' explanation for dismissing other single-source ideas, including Rend Lake and Devils Kitchen Lake. But the problems ran deeper, to the roots of the Corps' thinking. The Corps had dismissed certain alternatives because they supplied Marion and the Water District from separate sources. Why the Corps assumed the imperative of a single-source project, however, remained unexplained. "[T]he Corps never questioned the need for finding a water supply for both Marion and Lake of Egypt Water District," Judge Foreman wrote. "Yet there is no evidence that only Marion can supply Lake of Egypt Water District's water needs." (As we explain below, Judge Foreman's remarks remain just as true, and the Corps' analysis just as faulty, five years later.) Based on the flaws we mention above, plus others we do not, Judge Foreman vacated Marion's permit and forbade the Corps to issue another until it completed an environmental impact statement.

By late 1994, the Corps had a draft EIS ready. The Corps held a public hearing in December 1994 and received over a thousand written comments. The final EIS came out in July 1995. More comments followed. The Corps learned it had incorrectly assumed that Rend Lake was unavailable. (Rend Lake was one of the existing unitary water sources that the Corps had cursorily dismissed as an alternative in its environmental assessment.) The Corps prepared a supplement to the final EIS. Finally, on July 29, 1996, the Corps made its decision. Colonel Ralph Grieco (the decision-maker and a defendant in this action) wrote that building Sugar Creek Lake would be "environmentally sustainable." The project would not conflict with the public interest, he found. The Corps re-issued the permit.

The plaintiffs in the first action (minus the Sierra Club) contested the Corps' decision. This time, the case went before Chief Judge Gilbert. On cross-motions for summary judgment, the plaintiffs argued three points in the district court: one, the final EIS was inadequate; two, the Corps violated NEPA and the regulations promulgated thereunder by the Council on Environmental Quality; and three, the Corps violated its own regulations. In a carefully drafted opinion, the chief judge resolved all three points in favor of the Corps and Marion. The plaintiffs appealed, but only on the second point: whether the Corps had breached the strictures of NEPA by failing to consider all reasonable alternatives in its final EIS. We consider the merits of their appeal next.

### III.

Logic and law dictate that every time an agency prepares an environmental impact statement, it must answer three questions in order. First, what is the purpose of the proposed project (major federal action)? Second, given that purpose, what are the reasonable alternatives to the project? And third, to what extent should the agency explore each particular reasonable alternative? These are questions for an agency (the Corps) to resolve in the first instance. We owe and accord deference to the Corps on whether the Corps resolved those three questions in a permissible way. "[I]t is not our role to second-guess" the Corps. Van Abbema, 807 F.2d at 636. We ensure only that "the Corps followed required procedures, evaluated relevant factors and reached a reasoned decision." *Id.*

The Corps rigged the environmental impact statement on the question of purpose, contend the plaintiffs. The Corps defined the project's purpose as finding or creating a single source to supply both Marion and the Lake of Egypt Water District. (Actually, the Corps never did so explicitly; the district court had to "fill in the blanks" to ascribe this purpose to the Corps.) The Corps' imputed definition, the plaintiffs say, is unreasonable: the project's real purpose is supplying Marion and the Water District with more water, and there are reasonable alternatives to that beyond relying on a single reservoir. Marion, for instance, could hook its water-treatment plant up to an existing pipeline stemming from Rend Lake and lying only seven miles away. (Marion's water-treatment plant is twelve miles away from Sugar Creek Lake.)

As its first line of defense, the Corps essentially passes the buck to Marion. Marion wanted a single reservoir to supply it and the Lake of Egypt Water District. Since Marion is the proposer and will construct the project, the Corps must accept its definition. This is a losing position in the Seventh Circuit. Over a decade ago, we held that "the evaluation of 'alternatives' mandated by NEPA is to be an evaluation of alternative means to accomplish the general goal of an action." Van Abbema, 807 F.2d at 638; 40 C.F.R. § 1502.13 ("The [EIS] shall briefly specify the underlying purpose and need") (CEQ regulations). The general goal of Marion's application is to supply water to Marion and the Water District—not to build (or find) a single reservoir to supply that water. Indeed, in *Van Abbema*, we specifically rejected the Corps' present position. An agency cannot restrict its analysis to those "alternative means by which a particular applicant can reach his goals." Van Abbema, 807 F.2d at 638. This is precisely what the Corps did in this case. The Corps has "the duty under NEPA to exercise a degree of skepticism in dealing with self-serving statements from a prime beneficiary of the project." And that is exactly what the Corps has not shown in its wholesale acceptance of Marion's definition of purpose.

We turn then to probe the reasonableness of the Corps' looking only to single-source alternatives to damming Sugar Creek. Here the Corps argues that Marion and the Lake of Egypt Water District share the same problem—a shortage of water—and that they are contiguous. Hence, a single source is the obvious solution. Maybe, even probably, the Corps is right. Alternatives might fail abjectly on economic grounds. But the Corps and, more important, the public cannot know what the facts are until the Corps has tested its presumption. It is axiomatic that the Corps need not examine every conceivable alternative. Identifying, assessing and comparing alternatives costs time and money, and an agency should focus its energies only on the potentially feasible, not the unworkable. As a matter of logic, however, supplying Marion and the Water District from two or more sources is not absurd—which it must be to justify the Corps' failure to examine the idea at all. In fact, the plaintiffs have advanced at least one concrete alternative that seems reasonable: for Marion to build a shorter pipeline that would ultimately feed water from the extant Rend Lake. Alaska Wilderness Recreation & Tourism v. Morrison, 67 F.3d 723, 729 (9th Cir. 1995) ("The existence of a viable but unexamined alternative renders an environmental impact statement inadequate.") What other alternatives exist we do not know, because the Corps has not looked. Perhaps the Corps is relying on a contract between Marion and the Water District for Marion to supply the Water District with water if it succeeds in damming Sugar Creek. But this condition depends on meeting environmental requirements, which, in turn, demand exploration of alternatives free of contractual arrangements. The public interest in the environment cannot be limited by private agreements.

Perhaps cognizant of the weakness of the Corps' stance, co-defendant Marion argues that the Corps did look into separate-source alternatives—which the Corps itself does not even claim. This last ditch effort is unavailing. Marion cites to the EIS and the Corps' record of decision, but all we find are conclusory statements. Two separate projects would cost more than one, we are told, with no support: no mention of concrete proposals, no cost figures, no specifics at all. Even if we put aside that the Corps disclaims making this inquiry, the record offers precious little to show that the Corps ever paused to test its foundational assumption.

IV.

If NEPA mandates anything, it mandates this: a federal agency cannot ram through a project before first weighing the pros and cons of the alternatives. In this case, the officials of the Army Corps of Engineers executed an end-run around NEPA's core requirement. By focusing on the single-source idea, the Corps never looked at an entire category of reasonable alternatives and thereby ruined its environmental impact statement. We presume that the Corps' failure to satisfy NEPA was inadvertent, notwithstanding the Corps' failure to heed the admonitions of Judge Foreman on this point. We believe that Judge Foreman was right at the time of his decision, and remains right.

We regret that eight years have passed since the City of Marion first proposed to remedy its water shortage. Still no decision has been made. Better-oiled machinery for environmental policy-making would have long since decided yea or nay on the single-source rationale for Sugar Creek. Either way, Marion would probably have its extra water by now, from whatever source. But the specter of further delay cannot in itself justify setting aside the mandate of the law. The Corps failed to comply with the most basic terms of NEPA. If fault must be found, it lies with those who refused to consider patently reasonable alternatives and who ignored the explicit directions of the federal bench.

The opinion of the district court is REVERSED and the case REMANDED with instructions to enter summary judgment for the plaintiffs and to vacate the permit.

---

## WildEarth Guardians v. National Park Service

United States Court of Appeals for the 10th Circuit, 1997.
703 F.2d 1178.

■ TYMKOVICH, CIRCUIT JUDGE.

### I. Background

Rocky Mountain National Park (RMNP), located in northern Colorado, was established in 1915. The Rocky Mountain National Park Enabling Act (RMNP Act) bans hunting or killing wildlife within the park, with very limited exceptions. The park has always had a substantial elk population. But most elk predators, especially wolves and grizzly bears, were exterminated in the park area prior to its establishment, and Congress's decision to ban hunting in RMNP allowed the park's elk population to grow without constraint.

In the 1930s, the National Park Service (NPS) became concerned that the growing number of elk threatened the park's vegetation through overgrazing. In 1944, the NPS began to control the number of elk by relocating or killing them. This practice was the norm until 1969, when the NPS changed its elk management policy. The agency theorized that increased hunting in the areas around RMNP would sufficiently control the elk population, as elk tend to wander in and out of the park. This policy was not successful, however, as commercial and residential development near RMNP decreased the number of open spaces where hunting was allowed and RMNP's elk became habituated to residential areas. As a consequence, the number of elk in RMNP has more than tripled since 1969.

Several studies conducted in the 1990s found that the park's elk population is substantially larger, more sedentary, and more concentrated than it would be under natural conditions. As a result, elk overgraze much of the park's vegetation, eliminating some plant species and making it difficult for others to regenerate. In response, the NPS decided it needed a new elk management policy for the park, both to reduce the overall number of elk and to make the population fluctuate from year to year, as would occur under natural conditions. The NPS expected this would also have a beneficial effect on the park's vegetation.

In August 2002, the NPS assembled an interagency planning team to develop a new elk management plan. The participating agencies included the United States Forest Service, the Colorado Division of Wildlife (CDOW), and several nearby counties and municipalities, with the NPS designated as the lead agency.

In May 2003, the NPS published a notice in the Federal Register of its intent to prepare a new elk and vegetation management plan for RMNP and an environmental impact statement (EIS) for the plan. The NPS solicited public comments through a variety of channels, including newsletters, a website, and public meetings.

The NPS received around 1,100 public comments on its proposal, which it used to develop a preliminary draft of alternatives for the management plan. In July 2004, the agency publicly released these draft alternatives. One of the proposed alternatives was reintroducing a self-sustaining wolf population to RMNP (the natural wolf alternative). The NPS convened a meeting of biologists and other experts in March 2005 to discuss the feasibility of the natural wolf alternative. And once again, the agency sought public comments on the proposed alternatives.

Based on the second round of public comments and feedback from its experts, the NPS selected four alternative plans for analysis in an EIS. In a publicly released August 2005 newsletter discussing these alternatives, the NPS announced it would analyze the introduction of a small number of intensively managed wolves into the park, in conjunction with the use of sharpshooters, but would not include the natural wolf alternative in its EIS. The agency explained this alternative was infeasible due to lack of support from coordinating agencies, concerns by neighboring communities, the high potential for human-wolf conflicts, and the likelihood that management of wolves in the park would be expensive and time-consuming, distracting from the goal of the NPS's plan—managing elk.

In April 2006, the NPS publicly released a draft EIS that considered five alternative management plans: (1) the current plan (the no-action alternative); (2) rapid reduction of the elk population, which the agency identified as its preferred alternative; (3) gradual reduction of the elk population; (4) a combination of managed killing and elk contraception; and (5) a combination of managed killing and the introduction of a small number of intensively managed gray wolves. The draft EIS reiterated the NPS's reasons for excluding the natural wolf alternative.

The NPS again sought public comment on its draft EIS and held several public meetings during the comment period. The agency then considered the more than 3,100 comments it had received and prepared a final EIS.

The agency released its final EIS in December 2007. Although the agency had identified rapid reduction as its preferred alternative in the draft EIS, the final EIS selected a different alternative, gradual reduction. * * *

After the final EIS was released, WildEarth sought judicial review of the NPS's decision. WildEarth alleged the NPS acted arbitrarily and capriciously by excluding consideration of the natural wolf alternative from its EIS. . . . The district court entered judgment for the NPS, concluding the agency took a hard look at the relevant data and articulated a rational connection between that data and its conclusion that the natural wolf alternative was infeasible. * * *

## II. Discussion

### A. *Standard of Review*

We give no deference to a district court's review of agency action, reviewing its decision de novo. But our review of the NPS's actions is considerably more deferential. We review the NPS's compliance with NEPA under the Administrative Procedure Act (APA), which authorizes us to set aside agency action only when it is "arbitrary, capricious, an abuse of discretion, or otherwise not in accordance with law."

When reviewing agency action, our task is to ensure the agency examined the relevant data and articulated a rational connection between that data and its decision. Our deference to the agency is more substantial when the challenged decision involves technical or scientific matters within the agency's area of expertise. Accordingly, we will not set aside an agency's decision unless: the agency (1) entirely failed to consider an important aspect of the problem, (2) offered an explanation for its decision that runs counter to the evidence before the agency, or is so implausible that it could not be ascribed to a difference in view or the product of agency expertise, (3) failed to base its decision on consideration of the relevant factors, or (4) made a clear error of judgment.

"Deficiencies in an EIS that are mere `flyspecks' and do not defeat NEPA's goals of informed decisionmaking and informed public comment will not lead to reversal." *New Mexico ex rel. Richardson v. BLM,* 565 F.3d 683, 704 (10th Cir. 2009). And even if an agency violates the APA, this does not require reversal unless the appellant demonstrates prejudice resulting from the error. As these principles imply, a "presumption of validity attaches to the agency action and the burden of proof rests with the appellants who challenge such action." *New Mexico,* 565 F.3d at 704.

### *B. NEPA*

WildEarth's sole NEPA claim is that the NPS deviated from NEPA's required procedure by declining to consider the natural wolf alternative in its environmental impact statement. WildEarth argues the wolf alternative fit the purpose and need of the proposed action, and thus required the NPS to consider it in an EIS.

Agencies must consider alternatives to any project that might have a significant effect on the quality of the human environment. But agencies need not consider every possible alternative to a proposed action, only "reasonable" alternatives. A "rule of reason" applies to an agency's decision to prepare an EIS, as well as the agency's choice of alternatives to include in its analysis. In other words, agencies are not required to consider alternatives they have "in good faith rejected as too remote, speculative, or . . . impractical or ineffective." *Custer County Action Ass'n v. Garvey,* 256 F.3d 1024, 1039 (10th Cir. 2001). "Alternatives that do not accomplish the purpose of an action are not reasonable, and need not be studied in detail by the agency." *Citizens' Comm. to Save Our Canyons v. U.S. Forest Serv.,* 297 F.3d 1012, 1031 (10th Cir. 2002). Agencies must "briefly discuss the reasons" for eliminating unreasonable alternatives from an EIS.

WildEarth acknowledges that NEPA does not require an agency to consider impractical alternatives, but it argues the natural wolf alternative was practical. In particular, WildEarth points to studies, emails, and other documents in the record discussing the benefits of this alternative. The evidence WildEarth points to falls into three broad categories: (1) evidence of the biological benefits of wolf reintroduction, such as studies concluding that wolves not only reduce the number of elk but also prompt elk to congregate in smaller groups and spend less time grazing any particular area, further reducing their impact on vegetation; (2) information about successful wolf reintroduction in Yellowstone National Park and Banff National Park in Canada; and (3) evidence discussing the feasibility of wolf reintroduction, including a 1994 survey showing that 70.8% of Coloradans support wolf reintroduction and a 2004 report by CDOW's Wolf Management Working Group that discussed the potential benefits of wolf tourism and an offer by an environmental group to compensate livestock owners for wolf predation. While the record supports some benefits to a natural wolf option, that is not what guides us. What guides us is a rule of reason, where the agency explains its decision to take certain proposed options off the table because of a lack of practicality.

The NPS did that here. The agency found the natural wolf alternative would be impractical despite some marginal upside, and the record supports that decision. For example, wolf reintroduction may have been successful in Yellowstone and Banff, but the record reflects that those parks are not a good comparator for RMNP. RMNP is many times smaller than Banff and Yellowstone, and also much closer to residential and commercial developments at the park entrances, plus it is near a heavily populated urban area, Colorado's Front Range Urban Corridor. The NPS determined RMNP has relatively little suitable wolf habitat due to its small size and abundance of steep, high-altitude terrain, which wolves dislike. And as a consequence of the lack of habitat and wolves' natural tendency to disperse, NPS experts predicted that any wolves in RMNP would be very likely to leave the park boundaries, prompting conflicts with neighboring communities. Such conflicts would likely include predation on livestock and pets.

All this would require intensive, costly management of wolves by RMNP personnel, diverting the park's resources and attention from the very problem the NPS is trying to address—elk overpopulation and degraded vegetation. And given RMNP's relatively small size and the near certainty that wolves would leave park boundaries, the NPS would need the cooperation of Colorado wildlife agencies to manage wolves outside the park, where the NPS has no jurisdiction. Yet CDOW was unwilling and unable to do so. To add to the complexity of the proposal was the fact that the gray wolf species is endangered, lending a level of state management not required of other species. *See* Colo.Rev. Stat. § 33–2–105.5 (prohibiting any state or local agency from reintroducing threatened or endangered species into Colorado without authorization from the legislature).

WildEarth argues the NPS should not have considered CDOW's lack of support when determining the feasibility of the natural wolf alternative. WildEarth reads federal regulations to require NPS to ignore CDOW's opposition when determining which alternatives to include in its EIS. 40 C.F.R. § 1502.14(c) (requiring agencies to consider alternatives otherwise outside their jurisdiction in an EIS). We disagree with WildEarth's broad reading of § 1502.14(c). This regulation is intended to prompt agencies to consider otherwise appropriate alternatives that the agency lacks jurisdiction to authorize. But it is not meant to force an agency to consider alternatives rendered infeasible by the actions of another agency.

If the NPS concluded the natural wolf alternative was infeasible because it could not bring wolves to RMNP without CDOW's permission, then 40 C.F.R. § 1502.14(c) might require the NPS to include that alternative in its EIS if the alternative were otherwise feasible. But that is not the case. The NPS could bring wolves to RMNP with or without CDOW's approval. But without CDOW's cooperation in managing wolves outside RMNP's boundaries, the NPS estimated wolf reintroduction was unlikely to succeed. This is a question of feasibility, not jurisdiction. Consequently, the NPS did not violate § 1502.14(c) by excluding the natural wolf alternative from its EIS. * * *

WildEarth concludes by pointing to several emails and other internal communications from NPS employees expressing the opinion that the natural wolf alternative would be feasible, or at least should be included in the EIS. But the fact that some individual NPS employees believed the natural wolf alternative should be included in the EIS does not demonstrate that the agency ignored its own experts or inexplicably changed its mind. WildEarth cites no evidence showing this was a consensus view, rather than a recommendation from a few individual employees. Even if some NPS employees held this view, a diversity of opinion by local or lower-level agency representatives will not preclude the agency from reaching a contrary decision, so long as the decision is not arbitrary and capricious and is otherwise supported by the record. The NPS cites ample evidence supporting its decision, including the consensus opinion of the experts at its March 2005 meeting. Even the evidence WildEarth cites identifies factors both supporting and undermining the feasibility of the natural wolf alternative. Accordingly, WildEarth has not demonstrated that the NPS ignored its own experts when it decided to exclude the natural wolf alternative from its EIS.

Finally, it is worth reiterating that the NPS continued to consider wolves as a management tool at RMNP even after it eliminated the natural wolf alternative from its EIS. The agency included a modified wolf alternative in its EIS, combining a more limited role for wolves with the use of sharpshooters to cull elk. WildEarth suggests this alternative is not a substitute for the natural wolf alternative at least in part because these wolves would be sterilized, but this is not entirely accurate. Only the male wolves would be sterilized, and only at first. If wolves proved useful as a management tool and successfully established themselves in the park, they would later be allowed to breed. Under this plan, RMNP's wolf population would be more tightly regulated than under the natural wolf alternative, but this conclusion is appropriate given that the NPS's goal was not to reintroduce wolves but to manage elk.

In sum, we find that the NPS met NEPA's requirements when it excluded the natural wolf alternative from its EIS. The agency discussed the reasons for its decision in a newsletter it released prior to its release of the draft EIS, in the draft EIS, and in the final EIS, as required by 40 C.F.R. § 1502.14(a). The agency drew a rational connection between these reasons and its conclusion by examining the data in the record, consulting experts at its March 2005 meeting on wolf reintroduction, and repeatedly explaining why it excluded the natural wolf alternative from its EIS. This is all NEPA and the APA require. * * *

---

## QUESTIONS AND DISCUSSION

**1.** The relevant language from the CEQ rules for alternatives analysis is set out below. Are *Simmons* and *WildEarth Guardians* consistent with these rules?

> In this section agencies shall:
>
> (a) Rigorously explore and objectively evaluate all reasonable alternatives, and for alternatives which were eliminated from detailed study, briefly discuss the reasons for their having been eliminated.
>
> (b) Devote substantial treatment to each alternative considered in detail including the proposed action so that reviewers may evaluate their comparative merits.
>
> (c) Include reasonable alternatives not within the jurisdiction of the lead agency.
>
> (d) Include the alternative of no action.
>
> (e) Identify the agency's preferred alternative or alternatives, if one or more exists, in the draft statement and identify such alternative in the final statement unless another law prohibits the expression of such a preference.
>
> (f) Include appropriate mitigation measures not already included in the proposed action or alternatives.

40 C.F.R. § 1502.14.

How would you respond to the Corps of Engineers argument that the City of Marion wanted a single reservoir? What if the Marion City Council had told the Corps that a multiple sources alternative is simply not a politically viable option, and therefore section (a) allows them not to examine this alternative? If this would not be permissible, then why does the *WildEarth Guardians* court give so much deference to the Colorado Department of Wildlife's opposition?

**2.** *Simmons* and *WildEarth Guardians* reach very different holdings. Are the two cases consistent with one another? Why are the wolf relocation alternatives judged adequate but the water provision alternatives inadequate?

**3.** What must the Corps do to comply with the *Simmons* decision? Is it enough to create a supplemental EIS that simply adds a multiple sources section and then re-issue the same permit?

**4.** At the District Court level in *Simmons*, Judge Foreman found "Hundreds and hundreds of acres would be flooded. The bald eagle and two federally protected bats (the Indian bat and the gray bat) would lose habitats. Two aquatic creatures in Sugar Creek, the least brook lamprey and the Indiana crayfish, would be 'extirpated,' in the Corps' ominous phrase. And every state and federal agency with environmental competence called at a minimum for the Corps to write up an environmental impact statement." Despite this, the Corps of Engineers concluded there was no significant environmental impact and therefore no need for an EIS. Why do you think the Corps reached this conclusion? What does this suggest to you about the significance accorded to NEPA by the Corps and the importance of citizen suits to ensure agency compliance?

---

## PROBLEM EXERCISE:
## SUPPLEMENTATION OF ENVIRONMENTAL ANALYSES

The Forest Supervisor for the Medicine Bow National Forest has approved the Banner Timber Sale. In an environmental assessment of the sale, four options are considered. Under Alternative 1, no action would take place; Alternative 2 would allow logging 6.7 million board feet of timber; Alternative 3 provides for a smaller timber sale; and Alternative 4 provides for forest restoration projects. The Supervisor selects Alternative 2. In justifying his decision, he cites three "key" reasons:

(1) that Alternative 2 would do the most to help timber dependent communities;

(2) that the decision was consistent with the Forest Plan; and

(3) that Alternative 2 had the highest "benefit-cost" ratio of any of the alternatives considered.

After the timber sale was approved, the Forest Service conducted an inspection of the 362 acre sale area and determined that 55% fewer trees could be logged than had originally been assumed. The Forest Service therefore revised its estimate of the amount of timber available from the sale downward to 3 million board feet. As a result of this revision, the economics of the sale changed so that the approved sale no longer had the highest "benefit-cost ratio" of the alternatives that had been considered during the original analysis of the sale. Furthermore, the new data suggested that the sale would cost more than it would generate in revenue, so the government would actually lose money if it went forward with the sale.

Friends of the Bow filed a lawsuit alleging that the decision was arbitrary and capricious on the basis of the revised economic analysis. How should the Court analyze the agency's decision? What arguments can be made for or against the proposition that the decision approving the sale was arbitrary and capricious? Should the Forest Service conduct a supplemental EIS based on the inspection of the sale area? *See* Friends of the Bow v. Thompson, 124 F.3d 1210 (10th Cir. 1997).

---

## D. CHIPPING AWAY AT NEPA

### 1. NEPA AND NATIONAL SECURITY

As a result of the increased concern with national security following the attacks of September 11th, there has been a vigorous debate over whether the Department of Defense's and Department of Homeland Security's compliance with environmental laws compromise the nation's readiness. The claim that NEPA indirectly weakens our security is a powerful charge and raises difficult trade-offs. Should the military be given special exemptions from NEPA and, if so, under what circumstances?

The Real ID Act of 2005, attached as a rider to an appropriations bill to fund the wars in Iraq and Afghanistan, provided that

> Notwithstanding any other provision of law, the Secretary of Homeland Security shall have the authority to waive all legal requirements such Secretary, in such Secretary's sole discretion, determines necessary to ensure expeditious construction of the barriers and roads under this section.

Section 102(c)

Relying on this authority, the Secretary of Homeland Security, Michael Chertoff, granted a series of waivers in 2005–2008 from NEPA and a number of other environmental and historic preservation laws for projects in California, New Mexico, Arizona and Texas related to border protection. The waivers covered activities such as roads, over 470 miles of fence construction, towers, etc. The Department stated that it had conducted environmental reviews for many of the projects. Because of the waivers, however, they could not be challenged in court. Indeed, a number of lawsuits challenging these projects were dismissed in federal court. Randal Archibold, *Government Issues Waiver for Fencing Along Border,* NEW YORK TIMES April 2, 2008. Given the lengthy delays that NEPA litigation can cause, was this exemption appropriate?

The following case examines the application of NEPA in the disputed siting of a Navy landing field.

### Washington County, North Carolina v. U.S. Department of the Navy

United States District Court for the Eastern District of North Carolina, 2005.
357 F. Supp. 2d 861.

■ BOYLE, DISTRICT JUDGE:

This suit arises out of the Department of the Navy's ("Navy") plan to construct and operate a new Outlying Landing Field ("OLF") in Washington and Beaufort Counties, North Carolina ("Site C"). . . . Both the Environmental Plaintiffs and the County Plaintiffs allege that the Navy's decision to construct an OLF at Site C violates the National Environmental Policy Act ("NEPA") . . . and are seeking a permanent injunction barring Defendants from proceeding with the OLF at Site C until they comply with NEPA. * * *

[T]he OLF at Site C will be used to support the operation and training of new F/A-18 E/F ("Super Hornet") aircraft and for future military operational needs, including surge training. Current events teach that neither the government nor the law can be blind to the reality of military readiness and national security. The Court recognizes that this case invites a consideration of national security and raises an awareness of the military's special mission to protect the United States. Neither the defendants nor the law posit that the interest of military training invalidates federal law or the commitment to, and protection of, the environment established by the National Environmental Policy Act. The primary issue in this case is whether, upon full consideration of the evidence, the record shows that the Navy has thoroughly considered the environmental consequences of its proposed action as required by NEPA. In the final analysis, a fair and balanced application of the law must be achieved regardless of the outcome.

BACKGROUND

Site C is located in rural eastern North Carolina, within a few miles of the Pungo Unit of the nationally designated Pocosin Lakes National Wildlife Refuge ("Pocosin Lakes"). The Pungo Unit was established in 1963 to provide an undisturbed sanctuary for migratory waterfowl and is home to some of the most unspoiled habitat along the East Coast. The Pungo Unit is characterized by vast wetlands and areas of open water and serves a unique environmental role as host to one of the largest populations of migratory waterfowl along the Atlantic Flyway. Between November and March each year, nearly 100,000 waterfowl, including nearly 22,000 tundra swans and 44,000 snow geese, migrate to the Pungo Unit. During the migratory period, the waterfowl rest, forage, and feed in the safe harbor of the refuge and the rich feeding ground offered by the surrounding agricultural fields.

In this environment, highly populated by nature and thinly populated by man, the Navy has chosen to construct an OLF to support operation and training of new Super Hornet aircraft. Site C will have a 2,000 acre core area that will contain a runway and support structures, and 30,000 acres of land surrounding the core construction. The OLF at site C will be used primarily by the Super Hornet squadrons for Field Carrier Landing Practice ("FCLP"), pilot training consisting of "touch-and-go" operations. "Touch-and-go" operations are repetitive takeoffs and landings in which the pilot touches down on the runway and then immediately applies full power to lift-off. Once in the air, the pilots climb to approximately 600 feet and position the aircraft for subsequent "touch-

and-go" operations. Each aircraft conducting an FCLP flight will make eight to ten "touch-and-go" landings per training session.

The Navy projects that there will be approximately 31,650 FCLP operations annually at Site C. . . . The OLF is intended to have twenty-four hour capability and about 8,450 of the annual operations will occur between 10 p.m. and 7 a.m. If the Navy is required to surge more than one aircraft carrier at a time, there will be a concentrated period of operations until the squadrons are deployed, but the Navy states that it is impossible to predict the exact intensity, duration, and timing of surge operations. . . . However, portions of the eastern approach track and holding pattern are located within .2 mile of the Pungo Unit and flight altitudes in that area would be between 2,000 and 2,500 feet. * * *

In their Motion, Plaintiffs assert that the Navy has violated NEPA by: 1) failing to fairly and objectively consider available alternatives and instead, "reverse engineered" a predetermined objective; 2) minimizing the impact of the development of an OLF at Site C on the environment, particularly migratory birds and Pocosin Lakes; 3) failing to take a "hard look" at the cumulative environmental impacts associated with constructing an OLF at Site C; 4) failing to adequately discuss mitigation measures in the EIS; 5) failing to use appropriate methodology to determine the presence of wetlands; and, 6) failing to prepare a Supplemental EIS. * * *

Defendants contend that the FEIS complies with NEPA. They assert that they took the required "hard look" at the environmental consequences of an OLF at Site C, appropriately considered reasonable alternatives to an OLF at Site C, and appropriately considered the cumulative impacts associated with the project. * * *

A. Adequacy of Analysis of Impacts on Pocosin Lakes and Waterfowl

First, the Court considers whether the Navy took a "hard look" at the environmental impacts of an OLF at Site C on the migratory birds and Pocosin Lakes. Plaintiffs argue that the Navy improperly minimized the environmental impacts in the FEIS [Final EIS] and contend that the Navy's information is inadequate to support its conclusion. Plaintiffs argue that the Navy failed to consider relevant information, improperly characterized studies which contradicted the Navy's conclusion, failed to conduct adequate field visits or site studies to assess the issue, and failed to seek input from local experts. Finally, Plaintiffs argue that the Navy improperly relied on conclusions drawn from general observation of existing military operations in North Carolina.

The Navy asserts that the FEIS acknowledges and thoroughly analyzes the potential impacts of an OLF at Site C on wildlife in the area, including waterfowl—all that is required under NEPA. The Navy contends that it extensively reviewed scientific literature, consulted with experts, conducted site analysis, and considered the effects of aircraft overflight around existing facilities. In the ROD [Record of Decision] issued on September 10, 2003, the Navy states that "while there would be some impacts to migratory waterfowl, these impacts are mitigable and would be minor. Surrounding land use is primarily agricultural and is considered compatible with aircraft operations." The Navy contends that the issue before the Court is not whether the Plaintiffs, or even the Court, disagree with this conclusion, but only whether the Navy took a "hard look" at the issue prior to reaching its conclusion. * * *

1. Site Analysis

The ROD concludes that an OLF at Site C will have minimal impacts on Pocosin Lakes and its inhabitants. However, in reaching this decision, the team of Navy contractors hired to evaluate the impact of the various OLF sites on wildlife spent negligible time at the site. The first visit, part of the siting study on all of the proposed OLF sites, was made in the summer of 2001. The contractors overseeing the evaluation on wildlife, led by Greg Netti, did little more than drive around the area for several hours and made no effort to assess the environmental impacts associated with the waterfowl. Of course any assessment of the waterfowl population would have been futile in July, when the migratory population was not represented. Subsequently, without any site assessment to evaluate the unique situation posed by an OLF adjacent to the winter home of nearly one hundred thousand waterfowl, the Draft Environmental Impact Statement ("DEIS") was published on August 2, 2002, identifying Site C as one of two preferred OLF locations.

Nor was the inadequate site assessment rectified prior to the issuance of the FEIS in July 2003. The first and only visit to Site C for the purpose of assessing the potential environmental impacts on the waterfowl did not take place until January 2003. During the visit, Greg Netti, along with the FEIS project manager, Dan Cecchini, and other Navy representatives, met with members of environmental agencies to discuss information related to questions raised during the comment period on the EIS. During the meeting, the group drove around the refuge and Site C, and the visit provided an initial opportunity for the FEIS team to view the tundra swans and snow geese in the course of the migratory period. However, this visit, which was about five hours in total, offered little more than an introduction to the snow geese and tundra swans in their natural habitat. It was not the "hard look" envisioned by NEPA, and was the last visit to the site by Greg Netti, who authored the section on the proposed impacts on waterfowl, before the FEIS was issued in July 2003.

The incomplete evaluation resulting from the Navy's failure to spend adequate time in conducting site study is most visible in the Navy's handling of the Bird Aircraft Strike Hazard ("BASH") evaluation. Early during the siting process, Navy pilots were consulted and expressed disfavor of Site C for the proposed OLF because of the substantial BASH risk posed by its proximity to the Pungo Unit. Bird-aircraft collisions pose a serious concern for flight safety. As discussed, snow geese and tundra swans number in the tens of thousands in the land surrounding Site C. Furthermore, tundra swan and snow geese are large waterfowl and their size heightens the dangers of collision. Therefore, a thorough analysis of the risk of bird-aircraft strikes was essential to the NEPA analysis of an OLF at Site C. However, the BASH analysis conducted by the Navy demonstrates patently flawed methodology.

Despite Site C's proximity to the Pungo Unit and the migratory birds resting and foraging nearby, the Navy collected only limited radar data from the area. The on-site study was not conducted until February–March, a time when many of the migratory birds that winter at Pocosin Lakes have begun departing. Ronald Merritt, the contractor who led the BASH study for the Navy, cautioned that the study was conducted too late in the migratory period to establish meaningful data. Furthermore, even the Navy recognized that one month was insufficient to provide adequate data to assess the risk. In fact, after the ROD was published, Ronald Merritt wrote a letter to the Secretary of the Navy reiterating his concern that the BASH risk was understated in the FEIS and that a safer location for an OLF should be found.

In addition to a radar study that its experts consider inadequate in length and timing, the Navy based its BASH assessment on Bird Avoidance Modeling ("BAM") from other military facilities in eastern North Carolina and Virginia, and considered data on previous bird strikes from the Dare County Bombing Range and across the state. BAM relies on historical data on factors such as bird mass, flocking tendency, and flying behavior to assess the relative BASH risk of different species. Despite its recognition that BAM is limited because of its "inability to adjust for real-time bird movements or population fluctuations because it is derived from fixed, historical data," the Navy concluded the other facilities and areas considered posed similar risks. However, none of the sites considered in the BAM analysis or reviewed for previous incidences of bird strikes experience bird populations comparable in number or size to those at Site C. Tundra swans and snow geese number in the tens of thousands in the land surrounding site C, and nowhere else on the eastern seaboard is there a higher concentration of such birds. In contrast to the population of birds around the other sites, which include high numbers of ducks, the tundra swan and snow geese are significantly larger birds. An adult tundra swan weighs about sixteen pounds and flies with a wingspan of about seven feet. By comparison, a mature black duck weighs less than two pounds and has a wingspan of about two feet. Nonetheless, while recognizing the limits of modeling and with its own experts warning of the inadequacy of the radar study, the Navy asserts that the BASH risk is comparable to other military operation areas in eastern North Carolina and Virginia and is manageable. * * *

2. Scientific Literature

The disconnect between the Navy's conclusion and evidence is also found in its treatment of the scientific literature relied upon in the FEIS.

The Navy selectively cites studies and appears to discount, with no basis, information contrary to its conclusion. In other cases, the Navy appears to cite to scientific studies which simply do not support the premise for which they are being cited or, at best, provide a tenuous link to the Navy's conclusion.

A primary example is the Navy's treatment of the Gunn and Livingston materials cited in the FEIS. The FEIS states that the Gunn and Livingston study reports that "that snow geese on the North Slope were disturbed by Cessna 185 flights, with the greatest disturbances occurring when planes were under 1,000 feet." In relying on Gunn and Livingston in support of the proposition that aircraft flight will cause minimal impact to snow geese, the Navy made a conclusion that the materials do not support and is disconnected from the facts contained therein. As Plaintiffs note, a full consideration of the Gunn and Livingston materials indicates that aircraft overflights have significant negative effects on snow geese. Although not addressed in the FEIS, a chapter of the Gunn and Livingston materials, reproducing an article by Salter and Davis (1972) on snow geese disturbance, reports that a Cessna 185 flushed snow geese as much as nine miles away at 700 feet, up to five miles away at 300 to 400 feet, and up to five miles away at 5,000 feet. This is in great contrast to the Navy's selective citation of the materials suggesting snow geese were merely disturbed by flights less than 1,000 feet. Moreover, a comparison of the Cessna 185 and the Super Hornets show that the Navy's conclusion is not a reasonable extrapolation from the Gunn and Livingston materials considered in their entirety. * * *

Perhaps even more troubling and indicative of the inadequate methodology used by the Navy in assessing the potential environmental impacts in the FEIS, the Gunn and Livingston report was never read before being cited by the Navy in the FEIS. Greg Netti, the environmental scientist hired to oversee preparation of the section of the FEIS on impacts to wildlife, conceded that he had not read the actual materials and merely relied on an abstract. This is not the thorough analysis required by NEPA. * * *

C. Reverse Engineering

Plaintiffs argue extensively in the Motion for Summary Judgment that the FEIS and, ultimately, the selection of Site C for the OLF in the Record of Decision is the product of reverse engineering. In support, Plaintiffs have directed the Court to numerous emails and documents in the record which strongly suggest that Site C was foreordained as the site for an OLF as a political decision to appease the communities around Oceana and Naval Auxiliary Landing Field ("NALF") Fentress which were already concerned about jet noise. [NALF Fentress is located in Virginia approximately 7 miles southwest of Oceana.] Plaintiffs contend that the record shows the Navy then made the decision to go with the 8/2 split siting of the Super Hornets to help explain and justify the placement of an OLF at Site C and crafted an FEIS to support its decision. Although the Navy's failure to comply with NEPA is established by its inadequate environmental analysis, the selective examination of data and strained conclusions in the FEIS are more understandable when considered in light of the Navy's need to support a preordained determination that a new OLF would be constructed at Site C.

At the Motion for Summary Judgment hearing, while disputing that they started with a predetermined or preferred alternative for Site C, Defendants argued that the law does clearly not preclude an agency from preferring a certain course of action. Defendants assert that as long as they took the required "hard look" at all of the alternatives prior to reaching their decision, they have fulfilled their obligation under NEPA. However, Defendants themselves note in their memorandum in support of summary judgment that what NEPA requires is action and study based on "good faith objectivity rather than subjective impartiality." *Fayetteville Area Chamber of Commerce v. Volpe,* 515 F.2d 1021, 1026 (4th Cir. 1975). Furthermore, 40 C.F.R. § 1502.1 specifically states that an environmental impact statement is more than merely a "disclosure document" and an "environmental impact statement shall serve as the means of assessing the environmental impact of proposed agency actions, rather than justifying decisions already made." 40 C.F.R. §§ 1502.1, 1502.2(g). A predetermined conclusion affects the agency's evaluation and produces a selective consideration of the environmental consequences linked to the preferred course of action. This cannot be considered the "hard look" required by NEPA. * * *

III. Permanent Injunction

Plaintiffs seek a permanent injunction to bar the Navy from pursuing any activity associated with an OLF at Site C until it fulfills its obligations under NEPA. The Fourth Circuit standard for issuance of a permanent injunction is similar to its standard for issuance of a preliminary injunction. The standard for awarding interim injunctive relief is the "balance-of-hardships" test. *Blackwelder Furniture Co. v. Seilig Mfg. Co.,* 550 F.2d 189, 196 (4th Cir. 1977). Under the test for a preliminary injunction, the Court considers the balance of harms to plaintiff and defendant, the likelihood of plaintiff's success on the merits, and the public interest. The balance of irreparable harm to the plaintiff and the harm to the defendant if relief is granted is the most important aspect of that test. In determining whether to grant permanent injunctive relief, the Court again employs the hardship-balancing test, only it considers Plaintiffs' actual success on the merits, not the mere likelihood of their success evaluated on an incomplete record.

Plaintiffs have now shown no material facts exist that Defendants violated their NEPA obligations. Therefore, the Court must consider the balance of irreparable harm to Plaintiffs if the injunction is not granted against the likelihood of harm to the Navy if a permanent injunction is granted. The Court further considers the public interest.

In opposing an injunction, the Navy argues that it will not be able to meet its training goals in servicing carrier-based aircraft. They assert that this harm outweighs any harm that Plaintiffs allegedly will suffer if an injunction is not granted.

National security is paramount and deserving of the utmost consideration and deference in the balancing calculation. The Court is now faced with the reconciliation of an acute issue of national security with environmental concerns. Upon a full review of the record, it is apparent the national security interests at stake may still be protected, while at the same time first assuring that the Navy takes the time and makes the effort to recognize and consider the effects of their proposed action on the environment.

A review of the Navy's working documents about the inclusion of surge training in the FEIS demonstrates that NALF Fentress along with other existing facilities are capable of handling training if necessary, but were intentionally discredited in the drafting of the FEIS to justify the new OLF. The Navy has indicated that from an operational standpoint, single siting the Super Hornets, not split siting them, is preferable. . . . The record shows that while an OLF may increase operational flexibility, current military facilities, including NALF Fentress, are sufficient to accommodate training for the Super Hornets until a NEPA analysis can be completed. Therefore, Defendants fail to show that the Navy or the public will suffer irreparable harm if a permanent injunction is granted.

In contrast, irreparable harm will occur to the environment, wildlife patterns, and ultimately, the balance of nature in the absence of a permanent injunction. Plaintiffs have shown that the Navy has acted without complying with NEPA. NEPA was enacted to "protect and promote environmental quality." *Glickman,* 81 F.3d at 443. NEPA "mandates that action can be taken only following complete awareness on the part of the actor of the environmental consequences of his action and following his having taken the steps required by the Act." *Arlington Coalition on Transp. v. Volpe,* 458 F.2d 1323, 1332 (4th Cir.), *cert. denied,* 409 U.S. 1000, 34 L. Ed. 2d 261, 93 S. Ct. 312 (1972). Although Plaintiffs seek a permanent injunction, the term is misleading in this context. The reach of an injunction is limited. The Court's role is only to ensure that in the face of irreparable harm, the Navy not proceed without first complying with NEPA. In the event that the Navy chooses to proceed with the OLF project at Site C, it may do so if and when it has satisfied the mandates of NEPA.

Without an injunction, the Navy can continue to expend millions of dollars and other resources on the development of the OLF project at Site C without first complying with NEPA. If land acquisition is allowed to proceed, additional landowners will be permanently displaced, tax revenue permanently lost, and the fragile habitat around Site C will be disrupted. This irreparable harm will occur despite the fact that a proper EIS has never been completed. As this Court has noted, when an agency action governed by NEPA is made without the hard look that NEPA requires, "the harm that NEPA intends to prevent has been suffered." *Western North Carolina Alliance v. North Carolina Dept. of Transp.,* 312 F. Supp. 2d 765, 778 (E.D.N.C. 2003) (*quoting Massachusetts v. Watt,* 716 F.2d 946, 952 (1st Cir. 1983)). While this case has been pending, during the periods when an injunction has not been in place, the Navy has proceeded with the development of the OLF. The Navy's actions have been taken within a context that does not conform to the requirements of the law. If the Navy is allowed to continue with the development of the OLF, the Navy will be acting in contravention of NEPA and taking the uninformed action that NEPA was enacted to prevent.

In the face of the Navy's failure to comply with NEPA, and in consideration of the relative harms, the balance of equities weighs heavily in favor of a permanent injunction. The harm to the Navy will not be appreciable if its development of the OLF at Site C is enjoined until a proper NEPA assessment is completed, but without an injunction, Plaintiffs and the public will be irreparably harmed. Absent an injunction, the Navy will be permitted to undertake substantial and irreversible changes affecting the fragile wildlife refuges of the Pungo Unit and Pocosin Lakes without first thoroughly considering the consequences of its actions. Accordingly, Plaintiffs' request for a permanent injunction is GRANTED.

---

## QUESTIONS AND DISCUSSION

**1.** The history of this case provides a nice illustration of how local coalitions of unlikely partners can form around a NEPA challenge. The origins of the $193 million project to build the landing field lay in a deal between the head of the Armed Services Committee, Senator John Warner from Virginia, who wanted to address constituents' complaints over the noise complaints of jet landings, and Senator Elizabeth Dole from North Carolina who was trying to boost local jobs. The field was sited near the small town of Roper, North Carolina, with a population of 600. To impress the locals, in January, 2004, the Navy arranged for four Super Hornets to fly low over the nearby farms. As the *Wall Street Journal* later reported, this led to unanticipated consequences.

> The site was chosen, the admiral explained to onlookers, "because it is in the middle of essentially nowhere." "After that we started saying we're from 'Nowhere,' " said Buster Manning, whose family has farmed this land for five generations. Roper used to be part of the Great Dismal Swamp, but over the past 150 years, farmers have cleared and drained the land to plant crops.
>
> The farmers who owned the fields slated for the landing strip felt trapped. When they met with Navy officials in the winter of 2003, they were told that they could either sell their land or the Navy would condemn it. A real-estate firm hired by the Navy already had

> bought some area farms. Mr. Manning recalls one Navy officer at the meeting saying that a legal fight would be futile because: " 'We [the Navy] have more lawyers than you could ever afford to hire.' " The farmers consulted a group of lawyers from Virginia, but "they told us it was a hopeless case," recalls Gerald Allen, who raises corn and soybeans. "That's when the women took over."

John J. Fialka, *Navy Airstrip Plan Hits Local Head Winds,* WALL STREET JOURNAL, March 30, 2005, at A4.

A loose organization of farm wives joined together to start protesting against the airfield with roadside signs such as, "Danger: Falling Birds & 57 Million $$$ Jets." Over time, an unlikely coalition was formed of the local farmers who did not want to sell their land, bird watchers from the National Audubon Society and bird hunters from the National Rifle Association, both concerned over the impact of the field on the nearby bird populations, though for obviously different reasons.

Assisted by pro bono law firm efforts and the Southern Environmental Law Center, these groups brought the NEPA challenge described in the case. It is important to note, as well, the role played by 30 law students from Duke and the University of North Carolina. In response to discovery, the Navy provided 190,000 pages of unindexed documents. The law students read over all these documents and uncovered the reverse engineering, BAM and BASH analyses that played such a critical role in the court's decision.

**2.** Other than providing the judge the opportunity to use cool-sounding acronyms, why are the BASH assessment and BAM modeling relevant to this decision? These presumably focus on how well-suited the sites are for flying planes safely without "bash and bam" collisions in mid-air. There is no question that this should be a critically important consideration for siting the landing field, but if the EIS is supposed to consider the significant *environmental* impacts associated with the landing field, why should BASH and BAM be considered at all? A collision with a plane and goose may be dangerous, but why should the strength of this analysis play an important part in the NEPA analysis of whether the EIS is adequate?

**3.** Why is reverse engineering such a bad thing if there is a range of alternatives fully analyzed? Agencies have expertise and will sometimes have a clear policy preference by the time they prepare the EIS. Given this, is the court's requirement of "good faith objectivity rather than subjective impartiality" simply naive?

**4.** The court talks about "contractors" such as Greg Netti overseeing the EIS evaluation of wildlife. Who are these contractors? Given the sheer number of EAs and EIS's that must be prepared every year, most agencies simply do not have the internal capacity to handle the workload. As a result, NEPA is big business for consulting firms. The NEPA implementing regulations provide that an EIS may be prepared by agency staff, by working with a qualified consulting firm, or by using a "third party method," where the private applicant hires a third party contractor to prepare the EIS. 40 C.F.R. 1506(g).

One might expect that applicants would be likely to employ consultants who will write an EIS favorable to their project. To safeguard against this, the regulations provides that the agency must:

> (i) In consultation with the applicant, choose the third party contractor and manage that contract.
>
> (ii) Select the consultant based on his ability and an absence of conflict of interest. Third party contractors will be required to execute a disclosure statement prepared by the responsible official signifying they have no financial or other conflicting interest in the outcome of the project.
>
> (iii) Specify the information to be developed and supervise the gathering, analysis and presentation of the information. The responsible official shall have sole authority for approval and modification of the statements, analyses, and conclusions included in the third party EIS.

40 CFR § 6.60

In addition, the consulting firm must disclose whether it has any financial or other interest in the outcome of the project, including the promise of future construction or design work on the project. The firm may, however, bid for future work if the project is approved.

Are you persuaded that these safeguards will ensure credible and legitimate EIS preparation by third parties? Given the resource constraints on agencies, the use of third parties seems inevitable. Are there any further safeguards you would suggest?

**5.** *Subsequent Developments.* In 2005, the Fourth Circuit largely upheld the District Court's ruling. National Audubon Society v. Department of the Navy, 422 F.3d 174 (2005). The Court of Appeals agreed that the EIS was deficient and that the Navy must complete a supplemental EIS. It found that the injunction was overly broad, however, and allowed the Navy to proceed with limited pre-construction activities.

In accordance with the Fourth Circuit's ruling, the district court amended the injunction to allow the Navy to continue to conduct studies and develop plans necessary for the eventual construction of an OLF, including the purchase of land from willing sellers. However, no such sellers were identified. In March 2007, the Navy issued a draft SEIS (DSEIS), again selecting Site C in Washington and Beaufort Counties as its preferred alternative. The DSEIS included new information on wetlands, additional studies of bird movements and strike hazards, and a "conceptual" plan for managing strike hazards. The DSEIS also included new information on the endangered red wolf, whose population had expanded to include the site proposed for the OLF.

Perhaps the most significant development, however, was the refusal of the U.S. Fish and Wildlife Service to endorse the Navy's findings in the DSEIS. In the notice of intent the Navy issued in preparing the DSEIS, the Navy stated it had designated the Fish and Wildlife Service as the cooperating agency in accordance with CEQ regulations. Letters contained in the appendix to the DSEIS showed profound disagreement between the two agencies regarding the Navy's assessment of impacts to bird populations, the refuge itself, and red wolves. So severe were these disagreements that at the first public hearing on the DSEIS, the Director of the Fish and Wildlife Service appeared and read into the record a public statement that the Service did not concur with the Navy's conclusions and rejected the findings in the DSEIS.

The coalition that formed to oppose the OLF expanded to include sporting and hunting organizations, property rights organizations, and the NAACP. After the publication of the DSEIS, the Governor of North Carolina, Mike Easley, spoke out in opposition to the project at its proposed location and called upon the state's congressional delegation to remove funding for the OLF. In the following weeks, the North Carolina Secretary of Agriculture, Secretary of the Department of Health and Human Services, and Secretary of the Department of Environment and Natural Resources issued their own public statements supporting the Governor's call, as did numerous state legislators, community leaders and newspapers. One by one, most of the state's congressional delegation, including both Senators, also publicly objected to the Navy's action and called on the Navy to work with the state to develop a more prudent and acceptable alternative. Ultimately Congress pulled the funding authorization for the OLF at Site C and, as a result, the Navy withdrew the SDEIS and announced it would examine new sites for the OLF.

---

## PROBLEM EXERCISE:

### NRDC V. WINTER

In recent years, the U.S. Navy has been developing the use of "low frequency active" (LFA) sonar to detect the newest generation of quiet diesel submarines. In contrast to "passive" sonar, which listens for submarine engine noises, active sonar emits powerful sound waves and then listens for distinctive echoes to identify underwater objects. The Navy has been conducting LFA training exercises in the waters off southern California.

Animal rights and environmental groups have raised concerns that LFA can damage marine mammal hearing and disrupt their communication, thus affecting their breeding, feeding and other social interactions. Aware that it might face lawsuits alleging its activities resulted in a take under the Endangered Species Act (ESA) and the Marine Mammal Protection Act (MMPA), in the late 1990s the Navy requested a five-year take permit for impacts on marine mammals during testing of the LFA sonar over an area of roughly 14 million square miles in the northwestern Pacific. This was challenged by the Humane Society, NRDC, Cetacean Society International and other groups, who not only charged violations of the MMPA and ESA, but under NEPA, as well.

While this litigation was playing out, Congress passed a special exemption for National Security activities under the Marine Mammal Protection Act, excerpted below:

> (e) EXEMPTION OF ACTIONS NECESSARY FOR NATIONAL DEFENSE.—The Secretary of Defense, after conferring with the Secretary of Commerce, the Secretary of Interior, or both, as appropriate, may exempt any action or category of actions undertaken by the Department of Defense or its components from compliance with any requirement of the Marine Mammal Protection Act, 16 U.S.C. 1361 et seq., if he determines that it is necessary for national defense. Exemptions granted under this section shall be for a period of not more than two years. Additional exemptions for periods not to exceed two years each may be granted for the same action or category of actions upon the Secretary of Defense, after conferring with the Secretary of Commerce, the Secretary of Interior, or both as appropriate, making a new determination.

16 U.S.C. § 1371(f)(1)

In January 2007, the Department of Defense granted the Navy a two-year exemption from the MMPA for training purposes, subject to a number of mitigation measures:

> (1) training lookouts and officers to watch for marine mammals;
>
> (2) requiring at least five lookouts with binoculars on each vessel to watch for anomalies on the water surface (including marine mammals);
>
> (3) requiring aircraft and sonar operators to report detected marine mammals in the vicinity of the training exercises;
>
> (4) requiring reduction of active sonar transmission levels by 6 dB if a marine mammal is detected within 1,000 yards of the bow of the vessel, or by 10 dB if detected within 500 yards;
>
> (5) requiring complete shutdown of active sonar transmission if a marine mammal is detected within 200 yards of the vessel;
>
> (6) requiring active sonar to be operated at the "lowest practicable level"; and
>
> (7) adopting coordination and reporting procedures.

In *NRDC v. Winter*, five environmental groups requested a preliminary injunction to halt the Navy's use of mid-frequency active (MFA) sonar in fourteen large-scale training exercises in the Southern California Operating Area (SOCAL). 645 F. Supp. 2d 841 (C.D. Cal. 2007). The primary claim focused on the Navy's failure to prepare an Environmental Impact Statement. The Navy had prepared an

Environmental Assessment, concluding that the impacts were insufficient to require development of an EIS. In the face of litigation, the Navy subsequently agreed to prepare an EIS, but the plaintiffs moved for a preliminary injunction, trying to halt use of LFA sonar until the study was completed. The district court, agreed, finding that plaintiffs had demonstrated a probability of success on the merits and concluding that:

> From the numerous scientific studies, declarations, reports, and other evidence before the Court, Plaintiffs have established to a near certainty that use of MFA sonar during the planned SOCAL exercises will cause irreparable harm to the environment and Plaintiffs' standing declarants. The Court is also satisfied that the balance of hardships tips in favor of granting an injunction, as the harm to the environment, Plaintiffs, and public interest outweighs the harm that Defendants would incur if prevented from using MFA sonar, absent the use of effective mitigation measures, during a subset of their regular activities in one part of one state for a limited period. Accordingly, the Court grants Plaintiffs' requested relief and enjoins Defendants' use of MFA sonar during the remaining SOCAL exercises.

In January, 2008, the district court issued a preliminary injunction permitting the Navy to complete its remaining exercises so long as it employed measures to mitigate the harm to marine mammals from sonar use. In particular, the court modified the 5th mitigation measure, requiring the Navy to suspend its use of sonar if a marine mammal is detected within 2,200 yards of the sonar source (rather than 200 yards), and reducing the acoustic energy level of sonar by 6 decibels whenever significant surface ducting conditions were detected. These mitigation measures were stayed on appeal by the 9th Circuit if the sonar was being used "at a critical point in the exercise" but kept in place the court's preliminary injunction on future use of sonar in training exercises. *NRDC v. Winter*, 513 F.3d 920 (9th Cir. 2008).

The case was then appealed to the Supreme Court. In a decision focusing on the proper standard for issuing a preliminary injunction, the Court held for the Navy, concluding that:

> Plaintiffs contend that the Navy's use of MFA sonar will injure marine mammals or alter their behavioral patterns, impairing plaintiffs' ability to study and observe the animals.
>
> While we do not question the seriousness of these interests, we conclude that the balance of equities and consideration of the overall public interest in this case tip strongly in favor of the Navy. For the plaintiffs, the most serious possible injury would be harm to an unknown number of the marine mammals that they study and observe. In contrast, forcing the Navy to deploy an inadequately trained antisubmarine force jeopardizes the

> safety of the fleet. Active sonar is the only reliable technology for detecting and tracking enemy diesel-electric submarines, and the President—the Commander in Chief—has determined that training with active sonar is "essential to national security."
>
> The public interest in conducting training exercises with active sonar under realistic conditions plainly outweighs the interests advanced by the plaintiffs. Of course, military interests do not always trump other considerations, and we have not held that they do. In this case, however, the proper determination of where the public interest lies does not strike us as a close question.

Winter v. NRDC, 555 U.S. 7 (2008).

Justice Ginsburg's dissent argued that the 14 training exercises would be completed by the time the EIS has been drafted.

- How can the Court conclude that the balance of interests (including potential harm to the marine mammals) favors the Navy and therefore use of active sonar should continue until the EIS is prepared, without the information the EIS would provide?
- What do you think plaintiffs would need to have demonstrated in order to satisfy the Court?
- Considering the exemptions and cases described in this section, what do you think is the proper balance between marine mammal protection and military operations?
- What standard should a judge use in balancing the need for an injunction until an EIS has been prepared with the importance of particular Navy training programs to military readiness?

---

## 2. ENERGY, FORESTS, GRAZING, AND WATER

National security is not the only area where NEPA's requirements have been cut back in recent years. Following publication of the Cheney Energy Task Force's recommendations in 2001, President Bush issued Executive Order 13212 (May 18, 2001), titled "Actions To Expedite Energy-related Projects." The E.O. establishes an inter-agency group, headed by CEQ, to assist agencies in accelerating the completion of energy-related projects. A similar task force was created in Executive Order 13274 (Sept. 18, 2002), titled "Environmental Stewardship and Transportation Infrastructure Project Reviews." This inter-agency group, also headed by CEQ, is charged with expediting review of high priority transportation projects and streamlining the approval process.

While there have not been any serious efforts to amend NEPA directly, Congress has turned its attention to specific applications of NEPA. In an energy bill passed by the House of Representatives in 2003 (H.R. 6), for example, energy development decisions on tribal lands were exempted from NEPA. In 2004, the House passed a bill (H.R. 4513) that eliminated the requirement to consider a full range of alternatives for renewable energy projects. Neither measure was adopted by the Senate. The Senate, for its part, included language in the 2005 Department of Interior appropriations bill (S. 2804) preventing the Army Corps of Engineers from releasing reservoir water in Montana, North Dakota, and South Dakota into the Missouri River under certain drought conditions. This requirement to stop releasing water would have been binding regardless of NEPA's review and public participation mandates. *See* S. 2804, 108th Cong., § 338 (2004).

Other measures, however, have become law. In the 2004 Energy and Water appropriations bill, for example, a rider mandated construction of a road in the Izembek National Wildlife Refuge in Alaska. The rider stopped short the NEPA alternatives analysis, requiring construction of Alternative 1, "notwithstanding any other provision of law." NEPA has also been effectively amended through administrative action. The Bush Administration's "Healthy Forests Initiative," for example, exempts NEPA from certain types of commercial logging projects through new categorical exclusions. 68 Fed. Reg. 33813 (June 5, 2003). Congress has also passed legislation allowing the Forest Service and BLM to renew grazing permits without conducting an environmental review. Pub. Law 108–108 (Section 325); Pub. Law 108–447 (Section 339). And the economic stimulus package following the financial crisis of 2008 exempted a whole range of stimulus grants for renewable and carbon capture from NEPA compliance. Kristen Lombardi and John Solomon, *Big polluters freed from environmental oversight by stimulus* (Nov. 29, 2010, The Center for Public Integrity).

More recently, both Democrats and Republicans on the Senate Committee on the Environment unanimously approved a bill amending the Water Resources Development Act that would, among other things, create strict deadlines for NEPA compliance with Army Corps of Engineer water projects and fine agencies for failing to complete reviews on time. Barbara Boxer, Chair of the Committee and a California Senator with a strong environment track record, stated in response to criticism that "The environmentalists don't like to have deadlines set so that they can stall projects forever. I think it's wrong, and I have many cases in California where absolutely necessary flood control projects have been held up for so long that people are suffering from the adverse impacts of flooding." *Boxer Rejects Criticisms of NEPA Reform Push,* InsideEPA.com. April 29, 2013.

What do you think of project-specific NEPA exemptions passed by Congress? Is the legislature effectively saying that these projects are more important than the benefits provided by the review of information collected in the EIS? Are these types of exemptions inevitable political compromises in the face of lengthy NEPA litigation delays?

## E. DOES NEPA WORK?

Determining the effectiveness of NEPA is hard to do. Unlike the Clean Air Act or Clean Water Act, where one can simply measure air quality or water pollution over time, measuring the influence of environmental information on agency decisionmaking is no easy matter. Indeed it is not obvious how one would even go about assessing the cost-effectiveness of NEPA. At one extreme, the EIS could simply serve as a post hoc rationalization for decisions already taken—no more than going through the bureaucratic motions. And there certainly is reason to fear that this may happen in some instances, as in the *Washington County* landing field case, for example. After all, conflicts of interest run to the very core of NEPA. Placing agencies in charge of conducting an EIS that may challenge their proposed actions may be like placing the fox as guard of the hen house. As Professor Joe Sax memorably observed, "I think the emphasis on the redemptive quality of procedural reform is about nine parts myth and one part coconut oil." Joseph L. Sax, *The (Unhappy) Truth About NEPA*, 26 OKLA. L. REV. 239, 239 (1973).

Given the concrete statutory mission of an agency with dedicated budgets, organized lobbies and congressional pressure, on the one hand, and the requirements of NEPA to consider environmental impacts of a range of actions, on the other, one might reasonably be skeptical of NEPA's influence. After all, there have traditionally been few political rewards for forests not cut or range lands not grazed. If the decision has already been made, there are legitimate concerns over whether the benefit of generating information on impact analysis really outweighs the cost and delays of producing such information.

Despite all these reasons to dismiss NEPA, however, it has achieved a great deal. Compared to the state of agency transparency at the time of its passage, NEPA has played an important role in opening agency decision making to the public. NEPA has provided constant pressure on agencies to broaden their missions to consider and adopt environmental values. And it has spurred agencies to modify proposals and mitigate adverse impacts. Just look at the range of cases described in this section. The experience of the Atomic Energy Commission, preparing an EIS and simply refusing even to read it, simply could not happen today. Environmental impact analysis has become a standard part of federal decision making. Moreover, mindful of what an EIS will likely show, many projects are dropped before even conducting an EA, thus escaping measurement of effectiveness. Talk to litigators about NEPA and many say it is critical for providing data on agency actions they could not otherwise view or use. Public disclosure also creates its own dynamic. As former NEPA litigator, Professor Dave Owen, has blogged,

> NEPA generates many environmental benefits not from disclosure and open discussion, as Congress seems to have anticipated, but instead from project revisions designed to avoid the need to disclose and discuss adverse environmental impacts.... Though NEPA [may] not stop the project in question, [it can lead to] compelling project changes that substantially reduced the adverse environmental impacts that would have resulted from the original proposal. * * *
>
> If NEPA were simply a toothless wonder, a statute that required only meaningless disclosures, there would be no need for fraud and lies. Agencies could simply tell the truth, acknowledge the forthcoming environmental damage, and get on with their business. * * *
>
> I once asked a client, a good planner who bore the burden of working for a county high on massive-scale development and low on funds, about this dynamic. "Don't ever underestimate," he told me, "how much we fear that public reaction." For him, that fear was also leverage. The threat of controversy gave him at least a little ability to inject progressive planning principles into an otherwise headlong rush toward sprawl. I doubt his situation was unique.
>
> Dave Owen, *On NEPA and Duplicity,* Environmental Law Prof Blog, May 14, 2013

Despite its over thirty years of operation, NEPA still engenders controversy. In addition to the NEPA task forces described in the preceding section, the CEQ established an inter-agency group known as the "Modernizing NEPA Task Force." This committee received hundreds of comments from interested groups, issued a report, *Modernizing NEPA Implementation,* and subsequently hosted a series of regional roundtables. The House of Representatives Committee on Resources similarly created a bipartisan NEPA Task Force which conducted hearings on NEPA around the country. The House Task Force was charged with ensuring that the original intent of NEPA "is being fulfilled."

No significant legislative changes to NEPA have been adopted but widespread interest in "improving" NEPA, whatever that means, remains high. As the excerpt below from the CEQ's Task Force review of public comments makes clear, supporters and detractors of NEPA remain far apart.

### CEQ TASK FORCE, REVIEW OF THE NEPA PROCESS: SUMMARY OF PUBLIC COMMENT V–VI (2002)

> Many respondents believe that the general requirement to provide adequate analysis has been taken to an extreme, that documents have become unconscionably time-consuming and costly to produce, and that the resultant "analysis paralysis"

forestalls appropriate management of public lands and ultimately leaves the public distrustful and disengaged. People believe there are basically two related causes for this situation. First, they believe that NEPA analysis requirements are so vague that they are open to considerable interpretation; and thus, whatever amount of analysis is provided remains an easy target for litigation by groups opposed to a proposed management plan. Second, people believe that because the requirements are so vague and open to interpretation, that agencies themselves are not sure of what is expected and have therefore allowed court decisions throughout the country to dictate the process incrementally. The result is that agencies are not sure how much analysis will be considered adequate by the courts, and so feel under constant pressure to produce more. In short, a vicious cycle has developed: vague analysis requirements lead to both litigation and agency uncertainty over how much is enough; litigation and agency uncertainty cause agencies to produce more analysis which—due again to vague analysis requirements and open interpretation—leads to more litigation, which leads to more analysis . . . and so on. . . .

In response to this assessment of what has occurred since NEPA was originally enacted, many urge the Task Force to take control back from the courts—by providing clear and unambiguous guidance on the level of analysis required by NEPA; by clearly delineating the requirements for different NEPA documents, particularly environmental assessments (EAs) and environmental impact statements (EISs); and by working to rein in litigation through measures aimed either at restricting its reach or at mandating stiffer requirements for appellants. * * *

Many other respondents, however, assess NEPA differently in terms of analysis/documentation and litigation. According to these people, "analysis paralysis" is really a misnomer. Agencies are not required to produce unreasonable amounts of analysis, these respondents insist, they simply refuse to provide reasonable analysis the first time around. These respondents charge that agencies often predetermine the outcome of the planning process in virtue of the alternatives they offer; that they often fail to consider other reasonable alternatives; and that the analysis they provide is often wholly inadequate to support the management plan they propose. They feel that the environmental effects of proposed actions are often inadequately considered, particularly the cumulative effects; that agencies rely on inadequate or outdated data; and that agency research is not held to the same rigorous standards as research is in other fields, particularly in terms of scientific reference and peer review.

And so the debate goes on.

## II. PRIVATE INFORMATION DISCLOSURE STATUTES

Because of the limited ability of the law—and the limited resources of those charged with enforcing the law—to ensure that pollution is reduced or eliminated, much pollution control results not from legal mandates but from the decisions and acts of individuals and organizations. What drives these private decisions, though, is not always clear. The extremes are obvious: only the government can threaten a polluter with criminal sanctions; only a corporate executive can mandate voluntary actions within a company that are not required by law. In most cases, though, private and public choices interact—private pollution control decisions are made in the shadow of potential governmental regulation or are stimulated by information about pollution required by the government.

To be sure, the first step in addressing pollution must be to find out that the pollution is there, and this is not always easy. The residents who purchased houses on top of Love Canal surely did not know about the chemical nightmare that burbled just below them. Often we are simply left with questions. Why is my child sick? Does it have anything to do with the refinery two miles away, or the water from our well, or the hazy air surrounding the interstate highway? Or perhaps no one is sick, but there is more pollution in your community than you realize or desire. In each instance, we seek information concerning the presence of pollution and its dangers.

Most companies have been unwilling to provide information about their pollution voluntarily. The law, therefore, has mandated the disclosure of much information about pollution. Congress routinely includes provisions in statutes such as the Clean Water Act and the Clean Air Act that require studies of specific pollution problems. The Federal Insecticide, Fungicide, and Rodenticide Act (FIFRA) relies upon labels on registered pesticides as the principal means of ensuring that pesticides are not applied in a manner that pollutes the environment

Part II focuses on statutes that require generation of information by private parties on chemical releases to the environment or in products. The Toxics Release Inventory has been remarkably successful in reducing emissions despite its seemingly innocuous requirement that industries report the amount of specified toxic chemicals that they release. California's Proposition 65 requires businesses to disclose to the public both toxic releases and products containing toxic ingredients. Part II ends by considering the role of public disclosure of greenhouse gas emissions.

## A. THE TOXICS RELEASE INVENTORY

The Emergency Planning and Community Right-to-Know Act (EPCRA) was adopted in 1986 in response to public outcry over a series of tragic industrial toxic releases, most notably the 1984 release of methyl cyanate at the Union Carbide plant in Bhopal, India, which killed thousands of people and injured hundreds of thousands. Concerned communities throughout America demanded to know about nearby toxic threats and Congress responded by including in EPCRA a requirement for the Toxics Release Inventory (TRI). Unlike NEPA, which requires agencies to analyze and take a hard look at their proposed actions' environmental impacts, on its face TRI is little more than an accounting requirement. Facilities that "manufactured, processed, or otherwise used" chemicals listed on the TRI above threshold quantities in the past year must submit annual reports to EPA and certain state officials. 42 U.S.C. § 11023(b). These reports, known as "Section 313 reports," must disclose for each chemical:

> (1) whether the toxic chemical is manufactured, processed, or otherwise used, and the general categories of use of the toxic chemical;
>
> (2) an estimate of the maximum amount of the toxic chemical present at the facility during the preceding calendar year;
>
> (3) methods for treating and disposing of waste and an estimate of the treatment efficiency typically achieved through these methods; and
>
> (4) an estimate of the amount of toxic chemicals entering the environment.

42 U.S.C. § 11023(g)(1)(C).

TRI's coverage is limited to companies with ten or more employees that operate in particular industry categories (primarily manufacturing) and emit more than threshold amounts of listed chemicals (from the original 300 chemicals to now more than 650). The net result is over 20,000 Section 313 reports annually. EPA compiles data from the Section 313 reports onto a national toxic chemical inventory listing that is accessible to federal, state, and local governments as well as to the public. You can access it at http://www.epa.gov/triexplorer.

TRI has been far more influential than anyone imagined. Former EPA Administrators Carol Browner and Bill Reilly have held up TRI as one of the country's most effective laws. Year after year, there has been a steady increase of chemicals and industries added to TRI's coverage. Over the same period, reported releases of TRI toxics have steadily dropped, now to less than half of the amounts reported in 1988, when the program first began. To be sure, other factors have contributed to this impressive reduction, such as stricter regulations, changes in reporting requirements, and industry-specific developments, but TRI can rightfully claim a meaningful role. As the excerpt by Brad Karkkainen describes below, TRI has led to pollution reductions by providing information to both internal firm managers (giving proof to the business adage that "what gets measured gets done") and external private stakeholders, ranging from local communities, employees, and environmental groups to investors, consumers, and competitors. The net result has been a broad confluence of pressures, both inside and outside the firm, to reduce significant environmental impacts.

### Bradley C. Karkkainen, *Information as Environmental Regulation: TRI and Performance Benchmarking, Precursor to a New Paradigm?*

89 GEO. L.J. 257, 289–338 (2001).

TRI is the first regulatory statute of the contemporary "information age." It appears to have been the first, at any rate, to mandate that a federal agency compile information on a computerized database and provide that information directly to the public through online access. TRI thus exploits opportunities presented by the new information technology to trim information costs for reporting entities, regulators, and third-party information users, including the costs of reporting, storing, retrieving, aggregating, analyzing, and distributing environmental performance information. In many cases, TRI reporters are able to file electronically, shaving costly and cumbersome paperwork for both the reporting entity and the regulatory agency. With information storage and processing capacity increasing exponentially, this suggests almost limitless possibilities for expanding the role of the regulatory agency to collect, process, distribute, and access data. * * *

TRI achieves all this at a relatively low cost to the agency. EPA's direct administrative costs are approximately $25 million, a modest fraction of its $7 billion annual budget. TRI does not require the agency to produce the extensive, costly, and time-consuming studies necessary to establish quantified exposure levels, dose-response curves, and threshold levels of "significant" or "unreasonable" risk that are often required under other environmental statutes. Under TRI, the agency normally only needs to make the (relatively) low-threshold determination that a pollutant "can reasonably be anticipated to cause" cancer or other chronic health effects at *some* level of exposure. Moreover, TRI does not require the regulator to make complex and highly uncertain judgments about the technological feasibility or compliance costs associated with emission reductions to any particular target level, as is ordinarily required for both traditional command regulation and, implicitly, for market-based alternatives. * * *

Direct compliance costs are also quite low. EPA estimates that the average facility requires about fifty person-hours of labor annually to produce each required report. The cumulative paperwork burden on regulated firms is not trivial, of course. But it is consistent with the level of reporting required of firms under conventional regulatory approaches simply as an incident of compliance monitoring. Those approaches typically impose additional, and often quite heavy, direct compliance costs to achieve the mandated levels of emissions reductions.

In a sense this comparison is unfair, of course, for if TRI does induce real reductions in pollutant releases, then some firms must be incurring the costs of investing in new technologies or processes, even if these are not properly labeled "compliance costs." But since firms have absolute flexibility under TRI to determine how, when, and to what extent they will reduce emissions, they are generally free to adopt the improvement targets, timetables, and strategies that best suit their individual circumstances. This is almost certain to be cheaper than compliance with the costly "end-of-the-pipe" controls typically imposed by conventional regulation. Moreover, by creating pressures on firms to reduce *aggregate* emissions, TRI effectively creates a flexible "basket" of some 650 pollutants among which firms can make trade-offs. With this much discretion, it is fair to assume that firms will seek out the least-cost solutions, just as they would under tradeable permit schemes or Pigouvian taxes, but with added flexibility as to timetables and the precise mix of priority improvement targets. * * *

TRI works by establishing an objective, quantifiable, standardized (and therefore comparable), and broadly accessible metric that transforms the firm's understanding of its own environmental performance, while facilitating unprecedented levels of transparency and accountability. Firms and facilities are compelled to self-monitor and, therefore, to "confront disagreeable realities" concerning their environmental performance "in detail and early on," even prior to the onset of market, community, or regulatory reactions to the information they are required to make public. Simultaneously, they are subjected to the scrutiny of a variety of external parties, including investors, community residents, and regulators, any of whom may desire improved environmental performance and exert powerful pressures on poor performers to upgrade their performance as measured by the TRI yardstick. * * *

General availability of detailed, comparable TRI performance data further allows the firm to place each of its required reports in a variety of interpretive contexts. The firm can identify its own top-performing and under-performing facilities and processes, establish performance baselines and track process-, facility-, and firm-level performance trends over time. It can also compare its performance against that of its peers and competitors and set specific, objective performance targets to which it may hold itself and each of its operating units accountable. Analysis of TRI-derived comparative rankings of process-and facility-level performance may also facilitate the identification of environmentally superior processes and technologies and hasten their diffusion within and across firms. Very little of this information can be generated through conventional, fragmentary, frequently non-standardized, compliance-oriented environmental reporting.

TRI places information in the hands of corporate managers in the first instance. Consequently, it might be analogized to a private sector version of the National Environmental Policy Act (NEPA), requiring a process—the production and disclosure of environmental information relevant to decisionmaking—rather than substantive outcomes. In neither case does the regulatory approach require that anything in particular be done with the information once it is produced. But by compelling managers to examine environmental outcomes, it may influence their decisionmaking. Just as NEPA-generated information may prompt some governmental managers to mitigate the worst environmental consequences of their proposed actions, or even to choose less environmentally harmful alternatives, the performance monitoring mandated by TRI might also alert corporate managers to performance problems and opportunities for improvement that might otherwise have escaped their notice.

Many top corporate managers, previously unaware of the volumes of toxic pollutants their firms were generating, were indeed surprised by the information produced in the first rounds of TRI. In many cases, that knowledge prompted a swift and decisive response, as firms adopted ambitious improvement targets far above the levels required for compliance with regulatory requirements, often in the range of fifty, seventy, or even ninety percent reductions from initial TRI-reported levels. Beyond jarring firms into action, TRI also establishes the objective metric by which managers set firm-wide improvement targets and gauge progress toward their achievement. * * *

Because TRI compels polluting firms to monitor their own volumes of waste—in effect, to engage in a limited form of materials accounting—it may spur them to investigate pollution prevention options that may reduce materials and waste disposal costs, increase effective utilization of productive capacity, and simultaneously improve environmental performance. In some cases, investments in pollution prevention may be profitable even in the short run. But even when they are not, many leading firms now believe that their longterm competitive advantage lies in continuously pushing the envelope of innovation in both products and process efficiency, including pollution efficiency. * * *

Pollution prevention is not uniformly profitable or cheap, of course. Even where it is, investments in pollution prevention might be crowded out by more attractive investment alternatives, or the firm may lack the necessary capital, know-how, or commitment to make pollution prevention part of its overall business strategy. And for a variety of reasons, firms may not be equally responsive to the community, regulatory, and market pressures that figure into the long-range planning of the most sophisticated practitioners of pollution prevention. Put differently, the value of gains in these areas will vary by firm, depending on firm-specific circumstances. Consequently, we should expect that performance gains from TRI will be uneven across facilities, firms, and industries, generating a pattern of "leaders and laggards" * * *

TRI-generated performance data are readily available to regulators, as well as to environmentalists and other citizen-critics of regulatory policy. Regulators can use TRI data to establish baselines, profiles, and trends in the pollution performance of facilities, firms, industrial sectors, communities, and states, and to make benchmarking comparisons among them. Moreover, the data provide some indication of the effectiveness of regulatory and non-regulatory environmental policies, providing the basis for comparative analysis and benchmarking of program outcomes. TRI data thus help regulators identify regulatory gaps and shortcomings, set research and enforcement priorities, and identify the most effective programs so as to replicate or expand them. In perhaps the most widely cited instance, early rounds of TRI data revealed that much larger volumes of hazardous air pollutants were being released than had been previously recognized. This led Congress to amend the Clean Air Act in 1990 to strengthen its hazardous air pollutant (HAP) provisions, and to bypass and amend the cumbersome HAP regulatory listing procedure, which had resulted in the listing of only a small handful of pollutants.

Simultaneously, citizen-critics of governmental policies can use TRI-derived information to criticize or support current policies and programs, propose new ones, and benchmark and evaluate the achievements of regulated entities and regulators alike. * * *

Because TRI data allow easy comparisons among facilities, firms, and industries, a poor environmental performance record as reflected in TRI data can cause reputational damage, potentially affecting relations with customers, suppliers, employees, or investors. Unlike conventional regulations, which garner publicity for firms only in the breach, however, TRI may also generate opportunities for positive environmental image-building. No one credits a firm for being in compliance with mandatory environmental standards, but firms can use objective and comparable TRI data to document claims of "superior" performance or progress toward ambitious voluntary targets. These claims are otherwise difficult to verify and, therefore, subject to deep discounting. As a corollary, however, we should expect larger and more visible firms and those that invest most heavily in advertising and public relations to be more sensitive to TRI data because they have more reputational capital at stake—a result borne out in empirical research. * * *

[As Karkkainen goes on to point out, despite these benefits, one must keep in mind the shortcomings of such a simple measure of environmental performance.] TRI information provides, at best, one narrow and potentially highly misleading indicator of environmental performance, measuring releases from major point sources of substances on a short and far-from-complete EPA-compiled list of toxic pollutants.

A firm with superior TRI data might nonetheless produce large volumes of conventional pollutants or solid waste, or recklessly despoil valuable wildlife habitats—all beyond TRI's purview—while a firm with poor TRI data could nonetheless be a superior environmental performer along these other dimensions. Nor can we safely assume that every improvement in TRI data counts as an environmental gain because, in some cases, it might reflect a shift to activities that cause equal or greater environmental harm that is not reflected in TRI data. To that extent, TRI's very power to drive performance improvements *as measured by the TRI metric* makes it potentially misleading and possibly counterproductive if it is not matched and counterbalanced by a set of equally powerful metrics for other important dimensions of environmental performance.

Similarly, because all reported TRI releases are measured uniformly in pounds, regardless of the relative toxicity of the pollutant, a firm or facility might cut its reported emissions and transfers without reducing—and possibly even while increasing—health and environmental risks by substituting lower-volume, higher-toxicity pollutants. Because sulfuric acid, a relatively low-toxicity, high-volume pollutant, represented a large fraction of total TRI releases in the early rounds of reporting, some firms found they could achieve large TRI improvements by cutting their bulk sulfuric acid releases, although the net health and environmental benefits were in many cases thought to be quite modest. * * *

In addition, because TRI measures only the quantity of the pollutant released without factoring in proximity to population, exposure route, dispersion, persistence, sensitivity of exposed populations, or other important risk-related factors, it does not provide a very good guide to actual human and environmental risks. . . . Many users are tempted to rely on TRI data as a handy proxy for the environmental and health risks associated with toxic pollutants. In short, they use TRI as an indicator of environmental *quality* (which it is not), rather than as an indicator of the environmental *performance* of a limited class of sources (the only use the data can fairly support). But to do so may lead to serious overestimation or underestimation of risk.

Even understood narrowly as an indicator of toxic pollution performance, TRI has severe shortcomings. Although TRI's coverage extends to more toxic pollutants than are regulated under conventional standards, the TRI list is incomplete. While a final, comprehensive list of toxic pollutants is almost certainly an unattainable goal, our current level of toxic ignorance should be sobering. EPA acknowledges that even for the highest-volume organic chemicals, "the majority . . . lack the basic information needed to determine whether they should be listed on the TRI." * * *

A related problem is that arbitrary volumetric reporting thresholds keep some toxic pollutants off the TRI list, and in other cases understate the aggregate effects of numerous small releases that may cause serious cumulative harm. . . . Moreover, TRI requires reporting only by selected classes of pollution sources. Generally, these include manufacturers and other large point sources in specified SIC codes [Standard Industrial Classification, a standardized numerical coding of industry sectors], excluding most small businesses (those with fewer than ten employees), non-regulated sectors, and diffuse sources like automobiles and farms. As a result, TRI provides a radically underinclusive and consequently distorted picture of the extent, nature, and causes of toxic pollution and its associated health and environmental risks. Small "area sources" like dry cleaners are often an important source of local exposures. In large metropolitan areas automobiles are the leading source of many forms of airborne toxic pollution. Pesticide run-off is a leading contributor to groundwater and surface water contamination. Exclusion of these sources from community-level toxic profiles understates the aggregate and cumulative risks of toxic pollution, while feeding the commonplace but erroneous assumption that large industrial polluters are solely responsible for toxic risks faced by the public. * * *

Data quality is suspect. TRI does not require strict monitoring of emissions; instead, reporting entities may provide estimates. Though EPA provides guidance on estimation methods, the EPA estimation methods may be overinclusive, underinclusive, or both. Furthermore, EPA guidance is incomplete, leaving considerable discretion to reporting entities. Even firms in the same industry using similar production processes may use different estimation methods, and firms may change their methods from one reporting period to the next, creating opportunities to achieve "paper reductions." Nor does EPA make any systematic effort to verify reported figures, though it does some spot sampling to identify common problems and improve the agency's guidance to reporting entities. * * *

TRI's usefulness is further limited by problems with the timeliness of data. The usual time lag from the end of an annual reporting period to public release of the data is approximately two years—the period deemed necessary to allow reporting entities to complete and file their annual reports, and for EPA to compile, verify, and analyze the data. Consequently, at any given moment, users of the latest TRI data are actually analyzing conditions that prevailed two to three years in the past. In principle, real-time monitoring and electronic reporting could cure this problem, but again, at the price of sharply higher compliance costs. * * *

To generate the standardized data it needs to be effective, TRI must oversimplify, reducing a complex problem (environmental and health risk posed by toxic pollution) to a simple metric (pounds of emissions and transfers of listed substances from a limited set of reporting entities). In so doing, it distorts even as it informs, omitting much in the way of detail, dimension, and nuance. This is not to argue that the information TRI provides is not valuable. Indeed, despite its many deficiencies, we are certainly better informed, individually and collectively, with the information generated by TRI than we were without it. Nor is it to say, on the other hand, that TRI cannot be improved, or that more and better performance metrics cannot be devised over time. But it does suggest that TRI and similar performance metrics will be, always and at best, imperfect oversimplifications of a complex world, in need of constant reassessment, upgrading, and refinement.

---

## QUESTIONS AND DISCUSSION

**1.** In addition to the TRI database, there is an immense amount of environmental information currently available on EPA's website. Information on Superfund sites is available on EPA's CERCLIS Database. EPA's AirData Web provides information on criteria air pollutant and hazardous air pollutant concentrations across the country. And the STORET database provides data on water quality.

These are powerfully brought together, along with 400 other data sources, on the Scorecard website, www.scorecard.goodguide.com, which allows you to customize your search and identify the range of pollutants and environmental quality of where you live and work.

Go to the Scorecard website and type in your home zip code. See if you can identify:

- how many Superfund sites are located in your county;
- how your county compares with other counties for toxics, air pollution, and water pollution;
- how close local polluters are to where you live.

Were you surprised by any of the results? Did you find this information helpful? What further information would you like to be able to access on the web?

Environmental groups also use TRI data to shame polluters into reducing their emissions. Thus, for example, public interest groups have publicized the "MisFortune 100," a list of the nation's top corporate air polluters (as identified by TRI data and factoring in toxicity weights and the number of people exposed).

**2.** How can TRI encourage pollution prevention? Friendly critics of TRI have long argued that the disclosure requirements do not go far enough. By focusing on releases to the environment, they argued, TRI overlooked the more important goal of reducing the total amount of toxics used, generated, and disposed during the manufacturing process. In place of reporting on releases, they proposed a "materials accounting" approach. This would require facilities to track the use and flow of chemicals *throughout* the manufacturing processes, not just releases. Thus Section 313 reports would account for the quantity of the TRI chemical transported onto the site, produced on-site, consumed in the manufacturing process, contained in the product, released into the environment, transferred for off-site recycling and reclamation, etc. This would ensure a "mass balance," so the amount of chemical coming into the manufacturing process matched the amount coming out. Such information would provide a far more accurate, and useful, picture of the firm's hazard profile.

The 1990 Pollution Prevention Act took a step in this direction by requiring that amounts of TRI toxics recycled, treated, and recovered for energy (both on-and off-site) be included in the TRI annual reports alongside the TRI "release" (pollution & disposal) data. 42 U.S.C. § 13106. In 1996, EPA issued an Advanced Notice of Proposed Rulemaking to require materials accounting. 61 FED. REG. 51,322. Industry opposed the initiative, arguing that it would reveal confidential manufacturing process information to competitors and impose excessive reporting burdens. Over 40,000 comments were submitted on the proposed rule, but no further action was taken. Two states, New Jersey and Massachusetts, require materials accounting as part of their state right-to-know laws. *See* N.J. Stat. Ann. § 34:5A–1 to 3144; Mass. Gen. Laws ch. 21I, § 10.

**3.** In addition to increasing the lists of chemicals and industries covered by TRI since reporting first started, the type of reporting has changed, as well. In 1999, for example, reporting thresholds were lowered for specified Persistent Bioaccumulative Toxic (PBT) substances. 64 Fed. Reg. 58666. PBTs are not only toxic, but also remain in the environment for long periods and accumulate in organisms. As a result of this bioaccumulation, releases of very small amounts to the environment still pose health hazards. This type of initiative begins to address the concern that reported substances are not indexed for toxicity. While separate and additional reporting requirements for PBTs do not overcome that limitation—since all PBTs are treated alike regardless of relative toxicity—it is an important step toward more refined toxicity indexing.

EPA has also refined the types of environmental releases reported. Thus, for example, EPA now asks facilities to provide separate breakout data for releases, identifying quantities of waste sent to underground injection wells, hazardous waste landfills, other landfills, farm application, surface impoundments, etc. This differentiation of disposal routes is an important step toward providing information that correlates more closely to human exposures or health risks. It is much more useful, for example, to know that X pounds of solid waste are going to a landfill, Y pounds to a deep well, and Z pounds to farm application than that 1,500 pounds of solid waste were released. You can see how this is reported on EPA Form R, reproduced below and on the following page.

# FORM R

**Part II. CHEMICAL-SPECIFIC INFORMATION**

TRI Facility ID Number

Toxic Chemical, Category, or Generic Name

**SECTION 1. TOXIC CHEMICAL IDENTITY**
**(Important: DO NOT complete this section if you are reporting a mixture component in Section 2 below.)**

| | |
|---|---|
| 1.1 | CAS Number (Important: Enter only one number exactly as it appears on the Section 313 list. Enter category code if reporting a chemical category.) |
| 1.2 | Toxic Chemical or Chemical Category Name (Important: Enter only one name exactly as it appears on the Section 313 list.) |
| 1.3 | Generic Chemical Name (Important: Complete only if Part I, Section 2.1 is checked "Yes". Generic Name must be structurally descriptive.) |

**SECTION 2. MIXTURE COMPONENT IDENTITY** **(Important: DO NOT complete this section if you completed Section 1.)**

| | |
|---|---|
| 2.1 | Generic Chemical Name Provided by Supplier (Important: Maximum of 70 characters, including numbers, letters, spaces, and punctuation.) |

**SECTION 3. ACTIVITIES AND USES OF THE TOXIC CHEMICAL AT THE FACILITY**
**(Important: Check all that apply.)**

| 3.1 Manufacture the toxic chemical: | 3.2 Process the toxic chemical: | 3.3 Otherwise use the toxic chemical: |
|---|---|---|
| a. ☐ Produce b. ☐ Import | a. ☐ As a reactant | a. ☐ As a chemical processing aid |
| If Produce or Import | b. ☐ As a formulation component | b. ☐ As a manufacturing aid |
| c. ☐ For on-site use/processing | c. ☐ As an article component | c. ☐ Ancillary or other use |
| d. ☐ For sale/distribution | d. ☐ Repackaging | |
| e. ☐ As a byproduct | e. ☐ As an impurity | |
| f. ☐ As an impurity | | |

**SECTION 4. MAXIMUM AMOUNT OF THE TOXIC CHEMICAL ON-SITE AT ANY TIME DURING THE CALENDAR YEAR**

4.1 ☐ (Enter two digit code from instruction package.)

**SECTION 5. QUANTITY OF THE TOXIC CHEMICAL ENTERING EACH ENVIRONMENTAL MEDIUM ON-SITE**

| | | | **A. Total Release** (pounds/year*) (Enter a range code** or estimate) | **B. Basis of Estimate** (Enter code) | **C. Percent from Stormwater** |
|---|---|---|---|---|---|
| 5.1 | Fugitive or non-point air emissions | NA ☐ | | | |
| 5.2 | Stack or point air emissions | NA ☐ | | | |
| 5.3 | Discharges to receiving streams or water bodies (Enter one name per box) | NA ☐ | | | |
| | Stream or Water Body Name | Reach Code (optional) | | | |
| 5.3.1 | | | | | |
| 5.3.2 | | | | | |
| 5.3.3 | | | | | |

If additional pages of Part II, Section 5.3 are attached, indicate the total number of pages in this box ☐
and indicate the Part II, Section 5.3 page number in this box. ☐ (Example: 1, 2, 3, etc.)

**FORM R**

**Part II. CHEMICAL-SPECIFIC INFORMATION (CONTINUED)**

| TRI Facility ID Number |
|---|
| |
| Toxic Chemical, Category, or Generic Name |
| |



**SECTION 5. QUANTITY OF THE TOXIC CHEMICAL ENTERING EACH ENVIRONMENTAL MEDIUM ON-SITE (continued)**

| | | NA | **A. Total Release** (pounds/year*) (Enter a range code** or estimate) | **B. Basis of Estimate** (Enter code) |
|---|---|---|---|---|
| 5.4-5.5 | Disposal to land on-site | | | |
| 5.4.1 | Class I Underground Injection Wells | ☐ | | |
| 5.4.2 | Class II-V Underground Injection Wells | ☐ | | |
| 5.5.1A | RCRA Subtitle C landfills | ☐ | | |
| 5.5.1B | Other landfills | ☐ | | |
| 5.5.2 | Land treatment/application farming | ☐ | | |
| 5.5.3A | RCRA Subtitle C surface impoundments | ☐ | | |
| 5.5.3B | Other surface impoundments | ☐ | | |
| 5.5.4 | Other disposal | ☐ | | |

**SECTION 6. TRANSFER(S) OF THE TOXIC CHEMICAL IN WASTES TO OFF-SITE LOCATIONS**

6.1 **DISCHARGES TO PUBLICLY OWNED TREATMENT WORKS (POTWs)** NA ☐

6.1.__ POTW Name

POTW Address

City | County | State | ZIP

| A. Quantity Transferred to this POTW (pounds/year*) (Enter range code**or estimate) | B. Basis of Estimate (Enter code) |
|---|---|
| | |

If additional pages of Part II, Section 6.1 are attached, indicate the total number of pages in this box ☐ and indicate the Part II, Section 6.1 page number in this box. ☐ (Example: 1, 2, 3, etc.)

**SECTION 6.2 TRANSFERS TO OTHER OFF-SITE LOCATIONS** NA ☐

6.2.__ Off-Site EPA Identification Number (RCRA ID No.)

Off-Site Location Name:

Off-Site Address:

City | County | State | ZIP | Country (non-US)

Is this location under control of reporting facility or parent company? ☐ Yes ☐ No

**4.** Underreporting emissions is a potential danger in any program that relies on third party reporting, whether it be NPDES permits under the Clean Water Act or Section 313 reports under TRI. Section 325(c) of EPCRA provides for civil penalties of up to $25,000 per day for failure to comply with the reporting requirements. Given scarce resources, however, it is likely that EPA could undertake more enforcement actions for under-reporting than it currently does. This is no different than the situation with other environmental laws that rely on self-reporting, though, and one might expect citizen suits to help fill the enforcement gap and provide an additional incentive for compliance.

Citizen suits are particularly difficult to bring under EPCRA, however, for two reasons. The first, as described in the chapter on enforcement (Chapter 11) is the requirement of showing the likelihood of "continuing violations." In *Steel Co. v. Citizens for a Better Environment*, 523 U.S. 83 (1998), for example, Citizens for a Better Environment (CBE) alleged that Steel Company had failed to submit TRI reports for a number of years. By the time the case came to trial, though, Steel Company had filed its late reports. CBE continued the case, requesting the court to declare that Steel

Company's late filing had violated EPCRA, to allow CBE periodically to investigate the company's facility and records, to require the Steel Company to pay a civil fine to the U.S. Treasury, and to pay CBE's litigation costs. The Supreme Court rejected their claims, holding that none of these remedies could compensate the group for its injury suffered by the Steel Company's late reporting. Following the decision in *Friends of the Earth v. Laidlaw Environmental Services*, 528 U.S. 167 (2000), the Court held that civil penalties can act as a sufficient deterrent to satisfy the standing requirement of redressability, but plaintiffs must demonstrate that the violation is ongoing or likely to occur again. This obviously is difficult to demonstrate for a filing requirement such as TRI.

**5.** If nothing else, the TRI story shows the potential of voluntary industry pollution reduction efforts. Another example worth noting was the 33/50 Initiative. In 1990, EPA Administrator Bill Reilly sent letters to 1,300 companies operating 6,000 facilities in the United States. Reilly listed 17 priority chemicals and challenged the companies to reduce their emissions of these chemicals by 33% by 1993 and by 50% by 1995. Participation was high and EPA's 50% goal was achieved a year early. By the end of 1995 EPA reported emissions reductions of more than 750,000,000 pounds. EPA, 33/50 PROGRAM: THE FINAL RECORD (1999). Are you surprised that so many companies participated? Why do you think they were willing to meet and, in many cases, exceed EPA's challenge?

**6.** As with NEPA, success breeds imitation and the model of TRI has been adopted in many countries. Principle 10 of the Rio Declaration, adopted by over 170 countries at the 1992 United Nations Conference on Environment and Development, declares that:

> each individual shall have appropriate access to information concerning the environment that is held by public authorities, including information on hazardous materials and activities in their communities.

In the international community, systems that collect and publish data on pollution from industrial facilities are known as Pollutant Release and Transfer Registers (PRTRs). In addition to TRI and state programs in Massachusetts and New Jersey, PRTR programs are in place in Canada, the United Kingdom (England and Wales), and Australia. Initiatives are also underway in Mexico, Switzerland, the Czech Republic, the Slovak Republic, and Hungary. The European Union's program, the European Pollutants Emission Registrar, requires EU member states to report total emissions for 50 different pollutants above a minimum threshold. Details on these programs and international initiatives are available on the UN Environment Program's PRTR website at www.prtr.net.

## B. CALIFORNIA'S PROPOSITION 65

While Congress was passing EPCRA, California voters expressed their concern over exposure to toxics by passing the ballot initiative known as Proposition 65. Known as the Safe Drinking Water and Toxic Enforcement Act of 1986, Proposition 65 passed by a two-to-one margin.

Its basic requirement is that "no person in the course of doing business shall knowingly and intentionally expose any individual to a chemical known to the state [California] to cause cancer or reproductive toxicity without first giving a clear and reasonable warning. . . ." Cal. Health & Safety Code Sections 25249.5–13. As a result, businesses must disclose to the public both toxic releases and toxic ingredients in consumer products.

## James Salzman and Barton H. Thompson, Jr.

ENVIRONMENTAL LAW AND POLICY 225–226 (2014).

Under Proposition 65, the Governor of California publishes a list of those chemicals known to cause cancer or reproductive toxicity; this list currently contains approximately 750 chemicals. Businesses cannot knowingly discharge or release a listed chemical into water or onto or into land if the chemical probably would travel into a source of drinking water. More importantly, businesses cannot knowingly and intentionally expose someone to a listed chemical without first providing a "clear and reasonable" warning. Thus, if a consumer product contains a listed chemical, the seller must post a notice either on the product or in a location that purchasers will see. Factories emitting toxic air pollutants must warn neighboring residents.

Businesses are exempt from these rules if the amount of chemical at issue is "insignificant." Recognizing that whether a level of exposure is significant or not can be the source of considerable scientific debate, however, Proposition 65 reverses the normal burden of proof. In order to qualify for the exemption, the business has the burden to show that the exposure amount is insignificant. This led businesses to press California in the early days of Proposition 65 to quickly issue regulations specifying what would constitute an insignificant amount. The resulting regulations define an insignificant amount for carcinogens as an amount that presents a risk, assuming lifetime exposure, of less than one in 100,000. For reproductive toxins, a quantity is insignificant if the toxin would have no observable effect on people who are exposed over their lifetime to 1000 times that quantity.

Proposition 65 also was one of the first environmental statutes in the United States to include a "bounty" provision. Whoever brings a lawsuit for a violation of Proposition 65 receives 25 percent of any penalty imposed by the court. Courts can assess penalties of up to $2500 per day for each violation. Fearful that the bounty provision might be encouraging frivolous lawsuits, California in 2002 added a requirement that plaintiffs file a "certificate of merit" certifying that the plaintiff believes that there is good cause for the lawsuit. Plaintiffs must also give the California Attorney General 90 days notice of their intent to file a lawsuit, and the Attorney General can block the lawsuit by filing a governmental action at any point within that 90 day period.

When Proposition 65 originally passed, some people questioned whether consumers really would pay attention to warning labels and signs. Concern mounted when Proposition 65 warnings began to sprout up virtually everywhere—in liquor stores (potential for birth defects), bars and restaurants (alcohol and, before cigarettes were banned in California bars, second-hand smoke), and in gasoline stations (toxic fumes). Under Proposition 65, moreover, warning signs typically are quite generic. A typical warning reads, "Warning: This product contains a chemical known to the State of California to cause cancer." The warnings virtually never provide detailed information about the exact nature and size of the potential risk.

Proposition 65, however, has resulted in significant reductions in toxic exposures. Some producers have responded to Proposition 65 by reformulating their products. Producers simply do not want to take a chance on how consumers will respond to warning labels. Wine makers therefore no longer use lead foil for the tops of their bottles. Wite-Out Products removed trichloroethylene (TCE) from their correction fluid, the manufacturers of calcium supplements reduced the lead content in the supplements, and the maker of Progresso tomatoes stopped using lead solder in their cans. Because most manufacturers do not want to manufacture one version of a product for California and another version for the rest of the nation, moreover, these changes generally have benefited consumers nationwide.

---

## QUESTIONS AND DISCUSSION

**1.** In the nearly three decades since its adoption, Proposition 65 has become a standard cost of doing business in California. If you were asked to write a report assessing the law's success, what metrics would you use?

**2.** Proposition 65 has long been subject to the criticism that while information is a good thing, *too much* information can become the equivalent to no information, at all. In other words, the knowledge that so many products contain toxics can overwhelm an individual's ability to act in response to that unhappy information. As a result, critics charge, consumers simply block out the warnings as irrelevant background noise and ignore them. How would you respond to this concern if you were advocating the addition of new toxics to the Proposition 65 list?

**3.** As noted in the excerpt, the bounty provision of Proposition 65 was an innovation that sought to ensure greater enforcement capacity than could be provided solely by government officials. Despite the requirement of plaintiffs to file a "certificate of merit," some believe the bounty provision invites nuisance suits. As Michele B. Corash, a San Francisco environmental lawyer who represents defendants in Proposition 65 cases describes, the "bounty hunter" provision created a cottage industry for lawyers.

> [The bounty provision] is being used by people with no interest in the purpose of the statute in order just to line their pockets and

> bring cases that are frivolous. There are organizations that file hundreds of 60-day notices and demands for eight, ten, twelve thousand dollars—little enough that it's not worth fighting them. These cases are not litigated. There is not a single Proposition 65 case that has ever been litigated to judgment on the issue of whether or not there was a risk that required a warning. There has been only one case that has been litigated to judgment and that was simply on the issue of whether the warning on the label was good enough.

*A National Proposition?,* 103 ENVIRONMENTAL HEALTH PERSPECTIVES (July 1995)

This was written prior to the 2002 requirement that plaintiffs file a "certificate of merit" that the suit is legitimate. Do you expect this made a real difference? What other options would reduce the problem of nuisance suits? Would you support a requirement that plaintiffs post a bond at the time of filing?

**4.** It is worth noting the importance of Proposition 65's allocation of the burden of proof. As John Dwyer has observed,

> Under most statutes, the incentives are for the producers to delay, to have more studies, to think about the problem. It's paralysis by analysis, because all regulatory controls cost money, no matter how sensible they are. Proposition 65, however, says that you're vulnerable to litigation unless you get in there with the agency fast and figure out what is a significant risk level. I think that's had some impact in taking the delay out of the system. In a sense, it bypasses some of the normal administrative process by focusing on the litigation process. You don't see a big administrative agency here.

*A National Proposition?,* 103 ENVIRONMENTAL HEALTH PERSPECTIVES (July 1995)

**5.** At what point should information about pollution substitute for actions to prevent it? Consider a lawsuit filed against the City of Chesapeake, Virginia,. The city had advised pregnant women to boil their drinking water because of high levels of trihalomethanes. The city was then sued for allegedly causing miscarriages or birth defects in 214 local women. Plaintiffs contended that, rather than informing water consumers of the presence of toxics and advising how to remove them by boiling, the city should have taken steps to reduce the trihalomethane levels at the tap. How would you rule in such a case? At what point does provision of information about toxics remove or lessen the need for government to step in and mandate the removal or reduction of the toxics? *See* City of Chesapeake v. Cunningham, 604 S.E.2d 420 (Va. 2004).

---

## C. INFORMATION AND CLIMATE CHANGE

One of the most active areas of informational approaches to environmental protection has been in the climate field. The excerpt below describes the design issues and potential benefits of climate change information for retailers and consumers.

### Michael P. Vandenbergh and Jonathan Gilligan, *Beyond Gridlock*

40 COLUMBIA JOURNAL OF ENVTL. L. 217 (2015).

Disclosure of carbon footprints is another promising approach for private initiatives. Disclosure is often inexpensive and can harness existing drivers for corporate carbon emissions reductions. The examples below examine carbon disclosure at the corporate, lender and investor, project, and product levels.

a. Corporate Carbon Footprints

Several initiatives encourage corporations to disclose and reduce their corporate carbon footprints. Private organizations such as CDP, Ceres, and GRI focus on increasing the collection and disclosure of reliable emissions data. CDP (Carbon Disclosure Project) was established in 2000 through the collaborative efforts of U.K. businessman Paul Dickenson, institutional investors, and philanthropic foundations, and it uses investor pressure to create incentives for firms to disclose and reduce emissions. Over 700 institutional investors with $92 trillion in assets support the CDP, and it collects and discloses self-reported climate-change data from over 4,000 corporations and other entities. The responding corporations include more than 1,000 of the largest global corporations and include roughly 70% of the Standard & Poors 500. The CDP information disclosure initiatives provide corporations and investors with reputational and other incentives to reduce carbon emissions.

A number of opportunities exist to expand the types of information collection and disclosure efforts conducted by CDP and other organizations. For instance, the CDP has already reached many of the largest firms around the world, but hundreds of additional large firms could be subject to further pressure to participate, and thousands of the next tier of smaller firms could be the subject of additional initiatives. Efforts ranging from targeting by socially responsible investors, to NGO-led consumer reputation campaigns, to boycotts and other advocacy initiatives are all possible. A recent example is General Mills' 2014 announcement that it would participate in a Ceres disclosure initiative and join the CDP. These commitments occurred after a protest by Oxfam America at the New York Stock Exchange. In addition, as discussed in more detail in the supply chain section below, the CDP could continue to expand supply chain reporting efforts as a way to extend pressure to tens of thousands of small- and medium-sized firms around the world.

b. Investor and Lender Carbon Footprints

A related set of carbon disclosure initiatives target investors (including investment firms as well as pension funds, university endowments, foundations, religious organizations, and other organizations that have large stock holdings) and lenders. NGOs have developed campaigns to induce investors to disclose the carbon footprint of their investments. In turn, this has created opportunities for new types of private businesses, such as TruCost, a U.K. firm that assesses corporate carbon footprints and has released an analysis of the carbon footprint of investment firms' portfolios.

Disclosure campaigns are often coupled with pressure to divest, and in the last several years investors have pledged to divest more than $50 billion in assets from the fossil fuel sector. In addition, at least one NGO has participated in the formation of a low-carbon index fund. These initiatives may not involve sufficiently large amounts to adversely affect share prices, but they send normative signals that may influence corporate behavior in the near term, and they could affect share prices in the long term if they gain momentum.

Less commonly discussed are new efforts by NGOs to estimate and disclose the carbon footprint of lenders' loan portfolios. These initiatives are designed to motivate lenders to reduce their direct emissions and the emissions of their corporate borrowers. For instance, the Rainforest Action Network has estimated and disclosed the carbon footprints of the five largest Canadian banks' lending portfolios. Similarly, two Australian NGOs conducted a campaign in 2014 to induce retail consumers to move their bank accounts from several banks with large carbon footprints. Disclosure campaigns also may have played a role in several banks' decision not to fund a new coal port in Australia. These lender initiatives are nascent efforts, and lender carbon disclosure represents a promising area for new private initiatives.

c. Project Carbon Footprints

Other private initiatives have focused on disclosure at the project level. For example, advocacy groups have targeted major banks with naming and shaming campaigns based on the environmental effects of the banks' project finance lending in the developing world. The efforts of the advocacy groups, with support from the World Bank and International Monetary Fund, contributed to the formation of the Equator Principles, a private standard that requires participants to disclose the environmental harms of the projects funded through project finance loans. The vast majority of the project finance lending at a global level is now conducted by banks that have agreed to comply with the Equator Principles. As with many private governance initiatives, the effects of the project-level disclosure on carbon emissions are unclear, but the types of projects subject to Equator Principles disclosure (e.g., pipelines and other major infrastructure projects), suggest large effects if the disclosure affects decision making. * * *

Although these provisions do not prohibit funding of fossil fuel-fired power plants, they signal to utilities that lenders anticipate future restrictions on carbon emissions and will give serious consideration to the climate implications of plant emissions in the lending process. The Carbon Principles are limited to electric power generation within the United States, but there is room for growth: this type of initiative could be expanded to include additional lenders and additional countries, and to focus on other carbon-intensive industries.

d. Product Carbon Footprints

Private product carbon labeling is another area that is ripe for expansion. Government-sponsored carbon labeling systems exist in several countries, but a government carbon labeling program in the U.S. is probably no more likely in the near term than a national carbon price. Private carbon labeling systems have been attempted in several countries, however, and could extend their reach by targeting firms that stand to gain the most from demonstrating that their goods are low-carbon as compared to competitors. Climate considerations are included in several general eco-labels, but there is a risk that climate concerns will be under-valued in general ecolabeling systems, and product carbon disclosure has lagged behind corporate carbon footprint disclosure. This is due in part to the technical challenges of calculating product-specific labels for products that have complex or varying supply chains, but these challenges can be overcome for many products. For example, although some products have complex and varying inputs, others have well-understood carbon footprints. These footprints often differ dramatically from their substitutes (e.g., the carbon footprint of beef is often several times that of chicken), and the differences can be communicated through a well-designed label.

A common assumption is that labeling will only reduce emissions if it affects the direct purchasing behavior of retail consumers. If so, the prospects are limited. Although some consumers are willing to pay more for goods labelled as low carbon, many are not. Not surprisingly, this leads to pessimism about the effects of carbon labels.

Although consumer willingness to pay is important, carbon labeling may reduce emissions for a less intuitive reason: firms may reduce the carbon footprint of existing products and alter the selection of products they offer to consumers in anticipation of product carbon footprint disclosure. Food labeling studies suggest, for example, that consumers only respond to a limited extent to labels, but food labeling appears to change the products that food companies and restaurants offer to consumers, even if the direct consumer response is limited. In short, when retail food companies and restaurants know that they will be disclosing nutritional information, they appear to change the content and mix of products offered to consumers. In a similar way, firms may respond to private carbon labeling initiatives by looking for ways to reduce the carbon content of products or by changing the selection of products offered to consumers.

Many firms will not participate in a voluntary private carbon labeling initiative, but carbon labeling will be attractive to firms that anticipate competitive advantages from assessing and disclosing the carbon footprint of their products. For instance, a firm that offers fruit, vegetables, meat, or dairy products with a lower carbon footprint than competitors and sells through organic food stores may opt into a private carbon labeling program. Other firms may participate because of more generalized concerns about their reputation with consumers, investors, or lenders.

---

## QUESTIONS AND DISCUSSION

**1.** The excerpt discusses four different types of footprint disclosure—corporate, investor and lender, project, and product. Which do you think would prove more effective in reducing overall carbon emissions?

**2.** The authors claim that many consumers are not willing to pay for "climate-friendly" products. If consumer preferences for green goods are fairly weak, how do they argue that carbon labeling may still prove effective reducing companies' carbon footprints? What role might reputational concerns play?

**3.** Consistent with their argument about consumers' willingness to pay, it appears that interest in carbon labeling by retailers apparently has declined over time. Patagonia dropped carbon footprint information from its website in 2012. The leading British retailer, Tesco, dropped its carbon label pledge, as well. It's important to note that corporate interest in climate change action has remained strong over this period, focusing more on internal initiatives, so why do you think interest in labeling has declined?

Part of the answer may lie in the cost of calculating carbon footprints of individual products, estimated to be as much as $20,000–$60,000. It's also not clear that consumers care enough to influence their purchasing decisions. Bill Sheehan, *Whatever Happened to Carbon Labelling,* April 23, 2014, upstreampolicy.org.

Do you think laws should require greenhouse gas labeling or are we better served having the market develop voluntary standards? What are the potential downsides to mandating a labeling program for products' carbon footprints? Where would the data come from to assess the carbon footprints? What types of products should be included in this program (and, conversely, what should be exempted?) Should services be included, as well? If so, how would you measure the carbon footprint of a law firm?

**4.** As the excerpt notes, product labels risk running afoul of international trade rules and the WTO. This may seem odd, because labeling has long been proposed as an alternative to trade restrictions. Ecolabels can help consumers to exercise preferences for products whose production, use or disposal impose a lighter burden on the environment than competing products. Labeling and certification schemes are covered by the General Agreement on Tariffs and Trade (GATT) and the Technical Barriers to Trade (TBT) Agreement. The TBT Agreement applies both to both technical regulations, which are mandatory, and standards, which are voluntary, and seeks to reduce barriers to market access by harmonizing these to international standards.

There are three potential issues. The first is that ecolabels for greenhouse gas emissions would focus primarily on how the product was made and distributed, not the product itself. This raises concerns over the "PPM debate"—whether trade restrictions may be based on the product's process and production methods rather than on the product, itself. In the famous Tuna/Dolphin case under the GATT, for example, the question was whether the United States could ban the import of tuna based on whether or not the tuna had been harvested with "dolphin-friendly" gear. In the climate change context, is it permissible to treat two products differently based on how they were produced or distributed, even if the products themselves are indistinguishable?

The second issue is whether labeling rises to the level of an actionable trade restriction. The labeling schemes do not ban the sale of any products. They simply provide information to the consumer. Moreover, this is done in an evenhanded manner. High emissions products are treated the same, whether imported or produced domestically. What do you think is the strongest argument that this still amounts to a de facto restriction on trade for some products?

The last issue is whether WTO trade disciplines even apply to nongovernmental actions. They clearly apply to actions by national and state governments, but the situation is less clear for retailers and private labeling organizations. The TBT Agreement establishes a Code of Good Practice for local government and non-governmental standardizing and labeling bodies. It also provides that WTO Members must take "such reasonable measures as may be available" to ensure that local government and private standardizing bodies comply with the Code (TBT Agreement, Article 4.1). The precise scope of obligations in the Code, as well as the type of "reasonable measures" Members must take to enforce it, however, remains unclear. *See*, James Salzman, *Informing the Green Consumer: The Debate Over the Use and Abuse of Environmental Labels*, JOURNAL OF INDUSTRIAL ECOLOGY (Summer 1997).

# CHAPTER 7

# PUBLIC LANDS

**CHAPTER OUTLINE**

I. Multiple Use Management: The National Forests

II. Dominant Use Management: National Parks

III. Single Use Management: Wilderness Areas

---

Federal, state, and local governments own and manage vast amounts of land in the United States, with the federal government being the largest landholder in the nation. Federal public land management policy has gone through many phases. Initially, federal policy was to dispose of federal holdings, transferring them through a multitude of programs into private hands for settlement and resource development. As the public domain diminished increasingly over the 1800s, an era of "withdrawal and reservation" took hold in the late 1800s under which the federal government retained dominion over public lands and managed them under an increasing diversity of designations. With still almost one-third of the nation's land mass in federal hands, the formulation of public land management policy is of tremendous importance to many communities who depend on one or another use of the land. Over time, especially since the 1960s, the trend has unmistakably been to deemphasize resource extractive uses and to lean more toward recreational and conservation uses.

There are four primary federal land management agencies administering vast expanses of federally-owned land and natural resources. Three are within the Department of the Interior: the Bureau of Land Management (247 million acres); the National Park Service (80 million acres); and the United States Fish and Wildlife Service (89 million acres). The fourth agency is the United States Forest Service, a branch of the Department of Agriculture, which oversees 193 million acres of national forests and grasslands. These four agencies manage many different units of federal public lands, such as parks, wildlife refuges, forests, grasslands, rangelands, wilderness areas, and recreation areas. The agency that comes in a distant fifth in federal public land management is the Department of Defense, with a little over 14 million acres under its control, mostly as military base land.

The vast majority of the federal public lands are located west of the Mississippi River. Over 45 percent of the land mass of the 11 coterminous western states is owned by the federal government. Well over half of Alaska is federally owned, and almost half of California is federal land.

Only 4 percent of land outside the 11 western states and Alaska is federally owned.

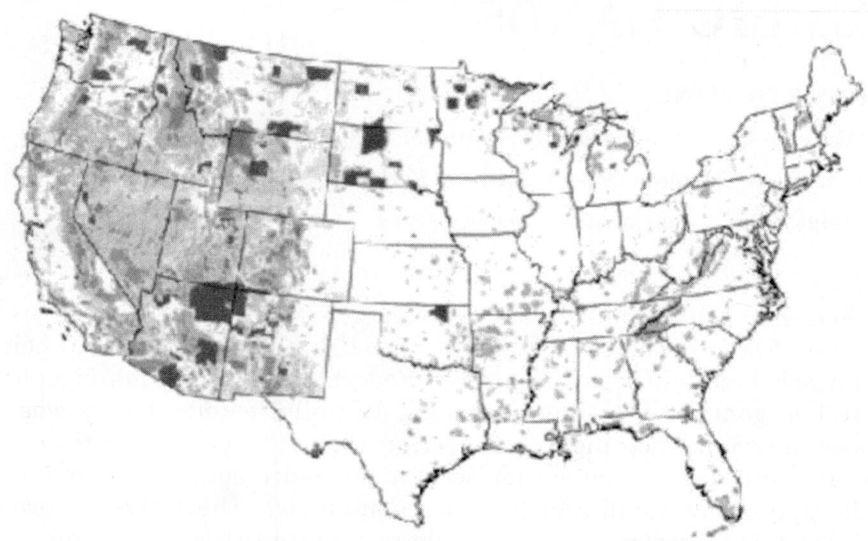

Map showing the 810,000 square miles of federal public lands in the lower 48 states, 90 percent of which are in 11 western states (source: University of Montana)

How these agencies decide to manage their combined total of over 620 million acres of federal land thus has played and will continue to play a prominent role in the development of environmental policy on public lands. Yet these agencies and their different land units serve many different purposes. There is, in other words, no single unifying federal land policy. Rather, different units of federal land are managed according to one of three principal types of mandate. *Multiple use* lands are managed to optimize a bundle of prescribed uses. *Dominant use* lands have a primary use specified, but may accommodate other uses so long as the primary use is not impeded. *Single use* lands have, as the name suggests, just one prescribed use. The vast majority of federal land is subject to a multiple use mandate of one form or another, and usually some of the uses involve an intensive human use, such as timber production, grazing, recreation, or mineral extraction, while others are more consistent with the goals of environmental policy, such as wildlife conservation. Congress usually leaves the agencies a fairly large policy space "box," meaning a wide variety of options is available to the agency. Nevertheless, given constant oversight by Congress, industry, conservation groups, and the public in general, the perpetual challenge federal land agencies face under these land management mandates is to balance the uses, particularly balancing the intense human uses against the resource conservation uses.

# I. MULTIPLE USE MANAGEMENT: THE NATIONAL FORESTS

About 46 percent of the contiguous United States was forested at the time of European settlement, and about 32 percent is today, but virtually none of the original tree stands—the so-called old growth forests—remain today. The biodiversity values of the secondary stands and managed plantations that replaced them, which do not count in most studies as deforested acres, are generally less than for primary stands. Moreover, the biodiversity capacity of many standing forests has been imperiled by industrial and agricultural pollution of air and water, invasive species introduced through inadvertent or purposeful human import, raging wildfires caused, ironically, by fuel buildup resulting from prior fire suppression, and other results of human management decisions both within and external to forests. And as overall forest health declines, natural threats such as insects and disease become more acute. For example, over 90 million acres of standing forests in the United States are threatened by seven major pests and diseases.

Thus, although headlines focus on loss of the tropical rainforests to agriculture and timber extraction, the United States has been no stranger to forest resource depletion and continues to suffer serious declines in the health of its remaining forest stands. Our nation's appetite for wood is voracious: we consume one fourth of the world's industrial timber; ten percent of the world's industrial timber is used in the U.S. construction industry, mostly for home building; and we produce 30 percent of the world's paper. These demands have taken their toll on American forests. Today, about 33 percent of the U.S. land area—747 million acres—is forest lands, but that is two-thirds of our forested area in 1600. More than 75 percent of the 307 million acres lost to other uses were converted in the 19th century, mostly to agricultural uses and mostly in the Midwest and lower Mississippi Valley. The net area of forested land has remained relatively stable since 1920, as the introduction of mechanized farm machines reduced the need to devote cropland to growing feed for farm draft animals. In short, we have little need for converting more forest land into farmland. Yet only a small fraction of what remains of our forested lands is primary old growth forest.

About two-thirds of the nation's remaining forested lands are classified as timberland suitable for production of lumber, paper, and other industrial goods. The federal government owns and manages about one-third of U.S. forested land. The rest is owned by nonfederal public agencies, forest industry firms, farmers, and some 6 million other private individuals. Forest lands, types, and ownership patterns are distributed unevenly. North Dakota, for example, is only one percent forested land, while Maine has the most at 89 percent. Most of the privately owned forest land is east of the Mississippi River, while most forest land to the west is publicly owned. Most hardwood timber stock is in the east;

western timber is mostly softwood. Private forest lands in the eastern states, particularly plantation forests in the southeast, will be our nation's primary source of timber in this century. This diversity of distribution, ownership, and type of forest lands makes formation of a national management policy for our forest ecosystems a difficult political and scientific undertaking.

Although the early North American colonists found a virtually boundless supply of forests, it was not long before the common practice of setting fire to forests as a means of opening the land to other uses became regarded as economically wasteful and environmentally unsound. For example, a 1626 ordinance of the Plymouth Colony in Massachusetts banned setting of open forest fires on the ground that an inconvenience might result from a depletion of the timber supply, and much later a North Carolina act of 1777 proscribed unlawful firing of the woods as being extremely prejudicial to the soil. By the early eighteenth century many colonial governments also forbade unnecessary cutting of timber on common lands, and shortly after the Revolutionary War concluded Massachusetts enacted a law requiring licenses for removal of large white pines from state lands.

The newly formed national government entered the forest policy scene quickly after the war as a result of repeated pirate attacks on American merchant vessels. Congress, realizing the need for a national navy, also realized the need for a national timber supply to build the navy's ships. By an act of February 25, 1799, 1 Stat. 622, Congress appropriated money to purchase a timber supply, which later was used to acquire Grover's and Blackbeard's Islands off the coast of Georgia to secure about 2000 acres of prime timber property. Later, after the navy proved instrumental to victory against the British in the War of 1812, an act of March 1, 1817, 3 Stat. 347, authorized the Secretary of the Navy to select vacant and unappropriated tracts on federal lands with prime timber resources and recommend that the President reserve them from sale.

Timber policy through 1850 thus was defined largely by ad hoc state laws regulating open fires and federal reservation of timber supplies on federal lands to meet the navy's shipbuilding needs. Reports of widespread theft of timber from federal, state, and private lands suggest that these laws were difficult to enforce. The development of iron shipbuilding technology in the mid-1800s, moreover, led Congress to return most of its naval timber reserves to the public domain, meaning they were once again open for sale. The federal and state land settlement policies of the 1800s then surged the transfer of title to federal and state lands from public to private ownership by sale, homestead laws, railroad laws, and other means, shifting most eastern forest lands to private hands by the late 1800s.

The first glimmer of forest conservation policy was lit when the American Forestry Congress of 1882, meeting in Cincinnati, created the

American Forestry Association to cooperate with the federal and state governments toward formulating a definite policy for managing public forest lands. In the following two decades, several states created state-level forestry agencies to regulate fires, encourage timber culture, and, in some cases, promote forest conservation, preservation, and extension. While in most cases the motivating force behind these laws was security of timber supply, laws such as one New York enacted in 1885, Session Laws, N.Y., 1885 ch. 283, p. 482, were among the first truly comprehensive forest management policies in America. The New York law established a system for designating, maintaining, and protecting state forests, complete with a state forest commission, wardens, forest inspectors, foresters, and other staff.

Federal policy witnessed a similar trend after the 1873 meeting of the American Society for the Advancement of Science appointed a committee to present to Congress a plan for the extension and preservation of forests, providing the impetus for a flurry of additional studies and proposals and even several federal laws promoting timber culture and the collection of forest statistics. The seeds of today's Forest Service also were planted in the Department of Agriculture through creation of the Division of Forestry, which began with one employee and an annual budget of $2000. By the late 1800s, though, federal forest policy remained a complete muddle—while promoting the extension of forest lands by subsidized plantings and other culture programs, albeit often in areas not suited to trees of any kind, the federal government was at the same time disposing of vast tracts of prime forest lands into private possession.

To resolve this inconsistency, a "rider" provision to the 1891 General Revision Act, known as the Forest Reserve Act of 1891, authorized the President to establish forest reservations on federal lands. *See* Act of March 3, 1891, ch. 561, 26 Stat. 1095, 1103 (repealed 1976). Fortunately, not all the federal lands had yet been given away or sold, and Presidents Harrison and Cleveland withdrew extensive areas in the Western states from sale or entry and declared them national forest reserves. But much remained uncertain: Western interests were quite bitter over the turn of events, there was debate over the actual authority of the president under the 1891 law, and there were no monies appropriated to manage what by 1896 amounted to millions of acres of national forests. Congress resolved the situation with the passage of the Forest Service Organic Act of 1897, 30 Stat. 11, 34–35 (Organic Act), which ratified the presidential reservations and authorized administration of the national forests, then called forest reserves, through a federal agency.

The Organic Act marks the beginning of the development of comprehensive federal forest policy and administration. Although it made no mention of biodiversity, ecosystems, or even wildlife, it provided that the national forests should be established "to improve and protect the forest within the boundaries, or for the purposes of securing favorable water flows, and to furnish a continuous supply of timber for the use and necessities of citizens of the United States." 15 U.S.C. § 473. For the latter purpose, the Organic Act authorized the Department of the Interior, then after 1905 the Forest Service in the Department of Agriculture, to

> cause to be designated and appraised so much of the dead, matured or large growth trees found upon such national forests as may be compatible with the utilization of the forests thereon, and may sell the same. . . . Such timber, before being sold, shall be marked and designated, and shall be cut and removed under the supervision of some person appointed for that purpose by the Secretary. . . .

Gifford Pinchot, who became head of the Forestry Service in 1898, envisioned the national forests as primarily a timber supply resource, and for nearly seventy years the Forest Service interpreted the Organic Act as allowing widespread extraction of timber. Indeed, after World War II, housing construction demands placed tremendous new pressure on the nation's timber supply, and on the Forest Service. Clearcutting became a common practice on private forest lands, thus depleting private timber supplies and causing the timber industry to pressure the Forest Service to increase the yield from national forests. The agency met this demand, but by doing so fueled a conflict between timber harvesting and another demand that boomed after the war—recreation. As clearcutting became common in the national forests, so too did the previously uncommon instance of public criticism of Forest Service decisions.

Congress nevertheless gave the Forest Service basically a free hand in all such matters of national forest policy, intervening only once to enact the Multiple Use and Sustained Yield Act of 1960 (MUSYA). MUSYA expanded the purposes of national forest management from water flows and timber supply to include "outdoor recreation, range, timber, watershed, and wildlife and fish purposes." 16 U.S.C. § 528. Recognizing that "some land will be used for less than all the resources," MUSYA required that the five multiple uses, which Congress deliberately named in alphabetical order, be treated as co-equal and managed "with consideration being given to the relative values of the various resources." *Id.* The statute described the core mandate of multiple use as meaning

> The management of all the various renewable surface resources of the national forests so that they are utilized in the combination that will best meet the needs of the American people; making the most judicious use of the land for some or all these resources or related services over areas large enough to provide sufficient latitude for periodic adjustments in use to conform to changing needs and conditions. . . .

*Id.* § 531.

Conservation and recreation interests opposed the legislation while the agency and timber industry actively supported it. Critics of the Forest Service charged that the agency had elevated timber extraction above the other uses and exercised widespread clearcutting without due regard to the Organic Act, and would continue to do both under MUSYA. Indeed, for all practical purposes MUSYA codified precisely the policy discretion the agency sought (and argued it had even without MUSYA). After MUSYA, the law of national forests explicitly recognized the breadth of the agency's discretion. While courts demanded that the agency give "due consideration" to each of the multiple use components, *see* Parker v. United States, 307 F. Supp. 685 (D. Colo. 1969), in the final analysis most courts agreed that "the decision as to the proper mix of uses within any particular area is left to the sound discretion and expertise of the Forest Service." Sierra Club v. Hardin, 325 F. Supp. 99, 123 (D. Alaska 1971). MUSYA's multiple use mandate was essentially rendered directionless, leaving it to the agency to decide where to go and providing no meaningful legislative or judicial check on the path chosen.

As Congress and the courts continued to afford the Forest Service wide latitude in setting policy after MUSYA, the agency began experimenting with planning as a way to resolve multiple use conflicts, requiring each national forest to develop a land use plan. Yet the agency used the end products as a vehicle to portray its policy of clearcutting as not merely a capitulation to the powerful timber industry, but the result a rational, scientifically sound policy decision making process. Neither congressional appropriations nor agency will would have supported any other outcome, thus leaving the growing recreational and conservation interests on the outside of the forest.

The first chink in this armor came in 1964 with passage of the Wilderness Act. 16 U.S.C. §§ 1131–36, which is explored in more detail later in this chapter. Since 1929 the Forest Service had regulations in place in one form or another for designating "primitive," "wilderness," and "wild" areas to be removed from timber harvesting and other resource extraction uses. Although this administrative policy had produced over 2 million mainly roadless acres of preserve acres and was well within the agency's discretion before and after MUSYA became part of national forest law, the agency could not satisfy conservationists that the agency would retain such designations in the face of increased demand for timber. After all, it would have been well within the agency's discretion and financial capability to withdraw the protected status, build roads, and open the lands to harvesting. After a decade of lobbying, these interests finally succeeded in convincing Congress to pass the Wilderness Act, in which the Forest Service was forced to place the protected lands into "The National Wilderness System" of wilderness and pristine lands, and thus out of the path of the timber industry. And although the Wilderness Act left MUSYA untouched for the remaining lands under Forest Service control, the new law required the agency to examine the eligibility of certain roadless national forest lands to be added to the National Wilderness System, a process that has embroiled the agency ever since and is discussed in more detail later in this chapter.

An incremental step toward wrestling the agency under control came with the Forest and Rangelands Renewable Resources Planning Act of 1974, Pub. L. No. 93–378, 88 Stat. 476. This law required the Forest Service to prepare a system-wide five-year plan for the national forests, known as the Renewable Resources Program, but also directed the agency to develop "land and resource management plans for units of the National Forest System." Yet the statute provided no direction as to procedure or content of such plans, leaving the agency in a position to continue the forest plan process it had already devised as a means of supporting the clearcutting program.

The next significant blow came in 1975, as the clearcutting age came to a screeching halt when the court in West Virginia Division of Izaak Walton League v. Butz, 522 F.2d 945 (4th Cir. 1975), used plain English meanings to interpret the Organic Act's "designated," "marked," "dead," "mature," and "large" terms to prohibit widespread clearcutting in most circumstances. The court simply noted that the Organic Act referred only to "dead, matured, or large growth" trees as eligible for harvesting, and that the statute required the Forest Service to designate and mark the trees before removal. MUSYA did not alter that basic starting point, so, the court concluded, clearcutting is illegal. In modern terms, this simply did not "compute" for the agency or the industry. As environmental groups seized the moment and filed suits around the nation to extend the Fourth Circuit's reasoning, the Forest Service and timber industry immediately sought congressional action to clear up what the agency could and could not do with respect to timber extraction policy.

Of course, what the agency sought and fully expected it would receive was legislative nullification of the court's opinion, but by this time criticism of the Forest Service had crept into Congress, focused initially through the so-called Bolle Report, commissioned by Senator Lee Metcalf of Montana, and the Church Commission hearings held in 1971 before the Senate Subcommittee on Public Lands of the Committee on Interior and Insular Affairs. At the request of Senator Metcalf, Arnold Bolle led a team of academics from the University of Montana in 1970 to study Forest Service practices. Their report, entitled *A University View of the Forest Service*, was sharply critical of the Forest Service's land management practices, concluding that the agency overemphasized timber production and thus undermined the multiple use mandate. At the Church Commission hearings the next year, numerous distinguished witnesses testified in those hearings as to the environmental harm Forest Service policies had caused. Amidst the emerging broad attention to environmental affairs that took hold in Congress during the early 1970s, this testimony proved critical in convincing Congress that the agency required more explicit direction. The result was the National

Forest Management Act of 1976 (NFMA), Pub. L. No. 94–588, 90 Stat. 2949, codified at 16 U.S.C. §§ 1601–14.

Adding to rather than replacing the Organic Act and MUSYA, the NFMA prescribed a set of substantive standards and planning requirements for the Forest Service. Generally it restricts timber harvests to only those national forest lands where "soil, slope, or other watershed conditions will not be irreversibly damaged" and which could "be adequately restocked within five years after harvest." 16 U.S.C. § 1604(g)(3)(E). In particular, clearcutting and other even-aged management techniques are specifically addressed and restricted by standards which, while loose, were more than had appeared in law previously. *Id.* § 1604(g)(3)(F). Also, the statute requires the Forest Service to "provide for diversity of plant and animal communities." *Id.* § 1604(g)(3)(B). These and other standards are to be coordinated for each national forest though individual "land and resources management plans" that require public input and are subject to judicial review. *Id.* §§ 1601–1604. Hence, although it was not without its detractors, the NFMA unquestionably charted a new direction for national forest policy, one in which, for the first time in Forest Service history, biodiversity values had to be taken into account. Although the NFMA provided vastly more detail to guide Forest Service policy than had the Organic Act and MUSYA, it left many more questions than it answered. A rich history of litigation helps fill in the details of such issues as where timber can be harvested under the "irreversible damage" standard, when clearcutting is allowed, and whether forest plans have been properly compiled.

There are other laws, of course, that play an important role in forest management, both within national forests and on state, local, and private forest lands. In the years preceding enactment of NFMA, Congress passed a flurry of other environmental laws, many with general application to federal agencies and some with general application to the public at large. Although the impact of these laws on forest management was not immediately apparent or felt substantially in the 1970s and 1980s, by the early 1990s it had become clear, primarily through citizen initiated litigation, that a web of federal environmental laws profoundly affects forest management decisions taken by federal, state, local, and even private forest managers. Indeed, as the materials in this chapter illustrate, in many circumstances statutes such as the Endangered Species Act, the National Environmental Policy Act, and the Clean Water Act have had a far more prescriptive effect on Forest Service policy than have the agency's trio of primary statutes—the Organic Act, MUSYA, and NFMA. Their effect on state, local, and private forest lands has been no less substantial.

---

## QUESTIONS AND DISCUSSION

**1.** Why have national forests? If the Forest Service identifies an area of federally-owned forest as most suitable for timber harvesting, why not auction the land—not just the timber—for sale to timber companies? If another area is deemed best suited to recreation, why not sell it to the Disney Corporation? Having paid for the land, won't these private interests have more incentive to manage it appropriately than does the federal government? Indeed, rather than having the federal government decide what use is suitable for particular parcels of forest, wouldn't a better way to determine "highest and best use" be to let the market decide through open auctions? Won't the successful bidder have the most incentive to manage the land in such a way as to maximize its realization of highest and best use, thus maximizing total social wealth? These are not idle questions. For decades federal land policy was one of disposition, not permanent retention. Only recently has the principal issue of federal land management become one of use rather than to whom to dispose and when. *See* GEORGE C. COGGINS ET AL., FEDERAL PUBLIC LAND AND RESOURCES LAW 39–148 (4th ed. 2001). And serious questions still are raised about the wisdom of the permanent retention approach. Some economists, for example, advocate privatizing the national forests to end many of the management issues that plague the Forest Service by replacing the incentives of negative-sum political dynamics with those of positive-sum private entrepreneurship. *See* RICHARD L. STROUP & JOHN A. BADEN, NATURAL RESOURCES: BUREAUCRATIC MYTHS AND ENVIRONMENTAL MANAGEMENT 118–27 (1983). As you delve into the materials on public lands, keep in mind that alternative ownership frameworks exist and consider whether they offer superior avenues to ecological management of forested lands.

**2.** Why have a Forest Service? Consider that the Forest Service has a workforce of over 30,000 employees. The agency is divvied up into 9 regions, within which are distributed 155 national forests, which together are comprised of a total of more than 600 ranger districts ranging in size from 50,000 to 1 million acres. Each district has a staff of 10 to 100 people. Overseeing the whole structure is the Chief, who reports directly to the USDA's Under Secretary for Natural Resources and Environment. Even if we maintain federal public lands as "national forests," are there alternatives we might consider for implementing national objectives for those lands other than through a large, centralized, hierarchical federal agency? Indeed, Professor Robert Nelson has characterized the Forest Service as bloated, anachronistic, and lacking a coherent vision, choosing instead to hop from one fashionable environmental solution to the next—most recently ecosystem management. He advocates abolishing the agency and replacing it with a decentralized system to manage protection of our national forests. *See* ROBERT NELSON, A BURNING ISSUE: A CASE FOR ABOLISHING THE U.S. FOREST SERVICE (2000). Other observers propose models that retain a role for the Forest Service in setting national forest management policy, but vesting greater power in local and private decision making bodies. *See* ROGER A. SEDJO, THE NATIONAL FORESTS: FOR WHOM AND FOR WHAT?, PERC POLICY SERIES NO. PS–23 (2001). Indeed, in 1987 New Zealand, which at one time managed its national forests under a system explicitly modeled after the Forest Service, replaced its centralized agency with a system of dominant-use management overseen by a conservation agency and a state-owned forestry corporation. *See* Robert L. Fischman & Richard L. Nagle, *Corporatisation: Implementing a Forest Management Reform in New Zealand*, 16 ECOLOGY L.Q. 719 (1989). For a spectrum of views about the role of national forests and the Forest Service, see A VISION FOR THE U.S. FOREST SERVICE (Roger A. Sedjo ed., 2000). For a comprehensive study finding that the Forest Service operates without a credible system to evaluate its performance and the results achieved from its annual $5 billion budget expenditures, see U.S. GENERAL ACCOUNTING OFFICE, FOREST SERVICE: LITTLE PROGRESS ON PERFORMANCE ACCOUNTABILITY UNLESS MANAGEMENT ADDRESSES KEY CHALLENGES (June 2, 2003).

**3.** All states have established agencies charged with duties similar to those of the Forest Service, and many states own substantial areas of land designated as state forests or devoted to similar purposes. In total, state and local governments own almost 70 million acres of forest land, or 8.75 percent of total national forested land. While this pales by comparison to federal and private holdings, much of the state and local forest lands provide valuable recreational opportunities or were acquired specifically to preserve sensitive resources.

Most states, however, have adopted forest management policies that put their forest management agencies in the same predicament as the Forest Service—having to satisfy a multiple-use mandate on public lands while responding to the increased focus on ecosystem management for protection of biodiversity. Florida, for example, maintains a state forest system covering over 830,000 acres in 36 state forests, as well as significant additional public land holdings devoted to forestry management. The Florida Forest Service, an arm of the Florida Department of Agriculture and Consumer Services, oversees these lands under the following mandate:

> The Florida Forest Service shall provide direction for the multiple-use management of forest lands owned by the state; serve as the lead management agency for state-owned land primarily suited for forest resource management; and provide to other state agencies having land management responsibilities technical guidance and management plan development for managing the forest resources on state-owned lands managed for other objectives. Multiple-use purposes shall include, but is not limited to, water-resource protection, forest-ecosystems protection, natural-resource-based low-impact recreation, and sustainable timber management for forest products.

Fla. Stat. § 589.04(3). Do these provisions give a clearer mandate to the Division of Forestry than the MUSYA and NFMA give the Forest Service?

**4.** The early history of federal and state forest policy is thoroughly explored in J. CAMERON, THE DEVELOPMENT OF GOVERNMENTAL FOREST CONTROL IN THE UNITED STATES (1972); J. P. KINNEY, THE DEVELOPMENT OF FOREST LAW IN AMERICA (1917); and James L. Huffman, *A History of Forest Policy in the*

*United States*, 8 ENVTL. L. 239 (1978). Excellent summaries of Forest Service policies prior to, leading to, and after the enactment of NFMA are found in MICHAEL J. BEAN AND MELANIE J. ROWLAND, THE EVOLUTION OF NATIONAL WILDLIFE LAW 340–56 (3rd ed.1997); Lawrence Ruth, *Conservation on the Cusp: The Reformation of National Forest Policy in the Sierra Nevada*, 18 J. ENVTL. L. 1 (2000); Federico Cheever, *Four Failed Forest Standards: What We Can Learn From the History of the National Forest Management Act's Substantive Timber Management Provisions*, 77 OR. L. REV. 601 (1998); and Oliver A. Houck, *On the Law of Biodiversity and Ecosystem Management*, 81 MINN. L. REV. 869, 883–929 (1997). The history of forests and of forest policy is also covered extensively by the Forest History Society. *See* www.foresthistory.org. Many of the statistics discussed in the text are described in more detail in the WorldWatch Institute's annual *State of the World* series, which provides additional information on the biodiversity values of forests, the historical losses of and current threats to them, and the effects of human economy on forests. *See* Janet N. Abramovitz & Ashley T. Mattoon, *Recovering the Paper Landscape*, in LESTER R. BROWN ET AL., STATE OF THE WORLD 2000 101 (2000); Janet N. Abramovitz & Ashley T. Mattoon, *Reorienting the Forest Products Economy*, *in* LESTER R. BROWN ET AL., STATE OF THE WORLD 1999 60 (1999); Janet N. Abramovitz, *Sustaining the World's Forests*, in LESTER R. BROWN ET AL., STATE OF THE WORLD 1998 21 (1998).

---

As the nation's largest single owner of forest lands, the federal government's decisions about forest management have lasting effects on the biodiversity and ecosystem values of our nation's forests. Of the federal land management agencies, the U.S. Forest Service controls the largest holding of federal forests—193 million acres of land in 42 states, the Virgin Islands, and Puerto Rico—through its jurisdiction over the National Forest System. The system is composed of 155 national forests, 20 national grasslands, and various other lands under the jurisdiction of the Secretary of Agriculture (the Secretary). The vast majority of the national forests acres are located west of Texas and the Great Plains states, though some other states have significant holdings.

According to the combined mandates of the Multiple-Use Sustained-Yield Act (MUSYA) and the National Forest Management Act (NFMA), the National Forest System lands are to be managed for a variety of uses on a sustained-yield basis to ensure a continued supply of products and services in perpetuity. Exactly what that management mandate means has been the subject of intense debate in Congress, the Forest Service, and the courts. The NFMA injects a biodiversity factor into the mix of overlapping and conflicting goals the Forest Service serves, requiring that the agency

> provide for diversity of plant and animal communities based on the suitability and capability of the specific land area in order to meet overall multiple-use objectives, and within the multiple-use objectives of a land management plan adopted pursuant to

> this section, provide, where appropriate, to the degree practicable, for steps to be taken to preserve the diversity of tree species similar to that existing in the region controlled by the plan.

16 U.S.C. § 1604(g)(3)(B). The Forest Service has implemented that statutory provision, complete with all its escape valves, qualifiers, and sources of discretion, through its regulation at 36 C.F.R. pt. 219.

Pursuant to that regulation, the diversity mandate, as well as all the other concerns the Forest Service must consider under its multiple use mandate, is factored into each national forest's land and resource management plan, or LRMP. Preparation of an LRMP is the first step in resource allocation within a national forest. In the case of timber harvesting, the LRMP outlines where, when, and under what conditions harvesting generally can occur. The Forest Service then authorizes harvesting in particular locations by selecting a timber sale area and preparing an environmental assessment subject to public review and comment. The agency must consider the environmental consequences of each sale and must determine that a decision to sell in a particular area complies with the LRMP. Only then can the agency award a timber harvest contract.

During the 1990s in particular, environmental groups pressed hard on the Forest Service to emphasize the biodiversity side of the agency's forest management mandate and de-emphasize the use of national forests for timber extraction. The groups initiated litigation challenging numerous LRMPs, through which they tried to force the agency to (1) use a new brand of science known as conservation biology as the guiding light for all forest management decisions; (2) manage forests to ensure the long-term viability of sensitive species above all else; and (3) perform rigorous population viability analyses for forest species before making forest management decisions. Although the suits largely failed in achieving the intended overhaul of Forest Service policy by judicial decree, the effort scored some modest successes in some courts and the relentless pressure the groups placed on the agency, coupled with recommendations from an independent body of experts, had by the end of the decade produced a proposal for change by the agency under the heading of "ecological sustainability."

Much activity transpired on the planning rule—or more accurately, planning *rules*—after the Committee issued its report, as changing political administrations engaged in a battle of contrasting visions. A brief history of the back-and-forth is provided in the following excerpt from one of the litigation matters that evolved along the way, Citizens for Better Forestry v. USDA, 632 F. Supp. 2d 968 (N.D. Cal. 2009):

> In 2000, the USDA amended the 1982 Rule. The USDA did not prepare an EIS in connection with the 2000 Rule, but it did prepare an EA. The EA found that the amendment had no significant impact on the environment.

The 2000 Rule modified its predecessor in a number of ways. First, it relaxed the species "viability" requirement by providing that "[p]lan decisions affecting species diversity must provide for ecological conditions that . . . provide a high *likelihood* that those conditions are capable of supporting over time the viability of . . . species well distributed throughout their ranges within the plan area." *National Forest System Land and Resource Management Planning,* 65 Fed. Reg. 67,514, 67,575 (Nov. 9, 2000) (amending 36 C.F.R. § 219.20(b)(2)) (emphasis added). The 1982 Rule had more stringently required that the USDA "insure" continued species existence. 47 Fed. Reg. at 43,038. The 2000 Rule also eliminated the requirement of developing and issuing "regional guides" to maintain regional consistency in forest management. *See* 65 Fed. Reg. at 67, 527. It further eliminated many of the "minimum specific management requirements." For example, in comments submitted in response to the draft 2000 Rule, the Environmental Protection Agency ("EPA") observed that "while [the 1982 Rule] contain[s] specific limits on clear cutting [of trees], the proposed [2000 Rule] would require only that individual forest plans 'provide standards and guidelines for timber harvest and regeneration methods,'" and asked "[h]ow will the proposed [2000 Rule] ensure requirements necessary for sustainability?"

Finally, the 2000 Plan Development Rule eliminated the post-decision appeal process of 36 C.F.R. pt. 217, and replaced it with a pre-decision "objection" process. 65 Fed. Reg. at 67,568 (removing 36 C.F.R. pt. 217); *id.* at 67,578–79 (creating 36 C.F.R. § 219.32). Under this new process, members of the public wishing to object to an amendment or revision of an LRMP have 30 days from the date an EIS is made available to do so. *See id.* Thus, this process can occur before the finalization of the planned amendment if the EIS is published more than 30 days before the amended LRMP becomes final.

Citizens and other environmental groups sued the USDA, challenging the substance of the 2000 Rule as contrary to the provisions of the NFMA and alleging that, in promulgating the Rule, the agency failed to adhere to procedures mandated by NEPA and the ESA. After the lawsuit was filed, the USDA announced its intention to revise the new rule. The parties agreed to stay Citizens' substantive challenges, but proceeded with the procedural challenges. The district court granted summary judgment against Citizens on the procedural claims, finding that they were not justiciable for lack of standing and ripeness. The Ninth Circuit reversed the district court on appeal and remanded the case for further proceedings. [The litigation] was dismissed pursuant to stipulation after remand.

In 2002, the USDA proposed amending the 2000 Rule. In its notice of proposed rulemaking, it found that, "[a]lthough the 2000 rule was intended to simplify and streamline the development and amendment of land and resource management plans, . . . the 2000 rule [was] neither straightforward nor easy to implement" and "did not clarify the programmatic nature of land and resource management planning." *National Forest System Land and Resource Management Planning,* 67 Fed. Reg. 72,770, 72,770 (Dec. 6, 2002). The proposed rule purported to retain "many of the basic concepts in the 2000 rule, namely sustainability, public involvement and collaboration, use of science, and monitoring and evaluation," but "attempted to substantially improve these aspects of the 2000 rule by eliminating unnecessary procedural detail, clarifying intended results, and streamlining procedural requirements consistent with agency staffing, funding, and skill levels." *Id.* at 72772.

The USDA did not publish the final version of the rule it proposed in 2002 until 2005. *National Forest System Land Management Planning,* 70 Fed. Reg. 1023 (Jan. 5, 2005). It did not conduct an EIS or an EA, asserting that the rule fell within a previously declared "categorical exclusion" to NEPA's requirements. A categorical exclusion is "a category of actions which do not individually or cumulatively have a significant effect on the human environment and which have been found to have no such effect in procedures adopted by a Federal agency . . . and for which, therefore, neither an environmental assessment nor an environmental impact statement is required." 40 C.F.R. § 1508.4. In the USDA's view, the 2005 Rule fell within an existing categorical exclusion that applied to "rules, regulations, or policies to establish Service-wide administrative procedures, program processes, or instruction." 70 Fed. Reg. at 1054. In addition, the USDA did not consult with the Fish and Wildlife Service (FWS) or the National Marine Fisheries Service (NMFS) to determine whether the 2005 rule would have an adverse effect on any endangered or threatened species.

Citizens and other environmental groups again sued the USDA, claiming procedural violations of NEPA and the ESA. In *Citizens for Better Forestry v. United States Department of Agriculture* (*Citizens II*), 481 F. Supp. 2d 1059 (N.D. Cal. 2007), the district court granted summary judgment in part against the USDA, finding that: 1) the agency had violated the Administrative Procedure Act by promulgating the 2005 Rule—a self-described "paradigm shift" from earlier rules, including the rule proposed in 2002—without first providing notice of the changes and allowing the public to submit comments; 2) the agency had violated NEPA by applying the categorical exclusion and failing to prepare either an EA or an EIS; 3) the agency had violated the ESA by failing to engage in consultations with other federal agencies or to publish a biological assessment (BA). The court enjoined the USDA from putting the 2005 rule into effect until the agency complied with these statutes.

In 2007, the USDA re-published the 2005 rule along with a draft EIS and sought public comment. *National Forest System Land Management Planning,* 72 Fed. Reg. 48,514 (Aug. 23, 2007). The agency published the final version of the EIS and the rule in 2008. *National Forest System Land Management Planning,* 73 Fed. Reg. 21,468 (April 21, 2008). The final version differs in some respects from the proposal, but adheres to the same basic approach to forest plan development. The EIS was undertaken in an effort to comply with the district court's decision in *Citizens II* and concluded, as the USDA had concluded previously, that the proposed rule would have no direct or indirect impact on the environment because the rule was programmatic in nature and did not, in itself, effect any predictable changes in the management of specific National Forest sites. In an effort to comply with the ESA, the USDA also published a BA in connection with the rule's promulgation. The BA concluded, similarly to the EIS, that the Rule would not have a direct or indirect effect on species protected by the Act.

The *Citizens* court invalidated the 2008 rule on procedural grounds, and the agency reinstated the 2000 rule given that it was the last version of the planning rule not invalidated by a court. *See* 74 Fed. Reg. 67062. The agency then published a proposed rule in 2010, yet again moving in an entirely new direction, *see* 76 Fed. Reg. 8480, and then promulgated a final rule in 2012. Like its predecessors, the 2012 rule might not withstand judicial review, congressional action, or a future administration, although it remains intact as of this writing. As the following excerpt suggests, the agency has high hopes for the current version of its planning rule.

## U.S. Forest Service, Department of Agriculture, National Forest System Land and Resource Management Planning; Final Rule

U.S. Forest Service, 2012.
77 Fed. Reg. 21162.

The mission of the Forest Service is to sustain the health, diversity, and productivity of the Nation's forests and grasslands to meet the needs of present and future generations. Responsible officials for each national forest, grassland, and prairie will follow the direction of the planning rule to develop, amend, or revise their land management plans.

The new planning rule provides a process for planning that is adaptive and science-based, engages the public, and is designed to be efficient, effective, and within the Agency's ability to implement. It meets the requirements under the National Forest Management Act (NFMA), the Multiple-Use Sustained-Yield Act (MUSYA), and the Endangered Species Act, as well as all other legal requirements. It was also developed to ensure that plans are consistent with and complement existing, related Agency policies that guide management of resources on the National Forest System (NFS), such as the Climate Change Scorecard, the Watershed Condition Framework, and the Sustainable Recreation Framework.

The planning rule framework includes three phases: Assessment, plan development/amendment/revision, and monitoring. The framework supports an integrated approach to the management of resources and uses, incorporates the landscape-scale context for management, and will help the Agency to adapt to changing conditions and improve management based on new information and monitoring. It is intended to provide the flexibility to respond to the various social, economic, and ecologic needs across a very diverse system, while including a consistent set of process and content requirements for NFS land management plans. The Department anticipates that the Agency will use the framework to keep plans current and respond to changing conditions and new information over time.

The planning rule requires the use of best available scientific information to inform planning and plan decisions. It also emphasizes providing meaningful opportunities for public participation early and throughout the planning process, increases the transparency of decision-making, and provides a platform for the Agency to work with the public and across boundaries with other land managers to identify and share information and inform planning.

The final planning rule reflects key themes expressed by members of the public, as well as experience gained through the Agency's 30-year history with land management planning. It is intended to create a more efficient and effective planning process and provide an adaptive framework for planning.

This final planning rule requires that land management plans provide for ecological sustainability and contribute to social and economic sustainability, using public input and the best available scientific information to inform plan decisions. The rule contains a strong emphasis on protecting and enhancing water resources, restoring land and water ecosystems, and providing ecological conditions to support the diversity of plant and animal communities, while providing for ecosystem services and multiple uses.

The 1982 planning rule procedures have guided the development, amendment, and revision of all existing Forest Service land management plans. However, since 1982 much has changed in our understanding of land management planning. The body of science that informs land management planning in areas such as conservation biology and ecology has advanced considerably, along with our understanding of the values and benefits of NFS lands, and the challenges and stressors that may impact them.

Because planning under the procedures of the 1982 rule is often times consuming and cumbersome, it has been a challenge for responsible officials to keep plans current. Instead of amending plans as conditions on the ground change, responsible officials often wait and make changes all at once during the required revision process. The result can be a drawn-out, difficult, and costly revision process. Much of the planning under the 1982 rule procedures focused on writing plans that would mitigate negative environmental impacts. The protective measures in the 1982 rule were important, but the focus of land management has changed since then and the Agency needs plans that do more than mitigate harm. The Agency needs a planning process that leads to plans that contribute to ecological, social, and economic sustainability to protect resources on the unit and maintain the flow of goods and services from NFS lands on the unit over time.

The instability created by . . . past planning rule efforts has caused delays in planning and confused the public. At the same time, the vastly different context for management and improved understanding of science and sustainability that have evolved over the past three decades have created a need for an updated planning rule that will help the Agency respond to new challenges in meeting management objectives for NFS lands.

This final rule is intended to ensure that plans respond to the requirements of land management that the Agency faces today, including the need to provide sustainable benefits, services, and uses, including recreation; the need for forest restoration and conservation, watershed protection, and wildlife conservation; and the need for sound resource management under changing conditions. The new rule sets forth a process that is adaptive, science-based, collaborative, and within the Agency's capability to carry out on all NFS units. Finally, the new rule is designed to make planning more efficient and effective.

---

## QUESTIONS AND DISCUSSION

**1.** Is the agency's focus on ecosystem sustainability a departure from the multiple use mandate of MUSYA? Based on this response to comments on the Bush Administration's 2005 rule, which also leaned heavily on the sustainability concept as part of overall "ecosystem management," the agency seems to think it has authority to follow the new approach:

> Comment: Multiple-Use Sustained-Yield Act (MUSYA). Some respondents pointed out that "multiple use" is part of the law and "ecosystem management" is not. Active forest management, they asserted, is necessary for forest health, maintaining biological diversity, and sustaining wildlife populations. These respondents requested that the final rule uphold what they believe are the active forest management principles mandated by the MUSYA. Further, they stated that timber harvesting is a goal of the MUSYA. They asked that the Forest Service provide a high-level sustained yield of renewable timber resources.
>
> Some respondents requested that the Forest Service comply with MUSYA by managing lands according to what they call its "wood, water, wildlife, range, and recreation" formula. Others stated that the 2002 proposed rule violates the MUSYA requirement that NFS lands be used to best meet the needs of the American people. These respondents requested that emphasis be placed on recreation, aesthetics, air and water quality, species habitat, and ecosystem integrity, rather than natural resource development.
>
> Response: The final rule is faithful to NFMA, which requires the use of the MUSYA to provide the substantive basis for forest planning. [S]ustainability embodies these Congressional mandates. The interrelated and interdependent elements of sustainability are social, economic, and ecological as described in § 219.10. The final rule sets the stage for a planning process that can be responsive to the desires and needs of both present and future generations of the Americans for the multiple uses of NFS lands. The final rule does not make choices among the multiple uses; it describes the processes by which those choices will be made as a preliminary step during development of plans. Later, the plan provides guidance for projects and activities.

If what the agency says is true about how ecosystem sustainability fits into the MUSYA and NFMA mandates, has it left itself any room for turning back from pursuing ecosystem sustainability? Would it violate the statutes were the agency to follow a "wood, water, wildlife, range, and recreation" formula?

**2.** Do we really know what is ecologically sustainable? Particularly in developing nations and areas of the United States where local populations depend on forests for economic well-being, are there income-producing uses of forests that are economically and ecologically sustainable? In many cases we won't know what is sustainable for a long time. For example, a major part of the rainforest economy in Brazil has been Brazil nut harvesting, and this was thought to be a sustainable way to prevent more destructive activities such as ranching. After 25 years of studying the practice, however, wildlife biologist Carlos Peres discovered that nut harvesting has been taken to ecologically unsustainable extremes—there are no nuts left on the ground to regenerate new Brazil nut trees. Peres advocates harvest quotas and rotating "no take" zones to allow new trees to take hold in the forest. Other researchers worry that it may take more invasive measures, such as clearing areas to open up sunlight to young trees, to ensure the survival of the Brazil nut tree. Either way, few people saw this coming. *See* Erik Stokstad, *Too Much Crunching on Rainforest Nuts*, 302 SCIENCE 2049 (2003). What other unanticipated consequences lurk behind today's prescriptions for sustainable uses of forest resources?

**3.** Notwithstanding it has been on the books over four years as of this writing, few national forests have developed new forest plans under the 2012 rule. The Forest Service did not issue more detailed "directives" explaining to national forest managers how to implement the rule until January 2015, *see* Land Management Planning Directives, 80 Fed. Reg. 6683 (Feb. 6, 2015), at which time 19 national forests were in the process of revising plans to conform to the new directives. See http://www.fs.fed.us/news/releases/forest-service-releases-final-land-management-planning-framework

---

One of the core themes of national forest planning has been the practice of designating a set of species to serve as the indicators of biodiversity. Once the Forest Service has designated the species for an area of national forest, the rules require it to develop a method of measuring the status of the species in order to develop and evaluate its multiple use planning. The following two decisions illustrate how the courts have grappled with their role in judicial review of the agency's chosen methodology. Although the second decision overrules the substance of the first, we ask you to read both to gain an appreciation of the underlying tensions in national forest management playing out through the courts.

## Ecology Center, Inc. v. Austin

United States Court of Appeals for the Ninth Circuit, 2005.
430 F.3d 1057.

■ FLETCHER, CIRCUIT JUDGE.

Ecology Center, Inc. ("Ecology Center") challenges the United States Forest Service's ("Forest Service" or "Service") Lolo National Forest Post Burn Project ("Project"), which was designed in the aftermath of the 2000 wildfires on the Lolo National Forest ("LNF"). Ecology Center raises a number of procedural and substantive claims under the . . . National Forest Management Act ("NFMA"). We have jurisdiction pursuant to 28 U.S.C. § 1291. Because we find that the Forest Service's decision to permit logging in critical old-growth forest and post-fire habitats was arbitrary and capricious, we reverse the grant of summary judgment to the Service and remand.

### I

In 2000, wildfires burned approximately 74,000 acres on the Lolo National Forest. While the fires caused considerable damage to the forest, they also created habitat for species that are dependent upon post-fire habitats, such as the black-backed woodpecker.

In response to the 2000 fires, the Forest Service began developing the Lolo National Forest Post Burn Project and preparing the requisite Environmental Impact Statement ("EIS"). The Forest Service considered four alternatives in detail, including a "no action alternative." In July 2002, the Forest Service selected a slightly modified version of "Alternative Number Five" for the Project. This alternative involves, *inter alia,* commercial thinning of small diameter timber and prescribed burning in old-growth forest stands, as well as salvage logging of burned and insect killed timber in various areas of the forest.

Ecology Center objects to the Forest Service's decision to permit commercial logging in old-growth forest stands, raising concerns about the impact of such logging on the viability of species that are dependent upon old-growth habitat, such as the pileated woodpecker and the northern goshawk. Similarly, Ecology Center questions the Service's impact analysis of salvage logging in post-fire habitat, particularly with respect to the black-backed woodpecker, a sensitive species.

## II

### A. *"Treatment" of Old-Growth Habitat*

The Project involves what the Forest Service characterizes as rehabilitative "treatment" of old-growth (and potential old-growth) forest stands; this treatment entails the thinning of old-growth stands via commercial logging and prescribed burning. The Forest Service cites a number of studies that indicate such treatment is necessary to correct uncharacteristic forest development resulting from years of fire suppression. The Service also points out that the treatment is designed to leave most of the desirable old-growth trees in place and to improve their health.

Ecology Center highlights the scientific uncertainty and debate regarding the necessity, design, and long-term effects of such old-growth treatment. In particular, Ecology Center alleges that the treatment of old-growth forest harms species that are dependent upon old-growth habitat. For example, Ecology Center claims that, even if treatment leaves most old-growth trees in place, it removes or alters other essential elements within old-growth habitat and disturbs bird species currently nesting or foraging within targeted stands. Although treatment may be designed to restore old-growth to "historic conditions," Ecology Center points out this can be a misleading concept: for example, information regarding historic conditions is incomplete; altering particular sections of forest in order to achieve "historic" conditions may not make sense when the forest as a whole has already been fundamentally changed; many variables can affect treatment outcomes; and the treatment process is qualitatively different from the "natural" or "historic" processes it is intended to mimic.

While Ecology Center does not offer proof that the proposed treatment causes the harms it fears, the Service does not offer proof that the proposed treatment benefits—or at least does not harm—old-growth dependent species. Ecology Center argues that because the Forest Service has not assessed the effects of old-growth treatment on dependent species, the Service cannot be reasonably certain that treating old-growth is consistent with NFMA's substantive mandate to ensure species diversity and viability. As a result, especially given the scientific uncertainty surrounding the treatment of old-growth stands, the Forest Service's decision to treat additional old-growth stands was arbitrary and capricious.

Although the Forest Service points to a report which notes that two species of woodpecker were observed foraging in treated old-growth forest, it does not otherwise dispute the charge that it has not directly monitored the impact of treating old-growth on dependent species. Instead, the Service maintains that it need not do so because (1) it has observed the short-term effects of thinning old-growth stands via commercial logging and prescribed burning on forest composition, (2) it has reason to believe that certain old-growth dependent species would prefer the post-treatment composition of old-growth forest stands, and (3) its assumption that treatment does not harm old-growth dependent species is therefore reasonable. The Service further argues that we must defer to its methodological choices regarding what to monitor and how to assess the impact of old-growth treatment.

An agency's choice of methodology is entitled to deference. *See, e.g., Salmon River Concerned Citizens v. Robertson,* 32 F.3d 1346, 1359 (9th Cir. 1994). However, there are circumstances under which an agency's choice of methodology, and any decision predicated on that methodology, are arbitrary and capricious. For example, we have held that in order to comply with NFMA, the Forest Service must demonstrate the reliability of its scientific methodology. Here . . . the Forest Service's conclusion that treating old-growth forest is beneficial to dependent species is predicated on an unverified hypothesis. While the Service's predictions may be correct, the Service has not yet taken the time to test its theory with any "on the ground analysis," despite the fact that it has already treated old-growth forest elsewhere and therefore has had the opportunity to do so. Just as it would be arbitrary and capricious for a pharmaceutical company to market a drug to the general population without first conducting a clinical trial to verify that the drug is safe and effective, it is arbitrary and capricious for the Forest Service to irreversibly "treat" more and more old-growth forest without first determining that such treatment is safe and effective for dependent species. This is not a case in which the Forest Service is asking for the opportunity to verify its theory of the benefits of old-growth treatment. Rather, the Service is asking us to grant it the license to continue treating old-growth forests while excusing it from ever having to verify that such treatment is not harmful.

Although the Service concedes that the opinions of well-qualified experts vary with respect to the appropriateness of management activities in old-growth areas, it also argues that it must have the "discretion to rely on the reasonable opinions of its own qualified experts even if, as an original matter, a court might find contrary views more persuasive." *Marsh v. Oregon Natural Resources Council,* 490 U.S. 360, 378 (1989). However, this is not a case in which different experts have studied the effects of commercial thinning and prescribed burning in old-growth forests and reached different conclusions. Here, experts have differing hypotheses regarding the effects that treating old-growth has on dependent species, yet the Forest Service proposes to continue treating old-growth without first taking the time to observe what those effects actually are. In light of its responsibilities under NFMA, this is arbitrary and capricious.

## The Lands Council v. McNair

United States Court of Appeals for the Ninth Circuit, 2008.
537 F.3d 981.

■ MILAN D. SMITH, JR., CIRCUIT JUDGE.

We took this case en banc to clarify some of our environmental jurisprudence with respect to our review of the actions of the United States Forest Service.

The Lands Council and Wild West Institute (collectively, Lands Council) moved for a preliminary injunction to halt the Mission Brush Project (the Project), which called for the selective logging of 3,829 acres of forest in the Idaho Panhandle National Forest (IPNF). As the basis for the preliminary injunction, Lands Council claimed that Ranotta McNair and the United States Forest Service (collectively, the Forest Service), failed to comply with the National Forest Management Act (NFMA), 16 U.S.C. § 1600 *et seq.,* the National Environmental Policy Act (NEPA), 42 U.S.C. § 4231 *et seq.,* and the Administrative Procedure Act (APA), 5 U.S.C. § 701 *et seq.,* in developing and implementing the Project.

Boundary County, City of Bonners Ferry, City of Moyie Springs, Everhart Logging, Inc., and Regehr Logging, Inc. (collectively, Intervenors) intervened on behalf of the Forest Service. The district court denied Lands Council's motion for a preliminary injunction. A three-judge panel of this court reversed the district court's decision and remanded for entry of a preliminary injunction in *Lands Council v. McNair,* 494 F.3d 771 (9th Cir. 2007). We vacate that decision and affirm the district court.

## FACTUAL AND PROCEDURAL BACKGROUND

### A. Mission Brush Area

The Mission Brush Area (or Project Area) encompasses approximately 31,350 acres and is located in the northeastern portion of the Bonners Ferry Ranger District. Approximately 16,550 acres of the Project Area are National Forest System lands, which are home to a variety of species (or their habitats), including the northern gray wolf, Canada lynx, grizzly bear, black-backed woodpecker, flammulated owl, fisher, western toad, pileated woodpecker, and the white-tailed deer. The Project Area is also home to old-growth trees.

The current structure and composition of the forest in the Project Area differs significantly from the forest's historic composition. While the Project Area previously consisted of relatively open ponderosa pine and Douglas-fir stands, today it is crowded with stands of shade-tolerant, younger Douglas-firs and other mid-to-late-successional species. The suppression of naturally occurring fires, past logging practices, and disease are primarily responsible for this shift in forest composition.

The increased density of trees has proven deleterious to the old-growth trees and the Project Area's ecology. First, old-growth trees need relatively open conditions to survive and maintain their growth rates. Second, the increased density is causing a decline in the health and vigor of all trees because they must compete for moisture, sunlight, and nutrients, and the densely clustered trees are less tolerant of insects and disease. Third, dense, dry forests are at risk for large, stand-replacing fires, due to the build-up of fuels. Lastly, wildlife species that prefer a relatively open forest composition with more old-growth trees have suffered a decline in habitat.

### B. Mission Brush Project

The Forest Service proposed the Project, in part, to restore the forest to its historic composition, which, in the Forest Service's assessment, is more likely to be sustainable over time. But this is not the Project's only objective. According to the Supplemental Final Environmental Impact Statement (SFEIS) that the Forest Service issued in April 2006, the overall "objectives of the project are to begin restoring forest health and wildlife habitat, improv[e] water quality and overall aquatic habitat by reducing sediment and the risk of sediment reaching streams, and provid[e] recreation opportunities that meet the varied desires of the public and the agency while reducing negative effects to the ecosystem." The Project proposes to accomplish these varied objectives through a number of actions, such as improving roads that presently contribute to sediment in the watersheds, decommissioning roads posing a great risk of contributing to sediment, ensuring that the Project Area has acceptable toilets and wheelchair accessible pathways to toilets, installing a boat ramp and fishing dock, and improving trails.

After considering multiple approaches on how best to accomplish the Project's goals with respect to forest composition, including one no-action alternative, the Forest Service chose to implement a modified version of Alternative 2. In relevant part, Alternative 2 calls for silvicultural treatments on 3,829 acres of forest, fuels treatments on 3,698 acres, and ecosystem burns without harvest on 238 acres. The silvicultural treatments proposed include commercial thinning, regeneration cuts, and sanitation salvage harvesting.

As a part of the Project, the Forest Service plans to treat 277 acres of dry-site old-growth stands in order to increase the overall quality of dry-site old-growth stands and scattered old-growth Douglas-fir, and to improve and maintain trees that could be old-growth in the future. Despite its plans to perform treatments within old-growth stands, the Project will not involve harvesting allocated old-growth trees. The Forest Service represented in the SFEIS that the allocated old-growth in the IPNF has not been harvested for several years, and that its "focus is on maintaining [existing] old growth stands . . . and allocating additional stands for future old growth as they mature." In those units containing old-growth trees, the Forest Service has identified those non-old-growth trees it plans to harvest.

The Project is expected to generate 23.5 million board feet of timber, which has been, or will be, sold pursuant to three timber sale contracts: the Brushy Mission Sale, the Haller Down Sale, and the Mission Fly By Sale. The Forest Service sold the Brushy Mission Sale to Everhart Logging, and the Haller Down Sale to Regehr Logging. The Forest Service received no bids for the Mission Fly By Sale, which contains all but fourteen of the old-growth acres that are part of the Haller Down Sale. Though logging under the Brushy Mission and Haller Down sales has already begun, the injunction imposed by the district court pursuant to the three-judge panel opinion in *Lands Council,* 494 F.3d 771, prohibits the Forest Service from logging in the fourteen acres of old-growth in the Haller Down Sale. The same injunction imposes other restrictions on the Forest Service, including a prohibition on taking any action in the area encompassed by the Mission Fly By Sale.

C. Procedural History

In late 2002, the Forest Service decided to undertake management activities in the Mission and Brush Creek areas. In 2003, the Forest Service issued a draft Environmental Impact Statement (EIS). After receiving public comments, the Forest Service released its final EIS and Record of Decision (ROD) in June 2004. Lands Council appealed the ROD. The Forest Service upheld the Project, but ordered the preparation of a supplemental EIS in light of this court's decision in *Lands Council v. Powell (Lands Council I),* 379 F.3d 738 (9th Cir. 2004), *amended by* 395 F.3d 1019 (9th Cir. 2005), which addressed the management of National Forest System lands in the IPNF in connection with a different Forest Service project. The Forest Service subsequently released a supplemental draft EIS for public comment, and issued the SFEIS and ROD in April 2006. Lands Council and other environmental groups filed an administrative appeal, which the Forest Service denied in July 2006. In October 2006, Lands Council filed this action and moved for a preliminary injunction.

DISCUSSION

Lands Council argues that, in developing the Project, the Forest Service violated the NFMA in two ways: (1) by failing to demonstrate the reliability of the scientific methodology underlying its analysis of the Project's effect on wildlife, (specifically the flammulated owl and its habitat),[FN4] and (2) by not complying with Standard 10(b) of the IPNF Forest Plan, which requires the Forest Service to maintain at least ten percent old-growth throughout the forest. Lands Council also argues that the Forest Service violated NEPA because, in Lands Council's view, the Forest Service did not adequately address the uncertainty concerning its proposed treatment as a strategy to maintain species viability.

In essence, Lands Council asks this court to act as a panel of scientists that instructs the Forest Service how to validate its hypotheses regarding wildlife viability, chooses among scientific studies in determining whether the Forest Service has complied with the underlying Forest Plan, and orders the agency to explain every possible scientific uncertainty. As we will explain, this is not a proper role for a federal appellate court. But Lands Council's arguments illustrate how, in recent years, our environmental jurisprudence has, at times, shifted away from the appropriate standard of review and could be read to suggest that this court should play such a role.

Below, we address each of Lands Council's arguments. We first discuss the language and purpose of the NFMA and how, in *Ecology Center, Inc. v. Austin,* 430 F.3d 1057 (9th Cir. 2005), we misconstrued what the NFMA requires of the Forest Service. We then turn to whether the Forest Service met the NFMA's requirements in this case; specifically, we consider the sufficiency of the Forest Service's analysis of the Project's effect on the flammulated owl and its habitat.

We are mindful, of course, that important environmental resources are at stake in cases such as this, and we strongly reaffirm that the Forest Service must fully comply with the requirements of the NFMA and NEPA. We conclude that the Forest Service has complied with those requirements in this case, and we affirm the district court's denial of Lands Council's request for a preliminary injunction.

A. The National Forest Management Act

1. Statutory Language And Purpose

The NFMA sets forth the statutory framework and specifies the procedural and substantive requirements under which the Forest Service is to manage National Forest System lands. Procedurally, the NFMA requires the Forest Service to develop a forest plan for each unit of the

National Forest System. 16 U.S.C. § 1604(a). In developing and maintaining each plan, the Forest Service is required to use "a systematic interdisciplinary approach to achieve integrated consideration of physical, biological, economic, and other sciences." *Id.* § 1604(b). After a forest plan is developed, all subsequent agency action, including site-specific plans such as the Mission Brush Project, must comply with the NFMA and be consistent with the governing forest plan. *Id.* § 1604(i); *see Idaho Sporting Cong., Inc. v. Rittenhouse,* 305 F.3d 957, 962 (9th Cir. 2002) ("[A]ll management activities undertaken by the Forest Service must comply with the forest plan, which in turn must comply with the Forest Act." (citing *Inland Empire Pub. Lands Council v. U.S. Forest Serv.,* 88 F.3d 754, 757 (9th Cir. 1996)).

Substantively, the NFMA requires the Secretary of Agriculture to develop guidelines "to achieve the goals of the Program," including:

> [P]rovid[ing] for diversity of plant and animal communities based on the suitability and capability of the specific land area in order to meet overall multiple-use objectives, and within the multiple-use objectives of a land management plan adopted pursuant to this section, provide, where appropriate, to the degree practicable, for steps to be taken to preserve the diversity of tree species similar to that existing in the region controlled by the plan . . .

The Project also must be consistent with the IPNF Forest Plan's provisions regarding wildlife viability. *See* 16 U.S.C. § 1604(i). In the IPNF Forest Plan, the Forest Service designated the flammulated owl, the only species at issue in this appeal, as a sensitive species. The IPNF Forest Plan requires the Forest Service to "[m]anage the habitat of species listed in the Regional Sensitive Species List to prevent further declines in populations which could lead to federal listing under the Endangered Species Act."

Congress has consistently acknowledged that the Forest Service must balance competing demands in managing National Forest System lands. Indeed, since Congress' early regulation of the national forests, it has never been the case that "the national forests were . . . to be 'set aside for non-use.' " *United States v. New Mexico*, 438 U.S. 696, 716 n.23 (1978) (citing 30 Cong. Rec. 966 (1897) (statement of Rep. McRae)). For example, in the Organic Administration Act of June 4, 1897, passed less than a decade after Congress began regulating the national forests, Congress identified two purposes for which it would reserve a national forest at that time: "[to] secur[e] favorable conditions of water flows, and to furnish a continuous supply of timber." *Id.* at 707–08 (quoting 16 U.S.C. § 475 (1976)).

Congress' current vision of national forest uses, a broader view than Congress articulated in 1897, is expressed in the Multiple-Use Sustained Yield Act of 1960, 16 U.S.C. §§ 528–31, which states that "[i]t is the policy of the Congress that the national forests are established and shall be administered for outdoor recreation, range, timber, watershed, and wildlife and fish purposes." *Id.* § 528. The NFMA references 16 U.S.C. §§ 528–531 and requires that plans developed for units of the National Forest System "provide for multiple use and sustained yield of the products and services obtained therefrom . . . and [must] include coordination of outdoor recreation, range, timber, watershed, wildlife and fish, and wilderness[.]" *Id.* § 1604(e)(1). Thus, the NFMA is explicit that wildlife viability is not the Forest Service's only consideration when developing site-specific plans for National Forest System lands.

2. We Overrule Ecology Center

Lands Council argues that the Forest Service violated the NFMA because it has not demonstrated the reliability of the scientific methodology underlying its analysis of the effect of the Project's proposed treatment on the flammulated owl and its habitat. Relying primarily on *Ecology Center,* Lands Council specifically contends that the Forest Service erred by not verifying its prediction regarding the effect of treatment on old-growth species' habitat with observation or on-the-ground analysis. We disagree, and hereby overrule *Ecology Center.* We also hold that the district court did not abuse its discretion in concluding that Lands Council is unlikely to succeed on the merits of this claim.

In *Ecology Center,* we applied an on-the-ground analysis requirement to our review of the Lolo National Forest Post Burn Project, in which the Forest Service proposed logging in old-growth forest and post-fire habitats. 430 F.3d at 1060. We held that in order to comply with the NFMA, the Forest Service was required to conduct on-the-ground analysis to verify its soil quality analysis and to establish the reliability of its hypothesis that "treating old-growth forest is beneficial to dependent species." *Id.* at 1064, 1070–71.

*Ecology Center* even suggests that such an analysis must be on-site, meaning *in the location of the proposed action.* There, we rejected the Forest Service's argument that its on-the-ground soil analysis was "sufficiently reliable because it utilized data from areas with ecological characteristics similar to the proposed harvest units." *Id.* at 1070. We noted that, as in *Lands Council I,* the Forest Service had not tested "much of *the activity area.*" *Id.*

We made three key errors in *Ecology Center.* First, we read the holding of *Lands Council I* too broadly. Second, we created a requirement not found in any relevant statute or regulation. And, third, we defied well-established law concerning the deference we owe to agencies and their methodological choices. Today, we correct those errors.

In *Lands Council I,* we expressly limited our holding that "on-site spot verification" was required for soil analysis to "the circumstances of [that] case." 395 F.3d at 1036. But in *Ecology Center,* we expanded the on-the-ground analysis requirement beyond the facts of *Lands Council I,* and even beyond the context of soil analysis. In holding that the Forest

Service violated the NFMA by not verifying its hypothesis that treating old-growth forest is beneficial to dependent species with on-the-ground analysis, *Ecology Center* established a far-reaching rule that the Forest Service must always verify its methodology with on-the-ground analysis, regardless of the context. 430 F.3d at 1064. We accept the description in *Lands Council I* that it was "limited to the circumstances of [that] case," and hold that it does not impose a categorical requirement of on-the-ground analysis or observation for soil analysis, or any other type of analysis.

The Forest Service is at liberty, of course, to use on-the-ground analysis if it deems it appropriate or necessary, but it is not required to do so. . . . The NFMA unquestionably requires the Forest Service to "provide for diversity of plant and animal communities . . . in order to meet overall multiple-use objectives." 16 U.S.C. § 1604(g)(3)(B). Similarly, the IPNF Forest Plan requires the Forest Service to "[m]anage the habitat of species listed in the Regional Sensitive Species List to prevent further declines in populations which could lead to federal listing under the Endangered Species Act." IPNF Forest Plan, *supra,* at II-28. However, despite imposing these substantive requirements on the Forest Service, neither the NFMA and its regulations nor the IPNF Forest Plan specify precisely how the Forest Service must demonstrate that its site-specific plans adequately provide for wildlife viability.

Granting the Forest Service the latitude to decide how best to demonstrate that its plans will provide for wildlife viability comports with our reluctance to require an agency to show us, by any particular means, that it has met the requirements of the NFMA every time it proposes action. . . . Thus, we defer to the Forest Service as to what evidence is, or is not, necessary to support wildlife viability analyses.

Were we to grant less deference to the agency, we would be ignoring the APA's arbitrary and capricious standard of review. Essentially, we assessed the quality and detail of on-site analysis and made "fine-grained judgments of its worth." It is not our proper role to conduct such an assessment. . . . Instead, our proper role is simply to ensure that the Forest Service made no "clear error of judgment" that would render its action "arbitrary and capricious." *See Marsh v. Or. Natural Res. Council,* 490 U.S. 360, 378 (1989). To do so, we look to the evidence the Forest Service has provided to support its conclusions, along with other materials in the record, to ensure that the Service has not, for instance, "relied on factors which Congress has not intended it to consider, entirely failed to consider an important aspect of the problem, offered an explanation for its decision that runs counter to the evidence before the agency, or [an explanation that] is so implausible that it could not be ascribed to a difference in view or the product of agency expertise." *Motor Vehicle Mfrs. Assn., Inc. v. State Farm Mut. Auto. Ins. Co.,* 463 U.S. 29, 43 (1983); *see Lands Council I,* 395 F.3d at 1026.

This approach respects our law that requires us to defer to an agency's determination in an area involving a "high level of technical expertise." *See Selkirk Conservation Alliance v. Forsgren,* 336 F.3d 944, 954 (9th Cir. 2003) (quoting *Marsh,* 490 U.S. at 377–78). We are to be "most deferential" when the agency is "making predictions, within its [area of] special expertise, at the frontiers of science." *Forest Guardians v. U.S. Forest Serv.,* 329 F.3d 1089, 1099 (9th Cir. 2003) (citations omitted).

Thus, as non-scientists, we decline to impose bright-line rules on the Forest Service regarding particular means that it must take in every case to show us that it has met the NFMA's requirements. Rather, we hold that the Forest Service must support its conclusions that a project meets the requirements of the NFMA and relevant Forest Plan with studies that the agency, in its expertise, deems reliable. The Forest Service must explain the conclusions it has drawn from its chosen methodology, and the reasons it considers the underlying evidence to be reliable. We will conclude that the Forest Service acts arbitrarily and capriciously only when the record plainly demonstrates that the Forest Service made a clear error in judgment in concluding that a project meets the requirements of the NFMA and relevant Forest Plan.

For these reasons, we overrule *Ecology Center* and affirm that *Lands Council I's* requirement of on-the ground analysis was limited to the circumstances of that particular case.

3. Reliability of the Forest Service's Analysis Concerning The Effects Of Treating Old-Growth Habitat On The Flammulated Owl

Today, as we have in the past, we approve, based on the record before us, of the Forest Service's use of the amount of suitable habitat for a particular species as a proxy for the viability of that species. We therefore find "eminently reasonable" the Forest Service's conclusion that the Project will maintain a viable population of flammulated owls because it will not decrease suitable flammulated owl habitat in the short-term and will promote the long-term viability of suitable flammulated owl habitat.

To always require a particular type of proof that a project would maintain a species' population in a specific area would inhibit the Forest Service from conducting projects in the National Forests. We decline to constrain the Forest Service in this fashion. Were we to do so, we may well be complicit in frustrating one or more of the other objectives the Forest Service must also try to achieve as it manages National Forest System lands.

Of course, a reviewing court still must ensure that the Forest Service's use of "habitat as a proxy" is not arbitrary and capricious. We therefore hold that when the Forest Service decides, in its expertise, that habitat is a reliable proxy for species' viability in a particular case, the Forest Service nevertheless must both describe the quantity and quality of habitat that is necessary to sustain the viability of the species in question and explain its methodology for measuring this habitat. We will defer to its decision to use habitat as a proxy unless the Forest Service makes a "clear error of judgment" that renders its decision arbitrary and capricious.

On the basis of the studies provided by the Forest Service and the Forest Service's reasonable assumption that maintaining suitable habitat for the flammulated owl will also maintain a viable population of flammulated owls, we conclude that the district court did not abuse its discretion in deciding that Lands Council is not likely to succeed on this aspect of its NFMA claim.

## QUESTIONS AND DISCUSSION

**1.** What *is* the Forest Service's substantive duty under the MUSYA and NFMA with respect to biodiversity and ecosystem management, and how much latitude does the agency have in choosing the method of implementing that duty? If the agency had settled *Lands Council* by agreeing to do everything the plaintiffs argued was necessary to comply with the statutes and regulations, could timber industry interests have challenged the agency's action as arbitrary and capricious? Indeed, the outcomes in the cases are of little surprise, as one would be hard-pressed to read the MUSYA and NFMA as making clear choices about which science to use, which species to designate as indicator species, and how to measure species viability. Who should make these decisions, Congress, the Forest Service, or the courts?

**2.** Why all the fuss? How much difference does it make? In other words, how altered would the Forest Service's planning process and decision making outcomes be for the national forests if it had to conduct "on the ground" population surveys to evaluate indicator species viability? Clearly, the plaintiffs in the cases believe the difference would be substantial, and apparently so did the Forest Service given how steadfastly it opposed the plaintiffs' arguments. But what would be the bottom line impact on Forest Service decisions for national forests?

**3.** The extensive discretion the Forest Service enjoys in the courts is neither an accident nor a recent phenomenon. As a leading expert in national forest law and policy explains, Gifford Pinchot, the progenitor of the national forests and first leader of the Forest Service, worked hard to steer Congress toward a statutory text for the Organic Act that appeared on its surface to impose mandates, but which had no depth of content or sense of direction. In other words, "Pinchot received *carte blanche*." *See* Federico Cheever, *The United States Forest Service and National Park Service: Paradoxical Mandates, Powerful Founders, and the Rise and Fall of Agency Discretion*, 74 DENV. U. L. REV. 625, 638 (1997). Congress since then has resisted efforts to enact prescriptive reform legislation, instead expanding the multiple use mandate through the MUSYA and adding planning layers through the NFMA.

**4.** As Professor Cheever further explains, the inherent tension in national forest policy between use and protection of biodiversity also was by design, as Pinchot extended the offer of a protection mandate to soften the use mandate that was his central goal in shaping the Organic Act. *See id.* at 631–35. A wealthy man used to acting as a strong leader, Pinchot used the Forest Service's wall of discretion to build agency prestige and pride. But over time the combination of multiple use mandate and extensive discretion became the agency's downfall. The environmental protection movement of the 1970s forged a powerful set of interest groups who clamored for more emphasis of the protection mandate. The agency thus was pulled between its use and protection mandates more forcefully than it had been in the past, though how to strike the balance was no more clear even after the NFMA was enacted. Gradually, each of the multiple uses became increasingly associated with strong interest groups demanding that their use be the dominant use. The agency's discretion then became more a burden than a benefit, for the open-ended statutes "allow those of us interested in public land management to project our vision and values onto the language Congress used to instruct [the agency]. This almost insures that some significant part of the interested public will believe that the [agency's] conduct is not only wrong but illegal." *Id.* at 629. It is no surprise that after decades of such battering from both sides, Forest Service prestige and morale have eroded. Indeed, in his assessment of the Forest Service, Michael Mortimer likens the agency's situation to that of purgatory, saddled with vague goal-setting laws that give it almost unbridled discretion but leave it "wallowing about, unable to define a consistent path or to stay on a path . . . in the rush to embrace management philosophies that may appease its varying critics." Michael J. Mortimer, *The Delegation of Law-Making Authority to the United States Forest Service: Implications for the Struggle for National Forest Management*, 54 ADMIN. L. 907, 914 (2002). He suggests that Congress either provide more definitive guidance to the agency or, if it lacks the political will to do so, consider the more radical approach of abolishing the agency and replacing it with a new institutional structure. In either case, it seems that the discretion Pinchot worked so hard to gain for the agency has become its curse.

## II. DOMINANT USE MANAGEMENT: NATIONAL PARKS

National parks are an American innovation dating to President Grant's approval of legislation to establish Yellowstone National Park in 1872. In addition to the 59 national parks, there are also a variety of national monuments, battlefields, military parks, historical parks, historic sites, lakeshores, seashores, recreation areas, scenic rivers and trails, all of which are under the authority of the National Park Service within the Department of the Interior. The National Park System now comprises 401 areas covering more than 84 million acres in every state except Delaware. These areas are governed by the Organic Act of 1916, which directs the National Park Service to:

> conform to the fundamental purpose of said parks, monuments, and reservations, which purpose is to conserve the scenery and the natural and historic objects and the wild life therein and to provide for the enjoyment of the same in such manner and by

such means as will leave them unimpaired for the enjoyment of future generations.

16 U.S.C. § 1. National parks often struggle with their dual mission of preservation and enjoyment, especially as the number of visitors has grown to over 300 million annually. Indeed, the question, "Are we loving our parks to death?", is no jest.

Professor Joseph Sax has observed "that most conflict over national park policy does not really turn on whether we ought to have nature reserves (for that is widely agreed), but on the uses that people will make of those places—which is neither a subject of general agreement nor capable of resolution by reference to ecological principles." JOSEPH L. SAX, MOUNTAINS WITHOUT HANDRAILS: REFLECTIONS ON THE NATIONAL PARKS 103 (1980). What principles should be employed to adjudicate the desires of those who favor greater human use of national parks versus those who favor preserving a park's natural environment? "The preservationists," says Sax, "are really moralists at heart," who "encourage people to immerse themselves in natural settings and to behave there in certain ways, because they believe such behavior is redeeming." *Id.* The advocates of greater usage see national parks as the quintessential venue for all sorts of recreational activities that should be made available to as many people as possible.

Consider, for example, the "firefall" in Yosemite National Park. For decades, crowds would gather every evening at 9 p.m. in Yosemite Valley at Camp Curry. A man in the Camp would shout up to the top of Glacier Point, "Let the Fire Fall!" On the signal, people on top would push a bonfire of red fir bark over the edge and those down below would be treated to the spectacle of a fiery waterfall. The practice stopped in 1968. This was a much-beloved event for much of the twentieth century, yet today most would likely argue that it is more appropriate in an amusement park than in a national park.

Conflicts over the competing goals of the Organic Act—providing for the enjoyment of the parks versus leaving them unimpaired for the enjoyment of future generations—much less how to define "enjoyment," continue today.

## River Runners for Wilderness v. Martin

United States Court of Appeals for the Ninth Circuit, 2010.
593 F.3d 1064.

■ PER CURIAM:

. . . Grand Canyon National Park ("Park") was established by Congress in 1919 and expanded in 1975. The Park consists of more than 1.2 million acres located on the southern end of the Colorado Plateau in Arizona.

. . . The waters of the Colorado River originate in the mountains of Colorado, Wyoming, and Utah and run 1,450 miles to the Gulf of California. The Colorado is the longest and largest river in the Southwestern United States. Once in the Grand Canyon, the river flows some 4,000 to 6,000 feet below the rim of the Canyon through cliffs, spires, pyramids, and successive escarpments of colored stone. Access to the bottom of the Grand Canyon can be gained only by hiking, riding mules, or floating the river. Those floating the river typically do so in motor-powered rubber rafts, oar- or paddle-powered rubber rafts, oar-powered dories, or kayaks. Floating the river through the Grand Canyon is considered one of America's great outdoor adventures and includes some of the largest white-water rapids in the United States.

Use of the Colorado River Corridor increased substantially after Glen Canyon Dam was completed in 1963 and produced a relatively steady flow through the Canyon. Because of this increased use, the Park Service initiated a series of river planning and management efforts, culminating in a December 1972 River Use Plan. The plan concluded that "motorized craft should be phased-out of use in the Grand Canyon." The plan also concluded that 89,000 commercial user days and 7,600 non-commercial user days would be allocated for the 1973 season, but that commercial use would be scaled down to 55,000 user days by 1977. A 1973 Draft Environmental Impact Statement concluded that "[t]he use of motors . . . should be eliminated as soon as possible from the river environment" and that "[t]he propose[d] elimination of motorized trips will . . . hav[e] a positive environmental impact."

The Park Service initiated a Colorado River Research Program in 1974 to examine, among other things, the impact of motorized activities on the river. In September of 1977, the Park Service issued a document suggesting that "the use of motors is contrary to established health and safety standards" and again opining that the "use of motorized craft should be eliminated." The document noted that "[n]on-motorized travel is more compatible with wilderness experience" and that "[m]otor noise levels may have adverse effects on pilot performance, resulting in potential safety hazards." The Park Service was unable, however, to document any difference in numbers and degree of injuries between the two types of craft.

The Park Service released the first Management Plan in December of 1979. Use of motorized watercraft between Lees Ferry and Separation Canyon was to be phased out over a five-year period. . . . Congress countermanded the 1979 Management Plan in a 1981 appropriations bill for the Department of the Interior. The bill prohibited the use of appropriated funds "for the implementation of any management plan for the Colorado River within the [Park] which reduces the number of user days or passenger-launches for commercial motorized watercraft excursions[.]" Members of Congress sent a letter to the Park Service expressing their "wish that the [1979 Management Plan] be amended to accommodate the 1978 level and pattern of commercial, motorized watercraft access while at the same time protecting the increased non-commercial allocation which the plan provides." The Park Service subsequently revised the 1979 Management Plan to "retain[ ] motorized use and the increase in user-days that had been intended as compensation for the phase-out of motors, resulting in more motorized use of the river."

. . . Planning for the 2006 Management Plan began in 1997 with the solicitation of public comments and a series of public workshops in Oregon, Utah, and Arizona. After this process was suspended and restarted following the filing of two lawsuits, the Park Service published in the Federal Register, on June 13, 2002, a notice of intent to prepare an environmental impact statement for a revised Management Plan. Seven additional public meetings and stakeholder workshops were held in Colorado, Utah, Arizona, Nevada, Maryland, and California. More than one thousand people attended the meetings and the Park Service received more than 13,000 written submissions.

In the Fall of 2004, the Park Service released for public review a Draft Environmental Impact Statement ("DEIS") for the revised Management Plan. The DEIS presented eight [that] included motorized and non-motorized options. Because of the complexity of the DEIS and the level of public interest, the Park Service extended the standard 90-day comment period for one additional month. The Park Service also hosted public meetings in Colorado, Utah, Washington, D.C., Nevada, Arizona, and California. The Park Service received some 10,000 written submissions, including approximately 6,000 substantive and 30,000 non-substantive comments on the DEIS. The Park Service coded, organized, analyzed, and responded to the substantive comments, and modified the DEIS where it felt modifications were warranted.

The Park Service received comments from a coalition of groups representing both commercial and non-commercial boaters of the Colorado River Corridor—groups often at odds with each other on issues of river management. The coalition included Intervenors, American Whitewater, and Grand Canyon River Runners Association. The coalition supported equal allocation of river time between commercial and non-commercial boaters and the continued authorization of appropriate levels of motorized use.

In November 2005, the Park Service issued the three-volume Final Environmental Impact Statement. . . . The selected alternatives permitted the use of motorized rafts, generators for emergencies and inflating rafts, and helicopters to make passenger exchanges at the Whitmore helipad. . . . [T]he Park Service issued a ROD that formally adopted Modified Alternatives H and 4 for the 2006 Management Plan.

### II. The District Court's Task

Plaintiffs argue that the 2006 Management Plan is unlawful and should be set aside. The court's task is not to make its own judgment about whether motorized rafts should be allowed in the Colorado River Corridor. Congress has delegated that responsibility to the Park Service. The court's responsibility is narrower: to determine whether the Park Service's 2006 Management Plan comports with the requirements of the APA, 5 U.S.C. § 701 et seq. . . .

### V. The Organic Act

The Organic Act provides that the Park Service "shall promote and regulate the use of . . . national parks . . . in such manner and by such means as will leave them unimpaired for the enjoyment of future generations." 16 U.S.C. § 1. The Act also provides that "[n]o natural curiosities, wonders, or objects of interest shall be leased, rented, or granted to anyone on such terms as to interfere with free access to them by the public[.]" 16 U.S.C. § 3. Plaintiffs contend that the 2006 Management Plan is arbitrary and capricious because it permits commercial boaters to use the river at levels that interfere with free access by the public, and because it concludes that motorized uses do not impair the natural soundscape of the Park.

#### A. Free Access

Plaintiffs argue that the allocation of river access between commercial and non-commercial users is inequitable and thus limits the free access of members of the public. As noted above, however, the Park Service has significantly increased the access of non-commercial users. The 2006 Management Plan allocates 115,500 user days to commercial users and an estimated 113,486 user days to non-commercial users. This is essentially the same allocation commercial users received under the 1989 Management Plan, but a substantial increase from the 58,048 user days that noncommercial boaters received under the 1989 plan. Stated in different terms, the allocation of river time between commercial and non-commercial user days changed from 66.5% commercial and 33.5% non-commercial under the 1989 Management Plan, to 50.4% commercial and 49.6% noncommercial under the 2006 Management Plan. The 2006 Management Plan also reduced the number of launches and passengers for commercial users while nearly doubling both categories for non-commercial users. It is noteworthy that neither GCROA, which consists of commercial river users, nor GCPBA, which consists of noncommercial users, agree with Plaintiffs. Both organizations contend that the Park Service's allocation of user days is reasonable.

Plaintiffs argue that non-commercial users are required to wait for permits to run the river—sometimes for 10 or more years—while clients of commercial rafting companies usually can book a trip within one year. They also assert that the current allocation favors the wealthy who can afford commercial trips, and they criticize the Park Service for not conducting a demand study that would have revealed the most equitable allocation. The court cannot conclude on this basis, however, that the Management Plan is arbitrary and capricious. The 2006 Management Plan significantly revised the system for private boaters to obtain permits by establishing a lottery system that is weighted to favor those who have not received a permit in previous years. Moreover, surveys show that 61% of private boaters have floated the Colorado River Corridor before, while only 20% of commercial boaters were on repeat trips. The existence of a waiting list therefore does not necessarily show that more private boaters than commercial customers are awaiting their first river trip. Finally, experts advised the Park Service that a demand study would cost more than $ 2 million and likely would be of limited value.

More generally, Plaintiffs tend to characterize the dispute as one between commercial companies and private citizens. This is not the true nature of the issue:

> Throughout these proceedings [plaintiff] has persisted in viewing the dispute as one between the recreational users of the river and the commercial operators, whose use is for profit. It asserts that by giving a firm allocation to the commercial operators to the disadvantage of those who wish to run the river on their own the Service is commercializing the park. [Plaintiff] ignores the fact that the commercial operators, as concessioners of the [Park] Service, undertake a public function to provide services that the [Park Service] deems desirable for those visiting the area. The basic face-off is not between the commercial operators and the non-commercial users, but between those who can make the run without professional assistance and those who cannot.

[Wilderness Public Rights Fund v. Kleppe, 608 F.2d 1250, 1253–54 (D.C. Cir. 1979) (internal citations omitted)].

As noted above, a coalition of commercial and private boater organizations submitted joint comments to the Park Service that supported an equal allocation of river time between commercial and non-commercial users on an annual basis. These users of the river apparently did not believe that such a system would interfere with free access.

### B. Impairment of the Natural Soundscape

Plaintiffs make several arguments in support of their claim that the Park Service acted arbitrarily and capriciously when it concluded that motorized uses of the Corridor do not impair the natural soundscape of the Park within the meaning of the Organic Act. These arguments are unpersuasive.

First, Plaintiffs contend that the Park Service used the wrong baseline—that it compared motor-generated sounds to the noise of the Corridor with aircraft flying overhead, rather than comparing motorized noises to the natural quiet of the Park. This argument is incorrect. The Park Service compared periods of noise from river traffic (motorized and non-motorized) to periods when there was no noise. The Park Service also evaluated the length of "noise-free intervals" when motorized traffic was in the Park. *See, e.g., id.* at 386.

Plaintiffs next contend that the Park Service failed to consider the cumulative effects of noise from river traffic. This also is incorrect. After comparing river traffic noise to natural background sounds, and evaluating noise-free intervals, the Park Service considered the cumulative effect of such noise when added to other sounds in the Park such as aircraft overflights. The Park Service then reached the following conclusion:

> Although Modified Alternative H would contribute to the overall cumulative effects of noise on the park's natural soundscape, even if all noise from all river recreation was eliminated from the park (including river-related helicopter flights at Whit-more), the cumulative effects of aircraft noise would still be adverse, short- to long-term, and major. There would still be 'significant adverse effects' on the natural soundscape due to frequent, periodic and noticeable noise from overflights, and 'substantial restoration of natural quiet' would not be achieved as required by Public Law 100–91 and other mandates.

*Id.* at 387 (emphasis omitted).

Plaintiffs contend that this cumulative analysis should have caused the Park Service to eliminate sounds from motorized river traffic. But if a cumulative analysis were to result in the elimination of all sounds that can be eliminated by the Park Service—in this case, all sounds other than aircraft overflights, which are not within the jurisdiction of the Park Service—then all human activity in the Park would be eliminated. And still the aircraft overflights would create substantial and adverse sound effects in the Park. Plaintiffs have articulated no principled basis upon which the court can conclude that the Park Service should have eliminated motorized noises on the basis of such cumulative analysis, but not other human-caused noises such as hiking or non-motorized raft trips. The court cannot conclude that the Park Service acted arbitrarily and capriciously when it concluded from a cumulative-effects analysis that motorized river traffic noise was not the source of serious sound problems in the Park and that elimination of such noise would not significantly improve the overall soundscape.

Finally, Plaintiffs argue that the Park Service failed to consider earlier environmental impact statements and a number of studies conducted in the 1970s, some of which found that river use impacted the soundscape within the Park. The Park Service relied primarily on studies conducted by noise experts in 1993 and 2003. These studies included field acoustic measurements, including sounds from motorized and non-motorized raft trips. The studies determined the distance at which motorized rafts could be heard and the length of time they were audible while traveling down-river, when measured from fixed points in the Park. The studies also evaluated the effects of other sounds such as water flow, wind, wildlife, human voices, helicopters, and aircraft overflights. The studies provide a reasonable basis for evaluating sound effects within the Park.

Plaintiffs argue that the Park Service failed to consider 28 previous studies, but they identify no specific studies for the court to consider. Nor do Plaintiffs cite any recent studies that call into question the findings of the 1993 and 2003 studies. Defendants also note that any studies conducted in the 1970s would have concerned louder two-stroke engines rather than the quieter and cleaner four-stroke engines now used in the Corridor. Finally, the 2003 study specifically considered and summarized the earlier studies relied on by Plaintiffs.

Given all of these considerations, the court cannot conclude that the Park Service acted arbitrarily and capriciously when it concluded that motorized uses do not impair the soundscape of the Park within the meaning of the Organic Act. . . .

---

## QUESTIONS AND DISCUSSION

**1.** Do you agree with the court that the Park Service's decision is consistent with the Organic Act? Would you want to take a motorized raft trip through the Grand Canyon? Would the presence of such rafts bother you if you were visiting the canyon on foot?

**2.** What type of natural resource is at issue here? Is it the Colorado River, the Grand Canyon National Park, or something else? How is the resource being threatened? How does the nature of the resource determine the appropriate policy approaches?

**3.** The plaintiffs raised a number of other substantive claims, including that the Park Service had violated (1) the Administrative Procedure Act by acting in an arbitrary and capricious manner, (2) the 2001 Park Service Management Policies, and (3) the Concessions Act. The Park Service policies contain much more detailed guidance concerning the management of all units of the national parks system; you can review them at http://concessions.nps.gov/document/policies.pdf. But the court held that the policies "are intended only to provide guidance within the Park Service, not to establish rights in the public generally." Additionally, the policies "do not prescribe substantive rules, nor were they promulgated in conformance with the procedures of the APA." Therefore, the plaintiffs could not rely on the policies to overturn the decision to permit motorized rafting in the Grand Canyon.

**4.** Why do you think Congress used the budget process to countermand the Park Service's 1979 Plan and mandate the continued use of motorized rafts?

Why didn't opponents of the 1979 Plan pass a bill or amendment through the House and Senate Committees on Natural Resources, instead? Which parties do you think lobbied Congress for this intervention?

**5.** The plaintiffs relied on yet another federal statute, the Concessions Act, which states a congressional policy that facilities and services must be "necessary and appropriate for public use and enjoyment of the unit of the National Park System in which they are located" and "consistent to the highest practicable degree with the preservation and conservation of the resources of the unit." 16 U.S.C. § 5951(b). The court held that the Park Service's conclusion that motorized rafting is consistent with the Concessions Act was supported by the administrative record, though the court pointedly opined that "[t]he question is not whether this court agrees with the Park Service's decision."

**6.** How would the Grand Canyon rafting case inform the NPS superintendent of Yellowstone National Park deciding whether to ban the use of snowmobiles or limit their use? Snowmobiling generally is prohibited in national parks. *See* 36 C.F.R. § 2.18(c) (1996). But Congress has specifically authorized snowmobiling in Yellowstone and some other national parks. In February 2013, the NPS proposed that it would allow up to 110 "transportation events" daily, meaning one snowcoach or a group of up to 10 snowmobiles, averaging seven snowmobiles per group per season the park would permit up to 110 "transportation events" daily, initially defined as one snowcoach or a group of up to 10 snowmobiles, averaging seven snowmobiles per group per season. See Yellowstone National Park Winter Use Plan/Supplemental EIS (Feb. 2013, available at http://parkplanning.nps.gov/document.cfm?parkID=111&projectID=40806&documentID=51874. But the permissible number of snowmobiles has yielded conflicting answers from the NPS, Congress, and the courts. Which of those federal entities should decide how many snowmobiles are allowed in Yellowstone? What weight should be given to the desires of the State of Wyoming and local communities? What weight should be given to the desires of national environmental organizations?

**7.** Snowmobiling is also permitted in Voyageurs National Park in northern Minnesota. *See* 16 U.S.C. § 160h (1994) ("The Secretary may, when planning for development of the park, include appropriate provisions for (1) winter sports, including the use of snowmobiles. . . ."). The use of snowmobiles in Voyageurs has been subject to much of the same criticism as in Yellowstone, and nearly as much litigation. In Mausolf v. Babbitt, 125 F.3d 661 (8th Cir. 1997), the court upheld the park's closure of some snowmobile trails because of the possible impact upon endangered gray wolves. Before it did so, though, the court held in an earlier ruling that the concerned environmental groups could formally intervene in the litigation. The district court had denied the motion to intervene because it concluded that the government could adequately represent the concerns of the environmentalists, but the Eighth Circuit disagreed:

> The Snowmobilers insist that the Government, like the Association, is interested in protecting wildlife and in upholding environmental regulations. This is true; it does not, however,

> answer the Association's objection that this interest is not adequately represented by the Government in this case. Unlike the Association, the Government is 'obliged to represent . . . all of its citizens." When managing and regulating public lands, to avoid what economists call the 'tragedy of the commons," the Government must inevitably favor certain uses over others. The Park was established for both recreational and conservationist purposes. Voyageurs National Park Act, 16 U.S.C. § 160 et seq. These purposes will sometimes, unavoidably, conflict, and even the Government cannot always adequately represent conflicting interests at the same time. In this case, the Government's interest in promoting recreational activity and tourism in the Park, an interest many citizens share, may be adverse to the Association's conservation interests, interests also shared by many.

Mausolf v. Babbitt, 85 F.3d 1295, 1303–04 (8th Cir. 1996). How do the government's responsibilities differ from other landowners? How should it avert the tragedy of the commons?

## National Parks & Conservation Association v. Babbitt

United States Court of Appeals for the Ninth Circuit, 2001.
241 F.3d 722.

■ REINHARDT, CIRCUIT JUDGE:

Glacier Bay National Park and Preserve is a place of "unrivaled scenic and geological values associated with natural landscapes" and "wildlife species of inestimable value to the citizens." The Bay was proclaimed a national monument in 1925 and a national park in 1980. UNESCO designated Glacier Bay an international biosphere reserve in 1986 and a world heritage site in 1992.

Not surprisingly, many people wish to visit the park. As there are no roads to Glacier Bay, most tourists arrive by boat. To be more specific, most—approximately 80% of the park's visitors—arrive on large, thousand-passenger cruise ships. In 1996 the National Park Service (Parks Service) commenced implementation of a plan that increased the number of times cruise ships could enter Glacier Bay each summer season immediately by 30% and overall by 72% if certain conditions were met. In its environmental assessments, the Parks Service acknowledged that this plan would expose the park's wildlife to increased multiple vessel encounters, noise pollution, air pollution, and an increased risk of vessel collisions and oil spills. The Parks Service also acknowledged that it did not know how serious these dangers to the environment were, or whether other dangers existed at all. Nevertheless, declaring that its plan would have "no significant impact" on the environment, the Parks Service put it into effect without preparing an environmental impact statement (EIS).

The plaintiff National Park and Conservation Association (NPCA), a nonprofit citizen organization, alleges that the Parks Service's failure to prepare an EIS violated the National Environmental Policy Act (NEPA), 42 U.S.C. § 4321 *et seq.* It seeks an order requiring the Parks Service to prepare an EIS and enjoining implementation of the plan pending its completion. The district court ruled that an EIS was not required because the Parks Service had made its findings after adequately "canvassing the existing knowledge base." We reverse the district court's ruling and remand with instructions to enjoin the plan's increases in vessel traffic, including any portion already put into effect, until the Parks Service has completed an EIS.

FACTUAL AND PROCEDURAL HISTORY

There may be no place on Earth more spectacular than the Glacier Bay. Located in the Alaskan panhandle, surrounded by snow-capped mountain ranges, Glacier Bay extends sixty miles inland and encompasses ten deep fjords, four of which contain actively calving tidewater glaciers, and approximately 940 square miles of "pristine" marine waters. The air quality, though fragile, is still unspoiled and permits those fortunate enough to be visitors a crisp, clear view of the Bay with its glacier faces as well as the opportunity to breathe the fresh and invigorating air. The park is the habitat for an extraordinary array of wildlife. On the land, pioneer plant communities grow in areas recently exposed by receding glaciers. Moose, wolves, and black and brown bears roam the park's spruce and hemlock rain forest. Bald eagles, kittiwakes, murrelets, and other seabirds nest along the shore; sea otters, harbor seals, Steller sea lions, harbor and Dall's porpoises, minke, killer, and humpback whales reside in the bay.

*Glacier Bay National Park*

The Steller sea lion and the humpback whale, two of the marine mammal species that inhabit Glacier Bay, are imperiled. The Steller sea lion was listed as a threatened species under the Endangered Species Act (ESA), 16 U.S.C. 1531 et seq., in 1990. The worldwide population of the species declined by as much as 48% in the thirty years prior to 1992. Glacier Bay has several "haul-out" sites where hundreds of Steller sea lions gather. The humpback whale, "the most gamesome and lighthearted of all the whales," Herman Melville, *Moby Dick,* 123 (Harrison Hayford & Hershel Parker, eds., W.W. Norton & Co. 1967) (1851), has been listed as an endangered species since the enactment of the ESA in 1973. Until a moratorium was instituted in 1965, commercial whaling decimated the worldwide population of humpback whales. Today only 10,000 to 12,000 remain. A subpopulation of humpbacks spends the summer feeding season in southeast Alaska, including the waters of Glacier Bay; other humpbacks remain there throughout the year.

Watercraft—cruise ships, tour boats, charter boats, and private boats—provide primary access to Glacier Bay's attractions. Approximately 80% of the park's visitors are cruise ship passengers. According to the Parks Service's environmental assessment, the "key attraction of the visit to Glacier Bay . . . [is] the glaciers at the head of the West Arm [of the Bay.] [They] are larger, more active, and considered by the [cruise-ship] companies to offer a more spectacular experience." The ships linger at the glaciers from between fifteen minutes to an hour and provide a large, high viewing platform from which to witness the crack and crash of the great ice masses as they cast off huge shards of floating ice. Although the ships' height permits an unobstructed view of the park's geologic features, it limits close views of the wildlife and vegetation that form such a significant feature of the park.

Between 1968 and 1978, vessel traffic in Glacier Bay increased dramatically. In 1978 the U.S. National Marine Fisheries Service (Fisheries Service) . . . recommended that the Parks Service regulate the number of vessels entering Glacier Bay; restrict vessels from approaching and pursuing whales; and conduct studies on whale feeding behavior, the effect of vessels on whale behavior, and the acoustic environment.

The Parks Service soon thereafter promulgated regulations governing the entry and activity of cruise ships and other vessels in Glacier Bay. The regulations provided that only two cruise ships could enter the bay each day, with a maximum of 89 cruise ship entries between June 1 and August 31. Smaller boats, designated "private/pleasure craft," were limited to twenty-one entries per day with a seasonal maximum of 538 entries. Vessels were prohibited from intentionally positioning themselves within a quarter of a nautical mile of a whale or attempting to pursue a whale. Within "designated whale waters," vessels had to operate at a constant speed of ten knots or less and follow a mid-channel course. [Over the next fifteen years, the Park

Service allowed an increasing number of vessels to enter Glacier Bay. Then, in] September 1992 the Parks Service completed an internal draft of a new Vessel Management Plan (VMP) that proposed to increase the then current level of cruise ship entries in Glacier Bay by an additional 72%. . . . As mandated by NEPA, the Parks Service investigated whether a substantial cruise-ship increase would significantly affect the environment in Glacier Bay. In May 1995 the Parks Service issued a combined proposed VMP and environmental assessment (EA). An EA is a document that, under NEPA, (1) provides "sufficient evidence and analysis for determining whether to prepare an environmental impact statement or a finding of no significant impact;" (2) aids an agency's compliance with NEPA when no EIS is necessary; and (3) facilitates preparation of an EIS when one is necessary. 40 C.F.R. § 1508.9(a). An EA is a "less formal and less rigorous" document than an EIS.

The combined VMP/EA . . . described and assessed six alternative approaches for managing vessels in Glacier Bay, ranging from Alternative Four's reduction in vessel traffic by between 14% and 22%, to Alternative One's maintenance of the status quo, to Alternative Five's increase of cruise ship entries by 72%. Notwithstanding the environmental problems it recognized, the Parks Service expressed its preference for Alternative Five. This alternative maintained the limit of two cruise ship entries per day, but increased the total number of seasonal entries from 107 to 184. It did not increase seasonal entries for other vessels.

The Parks Service conducted six public hearings on the VMP. The Parks Service received approximately 450 comments, approximately 85% of which opposed Alternative Five and favored Alternative Four. The Sierra Club, the Alaska Wildlife Alliance, and the plaintiff NPCA spoke out against Alternative Five at the hearings, and submitted expert opinion and evidence in opposition to the Parks Service's findings. On March 20, 1996, the Parks Service announced its decision to implement a modified version of Alternative Five as its new VMP. Under this modified plan, the seasonal entry quota for cruise ships would increase by 30% for 1996 and 1997, and by as much as 72% thereafter if certain conditions were met. Also, the entry quotas for charter boats and private/pleasure craft would increase by 8% and 15%, respectively. An accompanying revised EA, titled "Impacts of the Modified Alternative," discussed the effects of the new VMP on threatened and endangered marine mammals, other marine mammals, birds, and the human environment, including air quality. * * *

## ANALYSIS

### I. THE PARKS SERVICE VIOLATED NEPA. . . .

#### C. Uncertainty

An agency must generally prepare an EIS if the environmental effects of a proposed agency action are highly uncertain. Preparation of an EIS is mandated where uncertainty may be resolved by further collection of data, or where the collection of such data may prevent "speculation on potential . . . effects. The purpose of an EIS is to obviate the need for speculation by insuring that available data are gathered and analyzed prior to the implementation of the proposed action." Sierra Club [v. United States Forest Serv., 843 F.2d 1190, 1195 (9th Cir. 1988)].

Here, scientific evidence presented in the Parks Service's own studies revealed very definite environmental effects. The uncertainty was over the intensity of those effects. The FONSI reported increased daily and seasonal exposure of humpback whales and other denizens of the Bay to underwater noise (and predicted a range of adverse behavioral responses), "traffic effects" (including increased risk of collision, affecting whales, harbor seals, sea otters, murrelets, and molting waterfowl), and increased risk of oil pollution for all animal life in the Park. An increase in cruise ships would also "result in more violations of state air quality standards for cruise ship stack emissions." Among the specific effects set forth in the VMP/EA upon which the FONSI was based were that increased vessel entry into the Bay would: subject stellar sea lions to additional disturbance; increase the escape patterns of various types of whales; potentially increase mortality rates and change the social patterns of the harbor seal; preclude sea otters from colonizing the upper Bay; and increase disturbance of feeding murrelets, other seabird nesting colonies, and bald eagles.

The EA describes the intensity or practical consequences of these effects, individually and collectively, as "unknown." The uncertainty manifested through the EA stems from two sources: an absence of information about the practical effect of increased traffic on the Bay and its inhabitants; and a failure to present adequate proposals to offset environmental damage through mitigation measures. . . . [The EA] states that "little is known about the effects of the [cruise ship] disturbance" on steller sea lions; "the effect of increased levels of disturbance" on Glacier Bay's cetacean populations is "unknown"; and "the degree of increase [in oil spills as a result of increased traffic] is unknown." It also states that the effect of noise and air pollution on murrelets, bald eagles, and waterfowls remains "unknown" because unstudied. Moreover, the extent to which air pollution will diminish the beauty and quality of the natural environment is also unknown. The Parks Service's EA does, however, establish both that such information may be obtainable and that it would be of substantial assistance in the evaluation of the environmental impact of the planned vessel increase. The EA proposes a park research and monitoring program to "fill information needs, and understand the effects of vessel traffic on air quality, marine mammals [and] birds . . . to assist in the prediction, assessment, and management of potential effects on the human, marine, and coastal environments of Glacier Bay resulting from human use of the environment with particular emphasis on traffic." That is precisely the information and understanding that is required *before* a decision that may have a significant adverse impact on the environment is made, and precisely why an EIS must be prepared in this case.

The Parks Service proposes to increase the risk of harm to the environment and then perform its studies. It has in fact already implemented the first part of its VMP. This approach has the process exactly backwards. Before one brings about a potentially significant and irreversible change to the environment, an EIS must be prepared that sufficiently explores the intensity of the environmental effects it acknowledges. A part of the preparation process here could well be to conduct the studies that the Park Service recognizes are needed. That might be done here by performing the studies of the current vessel traffic and extrapolating or projecting the effects of the proposed increase. Ultimately, the Park Service may develop other means for obtaining the information it currently lacks. The point is, however, that the "hard look" must be taken before, not after, the environmentally-threatening actions are put into effect. . . .

The second source of uncertainty is the Parks Service's ability to offset the environmental impact of the increase in vessel traffic through its proposed mitigation measures. An agency's decision to forego issuing an EIS may be justified in some circumstances by the adoption of such measures. . . . There is a paucity of analytic data to support the Parks Service's conclusion that the mitigation measures would be adequate in light of the potential environmental harms. . . . The Parks Service first described its proposed mitigation measures in the initial EA. That document reflects the uncertainty that exists as to whether the mitigation measures would work: moreover, it is unclear from that document whether the measures are sufficiently related to the effects they are designed to cure. The Parks Service simply noted, for example, that mitigation measures *"could* mitigate some potential effects to humpbacks in concentrated whale-use areas"; *"could* reduce whale/vessel collisions and reduce the noise emanating from the ships"; "special-use-area closures and restrictions implemented under . . . alternative [five] *may* off-set some of the expected disturbance." Air pollution measures "would *be expected* to contribute to a reduction in cruise ship stack emissions *over time."* Further, the service stated that it:

> intends to institute a comprehensive research and monitoring program to fill informational needs and quantity the effects of vessel traffic on air quality, marine mammals, birds and visitor-use enjoyment. The monitoring program, developed within one year of the record of decision, will stipulate research and protection actions [Parks Service] will undertake to ensure that environmental effects do not exceed acceptable levels. . . .

The final EA was similarly uncertain with respect to the proposed measures' effects. It recognized that a 10-knot speed restriction to offset the increased vessel traffic might disturb the creatures in the park, but that "very little is known about the effects of the disturbance." The EA also stated that the increase in seasonal entries *"could* reduce whale/vessel collisions and reduce the noise level emanating from the ships . . . , follow-up research and monitoring will be essential to define humpback whale use patterns in Glacier Bay resulting from this alternative"; and that "requiring cruise ships to implement oil-spill response plans *could* mitigate the effects of oil spills." As for air pollution, "the magnitude of increased violations would presumably be reduced over time." There is no indication, however, as to how long any such reduction might take or how great a reduction might ultimately be accomplished. In short, there is no evidence that the mitigation measures would significantly combat the mostly "unknown" or inadequately known effects of the increase in vessel traffic. The EA's speculative and conclusory statements are insufficient to demonstrate that the mitigation measures would render the environmental impact so minor as to not warrant an EIS. * * *

NPCA has made the requisite showing for injunctive relief. As we concluded in Section I, an EIS is required. We so held because of the significant adverse impact on the environment that might result from the implementation of the VMP. Where an EIS is required, allowing a potentially environmentally damaging project to proceed prior to its preparation runs contrary to the very purpose of the statutory requirement. Here, the Parks Service has already undertaken a 30% increase in cruise-ship traffic preliminary to a seventy-two percent increase. The potential effects of its action extend beyond the endangered marine mammal population to the rest of the wildlife at Glacier Bay, as well as the Park's air quality. Kittiwakes, murrelet, eagles, sea otters, seals, sea lions, porpoises, and killer and minke whales, as well as the better known humpbacks, are affected. Until an EIS is prepared and the effects of increased vessel traffic on the inhabitants and air quality of Glacier Bay are properly examined, there is a sufficient possibility of environmental harm that the VMP may not be implemented.

Westours argues that the damage to its business should be considered when addressing injunctive relief, that its financial losses outweigh the potential damage to the environment, and that NPCA "is not entitled to an injunction against the 32 seasonal cruise ship entries" that the Parks Service authorized for the 2000–2004 seasons. As a general rule, only the federal government may be a defendant in a NEPA action. An exception may be made in the remedial phase of a case where the contractual rights of the applicant are affected by the proposed remedy. Here, Westours was permitted to intervene, and appears before us as a party-defendant. Westours has asserted financial damages premised upon its contracts of carriage. Its loss of anticipated revenues, however, does not outweigh the potential irreparable damage to the environment. Moreover, neither Westours nor those of its passengers who may be unable to view Glacier Bay at the time they originally planned have cause to claim surprise as a result of any injunction. The plaintiffs filed their objections to the plan approximately five years ago and just one year later sought an injunction. If the passengers who booked cruises on any "excess" tours were not warned by Westours of the pending litigation, their interests were not well served by that company. Thus, while Westours has standing to object to our grant of injunctive relief, its evidence fails to tilt the balance of harms in its favor.

CONCLUSION

Much of the briefing and argument in this appeal has focused on the impact of the VMP on the imperiled humpback whale population. However, a variety of other non-human inhabitants of the Park—bald eagles, kittiwakes, murrelets, sea otters, harbor seals, Steller sea lions, harbor and Dall's porpoises, minke, and killer whales—are, as the EA reflects, affected, and the already fragile air quality is as well. The existence of adverse effects is not uncertain. What is uncertain is the extent of the likely environmental injury, and the impact of the proposed mitigation measures. The Parks Service's own experts, whose integrity the government commended at oral argument, admitted both the likelihood of certain harms to the environment of Glacier Bay and their uncertainty about the likelihood of other harms. In giving insufficient respect to their experts' evaluation of harm, declaring that no significant environmental effects were likely, and implementing the vessel traffic increase without complying with the requirements of NEPA, the Parks Service's decision-makers made a "clear error of judgment." *Marsh v. Or. Natural Res. Council,* 490 U.S. 360, 378 (1989).

Glacier Bay Park is too precious an ecosystem for the Parks Service to ignore significant risks to its diverse inhabitants and its fragile atmosphere. We reverse the decision below and remand with instructions that the district court issue an injunction enjoining the granting of permits to vessels pursuant to the 1996 increase in vessel entry quotas pending the Parks Service's completion of an EIS. . . .

---

## QUESTIONS AND DISCUSSION

1. Reread the Organic Act's text directing the Park Service to:

> conform to the fundamental purpose of said parks, monuments, and reservations, which purpose is to conserve the scenery and the natural and historic objects and the wild life therein and to provide for the enjoyment of the same in such manner and by such means as will leave them unimpaired for the enjoyment of future generations.

Does this provide any guidance in addressing the conflict over vessel management at Glacier Bay?

2. Most litigation challenging the management of national parks relies on more general environmental statutes such as NEPA, the Endangered

Species Act, the Wilderness Act, and the Wild and Scenic Rivers Act. *See* John Copeland Nagle, *How National Park Law Really Works*, 86 U. COLO. L. REV. 861 (2015) (providing examples of each). Why is it so difficult to persuade a court that the Park Service has violated the Organic Act?

**3.** A history of Glacier Bay National Park identifies six contested management issues: wilderness protection, humpback whale protection, cruise-ship concession management, commercial fishing, subsistence, and wilderness access for scientific research. *See* THEODORE CATTON, LAND REBORN: A HISTORY OF ADMINISTRATION AND VISITOR USE IN GLACIER BAY NATIONAL PARK AND PRESERVE (1995). How should those issues be resolved? According to the park's historian:

> The traditionalist view of the wilderness park is of a nature preserve in which anthropogenic impacts on the environment are minimized, if not eliminated. . . . The "localist" conception of the Alaskan wilderness park is of a natural *and* cultural landscape in which the sparse human inhabitants live in dynamic balance with nature. . . . These two conceptions of Alaska's wilderness parks lead to different conclusions about the proper future course for Glacier Bay National Park and Preserve. From the traditionalist perspective, screening out human consumptive uses of the park should be a management priority. The traditionalist holds that consumptive uses are by definition disturbances of the natural environment. Commercial fishing is altering the biotic composition of the marine ecosystem and needs to be phased out, particularly since Glacier Bay National Park is one of the few protected areas in the world that includes offshore saltwater habitat within its jurisdiction. Subsistence use of the park needs to be resisted, as this, too, would alter the park's biota. The park's designation as a Biosphere Reserve and World Heritage Site, according to the traditionalist's way of thinking, should reinforce the Park Service's commitment to managing the park along these lines.
>
> The localist view of the wilderness park characterizes commercial fishing in Glacier Bay as small-scale, traditional, and a feature of the Alaskan wilderness lifestyle that ANILCA was designed to preserve. Rather than phase it out, they would like to see the NPS participate with other agencies and local citizens groups in ensuring that the fishery remains small. They do not want commercial fishing in the park to cause any resource depletion, but they maintain that harvest levels can conceivably remain low enough to have no significant effect. Subsistence use is central to the localist concept of Alaskan wilderness, and advocates view its absence in Glacier Bay as an anomaly and an injustice to the people of Hoonah that ought to be corrected.
>
> Interestingly, the traditionalist and localist perspectives are not really at odds over the problem of total park visitation. Neither perspective seems to have any advantages over the other in resolving the problem of limiting use to some reasonable amount

that equitably serves both the present and future generations of the American public.

*Id.* Who should resolve these conflicts? Those favoring greater access to the park favor legislative action, those favoring preservation favor judicial decisions, and the Park Service would like to resolve the disputes administratively.

**4.** Professor Joseph Sax's influential 1980 book on national park management was titled, *Mountains Without Handrails*. Do you think mountain paths in national parks should have handrails? Sax argues that the experience of climbing a mountain without handrails, without a care at the summit, is in itself an important experience. Accommodations should be made for those who are not strong or healthy enough to climb a peak, Sax contends, but not at national parks. How accessible do you think parks should be made for the full range of visitors?

Sax acknowledges that this perspective can be seen as elitist. He points out, however, that many of our society's most valued institutions are elitist, and it's a good thing. Top universities do not admit all applicants. If decisions were made solely by popular referendum, how many cities would have public libraries or museums?

**5.** In response to the Ninth Circuit's decision, Congress enacted legislation approving the 1996 increases in cruise vessel entries into Glacier Bay, pending the completion of an EIS. The EIS completed by the Park Service in 2003 identified six alternative courses of action. The Park Service preferred the alternative that maintained most of the existing vessel regulations, while the "environmentally preferred alternative" would have reduced cruise ship visits to Glacier Bay by 33%. NATIONAL PARK SERVICE, GLACIER BAY NATIONAL PARK AND PRESERVE, ALASKA, VESSEL QUOTAS AND OPERATING REQUIREMENTS FINAL ENVIRONMENTAL IMPACT STATEMENT 31 (2003).

New regulations governing cruise ships at Glacier Bay took effect on January 2, 2007. Under the new Glacier Bay regulations, all ships that weigh over 100 tons gross under the U.S. system (or over 2,000 tons gross using the international convention system) and are certified to carry over twelve passengers are considered cruise ships. A maximum of two cruise ships are allowed to enter Glacier Bay each day. Additionally, there are seasonal quotas: In May and September (the "shoulder season"), only 92 use days are allowed. In June, July, and August (the "prime season"), 153 use days are allowed. The seasonal quotas are reviewed annually.

**6.** Alaska has long mesmerized wilderness enthusiasts. The United States bought Alaska in 1867, ending a century and a half of Russian control. Within twelve years, John Muir arrived there for the first of seven visits. "For Muir," writes one historian, "Alaska was the epitome of nature's perfection." STEPHEN HAYCOX, ALASKA: AN AMERICAN COLONY 273–312 (2002). Muir was also the first American to popularize the beauties of Glacier Bay. More generally, he proclaimed that "[t]o the lover of pure wildness Alaska is one of the most wonderful countries in the world." A 1901 *National Geographic* article agreed that "[t]he scenery of Alaska is so much grander than anything else of its kind in the world, that, once beheld, all other scenery becomes flat and insipid." Henry Gannett, *The General Geography of Alaska*, 12 NATIONAL GEOGRAPHIC 182, 196 (1901). As early as 1937, Bob Marshall asked Congress to "keep northern Alaska largely a wilderness." Robert Marshall, *Comments on the Report of Alaska's Recreational Resources Committee*, Alaska—Its Resources and Development, House Doc. No. 485, 75th Cong., 3d Sess., App. B, at 213. Then, "[b]eginning in the 1950s, and increasing in the subsequent two decades, a flood of publicity called attention to the values of wild Alaska." NASH, *supra*, at 293. Justice William O. Douglas, for example, asserted in 1965 that "Alaska represents one last opportunity to preserve vast wilderness areas intact." WILLIAM O. DOUGLAS, A WILDERNESS BILL OF RIGHTS 134 (1965). Roderick Nash explains that "[t]he image of Alaska that emerges from the accounts of recreation-seekers and environmentalists is that of a wilderness mecca, a qualitatively wilder country that any that exists or, perhaps, ever existed in the lower forty-eight states." RODERICK FRAZIER NASH, WILDERNESS IN THE AMERICAN MIND 275 (4th ed. 2001).

Alaska did not become a state until January 1959. The federal statehood legislation promised that over one hundred million acres—or 28% of the state—would be given to the new state government, but precisely which land would be handed over to the state and the status of native land claims was both left unresolved. It wasn't until December 1980 when a lame-duck Congress approved ANILCA (the Alaska National Interest Lands Conservation Act), which afforded federal protection to vast amounts of land, provided for the transfer of other land to the state and to native corporations, and directed studies with respect to the status of additional lands. The statute created ten new national parks—including Wrangell—St. Elias National Park and Preserve, whose 13.2 million acres make it the largest national park—and expanded three others. ANILCA also established nine wildlife refuges and expanded seven others, designated 26 wild and scenic rivers, and produced various new conservation areas and national monuments.

**7.** The threat to Glacier Bay's wildlife became real when Princess Cruise Lines pled guilty "to a sole criminal charge of imperiling endangered humpback whales and agreed to pay at $200,000 fine plus a $550,000 contribution to the nonprofit National Park Foundation." Yereth Rosen, *Princess Cruise Lines Pays $750,000 for Threatening Endangered Whales*, 20 DAILY ENV'T REP. A–8 (Jan. 31, 2007). A pregnant humpback whale named "Snow" that had lived in Glacier Bay at least since 1975 was found dead from severe head trauma shortly after a cruise ship sailed through the area in 2001. The restitution paid to the National Park Foundation will be used for research and preservation activities at Glacier Bay.

**8.** Robert Keiter and Joseph Sax have twice studied the actual management of Glacier National Park. Glacier—not to be confused with Glacier Bay—is located in northwestern Montana, where it borders Waterton Lakes National Park in Canada. Glacier became the tenth national park in the United States in 1910. Professors Sax and Keiter wrote about the management of Glacier in 1987, *see* Joseph L. Sax & Robert B. Keiter, *Glacier National Park and Its Neighbors: A Study of Federal Interagency Relations*,

14 ECOLOGY L.Q. 207 (1987), and they explored those visited issues again in 2006. *See* Joseph L. Sax & Robert B. Keiter, *The Realities of Regional Resource Management: Glacier National Park and Its Neighbors Revisited*, 33 ECOLOGY L.Q. 233 (2006). The 2006 study concluded that "the past several decades have generated a good deal of progress, with wildlife management and other environmental issues becoming significant regional concerns." *Id.* at 239. Specifically,

> Environmental perils from timber harvesting and road development have sharply diminished, though increased recreational activity presents new challenges. These gains are impeded, however, by what is occurring on private land in the Flathead Valley. Here we encountered burgeoning population growth that includes newcomers attracted to the area's natural setting, and environmentally-suspicious residents who are building on sensitive habitat land, while resisting any intrusion on private property prerogatives under the rubric of zoning.

*Id.* Note that both the original challenges and the more recent ones often result from activities that take place outside the boundaries of the national park. "Despite various legislative proposals, Congress has been reluctant to give the Park Service authority beyond its park borders." *Id.* at 236. Absent such authority, how can the Park Service control what happens outside the park?

---

## III. SINGLE USE MANAGEMENT: WILDERNESS AREAS

Wilderness has long been a paradox in the United States. For early settlers, wilderness was a dangerous obstacle. For example, in 1814, the Supreme Court held that actual possession of a large tract of land in Kentucky was not necessary to confirm title under a state statute because, Justice Story explained, "[a]t the time of the passing of the act of 1779, Kentucky was a wilderness. It was the haunt of savages and beasts of pray. Actual entry or possession was impracticable; and, if practicable, it could answer no beneficial purpose." Green v. Liter, 12 U.S. (8 Cranch) 229, 248 (1814). But by the twentieth century, wilderness became valuable. *See generally* RODERICK FRAZIER NASH, WILDERNESS IN THE AMERICAN MIND 280 (4th ed. 2001). In 1964, Congress enacted the Wilderness Act, which provides for the management of designated federal public lands for their wilderness values. Today, the 765 wilderness areas comprise 109,129,657 acres of land, which is nearly five percent of the total land in the United States. *See* The National Wilderness Preservation System: Wilderness Fast Facts, http://www.wilderness.net/index.cfm?fuse=NWPS&sec=fastfacts. More than half of those lands were designated as wilderness by a single act, the Alaska National Interest Lands Conservation Act (ANILCA), passed by Congress in 1980. Most wilderness areas are in western states, but only Connecticut, Delaware, Iowa, Kansas, Maryland, and Rhode Island lack any federal wilderness areas. The management of wilderness areas, and the identification of new wilderness areas, present a variety of ongoing legal and policy controversies.

## Wilderness Watch and Public Employees for Environmental Responsibility v. Mainella

United States Court of Appeals for the Eleventh Circuit, 2004.
375 F.3d 1085.

■ BARKETT, CIRCUIT JUDGE:

Wilderness Watch appeals the grant of summary judgment to the National Park Service on its complaint seeking to enjoin the Park Service's practice of using motor vehicles to transport visitors across the designated wilderness area on Cumberland Island, Georgia. Wilderness Watch asserts that this practice violates the Wilderness Act, 16 U.S.C. §§ 1131–36. . . .

I. The Wilderness Act

A.

Mindful of our "increasing population, accompanied by expanding settlement and growing mechanization," Congress passed the 1964 Wilderness Act in order to preserve and protect certain lands "in their natural condition" and thus "secure for present and future generations the benefits of wilderness." 16 U.S.C. § 1131(a). The Act recognized the value of preserving "an area where the earth and its community of life are untrammeled by man, where man himself is a visitor who does not remain." *Id.* at § 1131(c). Congress therefore directed that designated wilderness areas "shall be administered for the use and enjoyment of the American people in such manner as will leave them unimpaired for future use and enjoyment as wilderness, and so as to provide for the protection of these areas, the preservation of their wilderness character, and for the gathering and dissemination of information regarding their use and enjoyment as wilderness." *Id.* at 1131(a).

Cumberland Island, which features some of the last remaining undeveloped land on the barrier islands along the Atlantic coast of the United States, was declared by Congress to be a National Seashore in 1972. Ten years later, Congress designated as wilderness or potential wilderness[2] some 19,000 acres, including most of the northern three-

[2] Potential wilderness areas contain certain temporary conditions that do not conform to the Wilderness Act. They are to receive full wilderness designation when the Secretary of the Interior determines that "uses prohibited by the Wilderness Act have ceased." P.L. 97–250 § 2(a). Park Service policy "is to treat potential wilderness in exactly the same manner as wilderness." R. at 2–17 Ex. 1 (declaration of Cumberland Island Superintendent Arthur Frederick). The Park Service wilderness manual states that:

> Management decisions made pertaining to lands qualifying as wilderness will be made in expectation of eventual wilderness designation. This policy also applies to potential wilderness, requiring it to be managed as wilderness to the extent that existing non-conforming uses allow. The National Park Service will seek to remove the temporary non-conforming conditions that preclude wilderness designation. All management decisions affecting wilderness will further

fifths of the island. See P.L. 97–250, 96 Stat. 709 (Sept. 8, 1982). Under the aegis of the Secretary of the Interior, the Park Service thus became responsible for administering the wilderness area "in accordance with the applicable provisions of the Wilderness Act." *Id.* at § 2(c). Today, visitors to Cumberland Island must leave their vehicles on the mainland and travel to the island by boat.

In addition to wilderness area, Park Service land includes several buildings and facilities on the southern end of the island as well as two historical areas on the northern and western coasts: Plum Orchard, just outside the wilderness boundary, and the Settlement, located in potential wilderness area.[3] Historically, these two locations have been reached via the "Main Road," a one-lane dirt road that has also been designated as part of the wilderness and potential wilderness areas.

*Plum Orchard*

Once federal land has been designated as wilderness, the Wilderness Act places severe restrictions on commercial activities, roads, motorized vehicles, motorized transport, and structures within the area, subject to very narrow exceptions and existing private rights. Specifically, the relevant section provides:

---

apply the concepts of "minimum requirements" for the administration of the area regardless of wilderness category.

National Park Service, Reference Manual 41: Wilderness Preservation and Management at 14 (1999).

[3] Plum Orchard, a mansion complex commissioned by Thomas Carnegie in the late nineteenth century, lies some two-and-one-half miles from the wilderness boundary on the western coast. The Settlement, the remnants of an area occupied by a group of freed slaves after the Civil War, lies another six miles north of Plum Orchard.

> Except as specifically provided for in this chapter, and subject to existing private rights, there shall be no commercial enterprise and no permanent road within any wilderness area designated by this chapter and, except as necessary to meet minimum requirements for the administration of the area for the purpose of this chapter (including measures required in emergencies involving the health and safety of persons within the area), there shall be no temporary road, no use of motor vehicles, motorized equipment or motorboats, no landing of aircraft, no other form of mechanical transport, and no structure or installation within any such area.

16 U.S.C. § 1133(c). Thus, aside from exceptions not relevant here,[4] the statute permits the use of motor vehicles and transport only "as necessary to meet minimum requirements for the administration of the area for the purpose of this chapter." *Id.*

Following the wilderness designation, the Park Service continued to use the existing one-lane dirt road to access the historical areas. Motorized transportation on Cumberland Island became a controversial issue in the 1990s, as the federal government sought to obtain remaining private tracts on the island and various groups called for greater public access to and support of the historical sites. An informal group of environmental organizations, historical societies, and local residents met several times in an attempt to discuss and ultimately to influence Park Service policy. Jack Kingston, the representative to Congress from the district including Cumberland, introduced legislation that would have removed the wilderness designation from the roads leading to the historical sites. This bill died in committee in 1998, but later that year the Park Service convened the first of two meetings with many of the same interested parties in an attempt to negotiate a solution to the conflict over its policies. In February 1999 the Park Service agreed to provide regular public access to Plum Orchard and the Settlement via Park Service motor vehicles until boat service could be established.

The Park Service claimed that it needed motorized access to the historical areas in order to "meet[ ] its obligations to restore, maintain, preserve and curate the historic resources . . . and permit visitor access and interpretation." The Service also claimed that permitting tourists to "piggyback" along on Park Service personnel trips to these locations would yield "no net increase in impact,"—that is, the number of trips and overall impact on the area would be no greater than if the Park Service were simply meeting its statutory obligations. For the first two months, the Park Service used vehicles that held four passengers, but the agency soon acquired a fifteen-person van in order to accommodate larger

---

[4] Neither "existing private rights" nor the exceptions "specifically provided for in this chapter" are relevant to this appeal. *See* 16 U.S.C. § 1133(d) (describing the special exceptions for aircraft, motorboats, fire, insects, disease, mining and mineral activities, water resources, certain specific commercial services, and state jurisdiction over wildlife).

numbers of visitors. The Park Service offered trips to Plum Orchard three times per week and to the Settlement once per month. Although the Park Service had not previously visited the sites on a regular schedule, the agency decided to establish a regular schedule in order to accommodate the transportation of visitors.

Wilderness Watch objects to this arrangement, arguing that the Wilderness Act restricts motorized vehicle use within wilderness areas to the minimum necessary for an agency to meet its administrative needs for the purpose of the Wilderness Act and not for any other purpose. Thus, Wilderness Watch argues, the statute prohibits the Park Service from offering these "piggybacked" tours to visitors.

The Park Service, on the other hand, reads the statute to allow visitors to ride along with its employees as they travel to Plum Orchard and the Settlement to perform what they claim is administrative and maintenance work on those properties. The Service claims that the Act allows land designated as wilderness to be devoted to multiple purposes, citing as authority 16 U.S.C. § 1133(b), which provides that "wilderness areas shall be devoted to the public purposes of recreational, scenic, scientific, educational, conservation, and historical use." Thus, the Park Service argues, because it has a separate duty to preserve the historical structures at the Settlement, the "preservation of historic structures in wilderness (or, as here, potential wilderness) is in fact administration to further the purposes of the Wilderness Act."

This dispute thus requires us to interpret the limitations imposed on motor vehicle use under the Wilderness Act, in particular the requirement that motor vehicle use be restricted to the level "necessary to meet minimum requirements for the administration of the area," 16 U.S.C. § 1133(c). We must also determine the effect of the Act upon the Park Service's obligations to maintain the historical structures on Cumberland Island and whether the Act can accommodate the Park Service's decision to transport tourists for the purpose of visiting those structures.

We analyze the Park Service's interpretation of the statutory phrase "except as necessary to meet minimum requirements for the administration of the area" under the two-step analysis described in Chevron, U.S.A., Inc. v. Natural Res. Def. Council, Inc., 467 U.S. 837 (1984), and clarified in United States v. Mead Corp., 533 U.S. 218 (2001). Under *Chevron*, we first ask whether congressional intent is clear, and if so, "that is the end of the matter; for the court, as well as the agency, must give effect to the unambiguously expressed intent of Congress." 467 U.S. at 842–43. We examine congressional intent through the plain language of the statute, understanding that "the words of a statute must be read in their context and with a view to their place in the overall statutory scheme." FDA v. Brown & Williamson Tobacco Corp., 529 U.S. 120, 133 (2000). If we find the statute silent or ambiguous, we defer to the agency interpretation "when it appears that Congress delegated authority to the agency generally to make rules carrying the force of law, and that the agency interpretation claiming deference was promulgated in the exercise of that authority." *Mead*, 533 U.S. at 226–27.

B.

As an initial matter, we cannot agree with the Park Service that the preservation of historical structures furthers the goals of the Wilderness Act. The Park Service's responsibilities for the historic preservation of Plum Orchard and the Settlement derive, not from the Wilderness Act, but rather from the National Historic Preservation Act (NHPA), 16 U.S.C. § 461, *et seq.* The NHPA requires agencies to "assume responsibility for the preservation of historic properties" they control. *Id.* at § 470h–2(a)(1). Plum Orchard and the historic district containing the Settlement have both been listed in the National Register of Historic Places,[8] though the congressional reports and early Park Service reports only mention Plum Orchard (which itself lies outside the designated wilderness area).

The agency's obligations under the Wilderness Act are quite different. The Wilderness Act defines wilderness as "undeveloped Federal land retaining its primeval character and influence, without permanent improvements or human habitation." 16 U.S.C. § 1131(c). A wilderness area should "generally appear[ ] to have been affected primarily by the forces of nature, with the imprint of man's work substantially unnoticeable." *Id.* Another section of the Act explicitly states that, except as necessary for minimal administrative needs that require occasional vehicle use, "there shall be . . . no structure or installation within any such [wilderness] area." 16 U.S.C. § 1133(c). As the Park Service notes, Section 1133(b) mentions "historical use" along with "recreational, scenic, scientific, educational, [and] conservation" uses. However, this list tracks the definition of wilderness areas in § 1131(c), which describes "a primitive and unconfined type of recreation" and "ecological, geological, or other features of scientific, educational, scenic, or historical value." 16 U.S.C. § 1131(c). Given the consistent evocation of "untrammeled" and "natural" areas, the previous pairing of "historical" with "ecological" and "geological" features, and the explicit prohibition on structures, the only reasonable reading of "historical use" in the Wilderness Act refers to natural, rather than man-made, features.

Of course, Congress may separately provide for the preservation of an existing historical structure within a wilderness area, as it has done through the NHPA. Congress wrote the wilderness rules and may create exceptions as it sees fit. Absent these explicit statutory instructions, however, the need to preserve historical structures may not be inferred from the Wilderness Act nor grafted onto its general purpose. Furthermore, any obligation the agency has under the NHPA to preserve

---

[8] *See* http://www.nationalregisterofhistoricplaces.com/GA/Camden/districts.html (accessed June 25, 2004).

these historical structures must be carried out so as to preserve the "wilderness character" of the area. *See* 16 U.S.C. § 1133(b). ("Each agency administering any area designated as wilderness shall be responsible for preserving the wilderness character of the area and shall so administer such area for such other purposes for which it may have been established as also to preserve its wilderness character.")

This appeal turns not on the preservation of historical structures but on the decision to provide motorized public access to them across designated wilderness areas. The Wilderness Act bars the use of motor vehicles in these areas "except as necessary to meet minimum requirements for the administration of the area for the purpose of this chapter [the Wilderness Act]." 16 U.S.C. § 1133(c). The Park Service's decision to "administer" the Settlement using a fifteen-passenger van filled with tourists simply cannot be construed as "necessary" to meet the "minimum requirements" for administering the area "for the purpose of [the Wilderness Act]." 16 U.S.C. § 1133(c). The plain language of the statute contradicts the Park Service position. When interpreting the language of a statute, "we generally give the words used their ordinary meaning." Griffith v. United States, 206 F.3d 1389, 1393 (11th Cir. 2000) (en banc) (citations and internal quotation marks omitted). If these words are unambiguous, our inquiry is complete, for "we must presume that Congress said what it meant and meant what it said." CBS, Inc. v. PrimeTime 24 Joint Venture, 245 F.3d 1217, 1222 (11th Cir. 2001) (citation omitted). In no ordinary sense of the word can the transportation of fifteen people through wilderness area be "necessary" to administer the area for the purpose of the Wilderness Act.

The Park Service argues that these trips affect the wilderness no more than would a standard Park Service vehicle with no additional passengers. Thus, the agency argues that the "use of motor vehicles" remains the same as what would be minimally necessary for administration. There are several problems with this interpretation. Most obviously, it still runs counter to the plain meaning of the provision. Under an ordinary, common-sense reading, people "use" motor vehicles when they ride in the Park Service van, thereby increasing the "use of motor vehicles" beyond the minimum necessary for administration of the Wilderness Act. The Park Service wishes to define the term based on the number of vehicles used rather than on the number of people using them, but even so, the acquisition and use of a large passenger van for transporting tourists cannot reasonably be squeezed into the phrase "necessary to meet minimum requirements" of administration. The language in this subsection is quite categorical, providing for "*no* motor vehicle use" except "as necessary" and labels this a "*prohibition.*" 16 U.S.C. § 1133(c) (emphasis added). Moreover, the same subsection provides that there shall be "no other form of mechanical transport" beyond what is necessary for administration of the Wilderness Act. *Id.* A passenger van certainly provides more "transport" than would a Park Service vehicle without extra passengers.

In addition, the overall purpose and structure of the statute argue against the agency interpretation. The prohibition on motor vehicle "use" in the Wilderness Act stems from more than just its potential for physical impact on the environment. The Act seeks to preserve wilderness areas "in their natural condition" for their "use and enjoyment *as wilderness*." 16 U.S.C. § 1131(a) (emphasis added). The Act promotes the benefits of wilderness "for the American people," especially the "opportunities for a primitive and unconfined type of recreation." *Id.* at § 1131(c). Thus, the statute seeks to provide the opportunity for a primitive wilderness experience as much as to protect the wilderness lands themselves from physical harm. *See also* National Park Service, Reference Manual 41 at 14 ("In addition to managing these areas for the preservation of the physical wilderness resources, planning for these areas must ensure that the wilderness character is likewise preserved."). Use of a passenger van changes the wilderness experience, not only for the actual passengers, but also for any other persons they happen to pass (more so than would be the case upon meeting a lone park ranger in a jeep). Of course, there is nothing wrong with appreciating natural beauty from inside a passenger van, and many other categories of public land administered by the federal government appropriately offer this opportunity. It simply is not the type of "use and enjoyment" promoted by the Wilderness Act.

Other documents in the record highlight the potential conflict between wilderness values and the transportation of passengers. The agency's Minimum Requirements Determination (MRD) for the Plum Orchard trips recognized "concerns over the van affecting the quality of the visitor experience for those seeking a wilderness experience." The House report accompanying the bill establishing the Cumberland wilderness area urged the Park Service to provide exclusive access to Plum Orchard by water "in the interests of minimizing unnecessary intrusion on wilderness values." H. Rep. No. 97–383 at 5. The agency itself previously stressed the need to limit mechanized transport to administrative purposes that promote wilderness values. *See, e.g.*, National Park Service, Reference Manual 41 at 16–17 ("Administrative use of motorized equipment or mechanical transport will be authorized only if determined by the superintendent to be the minimum requirement needed by management to achieve *the purposes of the area as wilderness*, including the preservation of *wilderness character and values*, or in emergency situations. . . .") (emphasis added).

The language of the specific provision at issue and the overall purpose and structure of the Wilderness Act demonstrate that Congress has unambiguously prohibited the Park Service from offering motorized transportation to park visitors through the wilderness area. . . .

---

## QUESTIONS AND DISCUSSION

**1.** Congress enacted the Wilderness Act to preserve those areas "where the earth and its community of life are untrammeled by man, where man himself is a visitor who does not remain." 16 U.S.C. § 1131(c). What activities are compatible with that purpose? Many users compete for acceptance in wilderness areas. "Recreational activities such as hunting, camping, canoeing, kayaking, swimming, picnicking, backpacking, bird watching, horseback riding, cross-country skiing, snowshoeing, spelunking, rock-climbing, and many other outdoor activities would be continued and encouraged in the new Wilderness Areas" proposed by the Virginia Ridge and Valley Act of 2005. 151 CONG. REC. E864 (daily ed. May 4, 2005) (statement of Rep. Boucher). Senator Diane Feinstein was careful to say that "horsepacking is an important use of wilderness" and that the state could still issue hunting and fishing licenses before Congress approved additional wilderness areas in California in 2004. 150 CONG. REC. S11794 (daily ed. Nov. 20, 2004) (statement of Sen. Feinstein). Grazing, the reintroduction of endangered species, fire suppression, mining, oil and gas exploration, dams, and aircraft use are at issue in other wilderness areas. *See generally* JOHN C. HENDEE & CHAD P. DAWSON, WILDERNESS MANAGEMENT: STEWARDSHIP AND PROTECTION OF RESOURCES AND VALUES (3d ed. 2002) (describing wilderness management issues). Which of those activities can coincide with the stated purposes of the Wilderness Act?

**2.** The Wilderness Act prohibits any "commercial enterprise" within any designated wilderness area. The Ninth Circuit construed the scope of that prohibition in two important cases. In The Wilderness Society v. FWS, 353 F.3d 1051 (9th Cir. 2003) (en banc), two environmental groups challenged a project by which the Cook Inlet Aquaculture Association (CIAA) added six million sockeye salmon fry to Tustumena Lake each year. Tustumena Lake is the largest freshwater lake within the Kenai wilderness area southwest of Anchorage, and the project was designed to enhance commercial fishing operations in the area. CIAA emphasized its non-profit status and the fact that the fishing occurred outside the wilderness area. But the Court held that the enhancement project was "literally a project related to commerce." *Id.* at 1061. The court acknowledged that "this fish-stocking program, whose antecedents were a state-run research project, is nothing like building a McDonald's restaurant or a Wal-Mart store on the shores of Tustumena Lake." *Id.* at 1062. Nor, however, was the project "aimed at preserving a threatened salmon run" or otherwise "furthering the goals of the Wilderness Act." *Id.* at 1062–63. So the court emphasized that "[t]he primary purpose of the Enhancement Project is to advance commercial interests of Cook Inlet fishermen by swelling the salmon runs from which they will eventually make their catch," *id.* at 1064, and "[t]he primary effect of the Enhancement Project is to aid commercial enterprise of fishermen." *Id.* at 1065.

High Sierra Hikers Association v. Blackwell, 390 F.3d 630 (9th Cir. 2004), involved the use of commercial horse and mule outfitters within the John Muir and Ansel Adams wilderness areas. The court explained that "[c]ommercial packstock operators provide the public with the opportunity to take guided trips into the wilderness areas, transport equipment for backcountry visitors, and enable access for people who would otherwise not be able to hike in those areas." *Id.* at 892. But the High Sierra Hikers Association claimed that the Forest Service's issuance of special-use permits to commercial packstock operators violated the Wilderness Act. The general prohibition on commercial enterprises in wilderness contains an exception "to the extent necessary for activities which are proper for realizing the recreational or other wilderness purposes of the areas." 16 U.S.C. § 1133(d)(5). Even so, the court held that the Forest Service failed to limit the packstock operations "to the extent necessary." According to the court, "[a]t best, when the Forest Service simply continued preexisting permit levels, it failed to balance the impact that the level of commercial activity was having on the wilderness character of the land. At worst, the Forest Service elevated recreational activity over the long-term preservation of the wilderness character of the land." *Id.* at 903–04. The court thus remanded the case "to the district court for a determination of appropriate relief under the Wilderness Act, including whether remediation of any degradation that has already occurred is appropriate." *Id.* at 905. What should the district court order?

**3.** Water rights have been a source of frequent controversy within wilderness areas. The Wilderness Act does not "constitute an express or implied claim or denial on the part of the Federal Government as to exemption from State water laws." 16 U.S.C. § 1133(d)(6). Given that congressional punt, claims to federal reserved water rights have arisen in Wilderness Act litigation, *see, e.g.*, In re SRBA, 12 P.3d 1260 (Idaho 2000) (holding that there were no federal reserved water rights in three wilderness areas in Idaho); and the issue has complicated debates over the proposed creation of new wilderness areas as well. *See* Karin P. Sheldon, *Water for Wilderness*, 76 DENVER U. L. REV. 555, 556–57 (1999) (blaming disputes over water rights for some of the congressional reluctance to establish new wilderness areas).

**4.** ANILCA designated 56.7 million acres of wilderness lands in Alaska, thus doubling the size of the national wilderness preservation system in one fell swoop. But the precise relationship between ANILCA's wilderness provisions and the provisions of the Wilderness Act remains unclear. Section 707 of ANILCA states that "except as otherwise expressly provided for in this Act, wilderness designated by this Act shall be administered in accordance with applicable provisions of the Wilderness Act governing areas designated by that Act as wilderness." *See* ANILCA § 707. ANILCA allows for subsistence activities, mineral assessment, access to inholdings, sport hunting and fishing, and motorized access for traditional activities in wilderness areas. *See* ANILCA § 811 (subsistence activities); *id.* at 1010 (mineral assessment); *id.* § 1109 (existing rights of access); *id.* § 1110(a) (access for traditional activities); *id.* § 1110(b) (access to inholdings); *id.* § 1313 (hunting and fishing). The extent of such activities, and the extent to which they can be regulated, is still contested.

**5.** Did the Eleventh Circuit correctly balance the interests of wilderness preservation and historical preservation on Cumberland Island? Both of the sites noted by the court have unique historical importance. The Settlement is a community built by freed slaves in the 1890s, and its church hosted the 1996 marriage off John F. Kennedy Jr. and Carolyn Bessette. Plum Orchard, built for Andrew Carnegie's nephew George in 1898, was one of several retreats built by nineteenth century industrial barons on Cumberland Island. Plum Orchard is currently undergoing a $3 million restoration of its interior. The island also contains the ruins of Dungeness, a mansion first built by Revolutionary War General Nathaniel Greene's widow in 1783 and rebuilt by the Carnegie family in 1884, which burned in 1959; along with numerous other sites dating from early Spanish explorers, African-Americans, and other wealthy vacationers. *See* http://www.cr.nps.gov/nr/travel/geo-flor/16.htm; *see also* NANCY C. ROCKEFELLER, THE CARNEGIES AND CUMBERLAND ISLAND (2007); LARY M. DILSAVER, CUMBERLAND ISLAND NATIONAL SEASHORE: A HISTORY OF CONSERVATION CONFLICT (2004).

**6.** After the Eleventh Circuit's decision, Representative Kingston persevered in his efforts to remove the Main Road from the Cumberland Island wilderness area. Kingston finally succeeded in adding a rider to the omnibus federal appropriations bill in December 2004. *See* Consolidated Appropriations Act, 2005, Pub. L. No. 447, § 145, 118 Stat. 2809, 3072–73 (2004). The resulting Cumberland Island Wilderness Boundary Adjustment Act of 2004 excluded the Main Road, two smaller roads, and a historic district from the wilderness area. The act also directed the Park Service to authorize visitor tours of the historic sites on the island. Representative Kingston said, "There's no divine right of the wilderness to come before the historic properties." Daniel Cusick, *Georgia Seashore Struggles with Balancing Conflicting Missions*, LAND LETTER, Aug. 4, 2005. Opponents insisted that more tours will bring more visitors who will compromise what makes the island's wilderness special. One newspaper editorialized that "[f]or staunch conservationists" the plan for motorized tours "is heresy. But if the tourism plan is handled correctly, their objections should prove unfounded." *Protect—And Enjoy; Strategic Plan Must Preserve Cumberland Island's Natural Essence, Allow More to Experience Its Beauty*, ATLANTA J.-CONST., Sept. 7, 2006, at 14A. How would you plan such tours?

## Norton v. Southern Utah Wilderness Alliance

Supreme Court of the United States, 2004.
542 U.S. 55.

■ JUSTICE SCALIA delivered the opinion of the Court.

In this case, we must decide whether the authority of a federal court under the Administrative Procedure Act (APA) to "compel agency action unlawfully withheld or unreasonably delayed," 5 U.S.C. § 706(1), extends to the review of the United States Bureau of Land Management's stewardship of public lands under certain statutory provisions and its own planning documents.

I

Almost half the State of Utah, about 23 million acres, is federal land administered by the Bureau of Land Management (BLM), an agency within the Department of Interior. For nearly 30 years, BLM's management of public lands has been governed by the Federal Land Policy and Management Act of 1976 (FLPMA), 90 Stat. 2744, 43 U.S.C. § 1701 et seq., which "established a policy in favor of retaining public lands for multiple use management." Lujan v. Nat'l Wildlife Fed'n, 497 U.S. 871, 877 (1990). "Multiple use management" is a deceptively simple term that describes the enormously complicated task of striking a balance among the many competing uses to which land can be put, "including, but not limited to, recreation, range, timber, minerals, watershed, wildlife and fish, and [uses serving] natural scenic, scientific and historical values." 43 U.S.C. § 1702(c). A second management goal, "sustained yield," requires BLM to control depleting uses over time, so as to ensure a high level of valuable uses in the future. § 1702(h). To these ends, FLPMA establishes a dual regime of inventory and planning. Sections 1711 and 1712, respectively, provide for a comprehensive, ongoing inventory of federal lands, and for a land use planning process that "project[s]" "present and future use," § 1701(a)(2), given the lands' inventoried characteristics.

Of course not all uses are compatible. Congress made the judgment that some lands should be set aside as wilderness at the expense of commercial and recreational uses. A pre-FLPMA enactment, the Wilderness Act of 1964, 78 Stat. 890, provides that designated wilderness areas, subject to certain exceptions, "shall [have] no commercial enterprise and no permanent road," no motorized vehicles, and no manmade structures. 16 U.S.C. § 1133(c). The designation of a wilderness area can be made only by Act of Congress, *see* 43 U.S.C. § 1782(b).

Pursuant to § 1782, the Secretary of the Interior has identified so-called "wilderness study areas" (WSAs), roadless lands of 5,000 acres or more that possess "wilderness characteristics," as determined in the Secretary's land inventory. § 1782(a); *see* 16 U.S.C. § 1131(c). As the name suggests, WSAs (as well as certain wild lands identified prior to the passage of FLPMA) have been subjected to further examination and public comment in order to evaluate their suitability for designation as wilderness. In 1991, out of 3.3 million acres in Utah that had been identified for study, 2 million were recommended as suitable for wilderness designation. 1 U.S. Dept. of Interior, BLM, Utah Statewide Wilderness Study Report 3 (Oct. 1991). This recommendation was forwarded to Congress, which has not yet acted upon it. Until Congress acts one way or the other, FLPMA provides that "the Secretary shall continue to manage such lands . . . in a manner so as not to impair the suitability of such areas for preservation as wilderness." 43 U.S.C. § 1782(c). This nonimpairment mandate applies to all WSAs identified under § 1782, including lands considered unsuitable by the Secretary.

Aside from identification of WSAs, the main tool that BLM employs to balance wilderness protection against other uses is a land use plan—

what BLM regulations call a "resource management plan." 43 C.F.R. § 1601.0–5(k) (2003). Land use plans, adopted after notice and comment, are "designed to guide and control future management actions," § 1601.0–2. *See* 43 U.S.C. § 1712; 43 C.F.R. § 1610.2 (2003). Generally, a land use plan describes, for a particular area, allowable uses, goals for future condition of the land, and specific next steps. § 1601.0–5(k). Under FLPMA, "[t]he Secretary shall manage the public lands under principles of multiple use and sustained yield, in accordance with the land use plans . . . when they are available." 43 U.S.C. § 1732(a).

Protection of wilderness has come into increasing conflict with another element of multiple use, recreational use of so-called off-road vehicles (ORVs), which include vehicles primarily designed for off-road use, such as lightweight, four-wheel "all-terrain vehicles," and vehicles capable of such use, such as sport utility vehicles. *See* 43 C.F.R. § 8340.0–5(a) (2003). According to the United States Forest Service's most recent estimates, some 42 million Americans participate in off-road travel each year, more than double the number two decades ago. United States sales of all-terrain vehicles alone have roughly doubled in the past five years, reaching almost 900,000 in 2003. The use of ORVs on federal land has negative environmental consequences, including soil disruption and compaction, harassment of animals, and annoyance of wilderness lovers. Thus, BLM faces a classic land use dilemma of sharply inconsistent uses, in a context of scarce resources and congressional silence with respect to wilderness designation.

In 1999, respondents Southern Utah Wilderness Alliance and other organizations (collectively SUWA) filed this action in the United States District Court for Utah against petitioners BLM, its Director, and the Secretary. In its second amended complaint, SUWA sought declaratory and injunctive relief for BLM's failure to act to protect public lands in Utah from damage caused by ORV use. SUWA made three claims that are relevant here: (1) that BLM had violated its nonimpairment obligation under § 1782(a) by allowing degradation in certain WSAs; (2) that BLM had failed to implement provisions in its land use plans relating to ORV use; (3) that BLM had failed to take a "hard look" at whether, pursuant to the National Environmental Policy Act of 1969 (NEPA), 42 U.S.C. § 4321 et seq., it should undertake supplemental environmental analyses for areas in which ORV use had increased. SUWA contended that it could sue to remedy these three failures to act pursuant to the APA's provision of a cause of action to "compel agency action unlawfully withheld or unreasonably delayed." 5 U.S.C. § 706(1).

The District Court [dismissed SUWA's three claims, but a divided panel of the Tenth Circuit reversed.]

II

All three claims at issue here involve assertions that BLM failed to take action with respect to ORV use that it was required to take. Failures to act are sometimes remediable under the APA, but not always. . . . [A] claim under § 706(1) can proceed only where a plaintiff asserts that an agency failed to take a *discrete* agency action that it is *required to take*. . . .

III

A

With these principles in mind, we turn to SUWA's first claim, that by permitting ORV use in certain WSAs, BLM violated its mandate to "continue to manage [WSAs] . . . in a manner so as not to impair the suitability of such areas for preservation as wilderness," 43 U.S.C. § 1782(c). SUWA relies not only upon § 1782(c) but also upon a provision of BLM's Interim Management Policy for Lands Under Wilderness Review, which interprets the nonimpairment mandate to require BLM to manage WSAs so as to prevent them from being "degraded so far, compared with the area's values for other purposes, as to significantly constrain the Congress's prerogative to either designate [it] as wilderness or release it for other uses."

Section 1782(c) is mandatory as to the object to be achieved, but it leaves BLM a great deal of discretion in deciding how to achieve it. It assuredly does not mandate, with the clarity necessary to support judicial action under § 706(1), the total exclusion of ORV use.

SUWA argues that § 1782 *does* contain a categorical imperative, namely the command to comply with the nonimpairment mandate. It contends that a federal court could simply enter a general order compelling compliance with that mandate, without suggesting any particular manner of compliance. It relies upon the language from the Attorney General's Manual quoted earlier, that a court can "take action upon a matter, without directing how [the agency] shall act," and upon language in a case cited by the Manual noting that "mandamus will lie . . . even though the act required involves the exercise of judgment and discretion." Safeway Stores v. Brown, 138 F.2d 278, 280 (Emerg. Ct. App. 1943). The action referred to in these excerpts, however, is *discrete* agency action, as we have discussed above. General deficiencies in compliance, unlike the failure to issue a ruling that was discussed in *Safeway Stores*, lack the specificity requisite for agency action.

The principal purpose of the APA limitations we have discussed—and of the traditional limitations upon mandamus from which they were derived—is to protect agencies from undue judicial interference with their lawful discretion, and to avoid judicial entanglement in abstract policy disagreements which courts lack both expertise and information to resolve. If courts were empowered to enter general orders compelling compliance with broad statutory mandates, they would necessarily be empowered, as well, to determine whether compliance was achieved—which would mean that it would ultimately become the task of the supervising court, rather than the agency, to work out compliance with the broad statutory mandate, injecting the judge into day-to-day agency management. To take just a few examples from federal resources management, a plaintiff might allege that the Secretary had failed to "manage wild free-roaming horses and burros in a manner that is designed to achieve and maintain a thriving natural ecological balance," or to "manage the [New Orleans Jazz National] [H]istorical [P]ark in such a manner as will preserve and perpetuate knowledge and understanding of the history of jazz," or to "manage the [Steens Mountain] Cooperative Management and Protection Area for the benefit of present and future generations." 16 U.S.C. §§ 1333(a), 410bbb–2(a)(1), 460nnn–12(b). The prospect of pervasive oversight by federal courts over the manner and pace of agency compliance with such congressional directives is not contemplated by the APA.

B

SUWA's second claim is that BLM failed to comply with certain provisions in its land use plans, thus contravening the requirement that "[t]he Secretary shall manage the public lands . . . in accordance with the land use plans . . . when they are available." 43 U.S.C. § 1732(a); *see also* 43 C.F.R. § 1610.5–3(a) (2003) ("All future resource management authorizations and actions . . . and subsequent more detailed or specific planning, shall conform to the approved plan"). The relevant count in SUWA's second amended complaint alleged that BLM had violated a variety of commitments in its land use plans, but over the course of the litigation these have been reduced to two, one relating to the 1991 resource management plan for the San Rafael area, and the other to various aspects of the 1990 ORV implementation plan for the Henry Mountains area.

The actions contemplated by the first of these alleged commitments (completion of a route designation plan in the San Rafael area), and by one aspect of the second (creation of "use supervision files" for designated areas in the Henry Mountains area) have already been completed, and these claims are therefore moot. There remains the claim, with respect to the Henry Mountains plan, that "in light of damage from ORVs in the Factory Butte area," a sub-area of Henry Mountains open to ORV use, "the [plan] obligated BLM to conduct an intensive ORV monitoring program." This claim is based upon the plan's statement that the Factory Butte area "will be monitored and closed if warranted." SUWA does not contest BLM's assertion in the court below that informal monitoring has taken place for some years, but it demands continuing implementation of a monitoring *program*. By this it apparently means to insist upon adherence to the plan's general discussion of "Use Supervision and Monitoring" in designated areas, which (in addition to calling for the use supervision files that have already been created) provides that "[r]esource damage will be documented and recommendations made for corrective action," "[m]onitoring in open areas will focus on determining damage which may necessitate a change in designation," and "emphasis on use supervision will be placed on [limited and closed areas]." *Id.*, at

149. SUWA acknowledges that a monitoring program has recently been *commenced.* In light, however, of the continuing action that existence of a "program" contemplates, and in light of BLM's contention that the program cannot be compelled under § 706(1), this claim cannot be considered moot.

The statutory directive that BLM manage "in accordance with" land use plans, and the regulatory requirement that authorizations and actions "conform to" those plans, prevent BLM from taking actions inconsistent with the provisions of a land use plan. Unless and until the plan is amended, such actions can be set aside as contrary to law pursuant to 5 U.S.C. § 706(2). The claim presently under discussion, however, would have us go further, and conclude that a statement in a plan that BLM "will" take this, that, or the other action, is a binding commitment that can be compelled under § 706(1). In our view it is not—at least absent clear indication of binding commitment in the terms of the plan.

FLPMA describes land use plans as tools by which "present and future use is *projected.*" 43 U.S.C. § 1701(a)(2) (emphasis added). The implementing regulations make clear that land use plans are a preliminary step in the overall process of managing public lands—"designed to guide and control future management actions and the development of subsequent, more detailed and limited scope plans for resources and uses." 43 C.F.R. § 1601.0–2 (2003). The statute and regulations confirm that a land use plan is not ordinarily the medium for affirmative decisions that implement the agency's "project[ions]." Title 43 U.S.C. § 1712(e) provides that "[t]he Secretary may issue management decisions to implement land use plans"—the decisions, that is, are distinct from the plan itself. Picking up the same theme, the regulation defining a land use plan declares that a plan "is not a final implementation decision on actions which require further specific plans, process steps, or decisions under specific provisions of law and regulations." 43 C.F.R. § 1601.0–5(k) (2003). The BLM's Land Use Planning Handbook specifies that land use plans are normally not used to make site-specific implementation decisions.

Plans also receive a different agency review process from implementation decisions. Appeal to the Department's Board of Land Appeals is available for "a specific action being proposed to implement some portion of a resource management plan or amendment." 43 C.F.R. § 1610.5–3(b). However, the Board, which reviews "decisions rendered by Departmental officials relating to . . . [t]he use and disposition of public lands and their resources," § 4.1(b)(3)(i), does not review the approval of a plan, since it regards a plan as a policy determination, not an implementation decision. Plans are protested to the BLM director, not appealed.

The San Rafael plan provides an apt illustration of the immense scope of projected activity that a land use plan can embrace. Over 100 pages in length, it presents a comprehensive management framework for 1.5 million acres of BLM-administered land. Twenty categories of resource management are separately discussed, including mineral extraction, wilderness protection, livestock grazing, preservation of cultural resources, and recreation. The plan lays out an ambitious agenda for the preparation of additional, more detailed plans and specific next steps for implementation. Its introduction notes that "[a]n [ORV] implementation plan is scheduled to be prepared within 1 year following approval of the [San Rafael plan]." Similarly "scheduled for preparation" are activity plans for certain environmentally sensitive areas, "along with allotment management plans, habitat management plans, a fire management plan, recreation management plans . . . , cultural resource management plans for selected sites, watershed activity plans, and the wild and scenic river management plan." *Ibid.* The projected schedule set forth in the plan shows "[a]nticipated [i]mplementation" of some future plans within one year, others within three years, and still others, such as certain recreation and cultural resource management plans, at a pace of "one study per fiscal year." *Id.*, at 95–102.

Quite unlike a specific statutory command requiring an agency to promulgate regulations by a certain date, a land use plan is generally a statement of priorities; it guides and constrains actions, but does not (at least in the usual case) prescribe them. It would be unreasonable to think that either Congress or the agency intended otherwise, since land use plans nationwide would commit the agency to actions far in the future, for which funds have not yet been appropriated. Some plans make explicit that implementation of their programmatic content is subject to budgetary constraints. While the Henry Mountains plan does not contain such a specification, we think it must reasonably be implied. A statement by BLM about what it plans to do, at some point, provided it has the funds and there are not more pressing priorities, cannot be plucked out of context and made a basis for suit under § 706(1).

Of course, an action called for in a plan may be compelled when the plan merely reiterates duties the agency is already obligated to perform, or perhaps when language in the plan itself creates a commitment binding on the agency. But allowing general enforcement of plan terms would lead to pervasive interference with BLM's own ordering of priorities. For example, a judicial decree compelling immediate preparation of all of the detailed plans called for in the San Rafael plan would divert BLM's energies from other projects throughout the country that are in fact more pressing. And while such a decree might please the environmental plaintiffs in the present case, it would ultimately operate to the detriment of sound environmental management. Its predictable consequence would be much vaguer plans from BLM in the future—making coordination with other agencies more difficult, and depriving the public of important information concerning the agency's long-range intentions.

We therefore hold that the Henry Mountains plan's statements to the effect that BLM will conduct "use supervision and monitoring" in designated areas—like other "will do" projections of agency action set forth in land use plans—are not a legally binding commitment enforceable under § 706(1). That being so, we find it unnecessary to consider whether the action envisioned by the statements is sufficiently discrete to be amenable to compulsion under the APA.

---

## QUESTIONS AND DISCUSSION

**1.** If BLM has a duty to "continue to manage [WSAs] in a manner so as not to impair the suitability of such areas for preservation as wilderness," then what difference does it make whether Congress actually designates the San Rafael or Henry Mountain areas as wilderness?

**2.** According to the unanimous Court's decision, when can SUWA sue to challenge BLM's policies with respect to ORVs in WSAs?

**3.** "SUWA's overarching goal is to protect Utah's remaining nine million acres of wild desert lands—lands owned by the American public and administered on our behalf by" BLM. Southern Utah Wilderness Alliance, http://www.suwa.org. Toward that end, SUWA supports the proposed America's Redrock Wilderness Act, which would designate nine million acres of Utah lands as wilderness. *See* America's Red Rock Wilderness Act, H.R. 1774, 109th Cong., 2d Sess. (2005). Thus far, the only significant wilderness designation in Utah occurred when Congress enacted, and President Bush signed, legislation to establish 100,000 acres in the Cedar Mountains west of Salt Lake City as wilderness. *See* National Defense Authorization Act for fiscal year 2006, 119 Stat. 3136, 3217. The future of Utah's remaining lands is still being debated, with SUWA pitted against the desires of many Utah counties that favor increased resource development activities. The various parties disagree about the amount of lands that should be designated as wilderness, with recommendations ranging from 1.9 million acres to 8.5 million acres. An initial BLM estimate identified 1.9 million acres in 1991, but a reinventory conducted by BLM eight years later (and in a different presidential administration) found 5.8 million acres. *See* Utah v. Babbitt, 137 F.3d 1193 (10th Cir. 1998) (holding that the State of Utah, the Utah School and Institutional Trust Lands Administration, and the Utah Association of Counties lacked standing to block the reinventory).

The issue is further complicated by a repealed—but grandfathered—provision of the General Mining Act of 1866 that granted right-of-ways for highway construction on public lands. *See* Act of July 26, 1866, § 8, 14 Stat. 253 (codified at REV. STAT. § 2477) (repealed in 1976). The so-called R.S. 2477 (named after its original codification section) provides a vested property right to anyone who built a highway on public lands before the statute was repealed in 1976, but the law neglected to define what constitutes a "highway." That has led to thousands of claims by Utah counties seeking to defeat any future wilderness claims based upon preexisting roads. *See* James

Rasband, *Questioning the Rule of Capture Metaphor for Nineteenth Century Public Land Law: A Look at R.S. 2477*, 35 Envtl. L. 1005 (2005). SUWA complains that "[m]ost of these proposed RS 2477 'highways' are not highways of any kind, but instead are remote jeep paths, desert streambeds, even cow paths." SUWA, Highway Robbery in America's Redrock Wilderness, www.suwa.org/page.php?page_name=Camp_2477_Home. The Tenth Circuit has held that the meaning of "highway" for purposes of R.S. 2477 is a question of state law, *see* SUWA v. BLM, 425 F.3d 735 (10th Cir. 2005); but that court has also held that R.S. 2477 claims must be judicially established before a county may treat roads as its own. *See* Wilderness Soc'y v. Kane County, 581 F.3d 1198 (10th Cir. 2009). For more on the Utah wilderness debate, see Sarah Krakoff, *Settling the Wilderness*, 75 U. COLO. L. REV. 1159 (2004); Michael C. Blumm, *The Bush Administration's Sweetheart Settlement Policy: A Trojan Horse Strategy for Advancing Commodity Production on Public Lands*, 34 ELR 10397, 10404–09 (2004); Stephen H.M. Bloch & Heidi J. McIntosh, *A View From the Front Lines: The Fate of Utah's Redrock Wilderness Under the George W. Bush Administration*, 33 GOLDEN GATE U. L. REV. 473 (2003); Kevin Hayes, *History and Future of the Conflict Over Wilderness Designations of BLM Land in Utah*, 16 J. ENVTL. L. & LITIG. 203, 207 (2001).

**4.** Congress enacted the Wilderness Act in 1964, culminating seven years of debates that began with the introduction of the first wilderness bill by Senator Hubert Humphrey. The act was the result of a congressional compromise. Many western officials and economic interests opposed wilderness legislation when it was first introduced during the 1950's. The principal fear was that the prohibition upon economic activities in lands designated by federal agency officials as wilderness would deprive local interests of the ability to provide for their economic well-being. Congress responded to the western concern about bureaucratic action by providing that "no Federal lands shall be designated as 'wilderness areas' except as provided for in this Act or by a subsequent Act." 16 U.S.C. § 1131(a). The creation of new wilderness areas is thus dependent upon further congressional legislation.

The Wilderness Act itself designated nine million acres of Forest Service land as wilderness areas. The more notable additions since then include the over two hundred million acres of federal lands in the eastern United States designated by the Eastern Wilderness Act of 1975, and the California Desert Protection Act of 1994, which designated 7.5 million acres of wilderness lands. Congress added another two million acres of wilderness areas in California, Colorado, Idaho, Michigan, New Mexico, Oregon, Utah, Virginia, and West Virginia in 2009. *See* Omnibus Public Land Management Act of 2009, Pub. L. No. 111–11, 123 Stat. 991, §§ 1001–1983 (2009). But other wilderness proposals await congressional approval, and many observers object to the slow pace of wilderness designations. *See, e.g.*, Sandra Zellmer, *A Preservation Paradox: Political Prestidigitation and an Enduring Resource of Wildness*, 34 ENVT. L. 1015, 1017–18 (2004) (asserting that "the cumbersome and compromise-ridden legislative process has not fulfilled the Wilderness Act's goal of 'securing an enduring resource of wilderness' ").

**5.** The Forest Service's roadless rule prompted litigation citing the exclusive congressional power to designate wilderness areas. During the last days of the Clinton Administration, the Forest Service announced a rule prohibiting most road construction within roadless areas of national forests. The State of Wyoming challenged the rule as an implied designation of wilderness in violation of Section 2(a) of the Wilderness Act. A federal district court agreed because "[t]o allow the Secretary of Agriculture and the Forest Service to establish their own system of de facto administrative wilderness through administrative rulemaking negates the system of wilderness designation established by Congress." Wyoming v. United States Dep't of Agriculture, 277 F. Supp. 2d 1197, 1236 (D. Wyo. 2003). But the dispute became moot once the Forest Service substituted a quite different rule the day after oral argument had been heard on the appeal in the Tenth Circuit. *See* Wyoming v. United States Dep't of Agriculture, 414 F.3d 1207 (10th Cir. 2005).

**6.** The Antiquities Act has served as another vehicle for protecting lands in Utah and elsewhere. Enacted in 1906, the Antiquities Act authorizes the President "in his discretion, to declare by public proclamation historic landmarks, historic and prehistoric structures, and other objects of historic or scientific interest that are situated upon the lands owned or controlled by the Government of the United States to be national monuments, and may reserve as a part thereof parcels of land, the limits of which in all cases shall be confined to the smallest area compatible with the proper care and management of the objects to be protected." 16 U.S.C. § 431. "On September 18, 1996, in the midst of his 1996 re-election campaign, President Clinton issued a Presidential Proclamation establishing the Grand Staircase-Escalante National Monument, a set-aside of approximately 1.7 million acres of land in southern Utah." Utah Ass'n of Counties v. Bush, 455 F.3d 1094, 1096 (10th Cir. 2006). Because the Antiquities Act allows the President to designate lands without congressional involvement, and then to restrict land uses within the designated area, this was seen by many in Congress, the state and local governments, and the private landowner community as an end run way of injecting enhanced conservation measures into public lands otherwise subject to the "multiple use" management mandate, but by many others as the only viable way of establishing ecosystem management regimes in those lands given Republican control of Congress. "Establishment of the Monument generated intense criticism, especially in some Congressional circles," but both legislative, administrative, and judicial attacks on the monument failed. *Id.* More generally, presidential decrees under the Antiquities Act were responsible for designation of significant protected areas within the Grand Canyon, Glacier Bay, Death Valley, and Carlsbad Caverns. For much more background on the recent use of the Antiquities Act, see Sandra Zellmer, *A Preservation Paradox: Political Prestidigitation and an Enduring Resource of Wildness*, 34 ENVTL. L. 1015 (2004); Mark Squillace, *The Monumental Legacy of the Antiquities Act of 1906*, 37 GA. L. REV. 473 (2003); Christine A. Klein, *Preserving Monumental Landscapes Under the Antiquities Act*, 87 CORNELL L. REV. 1333 (2002); James R. Rasband, *Moving Forward: The Future of the Antiquities Act*, 21 J. LAND RESOURCES & ENVTL. L. 619 (2001); Justin James Quigley, *Grand-Staircase Escalante National*

*Monument: Preservation or Politics*, 19 J. LAND, RESOURCES, & ENVT'L L. 55 (1999); Sanjay Ranchod, *The Clinton National Monuments, Protecting Ecosystems With the Antiquities Act*, 25 HARV. ENVT'L L. REV. 535 (2001).

# CHAPTER 8

# CLIMATE CHANGE

**CHAPTER OUTLINE**



---

## I. THE PROBLEM OF CLIMATE CHANGE

Climate change looms as a defining issue of the twenty-first century, pitting the potential disruption of our global climate system against the future of a fossil fuel-based economy. The possible environmental consequences are overwhelming, as are the measures that may be needed to avoid them. Yet there is substantial disagreement about the precise nature of the threats posed by climate change and the appropriate use of the law to respond to climate change. Policymakers and lawyers are the arbiters in this battle, attempting to negotiate among vastly different interests, and challenged by significant uncertainties in science and computer modeling.

### A. CLIMATE SCIENCE

Climate change refers to the response of the planet's climate system to altered concentrations of "greenhouse gases" such as carbon dioxide (CO2) in the atmosphere. These gases earn their name because, in some respects like a glass greenhouse, these gases allow sunlight to pass through the atmosphere while absorbing and re-radiating back heat from the earth's surface.

The basic mechanism of how CO2 and other greenhouse gases warm the planet (i.e. the "greenhouse effect") has been well known for decades.

Indeed, over a century ago, in 1896, the Swedish chemist Svante Arrhenius first advanced the theory that carbon dioxide emissions from combustion of coal would lead to global warming. Assuming all else is held constant (e.g., cloud cover, capacity of the oceans to absorb carbon dioxide, etc.), increases in greenhouse gases lead to "global warming"—an increase in global average temperatures—as well as other changes in the earth's climate patterns. (Climate is thus different from weather, which refers to meteorological conditions at a specific place and time). The debate regarding the science of climate change has not been over the proven warming potential of gases. If there were no greenhouse effect, the earth would be a frozen block of ice. The real debate concerns how much, at what rate, and where the planet will warm, and how such warming will affect human health and the environment.

The major man-made (or "anthropogenic") greenhouse gases include carbon dioxide (CO2), methane (CH4), nitrous oxide (NOx), and chlorofluorocarbons (CFCs). These gases account for only 3% of the earth's atmosphere, but concentrations have been steadily increasing over the last century (See figure below from the U.S. Department of Energy showing the contribution of anthropogenic emissions to total atmospheric concentrations). Not all greenhouse gases are created equally; different gases have different "global warming potentials" (GWPs). Thus, for example, the GWP of methane is 56 times that of CO2 (which has a GWP of 1.0) or, put another way, a molecule of methane is 56 times more potent in causing global warming than is CO2. The global warming potential for nitrous oxide is 280 and the global warming potential is in the thousands for the major CFC replacements (HFCs and PFCs). Thus emitting one ton of these compounds into the atmosphere has dramatically higher impacts than emitting one ton of CO2 or even methane.

Ice core samples taken from the Antarctic and Greenland ice caps show that atmospheric concentrations of anthropogenic greenhouse gases—carbon dioxide, methane, and nitrous oxide—have increased by about 30%, 145%, and 15%, respectively, in the industrial era. In short, our fossil fuel-based economy is unlocking and releasing greenhouse gases taken out of the atmosphere in prehistoric times and stored in fossil fuels such as coal, oil, and natural gas. Carbon dioxide and NOx remain in the atmosphere and contribute to the greenhouse effect for many decades to centuries. This means that we have "banked" substantial amounts of greenhouse gases already, and any reductions taken today will not reduce the overall impact for some time.

The atmosphere's resiliency in adjusting to variations from the status quo is remarkable, as only about three billion tons of the estimated total 6.5 billion to 8.5 billion metric tons of carbon emitted remains in the atmosphere every year. The additional carbon is assimilated, either through plants and the soil or through increased absorption by the oceans. Thus in addition to emissions of greenhouse gases by burning fossil fuels, many land-use and agricultural practices directly influence climate change. "Carbon sinks" refer to processes that remove a net amount of carbon from the atmosphere (e.g. through photosynthesis). Thus, carbon sinks present important opportunities for reducing the overall increase in atmospheric concentrations of greenhouse gases. The critical importance of sinks can be understood by recognizing that only 40% of the estimated man-made emissions of CO2 over the last century is showing up in the atmosphere; the remaining 60% has been absorbed either by the oceans, forests, or other sinks. See figure below showing the carbon cycle (in billion metric tons of carbon). "Carbon reservoirs" currently store carbon previously removed from the atmosphere. Carbon reservoirs are in equilibrium with the atmosphere unless disturbed, in which case they can release carbon and add to the concentrations of greenhouse gases in the atmosphere. Forests are perhaps the most well known carbon reservoirs and sinks. Mature forests tend to be carbon reservoirs. The relationship of forests to the global climate system is complex and not completely understood. Forests can act as reservoirs (storing carbon), sinks (actively sequestering carbon), or sources (emitting carbon), depending on the relative maturity of the forest as well as the human uses of the land. Over time, changes in forest cover, for example through deforestation and conversion to agriculture, have contributed significantly to the level of carbon in the atmosphere.

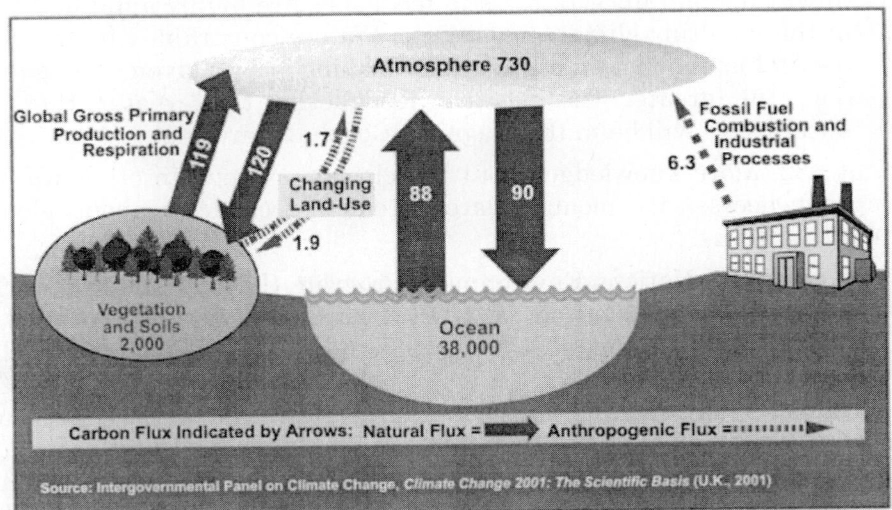


Climate change, it turns out, is not a one-variable, one-way phenomenon. Greenhouse gas emissions are not the only phenomena acting as a climate change "forcing." Dust, pollutant haze, and other aerosols in the atmosphere, for example, deflect incoming solar radiation and thus have a cooling effect. As temperatures rise, moreover, other positive and negative feedback effects are triggered that could amplify or impede further warming. Melting tundra, for example, releases more greenhouse gases, and researchers have found this effect, because of feedback properties, is far exceeding expected levels. On the other hand, increased duration and intensity of fire regimes may increase warming effects in the short-term because of carbon dioxide emissions but reduce temperatures in the long-term because of increased surface reflectivity (albedo). Even some human-induced phenomena deemed environmentally adverse in other contexts can prove helpful in the climate change context—for example, agricultural soil erosion sequesters organic carbon in stream and lake sediment—meaning feedback effects can cross policy realms with different outcomes in each. As climate change is increasingly studied, nonlinear positive and negative feedback loops like these are being uncovered, making it excruciatingly difficult to construct models of global trends over long time periods. Indeed, even as we learn more about the highly coupled, tightly interacting processes that comprise the climate, the likelihood is that we will realize with even greater clarity that it is inherently unpredictable. Consider that "the envelope of uncertainty in climate projections has not narrowed appreciably over the past 30 years, despite tremendous increases in computing power, in observations, and in the number of scientists studying the problem." Gerard H. Roe and Marcie B. Baker, *Why Is Climate Sensitivity So Unpredictable?*, 318 SCIENCE 629, 629 (2007). The emerging assessment is that things will not get better in this respect:

> [I]t is evident that the climate system is operating in a regime in which small uncertainties in feedbacks are highly amplified in the resulting climate sensitivity. We are constrained by the inevitable: the more likely a large warming is for a given forcing (i.e., the greater the positive feedbacks), the greater the uncertainty will be in the magnitude of that warming.

*Id.* at 632. More knowledge about the climate system, in other words, does not necessarily mean greater predictive capacity about global climate patterns.

The United Nations Environment Program (UNEP) and the World Meteorological Organization (WMO) created the Intergovernmental Panel on Climate Change (IPCC) in 1988. Following the example of the Ozone Trends Panel, the IPCC was assembled with over 2,000 accomplished natural and social scientists from around the globe and initially charged with assessing the scientific, technical and economic basis of climate change policy in preparation for the 1992 Earth Summit and the negotiations of the Climate Change Convention. After the Convention entered into force, the IPCC continued to provide technical reports to the Conference of the Parties and its scientific advisory body.

Although legitimate and important areas of uncertainty still exist with respect to the ultimate impacts of climate change, the range of uncertainty is narrowing over time. Perhaps most important, a global consensus now exists among the international scientific community that we are witnessing discernible impacts on our climate and natural systems due to human activities. The IPCC's Second Assessment concluded in 1995 that the observed warming trend was "unlikely to be entirely natural in origin" and that the balance of evidence suggested a "discernible human influence" on the Earth's climate. Given the conservative nature of the IPCC, this conclusion was critical for fueling the 1997 Kyoto negotiations. The IPCC compiled and released its Third Assessment in 2001, which concluded that "most of the warming observed over the last 50 years is likely to have been due to the increase in greenhouse gas concentrations" attributable to human activities. This conclusion was strengthened with the release of the Fourth Assessment in 2007, concluding that most of the warming is "very likely" due to human activities.

Despite variations in weather over the short-term, the long-term climate data suggest that the planet's average surface air temperature has increased by an estimated 1.1°F (0.6°C) since the 1970s and approximately 1.4°F (0.8°C) since 1900, with the most significant warming occurring in Alaska, Siberia, and the Antarctic Peninsula. A 2006 National Academy of Sciences report confirmed that the last few decades of the 20th century were the warmest in the past 400 years and likely over the past 1,000 years. The IPCC concluded in 2007 that "[e]leven of the last twelve years (1995–2006) rank among the twelve warmest years in the instrumental record of global surface temperature (since 1850)." In December 2009, the World Meteorological Organization reported that the year 2009 is likely to rank in the top 10 warmest on record since the beginning of instrumental climate records in 1850. Consistent with these results, recent satellite studies have found an estimated 10% loss in the extent of global snow cover since the 1960s. In 2004, the Arctic Climate Impact Assessment found that the Arctic was warming at nearly twice the rate as the rest of the planet. In 2006, Arctic winter ice reached the lowest coverage since records were first kept.

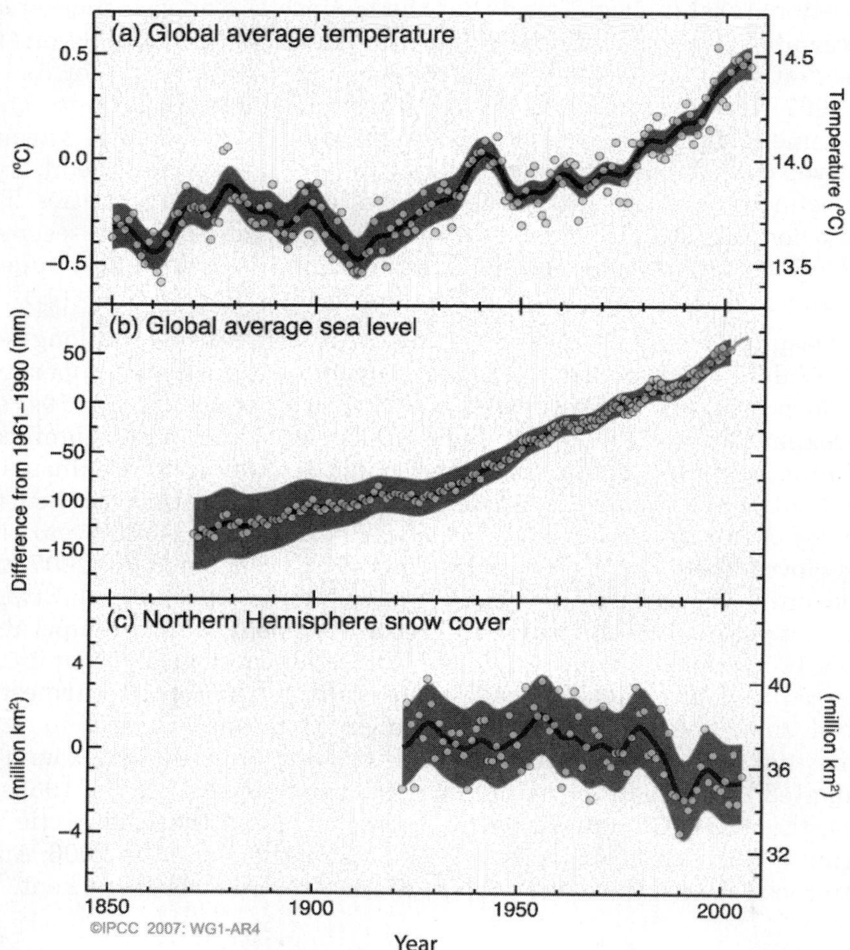


**Figure SPM.3.** *Observed changes in (a) global average surface temperature, (b) global average sea level from tide gauge (blue) and satellite (red) data and (c) Northern Hemisphere snow cover for March-April. All changes are relative to corresponding averages for the period 1961–1990. Smoothed curves represent decadal average values while circles show yearly values. The shaded areas are the uncertainty intervals estimated from a comprehensive analysis of known uncertainties (a and b) and from the time series (c). {FAQ 3.1, Figure 1, Figure 4.2, Figure 5.13}*

According to the IPCC, failure to mitigate greenhouse gases will result in a further projected increase of between 1.4° to 5.8° Celsius by the year 2100. Such a rate of warming is apparently without precedent for at least the last 10,000 years. Temperatures over land and particularly over the northern hemisphere are anticipated to increase even more than these global averages.

The greenhouse gases released from natural sources such as the respiration of animals and plants, evaporation from the oceans, and volcanoes far outweigh the emissions from anthropogenic—human—sources. But while the natural sources of greenhouse gases are relatively constant, human activities have changed in recent centuries, and even in recent decades. In 2007, the IPCC reported that "[t]he primary source of the increased atmospheric concentration of carbon dioxide since the pre-industrial period results from fossil fuel use, with land-use change providing another significant but smaller contribution."

Most greenhouse gas emissions come from industrial activity and thus, industrialized countries have been the primary contributors to the increase in atmospheric concentration of greenhouse gases over the past century. Historically, the United States has been by far the largest contributor to atmospheric levels of carbon dioxide. China passed the United States as the leading greenhouse gas emitter in 2006. National totals, however, represent only part of the picture, because they depend on both population size and the level of industrial activity. Per capita emissions allow a comparison of the average individual's contribution to emissions in each country. The United States has the highest per capita emissions among the nations that are the major sources of global emissions; the oil-rich middle eastern countries generally lead in per capita emissions. By contrast, per capita emissions in India and China were much lower. As developing countries raise their standard of living and industrial activity, however, absent changes in technology these per capita and absolute levels will surely change, dramatically increasing greenhouse gas emissions.

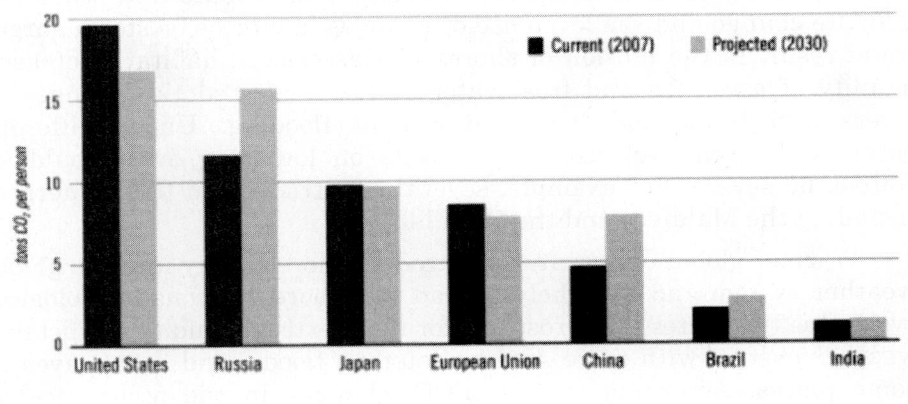


---

## B. IMPACTS OF CLIMATE CHANGE

But so what if the climate changes? So what if the planet's temperature increases? The ultimate impact, if any, of these changes on human health and the environment is the source of much of the uncertainty that has clouded policymaking with respect to climate change. The impacts from climate are expected to be significantly different across regions, with potentially dramatic environmental and social ramifications.

For starters, the impacts of climate change are already with us. Consider the following conclusion from the third IPCC Assessment in 2001.

> Examples of observed changes include shrinkage of glaciers, thawing of permafrost, later freezing and earlier break-up of ice on rivers and lakes, lengthening of mid- to high-latitude growing seasons, poleward and altitudinal shifts of plant and animal ranges, declines of some plant and animal populations, and earlier flowering of trees, emergence of insects, and egg-laying in birds.

Those effects could pale in comparison to the possible future results of climate change. The expected impacts of climate change include not only an increase in global temperature but a rise in the "energy" of storms and weather patterns, sea level rise, water availability, disease, and loss of biodiversity. The range of possible impacts is so broad and severe that many observers believe climate change to be the most significant long-term environmental problem facing the planet.

Global sea level has risen by between 10 and 20 cm over the past century, and this rise is very likely caused by this century's observed global warming. The IPCC estimates a sea-level rise of between 9 cm and 88 cm during the next century, caused in part by the melting of polar ice and in part by thermal expansion of water. Coastal systems are expected to vary widely in their response to changes in climate and sea level. Climate change and sea level rise or changes in storms or storm surges could result in the erosion of shores and associated habitat, increased salinity of estuaries and freshwater aquifers, altered tidal ranges in rivers and bays, and increased coastal flooding. Under different estimates of sea-level rise, the impacts on low-lying areas could, of course, be severe. For example, several countries could be submerged, including the Maldives and the Cook Islands.

Warmer global temperatures introduce more energy into the global weather system and are likely to lead to a more vigorous hydrological cycle; this translates into prospects for more extreme and unpredictable weather events, with more severe droughts, floods, and heat waves in some places. According to the IPCC, changes in the occurrence or geographical distribution of hurricanes and other tropical storms are possible, but still not certain. Changes in the total amount and frequency of precipitation directly affect the magnitude and timing of floods and droughts. Relatively small changes in temperature and precipitation can result in relatively large changes in runoff, especially in arid and semi-arid regions. More intense rainfall would tend to increase runoff and the risk of flooding. A warmer climate could decrease the proportion of precipitation falling as snow, leading to reductions in spring runoff and increases in winter runoff. Satellite data show an estimate 10% loss in the extent of snow cover since the 1960s, as well as a reduction of about two weeks in the annual duration of lake and river ice cover in the mid and high latitudes of the Northern hemisphere during the last century.

**Table SPM.2.** *Recent trends, assessment of human influence on the trend and projections for extreme weather events for which there is an observed late-20th century trend.* {Tables 3.7, 3.8, 9.4; Sections 3.8, 5.5, 9.7, 11.2–11.9}

| Phenomenon[a] and direction of trend | Likelihood that trend occurred in late 20th century (typically post 1960) | Likelihood of a human contribution to observed trend[b] | Likelihood of future trends based on projections for 21st century using SRES scenarios |
|---|---|---|---|
| Warmer and fewer cold days and nights over most land areas | *Very likely*[c] | *Likely*[d] | *Virtually certain*[d] |
| Warmer and more frequent hot days and nights over most land areas | *Very likely*[e] | *Likely* (nights)[d] | *Virtually certain*[d] |
| Warm spells/heat waves. Frequency increases over most land areas | *Likely* | *More likely than not*[f] | *Very likely* |
| Heavy precipitation events. Frequency (or proportion of total rainfall from heavy falls) increases over most areas | *Likely* | *More likely than not*[f] | *Very likely* |
| Area affected by droughts increases | *Likely* in many regions since 1970s | *More likely than not* | *Likely* |
| Intense tropical cyclone activity increases | *Likely* in some regions since 1970 | *More likely than not*[f] | *Likely* |
| Increased incidence of extreme high sea level (excludes tsunamis)[g] | *Likely* | *More likely than not*[f,h] | *Likely*[i] |

Table notes:
[a] See Table 3.7 for further details regarding definitions.
[b] See Table TS.4, Box TS.5 and Table 9.4.
[c] Decreased frequency of cold days and nights (coldest 10%).
[d] Warming of the most extreme days and nights each year.
[e] Increased frequency of hot days and nights (hottest 10%).
[f] Magnitude of anthropogenic contributions not assessed. Attribution for these phenomena based on expert judgement rather than formal attribution studies.
[g] Extreme high sea level depends on average sea level and on regional weather systems. It is defined here as the highest 1% of hourly values of observed sea level at a station for a given reference period.
[h] Changes in observed extreme high sea level closely follow the changes in average sea level. {5.5} It is *very likely* that anthropogenic activity contributed to a rise in average sea level. {9.5}
[i] In all scenarios, the projected global average sea level at 2100 is higher than in the reference period. {10.6} The effect of changes in regional weather systems on sea level extremes has not been assessed.

Recent trends, assessment of human influence on the trend and projections for extreme weather events for which there is an observed late-20th century trend

The increase in global temperatures may also have significant impacts on public health, particularly in developing countries. The World Health Organization has linked warmer temperatures with the spread of insect-borne diseases, such as malaria, increased illnesses and deaths from heat waves and air pollution, and increased cases of diarrhea and other water-borne diseases that are particularly dangerous in developing countries. The IPCC suggests that under most scenarios both malaria and dengue will expand their geographical and seasonal ranges. Existing studies further suggest that crop yields and changes in productivity could vary considerably across regions and among localities. Productivity is projected to increase in some areas and decrease in others, especially the tropics and subtropics. Many of the world's poorest people—particularly those living in subtropical and tropical areas and semi-arid and arid regions—may face the greatest risk of increased hunger. "More significantly," the Worldwatch Institute warns,

> Climatic disruption threatens the adequacy of the core 'building blocks' of health for large populations around the globe: sufficient food and nutrition, safe water for drinking and sanitation, fresh air to breathe, and secure homes to live in. As climate change dismantles these central elements of healthy societies, people with fewer resources will be forced to migrate in large numbers to lands where they may not be welcome. A likely result of all of these processes will be increased civic instability and strife.

Samuel S. Meyers, *Global Environmental Change: The Threat to Human Health*, WORLDWATCH REPORT 181, p. 7 (2009). Such concerns have prompted a growing understanding of climate change as a human rights issue, see Amy Sinden, *Climate Change and Human Rights*, 27 J. LAND RESOURCES & ENVTL. L. 255 (2009); Symposium, *Climate Change and Human Rights*, 18 TRANSNAT'L L. & CONTEMP. PROBS. 1 (2009); and as a national security issue, see United Nations General Assembly, Climate Change and Its Possible Security Implications: Report of the Secretary General (Sept. 11, 2009). Additionally, a proposed congressional resolution would find that "women will disproportionately face harmful impacts from climate change, particularly in poor and developing nations where women regularly assume increased responsibility for growing the family's food and collecting water, fuel, and other resources." H. Con. Res. 36, 113th Cong., 1st Sess. (2013).

Climate change could also cause quite substantial harm to biodiversity, since forests and other ecosystems will not be able to adapt to the rate of change in temperature. Indeed there is strong evidence that distributions, population sizes, population density, and behavior of wildlife already have already been affected directly by climate change. The plight of the polar bear as Arctic ice shrinks is already one of the most famous images of the possible effects of climate change. The IPCC reported in 2007 that "[t]he resilience of many ecosystems is likely to be exceeded this century by an unprecedented combination of climate change, associated disturbances (e.g. flooding, drought, wildfire, insects, ocean acidification) and other global change drivers (e.g. land use change, pollution, fragmentation of natural systems, overexploitation of resources). And this is not even considering low probability but catastrophic events such as significant slowing of the ocean circulation that transports warm water to the North Atlantic or large reductions in the Greenland and West Antarctic Ice Sheets.

Birds, for example, are already experiencing the effects of a changing climate. A 2008 Audubon Society report found:

> Analysis of four decades of Christmas Bird Count observations reveal that birds seen in North America during the first weeks of winter have moved dramatically northward—toward colder

> latitudes—over the past four decades. Significant northward movement occurred among 58% of the observed species—177 of 305. More than 60 moved in excess of 100 miles north, while the average distance moved by all studied species—including those that did not reflect the trend—was 35 miles northward. . . . There was also movement inland, from warmer coastal states into areas not long accustomed to winter temperatures suitable for their new arrivals.

Audubon, Birds and Climate Change: Ecological Disruption in Motion 3 (Feb. 2009), http://www.audubon.org/news/pressroom/bacc/pdfs/Birds_and_Climate_Report.pdf. Audubon also warns that many birds will suffer from decreased ranges as the climate continues to change:

Range Loss under three emission scenarios.

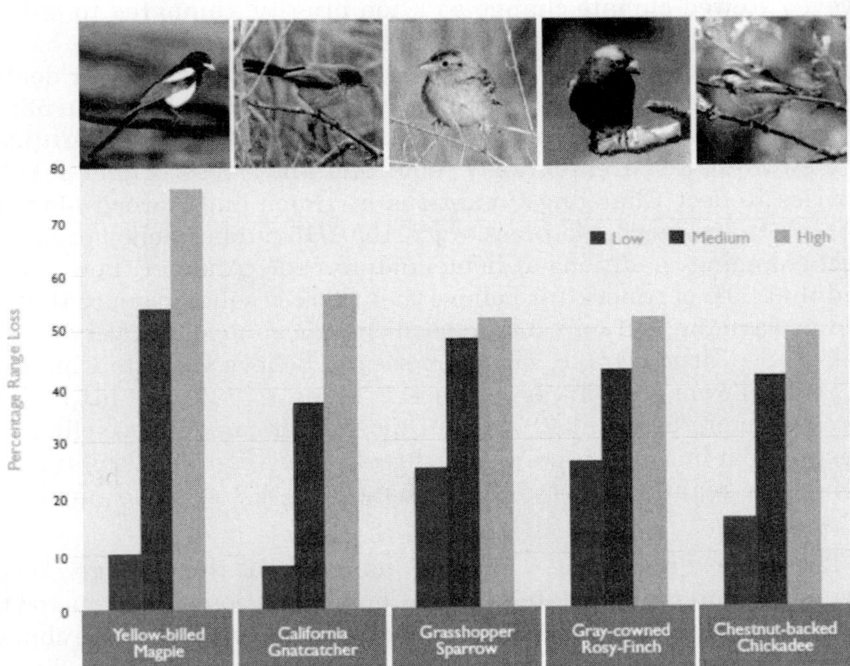


Figure 5, Source: Audubon California

These are just some of the harms that could result from a changing climate. But not every change to the climate is harmful. Residents of Buffalo or Siberia (not to equate the two!) may be delighted if their climate warmed. And an ideal climate for one purpose—say, cultivating grapes—is not an ideal climate for another purpose, such as polar bear habitat. It is thus likely "that climate change benefits will flow to substantial numbers of people and businesses and that many of the beneficiaries will perceive themselves to be climate change winners." J.B. Ruhl, *The Political Economy of Climate Change Winners*, 97 MINN. L.

REV. 206, 246 (2012). Additionally, some countries are more likely to experience the most severe harms of climate change while other countries are more likely to receive more of the benefits. Climate change, in short, can be expected to distribute its effects unevenly, which complicates the effort to respond to it.

## C. ATTITUDES TOWARD CLIMATE CHANGE

Former Vice President Al Gore testified before Congress in 2007 that climate change presents "a planetary emergency—a crisis that threatens the survival of our civilization and the habitability of the Earth." Gore and the IPCC won the 2007 Nobel Peace Prize for their efforts to combat climate change. But not everyone shares their perspective. A poll released by the Pew Research Center in January 2015 ranked climate change 22nd on a list of 23 issues of public concern. Only 28% of those surveyed viewed climate change as a top priority, compared to 86% for strengthening the economy, 71% for defending against terrorism, 57% for helping the poor, 40% for addressing moral decline, and 40% for dealing with illegal immigration. Climate change even fell far shy of the 52% of those who regarded "protecting the environment" as a top priority. *See* The Pew Research Center for People and the Press, Public's Policy Priorities Reflect Changing Conditions at Home and Abroad (Jan. 15, 2015), http://www.people-press.org/2015/01/15/publics-policy-priorities-reflect-changing-conditions-at-home-and-abroad/. Another Pew survey found that 69% of Americans believe that there is solid evidence that the world is warming, but only 33% regard climate change as a very serious problem. See Bruce Drake, Most Americans Believe Climate Change Is Real, But Fewer See It as a Threat (June 27, 2013), http://www.pewresearch.org/fact-tank/2013/06/27/most-americans-believe-climate-change-is-real-but-fewer-see-it-as-a-threat/. How can you explain such beliefs after reading about climate change science and the impacts of climate change?

The Yale Project on Climate Change and the George Mason University Center for Climate Change Communication has conducted the most sophisticated studies of American attitudes toward climate change. Their 2015 report divides the population into six groups depending on their views about climate change:

- The Alarmed (12%) are fully convinced of the reality and seriousness of climate change as a serious and urgent threat. The Alarmed are already making changes in their own lives and support an aggressive national response. They tend to be moderate to liberal Democrats who are active in their communities. They are more likely to be women, older middle-aged (55–64 years old), college educated, and upper income, and hold relatively strong egalitarian values, favoring government intervention to assure the basic needs of all people. They are less likely than other segments to use possessions as a measure of status. The Alarmed believe it is more important to protect the environment than privilege economic growth, and are the least likely to be evangelical Christians of the six segments.

- The Concerned (29%)—the largest of the six Americas—are also convinced that global warming is happening and a serious problem, but while they support a vigorous national response, they are distinctly less involved in the issue—and less likely to be taking personal action—than the Alarmed. They are very representative of the full diversity of America in terms of gender, age, incomes, education, and ethnicities—tend to be moderate Democrats who have an average rate of involvement in civic activities. They hold values and attitudes that in many ways are similar to the American norm, although they are somewhat more likely to hold moderate egalitarian values and prefer environmental protection over economic growth.
- The Cautious (26%) also believe that global warming is a problem, although they are less certain that it is happening than the Alarmed or the Concerned; they don't view it as a personal threat, and don't feel a sense of urgency to deal with it. They are evenly divided between moderate Democrats and Republicans, with relatively low levels of civic engagement, and have traditional religious beliefs. In general, their values and demographic characteristics closely track American averages.
- The Disengaged (7%) haven't thought much about the issue at all, don't know much about it, and are the most likely to say that they could easily change their minds about global warming. They tend to be moderate Democrats who are politically inactive. They hold egalitarian values, traditional religious beliefs, and are likely to prefer economic growth over environmental protection. They are more likely than average to be minority women with less education and lower incomes.
- The Doubtful (15%) are evenly split among those who think global warming is happening, those who think it isn't, and those who don't know. Many within this group believe that if global warming is happening, it is caused by natural changes in the environment, believe global warming won't harm people for many decades into the future, if at all, and say that America is already doing enough to respond to the threat. The Doubtful are more likely than average to be male, older, better educated, higher income, and white—tend to be Republicans with an average rate of involvement

in civic activities. They hold strongly individualistic values, are more likely than average to say they are "born again" or evangelical Christians, and are very likely to prefer economic growth over environmental protection.

- The Dismissive (11%) like the Alarmed, are actively engaged in the issue, but on the opposite end of the spectrum; the majority believe that warming is not happening, is not a threat to either people or non-human nature, and strongly believe it is not a problem that warrants a national response. are more likely than average to be high income, well-educated, white men. They are much more likely to be very conservative Republicans. The Dismissive are civically active, hold strongly traditional religious beliefs, and are the segment most likely to be evangelical Christian. They strongly endorse individualistic values, opposing any form of government intervention, antiegalitarian, and almost universally prefer economic growth over environmental protection.

See Yale Project on Climate Change and the George Mason University Center for Climate Change Communication, Global Warming's Six Americas, http://climatecommunication.yale.edu/about/projects/global-warmings-six-americas/. The "Six Americas" study shows that while opinions about climate change are polarized to some extent, there is actually a continuum of beliefs between the two opposite polls. The study, for example, noted the prevalence of evangelical Christians in some groups more than others, but evangelicals themselves are deeply divided about climate change and how to respond to it. *See* John Copeland Nagle, *The Evangelical Debate Over Climate Change,* 5 U. ST. THOMAS L. J. 53 (2008). Similarly, political party affiliation, geographic location, income, and other factors offer only partial explanations for the diverse beliefs regarding climate change. Why?

And what should we do about it? As we will see, efforts to respond aggressive to climate change have stalled both in the United States and worldwide. One response is to try to improve the communication of the scientific consensus that climate change is real and a real threat. *See, e.g.,* Center for Research and Environmental Decisions, The Psychology of Climate Change Communication: A Guide for Scientists, Journalists, Educators, Political Aides, and the Interested Public (2009). Al Gore agrees that "[i]t's increasingly clear that part of the challenge that we face in solving the climate change crisis stems from the way we think about it, both individually and collectively." AL GORE, OUR CHOICE: A PLAN TO SOLVE THE CLIMATE CRISIS 300 (2009). Is better education the solution to the inability to adopt the kinds of responses to climate change endorsed by Al Gore and others? What other actions are appropriate?

## II. RESPONDING TO CLIMATE CHANGE

There are two ways of responding to climate change. We can either try to prevent it from happening, or we can try to avoid the harms that it could cause. The first approach is known as *mitigation*, which refers to options for limiting climate change by reducing the emission of greenhouse gases, storing them underground (or even outer space), or removing greenhouse gases that are already in the atmosphere. So far, most efforts have concentrated on regulating the activities that release greenhouse gases. That task is complicated by the fact that a vast number of activities release gases from a vast number of sources. Rather than trying to promulgate rules that would regulate all of those sources, market-based mechanisms such as a cap-and-trade system have become the favorite way of seeking to reduce greenhouse gas emissions. Cap-and-trade approaches have been employed in the United States since Congress added the acid rain program to the CAA in 1990 (see Chapter 3). But former Alaska governor and vice presidential candidate Sarah Palin describes a cap-and-trade approach as "an environmentalist Ponzi scheme in which only the government benefits." SARAH PALIN, GOING ROGUE: AN AMERICAN LIFE 391 (2009). How would you answer her?

One alternative to a cap-and-trade system is a carbon tax. The idea of such a tax is that the demand for fossil fuels and other sources of carbon will be reduced if people have to pay more for them once they are taxed. Al Gore has "long advocated . . . a $CO_2$ tax that is offset by equal reductions in other tax burdens . . . as the simplest, most direct, and most efficient way of enlisting the market as an ally in saving the ecosystem of the planet." AL GORE, OUR CHOICE: A PLAN TO SOLVE THE CLIMATE CRISIS 343 (2009). But Gore laments that "one of the first casualties of the ascendance of market fundamentalism in the United States was in its success in creating massive opposition in the Congress to any new taxation—even taxation offset by reductions in other tax areas." *Id.* Is Gore right about the desirability of a carbon tax? Is he right about the obstacles to it?

Another alternative method of mitigating climate change is to encourage the development of new technologies that do not emit greenhouse gases. Wind power, solar energy, nuclear power, hydroelectric dams and other sources of renewable energy do not release many greenhouse gases, so climate change could be mitigated if we moved to such sources of energy instead of relying upon coal, oil, and other fossil fuels. Toward that end, Ted Nordhaus and Michael Shellenberger advocate a massive governmental investment in new energy technologies that would eliminate the need for generating energy by burning fossil fuels. They argue that such investment will drive down the costs of alternative energy sources and have a much greater likelihood of success than trying to regulate, tax, or otherwise raise the price of carbon. *See* TED NORDHAUS & MICHAEL SHELLENBERGER, BREAK THROUGH: FROM THE DEATH OF ENVIRONMENTALISM TO THE POLITICS OF

POSSIBILITY 111 (2007); Michael Shellenberger et al., *Fast, Clean, & Cheap: Cutting Global Warming's Gordian Knot*, 2 HARV. L. & POL'Y REV. 93, 94, 104–12 (2008); Ted Nordhaus & Michael Shellenberger, *Getting Real on Climate Change: We'll Never Succeed in Making Dirty Energy Too Expensive. Let's Make Clean Energy Cheap*, AM. PROSPECT, Dec. 2008, at 32, 33–35. Similarly, Congressman Jay Inslee has called for a commitment to public investment in renewable energy that matched the Apollo space program of the 1960s. *See* JAY INSLEE & BRACKEN HENDRICKS, APOLLO'S FIRE: IGNITING AMERICA'S CLEAN-ENERGY ECONOMY (2008). What are the advantages of such an approach? Is spending lots of government fund more likely to gain the popular support necessary to be enacted by Congress? Is spending on new technologies a substitute or a complement for a cap-and-trade or carbon tax system?

Carbon capture and sequestration (CCS) is another way of mitigating climate change. CCS is a promising technology that could enable the continued use of inexpensive fossil fuels while dramatically reducing accompanying greenhouse gas emissions. This technology drastically reduces emissions from power plants and industrial sources by capturing $CO_2$ emissions and injecting them into deep geologic formations, essentially sequestering them underground for long periods of time. Areas for potential $CO_2$ sequestration include oil and gas fields, saline aquifers, and deep coal seams. Natural geologic analogs, like geologic formations containing crude oil, natural gas, brine, and $CO_2$, have proven storage capabilities that will last for millions of years. CCS technologies would attempt to take advantage of these storage capacities to reduce $CO_2$ emissions into the atmosphere.

CCS, of course, is not free of risk. For CCS to have a real impact on climate change, projects must sequester millions of tons of $CO_2$ per year at each individual storage site, with injected $CO_2$ potentially spreading over tens of square miles for a single project and subsurface pressure effects felt over even greater distances. Moreover, the injected $CO_2$ should remain in the subsurface for hundreds to thousands of years for significant climate benefit, effectively using the subsurface property in perpetuity. Injected $CO_2$ will initially be more buoyant than the formation waters into which it is injected, making the possibility of leakage to the near surface or the surface a risk that must be managed through site selection, operation, monitoring, and remediation.

CCS thus presents both opportunities and challenges. The legal issues include possible tort liability for escaped $CO_2$, see Alexandra B. Klass and Elizabeth J. Wilson, *Climate Change and Carbon Sequestration: Assessing a Liability Regime for Long-Term Storage of Carbon Dioxide,* 58 EMORY L.J. 103 (2008), and the need to secure the necessary subsurface property rights, see Elizabeth J. Wilson & Alexandra B. Klass, *Climate Change, Carbon Sequestration, and Property Rights,* 2010 U. ILL. L. REV. 363 (2010). Those issues are quite modest, though, compared to the schemes that other scientists have suggested for disposing of $CO_2$. See, e.g., *A Stairway To Heaven?; Global Warming,* THE ECONOMIST, June 2, 2007 (describing a proposal to expel $CO_2$ into outer space).

Besides mitigation, *adaptation* is the second response to climate change. Adaptation refers to changes made to better respond to present or future climatic and other environmental conditions, thereby reducing harm or taking advantage of opportunity. Most of the efforts in recent years have emphasized mitigation, but adaptation is playing an increasing role as mitigation efforts have stalled and as some climate change is seen as inevitable even if mitigation efforts are to succeed. Regardless of the success of mitigation efforts, we are looking into a future of climate change that will last a century or more, and we've done very little in the United States to prepare ourselves for it. Yet adapt we must.

Indeed, the policy world's fixation on achieving, or blocking, federal greenhouse gas emission legislation as part of our national strategy for climate change mitigation has contributed to our neglect of national policy for climate change adaptation. This wrong turn happened early in the development of domestic climate change policy. As Professor Dan Tarlock observed in 1992, at the time there was "a growing split between environmentalists who advocate mitigation, and 'rational' resource policy analysts who have strongly endorsed adaptation." A. Dan Tarlock, *Now, Again Think About Climate Change,* 9 ARIZ. J. INT'L & COMP. L. 169, 169 (1992). Adaptation was winning the day, on the premise that "we should adopt the easy, low cost mitigation strategies to reduce energy use and then concentrate on selecting the most efficient adaptation strategies." *Id.* Tarlock insightfully suggested three reasons for exercising caution in pursuing that approach:

> First, adaptation is based on the ideology of scientific progress, a faith that is open to question. The principle message of environmentalism is that the tenets of Enlightenment thinking must be re-evaluated since science and technology may not always prevent serious harm or make things better. Second, the degree of friction in the proposed institutional responses is often underestimated so institutions may not perform as expected. Adaptation clearly exposes winners and losers in a reallocation. It is not reasonable to expect losers to accept all losses. More generally, institutional inflexibility is increasingly being adopted as a means to protect legitimate interests excluded from dominant resource allocation regimes. . . . Third, many institutions have no fair and adequate mechanism to deal with global warming. In these cases, adaptation is the adoption of a no action strategy, which may often be the most costly one.

*Id.* at 169–70.

As news about climate change grew steadily worse in the years after Tarlock's assessment, the domestic policy pendulum quickly swung sharply in mitigation's direction. Indeed, the challenge of climate change was portrayed as so exceptional, and the need for a new mitigation policy of sweeping dimensions thus so pressing, that talk of adaptation became taboo for fear it might knock the mitigation train off its tracks and lead to complacency. In their impressive book on the topic, ADAPTATION TO CLIMATE CHANGE, E. Lisa F. Schipper and Ian Burton sum up the tension that existed through the 1990s and well into the following decade:

> Interest in adaptation was overwhelmed by concern about the need to reduce greenhouse gas emissions and stabilize atmospheric greenhouse gas concentrations. Proponents of adaptation faced two obstacles that were attributed to adaptation: reducing the apparent need for mitigation; and playing down the urgency for action. For one, "adaptationists" were distrusted because their proposals seemed to undermine the need for mitigation. Critics felt that belief in the potential value of adaptation would soften the resolve of governments to grasp the nettle of mitigation and thus play into the hands of the fossil fuels interests and the climate change sceptics. In addition, because climate change was popularly perceived as a gradual process, adaptation was not considered urgent as there would be time to adapt when climate change and its impacts became manifest. These views dominated in the mid and late 1990s.

The problem is that mitigation policy soon ran into the same three problems Tarlock suggested would plague adaptation policy: institutions lack the political will to impose tough lifestyle sacrifices on people in general; those who expect to be losers were a mitigation regime to gear up have squawked loudly in objection to the anticipated regulatory measures; and no fair and adequate mechanism has been devised to deal with the distributional effects of a comprehensive regulatory regime even if the political will were there to put one in place. So, as with adaptation, mitigation is often portrayed as a scientific and technological challenge that eases us out of the climate change problem without sacrifices or losers—pump greenhouse gases into the ground; invent a cheap solar panel; launch mirrors into space; seed the oceans with iron.

Today it is abundantly clear that these drags on the formulation of our domestic climate change policy are persistent and debilitating. A comprehensive national strategy that successfully reduces greenhouse gas emissions to levels thought to be adequate to arrest climate change, a feat which the United States obviously could not accomplish alone even if it were known what those levels should be, quite clearly is not around the political corner. And it is just as clear that the miracle technological breakthrough is not past the research stage. Add to that the unavoidable reality of so-called committed warming—the climate change already built into the climate system as a result of past greenhouse gas emissions—which will play out for many decades even if one of these breakthroughs happened yesterday, and the cold war between mitigation and adaptation is finally thawing. Climate change is already happening, and more is yet to come no matter what, thus a consensus is building that mitigation needs adaptation, and vice versa, even if they fundamentally are different and sometimes competing policy thrusts.

It is not, in other words, an either-or choice between mitigation and adaptation. The time when such a choice could have been made—when starting to install a meaningful mitigation regime could have obviated the need ever to have to think about adaptation—is long since past by many decades. There certainly is room for argument over the relative mix of the two strategies and how much to spend respectively on them, questions I do not address here. But almost all recent legal scholarship and policy dialogue now recognizes that formulating and implementing adaptation strategies must in any case be a significant component of our domestic climate change law and policy.

The United States has struggled to identify the appropriate response to climate change. The initial congressional statement regarding climate change was a 97–0 vote in favor of a 1997 Senate resolution advising the Clinton Administration not to agree to an international climate change agreement that failed to limit the emissions from developing countries (think China) or that "would result in serious harm to the economy of the United States." S. Res. 98, 105th Cong., 1st Sess. § 1 (1997). Seeking to fill what they regard as a void in leadership on this issue, dozens of states, hundreds of local governments, environmental groups, and corporations stepped in with a range of innovative actions. Additionally, numerous organizations sought to rely upon existing federal laws to force the federal government to regulate greenhouse gas emissions.

The election of President Obama brought about significant changes in U.S. climate change policy as EPA and other federal agencies have demonstrated a greater willingness to impose governmental regulation designed to mitigate climate change. In June 2009, the U.S. House of Representatives approved H.R. 2454, the American Clean Energy and Security Act (ACES), by a vote of 219 to 212. ACES contained five key provisions that would

- Require electric utilities to meet 20% of their electricity demand through renewable energy sources and energy efficiency by 2020.
- Invest in new clean energy technologies and energy efficiency, including energy efficiency and renewable energy ($90 billion in new investments by 2025), carbon capture and sequestration ($60 billion), electric and other advanced technology vehicles ($20 billion), and basic scientific research and development ($20 billion).
- Establish new energy-saving standards for new buildings and appliances.

- Reduce carbon emissions from major U.S. sources by 17% by 2020 and over 80% by 2050 compared to 2005 levels. Complementary measures in the legislation, such as investments in preventing tropical deforestation, will achieve significant additional reductions in carbon emissions.
- Protect consumers from energy price increases. According to estimates from the Environmental Protection Agency, the reductions in carbon pollution required by the legislation will cost American families less than a postage stamp per day. The Congressional Budget Office (CBO) calculates that the legislation will cost the average household less than 50 cents per day.

But the Senate declined to pass the House bill or its own version of climate change legislation, and the ensuing 2010 midterm elections doomed further consideration of such proposals. It is widely assumed that Congress will not enact substantial climate change election within the foreseeable future.

The absence of federal climate change legislation has prompted reliance on existing federal laws, new state and local climate change laws, and international efforts to address climate change. President Obama relied on each approach in the climate action plan that he announced in June 2013. *See* Executive Office of the President, The President's Climate Action Plan 6 (June 2013). That plan "has three key pillars:

> 1) Cut Carbon Pollution in America: In 2012, U.S. carbon emissions fell to the lowest level in two decades even as the economy continued to grow. To build on this progress, the Obama Administration is putting in place tough new rules to cut carbon pollution—just like we have for other toxins like mercury and arsenic—so we protect the health of our children and move our economy toward American-made clean energy sources that will create good jobs and lower home energy bills.
>
> 2) Prepare the United States for the Impacts of Climate Change: Even as we take new steps to reduce carbon pollution, we must also prepare for the impacts of a changing climate that are already being felt across the country. Moving forward, the Obama Administration will help state and local governments strengthen our roads, bridges, and shorelines so we can better protect people's homes, businesses and way of life from severe weather.
>
> 3) Lead International Efforts to Combat Global Climate Change and Prepare for its Impacts: Just as no country is immune from the impacts of climate change, no country can meet this challenge alone. That is why it is imperative for the

> United States to couple action at home with leadership internationally. America must help forge a truly global solution to this global challenge by galvanizing international action to significantly reduce emissions (particularly among the major emitting countries), prepare for climate impacts, and drive progress through the international negotiations."

*Id.* at 5.

## A. THE CLEAN AIR ACT

The CAA may like seem the most obvious law to address climate change. The emission of greenhouse gases is responsible for much of the concern about climate change, and since the CAA is designed to control emissions into the air, it would seem to be well suited to the task. It took nearly a decade, though, for the Supreme Court to confirm that the CAA applies to the problem of climate change in a case that quickly became the most famous in the history of American environmental law. Even that case did not resolve the question, and EPA, concerned groups, and potentially regulated parties continue to struggle with the ways in which the CAA regulates greenhouse gas emissions.

### Massachusetts v. Environmental Protection Agency

Supreme Court of the United States, 2007.
549 U.S. 497.

■ JUSTICE STEVENS delivered the opinion of the Court.

A well-documented rise in global temperatures has coincided with a significant increase in the concentration of carbon dioxide in the atmosphere. Respected scientists believe the two trends are related. For when carbon dioxide is released into the atmosphere, it acts like the ceiling of a greenhouse, trapping solar energy and retarding the escape of reflected heat. It is therefore a species—the most important species—of a "greenhouse gas."

Calling global warming "the most pressing environmental challenge of our time," a group of States,[2] local governments,[3] and private organizations, alleged in a petition for certiorari that the Environmental Protection Agency (EPA) has abdicated its responsibility under the Clean Air Act to regulate the emissions of four greenhouse gases, including carbon dioxide. Specifically, petitioners asked us to answer two questions concerning the meaning of § 202(a)(1) of the Act: whether EPA has the statutory authority to regulate greenhouse gas emissions from new motor vehicles; and if so, whether its stated reasons for refusing to do so are consistent with the statute.

---

2 California, Connecticut, Illinois, Maine, Massachusetts, New Jersey, New Mexico, New York, Oregon, Rhode Island, Vermont, and Washington.

3 District of Columbia, American Samoa, New York City, and Baltimore.

In response, EPA, supported by 10 intervening States[5] and six trade associations, correctly argued that we may not address those two questions unless at least one petitioner has standing to invoke our jurisdiction under Article III of the Constitution. Notwithstanding the serious character of that jurisdictional argument and the absence of any conflicting decisions construing § 202(a)(1), the unusual importance of the underlying issue persuaded us to grant the writ.

I

Section 202(a)(1) of the Clean Air Act . . . provides:

> "The [EPA] Administrator shall by regulation prescribe (and from time to time revise) in accordance with the provisions of this section, standards applicable to the emission of any air pollutant from any class or classes of new motor vehicles or new motor vehicle engines, which in his judgment cause, or contribute to, air pollution which may reasonably be anticipated to endanger public health or welfare. . . ."

The Act defines "air pollutant" to include "any air pollution agent or combination of such agents, including any physical, chemical, biological, radioactive . . . substance or matter which is emitted into or otherwise enters the ambient air." § 7602(g). "Welfare" is also defined broadly: among other things, it includes "effects on . . . weather . . . and climate." § 7602(h).

When Congress enacted these provisions, the study of climate change was in its infancy. In 1959, shortly after the U. S. Weather Bureau began monitoring atmospheric carbon dioxide levels, an observatory in Mauna Loa, Hawaii, recorded a mean level of 316 parts per million. This was well above the highest carbon dioxide concentration—no more than 300 parts per million—revealed in the 420,000-year-old ice-core record. By the time Congress drafted § 202(a)(1) in 1970, carbon dioxide levels had reached 325 parts per million.

In the late 1970's, the Federal Government began devoting serious attention to the possibility that carbon dioxide emissions associated with human activity could provoke climate change. In 1978, Congress enacted the National Climate Program Act, 92 Stat. 601, which required the President to establish a program to "assist the Nation and the world to understand and respond to natural and man-induced climate processes and their implications," *id.*, § 3. President Carter, in turn, asked the National Research Council, the working arm of the National Academy of Sciences, to investigate the subject. The Council's response was unequivocal: "If carbon dioxide continues to increase, the study group finds no reason to doubt that climate changes will result and no reason to believe that these changes will be negligible. . . . A wait-and-see policy may mean waiting until it is too late."

---

[5] Alaska, Idaho, Kansas, Michigan, Nebraska, North Dakota, Ohio, South Dakota, Texas, and Utah.

Congress next addressed the issue in 1987, when it enacted the Global Climate Protection Act, Title XI of Pub. L. 100–204, 101 Stat. 1407, note following 15 U.S.C. § 2901. Finding that "manmade pollution—the release of carbon dioxide, chlorofluorocarbons, methane, and other trace gases into the atmosphere—may be producing a long-term and substantial increase in the average temperature on Earth," § 1102(1), 101 Stat. 1408, Congress directed EPA to propose to Congress a "coordinated national policy on global climate change," § 1103(b), and ordered the Secretary of State to work "through the channels of multilateral diplomacy" and coordinate diplomatic efforts to combat global warming, § 1103(c). Congress emphasized that "ongoing pollution and deforestation may be contributing now to an irreversible process" and that "[n]ecessary actions must be identified and implemented in time to protect the climate." § 1102(4).

. . . The first President Bush attended and signed the United Nations Framework Convention on Climate Change (UNFCCC), a nonbinding agreement among 154 nations to reduce atmospheric concentrations of carbon dioxide and other greenhouse gases for the purpose of "prevent[ing] dangerous anthropogenic [*i.e.*, human-induced] interference with the [Earth's] climate system." S. Treaty Doc. No. 102–38, Art. 2, p 5 (1992). The Senate unanimously ratified the treaty.

Some five years . . . the UNFCCC signatories met in Kyoto, Japan, and adopted a protocol that assigned mandatory targets for industrialized nations to reduce greenhouse gas emissions. Because those targets did not apply to developing and heavily polluting nations such as China and India, the Senate unanimously passed a resolution expressing its sense that the United States should not enter into the Kyoto Protocol. See S. Res. 98, 105th Cong., 1st Sess. (July 25, 1997) (as passed). President Clinton did not submit the protocol to the Senate for ratification.

II

On October 20, 1999, a group of 19 private organizations filed a rulemaking petition asking EPA to regulate "greenhouse gas emissions from new motor vehicles under § 202 of the Clean Air Act." . . . In 1998, Jonathan Z. Cannon, then EPA's General Counsel, prepared a legal opinion concluding that "$CO_2$ emissions are within the scope of EPA's authority to regulate," even as he recognized that EPA had so far declined to exercise that authority. Cannon's successor, Gary S. Guzy, reiterated that opinion before a congressional committee just two weeks before the rulemaking petition was filed.

Fifteen months after the petition's submission, EPA requested public comment on "all the issues raised in [the] petition," adding a "particular" request for comments on "any scientific, technical, legal, economic or other aspect of these issues that may be relevant to EPA's consideration of this petition." 66 Fed. Reg. 7486, 7487 (2001). EPA received more than 50,000 comments over the next five months. See 68 Fed. Reg. 52924 (2003). . . .

On September 8, 2003, EPA entered an order denying the rulemaking petition. 68 Fed. Reg. 52922. The agency gave two reasons for its decision: (1) that contrary to the opinions of its former general counsels, the Clean Air Act does not authorize EPA to issue mandatory regulations to address global climate change, see id., at 52925–52929; and (2) that even if the agency had the authority to set greenhouse gas emission standards, it would be unwise to do so at this time, id., at 52929–52931. . . .

### III

Petitioners, now joined by intervenor States and local governments, sought review of EPA's order in the United States Court of Appeals for the District of Columbia Circuit. Although each of the three judges on the panel wrote a separate opinion, two judges agreed "that the EPA Administrator properly exercised his discretion under § 202(a)(1) in denying the petition for rule making." 367 U.S. App. D.C. 282, 415 F.3d 50, 58 (2005). The court therefore denied the petition for review. . . .

### IV

EPA maintains that because greenhouse gas emissions inflict widespread harm, the doctrine of standing presents an insuperable jurisdictional obstacle. We do not agree. At bottom, "the gist of the question of standing" is whether petitioners have "such a personal stake in the outcome of the controversy as to assure that concrete adverseness which sharpens the presentation of issues upon which the court so largely depends for illumination." Baker v. Carr, 369 U.S. 186, 204 (1962). . . . To ensure the proper adversarial presentation, Lujan [v. Defenders of Wildlife, 504 U.S. 555, 560–61 (1992)] holds that a litigant must demonstrate that it has suffered a concrete and particularized injury that is either actual or imminent, that the injury is fairly traceable to the defendant, and that it is likely that a favorable decision will redress that injury. However, a litigant to whom Congress has "accorded a procedural right to protect his concrete interests," *id.*, at 572, n. 7—here, the right to challenge agency action unlawfully withheld, § 7607(b)(1)—"can assert that right without meeting all the normal standards for redressability and immediacy," *ibid.* When a litigant is vested with a procedural right, that litigant has standing if there is some possibility that the requested relief will prompt the injury-causing party to reconsider the decision that allegedly harmed the litigant. . . .

Well before the creation of the modern administrative state, we recognized that States are not normal litigants for the purposes of invoking federal jurisdiction. As Justice Holmes explained in Georgia v. Tennessee Copper Co., 206 U.S. 230, 237 (1907), a case in which Georgia sought to protect its citizens from air pollution originating outside its borders:

"The case has been argued largely as if it were one between two private parties; but it is not. The very elements that would be relied upon in a suit between fellow-citizens as a ground for equitable relief are wanting here. The State owns very little of the territory alleged to be affected, and the damage to it capable of estimate in money, possibly, at least, is small. This is a suit by a State for an injury to it in its capacity of quasi-sovereign. In that capacity the State has an interest independent of and behind the titles of its citizens, in all the earth and air within its domain. It has the last word as to whether its mountains shall be stripped of their forests and its inhabitants shall breathe pure air."

Just as Georgia's "independent interest . . . in all the earth and air within its domain" supported federal jurisdiction a century ago, so too does Massachusetts' well-founded desire to preserve its sovereign territory today. That Massachusetts does in fact own a great deal of the "territory alleged to be affected" only reinforces the conclusion that its stake in the outcome of this case is sufficiently concrete to warrant the exercise of federal judicial power.

When a State enters the Union, it surrenders certain sovereign prerogatives. Massachusetts cannot invade Rhode Island to force reductions in greenhouse gas emissions, it cannot negotiate an emissions treaty with China or India, and in some circumstances the exercise of its police powers to reduce in-state motor-vehicle emissions might well be pre-empted.

These sovereign prerogatives are now lodged in the Federal Government, and Congress has ordered EPA to protect Massachusetts (among others) by prescribing standards applicable to the "emission of any air pollutant from any class or classes of new motor vehicle engines, which in [the Administrator's] judgment cause, or contribute to, air pollution which may reasonably be anticipated to endanger public health or welfare." 42 U.S.C. § 7521(a)(1). Congress has moreover recognized a concomitant procedural right to challenge the rejection of its rulemaking petition as arbitrary and capricious. § 7607(b)(1). Given that procedural right and Massachusetts' stake in protecting its quasi-sovereign interests, the Commonwealth is entitled to special solicitude in our standing analysis. . . .

*The Injury*

The harms associated with climate change are serious and well recognized. . . . That these climate-change risks are "widely shared" does not minimize Massachusetts' interest in the outcome of this litigation. According to petitioners' unchallenged affidavits, global sea levels rose somewhere between 10 and 20 centimeters over the 20th century as a result of global warming. These rising seas have already begun to swallow Massachusetts' coastal land. Because the Commonwealth "owns a substantial portion of the state's coastal property," it has alleged a particularized injury in its capacity as a landowner. The severity of that injury will only increase over the course of the next century: If sea levels continue to rise as predicted, one Massachusetts official believes that a significant fraction of coastal property will be "either permanently lost through inundation or temporarily lost through periodic storm surge and flooding events." Remediation costs alone, petitioners allege, could run well into the hundreds of millions of dollars.

*Causation*

EPA does not dispute the existence of a causal connection between man-made greenhouse gas emissions and global warming. At a minimum, therefore, EPA's refusal to regulate such emissions "contributes" to Massachusetts' injuries.

EPA nevertheless maintains that its decision not to regulate greenhouse gas emissions from new motor vehicles contributes so insignificantly to petitioners' injuries that the agency cannot be haled into federal court to answer for them. For the same reason, EPA does not believe that any realistic possibility exists that the relief petitioners seek would mitigate global climate change and remedy their injuries. That is especially so because predicted increases in greenhouse gas emissions from developing nations, particularly China and India, are likely to offset any marginal domestic decrease.

But EPA overstates its case. Its argument rests on the erroneous assumption that a small incremental step, because it is incremental, can never be attacked in a federal judicial forum. Yet accepting that premise would doom most challenges to regulatory action. Agencies, like legislatures, do not generally resolve massive problems in one fell regulatory swoop. They instead whittle away at them over time, refining their preferred approach as circumstances change and as they develop a more-nuanced understanding of how best to proceed. That a first step might be tentative does not by itself support the notion that federal courts lack jurisdiction to determine whether that step conforms to law.

And reducing domestic automobile emissions is hardly a tentative step. Even leaving aside the other greenhouse gases, the United States transportation sector emits an enormous quantity of carbon dioxide into the atmosphere—according to the MacCracken affidavit, more than 1.7 billion metric tons in 1999 alone. That accounts for more than 6% of worldwide carbon dioxide emissions. To put this in perspective: Considering just emissions from the transportation sector, which represent less than one-third of this country's total carbon dioxide emissions, the United States would still rank as the third-largest emitter of carbon dioxide in the world, outpaced only by the European Union and China. Judged by any standard, U. S. motor-vehicle emissions make a meaningful contribution to greenhouse gas concentrations and hence, according to petitioners, to global warming.

*The Remedy*

While it may be true that regulating motor-vehicle emissions will not by itself reverse global warming, it by no means follows that we lack jurisdiction to decide whether EPA has a duty to take steps to slow or reduce it. Because of the enormity of the potential consequences associated with man-made climate change, the fact that the effectiveness of a remedy might be delayed during the (relatively short) time it takes for a new motor-vehicle fleet to replace an older one is essentially irrelevant. Nor is it dispositive that developing countries such as China and India are poised to increase greenhouse gas emissions substantially over the next century: A reduction in domestic emissions would slow the pace of global emissions increases, no matter what happens elsewhere. . . .

In sum—at least according to petitioners' uncontested affidavits—the rise in sea levels associated with global warming has already harmed and will continue to harm Massachusetts. The risk of catastrophic harm, though remote, is nevertheless real. That risk would be reduced to some extent if petitioners received the relief they seek. We therefore hold that petitioners have standing to challenge EPA's denial of their rulemaking petition.[24]

## V

The scope of our review of the merits of the statutory issues is narrow. As we have repeated time and again, an agency has broad discretion to choose how best to marshal its limited resources and personnel to carry out its delegated responsibilities. . . .

EPA concluded in its denial of the petition for rulemaking that it lacked authority under 42 U.S.C. § 7521(a)(1) to regulate new vehicle emissions because carbon dioxide is not an "air pollutant" as that term is defined in § 7602. In the alternative, it concluded that even if it possessed authority, it would decline to do so because regulation would conflict with other administration priorities. As discussed earlier, the Clean Air Act expressly permits review of such an action. § 7607(b)(1). We therefore "may reverse any such action found to be . . . arbitrary, capricious, an abuse of discretion, or otherwise not in accordance with law." § 7607(d)(9).

## VI

On the merits, the first question is whether § 202(a)(1) of the Clean Air Act authorizes EPA to regulate greenhouse gas emissions from new motor vehicles in the event that it forms a "judgment" that such emissions contribute to climate change. We have little trouble concluding that it does. In relevant part, § 202(a)(1) provides that EPA "shall by regulation prescribe . . . standards applicable to the emission of any air pollutant from any class or classes of new motor vehicles or new motor vehicle engines, which in [the Administrator's] judgment cause, or contribute to, air pollution which may reasonably be anticipated to endanger public health or welfare." 42 U.S.C. § 7521(a)(1). Because EPA believes that Congress did not intend it to regulate substances that contribute to climate change, the agency maintains that carbon dioxide is not an "air pollutant" within the meaning of the provision.

The statutory text forecloses EPA's reading. The Clean Air Act's sweeping definition of "air pollutant" includes "any air pollution agent or combination of such agents, including any physical, chemical . . . substance or matter which is emitted into or otherwise enters the ambient air. . . ." § 7602(g) (emphasis added). On its face, the definition embraces all airborne compounds of whatever stripe, and underscores that intent through the repeated use of the word "any." Carbon dioxide, methane, nitrous oxide, and hydrofluorocarbons are without a doubt "physical [and] chemical . . . substance[s] which [are] emitted into . . . the ambient air." The statute is unambiguous.

Rather than relying on statutory text, EPA invokes postenactment congressional actions and deliberations it views as tantamount to a congressional command to refrain from regulating greenhouse gas emissions. Even if such postenactment legislative history could shed light on the meaning of an otherwise-unambiguous statute, EPA never identifies any action remotely suggesting that Congress meant to curtail its power to treat greenhouse gases as air pollutants. That subsequent Congresses have eschewed enacting binding emissions limitations to combat global warming tells us nothing about what Congress meant when it amended § 202(a)(1) in 1970 and 1977. And unlike EPA, we have no difficulty reconciling Congress' various efforts to promote interagency collaboration and research to better understand climate change with the agency's pre-existing mandate to regulate "any air pollutant" that may endanger the public welfare. See 42 U.S.C. § 7601(a)(1). Collaboration and research do not conflict with any thoughtful regulatory effort; they complement it. . . .

VII

The alternative basis for EPA's decision—that even if it does have statutory authority to regulate greenhouse gases, it would be unwise to do so at this time—rests on reasoning divorced from the statutory text. While the statute does condition the exercise of EPA's authority on its formation of a "judgment," 42 U.S.C. § 7521(a)(1), that judgment must relate to whether an air pollutant "cause[s], or contribute[s] to, air pollution which may reasonably be anticipated to endanger public health or welfare," ibid. Put another way, the use of the word "judgment" is not a roving license to ignore the statutory text. It is but a direction to exercise discretion within defined statutory limits.

If EPA makes a finding of endangerment, the Clean Air Act requires the agency to regulate emissions of the deleterious pollutant from new motor vehicles. EPA no doubt has significant latitude as to the manner, timing, content, and coordination of its regulations with those of other agencies. But once EPA has responded to a petition for rulemaking, its reasons for action or inaction must conform to the authorizing statute. Under the clear terms of the Clean Air Act, EPA can avoid taking further action only if it determines that greenhouse gases do not contribute to climate change or if it provides some reasonable explanation as to why it cannot or will not exercise its discretion to determine whether they do. To the extent that this constrains agency discretion to pursue other priorities of the Administrator or the President, this is the congressional design.

EPA has refused to comply with this clear statutory command. Instead, it has offered a laundry list of reasons not to regulate. For example, EPA said that a number of voluntary executive branch programs already provide an effective response to the threat of global warming, 68 Fed. Reg. 52932, that regulating greenhouse gases might impair the President's ability to negotiate with "key developing nations" to reduce emissions, *id.*, at 52931, and that curtailing motor-vehicle emissions would reflect "an inefficient, piecemeal approach to address the climate change issue," ibid.

Although we have neither the expertise nor the authority to evaluate these policy judgments, it is evident they have nothing to do with whether greenhouse gas emissions contribute to climate change. Still less do they amount to a reasoned justification for declining to form a scientific judgment. In particular, while the President has broad authority in foreign affairs, that authority does not extend to the refusal to execute domestic laws. In the Global Climate Protection Act of 1987, Congress authorized the State Department—not EPA—to formulate United States foreign policy with reference to environmental matters relating to climate. *See* § 1103(c), 101 Stat. 1409. EPA has made no showing that it issued the ruling in question here after consultation with the State Department. Congress did direct EPA to consult with other agencies in the formulation of its policies and rules, but the State Department is absent from that list. § 1103(b).

Nor can EPA avoid its statutory obligation by noting the uncertainty surrounding various features of climate change and concluding that it would therefore be better not to regulate at this time. See 68 Fed. Reg. 52930–52931. If the scientific uncertainty is so profound that it precludes EPA from making a reasoned judgment as to whether greenhouse gases contribute to global warming, EPA must say so. That EPA would prefer not to regulate greenhouse gases because of some residual uncertainty . . . is irrelevant. The statutory question is whether sufficient information exists to make an endangerment finding.

In short, EPA has offered no reasoned explanation for its refusal to decide whether greenhouse gases cause or contribute to climate change. Its action was therefore "arbitrary, capricious, . . . or otherwise not in accordance with law." 42 U.S.C. § 7607(d)(9)(A). We need not and do not reach the question whether on remand EPA must make an endangerment finding, or whether policy concerns can inform EPA's actions in the event that it makes such a finding. We hold only that EPA must ground its reasons for action or inaction in the statute.

VIII

The judgment of the Court of Appeals is reversed, and the case is remanded for further proceedings consistent with this opinion.

It is so ordered.

■ CHIEF JUSTICE ROBERTS, with whom JUSTICE SCALIA, JUSTICE THOMAS, and JUSTICE ALITO join, dissenting.

Global warming may be a "crisis," even "the most pressing environmental problem of our time." Indeed, it may ultimately affect nearly everyone on the planet in some potentially adverse way, and it may be that governments have done too little to address it. It is not a problem, however, that has escaped the attention of policymakers in the Executive and Legislative Branches of our Government, who continue to consider regulatory, legislative, and treaty-based means of addressing global climate change.

Apparently dissatisfied with the pace of progress on this issue in the elected branches, petitioners have come to the courts claiming broad-ranging injury, and attempting to tie that injury to the Government's alleged failure to comply with a rather narrow statutory provision. I would reject these challenges as nonjusticiable. Such a conclusion involves no judgment on whether global warming exists, what causes it, or the extent of the problem. Nor does it render petitioners without recourse. This Court's standing jurisprudence simply recognizes that redress of grievances of the sort at issue here "is the function of Congress and the Chief Executive," not the federal courts. Lujan v. Defenders of Wildlife, 504 U.S. 555, 576 (1992). . . .

Relaxing Article III standing requirements because asserted injuries are pressed by a State, however, has no basis in our jurisprudence, and support for any such "special solicitude" is conspicuously absent from the Court's opinion. The general judicial review provision cited by the Court, 42 U.S.C. § 7607(b)(1), affords States no special rights or status. The Court states that "Congress has ordered EPA to protect Massachusetts (among others)" through the statutory provision at issue, § 7521(a)(1), and that "Congress has . . . recognized a concomitant procedural right to challenge the rejection of its rulemaking petition as arbitrary and capricious." The reader might think from this unfortunate phrasing that Congress said something about the rights of States in this particular provision of the statute. Congress knows how to do that when it wants to, *see, e.g.*, § 7426(b) (affording States the right to petition EPA to directly regulate certain sources of pollution), but it has done nothing of the sort here. Under the law on which petitioners rely, Congress treated public and private litigants exactly the same. . . .

III

Petitioners' reliance on Massachusetts's loss of coastal land as their injury in fact for standing purposes creates insurmountable problems for them with respect to causation and redressability. To establish standing, petitioners must show a causal connection between that specific injury and the lack of new motor vehicle greenhouse gas emission standards, and that the promulgation of such standards would likely redress that injury. . . . In light of the bit-part domestic new motor vehicle greenhouse gas emissions have played in what petitioners describe as a 150-year global phenomenon, and the myriad additional factors bearing on petitioners' alleged injury—the loss of Massachusetts coastal land—the connection is far too speculative to establish causation.

IV

Redressability is even more problematic. . . . What must be *likely* to be redressed is the particular injury in fact. The injury the Court looks to is the asserted loss of land. The Court contends that regulating domestic motor vehicle emissions will reduce carbon dioxide in the atmosphere, *and therefore* redress Massachusetts's injury. But even if regulation *does* reduce emissions—to some indeterminate degree, given events elsewhere in the world—the Court never explains why that makes it *likely* that the injury in fact—the loss of land—will be redressed. Schoolchildren know that a kingdom might be lost "all for the want of a horseshoe nail," but "likely" redressability is a different matter. The realities make it pure conjecture to suppose that EPA regulation of new automobile emissions will *likely* prevent the loss of Massachusetts coastal land. . . .

■ JUSTICE SCALIA, with whom THE CHIEF JUSTICE, JUSTICE THOMAS, and JUSTICE ALITO join, dissenting.

. . . "Air pollutant" is defined by the Act as "any air pollution agent or combination of such agents, including any physical, chemical, . . . substance or matter which is emitted into or otherwise enters the ambient air." 42 U.S.C. § 7602(g). The Court is correct that "[c]arbon dioxide, methane, nitrous oxide, and hydrofluorocarbons,", fit within the second half of that definition: They are "physical, chemical, . . . substance[s] or matter which [are] emitted into or otherwise ente[r] the ambient air." But the Court mistakenly believes this to be the end of the analysis. In order to be an "air pollutant" under the Act's definition, the "substance or matter [being] emitted into . . . the ambient air" must also meet the first half of the definition—namely, it must be an "air pollution agent or combination of such agents." The Court simply pretends this half of the definition does not exist.

. . . It is perfectly reasonable to view the definition of "air pollutant" in its entirety: An air pollutant can be "any physical, chemical, . . . substance or matter which is emitted into or otherwise enters the ambient air," but only if it retains the general characteristic of being an "air pollution agent or combination of such agents." This is precisely the conclusion EPA reached: "[A] substance does not meet the CAA definition of 'air pollutant' simply because it is a 'physical, chemical, . . . substance or matter which is emitted into or otherwise enters the ambient air.' It must also be an 'air pollution agent.' " 68 Fed. Reg. 52929, n. 3. Once again, in the face of textual ambiguity, the Court's application of *Chevron* deference to EPA's interpretation of the word "including" is nowhere to be found.[2] Evidently, the Court defers only to those reasonable interpretations that it favors.

. . . Unlike "air pollutants," the term "air pollution" is not itself defined by the CAA; thus, once again we must accept EPA's interpretation of that ambiguous term, provided its interpretation is a "permissible construction of the statute." *Chevron*, 467 U.S., at 843. In this case, the petition for rulemaking asked EPA for "regulation of [greenhouse gas] emissions from motor vehicles to reduce the risk of global climate change." 68 Fed. Reg. 52925. Thus, in deciding whether it had authority to regulate, EPA had to determine whether the concentration of greenhouse gases assertedly responsible for "global climate change" qualifies as "air pollution." EPA began with the commonsense observation that the "[p]roblems associated with atmospheric concentrations of $CO_2$," bear little resemblance to what would naturally be termed "air pollution". . . . [R]egulating the buildup of $CO_2$ and other greenhouse gases in the upper reaches of the atmosphere, which is alleged to be causing global climate change, is not akin to regulating the concentration of some substance that is *polluting* the *air*.

We need look no further than the dictionary for confirmation that this interpretation of "air pollution" is eminently reasonable. The definition of "pollute," of course, is "[t]o make or render impure or unclean." Webster's New International Dictionary 1910 (2d ed. 1949). And the first three definitions of "air" are as follows: (1) "[t]he invisible, odorless, and tasteless mixture of gases which surrounds the earth"; (2) "[t]he body of the earth's atmosphere; esp., the part of it near the earth, as distinguished from the upper rarefied part"; (3) "[a] portion of air or of the air considered with respect to physical characteristics or as affecting the senses." EPA's conception of "air pollution"—focusing on impurities in the "ambient air" "at ground level or near the surface of the earth"—is perfectly consistent with the natural meaning of that term. . . .

---

[2] Not only is EPA's interpretation reasonable, it is far more plausible than the Court's alternative. As the Court correctly points out, "all airborne compounds of whatever stripe," would qualify as "physical, chemical, . . . substance[s] or matter which [are] emitted into or otherwise ente[r] the ambient air," 42 U.S.C. § 7602(g). It follows that everything airborne, from Frisbees to flatulence, qualifies as an "air pollutant." This reading of the statute defies common sense.

## QUESTIONS AND DISCUSSION

**1.** According to Chief Justice Roberts, courts should refuse to decide climate change cases, both out of respect for separation of powers and comparative institutional competence concerns, because such topics are better left to the political arms of the government. How did the majority respond to that argument? Why did twelve states, several cities, and a bunch of environmental organizations take this case to the Supreme Court?

**2.** The Bush Administration consistently called for voluntary rather than regulatory approaches to climate change. In which sectors do you think voluntary reduction of greenhouse gases will be an effective approach? Do you think voluntary approaches work without the threat of possible regulations behind them?

**3.** Is Justice Scalia correct that the CAA now encompasses "*everything* airborne, from Frisbees to flatulence, qualifies as an 'air pollutant?' " Can you think of anything in the air that is not within the scope of the law? Frisbees have thus far eluded regulatory attention, but flatulence (from livestock, not humans) is a potential target of regulation. *See, e.g.*, Brian Duggan, *'Cow Tax' Angers Dorgan*, BISMARCK TRIB., Dec. 12, 2008 ("Sen. Byron Dorgan, D-N.D., is raising a stink over an idea stemming from the Environmental Protection Agency last week that would tax farmers with flatulence-producing livestock, which the agency suggested could be taxed to reduce climate change-inducing greenhouse gases.").

**4.** Water provides an even better example of the breadth of the CAA's understanding of pollution. After the Court decided *Massachusetts v. EPA*, the agency was petitioned to regulate water vapor as a pollutant under the CAA. *See* Letter from Friends of the Earth et al., to Stephen L. Johnson, Adm'r, Envtl. Prot. Agency (Dec. 14, 2007), *available at* http://oceana.org/fileadmin/oceana/uploads/Climate_Change/FINAL_Aircraft_GHG_Petition_FINAL.pdf. The petition focuses upon the "contrails"—condensation trails—of water vapor released by aircraft flying at high altitudes. Most of the twenty-six-page petition recites the disproportionate greenhouse gas effect of water vapor occurring at high altitudes and the ways in which aircraft could be changed to reduce such emissions. It took only one paragraph to argue that water vapor is a pollutant for purposes of the CAA. That paragraph simply quoted the statutory definition of "air pollutant," the history of broad judicial readings of that definition, and the Court's *Massachusetts v. EPA* conclusion that greenhouse gas emissions are pollutants. Water itself, it seems, is a pollutant.

## Utility Air Regulatory Group v. EPA

Supreme Court of the United States, 2014.
134 S. Ct. 2427.

■ JUSTICE SCALIA announced the judgment of the Court and delivered the opinion of the Court with respect to Parts I and II.

. . . In 2007, the Court held that Title II of the Act "authorize[d] EPA to regulate greenhouse gas emissions from new motor vehicles" if the

Agency "form[ed] a 'judgment' that such emissions contribute to climate change." Massachusetts v. EPA, 549 U.S. 497, 528 (2007) (quoting § 7521(a)(1)). In response to that decision, EPA embarked on a course of regulation resulting in "the single largest expansion in the scope of the [Act] in its history."

EPA first asked the public, in a notice of proposed rulemaking, to comment on how the Agency should respond to *Massachusetts*. In doing so, it explained that regulating greenhouse-gas emissions from motor vehicles could have far-reaching consequences for stationary sources. Under EPA's view, once greenhouse gases became regulated under any part of the Act, the PSD and Title V permitting requirements would apply to all stationary sources with the potential to emit greenhouse gases in excess of the statutory thresholds: 100 tons per year under Title V, and 100 or 250 tons per year under the PSD program depending on the type of source. Because greenhouse-gas emissions tend to be "orders of magnitude greater" than emissions of conventional pollutants, EPA projected that numerous small sources not previously regulated under the Act would be swept into the PSD program and Title V, including "smaller industrial sources," "large office and residential buildings, hotels, large retail establishments, and similar facilities." The Agency warned that this would constitute an "unprecedented expansion of EPA authority that would have a profound effect on virtually every sector of the economy and touch every household in the land," yet still be "relatively ineffective at reducing greenhouse gas concentrations."

In 2009, EPA announced its determination regarding the danger posed by motor-vehicle greenhouse-gas emissions. EPA found that greenhouse-gas emissions from new motor vehicles contribute to elevated atmospheric concentrations of greenhouse gases, which endanger public health and welfare by fostering global "climate change." 74 Fed. Reg. 66523, 66537 (hereinafter Endangerment Finding). It denominated a "single air pollutant" the "combined mix" of six greenhouse gases that it identified as "the root cause of human-induced climate change": carbon dioxide, methane, nitrous oxide, hydrofluorocarbons, perfluorocarbons, and sulfur hexafluoride. A source's greenhouse-gas emissions would be measured in "carbon dioxide equivalent units" (CO2e), which would be calculated based on each gas's "global warming potential."

Next, EPA issued its "final decision" regarding the prospect that motor-vehicle greenhouse-gas standards would trigger stationary-source permitting requirements. 75 Fed. Reg. 17004 (2010) (hereinafter Triggering Rule). EPA announced that beginning on the effective date of its greenhouse-gas standards for motor vehicles, stationary sources would be subject to the PSD program and Title V on the basis of their potential to emit greenhouse gases. As expected, EPA in short order promulgated greenhouse-gas emission standards for passenger cars, light-duty trucks, and medium-duty passenger vehicles to take effect on January 2, 2011. 75 Fed. Reg. 25324 (hereinafter Tailpipe Rule).

EPA then announced steps it was taking to "tailor" the PSD program and Title V to greenhouse gases. 75 Fed. Reg. 31514 (hereinafter Tailoring Rule). Those steps were necessary, it said, because the PSD program and Title V were designed to regulate "a relatively small number of large industrial sources," and requiring permits for all sources with greenhouse-gas emissions above the statutory thresholds would radically expand those programs, making them both unadministrable and "unrecognizable to the Congress that designed" them. EPA nonetheless rejected calls to exclude greenhouse gases entirely from those programs, asserting that the Act is not "ambiguous with respect to the need to cover [greenhouse-gas] sources under either the PSD or title V program." Instead, EPA adopted a "phase-in approach" that it said would "appl[y] PSD and title V at threshold levels that are as close to the statutory levels as possible, and do so as quickly as possible, at least to a certain point."

The phase-in, EPA said, would consist of at least three steps. During Step 1, from January 2 through June 30, 2011, no source would become newly subject to the PSD program or Title V solely on the basis of its greenhouse-gas emissions; however, sources required to obtain permits anyway because of their emission of conventional pollutants (so-called "anyway" sources) would need to comply with BACT for greenhouse gases if they emitted those gases in significant amounts, defined as at least 75,000 tons per year CO2e. During Step 2, from July 1, 2011, through June 30, 2012, sources with the potential to emit at least 100,000 tons per year CO2e of greenhouse gases would be subject to PSD and Title V permitting for their construction and operation and to PSD permitting for modifications that would increase their greenhouse-gas emissions by at least 75,000 tons per year CO2e. At Step 3, beginning on July 1, 2013, EPA said it might (or might not) further reduce the permitting thresholds (though not below 50,000 tons per year CO2e), and it might (or might not) establish permanent exemptions for some sources. Beyond Step 3, EPA promised to complete another round of rulemaking by April 30, 2016, in which it would "take further action to address small sources," which might (or might not) include establishing permanent exemptions. . . .

Numerous parties, including several States, filed petitions for review in the D. C. Circuit under 42 U.S.C. § 7607(b), challenging EPA's greenhouse-gas-related actions. The Court of Appeals dismissed some of the petitions for lack of jurisdiction and denied the remainder. Coalition for Responsible Regulation, Inc. v. EPA, 684 F. 3d 102 (D.C. Cir. 2012) (per curiam). . . . We granted six petitions for certiorari but agreed to decide only one question: " 'Whether EPA permissibly determined that its regulation of greenhouse gas emissions from new motor vehicles triggered permitting requirements under the Clean Air Act for stationary sources that emit greenhouse gases.' "

II. Analysis

This litigation presents two distinct challenges to EPA's stance on greenhouse-gas permitting for stationary sources. First, we must decide whether EPA permissibly determined that a source may be subject to the PSD and Title V permitting requirements on the sole basis of the source's potential to emit greenhouse gases. Second, we must decide whether EPA permissibly determined that a source already subject to the PSD program because of its emission of conventional pollutants (an "anyway" source) may be required to limit its greenhouse-gas emissions by employing the "best available control technology" for greenhouse gases. The Solicitor General joins issue on both points but evidently regards the second as more important; he informs us that "anyway" sources account for roughly 83% of American stationary-source greenhouse-gas emissions, compared to just 3% for the additional, non-"anyway" sources EPA sought to regulate at Steps 2 and 3 of the Tailoring Rule.

We review EPA's interpretations of the Clean Air Act using the standard set forth in Chevron U.S.A. Inc. v. Natural Resources Defense Council, Inc., 467 U.S. 837, 842–843 (1984). Under *Chevron*, we presume that when an agency-administered statute is ambiguous with respect to what it prescribes, Congress has empowered the agency to resolve the ambiguity. The question for a reviewing court is whether in doing so the agency has acted reasonably and thus has "stayed within the bounds of its statutory authority." Arlington v. FCC, 133 S. Ct. 1863 (2013) (emphasis deleted).

A. The PSD and Title V Triggers

We first decide whether EPA permissibly interpreted the statute to provide that a source may be required to obtain a PSD or Title V permit on the sole basis of its potential greenhouse-gas emissions.

1

. . . The Court of Appeals reasoned by way of a flawed syllogism: Under *Massachusetts*, the general, Act-wide definition of "air pollutant" includes greenhouse gases; the Act requires permits for major emitters of "any air pollutant"; therefore, the Act requires permits for major emitters of greenhouse gases. The conclusion follows from the premises only if the air pollutants referred to in the permit-requiring provisions (the minor premise) are the same air pollutants encompassed by the Act-wide definition as interpreted in *Massachusetts* (the major premise). Yet no one—least of all EPA—endorses that proposition, and it is obviously untenable.

The Act-wide definition says that an air pollutant is "any air pollution agent or combination of such agents, including any physical, chemical, biological, [or] radioactive . . . substance or matter which is emitted into or otherwise enters the ambient air." *§ 7602(g)*. In *Massachusetts*, the Court held that the Act-wide definition includes greenhouse gases because it is all-encompassing; it "embraces all airborne compounds of whatever stripe." But where the term "air pollutant" appears in the Act's operative provisions, EPA has routinely given it a narrower, context-appropriate meaning. . . .

*Massachusetts* does not strip EPA of authority to exclude greenhouse gases from the class of regulable air pollutants under other parts of the Act where their inclusion would be inconsistent with the statutory scheme. The Act-wide definition to which the Court gave a "sweeping" and "capacious" interpretation, is not a command to regulate, but a description of the universe of substances EPA may *consider* regulating under the Act's operative provisions. *Massachusetts* does not foreclose the Agency's use of statutory context to infer that certain of the Act's provisions use "air pollutant" to denote not every conceivable airborne substance, but only those that may sensibly be encompassed within the particular regulatory program. As certain *amici* felicitously put it, while *Massachusetts* "rejected EPA's categorical contention that greenhouse gases *could not* be 'air pollutants' for any purposes of the Act," it did not "embrace EPA's current, equally categorical position that greenhouse gases *must* be air pollutants for all purposes" regardless of the statutory context. . . .

In sum, there is no insuperable textual barrier to EPA's interpreting "any air pollutant" in the permitting triggers of PSD and Title V to encompass only pollutants emitted in quantities that enable them to be sensibly regulated at the statutory thresholds, and to exclude those atypical pollutants that, like greenhouse gases, are emitted in such vast quantities that their inclusion would radically transform those programs and render them unworkable as written.

2

Having determined that EPA was mistaken in thinking the Act *compelled* a greenhouse-gas-inclusive interpretation of the PSD and Title V triggers, we next consider the Agency's alternative position that its interpretation was justified as an exercise of its "discretion" to adopt "a reasonable construction of the statute." We conclude that EPA's interpretation is not permissible.

Even under *Chevron*'s deferential framework, agencies must operate "within the bounds of reasonable interpretation." And reasonable statutory interpretation must account for both "the specific context in which . . . language is used" and "the broader context of the statute as a whole." A statutory "provision that may seem ambiguous in isolation is often clarified by the remainder of the statutory scheme . . . because only one of the permissible meanings produces a substantive effect that is compatible with the rest of the law." Thus, an agency interpretation that is "inconsisten[t] with the design and structure of the statute as a whole," does not merit deference.

EPA itself has repeatedly acknowledged that applying the PSD and Title V permitting requirements to greenhouse gases would be inconsistent with—in fact, would overthrow—the Act's structure and design. In the Tailoring Rule, EPA described the calamitous consequences of interpreting the Act in that way. Under the PSD program, annual permit applications would jump from about 800 to nearly 82,000; annual administrative costs would swell from $12 million to over $1.5 billion; and decade-long delays in issuing permits would become common, causing construction projects to grind to a halt nationwide. The picture under Title V was equally bleak: The number of sources required to have permits would jump from fewer than 15,000 to about 6.1 million; annual administrative costs would balloon from $62 million to $21 billion; and collectively the newly covered sources would face permitting costs of $147 billion. Moreover, "the great majority of additional sources brought into the PSD and title V programs would be small sources that Congress did not expect would need to undergo permitting." EPA stated that these results would be so "contrary to congressional intent," and would so "severely undermine what Congress sought to accomplish," that they necessitated as much as a 1,000-fold increase in the permitting thresholds set forth in the statute.

Like EPA, we think it beyond reasonable debate that requiring permits for sources based solely on their emission of greenhouse gases at the 100- and 250-tons-per-year levels set forth in the statute would be "incompatible" with "the substance of Congress' regulatory scheme.". . . . The fact that EPA's greenhouse-gas-inclusive interpretation of the PSD and Title V triggers would place plainly excessive demands on limited governmental resources is alone a good reason for rejecting it; but that is not the only reason. EPA's interpretation is also unreasonable because it would bring about an enormous and transformative expansion in EPA's regulatory authority without clear congressional authorization. When an agency claims to discover in a long-extant statute an unheralded power to regulate "a significant portion of the American economy, we typically greet its announcement with a measure of skepticism. We expect Congress to speak clearly if it wishes to assign to an agency decisions of vast "economic and political significance." The power to require permits for the construction and modification of tens of thousands, and the operation of millions, of small sources nationwide falls comfortably within the class of authorizations that we have been reluctant to read into ambiguous statutory text. Moreover, in EPA's assertion of that authority, we confront a singular situation: an agency laying claim to extravagant statutory power over the national economy while at the same time strenuously asserting that the authority claimed would render the statute "unrecognizable to the Congress that designed" it. Since, as we hold above, the statute does not compel EPA's interpretation, it would be patently unreasonable—not to say outrageous—for EPA to insist on seizing expansive power that it admits the statute is not designed to grant.

3

EPA thought that despite the foregoing problems, it could make its interpretation reasonable by adjusting the levels at which a source's greenhouse-gas emissions would oblige it to undergo PSD and Title V permitting. Although the Act, in no uncertain terms, requires permits for sources with the potential to emit more than 100 or 250 tons per year of a relevant pollutant, EPA in its Tailoring Rule wrote a new threshold of *100,000* tons per year for greenhouse gases. Since the Court of Appeals thought the statute unambiguously made greenhouse gases capable of triggering PSD and Title V, it held that petitioners lacked Article III standing to challenge the Tailoring Rule because that rule did not injure petitioners but merely relaxed the pre-existing statutory requirements. Because we, however, hold that EPA's greenhouse-gas-inclusive interpretation of the triggers was *not* compelled, and because EPA has essentially admitted that its interpretation would be unreasonable without "tailoring," we consider the validity of the Tailoring Rule.

We conclude that EPA's rewriting of the statutory thresholds was impermissible and therefore could not validate the Agency's interpretation of the triggering provisions. An agency has no power to "tailor" legislation to bureaucratic policy goals by rewriting unambiguous statutory terms. Agencies exercise discretion only in the interstices created by statutory silence or ambiguity; they must always " 'give effect to the unambiguously expressed intent of Congress.' " It is hard to imagine a statutory term less ambiguous than the precise numerical thresholds at which the Act requires PSD and Title V permitting. When EPA replaced those numbers with others of its own choosing, it went well beyond the "bounds of its statutory authority."

The Solicitor General does not, and cannot, defend the Tailoring Rule as an exercise of EPA's enforcement discretion. The Tailoring Rule is not just an announcement of EPA's refusal to enforce the statutory permitting requirements; it purports to *alter* those requirements and to establish with the force of law that otherwise-prohibited conduct will not violate the Act. This alteration of the statutory requirements was crucial to EPA's "tailoring" efforts. Without it, small entities with the potential to emit greenhouse gases in amounts exceeding the statutory thresholds would have remained subject to citizen suits—authorized by the Act—to enjoin their construction, modification, or operation and to impose civil penalties of up to $37,500 per day of violation. EPA itself has recently affirmed that the "independent enforcement authority" furnished by the citizen-suit provision cannot be displaced by a permitting authority's decision not to pursue enforcement. The Solicitor General is therefore quite right to acknowledge that the availability of citizen suits made it necessary for EPA, in seeking to mitigate the unreasonableness of its greenhouse-gas-inclusive interpretation, to go beyond merely exercising its enforcement discretion. . . .

Were we to recognize the authority claimed by EPA in the Tailoring Rule, we would deal a severe blow to the Constitution's separation of powers. Under our system of government, Congress makes laws and the President, acting at times through agencies like EPA, "faithfully execute[s]" them. The power of executing the laws necessarily includes both authority and responsibility to resolve some questions left open by Congress that arise during the law's administration. But it does not include a power to revise clear statutory terms that turn out not to work in practice.

In the Tailoring Rule, EPA asserts newfound authority to regulate millions of small sources—including retail stores, offices, apartment buildings, shopping centers, schools, and churches—and to decide, on an ongoing basis and without regard for the thresholds prescribed by Congress, how many of those sources to regulate. We are not willing to stand on the dock and wave goodbye as EPA embarks on this multiyear voyage of discovery. We reaffirm the core administrative-law principle that an agency may not rewrite clear statutory terms to suit its own sense of how the statute should operate. EPA therefore lacked authority to "tailor" the Act's unambiguous numerical thresholds to accommodate its greenhouse-gas-inclusive interpretation of the permitting triggers. Instead, the need to rewrite clear provisions of the statute should have alerted EPA that it had taken a wrong interpretive turn. Agencies are not free to "adopt . . . unreasonable interpretations of statutory provisions and then edit other statutory provisions to mitigate the unreasonableness." Because the Tailoring Rule cannot save EPA's interpretation of the triggers, that interpretation was impermissible under *Chevron*.

B. BACT for "Anyway" Sources

For the reasons we have given, EPA overstepped its statutory authority when it decided that a source could become subject to PSD or Title V permitting by reason of its greenhouse-gas emissions. But what about "anyway" sources, those that would need permits based on their emissions of more conventional pollutants (such as particulate matter)?. . . . The question before us is whether EPA's decision to require BACT for greenhouse gases emitted by sources otherwise subject to PSD review is, as a general matter, a permissible interpretation of the statute under *Chevron*. We conclude that it is.

The text of the BACT provision is far less open-ended than the text of the PSD and Title V permitting triggers. It states that BACT is required "for each pollutant subject to regulation under this chapter" (*i.e.*, the entire Act), *§ 7475(a)(4)*, a phrase that—as the D. C. Circuit wrote 35 years ago—"would not seem readily susceptible [of] misinterpretation." Alabama Power Co. v. Costle, 636 F. 2d 323, 404 (D.C. Cir. 1979). Whereas the dubious breadth of "any air pollutant" in the permitting triggers suggests a role for agency judgment in identifying the subset of pollutants covered by the particular regulatory program at issue, the more specific phrasing of the BACT provision suggests that the necessary judgment has already been made by Congress. The wider statutory context likewise does not suggest that the BACT provision can bear a narrowing construction: There is no indication that the Act elsewhere uses, or that EPA has interpreted, "each pollutant subject to regulation under this chapter" to mean anything other than what it says.

Even if the text were not clear, applying BACT to greenhouse gases is not so disastrously unworkable, and need not result in such a dramatic expansion of agency authority, as to convince us that EPA's interpretation is unreasonable. We are not talking about extending EPA jurisdiction over millions of previously unregulated entities, but about moderately increasing the demands EPA (or a state permitting authority) can make of entities already subject to its regulation. And it is not yet clear that EPA's demands will be of a significantly different character from those traditionally associated with PSD review. In short, the record before us does not establish that the BACT provision as written is incapable of being sensibly applied to greenhouse gases.

We acknowledge the potential for greenhouse-gas BACT to lead to an unreasonable and unanticipated degree of regulation, and our decision should not be taken as an endorsement of all aspects of EPA's current approach, nor as a free rein for any future regulatory application of BACT in this distinct context. Our narrow holding is that nothing in the statute categorically prohibits EPA from interpreting the BACT provision to apply to greenhouse gases emitted by "anyway" sources.

However, EPA may require an "anyway" source to comply with greenhouse-gas BACT only if the source emits more than a *de minimis* amount of greenhouse gases. As noted above, the Tailoring Rule applies BACT only if a source emits greenhouse gases in excess of 75,000 tons per year CO2e, but the Rule makes clear that EPA did not arrive at that number by identifying the *de minimis* level. EPA may establish an appropriate *de minimis* threshold below which BACT is not required for a source's greenhouse-gas emissions. We do not hold that 75,000 tons per year CO2e necessarily exceeds a true *de minimis* level, only that EPA must justify its selection on proper grounds.

* * *

To sum up: We hold that EPA exceeded its statutory authority when it interpreted the Clean Air Act to require PSD and Title V permitting for stationary sources based on their greenhouse-gas emissions. Specifically, the Agency may not treat greenhouse gases as a pollutant for purposes of defining a "major emitting facility" (or a "modification" thereof) in the PSD context or a "major source" in the Title V context. To the extent its regulations purport to do so, they are invalid. EPA may, however, continue to treat greenhouse gases as a "pollutant subject to regulation under this chapter" for purposes of requiring BACT for "anyway" sources. The judgment of the Court of Appeals is affirmed in part and reversed in part.

■ JUSTICE BREYER, with whom JUSTICE GINSBURG, JUSTICE SOTOMAYOR, and JUSTICE KAGAN join, concurring in part and dissenting in part.

In *Massachusetts v. EPA*, 549 U.S. 497 (2007), we held that greenhouse gases fall within the Clean Air Act's general definition of the term "air pollutant." We also held, consequently, that the Environmental Protection Agency is empowered and required by Title II of the Act to regulate greenhouse gas emissions from mobile sources (such as cars and trucks) if it decides that greenhouse gases "contribute to . . . air pollution which may reasonably be anticipated to endanger public health or welfare." The EPA determined that greenhouse gases endanger human health and welfare, (Endangerment Finding), and so it issued regulations for mobile emissions, (Tailpipe Rule).

These cases take as a given our decision in *Massachusetts* that the Act's *general definition* of "air pollutant" includes greenhouse gases. One of the questions posed by these cases is whether those gases fall within the scope of the phrase "any air pollutant" as that phrase is used in the more specific provisions of the Act here at issue. The Court's answer is "no." I disagree. . . .

The Tailoring Rule solves the practical problems that would have been caused by the 250 tpy threshold. But what are we to do about the statute's language? The statute specifies a definite number—250, not 100,000—and it says that facilities that are covered by that number must meet the program's requirements. The statute says nothing about agency discretion to change that number. What is to be done? How, given the statute's language, can the EPA exempt from regulation sources that emit more than 250 but less than 100,000 tpy of greenhouse gases (and that also do not emit other regulated pollutants at threshold levels)?

The Court answers by (1) pointing out that regulation at the 250 tpy threshold would produce absurd results, (2) refusing to read the statute as compelling such results, and (3) consequently interpreting the phrase "*any* air pollutant" as containing an implicit exception for greenhouse gases. (Emphasis added.) Put differently, the Court reads the statute as defining "major emitting facility" to mean "stationary sources that have the potential to emit two hundred fifty tons per year or more of any air pollutant *except for those air pollutants, such as carbon dioxide, with respect to which regulation at that threshold would be impractical or absurd or would sweep in smaller sources that Congress did not mean to cover.*"

. . . But I do not agree with the Court that the only way to avoid an absurd or otherwise impermissible result in these cases is to create an atextual greenhouse gas exception to the phrase "any air pollutant.". . . . The implicit exception I propose reads almost word for word the same as the Court's, except that the location of the exception has shifted. To repeat, the Court reads the definition of "major emitting facility" as if it referred to "any source with the potential to emit two hundred fifty tons per year or more of any air pollutant *except for those air pollutants, such as carbon dioxide, with respect to which regulation at that threshold would be impractical or absurd or would sweep in smaller sources that Congress did not mean to cover*." I would simply move the implicit exception, which I've italicized, so that it applies to "source" rather than "air pollutant": "any *source* with the potential to emit two hundred fifty tons per year or more of any air pollutant *except for those sources, such as those emitting unmanageably small amounts of greenhouse gases, with respect to which regulation at that threshold would be impractical or absurd or would sweep in smaller sources that Congress did not mean to cover*."

From a legal, administrative, and functional perspective—that is, from a perspective that assumes that Congress was not merely trying to arrange words on paper but was seeking to achieve a real-world *purpose*—my way of reading the statute is the more sensible one. For one thing, my reading is consistent with the specific purpose underlying the 250 tpy threshold specified by the statute. The purpose of that number was not to prevent the regulation of dangerous air pollutants that cannot be sensibly regulated at that particular threshold, though that is the effect that the Court's reading gives the threshold. Rather, the purpose was to limit the PSD program's obligations to larger sources while exempting the many small sources whose emissions are low enough that imposing burdensome regulatory requirements on them would be senseless. . . .

I agree with the Court's holding that stationary sources that are subject to the PSD program because they emit other (non-greenhouse-gas) pollutants in quantities above the statutory threshold—those facilities that the Court refers to as "anyway" sources—must meet the "best available control technology" requirement of § 7475(a)(4) with respect to greenhouse gas emissions. I therefore join Part II-B-2 of the Court's opinion. But as for the Court's holding that the EPA cannot interpret the language at issue here to cover facilities that emit more than 100,000 tpy of greenhouse gases by virtue of those emissions, I respectfully dissent.

■ JUSTICE ALITO, with whom JUSTICE THOMAS joins, concurring in part and dissenting in part.

In *Massachusetts v. EPA*, 549 U.S. 497 (2007), this Court considered whether greenhouse gases fall within the Clean Air Act's general definition of an air "pollutant." The Environmental Protection Agency cautioned us that "key provisions of the [Act] cannot cogently be applied to [greenhouse gas] emissions," but the Court brushed the warning aside and had "little trouble" concluding that the Act's "sweeping definition" of a pollutant encompasses greenhouse gases. I believed *Massachusetts* v.

*EPA* was wrongly decided at the time, and these cases further expose the flaws with that decision. . . .

I do not agree, however, with the Court's conclusion that what it terms "anyway sources," *i.e.*, sources that are subject to PSD and Title V permitting as the result of the emission of conventional pollutants, must install "best available control technology" (BACT) for greenhouse gases. As is the case with the PSD and Title V thresholds, trying to fit greenhouse gases into the BACT analysis badly distorts the scheme that Congress adopted. . . .

---

## QUESTIONS AND DISCUSSION

**1.** Justice Scalia, Justice Breyer, and Justice Alito all agree that the CAA's 100,000 tpy provision does not make sense when applied to greenhouse gases. Why not? Should EPA have simply applied the standard as written even if "decade-long delays in issuing permits would become common, causing construction projects to grind to a halt nationwide?" Should EPA be allowed to choose a more sensible number (as Justice Breyer suggests)? Or does the mismatch between the 100,000 tpy provision and greenhouse gases suggest that the CAA should not be applied to climate change at all (as Justice Alito concludes)?

**2.** EPA's Clean Power Plan (CPP) would result in a much greater expansion of the CAA's application to climate change. *See* Carbon Pollution Emission Guidelines for Existing Stationary Sources: Electric Utility Generating Units; Final Rule, 80 Fed. Reg. 64661 (2015). The CPP contains final emission guidelines that states must follow in developing plans to reduce greenhouse gas emissions from existing fossil fuel-fired electric power plants. The CAA grandfathers the emission of traditional air pollutants from such power plants, and many of them have remained open long after Congress expected when it passed the CAA in 1970. In the CPP, EPA would direct states to regulate those power plants with specific requirements tailored to the unique characteristics of each state. The CPP has generated an enormous amount of commentary, pro and con, from those who regard the rule alternately as an essential step in addressing climate change and air pollution more generally and those who see it as an end run around Congress (which has declined to enact comprehensive climate change legislation) and as an unprecedented interference with state regulatory authority over energy production. The Supreme Court has stayed the application of the CPP pending the resolution of legal challenges in the D.C. Circuit. *See* North Dakota v. EPA, 136 S. Ct. 999 (U.S. 2016).

---

## PROBLEM EXERCISE

The Center for Biological Diversity (CBD) has petitioned EPA to establish national ambient air quality standards (NAAQS) for carbon dioxide and other greenhouse gas pollution under the Clean Air Act

(CAA). The petition seeks to have greenhouse gases designated as air pollutants and atmospheric $CO_2$ capped at 350 parts per million (ppm), the level leading scientists say is necessary to avoid the worst impacts of global warming.

"It's time to use our strongest existing tool for reducing greenhouse gas pollution—the Clean Air Act. The Act's provisions should cap carbon pollution at no more than 350 parts per million," said Kassie Siegel, an author of the petition and director of the CBD's Climate Law Institute. "For four decades, this law has protected the air we breathe—and it's done that through a proven, successful system of pollution control that saves lives and creates economic benefits vastly exceeding its costs. . . . Rather than perpetually wait for flawed and inadequate new climate legislation before taking meaningful action, the Obama administration can and must use the existing authorities under the Clean Air Act to set a target of 350 parts per million to protect the climate and our future," said Siegel.

The Administrator of EPA has asked you—the agency's general counsel—to write a memo explaining (1) the legal standards governing whether EPA should grant or deny the CBD's petition, (2) what actions the CAA requires or allows EPA to take if it grants the petition, and (3) the legal standards by which the courts will review EPA's decision to grant or deny the petition.

---

## B. THE ENDANGERED SPECIES ACT

We began this book by examining the ESA in the context of the Delhi Sands Flower-Loving Fly in chapter 1 and more generally in chapter 2. Historically, habitat loss has been the leading threat to the survival of listed species, and residential and commercial development has been responsible for much of that habitat loss. Increasingly, though, climate change threatens species as well. The Elkhorn coral and the Staghorn coral were the first species to be listed under the ESA because of the threat posed by climate change. See Endangered and Threatened Species: Final Listing Determinations for Elkhorn Coral and Staghorn Coral, 71 Fed. Reg. 26852 (2006). Other species have been listed since then, and many petitions to list many more species can be expected. Once listed, how does the ESA apply to a species, and how does it apply to the threat posed by climate change?

## Safari Club International v. Salazar

United States Court of Appeals for the District of Columbia Circuit, 2013.
709 F.3d 1.

■ EDWARDS, SENIOR CIRCUIT JUDGE:

In 2005, the Center for Biological Diversity petitioned the Secretary of the Interior and the Fish and Wildlife Service ("FWS" or "agency") to list the polar bear under the Endangered Species Act ("ESA" or "Act"). When a species such as the polar bear is listed as either "threatened" or "endangered" under the Act, it is then subject to a host of protective measures designed to conserve the species. After a three-year rulemaking process, FWS found that, due to the effects of global climate change, the polar bear is likely to become an endangered species and face the threat of extinction within the foreseeable future. *See generally* Determination of Threatened Status for the Polar Bear (Ursus maritimus) Throughout Its Range ("Listing Rule"), 73 Fed.Reg. 28,212 (May 15, 2008). The agency thus concluded that the polar bear should be listed as a threatened species.

A number of industry groups, environmental organizations, and states challenged the Listing Rule as either overly restrictive or insufficiently protective of the polar bear. These challenges were consolidated as a Multidistrict Litigation case in the U.S. District Court for the District of Columbia. After a hearing on the parties' submissions, the District Court granted summary judgment to FWS and rejected all challenges to the Listing Rule. *See generally In re Polar Bear Endangered Species Act Listing and § 4(d) Rule Litigation,* 794 F. Supp. 2d 65 (D.D.C.2011). Joint Appellants filed a timely appeal to contest the District Court's judgment. They contend that the Listing Rule is arbitrary and capricious under the Administrative Procedure Act ("APA"), 5 U.S.C. § 706(2)(A), and that FWS's action should be reversed because of a series of deficiencies in the rulemaking process and the Listing Rule itself.

The appellate court's task in a case such as this is a "narrow" one. *Motor Vehicle Mfrs. Ass'n of U.S., Inc. v. State Farm Mut. Auto. Ins. Co.,* 463 U.S. 29, 43 (1983). Our principal responsibility here is to determine, in light of the record considered by the agency, whether the Listing Rule is a product of reasoned decisionmaking. It is significant that Appellants have neither pointed to mistakes in the agency's reasoning nor adduced any data or studies that the agency overlooked. In addition, Appellants challenge neither the agency's findings on climate science nor on polar bear biology. Rather, the principal claim advanced by Appellants is that FWS misinterpreted and misapplied the record before it. We disagree.

In rejecting this appeal, we are guided by the Supreme Court's admonition that "a court is not to substitute its judgment for that of the agency," *id.,* particularly in cases where the issues "require[ ] a high level of technical expertise," *Marsh v. Or. Natural Res. Council,* 490 U.S. 360,

377 (1989). Given these considerations and the evident thoroughness and care of FWS's explanation for its decision, we can only conclude, as did the District Court, that Appellants' challenges "amount to nothing more than competing views about policy and science." Accordingly, we affirm the judgment of the District Court.

## I. Background

The District Court's opinion contains an extensive summary of the factual and procedural record, so it is unnecessary for us to recite all of that information here. Instead, we offer the following background statement for convenience and clarity.

### A. The Endangered Species Act

Congress passed the ESA in 1973 "to provide a means whereby the ecosystems upon which endangered species and threatened species depend may be conserved, [and] to provide a program for the conservation of such endangered species and threatened species." 16 U.S.C. § 1531(b). "The term 'endangered species' means any species which is in danger of extinction throughout all or a significant portion of its range. . . ." *Id.* § 1532(6). "The term 'threatened species' means any species which is likely to become an endangered species within the foreseeable future throughout all or a significant portion of its range." *Id.* § 1532(20). The Secretaries of Interior and Commerce are obligated to publish and maintain a list of all species determined to be endangered or threatened. *Id.* § 1533(c)(1). The Secretaries have delegated this authority to FWS and the National Marine Fisheries Service, depending on the species at issue. 50 C.F.R. § 402.01(b).

The ESA empowers an "interested person" to petition the appropriate agency for the listing of any species. 16 U.S.C. § 1533(b)(3)(A). Upon receiving such a petition, the agency "determine[s] whether [the] species is an endangered species or a threatened species because of *any* of the following factors: (A) the present or threatened destruction, modification, or curtailment of its habitat or range; (B) overutilization for commercial, recreational, scientific, or educational purposes; (C) disease or predation; (D) the inadequacy of existing regulatory mechanisms; or (E) other natural or manmade factors affecting its continued existence." *Id.* § 1533(a)(1) (emphasis added). The agency makes a listing determination "solely on the basis of the best scientific and commercial data available . . . after conducting a review of the status of the species and after taking into account those efforts, if any, being made by any State or foreign nation . . . to protect such species." *Id.* § 1533(b)(1)(A).

### B. The Listing Rule

On February 16, 2005, the Center for Biological Diversity petitioned the Secretary of the Interior to list the polar bear as threatened under the ESA because of the effects of global climate change on polar bear habitat. On December 21, 2006, following peer review and multiple opportunities for public comment, FWS completed a 262-page Status Review. *See generally* Scott Schliebe et al., Range-Wide Status Review of the Polar Bear (*Ursus Maritimus*) (Dec. 21, 2006). (The Status Review is posted on FWS's website at http://www.fws.gov/.) Shortly thereafter, on January 9, 2007, FWS published a proposed rule to list the species as threatened; this action triggered a 90-day public comment period. *See generally* 12-Month Petition Finding and Proposed Rule to List the Polar Bear (Ursus maritimus) as Threatened Throughout Its Range, 72 Fed.Reg. 1064 (Jan. 9, 2007). . . .

FWS published the final Listing Rule on May 15, 2008. The Listing Rule concludes that "the polar bear is likely to become an endangered species within the foreseeable future throughout all of its range" and should therefore be listed as threatened.

The Listing Rule explains in detail the taxonomy, evolution, and population of the species. Some of the principal findings are as follows:

Polar bears evolved in sea ice habitats and as a result are evolutionarily adapted to this habitat.

* * *

> Over most of their range, polar bears remain on the sea ice year-round or spend only short periods on land. However, some polar bear populations occur in seasonally ice-free environs and use land habitats for varying portions of the year.
>
> * * *
>
> Although polar bears are generally limited to areas where the sea is ice-covered for much of the year, they are not evenly distributed throughout their range on sea ice. They show a preference for certain sea ice characteristics, concentrations, and specific sea ice features. Sea-ice habitat quality varies temporally as well as geographically. Polar bears show a preference for sea ice located over and near the continental shelf, likely due to higher biological productivity in these areas and greater accessibility to prey in near-shore shear zones and polynyas (areas of open sea surrounded by ice) compared to deep-water regions in the central polar basin. Bears are most abundant near the shore in shallow-water areas, and also in other areas where currents and ocean upwelling increase marine productivity and serve to keep the ice cover from becoming too consolidated in winter.
>
> * * *
>
> Polar bears are distributed throughout the ice-covered waters of the circumpolar Arctic, and rely on sea ice as their primary habitat. Polar bears depend on sea ice for a number of purposes, including as a platform from which to hunt and feed upon seals; as habitat on which to seek mates and breed; as a

> platform to move to terrestrial maternity denning areas, and sometimes for maternity denning; and as a substrate on which to make long-distance movements.
>
> * * *
>
> The total number of polar bears worldwide is estimated to be 20,000–25,000. Polar bears are not evenly distributed throughout the Arctic, nor do they comprise a single nomadic cosmopolitan population, but rather occur in 19 relatively discrete populations. The use of the term "relatively discrete population" in this context is not intended to equate to the Act's term "distinct population segments." Boundaries of the 19 polar bear populations have evolved over time and are based on intensive study of movement patterns, tag returns from harvested animals, and, to a lesser degree, genetic analysis. The scientific studies regarding population bounds began in the early 1970s and continue today. [The Listing Rule adopts] the use of the term "population" to describe polar bear management units consistent with their designation by the World Conservation Union-International Union for Conservation of Nature and Natural Resources (IUCN), Species Survival Commission (SSC) Polar Bear Specialist Group (PBSG) with information available as of October 2006, and to describe a combination of two or more of these populations into "ecoregions." . . . Although movements of individual polar bears overlap extensively, telemetry studies demonstrate spatial segregation among groups or stocks of polar bears in different regions of their circumpolar range. These patterns, along with information obtained from survey and reconnaissance, marking and tagging studies, and traditional knowledge, have resulted in recognition of 19 relatively discrete polar bear populations. Genetic analysis reinforces the boundaries between some designated populations while confirming the existence of overlap and mixing among others.

The Listing Rule also explains that studies of the nineteen polar bear populations have divided the species into four "physiographically different functional groups or 'ecoregions' in order to forecast future polar bear population status on the basis of current knowledge of polar bear populations, their relationships to sea ice habitat, and predicted changes in sea ice and other environmental variables." The Listing Rule then discusses the Archipelago, Seasonal Ice, Divergent, and Convergent ecoregions in some depth.

FWS cited three principal considerations in determining that polar bears should be listed as a threatened species. *First,* the polar bear depends on sea ice for its survival. *Second,* sea ice is declining. On this point, the Listing Rule states:

> Polar bears evolved to utilize the Arctic sea ice niche and are distributed throughout most ice-covered seas of the Northern Hemisphere. We find, based upon the best available scientific and commercial information, that polar bear habitat—principally sea ice—is declining throughout the species' range, that this decline is expected to continue for the foreseeable future, and that this loss threatens the species throughout all of ***6** its range. Therefore, we find that the polar bear is likely to become an endangered species within the foreseeable future throughout all of its range.

*Third*, climatic changes have and will continue to reduce the extent and quality of Arctic sea ice.

FWS concluded that these findings satisfied two of the statutory listing factors: (A) the threatened destruction of the species' habitat or range, and (D) the inadequacy of existing regulatory mechanisms to preserve the species.

In aggregating data on climate change and sea ice, FWS relied on a variety of published studies and reports, including those of the Intergovernmental Panel on Climate Change ("IPCC"). FWS explained that

> [t]he rapid retreat of sea ice in the summer and overall diminishing sea ice throughout the year in the Arctic is unequivocal and extensively documented in scientific literature. Further extensive recession of sea ice is projected by the majority of state-of-the-art climate models, with a seasonally ice-free Arctic projected by the middle of the 21st century by many of those models.

Noting that sea ice had reached a record low in the summer of 2007, FWS also explained that "[t]he observational record indicates that current summer sea ice losses appear to be about 30 years ahead of the ensemble of modeled values, which suggests that a transition towards a seasonally ice-free Arctic might occur sooner than the models indicate."

The agency's assessment of the species' dependence on sea ice derives from peer reviewed studies on polar bear biology and behavior, observed polar bear demographics, and population modeling. As noted above, FWS explained that the bears are highly dependent on sea ice, "including as a platform from which to hunt and feed upon seals; as habitat on which to seek mates and breed; as a platform to move to terrestrial maternity denning areas, and sometimes for maternity denning; and as a substrate on which to make long-distance movements." The Listing Rule anticipates that changes to the polar bear's habitat will soon pose an existential threat to the species:

> Productivity, abundance, and availability of ice seals, the polar bear's primary prey base, would be diminished by the projected loss of sea ice, and energetic requirements of polar bears for

movement and obtaining food would increase. Access to traditional denning areas would be affected. In turn, these factors would cause declines in the condition of polar bears from nutritional stress and reduced productivity. As already evidenced in the Western Hudson Bay and Southern Beaufort Sea populations, polar bears would experience reductions in survival and recruitment rates. The eventual effect is that polar bear populations would decline. The rate and magnitude of decline would vary among populations, based on differences in the rate, timing, and magnitude of impacts. However, within the foreseeable future, all populations would be affected, and the species is likely to become in danger of extinction throughout all of its range due to declining sea ice habitat.

### C. The District Court's Decision

Soon after publication of the Listing Rule, nearly a dozen challenges were filed to contest FWS's action. Several plaintiffs argued that the listing was unwarranted because the agency failed to establish a foreseeable risk of extinction. Others argued the opposite—that the species should have been listed as endangered because it faced an imminent risk of extinction. These actions were consolidated before the District Court as a Multidistrict Litigation case. . . . After a lengthy review of Appellants' arguments, the District Court concluded that it was "simply not persuaded that [FWS's] decision to list the polar bear as a threatened species under the ESA was arbitrary and capricious." Appellants challenge this decision and several conservation groups have intervened on behalf of FWS.

## II. Analysis

Appellants' principal claim on appeal is that FWS misapplied the statutory criteria for a listing decision by ignoring or misinterpreting the record before it and failing to articulate the grounds for its decision. In particular, Appellants contend that: (1) FWS failed to adequately explain each step in its decisionmaking process, particularly in linking habitat loss to a risk of future extinction; (2) FWS erred by issuing a single, range-wide determination; (3) FWS relied on defective population models; (4) FWS misapplied the term "likely" when it determined that the species was likely to become endangered; (5) FWS erred in selecting a period of 45 years as the "foreseeable future"; (6) FWS failed to "take into account" Canada's polar bear conservation efforts; and (7) FWS violated Section 4(i) of the ESA by failing to give an adequate response to the comments submitted by the State of Alaska regarding the listing decision. For the reasons discussed below, we find these arguments meritless.

### A. Standard of Review

We will uphold an agency action unless we find it to be "arbitrary, capricious, an abuse of discretion, or otherwise not in accordance with law." 5 U.S.C. § 706(2)(A). This standard applies to our review of ESA listing decisions. Under the arbitrary and capricious standard, the reviewing court determines whether the agency "considered the factors relevant to its decision and articulated a rational connection between the facts found and the choice made." "The Supreme Court has explained that an agency acts arbitrarily or capriciously if it 'has relied on factors which Congress has not intended it to consider, entirely failed to consider an important aspect of the problem, offered an explanation for its decision that runs counter to the evidence before the agency, or is so implausible that it could not be ascribed to a difference in view or the product of agency expertise.'" "The scope of review under the 'arbitrary and capricious' standard is narrow and a court is not to substitute its judgment for that of the agency." Deference is especially warranted where the decision at issue "requires a high level of technical expertise." "In a case like the instant one, in which the District Court reviewed an agency action under the APA, we review the administrative action directly, according no particular deference to the judgment of the District Court."

### B. The Agency's Decision

The Listing Rule rests on a three-part thesis: the polar bear is dependent upon sea ice for its survival; sea ice is declining; and climatic changes have and will continue to dramatically reduce the extent and quality of Arctic sea ice to a degree sufficiently grave to jeopardize polar bear populations. No part of this thesis is disputed and we find that FWS's conclusion—that the polar bear is threatened within the meaning of the ESA—is reasonable and adequately supported by the record.

The Listing Rule is the product of FWS's careful and comprehensive study and analysis. Its scientific conclusions are amply supported by data and well within the mainstream on climate science and polar bear biology. Thirteen of the fourteen peer reviewers to whom FWS submitted the proposed rule found that it generally "represented a thorough, clear, and balanced review of the best scientific information available from both published and unpublished sources of the current status of polar bears" and that it "justified the conclusion that polar bears face threats throughout their range." Only one peer reviewer dissented, "express[ing] concern that the proposed rule was flawed, biased, and incomplete, that it would do nothing to address the underlying issues associated with global warming, and that a listing would be detrimental to the Inuit of the Arctic."

As we discuss below, several of Appellants' challenges rely on portions of the record taken out of context and blatantly ignore FWS's published explanations. Others, as the District Court correctly explained, "amount to nothing more than competing views about policy and science," on which we defer to the agency.

Significantly, Appellants point to no scientific findings or studies that FWS failed to consider in promulgating the Listing Rule. At oral argument, Appellants' counsel acknowledged that Appellants do not claim that FWS failed to use the "best scientific and commercial data available" as required by 16 U.S.C. § 1533(b)(1)(A). Rather, "Appellants merely disagree with the implications of the data for the species' continued viability."

Where, as here, the foundational premises on which the agency relies are adequately explained and uncontested, scientific experts (by a wide majority) support the agency's conclusion, and Appellants do not point to any scientific evidence that the agency failed to consider, we are bound to uphold the agency's determination. Therefore we affirm the District Court's decision to uphold the Listing Rule. . . .

## QUESTIONS AND DISCUSSION

**1.** The number of polar bears is generally stable, but climate change could drive polar bears to extinction. The listing of the polar bear, therefore, depended on the meaning of the ESA's terms "likely" and "foreseeable." The ESA provides that a species is "threatened" if it "is likely to become an endangered species within the *foreseeable* future throughout all or a significant portion of its range." 16 U.S.C. § 1532(20) (emphasis added). Neither "likely" nor "foreseeable" are defined in the ESA. The IPCC defines "likely" as 67-to-90 percent certainty, which the FWS acknowledged in its polar bear listing decision, but the court held that the FWS was permitted to adhere to follow a more generalized approach to the likelihood that the polar bear would become endangered. Similarly, the FWS determines foreseeability on a case-by-case basis, and the court deferred to the agency's choice of a 45-year period with respect to the polar bear.

**2.** Besides requiring the listing of new species, climate change may also keep already-listed species under the protection of the ESA. For example, the FWS declined to delist the marbled murrelet in part because "[w]hile seabirds such as the murrelet have life-history strategies adapted to variable marine environments, ongoing and future climate change could present changes of a rapidity and scope outside the adaptive range of murrelets." Endangered and Threatened Wildlife and Plants; 12-Month Finding on a Petition To Remove the Marbled Murrelet (Brachyramphus marmoratus) From the List of Endangered and Threatened Wildlife, 75 Fed. Reg. 3424, 3431 (2010). How will the prolonged application of the ESA affect the efforts to address climate change and to protect biodiversity?

**3.** Suppose that a species is listed because of concerns about climate change. As explained in chapter 2, the ESA requires a number of actions regarding listed species, including the designation of critical habitat, the preparation of a recovery plan, the avoidance of any federal agency actions that would jeopardize the survival of a species or its critical habitat, and a prohibition on the "take" of any species. The most important—and yet unanswered—question about how the ESA applies to climate change is whether a greenhouse gas emitter illegally jeopardizes or takes a species that may be many miles away. For example, would the EPA prohibit the construction of a coal-fired power plant in Virginia because the resulting greenhouse gases would harm the polar bear in the Arctic? That specific question has been answered, for now, by a FWS rule that exempts the polar bear from such legal scrutiny based on a so-called 4(d) rule available only for threatened species. *See* Special Rule for the Polar Bear Under Section 4(d) of the Endangered Species Act, 78 Fed. Reg. 11766 (2013). Environmental activists such as the Center for Biological Diversity hope to employ the ESA to regulate greenhouse gas emissions. By contrast, one of us has observed that

> it is difficult to conceive of how the agency would go about aggressively regulating greenhouse gas emissions through the jeopardy consultation program. The FWS does not have the pollution control expertise of the EPA, nor does any provision of the ESA explicitly provide authority to engage in emissions regulation. Given that all emission sources contribute to warming effects, the threat of jeopardy findings would have to be applied universally to all sources. This, in turn, might induce emission sources to engage in emission offsets (e.g., by purchasing forestation credits) or technological and operational emission reductions. But is the FWS equipped to assume the role of nation-wide regulator of farms, industrial facilities, auto emissions, and everything else? In short, the idea that all emission sources present jeopardy conditions to each and every climate-threatened species would prove too much, and likely render the ESA and the FWS political targets in the first degree.

J.B. Ruhl, *Climate Change and the Endangered Species Act: Building Bridges to the No-Analog Future*, 88 B.U. L. REV. 1, 44–47 (2008).

---

## C. NATIONAL ENVIRONMENTAL POLICY ACT

NEPA, as described in chapter 5, requires federal agencies to study the environmental impacts of their actions before they take them. NEPA does not impose any substantive obligations; instead, it produces information that can be used by federal agencies and other parties who are interested in whether to pursue a particular project. As applied to climate change, NEPA could provide insight both into activities that are responsible for climate change and activities that are affected by climate change. Again, federal agencies and courts are still trying to determine precisely what role NEPA should have in the response to climate change.

## Center for Biological Diversity v. Kempthorne

United States Court of Appeals for the Ninth Circuit, 2009.
588 F.3d 701.

■ FARRIS, CIRCUIT JUDGE:

### I. Background

In August 2006, the United States Fish and Wildlife Service promulgated five-year regulations under the Marine Mammal Protection Act § 101(a)(5) that authorize for a five-year period the non-lethal "take" of polar bears and Pacific walrus by oil and gas activities in and along the Beaufort Sea on the Northern Coast of Alaska. 50 C.F.R. § 18. The term "take" means "to harass, hunt, capture, or kill, or to attempt to harass, hunt, capture, or kill any marine mammal." 16 U.S.C. § 1362 (13). Under the regulations, individual oil and gas operators may apply to the Service for a "letter of authorization." The LOA, if granted, lasts for up to a year.

As of 2002, there were an estimated 2,200 polar bears in the South Beaufort Sea. Polar bears move according to the location of sea ice and prey, migrating south in the winter with the advance of the sea ice and returning north in the summer with the sea ice's retreat. They spend most of their time far offshore in the active ice zone, spending only a limited time on land to feed, to den, or to travel elsewhere. The pregnant females enter "maternity dens" in November, give birth to about two cubs around the new year and emerge from the den in March or April. A premature departure endangers the underdeveloped cubs. Most dens are located on pack ice, but some are located on land. Ringed seal pups are an essential source of food for polar bears, especially because adult polar bears require large quantities of seal fat to survive.

Polar bears are vulnerable to climate change. Acute threats posed by a warming climate include the loss of sea ice habitat; the resulting increased use of coastal environments and therefore more frequent encounters with humans; changes in body fitness, particularly reduction of fat stores in denning females; a decline in cub survival rate; reduction in available prey such as ringed seals; and increased energetic needs in hunting for seals as well as traveling and swimming longer distances due to reduced ice pack. Changes to the polar bear population have been observed. Distribution has shifted, with more frequent terrestrial denning, and there have been declines in physical condition, reproductive success, survival, and population.

A warming climate poses similar threats to Pacific walrus, but these threats are not emphasized in the record or in the party briefs.

The oil and gas industry has conducted exploration, development, and production along the Beaufort Sea and the Northern coast of Alaska since 1968. The 2006 incidental take regulations were preceded by similar regulations published in 1993, 1995, 1999, 2000 (twice), and 2003. 58 Fed. Reg. 60, 402 (1993); 60 Fed. Reg. 42, 805 (1995); 64 Fed.

Reg. 4, 328 (1999); 65 Fed. Reg. 5, 275 (2000); 65 Fed. Reg. 16, 828 (2000); and 68 Fed. Reg. 66, 744 (2003). Such past regulation yielded much information about the industry's interactions with polar bears and walrus.

Prior to issuing the 2006 regulations, the Service evaluated the impact of the oil and gas industry on polar bears and walrus. With respect to bears, it found that past interaction has been "minimal." Most industry activity is conducted on land, away from the ice floes that polar bears prefer. Therefore, most encounters are only short-term behavioral disturbances. It is unlikely that oil and gas activities will physically obstruct or impede polar bear movement. Since 1993, there have been no bears killed by industrial activities.

Nevertheless, from 1993 to 2004, there were more than 700 sightings of polar bears related to industrial activities. More recently, sightings have increased. Production facilities may negatively affect denning females, with industrial noise causing females to abandon their dens prematurely and endanger their offspring. However, industrial noise-producing activity may need to be very close to the den to cause such a response, and bears may even acclimate to such noises. The Service found that the impact would likely be consistent with that during previous periods of regulation. The impact would be negligible.

With respect to walrus, the Service also predicted that the impact would be negligible. Walrus are uncommon in the Beaufort Sea. Between 1993 and 2004, only nine were observed in the area, and there is no evidence that a walrus has been injured directly during an interaction with the oil and gas industry.

Pursuant to the National Environmental Policy Act, and before issuing the final 2006 regulations, the Service produced an environmental assessment but not an environmental impact statement. The purpose of the Service's EA in this context was not to evaluate "the impact of industry on polar bears and Pacific walrus"—the regulations themselves serve that purpose—but rather to "evaluate[ ] the impact of issuing incidental take regulations" as opposed to permitting industrial activities in the absence of such regulation. With this understanding, and based on the same information, the Service concluded that the incidental take regulation was likely to have no significant impact on the populations, recruitment, or survival of polar bears and walrus in the Beaufort Sea region. The EA acknowledged that climate change could affect the degree of impact on polar bears, but resolved that the magnitude of this effect was unclear.

Plaintiff Center for Biological Diversity is an organization devoted to protecting the habitat of endangered species. Plaintiff Pacific Environment is a similar organization. Their members have viewed polar bears and walrus in the region, enjoy doing so, and have plans to return. In February 2007, the Center, along with Pacific Environment, filed this action alleging that the Service regulations violate the MMPA and NEPA. Venue was transferred to the District of Alaska.

Following counter motions for summary judgment and briefing on the merits, the district court granted summary judgment to the defendants, upholding the regulations. The plaintiffs appeal. . . .

**VI. National Environmental Policy Act**

NEPA requires the production of an environmental impact statement for "major Federal actions significantly affecting the quality of the human environment." 42 U.S.C. § 4332(C). An environmental assessment is a "concise public document" that "[b]riefly provide[s] sufficient evidence and analysis for determining whether to prepare an [EIS] or a finding of no significant impact." 40 C.F.R. § 1508.9 (a); Anderson v. Evans, 371 F.3d 475, 488 (9th Cir. 2004).

If an agency issues a finding of no significant impact, "it must supply a 'convincing statement of reasons' to explain why a project's impacts are insignificant." Blue Mountains Biodiversity Project v. Blackwood, 161 F.3d 1208, 1212 (9th Cir. 1998). Such a statement is necessary to show that the agency took the requisite " 'hard look' at the consequences of its action." Environmental Protection Information Center v. U.S. Forest Serv., 451 F.3d 1005, 1009 (9th Cir. 2006). A finding of no significant impact violates NEPA if it "fail[s] to address certain crucial factors, consideration of which [is] essential to a truly informed decision." Found. for N. Am. Wild Sheep v. U.S. Dept. of Agr., 681 F.2d 1172, 1178 (9th Cir. 1982).

***A. Finding of No Significant Impact***

The plaintiffs argue that the Service's finding of no significant impact was arbitrary and capricious because it failed to address "the impacts to polar bears from disturbance by oil and gas activities in the context of a warming climate." The Service's EA did acknowledge climate change and enumerated its long term effects on polar bears, including "increased use of coastal environments, increased bear/human encounters, changes in polar bear body condition, decline in cub survival, and increased potential for stress and mortality, and energetic needs in hunting for seals, as well as traveling and swimming to denning sites and feeding areas."

The plaintiffs do not allege that the EA's list is incomplete, but rather that the EA failed to synthesize these concerns with the multiplying effects of oil and gas activities. However, the plaintiffs point merely to evidence that global warming poses a generalized threat to polar bear populations. Such evidence does not demonstrate that non-lethal takes within a particular industry and during a particular period of time are likely to have significant impact.

The plaintiffs next argue that the Service's conclusion "runs counter to the evidence before the agency" because negative impacts to the South Beaufort Sea polar bears were already well-documented. Assuming that such impacts were well-documented, their relationship to oil and gas activities was not. To the contrary, the administrative record tends to show that the oil and gas industry has little impact on polar bears. Not one polar bear death associated with Industry has occurred during the period covered by incidental take regulations. Interactions between bears and people associated with Industry have been rare. A typical incidental take provokes only short-term change and pose little threat to survival and recruitment.

Furthermore, the EA provides convincing reasons to believe that incidental take regulations will ameliorate the impact of takes. LOAs include mitigating guidelines that minimize disturbances to, among other things, denning females. These considerations, all explicitly analyzed in the EA, demonstrate that the Service took a "hard look" at the consequences of its actions. Its conclusion was reasonable and not arbitrary.

***B. Failure to produce an EIS***

Next, the plaintiffs argue that the Service acted arbitrarily in failing to produce an Environmental Impact Statement. Such statements are necessary where effects are "highly uncertain or involve unique or unknown risks." 40 C.F.R. § 1508.27(b)(5). We have held that "regulations do not anticipate the need for an EIS anytime there is some uncertainty, but only if the effects of the project are 'highly' uncertain." *EPIC*, 451 F.3d at 1011. The plaintiffs argue that effects of the incidental take regulation on polar bears were highly uncertain, because, compared to the circumstances of prior regulation, bears will be more vulnerable.

We have upheld agency predictions in spite of some uncertainty. In *EPIC*, predicted harm to spotted owls was not so uncertain as to require an EIS where the U.S. Forest Service forecasts were based on the extrapolation of existing owl nesting data. 451 F.3d at 1010. In Native Ecosystems Council v. U.S. Forest Serv., 428 F.3d 1233 (9th Cir. 2005), the effects of forest management projects could be reasonably predicted based on prior data.

Here, the Service made reasonable predictions on the basis of prior data, as did the agencies in *EPIC* and *Native Ecosystems*. Although the specter of climate change made the Service's prediction less certain than it would be otherwise, such uncertainty is not "high uncertainty," but only that quotient of uncertainty which is always present when making predictions about the natural world.

Again, we grant the Service great deference as it made a scientific prediction within the scope of its technical expertise. The Service committed no clear error in deciding not to produce an EIS.

**AFFIRMED**

———

## QUESTIONS AND DISCUSSION

**1.** Should the FWS prepared an EIS before issuing its MMPA regulations? What could such an EIS say about climate change?

**2.** The Ninth Circuit was less forgiving in Center for Biological Diversity v. National Highway Traffic Safety Administration, 538 F.3d 1172 (9th Cir. 2007). That case involved a challenge to the NHTSA's "Average Fuel Economy Standards for Light Trucks, Model Years 2008–2011," 71 Fed. Reg. 17,566 (Apr. 6, 2006), issued pursuant to the Energy Policy and Conservation Act of 1975 (EPCA), to set corporate average fuel economy (CAFE) standards for light trucks. The agency concluded that an EIS was unnecessary, but the court disagreed. First, the court held

> The impact of greenhouse gas emissions on climate change is precisely the kind of cumulative impacts analysis that NEPA requires agencies to conduct. Any given rule setting a CAFE standard might have an "individually minor" effect on the environment, but these rules are "collectively significant actions taking place over a period of time." 40 C.F.R. § 1508.7. Thus, NHTSA must provide the necessary contextual information about the cumulative and incremental environmental impacts of the Final Rule in light of other CAFE rulemakings and other past, present, and reasonably foreseeable future actions, regardless of what agency or person—undertakes such other actions.

538 F.3d at 1217. The court then held that the NHTSA failed to consider an adequate range of alternatives to the CAFÉ rule that it adopted. Accordingly, the court remanded to the agency to reconsider its finding of no significant impact, and if necessary, to prepare an EIS.

**3.** In February 2010, the Council on Environmental Quality (CEQ) issued proposed guidance for the consideration of climate change in the NEPA process. *See* Memorandum for Heads of Federal Departments and Agencies from CEQ Chair Nancy Sutley, Draft NEPA Guidance on Consideration of the Effects of Climate Change and Greenhouse Gas Emissions (Feb. 18, 2010), available at http://www.whitehouse.gov/sites/default/files/microsites/ceq/20100218-nepa-consideration-effects-ghg-draft-guidance.pdf. The proposed guidance suggests that "if a proposed action would be reasonably anticipated to cause direct emissions of 25,000 metric tons or more of $CO_2$-equivalent GHG emissions on an annual basis, agencies should consider this an indicator that a quantitative and qualitative assessment may be meaningful to decision makers and the public." *Id.* at 1. If an agency considers the direct effects of a proposed project on climate change, "it would be appropriate to: (1) quantify cumulative emissions over the life of the project; (2) discuss measures to reduce GHG emissions, including consideration of reasonable alternatives; and (3) qualitatively discuss the link between such GHG emissions and climate change. However, it is not currently useful for the NEPA analysis to attempt to link specific climatological changes, or the environmental impacts thereof, to the particular project or emissions, as such direct linkage is difficult to isolate and to understand." *Id.* at 3. The guidance remains a proposal as of July 2016.

## D. FEDERAL COMMON LAW & OTHER FEDERAL LAWS

### Native Village of Kivalina v. ExxonMobil Corporation

United States Court of Appeals for the Ninth Circuit, 2012.
696 F.3d 849.

■ THOMAS, CIRCUIT JUDGE:

The Native Village of Kivalina and the City of Kivalina (collectively "Kivalina") appeal the district court's dismissal of their action for damages against multiple oil, energy, and utility companies (collectively "Energy Producers").[1] Kivalina alleges that massive greenhouse gas emissions emitted by the Energy Producers have resulted in global warming, which, in turn, has severely eroded the land where the City of Kivalina sits and threatens it with imminent destruction. Kivalina seeks damages under a federal common law claim of public nuisance.

The question before us is whether the Clean Air Act, and the Environmental Protection Agency ("EPA") action that the Act authorizes, displaces Kivalina's claims. We hold that it does.

I

The City of Kivalina sits on the tip of a six-mile barrier reef on the northwest coast of Alaska, approximately seventy miles north of the Arctic Circle. The city, which was incorporated as a unified municipality under Alaska state law in 1969, has long been home to members of the Village of Kivalina, a self-governing, federally recognized tribe of Inupiat Native Alaskans. The City of Kivalina has a population of approximately four hundred residents, ninety-seven percent of whom are Alaska Natives.

Kivalina's survival has been threatened by erosion resulting from wave action and sea storms for several decades. The villagers of Kivalina depend on the sea ice that forms on their coastline in the fall, winter, and spring each year to shield them from powerful coastal storms. But in recent years, the sea ice has formed later in the year, attached later than usual, broken up earlier than expected, and has been thinner and less extensive in nature. As a result, Kivalina has been heavily impacted by storm waves and surges that are destroying the land where it sits.

[1] Defendants are: (1) ExxonMobil Corporation; (2) BP P.L.C.; (3) BP America, Inc.; (4) BP Products North America, Inc.; (5) Chevron Corporation; (6) Chevron U.S.A., Inc.; (7) Conocophillips Company; (8) Royal Dutch Shell PLC; (9) Shell Oil Company; (10) Peabody Energy Corporation; (11) The AES Corporation; (12) American Electric Power Company, Inc.; (13) American Electric Power Services Corporation; (14) Duke Energy Corporation; (15) DTE Energy Company; (16) Edison International; (17) Midamerican Energy Holdings Company; (18) Pinnacle West Capital Corporation; (19) The Southern Company; (20) Dynegy Holdings, Inc.; (21) Xcel Energy, Inc.; (22) Genon Energy, Inc.

Massive erosion and the possibility of future storms threaten buildings and critical infrastructure in the city with imminent devastation. If the village is not relocated, it may soon cease to exist.

Kivalina attributes the impending destruction of its land to the effects of global warming, which it alleges results in part from emissions of large quantities of greenhouse gases by the Energy Producers. Kivalina describes global warming as occurring through the build-up of carbon dioxide and methane (commonly referred to as "greenhouse gases") that trap atmospheric heat and thereby increase the temperature of the planet. As the planet heats, the oceans become less adept at removing carbon dioxide from the atmosphere. The increase in surface temperature also causes seawater to expand. Finally, sea levels rise due to elevated temperatures on Earth, which cause the melting of ice caps and glaciers. Kivalina contends that these events are destroying its land by melting the arctic sea ice that formerly protected the village from winter storms.

Kivalina filed this action against the Energy Producers, both individually and collectively, in District Court for the Northern District of California, alleging that the Energy Producers, as substantial contributors to global warming, are responsible for its injuries. Kivalina argued that the Energy Producers' emissions of carbon dioxide and other greenhouse gases, by contributing to global warming, constitute a substantial and unreasonable interference with public rights, including the rights to use and enjoy public and private property in Kivalina. Kivalina's complaint also charged the Energy Producers with acting in concert to create, contribute to, and maintain global warming and with conspiring to mislead the public about the science of global warming.

The Energy Producers moved to dismiss the action for lack of subject-matter jurisdiction, pursuant to Federal Rules of Civil Procedure 12(b)(1) and 12(b)(6). Native Vill. of Kivalina v. ExxonMobil Corp., 663 F. Supp. 2d 863, 868 (N.D.Cal.2009). They argued that Kivalina's allegations raise inherently nonjusticiable political questions because to adjudicate its claims, the court would have to determine the point at which greenhouse gas emissions become excessive without guidance from the political branches. They also asserted that Kivalina lacked Article III standing to raise its claims because Kivalina alleged no facts showing that its injuries are "fairly traceable" to the actions of the Energy Producers.

The district court held that the political question doctrine precluded judicial consideration of Kivalina's federal public nuisance claim. . . . The district court also held that Kivalina lacked standing under Article III to bring a public nuisance suit.

We review a district court's dismissal for lack of subject-matter jurisdiction de novo. The dismissal may be affirmed "on any basis fairly supported by the record." For the purpose of such review, this Court "must accept as true the factual allegations in the complaint."

II

A

In contending that greenhouse gases released by the Energy Producers cross state lines and thereby contribute to the global warming that threatens the continued existence of its village, Kivalina seeks to invoke the federal common law of public nuisance. We begin, as the Supreme Court recently did in American Electric Power Co., Inc. v. Connecticut ("AEP "), 131 S. Ct. 2527, 2535 (2011), by addressing first the threshold questions of whether such a theory is viable under federal common law in the first instance and, if so, whether any legislative action has displaced it. . . . In AEP, eight states, the city of New York, and three private land trusts brought a public nuisance action against "the five largest emitters of carbon dioxide in the United States." The AEP plaintiffs alleged that "defendants' carbon-dioxide emissions created a 'substantial and unreasonable interference with public rights,' in violation of the federal common law of interstate nuisance," and sought injunctive relief through a court-ordered imposition of emissions caps. Concluding that the Clean Air Act already "provides a means to seek limits on emissions of carbon dioxide from domestic power plants," the Supreme Court in AEP held "that the Clean Air Act and the EPA actions it authorizes displace any federal common law right to seek abatement" of such emissions.

This case presents the question in a slightly different context. Kivalina does not seek abatement of emissions; rather, Kivalina seeks damages for harm caused by past emissions. However, the Supreme Court has instructed that the type of remedy asserted is not relevant to the applicability of the doctrine of displacement. In Exxon Shipping Co. v. Baker, 554 U.S. 471 (2008), Exxon asserted that the Clean Water Act preempted the award of maritime punitive damages. The Supreme Court disagreed, noting that it had "rejected similar attempts to sever remedies from their causes of action." In Middlesex County Sewerage Authority v. National Sea Clammers Ass'n, 453 U.S. 1, 4 (1981), the Supreme Court considered a public nuisance claim of damage to fishing grounds caused by discharges and ocean dumping of sewage. The Court held that the cause of action was displaced, including the damage remedy. Thus, under current Supreme Court jurisprudence, if a cause of action is displaced, displacement is extended to all remedies.

Certainly, the lack of a federal remedy may be a factor to be considered in determining whether Congress has displaced federal common law. But if the federal common law cause of action has been displaced by legislation, that means that "the field has been made the subject of comprehensive legislation" by Congress. When Congress has acted to occupy the entire field, that action displaces any previously available federal common law action. Under Exxon and Middlesex, displacement of a federal common law right of action means displacement of remedies. Thus, AEP extinguished Kivalina's federal common law public nuisance damage action, along with the federal common law public nuisance abatement actions.

The Supreme Court could, of course, modify the Exxon/ Middlesex approach to displacement, and will doubtless have the opportunity to do so. But those holdings are consistent with the underlying theory of displacement and causes of action. Judicial power can afford no remedy unless a right that is subject to that power is present. If a federal common law cause of action has been extinguished by Congressional displacement, it would be incongruous to allow it to be revived in another form.

The fact that the damage occurred before the EPA acted to establish greenhouse gas standards does not alter the analysis. The doctrine of displacement is an issue of separation of powers between the judicial and legislative branches, not the judicial and executive branches. When the Supreme Court concluded that Congress had acted to empower the EPA to regulate greenhouse gas emissions, Massachusetts v. EPA, 549 U.S. 497, 528–29 (2007), it was a determination that Congress had "spoken directly" to the issue by legislation. Congressional action, not executive action, is the touchstone of displacement analysis. . . .

III

In sum, the Supreme Court has held that federal common law addressing domestic greenhouse gas emissions has been displaced by Congressional action. That determination displaces federal common law public nuisance actions seeking damages, as well as those actions seeking injunctive relief. The civil conspiracy claim falls with the substantive claim. Therefore, we affirm the judgment of the district court. We need not, and do not, reach any other issue urged by the parties.

Our conclusion obviously does not aid Kivalina, which itself is being displaced by the rising sea. But the solution to Kivalina's dire circumstance must rest in the hands of the legislative and executive branches of our government, not the federal common law.

PRO, District Judge, concurring:

. . . Kivalina alleges specifically with respect to Appellees that greenhouse gas emissions from Appellees' operations "no matter where such operations are located, rapidly mix in the atmosphere and cause an increase in the atmospheric concentration of carbon dioxide and other greenhouse gases worldwide. The heating that results from the increased carbon dioxide and other greenhouse gas concentrations to which defendants contribute cause specific, identifiable impacts in Kivalina." Kivalina further alleges that Appellees "knew that their individual greenhouse gas emissions were, in combination with emissions and conduct of others, contributing to global warming and causing injuries to entities such as the Plaintiffs."

Kivalina has not met the burden of alleging facts showing Kivalina plausibly can trace their injuries to Appellees. By Kivalina's own factual allegations, global warming has been occurring for hundreds of years and is the result of a vast multitude of emitters worldwide whose emissions mix quickly, stay in the atmosphere for centuries, and, as a result, are undifferentiated in the global atmosphere. Further, Kivalina's allegations of their injury and traceability to Appellees' activities is not bounded in time. Kivalina does not identify when their injury occurred nor tie it to Appellees' activities within this vast time frame. Kivalina nevertheless seeks to hold these particular Appellees, out of all the greenhouse gas emitters who ever have emitted greenhouse gases over hundreds of years, liable for their injuries.

It is one thing to hold that a State has standing to pursue a statutory procedural right granted to it by Congress in the CAA to challenge the EPA's failure to regulate greenhouse gas emissions which incrementally may contribute to future global warming. See Massachusetts, 549 U.S. at 516–20. It is quite another to hold that a private party has standing to pick and choose amongst all the greenhouse gas emitters throughout history to hold liable for millions of dollars in damages.

---

## QUESTIONS AND DISCUSSION

**1.** Who is responsible for Kivalina's plight? What should be done about it?

**2.** What rule should nuisance law play in responding to climate change? According to the Restatement of Torts § 821B(1), a public nuisance is an "interference with a right common to the general public." Is that a fair characterization of the effects of climate change? If so, who is responsible for the nuisance? Is there any reason that the plaintiffs sued only the five leading $CO_2$ emitters instead of the 50, 500, or 5,000,000 greatest emitters? Car makers, oil companies, utilities and others all have a duty to behave reasonably and avoid the unreasonable imposition of harm on others, of course, but what is the nature of this duty? What is the duty of fossil fuel companies in providing the energy source for a carbon-based economy? Even if we could identify a duty of care that might reduce greenhouse gas emissions, to whom should this duty be owed? For car companies, is it unreasonable to produce cars that fully comply with existing regulatory requirements? Have the impacts of auto emissions on the climate, and in turn on climatic events, been so foreseeable in the past that a reasonable car company should have accounted for them in their design? Is it sufficient that car companies have been conforming to general industry norms and customs? Indeed, given the consistently strong consumer demand for SUVs and cars with powerful engines, could a car company have reasonably produced low greenhouse gas emission vehicles and even stayed in business? Looking to the future, when will foreseeability and design options have progressed enough that the duty of car companies should evolve? Do the automobile companies' consistent lobbying against national fuel emissions standards or to oppose California's emissions standards in court have relevance to their potential liability? Similar questions could be posed of utilities and other potential defendants.

3. Many other federal laws may have a role to play with respect to climate change, including laws that are hard to imagine at this time. There are two obvious additional candidates, though, whose application to climate change are just beginning to be explored.

*The Clean Water Act*. According to Professor Robin Craig, the CWA can be instrumental in adapting to climate change, though it cannot prevent climate change from occurring. Craig describes the CWA as "a potentially very powerful tool for discovering, analyzing, providing information about, and responding to climate change impacts on the nation's water resources. More specifically, the Clean Water Act is and can be more expansively used as one tool for: (1) generating and compiling information about existing and projected climate change impacts and their effects on water availability, the variety of aquatic species and ecosystems, and the provision of ecosystem services, such as food, drinking water, water purification, and flood control; (2) generating expert recommendations regarding certain protective measures, such as climate-change-adjusted water quality criteria and best management practices for nonpoint sources; and (3) implementing a variety of measures that could mitigate, slow, or otherwise blunt the full impacts of climate change impacts on water quality, including more stringent requirements in NPDES permits for synergistic discharges or discharges into stressed aquatic ecosystems, increased use of best management practices to control nonpoint source pollution and some flooding problems, and increased or new protections for particular waters and aquatic ecosystems at risk." Robin Kundis Craig, *Climate Change Comes to the Clean Water Act: Now What?*, 1 WASH. & LEE J. ENERGY, CLIMATE & ENV'T 7 (2010).

*Federal land management laws*. National parks, forests, wildlife refuges, and other lands each have a statutory mandate describing the goal of their management. Climate change may complicate those goals as, for example, a refuge that was established to preserve one species finds that the species has migrated elsewhere. The glaciers of Glacier National Park are melting, the Saguaro of Saguaro National Park are confronting invasive species and wildfires, and half of the coral reefs of Virgin Islands National Park have died as a result of higher water temperatures since 2006. See Stephen Saunders et al., *National Parks in Peril: The Threats of Climate Disruption* vi (2009). How does the Park Service's duty to manage national parks for conservation and enjoyment apply in such situations? In 2012, NPS Director Jonathan Jarvis advised that the national parks "cannot be held accountable for impairment from external sources—particularly those of global dimensions—over which managers have no control. However, managers can be held accountable for engaging partners and using the best available science, including climate change science, to inform park planning and implementation of cooperative solutions." Memorandum from Director to National Leadership Council & All Superintendents, Applying National Park Management Policies in the Context of Climate Change, Mar. 6, 2012. Jarvis also advised that national parks should continue to strive to maintain "natural conditions" by "removing invasive species and other stressors;

maintaining natural processes and disturbance regimes; restoring naturally functioning ecosystems; supporting biodiversity and landscape connectivity; and continuing other actions that build and support system resilience." *Id.* Likewise, the Forest Service is pursuing its statutory multiple use mandate by emphasizing a research strategy designed to "to sustain ecosystem health, adjust management for ecosystem services ("adaptation"), and increase carbon sequestration ("mitigation"), all under changing climate conditions." U.S. Forest Serv., *Forest Service Global Change Research Strategy*, 2009–2019 4 (2009).

---

## E. STATE AND LOCAL LAWS

State and local governments have been active in responding to climate change, especially given the failure of Congress to enact federal legislation specifically targeting climate change. Every state had adopted some kind of climate change law or policy by 2006. *See* David Hodas, *State Initiatives*, in GLOBAL CLIMATE CHANGE AND U.S. LAW 343 (Michael B. Gerrard, ed., 2008). These laws govern emissions from state government activities, energy conservation, greenhouse gas inventories, agricultural policies, building codes, and regulation of private activities responsible for emitting greenhouse gases. In other instances, existing state laws have been employed to address climate change as well. These scattered approaches are collected in the climate action plans that 28 states had completed by 2006. *See id.* at 351.

### In re Otter Tail Power Company

Supreme Court of South Dakota, 2008.
744 N.W.2d 594.

■ KONENKAMP, JUSTICE:

Otter Tail Power Company, on behalf of several utilities, applied for a permit to construct Big Stone II, a coal-fired energy conversion facility. Certain non-profit environmental organizations intervened to oppose the application. They asserted that the carbon dioxide ($CO_2$) emissions from Big Stone II would contribute to global warming, thereby posing a threat of *serious* environmental injury. The South Dakota Public Utilities Commission (PUC) concluded that although the facility will emit $CO_2$, the amount will not pose a threat of serious injury to the environment. It found that $CO_2$ emissions are not currently regulated by Congress or South Dakota and that Big Stone II would only increase the national amount of emissions by seven hundredths of one percent. Because the PUC followed existing legal guidelines in approving the permit, and its findings were not clearly erroneous, we uphold its decision.

#### Background

The South Dakota Legislature acknowledged the significant impact energy development has on "the welfare of the population, the environmental quality, the location and growth of industry, and the use of the natural resources of the state." SDCL 49–41B–1. It enacted legislation to "ensure that [energy conversion and transmission] facilities are constructed in an orderly and timely manner so that the energy requirements of the people of the state are fulfilled." *Id.* The Legislature deemed it "necessary to ensure that the location, construction, and operation of facilities will produce minimal adverse effects on the environment and upon the citizens of this state by providing that a facility may not be constructed or operated in this state without first obtaining a permit from the [PUC]." *Id*; SDCL 49–41B–4.

A permit application must include:

(1) The name and address of the applicant;

(2) Description of the nature and location of the facility;

(3) Estimated date of commencement of construction and duration of construction;

(4) Estimated number of employees employed at the site of the facility during the construction phase and during the operating life of the facility. Estimates shall include the number of employees who are to be utilized but who do not currently reside within the area to be affected by the facility;

(5) Future additions and modifications to the facility which the applicant may wish to be approved in the permit;

(6) A statement of the reasons for the selection of the proposed location;

(7) Person owning the proposed facility and person managing the proposed facility;

(8) The purpose of the facility;

(9) Estimated consumer demand and estimated future energy needs of those consumers to be directly served by the facility;

(10) The potential short and long range demands on any estimated tax revenues generated by the facility for the extension or expansion of public services within the affected areas;

(11) Environmental studies prepared relative to the facility;

(12) Estimated construction cost of the facility.

SDCL 49–41B–11.

After a request for a permit is filed, the PUC must enlist a local review committee, which "shall meet to assess the extent of the potential social and economic effect to be generated by the proposed facility, to assess the affected area's capacity to absorb those effects at various stages of construction, and formulate mitigation measures." SDCL 49–41B–7. This committee issues a final report to the PUC with its findings and "recommendations of the committee as to mitigation measures and minority reports." SDCL 49–41B–10. The PUC may also "prepare or require the preparation of an environmental impact statement[.]" SDCL 49–41B–21. An applicant is required "to establish that: (1) The proposed facility will comply with all applicable laws and rules; (2) The facility will not pose a threat of serious injury to the environment nor to the social and economic condition of inhabitants or expected inhabitants in the siting area; (3) The facility will not substantially impair the health, safety or welfare of the inhabitants; and (4) The facility will not unduly interfere with the orderly development of the region with due consideration having been given the views of governing bodies of affected local units of government." SDCL 49–41B–22.

On November 8, 2004, in accord with SDCL 49–41B–5, the Otter Tail Corporation, doing business as Otter Tail Power Company, submitted a proposal to the PUC for permission to construct an energy conversion facility. Otter Tail submitted the proposal on behalf of Central Minnesota Municipal Power Agency, Great River Energy, Heartland Consumers Power District, Montana-Dakota Utilities Company, a division of MDU Resources Group, Inc., Southern Minnesota Municipal Power Agency, and Western Minnesota Municipal Power Agency (Applicants). As proposed, the facility would be a 600 megawatt (MW) coal-fired electric generating plant to be located in Grant County, South Dakota, east of Milbank and Northwest of Big Stone. The facility would be named Big Stone II and be situated next to an older facility, Big Stone I.

Several organizations sought to intervene: Clean Water Action; South Dakota Chapter Sierra Club; Union of Concerned Scientists; Mary Jo Stueve; Minnesotans for an Energy-Efficient Economy; Izaak Walton League of America, Midwest Office; and Minnesota Center for Environmental Advocacy (Intervenors). The Intervenors opposed the application on multiple grounds related to the environmental impact of Big Stone II. The PUC granted intervention to all parties.

The Applicants' petition to the PUC triggered SDCL 49–41B–6, and a local review committee was established to prepare a social and economic assessment of Big Stone II. The assessment (1) examined the potential impacts of Big Stone II; (2) addressed the area's ability to absorb those impacts; (3) identified a list of actions needed to ensure a smooth project; and (4) prepared a list of recommended mitigation measures. The committee's findings relate to issues not implicated in this appeal, and therefore, will not be discussed.

An environmental impact statement was also prepared. Among many other things, the impact statement assessed the air quality effects of Big Stone II. In so doing, the statement first identified the applicable regulations, stating

> The Clean Air Act, and its amendments (CAA), requires the Federal U.S. Environmental Protection Agency (USEPA) to set National Ambient Air Quality Standard (NAAQS) for pollutants

> considered harmful to public health and the environment. . . . The USEPA Office of Air Quality Planning and Standards has set NAAQS for six principal pollutants, which are called 'criteria' pollutants.

Draft Environmental Impact Statement May 2006 at 3–1, 3–2. The statement also recognized applicable regulations from Prevention of Significant Deterioration (PSD), New Source Performance Standards (NSPS), Best Available Control Technology (BACT), and the Clean Air Mercury Rule (CAMR).

Although $CO_2$ is not regulated, the statement recognized that Big Stone II was estimated to emit approximately 4.7 million tons of $CO_2$ per year. It remarked, however, that "[p]rojected emissions of all hazardous air pollutants from the existing and proposed plants would be reduced by approximately 41 [million] tons/year (from approximately 63 [million] tons/year by the existing plant to approximately 22 [million] tons/year by the combined existing and proposed plant operations)." Id. at ES–18. Moreover, the statement noted that "[t]he proposed super-critical combustion technology for the proposed Project is three-to-four percent more efficient, and would result in lower $CO_2$ emissions per MWh [megawatt hours] of electrical energy output as compared to the sub-critical boiler technology." Id. at 4–11.

The statement summarized the air quality effects of Big Stone II:

> Overall, no air quality impacts exceed significance criteria for air resources. The long-term impacts from the proposed Project for NAAQS and PSD increment would be less than significant. The Grant County, South Dakota area is in attainment or is unclassifiable for all criteria pollutants. Emissions from the proposed project would not conflict with or obstruct implementation of any applicable air quality plan. Since the increase in criteria pollutant emissions would either be less than the PSD significance levels or well within the NAAQS and PSD increments, the proposed Project long-term and short-term emissions impacts on distant air quality areas that are not in compliance with NAAQS is unlikely. In addition, visibility impacts to Class I and Class II areas would be less than significant. . . .

*Id.* at 4–13. Nevertheless, according to the statement, "[t]he proposed Big Stone II plant would generate unavoidable emissions of air pollutants that would be an adverse impact." *Id.* at 5–1. This was determined notwithstanding that Big Stone II "would operate under [an] appropriate air emission permit from the state of South Dakota that requires operation of the plant under regulatory limits. . . . Even with the permit requirements and air emission control equipment, these impacts would be adverse and unavoidable." *Id.*

In accord with SDCL 49–41B–16, the PUC is required to hold a public hearing near the proposed facility's location. Two public hearings were held. At the first hearing, fifteen people provided testimony. At the second hearing, twenty people attended, with twelve giving testimony. In addition to the public hearings, the Applicants, Intervenors, and the PUC exchanged substantial written discovery, with the Applicants answering more than 500 discovery requests and making available more than 47,000 pages of documents. All parties submitted pre-filed testimony and a formal evidentiary hearing was held on June 26–29, 2006. Oral argument was heard by the PUC on July 11, 2006.

Through their testimony, the Applicants asserted that Big Stone II would provide the energy necessary to serve consumers in South Dakota, North Dakota, Minnesota, Iowa, Montana, and Wisconsin. Big Stone II is projected to produce 4.6 million MW hours of electricity per year. The estimated cost to construct Big Stone II is $1 billion in 2011 dollars. The Applicants claimed that if construction of Big Stone II was delayed or prohibited, the member companies would not be able to generate sufficient energy, which would affect the reliability of their systems and harm consumers.

The Intervenors opposed construction of Big Stone II. They asserted that Big Stone II would pose a threat of serious injury to the environment under SDCL 49–41B–22 and should not be constructed. The threat of serious injury, the Intervenors alleged, would be caused by the amount of $CO_2$ Big Stone II would emit. These emissions, according to the Intervenors, would contribute to global warming, which they contend seriously harms the environment.

To support their contention that global warming harms the environment and $CO_2$ emissions contribute to global warming, the Intervenors submitted expert testimony from Dr. Ezra Hausman. Dr. Hausman is employed with Synapse Energy Economic, Inc., a company specializing in energy and environmental concerns. Dr. Hausman holds a Ph.D. in Atmospheric Science from Harvard University, a master's degree in Applied Physics from Harvard, and a master's degree in Water Resource Engineering from Tufts University.

Dr. Hausman testified that "[h]uman induced climate change is a grave and increasing threat to the environment and to human societies around the globe." According to Dr. Hausman, an increase in many greenhouse gases has caused a 0.6 [degrees] C increase in global temperature in the twentieth century. More notably, he opined, "This means that the planet as a whole does not lose heat to space as efficiently as it otherwise would, so the system as a whole is warming up. This is the phenomenon commonly referred to as 'global warming.' "

According to Dr. Hausman, the increase in global temperature "has come primarily from the burning of fossil fuels (coal, oil, and natural gas), and also from changes in land use such as deforestation." Of the fossil fuels, he stated that "coal emits the most $CO_2$ per unit of energy obtained." Dr. Hausman said that "[t]here is an unequivocal scientific consensus on many aspects of the issue of global climate change." Specifically, according to Dr. Hausman, there is a consensus that:

(1) "the $CO_2$ content of the atmosphere is increasing rapidly;"

(2) "this rate of increase, and resulting abundance of $CO_2$ in the atmosphere, is unprecedented in at least the past 200,000 years and probably much longer;"

(3) "the primary source of the increase is the combustion of fossil fuels by human industrialized societies, i.e., that is the anthropogenic $CO_2$;"

(4) "the increased abundance of $CO_2$ has a direct radiative forcing effect on climate by altering the heat transfer characteristics of the atmosphere;"

(5) "this change in the heat transfer properties of the atmosphere will have an impact on the climate of the planet;"

(6) "the climate of the earth is currently changing in ways that are consistent with model predictions based on the increased radiative forcing due to the anthropogenic increase in the atmospheric $CO_2$[;]"

(7) "the magnitude of climate impacts will increase with increasing atmospheric $CO_2$ content;" and

(8) "once the atmospheric abundance of $CO_2$ has been increased, it will only return to equilibrium levels through natural processes on a timescale of several centuries."

In regard to coal-fired power plants in general, Dr. Hausman testified that the ones "in the United States already emit almost one-third of the U.S. emissions, or 8% of all the world's anthropogenic $CO_2$ into the atmosphere, a staggering contribution to the global buildup of greenhouse gases." Moreover, he testified that because "base load coal plants in the United States are built to produce electricity for decades, as long as 70 years in the case of some of the older plants still operating today", the threat to the environment "is becoming increasingly obvious and severe."

With respect to Big Stone II, Dr. Hausman testified that it would "add over 4.5 million tons of $CO_2$ to the atmosphere every year of its operational life, inexorably and significantly contributing to the buildup of greenhouse gases in the atmosphere." This amount represents a 34% increase in South Dakota's emission record from the EPA in 2001. Further, he said that "[a]t 4.5 million tons per year, emissions from Big Stone II would be equivalent to emissions from almost 670,000 cars." The emissions from Big Stone II, Dr. Hausman explained, "would cause irreversible damage to the environment, especially considering its expected lifetime of 50 years or more and the slow recovery time for atmospheric $CO_2$." He stated, "Human societies and ecosystems will find themselves poorly adapted to their local climate and this will result in disruption of ecosystems[.]" He also predicted that the warming in a region like South Dakota will cause increased temperatures in the summer, resulting in more droughts and reduced crop yields.

He concluded that the emissions from Big Stone II will cause "a significant and irreversible impact on the environment, both globally and in South Dakota. . . . My opinion is that this facility will have a cumulative effect, in combination with other operating energy conversion facilities, both existing and under construction, of causing the level of atmospheric carbon dioxide to be significantly elevated relative to what it would be without this plant. . . . In my opinion, the environmental effects of this facility will pose a threat of serious injury to the environment in South Dakota and in the broader region."

In response to Dr. Hausman's testimony, the Applicants presented the rebuttal testimony of Ward Uggerud, Otter Tail's senior vice-president. Uggerud testified that Dr. Hausman's opinion that Big Stone II will have a significant adverse impact on South Dakota "lacks perspective, to say the least." Although he conceded that "Big Stone II will emit approximately 4.7 million short tons of carbon dioxide per year," Uggerud explained:

> The Energy Information Administration (EIA) reports that U.S. anthropogenic carbon dioxide emissions for 2010 are projected to be 6,365 million metric tons. . . . This means that Big Stone II's share of total U.S. anthropogenic carbon dioxide emissions in 2010 (assuming the plant came on line then) would be 0.0007 (0.07%, or seven hundredths of one percent). According to EIA, global anthropogenic $CO_2$ emissions in 2010 will be 30,005 million metric tons. Big Stone II's share of this amount will be 0.00014 (0.014% or less than two one-hundredths of one percent).

Moreover, Uggerud asserted that "[c]arbon dioxide is not the only greenhouse gas. Other gasses, such as methane and water vapor, also trap heat in the atmosphere. Water vapor is by far the most dominant greenhouse gas." He thought, therefore, that "the evidence is simply insufficient to conclude that $CO_2$ emissions associated with the proposed Big Stone II will cause [a] 'costly adverse impact on the environment both in South Dakota and throughout the region, the continent and the planet.' "

After considering Dr. Hausman's and Uggerud's testimony and the voluminous record, the PUC issued a thirty-four page letter decision, which, among other things, identified the applicable rules and regulations, the site description, alternative locations, and the impact of the plant on the environment. It also evaluated the regulatory and environmental costs associated with construction of Big Stone II. The PUC found that Big Stone II complied with all rules and regulations under SDCL Chapter 49–41B and ARSD Chapter 20:10:22. As for alternative energy sources, the PUC considered a study submitted by the Applicants from Burns & McDonnell Engineering Co. It examined alternative baseload generation technologies, such as wind, biomass, hydropower, solar, landfill gas, geothermal energy, distributed generation, atmospheric circulating fluidized bed, combined cycle natural gas turbine, and integrated coal gasification combined cycle. The PUC concluded that "there were no renewable generation options available to address the need for 600 MW of baseload power within the timeframe required, and that other fossil fuel sources were more expensive and less desirable." Further, according to the PUC, there was no single next best alternative source where the Applicants could obtain the needed energy and the "Intervenors have not proposed an alternative to provide base load capacity through natural gas or oil instead of coal" and "have not suggested any specific alternative to Big Stone II. . . ."

The PUC also addressed an issue that arose at the hearing where the Intervenors argued that the Applicants should pay the costs associated with possible future regulation of $CO_2$ emissions. Because neither Congress nor South Dakota has regulated $CO_2$ emissions, and the PUC found it speculative whether such regulations would be established, it concluded that imposing costs would be unwarranted.

The PUC considered the environmental impact statement filed by the Applicants. The statement indicated that Big Stone II would emit approximately 4.7 million tons of $CO_2$ each year and over 225 million tons of $CO_2$ over the expected life of the plant. But the plant would "produce about 18% less $CO_2$ than other existing coal-fired plants because the super-critical boiler proposed here is more efficient than other forms of coal-fired technologies." Thus, the PUC found that Big Stone II "will not contribute materially to the increase in the production of anthropogenic carbon dioxide[.]" The PUC also found that Big Stone II "would increase U.S. emissions of carbon dioxide by approximately .0007, or seven-hundredths of one percent[.]"

In sum, considering the voluminous record, including the pre-filed testimony, the committee report, the environmental impact statement, and the applicable rules and regulations, the PUC concluded that "if constructed in accordance with the terms and conditions" set forth in its decision, Big Stone II "will not pose a threat of serious injury to the environment or to the social and economic conditions of the inhabitants or expected inhabitants in the siting area."

Accordingly, the PUC granted the Applicants a permit to construct Big Stone II in compliance with the terms and conditions of the PUC's decision. In circuit court, the Intervenors' appeal was affirmed. They now appeal to this Court asserting that the PUC's decision (1) violated the plain language of SDCL 49–41B–22; and (2) was clearly erroneous in light of the evidence as a whole.

**Standard of Review**

Our review of the PUC's decision granting the Applicant's request for a permit to construct Big Stone II is controlled by SDCL 1–26–36. See Tebben v. Gil Haugan Const., Inc., 729 N.W.2d 166, 171 (S.D. 2007). The PUC's findings of fact are reviewed under the clearly erroneous standard, while its conclusions of law are reviewed de novo. See id. "A reviewing court must consider the evidence in its totality and set the [PUC's] findings aside if the court is definitely and firmly convinced a mistake has been made." Id.

**Analysis and Decision**

According to the Intervenors, the PUC erroneously applied SDCL 49–41B–22, and therefore, our review must be de novo, and we should accord no deference to the PUC's decision that Big Stone II will not pose a threat of serious injury to the environment. They argue that the PUC "was duty-bound to recognize" the findings by the scientific community concerning the impact of $CO_2$ emissions on global warming. Moreover, they argue that the PUC's finding that Big Stone II will emit 4.7 million tons of $CO_2$ each year clearly demonstrates that the plant will pose a threat of serious harm to the environment.

The Applicants respond that there are no regulations governing the emission of $CO_2$, and thus there are no standards by which to conclusively establish what amount of emission constitutes a threat of serious injury to the environment. According to the Applicants, the PUC was required to determine if Big Stone II, not all coal-fired facilities, will pose a threat of serious injury to the environment. Because Big Stone II is calculated to increase U.S. emissions by 0.0007, or seven hundredths of one percent, the Applicants contend that the PUC's conclusion is not clearly erroneous in light of all the evidence. Moreover, the PUC required that the Applicants report annually on any $CO_2$ regulations and their efforts to bring Big Stone II into compliance.

We review the PUC's decision and decide whether, based on the evidence as a whole, we are left with a definite and firm conviction that a mistake has been made. While we give due regard to an agency's well-reasoned and fully informed decision, we will not uphold clear errors of judgment or conclusions unsupported in fact. Our task in this appeal is to decide the narrow question of whether the PUC's conclusion that Big Stone II will not pose a threat of serious injury to the environment was clearly erroneous in light of all the evidence.

There were over 1,400 pages of documentary evidence submitted in this case. The Applicants offered evidence of studies conducted concerning the effect Big Stone II might have on the environment and the community. They also submitted evidence regarding the alternative sources of energy they considered, but ruled out. The Intervenors do not dispute the Applicants' need for the additional wattage. Nor do they present an argument that there exists a viable alternative to Big Stone

II's coal-fired facility. More significantly, the Intervenors suggest no standards by which the PUC may assess what amount of $CO_2$ emissions are tolerable. Rather, they maintain that $CO_2$ emissions, at any measurable level, seriously harm the environment.

Global warming presents a momentous and complex threat to our planet. A resolution for this problem, critical though it is, cannot be made in the isolation of judicial proceedings. The social, economic, and environmental consequences of global warming implicate policy decisions constitutionally reserved for the executive and legislative branches. To date, no $CO_2$ emission standards have been enacted by our political leaders. "Congress has recognized that carbon dioxide emissions cause global warming and that global warming will have severe adverse impacts in the United States, but it has declined to impose any formal limits on such emissions." Connecticut v. American Elec. Power Co., Inc., 406 F. Supp. 2d 265, 268–69 (S.D.N.Y. 2005) (citing The Global Climate Protection Act of 1987, PL 100–204, Title XI, §§ 1102–03, reprinted at 15 U.S.C. § 2901 note).

As members of the judiciary, we refrain from settling policy questions more properly left for the Governor, the Legislature, and Congress. No matter how grave our concerns on global warming, we cannot allow personal views to impair our role under the Constitution. In South Dakota, the Legislature designated the PUC as the responsible agency for this question of granting a permit. We must uphold the PUC's decision unless we conclude that the ruling was "clearly erroneous in light of the entire evidence in the record or arbitrary or capricious or characterized by abuse of discretion or clearly unwarranted exercise of discretion." See Korzan v. City of Mitchell, 708 N.W.2d 683, 686 (S.D. 2006) (citing SDCL 1–26–36).

The PUC, in its thirty-four page decision, entered several findings of fact concerning the issue of global warming and $CO_2$ emissions. It recognized that despite the asserted scientific consensus on the harm caused from global warming, neither Congress nor the South Dakota Legislature has chosen to regulate $CO_2$ emissions. Therefore, the PUC addressed the potential harm from Big Stone II by comparing the projected level of $CO_2$ emissions from Big Stone II to the level of emissions nationally. Because Big Stone II would increase $CO_2$ emissions by 0.0007, or seven hundredths of one percent, the PUC concluded the threat of harm would not result in serious injury. Nonetheless, as a condition on the permit, the PUC required that the Applicants submit annual reviews of any regulations on $CO_2$ emissions and their efforts to comply with those regulations.

Our review of the record shows the PUC entered a well-reasoned and informed decision when it concluded that Big Stone II would not pose a threat of serious injury to the environment. It addressed the parties' contentions regarding global warming and $CO_2$ emissions and also provided a detailed explanation of why it rejected the findings proposed by the Intervenors.

While global warming and $CO_2$ emissions are considered harmful by the scientific community, what will pose a threat of serious injury to the environment under SDCL 49–41B–22 is a judgment call initially vested with the PUC by the Legislature. Nothing in SDCL Chapter 49–41B so restricts the PUC as to require it to prohibit facilities posing any threat of injury to the environment. Rather, it is a question of the acceptability of a possible threat. Resolving what is acceptable for the people of South Dakota is not for this Court. The Legislature and Congress must balance the competing interests of economic development and protection of our environment. Based on all the evidence and our limited scope of review, the PUC's decision was not clearly erroneous.

Affirmed.

---

## QUESTIONS AND DISCUSSION

**1.** How does the South Dakota Supreme Court's view of its role compare to the United States Supreme Court's understanding of its role in *Massachusetts v. EPA?*

**2.** South Dakota's PUC sees its duty as "ensur[ing] utility companies in South Dakota provide safe, reliable service at fair and reasonable rates." Did its decision with respect to Big Stone II further that goal? More generally, the National Association of Regulatory Utility Commissioners resolved in 2007 that "during the nation's likely transition to greater reliance upon lower-carbon resources for the generation of electric power, State regulators should consider adopting policy approaches and regulatory tools that ensure continued electric system reliability and minimize economic dislocation and costs to consumers." Resolution on State Regulatory Policies Toward Climate Change, Nov. 14, 2007, http://www.naruc.org/Resolutions/ERE1%20 Resolution%20on%20State%20Regulatory%20Policies%20Toward%20 Climate%20Change.pdf.

**3.** Notwithstanding the court's decision, Big Stone II was abandoned in November 2009. The first hint of trouble occurred in September 2007, when the Central Minnesota Municipal Power Agency and Great River Energy withdrew from the project, leaving the projected capacity of the plant undersubscribed by about 27%. Three days after President Obama took office in 2009, EPA overturned its approval of the project. Then Otter Tail Power Co. quit the project on September 11, 2009, citing the economic downturn and uncertainty about pending federal regulations for carbon dioxide emissions. "This is happening in the context of coal plants around the country being abandoned," said Margaret Levin, state director for the Minnesota North Star chapter of the Sierra Club. "I would certainly attribute this outcome to an increased understanding . . . that we have got to switch away from coal and other dirty forms of power." See http://www.sourcewatch. org/index.php?title=Big_Stone_II.

4. The Sierra Club underscored its view of coal in the title of its 2008 report: "The Dirty Truth About Coal: Why Yesterday's Technology Should Not Be Part of Tomorrow's Energy Future." "Mining and burning coal scars lungs, tears up the land, pollutes water, devastates communities, and makes global warming worse," according to the report. Such attacks have generated complaints about a "war on coal" being waged by environmental organizations and EPA officials during the Obama Administration. One member of Congress introduced the "Stop the War on Coal Act of 2012" because "the Obama administration has waged a multi-front war on coal, on coal jobs, on the small businesses in the mining supply chain, and on the low cost energy that millions of Americans rely on." 158 CONG. REC. H6196 (daily ed. Sept. 20, 2012) (remarks of Rep. Hastings of Wash.). For his part, President Obama embraces an "all of the above" approach to energy development, including "clean coal." *See* Executive Office of the President, The President's Climate Action Plan 6 (June 2013) (listing "clean coal technology" as a type of clean energy technology). But the Sierra Club responds that "clean coal" is "America's lead energy misnomer." And remember that regardless of what the United States does about coal, China is opening a new coal-fired power plant every ten days. *See* Peter Galuszka, *With China and India Ravenous for Energy, Coal's Future Seems Assured*, N.Y. TIMES, Nov. 12, 2012.

## Association of Irritated Residents v. California Air Resources Board

California Court of Appeal, First District, Division 3, 2012.
206 Cal.App.4th 1487, 143 Cal.Rptr.3d 65.

■ POLLAK, J.

This appeal questions whether the "Climate Change Scoping Plan" adopted by the California Air Resources Board in 2009 complies with the requirements of the Global Warming Solutions Act of 2006. As did the trial court, we answer this question in the affirmative.

### Background

*The Legislation*

The Global Warming Solutions Act of 2006 (the Act or AB 32) (Health & Saf. Code, § 38500 et seq.) was conceived as groundbreaking legislation. The findings with which the Act begins declare that "[g]lobal warming poses a serious threat to the economic well-being, public health, natural resources, and the environment of California" (§ 38501, subd. (a)) and continues: "California has long been a national and international leader on energy conservation and environmental stewardship efforts, including the areas of air quality protections, energy efficiency requirements, renewable energy standards, natural resource conservation, and greenhouse gas emission standards for passenger vehicles. The program established by this division will continue this tradition of environmental leadership by placing California at the forefront of national and international efforts to reduce emissions of greenhouse gases" (§ 38501, subd. (c)).

The Act designates the California Air Resources Board (ARB or the Board) as "the state agency charged with monitoring and regulating sources of emission of greenhouse gases that cause global warming in order to reduce emissions of greenhouse gases", and imposes numerous directives and timelines on the Board. By June 30, 2007, the Board was to publish "a list of discrete early action greenhouse gas emission reduction measures that can be implemented prior to the measures and limits" to be adopted subsequently, and to adopt implementing regulations by January 1, 2010. By January 1, 2008, the Board was to "adopt regulations to require the reporting and verification of statewide greenhouse gas emissions and to monitor and enforce compliance with this program." By the same date and after receiving public input, the Board was required to "determine what the statewide greenhouse emissions level was in 1990, and approve . . . a statewide greenhouse emissions limit that is equivalent to that level, to be achieved by 2020."

The mandate central to the current litigation is contained in section 38561, which provides in part: "(a) On or before January 1, 2009, the [Board] shall prepare and approve a scoping plan as that term is understood by the [Board], for achieving the maximum technologically feasible and cost-effective reduction in greenhouse gas emissions from sources or categories of sources of greenhouse gases by 2020 under this division. . . . [¶] (b) The plan shall identify and make recommendations on direct emission reduction measures, alternative compliance mechanisms, market-based compliance mechanisms, and potential monetary and nonmonetary incentives for sources and categories of sources that the [Board] finds are necessary or desirable to facilitate the achievement of the maximum feasible and cost-effective reductions of greenhouse gas emissions by 2020. [¶] . . . [¶] (d) The [Board] shall evaluate the total potential costs and total potential economic and noneconomic benefits of the plan for reducing greenhouse gases to California's economy, environment, and public health, using the best available economic models, emission estimation techniques, and other scientific methods." The Board is required to update the scoping plan "at least once every five years." Section 38562 requires the Board to adopt implementing regulations by January 1, 2011, to become effective on January 1, 2012.

*Adoption of the Scoping Plan*

The process for developing and approving the scoping plan in compliance with the statutory mandate was extensive and rigorous. Since no challenge is made to the procedures followed by the Board, the process need not be elaborated in detail. The process involved more than 250 public workshops, more than 350 community meetings, and meetings by several specialized committees, including an environmental justice advisory committee, an economic and technology advancement advisory committee, and a market advisory committee. Technical analyses were submitted to academic peer review. In June 2008, the Board released a discussion draft of the scoping plan, in response to which it received some 5,000 pages of public comments. This was followed by several staff-led public workshops and community meetings. Additional public comments were received at Board meetings in June and October 2008. In October the Board released the "Proposed Scoping Plan" which elicited thousands of additional public comments. In all, more than 42,000 people commented on the draft scoping plan. The final public hearings took place over two days in December 2008, during which the Board made some modifications to the proposed scoping plan and, at the conclusion of the hearing, adopted Resolution No. 08–47. The resolution directed staff to take certain steps to finalize the plan and the functional equivalent document (FED) prepared to comply with the California Environmental Quality Act (CEQA) (Pub. Resources Code, § 21000 et seq.). The resolution recited that "[t]he recommendations in the *Proposed Scoping Plan* are necessary or desirable to facilitate the achievement of the maximum feasible and cost-effective reductions of greenhouse gas emissions by 2020." On May 7, 2009, the Board issued Executive Order No. G–09–001 adopting the final scoping plan.

*The Scoping Plan*

The final plan, entitled "Climate Change Scoping Plan: a framework for change," is 121 pages in length, plus many lengthy exhibits and appendices. The plan is preceded by a 14-page executive summary and consists of an introductory framework section, a section listing proposed emissions reduction measures, a section discussing methods used to evaluate those measures, a section discussing implementation of the plan, and a final section entitled "A Vision for the Future." The section on emissions reduction measures lists measures under 18 categories, including "California Cap-and-Trade Program Linked to Western Climate Initiative Partner Jurisdictions," energy efficiency, low carbon fuel standards, vehicle efficiency measures, a "Million Solar Roofs Program," industrial emissions, high speed rail, green building strategy, recycling and waste, sustainable forests, water, and agriculture. The plan summarizes the key elements of its recommendations, designed to reduce greenhouse gas emissions to 1990 levels by 2020, as follows:

- "Expanding and strengthening existing energy efficiency programs as well as building and appliance standards;
- Achieving a statewide renewable energy mix of 33 percent;
- Developing a California cap-and-trade program that links with other Western Climate Initiative partner programs to create a regional market system;
- Establishing targets for transportation-related greenhouse gas emissions for regions throughout California and pursuing policies and incentives to achieve those targets;

- Adopting and implementing measures pursuant to existing State laws and policies, including California's clean car standards, goods movement measures, and the Low Carbon Fuel Standard; and
- Creating targeted fees, including a public goods charge on water use, fees on high global warming potential gases, and a fee to fund the administrative costs of the state's long-term commitment to AB 32 implementation."

The scoping plan states that the emissions reduction measures that it recommends "will be developed over the next two years and be in place by 2012." The report concludes with the suggestion of additional measures to further reduce emissions beyond 2020 and to keep the state on track to meet the goal established by Governor Schwarzenegger in Executive Order No. S–3–05 of an 80 percent reduction below 1990 greenhouse gas emission levels by the year 2050.

*The Litigation*

On June 10, 2009, a petition for a writ of mandate was filed against the Board and its individual members by the Association of Irritated Residents, several other nonprofit organizations and several individuals (collectively AIR). The petition alleges that the scoping plan does not comply with the mandates of the Act—AB 32—and that the FED failed to comply with CEQA. With respect to the former, the petition alleges that the scoping plan "(a) fails to achieve the maximum technologically feasible and cost-effective reductions; (b) fails to require emissions reduction measures for significant sources of emissions, namely industrial and agricultural sources; (c) does not develop any policies to avoid the pitfalls of other greenhouse gas emission trading programs and fails to address how ARB will monitor and enforce reductions in a regional market; (d) fails to assess the likely impacts of proposed policy choices and regulatory programs and fails to propose policies to ensure that compliance with chosen measures will not disproportionately impact already overburdened communities; and (e) fails to prevent increases in criteria and toxic co-pollutant emissions. [¶] Instead, the Scoping Plan's analysis acts as a *post hoc* rationalization for the policy decisions already chosen by ARB." The petition alleges several respects in which the FED assertedly does not comply with CEQA, including the failure to adequately analyze alternatives to the regional cap-and-trade program included in the scoping plan.

[After extended proceedings before the trial court and the court of appeals,] what remains before the court is AIR's cross-appeal questioning whether the scoping plan satisfies the requirements of the Global Warming Solutions Act of 2006.

## Analysis

*Standard of Review*

. . . AIR characterizes its challenge as being directed to "'the fundamental legitimacy' of [ARB]'s quasi-legislative action to adopt the scoping plan" requiring the court to exercise its independent judgment. On that premise AIR asserts that the trial court erred in evaluating the plan under the arbitrary and capricious standard. However, the trial court implicitly satisfied itself that the plan "is within the scope of authority conferred," thus limiting its review of the plan's specifics to the more deferential arbitrary and capricious standard. We believe this is the correct standard.

"[I]f it can be inferred from the authorizing legislation that a [public agency] has been granted considerable discretion to determine what is necessary to accomplish a valid legislative goal, a more deferential standard of review is appropriate." ARB is explicitly directed by the Act to "prepare and approve a scoping plan, *as that term is understood by the [Board]*." (§ 38561, subd. (a), italics added.) The Board is directed to "consult with all state agencies with jurisdiction over sources of greenhouse gases" (*ibid.*) and to receive public input (§ 38561, subd. (g)), to "consider all relevant information pertaining to greenhouse gas emissions reduction programs" in other jurisdictions (*id.*, subd. (c)), to "evaluate the total potential costs and total potential economic and noneconomic benefits of the plan . . . to California's economy, environment, and public health, using the best available economic models, emission estimation techniques, and other scientific methods" (*id.*, subd. (d)) and, ultimately, to "identify and make recommendations on direct emission measures, alternative compliance measures, market-based mechanisms, and potential monetary and nonmonetary incentives for sources and categories of sources *that the [Board] finds are necessary and desirable* to facilitate the achievement of the maximum feasible and cost-effective reductions of greenhouse gas emissions by 2020" (*id.*, subd. (b)). These directives are exceptionally broad and open-ended. They leave virtually all decisions to the discretion of the Board, from determining the nature of a scoping plan, to determining the best available research techniques, to determining incentives for emissions reduction that are "necessary and desirable," to weighing economic, environmental and public health benefits, to determining what is most "feasible and cost-effective." Determining the content of the scoping plan plainly falls on the "deferential end of the continuum accorded quasi-legislative agency action" for which review under the arbitrary and capricious standard is appropriate.

*ARB did not disregard the statute or act arbitrarily or capriciously in adopting the scoping plan*

On appeal, AIR contends that ARB violated the terms of the Act in three principal respects: it assertedly "(1) limited the scoping plan measures to only those necessary to achieve the minimum reductions required by [the Act]; (2) failed to create and apply a standard criteria for cost-effectiveness; and (3) failed to include feasible and cost-effective direct regulations from the agricultural and industrial sectors in the scoping plan (choosing only to regulate industry through the cap and trade program and allow agricultural sources to provide offsets to industry)."

AIR's initial contention is that the Board violated the terms of the statute by failing to design the scoping plan to achieve "*maximum* technologically feasible and cost-effective reductions in greenhouse gas emissions." The scoping plan states repeatedly that it is designed "to achieve the 2020 greenhouse gas emissions limit." The emissions reduction measures in the draft scoping plan were calculated to achieve an aggregate reduction of 169 MMTCO$_2$E, which would reduce total emissions to what was determined to be the 1990 greenhouse gas emissions level. AIR contends that while this complies with section 38550 of the Act, requiring the Board to establish the statewide greenhouse gas emissions 1990 level as the limit to be achieved by 2020, it fails to comply with section 38561, which requires the Board to adopt a scoping plan to achieve "the *maximum* technologically feasible and cost-effective reductions" by 2020. AIR argues that rather than using the limit set under section 38550 as the minimum to be achieved by the scoping plan but seeking the maximum level of reductions possible, the Board has converted the limit into a ceiling.

AIR views the matter too narrowly. The goal that the plan sets for 2020 is but a step towards achieving a longer-term climate goal. As the plan states, "we must look beyond 2020 to see whether the emissions reduction measures set California on the trajectory needed to do our part to stabilize global climate. [¶] Governor Schwarzenegger's Executive Order S–3–05 calls for an 80 percent reduction below 1990 greenhouse gas emission levels by 2050. . . . Full implementation of the Scoping Plan will put California on a path toward these required long-term reductions. Just as importantly, it will put into place many of the measures needed to keep us on that path." The Board sought to define in the scoping plan measures that will permit the state to reach goals that are attainable by 2020, as a step toward the ultimate objective by 2050. It reasonably set those goals as the 1990 emissions level required by section 38550, but those goals are neither designed to limit nor do they have the effect of limiting emission reductions if greater reductions can be achieved. The draft scoping plan estimated that the measures proposed in the plan would bring emissions down to the 1990 level by reducing the level of emissions projected in 2020 in the absence of those measures ("business-as-usual") from 596 MMTCO$_2$E to 427 MMTCO$_2$E, a reduction of 169 MMTCO$_2$E. Modifications made subsequently provide a "margin of safety" by recommending additional strategies to account for measures in uncapped sectors of the economy that do not achieve estimated reductions. The modifications further increase estimated aggregate reductions in 2020 from 169 $MMTCO_2E$ to 174 $MMTCO_2E$. . . .

Even if other measures, such as inflexible emission limits or emission taxes might conceivably result in greater reductions, the Act does not call for maximum reductions without qualification, but for maximum reductions that are both feasible and cost-effective. The record reflects that the Board went to exceptional lengths to obtain informed and scholarly input on the complex scientific and economic issues that bear on these critical qualifications. While there are differences of opinion on many matters, AIR points to no recommendation included in the plan, and no rejection of a suggested recommendation, for which substantial evidence was not presented and considered.

AIR's principal contention is that the Board recommended implementing a cap-and-trade program to limit industrial greenhouse gas emissions without considering the feasibility and cost-effectiveness of alternative direct control measures. The record does not support this contention. The Board's economic analysis of the draft scoping plan, which recommended the cap-and-trade program, was submitted to independent peer reviewers for additional review. Two of those reviewers expressed the concern that the Board's analysis was designed too narrowly to allow identification of the most cost-effective approach to achieving the emissions limit. In response, the staff explained: "As the draft plan was developed, three major options—use of a cap-and-trade program together with complementary measures; use of a carbon fee together with complementary measures; and use of only sector-specific measures—were evaluated from a number of policy perspectives, which resulted in the preliminary recommendation to use a cap-and-trade program together with complementary measures." The record supports these statements.

The draft scoping plan included a section entitled "Other Measures Under Evaluation," which discussed potential measures under the headings "Other Sector-Based Measures," "Carbon Fees," and "Offsets." The discussion of carbon fees describes how such fees might be used, calculated, and implemented, and states: "Carbon fees, while supported by a number of interests, have received less attention during the development of the draft plan, in large part because they provide less certainty in California's ability to meet specific emission targets, as required under AB 32." A submission from a scholar at the Goldman School of Public Policy at the University of California at Berkeley explains that cap-and-trade sets a cap on the level of emissions but entails uncertainty as to the price that will be paid for a ton of emissions, while a carbon fee establishes the price but entails uncertainty as to the quantity of emissions that will result. Appendix C to the final scoping plan contains the following explanation with reference to several measures that were not recommended in the plan: "ARB has determined that some of the measures . . . that were still under evaluation in the draft scoping plan are not appropriate to pursue as regulations. However, for many of them, the types of reductions that were being evaluated are likely to be undertaken by facilities covered by the cap-and-trade program in the locations where they are most cost effective. ARB believes, based on the review of emission reduction opportunities conducted for the scoping plan, that significant reduction opportunities exist in the industrial sector that are more readily achieved through market mechanisms than through direct measures."

The final scoping plan explains the Board's rationale for recommending a cap-and-trade program in combination with the so-called "complementary measures" by citing the rationale outlined by the Market Advisory Committee and quoting from the report of the Economic and Technology Advancement Advisory Committee, in part, as follows: "A declining cap can send the right price signals to shape the behavior of consumers when purchasing products and services. It would also shape business decisions on what products to manufacture and how to manufacture them. Establishing a price for carbon and other GHG emissions can efficiently tilt decision-making toward cleaner alternatives. This cap and trade approach (complemented by technology-forcing performance standards) avoids the danger of having government or other centralized decision-makers choose specific technologies, thereby limiting the flexibility to allow other options to emerge on a level playing field. [¶] . . . Complementary policies will be needed to spur innovation, overcome traditional market barriers . . . and address distributional impacts from possible higher prices for goods and services in a carbon-constrained world." It is not for the court to re-evaluate ARB's judgment call, which is neither arbitrary nor unsupported in the record. Moreover, we note that the plan recommends numerous measures in addition to the cap-and-trade program which account for significantly more than half of the projected greenhouse gas emission reductions in 2020.

AIR faults the Board for failing to create and apply standard criteria for cost-effectiveness by which to evaluate alternative measures. Cost-effectiveness is not easily measured, however. The statute provides this definition: " 'Cost-effective' or 'cost-effectiveness' means 'the cost per unit of reduced emissions of greenhouse gases adjusted for its global warming potential.' " (§ 38505, subd. (d).) As the scoping plan observes, "This definition specifies the metric (i.e., dollars per ton) by which the Board must express cost-effectiveness, but it does not provide criteria to assess if a regulation is or is not cost-effective." Nor does it define what is to be included as a "cost" or how such costs are to be measured. As observed in a letter to the Board from the numerous environmental organizations identified below, "Because cost-effectiveness is merely a comparative tool, it is impossible to define cost-effectiveness in the abstract." The record shows that extended consideration was given to establishing a methodology for evaluating cost-effectiveness. Four possible approaches were studied by staff and described in a white paper presented to a

"Technical Stakeholder Working Group." Ultimately the Board adopted the so-called "Cost of a Bundle of Strategies" that was unequivocally endorsed in a letter to the Board from the Natural Resources Defense Council, the Union of Concerned Scientists, the Environmental Defense Fund, the Coalition for Clean Air, Californians Against Waste, the Center for Energy Efficiency and Renewable Technologies, California Wind Energy Association, and The Nature Conservancy. The scoping plan estimates the cost per ton of greenhouse gas emissions reductions from the measures recommended in the plan will range from $55 per ton to a net savings of $408 per ton. The plan concludes: "The criteria for judging cost-effectiveness will be updated as additional technological data and strategies become available. As ARB moves from adoption of the scoping plan to developing specific regulations, and as regulations continue to be adopted, updated cost-effectiveness estimates will be established in a rigorous and transparent process with full stakeholder participation."

. . . Determining the best means of identifying and implementing the most cost-effective and feasible measures to maximize greenhouse gas emissions reductions involves numerous highly technical and novel scientific, technical and economic issues. The voluminous administrative record makes clear that the Board approached this challenge by soliciting and obtaining knowledgeable input from industry, academia, environmental organizations, and members of the general public. It is not for the court to reweigh the conflicting views and opinions that were expressed on these complex issues, which in the end are largely matters of judgment in all events. We are satisfied that the record provides ample support for the recommendations on which the Board settled, and that its choices were thoughtfully considered, well within the scope of the Legislature's directive, and not arbitrary or capricious.

AIR contends that the scoping plan fails to "assess" available direct control measures in the agricultural sector and "fails to include them in the plan so as to maximize reductions." The record, however, reflects extensive analysis of numerous potential measures in the agricultural sector. Consideration was given to at least 11 different strategies applicable to this sector, ranging from agricultural pump efficiency and tractor tire inflation programs to manure management, fertilizer use efficiency, soil carbon sequestration and agricultural biomass utilization.

The final scoping plan recommends only voluntary measures in this sector at present. The single specific proposal included in the plan is "[e]ncouraging the capture of methane through use of manure digester systems at dairies," and reassessment of the voluntary approach at the five-year update "to determine if the program should become mandatory for large dairies by 2020." The plan also indicates that the Board has begun a research program to better understand the variables affecting fertilizer $N_2O$ emissions, "the other significant source of greenhouse gases in the agricultural sector." AIR faults the Board for not recommending a mandatory manure digester protocol and other mandatory agricultural measures. The explanation for not doing so, however, appears among other places in the record in an "Agriculture Sector Write-Up" prepared by staff for public distribution. The write-up explains: "The agriculture sector is unique in that nearly 82 percent of all greenhouse gas (GHG) emissions from the sector involve biological processes. . . . The gaps in scientific knowledge and scientific uncertainty in existing data on greenhouse gas emissions resulting from the complex biological process of agro ecosystems make the identification of real, permanent, additional, verifiable and enforceable reduction measures difficult to immediately implement. Research on understanding these systems, emissions, and rigorous quantification methodologies are needed to achieve the full reduction potential from this sector. . . . [¶] Due to scientific uncertainty resulting from complex biological process of agro ecosystems, traditional command and control regulations may not be feasible for many of the identified measures. In addition, implementation of many measures may not be cost effective without providing additional incentives or establishing an offset market." With specific reference to the recommendation that the manure digester protocol be voluntary, another document explains: "Establishing a voluntary protocol can help incentivize the installation of manure digesters by legitimizing the technology and offering a pathway to quantify and verify the GHG benefits. Keeping this protocol a voluntary measure helps avoid premature technology mandates which could have significant cost and environmental drawbacks due to digesters currently being a costly, combustion-driven technology." The Board's reasoning is neither arbitrary nor irrational. . . .

**Conclusion**

The Governor and the Legislature have set ambitious goals for reducing the level of greenhouse gas emissions in California and to do so by means that are feasible and most cost-effective. The challenges inherent in meeting these goals can hardly be overstated. ARB has been assigned the responsibility of designing and overseeing the implementation of measures to achieve these challenging goals. The scoping plan is but an initial step in this effort, to be followed by the adoption of regulations, the first of which are already in effect, and plan updates no less than every five years. As the plan itself indicates, there is still much to be learned that is pertinent to minimizing greenhouse gas emissions. It is hardly surprising that the scoping plan leaves some questions unanswered and that opinions differ as to many complex issues inherent in the task. After reviewing the record before us, we are satisfied that the Board has approached its difficult task in conformity with the directive from the Legislature, and that the measures that it has recommended reflect the exercise of sound judgment based upon substantial evidence. Further research and experience likely will suggest modifications to the blueprint drawn in the scoping plan, but the plan's adoption in 2009 was in no respect arbitrary or capricious.

---

### QUESTIONS AND DISCUSSION

**1.** Why is California such a leader among states addressing climate change? Why have so few states followed?

**2.** Numerous states have joined together to form regional greenhouse gas initiatives. See generally Eleanor Stein, Regional Initiatives to Reduce Greenhouse Gas Emissions, in GLOBAL CLIMATE CHANGE AND U.S. LAW 315 (Michael B. Gerrard, ed., 2008). The Northeast Regional Greenhouse Gas Initiative, for example, commits ten states to cap and reduce $CO_2$ emissions from the power sector 10% by 2018. Regulated power plants can use a $CO_2$ allowance issued by any of the ten participating states to demonstrate compliance with the state program governing their facility. *See* Bruce Huber, *How Did RGGI Do It?*, 39 ECOLOGY L.Q. 59 (2013). Taken together, the ten individual state programs function as a single regional compliance market for carbon emissions.

**3.** Over 1,000 mayors from across the United States have endorsed the U.S. Mayors Climate Protection Agreement, which in addition to calling for bipartisan federal response to climate change also commits their municipalities to meeting the reduction goals of the Kyoto Protocol and beyond. Many US cities have gone further, announcing substantial commitments to GHG reductions. Many cities have developed climate change adaptation plans, too.

## F. DEVELOPING RENEWABLE ENERGY

The laws that we have examined so far in this chapter attempt to discourage activities that emit greenhouse gases. Another group of laws seek to encourage activities that do not emit greenhouse gases. One-third of greenhouse gases come from the generation of electricity, so it is not surprising that there are many efforts to promote clean sources of energy production. The definition of what constitutes "renewable" or "green" energy is sometimes contested, especially as it related to nuclear and hydroelectric power, neither of which emit greenhouse gases but which cause other environmental harms. Wind and solar energy are the most favored types of renewable energy, while geothermal, tidal, and other technologies are at an earlier stage of development. The law encourages renewable energy by giving it favorable regulatory treatment, by mandating that utilities generate a specified amount of electricity with renewable sources, and by subsidizing renewable energy technology and projects. We consider the regulatory and mandate approaches in the following materials.

## Zimmerman v. Board of County Commissioners

Supreme Court of Kansas, 2009.
218 P.3d 400.

■ NUSS, JUSTICE:

This appeal results from the decision by the Board of County Commissioners of Wabaunsee County (Board) to amend its zoning regulations. Specifically, the Board prohibited the placement of Commercial Wind Energy Conversion Systems (CWECS, *i.e.,* commercial wind farms) in the county. . . . Plaintiffs are owners of land in Wabaunsee County who have entered into written contracts for the development of commercial wind farms on their properties. Intervenors are the owners of wind rights concerning other properties in the county.

Defendant is the three-member Board of County Commissioners of Wabaunsee County. The county is roughly 30 miles long and 30 miles wide, containing approximately 800 square miles and 7,000 people. It is located in the Flint Hills of Kansas, which contain the vast majority of the remaining Tallgrass Prairie that once covered much of the central United States.

In October 2002, the county zoning administrator told the Board that he had been contacted by a company desiring to build a wind farm in the county. At that time, the county had no zoning regulations relating specifically to wind farms. The next month, the Board passed a temporary moratorium on the acceptance of applications for conditional use permits for wind farm projects until the zoning regulations could be reviewed. The moratorium was extended on at least five occasions. . . .

[In 2004, the Board the county's Comprehensive Plan and amended its zoning code to prohibit CWECS but to allow Small Wind Energy Conversion Systems (SWECS, *i.e.,* small wind farms). Plaintiffs sued the Board, seeking to invalidate the prohibition on CWECS. District Court Judge Ireland dismissed the claims].

*Aesthetics*

As the court held in [Gump Rev. Trust v. City of Wichita, 131 P.3d 1268 (2006)], Kansas appellate courts have long allowed aesthetics to be considered in zoning matters. *See, e.g.,* Ware v. City of Wichita, 214 P. 99 (1923) (recognizing in a zoning case that "[t]here is an aesthetic and cultural side of municipal development which may be fostered within reasonable limitations. Such legislation is merely a liberalized application of the general welfare purposes of state and federal constitutions."). As our court acknowledged 60 years later: "[T]he current trend of the decisions is to permit regulation for aesthetic reasons. *See* Metromedia, Inc. v. San Diego, 453 U.S. 490, [1981]." Robert L. Rieke Bldg. Co. v. City of Overland Park, 657 P.2d 1121 (1983).

In addition to our long-standing case law, we further observe that K.S.A. 12–755(a) expressly provides that "[t]he governing body may adopt zoning regulations which may include, but not be limited to, provisions which: . . . (4) control the aesthetics of redevelopment or new development." As the Court of Appeals has observed when citing this statute, "regulation of redevelopment or new development is permitted for aesthetic reasons. K.S.A. 12–755." Blockbuster Video, Inc. v. City of Overland Park, 24 Kan. App. 2d 358, Syl. P 2, 948 P.2d 179 (1998).

Judge Ireland relied heavily on *Gump*. There, the city-county zoning code allowed construction of new communication facility towers up to 85 feet by administrative permit. According to the facts of that case, there was no prohibition against building new towers higher than 85 feet, but such towers required a conditional use permit approved by the city of Wichita.

Gump requested a conditional use permit to build a tower with an initial height of 135 feet, with a possible extension to 165 feet. The city denied the request, and Gump argued that the denial of the conditional use permit was unreasonable. The district court upheld the denial and a Court of Appeals panel affirmed, essentially holding that aesthetics alone was a reasonable basis for the city's action.

There are aesthetics considerations alleged in the instant case. The Board's Findings of Fact filed with the district court on October 6, 2006, included, *inter alia:*

> "10. The facts presented at various meetings indicate that Wind Farms would likely consist of complexes of a dozen or more turbines, *located on ridge lines within the county*. A single complex could have a footprint of 7500–20,000 acres. The turbines themselves would be from 260 to over 300′ tall, with blades 125′ in length. The mounting pad would be 14′ x 14′ x 28′ deep and made of concrete. The complexes could probably be seen from a distance of 20, or more miles. Wabaunsee County is approximately 30 miles, east to west, and 30 miles, north to south. The Zilkha Map (CR-270) shows potential sites that were being actively pursued by developers. These sites are located south of K-4 Highway between Alta Vista and Eskridge *along the ridge line*.
>
> "11. The Flint Hills of Kansas, of which Wabaunsee County is a part, contain the vast majority of the remaining Tallgrass Prairie, which once covered much of the central United States. The Tallgrass Prairie is considered one of the most endangered ecosystems in North America.
>
> "12. Wind Farms could have a detrimental effect on the ecology of the area. Prairie Chicken habitat may be altered so as to affect flight patterns, breeding grounds, nesting areas and feeding areas. Flora and Fauna may also be affected by industrial concentration of Wind Farms." (Emphasis added.)

The Board's Conclusions filed on October 6 included, *inter alia,* the following determinations regarding aesthetics and the closely related areas of ecology, flora, and fauna:

> 1. "The location of Wind Farms within Wabaunsee County would not be in the best interests of the general welfare of the County as a whole. In arriving at this conclusion, the Board is mindful of the fact that 'general welfare' includes a board spectrum of values, *including aesthetics. . . . Placing complexes of Wind Farms, of the size and scope necessary to accomplish their intended purpose, upon the ridge lines of the County would have a dramatic, and adverse, [e]ffect upon all of those general welfare issues [e.g.,* aesthetics].
>
> 2. ". . . *The size, and scope, of the proposed Wind Farms make them objectionable and unsightly,* partly as evidenced by the overwhelming opposition by the public. There is no question that the location of Wind Farms will have *an adverse effect on the scenic areas of the County. There is also evidence that their presence will have an adverse effect on wildlife.*
>
> 3. ". . . In addition to the support set forth in the preceding paragraphs, the Board would note that there was evidence presented that: . . . (b) *they* [Wind Farms] *would be harmful to the environment and the tallgrass ecosystem;* . . . [and] (d) they would have a *negative impact on wildlife.*
>
> 4. "Wind Farms would be incompatible with the rural, agricultural, and *scenic character of the County.*
>
> . . .
>
> 6. "Wind farms would be detrimental to property values and opportunities for agricultural and *nature based tourism. The Flint Hills are unique in their ecology, heritage and beauty.* The adverse effect Wind Farms will have on all of these things will also have an adverse effect on property values *and tourism."* (Emphasis added.)

Judge Ireland found that "[t]here is no doubt the County looked at the aesthetics of having the wind generators as a compatible or incompatible use with the Flint Hills area." We agree, particularly when the Board has cited its finding to the record for our review. We also agree that these Board's findings could reasonably have been found to justify its decision: that the commercial wind farms would adversely, if not dramatically, affect the aesthetics of the county and for that reason should be prohibited.

*Nonconformance with comprehensive plan and other considerations*

More than aesthetics considerations are alleged in the instant case. The Board's submitted Findings of Fact first referenced specifics of the county's Comprehensive Plan 2004:

"9. The final adopted Plan, Wabaunsee County Comprehensive Plan 2004, includes the following goals and objectives, which were developed as a direct result of a county-wide survey and focus groups by the Plan Preparation Class:

. . .

"b. *Maintain the rural character of the county with respect to its landscape, open spaces, scenery, peace, tranquility and solitude.*

. . .

"d. Develop realistic plans to protect *natural resources such* as the agricultural land, *landscape, scenic views, and Flint Hills* through regulatory policy

. . .

"h. *Develop tourism programs involving* historic properties, *nature of rural character, and scenic landscape.*" (Emphasis added.).

In the Board's Conclusions, it then determined that the commercial wind farms were not in conformance with the Comprehensive Plan 2004 for numerous reasons:

"5. The location of Wind Farms in Wabaunsee County would not conform to the Wabaunsee County Comprehensive Plan 2004, including the goals and objectives that were identified by the citizens of the County and incorporated as a part of the Plan. *The goals and objectives set forth in the Plan make it clear that maintaining the rural character of the County, and protecting the landscape, open spaces, scenery, peace, tranquility, and solitude of the County is of paramount important to the citizens. The size, scope and location of Wind Farms would be inconsistent with those goals.*" (Emphasis added.)

Judge Ireland found that "[t]he County also looked at the comprehensive plan . . . [and] found that placing the complexes of wind farms, of the size and scope necessary to accomplish their intended purpose, would have a dramatic, and adverse, effect upon all of the general welfare issues found in the comprehensive plan." We essentially agree with the judge, particularly when the Board has cited its finding to the record for our review.

We also agree that these Board findings could reasonably have been found to justify its decision: that the commercial wind farms would not be in conformance with the Comprehensive Plan 2004, *e.g.*, to "maintain the rural character of the County with respect to its landscape, open spaces, peace, tranquility and solitude" and to "develop tourism programs involving . . . [the] nature of rural character and scenic landscape." Consequently, the commercial wind farms should be prohibited. As aesthetics have been a valid consideration for a governing body's zoning decisions since at least 1923, conformance with the governing body's comprehensive plan has been a valid consideration since at least 1978.

*Wishes of the residents*

We agree with Judge Ireland that the Board not only took into consideration the commercial wind farms' impact upon county aesthetics and their nonconformance with the Comprehensive Plan 2004, but also considered the wishes of the citizens of Wabaunsee County. The Board's Findings of Fact reveal, *inter alia:*

> "4. In December 2002, the Planning Commission conducted its first meeting to discuss the pros and cons of wind farms. The Planning Commission conducted numerous public meetings on this topic from December 2002 until June 2004. In all, between the Planning Commission and the Board, this topic was discussed, in one form or another, at approximately 54 meetings over this period.
>
> "5. The first extensive public hearing on this issue was conducted by the Planning Commission on July 24, 2003. This meeting was well attended by the public and *a majority of the public attending expressed their opposition to allowing Wind Farms in Wabaunsee County*. . . .
>
> . . .
>
> "8. On December 11, 2003, the Planning Commission conducted a public hearing on the Comprehensive Plan, and approximately 200 people attended this hearing.
>
> "9. The final adopted Plan, Wabaunsee County Comprehensive Plan 2004, includes . . . goals and objectives, which were developed as a direct result of a county-wide survey and focus groups by the Plan Preparation Class. . . .
>
> . . .
>
> "13. In public meetings where the issue of Wind Farms was discussed, *the majority of those in attendance opposed allowing them. The vast majority of letters received by the Planning Commission and the Board expressed opposition to Wind Farms."* (Emphasis added.)

The Board's Conclusions provided to the district court included the following:

> "2. . . . The size, and scope, of the proposed Wind Farms make them objectionable and unsightly, *partly as evidenced by the overwhelming opposition by the public.*
>
> . . .
>
> "5. The location of Wind Farms in Wabaunsee County would not conform to the Wabaunsee County Comprehensive

Plan 2004, *including the goals and objectives that were identified by the citizens of the County and incorporated as a part of the Plan.*" (Emphasis added.)

In the words of Judge Ireland, "[o]ne can review the meetings and correspondence which the County conducted in its attempt to determine the wishes of the citizens of Wabaunsee County, Kansas. A large portion of the community's wishes were against the wind farms as proposed by the plaintiffs." Based upon our own examination of the record, including those places cited in support of the Board's findings, we agree. We also agree that these Board findings, while alone insufficient, could reasonably have been found to help justify its decision.

Intervenors take particular exception, however, to either the amount of the evidence presented in support of the commercial wind farm ban based on aesthetics or to the arguably greater amount of evidence presented in opposition to the ban. For example, they state: "Granted, some of the testimony and letters cited by the Board support finding CWECS may impact the aesthetic and scenic value of the Flint Hills. Nonetheless, the record also reveals an abundance of evidence CWECS would have minimal impact." They also acknowledge the Board's reliance upon a "Memorandum Re: Industrial Scale Wind Turbine Development Presented by the Tallgrass Ranchers, "which states that a landscape architect/attorney "has analyzed the visual impact of wind turbine complexes and . . . determined that they would be harmful to the stability and identity of the Flint Hills.". . . . As a result, the Intervenors conclude that "[a] reasonable zoning regulation would have accounted for the conflicting views by acknowledging CWECS can be placed in areas in which the current aesthetics would not be negatively impacted."

Intervenors misunderstand our limited review on this issue. [We are] limited to determining whether the given facts could reasonably have been found by the Board to justify its decision. We could not substitute our judgment for that of the Board, and we should "not declare the action unreasonable unless *clearly compelled to do so by the evidence.*" (Emphasis added.) Combined Investment Co. v. Board of Butler County Comm'rs, 605 P.2d 533 (1980).

The Intervenors also take exception to the Board's reliance upon the alleged nonconformance with the Comprehensive Plan 2004. They again, however, appear to make an argument that would require us to reweigh the evidence presented there. For example, they argue that the "Board's Findings of Fact cites testimony from the July 24, 2003, Planning Commission hearing of Roger Badeker and Larry Patton as evidence that CWECS would not conform to the . . . Comprehensive Plan 2004." They acknowledge "these individuals concluded these systems were not consistent with the Comprehensive Plan" but argue "their statements are mere conclusions and not actual evidence of nonconformance."

We must again disagree. Intervenors take no exception to the fact that these individuals provided testimony. Accordingly, their testimony is obviously evidence. Moreover, Badeker has written professionally on the subject of zoning. Consequently, the Board may have considered his "mere conclusions" as carrying additional weight, *i.e.,* approaching that of an expert witness. See Badeker, *"Tell it to the Judge: Appealing a Zoning Decision."* 67 J.K.B.A. 33 (September 1998); *K.S.A. 60–456* on expert witnesses. In any event, this testimony clearly supports the Board's finding of fact which could reasonably have been found by the Board to justify its decision: that the commercial wind farms were inconsistent with the Comprehensive Plan 2004 and therefore should be prohibited.

The Intervenors also take particular exception to the third factor relied upon by the Board as characterized by Judge Ireland: the concerns of county residents. Intervenors point out that the evidence reveals that some residents were for the commercial wind farms, others were against. They acknowledge that the Board should consider the objections of county residents but, quoting *Gump,* argue that " '[z]oning is not to be based upon a plebiscite of the neighbors.' " Intervenors argue that " 'although their wishes are to be considered, the final ruling is to be governed by consideration of the benefit or harm involved to the community at large.' " *Gump,* 35 Kan. App. 2d at 511. They argue the Board did not consider the community at large because it failed to consider "the impact upon [the] parties seeking to take advantage of their property rights."

Judge Ireland found that after reviewing the documents and the minutes of numerous meetings in the record, "the pros and cons of wind farms were discussed." He concluded that "the County has taken into account the benefit or harm involved to the community at large." We agree, and reject the position of the Intervenors.

Overall, we must acknowledge that several key points of appellate review dictate our result. We recognize that the Board—and not the court—has the right to change the zoning; that there is a presumption that the Board acted reasonably; that the Plaintiffs and Intervenors have the burden of proving the unreasonableness by a preponderance of the evidence; that this court may not substitute its judgment for the Board and should not declare the zoning amendment unreasonable unless *clearly* compelled to do so by the evidence; and that an act is unreasonable when "it is so arbitrary that it can be said it was taken without regard to the benefit or harm involved to the community at large, including all interested parties, and was so wide of the mark that its unreasonableness lies outside the realm of fair debate." Combined Investment Co. v. Board of Butler County Comm'rs, 605 P.2d 533 (1980). With these precepts in mind, we cannot hold that the Plaintiffs and Intervenors have met their burden of showing the Board acted unreasonably.

Finally, Plaintiffs' and Intervenors' repeated arguments that a county-wide ban on all commercial wind farms was unreasonable implies that the overall scope of the ban was somehow unreasonable *per se* and therefore improper. . . . In our view, however, the situation in the instant case does not involve such an absolute: The Board is allowing *some* wind farms, *i.e.,* small ones, and disallowing only the large, commercial wind farms. . . . More particularly, it allows a "*Small* Wind Energy Conversion System" (SWECS) consisting of a wind turbine, a tower and controls, which has a rated capacity of not more than 100 kilowatt and which is less than 120 feet in height and intended solely to reduce on-site consumption of purchased utility power. *See* Zoning Regulations, Article 1–104 (210); Article 31–109(i)(f).

By contrast, the Board has disallowed systems that exceed 100 kilowatt, exceed 120 feet in height, or that consist of more than one system of any size proposed or constructed by the same person or group of persons on the same or adjoining parcels or as a unified or single generating system. Zoning Regulations, Article 1–104 (208); Article 31–112(5). Consistent with this statutory authority, the Board further limits the small wind energy conversion systems by specifying parcel size, density, spacing, setback distance, blade height and advertising.

As for any argument that the important distinction is based not upon size, but rather upon commercial versus noncommercial, *i.e.,* so that any-sized commercial system is banned, we nevertheless believe that such a distinction, and therefore such restriction, is valid.

In sum, the Plaintiffs and Intervenors have not established that the Board acted unreasonably in amending its zoning regulations to prohibit commercial wind farms in its county.

---

## QUESTIONS AND DISCUSSION

**1.** Why don't the residents of the Flint Hills want large wind farms? Would you want to live near a wind farm? Where is the ideal place to locate a wind farm?

**2.** Wind is attractive to many environmentalists because it is a renewable source of energy. But wind turbines often generate as much controversy as they do electricity. Wind turbines are notorious for killing bats and birds (as we discuss in Part II of Chapter 10). Aesthetic complaints about wind turbines are also common. One of the most famous disputes has occurred in Nantucket. "A company known as Cape Wind, LLC has proposed the permanent installation of 130 wind turbines, each reaching 417 feet in height, on 24 square miles of Nantucket Sound in an area surrounded by three commercial airports, two busy ferry routes, and a major shipping channel." 152 CONG. REC. 6439 (daily ed. June 22, 2006) (statement of Sen. Stevens). That proposal has divided environmentalists, elicited complaints of elitism against the wealthy landowners on the island, and prompted efforts for congressional intervention. As one writer complained, the project "faces over-my-dead-body opposition from, among many others, two of the greatest environmental advocates of our time: Senator Edward Kennedy and his nephew, Robert F. Kennedy Jr., whose family compound has a view of the Nantucket Sound that would be forever changed by these giant windmills." Hamilton Kahn, *On Cape, Gales of Hypocrisy*, BOSTON GLOBE, May 16, 2007, at A9. That same writer asked "[w]hy aren't those likely to be affected first by global warming more eager to take the lead on alternative energy?" How would you answer that question?

The West Virginia Supreme Court of Appeals allowed a wind farm project to proceed despite aesthetic complaints in Mountain Communities for Responsible Energy v. Public Serv. Comm'n, 665 S.E.2d 315 (W. Va. 2008). The state's public service commission approved a wind farm consisting of 124 turbines spanning 23 miles along a ridge in Greenbrier County. On review, the state supreme court explained that the commission regarded the visual impact of the turbines as "a hotly contested issue." *Id.* at 329. The commission, quoted the court, asserted that, " 'what one person considers beautiful, another may consider ugly, while yet others are indifferent. The same goes for wind turbines. Some people consider them eyesores they do not want in their backyards. Others consider them elegant or beautiful.' " *Id.* The court also observed that the commission recognized "that while many expressed opposition to the project, other members of the public voice support of it for a variety of reasons including economic development and clean, renewable energy." *Id.* at 330. The court thus upheld the commission's decision as based upon substantial evidence and a proper weighing of the interests.

**3.** Wabaunsee County's solution is to restrict the size of wind farms. The State of Washington takes the opposite approach. Washington's solution is to give its governor the authority to override local zoning decisions to bar wind farms. In Residents Opposed to Kittitas Turbines v. State Energy Facility Site Evaluation Council, 197 P.3d 1153 (Wash. 2008), the court upheld the governor's approval of a wind farm despite the opposition of local residents. The governor acted pursuant to the state's energy facilities site locations act (EFSLA), which establishes a procedure for reviewing wind farm applications and authorizing the governor to decide whether to preempt local zoning regulations. The court held that the governor properly exercised such authority, and that the state-mandated EIS adequately considered the aesthetic impact of the proposed 121 wind turbines even though the EIS did "not list 'moving turbines away from every possible viewpoint' as a potential mitigation measure." *Id.* at 1172.

## Oregon Natural Desert Association v. Jewell

United States Court of Appeals for the Ninth Circuit, 2016.
2016 U.S. App. LEXIS 9642.

■ BERZON, CIRCUIT JUDGE:

Renewable energy projects, although critical to the effort to combat climate change, can have significant adverse environmental impacts, just as other large-scale developments do. Here, the Oregon Natural Desert Association and the Audubon Society of Portland (collectively, "ONDA") challenge a wind-energy development on the ground that the U.S. Bureau of Land Management's ("BLM") environmental review of the project did not adequately address impacts to the greater sage grouse, a relatively large ground-dwelling bird once abundant in the western United States. Greater sage grouse depend on sagebrush habitat for their survival. The challenged project entails the construction of wind turbines and a right-of-way across a sagebrush landscape in southeastern Oregon's Harney County.

We conclude that the BLM's review did not adequately assess baseline sage grouse numbers during winter at the Echanis site, where the wind turbines are to be installed. As to that point, we reverse the district court's entry of summary judgment in favor of the BLM, Harney County, and Columbia Energy Partners, the project developer. . . .

I.

**A. The Project**

The Echanis Wind Energy Project "is a 104-megawatt (MW) wind energy facility that would be constructed on a 10,500-acre privately-owned tract" on Steens Mountain in Harney County, Oregon. BLM, *North Steens 230-kV Transmission Line Project Final Environmental Impact Statement* (Oct. 2011) ("FEIS") ES–1. Between 40 and 69 wind turbines would be built on the Echanis site. FEIS ES–11, 2–21, 3.1–2; *see* FEIS 2–22–23. The North Steens 230-kV Transmission Line, which involves "the construction, operation, and maintenance of a new [230-kilovolt] overhead electric transmission line and associated facilities on BLM-administered land," would transport energy from the turbines to the electrical grid. FEIS ES–1–2. The entire undertaking—that is, both the transmission line and the turbine complex—("the Project"), was approved in the BLM's FEIS and Record of Decision ("ROD") here challenged.

Columbia Energy Partners received a conditional use permit from Harney County to develop the Project, commissioned several studies of the Project, and secured a 20-year agreement to sell energy generated by the wind facility. FEIS ES–1. Because the right-of-way for the transmission line crosses public lands administered by the BLM, and the construction of the turbines is a "connected action," 40 C.F.R. § 1508.25(a)(1), the entire Project is subject to environmental review under the National Environmental Policy Act ("NEPA"), 42 U.S.C. § 4321, *et seq. See* FEIS 1–1.

The Echanis site was chosen because "[i]nitial site reconnaissance revealed wind-swept areas well exposed to prevailing west winds and—where present—significant 'flagging' of vegetation, indicating a robust westerly wind resource." FEIS app. F at 6. This preliminary assessment was confirmed after a meteorological tower was erected at the site. *Id.* After considering three alternatives, the BLM chose a route for the transmission line and associated infrastructure that would cut across, in part, the Steens Mountain Cooperative Management and Protection Area ("Steens Protection Area"). *See, e.g.*, FEIS ES–3, ES–11, 1–4–5.

### B. Steens Mountain

Steens Mountain is many miles long and nearly 10,000 feet in elevation at its highest point. In 2000, Congress enacted the Steens Mountain Cooperative Management and Protection Act ("Steens Act"), which, among other things, established the Steens Protection Area and the Steens Mountain Wilderness Area. FEIS 1–19; *see* 16 U.S.C. § 460nnn, *et seq.* "The purpose of the [Steens Protection Area] is to conserve, protect, and manage the long-term ecological integrity of Steens Mountain for future and present generations." 16 U.S.C. § 460nnn–12(a). Under the Steens Act, the "ecological integrity" that must be conserved, protected, and managed includes "the maintenance of . . . genetic interchange." 16 U.S.C. § 460nnn(5)(B). Steens Mountain, home to many sagebrush communities, lies near the center of one of the last remaining "strongholds of contiguous sagebrush habitat essential for the long-term persistence of greater sage-grouse."

### C. Greater Sage Grouse

The greater sage grouse is a sagebrush-obligate bird, meaning that it relies on sagebrush for its survival year-round. Sage grouse use different aspects of sagebrush habitats for various purposes. For instance, at leks, "open areas surrounded by sagebrush," male sage grouse strut and compete for female mates, displaying their elaborate plumage. In addition, sage grouse use sagebrush habitats for nesting and brood rearing.

Sagebrush habitat is also essential for winter survival of sage grouse. "During the winter months, [the] greater sage-grouse's diet consists almost entirely of sagebrush leaves and buds." To facilitate sagebrush consumption, sage grouse in the winter months "tend toward areas with high canopy and taller sagebrush plants. . . . Sagebrush must be exposed at least 9.8 to 11.8 inches (25 to 30 cm) above the snow level to provide adequate forage and cover." "[I]f sagebrush is covered with snow, greater sage-grouse will move to areas where the sagebrush is exposed. . . . The availability of sagebrush above the snowpack is critical to the survival of greater sage-grouse through the winter." FEIS 3.5–23–24.

Once abundant across much of the western United States and Canada, the greater sage grouse now lives in "continually declining" and "increasingly separate" populations. FEIS 3.5–22. Since the 1950s, the overall population of sage grouse has declined by somewhere between 45% and 80%. *Id.* "Habitat loss and fragmentation are the primary cause[s] for long-term changes in [sage grouse] population abundance and distribution." As a consequence, "[m]aintenance of connectivity and reduction of fragmentation of sagebrush habitats is key to the long-term welfare of all . . . sagebrush associated species." Oregon is unique in that, "[c]ompared to other states within the range of sage-grouse, [it] has large expanses of contiguous habitat with minimal threats of fossil fuel exploration or development." "Oregon sage-grouse populations and sagebrush habitats likely comprise nearly 20% of the North American range wide distribution."

### D. Environmental Review

The impacts of the Project on sage grouse were by far the most significant concern during the environmental review process at issue here. In the draft environmental impact statement ("DEIS"), FEIS, and ROD, the BLM adopted information, guidance, and mitigation measures concerning the sage grouse from the Oregon Department of Fish & Wildlife's *Mitigation Framework* and *Sage Grouse Strategy* documents. FEIS ES–19, 3.5–21, 3.5–25–26; *see* C.A. Hagen, *Mitigation Framework for Sage-Grouse Habitats*, Aug. 23, 2011 ("*Mitigation Framework*").

In response to the DEIS, ONDA submitted to the BLM numerous comments on a variety of issues, supporting the comments with scientific studies, wildlife management materials, and other documents. After the comment period ended, the BLM issued the FEIS and ROD, selecting the North Route transmission line as the preferred alternative to be implemented. The North Route line would be approximately 46 miles long, connecting an electric substation at the Echanis site with an interconnection station near Crane, Oregon.

Of relevance here, the FEIS acknowledged the "potential conflict between wind energy development and greater sage-grouse winter foraging habitats, because the windswept ridges that keep sagebrush exposed during winter months could also be ideal locations for wind energy development." FEIS 3.5–25. Despite this concern, no surveys were conducted to determine if sage grouse are present at the Echanis site during the winter months of November through April. Instead, the BLM assumed, based on surveys done at the nearby East Ridge and West Ridge sites, that no grouse use the Echanis site during winter. The FEIS stated that "no greater sage-grouse were found" at the East and West Ridge sites between late December and April, during the period of snow accumulation. It explained:

> The East Ridge and West Ridge projects are similar but potentially at even lower elevations [than is the Echanis site]. . . . Because the Echanis Project area is generally covered with snow earlier and later in the season because of it's [sic] relatively higher elevation, it is reasonable to extrapolate winter use from the surveys at the East Ridge and West Ridge sites. Therefore, based upon these data, greater sage-grouse are assumed not to utilize the Echanis Project Area for winter habitat from the time that the vegetation is covered with snow until snowmelt, roughly December through April.

FEIS 3.5–25.

As to connectivity concerns, the transmission lines and associated access and maintenance roads would physically divide sage grouse habitat, and the lines would provide perches for predatory raptors (such as hawks and eagles) and corvids (such as ravens, crows, and jays). Accordingly, the FEIS assumed that grouse would avoid and be displaced from areas near transmission lines and poles. This displacement, combined with possible avoidance of some areas due to noise or other project-related disturbances, would result in habitat fragmentation, as the lines transect otherwise contiguous grouse habitat.

**E. This Litigation**

After the FEIS and ROD issued, ONDA filed a complaint in the U.S. District Court for the District of Oregon, challenging environmental review of the Project under NEPA. Harney County and Columbia Energy Partners intervened. The parties then filed cross-motions for summary judgment. Ultimately, the court granted the defendants' motions for summary judgment and denied ONDA's.

We reverse the district court's ruling.

II.

ONDA asserts that the BLM's review of the Project did not comply with NEPA, "our basic national charter for protection of the environment." The centerpiece of environmental review under NEPA is the environmental impact statement ("EIS"), in which the responsible federal agency describes the proposed project and its impacts, alternatives to the project, and possible mitigation for any impacts. NEPA imposes procedural requirements on federal agencies undertaking review; it does not mandate outcomes.

NEPA challenges are reviewed under the Administrative Procedure Act ("APA"). *Id.* Under the APA, we ask whether the agency's action was "arbitrary, capricious, an abuse of discretion, or otherwise not in accordance with law." 5 U.S.C. § 706(2)(A). An agency's action can be set aside as arbitrary and capricious only if the agency relied on factors Congress did not intend it to consider, entirely failed to consider an important aspect of the problem, or offered an explanation that runs counter to the evidence before the agency or is so implausible that it could not be ascribed to a difference in view or the product of agency expertise.

**A. Baseline Winter Conditions**

ONDA first contends that the BLM erred in failing directly to assess baseline conditions at the Echanis site, instead relying on an extrapolation from nearby sites to conclude that there is no greater sage grouse winter habitat at Echanis.

The establishment of a "baseline is not an independent legal requirement, but rather, a practical requirement in environmental analysis often employed to identify the environmental consequences of a proposed agency action." An EIS must "succinctly describe the environment of the area(s) to be affected . . . by the alternatives under consideration," 40 C.F.R. § 1502.15, and "insure that environmental information is available to public officials and citizens *before* decisions are made and *before* actions are taken," *id.* § 1500.1(b) (emphases added). "Accurate scientific analysis . . . [is] essential to implementing NEPA." *Id.*

Applying these principles, several cases have found environmental analyses insufficient for failing to establish an environmental baseline. Indeed, as to another project planned for sage grouse territory, the BLM submitted comments to the U.S. Department of Transportation ("DOT") urging DOT to assess baseline winter sage-grouse populations along a rail line. *See* N. Plains Res. Council v. Surface Transp. Bd. , 668 F.3d 1067, 1084 (9th Cir. 2011). Specifically, with regard to DOT's EIS, the BLM commented that "[w]ith the increasing importance of sage grouse, more discussion on sage grouse is needed, including discussion on wintering areas. . . . Sage grouse inventories need to be conducted at least two miles from any proposed disturbance." *Id. Northern Plains Resource Council* agreed with the BLM that DOT did not adequately assess baseline conditions for the challenged project. Similarly, *Half Moon Bay* ruled that analysis in an EIS was inadequate because it failed to assess baseline underwater conditions at a site where it was proposed dredged materials would be dumped. Half Moon Bay Fisherman's Marketing Ass'n v. Carlucci, 857 F.2d 505, 510 (9th Cir. 1988).

Under *Northern Plains Resource Council* and *Half Moon Bay*, the BLM had a duty to assess, in some reasonable way, the actual baseline conditions at the Echanis site. Baseline conditions were particularly important here because impacts to sage grouse were by far the most significant concern during environmental review, and the unique features of winter habitat are essential to sage-grouse survival. Baseline conditions at the Echanis site thus warranted comprehensive study in the FEIS.

The FEIS did not report on *any* observations of the Echanis site surveying winter sage grouse use of the area. Instead, the FEIS assumed that sage grouse are absent from the site during winter. FEIS 3.5–25. To justify this assumption, the FEIS relied on data from the East and West Ridge sites, located near the Echanis site but at generally lower elevations. *Id.* In doing so, the FEIS asserted that, although 36 sage grouse were found at the East Ridge site on December 17, 2008 and nine birds were found on the West Ridge site on December 11, "no greater sage-grouse were found later in December, or in January, February, March, or April, during the time that snow had accumulated." *Id.* The FEIS then explained that its extrapolation from surveys at these sites was reasonable because the "potentially" lower elevation of the sites, as compared to the Echanis site, indicated that it is more likely that snow would accumulate at Echanis earlier and dissipate later in winter. It is *less* likely, the FEIS asserted, that sage grouse use the Echanis site than the East and West Ridge sites in winter. A fundamental flaw infects this reasoning.

Contrary to what the FEIS stated, four sage grouse *were* found at the East Ridge site—the surveyed site closer to Echanis—during *February*, indicating that some sage grouse do spend the winter there. The FEIS thus did not comply with the requirement to provide "[a]ccurate scientific analysis," which is "essential to implementing NEPA," 40 C.F.R. § 1500.1(b), or with the agency's obligation to "insure the professional integrity, including scientific integrity, of the discussions and analyses in [EISs]," *id.* § 1502.24.

Further, that *some* grouse were found at the East Ridge site in mid-winter greatly undermines the validity of the BLM's assumed absence of sage grouse at the Echanis site. Given that grouse do use the East Ridge site during the winter, the BLM's own extrapolation method should have resulted in assuming the birds' *presence*, not their *absence*.

The record as a whole confirms the validity of this contrary assumption. Christian Hagen, the Oregon Department of Fish & Wildlife scientist who prepared the *Mitigation Framework*, suggested that, if grouse were still present at the East and West Ridge sites in December, the conditions were probably right to spend the entire winter there; in fact, as noted, grouse were present in February. Further, several sources on which the FEIS relied, and the FEIS itself, acknowledge that the wind-swept character of the Echanis site—the aspect of the site that makes it ideal for wind-energy generation—suggests it could be good winter habitat for sage grouse, despite its "potentially" higher elevation, as snow there may be blown off sagebrush and exposed for grouse to eat. And scientists and cooperating agencies recommended to the BLM either that actual winter surveys of sage grouse be conducted or, if not, that the BLM assume sage grouse were present at the Echanis site during the entire winter.

In short, the FEIS's inaccurate data concerning the closer East Ridge site that was surveyed rendered its assumption concerning the winter presence of sage grouse at the Echanis site arbitrary and capricious.

The defendants maintain that the BLM is owed special deference when undertaking scientific or technical analysis within its purview, which it is. But deference does not excuse the BLM from ensuring the accuracy and scientific integrity of its analysis, a NEPA requirement. The defendants also posit that invalidating the BLM's assessment of winter conditions at Echanis, and therefore requiring the BLM to gather better information, would essentially impose a procedural requirement not derived from NEPA. But we do not hold that habitat extrapolations from one site to another are impermissible. Instead, our holding is that any such extrapolation must be based on accurate information and defensible reasoning.

The errors in the BLM's analysis were not harmless. The inaccurate information and unsupported assumption materially impeded informed decisionmaking and public participation. Without appropriate data regarding sage grouse use of the Echanis site during the winter, whether direct or via a supportable extrapolation, it was not possible to begin to assess whether sage grouse would be impacted with regard to access to viable sagebrush habitat in the winter months.

In addition, had the BLM assumed the Echanis site provides winter sage grouse habitat, rather than that it does not, the site would be deemed "Category-1 Habitat" pursuant to the *Sage Grouse Strategy* and *Mitigation Framework*. Under that designation and the mitigation measures adopted in the FEIS and ROD, the Project would not go forward there. In that respect, the BLM's analysis materially affected the outcome of environmental review.

The defendants urge that the mitigation measures adopted in the FEIS cured any potential prejudice resulting from a faulty baseline analysis. Mitigation measures, however, while relevant to the adequacy of an environmental analysis, are not a panacea for inadequate data collection and analysis. More specifically, they do not address the concerns relevant to the prejudice analysis: the error's effect on informed decisionmaking and public participation, and on the outcome of the decision. Here, with baseline conditions inadequately established, the public was not able to tailor its comments to address concerns regarding the potential winter presence of sage grouse at the Echanis site. Nor was the BLM's explanation of the impacts to winter grouse habitat adequately informed. Having no reasonable assessment as to whether sage grouse are present at the Echanis site in winter, the BLM could not assess the Project's impacts to them, qualitatively or quantitatively. And with the impacts on sage grouse not properly established, the BLM did not know what impacts to mitigate, or whether the mitigation proposed would be adequate to offset damage to wintering sage grouse. Most importantly, had the BLM assumed the presence of sage grouse, rather than their absence, the Echanis site would be deemed Category-1 Habitat, and the mitigation measures adopted in the FEIS and ROD would not allow development to go forward there.

Given the BLM's prejudicial error, the district court's entry of summary judgment in favor of the defendants must be reversed. . . .

## Protect Our Communities Foundation v. Jewell

United States Court of Appeals for the Ninth Circuit, 2016.
2016 U.S. App. LEXIS 10269.

■ M. SMITH, CIRCUIT JUDGE:

Protect Our Communities Foundation (Protect), Backcountry Against Dumps (Backcountry), and Donna Tisdale (collectively, Plaintiffs) appeal the decision of the Bureau of Land Management to grant Defendant-Intervenor Tule Wind, LLC, (Tule) a right-of-way on federal lands in southeast San Diego County. Plaintiffs named several federal defendants in this action, including the Bureau of Land Management (BLM), the Department of the Interior, and various officials of those agencies (collectively, Defendants).

The BLM's right-of-way grant permits Tule to construct and operate a wind energy project, which Plaintiffs claim will harm birds in violation of the Migratory Bird Treaty Act (MBTA), 16 U.S.C. §§ 703–12, and the Bald and Golden Eagle Protection Act (Eagle Act), 16 U.S.C. §§ 668–668d. In addition, Plaintiffs challenge the adequacy of the BLM's Environmental Impact Statement (EIS) for the project, which was prepared pursuant to the National Environmental Policy Act (NEPA), 42 U.S.C. §§ 4321–70h. The district court rejected Plaintiffs' challenges and granted summary judgment to Defendants. We affirm.

## FACTS AND PRIOR PROCEEDINGS

### A. The Right-of-Way Grant

The BLM, which is an agency within the Department of the Interior, is charged with the management of federally owned land. Among the BLM's responsibilities is the determination of whether to grant rights-of-way for the use of such lands. Plaintiffs, which are a collection of environmental advocacy organizations and a local resident, challenge a right-of-way grant by the BLM that would permit Tule to construct and operate a wind energy facility on 12,360 acres of land in the McCain Valley, 70 miles east of San Diego (the Project).

Tule's original right-of-way proposal envisioned the construction of 128 wind turbines and supporting infrastructure, which could generate up to 200 megawatts of electricity. On December 23, 2010, the BLM released a lengthy draft EIS for public comment. The EIS discussed the environmental impacts of the Project and considered a range of alternative approaches.

Ultimately, the BLM decided to grant Tule a right-of-way for the development of a more modest wind-energy facility, which eliminated thirty-three of the originally proposed turbines from the Project. Moreover, in order to help reduce the risk of avian collisions with turbine blades, the approved Project repositioned several wind turbines that were originally proposed to be located on top of ridgelines. As modified, the Project was expected to generate up to 186 megawatts of electricity, thereby meeting the electrical energy needs of approximately 65,000 homes and businesses.

On October 3, 2011, the BLM released a final EIS reflecting these modifications. The agency published a Record of Decision (ROD) on December 19, 2011, memorializing its grant of a right-of-way for the Project. The ROD specified that the right-of-way grant would be issued for a thirty-year term, with an option to renew. It further provided that the grant of the right-of-way was expressly conditioned on the "implementation of mitigation measures and monitoring programs," as well as "the issuance of all other necessary local, state, and Federal approvals, authorizations, and permits."

Included among the mitigation measures required for the Project was the Project-Specific Avian and Bat Protection Plan (the Protection Plan). Tule developed the Protection Plan in conjunction with the BLM and the U.S. Fish and Wildlife Service (FWS), which is the federal agency responsible for enforcing the MBTA and the Eagle Act. The Protection Plan was based on scientific literature and research studies, including field surveys conducted by Tule over several years in the Project area. Based on this information, the Protection Plan outlines a number of measures that would, if implemented, mitigate the impacts of the Project on bird and bat species.

The Protection Plan provides for continuous monitoring and inspection of the Project's environmental impacts on bird and bat species as part of an adaptive-management plan. The FWS endorsed the Protection Plan, stating that it was "appropriate in its adaptive management approach to avoid and minimize take of migratory birds, bats and eagles." Although the FWS advised that the Protection Plan was not a "take permit," it acknowledged that it could serve as the basis for a future permit application with the FWS. The BLM incorporated the Protection Plan by reference into the final EIS and conditioned its right-of-way grant on Tule's adherence to the mitigation measures described therein.

### B. Procedural History

Plaintiffs jointly brought an action in federal district court, challenging the BLM's issuance of a right-of-way grant to Tule, and seeking injunctive and declaratory relief under the Administrative Procedure Act (APA), to address Defendants' alleged unlawful actions under NEPA, the MBTA, and the Eagle Act. Tule intervened as a defendant in the lawsuit.

The parties filed cross-motions for summary judgment, and the district court granted Defendants' motion for summary judgment on all claims. Specifically, the district court held that the final EIS had sufficiently articulated a proposed goal and need for the Project, properly reviewed a number of alternatives, and proposed reasonable mitigation measures. The district court also held that the final EIS complied with NEPA by taking a "hard look" at the environmental impacts of the Project, including impacts such as noise and electromagnetic energy or stray voltage, as well as effects on avian species and greenhouse-gas emissions. Finally, the district court concluded that the BLM was not responsible for ensuring that it or Tule obtain MBTA and Eagle Act permits from the FWS prior to issuing its right-of-way grant.

Plaintiffs filed two separate notices of appeal from the district court's judgment, with Plaintiff Protect addressing the MBTA issue, and

Plaintiffs Backcountry and Tisdale addressing all issues appealed. We consolidated these appeals from the district court's judgment.

## STANDARD OF REVIEW

We have jurisdiction pursuant to 28 U.S.C. § 1291. We review the district court's grant of summary judgment de novo. Under the APA, we review agency action to determine whether it is "arbitrary, capricious, an abuse of discretion, or otherwise not in accordance with law." An agency acts in an "arbitrary and capricious" manner when it "relie[s] on factors which Congress has not intended it to consider, entirely fail[s] to consider an important aspect of the problem, offer[s] an explanation for its decision that runs counter to the evidence before the agency, or is so implausible that it c[an]not be ascribed to a difference in view or the product of agency expertise." Motor Vehicle Mfrs. Ass'n v. State Farm Mut. Auto. Ins. Co. (1983). In general, a court will "uphold agency decisions so long as the agencies have 'considered the relevant factors and articulated a rational connection between the factors found and the choices made.'" This deference is particularly appropriate when a court is reviewing "issues of fact," "where analysis of the relevant documents requires a high level of technical expertise."

## DISCUSSION

### I. The Environmental Impact Statement's Compliance with NEPA

NEPA, which provides the statutory framework for federal agencies reviewing the environmental effects of a proposed action, requires the preparation of an EIS for "major Federal actions significantly affecting the quality of the human environment." The EIS must contain, among other things, a detailed discussion of "the environmental impact of the proposed action," "adverse environmental effects which cannot be avoided," "alternatives to the proposed action," and a statement of the purpose and need for the action.

NEPA outlines a series of procedural steps, but it does not impose any particular substantive result on an agency. Rather, compliance with NEPA involves the application of a "rule of reason," which involves "a pragmatic judgment whether the EIS's form, content, and preparation foster both informed decision-making and informed public participation." Specifically, a reviewing court will take a "hard look" at the EIS to determine whether it "contains a reasonably thorough discussion of the significant aspects of the probable environmental consequences." NEPA favors "coherent and comprehensive up-front environmental analysis to ensure . . . that the agency will not act on incomplete information, only to regret its decision after it is too late to correct."

Plaintiffs allege that Defendants failed to comply with NEPA in a number of respects in preparing the EIS. *First*, Plaintiffs maintain that the scope of the Project's purpose and need statement was too narrow. *Second*, Plaintiffs argue that the EIS failed to adequately examine viable alternatives, including a "distributed generation" alternative involving the use of rooftop solar panels. *Third*, Plaintiffs claim that the Project's proposed mitigation strategies are too vague and speculative to satisfy NEPA. *Finally*, Plaintiffs maintain that the EIS fails to take a "hard look" at the environmental impact of the Project in several distinct ways. Specifically, they note that the EIS omits a comprehensive discussion of the impacts of noise on bird species and fails to conduct a survey of nighttime migratory birds. In addition, Plaintiffs claim that the EIS does not fairly address the impacts of inaudible noise, electromagnetic fields, and stray voltage on humans, or the proposed consequences of the project on global warming. We address each of these arguments in turn.

### A. Statement of Purpose and Need

An agency tasked with preparing an EIS must prepare a statement that "briefly specif[ies] the underlying purpose and need to which the agency is responding." 40 C.F.R. § 1502.13. This statement should inform the agency's review of alternatives to the proposed action and guide its final selection. We accord the agency "considerable discretion to define a project's purpose and need" and review such statements for reasonableness. However, a statement of purpose and need "will fail if it unreasonably narrows the agency's consideration of alternatives so that the outcome is preordained." In a context, as here, where the agency is tasked with deciding whether to issue a permit or license, the statement of purpose and need may include "private goals" alongside statutory policy objectives. However, it is the statutory goal that "serve[s] as a guide by which to determine the reasonableness of the objectives outlined."

In this case, the district court properly determined that the EIS's purpose-and need-statement was adequately broad, such that the agency's decision was not foreordained. The statement specified that:

> [T]he purpose and need for the proposed action is to respond to a [Federal Land Policy and Management Act (FLPMA)] right-of-way application submitted by Tule Wind, LLC. . . . In conjunction with FLPMA, the BLM's applicable authorities include the following:
>
> - Executive Order 13212 . . . which mandates that agencies act expediently and in a manner consistent with applicable laws to increase the production and transmission of energy in a safe and environmentally sound manner.
> - Section 211 of the Energy Policy Act of 2005 . . . which established a goal for the [DOI] to approve at least 10,000 megawatts of nonhydropower renewable energy power on public lands by 2015.
> - Secretarial Order 3285A1, [which] establishes the development of renewable energy as a priority for the DOI [and] announced a policy goal of identifying and prioritizing

specific locations (study areas) best suited for large-scale production of solar energy.

The EIS's purpose-and-need statement reflects both the agency's immediate objective, "to respond" to Tule Wind's right-of-way request, as well as the broader policy goals that the agency considered in deciding among alternative proposals. This statement is fully consistent with the agency's duty to consider federal policies in fashioning its response to a right-of-way application, and constitutes a reasonable formulation of project goals. The purpose-and-need statement also permitted the agency to consider a range of alternatives to Tule's proposal, including one which it ultimately adopted in order to reduce the impact of the Project on the surrounding environment.

Although Plaintiffs also challenge the BLM's purported "need" for the action, the statement of need is adequately supported by the federal objectives outlined in the EIS. In particular, Section 211 of the Energy Policy Act of 2005 sets forth an agency goal of approving up to 10,000 watts of renewable energy development on public lands by 2015—a time frame which, the agency determined, would be most readily met through the development of a utility-scale energy project.

### B. Project Alternatives

Plaintiffs contend that the BLM dismissed viable alternative projects out of hand. Specifically, Plaintiffs challenge the BLM's decision to reject a "distributed generation" alternative, which would involve the use of rooftop solar panels. Having found the agency's statement of purpose and need to be reasonable, we also conclude that the BLM acted within its discretion in dismissing alternative proposals.

First, the range of alternatives considered in the EIS was not impermissibly narrow, as the agency evaluated all "reasonable [and] feasible" alternatives in light of the ultimate purposes of the project. An agency need not review "remote and speculative" alternatives. Instead, its review is guided by a "rule of reason." Accordingly, the EIS need only "briefly discuss" the reasons for eliminating an alternative not selected for detailed examination. 40 C.F.R. § 1502.14(a).

Here, the agency reviewed five action alternatives to the project originally proposed by Tule, as well as two no-action alternatives. The agency also briefly considered seven project-design alternatives and three energy-generation alternatives, including distributed generation. The distributed-generation alternative involved the use of rooftop solar panel systems on buildings in San Diego County and the development of other renewable-energy systems.

The BLM dismissed the distributed-generation alternative because it failed to satisfy the agency's goals and presented a number of feasibility challenges. First, the distributed generation alternative did not provide for utility-scale energy generation on public lands, and therefore would have been less effective at meeting the goals articulated by the agency.

Although an agency is not limited to considering alternatives within its jurisdiction, the agency is not required to give exhaustive consideration to an alternative that it appropriately deems remote and speculative. In this case, the private installation and use of rooftop solar systems presented significant feasibility issues that the agency decided to take into account when choosing among alternative proposals.

Specifically, the BLM found the implementation of this alternative to be "speculative" given the current status of solar technology and the regulatory and commercial landscape. According to the BLM, the installation of at least 100,000 new rooftop solar units, primarily on private residential or commercial properties, would be required in order to match the energy generation from the original wind-energy proposal. Even if such an outcome were feasible, however, the BLM concluded that a project of such scale might require "extensive upgrading" of infrastructure and generate uncertain environmental impacts. These technical determinations of the agency, reflecting the application of its specialized expertise, merit particular deference on review. We thus find that the BLM reasonably concluded that the overall effectiveness of a distributed-generation alternative, reliant on private installation and technical upgrading, remained speculative in practice. Similarly, Plaintiffs' final contention that the distributed-generation systems would present a cost-effective alternative must be weighed against the feasibility of the overall approach and its consistency with agency goals. Considered as a whole, therefore, the BLM did not act unreasonably in dismissing the distributed-generation alternative.

### C. Mitigation Measures

Pursuant to NEPA, an agency must also consider appropriate mitigation measures that would reduce the environmental impact of the proposed action. As noted, our review is guided by whether the agency's analysis is reasonable and offers "sufficient detail to ensure that environmental consequences have been fairly evaluated." "Perfunctory descriptions or mere lists of mitigation measures are insufficient." Rather, the agency must provide "an assessment of whether the proposed mitigation measures can be effective . . . [and] whether anticipated environmental impacts can be avoided." Because mitigation measures are projections that allow an agency to alleviate "impact *after* construction," the EIS may not use them "as a proxy for [collecting] baseline data" *before* construction that would enable the agency to "first understand[ ] the extent of the problem." On the other hand, the EIS's proposed mitigation measures "need not be legally enforceable, funded or even in final form to comply with NEPA's procedural requirements."

In this case, the agency drafted a comprehensive set of mitigation measures relying, in part, on field studies conducted by Tule over several years in the proposed Project area. These studies, in combination with scientific research, informed the BLM's development of a number of mitigation measures, including the creation of the lengthy Protection

Plan. The Protection Plan outlined additional methods of achieving environmental mitigation at each stage of the Project. The BLM incorporated the Protection Plan into the final EIS by reference.

Plaintiffs claim that the mitigation measures outlined in the EIS do not provide "sufficient detail," and that the EIS improperly defers the formulation of certain mitigation measures until post-development monitoring and inspection, notably through the use of an adaptive-management plan. Yet the mitigation measures, including the 85-page Protection Plan, provide ample detail and adequate baseline data for the agency to evaluate the overall environmental impact of the Project. Plaintiffs merely "fly speck" the EIS rather than identify consequential flaws that would prevent the agency from sufficiently grasping the Project's potential environmental consequences. Moreover, the EIS's inclusion of an adaptive-management plan, among other mitigation measures, provides flexibility in responding to environmental impacts through a regime of continued monitoring and inspection. That an agency decides to incorporate an adaptive management plan as one component of a comprehensive set of mitigation measures does not mean that the agency lacked a sufficient foundation of current baseline data from which to evaluate the Project's environmental effects. Rather, the use of such a continuous monitoring system may complement other mitigation measures, and help to refine and improve the implementation of those measures as the Project progresses.

### D. "Hard Look" at Environmental Impacts

Plaintiffs also raise a series of four substantive challenges to the BLM's investigation of the environmental impacts of the Project. [The court held that BLM had properly considered the effects of the project on birds, the environmental effects of inaudible noise, and the adverse health effects of electromagnetic fields and stray voltage that may be generated by the Project.]

#### 4. Greenhouse-Gas Emissions

The EIS also takes a "hard look" at the impact of the Project on greenhouse-gas emissions and global warming. The EIS analyzes projected emissions from the Project and concludes that these emissions, at 646 metric tons of carbon dioxide per year, fall below the level of significance required for further analysis under NEPA. In addition, the EIS states that "the project would create a renewable source of energy, thereby potentially decreasing overall emissions attributable to electrical generation in California." Contrary to Plaintiffs' contention, this passing projection of potential emissions reductions, simply by virtue of the Project's creation of a new source of renewable energy, is reasonable enough and does not mandate the provision of conclusive proof through additional evidence and analysis beyond that already provided in the EIS.

Finally, Plaintiffs contend that the BLM failed to take into account the emissions generated by the manufacture and transportation of equipment to the Project area. Instead, the BLM reasoned that these emissions levels were largely outside the control of Tule and that attempts to estimate these amounts would be overly speculative. The BLM was entitled to choose among various reasonable methodologies, as it did here, when estimating the emissions generated by the Project.

**II. Liability under the MBTA and Eagle Act**

Plaintiffs raise the novel argument that the BLM—by the mere act of granting Tule's right-of-way request—is complicit in future conduct by Tule that might result in violations of the MBTA and the Eagle Act (collectively, the Acts). Plaintiffs' theory of liability is two-fold. First, Plaintiffs assert that the BLM, acting in its regulatory capacity, is directly liable for the unlawful "take" of birds under the Acts, absent a permit from the FWS. Second, Plaintiffs assert that the agency's regulatory authorization is "not in accordance with law" within the meaning of the APA, because the BLM did not condition its right-of-way grant on Tule securing the appropriate permits from the FWS. We address each of these arguments in turn.

**A. The Migratory Bird Treaty Act**

The MBTA is a criminal statute that prohibits an individual, entity—or, in some cases, an agency—"at any time, by any means or in any manner, to pursue, hunt, take, capture [or] kill . . . any migratory bird, . . . nest, or egg of any such bird" in the absence of a permit or other exemption. 16 U.S.C. § 703(a). The FWS is the federal agency tasked with ensuring compliance with the MBTA, including issuing permits and prosecuting offenders. Through the APA's prohibition against unlawful agency action, a plaintiff may bring a civil suit to compel agency compliance with the MBTA.

. . . Plaintiffs' argument that the Project will inevitably result in migratory-bird fatalities, even if true, is unavailing because the MBTA does not contemplate attenuated secondary liability on agencies like the BLM that act in a purely regulatory capacity, and whose regulatory acts do not directly or proximately cause the "take" of migratory birds, within the meaning of 16 U.S.C. § 703(a). Here, the BLM only authorized Tule to construct and operate a wind energy facility on public lands, and therefore did not act to "take" migratory birds without a permit, within the meaning of the MBTA.

Similar to the MBTA, the Eagle Act provides that, absent a permit or other exemption, it is unlawful to "take, possess, sell, purchase, barter, offer to sell, purchase or barter, transport, export or import, at any time or in any manner, any bald eagle, common known as the American eagle, or any golden eagle, alive or dead, or any part, nest, or egg thereof." 16 U.S.C. § 668(b). The FWS also administers the Eagle Act, including overseeing the issuance of permits and ensuring compliance with the statute. Unlike the MBTA, the Eagle Act explicitly provides for both criminal and civil enforcement.

Despite some substantive differences between the MBTA and the Eagle Act, the same reasoning applies to defeat the imposition of liability on the BLM here. Further support for this conclusion is provided by a FWS regulation that pertains to permits for the "incidental take" of eagles. 50 C.F.R. § 22.26; *see* Eagle Permits; Take Necessary To Protect Interests in Particular Localities, 74 Fed. Reg. 46,836 (Sep. 11, 2009). There, the FWS explained that "[p]ersons and organizations that obtain licenses, permits, grants, or other such services from government agencies are responsible for their own compliance with the Eagle Act and should individually seek permits." It further explained, however, that "agencies must obtain permits for take that would result from agency actions that are implemented by the agency itself (including staff and contractors responsible for carrying out those actions on behalf of the agency)." We hold, in the narrow circumstances of this case, that the BLM did not, by granting Tule the referenced right-of-way, take "agency actions . . . implemented by the agency itself" that would directly or proximately result in the incidental take of eagles by it or Tule.

As a result, a requirement that the BLM independently seek a permit, or confirm that grantees seek permits before issuing a right-of-way grant, would impose an attenuated form of secondary liability on the BLM, an agency that is neither statutorily tasked with policing third-party compliance with the Eagle Act nor responsible for violations that might be independently committed by grantees, such as Tule.

## CONCLUSION

We hold that the BLM is not liable under NEPA, the MBTA, the Eagle Act, nor the APA for its regulatory decision to grant Tule a right-of-way to develop and operate a renewable wind energy project. The judgment of the district court is **AFFIRMED**.

---

## QUESTIONS AND DISCUSSION

**1.** Most of the best places for large renewable energy development are located on federal public lands. The federal Energy Policy Act of 2005 directs the Secretary of the Interior to approve 10,000 megawatts of electricity generated by renewable sources by 2015. See Energy Policy Act of 2005, Pub. L. No. 109–58, § 211, 119 Stat. 594, 660. The Obama Administration has prioritized the development of renewable energy on public lands, approving 25 solar energy facilities, nine wind farms, and eleven geothermal plants on public lands since 2009. *See* Executive Office of the President, The President's Climate Action Plan 7 (June 2013). President Obama's June 2013 climate change plan calls on the Department of the Interior to permit an additional 10 gigawatts of electricity by 2020. *Id.*

**2.** Like wind energy, solar energy presents its own environmental challenges. The presence of endangered desert tortoises was most significant issue affecting the nation's largest solar energy project, the Ivanpah Solar Electric Generating System located in the Mojave Desert forty miles southwest of Las Vegas just across the California border. The project displaced 49 tortoises during the first third of its construction, more than the 38 tortoises which FWS had estimated that the entire project would affect. FWS then prepared a revised biological opinion that listed a number of protective measures that the developer must follow to avoid harming tortoises, including removing trash and road-kill to avoid attracting ravens, installing extensive perimeter fencing to keep tortoises away from the project's operations, and acquiring up to 3,582 acres of land to compensate for the lost tortoise habitat. *See* U.S. Fish & Wildlife Serv., U.S. Dep't of the Interior, Biological Opinion on BrightSource Energy's Ivanpah Solar Electric Generating System Project (2011). Nonetheless, Western Watershed's local director contended that "[n]o project can be considered clean or green when it involves destruction of habitat for a species listed under Endangered Species Act on this scale." *Western Watershed Project Files Suit to Stop Ivanpah CSP Project*, SOLARSERVER. (Jan. 23, 2011).

Western Watersheds also alleged that BLM's approval of the Ivanpah project violated the Federal Land Management Policy Act (FLPMA). Enacted in 1976, FLPMA governs the use of what used to be called the "public domain," which are the federal public lands that were not otherwise disposed or designated as national parks, national forests, or otherwise reserved. BLM is responsible for managing those lands according to FLPMA. But Western Watersheds complained that BLM violated FLMPA regulations requiring reliance on multiple use and sustainable yield principles, use of a systematic interdisciplinary approach, and the weighing of " 'long-term benefits to the public against short-term benefits.' " The district court rejected all of those claims, too, in a later decision. *See* Western Watersheds Project v. Salazar, No. CV 11–00492, 2012 U.S. Dist. LEXIS 169097 (C.D. Cal. Nov. 5, 2012).

The district court rejected the plaintiff's motion for a preliminary injunction of the Ivanpah project after balancing the factors stated in Winter v. Natural Resource Defense Council, Inc., 555 U.S. 7, 23 (2008). On appeal, the Ninth Circuit affirmed:

> The district court did not abuse its discretion in its application of the *Winter* factors. In particular, the court properly analyzed the balance of equities and the public interest, and did not abuse its discretion in finding that these factors weighed against issuing a preliminary injunction. In balancing the equities, the district court properly weighed the environmental harm posed by the Ivanpah Solar Electric Generating System ("ISEGS") project against the possible damage to project funding, jobs, and the state and national renewable energy goals that would result from an injunction halting project construction, and concluded that the balance favored Appellees. The District Court also properly exercised its discretion in weighing Appellant's delay in seeking a preliminary

> injunction until after construction began, was temporarily halted, and begun anew, and some $712 million had been expended among the equitable factors. While Appellant maintains that it lacked facts supporting a preliminary injunction motion until the Bureau of Land Management ("BLM") revealed the greater tortoise impacts on April 19, 2011, many of Appellant's objections to the Final Environmental Impact Statement have nothing to do with BLM's disclosure of a greater-than-expected desert tortoise population.
>
> The district court also did not abuse its discretion in analyzing the public interests at stake. It properly concluded that Appellant's contention that rooftop solar panels were a preferable source of renewable energy amounted to a policy dispute and could not support a finding that an injunction was in the public interest. The district court properly took into account the federal government's stated goal of increasing the supply of renewable energy and addressing the threat posed by climate change, as well as California's argument that the ISEGS project is critical to the state's goal of reducing fossil fuel use, thereby reducing pollution and improving health and energy security in the state. Appellant has pointed to no clear factual error or mistake of law in the district court's analysis of the public interest factors. Accordingly, we affirm the denial of Appellant's preliminary injunction motion.

Western Watersheds v. Salazar, 692 F.3d 921 (9th Cir. 2012). How should Congress—which is not subject to the judicial test for injunctive relief—balance the benefits and harms of renewable energy projects such as Ivanpah? Should it exempt renewable energy projects from environmental regulations? Or should environmental regulations be enforced just as stringently against renewable energy projects as, for example, fossil fuel projects? *See generally* John Copeland Nagle, *Green Harms of Green Projects*, 27 N.D. J. L. ETHICS & PUB. POL'Y 59 (2013) (analyzing the different approaches to applying environmental law to renewable energy projects).

---

## G. INTERNATIONAL LEGAL RESPONSES

Climate change is a global problem, so it is not surprising that the international community sought to address to climate change ever since it was recognized as a problem. Those international efforts have yielded significant progress, but it is now uncertain how much more the existing approach will be able to accomplish. As in the United States, the diverse ways in which climate change will affect different actors complicates the effort to reach a comprehensive agreement.

Concern about climate change and calls for international action began in the 1970s and continued throughout the 1980s. Following the model of the ozone treaties, in 1990 the United Nations authorized an Intergovernmental Negotiating Committee on Climate to begin discussions of a global treaty. These negotiations culminated in the 1992

Framework Convention on Climate Change ("the Climate Change Convention") signed at the Earth Summit in Rio de Janeiro. 31 I.L.M. 849 (1992). The Climate Change Convention established a general framework, but delineated few specific or substantive obligations to curb climate change. While in many ways disappointing to environmentalists, the Convention was nonetheless a positive step in the control of greenhouse gases. Central to the Convention is the objective found in Article 2, requiring that Parties achieve "stabilization of greenhouse gas concentrations in the atmosphere at a level that would prevent dangerous anthropogenic interference with the climate system." The Conference of the Parties is charged with periodically evaluating implementation of the Convention to ensure that commitments are adequate to meet this overall objective. It was just such an evaluation that would ultimately lead to the recognition that binding targets were necessary in the Kyoto Protocol in 1997.

The most significant provisions of the Climate Change Convention addressed the specific commitments of the Parties. The Parties are essentially divided into three categories: all Parties; "Annex I," which includes all industrialized country Parties; and "Annex II," which includes all industrialized country Parties except those from the former Soviet bloc in a process of economic transition. In order to create a credible baseline, information and data collecting requirements are imposed on all Parties. Annex I countries are subjected to additional requirements, including most notably the obligation to "adopt national polices and take corresponding measures on the mitigation of climate change, by limiting anthropogenic emissions of greenhouse gases and protecting and enhancing greenhouse gas sinks and reservoirs." This requirement to adopt a national policy was not tied legally to any specific target, but Article 4(2)(b) requires the developed countries to provide detailed information on their policies as well as on their emissions "*with the aim of* returning individually or jointly to their 1990 levels. . . ." Environmentalists argued that these provisions reflected a commitment, albeit a non-binding one, by developed countries to stabilize their emissions at 1990 levels by the year 2000. No developed countries met this commitment.

In December 1997, the Parties responded negotiating the Kyoto Protocol to the Climate Change Convention, which established binding reduction targets for the United States and other developed countries. 37 I.L.M. 22 (1998). The core of the Kyoto Protocol was targets and timetables, or "quantified emissions limitation and reduction objectives" (QELROs), for industrialized (Annex I) Parties to reduce their net emissions of greenhouse gases. Most European countries agreed to lower their emission 8% below 1990 levels, while the United States agreed to a 7% reduction. Countries in economic transition were allowed to select a baseline year other than 1990, and several countries did so. In addition, all countries had the option of choosing 1995 as the baseline year for three relatively minor but potent greenhouse gases (hydrofluorocarbons, perfluorocarbons, and sulphur hexafluoride). All of the reduction targets must be met over a five-year commitment period—from 2008 to 2012—which is to be followed by subsequent commitment periods and presumably stricter emission targets. The issue of emission targets for developing countries was hotly contested during negotiations. Based on the reasoning that developed countries have been responsible for the lion's share of emissions to date and are better able to pay for reductions, the Kyoto Protocol does not address emission reductions for developing countries. Indeed a proposal that would have established procedures for developing countries to take on *voluntary* commitments for emission limits was not adopted.

The United States, however, never approved the Kyoto Protocol. While it was being negotiated, the Senate voted 97–0 vote in favor of a resolution advising the Clinton Administration not to agree to an international climate change agreement that failed to limit the emissions from developing countries or that "would result in serious harm to the economy of the United States." S. Res. 98, 105th Cong., 1st Sess. § 1 (1997). Despite voicing support during the 2000 presidential campaign for regulating GHGs, shortly after taking office President Bush declared that the Kyoto Protocol was unacceptable and would not be submitted to the Senate for ratification. President Obama vowed to reengage with international efforts to combat climate change, but he never submitted the Kyoto Protocol to the Senate either.

For several years, the UNFCCC's annual meeting in December 2009, to be held in Copenhagen, was targeted as the time at which a new agreement to replace the Kyoto Protocol would be approved. But things did not go as planned at "Hopenhagen." The tiny Pacific island nation of Tuvalu—whose very presence on the Earth is threatened by rising seas associated with climate change—insisted that developed countries should commit to a greater reduction in greenhouse gas emissions and a greater amount of adaptation funding for developing nations. Chinese premier Wen Jiabao told the delegates that "[t]he principle of 'common but differentiated responsibilities' represents the core and bedrock of international cooperation on climate change and it must never be compromised. . . . Developed countries, which are already leading an affluent life, still maintain a level of per capita emissions that is far higher than that of developing countries, and most of their emissions are attributed to consumption." The United States and Australia had both hoped to approve domestic climate change legislation before the Copenhagen meeting, both neither delivered. Copenhagen was widely regarded as a failure, with only a face-saving statement negotiated by President Obama preventing a complete collapse.

## Adoption of the Paris Agreement

United Nations Framework Convention on Climate Change,
Conference of the Parties, 2015.
https://unfccc.int/resource/docs/2015/cop21/eng/l09.pdf

*The Conference of the Parties,*

*Recalling* [various previous decisions and Articles 2, 3 and 4 of the Convention,]

*Welcoming* the adoption of United Nations General Assembly resolution A/RES/70/1, "Transforming our world: the 2030 Agenda for Sustainable Development", in local communities, migrants, children, persons with disabilities and people in vulnerable situations and the right to development, as well as gender equality, empowerment of women and intergenerational equity,

*Recognizing* that climate change represents an urgent and potentially irreversible threat to human societies and the planet and thus requires the widest possible cooperation by all countries, and their participation in an effective and appropriate international response, with a view to accelerating the reduction of global greenhouse gas emissions,

*Also recognizing* that deep reductions in global emissions will be required in order to achieve the ultimate objective of the Convention and emphasizing the need for urgency in addressing climate change,

*Acknowledging* that climate change is a common concern of humankind, Parties should, when taking action to address climate change, respect, promote and consider their respective obligations on human rights, the right to health, the rights of indigenous peoples, local communities, migrants, children, persons with disabilities and people in vulnerable situations and the right to development, as well as gender equality, empowerment of women and intergenerational equity,

*Also acknowledging* the specific needs and concerns of developing country Parties arising from the impact of the implementation of response measures. . . . ,

*Emphasizing* with serious concern the urgent need to address the significant gap between the aggregate effect of Parties' mitigation pledges in terms of global annual emissions of greenhouse gases by 2020 and aggregate emission pathways consistent with holding the increase in the global average temperature to well below 2 °C above preindustrial levels and pursuing efforts to limit the temperature increase to 1.5 °C,

*Also emphasizing* that enhanced pre-2020 ambition can lay a solid foundation for enhanced post-2020 ambition,

*Stressing* the urgency of accelerating the implementation of the Convention and its Kyoto Protocol in order to enhance pre-2020 ambition,

*Recognizing* the urgent need to enhance the provision of finance, technology and capacity-building support by developed country Parties, in a predictable manner, to enable enhanced pre-2020 action by developing country Parties,

*Emphasizing* the enduring benefits of ambitious and early action, including major reductions in the cost of future mitigation and adaptation efforts,

*Acknowledging* the need to promote universal access to sustainable energy in developing countries, in particular in Africa, through the enhanced deployment of renewable energy,

*Agreeing* to uphold and promote regional and international cooperation in order to mobilize stronger and more ambitious climate action by all Parties and non-Party stakeholders, including civil society, the private sector, financial institutions, cities and other subnational authorities, local communities and indigenous peoples,

**I. ADOPTION**

1. *Decides* to adopt the Paris Agreement under the United Nations Framework Convention on Climate Change (hereinafter referred to as "the Agreement"). . . .

**II. INTENDED NATIONALLY DETERMINED CONTRIBUTIONS**

12. *Welcomes* the intended nationally determined contributions that have been communicated by Parties. . . . ,

13. *Reiterates* its invitation to all Parties that have not yet done so to communicate to the secretariat their intended nationally determined contributions towards achieving the objective of the Convention as set out in its Article 2 as soon as possible and well in advance of the twenty-second session of the Conference of the Parties (November 2016) and in a manner that facilitates the clarity, transparency and understanding of the intended nationally determined contributions;

14. *Requests* the secretariat to continue to publish the intended nationally determined contributions communicated by Parties on the UNFCCC website;

15. *Reiterates* its call to developed country Parties, the operating entities of the Financial Mechanism and any other organizations in a position to do so to provide support for the preparation and communication of the intended nationally determined contributions of Parties that may need such support;

16. *Takes note* of the synthesis report on the aggregate effect of intended nationally determined contributions communicated by Parties by 1 October 2015, contained in document FCCC/CP/2015/7;

17. *Notes* with concern that the estimated aggregate greenhouse gas emission levels in 2025 and 2030 resulting from the intended nationally determined contributions do not fall within least-cost 2 °C scenarios but rather lead to a projected level of 55 gigatonnes in 2030, and also notes

that much greater emission reduction efforts will be required than those associated with the intended nationally determined contributions in order to hold the increase in the global average temperature to below 2 °C above pre-industrial levels by reducing emissions to 40 gigatonnes or to 1.5 °C above pre-industrial levels by reducing to a level to be identified in the special report referred to in paragraph 21 below;

18. *Also notes, in this context,* the adaptation needs expressed by many developing country Parties in their intended nationally determined contributions;

19. *Requests* the secretariat to update the synthesis report referred to in paragraph 16 above so as to cover all the information in the intended nationally determined contributions communicated by Parties pursuant to decision 1/CP.20 by 4 April 2016 and to make it available by 2 May 2016;

20. *Decides* to convene a facilitative dialogue among Parties in 2018 to take stock of the collective efforts of Parties in relation to progress towards the long-term goal referred to in Article 4, paragraph 1, of the Agreement and to inform the preparation of nationally determined contributions pursuant to Article 4, paragraph 8, of the Agreement;

21. *Invites* the Intergovernmental Panel on Climate Change to provide a special report in 2018 on the impacts of global warming of 1.5 °C above pre-industrial levels and related global greenhouse gas emission pathways;

---

## QUESTIONS AND DISCUSSION

**1.** The Paris Agreement relies on "intended nationally determined contributions" to achieve the necessary reduction in greenhouse gas emissions. In other words, each country gets to decide how much—and how—to reduce its emissions. The Kyoto Protocol, by contrast, prescribed the emissions reductions that must be achieved by the parties to the Convention, with different requirements for developed and developing countries. Why did the parties adopt a new approach in Paris? Will it work?

**2.** China believes that fairness requires that it be allowed to develop without bearing the costs that would result from greenhouse gas regulations. Many in the United States believe that fairness requires that all emitters be treated equally. Who is right? *See generally* John Copeland Nagle, *How Much Should China Pollute?*, 12 VT. J. ENVTL. L. 591 (2011) (analyzing the equitable arguments regarding China's emissions).

**3.** China has pursued a number of efforts to reduce its greenhouse gas emissions despite the absence of any regulatory strictures imposed by the Kyoto Protocol. Other nations have acted even more aggressively. The European Union boasts that it "leads the way" by agreeing "to cut its own greenhouse gas emissions by at least 20% by 2020 regardless of what other countries do." European Union, *Combating Climate Change: The EU Leads the Way 5* (2009). The EU has adopted a cap-and-trade system to achieve that goal, and it has been active in subsidizing clean energy and other programs in China and other developing countries pursuant to the CDM.

**4.** As described by the UNFCCC, the other essential elements of the Paris Agreement (besides those excerpted above) include

- *Sinks and reservoirs* (Art. 5)—The Paris Agreement also encourages Parties to conserve and enhance, as appropriate, sinks and reservoirs of greenhouse gases as referred to in Article 4, paragraph 1(d) of the Convention, including forests.
- *Market and non-markets* (Art. 6)—The Paris Agreement establishes a mechanism to contribute to the mitigation of greenhouse gas emissions and support sustainable development, as well as defining a framework for non-market approaches to sustainable development.
- *Adaptation* (Art. 7)—The Paris Agreement establishes a global goal to significantly strengthen national adaptation efforts—enhancing adaptive capacity, strengthening resilience and reduction of vulnerability to climate change—through support and international cooperation. It also recognizes that adaptation is a global challenge faced by all. All Parties should submit and update periodically an adaptation communication on their priorities, implementation and support needs, plans and actions. Developing country Parties will receive enhanced support for adaptation actions.
- *Loss and damage* (Art. 8)—The Paris Agreement significantly enhances the Warsaw International Mechanism on Loss and Damage, which will develop approaches to help vulnerable countries cope with the adverse effects of climate change, including extreme weather events and slow-onset events such as sea-level rise. The Agreement now provides a framework for Parties to enhance understanding, action and support with regard to loss and damage.
- *Support* (Arts. 9, 10 and 11)—The Paris Agreement reaffirms the obligations of developed countries to support the efforts of developing country Parties to build clean, climate-resilient futures, while for the first time encouraging voluntary contributions by other Parties. Provision of resources should also aim to achieve a balance between adaptation and mitigation. In addition to reporting on finance already provided, developed country Parties commit to submit indicative information on future support every two years, including projected levels of public finance. The agreement also provides that the Financial Mechanism of the Convention, including the Green Climate Fund (GCF), shall serve the Agreement. International cooperation on climate-safe technology development and transfer and building capacity in

the developing world are also strengthened: a technology framework is established under the agreement and capacity building activities will be enhanced through, inter alia, enhanced support for capacity building actions in developing country Parties and appropriate institutional arrangements.

- *Transparency* (Art. 13)—The Paris Agreement relies on a robust transparency and accounting system to provide clarity on action and support by Parties, with flexibility for their differing capabilities. In addition to reporting information on mitigation, adaptation and support, the agreement requires that the information submitted by each Party undergoes international review. The Agreement also includes a mechanism that will facilitate implementation and promote compliance in a non-adversarial and non-punitive manner, and will report annually to the COP.
- *Global Stocktake* (Art. 14)—A "global stocktake", to take place in 2023 and every 5 years thereafter, will assess collective progress toward meeting the purpose of the Agreement in a comprehensive and facilitative manner. Its outcomes will inform Parties in updating and enhancing their actions and support and enhancing international cooperation.

# PART 2

# THE PRACTICE OF ENVIRONMENTAL LAW

# CHAPTER 9

# ADMINISTRATIVE RULEMAKING AND PERMITTING

**CHAPTER OUTLINE**



---

## I. INTRODUCTION TO THE ADMINISTRATIVE STATE

It would be difficult, if not downright folly, to attempt to practice environmental law without a firm grounding in the law of administrative agencies, known shorthand as administrative law. While media-specific statutes such as the Clean Air Act or resource-specific laws such as the Endangered Species Act determine what regulated parties may or may not do, these operate within more general constraints on what the government is allowed to do. Administrative law sets the parameters for how agencies implement these statutes and constitutional law sets the limits of governmental authority. The chapters in Part I of the text survey an array of federal environmental laws that generally follow the same model: Congress adopts a statute defining goals and standards for an environmental regulatory program; the statute delegates implementation and enforcement authority to an administrative agency; the agency implements and enforces the statute; courts review the agency's activities when either the agency, citizens, an organized group, or a regulated entity obtains judicial review. Indeed, one cannot identify an environmental issue that is *not* managed by an agency. Air and water pollution? Look to EPA. Wetlands? The Department of Defense (through the Army Corps of Engineers). Forests? Department of Agriculture (Forest Service). Endangered Species? Department of Interior (Fish & Wildlife Service). Marine fisheries? Department of Commerce (National Marine Fisheries Service). The list could, and does, go on and on and on.

Agency action is where environmental protection happens. Much the same happens at state and local government levels as well. Hence, although not all of what environmental law encompasses fits within the administrative law process, the work product of administrative agencies dominates the day-to-day life of an environmental law practitioner.

At its broadest, administrative law is held up as one of the great inventions of the American experience and, in many respects, it truly is. Administrative law makes government activity more open, accountable, and responsive to the public than in any other country. Administrative law concerns *how agencies operate*—the processes and procedures they use to perform their functions—and the *separation of powers*—the competitive relationship and respective powers between the legislative and executive branches of government and the role of courts in refereeing this constant battle. Writ large, the field is about government, what government does, and what it can and can't do. In some ways, administrative law represents the flip side of corporate law. Just as corporate law regulates the conduct of private organizations, administrative law serves as the law of public organizations.

Hardly a new creation, the first three administrative departments were established in 1789 (State, Treasury, and War). Along the way, other well-known departments such as Interior, Treasury, Justice, Commerce, and Labor have been added with growth spurts during the New Deal in the 1930s and the Great Society in the 1960s. President Richard Nixon created the Environmental Protection Agency in 1970 in response to growing interest in the environment.

This alphabet soup of environmental and other agencies plays many different roles. Agencies can issue rules, conduct inspections, award licenses, adjudicate disputes, demand information, hold hearings, and give and take money, just to name a few activities. As a result of these varied roles, agencies maintain an uneasy position within the three branches of government. As we all learned in high school, the Executive Branch faithfully executes the laws, the Legislative Branch creates laws and controls the purse strings, and the Judicial Branch interprets the law and applies the Constitution. So where in this scheme do agencies fit in? All agency actions must be authorized by Congress, which effectively delegates some of its authorities. But, from the brief description above, it seems that agencies fit in all three branches—making rules, investigating compliance, punishing violations, and hearing appeals. This combination of tasks leads to tension within the Executive and Legislative branches as they compete with one another to influence agency behavior.

The judiciary is supposed to act as a referee in this turf war, determining if agencies (generally located within the Executive branch) have followed Congressional intent closely enough. Making this determination depends critically on the court's vision of the agency itself. Consider two very different models of administrative agencies. In one model, which is called *scientific expertise*, technocrats in white jackets populate the agency. These agency personnel are experts in what they do, faithfully carrying out the will of Congress by relying on their best professional judgment. This model views agencies as efficiently implementing the mandates of government.

The contrasting model, known as *interest group representation,* views agencies as mini-legislatures. As in Congress, special interests battle it out to influence the implementation of laws. In this model, agencies are simply a microcosm of the larger political debate, with the same political processes taking place within agencies. This is not necessarily a bad thing, but raises the specter of two dangers. The first is known as *agency capture*. Agencies may so closely align themselves with the industries they're supposed to regulate that the public interest is lost in the process. Perhaps the clearest example of this was the decision by the U.S. Forest Service that the best "multiple use" of the Tongass National Forest, given the competing interests of recreation, wildlife protection, preservation, and logging, was to dedicate *100%* of the forest to logging. *See* Sierra Club v. Hardin, 325 F. Supp. 99 (D. Alaska 1971), *rev'd sub nom.* Sierra Club v. Butz, 3 Envtl. L. Rep. 20292 (9th Cir. 1973). Such one-sided decisions can be explained by *public choice theory*, which predicts that the efforts of concentrated interests (e.g., timber companies) will more effectively influence the political process than more diffuse, though larger, interests (such as the general public).

A second danger is that of agency self-interest. In order to increase its power and perpetuate itself, the argument goes, agencies may act more out of bureaucratic self-interest than in the public interest. This charge is often levied against the Army Corps of Engineers, for example, for pushing environmentally harmful, expensive construction projects that are popular in Congressional members' home districts.

Which model one believes best describes agency action has a huge influence on the appropriate judicial role in administrative law. If scientific expertise is the accurate model, then judicial review should be deferential since, after all, the agency officials are the real experts. If, however, interest group representation better exemplifies agency action, then little deference should be granted by judges and strict review should be used to uncover hidden deals, rent seeking, and self-interested decisionmaking.

The last broad point to note about agencies is the importance of the Administrative Procedure Act (APA), 5 U.S.C. §§ 551 et seq. Passed in 1946, the APA operates for agencies in some respects the way the rules of civil procedure do for trial judges. For our purposes, the APA sets out procedures agencies must follow when promulgating rules and adjudicating conflicts. It also establishes the standard of judicial review (which varies depending on the type of action) when agency actions are challenged in court.

It is sound advice to steer you towards taking a course on administrative law. The survey course at most law schools focuses on federal administrative law, and many schools offer a course on state administrative law as well, usually focusing on the state in which the law school is located. This text cannot hope to cover all that is covered in such courses. Rather, our objective in this chapter is to introduce you to some of the overarching themes of administrative law and focus attention on processes and doctrines that have particular importance to environmental law practice. The first section examines the administrative law process at its two "ends." The beginning of the process involves the question of agency authority—what has the legislature empowered the agency to do? The conclusion of the process involves judicial review of the agency's action—did the agency properly do what the legislature authorized it to do? The remainder of the chapter examines two functions agencies perform between those two junctures that are of tremendous importance to environmental law practitioners—promulgating rules and issuing permits. With that foundation built, the Chapter 11 then is devoted to another administrative function of great consequence—enforcement of the rules and permits.

## A. THE SOURCE AND SCOPE OF AGENCY AUTHORITY

As mentioned in Chapter 5, one of the most controversial applications of liability under the Comprehensive Environmental Response, Compensation, and Liability Act (CERCLA) occurred in United States v. Fleet Factors Corp., 901 F.2d 1550 (11th Cir. 1990), *cert. denied*, 498 U.S. 1046 (1991). CERCLA § 101(20)(A) establishes the so-called secured lender exemption by defining "owner or operator" to include any person "owning or operating" a site of environmental contamination, but "not . . . a person who, without participating in the management of a vessel or facility, holds indicia of ownership primarily to protect his security interest in the vessel or facility." 42 U.S.C. § 9601(20)(A). This exception effectively removes most of the lending activities of financial institutions from the definition of "owner" and "operator," but it does not expressly exclude lenders who participate in the management of a business or take possession of business assets through loan foreclosure. Thus the court in *Fleet Factors* held that a lender who loaned money to a cloth printing business became an operator when the business went bankrupt and the lender foreclosed on its security interest in the business's equipment.

Several other judicial opinions followed similar reasoning, and the series of decisions provoked a panic among banks and other lenders who feared that they could become liable for the environmentally destructive activities of their clients. Indeed, some banks feared that the *Fleet Factors* approach to lender liability created a "Catch-22" situation: banks needed to become involved in the management of failing companies in order to protect their loans, but such involvement could make them liable for environmental cleanup costs under CERCLA. In response, the Environmental Protection Agency, to which Congress has delegated authority to implement CERCLA, promulgated a regulation limiting and clarifying the liability of lenders, after which the United States Court of Appeals for the District of Columbia Circuit gave EPA schooling in the source and scope of administrative authority.

## Kelley v. Environmental Protection Agency

United States Court of Appeals for the District of Columbia Circuit, 1994.
15 F.3d 1100.

■ SILBERMAN, CIRCUIT JUDGE:

Petitioners challenge an EPA regulation limiting lender liability under CERCLA. . . .

### I.

Congress enacted the Comprehensive Environmental Response, Compensation, and Liability Act (CERCLA), 42 U.S.C. 9601 *et seq.*, in 1980 to "provide for liability, compensation, cleanup, and emergency response for hazardous substances released into the environment and the cleanup of inactive hazardous waste disposal sites." Pub.L. No. 96–510, 94 Stat. 2767 (1980). . . . CERCLA also authorizes private parties and EPA to bring civil actions independently to recover their costs associated with the cleanup of hazardous wastes from those responsible for the contamination. 42 U.S.C. § 9607(a). Section 107 of CERCLA generally imposes strict liability on, among others, all prior and present "owners and operators" of hazardous waste sites. *Id.* § 9607(a)(1). Congress created a safe harbor provision for secured creditors, however, in the definition of "owner or operator," providing that "[s]uch term does not include a person, who, without participating in the management of a vessel or facility, holds indicia of ownership primarily to protect his security interest in the vessel or facility." 42 U.S.C. § 9601(20)(A).

Conflicting judicial interpretations as to the scope of this secured creditor exemption opened the possibility that lenders would be held liable for the cost of cleaning up contaminated property that they hold merely as collateral. Lenders lacked clear guidance as to the extent to which they could involve themselves in the affairs of a facility without incurring liability and also as to whether they would forfeit the exemption by exercising their right of foreclosure, which could be thought to convert their "indicia of ownership"—the security interest—into actual ownership. *See United States v. Maryland Bank & Trust Co.,* 632 F. Supp. 573, 578–80 (D. Md.1986). In *United States v. Fleet Factors Corp.,* 901 F.2d 1550 (11th Cir. 1990), the court, although adhering to the settled view that Congress intended to protect the commercial practices of secured creditors "in their normal course of business," *id.* at 1556, nevertheless stated that "a secured creditor will be liable if its involvement with the management of the facility is *sufficiently broad* to support the inference that it could affect hazardous waste disposal decisions if it so chose." *Id.* at 1558 (emphasis added).

This language, portending as it did an expansion in the scope of secured creditor liability, caused considerable discomfort in financial circles. Intervenor American Bankers Association points to survey data indicating that lenders curtailed loans made to certain classes of borrowers or secured by some types of properties in order to avoid the virtually unlimited liability risk associated with collateral property that may be contaminated. Some lenders, we are told, even chose to abandon collateral properties rather than foreclosing on them for fear of post-foreclosure liability.

EPA, responding to the understandable clamor from the banking community and in light of the federal government's increasing role as a secured creditor after taking over failed savings and loans, instituted a rulemaking proceeding, 56 Fed. Reg. 28,798 (1991), to define the secured creditor exemption when legislative efforts to amend CERCLA failed. *See, e.g.,* H.R. 4494, 101st Cong., 2d Sess. (1990), 136 Cong.Rec. H1505 (daily ed. Apr. 4, 1990). In April 1992, EPA issued the final regulation, which employs a framework of specific tests to provide clearer articulation of a lender's scope of liability under CERCLA. The rule provides an overall standard for judging when a lender's "[p]articipation in [m]anagement" causes the lender to forfeit its exemption. 40 C.F.R. § 300.1100(c)(1) (1992). A lender may, without incurring liability, undertake investigatory actions before the creation of a security interest, monitor or inspect the facility, and require that the borrower comply with all environmental standards. 40 C.F.R. § 300.1100(c)(2). When a loan nears default, the rule permits the lender to engage in work-out negotiations and activities, including ensuring that the collateral facility does not violate environmental laws. 40 C.F.R. § 300.1100(c)(2)(ii)(B). The rule also protects a secured creditor that acquires full title to the collateral property through foreclosure, as long as the creditor did not participate in the facility's management prior to foreclosure and undertakes certain diligent efforts to divest itself of the property. 40 C.F.R. § 300.1100(d). Lenders still face liability under Section 107(a)(3) and (4)—as opposed to liability as an "owner and operator" under Section 107(a)(1) and (2)—if they arrange for the disposal of hazardous substances at a facility or accept hazardous waste for transportation and disposal. 40 C.F.R. § 300.1100(d)(3).

In response to comments questioning whether the rule would apply in actions where the United States was not a party, EPA stated that the regulation is "a 'legislative' or 'substantive' rule that has undergone notice-and-comment pursuant to the Administrative Procedure Act" and as such "defines the liability of holders [of security interests] for CERCLA response costs in both the United States' and private party litigation." 57 Fed. Reg. 18,344, 18,368 (1992). The agency alternatively asserted that even if the rule were read as "a 'mere' interpretation of Section

101(20)(A)," it would affect third-party litigation since "EPA guidance and interpretations of laws administered by the Agency are given substantial deference by the courts." *Id.* (citations omitted).

Michigan and the Chemical Manufacturers Association filed petitions for review of the final regulation under Section 113(a) of CERCLA, 42 U.S.C. § 9613(a), which gives us exclusive jurisdiction to review any regulation promulgated under the statute. Petitioners are interested in the EPA rule because, as potential litigants under Section 107, they do not want to be foreclosed from suing lenders. Petitioners argue that EPA lacks statutory authority to define, through its regulation, the scope of lender liability under Section 107—an issue that they assert only federal courts may adjudicate. They also urge that the substance of the regulation contradicts the plain meaning of certain statutory language.

## II.

Although petitioners bring a general challenge to the authority of EPA to promulgate *any* substantive regulations under CERCLA, that issue is settled. We held in *Wagner Seed Co., Inc. v. Bush,* 946 F.2d 918, 920 (D.C. Cir. 1991), that the President had broadly delegated his statutory powers to EPA, and it is "the administering agency" for the statute. However, we had previously recognized that with respect to any specific regulation, EPA must demonstrate "either explicit or implicit evidence of congressional intent to delegate interpretive authority." *Linemaster Switch Corp. v. EPA,* 938 F.2d 1299, 1303 (D.C. Cir. 1991). . . . Here we encounter an issue not squarely decided in *Wagner Seed*—whether the EPA can, by regulation, define and limit a party's liability under Section 107. But the reasoning of *Wagner Seed,* or at least its dicta, cuts against the government.

EPA looks to several different portions of CERCLA to find the specific authority we have required. The agency points to Section 105 of CERCLA, which provides that the agency has responsibility to promulgate the national contingency plan setting forth the actions and procedures to be taken in response to a contamination. It is argued that the broad language of Section 105, authorizing EPA "to reflect and effectuate the responsibilities and powers created by this chapter," 42 U.S.C. § 9605(a); Exec. Order No. 12,580 § 1(b)(1), gives it power to define Section 107 liability—which the agency characterizes as a "responsibility and power" under the chapter. Although the mandate of Section 105 does "provide[ ] the EPA with broad rulemaking authority to craft the NCP," *Ohio v. EPA,* 838 F.2d 1325, 1331 (D.C. Cir. 1988), it is hardly a specific delegation of authority to EPA to interpret Section 107. We must still determine whether defining the scope of liability is among the "responsibilities and powers" Congress delegated to EPA under CERCLA.

EPA points to specific provisions of that section, paragraphs 105(a)(4) and 105(a)(3). The former authorizes the agency to prescribe "appropriate *roles* and responsibilities . . . of nongovernmental entities in effectuating the plan." 42 U.S.C. § 9605(a)(4) (emphasis added). EPA claims that the lender liability rule accomplishes just that by defining the "role" of security creditors. That is an imaginative use of the word role, but EPA's argument is hardly persuasive since Section 105 refers to the nature of actions parties must take in response to contamination—not their ultimate liability for the contamination set forth in Section 107. If EPA's position were correct, Congress would have had no need to provide for a party's liability in Section 107; EPA would have been authorized to develop those standards under Section 105. For similar reasons, paragraph 105(a)(3) does not help EPA. That provision obliges the agency to issue "methods and criteria for determining the appropriate extent of removal, remedy, and other measures authorized by [CERCLA]," but it does not speak to liability. As discussed below, a party might be obliged to provide a remedy and be entitled to reimbursement when determined subsequently not to be liable.

EPA also relies on those statutory provisions which grant it authority to seek enforcement. The agency may choose to contract to clean up a contaminated site (financed through the Superfund), and then bring action in federal court under Section 107(a)(4)(A) to recover its costs from a liable party. It is argued that the agency must first decide whether a party is actually liable before bringing such an action. That is no different, however, than any government "prosecutor" who must in good faith determine for itself whether a civil action in federal court should be brought—which necessarily includes a judgment whether a potential defendant violated the law or is "liable." The court is, nevertheless, the first body to formally determine liability, and therefore a civil prosecutor typically lacks authority to issue substantive regulations to interpret a statute establishing liability. *See, e.g., EEOC v. Arabian Am. Oil Co.,* 499 U.S. 244, 256 (1991); *Skidmore v. Swift & Co.,* 323 U.S. 134, 137–38 (1944).

To be sure, the agency also has authority, when imminent danger of harm exists, to issue administrative orders under Section 106(a) requiring private parties to clean up a site. And, if the party refuses, Section 106(b)(1) authorizes EPA to seek compliance in federal court. But, under the statute, a respondent must comply with such orders whether or not it is liable. Liability issues are resolved when the party against whom the order was levied seeks reimbursement under Section 106(b)(2). The statutory scheme might be described as requiring parties to shoot first (clean up) and ask questions (determine who bears the ultimate liability) later.

### III.

There remains the question of whether the regulation can be sustained as an interpretative rule. The preamble to the final regulation suggests that EPA attempted to straddle two horses—issuing the rule as a legislative regulation but asserting in the alternative that as an interpretative rule, it would still be entitled to judicial deference and therefore affect private party litigation. 57 Fed. Reg. 18,344, 18,368 (1992). Although we have admitted that the distinction between legislative and interpretative rules is "enshrouded in considerable smog," *General Motors Corp. v. Ruckelshaus,* 742 F.2d 1561, 1565 (D.C. Cir. 1984) (en banc) (quotations omitted), it is commonly understood that a rule is legislative if it is "based on an agency's power to exercise *its judgment* as to how best to implement a general statutory mandate," *American Mining Congress v. Mine Safety & Health Admin.,* 995 F.2d 1106, 1110 (D.C. Cir. 1993) (quotations omitted) (emphasis added), and has the binding force of law. *Id.* at 1109. By contrast, an interpretative rule "is based on specific statutory provisions," *United Technologies Corp. v. EPA,* 821 F.2d 714, 719 (D.C. Cir. 1987), and represents the agency's construction of the statute that is—while not binding—entitled to substantial judicial deference under *Chevron U.S.A. Inc. v. Natural Resources Defense Council, Inc.,* 467 U.S. 837, 842–43 (1984).

The rule bears little resemblance to what we have traditionally found to be an interpretative regulation. EPA does not really define specific statutory terms, but rather takes off from those terms and devises a comprehensive regulatory regimen to address the liability problems facing secured creditors. This extensive quasi-legislative effort to implement the statute does not strike us as merely a construction of statutory phrases, as was so in *Wagner Seed. See National Family Planning & Reproductive Health Ass'n, Inc. v. Sullivan,* 979 F.2d 227, 237 (D.C. Cir. 1992); *Chamber of Commerce v. OSHA,* 636 F.2d 464, 469 (D.C. Cir. 1980).

In any event, the same reason that prevents the agency from issuing the rule as a substantive regulation precludes judicial deference to EPA's offered "interpretation." If Congress meant the judiciary, not EPA, to determine liability issues—and we believe Congress did—EPA's view of statutory liability may not be given deference. "A precondition to deference under *Chevron* is a congressional delegation of administrative authority." *Adams Fruit Co. v. Barrett,* 494 U.S. 638, 649 (1990). *Chevron,* which sets forth the reigning rationale for judicial deference to agency interpretation of statutes, is premised on the notion that Congress implicitly delegated to the agency the authority to reconcile reasonably statutory ambiguities or to fill reasonably statutory interstices. Where Congress does not give an agency authority to determine (usually formally) the interpretation of a statute in the first instance and instead gives the agency authority only to bring the question to a federal court as the "prosecutor," deference to the agency's interpretation is inappropriate. *See United States v. Western Elec. Co.,* 900 F.2d 283, 297 (D.C. Cir. 1990). As we have explained, that is all that EPA can do regarding liability issues. Moreover, even if an agency enjoys authority to determine such a legal issue administratively, deference is withheld if a private party can bring the issue independently to federal court under a private right of action. *See Litton Fin. Printing Div. v. NLRB,* 501 U.S. 190, 197 (1991) (citing *Local Union 1395, International Brotherhood of Elec. Workers v. NLRB,* 797 F.2d 1027, 1030–31 (D.C. Cir. 1986)) (NLRB's interpretation of a collective bargaining agreement not entitled to deference since private parties can come to federal court independently to enforce those agreements). Petitioners are such private parties; they wish to preserve the right to sue lenders when, in petitioners' view, a lender's behavior transgresses the statutory test—whether or not EPA would regard the lender as liable. As we read the statute, Congress intended that petitioners' claim in such an event should be evaluated by the federal courts independent of EPA's institutional view.

Petitioners conceded that the regulation could be sustained as a policy statement that would guide EPA's enforcement proceedings across the country, but EPA has not asked that its regulation be so regarded. Furthermore, intervenors point out that if the regulation were to affect only EPA's enforcement proceedings, lenders would still face potentially staggering liability because of the generality of the statutory language and the prospect of private suits. That potential liability would force lenders to behave cautiously even if EPA were to adhere to the regulation as its policy. Given our uncertainty as to EPA's wishes, we think the proper course is to vacate the rule and leave EPA free to take whatever steps it thinks appropriate.

We well recognize the difficulties that lenders face in the absence of the clarity EPA's regulation would have provided. Before turning to this rulemaking, EPA sought congressional relief and was rebuffed. We see no alternative but that EPA try again. The petition for review is granted and the regulation is hereby vacated.

■ MIKVA, CHIEF JUDGE, dissenting:

. . . Petitioners argue, and the majority agrees, that the Final Rule is invalid because Congress delegated to the courts, rather than to the Executive branch, authority to interpret the scope of CERCLA's secured lender exemption. I disagree. CERCLA's language, structure and legislative history suggest that Congress implicitly delegated to the President (who in turn delegated to the EPA) the authority to interpret who falls within the scope of CERCLA's regulatory regime. . . .

### A. Delegation of Authority

When Congress enacted CERCLA in 1980, it implicitly delegated authority to the EPA to define which parties fell within the statute's regulatory regime. For example, CERCLA charged the EPA Administrator with responsibility for prescribing the manner and form by which owners and operators were to notify the agency of hazardous waste storage, treatment or disposal at their facilities. 42 U.S.C. 9603(c). CERCLA also authorized the EPA Administrator to promulgate rules and regulations specifying the recordkeeping requirements to which owners and operators of hazardous waste facilities were subject and vested the EPA Administrator with discretion to waive those requirements on petition from those parties. 42 U.S.C. § 9603(d). In addition, CERCLA authorized the President, who in turn authorized the EPA, to undertake those remedial actions necessary to contain or remove hazardous substances at-risk of release "unless the President determine[d] that such removal and remedial action w[ould] be done properly by the owner or operator of the vessel or facility from which the release or threat of release emanate[d]." 42 U.S.C. § 9604(a)(1). CERCLA also authorized the EPA to issue abatement orders to those parties responsible for particularly dangerous hazardous wastes. 42 U.S.C. § 9606. To administer each of these subsections effectively, the EPA was obliged to construe the term "owner or operator" within the meaning of CERCLA; Congress implicitly delegated authority to the EPA, as the administering agency, to do so. *See Wagner Seed Co., Inc. v. Bush,* 946 F.2d 918, 923 (D.C. Cir. 1991). . . . I would uphold the rule.

---

## QUESTIONS AND DISCUSSION

**1.** CERCLA establishes the framework for EPA to administer remediation of contaminated sites and creates both a public and a private right of action for recovery of remedial costs. As Judge Mikva reasoned in dissent, to administer the remedial program effectively, EPA was obliged to construe the term "owner or operator" within the meaning of CERCLA, and thus Congress implicitly delegated authority to the EPA, as the administering agency, to do so. But the majority drew the line on EPA's authority at the point at which EPA attempted to define "owner and operator" outside of the administrative domain in such a way as to constrain the cost recovery liability cause of action available to public and private parties other than EPA. Is it likely that Congress meant for it to be possible that there to be two different meanings of "owner or operator" for purposes of the statute—one for the regulatory program defined by EPA's institutional view and one for the liability regime defined by the courts?

**2.** Note that the *Kelley* court did not reach the question whether EPA's interpretation of the scope of "owner or operator" would have been upheld had Congress authorized EPA to interpret the term for purposes of defining the scope of CERCLA liability. As is explored more later in this chapter as well as in Chapter 10, it is a basic principle of administrative law that an agency's construction of the statute it has been delegated to administer is entitled to substantial judicial deference. Chevron U.S.A., Inc. v. Natural Resources Defense Council, Inc., 467 U.S. 837, 842–43 (1984). But as the majority observed, the rationale for judicial deference to agency interpretation of statutes is premised on the notion that Congress implicitly delegated to the agency the authority to reconcile reasonably statutory ambiguities or to fill reasonably statutory interstices. Under CERCLA, Congress gave EPA authority only to bring the question to a federal court as the "prosecutor," for which deference to the agency's interpretation is inappropriate.

**3.** The practical lesson of *Kelley*, therefore, is to start at the beginning when an agency and a regulated party (or other interest) dispute the outcome of agency action. Square one is to consider whether the agency was legislatively authorized to perform the action procedurally and substantively. EPA surely was procedurally authorized to conduct rulemakings under CERCLA, but not with respect to defining the substantive scope of liability in judicial cost recovery actions.

**4.** Congress subsequently adopted EPA's approach by amending CERCLA's definition of "owner or operator" to exclude lenders not participating in management on substantially the same terms as had EPA's vacated regulation. *See* 42 U.S.C. § 9601(20)(E) and Chapter 5. Does this suggest the *Kelley* court decided the question of EPA's authority incorrectly?

---

## B. JUDICIAL REVIEW OF AGENCY ACTION

The *Kelley* court determined that EPA had no authority to dictate CERCLA liability rules applicable between private parties, but from where did the *Kelley* court derive its judicial authority to decide the scope of EPA's administrative authority? The answer, as with EPA's authority, is Congress. Congress defines the rules of judicial review of agency action—who may pursue it, when, where, and under what standards.

The Administrative Procedure Act (APA), 5 U.S.C. §§ 551 et seq., establishes the default rules for federal administrative law. Chapter 5 of the APA governs the "internal procedures" of agencies, everything from public information, open meetings, rulemaking, adjudications, permitting, and sanctions. More on those provisions later. Chapter 7 of the APA governs judicial review. Section 701 precludes judicial review when "(1) statutes preclude judicial review; or (2) agency action is committed to agency discretion by law." Section 702 establishes the right of review for all other cases: "A person suffering legal wrong because of agency action, or adversely affected or aggrieved by agency action within the meaning of a relevant statute, is entitled to judicial review thereof." Section 704 limits this right of review to "agency action made reviewable by statute and final agency action for which there is no other adequate remedy in court." Hence, unless another statute precludes review, if a person challenging agency action not "committed to agency discretion by law" can demonstrate the action was "final agency action" that caused "legal wrong," the door is open to judicial review.

Section 706 in turn governs the scope of such judicial review, providing that a "reviewing court shall . . . hold unlawful and set aside agency action, findings, and conclusions found" not to meet six separate standards. In all cases agency action must be set aside if the action was "arbitrary, capricious, an abuse of discretion, or otherwise not in accordance with law" or if the action failed to meet statutory, procedural, or constitutional requirements. In certain narrow, specifically limited situations, the agency action is to be set aside if the action was not supported by "substantial evidence." And in other equally narrow circumstances the reviewing court is to engage in a *de novo* review of the action and set it aside if it was "unwarranted by the facts." The provision reads in full as follows:

> To the extent necessary to decision and when presented, the reviewing court shall decide all relevant questions of law, interpret constitutional and statutory provisions, and determine the meaning or applicability of the terms of an agency action. The reviewing court shall—
>
> (1) compel agency action unlawfully withheld or unreasonably delayed; and
>
> (2) hold unlawful and set aside agency action, findings, and conclusions found to be—
>
> (A) arbitrary, capricious, an abuse of discretion, or otherwise not in accordance with law;
>
> (B) contrary to constitutional right, power, privilege, or immunity;
>
> (C) in excess of statutory jurisdiction, authority, or limitations, or short of statutory right;
>
> (D) without observance of procedure required by law;
>
> (E) unsupported by substantial evidence in a case subject to Sections 556 and 557 of this title or otherwise reviewed on the record of an agency hearing provided by statute; or
>
> (F) unwarranted by the facts to the extent that the facts are subject to trial de novo by the reviewing court.
>
> In making the foregoing determinations, the court shall review the whole record or those parts of it cited by a party, and due account shall be taken of the rule of prejudicial error.

Most states have a state APA that follows a similar model, though by no means can one assume that the state APA is a carbon copy of the federal regime in text or application. At both the federal and state levels, moreover, a not insubstantial body of administrative law is about specific exceptions to the APA default rules that the legislature has inserted in other statutes or that courts have devised in particular circumstances based on constitutional and prudential concerns. For the most part, however, administrative law is the law of the federal or relevant state APA. And among the fields of practice touched by administrative law, environmental law cases have provided more than ample fodder for testing and interpreting agency action. Indeed, one of the seminal cases on access to and the scope of judicial review under the federal APA involved an environmental protection statute.

## Citizens to Preserve Overton Park, Inc. v. Volpe

Supreme Court of the United States, 1971.
401 U.S. 402.

■ Opinion of the Court by MR. JUSTICE MARSHALL, announced by MR. JUSTICE STEWART.

The growing public concern about the quality of our natural environment has prompted Congress in recent years to enact legislation designed to curb the accelerating destruction of our country's natural beauty. We are concerned in this case with 4(f) of the Department of Transportation Act of 1966, as amended, and § 18(a) of the Federal-Aid Highway Act of 1968, 82 Stat. 823, 23 U.S.C. § 138 (1964 ed., Supp. V) (hereafter § 138). These statutes prohibit the Secretary of Transportation from authorizing the use of federal funds to finance the construction of highways through public parks if a "feasible and prudent" alternative route exists. If no such route is available, the statutes allow him to approve construction through parks only if there has been "all possible planning to minimize harm" to the park.

Petitioners, private citizens as well as local and national conservation organizations, contend that the Secretary has violated these statutes by authorizing the expenditure of federal funds for the construction of a six-lane interstate highway through a public park in Memphis, Tennessee. Their claim was rejected by the District Court, which granted the Secretary's motion for summary judgment, and the Court of Appeals for the Sixth Circuit affirmed. After oral argument, this Court granted a stay that halted construction and, treating the application for the stay as a petition for certiorari, granted review. We now reverse the judgment below and remand for further proceedings in the District Court.

Overton Park is 342-acre city park located near the center of Memphis. The park contains a zoo, a nine-hole municipal golf course, an outdoor theater, nature trails, a bridle path, an art academy, picnic areas, and 170 acres of forest. The proposed highway, which is to be a sixlane, high-speed, expressway, will sever the zoo from the rest of the park. Although the roadway will be depressed below ground level except where it crosses a small creek, 26 acres of the park will be destroyed. The highway is to be a segment of Interstate Highway I-40, part of the National System of Interstate and Defense Highways. I-40 will provide Memphis with a major east-west expressway which will allow easier access to downtown Memphis from the residential areas on the eastern edge of the city.

Although the route through the park was approved by the Bureau of Public Roads in 1956 and by the Federal Highway Administrator in 1966, the enactment of § 4(f) of the Department of Transportation Act prevented distribution of federal funds for the section of the highway designated to go through Overton Park until the Secretary of Transportation determined whether the requirements of § 4(f) had been met. Federal funding for the rest of the project was, however, available; and the state acquired a right-of-way on both sides of the park. In April 1968, the Secretary announced that he concurred in the judgment of local officials that I-40 should be built through the park. And in September 1969 the State acquired the right-of-way inside Overton Park from the city. Final approval for the project—the route as well as the design—was not announced until November 1969, after Congress had reiterated in § 138 of the Federal-Aid Highway Act that highway construction through public parks was to be restricted. Neither announcement approving the route and design of I-40 was accompanied by a statement of the Secretary's factual findings. He did not indicate why he believed there were no feasible and prudent alternative routes or why design changes could not be made to reduce the harm to the park.

Petitioners contend that the Secretary's action is invalid without such formal findings and that the Secretary did not make an independent determination but merely relied on the judgment of the Memphis City Council. They also contend that it would be "feasible and prudent" to route I-40 around Overton Park either to the north or to the south. And they argue that if these alternative routes are not "feasible and prudent," the present plan does not include "all possible" methods for reducing harm to the park. Petitioners claim that I-40 could be built under the park by using either of two possible tunneling methods, and they claim that, at a minimum, by using advanced drainage techniques the expressway could be depressed below ground level along the entire route through the park including the section that crosses the small creek.

Respondents argue that it was unnecessary for the Secretary to make formal findings, and that he did, in fact, exercise his own independent judgment which was supported by the facts. In the District Court, respondents introduced affidavits, prepared specifically for this litigation, which indicated that the Secretary had made the decision and that the decision was supportable. These affidavits were contradicted by affidavits introduced by petitioners, who also sought to take the deposition of a former Federal Highway Administrator who had participated in the decision to route I-40 through Overton Park.

The District Court and the Court of Appeals found that formal findings by the Secretary were not necessary and refused to order the deposition of the former Federal Highway Administrator because those courts believed that probing of the mental processes of an administrative decisionmaker was prohibited. And, believing that the Secretary's authority was wide and reviewing courts' authority narrow in the approval of highway routes, the lower courts held that the affidavits contained no basis for a determination that the Secretary had exceeded his authority.

We agree that formal findings were not required. But we do not believe that in this case judicial review based solely on litigation affidavits was adequate.

A threshold question—whether petitioners are entitled to any judicial review—is easily answered. Section 701 of the Administrative Procedure Act, 5 U.S.C. § 701 (1964 ed., Supp. V), provides that the action of "each authority of the Government of the United States," which includes the Department of Transportation, is subject to judicial review except where there is a statutory prohibition on review or where "agency action is committed to agency discretion by law." In this case, there is no indication that Congress sought to prohibit judicial review and there is most certainly no "showing of 'clear and convincing evidence' of a * * * legislative intent" to restrict access to judicial review. Abbott Laboratories v. Gardner, 387 U.S. 136 (1967).

Similarly, the Secretary's decision here does not fall within the exception for action "committed to agency discretion." This is a very narrow exception. The legislative history of the Administrative Procedure Act indicates that it is applicable in those rare instances where "statutes are drawn in such broad terms that in a given case there is no law to apply." S.Rep. No. 752, 79th Cong., 1st Sess., 26 (1945).

Section 4(f) of the Department of Transportation Act and § 138 of the Federal-Aid Highway Act are clear and specific directives. Both the Department of Transportation Act and the Federal-Aid to Highway Act provide that the Secretary "shall not approve any program or project" that requires the use of any public parkland "unless (1) there is no feasible and prudent alternative to the use of such land, and (2) such program includes all possible planning to minimize harm to such park * * * ." 23 U.S.C. § 138 (1964 ed., Supp. V); 49 U.S.C. § 1653(f) (1964 ed., Supp. V). This language is a plain and explicit bar to the use of federal funds for construction of highways through parks—only the most unusual situations are exempted.

Despite the clarity of the statutory language, respondents argue that the Secretary has wide discretion. They recognize that the requirement that there be no "feasible" alternative route admits of little administrative discretion. For this exemption to apply the Secretary must find that as a matter of sound engineering it would not be feasible to build the highway along any other route. Respondents argue, however, that the requirement that there be no other "prudent" route requires the Secretary to engage in a wide-ranging balancing of competing interests. They contend that the Secretary should weigh the detriment resulting from the destruction of parkland against the cost of other routes, safety considerations, and other factors, and determine on the basis of the importance that he attaches to these other factors whether, on balance, alternative feasible routes would be "prudent."

But no such wide-ranging endeavor was intended. It is obvious that in most cases considerations of cost, directness of route, and community disruption will indicate that parkland should be used for highway construction whenever possible. Although it may be necessary to transfer funds from one jurisdiction to another, there will always be a smaller outlay required from the public purse when parkland is used since the public already owns the land and there will be no need to pay for right-of-way. And since people do not live or work in parks, if a highway is built on parkland no one will have to leave his home or give up his business. Such factors are common to substantially all highway construction. Thus, if Congress intended these factors to be on an equal footing with preservation of parkland there would have been no need for the statutes.

Congress clearly did not intend that cost and disruption of the community were to be ignored by the Secretary. But the very existence of the statutes indicates that protection of parkland was to be given paramount importance. The few green havens that are public parks were not to be lost unless there were truly unusual factors present in a particular case or the cost or community disruption resulting from alternative routes reached extraordinary magnitudes. If the statutes are to have any meaning, the Secretary cannot approve the destruction of parkland unless he finds that alternative routes present unique problems.

Plainly, there is "law to apply" and thus the exemption for action "committed to agency discretion" is inapplicable. But the existence of judicial review is only the start: the standard for review must also be determined. For that we must look to § 706 of the Administrative Procedure Act, 5 U.S.C. § 706 (1964 ed., Supp. V), which provides that a "reviewing court shall * * * hold unlawful and set aside agency action, findings, and conclusions found" not to meet six separate standards. In all cases agency action must be set aside if the action was "arbitrary, capricious, an abuse of discretion, or otherwise not in accordance with law" or if the action failed to meet statutory, procedural, or constitutional requirements. 5 U.S.C. §§ 706(2)(A), (B), (C), (D) (1964 ed., Supp. V). In certain narrow, specifically limited situations, the agency action is to be set aside if the action was not supported by "substantial evidence." And in other equally narrow circumstances the reviewing court is to engage in a de novo review of the action and set it aside if it was "unwarranted by the facts." 5 U.S.C. §§ 706(2)(E), (F) (1964 ed., Supp. V).

Petitioners argue that the Secretary's approval of the construction of I-40 through Overton Park is subject to one or the other of these latter two standards of limited applicability. First, they contend that the "substantial evidence" standard of § 706(2)(E) must be applied. In the alternative, they claim that § 706(2)(F) applies and that there must be a de novo review to determine if the Secretary's action was "unwarranted by the facts." Neither of these standards is, however, applicable.

Review under the substantial-evidence test is authorized only when the agency action is taken pursuant to a rulemaking provision of the Administrative Procedure Act itself, 5 U.S.C. § 553 (1964 ed., Supp. V), or when the agency action is based on a public adjudicatory hearing. *See* 5 U.S.C. §§ 556, 557 (1964 ed., Supp. V). The Secretary's decision to allow the expenditure of federal funds to build I-40 through Overton Park was plainly not an exercise of a rulemaking function. And the only hearing that is required by either the Administrative Procedure Act or the statutes regulating the distribution of federal funds for highway construction is a public hearing conducted by local officials for the purpose of informing the community about the proposed project and eliciting community views on the design and route. 23 U.S.C. § 128 (1964 ed., Supp. V). The hearing is nonadjudicatory, quasi-legislative in nature. It is not designed to produce a record that is to be the basis of agency action—the basic requirement for substantial-evidence review.

Petitioners' alternative argument also fails. De novo review of whether the Secretary's decision was "unwarranted by the facts" is authorized by § 706(2)(F) in only two circumstances. First, such de novo review is authorized when the action is adjudicatory in nature and the agency factfinding procedures are inadequate. And, there may be independent judicial factfinding when issues that were not before the agency are raised in a proceeding to enforce nonadjudicatory agency action. Neither situation exists here.

Even though there is no de novo review in this case and the Secretary's approval of the route of I-40 does not have ultimately to meet the substantial-evidence test, the generally applicable standards of § 706 require the reviewing court to engage in a substantial inquiry. Certainly, the Secretary's decision is entitled to a presumption of regularity. But that presumption is not to shield his action from a thorough, probing, in-depth review.

The court is first required to decide whether the Secretary acted within the scope of his authority. This determination naturally begins with a delineation of the scope of the Secretary's authority and discretion. As has been shown, Congress has specified only a small range of choices that the Secretary can make. Also involved in this initial inquiry is a determination of whether on the facts the Secretary's decision can reasonably be said to be within that range. The reviewing court must consider whether the Secretary properly construed his authority to approve the use of parkland as limited to situations where there are no feasible alternative routes or where feasible alternative routes involve uniquely difficult problems. And the reviewing court must be able to find that the Secretary could have reasonably believed that in this case there are no feasible alternatives or that alternatives do involve unique problems.

Scrutiny of the facts does not end, however, with the determination that the Secretary has acted within the scope of his statutory authority.

Section 706(2)(A) requires a finding that the actual choice made was not "arbitrary, capricious, an abuse of discretion, or otherwise not in accordance with law." 5 U.S.C. § 706(2)(A) (1964 ed., Supp. V). To make this finding the court must consider whether the decision was based on a consideration of the relevant factors and whether there has been a clear error of judgment. Although this inquiry into the facts is to be searching and careful, the ultimate standard of review is a narrow one. The court is not empowered to substitute its judgment for that of the agency.

The final inquiry is whether the Secretary's action followed the necessary procedural requirements. Here the only procedural error alleged is the failure of the Secretary to make formal findings and state his reason for allowing the highway to be built through the park.

Undoubtedly, review of the Secretary's action is hampered by his failure to make such findings, but the absence of formal findings does not necessarily require that the case be remanded to the Secretary. Neither the Department of Transportation Act nor the Federal-Aid Highway Act requires such formal findings. Moreover, the Administrative Procedure Act requirements that there be formal findings in certain rulemaking and adjudicatory proceedings do not apply to the Secretary's action here. See 5 U.S.C. §§ 553(a)(2), 554(a) (1964 ed., Supp. V). And, although formal findings may be required in some cases in the absence of statutory directives when the nature of the agency action is ambiguous, those situations are rare. Plainly, there is no ambiguity here; the Secretary has approved the construction of I-40 through Overton Park and has approved a specific design for the project. . . .

Thus it is necessary to remand this case to the District Court for plenary review of the Secretary's decision. That review is to be based on the full administrative record that was before the Secretary at the time he made his decision. But since the bare record may not disclose the factors that were considered or the Secretary's construction of the evidence it may be necessary for the District Court to require some explanation in order to determine if the Secretary acted within the scope of his authority and if the Secretary's action was justifiable under the applicable standard.

The court may require the administrative officials who participated in the decision to give testimony explaining their action. Of course, such inquiry into the mental processes of administrative decisionmakers is usually to be avoided. United States v. Morgan, 313 U.S. 409, 422 (1941). And where there are administrative findings that were made at the same time as the decision, as was the case in *Morgan*, there must be a strong showing of bad faith or improper behavior before such inquiry may be made. But here there are no such formal findings and it may be that the only way there can be effective judicial review is by examining the decisionmakers themselves. *See* Shaughnessy v. Accardi, 349 U.S. 280 (1955).

The District Court is not, however, required to make such an inquiry. It may be that the Secretary can prepare formal findings . . . that will provide an adequate explanation for his action. Such an explanation will, to some extent, be a "post hoc rationalization" and thus must be viewed critically. If the District Court decides that additional explanation is necessary, that court should consider which method will prove the most expeditious so that full review may be had as soon as possible.

Reversed and remanded.

---

*Overton Park* provides a practical anatomy lesson on the structure of administrative action and judicial review. Distilling the case to its basic elements, the Court explained that a reviewing court has to make five inquiries before turning to the merits: (1) what findings was the agency required to make; (2) what discretion did the agency have in making those findings; (3) what procedures was the agency required to conduct in order to exercise that discretion; (4) what standard of review must the court apply to determine whether the agency properly exercised its discretion; and (5) based on what body of evidence must the court apply its review? As *Overton Park* suggests, of course, there are innumerable different ways legislatures have defined agencies' findings, discretion, and procedures. Our objective is not to provide examples of all or even a limited sample of the different models, but rather to illustrate how a court defines the scope of judicial review based on the characterization of these attributes of agency action, and thus how important it is for practitioners to be familiar with the rules of judicial review in general, and with the particular construction of agency action used by agencies for which, or before which, the attorney practices.

*Findings.* The first question the Court had to consider in *Overton Park* was what findings Congress required the relevant agency authorities to make in order to approve construction through the park. The Court explained that Congress prohibited the Secretary of Transportation from authorizing the use of federal funds to finance the construction of highways through public parks if a "feasible and prudent" alternative route exists; if no such route is available, the Secretary can approve construction through parks only if there has been "all possible planning to minimize harm" to the park. Were any other findings necessary to approve construction through the park?

*Discretion.* Once the Court isolated the relevant findings, the next question was how much discretion Congress delegated to the Secretary in making them. The government agreed that the no "feasible" alternative route finding admits of little administrative discretion, but argued that the requirement that there be no other "prudent" route requires the Secretary to engage in a wide-ranging balancing of competing interests. But as the Court observed, the government's position reduced the entire "feasible and prudent" test to a cost-benefit analysis, whereas if Congress intended factors such as cost and safety to be on an equal footing with preservation of parkland there would have been no need for the statutory restrictions. Rather, while Congress did not require the Secretary to ignore cost and safety, the point of having the agency go through the findings process indicates that protection of parkland was to be given paramount importance. Yet, even given that park protection is the paramount goal, presumably it is not the exclusive goal, or Congress would simply have dispensed with the "feasible and prudent" test and banned construction through parks in all cases. Does the Court provide any insight for knowing when an alternative route is or is not prudent?

*Procedure.* Next the Court had to characterize the procedure Congress required the Secretary to use to make the findings within the applicable scope of discretion. As the Court observed, the decision to allow the expenditure of federal funds for construction through the park was plainly not an exercise of a rulemaking function. A hearing was required, but only in the form of public forum conducted by agency officials for the purpose of informing the community about the proposed project and eliciting community views on the design and route. The Court described the hearing as nonadjudicatory, quasi-legislative in nature and *not* designed to produce a record that is to be the basis of agency action. So what is the purpose of the hearing, and what is the status of information the agency obtains through it?

*Standard of Review.* The park advocates argued that the courts should have applied a probing review of the agency's findings. First, they contended that the "substantial evidence" standard of § 706(2)(E) must be applied. In the alternative, they claimed that § 706(2)(F) applies and that there must be a de novo review to determine if the Secretary's action was "unwarranted by the facts." But neither standard matched up with the applicable procedure the Secretary was authorized to use. The substantial evidence test is employed when the agency action is based on a public *adjudicatory* hearing. *See* 5 U.S.C. §§ 556, 557 (1964 ed., Supp. V). *De novo* review is even more limited, authorized only when the action is adjudicatory in nature and the agency factfinding procedures are inadequate. None of these conditions was present in *Overton Park*.

Rather, as in the *Kelley* case excerpted in the previous section of this chapter, the Court started at the beginning, observing that it must first decide whether the Secretary acted within the scope of delegated authority. Where such authority exists—which it clearly did in the case—Section 706(2)(A) of the APA requires a finding that the actual choice made was not "arbitrary, capricious, an abuse of discretion, or otherwise not in accordance with law." As the Court explained, to make this finding the court must consider whether the decision was based on a consideration of the relevant factors and whether there has been a clear error of judgment. Although this inquiry into the facts is to be searching and careful, the ultimate standard of review is a narrow one, and the court is not empowered to substitute its judgment for that of the agency.

*The Administrative Record.* To what does a court apply the applicable standard of review? In rulemakings, adjudications, and quasi-legislative actions like the one in *Overton Park*, generally the agency must compile some form of administrative record defining the body of "evidence" for purposes of judicial review. In *Overton Park* the Secretary had made no formal findings or statement explaining the reason for allowing the highway to be built through the park. The Court acknowledged that the lack of formal findings "hampered" judicial review, but was not fatal. Rather, the Court remanded the matter to the lower court and suggested alternatives for applying the standard of review—from using the record available from the agency to hearing testimony designed to explain the reasons for the decision.

## II. RULEMAKING PROCEEDINGS

The *Kelly* case excerpted above in Section I.A. involved a rulemaking the court determined should never have happened because of a lack of agency authority. But do not get the wrong impression: what Congress states in statutes, it usually intends for agencies to flesh out in rulemakings. Congress, and state and local legislatures, delegate environmental agencies extensive authority to implement statutory provisions through the promulgation of agency rules. As you look back over the programs surveyed in Part I of the text, for example, you find rules covering a broad array of topics:

- Emission standards under the Clean Air Act
- Remediation standards under CERCLA
- Listing of endangered species under the Endangered Species Act
- Procedures for environmental assessment under NEPA
- Rules governing access to and use of federal public lands

The volume of federal agency administrative rulemaking alone is staggering. It is not uncommon to have over 4000 final rules issued in one year. Agencies explain what their proposed and final rules mean in the daily *Federal Register*, which typically runs over 50,000 pages a year. The current text of all final rules is compiled in the *Code of Federal Regulations*, which exceeds 130,000 pages in length. Environmental agencies contribute a large dose of this activity each year. In short, agencies rules make up most of the meat of environmental law. Environmental law practitioners, both within and outside of agencies, thus appreciate the importance of involvement in the rulemaking process as a means to influence the outcome as well as to prepare for post-promulgation litigation seeking judicial review of the validity of the rule and its application.

The APA provides the default rules for the agency rulemaking process. Under Section 533 of the APA, federal agencies generally must publish notice of proposed rulemaking in the *Federal Register* to give interested persons an opportunity to comment and participate in the rulemaking. The notice-and-comment provision applies to "legislative" or "substantive" rules that establish legal requirements, but not to "interpretive rules, general statements of policy, or rules of agency organization, procedure, or practice." 5 U.S.C. 553(b)(A). After the notice and comment period concludes, the agency "shall incorporate in the rules adopted a concise general statement of their basis and purpose."

Agency rulemaking presents a wide variety of practice settings and functions for environmental attorneys. Obviously, agencies employ attorneys to draft regulations. But attorneys for other public agencies, for private industry, and for non-governmental organizations that have a stake in a particular agency's rulemaking are likely to be enlisted to monitor and weigh in on the agency's promulgation process and to interpret the agency's final rulemaking product. The following materials provide an overview of how that process is *supposed* to work and a case study of how it more often plays out in practice. The following 2005 web posting from the EPA (no longer available) explains the process in its ideal state:

## U.S. Environmental Protection Agency, Developing Regulations: From Start to Finish

When EPA identifies the potential need for a regulation, staff meet to form a *workgroup*. The workgroup is led by the EPA office that will be writing the regulation and includes members from other parts of the Agency with related interests or responsibilities. This process can take months before an appropriate course of action is carefully and methodically decided. It generally goes like this:

- **Analyze the Problem.** The workgroup studies the origin, magnitude, and impacts of the problem. It may draw information from EPA's own research, scientific literature, or from other researchers in the United States and abroad.

- **Identify Options.** The workgroup then considers the available options for addressing the problem. This may require evaluating environmental technologies, changes in environmental management practices, and incentives that can motivate better environmental performance. The workgroup also takes related issues into account at this stage, such as the impact of various options on small businesses, on children's health, or on state and local governments. Sometimes the workgroup might find there is no need for regulation.

- **Publish Proposal.** Once the preliminary analysis is complete and the need for regulation is determined, the workgroup drafts a proposed regulation for publication in the *Federal Register*. A law called the Administrative Procedure Act generally requires EPA (and other federal regulatory agencies) to request comments from the public before finalizing the regulation. The public comment period typically lasts 60 to 90 days.

• **Review Public Comments.** Next, the workgroup reviews and evaluates all the comments received. Depending on the regulation, these comments may range from minimal to extensive. In any case, the workgroup carefully weighs and evaluates the comments before developing a draft final regulation for review and approval by EPA senior management.

• **Issue Regulation.** After approval by senior management, the EPA Administrator reviews the draft regulation and decides whether it should be issued. If the Administrator decides to issue the regulation, it is published in the *Federal Register* and goes into effect soon afterwards. In accordance with the Congressional Review Act, Congress may overturn a regulation even after the Administrator has issued it, however, this is an extremely rare occurrence.

Occasionally there are interim steps in this process. For instance, if the workgroup receives new data from the public during a comment period, the workgroup might publish in the *Federal Register* a "Notice of Data Availability" so interested parties can learn more and submit additional comments. Sometimes the workgroup might decide to take a new direction after receiving new data, which can result in a "Supplemental Notice of Proposed Rulemaking." Finally, the workgroup might decide to draft a notice seeking public comment and information before the proposal is even developed. This pre-proposal is called an "Advanced Notice of Proposed Rulemaking" and is also published in the *Federal Register*.

EPA maintains a central staff within the Administrator's office to track all the regulations under development. The Regulatory Management Division monitors the status of workgroups, helps with *Federal Register* publication, and ensures that EPA is following the various laws and mandates that govern regulation writing.

Because EPA is part of the Executive Branch, the White House's Office of Management and Budget (OMB) reviews some before they are published in the *Federal Register*. Generally, OMB reviews regulations that could potentially impose more than $100 million in annual costs on society or present controversial legal or policy issues. OMB also ensures rules are consistent with the Administration's environmental priorities and policies, and coordinates review by other federal agencies that might have an interest in the issue.

### Making It Official—Where To Look for Regulations

EPA publishes its proposed regulations, final regulations, and notices in the *Federal Register*. Final regulations are also published in the *Code of Federal Regulations*. Known as the *CFR*, this compilation of government regulations is divided up into 50 titles that represent topics of federal authority, such as education, transportation, and agriculture. *CFR* Title 40: Protection of the Environment, is retrievable by Chapter I (Parts 1–799), Chapter V (Parts 1500–1517), and Chapter VI (Part 1700).

---

If only it were that simple! The following materials, built around a case study of the promulgation of a regulation implementing the Endangered Species Act (ESA), provide a more representative example of what *really* happens during and after environmental law rulemaking proceedings.

As you learned in Chapter 2, Section 9 of the Endangered Species Act (ESA) generally prohibits the "take" of species listed under the ESA as endangered. Pursuant to the broad grant of regulatory authority over threatened species in Section 4(d) of the ESA, regulations implementing the ESA, promulgated by the U.S. Fish and Wildlife Service (FWS) and the National Marine Fisheries Service (NMFS), also generally prohibit take of species listed as threatened. *See, e.g.*, 50 C.F.R. 17.31 and 17.21. Section 3(18) of the ESA defines take to mean "to harass, harm, pursue, hunt, shoot, wound, kill, trap, capture, or collect, or to attempt to engage in any such conduct." FWS regulations in turn define "harm" to include "significant habitat modification or degradation where it actually kills or injures wildlife by significantly impairing essential behavioral patterns, including breeding, feeding or sheltering." 50 C.F.R. 17.3.

Section 10(a) of the ESA allows the FWS and NMFS to issue permits authorizing the incidental take of listed species in the course of otherwise lawful activities, provided activities are conducted according to a conservation plan (also known as a habitat conservation plan or HCP) designed to further the long-term conservation of the species and to avoid jeopardy to the continued existence of the species. In adding this permitting program to the ESA in 1982 amendments to the statute, Congress indicated it was acting to "address the concerns of private landowners who are faced with having otherwise lawful actions not requiring Federal permits prevented by Section 9 prohibitions against taking." H.R. Rep. No. 835, 97th Cong., 2d Sess. 29 (1982). Indeed, Congress modeled the 1982 HCP amendments after the conservation plan developed by private landowners and local governments to protect the habitat of two listed butterflies on San Bruno Mountain in San Mateo County, while allowing development activities to proceed. *See* H.R. Conf. Rep. No. 835, 97th Cong., 2d Sess. 30–31 (1982), *reprinted in* 1982 U.S.C.C.A.N. 2860, 2872 (Conf. Rep.)

By the early 1990s, the number and geographic range of listed species had increased dramatically and demand for HCP permits grew among landowners affected by the take prohibition, but there was concern in the land development and real estate communities that HCP permits did not protect against escalating demands for habitat conservation as a species continued to decline. To respond to that concern, in an August 11, 1994 public statement, the FWS and NMFS announced, without any prior public notice and comment, a "No Surprises" policy which was to go into effect immediately. The policy required the agency when approving an HCP to provide landowners with "assurances" that, once approved, even if circumstances subsequently changed in such a way as to render the HCP inadequate to conserve listed species, the agency would not impose additional conservation and mitigation requirements which would increase costs or further restrict the use of natural resources beyond the original plan. The stated purpose of the policy was to "provid[e] regulatory certainty in exchange for conservation commitments." Pursuant to the policy, upon an applicant's request, No Surprises "assurances" were incorporated in all HCPs approved after August of 1994.

After the No Surprises policy was issued, it was the subject of a public comment process when it was released as a key component of the draft 1994 Habitat Conservation Planning Handbook FWS and NMFS published in late 1994. *See* 59 Fed. Reg. 65782 (Dec. 21, 1994). The No Surprises policy was included in slightly revised form in the final 1996 Habitat Conservation Planning Handbook. Starting with that publication of the policy, things began to unwind for the agencies as their policy worked its way through the rulemaking labyrinth.

## A. THE NOTICE AND COMMENT PROCESS

### Department of the Interior, Fish and Wildlife Service, and Department of Commerce, National Oceanic and Atmospheric Administration, Notice of Availability of Final Handbook for Habitat Conservation Planning and Incidental Take Permitting Process

61 Fed. Reg. 63854 (1996).

**SUMMARY:** The Fish and Wildlife Service and National Marine Fisheries Service (hereafter referred to as the Services) announce the availability of their final Handbook for Habitat Conservation Planning and Incidental Take Permitting Process. This final guidance document provides internal guidance for conducting the incidental take permit program under Section 10(a)(1)(B) of the Endangered Species Act of 1973, as amended (Act). Its purpose is to provide policy and guidance for Section 10(a)(1)(B) procedures to promote efficiency and nationwide consistency within and between the Services. Although intended primarily as internal agency guidance, this Handbook is fully available for public evaluation, and use, as appropriate.

* * *

## SUPPLEMENTARY INFORMATION:

### Background

This final Handbook provides consistent procedures for Service compliance with the incidental take permit provisions of Section 10(a)(1)(B) of the Act. Consistency in the Section 10(a)(1)(B) program will be achieved by:

(1) providing national procedural and policy guidance;

(2) providing standardized guidance to Service offices and personnel who participate in conservation planning programs under Section 10(a)(1)(B) and review and process incidental take permit applications;

(3) providing assistance to applicants in the non-Federal sector who wish to apply for incidental take permits; and

(4) providing for conservation of federally listed, proposed, and candidate species.

### Public Comments Addressed

The Services considered all information and recommendations from earlier comments submitted on the Handbook. The major issues advanced by commenters have been combined, paraphrased, and responded to below.

Issue: Several issues were raised regarding the "No Surprises" policy included in the draft HCP Handbook. These include: a request to clarify the fact that net benefit to the species is not required to obtain "No Surprises" assurances; the suggestion that the "extraordinary circumstances" provision in the policy is not consistent with the promise of long-term certainty under HCPs; and the conflicting suggestions that the "No Surprises" policy should be codified as a regulation and that the "No Surprises" policy exceeds FWS and NMFS authority under the ESA.

Response: The first issue pertains to the assurances provided to an applicant with an HCP that does not provide a net benefit to the species covered in the HCP. The HCP Handbook describes the differing assurances provided applicants depending upon whether the HCP is designed to provide a net benefit to the species. The following two assurances are provided regardless of whether an HCP provides an overall net benefit to a species:

1. If additional mitigation measures are subsequently deemed necessary to provide for the conservation of a species that was otherwise adequately covered under the terms of a properly functioning HCP, the obligation for such measures shall not rest with the HCP permittee.

2. If extraordinary circumstances warrant the requirement of additional mitigation from an HCP permittee who is in compliance with the HCP's obligations, such

> mitigation shall maintain the original terms of the HCP to the maximum extent possible. Further, any such changes shall be limited to modifications within any Conserved Habitat areas which might be established under the HCP or to the HCP's operating conservation program for the affected species. In all cases, additional mitigation requirements shall not involve the payment of additional compensation or apply to parcels of land available for development or land management under the original terms of the HCP without the consent of the HCP permittee.

In addition, even in the event of unforeseen circumstances, the FWS and NMFS will not seek additional mitigation from an HCP permittee where the terms of a properly functioning HCP agreement were designed to provide an overall net benefit for that species and contained measurable criteria for the biological success of the HCP which have been or are being met. This means that the Services will not attempt to impose additional mitigation measures of any type under the terms stated. It is intended to encourage HCP applicants to develop HCPs that provide an overall net benefit to affected species. It does not mean that any HCP must in fact have already achieved a net benefit before the "No Surprises" policy applies, but instead that the HCP must have been designed to achieve an overall net benefit and is being implemented fully by the HCP permittee.

The second issue, which pertains to the promise of long-term certainty under HCPs and the "extraordinary circumstances" provision in the policy, has been clarified in the final Handbook. The "No Surprises" policy provides certainty for private landowners in HCPs through the following assurances: In negotiating "unforeseen circumstances" provisions for HCPs, the Services will not require the commitment of additional land or financial compensation beyond the level of mitigation which was otherwise adequately provided for a species under the terms of a properly functioning HCP. Moreover, the Services will not seek any other form of additional mitigation from an HCP permittee except under extraordinary circumstances. Thus, the long-term certainty that is provided is the assurance that under no circumstances, including extraordinary circumstances, shall an HCP permittee who is abiding by the terms of their HCP be required to provide a greater financial commitment or accept additional land use restrictions on property available for economic use or development.

The third issue pertains to the codification of the "No Surprises" policy into a regulation. The Services do not believe it is necessary to codify the "No Surprises" policy as a specific regulation, because it is simply a statement of policy. Nevertheless, the policy has been subjected to procedures similar to those used to codify regulations. The policy was incorporated into the draft Handbook for Habitat Conservation Planning and Incidental Take Permitting Process to help address the problem of maintaining regulatory assurances for applicants applying for incidental take permits through the HCP process. This policy was subjected to a public review process when a notice of availability was published in the Federal Register for the draft Handbook for Habitat Conservation Planning and Incidental Take Permitting Process on December 21, 1994 and the FWS solicited comments through this availability announcement.

The final issue concerns the fact that commenters objected to the "No Surprises" policy because it is seen as exceeding FWS and NMFS authority under the ESA. The Services believe this policy is fully consistent with their authority under the ESA and is based on legislative history. Congress recognized in enacting the habitat conservation plan/incidental take provision in Section 10 of the ESA that ". . . the Secretary may utilize this provision [on HCPs] to approve conservation plans which provide long-term commitments regarding the conservation of listed as well as unlisted species and long-term assurances to the proponent of the conservation plan that the terms of the plan will be adhered to and that further mitigation requirements will only be imposed in accordance with the terms of the plan. In the event that an unlisted species addressed in an approved conservation plan is subsequently listed pursuant to the Act, no further mitigation requirements should be imposed if the conservation plan addressed the conservation of the species and its habitat as if the species were listed pursuant to the Act" (H.R. Rep. No. 835, 97th Cong., 2d Sess. 30–31 (1982)). Accordingly, Federal regulation requires such procedures to be detailed in the HCP [50 CFR 17.22(b)(1)(iii)(C)].

Moreover, as the discussion of the "No Surprises" policy in the final Handbook makes clear, the commitment by the Services in the policy is a commitment "to the extent consistent with the requirements of the Endangered Species Act and other Federal laws," like the Anti-Deficiency Act. However, the policy also makes clear that "methods of responding to the needs of affected species [other than exacting additional mitigation from the permittees], such as government action and voluntary conservation measures by the permittee, remain available to assure the requirements of the ESA are satisfied."

---

## QUESTIONS AND DISCUSSION

**1.** Although most of the agencies' "notice of availability" focused on the substance of the No Surprises policy, the glimmer of a *procedural* issue lurked in the notice for some of the commenters. As the agencies explained, they did not believe it was necessary to codify the "No Surprises" policy as a regulation, because it is simply a statement of policy. Nevertheless, the agencies subjected the policy to procedures "similar to" those used to codify regulations. The saying "Close but no cigar" comes to mind. If the agencies were certain that the policy did not require codification as a formal regulation, then why bother using procedures "similar to" rulemaking procedures? On the other hand, if the agency took the trouble to use procedures "similar to" rulemaking procedures, why not go the full distance by using the procedures that would satisfy those required for codification of a rule? Some commenters did not pass up the opportunity to argue that the agency fell short in this regard. How would you have advised the agency to respond to this concern?

**2.** A key *substantive* issue for the No Surprises policy—i.e., regardless of whether the agencies could adopt it as a policy or as a rule—was whether they were authorized to adopt it at all? This is the theme of the *Kelley* case excerpted in Part I.A. of this chapter—an agency must have authority to act before a court need examine whether it adopted the correct procedure or reached a valid substantive decision. Acknowledging that the ESA does not expressly authorize a No Surprises provision in HCP permits, the agencies responded that the legislative history of Section 10(a)(1)(B) made it clear that "the Secretary may utilize this provision [on HCPs] to approve conservation plans which provide . . . long-term assurances to the proponent of the conservation plan that the terms of the plan will be adhered to and that further mitigation requirements will only be imposed in accordance with the terms of the plan. In the event that an unlisted species addressed in an approved conservation plan is subsequently listed pursuant to the Act, no further mitigation requirements should be imposed if the conservation plan addressed the conservation of the species and its habitat as if the species were listed pursuant to the Act." *See* H.R. Rep. No. 835, 97th Cong., 2d Sess. 30–31 (1982). Would you have advised the agencies to hang their hat on this passage from the legislative history? Does the policy they outline in the *Handbook* notice comport with the parameters of the quoted passage?

---

In October 1996, environmental groups filed an action challenging the "No Surprises" policy on a number of grounds, including that it had been promulgated without complying with the Administrative Procedure Act's notice and comment requirements for rulemakings. Spirit of the Sage v. Babbitt, No. 1:96CV02503 (D.D.C.). The parties reached a settlement agreement requiring the FWS and NMFS to solicit and consider public comment before publishing a final decision with respect to No Surprises assurances as a rule, not a policy. They did so in the following promulgation, which not surprisingly is considerably more detailed than the explanation given when the policy was announced in connection with the *Handbook*.

## Department of the Interior, Fish and Wildlife Service, and Department of Commerce, National Oceanic and Atmospheric Administration, No Surprises Policy, Proposed Rule

62 Fed. Reg. 29091 (1997).

**SUMMARY:** This proposed rule will codify the substance of the Endangered Species Act (ESA) "No Surprises" policy issued by the Fish and Wildlife Service (FWS) and the National Marine Fisheries Service (NMFS) in 1994 and included in the joint FWS and NMFS Endangered Species Habitat Conservation Planning Handbook issued in November 1996 (61 FR 63854). The No Surprises policy provides regulatory assurances to the holder of an incidental take permit issued under Section 10(a) of the ESA that no additional land use restrictions or financial compensation will be required of the permit holder with respect to species adequately covered by the permit, even if unforeseen circumstances arise after the permit is issued indicating that additional mitigation is needed for a given species covered by a permit. The proposed rule contains proposed revisions to parts 17 (FWS) and 222 (NMFS) of Title 50 of the Code of Federal Regulations necessary to implement the substance of the No Surprises policy.

**SUPPLEMENTARY INFORMATION:** The Services firmly believe that they have had sufficient authority under the Endangered Species Act (ESA) to issue Habitat Conservation Plan (HCP) permits with No Surprises assurances and continue to believe in the validity of those permits. The Services also believe that the current process and those permits issued in the past with the No Surprises assurances are legally adequate and continue to assert the Services' authority to issue individual HCP permits with the No Surprises assurances. Nevertheless, the Services recognize the benefits of permanently codifying the No Surprises policy as a rule in 50 CFR, as well as the value of soliciting additional comments on the policy itself. Therefore, the Services believed it served their purposes to settle the Spirit of the Sage Council v. Babbitt, No. 1:96CV02503 (SS) (D. D.C.), lawsuit, which challenged the procedures under which the No Surprises policy was adopted and under which subsequent HCP permits were issued, by agreeing to submit the No Surprises Policy to further public comment and to consider public comment in drafting a final No Surprises rule. . . .

### Background

Congress recognized in enacting the Section 10 HCP amendments that significant development projects often take many years to complete and permits applicants may need long-term permits. In this situation, and in order to provide sufficient incentives for the private sector to participate in the development of such long-term conservation plans, plans which may involve the expenditure of hundreds of thousands if not millions of dollars, adequate assurances must be made to the financial and development communities that a Section 10(a) permit can be made available for the life of the project. Thus, the Secretary should have the discretion to issue Section 10(a) permits that run for periods significantly longer than are commonly provided [for other types of permits]. (Conf. Report at 31).

Congress also recognized that long term HCP permits would present unique issues that would have to be addressed if the permits were to function properly to protect the interests of both the species involved and the development community. For instance, Congress realized that "circumstances and information may change over time and that the original [habitat conservation] plan might need to be revised. To address this situation the Committee expects that any plan approved for a long-term permit will contain a procedure by which the parties will deal with unforeseen circumstances." (Conf. Report at 31). More importantly, Congress recognized that non-Federal property owners seeking HCP permits would need to have economic and regulatory certainty regarding the overall cost of species mitigation over the life of the permit. As stated in the Conference Report on the 1982 ESA amendments:

> The Committee intends that the Secretary may utilize this provision to approve conservation plans which provide long-term commitments regarding the conservation of listed as well as unlisted species and long-term assurances to the proponent of the conservation plan that the terms of the plan will be adhered to and that further mitigation requirements will only be imposed in accordance with the terms of the plan. In the event that an unlisted species addressed in the approved conservation plan is subsequently listed pursuant to the Act, no further mitigation requirements should be imposed if the conservation plan addressed the conservation of the species and its habitat as if the species were listed pursuant to the Act. (Conf. Report at 30 and 50 FR 39681–39691 (Sept. 30, 1985)).

Congress thus allowed the Federal government to provide assurances to non-Federal property owners through the Section 10 incidental take permit process. Non-Federal property owners would have economic and regulatory certainty regarding the overall cost of species mitigation, provided that the conservation plan adequately provided for the affected species in the first instance, the permittee was complying in good faith with the terms and conditions of the permit and the HCP, and that the HCP was properly functioning.

**Description/Overview of Proposed No Surprises Rule**

The information presented below briefly describes the No Surprises policy and this proposed rule.

To address the problem of maintaining regulatory assurances and providing regulatory certainty in exchange for conservation commitments, the FWS and the NMFS jointly established a "No

Surprises" policy for HCPs on August 11, 1994. The No Surprises policy set forth a clear commitment by the FWS and the NMFS that, to the extent consistent with the requirements of the ESA and other Federal laws, the government will honor its agreements under a negotiated and approved HCP for which the permittee is in good faith implementing the HCP's terms and conditions. The specific nature of these provisions will vary among HCPs depending upon individual habitat and species needs.

The No Surprises policy and this proposed rule provide certainty for non-Federal property owners in ESA HCP planning through the following assurances:

> — In negotiating "unforeseen circumstances" provisions for HCPs, the Services will not require the commitment of additional land or financial compensation beyond the level of mitigation which was otherwise adequately provided for a species under the terms of a properly functioning HCP. Moreover, the Services will not seek any other form of additional mitigation from an HCP permittee except under unforeseen circumstances.

This means that if unforeseen circumstances occur during the life of an HCP, the Services will not require additional lands or property interests, additional funds, or additional restrictions on lands or other natural resources released under an HCP for development or use from any permittee who, in good faith, is adequately implementing or has fully implemented their commitments under an approved HCP. Once an HCP permit has been issued and its terms are being complied with, the permittee may remain secure regarding the agreed upon cost of mitigation, because no additional mitigation land or property interests, funding, or land use restrictions will be requested by the issuing Service. The permittee would not be responsible for any other forms of additional mitigation, unrelated to the categories noted in the previous sentence, except where unforeseen circumstances exist.

The legislative history of the 1982 ESA amendments noted above in the "Background" section illustrates the two primary goals of the HCP program: (1) adequately minimizing and mitigating for the incidental take of listed species; and (2) providing regulatory assurances to Section 10 permittees that the terms of an approved HCP will not change over time, or that necessary changes will be minimized to the maximum extent possible, and will be mutually agreed to by the applicant. How to reconcile these objectives remains one of the central challenges of the HCP program.

"Unforeseen circumstances" has been broadly defined to include a variety of changing circumstances that may occur over the life of an ongoing HCP. However, it is important to distinguish between "unforeseen circumstances" and "changed circumstances." "Changed circumstances" are not uncommon during the course of an HCP and can reasonably be anticipated and planned for (e.g., the listing of new species, modifications in the project or activity as described in the original HCP, or modifications in the HCP's monitoring program). "Unforeseen circumstances," however, means changes in circumstances surrounding an HCP that were not, or could not, be anticipated by HCP participants and the Services at the time of the HCP's negotiation and development and that result in a substantial and adverse change in the status of a covered species.

Consequently, the No Surprises policy and this proposed rule also provide that:

> — If additional mitigation measures are subsequently deemed necessary to provide for the conservation of a species that was otherwise adequately covered under the terms of a properly functioning HCP, the obligation for such measures will not rest with the HCP permittee.

This means that in cases where the status of a species addressed under an HCP unexpectedly worsens, the primary obligation for implementing additional conservation measures would be borne by the Federal government, other government agencies, private conservation organizations, or other private landowners who have not yet developed an HCP.

> — If unforeseen circumstances warrant the requirement of additional mitigation from an HCP permittee who is in compliance with the HCP's obligations, such mitigation will maintain the original terms of the HCP to the maximum extent possible. Further, any such changes will be limited to modifications within Conserved Habitat areas or to the HCP's operating conservation program for the affected species. Additional mitigation requirements will not involve the payment of additional compensation or apply to parcels of land available for development or land management under the original terms of the HCP without the consent of the HCP permittee.

This means that if unforeseen circumstances are found to exist, the Services will consider additional mitigation measures. However, such measures must be as close as possible to the terms of the original HCP and must be limited to modifications within any Conserved Habitat area or to adjustments in lands that are already set aside by the HCP in the HCP's operating conservation program. Any such adjustments or modifications will not include requirements for additional land protection, payment of additional funds, or apply to lands otherwise available for development or use under the HCP, unless the permittee consents to such additional measures.

For the reasons set out in the preamble, the Services propose to amend title 50, chapter I, subchapter B; and to amend title 50, chapter II, subchapter C of the Code of Federal Regulations, as set forth below:

PART 17—[AMENDED]

Subpart C—Endangered Wildlife

50 CFR § 17.22

§ 17.22 Permits for scientific purposes, enhancement of propagation or survival, or for incidental taking.

(b) * * *

(5) Permit assurances. (i) Permit assurances will apply to incidental take permits that are issued in accordance with paragraph (b)(2) of this section for those species that are adequately provided for under properly functioning conservation plans. Such assurances will apply to those permittees who in good faith have complied with the required terms and conditions of the permit and the conservation plan.

(ii) In negotiating unforeseen circumstances provisions for conservation plans, the Director will not require the commitment of additional land, property interests, or financial compensation beyond the level of mitigation which was otherwise adequately provided for a species under the terms of a properly functioning conservation plan. Moreover, the Director will not seek any other form of additional mitigation from a permittee except under unforeseen circumstances.

(iii) If additional mitigation measures are subsequently deemed necessary to provide for the conservation of a species that was otherwise adequately covered under the terms of a properly functioning conservation plan, the obligation for such measures will not rest with the permittee.

(iv) If unforeseen circumstances warrant the requirement of additional mitigation from a permittee who is in compliance with the conservation plan's obligations, such mitigation will maintain the original terms of the conservation plan to the maximum extent possible. Further, any such changes will be limited to modifications within Conserved Habitat areas, if any, or to the conservation plan's operating conservation program for the affected species. Additional mitigation requirements will not involve the payment of additional compensation or apply to parcels of land or property interests available for development or land management under the original terms of the conservation plan without the consent of the permittee.

* * *

(vi) The Director will not seek additional mitigation for a species from a permittee where the terms of a properly functioning conservation plan agreement were designed to provide an overall net benefit for that species and contained measurable criteria for the biological success of the conservation plan which have been or are being met.

(vii) Nothing in this rule will be construed to limit or constrain the Director or any other governmental agency from taking additional actions at its own expense to protect or conserve a species included in a conservation plan.

---

## QUESTIONS AND DISCUSSION

**1.** How would you compare the overall depth and breadth of the discussion in the proposed *regulation* publication to the discussion in the *Handbook policy* notice? Why the difference?

**2.** What are the "benefits of permanently codifying the No Surprises policy as a rule in 50 CFR," and why did the agency not take advantage of them from the start?

**3.** If you were advising a client seeking an HCP permit in 1997 around the time the agencies proposed the No Surprises regulation, would you advise the client to request No Surprises security in the permit, and if so how would you propose securing it? If you were advising FWS or NMFS at the time, how would you advise the agency to respond to such a request?

---

In the proposed No Surprises rule the agencies asked for public comments. They received many, some in support and some condemning the proposal. An example from each end of the spectrum follows.

## National Association of Home Builders, Letter to Laverne Smith, Chief, Division of Endangered Species, U.S. Fish and Wildlife Service

July 21, 1997.

Dear Ms. Smith:

On behalf of the 190,000 member firms of the National Association of Home Builders (NAHB), I am pleased to submit comments on the Endangered Species Act (ESA) No Surprises regulations proposed by the U.S. Fish & Wildlife Service (FWS). NAHB's membership consists of individuals and firms who develop land and construct homes and apartments, as well as commercial and individual projects. NAHB strongly supports the promulgation of the No Surprises rule as proposed in the *Federal Register*. The No Surprises proposed rule is crucial to provide certainty to the building industry.

The No Surprises proposed rule codifies FWS's policy that the government will honor its agreements under a negotiated and approved Habitat Conservation Plan (HCP) for which the permittee is in good faith implementing the HCP's terms and conditions. The No Surprises rule will provide needed certainty for non-federal property owners in ESA HCP planning.

The interests of the home building industry are clear. Builders and developers seek to be regulated in a predictable, reasonable, and consistent manner. At a basic level, builders need to know under what conditions their activities are regulated. No business can succeed when it is uncertain that its operations and functions may, as under the ESA, result in a $25,000 per day liability. When builders need to obtain a permit, they want to know the application's requirements, the standards by which the permit will be judged, the timetable by which a decision will be rendered, and that no enforcement action will be taken if they maintain compliance with the permit. These are not idle or frivolous requests. Most financial institutions will not lend money when regardless of a permit approval, an applicant may still face prosecution from the federal government at any time during the life of the project. Consequently, the livelihood of many of our members depends on the federal government's promise that they will not renege on a previously made agreement.

**Support for the No Surprises Policy**

NAHB believes that the proposed regulation satisfies the public notice and comment requirements under both the Administrative Procedure Act and the ESA. In fact, NAHB applauds FWS for gathering input on this proposed policy from all interested parties.

Since Congress authorized HCPs in 1982, they have proven to be an invaluable tool for species conservation and the accomplishments of HCPs developed in the past are substantial. First, HCPs encourage landowners to preserve private property for the benefit of endangered species, which are considered a public resource. This is critical to the endangered species program. Over 60% of listed species occur on non-federal land. Consequently, it would be impossible to recover listed species without the assistance of the private landowner. Second, HCPs help to infuse the chronically underfunded federal species preservation program with significant private funds. To date, Congress has been unwilling to back the ambitious mission of the ESA with sufficient budget resources. As a result, many of the strategies undertaken to recover listed species have been developed as part of an HCP. Third, many listed species would be worse off had an HCP not been prepared. In the case of the mission blue butterfly, for example, its habitat was gradually declining as native grasslands were replaced by non-native vegetation. The San Bruno HCP provided for the gradual restoration of native grasslands. Similar restorative activities are components of other HCPs. . . .

In the past, without No Surprises, the HCP process was problematic for builders. Once a permit was issued there was no guarantee that the federal government would not come back and request additional land or financial resources. This lack of certainty was crippling to many businesses involved in land development. The current HCP process is not perfect, but changes such as the No Surprises proposed rule represent a significant improvement. Chief among those improvements is the No Surprises policy. The importance of the No Surprises policy is evident by the number of HCPs developed since the 1982 ESA amendments under which they were authorized. Between 1982 and 1993 FWS approved less than 58 HCPs. Since 1994, when FWS issued the No Surprises policy, 285 HCPs were issued, a nearly 400% increase. Without question, the No Surprises Policy was instrumental in encouraging landowners and more importantly, banks and mortgage companies to embrace private conservation plans.

FWS's authority to promulgate the No Surprises policy arises from Congress' 1982 ESA amendments. In 1982, Congress authorized the Secretary to permit prohibited takings of endangered species if they are "incidental to, and not the purpose of carrying out of an otherwise lawful activity" upon the approval of a HCP. Congress deemed that the development of a conservation plan, which would provide for the protection and/or enhancement of endangered species habitat, would be a beneficial trade-off for the potential loss of a few individuals of a listed species. In particular, potential losses would be justified if long-term habitat conservation provided improved prospects for the species that a short-term prohibition on species population depletion could not provide. In authorizing HCPs, Congress recognized that certainty would be necessary to trigger long-term private sector funding and land use commitments for species conservation. . . .

The proposal provides long term assurances to permittees who are in compliance with an approved HCP that additional mitigation and/or financial resources will not be imposed by the federal government. However, the proposal also contains a procedure to deal with unforeseen circumstances, as [Congress] envisioned.

**Consideration of Comments in Opposition to the Rule**

The ESA states that all federal agencies shall seek to conserve endangered and threatened species. 16 U.S.C. § 1531(c). "Conserve" under the ESA means "to use and the use of all methods and procedures which are necessary to bring any endangered species or threatened species to the point at which the measures provided . . . are no longer necessary. Such methods and procedures include . . . all activities associated with scientific resources management such as research, census, law enforcement, habitat acquisition and maintenance, propagation, live trapping, and transplantation. . . ." 16 U.S.C. § 1532(3). The creation of a HCP with a No Surprises clause does not preclude a federal agency from fulfilling its duty under the statute. In fact, nothing in the proposal says that a federal agency may take no further action of its own. A federal agency may, for example, acquire habitat later through eminent domain. No Surprises simply prevents the federal agency from returning to the landowner for greater mitigation. This is consistent with the legislative history:

> The terms of this provision require a unique partnership between the public and private sectors in the interest of species and habitat conservation. However, it is recognized that

> significant development projects often take many years to complete and permit applicants may need long-term permits. In this situation, and in order to provide sufficient incentives for the private sector to participate in the development of such long-term conservation plans, plans which may involve the expenditure of hundreds of thousands if not millions of dollars, adequate assurances must be made to the financial and development communities that a Section 10(a) permit can be made available for the life of the project.
>
> Thus, the Secretary should have the discretion [sic] to issue Section 10(a) permits that run for periods significantly longer than are commonly provided for under current administration practices. It is also recognized that circumstances and information may change over time and that the original plan might need to be revised. To address this situation the committee expects that any plan approved for a long-term permit will contain a procedure by which the parties will deal with unforeseen circumstances.

H.R. Conf. Rep. No. 835, 97th Cong., 2d Sess. 30–31 (1982), *reprinted in* 1982 U.S.C.C.A.N. 2860, 2872.

As proposed, the No Surprises rule will not cause long-term harm to species. In fact, the No Surprises rule also provides species with long term assurances for their existence. As mentioned above, prior to implementation of the No Surprises policy, few HCPs were developed. Many landowners believed that the HCP process was so onerous that they would take whatever steps necessary to ensure that their land was not considered habitat rather than navigate the permit procedure. In addition, before FWS carried out the No Surprises policy, most HCPs were for planning areas less than 1,000 acres. In the past few years, however, approximately 25 HCPs exceed 10,000 acres in size, 25 exceed 100,000 acres, and 18 exceed 500,000 acres. According to FWS documents, these numbers suggest that HCPs have evolved from a process once used primarily to address single developments to a more broad-based landscape level planning tool which can help achieve long term species conservation goals. NAHB firmly believes that the No Surprises policy encourages landowners to participate in regional HCPs.

Parties to an HCP can anticipate most of the circumstances up front. The proposed rule states that an HCP should discuss the measures developed by the applicant and FWS to meet changes in circumstances over time, possibly incorporating adaptive management measures for covered species in the HCP. When problems do arise, FWS has the authority to take whatever agency actions are needed to protect the species of concern. Moreover, FWS will always have myriad options available, ranging from voluntary conservation measures to government action to address the "unforeseen circumstances."

Some individuals oppose the No Surprises policy because ecological systems are uncertain, dynamic, and in flux. Consequently, they reason that FWS should maintain the right to exact additional mitigation or financial resources from the permittee throughout the term of an HCP. This is unrealistic and unfair. Many land development projects take years to complete. Therefore, adequate assurances must be made to the financial and developmental communities that an HCP will remain valid for the life of the project. If the federal government can not make adequate assurances that an HCP will remain valid for the permit's term landowners will simply choose not to enter into HCPs. Others cite "political uncertainty" as a reason to deny private landowners the assurances of the No Surprises policy. Political uncertainty is the main reason why FWS must codify the No Surprises Policy as regulation. If No Surprises remains merely as a policy, it exists at the whim of the current Administration. Landowners will continually fear that the policy will be revoked if the next Administration is not equally committed to private strategies for species conservation.

Another criticism is that the No Surprises Policy deprives the public of meaningful comment on individual HCPs. This is absolutely untrue. FWS provides a minimum of a 30-day comment period for each HCP, longer if the HCP requires an Environmental Impact Statement. The No Surprises Policy will not change that requirement.

In conclusion, NAHB applauds Secretary Babbitt and the Department of Interior's commitment to carry out the ESA in a fair, efficient, and scientifically sound manner. Implementation of the ESA can be improved with stronger partnerships with private landowners and the building industry. Codifying the No Surprises policy as a regulation is an important step in fostering such partnerships.

If you have any questions about our comments please do not hesitate to call Michelle Desiderio at (202) 822–0485.

Best regards, Kent W. Colton Executive Vice-President & Chief Executive Officer

## Spirit of the Sage Council, Letter to Laverne Smith, Chief, Division of Endangered Species, U.S. Fish and Wildlife Service

July 24, 1997.

Dear Ms. Smith:

On behalf of Spirit of the Sage Council, Biodiversity Legal Foundation, and National Endangered Species Network, I am submitting the following comments on the Services' proposed "No Surprises" rule, as set forth at 62 Fed. Reg. 29091. This comment supplements any individual comments submitted by these organizations or their representatives.

This letter will not exhaustively detail the reasons why the proposed No Surprises rule is legally untenable and biologically insupportable. Many of our legal objections are set forth in our June 13, 1996 60-day notice letter regarding the No Surprises policy, as well as in Congressional testimony on the same subject. Copies of those documents are attached for your convenience and all of the points raised in them are incorporated in this comment letter by reference.

In this letter, we will focus instead on several glaring anomalies and omissions in the proposed rule and the preamble purporting to explain it.

**1. The Services Do Not Articulate What Will Happen When, As A Result Of "Unforeseen Circumstances," An ITP/HCP Is Contributing To The Extinction Of A Species And The Permit Holder Does Not Wish to Voluntarily Alter The Terms of the ITP/HCP.**

The assumption underlying the proposed rule is that, following the approval of Incidental Take Permits ("ITPs") and Habitat Conservation Plans ("HCPs"), "unforeseen circumstances" upon occasion, occur which render an HCP inadequate to "conserve" a species whose incidental taking is being permitted by the Services. Indeed, if that assumption were being made, then the No Surprises rule would, of course, be entirely unnecessary.

But if it is assumed that "unforeseen circumstances" will occur which render an HCP inadequate to conserve a species whose ongoing taking is being authorized by the federal government, the obvious, critical question becomes—what sort of remedial action will be taken when such circumstances arise, i.e., what will be done when a previously approved ITP/HCP is, because of unanticipated developments, found to be contributing to the extinction of a species? Even more specifically, what, precisely, will happen under the very scenario which the Services themselves describe as the paradigm of unforeseen circumstances—"if a species is declining rapidly and if the HCP encompasses a majority of the species' range." 62 Fed. Reg. 29094 (emphasis added).

The proposed rule declares emphatically what will not be done under such circumstances—even if "unforeseen circumstances warrant the requirement of additional mitigation from an HCP permittee," the Service will require the "payment of additional compensation" or impose new requirements on "parcels of land available for development or land management under the original terms of the HCP. . . ." 62 Fed. Reg. 29094 (emphasis added). But what the Services have studiously avoided explaining in any coherent, detailed fashion is what alternative framework they will use under such circumstances, or why they have any reason for believing that such an alternative framework will be more, or even as, effective in conserving species as amendments to HCPs/ITPs. Instead of providing any meaningful insight into this critical question, the Services mention in passing two alternative "remedies" which simply beg the necessary questions. First, the Services state the obvious point that "[n]either is there anything in the No Surprises policy or this proposed rule that prevents the Services from requesting a permittee to voluntarily undertake additional mitigation on behalf of affected species. . . ." 62 Fed. Reg. 29094 (emphasis in original).

Obviously, ITP holders and any associated local governmental bodies which are truly concerned with the conservation of endangered species can do more than they are required to do by the conditions of their permits—just as holders of NPDES permits or Clean Air Act permits could voluntarily adopt far more stringent restrictions on air or water emissions. Once again, however, the necessary assumption of the No Surprises Policy and proposed rule is that the vast majority of permit holders (as in other regulatory contexts) will opt voluntarily to impose additional restrictions on their activities, and will almost never agree to pay "additional compensation" or accept restrictions on "parcels of land available for development or land management under the original terms of the HCP." 62 Fed. Reg. 29094. The only other suggestion in the proposal is that the "FWS and NMFS have a wide array of authorities and resources that can be utilized to provide additional protection for threatened and endangered species included in an HCP." 62 Fed. Reg. 29094. But the Services do not further delineate this "wide array of authorities and resources," nor, more important, does the preamble or proposed rule provide a clue as to how they would actually be used to respond to unanticipated circumstances which have rendered an ITP/HCP far more damaging than previously believed. . . .

What, for example, will be done if the Services' own biologists conclude that they (and all other experts regarding the species at issue) badly underestimated, at the time of an HCP's approval, the vital importance of particular habitat available for development under the HCP, and they further concede that this development was entirely unanticipated, because they did not fully understand the habitat needs of the species at the time of the HCP's approval? If the landowner is also unwilling to sell the property to the government—and again keeping in mind the Service's own example of an "HCP [that] encompasses a majority of the species' range"—then there will literally be nothing that could be done under the proposed rule to forestall the extinction of the species.

And even if landholders were willing to sell under such circumstances, where will the Services obtain the money to engage in large-scale purchases of non-federal landholdings? Predictably, the proposed rule hints at no answer to that question, although it does contain the unsubstantiated assertion that "it is extremely unlikely that the Services would have to resort to protective or conservation action requiring new appropriations of funds by Congress." 62 Fed. Reg. 29094 (emphasis added).

If, as appears to be the case, that statement is intended to suggest that the Services already [have] sufficient appropriations to purchase huge amounts of habitat in the event of "unforeseen circumstances," then we urge the agencies, in their final rule, to explain the basis for that remarkable development. We further request that the Services explain how that proposition can be reconciled with the agencies' repeated statements in the last several years—including in numerous sworn affidavits filed in federal court—that the agencies' current appropriations are woefully inadequate even to implement the most basic requirements of the ESA, such as listing all of the species which the Services concede warrant protection under the Act.

At bottom, while eliminating the most clear cut, direct vehicle for dealing with the inevitable unanticipated circumstances—i.e., simply altering, as necessary, the terms of a federally issued permit for killing or harming an endangered species—the proposed rule substitutes only generic, empty, and facially absurd rhetoric. That is not reasoned agency decisionmaking in accordance with the Administrative Procedure Act and, more important, it is utterly impossible to reconcile with the overarching purposes of the ESA "to provide a means whereby the ecosystems upon which endangered species and threatened species depend may be conserved" and to "provide a program for the conservation of such endangered species and threatened species." 16 U.S.C. § 1531(b).

**2. The Services Have Proposed a "Rule" But Have Provided No Rationale For It.**

A related, equally glaring omission from the proposed rule is that it simply provides no coherent explanation as to why the Services have opted to adopt this particular approach to implementation of the ESA. The preamble sets forth an analysis of the legislative history which is designed merely to demonstrate that Congress "allowed the Federal government to provide assurances to non-Federal property owners through the Section 10 incidental take permit process." 62 Fed. Reg. 29092 (emphasis added).

As discussed in the accompanying 60-day notice letter and Congressional testimony, even this discussion of the background of Section 10 is based on a highly selective, erroneous reading of the legislative history. But even if it were accurate, the mere fact that Congress "allowed"—i.e., did not prohibit—a particular approach to implementation of the ESA does not mean that such an approach should, in fact, be adopted as general agency policy. Simply put, however, there is no analysis in the proposed rule as to how the No Surprises policy will "further the purposes of the ESA."

In short, the public does not have the slightest clue—at least based on the preamble provided here—as to the factors motivating the fundamental policy choice embodied in the proposed rule. At an absolute minimum, the Services must admit that, in the event of unforeseen circumstances, the proposed rule increases the risk of extinction of species by removing one of the legal tools—indeed, the most direct tool—that would otherwise be available for responding to new circumstances which, according to the Services' own description, "result in substantial and adverse change in the status of a covered species." 62 Fed. Reg. 29093 (emphasis added). But the public is simply left to guess as to why the risk of extinctions *should* be increased in this fashion, especially in view of the overall design of the ESA. See TVA v. Hill, 437 U.S. 153, 194 (1977) ("Congress has spoken in the plainest of words, making it abundantly clear that the balance has been struck in favor of affording endangered species the highest of priorities, thereby adopting a policy which it described as 'institutionalized caution' ") (emphasis added). Where an agency fails to articulate the rationale underlying its policy choice, there is usually a straightforward explanation for the omission—the agency knows that the more it says about its reasons, the more flimsy and improper they must appear. The No Surprises proposal is a textbook illustration of that principle.

For example, the agencies' passing reference to landowners' ostensible "need" for No Surprises assurances simply raises more questions than it answers, especially in view of the particular rule proposed by the Services. Thus, the preamble purports to distinguish "[u]nforeseen circumstances" from "changed circumstances," and suggests that HCPs may impose new measures on landowners in the case of the former—including the "listing of new species, modifications in the project or activity as described in the original HCP, or modifications in the HCP's monitoring program"—but not in the case of the latter. 62 Fed. Reg. 29093.

Once again, however, the proposal utterly fails to explain why this distinction makes any sense from anyone's standpoint, including that of the permit holder. Presumably, a "changed circumstance," as defined by the Services, could entail a far more expensive and burdensome modification of an HCP than an "unforeseen circumstance." Yet, under the proposed rule, the permit holder would be liable for the more expensive, burdensome change, while avoiding liability entirely for the less expensive one—because of whether the particular kind of "change" happened to be, in some sense, "anticipated by HCP participants and the Services at the time of the HCP's negotiation and development." 62 Fed. Reg. 29093.

More important, there is no explanation in the preamble as to why that distinction is at all relevant to the conservation of endangered and threatened species. In stark terms, there is no conceivable reason why a species' relative risk of extinction should depend on whether a particular kind of "change in circumstances surrounding an HCP" is labeled an "unforeseen" or an "anticipated" change. Yet that is precisely the bizarre approach proposed by the Services.

It is even more peculiar in light of the fact that any distinction between "changed" and "[u]nforeseen circumstances" largely reduces to a difference, at the time of HCP approval, in the mount of information available to scientists regarding the species at issue and the effects of a particular HCP. Plainly, the more information available to scientists, the more they can make predictions regarding a species' fate and the more they can plan for "changed circumstances" that might affect the species. Conversely, the less scientists know at the time of HCP approval, the less they can make predictions regarding potential changes, the more likely that adverse changes will be "unforeseen" and hence, by regulatory fiat, not susceptible to mandatory remedial action through Section 10 of the ESA.

There is, once again, no rational reason why the extent of information regarding a species at the time of HCP approval should have an enormous bearing on the risk of extinction in the event of an "adverse change in the status of a covered species." Yet that is one of the most perverse consequences of the rule proposed by the Services.

[Spirit of the Sage also argued in the letter that adoption of the proposed rule would undermine the overriding purpose of the ESA to recover species, and that there were alternatives to the proposed rule that could meet the agencies' objectives without posing risks to species]

Even a cursory review of the proposed rule necessitates the conclusion that it is riddled with serious omissions, inconsistencies, anomalies, and flaws. We urge that it not be adopted and that the Services instead fundamentally reconsider their approach to this critical issue before it is too late for the multitude of species whose very existence may depend on the Services' decision.

Sincerely, Eric R. Glitzenstein

---

## QUESTIONS AND DISCUSSION

**1.** Why did the National Home Builders Association (NAHB) and Spirit of the Sage Council (SOSC) submit comments? Did SOSC believe its comments would lead the agencies to withdraw the proposal or to modify the rule substantially? Did NAHB believe the agencies might waver in that regard and try to bolster the agencies' resolve to issue the rule as proposed? Were both simply posturing for their constituencies, or perhaps preparing for post-promulgation litigation?

**2.** Richard Stoll, a prominent environmental law practitioner, advises that in designing your rulemaking comments, you should consider three principal roles your comments may play. First, they may be useful in convincing the agency to shape its final rule in a certain way. Second, your comments may be critical in laying the groundwork for judicial review of the final rule. Finally, for the parts of the proposed rule your client favors, your comments may play a supportive or even buttressing role to the agency's position. *See* Richard G. Stoll, *Effective Written Comments in Informal Rulemaking*, ADMINISTRATIVE AND REGULATORY LAW NEWS, Summer 2007, at 15. Which set of comments do you think did a better job of fulfilling these roles, those from SOSC or from NAHB?

Stoll goes on to provide some maxims for rulemaking comment strategies:

1. Discretion over valor, meaning keep track of winning ground for your client, such as by suggesting ways to improve the rule rather than suggesting it be thrown in the trash pile.
2. Frame opposition comments to anticipate judicial review.
3. Consider framing supporting comments to anticipate opponents' judicial review.
4. Specificity is golden.
5. Authenticity is golden; both for your sources and for yourself.
6. Err on the side of inclusion with relevant and bona fide arguments.
7. Follow and respond to your opponents' comments.
8. Follow the agency's directions.
9. Stay cool—edit all the venting, sarcasm, and nastiness out of your first draft.
10. Make it easier for any reader to follow.
11. Make it easier for each reader to find the parts of interest to him or her.
12. If the agency asks for certain questions and issues to be addressed in certain order or format, do it.
13. Summarization is also golden.

Which set of comments do you think did a better job of fulfilling these maxims, those from SOSC or from NAHB? If you were counsel to NAHB, how would you improve on the comments submitted? Consider the same question for SOSC.

**3.** To prepare rulemaking comment letters competently, one must have a thorough knowledge of the statute being implemented, the existing body of administrative rules, the congressional purposes and legislative history, and the objectives of your client. Do both sets of comments strike you as evidencing that level of expertise? Is it possible for both sets of attorneys to have that thorough foundation in the legal and policy context and disagree so radically on the merits of the proposed rule?

**4.** Which of SOSC's comments strikes you as presenting a concern that the agencies should have taken seriously in terms of either adjusting or withdrawing all or part of the rule? To put it another way, if you were advising a client seeking an HCP permit in 1997 and had just read SOSC's comments on the proposed rule, would you advise the client to request No Surprises security in the permit, and if so how would you propose securing it? If you were advising FWS or NMFS, how would you advise the agency to respond to such a request? Is your answer to this and the questions in the previous notes influenced by your personal assessment of the No Surprises concept?

---

## B. POST-PROMULGATION LITIGATION

On February 23, 1998, the FWS and NMFS jointly promulgated the final No Surprises Rule in substantially the same form as proposed. *See* 63 Fed. Reg. 8859 (1998). In July 1998, a group of environmental interest groups challenged the No Surprises Rule in Spirit of the Sage Council v. Norton, 2004 WL 1326279 (D. D.C.). An odd twist in the litigation came in the form of another rule regarding revocation of permits the FWS proposed in 1997 (after publication of the proposed No Surprises rule) and adopted in 1998 (after the promulgation of the final No Surprises rule).

The FWS administers a variety of conservation laws that authorize the issuance of permits for otherwise prohibited activities. In 1974, the agency published 50 CFR Part 13 to consolidate the administration of various permitting programs. Part 13 established a uniform framework of general administrative conditions and procedures that would govern the application, processing, and issuance of all permits FWS issues. The agency intended the general Part 13 permitting provisions to be in addition to, and not in lieu of, other more specific permitting requirements of Federal wildlife laws. For example, the regulations at 50 C.F.R. Part 17 contain specific permitting requirements for the ESA that supplement the general permitting provisions of Part 13.

According to the agency, the combination of the general permitting provisions in Part 13 and the specific permitting provisions in Part 17 worked well in most instances. However, FWS took the position that, in some areas of permitting policy under the Act, the "one size fits all" approach of Part 13 has been inappropriately constraining and narrow. The agency identified incidental take permitting under Section 10(a)(1)(B) of the ESA as one such area.

On June 12, 1997, FWS published proposed revisions to the Part 13 general permitting regulations to identify, among other things, the situations in which the permit provisions in Part 13 would not apply to individual incidental take permits. *See* 62 Fed. Reg. 32189 (1997). On June 17, 1999, the agency published a final set of regulations, which the agency described as *interpretive* rules, that included two provisions that relate to revocation of incidental take permits. *See* 64 Fed. Reg. 32706 (1999). The first provided that the general revocation standard in 50 CFR 13.28(a)(5) will not apply to several types of ESA permits, including incidental take permits. The second provision, referred to as the Permit Revocation Rule, described circumstances under which incidental take permits, including permits with No Surprises assurances, could be revoked.

The Permit Revocation Rule, which was codified at 50 CFR 17.22(b)(8) (endangered species) and 17.32(b)(8) (threatened species), clarified that an incidental take permit "may not be revoked . . . unless continuation of the permitted activity would be inconsistent with the criterion set forth in 16 U.S.C. 1539(a)(2)(B)(iv) and the inconsistency has not been remedied in a timely fashion." The referenced "criteria set forth," that "the taking will not appreciably reduce the likelihood of the survival and recovery of the species in the wild," is one of the statutory standards that incidental take permit applicants must meet in order to obtain a permit.

The plaintiffs in the No Surprises lawsuit promptly amended their complaint to challenge the Permit Revocation Rule as well. The government explained in its briefs that the ESA itself authorizes the FWS to revoke incidental take permits, and that the Permit Revocation Rule simply confirmed that the agency would employ its statutory authority if the need arose, so it was not necessary to promulgate the rule as a legislative rule subject to notice and comment. (Where have we heard this line of reasoning before?) The following judicial opinion—issued almost *ten years* after the No Surprises policy first surfaced—added a new chapter to the rulemaking saga.

## Spirit of the Sage Council v. Norton

United States District Court for the District of Columbia, 2003.
294 F. Supp. 2d 67.

■ SULLIVAN, DISTRICT JUDGE:

This action challenges the validity of two administrative regulations promulgated by the Department of the Interior ("DOI"), the U.S. Fish and Wildlife Service ("FWS"), the Department of Commerce ("DOC"), and the National Marine Fisheries Service ("NMFS") (collectively, "the Services"): the so-called "No Surprises Rule," 63 Fed. Reg. 8,859 (Feb. 23, 1998) (codified at 50 C.F.R. § 17.22, 17.32, 222.2) and the "Permit Revocation Rule" ("PRR"), 64 Fed. Reg. 32,712, 32,714 (Jun. 17, 1999) (codified at 50 C.F.R. §§ 17.22(b), 17.32(b)).

The first resolution provides regulatory assurances to holders of Incidental Take Permits ("ITPs") issued pursuant to the Endangered Species Act ("ESA"), 16 U.S.C. § 1532 *et seq.* (2003), that they will not be required to commit funds or resources beyond those contemplated at the time the permit was issued to mitigate the effects of unforeseen circumstances on threatened or endangered species and their habitats.

The second resolution describes the circumstances under which ITPs may be revoked in light of the No Surprises Rule. The Services' promulgation of these regulations is alleged to violate the ESA and the Administrative Procedure Act ("APA"), 5 U.S.C. § 706 (2003). The parties' cross-motions for summary judgment are now pending before the Court.

## Introduction

Plaintiffs are six organizations, a Native American Tribe, and three individuals, one of whom is the Chief of the Shoshone Gabrielino Nation. They contend that the No Surprises Rule, by limiting the obligations of ITP holders to protect threatened and endangered species, flagrantly violates the letter and purpose of the ESA. Plaintiffs further submit that both the No Surprises Rule and the PRR, which was announced during the pendency of this action and sets forth the standards governing revocation of ITPs issued pursuant to the No Surprises Rule, were promulgated in a manner which impermissibly violates the APA's notice and comment requirements, and therefore should be struck down and remanded as procedurally infirm. Defendants' principal arguments on summary judgment are that plaintiffs lack standing and the claims presented in their Second Amended Complaint are not ripe for review.

The Court finds that plaintiffs have standing to assert their claims, and that, at a minimum, plaintiffs' challenge to the PRR is ripe for review. It further concludes that the public notice and comment procedures followed by the Services when promulgating the PRR were deficient as a matter of law. Accordingly, the Court will vacate and remand the PRR to the Services for further consideration consistent with the APA. Moreover, the Court finds that the relationship between the PRR and the No Surprises Rule is such that remand of the former requires remand of the latter without further inquiry into the merits of plaintiffs' substantive challenges.

[The court described the procedural history and the parties]

During the pendency of this litigation, the FWS promulgated the Permit Revocation Rule ("PRR"). 64 Fed. Reg. 32,712, 32,714 (Jun. 17, 1999), (codified at 50 C.F.R. §§ 17.22(b), 17.32(b)). The PRR amends the regulations specifically applicable to ITPs, which now include the No Surprises Rule, and provides, in pertinent part, that an ITP "may not be revoked . . . unless continuation of the permitted activity would be inconsistent with the criterion set forth in 16 U.S.C. § 1539(a)(2)(B)(iv)," and the "inconsistency has not been remedied [by the Services] in a timely fashion." 64 Fed. Reg. 32,712, 32,714, codified at 50 C.F.R. §§ 17.22(b), 17.32(b). The defendants submit that the purpose of the PRR was simply to "explain" how the Services' pre-existing permit revocation power would apply to ITPs issued pursuant to the No Surprises Rule.

Plaintiffs maintain that the PRR represented a substantive change in the regulations, and therefore was subject to the notice and comment requirements of the APA. *See* 5 U.S.C. § 553. They further submit that the public was not afforded any opportunity to comment on the rule. Plaintiffs also argue that the PRR further undermines the conservation and protection of endangered and threatened species by imposing a higher threshold for revocation of ITPs compared to that applicable to other permits issued by the Services.

### Merits

The Court need only address the procedural challenges to PRR, as resolution of those claims effectively disposes of the entire case. Finding that the PRR was promulgated in violation of the APA's notice and comment requirements, the Court will vacate and remand the PRR for further consideration by the Services. Moreover, because the government explicitly relies on the PRR to bolster its contention that the No Surprises Rule is consistent with the requirements of the ESA, the Court will not reach the merits of plaintiffs' substantive challenges to the No Surprises Rule, and instead remands the No Surprises Rule for consideration as a whole with the PRR.

1. *Public Notice and Comment*

Under the APA, federal agencies generally must publish notice of proposed rulemaking in the Federal Register to give interested persons an opportunity to comment and participate in the rulemaking. 5 U.S.C. § 553(b). That notice-and-comment provision applies to "legislative" or "substantive" rules that establish legal requirements, but not to "interpretive rules, general statements of policy, or rules of agency organization, procedure, or practice." 5 U.S.C. § 553(b)(A).

The D.C. Circuit has described the distinction between an interpretive and substantive rule: the "critical" feature of the procedural exception "is that it covers agency actions that do not themselves alter the rights or interests of parties, although it may alter the manner in which the parties present themselves or their viewpoints to the agency. . . ." The issue, therefore, "is one of degree," and our task is to identify which substantive effects are "sufficiently grave so that notice and comment are needed to safeguard the policies underlying the APA." *JEM Broadcasting Co. v. FCC,* 22 F.3d 320, 326–27 (D.C. Cir. 1994). "[A] legislative or substantive rule is one that does more than simply clarify or explain a regulatory term, or confirm a regulatory requirement, or maintain a consistent agency policy." *National Family Planning and Reproductive Health Ass'n, Inc. v. Sullivan,* 979 F.2d 227, 237 (D.C. Cir. 1992). Of particular relevance to this case, the Circuit has stated that a rule intended to "grant rights, impose obligations, or produce other significant effects on private interests," or which " 'substantially curtails [an agency's] discretion in . . . decisions and accordingly has present binding effect,' is a legislative rule." *Id.* at 238, 239.

It is clear under this Circuit's precedent that the PRR represents a legislative rule subject to the notice and comment requirements of the APA. It narrows the Services' discretion to revoke ITPs, adds a threshold precondition to permit revocation where ITPs are concerned, and significantly raises the bar as to the degree of harm to listed species which must be likely to occur in the absence of corrective action before an ITP permit can be revoked. Prior to promulgation of the PRR, the Services could revoke an ITP once "the population(s) of the wildlife or plant that is the subject of the permit declines to the extent that continuation of the permitted activity would be detrimental to maintenance *or* recovery of the affected *population.*" *See* 50 C.F.R. § 13.28(a)(5) (emphasis added). It appears beyond dispute that, following promulgation of the PRR, the Services can no longer revoke an ITP under these circumstances. 50 C.F.R. § 17.22 (An ITP "may not be revoked for any reason except those set forth in § 13.28(a)(1) through (4) or unless continuation of the permitted activity would be inconsistent with the criterion set forth in 16 U.S.C. 1539(a)(2)(B)(iv) and the inconsistency has not been remedied in a timely fashion."). Instead, so long as "the taking will not appreciably reduce the likelihood of the survival *and* recovery of the *species* in the wild," the permittee commits no procedural violations, and the law does not change, the PRR precludes the Services from revoking an ITP.

The difference between the two standards is significant: the first refers to maintenance and recovery in the disjunctive, and focuses on specific populations of listed species, whereas the second requires a showing that both *survival* and recovery of an entire *species* be affected by an activity authorized by an ITP before permit revocation can even be contemplated. As stated in the final rule itself, "[i]n keeping with the 'No Surprises' rule . . . these provisions would allow the Service to revoke an HCP permit as a last resort in the narrow and unlikely situation in which an unforeseen circumstance results in likely jeopardy to a species covered by the permit and the Service has not been successful in remedying the situation through other means." As a result, it is apparent that the PRR vests private ITP holders with a new right not to have their ITPs revoked under circumstances for which revocation would have been available under the previous regulatory regime, and for which revocation remains possible for other types of permits.

Furthermore, by precluding ITP revocation "unless continuation of the permitted activity would be inconsistent with the criterion set forth in 16 U.S.C. § 1539(a)(2)(B)(iv) *and* the *inconsistency has not been remedied in a timely fashion,*" 50 C.F.R. § 17.22 (emphasis added), the PRR adds a new precondition to revocation of an ITP which does not apply to revocation of other permits, namely that "the Service has not been successful in remedying the situation through other means." *See* 64 C.F.R. § 32.709. "When an agency changes the rules of the game—such that one source becomes solely responsible for what had been a dual responsibility and then must assume additional obligations . . . more than a clarification has occurred." *Sprint Corp. v. FCC,* 315 F.3d 369, 374 (D.C. Cir. 2003).

Defendants themselves concede that the final No Surprises rule "did not exempt ITPs from the . . . permit revocation provisions in 50 C.F.R. § 13.28(a)(5)," thus confirming that the PRR amended the pre-existing substantive rules for revocation of ITPs with No Surprises assurances. *National Family Planning and Reproductive Health Ass'n, Inc. v. Sullivan,* 979 F.2d at 235 ("It is a maxim of administrative law that: 'If a second rule repudiates or is irreconcilable with [a prior legislative rule], the second rule must be an amendment of the first; and, of course, an amendment to a legislative rule must itself be legislative.' "); *Paralyzed Veterans of America v. D.C. Arena L.P.,* 117 F.3d 579, 582 (D.C. Cir. 1997) (an agency's "change in interpretation is contrary to the Administrative Procedure Act because it circumvents Section 553, which requires that notice and comment accompany the amendment of regulations.") ("Even if not a change, it constitutes a substantive addition which itself requires notice and comment."). Defendants nevertheless maintain that the PRR does not announce a new substantive rule with the force of law, but rather "merely conformed FWS agency regulations to the statute" by specifying that revocation of ITPs would be conducted by reference to statutory issuance criteria. The Services' self-serving statements in this regard hold no persuasive weight in the face of the language of the regulation itself, which clearly imposes new obligations, vests new rights, and further restricts agency discretion.

Finally, plaintiffs refer to an e-mail message from the Solicitor of the DOI noting that the previous regulatory regime allowed revocation of an ITP when it threatened the recovery of a listed species, without requiring that the species be placed in jeopardy of extinction before revocation is authorized, and noting that "there can be a considerable difference between the two" standards. Defendants submit that these e-mail communications do not represent agency "admissions," but rather, informal, pre-decisional documents of no binding effect on the agency. The Court need not resolve the question of how much weight can be given to these communications, as the undisputed record before it clearly supports a finding that the PRR was a substantive rule.

Accordingly, the Court concludes that the PRR is a substantive rule subject to the notice and comment requirements of the APA.

[The court held further that the final PRR was neither a "logical outgrowth" of prior regulatory promulgations, in which case independent notice and comment would not have been necessary, and that notice and comment provided after the final PRR was promulgated, even if it could have cured defects in the PRR, could not cure any defects it might have caused with respect to the No Surprises rulemaking. The court thus vacated the PRR and then turned to the connection between the two rulemaking proceedings.]

2. *Relationship between PRR and No Surprises Rule*

Having concluded that PRR promulgated during the pendency of this litigation should be set aside and remanded for public notice and comment, the Court further finds that the No Surprises Rule is sufficiently intertwined with the PRR that it must also be remanded to the agency for consideration as a whole with the PRR without further inquiry into its substantive validity.

Plaintiffs submit that "[s]ince defendants have expressly relied on the Revocation rule changes to defend the No Surprises rule . . . the No Surprises rule must, at minimum, also be set aside and remanded, so that defendants can consider both of these interrelated regulatory actions at the same time, and provide the public with the input mandated by law." The defendants relied on the PRR in the course of a prior cross-motion for summary judgment in this case, stating that the PRR would amend ITP regulations to "clarify" that the Services may "revoke a[ ] permit for which there has been an unforeseen circumstance resulting in likely jeopardy to a covered species. . . ."

In so doing, defendants effectively conceded that the PRR is relevant to the Court's review of the No Surprises Rule. Although defendants maintain that No Surprises Rule withstands plaintiffs' APA and ESA challenges without reference to the PRR, they further concede that remand of both rules to determine the impact of the PRR on the No Surprises rule is one course of action available to the Court.

This Court has already preliminarily found, at least for purposes of ordering production of the administrative record, that the defendants are relying on the PRR to defend the No Surprises rule. Defendants have advanced neither argument nor evidence persuading the Court to revisit the issue. Accordingly, remand of the No Surprises Rule for consideration in tandem with the now-vacated PRR over the course of any new rulemaking procedures concerning revocation of ITPs No Surprises with No Surprises assurances is in order.

**Conclusion**

The history of the two regulatory provisions challenged in this action has indeed been full of surprises. The public has consistently been denied the opportunity, absent a court order, to be notified of substantive changes to regulations enforcing the ESA, and to weigh in on decisions likely to have significant effects on public resources.

First, the No Surprises Rule was announced as a "policy" without any prior notice or opportunity to comment on its wisdom. It was only pursuant to a settlement agreement spurred by litigation and approved by Judge Sporkin of this Court that members of the public were finally afforded an opportunity to have their say with respect to the proposed policy.

Similarly, the Services promulgated the PRR during the pendency of this litigation without prior public notice or opportunity to provide meaningful comment, only to turn around and rely on the recently issued rule in their motion for summary judgment on plaintiffs' claims relating to the No Surprises Rule.

Flagrant violations of the APA's notice and comment requirements such as those involved in the promulgation of the PRR can neither be countenanced nor cured by *post hoc* proceedings which merely go through the motions.

Finally, with respect to the No Surprises Rule, defendants cannot have it both ways. They cannot, in one breath, cite to the PRR in its pleadings in support of summary judgment as evidence that the No Surprises Rule does not violate the ESA, and in the next contend that the No Surprises Rule can stand on its own without reference to the PRR such that judicial review of one without the other is appropriate. The Court therefore **REMANDS** the No Surprises Rule, 63 Fed.Reg. 8,859 (Feb. 23, 1998), for further consideration along with the Permit Revocation Rule.

---

## QUESTIONS AND DISCUSSION

**1.** Having acknowledged the "benefits" of rulemaking notice-and-comment procedures and commenced them for the No Surprises Rule, why did FWS not do the same for the Permit Revocation Rule? To compound the matter, why did FWS point to the Permit Revocation Rule as evidence of the validity of the No Surprises Rule, thus risking the possibility that the fall of the Permit Revocation could drag down the No Surprise Rule with it? Do you think the agency saw any of this coming?

**2.** One argument the FWS made in *Spirit of the Sage*, as did EPA in the *Kelley* case excerpted in Part I.A. of this chapter, is that notice-and-comment rulemaking was not required of the Permit Revocation Rule because it was merely "interpretive." In *Kelly* the question whether the CERCLA rule was legislative or interpretive was moot, because the court found the agency had no authority to issue either kind of rule with respect to CERCLA's liability regime. In *Spirit of the Sage* the court found the rule was legislative because it altered the substantive standards on which the agency could justify permit revocation. After observing the pitfalls of relying on the "interpretive rule" exception to notice-and-comment procedures, how conservative would you be in advising an agency whether to go that route or use full rulemaking procedures?

**3.** If, as *Spirit of the Sage* and *Kelley* suggest, agencies seem eager to promulgate "interpretive rules," they are even more prolific in issuing "guidance"—ostensibly non-binding text agencies issue to "help" the regulated community understand and comply with the "official" found in the Code of Federal Regulations. This body of "gray law" has grown to gargantuan proportions in environmental law, overshadowing by far the "official" law. For example, even as early as the mid-1990s EPA's hazardous waste regulatory program filled 697 pages of the Code of Federal Regulations, but over *19,500 pages* of informal guidance. *See* William H. Rodgers, *Environmental Law Trivia*, 22 B.C. ENVTL. AFF. L. REV. 807, 812, 816 (1995). Several features of this informal, shifting, buried universe of guidance leads to difficulty in divining the "law" applicable to particular circumstances. It is not binding, yet agencies routinely act as if it is. Notice and comment procedures are not necessary for issuing guidance, and there usually is no organized repository for an agency's "final" guidance. It can change rapidly—new guidance need not be the "logical outgrowth" of prior guidance. For a spirited debate on the propriety of the growth of agency guidance, *compare* George B. Wyeth, *The "Regulation by Guidance" Debate: An Agency Perspective*, NAT. RESOURCES & ENV'T, Spring 1995, at 52, *with* F. William Brownell, *"Regulation by Guidance": A Response to EPA*, NAT. RESOURCES & ENV'T, Winter 1996, at 56. *See also* Robert A. Anthony, *Interpretive Rules, Policy Statements, Guidances, Manuals, And The Like—Should Federal Agencies Use Them To Bind The Public?*, 41 DUKE L.J. 1311 (1992); James W. Conrad, Jr., *Draft Guidance on the Appropriate Use of Rules vs. Guidance*, 32 ENVTL. L. REP. (Envtl. L. Inst.) 10721 (2002). Indeed, some courts have suggested limits to the agencies' ability to side-step rule promulgation in this manner and still use the guidance as a surrogate for regulation. *See* General Electric Co. v. EPA, 290 F.3d 377 (D.C. Cir. 2002); Appalachian Power Co. v. EPA, 208 F.3d 1015 (D.C. Cir. 2000). The phenomenon has also surfaced at the state regulatory level, *see* Michael Asimow, *Guidance Documents in the States: Toward a Safe Harbor*, 54 ADMIN. L. REV. 631 (2002), and is presented as well in the phenomenon of informal agency "advice," *see* William R. Andersen, *Informal Agency Advice—Graphing the Critical Analysis*, 54 ADMIN. L. REV. 595 (2002).

**4.** On June 10, 2004, the *Spirit of the Sage* court further ordered FWS and NMFS to complete the rulemaking on any new Permit Revocation Rule no later than December 10, 2004, and to refrain from approving new incidental take permits or related documents containing "No Surprises" assurances until the agency completed all proceedings remanded by the court's order. The agencies published a notice in the Federal Register on May 25, 2004, requesting public comment on a proposed new Permit Revocation Rule that was in all respects the same as the vacated rule. *See* 69 Fed. Reg. 29681. The agencies also requested comments on the proposed rule and its interrelationship with the No Surprises Rule. On December 10, 2004, the agencies issued this same version of the Permit Revocation Rule as a final rule. *See* 69 Fed Reg. 71723. The D.C. Circuit held that this promulgation rendered moot the government's appeal from the district court ruling. Spirit of the Sage Council v. Norton, 411 F.3d 225 (D.C. Cir. 2005). And we assume you will not be surprised to learn that the Spirit of the Sage Council then commenced a new lawsuit against the No Surprises Rule. All that had been resolved, more than *ten years* after the No Surprises policy first surfaced, was that it was ruled *procedurally* sound. The questions of whether the agencies had authority to issue the rule and, if so, whether the rule was an acceptable implementation of the ESA, had never been considered in the litigation and thus remained fair game for challenge.

**5.** On August 30, 2007, the court ruled that the No Surprises and Permit Revocation rules are reasonable interpretations of the ESA and in no way beyond the agencies' authority. *See* Spirit of the Sage Council v. Kempthorne, 511 F. Supp. 2d 31 (D.D.C. 2007). In just over *thirteen years* from their unveiling of the No Surprises Policy, the agencies had completed the process. This seems a far cry from the tidy process EPA outlined in its *Start to Finish* primer on rulemaking!

**6.** Although the No Surprises policy saga was resolved almost a decade ago, its lessons remain as relevant today as then, and the practice of rulemaking comments and litigation have changed very little. Perhaps the most significant change has been the federal government's creation of an online portal for tracking rulemakings and submitting comments. *See* www.reg.gov.

## III. PERMITTING PROCEEDINGS

One of the grist mills of environmental agency work is permitting—the granting of permission, under specified conditions, for a proposed activity to be carried out consistent with the dictates of an environmental statute and the agency's implementing regulations. Environmental statutes that use the permitting approach usually contain several components: (1) a general prohibition of specified activities or impacts; (2) the creation of a permit program to allow activities to carry out the specified activities or impacts under prescribed conditions; and (3) delegation of authority to issue such permits to an administrative agency. Usually the legislative delegation of authority is to the head of the agency, such as the EPA Administrator or the Interior Department Secretary, who in turn delegates his or her authority to other officials of the agency. The following excerpt is from an Army Corps of Engineers' explanation of how these three components work under the laws the agency administers.

### U.S. Army Corps of Engineers, Regulatory Program Overview

INTRODUCTION

The Department of the Army regulatory program is one of the oldest in the Federal Government. Initially it served a fairly simple, straightforward purpose: to protect and maintain the navigable capacity of the nation's waters. Time, changing public needs, evolving policy, case law, and new statutory mandates have changed the complexion of the program, adding to its breadth, complexity, and authority.

LEGISLATIVE AUTHORITIES

The legislative origins of the program are the Rivers and Harbors Acts of 1890 (superseded) and 1899 (33 U.S.C. 401, et seq.). Various sections establish permit requirements to prevent unauthorized obstruction or alteration of any navigable water of the United States. The most frequently exercised authority is contained in Section 10 (33 U.S.C. 403) which covers construction, excavation, or deposition of materials in, over, or under such waters, or any work which would affect the course, location, condition, or capacity of those waters. The authority is granted to the Secretary of the Army. Other permit authorities in the Act are Section 9 for dams and dikes, Section 13 for refuse disposal, and Section 14 for temporary occupation of work built by the United States. Various pieces of legislation have modified these authorities, but not removed them.

In 1972, amendments to the Federal Water Pollution Control Act added what is commonly called Section 404 authority (33 U.S.C. 1344) to the program. The Secretary of the Army, acting through the Chief of Engineers, is authorized to issue permits, after notice and opportunity for public hearings, for the discharge of dredged or fill material into waters of the United States at specified disposal sites. Selection of such sites must be in accordance with guidelines developed by the Environmental Protection Agency (EPA) in conjunction with the Secretary of the Army; these guidelines are known as the 404(b)(1) Guidelines. The discharge of all other pollutants into waters of the U.S. is regulated under Section 402 of the Act which supersedes the Section 13 permitting authority mentioned above. The Federal Water Pollution Control Act was further amended in 1977 and given the common name of "Clean Water Act" and was again amended in 1987 to modify criminal and civil penalty provisions and to add an administrative penalty provision.

Also in 1972, with enactment of the Marine Protection, Research, and Sanctuaries Act, the Secretary of the Army, acting through the Chief of Engineers, was authorized to issue permits for the transportation of dredged material to be dumped in the ocean. This authority also carries with it the requirement of notice and opportunity for public hearing. Disposal sites for such discharges are selected in accordance with criteria developed by EPA in consultation with the Secretary of the Army.

GEOGRAPHIC EXTENT

The geographic jurisdiction of the Rivers and Harbors Act of 1899 includes all navigable waters of the United States which are defined (33 CFR Part 329) as, "those waters that are subject to the ebb and flow of the tide and/or are presently used, or have been used in the past, or may be susceptible to use to transport interstate or foreign commerce." This jurisdiction extends seaward to include all ocean waters within a zone three nautical miles from the coast line (the "territorial seas"). Limited authorities extend across the outer continental shelf for artificial islands, installations and other devices (see 43 U.S.C. 333(e)). Activities requiring Section 10 permits include structures (e.g., piers, wharfs, breakwaters, bulkheads, jetties, weirs, transmission lines) and work such as dredging or disposal of dredged material, or excavation, filling, or other modifications to the navigable waters of the United States.

The Clean Water Act uses the term "navigable waters" which is defined (Section 502(7)) as "waters of the United States, including the territorial seas." Thus, Section 404 jurisdiction is defined as encompassing Section 10 waters plus their tributaries and adjacent wetlands and isolated waters where the use, degradation or destruction of such waters could affect interstate or foreign commerce.

Activities requiring Section 404 permits are limited to discharges of dredged or fill materials into the waters of the United States. These discharges include return water from dredged material disposed of on the upland and generally any fill material (e.g., rock, sand, dirt) used to construct fast land for site development, roadways, erosion protection, etc.

The geographic scope of Section 103 of the Marine Protection Research and Sanctuaries Act of 1972 is those waters of the open seas lying seaward of the baseline from which the territorial sea is measured. Along coast lines this baseline is generally taken to be the low water line. Thus, there is jurisdiction overlap with the Clean Water Act. By interagency agreement with EPA, the discharge of dredged material in the territorial seas is regulated under the Section 103 criteria rather than those developed for Section 404.

DELEGATION OF AUTHORITY

Most of these permit authorities (with specific exception of Section 9) have been delegated by the Secretary of the Army to the Chief of Engineers and his authorized representatives. Section 10 authority was formally delegated on May 24, 1971, with Section 404 and 103 authorities delegated on March 12, 1973. Those exercising these authorities are directed to evaluate the impact of the proposed work on the public interest. Other applicable factors (such as the 404(b)(1) Guidelines and ocean dumping criteria) must also be met, of course. In delegating this authority, the Secretary of the Army qualified it to ". . . [be] subject to such conditions as I or my authorized representatives may from time to time impose."

Additional clarification of this delegation is provided in the program's implementing regulations (33 CFR 320–331). Division and district engineers are authorized to issue conditioned permits (Part 325.4) and to modify, suspend, or revoke them (Part 325.7). Division and district engineers also have authority to issue alternate types of permits such as letters of permission and regional general permits (Part 325.2). In certain situations the delegated authority is limited (Part 325.8).

This delegation recognizes the decentralized nature and management philosophy of the Corps of Engineers organization. Regulatory program management and administration is focused at the district office level, with policy oversight at higher levels. The backbone of the program is the Department of the Army regulations (33 CFR 320–331) which provide the district engineer the broad policy guidance needed to administer day-to-day operation of the program. These regulations have evolved over time, changing to reflect added authorities, developing case law, and in general the concerns of the public. They are developed through formal rule making procedures.

If a district engineer has the authority under Part 325.8 to make a final decision on a permit application and he makes that decision in accordance with the procedures and authorities contained in the regulations, there is no formal administrative appeal of that decision.

---

The role of the attorney in permitting proceedings can be quite substantial and extend well beyond the direct application of legal knowledge. It is not uncommon for an attorney in an environmental permit case—whether representing the agency, the applicant, or a third party in favor or in opposition to permit issuance—to perform many or all of the following tasks:

- Identify the jurisdictional need for the permit
- Identify the relevant findings the agency must make to issue or deny the permit
- Meet with agency decision makers prior to the permit application to discuss jurisdiction, findings, and procedures
- Coordinate community information and outreach meetings to convey the client's positions
- Identify the evidentiary submissions to the agency decision maker that will support the client's position
- Identify, hire, and coordinate scientific and other consulting services needed to compile the relevant evidence
- Prepare written and oral testimony of experts for submission to the record or at a hearing
- Conduct the client's case at any hearings
- Draft written arguments to submit to the agency
- Monitor the progress of the permit application through all stages
- Coordinate any settlement and mediation proceedings with other parties
- Prepare for post-decision judicial review

The materials in this part of the chapter provide an overview of the environmental permitting process and examples of the two major approaches to permitting: (1) the conventional project specific "individual" permit; and (2) an alternative to project specific permitting known as "general" permits.

## A. THE PERMITTING PROCESS

There is no one type of or way to issue an environmental permit. At one extreme are discrete "quasi-legislative" decisions, such as the highway authorization decision involved in the *Overton Park* case excerpted above in Section I.B., that involve minimal process to issue a one-time license to do something. Once the Secretary of Transportation made the necessary findings, which were not even required to be formally documented, federal money could be devoted to the highway project and that was that. At the other extreme are permits issued only after "quasi-judicial" adjudicatory hearings that assume trial-like procedures to define numerous long-term compliance, reporting, and other obligations. These permits are often hotly contested and amount to a permit to remain subject to the agency's continuing oversight and authority. Of course, the agency's ultimate goal is to make a substantive decision that will fulfill its statutory mandates and policy objectives and withstand judicial review in that regard. But it is essential that the agency conduct the permitting procedure properly along the way toward its final decision, for procedural error, if committed, often leads a reviewing court to vacate the substantive decision and remand the matter to the agency to decide again using the correct procedures. The general chronology of permitting procedures is explored in the following excerpt from a handbook designed as a generic primer for government agencies and industry involved in the development of wind power generation facilities, or "wind farms."

## National Wind Coordinating Committee, Handbook on Permitting of Wind Energy Facilities

August 2002.

### Chapter 1

Overview of the Permitting Process

This chapter describes the typical steps in wind farm permitting, and presents several principles common to many successful permitting processes. . . . Nothing in this handbook is intended to prescribe a specific permitting process or determine which level of government should be responsible for permitting. Each state and local government is encouraged to develop the process best suited to its needs and determine which decision-making considerations are applicable and appropriate.

### TYPICAL STEPS IN PERMITTING

Most permitting processes for energy facilities, including wind turbines and associated transmission facilities, consist of five basic phases:

1) Pre-application
2) Application Review
3) Decision-making
4) Administrative and Judicial Review
5) Permit Compliance

### Pre-application

The pre-application phase occurs before a permit application is officially filed with the permitting agency. This phase may be formal or informal and may be a required part of an agency's permitting process or at the project developer's option. It may occur from a few days to as much as a year prior to filing a permit application. During this phase, a project developer and permitting agencies typically meet to help ensure that both understand the project concept, permitting process, and possible issues. The permitting agency should clearly specify whether environmental analysis or surveys are required or what other information must be submitted with the permit application. The permitting agency may also take this opportunity to become familiar with the project site, establish working relationships with other agencies, and acquaint community leaders and interest groups with the permitting process. Some agencies may review drafts of the permit application, environmental analyses, or other materials during this phase if time allows. During the pre-application phase, project developers often meet with nearby landowners, community leaders, environmental groups, and other potentially affected interests. This acquaints the developer with their initial concerns and allows the developer to respond to questions regarding the project. In some jurisdictions, the project developer is required to hold public meetings or submit a public notice regarding the project during this phase.

**Application Review**

For most agencies, the application review begins when the project developer files a permit application. Many agencies may review the filing to ensure that it contains sufficient information for the agency and the public to adequately understand the project and its consequences. If the agency has a time requirement for making a decision on the project, the "clock" often starts once the agency has determined that the application is complete, in that it contains the appropriate type and amount of information. The activities and time frames of the application review phase vary according to each agency's permitting process requirements. Some processes require public issue identification sessions, meetings, and site visits. Others also allow a "discovery" period where any formal participants in the process can question other participants regarding the project, potential impacts, and mitigation measures or possible alternatives. If a formal process is in place, the "lead" permitting agency may be required to evaluate the short- and long-term consequences of the proposed wind farm. This evaluation and the agency's recommendations on alternatives and requirements for mitigating the impacts, if necessary, frequently are presented to the project developer and the public in an environmental assessment document. These documents may be prepared by the appropriate federal, state, or local permitting agency staff, or by consultants for the agency.

**Decision-making**

In its decision-making, the agency not only determines whether or not to allow a proposed wind farm to be constructed and operated, but also whether environmental mitigation and other construction, operation, or wind farm decommissioning requirements are needed. This phase frequently includes one or more public hearings. Some permitting processes require that these hearings take place in the community most directly affected by the proposed project, while others are held in the county seat or state capital. For many state agencies, the final decision-maker is a siting board or commission. The City Council, County Board of Supervisors or Township Board of Supervisors is the final decision-maker for most local agencies. However, in some places the local decision-making body may consider a project only after it has been reviewed by a separate Planning Commission.

### Administrative Appeals and Judicial Review

Appeals of all or a portion of a final decision are considered during the administrative and judicial review phase. The first avenue of appeal is directed to the decision-maker. Only after all administrative appeals have been exhausted are challenges to the decision reviewed by the courts. Appeals to the courts most frequently are directed at determining whether the permitting process was executed fairly and in accordance with the review requirements. In addition to considering such "procedural errors," the courts occasionally are also asked to consider factual errors that may have arisen during the permitting process.

### Permit Compliance

The permit compliance phase extends throughout a wind project's lifetime, and may include inspection or monitoring to ensure that the project is constructed, operated, and decommissioned in compliance with the terms and conditions of its permit and all applicable laws. For some agencies, the permit compliance phase also includes resolving public complaints and expeditiously considering changes or amendments to a previously permitted project. Wind farm closure or decommissioning may also be monitored to ensure that a non-operating project does not represent a health or safety risk or pose environmental concerns, and that it is disposed of either in conformance with the permit conditions, or as warranted at the time operations cease. Agencies may: 1) require wind developers to post bonds after permitting to ensure that decommissioning costs are covered; 2) rely on the project developer to contribute to a decommissioning fund as the project generates revenue; or 3) rely on the salvage value of any abandoned equipment.

## PRINCIPLES COMMON TO SUCCESSFUL PERMITTING PROCESSES

The following eight elements are suggested as keys to a successful process for permitting wind farms:

1) Significant Public Involvement
2) Issue-Oriented Process
3) Clear Decision Criteria
4) Coordinated Permitting Process

5) Reasonable Time Frames
6) Advance Planning
7) Timely Administrative and Judicial Review
8) Active Compliance Monitoring

While each of these guidelines may be applied individually, collectively they represent principles for structuring a permitting process to allow for timely agency review, meaningful public involvement, and sound decisions.

**Significant Public Involvement**

A key feature of a successful permitting process is providing opportunities for early, significant, and meaningful public involvement. The public has a right to have its interests considered in permitting decisions, and without early and meaningful public involvement there is a much greater likelihood of subsequent opposition and costly and time-consuming administrative reviews and judicial appeals. While each agency's permitting process is likely to differ in the timing, location, and forum for public involvement, methods that have been used to facilitate public participation in a permitting process include:

- developers consulting with potentially affected or interested persons and giving them the opportunity to comment before proposals are submitted for permit approval;
- permitting agencies notifying potentially affected persons (adjacent landowners and the community at large) at the time of filing to inform them that a permitting process is beginning and describing how they can participate;
- permitting agencies holding public information meetings at the beginning of the permitting process to inform the public of the project, the permitting process, possible issues, and ways they can provide input;
- permitting agencies holding meetings or workshops in the community at times when the most people can attend to allow meaningful public involvement throughout the application and review phase;
- permitting agencies sending copies of any analyses or pre-decision documents to affected or interested persons and requesting formal comments;
- permitting agencies providing advanced notice to all affected or interested persons and the community in general of any decision-making hearings or meetings; and
- decision-making agencies allowing formal public involvement in open hearings when making the decision on

the proposed project or considering appeals to the decision on the project.

### Issue-Oriented Process

Successful siting processes often focus the decision on issues that can be dealt with in a factual and logical manner. No project, whether it is a wind turbine or any other type of development, is without issues. Chapter 3 of this handbook discusses the issues that are most likely to be encountered in permitting wind farms.

A key to dealing with issues objectively and in a timely manner is having appropriate information available early in the permitting process. Because the collection of information or data represents a major up-front cost, agencies need to provide opportunities for project developers to learn about information requirements well in advance of the permitting process. The requirements should be clear, reasonable, consistently applied to all projects (and all developers), and reflect information that actually will be used in the process.

Even with a focus on issues and the development of consistent, up-front information requirements, some issues may not be easily solved from a purely analytical perspective. Issues such as real or perceived public health effects associated with magnetic fields, fear of possible changes in property values, and visual impacts can become emotional. An issue-oriented approach can help focus the debate, educate the public and decision-makers, and ensure an analytic basis for the eventual decision. While this approach may not eliminate all opposition to a proposed project, a focus on issues allows for a clearer understanding of the objections to a project and a decision that is more likely to withstand any administrative or legal appeals of the facts associated with those objections.

### Clear Decision Criteria

Knowing in advance the criteria the decision-makers will use in making their decisions is an important feature of a fair and efficient permitting process. To help provide clear criteria and also more certainty on the likely outcome of a project, some decision-makers have taken one or more of the following steps in drafting ordinances or regulations:

- list all of the findings that need to be made in the decision;
- identify specific criteria to be used in decisionmaking;
- define which factors will be considered in a decision and how they will be considered and/or weighted;
- specify how environmental impacts, both positive and negative, and mitigation measures, economic considerations and other factors will be balanced in the decision-making process; and
- set minimum requirements to be met by a proposed project.

Specific decision-making criteria or factors will vary depending on the permitting agency involved, the issues or concerns within their jurisdiction, and the resources likely to be affected by wind development. Most representatives of agencies, environmental interest groups, and members of the public indicate that the primary permitting criterion is a finding that the project either has no significant environmental or public health and safety impacts or that these impacts have been mitigated so that they are not significant.

Participants in the permitting process generally rely on existing federal or state laws requiring an environmental assessment document prepared by the permitting agency as the basis for the evaluation of project impacts. However, the type of issues considered and the scope of the analysis can vary depending on: the agency, group, or local public involved; familiarity with the area, the project and the technology proposed; and the impact potential.

Many agencies also stress the importance of making a finding that the project complies with all applicable laws, ordinances, regulations, or standards. These include Federal Aviation Administration standards, Public Utility or Public Service Commission standards for electrical lines, state or federal endangered species laws, and local land use ordinances. Some local agencies believe that the requirements for Conditional Use Permits (CUP) are adequate for wind developments and feel the CUP process is well understood by all of the participants. Other local agencies have determined that their CUP process does not readily apply to wind energy developments and have modified their permit processes to better fit the characteristics and issues of wind projects.

Anticipating the potential for future wind development, some agencies have identified preferred siting areas for wind projects prior to receiving permit applications. In this manner, they have been able to guide development of the initial wind projects toward the least environmentally sensitive lands. This allows wind projects and their potential impacts to be better understood before development is permitted in more sensitive areas. Some agencies use economic development considerations as decision-making criteria. Agency staff, public interest groups and wind developers have stressed the importance of including economics in the decision-making process and openly presenting the property tax, jobs, and economic development benefits as well as any costs associated with a project. Wind developers indicate that they generally seek the highest wind sites in known wind resource areas that are economically feasible to construct, close to existing transmission facilities, and have low potential for significant environmental impacts.

The developer is responsible for mitigating project related impacts. With proper construction techniques and restoration practices, the need for additional mitigation may be limited. Along with criteria related to integrating wind generation into the regional or state electrical system, some agencies also include the "need" for additional generation facilities in their decisions. This may be considered in the context of a state or utility service area "integrated resource plan" or other energy policies or goals such as energy diversity. In moving to a competitive electricity market structure, some states have discontinued the requirement to evaluate "need" because the project's financial risk is not borne by the electricity ratepayers. Others have dropped the "need" process in cases where wind projects have been mandated by state law.

### Coordinated Permitting Process

Project permitting can be one of the significant costs associated with developing wind resources and one of the major sources of uncertainty. Projects can be delayed and developers and agencies can incur significant costs when multiple agencies require separate processes, or where environmental impact assessment and mitigation requirements are inconsistent. This problem may be particularly significant where the wind resource area includes more than one jurisdiction or the proposed wind project and related facilities such as transmission lines or access roads affect multiple agencies with land use or permitting authority. The most efficient permitting process for energy facilities would be one in which there is little or no duplication of documents or review by permitting entities, no conflicts between the different agencies in resolving issues, and no inconsistencies in permit requirements. Coordinated permitting has been achieved by:

- issuing all state and local permits by one agency in one process;
- making one agency responsible for coordinating the permit review by all other agencies;
- having all agencies agree on concurrent review processes and schedule and on a method for resolving any differences or disputes; or by
- establishing a multi-agency decision-making authority to consider the review and permit requirements of all agencies in one forum.

Coordination also is important in implementing permit requirements, monitoring during construction and operation, and decommissioning wind farms. Inconsistencies can develop when responsibilities shift from one agency or department to another. For example, the applicability of permit conditions and agreements can become confused when responsibilities are transferred from a local Planning Department that had the responsibility for permitting to the Building Department that had no previous involvement in the project but is now expected to monitor a project's compliance. If possible, the agency that developed the permit conditions should also be responsible for monitoring compliance. Wind developers and agencies within some wind resource areas have found it beneficial to pool their resources to resolve issues and problems that arise during project development, site planning, construction, or operation. Pooled resources have led to ongoing studies of avian mortality, erosion control, noise, and other issues of local concern. For example, Minnesota's avian requirements were pooled so that there was one study that all developers paid for on a per-megawatt basis.

### Reasonable Time Frames

In addition to close coordination between regulatory agencies, certainty in permitting can also be provided by establishing clear and reasonable time frames for completing the various steps in the permitting process and reaching a final decision. A principal concern of any developer is that the final decision on their proposed project will be subject to lengthy, unnecessary delays. Developers prefer known "stop points" for providing project information and making significant project changes so they can complete project design and financing arrangements. Agencies, representatives of interest groups and the general public also need to have some certainty about the permitting schedule so they can plan their activities and make the best use of their resources. In general, the timing of a permitting process is the responsibility of the permitting agency or agencies. Timing usually can be controlled if either one agency is in the lead for all permitting activities or all agencies involved have agreed to coordinate permitting activities and meet specific time goals. Many permitting agencies have found that the best way to address the concern about unnecessary delay is to specify reasonable time frames for each of the major phases of a permitting process leading to a final permitting decision. They clearly communicate the time frames to all participants throughout the process so that all involved have common expectations on the time available and how it is to be used.

### Advance Planning

The successful permitting of any energy facility requires early planning and communication on the part of the developers and the permitting agencies. Some state and local agencies have geographic based information systems that identify land use and environmental resources. These may include zoning and land use designations, transmission lines, roads and highways including scenic designations, biological resources, parks, and recreation areas. A few agencies have discussed using this information to identify in advance geographic areas that: have developable wind resources or present opportunities for locating wind farms; are likely to pose permitting problems for wind farms; or where wind development would not be allowed. Establishing communications is another critical function of advance planning. Most participants involved in permitting wind farm—developers, agencies and the public—concur that identifying the key players and initiating communications is important to successful permitting and should be done before the formal permitting process begins whenever possible.

### Timely Administrative and Judicial Review

If issues or conflicts raised during a permitting process are not satisfactorily resolved, the dissatisfied party—project developer, concerned public, or even agency staff—typically has an opportunity to appeal the decision to the decision-makers or to a higher administrative body. If the appeal is not resolved or if an administrative appeal process is not available, the conflict can be raised in local, state, or federal courts. While judicial appeals may be filed because of alleged factual or procedural errors, most successful appeals are the result of errors in the actual permitting process. Consequently a major goal of most wind permitting processes is to follow established procedures and produce factually-based decisions so that subsequent judicial appeals may be minimized. Should legal appeals occur, whether in an administrative or a judicial forum, the goal becomes to proceed efficiently and reach a conclusion in a reasonable amount of time.

One method used by many jurisdictions to increase the efficiency of handling appeals is to design the permitting process to systematically narrow the issues of concern. While all potential issues may be reviewed at the beginning of the process, issues that are either not of concern or that can be readily resolved in a manner acceptable to the developer, permitting agency staff, and concerned public may be set aside early in the process through meetings, workshops, or initial environmental documents. As a result, only those issues specifically identified by the parties as being in dispute need to be considered in hearings before the decision-makers. Both the hearings and preliminary decision documents can also be used to further focus the issues. Using a "scoping process," the permitting agency can produce a focused and detailed administrative record which can be used to support their decision. This can significantly limit any administrative or judicial appeals and allow them to proceed more efficiently.

Some of the methods agencies have used to enhance an efficient administrative and judicial review process include:

- using an issue-oriented public hearing process incorporating significant public involvement to reach a permitting decision;
- using a contested case or trial-type hearing process for an administrative review or appeal of the final permitting action;
- allowing consideration only of the record of the contested case proceeding in a judicial appeal;
- limiting the judicial appeal to only those issues identified and unresolved in the administrative appeal;
- defining who has standing to initiate the review;

- specifying time limits within which appeals must be initiated;
- setting standards for review;
- specifying how the costs of appeals will be paid and whether costs can be awarded to a prevailing party; and
- directing that judicial review will be to the highest state court of competent jurisdiction, thereby eliminating any intermediate appellate court review.

---

## QUESTIONS AND DISCUSSION

**1.** The National Wind Coordinating Committee's generic description of the permitting process corresponds well with how environmental agencies describe their particular processes. For example, the Army Corps of Engineers has explained its permitting procedures for developments in wetlands as follows:

> PROCESSING STEPS
>
> The basic form of authorization used by Corps districts is the individual permit. Processing such permits involves evaluation of individual, project specific applications in what can be considered three steps: pre-application consultation (for major projects), formal project review, and decision making.
>
> Pre-application consultation usually involves one or several meetings between an applicant, Corps district staff, interested resource agencies (Federal, state, or local), and sometimes the interested public. The basic purpose of such meetings is to provide for informal discussions about the pros and cons of a proposal before an applicant makes irreversible commitments of resources (funds, detailed designs, etc.). The process is designed to provide the applicant with an assessment of the viability of some of the more obvious alternatives available to accomplish the project purpose, to discuss measures for reducing the impacts of the project, and to inform him of the factors the Corps must consider in its decision making process.
>
> Once a complete application is received, the formal review process begins. Corps districts operate under what is called a project manager system, where one individual is responsible for handling an application from receipt to final decision. The project manager prepares a public notice, evaluates the impacts of the project and all comments received, negotiates necessary modifications of the project if required, and drafts or oversees drafting of appropriate documentation to support a recommended permit decision. The permit decision document includes a discussion of the environmental impacts of the project, the findings of the public interest review process, and any special evaluation required by the

type of activity such as compliance determinations with the Section 404(b)(1) Guidelines or the ocean dumping criteria.

The Corps supports a strong partnership with states in regulating water resource developments. This is achieved with joint permit processing procedures (e.g., joint public notices and hearings), programmatic general permits founded on effective state programs, transfer of the Section 404 program in non-navigable waters, joint EISs, special area management planning, and regional conditioning of nationwide permits.

PERMIT DECISION

Of great importance to the project evaluation is the Corps public interest balancing process. The public benefits and detriments of all factors relevant to each case are carefully evaluated and balanced. Relevant factors may include conservation, economics, aesthetics, wetlands, cultural values, navigation, fish and wildlife values, water supply, water quality, and any other factors judged important to the needs and welfare of the people. The following general criteria are considered in evaluating all applications:

1. the relevant extent of public and private needs;

2. where unresolved conflicts of resource use exist, the practicability of using reasonable alternative locations and methods to accomplish project purposes; and

3. the extent and permanence of the beneficial and/or detrimental effects the proposed project may have on public and private uses to which the area is suited.

No permit is granted if the proposal is found to be contrary to the public interest.

PUBLIC INVOLVEMENT

Public involvement plays a central role in the Corps' administration of its regulatory program. The major tools used to interact with the public are the public notice and public hearing. The public notice is the primary method of advising all interested parties of a proposed activity for which a permit is sought and of soliciting comments and information necessary to evaluate the probable beneficial and detrimental impacts on the public interest. Public notices on proposed projects always contain a statement that anyone commenting may request a public hearing. Public hearings are held if comments raise substantial issues which cannot be resolved informally and the Corps decision maker determines that information from such a hearing is needed to make a decision. Public notices are used to announce hearings. The public is also informed by notice on a monthly basis of permit decisions.

U.S. ARMY CORPS OF ENGINEERS, REGULATORY PROGRAM OVERVIEW.

**2.** One feature that will dramatically alter the nature of the permitting proceeding, and the attorney's role in it, is whether it is adjudicatory in nature and, if so, whether full-fledged "contested case" trial-like procedures are employed to compile the record. Notice that the National Wind Coordinating Committee's description mentions the contested case method, but that the Corps' overview of its permit processes does not mention such an approach. The federal Administrative Procedure Act defines "license" to include any "agency permit, certificate, approval, registration . . . or other form of permission," 5 U.S.C. § 551(7), but does not require trial-like adjudication of license decisions except when the relevant statute requires the decision be "determined on the record after opportunity for an agency hearing." *Id.* § 554(a). As in the *Overton Park* case excerpted in Part I.B. of this chapter, most federal environmental statutes do not require this kind of adjudicatory hearing. For example, Section 404 of the Clean Water Act, under which federal regulation of fill of wetlands is administered, states that the Army Corps of Engineers "may issue permits . . . after notice and opportunity for public hearings." The absence of the "on the record" condition removes this permitting decision from the adjudication procedures of the APA. The great bulk of federal environmental permitting follows this model and thus is "quasi-legislative" in nature.

---

## B. INDIVIDUAL PERMITS

The basic form of authorization used by environmental agencies is the individual permit. Processing such permits involves evaluation of individual, project-specific applications in a multi-stage review process involving potentially many parties other than the applicant and the permitting agency. For example, here are the typical processing steps for a standard individual permit the Army Corps of Engineers issues under Section 404 of the Clean Water Act for fill in wetlands:

1. Pre-application consultation between applicant and district regulatory office.
2. Applicant submits "ENG Form 4345" to district regulatory office.
3. Application received and assigned identification number.
4. Public notice issued (within 15 days of receiving all information).
5. 15 to 30 day comment period depending upon nature of activity.
6. Proposal is reviewed by Corps and:

    Public

    Special interest groups

    Local agencies

    State agencies

    Federal agencies

7. Corps considers all comments.

8. Other Federal agencies consulted, if appropriate or required by law.
9. District engineer may ask applicant to provide additional information.
10. Public hearing held, if needed.
11. District engineer makes decision.
12. Permit issued or permit denied and applicant advised of reason.

Individual permits can cover significant projects with potentially extensive environmental and other impacts. Frequently the proposed activity has attracted opposition from neighborhood, environmental, and other interests. Assuming the proper procedures are followed when issuing such a permit, judicial review litigation focuses on the substantive quality of the agency's decision.

## Airport Communities Coalition v. Graves

United States District Court for the Western District of Washington, 2003.
280 F. Supp. 2d 1207.

■ ROTHSTEIN, DISTRICT JUDGE:

### I. BACKGROUND

As part of its Master Plan Update ("MPU") to the Seattle-Tacoma International Airport, the Port of Seattle has proposed the construction of an 8,500 foot third runway and related improvements collectively known as the Third Runway Project ("3RW Project"). The proposed project requires 23.64 million cubic yards of fill, *see* AR 62374, and will fill all or portions of 50 wetlands. AR 52375. Before such filling takes place, however, the Army Corps of Engineers must first issue a Clean Water Act ("CWA") Section 404 permit to the Port. 33 U.S.C. § 1344.

On December 13, 2002, the Army Corps of Engineers issued such a permit to the Port. Plaintiff, the Airport Communities Coalition ("ACC"), immediately filed this suit seeking judicial review under the Administrative Procedures Act, 5 U.S.C. §§ 701–706. The parties agreed that no work would proceed on the project pending the outcome of this case. The parties have now moved for summary judgment. The parties also have moved to strike various extra-record submissions.

### II. DISCUSSION

A. *Standard of review*

A court may reverse a final decision of an administrative agency where the final action is "arbitrary, capricious, an abuse of discretion or otherwise not in accordance with the law." 5 U.S.C. § 706(2)(A). The scope of review under this standard "is narrow and a court is not to substitute its judgment for that of the agency." *Motor Vehicle Mfrs. Ass'n v. State Farm Mut. Auto. Ins. Co.*, 463 U.S. 29, 43 (1983). An agency decision will be upheld as long as there is a "rational connection between the facts found and the choice made." *Id.* In reviewing the agency's explanation, the court must "consider whether the decision was based on a consideration of the relevant factors and whether there has been a clear error of judgment." *State Farm,* 463 U.S. at 43.

In conducting this review, the "focal point . . . should be the administrative record already in existence, not some new record made initially in the reviewing court." *Camp v. Pitts,* 411 U.S. 138, 142 (1973). Review may be expanded beyond the record, however, if it is necessary to explain agency decisions. *Animal Def. Council v. Hodel,* 840 F.2d 1432, 1436 (9th Cir. 1988). In the Ninth Circuit, extra-record materials are allowed (1) if necessary to determine whether the agency has considered all relevant factors and has explained its decision, (2) when the agency has relied on documents not in the record, or (3) when supplementing the record is necessary to explain technical terms or complex subject matter. *Inland Empire Pub. Lands Council v. Glickman,* 88 F.3d 697, 704 (9th Cir. 1996). Extra-record documents may also be admitted "when plaintiffs make a showing of agency bad faith." *Nat'l Audubon Soc. v. United States Forest Serv.*, 46 F.3d 1437, 1447 n.9 (9th Cir. 1993). All of these exceptions are provided in order to ensure the integrity of the administrative process.

C. *Corps' decision to issue permit*

ACC contends that the Corps' decision to issue the 404 permit was arbitrary and capricious because (1) the Corps failed to incorporate into the permit various conditions placed on the project by the state Pollution Control Hearing Board ("PCHB"); (2) the Corps failed to issue a supplemental environmental impact statement regarding new information about future aircraft operations at the airport and possible arsenic contamination of the topsoil in the project area; and (3) the Corps failed to conduct an adequate public interest review before issuing the Section 404 permit.

[The court found no error in the Corps' treatment of the state agency findings or in the Corps' decision not to issue a supplemental environmental impact statement.]

3. *Failure to conduct adequate public interest analysis*

Corps regulations require it to evaluate the probable impacts of a proposed activity on the public interest. 33 C.F.R. § 320.4(a)(1). Such an evaluation requires a careful weighing of all those factors which become relevant in each particular case. The benefits which reasonably may be expected to accrue from the proposal must be balanced against its reasonably foreseeable detriments. The decision whether to authorize a proposal, and if so, the conditions under which it will be allowed to occur, are therefore determined by the outcome of this general balancing process. *Id.* If a permit would be contrary to the public interest, it must be denied. *Id.*

In the present case, ACC contends that the Corps failed to conduct an adequate public interest analysis because the Corps failed (1) to independently evaluate the need for the 3RW Project; (2) to properly conduct an alternatives analysis; (3) to consider current cost data for the project; (4) to adopt fill criteria adequate to protect water quality; and (5) to properly assess the impacts of the project on wetlands.

As a reviewing court, this court must give the Corps' determinations substantial deference. *Town of Norfolk v. United States Army Corps of Eng'rs,* 968 F.2d 1438, 1454 (1st Cir. 1992) ("Under the 'public interest' review, the Corps conducts a general balancing of a number of economic and environmental factors and its ultimate determinations are entitled to substantial deference."); *Envtl. Coalition of Broward County, Inc. v. Myers,* 831 F.2d 984, 986 (11th Cir. 1987). "In reviewing this public interest determination by the Corps, it is not [the court's] role to second-guess. . . . [but to] merely consider whether the Corps followed required procedures, evaluated relevant factors and reached a reasoned decision." *Van Abbema v. Fornell,* 807 F.2d 633, 636 (7th Cir. 1986).

a. *The need for the 3RW Project*

According to ACC, the Corps failed to conduct an adequate and independent analysis of the need for the 3RW Project. *See* 33 C.F.R. § 320.4(a)(2)(i) (public interest analysis must include a determination of "the relative extent of the public and private need for the proposed structure or work"). ACC points to the effect of September 11, 2001 and the subsequent and sustained dramatic drop in flights and the reduction of airline operations to support its claim that the project is not needed. ACC further contends that the project is not needed given technology that can reduce delays despite increased flight operations.

*In conducting its public interest analysis, the Corps had before it the FAA*'s conclusions that the 3RW Project was necessary to ensure safety and reduce delays given the fact that the airport's current two runways are located only 800 feet apart and that poor weather, not aircraft operations, is the main cause of delays. Such an opinion is entitled to great deference from the Corps. 33 C.F.R. § 320.4(j)(4) ("another federal agency's determination to proceed is entitled to substantial consideration in the Corps' public interest review"); *Crutchfield v. County of Hanover,* 325 F.3d 211 (4th Cir. 2003) (Corps may rely on proponent studies regarding the project need). It was not arbitrary and capricious for the Corps to accept these conclusions. *See City of Los Angeles v. FAA,* 138 F.3d 806, 807 (9th Cir. 1998) (predicting demand for an airport in 15 years is a prognostication that is due deference).

Despite the fact that the Corps could have given deference to the FAA's needs determination, the record reveals that the Corps did in fact conduct an independent review of the project need. The Corps took note of ACC's criticisms, noting the concerns about the effect of September 11, the economic downturn in the airline industry, and the reduction in number of aircraft operations. The Corps asked the Port to respond. The

Port did. The Corps also sought the FAA's analysis of these issues. The FAA also responded. Clearly, ACC and their expert, Dr. Stephen Hockaday, paint a different picture of the future of air travel than the Port and the FAA. However, it is not the role of this court to resolve scientific disagreements between ACC's expert and the Corps' experts. *Friends of the Earth v. Hall,* 693 F. Supp. 904, 922 (W.D. Wash. 1988). The record makes clear that the Corps followed required procedures, evaluated relevant factors and reached a reasoned decision.

b. *Failure to conduct adequate alternatives analysis*

By law, the Corps must evaluate alternatives to a proposed project in deciding whether a permit should issue. 42 U.S.C. § 4332(2)(E); 33 C.F.R. § 320.4(a). According to ACC, had the Corps properly examined alternatives, it would have found one that is less environmentally harmful. The specific alternative that ACC contends the Corps neglected is one where the FAA would utilize technology and various demand-management techniques to handle increased capacity and reduce poor-weather delays. The record reflects, however, that the Corps did consider these alternatives and concurred with the Port that they did not meet the project need. ACC fails to point to any evidence in the record to challenge these conclusions. In fact, the source of ACC's proposed alternative is the FAA itself, which after raising the alternative, discounted it as not being a viable solution to solving the *total* poor weather problem. Furthermore, the Corps specifically requested additional information from both the Port and FAA regarding alternatives on several occasions. Consequently, the Corps conducted an adequate alternatives analysis.

c. *Failure to request current cost estimates*

In line with its attack on the Corps' decision not to issue a supplemental EIS, ACC also attacks the Corps' decision not to require the Port to submit updated costs estimates for the project. According to ACC, without those costs estimates, the Corps could not have properly conducted that analysis, which is required to include a consideration of the economics of the project. 33 C.F.R. § 320.4(a)(1). Where "a proposal's benefits are entirely economic and its costs environmental, the Corps must make at least a minimally reliable effort to establish economic benefit." *Van Abbema,* 807 F.2d at 639.

Here, however, the benefits are not entirely economic. Rather they include such intangibles as air travel safety, increased traveler convenience, and reduced poor-weather delays. Furthermore, cost was not a determinative factor in comparing practicable alternatives. Consequently, the economics of the project were not as relevant to the Corps' public interest analysis than if cost had been a determinative factor. Therefore, the court finds that the Corps did not act arbitrarily and capriciously when it did not ask the Port for updated cost estimates. *Van Abbema,* 807 F.2d at 636 (court cannot second-guess the Corps where the Corps followed the required procedures, evaluated relevant factors, and reached its own reasoned decision).

d. *Failure to require adequate fill contamination criteria*

ACC contends that the Corps did not properly assess the impact of the use of contaminated fill and did not properly impose stricter limitations on the use of such fill. Under the Section 404(b)(1) Guidelines, the Corps must prohibit any discharge of fill material that "causes or contributes . . . to violations of any applicable State water quality standard" or "[v]iolates any applicable toxic, effluent standard or prohibition." 40 C.F.R. § 230.10(b). In its permit, the Corps deemed the fill criteria that were provided in Ecology's original certification sufficiently protective of the aquatic environment. In doing so, the Corps rejected more stringent criteria that were announced by the PCHB in its ruling on the appeal of Ecology's certification. ACC contends that the Corps should have adopted PCHB's stricter criteria and that it acted arbitrarily and capriciously by "concluding without analysis" that Ecology's standards were sufficiently protective.

This court will uphold the Corps' decision regarding the fill criteria provided there is a rational basis for that decision in the record. *Hintz,* 800 F.2d at 831. Certainly there is disagreement in the record among the experts over which requirements—the Corps' or PCHB's—adequately protect aquatic resources. Again, this court "is not in the business of resolving scientific disagreements between plaintiffs' experts and the Corps' experts." *Friends of the Earth,* 693 F. Supp. at 922. Here, the Corps' analysis relied on the judgment of the experts at Ecology. Such reliance is not arbitrary and capricious even in light of PCHB's imposition on appeal of stricter standards. In the present case, the record reveals that the district engineer considered the stricter standards and rejected them. There is a rational basis for this decision. For example, PCHB's requirements for selenium, chromium, and silver are lower than local natural background levels in the Puget Sound area. In setting those requirements, PCHB used *statewide* rather than *regional* background levels. The result would be that the Port would have to use fill that is cleaner than the soils in the surrounding area. The Corps correctly rejected those criteria as being unreasonable. The Corps also considered PCHB's other criteria and likewise rejected the stricter criteria as not being necessary to protect aquatic resources. Instead, the Corps deemed the criteria proffered by Ecology and by the Fish and Wildlife Service to be adequate and adopted them. ACC fails, therefore, to demonstrate that the Corps acted arbitrarily and capriciously in setting fill criteria for the permit. . . .

e. *Failure to assess impacts to wetlands*

ACC contends that the Corps failed to require sufficient mitigation to assure no net loss of wetland function. According to ACC, the Corps failed to properly calculate the net areal loss that will occur as a result of the 3RW Project and failed to provide an adequate functional analysis of the wetlands mitigation plan. ACC also argues that the Corps improperly set the width of upland buffers and that the Corps failed to properly engage in a cumulative impact analysis.

(1) *Failure to properly calculate net areal loss*

Under the CWA, the Corps must minimize the damage to wetlands that result from the issuance of a Section 404 permit. One way to accomplish this is through compensatory mitigation, such as restoration of existing degraded wetlands or creation of manmade wetlands. Memorandum of Agreement Between the Environmental Protection Agency and the Department of the Army Concerning the Determination of Mitigation Under the Clean Water Act Section 404(b)(1) Guidelines § II.C.3 ("Mitigation MOA"). Toward that end, the Port submitted its Natural Resource Mitigation Plan ("NRMP").

ACC contends that the Corps improperly calculated the amount of wetlands that will be lost as a result of the 3RW Project. There is, however, no requirement that the Corps consider the *area* of wetlands lost in evaluating a mitigation plan, only that there be no net loss of wetlands *function*. Mitigation MOA § II.B (the Corps must strive "to achieve a goal of no overall net loss of [wetland] values and functions").

Despite this, ACC alleges that the Corps undercounted the acreage of impacted wetlands by 1.75 acres. ACC makes much of a statement by the Corps that "[i]n some instances, areal impacts will occur to a wetland to such an extent (e.g. 70% or more of the wetland is impacted) the remaining portion of the wetland becomes substantively impaired." AR 53826. According to ACC, the Corps should have considered three wetlands as being completely impacted given the fact that the actual impacts exceed 70 percent of the wetlands' acreage.

However, it is clear from the Corps' statement that it is not meant to be a bright-line rule. First, the statement is prefaced with a condition that it only applies "in some instances." Second, the "rule" does not provide any bright-line cutoff for the percentage of acreage that must be impacted but rather suggests ("e.g.") one such value as an example. Furthermore, whether a wetland is indirectly impacted when a large portion of it has been directly affected is specific to each wetland. ACC produces no specific evidence that the Corps undercounted impacted wetlands. Consequently, this court defers to the Corps' determination. *Friends of the Clearwater v. Dombeck,* 222 F.3d 552, 556 (9th Cir. 2000) (deference "is especially appropriate where . . . the challenged decision implicates substantial agency expertise").

(2) *Failure to properly account for net functional loss*

ACC also contends that the Corps' functional analysis is flawed because it fails to sufficiently quantify the net gain or loss of wetlands functions for the Port's mitigation plan. First, ACC contends that the Corps merely deferred to the Port's NRMP. It is readily apparent from the record, however, that the Corps initially found the Port's NRMP inadequate. AR 53833–32. The Corps repeatedly requested more information and analysis from the Port. *Id.* at 53832. The Corps finally undertook its own independent functional assessment and impact analysis. *Id.* The Port eventually incorporated the Corps' concerns in a revised mitigation plan. *Id.* The record, therefore, does not support ACC's contention that the Corps simply deferred to the Port.

Furthermore, there is no evidence in the record to support ACC's contention that the Corps acted arbitrarily and capriciously by performing a purely qualitative functional analysis. In performing its analysis, the Corps utilized a methodology that consisted of a series of subjective descriptions of the wetlands and the functions they serve. According to ACC, the Corps should have used a quantitative methodology that would more accurately calculate the loss or gain in wetlands function. ACC points to a National Research Council study titled *Compensating for Wetlands Losses Under the Clean Water Act,* which rejects the subjective approach used by the Corps in favor of a more "science-based" quantitative numeric indexing approaching to compare wetlands functions to ensure the equivalency of the compensatory mitigation.

The Corps' selection of methodology, however, is not plainly wrong in light of the guidance provided within the Corps' Ecosystem Management and Restoration Information System ("EMRIS"). Through that guidance, Corps personnel wishing to establish mitigation/compensation ratios are instructed to select from up to 10 different methodologies. . . . The choice of methodology is clearly an area within the Corps' expertise to which this court defers. Accordingly, the court finds that the Corps adequately accounted for net functional loss of wetlands.

(3) *Failure to provide adequate upland buffers*

As part of the mitigation package, the Corps required the Port to set aside and/or enhance buffer zones around the impacted wetlands. The Corps gave credit for the value of these upland buffers in determining the extent of the need for compensatory mitigation. ACC challenges these credits. First, ACC points out that the land in those buffers is already protected by local and state law so that there is no added environmental value to these buffers. However, ACC does not point to any statute or regulation prohibiting the Corps from giving credit for buffers that are already protected by local and state law, especially where the Corps requires that those buffers be enhanced. . . .

Next, ACC takes issue with the Corps' selection of 100 foot buffers rather than the 150 foot buffers recommended by the Fish and Wildlife Service ("FWS"). The conservation measures recommended by FWS, however, are "nonbinding suggestions that a Federal agency may elect to implement in its proposed action." 51 Fed. Reg. 19,926, 19,931 (June 3, 1985). Moreover, 100-foot buffers are supported by the scientific literature. Contrary to ACC's assertion that the Port and Corps fail to follow the recommendations embodied in that literature, the court finds that the literature adequately supports the position that 100-foot buffers provide ecological benefits.

Put simply, this court will not substitute its judgment as to the effectiveness of the mitigation measures for that of the Corps. *Sierra Club v. Alexander,* 484 F. Supp. 455, 468 (N.D.N.Y. 1980). Given the studied and expert decision announced by the Corps that the mitigation measures are adequate, and given that the record demonstrates that the Corps considered the relevant environmental data and factors in reaching that decision, the court finds that the Corps did not act arbitrarily and capriciously regarding the adequacy of the buffers.

(4) *Corps' approval of out-of-basin mitigation*

Under the Corps' regulations, the Corps is authorized to employ off-site mitigation. 33 C.F.R. §§ 320.4(r)(1), 325.4(a)(3); *see also* Mitigation MOA § II.C.3 ("If on-site compensatory mitigation is not practicable, off-site compensatory mitigation should be undertaken in the same geographic area if practicable."). ACC contends that the Corps' decision to use the Auburn site was arbitrary and capricious given that the Auburn wetland is not in physical proximity to the impacted areas, is not in the same watershed, and is not a similar wetland. ACC further contends that there are sufficient and adequate in-basin alternatives that should have been adopted instead.

The record demonstrates, however, that the Corps considered the relevant environmental data in reaching its decision. The purpose of the Auburn wetland is to provide displaced avian habitat. Such habitat cannot easily be located near the impacted area because birds pose a threat to aircraft operations. *See* FAA Advisory Circular No. 150/5200–33 at § 1–3 (mitigation projects within 10,000 feet of an airport that have the potential to attract birds that might pose a threat to aircraft should not be approved). . . .

Furthermore, it was not arbitrary and capricious to reject other areas for mitigation in light of a finding that those areas are unsuitable or impracticable. ACC takes issue with the Port's and the Corps' consideration of only those sites that are 10 or more acres in size. According to ACC, many smaller sites are suitable for mitigation and should have been included in lieu of the off-site mitigation. ACC points to their own expert's testimony that numerous smaller wetland areas may provide more overall wetland functions than concentrating mitigation in a single large site. While this may be true, it is also the case that the areas that ACC suggests are already heavily developed. The Port and the Corps found that a network of small and fragmentary mitigation sites would not adequately compensate for the functional losses associated with the development. Given the impracticability of in-basin mitigation, it was entirely reasonable for the Corps to require out-of-basin mitigation.

(5) *Failure to properly perform cumulative impacts analysis*

Finally, ACC contends that the Corps merely rubber-stamped the Port's cumulative impacts analysis, thereby failing to provide a competent analysis as required by its own regulations. After EPA noted that the Port's submission to the Corps lacked any cumulative impacts analysis, both the Port and the Corps conducted such an analysis. In light of its analysis, the Corps concluded that "while the proposed project and mitigation does not reverse the past adverse impacts having occurred in these watersheds, it does not further contribute to the degradation of the aquatic environment, except for passerine bird and waterfowl habitat. Mitigation for these impacts are provided at the off-site mitigation in Auburn." There is simply no evidence in the record that the Corps adopted the Port's analysis without any consideration. A cursory analysis of the Port's and Corps' assessments reveals that they are quite different. While the Corps may have used the underlying information in the Port's analysis as a foundation for its own assessment, such reliance is not an unlawful shirking of responsibility. *Friends of the Earth v. Hintz,* 800 F.2d 822, 834 (9th Cir. 1986).

III. CONCLUSION

For the foregoing reasons, the court finds that the Corps did not act arbitrarily and capriciously in issuing the Section 404 permit to the Port of Seattle. The Corps' and Port's motions for summary judgment are GRANTED. ACC's motion for summary judgment is DENIED.

---

**QUESTIONS AND DISCUSSION**

**1.** Challenging an agency permit decision is an uphill battle, as the standard of review is tilted decidedly in favor of the agency decision. As the *Airport Communities* court explains, the reviewing court's primary role is to explore three questions: (1) did the agency follow required procedures; (2) did the agency evaluate relevant factors; and (3) did the agency reach a reasoned decision. Although this is not to suggest that courts never overturn agency permitting decisions under this test, it is more often the case that the agency decision to deny or issue a permit is upheld on judicial review.

**2.** Environmental permit decisions often demand that the agency base decisions on data and information derived from scientific inquiries using experimental, field study, and empirical methods, such as the Corps had to do to reach decisions about appropriate compensatory mitigation for the permit challenged in the *Airport Communities* case. It often is the case that more than one method is employed by different scientists for particular questions, and that there may be a dispute within the scientific community as to which method is superior. This "selection of methodology" issue is often raised as a basis for challenging the substantive merits of an agency's permitting decision. As did the *Airport Communities* court, however, the choice of methodology is usually treated as an area within the permitting agency's expertise to which the courts defer.

3. Scientists who agree on the appropriate method might disagree over the proper interpretation of the results. In environmental permitting proceedings involving many parties it is not unusual to find this "battle of the experts" in full swing. Yet, so long as the agency reasonably relies on the expert that supports its decision, the courts generally follow the *Airport Communities* court's observation that a reviewing court is "not in the business of resolving scientific disagreements between one party's experts and the agency's experts."

4. Another common attack point in challenges to agency permit decisions—usually decisions granting a permit—is that the permitting agency unreasonably relied on reports or analyses prepared by other parties or agencies. In *Airport Communities*, for example, the plaintiff objected that the Corps merely "rubber-stamped" the Port's cumulative impacts analysis, thereby failing to provide a competent analysis as required by its own regulations. But out of administrative necessity it is often the case that the permitting agency reviews and incorporates information contained in reports prepared outside of the agency, either by the permit applicant, one of the other parties, or other agencies. Again, most courts follow the *Airport Communities* court's approach that "such reliance is not an unlawful shirking of responsibility."

## NOTE ON MITIGATION POLICY

As discussed in detail in the materials on protecting wetlands in Chapter 4, the practice of requiring permit applicants to "mitigate" the impacts of the actions approved in a Corps permit has been standard practice for several decades. Indeed, mitigation is a ubiquitous feature of environmental law permitting. For the most part, however, there has never been a coherent federal policy to guide the evolution and implementation of mitigation. Different federal and state agencies have designed and managed their own mitigation programs and fought their own battles. The Corps and EPA essentially invented mitigation banking in the mid-1990s to facilitate implementation of CWA Section 404, but until 2008 had no comprehensive regulatory approach for compensatory mitigation, relying instead on a collection of memorandums and other guidance. *See* Compensatory Mitigation for Losses of Aquatic Resources, 70 Fed. Reg. 19594 (Apr. 10, 2008). The Council on Environmental Quality, has grappled for decades with how to integrate project mitigation into the decision under the National Environmental Policy Act whether to require a full-blown environmental impact statement (see Chapter 6). *See* Final Guidance for Federal Departments and Agencies on the Appropriate Use of Mitigation and Monitoring and Clarifying the Appropriate Use of Mitigated Findings of No Significant Impact, 76 Fed. Reg. 3843 (Jan. 21, 2011). And the Fish and Wildlife Service, which geared up its Endangered Species Act incidental take permit program in the early 1990s (see Chapter 2), did not develop its own guidance on habitat conservation banking until 2003. *See* Guidance for the Establishment, Use, and Operation of Conservation Banks, 68 Fed. Reg.

24753 (May 8, 2003). This decentralized, ad hoc approach to agencies' mitigation policies, however, may have seen its last days at the federal level.

On November 3, 2015, President Obama issued a Presidential Memorandum aimed at unifying the mitigation practice and policy for activities carried out and approved by the Departments of Defense, Interior, and Agriculture, the EPA, and the National Oceanic and Atmospheric Administration. *See* Mitigating Impacts on Natural Resources from Development and Encouraging Related Private Investment, 80 Fed. Reg. 68743 (Nov. 6, 2015). The broad policy goal of the Memorandum is to facilitate the win-win of promoting environmental protection and economic development by ensuring that the agencies' mitigation policies "are clear, work similarly across agencies, and are implemented consistently within agencies." *Id.* at 68743. The Memorandum also emphases the need for transparency, measurable performance standards, and clear policies regarding who is responsible for what. *Id.* at 687465. The Memorandum develops four key themes working towards those goals.

*Sequencing*. First, the Memorandum unambiguously adopts the sequencing approach. Mitigation is defined as using "avoidance, minimization, and compensation. These three actions are generally applied sequentially." *Id.* at 68745. The Memorandum's substantive directive further explains that it shall be the agencies' policy "to avoid and then minimize harmful effects to land, water, wildlife, and other ecological resources (natural resources) caused by land- or water-disturbing activities, and to ensure that any remaining harmful effects are effectively addressed" through compensatory mitigation where appropriate. *Id.* at 68743. Indeed, the Memorandum proposes that some statutory programs protect resources that "are of such irreplaceable character that minimization and compensation measures, while potentially practicable, may not be adequate or appropriate," in which case the agency shall promote avoidance. *Id.* at 68744. In short, unless a statutory program imposes another approach, the subject agencies must adopt the sequencing approach and in some cases may be required to demand that projects emphasize avoidance. But the Memorandum does not provide standards, such as feasibility, practicability, or cost-effectiveness, for determining when a project may move along the sequence from avoidance to minimization to compensation. Also, although the Memorandum defines irreplaceable resources as those which existing legal authorities recognize as "requiring particular protection" and thus "because of their high value or function and unique character, cannot be restored or replaced," *id.*, it leaves unclear what an agency must do in cases where an avoidance-only approach is not technologically or economically available for the project to proceed.

*Net Outcome*. The second major theme goes to the question of net outcome. The Memorandum requires that agency mitigation policies "should establish a net benefit goal or, at a minimum, a no net loss goal for natural resources the agency manages." *Id.* at 68745. This ambitious goal is tempered with the qualifications that it applies only to resources that are "important, scarce, or sensitive, or wherever doing so is consistent with agency mission and established natural resources objectives." *Id.* Those key terms, however, are not defined.

*Advance Compensation*. In its third major theme, the Memorandum directs agencies to "encourage advance compensation, including mitigation bank-based approaches, in order to provide resource gains before harmful impacts occur." *Id.* at 68744. The Memorandum's definition of "advance compensation" does not provide more details, but in a specific directive to the Fish and Wildlife Service the Memorandum requires the agency to develop a policy—which it had already begun exploring—to provide clarity regarding actions landowners take to conserve species in advance of potential listing under the Endangered Species Act and to "provide a mechanism to recognize and credit such action as avoidance, minimization, and compensatory mitigation." *Id.* at 68746. This suggests a broad meaning for advance compensation programs designed to promote, and reward, conservation measures implemented even before regulatory restrictions attach to an activity.

*Large-Scale Planning*. The fourth major theme of the Memorandum incorporates the directives into the front end of agency land management planning. The Memorandum explains that agencies' "large-scale plans and analysis should inform the identification of areas where development may be most appropriate, where high natural resource values result in the best locations for protection and restoration, or where natural resource values are irreplaceable." *Id.* at 68744. Large-scale planning is defined broadly, but clearly has in mind in particular the planning required of the federal public land management agencies. *Id.* at 68744. By incorporating mitigation at the front end of planning, the effect of this directive would be to reduce the need to apply mitigation at the back end to specific land permitting and approval decisions, such as timber harvesting or grazing, by designating which areas are off limits and which are open for resource development. Whether that has any practical impact on the allocation of uses versus the existing planning practices of agencies remains to be seen.

Agencies quickly began implementing the Memorandum directives. Their efforts as of this writing range from exploratory to far along in developing proposals. For example, the Forest Service issued a white paper in March 2016 announcing its intention to publish a policy implementing the Memorandum in late 2017 and requesting input on over a dozen implementation questions. *See* U.S. Forest Service, Seeking Recommendations in Formulating Agency Policy on Mitigating Adverse Impacts on National Forests and Grasslands (Mar. 2016), available at http://www.fs.fed.us/emc/nepa/FSMitigationPolicy.htm. By contrast, that same month the Fish and Wildlife Service issued an extensive set of proposed revisions to its mitigation policies, including for Endangered Species Act Section 10 permitting, which closely tracks and expands upon the Memorandum directives. *See* Proposed Revisions to the U.S. Fish and Wildlife Service Mitigation Policy, 81 Fed. Reg. 12380 (Mar. 8, 2016). Nor did the Memorandum escaped the attention of Congress, as the House Committee on Natural Resources held hearings to air out concerns on what it described as the "Obama Administration's new environmental mitigation regulations." *See* House Committee on Natural Resources, Press Release

(Feb. 24, 2016), available at http://naturalresources.house.gov/newsroom/documentsingle.aspx?DocumentID=400005.

The Memorandum clearly represents a milestone in federal natural resources mitigation policy. If all agencies were to maximize implementation of the sequencing, net outcome, advance compensation, and large-scale planning directives, and do so consistently, transparently, and with measurable performance standards, mitigation in the United States would look considerably different from its present practice.

---

## C. GENERAL PERMITTING

Another form of authorization is the general permit authorized in many environmental statutes as an alternative to individual permits. General permits are not normally developed for an individual applicant, but cover activities the agency has identified as being substantially similar in nature and causing only minimal individual and cumulative environmental impacts. These permits may cover activities in a limited geographic area (e.g., county or state), a particular region of the county (e.g., group of contiguous states), or the nation. The general permit specifies the conditions a particular activity must meet to qualify for its "umbrella" of authorization. General permits are adopted by a rulemaking and applied to individual projects with minimal or no additional procedure. Clearly, if a planned activity can qualify for a general permit, it often represents considerable time and costs savings to do so. On the other hand, the reduced procedural component represents less opportunity for public involvement in particular applications of the general permit. Interest groups thus take great interest in a general permit rulemaking proceeding, as once it is final the line between general and individual permits is fixed.

### National Association of Home Builders v. United States Army Corps of Engineers

United States District Court for the District of Columbia, 2006.
453 F. Supp. 2d 116.

■ LEON, DISTRICT JUDGE:

Before the Court on remand are the parties' Cross Motions for Summary Judgment. In these three consolidated cases, the plaintiffs challenge nationwide permits ("NWPs") issued under Section 404(e) of the Clean Water Act ("CWA") by the defendant U.S. Army Corps of Engineers ("Corps") in March 2000 and January 2002. . . .

BACKGROUND

Congress enacted the CWA to "restore and maintain the chemical, physical, and biological integrity of the Nation's waters." 33 U.S.C. § 1251(a). To that end, the CWA prohibits a party from discharging pollutants, such as dredged or fill material, into navigable waters of the United States. *Id.* § 1311(a). Under the CWA, however, the Corps is authorized to allow such discharges through the issuance of permits, both general and individual. *Id.* § 1344. The purpose of general permits, including nationwide permits ("NWP"), issued under Section 404(e) of the CWA is to allow projects that cause minimal environmental impact to go forward with little delay or paperwork. 33 C.F.R. § 330.1(b) (explaining that general permits are "designed to regulate with little, if any, delay or paperwork certain activities having minimal impacts"). If a proposed activity meets the conditions for general permits, it need not be subjected to the individualized permit process through which the Corps makes determinations on discharges on a case-by-case basis. 33 U.S.C. § 1344. Specifically, Section 404(e) states that:

> the Secretary may, after notice and opportunity for public hearing, issue general permits on a State, regional, or nationwide basis for any category of activities involving discharges of dredged or fill material if the Secretary determines that the activities in such category are similar in nature, will cause only minimal adverse environmental effects when performed separately, and will have only minimal cumulative adverse effect on the environment.

*Id.* § 1344(e)(1). Thus, the Corps has the discretion to issue such general permits if the polluting activities are similar in nature and will only cause minimal environmental effects. *Id.* If a party discharges pollutants into navigable waters without meeting the conditions of a general permit or otherwise acquiring an individual permit, then the party can be subject to enforcement actions, such as a civil administrative action by the Corps or a civil and criminal proceeding by the Department of Justice. *Id.* § 1319(g); 33 C.F.R. §§ 326.5–326.6.

For five-year intervals, beginning in 1977, the Corps has issued NWPs, including the most widely used permit, NWP 26. 61 Fed. Reg. 65,874, 65,893 (Dec. 13, 1996). Before the relevant changes to the NWPs made in 2000, NWP 26 authorized discharges that affected up to ten acres of waters without requiring a party to acquire an individual permit, and required that a party notify a Corps' district engineer of any discharges causing loss or substantial adverse modification of one to ten acres of wetlands (this second requirement is known as a "pre-construction notification"). 61 Fed. Reg. 30,781, 30,783 (June 17, 1996). On June 17, 1996, the Corps proposed reissuing many of the NWPs, including NWP 26, which was to expire on January 21, 1997. *Id.* at 30,780. On December 13, 1996, the Corps reissued NWP 26 for a period of two years, with somewhat different conditions. 61 Fed. Reg. at 65,874, 65,877, 65,891, 65,895. In July 1998, the Corps published its proposed replacement permits, and extended the term of NWP 26 again. 63 Fed. Reg. 36,040 (July 1, 1998). Following a public comment period in which it received approximately 10,000 comments on the proposal, 64 Fed. Reg.

39,257 (July 21, 1999), the Corps set forth a second proposal regarding the other new permits in July 1999. *See* 64 Fed. Reg. 39,252 (July 21, 1999). On March 9, 2000, after considering even more comments, the Corps issued the permits that replaced NWP 26. *See* 65 Fed. Reg. 12,818. 12.818 (Mar. 9, 2000).

Overall this process resulted in five new NWPs (known collectively as "Replacement Permits"), modification of six existing NWPs, two new General Conditions ("GC"), and modification of nine existing GCs. *Id.* These changes to the NWPs process authorized many of the same activities allowed under NWP 26, but the new and modified NWPs were activity-specific. *See id.* Among the controversial changes, the Corps narrowed the maximum per-project acreage impact from ten acres to a half acre, and pre-construction notification was required for impacts greater than one-tenth of an acre instead of one acre. The new NWPs became effective on June 7, 2000, and NWP 26 expired the same day. 65 Fed. Reg. 14,255, 14,255 (Mar. 16, 2000).

. . . The plaintiffs argue, *inter alia,* that the NWPs exceed the Corps' authority under the CWA because the Corps only has jurisdiction over "discharges" of "pollutants," including dredged or fill material, into "waters of the United States," the NWPs exceed the Corps' authority under the CWA because the Corps can only issue NWPs for categories of activities that are similar in nature and will cause only minimal adverse environmental impacts, that the Corps acted arbitrarily and capriciously in the issuance of the replacement permit NWPs, that the Corps did not conduct a flexibility analysis as required by the Regulatory Flexibility Act ("RFA"), 5 U.S.C. §§ 601 *et. seq.,* and that the NWPs violated the National Environmental Policy Act ("NEPA"), 42 U.S.C. §§ 4321 *et seq.,* because the Corps did not conduct a Programmatic Environmental Impact Statement. On February 15, 2001, all three sets of plaintiffs filed motions for summary judgment, and the defendants and intervenors responded with cross-motions for summary judgment on June 14, 2001. . . . While the parties' cross-motions for summary judgment were pending, on January 15, 2002, the Corps re-issued all existing NWPs and GCs with some modifications. *See* 67 Fed. Reg.2020 (Jan. 15, 2002).

DISCUSSION

Plaintiffs raise a myriad of challenges to the Corps' issuance of the replacement NWPs and GCs in 2000 and the re-issuance of the NWPs and General Conditions in 2002 and several underlying claims. The main claims, however, can be boiled down to the following: 1) that the Corps did not provide adequate notice and opportunity to comment before issuing the NWPs challenged by plaintiffs and that the NWPs and GCs are not the logical outgrowth of the proposals; 2) that the Corps acted arbitrarily and capriciously and abused its discretion in performing a regionalized analysis of the "minimal adverse environmental effects" the NWPs would have on the environment; 3) that the Corps did not provide a reasonable basis for the acreage limitations and pre-construction notification requirements for NWPs; 4) that the restrictions in the use of NWPs in the 100-year floodplains were arbitrary and capricious and are not consistent with the Corps' authority; 5) that the regulation of aggregate and hard rock/mineral mining as activities "similar in nature" is arbitrary and capricious; 6) that the Corps did not have the statutory authority to condition NWPs to assure protection of water quality; 7) that the utilization of vegetated buffers in mitigation as referenced in GC 19 is not reasonably related to the disposal of dredged and fill material and, therefore, is beyond the Corps' authority; and 8) that the issuance of NWP 29 is arbitrary and capricious. The Corps counters, in essence, that the issuance of the replacement NWPs and GCs and the re-issuance of the NWPs and GCs in 2002 were in accordance with Section 404 of the CWA, were proper under the APA, and were neither arbitrary and capricious, nor contrary to law. For the following reasons, the Court agrees with the Corps and GRANTS its motion for summary judgment.

[The court held that the Corps did provide adequate notice and opportunity to comment on NWP proposals before issuing the NWPs challenged by the plaintiffs and that the final NWPs were the logical outgrowth of the proposals.]

*II. The Corps Did Not Act Arbitrarily or Capriciously or Abuse Its Discretion in Performing a Regionalized Analysis of the "Minimal Adverse Environmental Effects" the NWPs Would Have on the Environment.*

Plaintiffs allege that the Corps acted arbitrarily and capriciously, and abused its discretion, in performing a regionalized analysis of the "minimal adverse environmental effects" the NWPs would have on the environment. The Corps argues that the NWPs and GCs issued by the Corps do not violate the APA in their regionalized analysis of the "minimal adverse environmental effects" and that the Corps did not violate the APA by not defining the term "minimal adverse environmental effects." For the following reasons, the Court agrees with the Corps that the NWPs and GCs do not violate the provisions of the APA.

A court must set aside an agency decision if it lacks "substantial evidence" in the record to support the conclusion. 5 U.S.C. § 706(2)(E); *AT&T Corp. v. FCC,* 86 F.3d 242, 247 (D.C. Cir. 1996). In deciding if there is "substantial evidence" in the record to support an agency's position, the Court's analysis is limited to determining whether the agency's decision was "rational and based on consideration of the relevant factors." *FCC v. Nat'l Citizens Comm. for Broad.,* 436 U.S. 775, 803 (1978). That said, an agency must provide a "clear and coherent explanation" for its ruling. *Cf. Tripoli Rocketry Ass'n, v. ATF,* 437 F.3d 75, 81 (D.C. Cir. 2006). Section 706 of the APA requires this Court to consider the administrative record in its entirety to determine the factors the agency considered in making its decision. 5 U.S.C. § 706; *see Citizens to Pres. Overton Park, Inc. v. Volpe*, 401 U.S. 402, 419–21 (1971). "To survive review under the 'arbitrary and capricious' standard, an agency must 'examine the relevant data and articulate a satisfactory explanation for its action including a rational connection between the facts found and the choice made.'" *PPL Wallingford Energy LLC v. FERC,* 419 F.3d 1194, 1198 (D.C. Cir. 2005) . . . However, the agency's decision need not be a "model of analytical precision," *Dickson v. Sec'y of Def.,* 68 F.3d 1396, 1404 (D.C. Cir. 1995), and the agency's decision will be upheld even if it is not ideally clear as long as the "agency's path may be reasonably be discerned," *id.* The agency's decision must contain "'a rational connection between the facts found and the choice made,'" *Motor Vehicle Mfrs.,* 463 U.S. at 43; yet, if the decision "merely parrots the language of the statute without providing an account of how it reached its results," then the agency has not provided an adequate explanation for its actions, *Dickson,* 68 F.3d at 1405.

The CWA was enacted in order to "restore and maintain the chemical, physical, and biological integrity of the Nation's waters." 33 U.S.C. § 1251(a). In passing the Act, Congress provided the Corps the ability to issue general, and individual permits, to parties to discharge pollutants, such as dredged or fill material, into navigable waters of the United States. *Id.* § 1344. However, the Corps can only issue general permits that "will cause only minimal adverse environmental effects when performed separately" or cumulatively. *Id.* § 1344(e)(1).

In the Corps' March 9, 2000 Final Notice that issued five new NWPs and two new GCs and modified six NWPs and nine GCs which were to replace NWP 26 when it expired, the Corps made it clear that it appreciated:

> that the terms and conditions of the new and modified NWPs may cause some activities with minimal adverse effects on the aquatic environment to be subject to the individual permit process. It is important to note that aquatic resource functions and values differ greatly across the country. When developing NWPs that have national applicability, there will be many parts of the country where the terms and limits of the NWPs will not authorize some activities that have minimal adverse effects on the aquatic environment.

65 Fed. Reg. at 12,820. Thus, it is clear from this statement that the Corps purposefully set the NWPs at a low level in order to err on the side of protecting the environment when allowing the discharge of pollutants into the navigable waters of the United States. This approach, although disagreeable to the plaintiffs, is not only natural, but reasonable in light of the industrial permit options available to those whose activities will have minimal adverse effects on the environment.

Indeed, in the January 15, 2002 Final Notice that re-issued all existing NWPs and GCs, modified some definitions, and issued one new GC, the Corps specifically stated as a part of its reasoning that because aquatic resources and values differ so greatly across the country, "minimal effects determinations for proposed NWP activities should be made at the local level by district engineers." 67 Fed. Reg. at 2027–28. Thus, the Corps, in essence, concluded that questions necessitating technical certainty should be developed at the local, not national, level.

By setting a baseline that is low and more protective of these waters against the discharge of pollutants, the Corps chose to protect the waters of the United States that are more sensitive to discharged pollutants than waters that are less affected by a similar discharge. This "path" is reasonably discernable from the final notices the Corps has issued. *See Dickson,* 68 F.3d at 1404; 65 Fed. Reg. 12,818 (Mar. 9, 2000); 67 Fed. Reg. 2020 (Jan. 15, 2002). Indeed, if the national baseline is not protective enough for certain areas, regional district engineers can "add special conditions to the NWP authorization to ensure that the activity results in no more than minimal adverse environmental effects." 67 Fed. Reg. at 2027; *see* 65 Fed. Reg. at 12, 821.

While the Corps acknowledges that the lower acreage limits and pre-construction notification thresholds may require "certain activities that were previously authorized by NWPs" to "require individual permits, and that it takes more time to authorize those activities," 67 Fed. Reg. at 2022, the limits and thresholds, as well as all the new or modified NWPs, were "necessary to ensure compliance with Section 404(e) of the Clean Water Act," *id.* The decision documents for each of the NWPs, which were issued on January 4, 2002, and are part of the administrative record, discuss the impacts that the activities governed by these NWPs and GCs will have on the environment and the associated aquatic life. The different activities authorized by the NWPs and the different conditions of the aquatic environment in the United States require rules that can account for the complexities of protecting the diverse aquatic environment of the United States. *See* 65 Fed. Reg. at 12,819 ("Some complexity is unavoidable because different activities in waters of the United States do not have the same effects on the aquatic environment and each NWP must have different conditions to address those dissimilar impacts.").

A review of the record makes it clear that the Corps has adequately explained its reasoning behind the issuance and re-issuance of the NWPs and GCs. While the Corps' reasoning may be unnecessarily lengthy, it is reasonable, supported by the facts, and its explanation clearly and adequately lays out the "path" of the Corps' logic and that logic has been adequately explained. *See Motor Vehicle Mfrs.,* 463 U.S. at 43 (quoting *Bowman Transp., Inc.,* 419 U.S. at 286); *Dickson,* 68 F.3d at 1404 (quoting *Bowman Transp., Inc.,* 419 U.S. at 286) Accordingly, this Court finds that the Corps did not act arbitrarily or capriciously, or abuse its discretion, in performing a regionalized analysis of the "minimal adverse environmental effects" the NWPs would have on the environment.

Plaintiffs also claim, in essence, that the Corps' failure to define the term "minimal adverse environmental effect" is arbitrary, capricious, and an abuse of discretion. Conversely, the Corps claims that it is not only not required to define this term, but that such a definition is impossible to determine on a national level due to the diversity of the aquatic environments of the waters of the United States. The Court agrees with the Corps. *See* 65 Fed. Reg. at 12,862–63. What is a minimally adverse environmental impact in Arizona, for example, will not be the same as the effect on the bayous of Louisiana. Thus, the Corps has reasonably articulated its reasoning behind the promulgation of the NWPs and the GCs and that reasoning is supported by the record. Therefore, the Corps is not required to define the term "minimal adverse environmental effect," and, thus, did not act arbitrarily or capriciously or contrary to law.

---

## QUESTIONS AND DISCUSSION

**1.** Why is the National Association of Home Builders, members of which are likely to use many of the Nationwide Permits the Corps promulgated, challenging the permits? Environmental interest groups also have problems with some of the Corps' general permits. *See, e.g.*, Black Warrior Riverkeeper v. U.S. Army Corps of Engineers, 781 F.3d 1271 (11th Cir. 2015) (finding general permit for coal mining operations invalid).

**2.** Although the NWPs are adopted by rulemaking, not by a permitting proceeding, notice that the court adopts roughly the same approach to judicial review and deference to the agency as the *Airport Communities* court did for an individual permit. The court in the NWPs case drove the point home in its explanation that to uphold the agency decision, the reviewing court must merely satisfy itself that the agency examined the relevant data and articulated a satisfactory explanation for its action, including a rational connection between the facts found and the choice made. Going further, the court added that the agency's decision need not be a "model of analytical precision," and will be upheld even if it is not ideally clear as long as the "agency's path may be reasonably be discerned."

**3.** Most litigation over general permits focuses on the two findings most statutes authorizing general permits require the agency make to issue them: that the general permit applies to actions that are similar in nature and will have only minimal separate and cumulative adverse effects. Usually challenges to general permits argue that the agency included actions that are not similar and that will have excessive impacts, whereas the litigation over the Corps' NWPs involved allegations that the Corps had been too restrictive in defining the availability of the general permits. Given the applicable standard of review and the "similar in nature" and "minimal effects" findings that support general permitting, how likely was it that the court would overturn the NWPs for being too limited in scope? For a thorough review of general permitting programs, focusing in detail on the Corps' Section 404 program, see Eric Biber & J.B. Ruhl, *The Permit Power Revisited: The Theory and Practice of Regulatory Permits in the Administrative State*, 64 DUKE L.J. 133, 150 (2014).

4. There has been considerable effort by federal and many state environmental agencies in recent years to cut out the red tape and unnecessary process of individual permitting while retaining the particularized focus that is lost in general permitting. Many times this "streamlining" is focused on reducing the time and expense needed to complete the permitting process, with no changes to the substance or procedure of permitting. For example, the Massachusetts Department of Environmental Protection embarked on such an effort in 2007:

> MassDEP's 2007 Permit Efficiency Initiatives
>
> The Massachusetts Department of Environmental Protection is committed to focusing on protecting the environment. To achieve the goal of speeding regulatory decisions while ensuring that strict environmental standards are upheld, MassDEP has launched the following initiatives:
>
> Reduction of Permit Timelines: In February 2007, MassDEP proposed regulations that will reduce timelines for the majority of its permit categories by 20%. MassDEP has also committed to issuing 90% of all permit decisions in 180 days or less. These proposed regulations will be available for public review and comment in March and April 2007. (Draft regulations/hearings for draft Timely Action & Fees Regs).
>
> Specific Permit Categories Targeted for Streamlining Opportunities: MassDEP has targeted three permit categories for detailed analysis to identify ways to shorten the decision time. These permit categories were selected for in-depth review because they are generally associated with significant economic development opportunities, have a history of customer concerns about decision delays, are relatively high-volume, and more than 20% of the permit decisions exceed the 180 day goal. The three permit categories are:
>
> > Air Quality Permits—Air quality permits, particularly those referred to as "non-major" comprehensive plan approvals, which are commonly required for new or expanded business activities. These permits also require a resource intensive "Best Available Control Technology" (BACT) analysis. The initial focus will be on energy-related projects followed by a more inclusive review of other business activities. Learn more. . . .
> >
> > Chapter 91 Licenses for Land-Based Development Projects—Permits for non-water dependent developments in filled or flowed tidelands (Chapter 91 Licenses).
> >
> > Permits for Groundwater Discharge of Wastewater—Permits for groundwater discharge of wastewater for major new and/or expanded development projects.
>
> Streamlining of the Adjudicatory Appeals Process: MassDEP is proposing to further streamline its adjudicatory appeals process, building on its efforts in 2005 & 2007 to institute an effective

> appeals prescreening program. This next phase is a two-part strategy that will streamline processing of cases currently in the system and create a revised intake for new appeals. As part of this effort, MassDEP has re-convened its Appeals Advisory Stakeholder Group to seek input on potential streamlining for appeals of wetlands decisions, enforcement actions, and other permits.

MassDEP, Service Center, Permitting Efficiencies: More Protection, Less Process (2007).

# CHAPTER 10

# COMPLIANCE COUNSELING

## CHAPTER OUTLINE



---

The practice of law is about far more than knowing the law. Mastering every nuance of the myriad of statutory, regulatory, and judicial entries in the field of environmental law would not, by itself, fully equip one to evaluate the compliance status and options of a particular activity. As two veteran government environmental lawyers have observed, "knowing what constitutes the rule of law and whether a particular rule applies to a given situation provides most billable hours. Current U.S. law school curriculum trains lawyers in this analysis quite well." Paul B. Smyth and Milo C. Mason, *Making Tough Choices Easier: Compliance and Enforcement 102*, NATURAL RESOURCES & ENV'T, Spring 2004, at 3, 9. But they go on to explain the difficult aspects of what many environmental lawyers get paid "the big bucks" to do—compliance counseling:

> Lawyers are constantly put on the spot to explain not only what the law is, but why or whether it is important to comply. Counseling roguish clients on what constitutes the rule of law, say 55 parts per million or 55 mph, and why one must comply can get quite tricky. Yet the question of compliance is at the heart of our legal system, our civil peace, and the sense of a just society. It is as important, if not more so, as teaching the nuts and bolts of what constitutes the law, although few, if any, of our law schools teach even one course in what causes compliance

with the rule of law. Law schools need to teach courses in the reason for the rule of law and compliance theory. We lawyers need to be perceived as compliance counselors, not as mainly noncompliance counselors.

While this chapter cannot fulfill all of what Smyth and Mason hope for, it is designed to introduce the topic of compliance counseling in its practical dimensions. Part I of the chapter explores the difficulties of knowing what the law is given the challenges involved in statutory and regulatory interpretation. Assuming one gains confidence about the proper interpretation of the law, the next task is applying it to the dynamic sets of facts different clients present in different stages of compliance. Part II of the chapter thus walks through different roles the compliance counselor is asked to assume in the planning, monitoring, and disclosure of compliance performance. Part III closes the discussion with a survey of different compliance strategies government agencies and private companies have devised to facilitate compliance.

## I. INTERPRETING STATUTES AND REGULATIONS

As you have no doubt noticed, much of today's environmental law is the result of statutes enacted by Congress, state legislatures, city councils, and other legislative bodies. These statutes, in turn, empower administrative agencies to promulgate detailed regulations further prescribing conduct that affects the environment. Like other written documents, statutes and regulations require interpretation. Congress may have had one problem in mind when it enacted a statute, only to have an entirely new issue later arise that may or may not fall within the scope of the law. Or the words that the legislature writes into a statute may be ambiguous, vague, confusing, or contrary to what the legislature was really trying to do. Or the different parties affected by a statute may simply have strikingly distinct views of what the statute requires. In each instance, the statute must be interpreted.

Debates about theories of statutory interpretation have flourished in recent years. Most observers trace the increased interest in the topic to Justice Scalia, who has advocated a textualist theory that emphasizes the plain meaning of the statutory text. *See* ANTONIN SCALIA & BRIAN GARDNER, READING LAW: THE INTERPRETATION OF LEGAL TEXTS (2012); ANTONIN SCALIA, A MATTER OF INTERPRETATION (1997). The traditional view posits that what the enacting (*i.e.*, original) legislature wanted is key to statutory interpretation. There are three originalist theories of statutory interpretation: intentionalism, purposivism, and textualism. *Intentionalism* looks to the intent of the legislature that enacted the statute. That could mean the actual intent of the legislature (which asks what the enacting legislature had in mind, and often relies upon evidence from the bill's sponsors, reviewing committees, or other legislative leaders), or imaginative reconstruction (which asks how the enacting legislature would have decided a specific question). *Purposivism*, in turn, inquires more broadly into the purposes of the legislature that enacted the statute, and seeks to interpret the statute to best achieve those purposes. *Textualism* claims that the statutory text controls both because that is what the legislators actually voted on and because the subjective intent of the legislature is impossible to ascertain. As Justice Holmes once put it, "we ask what the law means, not what the legislature intended." Oliver Wendell Holmes, *The Theory of Legal Interpretation*, 12 HARV. L. REV. 417, 419 (1899). Textualism relies upon dictionaries, grammatical presumptions, structural arguments, and substantive canons to help understand the meaning of the statutory text. Each of these originalist theories—and especially textualism—face a variety of criticisms. Numerous scholars and some judges object that statutory texts do not yield objective and determinate answers because words lack meaning until interpreted, and they contend that current values are useful in interpreting the current application of statutes whenever they were enacted.

The doctrines of statutory interpretation move from theory to specific rules for deciding cases. The accepted doctrines include textual canons, such as rules of grammar, punctuation and structure; substantive canons, which establish presumptions about statutory meaning based upon particular policies; evidence of statutory context, such as the placement of a provision within a broader statute or the relationship to analogous statutes; evidence of historical context, which can be drawn from the common law or the debates and committee reports comprising a statute's formal legislative history. *See generally* NORMAN J. SINGER, SUTHERLAND ON STATUTES AND STATUTORY CONSTRUCTION (6th ed. 2000) (the four volume treatise that is the best source detailing all of the doctrines).

---

## A. OVERVIEW OF STATUTORY INTERPRETATION

### BedRoc Limited, LLC v. United States

Supreme Court of the United States, 2004.
541 U.S. 176.

■ CHIEF JUSTICE REHNQUIST announced the judgment of the Court and delivered an opinion, in which JUSTICE O'CONNOR, JUSTICE SCALIA, and JUSTICE KENNEDY join.

The question here is whether sand and gravel are "valuable minerals" reserved to the United States in land grants issued under the Pittman Underground Water Act of 1919 (Pittman Act or Act), ch. 77, 41 Stat. 293. We hold they are not.

Beginning with the Homestead Act of 1862, ch. 75, 12 Stat. 392, and stretching into the early 20th century, Congress enacted a series of land-grant statutes aimed at settling the American frontier. One of these was the Pittman Act. That Act sought to succeed where earlier homestead laws had failed: promoting development and population growth in the State of Nevada. H. R. Rep. No. 286, 66th Cong., 1st Sess., 2 (1919). It was thought that Nevada's lack of surface water resources was hindering its agricultural progress. After rejecting various proposals to directly fund exploration for underground water, Congress enacted the Pittman Act to encourage private citizens to prospect for water in Nevada.

Nevada lies in the heart of the Great Basin, that part of the United States lying roughly between the Sierra Nevada Range on the west and the Wasatch and other mountain ranges on the east. The western face of the Sierra Nevada blocks rain-bearing winds off the Pacific Ocean from reaching the Great Basin, forming a rain shadow over the entire region. Nevada has, on the average, less precipitation than any other State in the Union. This is one reason why most of its rivers, instead of eventually flowing into the sea, disappear into "sinks."

The Pittman Act authorized the Secretary of the Interior to designate certain "nonmineral" lands[2] in Nevada, on which settlers could obtain permits to drill for water. §§ 1–2, 41 Stat. 293–294. Any settler who could demonstrate successful irrigation of at least 20 acres of crops was eligible for a land grant, or patent, of up to 640 acres. § 5, *id.,* at 294. Of central importance here, each patent issued under the Act was required to contain "a reservation to the United States of all the coal and other valuable minerals in the lands . . . , together with the right to prospect for, mine and remove the same." § 8, *id.,* at 295. By virtue of this reservation, the United States was free to dispose of the "coal and other valuable mineral deposits in such lands" in accordance with "the provisions of the coal and mineral land laws in force at the time of such disposal." *Ibid.*

The Pittman Act failed to significantly advance agricultural development in Nevada, and Congress repealed it in 1964. The repealing legislation, however, expressly reserved the rights of existing patentees.

Two such patentees, Newton and Mabel Butler, were the predecessors-in-interest of the petitioners in this case. In 1940, the Butlers obtained a patent for 560 acres of land in Lincoln County, some 65 miles north of Las Vegas. As required by the Act, the patent reserved the "coal and other valuable minerals" to the United States. Common sand and gravel were plentiful and visible on the surface of the Butlers' land, but there was no commercial market for them due to Nevada's sparse population and the land's remote location.

Earl Williams acquired the Butler property in 1993. By that time, the expansion of Las Vegas had created a commercial market for the sand and gravel on the land. Shortly after Williams began extracting the sand and gravel, however, the Bureau of Land Management (BLM) served him

[2] "Nonmineral" lands are "more valuable for agricultural or other purposes than for the minerals [they] contai[n]." Watt v. Western Nuclear, Inc., 462 U.S. 36, 48, n.9 (1983).

with trespass notices pursuant to 43 CFR § 9239.0–7 (1993) (providing that any unauthorized removal of "mineral materials" from public lands is "an act of trespass"). When Williams challenged the notices, the BLM ruled that by removing sand and gravel Williams had trespassed against the Government's reserved interest in the "valuable minerals" on the property. The Interior Board of Land Appeals affirmed that decision. Earl Williams, 140 IBLA 295 (1997). Meanwhile, petitioner BedRoc Limited, LLC (BedRoc), acquired the Butler property from Williams in 1995. BedRoc continued to remove sand and gravel under an interim agreement with the Department of the Interior, pending final resolution of the ownership dispute.

Petitioners filed an action in the United States District Court seeking to quiet title to the sand and gravel on the Butler property. The District Court granted summary judgment to the Government, holding that the contested sand and gravel are "valuable minerals" reserved to the United States by the Pittman Act. 50 F. Supp. 2d 1001 (Nev. 1999). The United States Court of Appeals for the Ninth Circuit affirmed, relying primarily on the legislative history of the Pittman Act and our decision in Watt v. Western Nuclear, Inc., 462 U.S. 36 (1983). We granted certiorari, and now reverse.

In *Western Nuclear, supra*, we construed the mineral reservation in the Stock-Raising Homestead Act of 1916 (SRHA), 39 Stat. 862, 43 U.S.C. § 291 et seq.—"the most important . . . land-grant statut[e] enacted in the early 1900's." 462 U.S. at 47. Unlike the Pittman Act, the SRHA was not limited to Nevada; it applied to any "public lands" the Secretary of the Interior designated as " 'stock-raising lands.' " 43 U.S.C. § 291 (1976 ed.) (repealed by Pub. L. 94–579, 90 Stat. 2787). A person could obtain a patent under the SRHA if he resided on stock-raising lands for three years, and "ma[de] permanent improvements upon the land . . . tending to increase the value of the [land] for stock-raising purposes," § 293 (repealed by Pub. L. 94–579, 90 Stat. 2787). The SRHA's mineral reservation was identical to the Pittman Act's in every respect, save one: Whereas the SRHA reserved to the United States "all the coal and other minerals," § 299 (2000 ed.), the Pittman Act reserved "all the coal and other *valuable* minerals," § 8, 41 Stat. 295 (emphasis added).

The question before us in *Western Nuclear* was "whether gravel found on lands patented under the [SRHA] is a mineral reserved to the United States." 462 U.S. at 38. A closely divided Court held that it is. After determining that "neither the dictionary nor the legal understanding of the term 'minerals' that prevailed in 1916 sheds much light on the question before us," we turned to the purpose and history of the SRHA. 462 U.S. at 46–47. We observed that the SRHA, like other land-grant Acts containing mineral reservations, sought to "facilitate development of both surface and subsurface resources." 462 U.S. at 49–52. We therefore reasoned that "the determination of whether a particular substance is included in the surface estate or the mineral estate should be made in light of the use of the surface estate that Congress contemplated." 462 U.S. at 52. Accordingly, we interpreted the SRHA's mineral reservation to include "substances that are mineral in character (*i.e.*, that are inorganic), that can be removed from the soil, that can be used for commercial purposes, and that there is no reason to suppose were intended to be included in the surface estate." 462 U.S. at 53. Because we thought it unlikely that Congress would have made the exploitation of gravel deposits dependent on farmers and ranchers "whose interests were known to lie elsewhere," and because gravel met our other criteria, we concluded that it is indeed a "mineral" reserved to the United States. 462 U.S. at 55–60.[4]

The Government argues that our rationale in *Western Nuclear* compels the outcome in this case, notwithstanding the Pittman Act's seemingly narrower reservation of "valuable" minerals. Petitioners, for their part, argue that *Western Nuclear* should be distinguished on this ground or, in the alternative, overruled altogether. While we share the concerns expressed in the *Western Nuclear* dissent, we decline to overrule our recent precedent. By the same token, we will not extend *Western Nuclear*'s holding to conclude that sand and gravel are "*valuable* minerals."

Whatever the correctness of *Western Nuclear*'s broad construction of the term "minerals," we are not free to so expansively interpret the Pittman Act's reservation. In *Western Nuclear*, we had no choice but to speculate about congressional intent with respect to the scope of the amorphous term "minerals." Here, by contrast, Congress has textually narrowed the scope of the term by using the modifier "valuable."

The preeminent canon of statutory interpretation requires us to "presume that [the] legislature says in a statute what it means and means in a statute what it says there." Connecticut Nat. Bank v. Germain, 503 U.S. 249, 253–254 (1992). Thus, our inquiry begins with the statutory text, and ends there as well if the text is unambiguous. We think the term "valuable" makes clear that Congress did not intend to include sand and gravel in the Pittman Act's mineral reservation.

"In interpreting statutory mineral reservations like the one at issue here, we have emphasized that Congress 'was dealing with a practical subject in a practical way' and that it intended the terms of the reservation to be understood in 'their ordinary and popular sense.'" Amoco Production Co. v. Southern Ute Tribe, 526 U.S. 865, 873 (1999) (quoting Burke v. Southern Pacific R. Co., 234 U.S. 669, 679 (1914)).

---

[4] Four Justices vigorously disagreed with the Court's approach. 462 U.S. at 60–72 (Powell, J., joined by Rehnquist, Stevens, and O'Connor, JJ., dissenting). The dissenters pointed out that at the time the SRHA was enacted the Department of the Interior "had ruled consistently that gravel was not a mineral under the general mining laws." 462 U.S. at 62–67. Furthermore, the ultimate congressional purpose behind the SRHA was settling the West, not stockraising, the dissenters argued, and this purpose would have been thwarted if potential settlers thought the Government had reserved "commonplace substances that actually constitute much of the soil." 462 U.S. at 71–72.

Importantly, the proper inquiry focuses on the ordinary meaning of the reservation at the time Congress enacted it. *Amoco Production Co., supra*, 526 U.S. at 874; Leo Sheep Co. v. United States, 440 U.S. 668, 682 (1979) (land-grant statutes should be interpreted in light of "the condition of the country when the acts were passed" (internal quotation marks omitted)); *see also* Perrin v. United States, 444 U.S. 37, 42 (1979) ("[U]nless otherwise defined, words will be interpreted as taking their ordinary, contemporary, common meaning" at the time Congress enacted the statute). Because the Pittman Act applied only to Nevada, the ultimate question is whether the sand and gravel found in Nevada were commonly regarded as "valuable minerals" in 1919.

Common sense tells us, and the Government does not contest, that the answer to that question is an emphatic "No." Sand and gravel were, and are, abundant throughout Nevada; they have no intrinsic value; and they were commercially worthless in 1919 due to Nevada's sparse population and lack of development.[6] Thus, even if Nevada's sand and gravel were regarded as minerals, no one would have mistaken them for *valuable* minerals. The Government argues only that sand and gravel were commercially marketable in other parts of the United States during World War I and that there is now a market for sand and gravel in some parts of Nevada. As we have explained, this evidence is simply irrelevant to the proper inquiry into the meaning of the statutory mineral reservation. *Cf. Amoco Production Co.*, 526 U.S. at 873–880 (relying on the popular meaning of "coal" in 1909 and 1910 to hold that a reservation of "coal" does not include coalbed methane gas). Because we readily conclude that the "most natural interpretation" of the mineral reservation does not encompass sand and gravel, we "need not consider the applicability of the canon that ambiguities in land grants are construed in favor of the sovereign." 526 U.S. at 880.

The statutory context of the Pittman Act's mineral reservation further confirms its ordinary meaning. The sentence directly following the reservation provides that the reserved "valuable mineral deposits . . . shall be subject to disposal by the United States in accordance with the provisions of the . . . mineral land laws in force at the time of such disposal." § 8, 41 Stat. 295. Here, Congress was explicitly cross-referencing the General Mining Act of 1872. Then, as now, the General Mining Act provided that "all valuable mineral deposits in lands belonging to the United States . . . shall be free and open to exploration and purchase . . . under regulations prescribed by law." We can therefore infer that the reserved "valuable minerals" in Pittman Act lands were the same class of minerals that could be located and disposed of under the General Mining Act.

It is beyond dispute that when the Pittman Act became law in 1919, common sand and gravel could not constitute a locatable "valuable

[6] Indeed, as petitioners aptly point out, "[e]ven the most enterprising settler could not have sold sand in the desert."

mineral deposit" under the General Mining Act. . . . Thus, in the unlikely event that some ambitious prospector had sought a patent from the United States in 1919 to extract sand and gravel from Pittman Act lands, the Secretary of the Interior would have flatly refused him. . . .

Notwithstanding the contemporaneous plain meaning of the Pittman Act's mineral reservation, the Government argues that the Act's legislative history counsels us to give "valuable minerals" precisely the same meaning we ascribed to "minerals" in *Western Nuclear*. Because we have held that the text of the statutory reservation clearly excludes sand and gravel, we have no occasion to resort to legislative history. Having declined to extend *Western Nuclear*'s rationale to a statute where the plain meaning will not support it, we will not allow it in through the back door by presuming that "the legislature was ignorant of the meaning of the language it employed." Montclair v. Ramsdell, 107 U.S. 147, 152 (1883).[8]

The judgment of the United States Court of Appeals for the Ninth Circuit is therefore reversed, and the case is remanded for further proceedings.

■ JUSTICE THOMAS, with whom JUSTICE BREYER joins, concurring in the judgment.

I agree with Justice Stevens that the mineral reservation provision in the Pittman Underground Water Act of 1919 (Pittman Act or Act) cannot be meaningfully distinguished from the analogous provision in the Stock-Raising Homestead Act of 1916 (SRHA). As Justice Stevens points out, the term "minerals" in the Pittman Act provision is only twice modified by the adjective "valuable," which "suggest[s] that the terms 'valuable minerals' and 'minerals' were intended to be synonymous." I concur in the judgment, however, because I believe that mineral reservations pursuant to both the Pittman Act and the SRHA do not include sand and gravel. . . .

Although the Court in *Western Nuclear* incorrectly applied its definition of "minerals" to include sand and gravel, the Court is typically reluctant to overrule decisions involving statute interpretation because

---

[8] While Justice Stevens does not contest the plain meaning of the Pittman Act's mineral reservation, he nonetheless takes us to task for "refusing to examine" the legislative history proffered by the Government and thereby engaging in a "deliberately uninformed" and "unconstrained" method of statutory interpretation. Of course, accepting Justice Stevens' approach would require a radical abandonment of our longstanding precedents that permit resort to legislative history only when necessary to interpret ambiguous statutory text. Chief Justice Marshall in 1805 stated the principle that definitively resolves this case nearly 200 years later: "Where a law is plain and unambiguous, whether it be expressed in general or limited terms, the legislature should be intended to mean what they have plainly expressed, and consequently no room is left for construction." United States v. Fisher, 6 U.S. 358, 2 Cranch 358, 399. We thus cannot accept Justice Stevens' invitation to presume that Congress expressed itself in a single House Committee Report rather than in the unambiguous statutory text approved by both Houses and signed by the President. We fail to see, moreover, how a court exercises unconstrained discretion when it carries out its "sole function" with respect to an unambiguous statute, namely, to "enforce it according to its terms." Caminetti v. United States, 242 U.S. 470, 485 (1917).

"*stare decisis* concerns are at their acme in cases involving property and contract rights." State Oil Co. v. Khan, 522 U.S. 3, 20 (1997). Because the Government identifies significant reliance interests that would be upset by overruling *Western Nuclear*, I do not advocate doing so. The Pittman Act, however, involves substantially less land than the SRHA, and the Government does not identify any significant reliance interests that would be unsettled by our failing to extend *Western Nuclear*'s reasoning. I would therefore reverse the judgment of the Court of Appeals and decline to extend *Western Nuclear*'s faulty reasoning beyond the SRHA.

■ JUSTICE STEVENS, with whom JUSTICE SOUTER and JUSTICE GINSBURG join, dissenting.

. . . Today the Court decides that the reservation of minerals in § 8 of the Pittman Act does not include gravel. I think it highly unlikely that Congress would reserve its ownership of sand and gravel in the millions of acres of land in the West that were covered by the SRHA and not do so for the land in Nevada covered by the Pittman Act. Indeed, the House Committee Report describing the scope of the mineral reservation in § 8 of the Pittman Act plainly states: "Section 8 of the bill contains the same reservations of minerals, with the facility for prospecting for and developing and mining such minerals as was provided in the [SRHA]." *Ibid.* A clearer expression of Congress' intent would be hard to find.

The plurality opinion rests entirely on the textual difference between the SRHA's reservation of " 'all the coal and other minerals' " and the Pittman Act's reservation of " 'all the coal and other *valuable* minerals.' " But that holding ignores the fact that in *Western Nuclear* the Court's interpretation of the term "mineral" in the SRHA included the requirement that the material be valuable. Moreover, the term "mineral" or "minerals" appears eight times in § 8 of the Pittman Act, and only twice is it modified by the adjective "valuable," strongly suggesting that the terms "valuable minerals" and "minerals" were intended to be synonymous. Thus, the text of § 8 and its legislative history, as well as both the reasoning and the result in *Western Nuclear*, all support the conclusion that Congress intended the mineral reservation in these two statutes to be the same. The single word "valuable," in short, cannot support the weight the Chief Justice places on it.

As a matter of public policy, there is no reason why Congress would enact a broader reservation in either statute. The policy of including sand and gravel in the reservation may well be unwise, and, indeed, the majority in *Western Nuclear* may have misinterpreted Congress' intent in 1916. Neither of those possibilities, however, provides an adequate justification for substituting the plurality's appraisal today of Congress' judgment for the view that prevailed in a decision that has been settled law for two decades. This conclusion is fortified by the well-recognized "need for certainty and predictability where land titles are concerned." Leo Sheep Co. v. United States, 440 U.S. 668, 687 (1979).

In refusing to examine the legislative history that provides a clear answer to the question whether Congress intended the scope of the mineral reservations in these two statutes to be identical, the plurality abandons one of the most valuable tools of judicial decisionmaking. As Justice Aharon Barak of the Israel Supreme Court perceptively has explained, the "minimalist" judge "who holds that the purpose of the statute may be learned only from its language" retains greater discretion than the judge who "will seek guidance from every reliable source." Judicial Discretion 62 (Y. Kaufmann transl. 1989). A method of statutory interpretation that is deliberately uninformed, and hence unconstrained, increases the risk that the judge's own policy preferences will affect the decisional process. The policy choice at issue in this case is surely one that should be made either by Congress itself or by the executive agency administering the Pittman Act. Congress' acceptance of the holding in *Western Nuclear* for the past two decades should control our decision, and any residual doubt should be eliminated by the deference owed to the executive agency that has consistently construed the mineral reservations in land grant statutes as including sand and gravel.

Accordingly, I respectfully dissent.

---

## QUESTIONS AND DISCUSSION

**1.** What is the correct interpretation of Section 8 of the Pittman Act? How do you know? Why do Chief Justice Rehnquist and Justice Stevens interpret the statute in different ways?

**2.** Which doctrines of statutory interpretation did the various members of the Court rely upon in *BedRoc Limited*?

**3.** Environmental law offers abundant examples of the application of contested understandings of statutory interpretation. Two of the most famous statutory interpretation cases involve the Endangered Species Act and are contained in Chapter 2 above. In Tennessee Valley Authority v. Hill, 437 U.S. 153 (1978), a majority of the Court followed the plain meaning of the ESA and held that the Tellico Dam could not be completed because it would cause the extinction of the snail darter. *But see* RONALD DWORKIN, LAW'S EMPIRE 317–54 (1986) (concluding that "the statute [is] unclear about projects already begun because it strikes many people as silly that so much money should be wasted to save an unappealing and scientifically unimportant species"). Seventeen years later, the members of the Court again disagreed about the interpretation of the ESA in Babbitt v. Sweet Home Chapter of Communities for a Great Oregon, 515 U.S. 687 (1995). What are the different sources of statutory meaning that the majority, concurrence, and dissent consulted to understand the ESA's terms "take" and "harm" in *Sweet Home*?

Another famous statutory interpretation case considers federal mineral rights such as those at issue in *BedRoc Limited*. In United States v. Locke, 471 U.S. 84 (1985), the Court interpreted the Federal Land Policy and

Management Act's (FLPMA) requirement that the holders of certain mining claims on federal land must file documents with the federal Bureau of Land Management (BLM) "prior to December 31" each year. 43 U.S.C. § 1744(c). The Locke family had held mining claims since the 1950s, but when a local BLM employee told their daughter that the papers had to be filed *by* December 31, they filed their claim on December 31. BLM refused to accept the papers as untimely, so the Lockes lost their claim and sued. The Court ruled for the government. Justice Marshall observed that filing deadlines must be read literally. He explained that "deference to the supremacy of the Legislature, as well as recognition that Congressmen typically vote on the language of a bill, generally requires us to assume that 'the legislative purpose is expressed by the ordinary meaning of the words used.'" *Id.* at 95 (quoting Richards v. United States, 369 U.S. 1, 9 (1962)). Moreover, looking for the actual congressional intent would be futile because Congress could have chosen any date. Justice Stevens, by contrast, believed that Congress simply meant to require the filing by "the end of the year." Justice Stevens also pointed to the other drafting errors contained in FLPMA as evidence that the statute need not always be interpreted literally. *See id.* at 117–18 (Stevens, J., dissenting).

What is the proper interpretation of FLPMA's deadline? The leading statutory interpretation casebook claims that "this is the quintessential trap for the unwary, since it seems wholly illogical to require someone to file something, under severe penalty for default, the day *before* the last day of the year." WILLIAM N. ESKRIDGE, JR., PHILIP P. FRICKEY & ELIZABETH GARRETT, CASES AND MATERIALS ON LEGISLATION: STATUTES AND THE CREATION OF PUBLIC POLICY 705 (3d ed. 2001). But could Congress have wanted to require the filing before New Year's Eve, when many government employees take the day off? Hundreds of federal and state statutes require certain actions "prior to December 31." *See, e.g.*, Cal. Food & Agr. Code § 599 (providing that new agricultural chemical reduction pilot demonstration projects "may not be commenced *on or after* December 31, 2010") (emphasis added); Fla. Stat. § 316.6145(1)(a) (providing that new school buses purchased "after December 31, 2000" must have seat belts, while new school buses purchased "prior to December 31, 2000" need not have seat belts). Is there a difference between those provisions?

The other issue in *Locke* was the extent to which the Lockes should have relied upon the (erroneous?) advice of the BLM employee. Generally, the courts are reluctant to hold that the conduct of an individual government employee estops the government from acting. In *Locke*, Justice Marshall noted that the Court need not reach the estoppel question. *Locke*, 471 U.S. at 73 n.7. But on remand, the government settled the case and allowed the Lockes to keep their claims. See Lawrence M. Solum, *Learning our Limits: The Decline of Textualism in Statutory Cases*, 1997 WIS. L. REV. 235, 242 (citing an interview with the attorney who represented the Lockes).

**4.** State courts confront many statutory interpretation problems as well. In Alaska Center for the Environment v. Alaska Department of Fish and Game, 95 P.3d 924 (Alaska 2004), the Alaska Supreme Court revisited the same distinction between ordinary meaning and technical meaning that the

U.S. Supreme Court considered in *BedRoc Limited*. The question addressed by the Alaska court was whether the Cook Inlet Beluga whale was a distinct subspecies that could be listed under the state's endangered species act. The state Commissioner of Fish and Game read the state's law to require that a "subspecies" be recognized by "formal taxonomic classifications accepted in the published literature." *Id.* at 931. The court disagreed:

> The commissioner's reliance on this narrow definition is problematic, since it conflicts with the legislature's intent to use "species" and "subspecies" as they are commonly understood. The narrow "technical" meaning of these words may well be the one commonly applied by scientists engaged in taxonomy—a scientific discipline devoted to the systematic classification of plants and animals. But we doubt that scientists working outside the specialized realm of taxonomy—particularly those engaged in actively developing areas of biological study involving fish and wildlife management—would commonly restrict these words to the narrow meanings taxonomists agree to give them in published articles. Nor does it seem realistic to assume that the Alaska Legislature chose to assign these words such a static and constricted "technical meaning" when it adopted the act. After all, the act's stated purpose is to establish a program that will effectively protect fish and wildlife against dynamic new threats of extinction—new dangers attributable "to growth and development." It seems unlikely that the legislature could have expected the act to function effectively in averting such threats if the act protected "species" or "subspecies" of fish and wildlife only after they gained formal recognition by an isolated scientific discipline that devotes itself to abstract "technical" matters of classification that are largely unrelated to fish and game management.

*Id.* How would you interpret the term "subspecies" in a state endangered species law?

**5.** Justice Thomas was unwilling to overrule *Western Nuclear* because of general judicial reluctance to overrule prior interpretations of a statute. Why should statutory precedents be entitled to greater respect than, say, constitutional decisions? Should it matter whether the Supreme Court is considering one of its previous decisions, as opposed to the authority that stare decisis should receive from a lower federal court considering one of its previous decisions? *See generally* Amy Coney Barrett, *Statutory Stare Decisis in the Courts of Appeals*, 73 GEO. WASH. L. REV. 317 (2005) (arguing that the justifications for stare decisis do not apply to federal courts of appeals).

**6.** Justice Stevens draws support from his interpretive theory from Israeli Supreme Court Justice Aharon Barak. Should the views of foreign judges be relevant to statutory interpretation in the United States? Citations to foreign law have both increased and become controversial in recent years, especially in federal constitutional cases. *Compare, e.g.*, Roper v. Simmons, 543 U.S. 551 (2005) (consulting foreign laws when interpreting the eighth amendment); *with id.* at 622–28 (Scalia, J., dissenting) (objecting to reliance on foreign sources).

---

## B. A GREEN CANON OF STATUTORY INTERPRETATION

### Daniel A. Farber, *Eco-pragmatism*

Pages 124–127 (University of Chicago Press, 1999).

In interpreting statutes today, courts apply a number of "canons" of interpretation: for instance, that waivers of sovereign immunity must be express and that ambiguous criminal statutes are construed in favor of the defendant. But there is no particular canon dealing with environmental issues. The hybrid approach would suggest interpreting ambiguous statutes to cover significant environmental risks (with an escape hatch for infeasibility). Should such a "green" canon be recognized?

Statutory interpretation, as a topic, is the subject of vigorous scholarly and judicial debate. In general, there seem to be three basic positions current in the literature. First, the conventional view is that judges should attempt to apply statutes in accordance with the legislative intent. (The whole concept of legislative intent is itself subject to vigorous attack, based largely on skepticism about whether groups of legislators share a coherent, let alone public-spirited, set of intentions. Nevertheless, this approach still has its adherents.) Second, advocates of dynamic interpretation believe that judges should apply evolving public values when interpreting statutes. Advocates of this perspective also call on courts to use their rulings to improve the deliberative aspects of the legislative process. Third, formalists such as Justice Scalia argue that interpretation should be based not on current values or legislative intentions, but on the language actually enacted by the legislature, construed in light of general rules and canons of interpretation. Although the question is obviously a complex one, under each of these three views there is an argument to be made in favor of a green canon of interpretation.

The argument is straightforward in terms of the "legislative intent" approach. One justification for canons of interpretation is that they mirror the likely intentions of the legislature. Courts assume that the legislature would have been explicit if it had wanted to deviate sharply from well-established legal principles. After all, legislators are likely to share in the general acceptance of those principles, at least to the extent that a decision to deviate would be hotly debated. Even critics who believe that Congress has been unduly responsive to environmental concerns, despite their normative qualms, are endorsing the empirical proposition that this is indeed what Congress often intended. Thus, given the frequency with which Congress has applied some form of the hybrid approach, it seems plausible to assume that this was the legislative intent in a given case even if the language used is somewhat ambiguous.

In terms of dynamic interpretation, the argument is also straightforward, at least if we assume that judges are supposed to look to evolving community norms rather than their own personal preferences when construing statutes. For, as I have argued, the environmentalist baseline is clear and well established. As the community's considered judgment, reached after considerable political deliberation, this norm is well deserving of judicial respect. Moreover, forcing Congress to be explicit when it wishes to depart from the prevailing baseline has the advantage of making it more politically accountable and less prone to behind-the-scenes manipulation by private interest.

Perhaps more surprisingly, there is also a formalist argument for a green canon. The argument is grounded on the National Environmental Policy Act (NEPA), the statute that mandates environmental impact statements. Although the statute is best known for that mandate, it also contains other provisions, including a broad statement of environmental policy. NEPA calls on the government to use "all practicable means, consistent with essential considerations of national policy." to achieve a list of environmental goals. These goals include directives to "fulfill the responsibilities of each generation as trustee of the environment for succeeding generations" and to "assure for all Americans safe, healthful, productive, and esthetically and culturally pleasing surroundings." The statute also declares the "critical importance of restoring and maintaining environmental quality to the overall welfare and development of man." The Supreme Court has ruled that a court has no power to review whether a particular agency action comports with these policies, assuming a valid impact statement exists. Nevertheless, there is a strong argument in favor of applying these policies to the interpretation of ambiguous statutes.

For a formalist, statutory text is the decisive consideration. NEPA itself expressly establishes a canon of statutory interpretation. Section 102(1) contains the following unmistakable mandate: "The Congress authorizes and directs that, to the fullest extent possible (1) the policies, regulations and public laws of the United States shall be interpreted and administered in accordance with the policies set forth in this chapter." If this language is not clear enough to establish a canon of interpretation, it is hard to imagine what would be required to do so. Note that this mandate has two parts—it endorses environmentalist goals, but subjects them to a qualification ("to the fullest extent possible"). This language seems virtually identical with the hybrid approach that I have endorsed in this chapter.

Thus, regardless of whether we think judges should implement legislative intent, evolving community values, or textual commands, a strong case can be made for a "green" canon of interpretation. Statutory interpretation is a knotty subject, and the issues cannot be fully resolved in the course of a few paragraphs. But what I have presented here will, I hope, be enough to put the possibility of an environmental canon of interpretation on the table.

---

## QUESTIONS AND DISCUSSION

**1.** Should there be a green canon? How would such a canon affect the resolution of *BedRoc?*

**2.** Some statutes are harder to interpret than others. "CERCLA confounds every theory of statutory interpretation." John Copeland Nagle, *CERCLA's Mistakes*, 38 WM. & MARY L. REV. 1405, 1410 (1997). Congress enacted CERCLA, covered in Chapter 5, during the hurried lame-duck session following the defeat of President Carter and the Democratic Senate in November 1980 but before President Reagan and the Republican Senate took office in January 1981.

> The circumstances of CERCLA's enactment present formidable challenges to any theory of statutory interpretation. You favor a textualist theory that examines the statutory language alone? "CERCLA is not a paradigm of clarity or precision. It has been criticized frequently for inartful drafting and numerous ambiguities attributable to its precipitous passage." You rely on canons of construction from which to glean statutory meaning? "Because of the inartful crafting of CERCLA . . . reliance solely upon general canons of statutory construction must be more tempered than usual." You prefer to rely on the legislative history of a statute's enactment? "[T]he legislative history of CERCLA gives more insight into the 'Alice-in-Wonderland'-like nature of the evolution of this particular statute than it does helpful hints on the intent of the legislature." You seek to implement congressional intent? "[C]ongressional intent may be particularly difficult to discern with precision in CERCLA." You try to interpret statutes to promote good public policy? "CERCLA 'can be terribly unfair in certain instances in which parties may be required to pay huge amounts for damages to which their acts did not contribute'." You consider the current attitude toward a statute? "CERCLA is now viewed nearly universally as a failure." Those who emphasize the purpose of a statute have found CERCLA more to their liking, but there is an increasing awareness that purpose alone cannot solve all of CERCLA's riddles.

*Id.* at 1406–07 (quoting cases interpreting CERCLA). Would a green canon help with the interpretation of CERCLA?

**3.** *Romer v. Carlucci*, 847 F.2d 445 (8th Cir. 1988) (en banc), offers a rare example of a judge invoking the interpretive canon contained in NEPA § 102(1), covered in Chapter 6. The State of Colorado and environmental groups sued the Air Force for failing to conduct an adequate environmental impact statement before placing MX missiles in old missile silos in Colorado and Nebraska. The court held that the Air Force had conducted a satisfactory EIS. Judge Arnold agreed that the EIS did not need to consider the environmental effects of nuclear war, but he dissented because he thought the Air Force should consider alternative basing modes for the missiles (for example, placement in silos versus on a railroad car). "This is a Congressionally mandated rule of construction, addressed to all agencies of the Executive Branch and to the courts. It must mean, at least, that legitimate differences of opinion as to the interpretation of statutes should be resolved in favor of the policies expressed in NEPA, one of which is that major federal actions significantly affecting the quality of the human environment should not go forward until their effects have been fully explored in an EIS." *Id.* at 468 (Arnold, J., concurring in part & dissenting in part).

**4.** "Federal statutes do not come with instructions, but maybe they should." Nicholas Quinn Rosenkranz, *Federal Rules of Statutory Interpretation*, 115 HARV. L. REV. 2085, 2085 (2002). Should the legislature enact statutes indicating how other statutes should be interpreted? Are such statutory directions binding upon the courts? Many states have codified certain rules of statutory interpretation. *See, e.g.*, Minn. Stat. § 645.16 (stating that "[t]he object of all interpretation and construction of laws is to ascertain and effectuate the intention of the legislature," and listing factors to be considered to identity legislative intent). Federal law contains fewer such provisions. *See* 1 U.S.C. §§ 1–8. But critics assert that legislative directions regarding statutory interpretation violate the constitutional separation of powers or such directions unconstitutionally delegate lawmaking power to the courts. Rosenkranz rejects those claims, and advocates Federal Rules of Statutory Interpretation—akin to the Federal Rules of Civil Procedure—that would instruct courts how to interpret all federal statutes, including environmental laws. What rules would you include in such a law? Would you support Rosenkranz's proposal? Or should courts continue to interpret to interpret environmental statutes according to their traditional doctrines, canons, and other tools?

---

## C. AGENCY INTERPRETATIONS OF ENVIRONMENTAL STATUTES

### Chevron U.S.A. Inc. v. Natural Resources Defense Council, Inc.

Supreme Court of the United States, 1984.
467 U.S. 837.

■ JUSTICE STEVENS delivered the opinion of the Court.

In the Clean Air Act Amendments of 1977, Congress enacted certain requirements applicable to States that had not achieved the national air quality standards established by the Environmental Protection Agency (EPA) pursuant to earlier legislation. The amended Clean Air Act required these "nonattainment" States to establish a permit program regulating "new or modified major stationary sources" of air pollution. Generally, a permit may not be issued for a new or modified major stationary source unless several stringent conditions are met.[1] The EPA regulation promulgated to implement this permit requirement allows a State to adopt a plantwide definition of the term "stationary source."[2] Under this definition, an existing plant that contains several pollution-emitting devices may install or modify one piece of equipment without meeting the permit conditions if the alteration will not increase the total emissions from the plant. The question presented by these cases is whether EPA's decision to allow States to treat all of the pollution-emitting devices within the same industrial grouping as though they were encased within a single "bubble" is based on a reasonable construction of the statutory term "stationary source."

I

The EPA regulations containing the plantwide definition of the term stationary source were promulgated on October 14, 1981. 46 Fed. Reg. 50766. Respondents filed a timely petition for review in the United States Court of Appeals for the District of Columbia Circuit pursuant to 42 U.S.C. § 7607(b)(1). The Court of Appeals set aside the regulations. Natural Resources Defense Council, Inc. v. Gorsuch, 685 F.2d 718 (D.C. Cir. 1982).

The court observed that the relevant part of the amended Clean Air Act "does not explicitly define what Congress envisioned as a 'stationary source', to which the permit program . . . should apply," and further stated that the precise issue was not "squarely addressed in the legislative history." *Id.* at 723. In light of its conclusion that the legislative history bearing on the question was "at best contradictory," it reasoned that "the purposes of the non-attainment program should guide our decision here." *Id.* at 726, n.39. Based on two of its precedents concerning the applicability of the bubble concept to certain Clean Air Act programs, the court stated that the bubble concept was "mandatory" in programs designed merely to maintain existing air quality, but held that it was "inappropriate" in programs enacted to improve air quality. *Id.* at 726. Since the purpose of the permit program—its *"raison d'etre,"* in the court's view—was to improve air quality, the court held that the

---

1 Section 172(b)(6) provides:

"The plan provisions required by subsection (a) shall—"

. . . .

"(6) require permits for the construction and operation of new or modified major stationary sources in accordance with Section 173 (relating to permit requirements)." 91 Stat. 747.

2 "(i) 'Stationary source' means any building, structure, facility, or installation which emits or may emit any air pollutant subject to regulation under the Act."

"(ii) 'Building, structure, facility, or installation' means all of the pollutant-emitting activities which belong to the same industrial grouping, are located on one or more contiguous or adjacent properties, and are under the control of the same person (or persons under common control) except the activities of any vessel." 40 CFR §§ 51.18(j)(1)(i) and (ii) (1983).

bubble concept was inapplicable in these cases under its prior precedents. *Ibid.* It therefore set aside the regulations embodying the bubble concept as contrary to law. We granted certiorari to review that judgment, and we now reverse.

The basic legal error of the Court of Appeals was to adopt a static judicial definition of the term "stationary source" when it had decided that Congress itself had not commanded that definition. Respondents do not defend the legal reasoning of the Court of Appeals. Nevertheless, since this Court reviews judgments, not opinions, we must determine whether the Court of Appeals' legal error resulted in an erroneous judgment on the validity of the regulations.

II

When a court reviews an agency's construction of the statute which it administers, it is confronted with two questions. First, always, is the question whether Congress has directly spoken to the precise question at issue. If the intent of Congress is clear, that is the end of the matter; for the court, as well as the agency, must give effect to the unambiguously expressed intent of Congress.[9] If, however, the court determines Congress has not directly addressed the precise question at issue, the court does not simply impose its own construction on the statute, as would be necessary in the absence of an administrative interpretation. Rather, if the statute is silent or ambiguous with respect to the specific issue, the question for the court is whether the agency's answer is based on a permissible construction of the statute.[11]

"The power of an administrative agency to administer a congressionally created . . . program necessarily requires the formulation of policy and the making of rules to fill any gap left, implicitly or explicitly, by Congress." Morton v. Ruiz, 415 U.S. 199, 231 (1974). If Congress has explicitly left a gap for the agency to fill, there is an express delegation of authority to the agency to elucidate a specific provision of the statute by regulation. Such legislative regulations are given controlling weight unless they are arbitrary, capricious, or manifestly contrary to the statute. Sometimes the legislative delegation to an agency on a particular question is implicit rather than explicit. In such a case, a court may not substitute its own construction of a statutory provision for a reasonable interpretation made by the administrator of an agency.

We have long recognized that considerable weight should be accorded to an executive department's construction of a statutory scheme

---

[9] The judiciary is the final authority on issues of statutory construction and must reject administrative constructions which are contrary to clear congressional intent. If a court, employing traditional tools of statutory construction, ascertains that Congress had an intention on the precise question at issue, that intention is the law and must be given effect.

[11] The court need not conclude that the agency construction was the only one it permissibly could have adopted to uphold the construction, or even the reading the court would have reached if the question initially had arisen in a judicial proceeding.

it is entrusted to administer, and the principle of deference to administrative interpretations

> "has been consistently followed by this Court whenever decision as to the meaning or reach of a statute has involved reconciling conflicting policies, and a full understanding of the force of the statutory policy in the given situation has depended upon more than ordinary knowledge respecting the matters subjected to agency regulations.
>
> ". . . If this choice represents a reasonable accommodation of conflicting policies that were committed to the agency's care by the statute, we should not disturb it unless it appears from the statute or its legislative history that the accommodation is not one that Congress would have sanctioned." United States v. Shimer, 367 U.S. 374, 382, 383 (1961).

In light of these well-settled principles it is clear that the Court of Appeals misconceived the nature of its role in reviewing the regulations at issue. Once it determined, after its own examination of the legislation, that Congress did not actually have an intent regarding the applicability of the bubble concept to the permit program, the question before it was not whether in its view the concept is "inappropriate" in the general context of a program designed to improve air quality, but whether the Administrator's view that it is appropriate in the context of this particular program is a reasonable one. Based on the examination of the legislation and its history which follows, we agree with the Court of Appeals that Congress did not have a specific intention on the applicability of the bubble concept in these cases, and conclude that the EPA's use of that concept here is a reasonable policy choice for the agency to make. . . .

IV

The Clean Air Act Amendments of 1977 are a lengthy, detailed, technical, complex, and comprehensive response to a major social issue. A small portion of the statute—91 Stat. 745–751 (Part D of Title I of the amended Act, 42 U.S.C. §§ 7501–7508)—expressly deals with nonattainment areas. The focal point of this controversy is one phrase in that portion of the Amendments.[22]. . . .

*Statutory Language*

The definition of the term "stationary source" in § 111(a)(3) refers to "any building, structure, facility, or installation" which emits air pollution. See *supra*, at 846. This definition is applicable only to the NSPS program by the express terms of the statute; the text of the statute does not make this definition applicable to the permit program. Petitioners therefore maintain that there is no statutory language even

---

[22] Specifically, the controversy in these cases involves the meaning of the term "major stationary sources" in § 172(b)(6) of the Act. The meaning of the term "proposed source" in § 173(2) of the Act is not at issue.

relevant to ascertaining the meaning of stationary source in the permit program aside from § 302(j), which defines the term "major stationary source." We disagree with petitioners on this point.

The definition in § 302(j) tells us what the word "major" means—a source must emit at least 100 tons of pollution to qualify—but it sheds virtually no light on the meaning of the term "stationary source." It does equate a source with a facility—a "major emitting facility" and a "major stationary source" are synonymous under § 302(j). The ordinary meaning of the term "facility" is some collection of integrated elements which has been designed and constructed to achieve some purpose. Moreover, it is certainly no affront to common English usage to take a reference to a major facility or a major source to connote an entire plant as opposed to its constituent parts. Basically, however, the language of § 302(j) simply does not compel any given interpretation of the term "source."

Respondents recognize that, and hence point to § 111(a)(3). Although the definition in that section is not literally applicable to the permit program, it sheds as much light on the meaning of the word "source" as anything in the statute. As respondents point out, use of the words "building, structure, facility, or installation," as the definition of source, could be read to impose the permit conditions on an individual building that is a part of a plant. A "word may have a character of its own not to be submerged by its association." Russell Motor Car Co. v. United States, 261 U.S. 514, 519 (1923). On the other hand, the meaning of a word must be ascertained in the context of achieving particular objectives, and the words associated with it may indicate that the true meaning of the series is to convey a common idea. The language may reasonably be interpreted to impose the requirement on any discrete, but integrated, operation which pollutes. This gives meaning to all of the terms—a single building, not part of a larger operation, would be covered if it emits more than 100 tons of pollution, as would any facility, structure, or installation. Indeed, the language itself implies a "bubble concept" of sorts: each enumerated item would seem to be treated as if it were encased in a bubble. While respondents insist that each of these terms must be given a discrete meaning, they also argue that § 111(a)(3) defines "source" as that term is used in § 302(j). The latter section, however, equates a source with a facility, whereas the former defines "source" as a facility, among other items.

We are not persuaded that parsing of general terms in the text of the statute will reveal an actual intent of Congress. We know full well that this language is not dispositive; the terms are overlapping and the language is not precisely directed to the question of the applicability of a given term in the context of a larger operation. To the extent any congressional "intent" can be discerned from this language, it would appear that the listing of overlapping, illustrative terms was intended to enlarge, rather than to confine, the scope of the agency's power to regulate particular sources in order to effectuate the policies of the Act.

*Legislative History*

In addition, respondents argue that the legislative history and policies of the Act foreclose the plantwide definition, and that the EPA's interpretation is not entitled to deference because it represents a sharp break with prior interpretations of the Act.

Based on our examination of the legislative history, we agree with the Court of Appeals that it is unilluminating. The general remarks pointed to by respondents "were obviously not made with this narrow issue in mind and they cannot be said to demonstrate a Congressional desire. . . ." Jewell Ridge Coal Corp. v. Mine Workers, 325 U.S. 161, 168–169 (1945). Respondents' argument based on the legislative history relies heavily on Senator Muskie's observation that a new source is subject to the LAER requirement. But the full statement is ambiguous and like the text of § 173 itself, this comment does not tell us what a new source is, much less that it is to have an inflexible definition. We find that the legislative history as a whole is silent on the precise issue before us. It is, however, consistent with the view that the EPA should have broad discretion in implementing the policies of the 1977 Amendments.

More importantly, that history plainly identifies the policy concerns that motivated the enactment; the plantwide definition is fully consistent with one of those concerns—the allowance of reasonable economic growth—and, whether or not we believe it most effectively implements the other, we must recognize that the EPA has advanced a reasonable explanation for its conclusion that the regulations serve the environmental objectives as well. Indeed, its reasoning is supported by the public record developed in the rulemaking process, as well as by certain private studies.

Our review of the EPA's varying interpretations of the word "source"—both before and after the 1977 Amendments—convinces us that the agency primarily responsible for administering this important legislation has consistently interpreted it flexibly—not in a sterile textual vacuum, but in the context of implementing policy decisions in a technical and complex arena. The fact that the agency has from time to time changed its interpretation of the term "source" does not, as respondents argue, lead us to conclude that no deference should be accorded the agency's interpretation of the statute. An initial agency interpretation is not instantly carved in stone. On the contrary, the agency, to engage in informed rulemaking, must consider varying interpretations and the wisdom of its policy on a continuing basis. Moreover, the fact that the agency has adopted different definitions in different contexts adds force to the argument that the definition itself is flexible, particularly since Congress has never indicated any disapproval of a flexible reading of the statute.

Significantly, it was not the agency in 1980, but rather the Court of Appeals that read the statute inflexibly to command a plantwide definition for programs designed to maintain clean air and to forbid such a definition for programs designed to improve air quality. The distinction the court drew may well be a sensible one, but our labored review of the problem has surely disclosed that it is not a distinction that Congress ever articulated itself, or one that the EPA found in the statute before the courts began to review the legislative work product. We conclude that it was the Court of Appeals, rather than Congress or any of the decisionmakers who are authorized by Congress to administer this legislation, that was primarily responsible for the 1980 position taken by the agency.

*Policy*

The arguments over policy that are advanced in the parties' briefs create the impression that respondents are now waging in a judicial forum a specific policy battle which they ultimately lost in the agency and in the 32 jurisdictions opting for the "bubble concept," but one which was never waged in the Congress. Such policy arguments are more properly addressed to legislators or administrators, not to judges.

In these cases the Administrator's interpretation represents a reasonable accommodation of manifestly competing interests and is entitled to deference: the regulatory scheme is technical and complex, the agency considered the matter in a detailed and reasoned fashion, and the decision involves reconciling conflicting policies. Congress intended to accommodate both interests, but did not do so itself on the level of specificity presented by these cases. Perhaps that body consciously desired the Administrator to strike the balance at this level, thinking that those with great expertise and charged with responsibility for administering the provision would be in a better position to do so; perhaps it simply did not consider the question at this level; and perhaps Congress was unable to forge a coalition on either side of the question, and those on each side decided to take their chances with the scheme devised by the agency. For judicial purposes, it matters not which of these things occurred.

Judges are not experts in the field, and are not part of either political branch of the Government. Courts must, in some cases, reconcile competing political interests, but not on the basis of the judges' personal policy preferences. In contrast, an agency to which Congress has delegated policymaking responsibilities may, within the limits of that delegation, properly rely upon the incumbent administration's views of wise policy to inform its judgments. While agencies are not directly accountable to the people, the Chief Executive is, and it is entirely appropriate for this political branch of the Government to make such policy choices—resolving the competing interests which Congress itself either inadvertently did not resolve, or intentionally left to be resolved by the agency charged with the administration of the statute in light of everyday realities.

When a challenge to an agency construction of a statutory provision, fairly conceptualized, really centers on the wisdom of the agency's policy, rather than whether it is a reasonable choice within a gap left open by Congress, the challenge must fail. In such a case, federal judges—who have no constituency—have a duty to respect legitimate policy choices made by those who do. The responsibilities for assessing the wisdom of such policy choices and resolving the struggle between competing views of the public interest are not judicial ones: "Our Constitution vests such responsibilities in the political branches." TVA v. Hill, 437 U.S. 153, 195 (1978).

We hold that the EPA's definition of the term "source" is a permissible construction of the statute which seeks to accommodate progress in reducing air pollution with economic growth. "The Regulations which the Administrator has adopted provide what the agency could allowably view as . . . [an] effective reconciliation of these twofold ends. . . ." United States v. Shimer, 367 U.S., at 383.

---

## QUESTIONS AND DISCUSSION

**1.** What did the D.C. Circuit—in an opinion written by then-Judge Ruth Bader Ginsburg—do wrong?

**2.** Why should a court care how an agency interprets a statute? Are there some circumstances in which an agency's interpretation should be entitled to more deference than others?

**3.** At first, *Chevron* was viewed as revolutionary decision in administrative law—and thus in environmental law, too—but its consequences have not been as dramatic as initially hoped or feared. The courts have struggled with a number of questions about how to apply *Chevron*. What evidences that Congress has spoken to the precise issue under Step 1? A clear statement in the statutory text? The plain meaning of statute in context? Other interpretive canons? The legislative history of the statute? Which interpretations are unreasonable under Step 2? And how does one's overall approach to statutory interpretation affect the task of applying *Chevron*'s Steps 1 and 2?

**4.** The Supreme Court continues to define the deference that courts must afford to administrative interpretations. The Court narrowed the scope of *Chevron* in *United States v. Mead Corp.*, 533 U.S. 218 (2001), which held that a tariff classification ruling of the United States Custom Service is not entitled to the judicial deference afforded by *Chevron*. Justice Souter explained that different statutes present different reasons for receiving judicial deference. Thus, the courts should look to see if Congress delegated power to the agency to "make rules carrying the force of law" and that the challenged action was taken "in the exercise of that authority." *Id.* at 526–27. Indeed, the courts should presume that the agency is not afforded interpretive discretion unless the statute expressly or implicitly says so. As such, an agency's interpretation is given weight by the court, but only to the extent that it is thorough, rational, and consistent with the agency's other interpretations. Only Justice Scalia dissented. He contended that *Chevron* requires deference to all agency interpretations, and he defended *Chevron* as relying upon a presumption of legislative intent that was consistent with separation of powers and as encouraging administrative experimentation with different policies. The impact of *Mead* is illustrated in *The Wilderness Society v. United States Fish & Wildlife Service*, 353 F.3d 1051 (9th Cir. 2003) (en banc), which presented a challenge to a permit issued by the FWS to authorize a state salmon stocking operation within a federal wilderness area. The Ninth Circuit applied *Mead* instead of *Chevron* because the case involved "only an agency's application of law in a particular permitting context, and not an interpretation of a statute that will have the force of law generally for others in similar circumstances." *Id.* at 1067.

Also, in *Decker v. Northwest Environmental Defense Center*, 133 S. Ct. 1326 (2013), the Court considered its related doctrine affording judicial deference to an agency's interpretation of its own regulations. Decker involved a regulation interpreting the Clean Water Act's application to runoff from logging roads that EPA promulgated just days before oral argument in the Supreme Court on that question. The Court held it was "well established that an agency's interpretation need not be the only possible reading of a regulation—or even the best one—to prevail. When an agency interprets its own regulation, the Court, as a general rule, defers to it 'unless that interpretation is "plainly erroneous or inconsistent with the regulation.'" *Id.* at 1337 (quoting Chase Bank USA, N. A. v. McCoy, 131 S. Ct. 871 (2011)). Justice Scalia, however, objected that allowing an agency to first issue a regulation and then later interpret it "contravenes one of the great rules of separation of powers: He who writes a law must not adjudge its violation." *Id.* at 1342 (Scalia, J., concurring in part & dissenting in part).

**5.** After several decades of generating mostly only academic interest, *Chevron* has become a political issue. One recent congressional hearing featured contrasting views of *Chevron* as facilitating executive aggrandizement versus facilitating agency expertise. Compare *The Chevron Doctrine: Constitutional and Statutory Questions in Judicial Deference to Agencies: Hearing Before the Subcomm. on Regulatory Reform, Commercial and Antitrust Law of the House Judiciary Comm.,* 114th Cong., 2d Sess. 2 (2016) (statement of Rep. Marino) ("Over 30 years of *Chevron* deference, we have seen the gradual creep of executive agencies from administrators of the legislative process to becoming legislators themselves.") *with id.* at 3 (statement of Rep. Johnson) (objecting to efforts to "enlist generalist courts to supplant the expertise and political accountability of agencies in the rulemaking process"). The proposed Separation of Powers Restoration Act of 2016 would instruct courts to "decide de novo all relevant questions of law, including the interpretation of constitutional and statutory provisions, and rules made by agencies." H.R. 4768, 114th Cong., 2d Sess. § 2(3) (2016). Should Congress enact such legislation?

## II. STAGES OF COMPLIANCE

Compliance counseling is a dynamic process that depends on the circumstances of a particular activity, including its stage of development. For example, a client might have a *proposed* land use in mind and seek advice about what regulatory restrictions might apply under the Endangered Species Act. Or a client might operate an *ongoing* industrial use and seek advice about how new Clean Air Act rules apply or what the legal implications would be under the Clean Water Act of changing the type of equipment or processes used at the facility. And given that noncompliance occurs, an environmental lawyer might be asked whether disclosure to the government or third parties of known *past* noncompliance events or environmental liabilities is necessary.

### A. PLANNING: IDENTIFYING COMPLIANCE ISSUES AND OPTIONS

Congratulations! You've recently made partner at your law firm and are enjoying the idea of leaving the office early on a glorious Friday afternoon. But then you make the mistake of answering the phone. On the line is the General Counsel of Energena, a large electricity generation company that has been a long-time client of the firm. Energena, you learn, sees the writing on the wall and is hoping to move more of its production capacity into renewable energy sources. One of the company's major initiatives will be wind power generation. The General Counsel explains that Energena anticipates becoming the nation's largest wind energy producer, with large-scale "wind farms" in many different states. Siting and operating wind farms, however, can present environmental compliance issues, for which they will need your help. You gladly offer your services and express great enthusiasm about being a part of this new and exciting initiative. The two of you agree to meet the following Monday to discuss the game plan further and then hang up.

The first step in compliance counseling in environmental law is understanding the nature of the activity about which you are providing advice. In other words, get the facts. Unfortunately, all the firm's associates have left the office ahead of you, so you'll need to do some background research. After a while you come across the following:

#### National Wind Coordinating Committee, Handbook on Permitting of Wind Energy Facilities

August 2002.

#### INTRODUCTION

This chapter describes the basic features of a wind project and the steps developers take to get a project on line. Wind energy and other renewable energy sources, such as solar and geothermal energy, offer the prospect of producing an increasing share of US electricity production with greatly reduced effects on the environment. The recoverable portion of the total wind resource in the contiguous US is approximately 1,230,300 average [Megawatts (MW)]. . . . This is almost 3.5 times the 48 states' total electricity consumption in 1990. While technical and other issues may limit the contribution of wind energy, its potential is quite large.

## ANATOMY OF A WIND PROJECT

Wind projects vary greatly in size, from a few wind turbines ("distributed wind systems") serving individual customers or operating either at substations or at the end of a utility's distribution system, to large arrays of wind turbines ("wind farms") designed for providing wholesale bulk electricity to utilities or to an electricity market.

The role wind generation plays in the electric power system depends on the nature of that system and the relationship between daily and seasonal system needs and wind patterns. In some locales, however, periods of significant electricity demand correlate with periods of high and consistent wind conditions. In the same manner, some electric power systems, such as those that use a significant amount of hydroelectric power, can use wind generation not only to produce power but to help manage other limited resources.

**Distributed wind systems.** Most distributed wind systems range in size from one [kilowatt (kW)] to about 5 MW, providing on-site power in either stand-alone or grid-connected configurations. When grid-connected, these systems are interconnected to the electricity distribution system rather than to the higher voltage electricity transmission system. Such systems are used by industry, water districts, schools, rural residences, farms, and other remote power users. In cases where wind patterns match well with electricity load patterns on distribution feeder lines, distributed wind systems also can be used by utilities to reduce line loads and voltage variations.

**Wind farms.** Larger arrays usually are owned and operated by independent power producers which traditionally have sold their power to—or by—electric utilities. These facilities are grid-connected, and are interconnected to the electrical transmission system. Wind farms vary in generating capacity anywhere from five to more than several hundred megawatts and may consist of a few to several thousand wind turbines of the same or different models. The turbines are mounted on towers and often are placed in linear arrays along ridge tops, or sited in uniform patterns on flat or hilly terrain.

The wind turbine on its tower is the most noticeable feature of a wind project. Other components may include anemometers (wind measuring equipment), an electrical power collection and transmission system (transformers, substation, underground and/or overhead lines), control and maintenance facilities, and site access and service roads. Each component is described in the paragraphs that follow.

**Wind Turbines.** Wind turbines capture the kinetic energy of the wind and convert it into electricity. The primary components of a wind turbine are the rotor (blade assembly), electrical generator, and tower. As the wind blows it spins the wind turbine's rotor, which turns the generator to produce electricity.

The rotor is the part that captures the wind. On most wind turbines the rotor consists of two or three blades which spin about a horizontal axis. "Upwind" turbines have the blades facing into the wind, in front of the generator and tower. The blades on "downwind" turbines are located behind the generator and tower as viewed from the direction of the prevailing wind. Increasingly rare, but still occasionally seen, are the Darrieus (or "eggbeater") wind turbines, whose rotors spin about a vertical axis. New turbine manufacturers enter the market from time to time with a variety of other designs, but to date, none of these machines has achieved significant commercial sales.

The nacelle, mounted on top of the tower, houses the wind turbine's electrical generator. A generator's rating, in kilowatts or megawatts, indicates its potential power output. Actual generation, as kilowatt—or megawatt—hours, will depend on rotor size and wind speed. Larger rotors allow turbines to intercept more wind, increasing power output. The amount of power in the wind is a cubic function of wind speed; thus wind turbines produce an exponentially increasing amount of power as wind speeds increase. For example, if the wind speed doubles, wind power increases eight-fold. Also, since the rotor's swept area (the area of a circle) is a function of the square of the blade length (the radius of the circle), a small increase in blade length leads to a large increase in swept area and energy capture. Economies of scale are quite significant in wind turbines.

A wind turbine's blades typically begin spinning as wind speeds reach approximately seven miles per hour (mph). At nine to 10 mph ("cut-in" speed), they will start generating electricity. Rated output is usually reached in 27- to 35-mph winds. To avoid damage, most turbines automatically shut themselves down when wind speeds exceed 55 to 65 mph ("cut-out" speed). Because wind is intermittent, wind turbines will seldom operate at their rated power output for long periods of time. A typical large-scale turbine, however, will generate some electricity 60% to 80% of the time.

**Maintenance Facility.** A large wind project will require a maintenance facility for storing trucks, service equipment, spare parts, lubricants, and other supplies. The maintenance facility may be located on-or off-site. Some wind farms combine control and maintenance functions in one building.

**Access Roads.** There usually will be one or more access roads into and around a wind project. These service roads provide access to each wind turbine, and typically run parallel to a string of turbines.

## STEPS AND PARTICIPANTS IN WIND FARM DEVELOPMENT

Development of a wind farm is a complex process involving developers, landowners, utilities, the public, and various local, state, and federal agencies. The amount of time required from initial planning to project operation in an area without existing wind projects will vary, and can range from one to two years or more. The development time for subsequent projects at the same or a nearby site may be reduced by several months, provided that:

- permits are issued for the project as a whole and construction is done in phases;
- a comprehensive environmental review [environmental assessment (EA) or impact statement (EIS)], is prepared in compliance with the National Environmental Policy Act, or a state equivalent. Should the analysis show that the impacts of the first project do not suggest a significant adverse cumulative impact, an equivalent environmental review may not be needed for later projects;
- additional experience and knowledge about wind energy projects removes some of the uncertainties that contribute to lengthy analyses and processes.

### Planning

A wind project may be proposed by an independent company, a local government agency, or a unit of a traditional electric utility. The first step in developing a wind project is to identify a suitable site for the turbine or turbines and a likely market for the project's output. To identify possible wind development areas, developers usually consult published wind resource studies or wind resource maps such as Pacific Northwest Laboratory's Wind Energy Resource Atlas of the United States. The developer also will study maps of the electric power system and the local area. To select a specific site within a region, developers may gather long-term wind information from the nearest wind measurement station. They will also visit project site locations to collect general information, including obvious signs of strong winds (e.g., flagged trees, sand dunes and scours), accessibility of terrain, proximity to an electrical transmission line, and any potential environmental constraints.

After finding a potentially suitable site, the developer negotiates to gain access to or control of the properties to conduct further investigations. Developers may secure options for long-term leases or simple anemometer agreements from the landowners. During the option period the developer obtains the landowner's permission to erect anemometers for making site-specific wind measurements. The developer usually collects data at the property for at least one full year to determine the average annual wind speed. More than one year may be needed if site measurements do not correlate well with those made by the closest wind measurement station. If wind data show that the site has economic potential for wind energy generation, the developer will prepare an initial site plan which proposes where to put the wind turbines and electrical facilities that connect to the power grid. In some instances, the ability of the local electrical system to handle the output of the wind farm may have a substantive effect on its location and design. Depending on market prospects, an anemometer agreement may be upgraded to an option or lease at this point if an option or lease has not already been signed.

**Permitting**

Typically, wind projects are required to obtain a permit from one or more government agencies. A wind project typically can be permitted within 12 months. Early in the project planning and development process, the wind developer should contact all relevant permitting agencies or authorities. Permitting entities at the federal, state, and local levels may have jurisdiction over a wind development. The number of agencies and the level of government involvement will depend on a number of factors particular to each development. These factors primarily include: applicable existing laws and regulations, location of the wind turbines and associated facilities or equipment, need for transmission lines and access roads, size of the wind farm, ownership of the project, and ownership of the land.

**Local permitting authorities.** In many states the primary permitting jurisdiction for wind farms is the local planning commission, zoning board, city Council, or county board of supervisors or commissioners. Typically, these local jurisdictional entities regulate through zoning ordinances. In addition to local zoning approval, permitting under local jurisdiction may require a developer to obtain some form of local grading or building permit to ensure compliance with structural, mechanical, and electrical codes.

**State permitting authorities.** In some states, one or more state agencies may have siting or review responsibilities for wind developments. State authorities may include natural resource and environmental protection agencies, state historic preservation offices, industrial development and regulation agencies, public utility commissions, or siting boards. Depending on the state where the wind development is proposed, state permits may be required in addition to local or conditional use permits. In other states, state law may supersede some or all local permitting authorities. Where there is state level regulation there may be a lead agency to coordinate the regulatory review process or a "onestop" siting process housed under one agency. . . .

**Federal permitting authorities.** In some cases (notably in the West), federal land management agencies such as the Bureau of Land Management or the United States Forest Service may be both the manager and the permitting authority. Additionally, agencies such as the Bonneville Power Administration (BPA) or Western Area Power

Administration (WAPA) may be either a wind developer or the customer for the power. If the proposed wind farm has the potential to impact aviation, the Federal Aviation Administration (FAA) may be involved. Generally, when structures exceed 200 feet (about 61 m), the FAA is involved. If the project poses potential impacts on wildlife habitat and species protected under the Endangered Species Act, the Bald and Golden Eagle Protection Act, or the Migratory Bird Treaty Act, wind project permitting may involve coordination and consultation with the United States Fish and Wildlife Service and state wildlife agencies.

Federal actions are subject to the requirements of the National Environmental Policy Act (NEPA). Depending on the type of actions and the potential for impacts, the federal agency may have to prepare an environmental assessment or environmental impact statement for the project before it can act. The NEPA process requires public involvement in identifying issues to be considered and in commenting on the agency's analysis. The reviewing agency may use the results of the NEPA review to clarify requirements for mitigation and monitoring to address the project's environmental impacts.

---

## QUESTIONS AND DISCUSSION

**1.** Based on what you have learned from the foregoing summary, draft what you consider to be the five most important questions you would ask your client at your meeting on Monday.

**2.** Based on what you have learned from the foregoing summary, draft a research assignment for one of your law firm's associates or paralegals to begin working on bright and early Monday morning (or over the weekend if you can track one of them down!).

**3.** Using what you have learned about environmental laws in Part I of this book, brainstorm about potential legal issues you anticipate might arise in connection with the siting, development, and operation of a wind farm.

---

Now that you know something about wind farms and that, in general, they face some level of environmental compliance issues, the job is to identify with more particularity the nature and magnitude of those issues. It appears from the description of wind farms that one general area of concern is impact on wildlife, and you know from your familiarity with the Endangered Species Act (ESA) and other wildlife management laws (see Chapter 2) that the U.S. Fish and Wildlife Service (FWS) is responsible for implementing the ESA and several similar federal laws. Does FWS have anything to say about which of these laws might have applications to wind farms? Indeed the agency does, and they have provided this convenient synopsis:

## United States Fish and Wildlife Service, Wildlife Laws Relevant To Wind Power Development Projects

May 13, 2003.

**The Migratory Bird Treaty Act** (16 U.S.C. 703–712; MBTA), which is administered by the Fish and Wildlife Service (FWS), is the cornerstone of migratory bird conservation and protection in the United States. The MBTA implements four treaties that provide for international protection of migratory birds. It is a strict liability statute wherein proof of intent is not an element of a taking violation. Wording is clear in that most actions that result in a "taking" or possession (permanent or temporary) of a protected species can be a violation. Specifically, the MBTA states: "Unless and except as permitted by regulations . . . it shall be unlawful at any time, by any means, or in any manner to pursue, hunt, take, capture, kill . . . possess, offer for sale, sell . . . purchase . . . ship, export, import . . . transport or cause to be transported . . . any migratory bird, any part, nest, or eggs of any such bird . . . (The Act) prohibits the taking, killing, possession, transportation, and importation of migratory birds, their eggs, parts, and nests, except when specifically authorized by the Department of the Interior." The word "take" is defined as "to pursue, hunt, shoot, wound, kill, trap, capture, or collect, or attempt to pursue, hunt, shoot, wound, kill, trap, capture, or collect." . . . A violation of the MBTA by an individual can result in a fine of up to $15,000, and/or imprisonment for up to 6 months, for a misdemeanor, and up to $250,000 and/or imprisonment for up to 2 years for a felony. Fines are doubled for organizations. Penalties increase greatly for offenses involving commercialization and/or the sale of migratory birds and/or their parts. Under authority of the Bald and Golden Eagle Protection Act (16 U.S.C. 668–668d; BGEPA), Bald and Golden Eagles are afforded additional legal protection. Penalties for violations of the BGEPA are up to $250,000 and/or 2 years imprisonment for a felony, with fines doubled for an organization.

While these Acts have no provision for allowing unauthorized take, the FWS realizes that some birds may be killed even if all reasonable measures to avoid the take are implemented. The FWS Office of Law Enforcement carries out its mission to protect migratory birds not only through investigations and enforcement, but also through fostering relationships with individuals, companies, and industries who seek to eliminate their impacts on migratory birds. Unless the activity is authorized, it is not possible to absolve individuals, companies, or agencies from liability even if they implement avian mortality avoidance or similar conservation measures. However, the Office of Law Enforcement focuses on those individuals, companies, or agencies that take migratory birds with disregard for their actions and the law, especially when conservation measures have been developed but are not properly implemented.

**The Endangered Species Act** (16 U.S.C. 1531–1544; ESA) was passed by Congress in 1973 in recognition that many of our Nation's native plants and animals were in danger of becoming extinct. The purposes of the Act are to protect these endangered and threatened species and to provide a means to conserve their ecosystems. To this end, Federal agencies are directed to utilize their authorities to conserve listed species, as well as "Candidate" species which may be listed in the near future, and make sure that their actions do not jeopardize the continued existence of these species. . . .

Section 9 of the ESA makes it unlawful for a person to "take" a listed species. Take means " . . . to harass, harm, pursue, hunt, shoot, wound, kill, trap, capture, or collect or attempt to engage in any such conduct." The Secretary of the Interior, through regulations, defined the term "harm" as "an act which actually kills or injures wildlife by significantly impairing essential behavioral patterns, including breeding, feeding, or sheltering." However, permits for "incidental take" can be obtained from the FWS for take which would occur as a result of an otherwise legal activity, such as construction of wind turbines, and which would not jeopardize the species.

Section 10 of the ESA allows for the development of "Habitat Conservation Plans" for endangered species on private lands. This provision is designed to assist private landowners in incorporating conservation measures for listed species with their land and/or water development plans. Private landowners who develop and implement an approved habitat conservation plan can receive an incidental take permit that allows their development to go forward.

**The National Environmental Policy Act of 1969** (42 U.S.C. 4371 et seq.; NEPA) requires that Federal agencies prepare an environmental impact statement (EIS) for Federal actions significantly affecting the quality of the human environment. "Federal Actions" are those actions in which a Federal agency is conducting the activity, providing funding for the activity, or licensing or permitting the activity. An EIS must describe the proposed action, present detailed analyses of the impacts of the proposed action and alternatives to that action, and include public involvement in the decision making process on how to proceed to accomplish the purpose of the action. The purpose of NEPA is to allow better environmental decisions to be made. The Council on Environmental Quality, established by NEPA, has promulgated regulations in 40 CFR 1500–1508 that include provisions for 1) preparing EISs and Environmental Assessments, 2) considering categorical exclusions from NEPA documentation requirements for certain agency actions, and 3) developing cooperating agency agreements between Federal agencies.

Other Federal agencies may be required by NEPA to review and comment on proposed activities as a cooperating agency with the action agency under Section 1501.6, or because of a duty to comment on federally-licensed activities for which the agency has jurisdiction by law (Section 1503.4). For the FWS, this would be the MBTA and BGEPA. Other agencies may also be called on for review and comment because of special expertise.

**The National Wildlife Refuge System Administration Act** (16 U.S.C. 668dd), as amended, serves as the "organic act" for the National Wildlife Refuge System. It consolidates the various categories of lands administered by the Secretary of the Interior (Secretary) through the FWS into a single National Wildlife Refuge System. The Act establishes a unifying mission for the Refuge System, a process for determining compatible uses of refuges, and a requirement for preparing comprehensive conservation plans. The Act states first and foremost that the mission of the National Wildlife Refuge System will be focused singularly on wildlife conservation. The Act identifies six priority wildlife-dependent recreation uses; clarifies the Secretary's authority to accept donations of money for land acquisition; and places restrictions on the transfer, exchange, or other disposal of lands within the Refuge System. Most importantly, the Act reinforces and expands the "compatibility standard" of the Refuge Recreation Act, authorizing the Secretary, under such regulations as he may prescribe, to "permit the use of any area within the System for any purpose, including but not limited to hunting, fishing, public recreation and accommodations, and access whenever he determines that such uses are compatible with the major purposes for which such areas were established." This section applies to any proposed development of wind energy on Refuge System lands; such development must be compatible with the major purpose for which that Refuge was established.

**The National Historic Preservation Act of 1966** (16 U.S.C. 470–470b, 470c–470n) approved October 15, 1966 and repeatedly amended, provides for preservation of significant historical features (buildings, objects, and sites) through a grant-in-aid program to the States. It established a National Register of Historic Places and a program of matching grants under the existing National Trust for Historic Preservation (16 U.S.C. 468–468d). The Act also requires Federal agencies to take into account the effects of their actions on items or sites listed or eligible for listing in the National Register. Thus, the Act functions similarly to NEPA, requiring a determination of the presence of any such items or sites, and an evaluation of the effects of proposed developments (such as wind energy facilities) on them, if the facility would be built, funded, licensed or permitted by a Federal agency. This includes State lands purchased or improved with Federal Aid in Wildlife Restoration funds.

---

## QUESTIONS AND DISCUSSION

1. Based on the foregoing summary of laws the Fish and Wildlife Service believes are relevant to wind farms, would you change the questions you plan to pose to your client (see note 1 from the prior set of questions) or the research assignment you have drafted for your associate (see note 2 from the prior set of questions)?

2. Is the Fish and Wildlife Service's summary of laws relevant to wind farms exhaustive of laws that might heave a bearing? Is it binding? Would you forward this summary to your client without first confirming that the agency is correct? How would you confirm that?

3. The Fish and Wildlife Service's focus clearly is on laws relevant to wind farms with which it as an agency has some connection. Yet as you know from your prior research, other federal, state, and local agencies might administer laws applicable to wind farm siting, development, and operation. Also, what if your client plans to purchase real estate on which to develop a wind farm, or plans to acquire an existing wind farm facility or a company that already owns and operates several wind farms. What advice would you have for your client in those situations? See Chapter 13.

---

Now that you have developed a sense of the wind farm business and knowledge about what laws are likely to apply to wind farm facilities, the real task at hand can begin—how do these law apply? What must wind farms do or not do to comply with them? Your research on that front would find no part of the Code of Federal Regulations devoted to environmental regulation of wind farms. There is no Federal Wind Farm Agency that issues such rules, and indeed there is no federal agency whatsoever that issues such rules specifically for wind farms. Instead, you are about to enter the world of "guidance."

As discussed in Chapter 9, administrative agencies issue guidance to serve the interpretation function discussed in Part I of this chapter. The FWS, for example, issues rules under the Endangered Species Act to define statutory terms and provisions, as covered in Chapter 2, but does so at a fairly general level. The agency does not have one set of rules for housing subdivisions, another for commercial buildings, another for wind farms, and so on. Compliance counseling involves interpreting how the general rules apply in specific settings. In some cases, however, the agency issuing the rules will develop guidance designed to inform the regulated public how it interprets the general rules to apply in specific settings. Indeed, FWS has issued guidance for wind farms that contains some rather detailed steps the agency believes wind farms should take to comply with the set of laws described in the previous summary of laws.

## United States Fish and Wildlife Service, Land-Based Wind Energy Guidelines

March 23, 2012.

Executive Summary

As the Nation shifts to renewable energy production to supplant the need for carbon-based fuel, wind energy will be an important source of power. As wind energy production increases, both developers and wildlife agencies have recognized the need for a system to evaluate and address the potential negative impacts of wind energy projects on species of concern. These voluntary Guidelines provide a structured, scientific process for addressing wildlife conservation concerns at all stages of land-based wind energy development. They also promote effective communication among wind energy developers and federal, state, and local conservation agencies and tribes. When used in concert with appropriate regulatory tools, the Guidelines form the best practical approach for conserving species of concern. The Guidelines have been developed by the Interior Department's U.S. Fish and Wildlife Service (Service) working with the Wind Turbine Guidelines Advisory Committee. They replace interim voluntary guidance published by the Service in 2003.

The Guidelines discuss various risks to "species of concern" from wind energy projects, including collisions with wind turbines and associated infrastructure; loss and degradation of habitat from turbines and infrastructure; fragmentation of large habitat blocks into smaller segments that may not support sensitive species; displacement and behavioral changes; and indirect effects such as increased predator populations or introduction of invasive plants. The Guidelines assist developers in identifying species of concern that may potentially be affected by their proposed project, including migratory birds; bats; bald and golden eagles and other birds of prey; prairie and sage grouse; and listed, proposed, or candidate endangered and threatened species. Wind energy development in some areas may be precluded by federal law; other areas may be inappropriate for development because they have been recognized as having high wildlife value based on their ecological rarity and intactness.

The Guidelines use a "tiered approach" for assessing potential adverse effects to species of concern and their habitats. The tiered approach is an iterative decisionmaking process for collecting information in increasing detail; quantifying the possible risks of proposed wind energy projects to species of concern and their habitats; and evaluating those risks to make siting, construction, and operation decisions. During the pre-construction tiers (Tiers 1, 2, and 3), developers are working to identify, avoid and minimize risks to species of concern. During postconstruction tiers (Tiers 4 and 5), developers are assessing whether actions taken in earlier tiers to avoid and minimize impacts are successfully achieving the goals and, when necessary, taking additional steps to compensate for impacts. Subsequent tiers refine and build upon issues raised and efforts undertaken in previous tiers. Each tier offers a set of questions to help the developer evaluate the potential risk associated with developing a project at the given location.

Briefly, the tiers address:

- Tier 1—Preliminary site evaluation (landscape-scale screening of possible project sites)
- Tier 2—Site characterization (broad characterization of one or more potential project sites)
- Tier 3—Field studies to document site wildlife and habitat and predict project impacts
- Tier 4—Post-construction studies to estimate impacts
- Tier 5—Other postconstruction studies and research

The tiered approach provides the opportunity for evaluation and decision-making at each stage, enabling a developer to abandon or proceed with project development, or to collect additional information if required. This approach does not require that every tier, or every element within each tier, be implemented for every project. The Service anticipates that many distributed or community facilities will not need to follow the Guidelines beyond Tiers 1 and 2. Instead, the tiered approach allows efficient use of developer and wildlife agency resources with increasing levels of effort.

If sufficient data are available at a particular tier, the following outcomes are possible:

1. The project proceeds to the next tier in the development process without additional data collection.
2. The project proceeds to the next tier in the development process with additional data collection.
3. An action or combination of actions, such as project modification, mitigation, or specific post-construction monitoring, is indicated.
4. The project site is abandoned because the risk is considered unacceptable.

If data are deemed insufficient at a tier, more intensive study is conducted in the subsequent tier until sufficient data are available to make a decision to modify the project, proceed with the project, or abandon the project.

The most important thing a developer can do is to consult with the Service as early as possible in the development of a wind energy project. Early consultation offers the greatest opportunity for avoiding areas where development is precluded or where wildlife impacts are likely to be high and difficult or costly to remedy or mitigate at a later stage. By consulting early, project developers can also incorporate appropriate wildlife conservation measures and monitoring into their decisions about project siting, design, and operation. Adherence to the Guidelines is voluntary and does not relieve any individual, company, or agency of the responsibility to comply with laws and regulations. However, if a violation occurs the Service will consider a developer's documented efforts to communicate with the Service and adhere to the Guidelines. The Guidelines include a Communications Protocol which provides guidance to both developers and Service personnel regarding appropriate communication and documentation.

The Guidelines also provide Best Management Practices for site development, construction, retrofitting, repowering, and decommissioning:

[a sampling of these Best Management Practices (BMPs) follows]

1. Minimize, to the extent practicable, the area disturbed by pre-construction site monitoring and testing activities and installations.

2. Avoid locating wind energy facilities in areas identified as having a demonstrated and unmitigatable high risk to birds and bats.

3. Use available data from state and federal agencies, and other sources (which could include maps or databases), that show the location of sensitive resources and the results of Tier 2 and/or 3 studies to establish the layout of roads, power lines, fences, and other infrastructure.

4. Minimize, to the maximum extent practicable, roads, power lines, fences, and other infrastructure associated with a wind development project. When fencing is necessary, construction should use wildlife compatible design standards.

5. Use native species when seeding or planting during restoration. Consult with appropriate state and federal agencies regarding native species to use for restoration.

6. To reduce avian collisions, place low and medium voltage connecting power lines associated with the wind energy development underground to the extent possible, unless burial of the lines is prohibitively expensive (e.g., where shallow bedrock exists) or where greater adverse impacts to biological resources would result.

7. Avoid guyed communication towers and permanent met towers at wind energy project sites. If guy wires are necessary, bird flight diverters or high visibility marking devices should be used.

8. Where permanent meteorological towers must be maintained on a project site, use the minimum number necessary.

9. Use construction and management practices to minimize activities that may attract prey and predators to the wind energy facility.

10. Employ only red, or dual red and white strobe, strobe-like, or flashing lights, not steady burning lights, to meet Federal Aviation Administration (FAA) requirements for visibility lighting of wind turbines, permanent met towers, and communication towers. Only a portion of the turbines within the wind project should be lighted, and all pilot warning lights should fire synchronously.

11. Keep lighting at both operation and maintenance facilities and substations located within half a mile of the turbines to the minimum required:

a. Use lights with motion or heat sensors and switches to keep lights off when not required.

b. Lights should be hooded downward and directed to minimize horizontal and skyward illumination.

c. Minimize use of high-intensity lighting, steady-burning, or bright lights such as sodium vapor, quartz, halogen, or other bright spotlights.

d. All internal turbine nacelle and tower lighting should be extinguished when unoccupied.

12. Establish non-disturbance buffer zones to protect sensitive habitats or areas of high risk for species of concern identified in pre-construction studies. Determine the extent of the buffer zone in consultation with the Service and state, local and tribal wildlife biologists, and land management agencies (e.g., U.S. Bureau of Land Management (BLM) and U.S. Forest Service (USFS)), or other credible experts as appropriate.

13. Locate turbines to avoid separating bird and bat species of concern from their daily roosting, feeding, or nesting sites if documented that the turbines' presence poses a risk to species.

14. Avoid impacts to hydrology and stream morphology, especially where federal or state-listed aquatic or riparian species may be involved. Use appropriate erosion control measures in construction and operation to eliminate or minimize runoff into water bodies.

15. When practical use tubular towers or best available technology to reduce ability of birds to perch and to reduce risk of collision.

16. After project construction, close roads not needed for site operations and restore these roadbeds to native vegetation, consistent with landowner agreements.

---

## QUESTIONS AND DISCUSSION

**1.** Do the Fish and Wildlife Service's guidelines seem to impose onerous constraints on wind farm siting and design? Are they binding? What law or laws does the Service suggest mandate any of the suggested guidelines in particular? How would you describe the effect of these guidelines to your client? Presumably, in some cases a wind farm might find a particular guideline innocuous, but in other cases following them could prove costly in terms of the expense of implementation or the effect on wind power generation performance. What would you describe to your client as being the "upside" and the "downside" of following the guidelines in those cases?

**2.** The agency guidelines elsewhere recognize that "each site poses its own set of possibilities for negative effects on wildlife." If Energena were to ask you to design a site feasibility checklist it could use to compare the legal constraints posed by wildlife conservation laws at prospective wind farm sites, how would you structure its content and implementation method?

**3.** The guidelines elsewhere include the caveat that they "are not intended nor shall they be construed to limit or preclude the Service from exercising its authority under any law, statute, or regulation, and to take enforcement action against any individual, company, or agency, or to relieve any individual, company, or agency of its obligations to comply with any applicable Federal, State, or local laws, statutes, or regulations." Does that mean if Energena follows the guidelines to the letter, there is still the possibility it could violate one of the laws the Fish and Wildlife Service administers? So what do you suggest Energena do?

**4.** The wind energy industry takes the position that wind farms present generally low-level compliance difficulties:

> Experience has shown that unless protected plants, animals or their habitat are destroyed or displaced during construction, permitting agencies are likely to find the non-collision consequences of wind development on wildlife to be insignificant. Constructing wind farms to disturb only a small amount of surface area confines habitat losses to only a small part of the entire project. In many cases, impacts on protected plant species can be avoided or minimized by carefully planning and constructing the project. The impact of collisions between birds and wind farms has been the most controversial biological consideration affecting wind farm siting. In North America, only one wind resource area, with thousands of turbines, combined with site characteristics that attract some types of birds, has produced enough bird collisions and deaths to raise concerns by fish and wildlife agencies and conservation groups. On the other hand, most large wind farms have been operating for years with only minor impacts on birds and bats. To date, the only known concern regarding population effects has arisen in the Altamont Pass [Wind Resource Area (WRA)]. Population effects are a function not of the absolute number or birds or bats killed, but of the number killed relative to the size of the total species population in the region. Estimates of annual bird fatalities due to collisions with man-made structures in the United States range from 100 million to greater than 1 billion. These structures include vehicles, buildings and windows, power lines, communication towers and wind turbines. Structures such as smokestacks, power lines, and radio and television towers have been associated with far larger numbers of bird kills than have

> wind farms. Other sources of bird fatalities, such as motor vehicles and pollution, are responsible for a much higher proportion of total bird deaths. Even cats (domestic and feral) account for an estimated 100 million bird deaths per year. Based upon an estimate of 15,000 operating wind turbines in the US, estimates of birds killed by wind turbines are projected at 33,000 bird fatalities per year for all species combined. Many of the bird fatalities tend to come from common species (many of which are non-natives) such as house sparrows, starlings, gulls and rock doves (pigeons). Raptors are a special concern, due to their low numbers and the protected status of most species. With the exception of Altamont Pass WRA, even the numbers of this group killed by wind turbines are quite small. Shore and water birds are occasional fatalities at locations near seasonal or year-round water features.

National Wind Coordinating Committee, Handbook on Permitting of Wind Energy Facilities, Chapter 3—Specific Permitting Considerations (Aug. 2002). Would you rely on these observations in advising Energena? If not, what would you advise Energena do to obtain a reliable profile of the range and magnitude of compliance issues wind farms might face? Are your answers different on learning that a National Academy of Sciences scientific panel reached the same conclusions as the industry? *See* NATIONAL RESEARCH COUNCIL, ENVIRONMENTAL IMPACTS OF WIND-ENERGY PROJECTS (2007).

---

Illustrating the importance of careful planning and assessment of potential liabilities for your client, consider these excerpts from a court decision enjoining a wind farm because of noncompliance with the Endangered Species Act.

## Animal Welfare Institute v. Beech Ridge Energy LLC

United States District Court for the District of Maryland, 2009.
675 F. Supp. 2d 540.

■ ROGER W. TITUS, DISTRICT JUDGE.

CALVIN:

My report is on bats. . . . Ahem . . . "Dusk! With a creepy, tingling sensation, you hear the fluttering of leathery wings! Bats! With glowing red eyes and glistening fangs, these unspeakable giant bugs drop onto . . ."

Bill Watterson, Scientific Progress Goes "Boink": A Calvin and Hobbes Collection 26 (Andrews and McMeel 1991) (explaining that "Bats aren't bugs!").

This is a case about bats, wind turbines, and two federal polices, one favoring protection of endangered species and the other encouraging development of renewable energy resources. It began on June 10, 2009, when Plaintiffs Animal Welfare Institute ("AWI"), Mountain Communities for Responsible Energy ("MCRE"), and David G. Cowan (collectively, "Plaintiffs") brought an action seeking declaratory and injunctive relief against Defendants Beech Ridge Energy LLC ("Beech Ridge Energy") and Invenergy Wind LLC ("Invenergy") (collectively, "Defendants"). Plaintiffs allege that Defendants' construction and future operation of the Beech Ridge wind energy project ("Beech Ridge Project"), located in Greenbrier County, West Virginia, will "take" endangered Indiana bats, in violation of § 9 of the Endangered Species Act ("ESA"), 16 U.S.C. § 1538(a)(1)(B).

**The Endangered Species Act**

Section 9 of the ESA, the cornerstone of the Act, makes it unlawful for any person to "take any [endangered] species within the United States." 16 U.S.C. § 1538(a)(1)(B). The ESA defines the term "take" as "to harass, harm, pursue, hunt, shoot, wound, kill, trap, capture, or collect, or to attempt to engage in any such conduct." 16 U.S.C. § 1532(19).

The U.S. Fish and Wildlife Service ("FWS" or the "Service") has passed regulations implementing the ESA that further refine what activities constitute an impermissible "take." The regulations define the term "harass" as:

> an intentional or negligent act or omission which creates the likelihood of injury to wildlife by annoying it to such an extent as to significantly disrupt normal behavioral patterns which include, but are not limited to, breeding, feeding, or sheltering.

50 C.F.R. § 17.3. The regulations also define the term "harm" as:

> an act which actually kills or injures wildlife. Such act may include significant habitat modification or degradation where it actually kills or injures wildlife by significantly impairing essential behavioral patterns, including breeding, feeding or sheltering.

Id. In 1981, the FWS added to its definition of the term "harm" the "word 'actually' before the words 'kills or injures' . . . to clarify that a standard of actual, adverse effects applies to section 9 takings." 46 Fed.Reg. 54,748, 54,750 (Nov. 4, 1981). See also Babbitt v. Sweet Home Chapter of Communities for a Great Or., 515 U.S. 687 (1995) (rejecting a facial challenge to invalidate the regulation and concluding that the Secretary's definition of harm to include habitat modification was consistent with "Congress' clear expression of the ESA's broad purpose to protect endangered and threatened wildlife").

Anyone who knowingly "takes" an endangered species in violation of § 9 is subject to significant civil and criminal penalties. 16 U.S.C. § 1540(a) (authorizing civil fines of up to $25,000 per violation); § 1540(b) (authorizing criminal fines of up to $50,000 and imprisonment for one year). In order to provide a safe harbor from these penalties, Congress amended the ESA in 1982 to establish an incidental take permit ("ITP") process that allows a person or other entity to obtain a permit to lawfully take an endangered species, without fear of incurring civil and criminal penalties, "if such taking is incidental to, and not the purpose of, the carrying out of an otherwise lawful activity." § 1539(a)(1)(B). Some wind energy companies have obtained or are in the process of pursuing ITPs.

Congress also provided under Section 11 of the ESA that "any person" may bring a citizen suit in federal district court to enjoin anyone who is alleged to be in violation of the ESA or its implementing regulations. 16 U.S.C. § 1540(g).

The ESA's plain language, citizen-suit provision, legislative history, and implementing regulations, as well as case law interpreting the Act, require that this Court carefully scrutinize any activity that allegedly may take endangered species where no ITP has been obtained.

**The Indiana Bat**

The FWS originally designated the Indiana bat (Myotis sodalis) as in danger of extinction in 1967 under the Endangered Species Preservation Act of 1966, the predecessor to the ESA. 32 Fed.Reg. 4,001 (Mar. 11, 1967). The species has been listed as endangered since that time. An Indiana bat weighs approximately one quarter of an ounce (approximately seven grams), its forearm length is 1 3/8 inches to 1 5/8 inches (35–41 millimeters), and its head and body length is 1 5/8 inches to 1 7/8 inches (41–49 millimeters). . . . Approximately three percent of Indiana bats are located in West Virginia.

The Indiana bat is an insectivorous, migratory bat whose behavior varies depending on the season. In the fall, Indiana bats migrate to caves, called hibernacula. The bats engage in a "swarming" behavior in the vicinity of the hibernacula, which culminates in mating. Indiana bats ordinarily engage in swarming within five miles of hibernacula, but may also engage in swarming beyond the five mile radius. During swarming, the bats forage for insects in order to replenish their fat supplies. In mid-November, Indiana bats typically enter hibernation and remain in hibernacula for the duration of winter.

In April and May, Indiana bats emerge from hibernation. After engaging in "staging," typically within five miles of the hibernacula, they fly to summer roosting and foraging habitat. In the summer, female Indiana bats form maternity colonies in roost trees, where they give birth to "pups," and raise their young. Studies suggest that reproductive female Indiana bats give birth to one pup each year. Male Indiana bats spend their summers alone or in small temporary groups in roost trees, changing roost trees and locations throughout the summer. Roost trees generally consist of snags, which are dead or dying trees with exfoliating bark, or living trees with peeling bark. Like other bats, Indiana bats navigate by using echolocation. Specifically, bats emit ultrasonic calls and determine from the echo the objects that are within their environment. Call sequences are typically composed of multiple pulses.

**Wind Turbines and Bat Mortality**

Research shows, and the parties agree, that wind energy facilities cause bat mortality and injuries through both turbine collisions and barotrauma. Barotrauma is damage caused to enclosed air-containing cavities (e.g., the lungs, eardrums, etc.) as a result of a rapid change in external pressure, usually from high to low. The majority of bat mortalities from wind energy facilities has occurred during fall dispersal and migration, but bat mortalities have also occurred in the spring and summer. At the Mountaineer wind energy facility in West Virginia, which is located approximately 75 miles from the Beech Ridge Project, a post-construction mortality study resulted in an estimated annual mortality rate of 47.53 bats per turbine.

The construction of wind energy projects may also kill, injure, or disrupt bat behavior. For example, the cutting of trees may kill or injure roosting bats and destroy potential roosting sites. House v. U.S. Forest Serv., 974 F. Supp. 1022, 1032 (E.D.Ky.1997) (finding that the cutting of trees will destroy Indiana bat roosting habitat).

**The Beech Ridge Project**

Defendant Invenergy is the fifth largest wind developer in the United States, with an aggregate wind-energy generating capacity of nearly 2,000 megawatts. Beech Ridge Energy, a wholly-owned subsidiary of Defendant Invenergy, intends to construct and operate 122 wind turbines along 23 miles of Appalachian mountain ridgelines, in Greenbrier County, West Virginia. The first phase of the project currently consists of 67 turbines and the second phase consists of 55 turbines.

The footprint for the transmission line will be approximately 100 acres and the footprint for the wind turbines will be approximately 300 acres. . . . The Beech Ridge Project will cost over $300 million to build and will produce 186 megawatts of electricity, equivalent to the amount of electricity consumed by approximately 50,000 West Virginia households in a typical year. The project is projected to operate for a minimum of twenty years. Invenergy has signed a twenty-year contract with Appalachian Power Company to sell all output from the first 105 megawatts of power. Sixty-seven turbines, the number of turbines in the first phase of the project, are required to produce this amount of electricity.

**The Beech Ridge Project Development History and Environmental Studies**

In 2005, David Groberg, Vice President of Business Development for Invenergy and the lead developer of the Beech Ridge Project, hired BHE Environmental, Inc. ("BHE") as environmental consultant to the Beech Ridge Project. BHE provides a variety of services to its clients, including agency coordination, study design and implementation, biological assessment and HCP preparation, as well as expert witness services.

Russ Rommé, then Director of the Natural Resources Group at BHE, became the BHE project manager and was responsible for, among other things, assessing potential risks to bat species at the Beech Ridge Project site and consulting with state and federal regulatory agencies.

In July 2005, Rommé contacted Frank Pendleton, an employee at the FWS Field Office in Elkins, West Virginia ("FWS West Virginia Field Office"). Rommé then wrote an e-mail to Pendleton to "create a record of our phone conversation," in which Pendleton told Rommé that BHE's proposal to conduct a preconstruction bat presence survey consisting of fifteen mist-net sites "was a reasonable level of effort" but with the specific caution that the proposed mist-netting survey would only reflect the presence of bats in the area during the summer. Pendleton also stated that Thomas Chapman, Field Supervisor at the FWS West Virginia Field Office, would have the lead on any further discussions with the FWS regarding the Beech Ridge Project.

From July 22–26, 2005, BHE conducted a mist-net survey at fifteen sites near proposed turbine locations. The summer survey consisted of sixty-two net nights, and was conducted during full moon or near full moon conditions. At the time, the FWS recommended a minimum of three net nights per site, a minimum of two net locations at each site, and a minimum of two nights of netting.

During the July survey, BHE captured a total of seventy-eight bats, representing six species. Among those bats captured were post-lactating females and juveniles of Myotis species. Several bats escaped prior to being identified, including at least one Myotis species. BHE captured no Indiana bats in the mist nets.

Based on post-construction mortality studies conducted at the Mountaineer wind energy facility, the draft Chiropteran Risk Assessment estimated that the Beech Ridge Project will cause approximately 6,746 annual bat deaths as the result of turbine collisions. The draft Chiropteran Risk Assessment also raised the possibility that Indiana bats are present at the Project site and that they may be injured or killed by the turbines once they are in operation.

On November 10, 2005, BHE and Invenergy participated in a conference call with Barbara Douglas, from the FWS, and Craig Stihler, from the [West Virginia Department of Natural Resources (WV DNR)]. The meeting minutes indicate that after a preliminary review of the mist-net report, the regulators believed that BHE properly conducted the summer mist-net survey and that the clearing of land is unlikely to adversely affect Indiana bat maternity colonies. . . . However, the meeting minutes also reveal that the regulators believed that potential impact on "migrating and swarming Ibats [Indiana bats] will still need to be addressed," id., and that they remained concerned about the risks posed by the Beech Ridge Project to Indiana bats:

On March 7, 2006, Chapman, the Field Supervisor of the FWS West Virginia Field Office and lead contact regarding the Beech Ridge Project, sent the first of three formal letters to Rommé. The letter begins by summarizing the November 10, 2005 conference call, stating that during the teleconference the FWS and the WV DNR recommended preconstruction surveys as well as post construction minimization measures. The Service remained concerned that Indiana bats may be adversely affected by construction and operation of the project, and "strongly encouraged [BHE] to continue to determine the temporal and spatial use of the project area by bats so that such use by bats can be reported to us and others prior to construction." The FWS recommended "conducting multi-year studies (usually for three years)" as well as springtime emergence studies. The Service also stated that BHE should employ "[r]adar, thermal imaging, acoustical studies, mist-netting and other appropriate sampling techniques. . . .".

On June 19, 2006, while the second mist-net survey was being conducted, BHE provided the FWS and the WV DNR a final Chiropteran Risk Assessment. The final Chiropteran Risk Assessment concluded that the Beech Ridge Project poses a low risk of harm to Indiana bats because the species is unlikely to be present at the site.

In response to BHE's final Chiropteran Risk Assessment, Chapman sent the second of three formal letters from the FWS West Virginia Field Office to Rommé on August 10, 2006. The letter states that the FWS remained "concerned that the proposed Breech Ridge wind power project may harm or kill federally-listed Indiana bats (Myotis sodalis). . . ." The FWS again recommended that BHE conduct a minimum of three years of pre-construction surveys and studies, as described in the Service's 2003 interim guidance, and conduct mist-net surveys during fall and spring migration. The Service also encouraged the developers to formulate and implement an adaptive management plan to minimize the risk of harm to federally-listed species.

On July 31, 2007, Chapman sent the third and final formal letter from the FWS West Virginia Field Office to Rommé regarding the Beech Ridge Project. The letter reiterates that the Service remained "concerned about annual and cumulative mortality of migratory bats. . . ." Furthermore, the letter again states that one summer season of mist-netting surveys is likely insufficient to determine species presence. . . . While expressing these reservations, the FWS noted that the decision to obtain an ITP under § 10 of the ESA "lies with the prospective applicant."

On February 13, 2009, the [West Virginia Public Service Commission] authorized construction at the Beech Ridge Project site . . . At the time of trial, foundations for 67 turbines had been poured, turbine deliveries had commenced, and transmission lines were being strung in agreed upon areas. Beech Ridge Energy has not applied for an ITP which would allow it to incidentally take an endangered species.

**Wholly-Future Violations Under the ESA**

The Court holds that the ESA's citizen-suit provision allows actions alleging wholly-future violations of the statute, where no past violation has occurred. The Court's holding is consistent with the text of the citizen-suit provision, the legislative history, the purpose of the ESA, as well as decisions from the Ninth Circuit squarely addressing the issue. See Forest Conservation Council v. Rosboro Lumber Co., 50 F.3d 781, 783 (9th Cir. 1995) ("The language and legislative history of the ESA, as well as applicable case law support our holding today that a showing of a future injury to an endangered or threatened species is actionable under the ESA."); Marbled Murrelet v. Pacific Lumber Co., 83 F.3d 1060, 1064–65 (9th Cir. 1996) (concluding that Sweet Home did not overrule Rosboro and that "an imminent threat of future harm is sufficient for the issuance of an injunction under the ESA").

**Requisite Degree of Certainty Under the ESA**

The Court . . . holds that in an action brought under § 9 of the ESA, a plaintiff must establish, by a preponderance of the evidence, that the challenged activity is reasonably certain to imminently harm, kill, or wound the listed species. To require absolute certainty, as proposed by Defendants, would frustrate the purpose of the ESA to protect endangered species before they are injured and would effectively raise the evidentiary standard above a preponderance of the evidence.FN30 The reasonable certainty standard, in combination with the temporal component, is consistent with the purpose of the Act, its legislative history, the implementing regulations, and Supreme Court precedent.

**Likelihood of a Take of Indiana Bats at the Beech Ridge Project Site**

It is uncontroverted that wind turbines kill bats, and do so in large numbers. Defendants contend, however, that Indiana bats somehow will escape the fate of thousands of their less endangered peers at the Beech Ridge Project site.

Plaintiffs' experts opined as follows regarding the likelihood that Indiana bats will be harmed by the Beech Ridge Project:

- Robbins: "Because the only logical scientific conclusion based on the foregoing is that Indiana bats are very likely-if not certainly-present on the Beech Ridge project site during spring, summer, and fall, it is still my opinion that there is a high likelihood that Indiana bats will be killed and injured by this project."
- Gannon: "Since, in my opinion, there exists an extremely high likelihood of Indiana bat presence on the project site during spring, summer, and fall based on the current

evidence, my position remains that Indiana bats are very likely to be killed and injured by the [Beech Ridge Project]."

- Kunz: "Because Indiana bats are very likely to be present on the Beech Ridge project site during three seasons of each year when turbines operate, it continues to be my opinion that there is a high likelihood that Indiana bats will be killed and/or injured by this project during its twenty-year lifespan."

The Court agrees with these very credible expert opinions. Based on the evidence in the record, the Court therefore concludes, by a preponderance of the evidence, that, like death and taxes, there is a virtual certainty that Indiana bats will be harmed, wounded, or killed imminently by the Beech Ridge Project, in violation of § 9 of the ESA, during the spring, summer, and fall.

**Injunctive Relief**

Because the Court has found that the Beech Ridge Project will take Indiana bats, injunctive relief is appropriate under § 11 of the ESA. The question, then, is what form that injunctive relief should take. The ITP process is available to Defendants to insulate themselves from liability under the ESA and, while this Court cannot require them to apply for or obtain such a permit, it is the only way in which the Court will allow the Beech Ridge Project to continue.

The Court sees little need to preclude the completion of construction of those forty turbines already under construction, but does believe that any construction of additional turbines should not be commenced unless and until an ITP has been obtained. The simple reason for this is that the ITP process may find that some locations for wind turbines are entirely inappropriate, while others may be appropriate.

There is, by the same token, no reason to completely prohibit Defendants from operating wind turbines now under construction once they are completed. However, in light of the record developed before this Court, that operation can only occur during the periods of time when Indiana bats are in hibernation, i.e., from November 16 to March 31. Outside this period, determining the timing and circumstances under which wind turbine operation can occur without danger of the take of an Indiana bat is beyond the competence of this Court, but is well within the competence of the FWS under the ITP process.

Accordingly, the Court will enjoin all operation of wind turbines presently under construction except during the winter period enumerated above. However, the Court invites the parties to confer with each other and return to the Court, if agreement can be reached, on the conditions under which the wind turbines now under construction would be allowed to operate, if at all, during any period of time outside of the hibernation period of Indiana bats.

## Conclusion

As noted at the outset, this is a case about bats, wind turbines, and two federal policies, one favoring the protection of endangered species, and the other encouraging development of renewable energy resources. Congress, in enacting the ESA, has unequivocally stated that endangered species must be afforded the highest priority, and the FWS long ago designated the Indiana bat as an endangered species. By the same token, Congress has strongly encouraged the development of clean, renewable energy, including wind energy. It is uncontroverted that wind turbines kill or injure bats in large numbers, and the Court has concluded, in this case, that there is a virtual certainty that construction and operation of the Beech Ridge Project will take endangered Indiana bats in violation of Section 9 of the ESA.

The two vital federal policies at issue in this case are not necessarily in conflict. Indeed, the tragedy of this case is that Defendants disregarded not only repeated advice from the FWS but also failed to take advantage of a specific mechanism, the ITP process, established by federal law to allow their project to proceed in harmony with the goal of avoidance of harm to endangered species.

Sadly, Defendants' environmental consultant, Russ Rommé, viewed formal communications from the FWS through rose-colored glasses and simply disregarded what he was told repeatedly. . . . Had Rommé listened more carefully to what he was told repeatedly, Defendants would not be in the unfortunate situation in which they now find themselves. It is clear that Rommé adopted a "minimalist" approach to his responsibilities and that he neither strained very hard nor looked very far in his effort to find Indiana bats. Searching for bats near proposed wind turbine locations for one year instead of three, looking in one season rather than three, and using only one method to detect bats was wholly inadequate to a fair assessment.

This Court has concluded that the only avenue available to Defendants to resolve the self-imposed plight in which they now find themselves is to do belatedly that which they should have done long ago: apply for an ITP. The Court does express the concern that any extraordinary delays by the FWS in the processing of a permit application would frustrate Congress' intent to encourage responsible wind turbine development. Assuming that Defendants now proceed to file an application for an ITP, the Court urges the FWS to act with reasonable promptness, but with necessary thoroughness, in acting upon that application.

The development of wind energy can and should be encouraged, but wind turbines must be good neighbors. Accordingly, the Court will, albeit reluctantly, grant injunctive relief as discussed above.

### QUESTIONS AND DISCUSSION

**1.** Had you been the lawyer representing Invenergy as it wound its way through the various state and federal approval processes, and had you received a copy of the three letters the FWS sent to Rommé of the BHE consulting company assisting on the project, what would you have advised Invenergy to do? Consider that preparing an HCP permit application for submission to FWS typically takes at least six months and that it will take at least six additional months for FWS to review the HCP and process a final permit. In other words, assume that telling Invenergy it should seek an incidental take permit would have added at least one year to the project's completion time line. Moreover, the FWS might demand that many of the "voluntary" best management practices detailed in the Land-Based Wind Energy Guidelines excerpted above be made conditions of the permit, adding substantially to the cost of the project and reducing wind power generation potential.

**2.** Clearly, Energena does not want the same thing to happen to them as happened to the Beech Ridge project. It's Sunday evening, the night before your meeting with Energena's General Counsel, and you've managed to find two associates to join you at the office. Do you now have more specific legal research questions to assign to them? Do you now have more specific questions you'd like to ask of Energena? How will you communicate what you have learned thus far to your client? And what will you suggest to Energena it hire your firm to do over the next month to prepare for its move into the wind power industry?

**3.** Rather than appeal the district court's opinion, Invenergy settled with the plaintiffs after agreeing to project modifications, allowing it to continue construction and operations while pursuing its ESA HCP permit. FWS approved Invenergy's permit application in December 2013. *See* http://www.fws.gov/westvirginiafieldoffice/beech_ridge_wind_power.html.

**4.** As of this writing, no Indiana bat has been seen on the Beech Ridge project site, although calls similar to those of the Indiana bat were acoustically detected in 2011, and as of 2015 there have been only *seven* documented incidents in the entire nation of Indiana bat mortality associated with wind power facilities.

---

## B. MONITORING: ASSESSING COMPLIANCE STATUS

Why does noncompliance occur? More to the point, is anyone who fails to comply with an environmental law a "bad apple," meaning noncompliance is simply the product of malfeasance and wanton disregard for the law? Or are even "good apples" thwarted in their efforts to comply by confusion about the rules or the possibility that the rules simply ask for too much? There is something to be said for the observation by Smyth and Mason, which opened this chapter, that some understanding of compliance theory is useful to understanding the challenges of compliance counseling.

In that pursuit, two of your authors have explored what environmental lawyers for government and private entities think about compliance. Their research was designed to test conventional theory that "compliance is simply a matter of (1) investing the appropriate level of resources toward gathering the information needed to perform the tasks required to comply (information burden) and (2) performing those tasks (effort burden)." J.B. Ruhl & James Salzman, *Mozart and the Red Queen: The Problem of Regulatory Accretion in the Administrative State*, 91 GEO. L. J. 757, 763 (2003). Under this theory, the good apples expend the resources necessary to fulfill the information and effort burdens needed to comply (implying a healthy dose of compliance counseling from lawyers) and the bad apples don't. But what if the sheer volume and complexity of the rules adds a third kind of burden, which might be called the "system burden," that arises as feedback between the burgeoning mass of rules creates conflicting demands and unpredictable outcomes. After all, the Code of Federal Regulations is now well over 140,000 pages long, and each year the Federal Register publishes well over 60,000 pages of administrative pronouncements of one kind or another. The volume of "guidance" like that included in the previous section on wind farms dwarfs even those numbers. In short, Part I of this book covers the miniscule tip of an enormous iceberg. It seems improbable that all these rules will work together seamlessly and efficiently, never presenting contradictions or inconsistencies. Is it possible that even good apples might not be able to comply all the time in such a setting given compliance means complying with a dynamic system of rules? To test for the presence and consequences of this kind of compliance burden, the research team surveyed a group of environmental lawyers about their impressions and experience with compliance and found some interesting patterns in the results. A summary of their findings follows:

### J.B. Ruhl, James Salzman, Kai-Sheng Song, & Han Yu, *Environmental Compliance: Another Corporate Integrity Crisis or Too Many Traps for the Unwary?*

NATURAL RESOURCES & ENV'T, Summer 2002, at 24.

[A] wave of suspicion is affecting attitudes about all aspects of corporate behavior, including environmental compliance. Public skepticism about corporate environmental compliance is not new. If the popular media is any indication, the public's baseline assumption is that many companies break the rules, the only question being the degree of non-compliance and whether it will be discovered. And even among the "insiders"—the regulated businesses and government officials who regulate them—it has become almost a given that no industrial facility is in compliance with all environmental regulations all of the time. But why? Would full compliance be too costly? Are the regulations too difficult to follow? Do companies just not care? Are regulators too lenient?

These questions, raised as modern environmental law enters its fourth decade, have spawned a great deal of introspection regarding the issue of compliance. As a step to finding answers to these questions, the authors conducted a survey of randomly-selected members of the American Bar Association's Section of the Environment, Energy, and Resources (SEER). Underlying the survey's questions were the competing models of the behavioral dimension of compliance that have emerged in the quest to improve compliance performance. One school of thought portrays compliance as simply the result of rational actor behavior—that is, profit-maximizing companies weigh the costs and benefits of complying and comply just as much as makes sense from the perspective of the bottom line. All noncompliance is voluntary under this "rational polluter" model. An opposing view is that many companies are "good apples" to the core and would comply at higher rates than experienced but for obstacles put in the way, such as ambiguous regulations, constantly shifting rules, and conflicting mandates. Noncompliance, in this alternative model, has voluntary and involuntary components. Yet a third model portrays companies not as single-minded black boxes, but as amalgams of a wide variety of officer, manager, employee, and shareholder interests that produces complex resource allocation problems, of which compliance is but one among many. Much of the ongoing debate in the compliance introspection dialogue that is unfolding today is over which of these models should guide the design of compliance and enforcement policy.

But if, in fact, there are systemic obstacles to compliance that lead to involuntary noncompliance, it is not enough to know whether companies generally fit the rational polluter, good apple, or resource allocation model, as in either case at least some companies will seek to comply at some level and may face externally-imposed barriers to doing so. Hence, whichever behavioral model regulators choose for policy design, they ought to pay attention to identifying and accounting for sources of involuntary noncompliance.

To facilitate that effort, we conducted a survey of [500] randomly-selected environmental law attorneys to detect their level of concern about involuntary noncompliance and to identify its possible sources. Among the many sources that have been postulated in compliance literature, the one of particular concern to us is perhaps the most obvious but least understood of all—the sheer number of regulations. No practitioner of environmental law would describe the field as lean in terms of number of rules and standards. Usually, however, the complaints one hears about environmental law are that the rules are too complex, they are unclear, they require unreasonable expenditures, and they change too often. These traits may or may not correlate with number of rules. One could envision a world of few environmental rules, all of which are unclear, overly expensive, and so on. And it would be possible (though we have heard no one suggest it to be the case) that a multitude of environmental rules could consist entirely of rules that are clear, cost-efficient, and stable. So, in addition to exploring the presence and sources of environmental noncompliance generally, we designed our survey to identify whether practitioners perceive the number or rules as an independent factor contributing to involuntary noncompliance.

*Study Population*

We grouped our respondent population using several personal characteristics called for in the survey's opening questions. First, because of our interest in determining the influence of government work on perceptions of regulatory compliance, we divided respondents into three practice setting categories: (1) 50 percent of respondents had spent their entire practice careers representing industry in positions such as private law firms, in-house counsel, or trade associations; (2) 33 percent had spent all or a part of their practice careers in a government position, regardless of other experience; and (3) the remaining respondents were those who had no government work but also some experiences other than representing industry, such as in judicial or academic settings. . . .

*Survey Results*

We designed our survey to elicit the respondents' perceptions for three topics relevant to compliance policy. First, a series of questions asked respondents to describe their perceptions of their own ability to assess environmental compliance and of their clients' ability to achieve compliance. Expecting that at least some respondents would report significant levels of noncompliance, another group of questions probed the respondents' perceptions of the institutional effects noncompliance has on businesses. We did so to determine whether respondents would identify effects other than those consistent with the rational polluter model, as well as simply to see whether the respondents believe noncompliance is a serious concern. Turning to the heart of the matter, a group of questions then asked respondents to identify the sources of noncompliance. We closed the survey with questions about the solutions the respondents would recommend for reducing noncompliance, both within businesses and as a matter of policy. Overall, we found support for all of the compliance models in the responses, and we believe our core hypothesis—that the number of environmental regulations has become so large as to lead to involuntary noncompliance—is resoundingly supported by the results.

*Compliance Assessment and Performance.* Environmental lawyers representing business clients have the unenviable task, day in and day out, of assessing their clients' level of compliance for past, present, and future activities. We designed a series of questions, limited to respondents who currently represent businesses or did so in the past, to capture what environmental attorneys think about regulation and compliance. We were not surprised to find that, overall, they think compliance is difficult both to assess and to achieve.

With respect to compliance assessment, a significant portion of the respondents said they find the task difficult for paperwork regulations (e.g., record keeping and reporting) and physical violations (e.g., discharge and disposal violations). Indeed, when asked whether they agree with the statement that they can confidently assess absolute levels of compliance, roughly equal numbers agreed and disagreed:

| | strongly agree | agree | indifferent | disagree | strongly disagree |
|---|---|---|---|---|---|
| paperwork | 13 | 36 | 12 | 28 | 11 |
| physical | 9 | 38 | 13 | 31 | 9 |

The volume of regulation appears to play a role in making compliance assessment this challenging. The vast majority of respondents said they find keeping track of environmental regulations difficult. None described the task as easy, and only 14 percent found it moderately difficult, whereas 40 percent said it is a difficult task and 43 percent found it very difficult.

As difficult as they believe it is to assess compliance, many respondents also believe businesses often fall short of the goal both for all regulations generally and for regulations of major significance. When asked how consistently their clients achieved full compliance, a startling number of respondents said they believe their clients did so less than two-thirds of the time:

| | always | 90 percent | 66 to 25 percent | never | can't estimate |
|---|---|---|---|---|---|
| all paperwork | <1 | 40 | 34 | 11 | 14 |
| major paperwork | 11 | 60 | 24 | 1 | 4 |
| all physical | 2 | 46 | 28 | 8 | 16 |
| major physical | 12 | 61 | 18 | 0 | 9 |

Responses to this series of questions on compliance assessment and compliance rates revealed remarkably uniform perceptions shared by our different respondent groups. Response distributions generally held true regardless of the respondent's practice background or type of business client. Of particular interest is that exposure to government work did not measurably affect response distributions.

It is encouraging that over 70 percent of the respondents believe their clients achieved full compliance at least 90 percent of the time for major paperwork and physical regulations. Of course, 30 percent believe that noncompliance prevails *at least* a third of the time. Moreover, the respondents' estimates of compliance rates were considerably higher for major regulations than for all regulations, which means that respondents believe business compliance rates for non-major paperwork and physical regulations are quite low. Like many of the findings discussed below, this result can be interpreted consistent with any of the three compliance behavior models. A rational polluter may view the consequences of violating major rules as more significant than for violations of non-major rules, and thus devote more compliance effort to major rules. A good apple may view major rules as having the most important environmental protection benefits and thus make complying with them a more unyielding corporate ethic. Managers and employees in a resource allocation scenario may seek to work on major compliance issues, or to be associated with high-budget allocations of corporate resources, and thus the major rules get more attention. In either case, however, the findings suggest high levels of noncompliance with non-major rules and not insubstantial levels of noncompliance with major rules.

*Institutional Effects of Noncompliance.* We know that it occurs and is hard to assess, but how serious an institutional concern to businesses is the problem of regulatory noncompliance? The rational polluter model predicts that businesses will perceive of noncompliance as simply a cost of doing business, whereas the good apple model suggests that businesses will suffer institutional discordance if noncompliance rates become significant. The resource allocation model suggests that employees associated with high noncompliance may feel threatened. Our survey results suggest that each of the models has some explanatory value. First, the vast majority of respondents identified significant institutional costs associated with noncompliance. Respondents agreed or strongly agreed that noncompliance hurts the corporate public image (85 percent), creates friction between businesses and government (81 percent), increases administrative costs (82 percent), and demoralizes company personnel (74 percent). These response rates sound like the worries of good apples. On the other hand, consistent with the rational polluter model, 68 percent of respondents agreed or strongly agreed that noncompliance is simply another business risk to manage. Perhaps the prevailing compliance behavior is that of a rational good apple—concerned about the psychic and other nonpecuniary costs of involuntary noncompliance, but also confronting its consequences as a risk management issue. In any event, very few respondents—less than 9 percent—agreed that noncompliance is not a significant concern. It is difficult to square these results with the notion that all noncompliance is the result of voluntary, calculated decisions about what is best for the bottom line.

Respondents with at least some government experience tended to rate the demoralizing effects of noncompliance as less significant a consequence, but otherwise conformed with results for the study population as a whole. Response distributions also were unaffected by client size and sector, once again demonstrating remarkable uniformity of perception about compliance matters.

*Sources of Involuntary Noncompliance.* The respondents generally agreed that involuntary noncompliance presents an array of institutional harms for businesses. Agreement on what to do about it may be more elusive. Taking action, both by government and businesses, will require first identifying the sources of noncompliance. This is an important question for both behavioral models. Under the rational polluter model, any negative consequences of noncompliance that can be efficiently reduced will allow a company to improve the bottom line. Under the good apple model, noncompliance is involuntary, but not necessarily beyond the company's control if it can be better understood and thus more effectively combated. The resource allocation model suggests that noncompliance can be weeded out if managers and employees value doing so high enough compared to competing corporate goals. So what, other than the deliberate decision not to comply, causes noncompliance?

To explore that question more deeply, we culled explanations for noncompliance found in the compliance behavior literature, particularly the body of work developing the rational polluter and good apple models, and asked our survey population to rate each in terms of its importance in contributing to noncompliance. As shown below, the overwhelming majority of our respondents found many of the factors associated with *involuntary* noncompliance at least relevant; indeed, most were rated important to very important by a majority of respondents.

| | Very important | Important | Relevant | Minor | Not significant |
|---|---|---|---|---|---|
| Sheer number of regulations | 64 | 26 | 8 | 2 | <1 |
| Complexity of regulations | 44 | 36 | 19 | 1 | 0 |
| Ambiguity of regulations | 39 | 31 | 21 | 7 | 1 |
| Too many different and conflicting requirements | 36 | 40 | 13 | 8 | 3 |
| Keeping track of changes in regulations | 32 | 42 | 22 | 5 | 0 |
| Size of business operation | 32 | 39 | 21 | 6 | 2 |
| Agencies relying on informal guidance | 25 | 28 | 32 | 14 | 1 |
| Unpredictability of inspectors and enforcement | 24 | 21 | 30 | 20 | 5 |

| | Very important | Important | Relevant | Minor | Not significant |
|---|---|---|---|---|---|
| Too many levels of government authority | 16 | 35 | 30 | 16 | 4 |
| Costs of compliance | 13 | 25 | 39 | 22 | 1 |

Clearly, the most important factor by far was the sheer number of regulations, and the least important factor was costs of compliance. Most of the literature supporting the good apple model of environmental compliance behavior focuses on the complexity, ambiguity, inconsistency, and fluidity of regulations, qualitative factors that can operate independent of the quantitative number of regulations. We would not have been surprised to find number of regulations scoring roughly the same as these other factors, but to have it rated significantly more important suggests that the *quantity* of regulations has an effect on compliance at least partly independent of the *quality* of the regulations. This suggests that advocates of the good apple model have been missing an important factor in support of their position.

Given how prominent the cost of compliance in environmental policy dialogue generally, the low score that costs of compliance received in the responses was also a curious result. To be sure, cost of compliance was rated as at least relevant by three quarters of the respondents, but the rational polluter model predicts that cost of compliance should be rated the *most* important factor, as compliance behavior is purely a cost-benefit decision process. Yet almost a quarter of respondents described cost of compliance as of minor or no significance, and its scores for very important and important pale in comparison to the ratings for number of regulations and the factors focusing on qualities of regulation.

Nevertheless, these results could be interpreted consistent with either behavioral model. On the one hand, the prominence of factors such as number and complexity of regulations supports the good apple model, as it points primarily to sources of noncompliance that are external to the business. On the other hand, it may simply be that businesses generally have arranged their internal affairs as they see fit for purposes of overall profit efficiency, so that the external sources of noncompliance have become the driving factors in the rational pollution decision. Or, under the resource allocation model, one would expect a wide variety of factors to influence resource allocation decisions by the numerous managers and employees involved. For us, the important message is that, regardless of which model one espouses, the results point strongly toward external sources of noncompliance that are largely outside the control of businesses and their employees, thus supporting the notion that a significant component of noncompliance is in fact involuntary in character.

While respondents with government experience did tend to rate conflicting requirements and regulatory ambiguity as less important than did industry lawyers, they did not depart from the general study population in their perception of which factors were the most and least important. And, once again, client size and sector did not affect response distributions. It appears that environmental attorneys of all flavors share a common perception about the sources of noncompliance, and that the sheer number of rules is foremost on all their minds as a chief cause.

*Remedies.* The sources of environmental noncompliance are numerous, varied, and complex, suggesting no easy solutions. Nevertheless, one frequently heard maxim, particularly from advocates of the rational polluter model, is that companies simply need to devote more budget resources to compliance in order to improve compliance performance. Of course, this sweeping generality doesn't answer how companies should deploy the money, something the resource allocation model attempts to solve. But in any event, this view was not widely held among our respondents. When asked whether a two-fold increase in environmental regulation compliance budgets would ensure full compliance at least 90 percent of the time, only 40 percent of respondents agreed it would. Thirty percent disagreed, and 30 percent were indifferent. Ironically, respondents with at least some government experience were more likely to disagree—i.e., to have less faith that more money means more compliance. At the very least, these responses suggest that something in addition to budget increases will be needed to boost compliance rates.

Another commonly-held notion our respondents' answers did not support is that the federal government is the principal source of regulatory overload. Although EPA clearly is the most prominent (and perhaps prolific) environmental agency, a significant majority of the respondents (63 percent) agreed that levels of noncompliance are the same for federal, state, and local regulations. Of those who identified a particular level of regulation as spawning more noncompliance, roughly equal numbers identified federal (19 percent) and state (13 percent) regulations, while local regulations were identified the least (5 percent). Whatever its source, therefore, noncompliance does not appear to be a problem isolated to a particular level of government regulation. The problem, in other words, is system-wide.

If the simple answers of budget increases and wrestling EPA under control are not enough, what should companies do to control involuntary noncompliance? Once again, we culled through the environmental compliance literature to compile a list of remedies for respondents to rate in terms of importance. We first asked respondents to rate the importance of different compliance resources. The emphasis on internal compliance mechanisms such as technical staff, versus external resources such as trade associations, was pronounced:

| | Very Important | Important | Relevant | Minor | Not significant |
|---|---|---|---|---|---|
| In-house technical staff | 77 | 19 | 4 | 1 | 0 |
| Contact with agency officials | 38 | 35 | 21 | 5 | <1 |
| In-house legal staff | 33 | 36 | 27 | 1 | 0 |
| Outside technical consultants | 22 | 44 | 28 | 1 | 0 |
| Outside legal counsel | 21 | 53 | 26 | 1 | 0 |
| Educational programs/ seminars | 20 | 36 | 33 | 11 | 0 |
| Trade association support | 13 | 44 | 28 | 13 | <1 |

These responses were remarkably consistent with the answers we received to a question asking how respondents would deploy a two-fold increase in regulatory compliance budgets among a variety of options, with the goal of maximizing compliance. The emphasis, once again, was on devoting more dollars to internal compliance resources, followed by physical facility improvements, and then, of least importance, expenditures on external resources:

| | High Priority | Medium Priority | Low Priority | No Investment |
|---|---|---|---|---|
| Increase employee education on regulatory requirements | 67 | 29 | 4 | 0 |
| Hire more in-house technical staff | 61 | 34 | 5 | 1 |
| Increase environmental compliance monitoring | 59 | 31 | 9 | 1 |
| Invest in facility repair and renovation | 53 | 39 | 7 | 1 |

| | High Priority | Medium Priority | Low Priority | No Investment |
|---|---|---|---|---|
| Invest in new pollution control and other new technology | 42 | 40 | 16 | 3 |
| Increase contacts and relations with government agencies | 22 | 44 | 25 | 8 |
| Hire more in-house legal staff | 13 | 43 | 40 | 4 |
| Increase retention of outside technical consultants | 10 | 53 | 35 | 2 |
| Increase retention of outside legal counsel | 7 | 45 | 43 | 6 |

There was no significant difference in response distributions to any of these questions between respondents who had at least some government experience and those who had none. Likewise, client size and sector had no influence on the results.

These results suggest that the highest priority environmental compliance resources are those devoted to internal compliance problem-solving, a result that is entirely consistent with the finding that the primary sources of noncompliance are the quantity and qualities of environmental regulation. This finding also favors the resource allocation model as explaining what really transpires in the corporate "black box." First and foremost, human resources are needed to confront the challenge of understanding and complying with the vastness and complexity of environmental law. When their work identifies the need for capital investments, that becomes a priority. Where greater expertise levels are needed to solve compliance problems or address conflicts with government or citizens, outside technical and legal resources can be employed.

*Conclusions*

Our interest in describing involuntary environmental noncompliance is motivated by the debate between the rational polluter, good apple, and resource allocation models of environmental compliance behavior, but is not intended to settle it. The debate whether corporations are bad actors or just caught in a web of complex regulations (or a combination of both) will continue, particularly when fueled by stories of corporate misconduct. Having said that, after analyzing our survey results we do, however, have a clearer picture of the issue. We believe each of the models underestimate the importance of involuntary noncompliance and thus fails adequately to address its sources and solutions. Many of the results of our survey could be interpreted to support either model, but they also support our hypothesis that much environmental noncompliance is involuntary and that a significant source of that component of noncompliance is the quantity of regulations.

Perhaps the most curious results of the survey, therefore, are the responses to the final two questions. First, we asked what clients thought of the statement that additional specificity in environmental regulations would facilitate compliance. Over half the respondents agreed or strongly agreed it would, almost one-third disagreed or strongly disagreed, and the rest were indifferent. Clearly, there is a strong yearning among environmental attorneys for more specificity in environmental regulation. But in the final survey question we asked respondents whether they agree or disagree that reducing the number of environmental regulations would improve compliance without reducing environmental quality. Over two-thirds agreed (42 percent), and almost one-third strongly agreed (27 percent), while only 20 percent disagreed or strongly disagreed. This result, of course, further supports our hypothesis that the number of regulations has become a compliance impediment, but it also leads to another research question: How can so many respondents desire and believe that the specificity of regulations can be increased while the number of regulations decreased? Alas, that is for another day.

---

## QUESTIONS AND DISCUSSION

**1.** Based on the foregoing, what advice would you have for Energena about the importance of identifying all regulatory provisions that could apply to its planned wind farm initiatives? What advice would you have for Energena about how most effectively to deploy its compliance efforts and expenditures? Would it be useful to conduct a study of the compliance practices and experiences of the wind power industry in general?

**2.** For a probing examination of compliance theory and the "rational polluter" model, see David Spence, *The Shadow of the Rational Polluter: Rethinking the Role of Rational Actor Models in Environmental Law*, 89 CAL. L. REV. 917 (2001). Like Ruhl et al., Spence advocates the "complex resource allocation" model as the most useful for developing compliance theory. Is that model, however, too complex? Will government agencies be better off using the rational polluter model for compliance policy, even if it is inaccurate at the margins, if adopting the complex resource allocation model would make compliance policy too complicated and expensive to design and implement?

---

Given the combined effects of information burdens, effort burdens, and system burdens associated with compliance under environmental laws, it would make sense for regulated entities to have a protocol for checking a facility's compliance performance status. Indeed, note that the findings from Ruhl et al. discussed in the previous article suggest that lawyers who advise regulated entities place very high emphasis on increasing employee education on regulatory requirements, hiring more in-house technical staff, and increasing environmental compliance monitoring, far more than they do hiring more inside and outside compliance counsel.

The basic instrument of compliance monitoring has come to be known as the "environmental compliance audit," a systematic, documented, periodic, and objective review by regulated entities of facility operations and practices related to meeting environmental requirements. An environmental compliance audit in essence takes a snapshot of compliance performance at ongoing operations. Its purpose is similar in this respect to the "pre-transfer environmental audit" (also known as "all appropriate inquiries") conducted in many business transactions involving the transfer of real estate and other assets, which is designed to detect instances of noncompliance as well as the presence of contamination and of regulatory constraints to future planned uses of the assets (see Chapter 13).

As the enforcement consequences of regulatory noncompliance grew over the 1980s in terms of monetary penalties and negative reputation effects (see Chapter 11), the practice of environmental compliance auditing became more common and routinized. The participation of environmental counsel on the audit team also became standard operating procedure to assist in identifying applicable standards, designing auditing protocols, evaluating the gravity and potential enforcement consequences of any instance of noncompliance, and assessing options for responding to such instances.

As part of its effort to provide compliance guidance, the U.S. EPA has promulgated a set of auditing protocols for determining compliance with a variety of laws EPA administers (available at http://cfpub.epa.gov/compliance/resources/policies/incentives/auditing/). The following is an excerpt from a protocol for hazardous waste regulations under the Resource Conservation and Recovery Act (see Chapter 5) providing general instructions for using the protocols' "checklist" system and an example of the specific step-by-step inquiries an entity would conduct to determine compliance with RCRA standards (*available at* http://www.epa.gov/compliance/resources/policies/incentives/auditing/apcol-rcrad.pdf)

## U.S. Environmental Protection Agency, Protocol for Conducting Environmental Compliance Audits for Hazardous Waste Generators under RCRA

(June 2001).

### How to Use the Protocols

Each protocol provides guidance on key requirements, defines regulatory terms, and gives an overview of the federal laws affecting a particular environmental management area. They also include a checklist containing detailed procedures for conducting a review of facility conditions. The audit protocols are designed to support a wide range of environmental auditing needs; therefore several of the protocols in this set or sections of an individual protocol may not be applicable to a particular facility. . . .

The protocols are not intended to be an exhaustive set of procedures; rather they are meant to inform the auditor, about the degree and quality of evaluation essential to a thorough environmental audit. EPA is aware that other audit approaches may also provide an effective means of identifying and assessing facility environmental status and in developing corrective actions.

It is important to understand that there can be significant overlap within the realm of the federal regulations. For example, the Department of Transportation (DOT) has established regulations governing the transportation of hazardous materials. Similarly, the Occupational Safety and Health Administration (OSHA) under the U.S. Department of Labor has promulgated regulations governing the protection of workers who are exposed to hazardous chemicals. There can also be significant overlap between federal and state environmental regulations. In fact, state programs that implement federally mandated programs may contain more stringent requirements that are not included in these protocols. There can also be multiple state agencies regulating the areas covered in these protocols. The auditor also should determine which regulatory agency has authority for implementing an environmental program so that the proper set of regulations is consulted. Prior to conducting the audit, the auditor should review federal, state and local environmental requirements and expand the protocol, as required, to include other applicable requirements not included in these documents.

<u>Review of Federal Legislation and Key Compliance Requirements:</u>

These sections are intended to provide only supplementary information or a "thumbnail sketch" of the regulations and statutes. These sections are not intended to function as the main tool of the protocol (this is the purpose of the checklist). Instead, they serve to remind the auditor of the general thrust of the regulation and to scope out facility requirements covered by that particular regulation. For example, a brief paragraph describing record keeping and reporting requirements and the associated subpart citations will identify and remind the auditor of a specific area of focus at the facility. This allows the auditor to plan the audit properly and to identify key areas and documents requiring review and analysis.

State and Local Regulations:

Each EPA Audit Protocols contains a section alerting the auditor to typical issues addressed in state and local regulations concerning a given topic area (e.g., RCRA and used oil). From a practical standpoint, EPA cannot present individual state and local requirements in the protocols. However, this section does provide general guidance to the auditor regarding the division of statutory authority between EPA and the states over a specific media. This section also describes circumstances where states and local governments may enact more stringent requirements that go beyond the federal requirements.

EPA cannot overemphasize how important it is for the auditor to take under consideration the impact of state and local regulations on facility compliance. EPA has delegated various levels of authority to a majority of the states for most of the federal regulatory programs including enforcement. For example, most facilities regulated under RCRA, and/or CWA have been issued permits written by the states to ensure compliance with federal and state regulations. In turn, many states may have delegated various levels of authority to local jurisdictions. Similarly, local governments (e.g., counties, townships) may issue permits for air emissions from the facility. Therefore, auditors are advised to review local and state regulations in addition to the federal regulations in order to perform a comprehensive audit.

The Checklists:

The checklists delineate what should be evaluated during an audit. The left column states either a requirement mandated by regulation or a good management practice that exceeds the requirements of the federal regulations. The right column gives instructions to help conduct the evaluation. These instructions are performance objectives that should be accomplished by the auditor. Some of the performance objectives may be simple documentation checks that take only a few minutes; others may require a time-intensive physical inspection of a facility. The checklists contained in these protocols are (and must be) sufficiently detailed to identify any area of the company or organization that would potentially receive a notice of violation if compliance is not achieved. For this reason, the checklists often get to a level of detail such that a specific paragraph of the subpart (e.g., 40 CFR 262.34(a)(1)(i)) contained in the CFR is identified for verification by the auditor. The checklists contain the following components:

- **"Regulatory Requirement or Management Practice Column:"** The "Regulatory Requirement or Management Practice Column" states either a requirement mandated by regulation or a good management practice that exceeds the requirements of the federal regulations. The regulatory citation is given in parentheses after the stated requirement. Good management practices are distinguished from regulatory requirements in the checklist by the acronym (MP) and are printed in italics.

- **"Reviewer Checks" Column:** The items under the "Reviewer Checks:" column identify requirements that must be verified to accomplish the auditor's performance objectives. (The key to successful compliance auditing is to verify and document site observations and other data.) The checklists follow very closely with the text in the CFR in order to provide the service they are intended to fulfill (i.e., to be used for compliance auditing). However, they are not a direct recitation of the CFR. Instead they are organized into more of a functional arrangement (e.g., record keeping and reporting requirements vs. technical controls) to accommodate an auditor's likely sequence of review during the site visit. Wherever possible, the statements or items under the "Reviewer Checks" column, will follow the same sequence or order of the citations listed at the end of the statement in the "Regulatory Requirement" column.
- **"NOTE:" Statements "Note:"** Statements contained in the checklists serve several purposes. They usually are distinguished from "Verify" statements to alert the auditor to exceptions or conditions that may affect requirements or to referenced standards that are not part of Title 40 (e.g., American Society for Testing and Materials (ASTM) standards). They also may be used to identify options that the regulatory agency may choose in interacting with the facility (e.g., permit reviews) or options the facility may employ to comply with a given requirement.
- **Checklist Numbering System:** The checklists also have a unique numbering system that allows the protocols to be more easily updated by topic area (e.g., RCRA Small Quantity Generator). Each topic area in turn is divided into control breaks to allow the protocol to be divided and assigned to different teams during the audit. This is why blank pages may appear in the middle of the checklists. Because of these control breaks, there is intentional repetition of text (particularly "Note" Statements) under the "Reviewer Checks" column to prevent oversight of key items by the audit team members who may be using only a portion of the checklist for their assigned area.

Updates:

Environmental regulations are continually changing both at the federal and state level. For this reason, it is important for environmental auditors to determine if any new regulations have been issued since the publication of each protocol document and, if so, amend the checklists to reflect the new regulations. Auditors may become aware of new federal regulations through periodic review of Federal Register notices as well as public information bulletins from trade associations and other compliance assistance providers. In addition, EPA offers information on new regulations, policies and compliance incentives through several Agency Websites. Each protocol provides specific information regarding EPA program office websites and hotlines that can be accessed for regulatory and policy updates.

[example of checklist item]

**COMPLIANCE CATEGORY: HAZARDOUS WASTE MANAGEMENT**

| REGULATORY REQUIREMENT OR MANAGEMENT PRACTICE | REVIEWER CHECKS |
|---|---|
| **HW.440.5.** An owner/operator of a U.S. recovery facility must send signed copies of the tracking document to the notifier, to U.S. EPA, and to the exporting and transit countries within three days of receipt of imports (40 CFR 262.84(e)). | Verify that the facility sends signed copies of the tracking document to the notifier, to U.S. EPA, and to the competent authorities of the exporting and transit countries within the three days. |
| **HW.440.6.** A facility that has arranged to receive hazardous waste from a foreign source must notify U.S. EPA (40 CFR 264.12(a)(1) and 265.12(a)(1)). | Verify that the facility notifies the appropriate U.S. EPA Regional Administrator in writing at least four weeks prior to the date the waste is expected to arrive at the facility. |

**COMPLIANCE CATEGORY: HAZARDOUS WASTE MANAGEMENT**

| REGULATORY REQUIREMENT OR MANAGEMENT PRACTICE | REVIEWER CHECKS |
|---|---|
| | (NOTE: Notice of subsequent shipments of the same waste from the same foreign source is not required.) |

**QUESTIONS AND DISCUSSION**

**1.** As EPA explains, this set of checklists covers just the regulations EPA administers for hazardous waste generators. EPA and other federal, state, and local agencies might have additional regulatory requirements applicable to a facility using the hazardous waste generator checklists. At a major industrial facility, therefore, effective environmental compliance auditing requires preparation of a comprehensive set of checklists covering all applicable regulatory provisions.

**2.** Do you think the EPA's "checklist" approach would be useful for Energena to employ at its wind farm facilities? Based on what you know from the materials on wind farms in the previous section of the text, design a set of checklists and draft a memorandum to Energena explaining their purpose and use.

———

## C. DISCLOSING: REPORTING NONCOMPLIANCE

Compliance auditing is designed to improve overall compliance performance by detecting instances of noncompliance. As compliance auditing became more common, therefore, the question inevitably arose, what disclosure obligations apply when instances of noncompliance are detected? This question has played out in two forums. First, environmental enforcement agencies faced a double-edged sword in that they wished to encourage environmental compliance auditing as a means of improving compliance performance, but also wished to know about, and punish, events of noncompliance. The more they did the latter, of course, the more they discouraged auditing. The U.S. EPA and state environmental agencies differed markedly over how to strike the balance between encouraging auditing and facilitating enforcement.

On the other front, the Securities and Exchange Commission, which regulates publicly traded companies, became increasingly concerned about how companies reported their environmental compliance performance obligations. Compliance with environmental regulations can be expensive, and noncompliance can have serious enforcement consequences. Unlike the EPA, however, the SEC has a singular mission in this regard—ensuring the investing public has complete and reliable information relevant to investment decisions. Over time, therefore, the SEC became the primary regulator of compliance performance disclosure for publicly traded companies.

1. COMPLIANCE AUDIT RESULT DISCLOSURES

Other than mandated monitoring of specific compliance events, such as emission monitoring under the Clean Air Act (see Chapter 3), comprehensive environmental compliance auditing is not required by any environmental law. The practice arose initially largely through the initiative of private regulated entities attempting to get a handle on compliance performance. By the end of the 1980s, the practice was widespread and environmental enforcement agencies were confronted with the dilemma of how to take advantage of the information revealed by audits while at the same time encouraging auditing as a practice. The initial responses in this regard from federal enforcement agencies focused on providing limited relief from enforcement penalties for the voluntary disclosure of noncompliance.

For example, on July 1, 1991, the Department of Justice issued guidance on environmental auditing describing the goal of "encourage[ing] self-auditing, self-policing and voluntary disclosure of environmental violations by the regulated community. Such factors as the defendant's voluntary disclosure of violations, cooperation with government investigation of the violations, use of environmental audits and other procedures to ensure compliance with applicable environmental laws and regulations, and use of measures to remedy expeditiously . . . any violations are viewed as mitigating factors in the Departments exercise of criminal enforcement discretion." Factors in Decisions on Criminal Prosecutions for Environmental Violations: In the Context of Significant Voluntary Compliance or Disclosure Efforts by the Violator. Later, Section 9A1.1 of the 1993 Draft Corporate Sentencing Guidelines for Environmental Violations provided for the mitigation of sentences where a court finds that the following factors for environmental compliance are satisfied: Line management attention to compliance; integration of environment policies, standards, and procedures; auditing, monitoring, reporting and tracking systems; regulatory expertise, training and evaluation; incentives for compliance; disciplinary procedures; continuing evaluation and improvement.

On January 12, 1994, EPA's Criminal Enforcement division issued guidance identifying specific factors that distinguish cases meriting criminal investigation from those more appropriately pursued under administrative or civil judicial authorities. With respect to corporations conducting environmental audits, the guidance explained that

> EPA policy strongly encourages self-monitoring, self-disclosure and self-correction. When self auditing has been conducted and

> full, complete disclosure has occurred, the company's constructive activities should be considered as mitigating factors in EPA's exercise of investigative discretion. Therefore, a violation that is voluntarily revealed and fully and promptly remediated as part of a corporation's systematic and comprehensive self evaluation program generally will not be a candidate for the expenditure of scarce criminal resources.

U.S. EPA, Office of Enforcement, Guidance on EPA's Exercise of Investigative Discretion for Environmental Crimes (Jan. 12, 1994).

On December 22, 1995, EPA issued its final policy on "Incentives for Self-Policing: Discovery, Disclosure, Correction and Prevention of Violations." 60 Fed Reg. 66,706. The agency described the purpose of the policy as being to enhance protection of human health and the environment by encouraging regulated entities to voluntarily discover, disclose, correct and prevent violations of Federal environmental law. Benefits available to entities that make disclosures under the terms of the policy included reductions in the amount of civil penalties and a determination not to recommend criminal prosecution of disclosing entities.

In stark contrast to the federal response, states favored encouraging compliance audits far more than they did taking advantage of them for enforcement purposes. Rather than simply reducing enforcement exposure, many states took the approach of treating environmental audits as being protected by evidentiary privileges and as conferring enforcement immunity on the reporting entity. One such statute is the Texas Environmental, Health, and Safety Audit Privilege Act, TEX. REV. CIV. STAT. Art. 4447cc. Soon after its enactment in 1995, EPA objected to the scope of safe harbors the state provided and threatened to withdraw Clean Water Act delegation. The state amended the Act in 1997 to reflect a compromise with EPA. .The Texas Council on Environmental Quality provides the following guidance on the statute's provisions:

## Texas Council on Environmental Quality, Guidance on the Texas Environmental, Health, and Safety Audit Privilege Act

Aug. 2009.

### GUIDANCE

The Audit Act gives incentives for persons to conduct voluntary audits, at regulated facilities or operations, of their compliance with environmental, health, and safety regulations and to implement prompt corrective action. The two primary incentives are a limited evidentiary privilege for certain information gathered in a voluntary self-audit and an immunity from administrative and civil penalties for certain violations voluntarily disclosed as a result of such an audit. Neither the privilege nor the immunity applies if an audit was conducted in bad faith, or if the person fails to take timely, appropriate action to achieve compliance, among other conditions.

Many violations disclosed under the Audit Act would not have been discovered in an ordinary inspection, since they could be discovered only through expensive sampling and testing protocols, or time-consuming data reviews.

### Submissions Required under the Audit Act

Three types of notices are anticipated under the Audit Act: a Notice of Audit, a Disclosure of Violation, and a Request for Extension. In order to take advantage of the immunity offered by the Audit Act, a "person" (defined in the Audit Act as an individual, corporation, partnership, or any other legal entity) must give notice to the TCEQ prior to the initiation of an environmental audit and must disclose to the agency any violations for which immunity is being sought. However, if an auditing person does not intend to take advantage of potential immunity, no notice of intent to initiate an audit is necessary; in such cases the audit report will still be privileged, but no immunity can attach to any violations discovered. A person must request the written approval of the TCEQ if it seeks to extend the audit more than six months beyond the date it was begun.

***Guidance***. The Notice of Audit and Disclosure of Violation are not privileged documents and are available to the public.

#### *Notice of Audit (NOA)*

A *Notice of Audit* is the letter a person submits to the TCEQ before the person begins an environmental audit. Although the person is not required to give this notice to the TCEQ, the person cannot take advantage of the immunity provision of the Audit Act if it fails to give proper notice to the TCEQ that it is *planning to commence* an environmental audit [Audit Act § 10(g)].

An NOA should be submitted in writing by certified mail. Certified mail is not required, but using certified mail is in the person's best interest, in part because it provides a positive identification of the time the NOA was mailed.

#### *Disclosure of Violations (DOV)*

A *Disclosure of Violations* is the notice or disclosure made by a person to the TCEQ promptly upon discovery of a violation as a result of an environmental audit. A person wishing to take advantage of the immunity from penalty must make a proper voluntary disclosure of the violation.

#### *Request for Extension*

The person may submit a letter requesting an extension of the deadline for the completion of the audit investigation. The Audit Act explicitly limits the audit period to "a reasonable time not to exceed six months" unless an extension is approved "based on reasonable grounds."

### Privilege and the Audit Act

#### *Evidentiary Privilege*

Section 5 of the Audit Act grants a limited evidentiary privilege for audit reports developed according to the statute. The audit privilege applies to the admissibility and discovery of audit reports in civil and administrative proceedings. The privilege does not apply to documents, reports, and data required to be collected, developed, maintained, or reported under state or federal law or to information obtained independent of the audit process. The privilege also does not apply to criminal proceedings.

The effects of the audit privilege extend beyond admissibility and discovery in legal proceedings. The TCEQ will not routinely receive or review privileged audit report information, and such information should not be requested, reviewed, or otherwise used during an inspection. If the review of privileged information is necessary to determine compliance status, that information and information derived from its use will remain privileged and inadmissible in administrative or civil proceedings. Such review will occur under the terms of a confidentiality agreement between the TCEQ and the auditing person, where appropriate.

Note that information required for a Disclosure of Violations (violation, citation, violation start and end dates, corrective-action plan, and corrective-action target completion date) is considered basic information required to be voluntarily disclosed in order for a person to claim immunity pursuant to Audit Act § 10. The Disclosure of Violations is not considered to be a privileged audit report pursuant to Audit Act § 4.

***Guidance.*** All privileged information contained in an audit report should be clearly labeled COMPLIANCE REPORT: PRIVILEGED DOCUMENT. The TCEQ accepts Disclosures of Violations and considers them to be non-privileged; it does not accept audit reports submitted under *claims of confidentiality* unless there is also a confidentiality agreement already in place.

#### *Waiver of Privilege*

The Audit Act privilege is waivable and will be lost if privileged information is communicated to others except in limited situations described in the legislation. This section discusses the potential consequences of disclosure in some foreseeable circumstances.

### Disclosure to Government Officials

**No waiver** for disclosure of an audit report to TCEQ personnel pursuant to a confidentiality agreement or under a claim of confidentiality

Disclosure of an audit report to applicable TCEQ personnel ("government official of a state") does *not* waive the privilege if disclosure is made under the terms of a confidentiality agreement between the owner or operator of the audited facility (or the person for whom the report was prepared) and the TCEQ. [Audit Act § 6(b)(2)(D)].

***Guidance.*** TCEQ personnel will not accept any information offered under a claim of confidentiality. Any TCEQ employee who receives a document offered under such a claim should return it immediately, without review. Also, no employee should request, review, accept, or use an audit report during an inspection without first consulting the Litigation Division.

**No waiver** for disclosure to a state regulatory agency of information required to be made available under state or federal law

The disclosure for agency review of information required "to be made available" [Audit Act § 9(b)] as opposed to information required "to be collected, developed, maintained, or reported" under a federal or state environmental or health and safety law [Audit Act § 8(a)(1)] does *not* result in waiver of any applicable privilege.

If the TCEQ requests the review of such material, it accepts the responsibility to maintain confidentiality. The use of any such information obtained is strictly limited. Evidence that arises or is derived from review, disclosure, or use of such information can be suppressed in a civil or administrative proceeding [Audit Act § 9(d)]. If such a request for review could result in public disclosure as the result of any specific state or federal law requiring public access to information in the TCEQ's possession, TCEQ personnel must affirmatively notify the person claiming the privilege before the agency obtains the material for review [Audit Act § 9(c)].

**Waiver** for disclosure of privileged information to the EPA or other federal agencies

Information privileged under the Audit Act cannot be disclosed to the EPA or other federal agencies without resulting in waiver of the privilege. Federal agencies are *not* included among entities to which privileged information can be disclosed under Audit Act § 6(b).

Likewise, disclosure to the EPA or other federal agencies of information "required to be made available" under state or federal law will result in waiver of any applicable Audit Act privilege even though the disclosure of such information exclusively for TCEQ review would not waive the privilege under Audit Act § 9(b).

**Disclosure to Private Parties**

**No waiver** for disclosure to certain nongovernmental parties in order to address an issue identified through an audit

The Audit Act authorizes the disclosure of privileged information to the following nongovernmental parties for addressing or correcting a matter raised by the audit:

- a person employed by the owner or operator, including a temporary or contract employee;
- a legal representative of the owner or operator;

- an officer or director of the regulated facility or a partner of the owner or operator; or
- an independent contractor retained by the owner or operator. [Audit Act § 6(b)(1)]

**No waiver** for disclosure to certain nongovernmental parties pursuant to the terms of a confidentiality agreement

If the disclosure is made under the terms of a confidentiality agreement, the Audit Act authorizes disclosure of privileged information to the following nongovernmental parties:

- a partner or potential partner of the owner or operator;
- a transferee or potential transferee of the facility or operation;
- a lender or potential lender for the facility or operation; or
- a person who insures, underwrites, or indemnifies the facility or operation. [Audit Act § 6(b)(2)]

**Criminal Proceedings**

**No waiver** relative to civil or administrative proceedings where an audit report is obtained, reviewed, or used in a criminal proceeding. [Audit Act § 9(a)]

**Immunity and the Audit Act**

Immunity under Audit Act § 10 is from administrative and civil penalties relating to certain self-disclosed violations. This limited immunity does not affect the TCEQ's authority to seek injunctive relief, make technical recommendations, or otherwise enforce compliance. In order to receive immunity, the disclosure must be both voluntary *and* preceded by a proper Notice of Audit that notified the TCEQ of the intent to initiate the environmental audit.

A disclosure will be deemed voluntary under Audit Act § 10 only if the following conditions apply. ("PINNACLE" can serve as a mnemonic device.)

**P**—the disclosure was made *promptly* after the violation was discovered;

**I**—the disclosure was made *in writing by certified mail* to the TCEQ;

**N**—the violation was *not independently detected,* or an investigation of the violation was not initiated, before the disclosure was made in writing by certified mail;

**N**—the violation was *noted and disclosed as the result* of a voluntary environmental audit;

**A**—*appropriate efforts to correct* the noncompliance are initiated, pursued, and completed within a reasonable amount of time;

**C**—the disclosing person *cooperates in the investigation* of the issues identified in the disclosure;

L—the violation *lacks injury or imminent and substantial risk of injury*; and

E—the disclosure is not required by an *enforcement order or decree.*

Audit Act § 10(d) further limits the availability of the immunity for certain violations. Immunity does not apply, and a civil or administrative penalty may be imposed, if the violation was intentionally or knowingly committed; was recklessly committed; or resulted in a "substantial economic benefit which gives the violator a clear advantage over its business competitors." Furthermore, the immunity does not apply if a court or administrative law judge finds that the person claiming immunity has repeatedly or continuously committed significant violations and has not attempted to bring the facility into compliance, resulting in a pattern of disregard of environmental or health and safety laws. A three-year period will be used to determine whether a pattern exists [Audit Act § 10(h)].

***Guidance.*** TCEQ enforcement programs should take appropriate steps in coordination with the Environmental Audit Coordinators when a violation is disclosed as a result of an environmental audit. *The TCEQ's enforcement authority remains unaltered by the Audit Act, except for the exclusion of penalties.*

**The Texas Audit Act and the EPA**

1. How does the Audit Act apply to EPA inspectors operating in Texas? The Audit Act does not apply to federal agencies, including the EPA. The EPA has its own audit policy, and EPA inspectors operate within that policy.

2. If an EPA inspector requests a copy of an audit during a joint inspection, should the TCEQ inspector continue to participate?

The EPA has explicitly stated that it "will not request an environmental audit report in routine inspections." However, if an EPA inspector does request and obtain a copy of an audit report privileged under the Texas Audit Act, the TCEQ inspector should continue to participate, but should not receive, review, or otherwise use such information. The inspector should refer the issue to the Litigation Division as soon as possible.

---

## QUESTIONS AND DISCUSSION

1. How easy do you think it is for facilities that engage in periodic environmental compliance audits to satisfy the "PINNACLE" standard of disclosure? Does PINNACLE define "good apple" behavior, and if so, then why does the Texas statute extend the evidentiary privileges and enforcement immunities to PINNACLE disclosures? Is it to reward "good apple" behavior or provide incentives to sway facilities into becoming "good apples."

**2.** Are the privileges and immunities advantages of the Texas statute sufficiently attractive to turn a "bad apple" into a diligent compliance auditor? How would you advise a client that asks whether the costs of engaging in more rigorous and frequent environmental compliance auditing and PINNACLE disclosure are offset by the benefits? Indeed, what *are* the costs of engaging in more rigorous and frequent environmental compliance auditing and PINNACLE disclosure?

**3.** In June 2013 Texas enacted amendments to the Audit Act to extend its privileges and immunities, under specified conditions, to due diligence audits conducted prior to closing of a business asset acquisition transaction (this kind of audit is described in Part I of Chapter 13). *See* Act of May 8, 2013, 83rd Leg., S.B No. 1300. Why? TCEQ updated its guidance in November 2013, but found that nothing in the 2013 legislation altered the approach the agency outlined in the 2009 version excerpted above. See https://www.tceq.texas.gov/publications/rg/rg-173.html.

---

As outlined above, EPA had been taking a very different approach than the one represented by the Texas statute, focusing on mitigation of enforcement penalties, and it became concerned that the privilege and immunity approach would provide too much safe harbor for violators and reduce compliance incentives. Although EPA was criticized for its approach, the agency remained firm, continuing penalty reduction incentives for disclosure but rejecting privileges and immunities. In April 2000, however, EPA issued a revised audit disclosure incentives guidance. *See* Incentives for Self-Policing Discovery, Disclosure, Correction and Prevention of Violations Environmental Auditing, 65 Fed. Reg. 19,618 (Apr. 11, 2000). The revised policy provides incentives for regulated entities to detect, promptly disclose, and expeditiously correct violations of federal environmental requirements. The policy contains nine specified conditions. Entities that meet all of them are eligible for 100 percent mitigation of the punitive component of any penalties that otherwise could be assessed, known as the "gravity-based" component (the portion of the penalty designed to disgorge the cost-saving benefits of noncompliance is not mitigated). EPA also generally will elect not to recommend criminal prosecution by DOJ or any other prosecuting authority of a disclosing entity as long as its self policing, discovery, and disclosure were conducted in good faith and the entity adopts a systematic approach to preventing recurrence of the violation. EPA has summarized its audit incentives policy as follows:

## EPA Summary of Audit Policy

http://www.epa.gov/compliance/incentives/auditing/auditpolicy.html.

The EPA Audit Policy, formally titled "Incentives for Self-Policing: Discovery, Disclosure, Correction and Prevention of Violations," safeguards human health and the environment by providing several major incentives for regulated entities to voluntarily come into compliance with federal environmental laws and regulations.

To take advantage of these incentives, regulated entities must voluntarily discover, promptly disclose to EPA, expeditiously correct, and prevent recurrence of future environmental violations. Disclosures are often preceded by consultation between EPA and the regulated entity, so that they can discuss mutually acceptable disclosure details, compliance, and audit schedules can be discussed.

**Summary of Incentives**

**Significant penalty reductions.** Civil penalties under the environmental laws generally have two components, an amount assessed based upon the severity or "gravity" of the violation, and the amount of economic benefit a violator received from failing to comply with the law.

- **No gravity-based penalties if all nine of the Policy's conditions are met.** EPA retains its discretion to collect any economic benefit that may have been realized as a result of noncompliance.
- **Reduction of gravity-based penalties by 75%** where the disclosing entity meets all of the Policy's conditions except detection of the violation through a systematic discovery process.

**No recommendation for criminal prosecution** for entities that disclose criminal violations if all of the applicable conditions under the Policy are met. "Systematic discovery" is not a requirement for eligibility for this incentive, although the entity must be acting in good faith and adopt a systematic approach to preventing recurring violations. Refer to the Audit Policy for a complete discussion of issues relating to disclosure of criminal violations.

**No routine requests for audit reports would be made.**

Conditions for Penalty Mitigation

Entities that satisfy the following conditions are eligible for Audit Policy benefits. Even if your entity fails to meet the first condition—systematic discovery—you can still be eligible for 75% penalty mitigation, and a recommendation for no criminal prosecution of the violations against your entity.

- **Systematic discovery** of the violation through an environmental audit or the implementation of a compliance management system.
- **Voluntary discovery** of the violation was not detected as a result of a legally required monitoring, sampling or auditing procedure.
- **Prompt disclosure** in writing to EPA within 21 days of discovery or such shorter time as may be required by law. Discovery occurs when any officer, director, employee or agent of the facility has an objectively reasonable basis for believing that a violation has or may have occurred.

• **Independent discovery and disclosure** before EPA or another regulator would likely have identified the violation through its own investigation or based on information provided by a third-party.

• **Correction and remediation** within 60 calendar days, in most cases, from the date of discovery.

• **Prevent recurrence** of the violation.

• **Repeat violations are ineligible**, that is, the specific (or closely related) violations have occurred at the same facility within the past 3 years or those that have occurred as part of a pattern at multiple facilities owned or operated by the same entity within the past 5 years; if the facility has been newly acquired, the existence of a violation prior to acquisition does not trigger the repeat violations exclusion.

• **Certain types of violations are ineligible** such as those that result in serious actual harm, those that may have presented an imminent and substantial endangerment, and those that violate the specific terms of an administrative or judicial order or consent agreement.

• **Cooperation** by the disclosing entity is required.

---

## QUESTIONS AND DISCUSSION

**1.** With respect to state audit privilege and immunity statutes, EPA hung firm with its opposition and had the following to say in its guidance:

> *Opposition to Audit Privilege and Immunity*
>
> The Agency believes that the Audit Policy provides effective incentives for self-policing without impairing law enforcement, putting the environment at risk or hiding environmental compliance information from the public. Although EPA encourages environmental auditing, it must do so without compromising the integrity and enforceability of environmental laws. It is important to distinguish between EPA's Audit Policy and the audit privilege and immunity laws that exist in some States. The Agency remains firmly opposed to statutory and regulatory audit privileges and immunity. Privilege laws shield evidence of wrongdoing and prevent States from investigating even the most serious environmental violations. Immunity laws prevent States from obtaining penalties that are appropriate to the seriousness of the violation, as they are required to do under Federal law. Audit privilege and immunity laws are unnecessary, undermine law enforcement, impair protection of human health and the environment, and interfere with the public's right to know of potential and existing environmental hazards.
>
> Statutory audit privilege and immunity run counter to encouraging the kind of openness that builds trust between regulators, the regulated community and the public. For example, privileged information on compliance contained in an audit report may

include information on the cause of violations, the extent of environmental harm, and what is necessary to correct the violations and prevent their recurrence. Privileged information is unavailable to law enforcers and to members of the public who have suffered harm as a result of environmental violations. The Agency opposes statutory immunity because it diminishes law enforcement's ability to discourage wrongful behavior and interferes with a regulator's ability to punish individuals who disregard the law and place others in danger. The Agency believes that its Audit Policy provides adequate incentives for self-policing but without secrecy and without abdicating its discretion to act in cases of serious environmental violations.

Privilege, by definition, invites secrecy, instead of the openness needed to build public trust in industry's ability to self-police. American law reflects the high value that the public places on fair access to the facts. The Supreme Court, for example, has said of privileges that, "[w]hatever their origins, these exceptions to the demand for every man's evidence are not lightly created nor expansively construed, for they are in derogation of the search for truth." United States v. Nixon, 418 U.S. 683, 710 (1974). Federal courts have unanimously refused to recognize a [common law self-evaluation] privilege for environmental audits in the context of government investigations. See, e.g., United States v. Dexter Corp., 132 F.R.D. 8, 10 (D. Conn. 1990) (application of a privilege "would effectively impede [EPA's] ability to enforce the Clean Water Act, and would be contrary to stated public policy.") Cf. In re Grand Jury Proceedings, 861 F. Supp. 386 (D. Md. 1994) (company must comply with a subpoena under Food, Drug and Cosmetics Act for self-evaluative documents).

*Effect on States*

The revised final Policy reflects EPA's desire to provide fair and effective incentives for self-policing that have practical value to States. To that end, the Agency has consulted closely with State officials in developing this Policy. As a result, EPA believes its revised final Policy is grounded in commonsense principles that should prove useful in the development and implementation of State programs and policies.

EPA recognizes that States are partners in implementing the enforcement and compliance assurance program. When consistent with EPA's policies on protecting confidential and sensitive information, the Agency will share with State agencies information on disclosures of violations of Federally-authorized, approved or delegated programs. In addition, for States that have adopted their own audit policies in Federally-authorized, approved or delegated programs, EPA will generally defer to State penalty mitigation for self-disclosures as long as the State policy meets minimum requirements for Federal delegation. Whenever a State provides a penalty waiver or mitigation for a violation of a requirement

> contained in a Federally-authorized, approved or delegated program to an entity that discloses those violations in conformity with a State audit policy, the State should notify the EPA Region in which it is located. This notification will ensure that Federal and State enforcement responses are coordinated properly.
>
> As always, States are encouraged to experiment with different approaches to assuring compliance as long as such approaches do not jeopardize public health or the environment, or make it profitable not to comply with Federal environmental requirements. The Agency remains opposed to State legislation that does not include these basic protections, and reserves its right to bring independent action against regulated entities for violations of Federal law that threaten human health or the environment, reflect criminal conduct or repeated noncompliance, or allow one company to profit at the expense of its law-abiding competitors.

65 Fed. Reg. 19618, 19623–24 (Apr. 11, 2000).

**2.** EPA's leverage over states is limited to the "adequate authority" standard for delegation of federal programs to states. EPA has threatened to withdraw delegation of programs based on its conclusion that a state has adopted privilege and immunity policies inconsistent with EPA's criteria, which has usually led to the state agreeing to apply its policy as EPA has outlined. *See, e.g.*, 66 Fed. Reg. 49,839 (Oct. 1, 2001) (Rhode Island Clean Air Act delegation decision). But not all states seek delegation of federal programs, not all federal programs are eligible for delegation to states, and not all state environmental programs are counterparts to federal programs. So EPA's policy does not cover the waterfront of state programs that could employ privilege and immunity incentives for environmental compliance audit disclosures. When all is said and done, therefore, what advice would you have for a client, such as Energena, about how to approach the questions of whether to engage in environmental compliance auditing and, if so, whether to disclose noncompliance events detected through such audits?

**3.** For contrasting assessments of EPA's audit disclosure policy, see Lawrence Culleen and Thomas Glazer, *Let's Make a Deal: Twenty Years of EPA's Audit Policy*, NATURAL RESOURCES & ENV'T, Winter 2016, at 3 (noting that between 1995 and 2010 6,200 companies voluntarily disclosed under the policy violations at over 17,000 facilities); Gregory F. Linsin, *Environmental Self-Audit and Voluntary Disclosure to what End?*, NATURAL RESOURCES & ENV'T, Winter 2009, at 50. For early history and practical implications of the squabble between EPA and the states over the state privilege and immunity laws, see James M. Weaver et al., *State Environmental Audit Laws Advance Goal of a Cleaner Environment*, NAT. RES. & ENV'T, Spring 1997, at 6. A survey of state laws is available at Special Report, *Environmental Audit Immunity Laws and Self-Disclosure Policies: A State-by-State Comparison*, 35 ENV'T REP. S–53 (2004). A preliminary empirical study of the impacts of the differing EPA and state policies suggests that the states may be onto something—the evidence is that compliance is improved somewhat by the state policies as compared to the EPA approach. *See* Sarah Stafford, *Does*

*Self-Policing Help the Environment? EPA's Audit Policy and Hazardous Waste Compliance*, 6 VT. J. ENVTL. L. 14 (2004–05).

**4.** EPA sweetened the disclosure pot by proposing a set of penalty reduction incentives for new owners of facilities that investigate, self-disclose, and correct violations. Believing new owners are "particularly well-situated and highly motivated to focus on and invest in making a 'clean start,' " EPA asked for public input on the kind of "tailored" incentives going beyond the standard audit policy incentives that could be used to make it attractive for purchasers of facilities promptly to disclose and correct. violations. *See* Enhancing Environmental Outcomes from Audit Policy Disclosures through Tailored Incentives for New Owners: Notice, 72 Fed. Reg. 27116 (May 14, 2007). What would you have proposed?

EPA followed through with this concept and in 2008 developed its Interim Approach to Applying the Audit Policy to New Owners, 73 Fed. Reg. 44991 (Aug 1, 2008). The incentives are for the most part tweaks to the Audit Policy that recognize the goal of incentivizing a "clean start." For example, the policy provides:

> The uncertainties associated with the calculation and assessment of economic benefit may be factors that new owners otherwise interested in using the Audit Policy perceive as disincentives. In this section, EPA discusses an approach to calculating and assessing economic benefit in the new owner context.
>
> 1. Interim Approach to the Calculation and Assessment of Penalties
>
> a. No penalties for economic benefit or gravity will be assessed against the new owner for the period before the date of acquisition.
>
> b. Penalties for economic benefit associated with avoided operation and maintenance costs will be assessed against the new owner from the date of acquisition.
>
> c. Penalties for economic benefit associated with delayed capital expenditures or with unfair competitive advantage will not be assessed against the new owner if violations are corrected in accordance with the Audit Policy (i.e., within 60 days of the date of discovery or another reasonable timeframe to which EPA has agreed).

Do these strike you as significant incentives?

## 2. SECURITIES REGISTRATION DISCLOSURES

The federal securities regulatory system relies upon Securities and Exchange Commission (SEC) registrants, such as publicly traded companies, to fully disclose material information to actual and potential shareholders to ensure they can make informed investments and for proper market functioning. The SEC's regulations do not promote any particular type of investment over another, but facilitate the free flow of information between regulated companies and the public. The SEC has several regulatory provisions that specifically require registrant companies to publicly disclose environmental compliance performance information:

**Securities and Exchange Commission Regulation S–K, Item 101**, Description of Business, 17 CFR 229.101. This provision requires SEC registrants to disclose, among other things, the material effects of complying or failing to comply with environmental requirements on the capital expenditures, earnings and competitive position of the registrant and its subsidiaries.

**Securities and Exchange Commission Regulation S–K, Item 103**, Legal Proceedings, 17 CFR 229.103. This provision requires SEC registrants to disclose, on at least a quarterly basis, pending environmental legal proceedings or proceedings known to be contemplated, which meet any of three qualifying conditions: (1) a materiality threshold, (2) 10% of current assets, or (3) a monetary sanctions threshold.

**Securities and Exchange Commission Regulation S–K**, Item 303, Management's Discussion and Analysis of Financial Condition and Results of Operations, 17 CFR 229.303. This provision requires SEC registrants to disclose environmental contingencies that may reasonably have material impact on net sales, revenue, or income from continuing operations.

Of course, the SEC does not promulgate, administer, or enforce environmental regulations, but the EPA does. In 2001, EPA gave the industry a clear message about how serious it was about the SEC disclosures.

## Environmental Protection Agency, Guidance on Distributing the "Notice of SEC Registrants' Duty to Disclose Environmental Legal Proceedings" in EPA Administrative Enforcement Actions

Jan. 19, 2001.

The purpose of this memorandum is to request Regional and Headquarters enforcement personnel to distribute the attached "Notice of SEC Registrants' Duty to Disclose Environmental Legal Proceedings" in EPA-initiated administrative enforcement actions. As outlined below, distribution of the Notice has the potential to increase public access to corporate environmental information, and encourage improved corporate environmental performance.

### Application of this Guidance

Who Should Receive the Notice

Any enforcement action initiated by the EPA is potentially a "legal proceeding" that is subject to the SEC's environmental disclosure requirements. However, SEC Regulation S–K applies only to companies that are SEC "registrants" within the meaning of the term as defined by the SEC. OECA does not expect EPA enforcement staff to make a determination of whether or not the party to an environmental legal proceeding is, indeed, an SEC registrant. Rather, the Notice seeks to inform recipients that they are *potentially* subject to Regulation S–K, Item 103 and should themselves determine its applicability to their company and the relevant legal proceeding. There is one exception. Because governmental entities (federal, state, or local) are not subject to SEC regulation, the Notice should not be distributed to them. However, if enforcement personnel have information that leads them to reasonably believe that a party to a legal proceeding is not an SEC registrant, then the Notice does not have to be distributed.

Additionally, the Notice only should be distributed to parties to an environmental legal proceedings when the EPA has initiated the enforcement action, and the Agency has the lead for prosecuting the case. The Notice should not be distributed if a case has been, or is expected to be, referred to the Department of Justice (DOJ).

NOTICE OF SECURITIES AND EXCHANGE COMMISSION REGISTRANTS' DUTY TO DISCLOSE ENVIRONMENTAL LEGAL PROCEEDINGS

Securities and Exchange Commission regulations require companies registered with the SEC (e.g., publicly traded companies) to disclose, on at least a quarterly basis, the existence of certain administrative or judicial proceedings taken against them arising under Federal, State or local provisions that have the primary purpose of protecting the environment. Instruction 5 to Item 103 of the SEC's Regulation S–K (17 CFR 229.103) requires disclosure of these environmental legal proceedings. For those SEC registrants that use the SEC's "small business issuer" reporting system, Instructions 1–4 to Item 103 of the SEC's Regulation S–B (17 CFR 228.103) requires disclosure of these environmental legal proceedings.

If you are an SEC registrant, you have a duty to disclose the existence of pending or known to be contemplated environmental legal proceedings that meet any of the following criteria (17 CFR 229.103(5)(A)–(C)):

A. Such proceeding is material to the business or financial condition of the registrant;

B. Such proceeding involves primarily a claim for damages, or involves potential monetary sanctions, capital expenditures, deferred charges or charges to income and the amount involved, exclusive of interest and costs, exceeds 10 percent of the current assets of the registrant and its subsidiaries on a consolidated basis; or

C. A governmental authority is a party to such proceeding and such proceeding involves potential monetary sanctions, unless the registrant reasonably believes that such proceeding will result in no monetary sanctions, or in monetary sanctions, exclusive of interest and costs, of less than $100,000; provided, however, that such proceedings which are similar in nature may be grouped and described generically.

Specific information regarding the environmental legal proceedings that must be disclosed is set forth in Item 103 of Regulation S–K or, for registrants using the "small business issuer" reporting system, Item 103(a)–(b) of Regulation S–B. If disclosure is required, it must briefly describe the proceeding, "including the name of the court or agency in which the proceedings are pending, the date instituted, the principal parties thereto, a description of the factual basis alleged to underlie the proceedings and the relief sought."

You have been identified as a party to an environmental legal proceeding to which the United States government is, or was, a party. If you are an SEC registrant, this environmental legal proceeding may trigger, or may already have triggered, the disclosure obligation under the SEC regulations described above.

This notice is being provided to inform you of SEC registrants' duty to disclose any relevant environmental legal proceedings to the SEC. This notice does not create, modify or interpret any existing legal obligations, it is not intended to be an exhaustive description of the legally applicable requirements and it is not a substitute for regulations published in the Code of Federal Regulations. This notice has been issued to you for information purposes only. No determination of the applicability of this reporting requirement to your company has been made by any governmental entity. You should seek competent counsel in determining the applicability of these and other SEC requirements to the environmental legal proceeding at issue, as well as any other proceedings known to be contemplated by governmental authorities.

If you have any questions about the SEC's environmental disclosure requirements, please contact the SEC Office of the Special Senior Counsel for Disclosure Operations at (202) 942–1888.

---

## QUESTIONS AND DISCUSSION

**1.** Assuming Energena is a publicly traded company, do its plans to enter the wind power industry trigger any reporting obligations under SEC rules? Consider in particular Item 101, description of business, and Item 303, management's discussion and analysis. Item 101 generally requires disclosure of the material effects of complying with environmental regulations upon capital expenditures and earnings, and Item 303 requires a narrative description of management's discussion and analysis (known as the MD & A) of, among other things, forward-looking information that will enable investors to see the company through the eyes of management. Draft a disclosure statement describing in general the environmental compliance issues and potential enforcement liabilities Energena will face as it embarks on its new wind power initiative. Consider in particular the possibility that Energena might locate wind farms where winds are suitable today, but that global climate change might significantly alter wind patterns in those areas over time. Should Energena disclose the effects of such changes pursuant to Items 101 and 303? *See Survey Finds Most Publicly Traded Firms Not Disclosing Climate Risks to Investors*, 38 ENV'T REP. (BNA) 238 (Feb. 2, 2007).

**2.** In September 2007, New York Attorney General Andrew Cuomo subpoenaed five power companies with charges that they had failed adequately to disclose to investors the carbon dioxide emissions that will be emitted by several planned coal-fired power plants, and a coalition of pension funds and other investors petitioned the SEC to investigate the adequacy of disclosures regarding the impacts of climate change and climate change regulation (see Chapter 8) on business. The SEC in January 2010 voted to provide public companies with interpretive guidance on existing SEC disclosure requirements as they apply to business or legal developments relating to the issue of climate change. It summarized the guidance in this press statement:

> Federal securities laws and SEC regulations require certain disclosures by public companies for the benefit of investors. Occasionally, to assist those who provide such disclosures, the Commission provides guidance on how to interpret the disclosure rules on topics of interest to the business and investment communities. The Commission's interpretive releases do not create new legal requirements nor modify existing ones, but are intended to provide clarity and enhance consistency for public companies and their investors.
>
> The interpretive release approved today provides guidance on certain existing disclosure rules that may require a company to disclose the impact that business or legal developments related to climate change may have on its business. The relevant rules cover a company's risk factors, business description, legal proceedings, and management discussion and analysis.
>
> "We are not opining on whether the world's climate is changing, at what pace it might be changing, or due to what causes. Nothing that the Commission does today should be construed as weighing in on those topics," said SEC Chairman Mary Schapiro. "Today's guidance will help to ensure that our disclosure rules are consistently applied."

Specifically, the SEC's interpretative guidance highlights the following areas as examples of where climate change may trigger disclosure requirements:

- **Impact of Legislation and Regulation:** When assessing potential disclosure obligations, a company should consider whether the impact of certain existing laws and regulations regarding climate change is material. In certain circumstances, a company should also evaluate the potential impact of pending legislation and regulation related to this topic.
- **Impact of International Accords:** A company should consider, and disclose when material, the risks or effects on its business of international accords and treaties relating to climate change.
- **Indirect Consequences of Regulation or Business Trends:** Legal, technological, political and scientific developments regarding climate change may create new opportunities or risks for companies. For instance, a company may face decreased demand for goods that produce significant greenhouse gas emissions or increased demand for goods that result in lower emissions than competing products. As such, a company should consider, for disclosure purposes, the actual or potential indirect consequences it may face due to climate change related regulatory or business trends.
- **Physical Impacts of Climate Change:** Companies should also evaluate for disclosure purposes the actual and potential material impacts of environmental matters on their business.

Does it strike you as odd that the SEC would issue guidance for how to report these business impacts while professing that it was "not opining on whether the world's climate is changing, at what pace it might be changing, or due to what causes"? Regardless of the agency's neutrality on that subject at the time, its follow through on the policy has been mixed. In 2015 a coalition of institutional investors known as CERES studied public company disclosures and found them wanting, writing to the SEC:

> As institutional investors representing over $1.9 trillion in assets under management, we are concerned that oil and gas companies are not disclosing sufficient information about several converging factors that, together, will profoundly affect the economics of the industry. They include capital expenditures on increasingly high cost, carbon intensive oil and gas exploration projects, government efforts to limit carbon emissions, and the possibility of reduced global demand for oil as early as 2020 (collectively "carbon asset risks").
>
> We have found an absence of disclosure in SEC filings regarding these material risks, which constitute "known trends" under SEC rules, and respectfully ask the Commission to address this issue in comment letters to issuers.

Letter from CERES to Mary Jo White, SEC Chair (April 17, 2015), available at https://www.ceres.org/files/confidential/investor-sec-letter-inadequate-carbon-asset-risk-disclosure-by-oil-and-gas-companies.

The climate got hotter after that (pun intended), with similar demands from Members of Congress and the New York State Attorney General for more robust scrutiny and enforcement by the SEC of its climate change related disclosure policy. Matters peaked in late 2015 when the New York State Attorney General obtained assurances from Peabody Coal Company that it would end misleading statements in its corporate disclosures. *See* http://www.ag.ny.gov/press-release/ag-schneiderman-secures-unprecedented-agreement-peabody-energy-end-misleading. How would you advise your client Energena to design its disclosures given these developments?

**3.** For more background on and assessment of the SEC climate risks disclosure policy, see Sudhir Lay Burgaard, *Time to Issue a New Climate Disclosure Guidance*, NATURAL RESOURCES & ENV'T, Fall 2014, at 56; Scott D. Deatherage, *The SEC Enters the Fray on Climate Risk Disclosure*, NATURAL RESOURCES & ENV'T, Winter 2011, at 35. For a thorough explanation of the legal basis and practical effects of SEC's environmental liabilities disclosure rules, see Joseph J. Armao and Brian J. Griffith, *The SEC's Increasing Emphasis on Disclosing Environmental Liabilities*, NATURAL RESOURCES & ENV'T, Spring 1997, at 31, and for a more current prognosis, see Ann Johnston and Angeles T. Rodriguez, *Environmental Disclosure: Come Clean in the Green Wave or Face the Heat*, Natural Resources & Env't, Winter 2006, at 3, and Caroline B.C. Hermann, *Corporate Environmental Disclosure Requirements*, 35 Envtl. L. Rep. 10308 (2005). For a critique of the SEC rules, arguing they contain too many loopholes and are not sufficiently demanding, see Sanford Lewis and Tim Little, The Rose Foundation for Communities and the Environment, Fooling Investors and Fooling Themselves: How Aggressive Corporate Accounting & Asset Management Tactics Can Lead to Environmental Accounting Fraud (July 2004), *available at* http://www.rosefdn.org/fooling.pdf. In 2004, the U.S. Government Accountability Office also concluded that the SEC had not been systematically tracking disclosures or adequately keeping track of environmental issues that should lead to disclosure. *See* GAO, Environmental Disclosure: SEC Should Explore Ways to Improve Tracking and Transparency of Information, GAO–04–808 (July 2004).

## III. COMPLIANCE STRATEGIES

The materials in Part II of this chapter describe compliance mechanisms applied in discrete settings, such as an assessment of compliance issued when a project is proposed or a snapshot environmental compliance audit of ongoing industrial operations. To the extent that these one-time compliance efforts "pay off" in the sense that their costs are outweighed by the reduced enforcement penalties that can result from better compliance performance as well as from federal and state voluntary disclosure policies, it would make sense to engage in a more systematic compliance assessment process. Indeed, increased compliance might also have a pay off for government by reducing enforcement costs, possibly justifying providing cost-saving incentives beyond reduced penalties, such as fewer facility inspections and expedited permit review, to regulated entities that engage in such systematic compliance initiatives. Going even further, it may be the case that the pay off for companies of boosting compliance through systematic assessment programs goes beyond the enforcement and permitting context—i.e., beyond just lower penalties and preferred treatment. Perhaps going "green" by maximizing compliance with environmental regulations, or even going beyond compliance, is in itself good for a business's financial bottom line. This part considers all three possibilities.

## A. ENVIRONMENTAL MANAGEMENT SYSTEMS

### New York Department of Environmental Conservation, Environmental Management Systems

http://www.dec.state.ny.us/website/ppu/p2ems.html.

**What is an EMS?**

An Environmental Management System (EMS) is a set of management tools and principles designed to create the administrative procedures that an organization needs to integrate environmental concerns into its daily business practices. Basically, an EMS provides a framework for managing environmental responsibilities in a more systematic manner. A properly developed EMS is built on the "Plan, Do, Check, Act" model for continual improvement. In an EMS Standard, the "plan, do, check, act" steps have been expanded into the following five steps: 1) environmental policy, 2) planning, 3) implementation, 4) checking/ corrective action and 5) management review. . . .

**What types of organizations can have an EMS?**

Essentially any organization can benefit from an EMS. The highly regulated industrial facility is an obvious candidate for an EMS, but even the most service orientated office operation can make effective use of an EMS. The emissions from smokestacks and discharges from pipes are clear interactions with the environment. However, even the way we travel to work, procure office materials, or plan meetings and conferences can impact the environment. Thus, the EMS is not solely the domain of large private sector manufacturers. To the contrary, EMSs are being implemented at private sector businesses of all shapes and sizes, and at government organizations of all levels.

### Why should you have an EMS?

Increasingly businesses have realized that environmental problems would be better managed in a systematic way. Just as businesses develop financial management systems to promote the efficient use and management of monetary resources, they realize that EMSs developed and integrated into the organizational structure will reduce risks from pollution and will help provide an opportunity to be more efficient and organized. First, an effective EMS makes good business sense. By helping you identify the causes of environmental problems (and then eliminating them), an EMS can help you save money. In addition, the EMS will help your organization identify opportunities to prevent pollution, mitigate occupational hazards, and better control those operations that pose the most risk. Second, a properly implemented and audited EMS will aid a facility in maintaining compliance. By requiring an organization to identify each of its compliance requirements and monitoring their ability to meet these obligations the facility is better positioned to stay in compliance.

## Environmental Protection Agency, Position Statement on Environmental Management Systems

71 Fed. Reg. 5664 (Feb. 2, 2006).

### Background

During the past decade, public and private organizations have increasingly adopted formal Environmental Management Systems (EMSs) to address their environmental responsibilities. The most common framework an EMS uses is the plan-do-check-act process, with the goal of continual improvement. EMSs provide organizations of all types with a structured system and approach for managing environmental and regulatory responsibilities to improve overall environmental performance and stewardship, including areas not subject to regulation such as product design, resource conservation, energy efficiency, and other sustainable practices. EMSs can also facilitate the integration of the full scope of environmental considerations into the mission of the organization and improve environmental performance by establishing a continual process of checking to ensure environmental goals are set and met. A well-designed EMS includes procedures for taking corrective action if problems occur and encourages preventive action to avoid problems.

Over the last several years, EPA has been involved in a wide range of voluntary activities to facilitate EMS adoption. EPA has learned through our work with other organizations that EMSs can improve organizational efficiency and competitiveness, provide an infrastructure for public communication and engagement, and provide a platform to address other important issues such as security. EMSs do not replace the need for regulatory and enforcement programs, but they can complement them. Although EMSs cannot guarantee any specific level of environmental performance, EPA has learned that, when properly implemented, EMSs can help facilities achieve significantly improved environmental results and other benefits.

**Statement of Principles**

EPA's overall policy on EMSs, as with the EMS approach itself, will continue to be guided by the principles of continual improvement and learning, flexibility, and collaboration.

- EPA will encourage widespread use of EMSs across a range of organizations and settings, with particular emphasis on adoption of EMSs to achieve improved environmental performance and compliance, pollution prevention through source reduction, and continual improvement. The Agency will support EMSs that are appropriate to the needs and characteristics of specific sectors and facilities and encourage the use of EMSs as a means of integrating other facility management programs.
- EPA will promote the voluntary adoption of EMSs. To encourage voluntary adoption of EMSs, EPA will rely on public education and voluntary programs.
- EPA will encourage organizations that use EMSs to obtain stakeholder input on matters relevant to the development and implementation of an EMS and to demonstrate accountability for the performance outcomes of their EMSs through measurable objectives and targets. Additionally, the Agency will encourage organizations to share information on the performance of their EMSs with public and government agencies and facilitate this process where practicable.
- EPA will encourage the use of recognized environmental management frameworks, such as the ISO 14001 Standard, as a basis for designing and implementing EMSs that aim to achieve outcomes aligned with the nation's environmental policy goals and the principles of this Position Statement.
- EPA will collaborate with other key partners—including states, other federal agencies, tribes, local governments, industry, and non-governmental organizations—as it implements this policy. EPA will support international EMS initiatives that facilitate the increased use of EMSs in the United States. The Agency will ensure that as it implements this policy, its decisions and work are transparent to all interested parties.

- EPA will lead by example, by developing, implementing, and maintaining EMSs at appropriate EPA facilities.
- EPA will foster continual learning by supporting research and public dialogue on EMSs that help improve the Agency's understanding of circumstances where EMSs can advance the nation's environmental policy goals. EPA will continue to collect improved data on the application of EMSs as it becomes available, including the efficacy of EMSs in improving environmental performance and the costs and benefits of an EMS to an organization and the environment.

## QUESTIONS AND DISCUSSION

**1.** It is important to distinguish between the kind of snapshot environmental compliance audit described in Part I of Chapter 13 for business transactions and the environmental management system described by the New York DEC and EPA in the foregoing policy excerpts. The latter is *systematic* in that it is designed not only to identify noncompliance, but also to ferret out its causes and develop options for correcting them. As the EPA has explained:

> An environmental auditing program is an integral part of any organization's environmental management system (EMS). Audit findings generated from the use of these protocols can be used as a basis to implement, upgrade, or benchmark environmental management systems. Regular environmental auditing can be the key element to a high quality environmental management program and will function best when an organization identifies the "root causes" of each audit finding. Root causes are the primary factors that lead to noncompliance events. For example a violation of a facility's wastewater discharge permit may be traced back to breakdowns in management oversight, information exchange, or inadequate evaluations by untrained facility personnel.
>
> [A] typical approach to auditing involves three basic steps: conducting the audit, identifying problems (audit findings), and fixing identified deficiencies. When the audit process is expanded, to identify and correct root causes to noncompliance, the organization's corrective action part of its EMS becomes more effective. In the expanded model, audit findings (exceptions) undergo a root cause analysis to identify underlying causes to noncompliance events. Management actions are then taken to correct the underlying causes behind the audit findings and improvements are made to the organizations overall EMS before another audit is conducted on the facility. Expanding the audit process allows the organization to successfully correct problems, sustain compliance, and prevent discovery of the same findings again during subsequent audits.

> Furthermore, identifying the root cause of an audit finding can mean identifying not only the failures that require correction but also successful practices that promote compliance and prevent violations. In each case a root cause analysis should uncover the failures while promoting the successes so that an organization can make continual progress toward environmental excellence.

U.S. Environmental Protection Agency, Protocol for Conducting Environmental Compliance Audits for Hazardous Waste Generators under RCRA (June 2001).

**2.** In his thought-provoking exploration of EMSs as an agent of change in corporate compliance behavior, David Case provides this brief history of the emergence through private sector initiatives—i.e., not from government mandate—of standardized approaches to EMS implementation:

> In the early 1990s, a number of business-oriented, non-governmental organizations sought to influence the environmental behavior of business organizations. These non-governmental organizations provided early momentum to the standardization movement by creating guidelines for the development of EMSs. Particularly celebrated examples include environmental management principles and guidelines published by the Global Environmental Management Initiative ("GEMI"), the Coalition for Environmentally Responsible Economies ("CERES"), and the International Chamber of Commerce ("ICC"). Public and social pressures on this issue influenced these business-oriented groups. Environmental advocacy groups such as Greenpeace, the Sierra Club, the Natural Resources Defense Council and others encouraged these organizations to develop environmental management guidelines.
>
> By 2000, seven trade associations had developed codes of environmental management practices and required their member to adopt these practices. Notable trade-association EMS initiatives and guidance documents include the American Chemistry Counsel's "Responsible Care" program and the American Petroleum Institute's Strategies for Today's Environmental Partnership program. The Responsible Care initiative is considered "a direct attempt by U.S. chemical manufacturers to institutionalize new norms of behavior for participants." Other trade association adopting similar EMS guidelines include those for chemical distribution, forestry and textile industries.
>
> By far, however, the most well known and influential standardization initiative is ISO 14001, "the voluntary international EMS standard [first] published by the Geneva-based International Organization for Standardization ('ISO') in 1996." The initial objective underlying publication of ISO 14001 was to create a single, international EMS standard applicable to organizations of all types and sizes. Early predictions that ISO 14001 would become the leading voluntary EMS standard around

> the globe have proven accurate. From 1996 to the end of 2001, at least 1,645 United States businesses and firms "were registered as conforming to this standard." At that time, United States registrations were increasing at a rate exceeding fifty percent per year. By the end of the 2001, "an estimated 36,765 organization were registered" worldwide. By the end of 2004, the estimated number of worldwide ISO 14001 registrations had increased to 90,569. This number includes an estimated 4,759 businesses and firms in the United States.

David W. Case, *Changing Corporate Behavior Through Environmental Management Systems*, 31 WM. & MARY ENVTL. L. & POL'Y REV. 75, 87–88 (2006). For additional history and analysis, see REGULATING FROM THE INSIDE: CAN ENVIRONMENTAL MANAGEMENT SYSTEMS ACHIEVE POLICY GOALS? (Cary Coglianese and Jennifer Nash eds., 2001). For more information on the Global Environmental Management Initiative and ISO 14001, see GEMI's website at http://www.gemi.org. For a diversity of views about whether ISO 14001 and other voluntary, industry-driven EMS initiatives are effective, see The Forum, *Are Voluntary Standards Working?*, The Environmental Forum, Sept.–Oct. 2006, at 42.

**3.** How would you describe EPA's position in the EMS position statement? Is it cautious or ambitious? Does it outline an incentive-based approach or an education-based approach? To what has the agency committed? How meaningful to industry are the "positions" EPA assumes? What should EPA's position be? In particular, if EMSs are so beneficial and have been driven largely by private sector initiative, should EPA mandate their use, or should it "get out of the way" and let the movement flourish?

**4.** Why should an environmental lawyer care about the previous questions? Two veteran environmental attorneys suggest why:

> What do the growth in EMSs and the use of the ISO 14001 Standard as an EMS model mean to an environmental lawyer? Most managers believe that what gets attention, gets improved—so, if a client wants to see improvement he or she needs to devote the appropriate attention. Thus, it makes sense to know exactly what constitutes an EMS and how to evaluate it. In recognizing that an EMS is one of the management systems and quality systems that constitutes an organization's overall management approach, one should become sufficiently comfortable with its application to be able to counsel on its wise use.

Henry Balikov & David Soltis, *Environmental Management Systems: Part of Doing Business in the 21st Century*, 35 TRENDS 12, 13 (2003).

---

## B. COMPLIANCE INCENTIVE PROGRAMS

Given the expected benefits of EMS programs in terms of compliance performance, many commentators have advocated that EPA and other government agencies should do more to provide incentives for companies to adopt rigorous EMS practices. *See, e.g.*, David W. Case, *Changing Corporate Behavior Through Environmental Management Systems*, 31 WM. & MARY ENVTL. L. & POL'Y F. 75 (2006); Allison F. Gardner, *Beyond Compliance: Regulatory Incentives to Implement Environmental Management Systems*, 11 N.Y.U. ENVTL. L.J. 662 (2003); Timothy F. Malloy, *Regulation, Compliance and the Firm*, 76 TEMPLE L. REV. 451 (2003). The idea that compliance incentives should go beyond promoting disclosure of noncompliance picked up steam in the 1990s in the Clinton Administration's so-called "reinvention" initiative. Key components of that movement are described in the following article:

## Dennis D. Hirsch, *Lean and Green? Environmental Law and Policy and the Flexible Production Economy*

79 INDIANA L.J. 611 (2004).

Launched with great fanfare in the mid-1990s, Environmental Regulatory Reinvention was the signature environmental initiative of the Clinton Administration and of several state environmental agencies. It consisted of a set of pilot programs that experimented with new approaches to environmental regulation, some of which continue to operate today. The leading Reinvention programs shared three core themes: (1) they provided flexibility to participating facilities as to how they should go about meeting environmental standards (including flexibility as to permit requirements); (2) they set ambitious environmental standards for these facilities and required them to deliver environmental performance superior to that which would otherwise be required under traditional regulatory requirements; and (3) they required participating facilities to reach out to interested parties (community members, environmental groups, local regulators, etc.) and engage these stakeholders in a discussion of the facility's environmental management and performance. The hope was that aggressive performance measures combined with flexibility in implementation and greater stakeholder involvement might offer improved environmental protection for less cost, and with greater accountability than traditional regulation. Or, as the Clinton administration liked to say, Reinvention would provide a "cheaper, cleaner and smarter" approach to environmental regulation.

The Clinton Administration billed the Reinvention effort as a way to bring "common sense" to environmental regulation and develop fundamentally new and more effective approaches to the field. Some commentators agree with this characterization. Others have come to view Reinvention more cynically. They see it as an attempt by the Clinton Administration to portray environmental policies as being less costly, and so to deflect the recently-elected (in 1994) Republican Congress's attacks on environmental regulation.

### 1. Environmental Contracting Under Project XL

The flagship program of the Clinton Administration's Reinvention effort was Project XL. This initiative experimented with a regulatory method known as environmental contracting. Under this approach, the EPA invited regulated parties to design their own strategies for achieving pollution control. It then offered to provide them with the flexibility to implement these new compliance methods, even where this required a departure from existing regulatory requirements. In exchange, participating facilities had to do two things. Following the basic Reinvention model, they had to commit to levels of environmental performance that were more stringent than those that they would have achieved under existing requirements, and they had to seek out and engage a diverse group of stakeholders and attempt to gain their support for the project. This bargain—regulatory flexibility from the government in exchange for better environmental performance and increased stakeholder participation from the facility—constituted the "environmental contract."

While the XL projects are quite varied in nature, one theme that emerges from them is that participating companies seem interested in obtaining regulatory flexibility with respect to air permitting requirements. These requests appear to be generated by companies engaged in rapid process change whose main concern is regulatory speed. For example, Intel Corporation turned to Project XL to resolve the conflict between its fast-cycle operation and [Clean Air Act New Source Review (NSR)] permitting requirements. The project . . . concerned a new Intel chip manufacturing plant located in Chandler, Arizona, that produced Pentium microprocessors. The company represented that, in its globally competitive business, success depended on its ability to develop new chips faster than its competitors. The company developed an entirely new generation of microprocessors every two to three years, and undertook thirty to forty-five meaningful changes to its manufacturing process per year. . . . Intel maintained that [the NSR] requirements, with their delays on new constructions and modifications, were fundamentally incompatible with its fast-change business model. According to the company, permitting delays cost it millions of dollars in lost revenue per day.

The company and the EPA used Project XL to develop a solution. Under the terms of the environmental contract, Intel agreed to cap pollutant emissions from the facility at a level more stringent than that which existing standards would otherwise have required and to take steps to increase public involvement. So long as the company remained within this emissions limit, the regulatory authorities would allow it to change its manufacturing process without obtaining a permit—the plantwide emissions limit approach to permitting. According to the company, it was able to meet the stringent plantwide limit by using a "design for the environment" approach that allowed it to build pollution prevention into the design of its products.

While the Intel XL Project demonstrates the potential benefits of such an approach, it also brings out some weaknesses, particularly with respect to the superior environmental performance and stakeholder participation aspects. Intel's XL agreement set a number of caps on different types of emissions. One of these governed the emission of a specific category of pollutants known as hazardous air pollutants ("HAPs"). Some hazardous air pollutants are more dangerous than others. Critics argued that, by grouping these pollutants as a category and setting an overall cap, the agreement would allow Intel to increase emissions of a more toxic pollutant while decreasing emissions of a less dangerous one. This could result in worse, not better, environmental performance. This dispute almost derailed the project. This experience argues in favor of defining superior environmental performance on a pollutant-by-pollutant basis, rather than for categories of pollutants. Except where they are manifestly beneficial to the environment, cross-pollutant "trades" (such as increasing emissions of one pollutant in exchange for decreased emissions of another) should be avoided.

With respect to stakeholder involvement, a concern emerged that national environmental groups would not have the resources to monitor a large number of site-specific XL agreements such as the one negotiated with Intel, while local groups do not have sufficient expertise to make their participation meaningful. The EPA tried to address this problem by providing these groups (local or national) with a $25,000 grant for the hiring of experts. Another issue is that, in Intel's XL project and others, the EPA has let the company convene and run the stakeholder group. This poses an obvious conflict of interest. A better approach would be to have the EPA itself choose and moderate the stakeholder group. In sum, the Intel project provides some cautionary lessons about the emissions cap method. Yet it also points up the need for such an approach, and the role of Reinvention in addressing that need.

### 2. The Pollution Prevention in Permitting Program (P4)

A second Reinvention pilot program, the Pollution Prevention in Permitting Project (P4), also demonstrates a connection to fast-cycle industry. The P4 initiative focused on permit modification requirements under the [Clean Air Act] Title V Operating Permit Program. The EPA invited facilities to submit a list of upcoming physical and process changes that would typically trigger review and modification of these facility air permits. The agency then offered to pre-approve these changes if the facility, in return, would agree to an emissions cap set below the level traditionally required, and would use pollution prevention measures to achieve this more ambitious level of performance. This allowed facilities to have all their anticipated changes approved at once, rather than going through a separate permitting process for each and so created an incentive for pollution prevention and for better environmental results. A later EPA report found that all the participating facilities reduced their emissions during the terms of their P4 permits, some by substantial amounts, although others have disputed these results.

Six facilities participated in the P4 pilot. According to a later study, the common themes that linked them were a commitment to rapid process change and the ability to implement upstream design and process changes in order to achieve pollution reductions elsewhere in the operation. The EPA's own statements further demonstrate the link to flexible production. An agency official explained that the program is not designed for "a slowly changing company that needs to make only one facility permit revision per year. . . . But if you're making a change every month, all of a sudden the scale changes. The need for predictability increases the value of the P4 permit." Elsewhere, the EPA described the P4 program as designed for "sources in highly competitive industries characterized by frequent and/or unpredictable movement within product lines" that are "technically capable of . . . promot[ing] P2."

While the P4 program appears to have worked for certain . . . facilities, it too provides some cautionary lessons. Stakeholder involvement was insufficient. The pre-approval agreement encompassed an array of future changes, yet the EPA granted no more public review than it does for standard permits that involve only a single change. In addition, . . . it will often be hard, if not impossible, to predict the precise future process changes that a facility will want to make. This means that the list of anticipated changes (pre-approved so long as the facility remains within its emissions cap) will have to be broadly worded and short on detail. But this will hamper the Agency's (and the public's) ability to determine exactly what the facility has in mind, and what the emissions implications of these changes will be. The pre-approval approach accordingly introduces an element of uncertainty into the regulatory process.

### 3. The Performance Track Approach

Performance track programs at the state and federal levels are among the most significant Reinvention initiatives. These programs create a separate, more flexible regulatory pathway for facilities that can demonstrate that they are top environmental performers. They thereby seek to encourage better environmental stewardship. This section will offer a view of Reinvention at the state level by focusing on Oregon's performance track initiative, known as the Green Permits program.

To be admitted to the Green Permits program, a facility must achieve environmental results "significantly better than otherwise required by law;" engage stakeholders in a discussion of the facility's environmental planning; "consider [the] results of stakeholder involvement in decisionmaking, and respond to comments received;" and implement an environmental management system. The benefits to participating companies range from public recognition, to technical assistance, to the designation of a single point of contact with the agency. Of greater relevance here, facilities also can receive "regulatory flexibility" with respect to existing environmental requirements, including the replacement of traditional state air permitting requirements with plantwide emission limits (as were used in the Intel XL project) and pre-approvals (as in the P4 program). In short, the Green Permits program—much like Project XL and the P4 program—offers permit flexibility (among other regulatory benefits) in exchange for improved environmental performance and increased stakeholder involvement.

As with Project XL, the Green Permits experience points up the difficulty in defining superior environmental performance. The Oregon DEP's rules require that all participating facilities "achieve environmental results that are significantly better than otherwise required by law," but leaves it entirely up to the agency to determine what counts as "significant." According to an early report, this open-ended definition of better performance has allowed participating facilities to be vague in defining just how their performance would be "superior." Green Permits also provides some lessons with respect to stakeholder involvement. Here too, the regulations are broadly worded. They require participating facilities to "encourage public inquiries and comments" and "provide mechanisms" for public input on environmental performance, but do not specifically define how this is to occur. This has led to under-inclusive stakeholder participation that, in some cases, has excluded environmental groups.

---

## QUESTIONS AND DISCUSSION

**1.** Notwithstanding his general enthusiasm for the Reinvention programs, Hirsch identified several tensions between them and conventional enforcement policy. One is that stakeholder participation, which is made more difficult by the "contractarian" approach used in programs that tailor incentives to the particular compliance profiles of individual facilities. Even more problematic is the concern that the baseline of expected compliance can be difficult to define precisely, making it all the more difficult to identify when incentives for going "beyond" compliance are appropriate. Concerns such as these led some commentators to question the wisdom, and even the legality, of the Reinvention programs. *See, e.g.*, Rena Steinzor, *Regulatory Reinvention and Project XL: Does the Emperor Have Any Clothes?*, 26 ENVTL. L. REP. 10527 (1996).

**2.** Assuming programs like those Hirsch describes were available to the wind energy industry, would you advise Energena to participate in them? How would you evaluate for Energena the costs and benefits of such programs? Are there hidden costs if a company decides to participate in a program and then either backs out because the program was not what it appeared to be or because the company simply fails to live up to the program's demands?

**3.** Assuming no such programs currently exist for wind energy production facilities, would you advise EPA or a state environmental agency to design such programs for the wind energy industry? If so, what programs do you believe would be most effective?

**4.** Hirsch describes "performance track" programs as the "most significant" of the Reinvention initiatives. The benefit of participating in such programs is supposed to be "regulatory flexibility." Indeed, EPA touted just over 400 participants in its Performance Track program by October 2006, six years into the program's history. Does that seem like a lot of participants, or surprisingly few? EPA even sweetened the pot for participation in Performance Track by specifically reducing paperwork and inspection burdens for participant companies under hazardous waste regulations. *See* Resource Conservation and Recovery Act Burden Reduction Initiative, 71 Fed. Reg. 16862 (Apr. 4, 2006). But in 2007 EPA's Inspector General concluded that the voluntary Performance Track program does not adequately link actions with goals and does not itself have sufficient performance measures to determine whether the program is succeeding. *See* Office of Inspector General, USEPA, Performance Track Could Improve Program Design and Management to Ensure Value (Mar. 29, 2007), *available at* http://www.epa.gov/oig/reports/2007/20070329–2007–P–00013.pdf. EPA terminated Performance Track on May 14, 2009. At the time of termination, the program had a membership base of 547 facilities in 49 states and Puerto Rico.

**5.** If you were charged with designing a compliance incentive program for a federal or state agency, what approach would you take?

**6.** Looking into the future, what are the compliance counseling challenges for environmental lawyers? This description of the opening general session at a major conference the American Bar Association holds each March for environmental lawyers suggests a vision:

> As the importance of multinational corporations in the global economy grows, so too does scrutiny of their potential to exacerbate or ameliorate global environmental threats such as climate change, water quality and scarcity, and loss of biological diversity. Similarly, deepening public reservations about resource scarcity, poverty, consumption patterns and urbanization are prompting CEOs to demonstrate that profits at home and abroad have not come at the expense of workers, supply chains, and host countries and communities. Others are deeply concerned with whether current business growth will be limited by natural resource constraints, be they oil or water or the atmosphere's capacity to absorb greenhouse gases. With globalization affecting corporate sustainability and reshaping perceptions of corporate virtue and competitiveness, this session will explore the role of business in furthering, or impeding, environmentally sustainable

> globalization, as well as the implications of these trends for policy makers, the bar and other interested stakeholders.

American Bar Association, Program Brochure, 36th Annual Conference on Environmental Law (2007). It appears that environmental compliance counseling work is in no danger of going out of demand. For thoughts on the role of corporate counsel in responding to that need, see Craig D. Galli, *A Compliance Crisis is a Terrible Thing to Waste: Counsel's Role to Enhance Corporate Culture*, NATURAL RESOURCES & ENV'T, Winter 2016, at 8.

# CHAPTER 11

# ENFORCEMENT

## CHAPTER OUTLINE



---

*Enforcement is where the rubber meets the road,*
*and everything else hits the fan.*
—attributed to Douglas Farnsworth

# I. OVERVIEW OF THE ENFORCEMENT PROCESS

## A. INTRODUCTION

Environmental enforcement is a critically important topic. While law students spend a great deal of time studying the laws on the books, one must keep clearly in mind that the mere fact of a law's existence is no assurance of its implementation. Rules on the books can prove toothless if they are not enforced. At a minimum, an effective system of enforcement should seek to achieve both the force of law—to ensure the law is effectively applied—and the rule of law—to ensure the law is justly applied. Yet ensuring the force and rule of law is by no means a given. Indeed, this is a very real challenge faced daily in many countries around the world.

It is assumed among regulators and regulated alike that few parties, if any, are in compliance with all relevant regulations all of the time. What taxpayer does not blanch when receiving notification of an Internal Revenue Service audit? A fine-tooth inspection of any tax return will likely reveal some filing or calculation error, as will most searching audits in any highly regulated field, whether securities, insurance, or others. Some noncompliance may be unintentional, and some knowing. Just think about your own driving. How often do you drive above the speed limit when the road is empty? Do you drive above the speed limit when everyone else seems to be driving 10 miles above the limit? Our own behavior raises larger law enforcement issues—How can the law be fairly enforced when everyone is driving over the speed limit? Given that speeding causes more deaths than violations of environmental laws, should more resources be dedicated to traffic enforcement than environmental enforcement?

Ensuring effective environmental enforcement is complex. As economist Gary Becker famously observed in the context of criminal enforcement, decisions whether to break the law turn largely on a calculus of four factors—the benefit of noncompliance weighed against the probability of apprehension, likelihood of conviction, and severity of punishment. Gary Becker, *Crime and Punishment: An Economic Approach,* 76 J. OF POL. ECON. 169 (1968). Breaking this down, effective enforcement depends on three very different tasks: (1) monitoring to ensure the party is in compliance, (2) administrative and judicial processes that convert observed noncompliance into a legal judgment against the offending party, and (3) sanctions that are significant enough to achieve the rule's objective.

Enforcement speaks to several parties. Most obvious, enforcement efforts seek to punish the offending party such that they do not profit from their noncompliance. This helps ensure a level playing field for those who comply with the law. Nobody wants to feel like a chump, being effectively punished for law-abiding behavior because lawbreakers "get away with it." Enforcement also speaks volumes to parties *outside* the particular action. That is, enforcement not only deters the particular lawbreaker who was punished, but it should also deter potential lawbreakers from violating the law. Punishing a speeding motorist with a heavy fine not only deters that motorist but others, as well, who do not want to pay a fine in the future. These two aspects are known as specific deterrence and general deterrence. And, finally, these goals of enforcement need to be tempered with justice. Compliance will be easier to obtain if the enforcement process is widely regarded as legitimate. This may involve, often in subtle ways, informal norms of the community or industry sector that guide behavior. *See generally,* Michael P. Vandenbergh, *Beyond Elegance: A Testable Typology of Social Norms in Corporate Environmental Compliance,* 22 STANFORD ENVTL. L. J. 55 (2003).

How well does U.S. environmental enforcement work? In terms of overall environmental metrics, the answer appears to be quite positive. With few exceptions, the air is cleaner, water less polluted, and waste more safely handled than twenty and thirty years ago. In 2015, the EPA initiated 2,380 civil and administrative enforcement cases and opened over 200 new environmental crime cases, not to mention the many actions filed by state authorities and many more independently-filed citizen suits. EPA claimed its enforcement actions resulted in 1.8 billion pounds of reduced pollution and over $7 billion of investments by regulated parties to reduce pollution, clean up contamination, and fund environmentally beneficial projects. Criminal fines, restitution and court-ordered projects comprised an additional $4 billion. Taken together, these are big numbers, and indicate a lot of enforcement activity. EPA, FY2015 COMPLIANCE AND ENFORCEMENT ANNUAL RESULTS 10 (2015).

Yet, if one focuses on noncompliance, the success of our enforcement efforts becomes less clear. Consider, for example, monitoring activities. In 2015, EPA conducted about 15,400 inspections leading to over 2,300 civil actions. States (who do the lion's share of enforcement) will conduct roughly 140,000 inspections and 9,000 enforcement actions. Jon Silberman, *Does Environmental Deterrence Work? Evidence and Experience Say Yes, But We Need to Understand How and Why*, 30 ENVTL. L. REP. 10,523, 10,528 (2000); EPA, FY2015 COMPLIANCE AND ENFORCEMENT ANNUAL RESULTS (2015). Impressive numbers, until one realizes that there are roughly eight *million* regulated parties subject to environmental laws. In other words, a regulated party has about a 2% chance of being inspected (and a 0.16% chance of being sanctioned) in any given year.

Indeed, there still exist areas of U.S. environmental law with significant levels of noncompliance. A 2009 series of articles in the *New York Times* reported more than half a million violations of the Clean Water Act by 23,000 different companies since 2004. Roughly 40 percent of the nation's water systems had violated the Safe Drinking Water Act. The newspaper's conclusion was damning: "The violations range from failing to report emissions to dumping toxins at concentrations regulators say might contribute to cancer, birth defects and other illnesses. However, the vast majority of those polluters have escaped punishment. State officials have repeatedly ignored obvious illegal dumping, and the Environmental Protection Agency, which can prosecute polluters when states fail to act, has often declined to intervene." Charles Duhigg, *Clean Water Laws Are Neglected, at a Cost in Suffering,* N.Y. TIMES, Sept. 12, 2009, at 1. Nor is this a new problem. A 2012 General Accounting Office study concluded that "because of incomplete or unreliable data on compliance in some programs, such as the NPDES [permitting program under the Clean Water Act], EPA cannot determine the full extent of entities' compliance." GAO, ENVIRONMENTAL PROTECTION: EPA SHOULD DEVELOP A STRATEGIC PLAN FOR ITS NEW COMPLIANCE INITIATIVE (2012).

Should we be troubled by this noncompliance? Are these mostly paperwork violations or real harm to the environment and public health? Does it mean the enforcement system is not working, and what could be done to strengthen compliance?

We will address these questions and many others throughout this chapter as we explore the fascinating and fundamental topic of environmental enforcement. As we shall see, there are many steps in the enforcement process, involving significant discretion and judgment along the way by the attorneys and officials involved. Section I focuses on the players in enforcement—the Environmental Protection Agency, the Department of Justice, and state authorities. Environmental enforcement relies on a complex relationship between state and federal agencies that is both supportive and, at times, deeply conflicted. Section II turns to the enforcement process, walking through compliance monitoring, decisions to enforce, and the different avenues available to enforcement authorities—administrative, civil, or criminal processes. The section ends by reviewing the wide range of sanctions available, from fines and injunctions to jail time and supplemental environmental projects. Section III turns to one of the greatest innovations of environmental law and perhaps the most significant guarantor of environmental enforcement—the citizen suit. Section IV provides an extensive case study involving violations of the Clean Air Act.

## B. WHO ARE THE PLAYERS?

As described above, enforcement of federal environmental law involves the close cooperation of different actors at both the federal and state level. In simple terms, the U.S. EPA wields the primary implementation and enforcement authority for most environmental statutes. EPA interprets how the laws and regulations should be applied, determines enforcement priorities, issues penalty guidelines, and serves as the institutional check on state enforcement of federal environmental laws. EPA, however, has neither the independent authority to litigate cases nor the resources to administer all the federal laws. As a result, the Department of Justice serves as EPA's lawyer and many of the states have been delegated significant implementation and enforcement authority for most of the statutes. As you might expect with this many parties engaged in a common enterprise, disagreements among these agencies and divisions are not uncommon. As you read the description of these various roles below, consider how the different internal incentives of these actors can improve or obstruct enforcement efforts.

## Joel A. Mintz, *Civil Enforcement,* in PRACTICAL GUIDE TO ENVIRONMENTAL LAW (Michael Gerrard, ed.)

12–65 to 12–72 (2004).

### ENVIRONMENTAL PROTECTION AGENCY (EPA)

The U.S. EPA was formed in 1970, and has experienced rapid growth. It is today the largest regulatory agency in the United States, with approximately 18,000 employees [the number was down to 15,000 in 2015]. Most of those employees are located in the EPA's Washington, D.C., headquarters, and in its ten regional offices located in Boston, New York, Philadelphia, Atlanta, Chicago, Dallas, Kansas City Denver, San Francisco, and Seattle. It is charged by Congress with the administration and enforcement of the major environmental statutes. The organizational structure of EPA is very complex, particularly for enforcement. * * *

EPA's ten regional offices are organized into units, called "divisions," that generally correspond to the major environmental programs that EPA is charged with administering and enforcing. There are divisions that separately administer and enforce the air, water, solid and hazardous waste, and pesticide and toxic substance programs. Because they are program-specific, they are referred to as "program" divisions, and consist primarily of technical or scientific personnel. They are headed by Division Directors.

In some EPA regions, each program division has an enforcement subdivision that has primary authority for administrative enforcement of the program. This is an important responsibility as a high proportion of all of EPA's enforcement actions are administrative proceedings. This arrangement sometimes results in nonlegal personnel taking the lead in development or negotiation of some administrative enforcement cases, although the regional attorneys are frequently called into matters that are likely to be contested.

In other EPA regions, administrative enforcement and judicial case investigation and development are handled by technically trained personnel who are stationed in a regional enforcement division. Such enforcement divisions are often subdivided into branches that have sole responsibility for the enforcement of regulations concerning specific environmental media under particular federal environmental statutes (*e.g.*, Clean Air Act enforcement branches and Clean Water Act enforcement branches). Some EPA regional enforcement divisions also have separate branches that take the lead in regional development of multi-media enforcement cases against facilities, companies and/or industrial sectors. * * *

The EPA's enforcement functions and activities are centralized in the Office of Enforcement and Compliance Assurance (OECA). OECA contains two broad sub-units: an Office of Regulatory Enforcement and an Office of Compliance. The former, which is organized along media-lines and contains a mix of attorneys and technical enforcement staff, is responsible (along with the Office of Compliance, EPA regional enforcement personnel, cooperating states and the U.S. Department of Justice) for the development and pursuit of national enforcement initiatives that target particular companies and industrial sectors for large-scale enforcement actions. Targeting is usually premised on the extent to which discharges or emissions from those entities harm human health and the environment. Such strategic determinations are made following extensive EPA investigations into a wide variety of social, financial and environmental data. * * *

In their oversight of the enforcement activities of EPA's regional offices, OECA personnel sometimes become aware of or involved in cases presenting unique or important policy issues that arise in the course of enforcement actions. Their influence in the resolution of such issues is enhanced by the requirement that the Assistant Administrator for the OECA must approve the filing of all judicial cases and all consent decrees entered into by EPA.* * *

Since the headquarters offices' role in enforcement is, in part, one of oversight, the target of an enforcement action will find that appeals to those offices may be valuable when the regional offices have acted in an arbitrary, capricious, or illegal way, or have violated one of EPA's own policy or guidance documents. While EPA headquarters offices are usually reluctant to overrule a regional office action in an enforcement case, they will do so when it is clear that the regional office has acted improperly or unwisely from a national perspective.

*Practice Tip:* The enforcement target must be cautious in appealing a regional office action to EPA headquarters, particularly in doing so without informing the regional office enforcement personnel. As noted above, EPA headquarters will rarely overrule a regional office action, and the regional office enforcement personnel may take umbrage at having the enforcement target complain to headquarters. Considering the substantial discretion vested in the regional offices in various enforcement decisions (*e.g.*, penalty assessments), it may not be wise to unduly antagonize them. Appeals to headquarters should be based on clear abuses by the regional office, and the regional office usually should be advised that the appeal will be made. * * *

UNITED STATES DEPARTMENT OF JUSTICE (DOJ)

DOJ plays a major role in environmental judicial enforcement. Some environmental statutes require EPA, should it desire to file a civil judicial action, to use DOJ as its attorney, while other statutes would seem to empower EPA to file its own actions. However, in all cases EPA uses DOJ to file judicial actions on its behalf pursuant to a memorandum of understanding entered into between the two agencies in 1977.

While DOJ enlists the assistance of the U.S. attorneys in filing cases and in local management of the cases, most of the cases are actually managed, negotiated and, if necessary, tried by the attorneys from DOJ's Environmental Enforcement Section (EES) in Washington, DC, or one of the Section's five field offices (located in San Francisco, Denver, Boston, Anchorage and Seattle). * * *

DOJ's influence in environmental judicial enforcement goes beyond merely acting as EPA's legal counsel. DOJ claims a "national perspective" in court decisions, and frequently objects to the filing of cases in which the potential is high for a decision that may create an adverse national precedent or would be inconsistent with EPA's program goals. DOJ also sometimes involves itself in the development of EPA's regulations, and in the development of environmental legislation through working with EPA and congressional committees. * * *

*Practice Tip:* The enforcement target should be alert as to whether its case may involve issues that are precedential or important to EPA, and carefully evaluate the potential for successfully defending the case. If such issues are present, and the facts of the case are favorable to the target, contact with the DOJ attorney assigned to the case or that attorney's supervisors to discuss the merits and the effect of a successful defense may be important. * * *

FEDERAL-STATE RELATIONSHIP

Notwithstanding the high profile of EPA's enforcement actions, much of the country's environmental enforcement is conducted by state environmental agencies. Federal and state environmental laws frequently overlap, so that both may have jurisdiction over the same violation. In addition, EPA delegates some programs (*e.g.,* RCRA, NPDES) to the states to administer and enforce in lieu of EPA, but retains authority to oversee the enforcement of the program and to take federal enforcement action, if necessary. States may also enact laws covering much the same subject matter as federal environmental law. This gives both federal and state environmental agencies possible jurisdiction over a particular violation, although if the federal statute is comprehensive, EPA may claim preemption in the area. In such cases, the relationship between the federal and state agencies is often confusing, and there is no clear line dividing responsibility between federal and state enforcement.

Beginning in the mid-1990s, the U.S. Department of Justice and EPA began urging state environmental agencies and state attorneys general to join them, as co-plaintiffs, in civil environmental enforcement cases in federal district courts. These efforts bore fruit. A number of civil judicial actions have been filed, and continue to be filed, under such arrangements. At times, they provide the governmental co-plaintiffs who have acted in tandem with added leverage in settlement negotiations with defendants. * * *

Generally, EPA tends to focus its enforcement efforts on facilities that it defines as "majors" under most of its programs. For example, in the water area, it concentrates on wastewater treatment facilities that discharge more than one million gallons per day effluent, and in the air program, on stationary sources that emit more than 100 tons per year of conventional pollutants. EPA leaves to the states the primary responsibility of enforcing against smaller facilities, although this major/minor classification system is merely a resource planning system, and EPA may take action against any facility over which it has statutory authority.

Moreover, as adverted to above, in recent years EPA and DOJ have focused many more of their enforcement resources on industrial sector-based initiatives, undertaken following far-reaching EPA investigations of major national companies and polluting industries (*e.g.,* wood products, petroleum refining, and diesel engine manufacturing) that revealed widespread violations of applicable environmental requirements. States were frequently invited to participate in those federal lawsuits as well, in the role of co-plaintiffs. Many of them did so, often with favorable results for the cooperating governmental parties.

---

## QUESTIONS AND DISCUSSION

**1.** While the Department of Justice serves as EPA's lawyer, the relationship is more complicated than the standard attorney-client model, for DOJ is first and foremost the government's lawyer. This dual loyalty can quickly become problematic in three circumstances: (1) when EPA wants to file an action that DOJ believes is inconsistent with other governmental priorities, (2) when EPA and another agency (such as the Department of Transportation) take different views on litigation, and (3) when EPA wants DOJ to appeal an adverse decisions but DOJ lawyers decide not to, concerned over the precedential effect of an adverse ruling at the appellate level. It is not surprising that agencies take different views on what constitutes the best interests of the government, but DOJ must ultimately exercise its judgment and not defer to the view of any single agency.

2. Are you surprised that EPA does not have independent litigating authority? What would be the benefits of allowing the agency to decide for itself which cases to bring and which to appeal?

3. EPA has been under considerable budgetary constraints for well over the past decade. This has led to reductions in personnel and hard choices over the priority areas to dedicate scarce resources. The chart below shows EPS budget and employees through 2013. The number of employees has continued to drop. Professor Joel Mintz has warned that this forced austerity will be harmful to the agency's missions, that "any form of budget cutting in EPA's severely understaffed enforcement program is likely to have an adverse effect on the robustness and effectiveness of the Agency's critical enforcement work." Joel Mintz, *Cutting EPA's Enforcement Budget: What It Might Mean*, CENTER FOR PROGRESSIVE REFORM BLOG (Apr. 12, 2012).

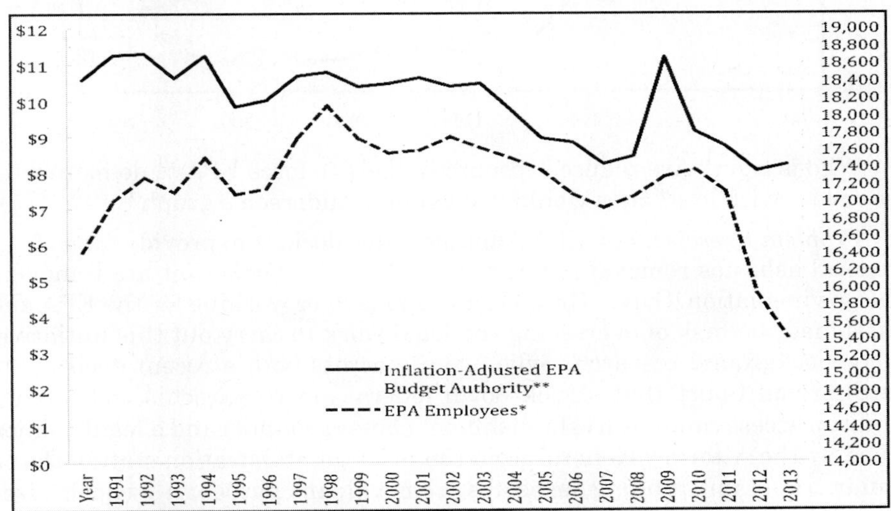


Others, though, have countered that EPA remains a bloated bureaucracy and that it should do more with less. The chart below, created by Terry Anderson, suggests that environmental quality has continued to improve despite steady and declining EPA budgets.

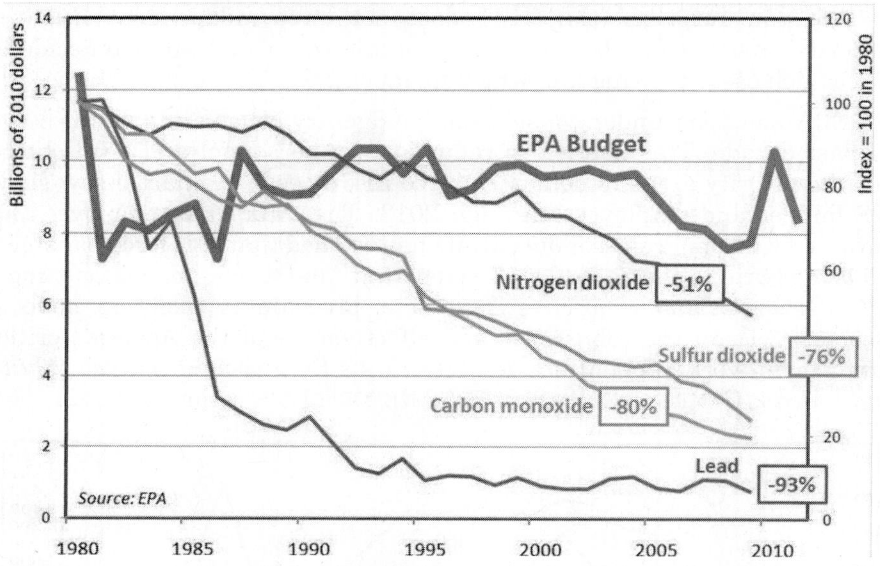


Who is right? Are reduced resources likely to force EPA to do more with less or less with less? How would you explain Anderson's graph?

**4.** *Problem Exercise*: The EPA Administrator decides to provide funds from a federal asbestos removal program to parochial schools that are removing asbestos insulation. Sylvia Green is a young lawyer working for the EPA and is assigned the task of overseeing the legal work to carry out this initiative. In her background research, Sylvia comes across both a recent decision by the Supreme Court that struck down federal aid to parochial schools for handicap access ramps (on establishment clause grounds) and a legal opinion issued by the Attorney General from the prior administration stating that a similar program funding asbestos removal in parochial schools was unconstitutional. Sylvia believes that the EPA Administrator has been told by the President's campaign manager that this initiative is important to garner votes from parents of parochial school children in the upcoming election. Is it unethical for Sylvia Green to work on this matter? *See* Geoffrey P. Miller, *Government Lawyers' Ethics in a System of Checks and Balances,* 54 U. CHI. L. REV. 1293 (1987) (from which this hypothetical is adapted).

**5.** How does enforcement affect you? The EPA has created a searchable map website of enforcement actions, "Enforcement Annual Results," at http://www.epa.gov/enforcement/data/eoy2012/casemap.html

Check out the compliance activities near where you live. Do you think this type of publicly available information can affect compliance behavior?

---

## 1. FEDERAL-STATE TENSIONS

As noted above, EPA has delegated significant enforcement authority to the states for the administration and enforcement of many of its statutes. *See, e.g.,* 15 U.S.C. § 2684 (Toxic Substances Control Act:

EPA Administrator and State enforcement of lead-based paint training and certification requirements and lead hazard pamphlet); 42 U.S.C. § 7413 (Clean Air Act: EPA Administrator and State enforcement of the State Implementation Plan); 33 U.S.C. § 1319 (Clean Water Act: EPA Administrator and State enforcement of permits). These delegations are premised on the adoption of state statutes and regulations that are substantially equivalent to or no less stringent than EPA's program under the federal statute. In many respects, this arrangement benefits both parties. EPA has limited resources and cannot practically carry out the inspections and enforcement actions necessary to ensure adequate deterrence throughout the country. State and local authorities not only can provide these resources, but are closer to both the actors and the impacts of pollution, and thus are likely to have a better understanding of the specific challenges and opportunities surrounding particular enforcement actions. At the same time, however, over the last decade there has been increasing tension between EPA and many state environmental agencies from concerns over the proper approach to noncompliance. This grows out of a broader tension over the fundamental causes of noncompliance. The excerpt below describes the contrasting "good apple" and "bad apple" views of noncompliance. It is followed by the Senate testimony of the Delaware Secretary of the Environment, explaining how these differing views play out in EPA/state compliance and enforcement strategies.

### J.B. Ruhl, James Salzman, and Kai-Sheng Song
### *Regulatory Traffic Jams*

2 WYOMING L. REV. 253, 256–265 (2002).

Both the enforcement literature and practice have been dominated by two models. One, which we will call the "rational polluter model," favors an adversarial, deterrence-based approach. The other, the good apple or "facilitation model," rests on collaborative assistance.

Traditionally, enforcement in the environmental field (as in others) has been based on strategic deterrence. In this model of behavior, the rational actor will comply when it is in his economic self-interest to do so, but will otherwise violate the law. A profit-maximizing company's decision to comply simply comes down to comparing the costs and benefits of noncompliance (i.e., because in some instances crime *does* pay). This notion of regulated behavior rests on the assumption that most noncompliance is due to "bad apples" and, as a result, the appropriate enforcement strategy is one of sanction. Malefactors respond most effectively to punishment.

This approach is so prevalent that it seems obvious to us, whether by imposing fines at a chemical facility or adding points to the license of a speeding driver. Both settings employ a deterrence-based remedy because, this model predicts, only when the sanction is painful enough, and the likelihood of detection high enough, will the regulated party comply. In the environmental field, the sufficient pain can take any number of forms, ranging from public notice of violations, ineligibility for government contracts, civil penalties and supplemental environmental projects to injunctions or even jail time. Regardless of the final penalty, though, under this behavioral model it goes without saying that noncompliance is intentional.

With the rational polluter behavioral model as the premise, therefore, the deterrence-based sanction approach to enforcement is inevitable. As Chester Bowles, the famous New Deal administrator, memorably observed: "Twenty percent of the regulated population will automatically comply with any regulation, five percent will attempt to evade it, and the remaining seventy-five percent will comply as long as they think that the five percent will be caught and punished."

Advocates of the rational polluter model may quibble over the appropriate percentages, but their approach is consistent. Enforcement against the critical five percent of bad apples through sanctions (known as "specific deterrence") will ensure that compliance by the rest ("general deterrence") will follow. The implication, of course, is that the remaining seventy-five percent, while perhaps not rotten to the core, are certainly willing to skirt the law if they can get away with it.

Evidence of this approach to enforcement is easy to find. The recent rise of criminal sanctions in environmental law demonstrates the desire both to increase compliance and send the message that pollution is serious business. EPA's penalty policy clearly states that penalties must go beyond any economic benefits gained from noncompliance. The agency's proud publications of enforcement statistics every year—the number of site inspections, suits filed, dollars collected, jail sentences served—is regarded as an important proxy for environmental protection. Whether EPA or Congress has primarily been responsible for this emphasis on bean-counting is unclear, but the underlying message is not. More inspections, fines and punishment means better deterrence and, therefore, better enforcement. * * *

This description of compliance has not gone unchallenged, however. While the sanction model is based on the assumption of regulating "bad apples," the competing approach assumes that most companies are "good apples" to the core and would comply at higher rates than experienced but for obstacles put in their way. It's not hard to imagine why this might be the case and may, in fact, better describe reality than the sanction model.

The most obvious reason for corporate compliance, of course, is to avoid one or more of the sanctions described above, the "sticks" of deterrence. But it is important to acknowledge, as well, that the senior management of some companies is personally committed to conducting business in an environmentally responsible manner. Reputation matters, too. Some companies operate in sectors where a poor environmental reputation can harm them in the marketplace or with their shareholders. Others manage environmental reputation as a positive business asset for corporate image or marketing. And, finally, a growing number of companies are realizing that high levels of environmental management actually contribute to the bottom line through increased efficiencies. There clearly is something to these arguments when one recalls that, despite the well-publicized big penalties by EPA, these are relatively infrequent and the size of most environmental fines is too small, in itself, to change the bottom line profits for most companies.

So, if many companies have good selfish reasons to comply, why are they so often in noncompliance? Sanction advocates would point out that rational polluters, despite the potential benefits listed above, may still find that crime pays. And, to be sure, no one with experience in environmental protection would deny that there are bad apples out there. Much noncompliance *is* voluntary. One cannot sprinkle pixie dust on bad apples, hold your breath, and wish them to go away. But if they are in the small minority, what about the good apples? It turns out that the reasons for well-intentioned failure are numerous. As many have pointed out, environmental law is complicated. Regulations can be difficult to understand because they are highly technical. They may be ambiguous, whether intentionally or because of poor drafting. They may appear to contradict other requirements. Given the combination, and occasional overlap, of federal, state and local regulation of many polluting activities, this is not hard to imagine. Because of such federalism in practice, as well as EPA's increasing reliance on guidance documents and other nonlegislative rules, the relevant requirements may be hard to find. And, finally, there are a lot of rules, and more so for EPA than other agencies. Consider that there are over 10,000 pages of *federal* environmental laws on the books, not including guidance documents and state laws. When corporate counsels say they can't keep track of all the requirements of compliance, it is not false modesty.

If the logical consequence of the rational polluter model is the punitive deterrence of enforcement, the obvious response to the good apple model of behavior is compliance facilitation. Helping regulated parties come into compliance, rather than threatening them to do so, not only seems more appropriate if parties truly want to comply, but equitable as well. After all, compliance facilitation simply asks that government help the good apples overcome obstacles that government largely created in the first place. And practical evidence of this enforcement approach is as easy to find as that for the sanction model. The Clinton Administration launched an effort to reinvent regulation writing, expressing the rules in plain English. EPA has dedicated considerable resources to outreach and education efforts, publishing numerous reports such as the *Small Business Ombudsman Update* and 1–800 toll free help lines. Congressional passage of the Small Business Regulatory Enforcement Fairness Act (SBREFA) requires forgiveness for small violations by small businesses. And, over the last decade, at least 23 states have passed laws providing evidentiary privileges or immunity to corporations that uncover and correct violations through internal environmental audits. The goal of all these initiatives, and many more, is to rely on carrots rather than sticks, cooperation rather than confrontation, either by education or reducing penalties in exchange for coming into compliance.

Not surprisingly, proponents of the sanction model remain unconvinced. While many scholars and environmental enforcement personnel acknowledge that numerous challenges to compliance like those listed above do exist, they reject any conclusion that reliance on sanctions as the principal compliance-inducing mechanism may be inappropriate. As Cliff Rechtschaffen has bluntly observed, "you don't get to drive drunk or hold up a store one time for free."

In practice, of course, enforcement in the field rarely follows solely the sanction or facilitation approach but, rather, a hybrid depending on the situation. To paraphrase Teddy Roosevelt, compliance facilitation may prove effective because the big stick of potential sanction is held at the ready. . . . Thus deterrence-based sanction and compliance facilitation can be, and often are, combined. And, in certain cases, they may not be very useful categories for sorting purposes. But make no mistake. They represent very different views of compliance with far-reaching implications for immunity for violations found in self-audits, criminal sanctions, and the very relationship of regulators and regulated parties. Through the eyes of a sanction-based enforcer, compliance facilitation efforts too often mask examples of agency capture, letting regulated industries off the hook. Through the lens of compliance facilitation, though, sanctions can seem heavy-handed and ineffective. Government resources, many state agencies argue, would be better spent by working with rather than against regulated parties, preventing noncompliance events and saving sanctions for the truly bad apples. Moreover, the *balance* of sanction versus facilitation remains hotly contested. Thus much of the debate in environmental enforcement today is over which of these models should guide enforcement policy.

## Statement of Christophe A.G. Tulou, Secretary, Delaware Dept. of Natural Resources and Environmental Control Before the Senate Committee on Environment and Public Works

June 10, 1997.

Delaware's enforcement relationship with EPA Region III is very good. Though the relationship continues to be positive, our development of a Performance Partnership Agreement (PPA) with Region III has created some friction regarding the role of enforcement in environmental management. * * *

Despite these assurances in our Agreement, I fear that EPA will insist on greater reliance on enforcement-specific activities, focusing on enforcement for enforcement's sake.

We have argued since the beginning of the PPA process that enforcement should be a part of all our environmental goals, not a stand-alone end unto itself. In short, we view enforcement as an important tool to achieve our environmental goals, not a goal in its own right. That disagreement continues.

We also contend that compliance is a more relevant and important programmatic goal than enforcement. We should be striving—through whatever means—to get all our polluters in compliance. This distinction between compliance and enforcement is crucial in determining what States and EPA should be measuring and reporting. If enforcement is a goal, then we should continue to count beans such as penalty dollars collected or enforcement actions taken. If compliance is the goal, then we should be measuring and reporting who is in, and who is out, of compliance. The traditional measures of dollars and enforcement actions are less important if compliance is the true goal. Measuring compliance is feasible and relevant. Last year, just over 70% of facilities in Delaware complied with hazardous waste regulations at the time of inspection. Within 30 days of the inspection, the percentage rose to 85%. Within 180 days, 100% of facilities were in compliance.

In Delaware, we work with violators to get them back into compliance as quickly as possible. Using compliance assistance as an option of first choice, we can usually achieve that goal much faster, cheaper, and with far greater goodwill than through aggressive enforcement. We also create allies for our environmental efforts. In fact, several of our companies are moving beyond mere compliance by adopting forward-looking environmental management strategies such as continuous improvement, pollution prevention, and enhanced product stewardship.

Overly aggressive and ill-timed enforcement is a dare: it inspires polluters to assume an adversarial relationship with their environment and regulatory agencies, and to challenge enforcers to discover their misdeeds. Neither the States nor EPA can afford that cat-and-mouse approach to environmental management; neither can our environment.

---

## 2. OVERFILING

While EPA has delegated much administrative and enforcement authority to the states, it retains the ability to step in and intervene in enforcement actions, even if the state has already imposed a sanction. In a practice known as "overfiling," EPA can seek to impose penalties in addition to the state's sanctions if the state has not taken "timely" and "appropriate" enforcement action. In simple terms, if EPA officials determine that the state's response to noncompliance was too slow (i.e., not within 90–120 days from the date of discovery of the violation) or too lenient (i.e., an inadequate response given the severity of the violation), it can seek to increase the penalties or impose other appropriate remedies, so long as they are consistent with the substantive law of the state in which the violation took place (since the state program was approved by EPA in lieu of the federal program). Overfiling authority is generally provided both by the statute authorizing delegation and a memorandum of understanding between EPA and the state at the time of delegation. In practice, this has proven controversial and, as the case below explains, its application remains contested.

## Harmon Industries, Inc. v. Browner

United States Court of Appeals for the Eighth Circuit, 1999.
191 F.3d 894.

■ HANSEN, CIRCUIT JUDGE:

. . . Harmon Industries operates a plant in Grain Valley, Missouri, which it utilizes to assemble circuit boards for railroad control and safety equipment. In November 1987, Harmon's personnel manager discovered that maintenance workers at Harmon routinely discarded volatile solvent residue behind Harmon's Grain Valley plant. This practice apparently began in 1973 and continued until November 1987. Harmon's management was unaware of its employees' practices until the personnel manager filed his report in November 1987. Following the report, Harmon ceased its disposal activities and voluntarily contacted the Missouri Department of Natural Resources (MDNR). The MDNR investigated and concluded that Harmon's past disposal practices did not pose a threat to either human health or the environment. The MDNR and Harmon created a plan whereby Harmon would clean up the disposal area. Harmon implemented the clean up plan. While Harmon was cooperating with the MDNR, the EPA initiated an administrative enforcement action against Harmon in which the federal agency sought $2,343,706 in penalties. Meanwhile, Harmon and the MDNR continued to establish a voluntary compliance plan. In harmonizing the details of the plan, Harmon asked the MDNR not to impose civil penalties. Harmon based its request in part on the fact that it voluntarily self-reported the environmental violations and cooperated fully with the MDNR.

On March 5, 1993, while the EPA's administrative enforcement action was pending, a Missouri state court judge approved a consent decree entered into by the MDNR and Harmon. In the decree, MDNR acknowledged full accord and satisfaction and released Harmon from any claim for monetary penalties. MDNR based its decision to release Harmon on the fact that the company promptly self-reported its violation and cooperated in all aspects of the investigation. After the filing of the consent decree, Harmon litigated the EPA claim before an administrative law judge (ALJ). The ALJ found that a civil penalty against Harmon was

appropriate in this case. The ALJ rejected the EPA's request for a penalty in excess of $2 million but the ALJ did impose a civil fine of $586,716 against Harmon. A three-person Environmental Appeals Board panel affirmed the ALJ's monetary penalty. Harmon filed a complaint challenging the EPA's decision in federal district court on June 6, 1997.
* * *

A. *The Permissibility of Overfiling*

. . . The Resource Conservation and Recovery Act (RCRA) permits states to apply to the EPA for authorization to administer and enforce a hazardous waste program. If authorization is granted, the state's program then operates "in lieu of" the federal government's hazardous waste program. The EPA authorization also allows states to issue and enforce permits for the treatment, storage, and disposal of hazardous wastes. "Any action taken by a State under a hazardous waste program authorized under [the RCRA] [has] the same force and effect as action taken by the [EPA] under this subchapter." Once authorization is granted by the EPA, it cannot be rescinded unless the EPA finds that (1) the state program is not equivalent to the federal program, (2) the state program is not consistent with federal or state programs in other states, or (3) the state program is failing to provide adequate enforcement of compliance in accordance with the requirements of federal law. *See* 42 U.S.C. § 6926(b). Before withdrawing a state's authorization to administer a hazardous waste program, the EPA must hold a public hearing and allow the state a reasonable period of time to correct the perceived deficiency.

Missouri, like many other states, is authorized to administer and enforce a hazardous waste program pursuant to the RCRA. Despite having authorized a state to act, the EPA frequently files its own enforcement actions against suspected environmental violators even after the commencement of a state-initiated enforcement action. The EPA's process of duplicating enforcement actions is known as overfiling. The permissibility of overfiling apparently is a question of first impression in the federal circuit courts. After examining this apparent issue of first impression, the district court concluded that the plain language of Section 6926(b) dictates that the state program operate "in lieu" of the federal program and with the "same force and effect" as EPA action. Accordingly, the district court found that, in this case, the RCRA precludes the EPA from assessing its own penalty against Harmon.

The EPA contends that the district court's interpretation runs contrary to the plain language of the RCRA. Specifically, the EPA cites Section 6928 of the RCRA, which states that:

> (1) Except as provided in paragraph (2), whenever on the basis of any information the [EPA] determines that any person has violated or is in violation of any requirement of this subchapter, the [EPA] may issue an order assessing a civil penalty for any past or current violation, requiring compliance

> immediately or within a specified time period, or both, or the [EPA] may commence a civil action in the United States district court in the district in which the violation occurred for appropriate relief, including a temporary or permanent injunction.
>
> (2) In the case of a violation of any requirement of [the RCRA] where such violation occurs in a State which is authorized to carry out a hazardous waste program under Section 6926 of this title, the [EPA] shall give notice to the State in which such violation has occurred prior to issuing an order or commencing a civil action under this section.

The EPA argues that the plain language of Section 6928 allows the federal agency to initiate an enforcement action against an environmental violator even in states that have received authorization pursuant to the RCRA. The EPA contends that Harmon and the district court misinterpreted the phrases "in lieu of" and "same force and effect" as contained in the RCRA. According to the EPA, the phrase "in lieu of" refers to which regulations are to be enforced in an authorized state rather than who is responsible for enforcing the regulations. The EPA argues that the phrase "same force and effect" refers only to the effect of state issued permits. The EPA contends that the RCRA, taken as a whole, authorizes either the state or the EPA to enforce the state's regulations, which are in compliance with the regulations of the EPA. The only requirement, according to the EPA, is that the EPA notify the state in writing if it intends to initiate an enforcement action against an alleged violator. * * *

There is no support either in the text of the statute or the legislative history for the proposition that the EPA is allowed to duplicate a state's enforcement authority with its own enforcement action. The EPA argues that the statute and legislative history support its contention that it may initiate an enforcement action if it deems the state's enforcement action inadequate. The EPA's argument misses the point. Without question, the EPA can initiate an enforcement action if it deems the state's enforcement action inadequate. Before initiating such an action, however, the EPA must allow the state an opportunity to correct its deficiency and the EPA must withdraw its authorization. Consistent with the text of the statute and its legislative history, the EPA also may initiate an enforcement action after providing written notice to the state when the authorized state fails to initiate any enforcement action. The EPA may not, however, simply fill the perceived gaps it sees in a state's enforcement action by initiating a second enforcement action without allowing the state an opportunity to correct the deficiency and then withdrawing the state's authorization.

A contrary interpretation would result in two separate enforcement actions. Such an interpretation, as explained above, would derogate the RCRA's plain language and legislative history. Companies that reach an agreement through negotiations with a state authorized by the EPA to act in its place may find the agreement undermined by a later separate enforcement action by the EPA. While, generally speaking, two separate sovereigns can institute two separate enforcement actions, those actions can cause vastly different and potentially contradictory results. Such a potential schism runs afoul of the principles of comity and federalism so clearly embedded in the text and history of the RCRA. When enacting the RCRA, Congress intended to delegate the primary enforcement of EPA-approved hazardous waste programs to the states. In fact, as we have noted above, the states' enforcement action has the "same force and effect as an action taken by" the EPA. In EPA authorized states, the EPA's action is an alternative method of enforcement that is permitted to operate only when certain conditions are satisfied. The EPA's interpretation simply is not consistent with the plain language of the statute, its legislative history, or its declared purpose. Hence, it is also an unreasonable interpretation to which we accord no deference. Therefore, we find that the EPA's practice of overfiling, in those states where it has authorized the state to act, oversteps the federal agency's authority under the RCRA.

---

## QUESTIONS AND DISCUSSION

**1.** It is important to note that *Harmon* has not been followed outside the Eighth Circuit. The Tenth Circuit, for example, in *United States v. Power Engineering*, 303 F.3d 1232 (10th Cir. 2002), firmly rejected *Harmon*, concluding that EPA could file a civil enforcement action against a metal finisher despite the fact that the state of Colorado had already issued an administrative compliance order and civil penalty for the same violation.

Other decisions have distinguished *Harmon* by stating that it only applies to RCRA. Thus in *United States v. LTV Steel Company*, 118 F. Supp. 2d 827 (N.D. Ohio 2000), for example, the court rejected the steel company's argument that settlement with the city of Cleveland precluded EPA enforcement actions, concluding that "Unlike RCRA, the Clean Air Act contains language in its enforcement section which seems to anticipate overfilling."

**2.** While overfiling represents a potential stick for the EPA to bring states in line, EPA also has a big club that it can swing in the form of withdrawing a state's delegated authority to operate a program. EPA giveth and EPA can taketh away. . . . In practice, however, EPA only rarely threatens to exercise this authority. What do you think EPA considers the downsides to withdrawing delegated authority?

**3.** Would you expect states to systematically over-enforce or under-enforce environmental regulations, compared to federal agencies? What might explain this tendency? In answering this question, consider the background of the *Laidlaw* case we will read later in this chapter. In *Laidlaw,* South Carolina Department of Health and Environmental Control (DHEC) entered into a settlement with Laidlaw for hundreds of Clean Water Act violations. Laidlaw agreed to pay a $100,000 civil penalty. Digging deeper into the issue, the District Court found that "Laidlaw drafted the state-court complaint and settlement agreement, filed the lawsuit against itself, and paid the filing fee. . . . [T]he settlement agreement between DHEC and Laidlaw was entered into with unusual haste, without giving the Plaintiffs the opportunity to intervene. . . . [And, the court concluded,] in imposing the civil penalty of $100,000 against Laidlaw, DHEC failed to recover, or even to calculate, the economic benefit that Laidlaw received by not complying with its permit." Friends of the Earth v. Laidlaw Envtl. Serv., 890 F. Supp. 470, 491 (D.S.C. 1995).

**4.** Given its limited resources. EPA must choose its enforcement targets carefully. Every three years, it develops the National Enforcement Initiatives (NEIs) to guide enforcement priorities. These are the result of stakeholder discussions and seek to identify those opportunities where federal intervention will make the biggest difference. For 2017–2019, the NEIs are:

*Air*

- Reducing Air Pollution from the Largest Sources
- Cutting Hazardous Air Pollutants

*Energy Extraction*

- Ensuring Energy Extraction Activities Comply with Environmental Laws

*Hazardous Chemicals*

- Reducing Risks of Accidental Releases at Industrial and Chemical Facilities

*Water*

- Keeping Raw Sewage and Contaminated Stormwater Out of Our Nation's Waters
- Preventing Animal Waste from Contaminating Surface and Ground Water
- Keeping Industrial Pollutants Out of the Nation's Waters

**5.** As noted in the text, EPA pursues both sanction and facilitation strategies. Indeed, the title of the Office of Enforcement was changed during the Clinton Administration to the Office of Enforcement and Compliance Assurance. In its annual performance assessment, the Office has included metrics such as "Users reporting increased understanding of regulations," "Users reporting environmental management practices adopted," and "Users reporting pollution reductions." What metrics would you try to collect to measure whether the Office's compliance assurance activities were effective?

## II. THE ENFORCEMENT PROCESS

The enforcement process involves a series of discretionary decisions—how to monitor for and detect noncompliance; whether to prosecute noncompliance; whether to rely on administrative or judicial processes; whether to pursue civil or criminal sanctions. And each of these individual decisions masks many smaller decisions (e.g., which type of civil sanction to pursue, and at what level).

### A. MONITORING AND DETECTING NONCOMPLIANCE

While discussions of enforcement generally focus on punishment—whether to impose fines, an injunction, or criminal sanctions—it is important to keep in mind that enforcement authorities must first be aware that a violation has even occurred. Though often taken for granted, monitoring for and detecting noncompliance are two essential, initial steps in the enforcement process.

> EPA typically becomes aware of violations of environmental requirements in one or more of several ways. These include reports from neighbors, disgruntled employees or local response agencies such as police or fire departments, self-reporting by a company in compliance with statutory or regulatory reporting requirements, and referrals from state regulatory personnel. Additionally or alternatively, EPA may discover enforceable violations during random in-person compliance inspections of facilities in response to written requests for information, or as part of a broader investigation of a targeted industrial-sector or multi-facility company.

Joel A. Mintz, *Civil Enforcement,* in MICHAEL GERRARD, ED., PRACTICAL GUIDE TO ENVIRONMENTAL LAW 12–81 (2004)

Under Section 308(a)(B) of the Clean Water Act, for example, EPA officials and their authorized representatives:

> (i) shall have a right of entry to, upon, or through any premises in which an effluent source is located or in which any records required to be maintained . . . and
>
> (ii) may at reasonable times have access to and copy any records, inspect any monitoring equipment or method required . . . and sample any effluents which the owner or operator of such source is required to sample under such clause.

EPA's access to records and right of entry under the Clean Air Act are virtually identical to the Clean Water Act. *See* 42 U.S.C. 7414(a)(2).

Perhaps surprisingly, however, the primary source of information on environmental noncompliance is not gained through government inspections but, rather, through the polluters, themselves. Self-reporting requirements are found throughout environmental law. Under Section

308(a)(A) of the Clean Water Act, for example, owners or operators of point sources (i.e., discrete sources of water pollution such as pipes), must:

(i) establish and maintain such records,

(ii) make such reports,

(iii) install, use, and maintain such monitoring equipment or methods (including where appropriate, biological monitoring methods),

(iv) sample such effluents (in accordance with such methods, at such locations, at such intervals, and in such manner as the Administrator shall prescribe), and

(v) provide such other information as he may reasonably require

Section 114 of the Clean Air Act operates in a similar manner, providing EPA the authority to require any person who owns or operates an emission source to establish and maintain records, make reports, install, use and maintain monitoring equipment or methods, sample emissions as EPA prescribes, and provide such other information as EPA may reasonably require.

As a result of these requirements, inspections are much more likely to find so-called "paperwork violations" than physical violations such as finding illegal pollution occurring during the inspection. Such a heavy reliance on self-reporting reduces the burden on EPA and the state agencies in terms of physically monitoring every source of pollution but a moment's reflection makes clear that it also creates the potential for cheating. Why should a company admit it has violated the law when no one is looking?

There are two basic strategies to address the incentives for cheating when self-reporting. The first is to require facilities to use monitoring technologies that are tamper-proof or provide real-time reporting. This has been difficult in the past, but with technological developments is increasingly viable. The second, and more common strategy, is to make cheating extremely painful (i.e., following the rational polluter or "bad apple" model). Thus under the major environmental statutes, paperwork violations are treated no different than physical violations. Section 113 of the Clean Air Act, for example, provides for civil penalties of up to $25,000 *per day of violation*. Knowing violations can lead to criminal penalties.

As described in the earlier section on federal/state tensions, compliance facilitation is an important aspect of enforcement policy. Ideally, companies should be able to understand the applicable environmental requirements and audit their own operations to ensure they are in compliance. In practice, however, perfect compliance is rare, even for companies that fully want to comply. Thus both EPA and state environmental agencies have increasingly dedicated resources to compliance assistance. Indeed it is no coincidence that EPA's enforcement office changed its name in the 1990s to the Office of Enforcement and Compliance Assurance. To gain a sense of the wide range of compliance assistance programs and materials, check out EPA's impressive website resources for the regulated community at the website, www.epa.gov/compliance.

The internal audit is a key aspect of compliance assurance. Knowing the law is important, but knowing whether or not you are in compliance is even more important. Internal audits are investigations that a company conducts of its own operations to ensure that it is in compliance with all the relevant environmental laws. In some respects, it is analogous to the annual tune-up you give your car. It is not required by law, but provides reassurance that your car is in good working order. If a company's review of its records, operating policies, and personnel uncovers violations, presumably it will then remedy them. Moreover, audit procedures allow management to set environmental performance goals. A manufacturing team cannot be rewarded for reducing waste by 20% if there are no tracking mechanisms in place both to establish a baseline and to measure performance over time. The old business adage, "What gets measured gets done," is surely true in the case of environmental management.

The challenge for enforcement officials is what to do about past periods of noncompliance revealed by voluntary audits. Over the last decade, EPA and state environmental agencies have wrestled with the issue of how to treat internal environmental audits when prosecuting a company. If companies expect to be punished for violations uncovered by audits, then there will be a strong incentive never to carry out voluntary audits. Willful ignorance may be more attractive than punishment. At the same time, granting full immunity for violations uncovered by audits presents obvious problems, as well. As a general matter, enforcement authorities have conflicting goals. They want to encourage audits by companies but, at the same time, do not want to undermine their enforcement efforts.

---

## QUESTIONS AND DISCUSSION

**1.** Given the sheer size of many facilities and the voluminous records, inspectors often rely on inside information to identify potential violations. Such tip-offs may come from fired or disgruntled employees, competitors, or even neighbors. Environmental law encourages this type of information through two mechanisms. A number of laws provide explicit protection for whistle-blowers. Under Section 322 of the Clean Air Act, for example,

> No employer may discharge any employee or otherwise discriminate against any employee with respect to his

compensation, terms, conditions, or privileges of employment because the employee (or any person acting pursuant to a request of the employee):

(1) commenced, caused to be commenced, or is about to commence or cause to be commenced a proceeding under this chapter or a proceeding for the administration or enforcement of any requirement imposed under this chapter or under any applicable implementation plan,

(2) testified or is about to testify in any such proceeding, or

(3) assisted or participated or is about to assist or participate in any manner in such a proceeding or in any other action to carry out the purposes of this chapter.

A number of laws also provide bounty rewards for information that leads to successful enforcement actions. The Act to Prevent Pollution From Ships (APPS), for example, has greatly benefited from its bounty provisions. In 2009, Polembros Shipping, a shipping company based in Greece, paid a fine of $2.7 million dollars and had its ships banned from U.S. ports for three years for concealing an oil leak in its ballast. Nine crew members shared a bounty of $540,000. Using a bounty system to improve enforcement efforts can be particularly effective when monitoring is practically difficult, as is the case with ocean pollution from ships. As one prosecutor described, "I want every chief engineer in every ship in the world wondering if they [the crew] are trying to get rich off him." JUDSON STARR ET AL., ENVIRONMENTAL CRIMES DESKBOOK 143 (2nd ed. 2014). What are the disadvantages of such a reward system for information leading to prosecutions?

**2.** Given the wide-ranging discretion of enforcement officials over the type and size of penalty, it should come as no surprise that the threatened penalty generally differs from the final sanction as a result of negotiation, sometimes protracted negotiation. One of this book's co-authors served as a corporation's environmental manager prior to becoming a professor and experienced a high-profile EPA announcement that the agency was seeking a $1.25 million fine against his company, only to find a year later that the penalty had been reduced to less than $250,000 (this time with no triumphant press release).

**3.** While the major pollution statutes often provide for civil penalties of up to $25,000 per violation per day, the limit is now higher. The Debt Collection Improvement Act of 1996 allows enforcement agencies to increase their civil penalties to account for inflation. 31 U.S.C. § 3701. Thus statutes that originally authorized maximum penalties of $25,000 may now be used to impose maximum penalties of $37,500 per day. 73 Fed. Reg. 75,340 *et seq.* (Dec. 11, 2008).

---

## PROBLEM EXERCISE:
### AUDIT IMMUNITY POLICIES

You have been asked to write a memo analyzing the implications of creating an "audit immunity" policy. There exists a number of possible audit immunity approaches, ranging from total protection from prosecution for violations discovered by an internal audit, to lesser penalties, to no protection at all. Not surprisingly, at one end of the spectrum, industry lobbyists are pushing for total protection from penalties while, on the other end, some prosecutors are arguing for no protection at all.

Moreover, there are many factors that may counsel in favor of greater or lesser immunity. Your memo should consider, for example, how (or whether) the level of immunity should be dependent on each of the following specific concerns:

- Whether the audit was voluntary or legally required;
- Whether the noncompliance was discovered through a systematic audit or by chance;
- Whether the environmental agency had already commenced an investigation and likely would have uncovered the noncompliance on its own;
- How soon after discovery the noncompliance was reported to the environmental authorities;
- How soon after discovery the noncompliance was corrected;
- Whether the facility is a small business;
- Whether there have been past violations of the same type at the facility;
- How cooperative the violating party was with the environmental agency.

Please also address the type of immunity and:

- Whether certain types of violations should be treated differently (or perhaps never be eligible for immunity);
- Whether the type of immunity should vary depending on the statute (i.e., whether audit immunity should provide the same kinds of protection for Clean Air Act, Clean Water Act, or CERCLA violations uncovered by audits);
- In which circumstances immunity should include a reduction in civil penalty, a reduction in criminal penalty, and/or inadmissibility of the audit in a civil or criminal proceeding.

*Note: According to EPA, over twenty states have adopted policies for privilege or immunity for self-disclosure of environmental violations.*

---

## B. CIVIL ENFORCEMENT

Once a potential violation has been detected, the enforcement agency must decide whether and how to proceed. With limited resources, neither EPA nor the state can pursue every violation through administrative or judicial processes. For many violations, simply notifying the manager of the violation and how it can be corrected may be all that is needed. Informal communication as simple as phone calls, site visits, or notice of violation letters may be sufficient to return the party into compliance. One would be hard-pressed, however, to assume that light slaps on the wrist alone will always be sufficient to ensure widespread compliance. To help determine which violations should be subject to formal enforcement mechanisms, EPA has developed a series of enforcement policies. These policies are internal agency documents with the status of nonlegislative rules. The decision to pursue a violation turns on a number of factors, including the seriousness of the violation, the magnitude of the harm and its threat of harm to human health and the environment, past record of noncompliance, degree of cooperation, and others.

Enforcement policies are not binding, even on the agency that issued the policy, but in practice they are closely followed and lawyers defending clients in enforcement actions need to be familiar with their requirements.

### 1. ADMINISTRATIVE PROCEEDINGS

The majority of enforcement actions are civil, and the vast majority of these are administrative rather than judicial (i.e., handled within the agency rather than in the court system). In 2011, only 5.5% of civil enforcement proceedings went before a judge. All the others, well over 90%, went through the EPA's administrative enforcement process. EPA, FY2011 COMPLIANCE AND ENFORCEMENT ANNUAL RESULTS 10 (2011).

As with any legal proceeding, seeking enforcement through an administrative process follows a strict set of procedures, though the scope and complexity of these proceedings can vary depending on the agency and the statute. The benefits of relying on internal agency adjudication rather than courts are obvious—easier to administer, less costly in terms of time and personnel, no need to coordinate with the Department of Justice, and a judge who is familiar with environmental statutes. Failure to follow administrative procedure, however, can result in a dismissal of an appeal. *See, e.g., In the Matter of: Apex Microtechnology, Inc.*, 1994 WL 412929 (1994) (where EAB denied an appeal not because the claim was without merit, but because the appeal was not filed in a timely fashion).

> Typically, an EPA Regional Office (or, occasionally an EPA headquarters office) begins an enforcement proceeding by filing a complaint charging that a person (which can include a corporation or government entity) violated an environmental law or regulation. The complaint proposes the amount of the

> financial penalty that EPA should assess for the violation and, where necessary, what actions EPA believes the person should take to remedy the violation. The EPA office that filed the complaint is called "the Complainant." The person who is charged with the violation is called the "Respondent." A complaint may charge, for example, that the Respondent violated FIFRA by selling pesticides that were not labeled with adequate instructions for use. As another example, a complaint may charge that the Respondent violated RCRA by improperly disposing of hazardous waste. The Respondent may dispute the charges in the Complaint, or the amount of the proposed financial penalty, by filing an Answer.
>
> After the Answer has been filed, the case is assigned to an ALJ [Administrative Law Judge], who reviews the written legal arguments (called "briefs") that both parties submit. If the ALJ thinks that the case presents genuine factual issues that are material to a decision in the case, he or she will schedule a hearing, during which each side may present witnesses and introduce documentary evidence. The ALJ then issues a decision that resolves the issues in the case, based on the parties' briefs and the evidence introduced at the hearing. The ALJ's decision is called an "Initial Decision."
>
> Within the timeframe specified in the regulations . . . both the Complainant and the Respondent have the right to file an appeal with the Environmental Appeal Board (EAB) from the Initial Decision, challenging the ALJ's conclusions regarding liability for the violations or the amount of the penalty, or both. [Like the various courts of appeal in federal and state court systems, the EAB is bound by precedent and standards of review.] The Respondent may argue that he or she did not violate the law or that the ALJ assessed too high a financial penalty for the violation. The Regional office that filed the original complaint against the Respondent may argue that the ALJ acted in error when he or she concluded that the Respondent did not violate the law, or may argue that the ALJ should have assessed a higher penalty. . . . If no one files an appeal, the Initial Decision becomes a final EPA decision, unless the EAB decides on its own initiative to review the decision.

EPA, A CITIZEN'S GUIDE TO EPA'S ENVIRONMENTAL APPEALS BOARD 21–22 (2005).

An administrative decision can take a number of forms. Notices of violation are usually issued by the staff of an enforcement agency. Administrative compliance orders may be issued either by the agency staff or by an ALJ after a hearing to declare a party is in noncompliance or to prevent further action. Administrative compliance orders (whether issued by an agency staff or an ALJ) are similar to judicial injunctions in that they mandate that the party subject to them take specific, affirmative actions to achieve compliance with applicable environmental standards. They are not, however, self-enforcing. If the regulated party does not comply with the administrative order, it is enforceable in the courts.

Sometimes immediate action must be taken even before the hearing. The timing depends on the statute. Under CERCLA, if EPA orders potentially responsible parties to clean up a site, they must do so and challenge the order later. Section 113 of the statute explicitly rules out "pre-enforcement review," and parties who fail to comply with the cleanup order risk penalties up to $25,000 per day of violation and up to triple the cleanup costs. 42 U.S.C. § 9606(b)(1). In *Sackett v. EPA,* 132 S. Ct. 1367 (2012), the Supreme Court unanimously held that administrative compliance orders are final agency actions subject to judicial review.

### 2. CIVIL PROCEEDINGS

After exhausting administrative proceedings, parties in an enforcement action may end up in court litigating civil judicial enforcement actions, or enforcement officials may choose to go to court directly, bypassing the administrative process.

> When the appropriate regional program office or the regional enforcement division determines that a violation merits judicial response, the case file, consisting of the technical information developed to date, is then forwarded to the regional counsel's office for review and development of the legal basis for the case. This may be the first legal review of the case, although, as mentioned above, in most regional offices, the program offices consult the regional attorneys, at least about the more complicated cases, at an early date.
>
> The regional attorney will confirm the legal basis for the violation and whether a judicial response is the appropriate course of action, develop the legal theories of the case, request additional technical data or reports, if any, needed to support the violation, and put all of that information together into a document called a "referral package." . . . After the case is referred to DOJ for filing, the regional attorney will frequently continue to assist in development of the case by assisting in discovery and negotiation of settlement, and by acting as liaison between EPA technical personnel and DOJ. In some cases, by agreement with the DOJ attorney assigned to the case, he or she will serve as the lead negotiator for the federal government.

Joel A. Mintz, *supra,* at 12–82 to 12–83.

As noted above, civil litigation generally takes longer and is more expensive than administrative enforcement. As a result, far fewer cases are resolved through judicial enforcement than administrative enforcement. Why, then, would the government choose to go to court rather than seek relief through the administrative process?

A key reason turns on the different range of civil options available to a district court judge and administrative law judge. Environmental laws often provide for imposition of higher penalties in civil cases than administrative cases. Civil judicial penalties are often higher than the administrative penalties, despite many more enforcement actions pursued in court. Moreover, EPA retains complete control over administrative cases, with no role played by Department of Justice lawyers. Once the Justice Department takes over civil judicial cases, EPA attorneys usually step back and play a secondary role.

### 3. REMEDIES

Remedies represent the "so what" of the enforcement process. At the end of the day, regulated parties need to understand what the potential consequences of noncompliance will be. Even with constraints imposed by the respective statutes, EPA and the states retain a great deal of discretion over both the type and amount of remedy. After all, $32,500 per day adds up pretty quickly.

One can think of environmental penalties in four basic categories—monetary fines, criminal sanctions, injunctions, or supplemental environmental projects. If one is most concerned with returning the violators to compliance immediately, then a tailored injunction may be appropriate. If one seeks to punish the party then criminal or economic sanctions will suffice. If one seeks to restore the harmed environment, then supplemental projects may be necessary. And if the goal is simply to remove the economic benefit of noncompliance, then fines will work. Drawing on our earlier discussion of good apple and bad apple theories of enforcement, one may instead want to craft a remedy that fosters compliance facilitation. As you read the table below showing the wide range of potential remedies, consider how each remedy furthers a particular enforcement goal. INECE, PRINCIPLES OF ENVIRONMENTAL ENFORCEMENT (1992).

**Remedial Actions**

- Authority to impose a schedule for compliance
- Authority to permanently shut down part of an operation
- Authority to temporarily shut down certain parts of operations or practices
- Authority to permanently shut down an entire facility
- Authority to temporarily shut down an entire facility
- Authority to deny a permit
- Authority to revoke a permit

■ Authority to require a facility to clean up part of the environment

■ Emergency powers to enter and correct immediate dangers to the local population or environment

■ Authority to seek compensation for damage caused by the violation

**Sanctions**

■ Authority to impose a monetary penalty with specified amounts per day per violation

■ Authority to seek imprisonment (a jail term)

■ Authority to seek punitive damages or fines within specified limits

■ Authority to seize property

■ Authority to seek reimbursement for government clean-up expenses

■ Authority to bar a facility or company from government loans, guarantees, or contracts

■ Authority to require service or community work to benefit the environment

■ Limitations on financial assistance

**Other**

■ Authority to require specific testing and reporting

■ Authority to impose specific labeling requirements

■ Authority to require monitoring and reporting

■ Authority to request information on industrial processes

■ Authority to require specialized training (e.g., in emergency response to spills) for facility employees

■ Authority to require a facility to undergo an environmental audit

■ Authority to require environmental restoration or offsite mitigation

The following sections address civil penalties in more detail, focusing on civil penalty policies, injunctions, and supplemental environmental projects. Criminal sanctions are then addressed in Section C.

*a. Civil Penalty Policies*

When the government decides to seek civil penalties, it must also calculate the appropriate dollar figure. The maximum is usually set by the statute. The minimum is the lowest level that can still be considered a deterrent, i.e., eliminating any economic benefit achieved by violating the statute. The proposed damages are important not only for the court case but also for the negotiations preceding a trial, particularly since few enforcement actions ever go to trial.

### Joel A. Mintz, *Civil Enforcement*, in MICHAEL GERRARD, ED. PRACTICAL GUIDE TO ENVIRONMENTAL LAW

12–75 to 12–77, 12–88, 12–93 to 12–94 (2004).

Due to the intense scrutiny that environmental case settlements frequently receive from legislative oversight committees, the news media, environmental groups and the public, some rather detailed settlement procedures have been developed by government enforcement agencies. * * *

Federal environmental statutes typically provide EPA the authority to impose civil penalties up to $37,500 per day of noncompliance for each violation. Many statutes also include some general criteria for EPA or the courts to follow in assessing penalties. For example, Clean Air Act § 113(e) requires EPA or the court to consider the following factors in assessing a penalty:

- the size of the business;
- the violator's full compliance history and good faith efforts to comply;
- the duration of the violation;
- payment by the violator of penalties previously assessed for the same violation;
- the economic benefit of noncompliance;
- the seriousness of the violation; and
- other factors as justice may require.

The statutory ceilings and penalty assessment criteria leave EPA with considerable discretion in setting penalties. EPA has taken the approach of issuing informal civil penalty policies to guide its calculation of appropriate penalties. These policies generally do not address whether a civil penalty action is the appropriate enforcement response to a particular violation, but simply help EPA determine the appropriate civil penalty once it has decided to seek a civil penalty.

EPA uses the civil penalty policies primarily to calculate penalties that it will seek in administrative enforcement actions and that would be acceptable in settlement of administrative and judicial actions. Some policies apply only to administrative enforcement actions, while others focus solely on settlement of judicial enforcement actions. Most of the penalty policies include prominent disclaimers to emphasize that they are internal agency guidance documents and the Agency reserves the right to act at variance with the policies.

Despite these disclaimers, EPA enforcement personnel rely heavily on these policies. To a lesser extent, the policies are relied upon by parties outside EPA's enforcement office. EPA's consolidated rules governing the administrative assessment of civil penalties require the Agency's administrative law judges (ALJs) to consider "civil penalty guidelines" when assessing a civil penalty, although the ALJs may deviate from the penalty policies. Courts have sometimes used the policies to calculate appropriate penalties, and plaintiffs in citizen suits have used the policies in negotiating penalties with defendants. Some state environmental agencies have adopted EPA's civil penalty policies or similar policies.

EPA issued its General Civil Penalty Policy in 1984 to bring more consistency to its penalty assessment process. The General Policy provided that penalties should include an "economic benefit" component and a "gravity" component. The economic benefit component is intended to remove any significant economic benefit the violator received from failure to comply with the law. It includes both benefits from delayed costs and costs the violator avoided completely by noncompliance. The General Policy also provided that a penalty must also include an additional amount to punish the violator—the gravity component. The gravity component reflects the seriousness of the violation.

The sum of the economic benefit and gravity components yields a preliminary deterrence figure. The General Policy states that EPA will apply various adjustment factors (such as degree of willfulness, history of noncompliance, ability to pay, and degree of cooperation) to arrive at an initial penalty target figure. This figure would be the amount that EPA would assess in administrative complaints. In judicial actions, it would be EPA's first settlement goal. EPA will apply additional adjustments to this initial penalty target after settlement negotiations have begun to arrive at an adjusted penalty target figure.

On the same day that it issued the General Policy, EPA also issued a document that provides a framework for individual EPA offices to follow in developing statute-specific penalty policies. EPA has since issued or updated civil penalty policies for most of its programs where civil penalties are authorized by statute. The statute-specific policies typically begin with a discussion of EPA's statutory penalty authority and an overview of the enforcement process for that program. The policies then include sections on determining the economic benefit and gravity components of the penalty. The gravity section will often include a penalty assessment matrix. The policies then often discuss how the initial penalty figure should be adjusted, and how to calculate penalties for multiple and multi-day violations. Many policies include helpful examples of penalty calculations. * * *

### b. *Enforcement Against Federal Facilities*

The United States government is much bigger than the world's largest companies and undertakes many, many activities that can cause significant environmental impacts, from nuclear weapons production to building a dam. As a straight matter of law, enforcement against federal facilities should not be problematic. The Clean Water Act and RCRA, for example, both explicitly provide that the federal government and its agents shall be subject to the same requirements as nongovernmental parties. *See* CWA Section 313(a), RCRA Section 6001. But, in practice, effective enforcement is a far different matter. Beyond the basic political difficulty within the Executive branch of managing one sister agency suing another sister agency, the threat of monetary penalties is muted. Having one part of the government pay a fine to the U.S. Treasury does not send nearly the same message as a company taking a hit on its bottom line. If a government facility is funded out of an agency's overall budget, fines may have little or no impact on the facility's operating budget. You can threaten to drive a company out of business, but not the U.S. government.

In the 1992 case, *Department of Energy v. Ohio,* 503 U.S. 607 (1992), the Supreme Court changed the landscape of enforcement, holding that federal agencies were immune from civil penalties for violations of the Clean Water Act and RCRA. Moreover, federal agencies were only liable for fines to change behavior prospectively, not penalties for past behavior. Congress responded soon after with passage of the Federal Facility Compliance Act of 1992 (FFCA), waiving the government's immunity from civil penalties for RCRA violations. Pub. L. No. 102–386 (1992). Fines collected from agencies by states could only be used for environmental protection. While the FFCA effectively reverses *Department of Energy v. Ohio*'s holding for RCRA, immunity still appears to be in place for Clean Air Act and Clean Water Act violations. Kenneth M. Murchiso, *Waivers of Immunity in Federal Environmental Statutes of the Twenty-First Century: Correcting a Confusing Mess*, 32 WM. & MARY ENVTL. L. & POL'Y REV. 359 (2008).

### c. *Injunctions*

In some circumstances, an injunction can be far more damaging than even heavy fines, particularly for a large development project where loans must continue to be paid, permits may expire, and stopping one action may result in halting many more related activities. The scope of an injunction can vary. A permanent injunction ceases all activity indefinitely. A temporary injunction might be issued until an Environmental Impact Statement or some other process has been completed. And some courts may choose not to issue an injunction when other effective remedies are available.

## Weinberger v. Romero-Barcelo

Supreme Court of the United States, 1982.
456 U.S. 305.

■ JUSTICE WHITE delivered the opinion of the court:

The issue in this case is whether the Federal Water Pollution Control Act (FWPCA or Act) requires a district court to enjoin immediately all discharges of pollutants that do not comply with the Act's permit requirements or whether the district court retains discretion to order other relief to achieve compliance. The Court of Appeals for the First Circuit held that the Act withdrew the courts' equitable discretion. We reverse.

I

For many years, the Navy has used Vieques Island, a small island off the Puerto Rico coast, for weapons training. Currently all Atlantic Fleet vessels assigned to the Mediterranean Sea and the Indian Ocean are required to complete their training at Vieques because it permits a full range of exercises under conditions similar to combat. During air-to-ground training, however, pilots sometimes miss land-based targets, and ordnance falls into the sea. That is, accidental bombings of the navigable waters and, occasionally, intentional bombings of water targets occur. The District Court found that these discharges have not harmed the quality of the water.

In 1978, respondents, who include the Governor of Puerto Rico and residents of the island, sued to enjoin the Navy's operations on the island. Their complaint alleged violations of numerous federal environmental statutes and various other Acts. After an extensive hearing, the District Court found that under the explicit terms of the Act, the Navy had violated the Act by discharging ordnance into the waters surrounding the island without first obtaining a permit from the Environmental Protection Agency (EPA). *Romero-Barcelo v. Brown*, 478 F. Supp. 646 (P.R. 1979). * * *

As the District Court construed the FWPCA, the release of ordnance from aircraft or from ships into navigable waters is a discharge of pollutants, even though the EPA, which administers the Act, had not promulgated any regulations setting effluent levels or providing for the issuance of an NPDES permit for this category of pollutants. Recognizing that violations of the Act "must be cured," 478 F. Supp., at 707, the District Court ordered the Navy to apply for an NPDES permit. It refused, however, to enjoin Navy operations pending consideration of the permit application. It explained that the Navy's "technical violations" were not causing any "appreciable harm" to the environment. *Id.*, at 706. Moreover, because of the importance of the island as a training center, "the granting of the injunctive relief sought would cause grievous, and perhaps irreparable harm, not only to Defendant Navy, but to the general welfare of this Nation." *Id.*, at 707. The District Court concluded that an injunction was not necessary to ensure suitably prompt compliance by the Navy. To support this conclusion, it emphasized an equity court's traditionally broad discretion in deciding appropriate relief and quoted from the classic description of injunctive relief in *Hecht Co. v. Bowles*, 321 U.S. 321, 329–330 (1944): "The historic injunctive process was designed to deter, not to punish."

The Court of Appeals for the First Circuit vacated the District Court's order and remanded with instructions that the court order the Navy to cease the violation until it obtained a permit. 643 F.2d 835 (1981). Relying on *TVA v. Hill*, 437 U.S. 153 (1978), in which this Court held that an imminent violation of the Endangered Species Act required injunctive relief, the Court of Appeals concluded that the District Court erred in undertaking a traditional balancing of the parties' competing interests. "Whether or not the Navy's activities in fact harm the coastal waters, it has an absolute statutory obligation to stop any discharges of pollutants until the permit procedure has been followed and the Administrator of the Environmental Protection Agency, upon review of the evidence, has granted a permit." 643 F.2d, at 861. "The court suggested that if the order would interfere significantly with military preparedness, the Navy should request that the President grant it an exemption from the requirements in the interest of national security."

Because this case posed an important question regarding the power of the federal courts to grant or withhold equitable relief for violations of the FWPCA, we granted certiorari. We now reverse.

II

It goes without saying that an injunction is an equitable remedy. It "is not a remedy which issues as of course," or "to restrain an act the injurious consequences of which are merely trifling." An injunction should issue only where the intervention of a court of equity "is essential in order effectually to protect property rights against injuries otherwise irremediable." The Court has repeatedly held that the basis for injunctive relief in the federal courts has always been irreparable injury and the inadequacy of legal remedies.

Where plaintiff and defendant present competing claims of injury, the traditional function of equity has been to arrive at a "nice adjustment and reconciliation" between the competing claims, *Hecht Co. v. Bowles, supra*, at 329. In such cases, the court "balances the conveniences of the parties and possible injuries to them according as they may be affected by the granting or withholding of the injunction." *Yakus v. United States*, 321 U.S. 414, 440 (1944). "The essence of equity jurisdiction has been the power of the Chancellor to do equity and to mould each decree to the necessities of the particular case. Flexibility rather than rigidity has distinguished it." *Hecht Co. v. Bowles, supra*, 321 U.S., at 329.

In exercising their sound discretion, courts of equity should pay particular regard for the public consequences in employing the extraordinary remedy of injunction. *Railroad Comm'n v. Pullman Co.*, 312 U.S. 496, 500 (1941). Thus, the Court has noted that "[t]he award of an interlocutory injunction by courts of equity has never been regarded as strictly a matter of right, even though irreparable injury may otherwise result to the plaintiff," and that "where an injunction is asked which will adversely affect a public interest for whose impairment, even temporarily, an injunction bond cannot compensate, the court may in the public interest withhold relief until a final determination of the rights of the parties, though the postponement may be burdensome to the plaintiff." *Yakus v. United States, supra*, 321 U.S., at 440. The grant of jurisdiction to ensure compliance with a statute hardly suggests an absolute duty to do so under any and all circumstances, and a federal judge sitting as chancellor is not mechanically obligated to grant an injunction for every violation of law. *TVA v. Hill*, 437 U.S., at 193.

These commonplace considerations applicable to cases in which injunctions are sought in the federal courts reflect a "practice with a background of several hundred years of history," *Hecht Co. v. Bowles, supra*, at 329, a practice of which Congress is assuredly well aware. Of course, Congress may intervene and guide or control the exercise of the courts' discretion, but we do not lightly assume that Congress has intended to depart from established principles. * * *

In *TVA v. Hill*, we held that Congress had foreclosed the exercise of the usual discretion possessed by a court of equity. There, we thought that "[o]ne would be hard pressed to find a statutory provision whose terms were any plainer" than that before us. 437 U.S., at 173, 98 S. Ct., at 2291. The statute involved, the Endangered Species Act, 87 Stat. 884, 16 U.S.C. § 1531 *et seq.*, required the District Court to enjoin completion of the Tellico Dam in order to preserve the snail darter, a species of perch. The purpose and language of the statute under consideration in *Hill*, not the bare fact of a statutory violation, compelled that conclusion. Section 7 of the Act, 16 U.S.C. § 1536, requires federal agencies to "insure that actions authorized, funded, or carried out by them do not jeopardize the continued existence of [any] endangered species . . . or result in the destruction or modification of habitat of such species which is determined . . . to be critical." The statute thus contains a flat ban on the destruction of critical habitats.

It was conceded in *Hill* that completion of the dam would eliminate an endangered species by destroying its critical habitat. Refusal to enjoin the action would have ignored the "explicit provisions of the Endangered Species Act." 437 U.S., at 173. Congress, it appeared to us, had chosen the snail darter over the dam. The purpose and language of the statute limited the remedies available to the District Court; only an injunction could vindicate the objectives of the Act.

That is not the case here. An injunction is not the only means of ensuring compliance. The FWPCA itself, for example, provides for fines and criminal penalties. 33 U.S.C. §§ 1319(c) and (d). Respondents suggest that failure to enjoin the Navy will undermine the integrity of the permit process by allowing the statutory violation to continue. The integrity of the Nation's waters, however, not the permit process, is the purpose of the FWPCA. As Congress explained, the objective of the FWPCA is to "restore and maintain the chemical, physical, and biological integrity of the Nation's waters." 33 U.S.C. § 1251(a).

This purpose is to be achieved by compliance with the Act, including compliance with the permit requirements. Here, however, the discharge of ordnance had not polluted the waters, and, although the District Court declined to enjoin the discharges, it neither ignored the statutory violation nor undercut the purpose and function of the permit system. The court ordered the Navy to apply for a permit. It temporarily, not permanently, allowed the Navy to continue its activities without a permit.

In *Hill*, we also noted that none of the limited "hardship exemptions" of the Endangered Species Act would "even remotely apply to the Tellico Project." 437 U.S., at 188. The prohibition of the FWPCA against discharge of pollutants, in contrast, can be overcome by the very permit the Navy was ordered to seek. The Senate Report to the 1972 Amendments explains that the permit program would be enacted because "the Committee recognizes the impracticality of any effort to halt all pollution immediately." S.Rep.No. 92–414, p. 43 (1971). That the scheme as a whole contemplates the exercise of discretion and balancing of equities militates against the conclusion that Congress intended to deny courts their traditional equitable discretion in enforcing the statute. * * *

The FWPCA directs the Administrator of the EPA to seek an injunction to restrain immediately discharges of pollutants he finds to be presenting "an imminent and substantial endangerment to the health of persons or to the welfare of persons." 33 U.S.C. § 1364(a). This rule of immediate cessation, however, is limited to the indicated class of violations. For other kinds of violations, the FWPCA authorizes the Administrator of the EPA "to commence a civil action for appropriate relief, including a permanent or temporary injunction, for any violation for which he is authorized to issue a compliance order. . . ." 33 U.S.C. § 1319(b). The provision makes clear that Congress did not anticipate that all discharges would be immediately enjoined. Consistent with this view, the administrative practice has not been to request immediate cessation orders. "Rather, enforcement actions typically result, by consent or otherwise, in a remedial order setting out a detailed schedule of compliance designed to cure the identified violation of the Act." * * *

### III

This Court explained in *Hecht Co. v. Bowles*, 321 U.S. 321 (1944), that a major departure from the long tradition of equity practice should not be lightly implied. As we did there, we construe the statute at issue "in favor of that interpretation which affords a full opportunity for equity courts to treat enforcement proceedings . . . in accordance with their traditional practices, as conditioned by the necessities of the public interest which Congress has sought to protect." *Id.* We do not read the FWPCA as foreclosing completely the exercise of the court's discretion. Rather than requiring a district court to issue an injunction for any and all statutory violations, the FWPCA permits the district court to order that relief it considers necessary to secure prompt compliance with the Act. That relief can include, but is not limited to, an order of immediate cessation.

The exercise of equitable discretion, which must include the ability to deny as well as grant injunctive relief, can fully protect the range of public interests at issue at this stage in the proceedings. The District Court did not face a situation in which a permit would very likely not issue, and the requirements and objective of the statute could therefore not be vindicated if discharges were permitted to continue. Should it become clear that no permit will be issued and that compliance with the FWPCA will not be forthcoming, the statutory scheme and purpose would require the court to reconsider the balance it has struck.

Because Congress, in enacting the FWPCA, has not foreclosed the exercise of equitable discretion, the proper standard for appellate review is whether the District Court abused its discretion in denying an immediate cessation order while the Navy applied for a permit. We reverse and remand to the Court of Appeals for proceedings consistent with this opinion.

---

## QUESTIONS AND DISCUSSION

**1.** Review the case, *Washington County, North Carolina v. U.S. Department of the Navy,* excerpted in Chapter 6 at page 533. There, as here, the U.S. Navy was sued for its flight activities and the plaintiffs requested an injunction for a violation of environmental laws (the Clean Water Act here, and NEPA in *Washington County*). Here an injunction is denied yet in *Washington County* it is granted, despite the Navy's assertion that "it will not be able to meet its training goals in servicing carrier-based aircraft." How can you explain the different results? What if the Navy had asserted that compliance with the Clean Water Act would weaken its training activities and harm national security?

Is this case consistent with the *Winter v. NRDC* decision described in Chapter 6? *Winter* is a more recent Supreme Court case. Does it affect the *Romero-Barcelo* precedent?

**2.** In its conclusion, the court engages in a triple-negative, saying:

> The District Court did not face a situation in which a permit would very likely not issue, and the requirements and objective of the statute could therefore not be vindicated if discharges were permitted to continue.

What does this mean in plain English? What type of situation is the court suggesting *would* have justified enjoining the challenged activity?

**3.** One of the signature initiatives of the Obama Administration's EPA has been Next Generation Compliance. As EPA describes:

> Today's pollution challenges require a modern approach to compliance, taking advantage of new tools and approaches while strengthening vigorous enforcement of environmental laws. Next Generation Compliance is EPA's integrated strategy to do that, designed to bring together the best thinking from inside and outside EPA.

Next Generation Compliance consists of five interconnected components, each designed to improve the effectiveness of our compliance program:

- **Design regulations and permits** that are easier to implement, with a goal of improved compliance and environmental outcomes.
- Use and promote **advanced emissions/pollutant detection technology** so that regulated entities, the government, and the public can more easily see pollutant discharges, environmental conditions, and noncompliance.
- Shift toward **electronic reporting** to help make environmental reporting more accurate, complete, and efficient while helping EPA and co-regulators better manage information, improve effectiveness and transparency.
- Expand **transparency** by making information more accessible to the public.
- Develop and use **innovative enforcement** approaches (e.g., data analytics and targeting) to achieve more widespread compliance.

This strategy has been adopted in settlements. In a 2012 consent decree, for example, the defendant agreed to install an Optical Gas Imaging Camera to provide real-time tracking of emissions from its vents and to inspect and repair any leaks detected. *U.S. v. BP Products North America,* Civil No. 2:12 CV 207 (N.D. Ind. 2012). In a 2015 consent decree, the defendant agreed to institute a third-party inspection program to improve and confirm compliance. This requires four separate inspections by a qualified auditor over the course of a year, three of which are unannounced, with the results reported to the local fire department and EPA. *In the matter of Mann Distribution,* Administrative Order on Consent, Docket Nos. RCRA 001–2015–0028. For a detailed review and assessment of the Next Generation Compliance program, see David A. Markell and Robert L. Glicksman, *Next Generation Compliance*, NATURAL RESOURCES & ENV'T, Winter 2016, at 22.

---

### *d. Supplemental Projects and Nontraditional Remedies*

The past ten years have witnessed significant growth of nontraditional, flexible agreements between environmental enforcement agencies and regulated parties. Habitat conservation plans—negotiated agreements between landowners with endangered species habitat and the government for planned development—have become a significant aspect of the Endangered Species Act (described in Part I of Chapter 2). The Superfund program has been greatly influenced by state brownfields programs that accelerate the development of inner city sites lying vacant, bereft of economic development because of liability fears (described in Chapter 5). Similar movement has been underway in the enforcement arena, as well, with the growth of supplemental environmental projects (SEPs) to settle enforcement actions. In general, SEPs are part of negotiated settlements between the government and violators for "beyond compliance" environmental activities either in place of or in addition to monetary penalties. Put simply, SEPs represent a negotiated deal that trades off a reduced penalty for the violator in exchange for an environmentally beneficial action that is not mandated by law. SEPs have ranged from purchasing lead paint abatement kits for schools and restoring endangered species habitat to installing a closed-loop wastewater recycling system. As David Dana has described,

> SEPs entail the replacement of relatively general standards (in this case, standards for the calculation and payment of monetary penalties) with negotiated, mutually agreed upon, site-specific measures. And like the other reform programs, the SEPs program lacks a firm statutory basis. SEPs, not surprisingly, have proponents and detractors. Proponents view the SEPs program as a win-win opportunity for business and the environmental community alike; critics view SEPs as potentially undermining the deterrence power of environmental enforcement programs by, in effect, giving violators a low cost or costless way to pay for violations. In any event, the use of SEPs continues to increase. It is now commonplace for the violator's counsel to propose and attempt to negotiate a SEP as part of the resolution of a major enforcement action under state and federal pollution control statutes.

David A. Dana, *Innovations In Environmental Policy: The New "Contractarian" Paradigm In Environmental Regulation,* 2000 U. ILL. L. REV. 35, 43–44 (2000).

The importance of SEPs as a remedy is evident in the chart below. EPA, FY2015 COMPLIANCE AND ENFORCEMENT ANNUAL RESULTS 13 (2015).

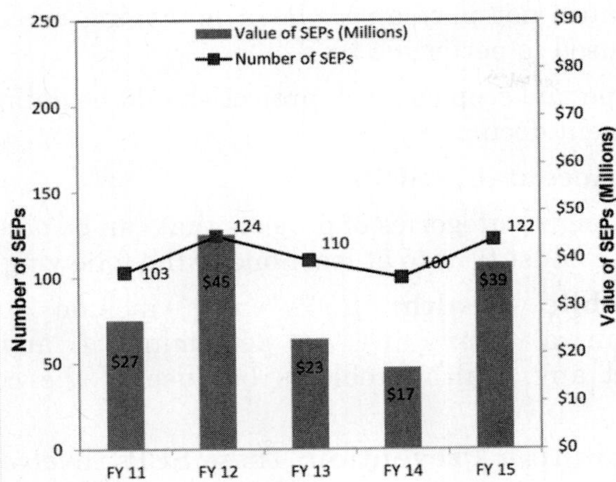


In 1998, EPA issued a revised policy on SEPs, increasing the number of categories of projects, establishing guidelines for their use, and providing procedures for calculating the cost of these projects. The following excerpt outlines the main features of the Policy.

## EPA, Final Supplemental Environmental Projects Policy

1998.

### Characteristics of SEPs

- Because SEPs are part of an enforcement settlement, they must meet certain legal requirements.
- There must be a relationship between the underlying violation and the human health or environmental benefits that will result from the SEP.
- A SEP must improve, protect, or reduce risks to public health or the environment, although in some cases a SEP may, as a secondary matter, also provide the violator with certain benefits.
- The SEP must be undertaken in settlement of an enforcement action as a project that the violator is not otherwise legally required to perform.

### SEP Guidelines

In addition, there are several guidelines that a SEP must meet.

- A project cannot be inconsistent with any provision of the underlying statute(s).
- A SEP must advance at least one of the objectives of the environmental statute that is the basis of the enforcement action.

- EPA must not play any role in managing or controlling funds used to perform a SEP.
- The type and scope of each project should be defined in the settlement document.

**Categories of Acceptable SEPs**

EPA has set out eight categories of projects that can be acceptable SEPs. To qualify, a SEP must fit into at least one of the following categories:

1. **Public Health:** SEPs may include examining residents in a community to determine if anyone has experienced any health problems because of the company's violations.

2. **Pollution Prevention:** These SEPs involve changes so that the company no longer generates some form of pollution. For example, a company may make its operation more efficient so that it avoids making a hazardous waste along with its product.

3. **Pollution Reduction:** These SEPs reduce the amount and/or danger presented by some form of pollution, often by providing better treatment and disposal of the pollutant.

4. **Environmental Restoration and Protection:** These SEPs improve the condition of the land, air or water in the area damaged by the violation. For example, by purchasing land or developing conservation programs for the land, a company could protect a source of drinking water.

5. **Emergency Planning and Preparedness:** These projects provide assistance to a responsible state or local emergency response or planning entity to enable these organizations to fulfill their obligations under the Emergency Planning and Community Right-to-Know Act (EPCRA.) Such assistance may include the purchase of computers and/or software, communication systems, chemical emission detection and inactivation equipment, HAZMAT equipment, or training. Cash donations to local or state emergency response organizations are not acceptable SEPs.

6. **Assessments and Audits:** A violating company may agree to examine its operations to determine if it is causing any other pollution problems or can run its operations better to avoid violations in the future. These audits go well beyond standard business practice.

7. **Environmental Compliance Promotion:** These are SEPs in which an alleged a violator provides training or technical support to other members of the regulated community to achieve, or go beyond, compliance with applicable

environmental requirements. For example, the violator may train other companies on how to comply with the law.

8. **Other Types of Projects:** Other acceptable SEPs would be those that have environment merit but do not fit within the categories listed above. These types of projects must be fully consistent with all other provisions of the SEP Policy and be approved by EPA.

---

Another sanction available to EPA includes so-called "contractor listing." Under both the Clean Air Act and Clean Water Act, and elaborated in Executive Order 11738 (Sept. 10, 1973, 38 Fed.Reg. 25161), facilities with convictions under Clean Air Act Section 113(c) and Clean Water Act Section 309(c) can be placed on EPA's "List of Violating Facilities." Facilities on this list are barred from receiving contracts, subcontracts, grants or loans from the federal government. The sanction applies only to the facility, not the entire company, but if a facility depends on government contracts this can be a severe punishment.

> A listing for civil violations must be preceded by a hearing conducted by an EPA hearing examiner. If the hearing examiner recommends listing of the violator, a determination for listing must then be signed by the Assistant Administrator for Enforcement and Compliance Assurance at EPA headquarters at which time the listing becomes effective. A listing for civil violations is effective for a period of one year, although it may be renewed by EPA. Placement on the List is automatic without additional hearing following a criminal conviction (including a plea of guilty), and the violator remains on the List until a determination for removal is signed by the Assistant Administrator for Enforcement and Compliance Assurance following a showing by the violator that the conditions that gave rise to the violation have been removed, or the conviction is reversed

Joel A. Mintz, *Id.* at 12–43 to 12–44.

The head of a Federal agency can exempt any contract, grant, or loan from listing so long as he promptly notifies the EPA of the exemption and its justification and reviews the necessity of the exemption annually.

---

## QUESTIONS AND DISCUSSION

**1.** While SEPs may provide more direct environmental benefit than payment of a fine to the U.S Treasury, concerns have been expressed over companies gaining inappropriate benefits. As a result, violators whose SEPs involve public awareness projects are required to state that the project is part of the settlement of a government lawsuit. Moreover, funds paid for

SEPs are not tax deductible. *See* Allied-Signal Inc. v. Internal Revenue Service, 54 F.3d 767 (3d Cir. 1995) ($8 million payment to private fund for remedying environmental contamination is not a deductible business expense).

**2.** Others are concerned with the very flexibility of SEPs. Consider, for example, SEPs performed by Citgo in Port Arthur, Texas, for unauthorized benzene emissions.

> [R]efinery-reform advocates and the government and industry watchdog Public Citizen argued that SEPs in Texas serve mainly as public-relations gestures. Recent citations for pollution violations by Citgo, for instance, have resulted in a program to monitor car pollution and a donation to a local bird refuge—projects environmentalists have blasted as patently irrelevant to the people exposed to toxic refinery emissions.

Michelle Chen, *Citgo Indictment Hints at Pollution Scourge, Texas Activists Say,* THE NEW STANDARD, Sept. 1, 2006.

If Citgo ended up paying the same amount for the car monitoring program and bird refuge as it would have paid in civil fines, is this not a better outcome for the environment? What would have been a better SEP?

**3.** Enforcement officials can be very creative with remedies. Allegheny County, Pennsylvania, negotiated the following innovative consent decrees with polluters.

- Performance Bonds. Some companies are asked to post a performance bond. They forfeit the bond if they subsequently fail to meet the terms of the consent decree.
- Escrow Accounts. Some companies were required to establish special escrow accounts to ensure that monies would be available to pay any penalties that might accrue.
- Research Requirements. In some cases, facilities are asked to perform a study to determine how they could best come into compliance.
- Credit Projects. As a substitute for payment of a penalty, companies sometimes agreed to reduce emissions beyond the levels required by the regulations.
- Delayed Compliance Orders. These orders set forth schedules for pollution sources to achieve compliance but protect the sources from further enforcement action as long as the sources remain on schedule with the orders.
- Stipulated Penalties. Some consent decrees and consent orders contain provisions for the payment of stipulated penalties if the decrees or orders are violated. Such provisions set forth agreed-upon fixed or graduated penalties for various types of violations.
- Self-monitoring. Consent decrees often contain provisions for self-monitoring. The goal of self-monitoring requirements is to

> increase the company's awareness about their state of compliance with the hope that the company will then take steps on their own to correct any violations. To encourage companies to accurately record the data, self-monitoring data are rarely used by the County for enforcement. Companies are required to report any violations they detect and, at times, are permitted to reduce the amount of self-monitoring as a reward for, or in recognition of, good performance. Self-monitoring, in effect, extends the limited inspection resources of the County.

EPA, PRINCIPLES OF ENVIRONMENTAL ENFORCEMENT 11–5 (1992).

SEPs for air pollution violations in Texas have included requiring the railroad commission to "Provide up to 100% of the purchase price of a propane or natural gas powered school bus that is model year 2010 or newer to public and public charter schools to replace a diesel school bus that is 2002 or older" and requiring the city of El Paso to establish "collection events to collect, properly dispose, or recycle household non-hazardous materials such as used tires, motor oil, batteries, antifreeze, and bulky solid waste." TEXAS COUNCIL OF ENVIRONMENTAL QUALITY PRE-APPROVED SEPS, June 11, 2013.

---

## C. CRIMINAL ENFORCEMENT

> **Question:** What do the following companies all have in common? Royal Caribbean, British Petroleum, American Airlines, International Paper, Pillsbury, Nabisco, Ralston-Purina, Bristol-Myers, and Exxon?
>
> **Answer:** All have been convicted of environmental crimes.

A range of environmental statutes, including the key statutes governing air, water and solid waste, provide for criminal sanctions. Over the past fifteen years, enforcement of criminal violations has become commonplace. Heavy civil fines and injunctions can provide powerful deterrents to regulated parties, so why include criminal provisions in environmental laws? Most important, criminal sanctions send a very different message both to the regulated community and to the public. Put simply, criminal sanctions are not regarded as just another cost of doing business. Criminal sanctions, whether in the form of imprisonment or monetary penalties, are the exclamation point at the end of the sentence, "You will comply, or else!" Recent criminal enforcement action statistics are set out in the graph below. EPA, FY2015 COMPLIANCE AND ENFORCEMENT ANNUAL RESULTS 14 (2015).

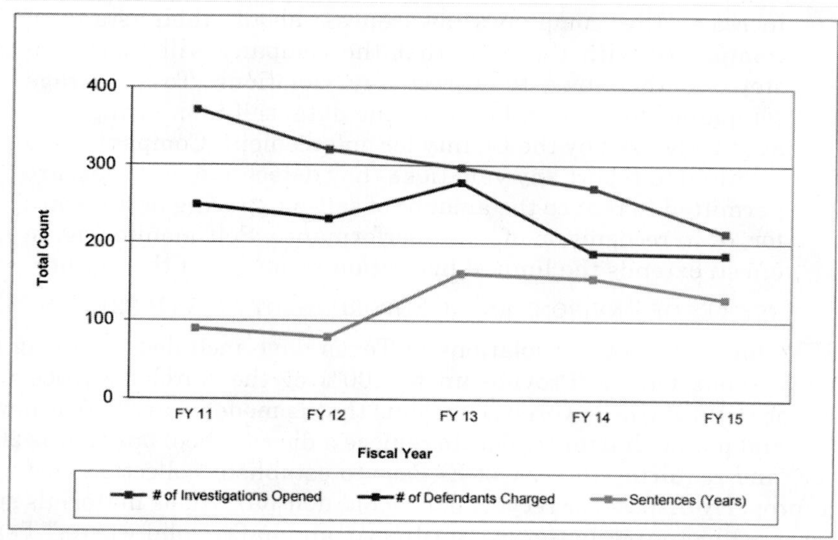


Despite their greater deterrent force and powerful rhetoric, criminal sanctions can also prove problematic in an environmental context. We have already discussed the difficulty of achieving full compliance all of the time. Federal environmental regulations mandate hundreds of thousands of discrete obligations, so if enforcement officials want to find instances of noncompliance at a company, chances are they can. The key question then becomes when criminal charges should be brought instead or in addition to civil charges.

1. INTENT

If one looks across the criminal cases that have been brought, typical cases include falsifying documents, tampering with monitoring or control equipment, and repeated violations. But this doesn't tell us why criminal charges were brought rather than civil. As all law students learn in their criminal law class discussion of *scienter* and *mens rea*, the key to criminal enforcement is intent—a person or organization has knowingly and willingly committed the illegal act. This simple requirement can be problematic in a technical, highly regulated field such as environmental law, however. More specifically, does criminal sanction for environmental violations require intent only to commit the act, or is it necessary to commit an act *and* have knowledge that the act is illegal, as well?

## United States v. Ahmad

United States Court of Appeals for the Fifth Circuit, 1996.
101 F.3d 386.

■ SMITH, CIRCUIT JUDGE:

. . . This case arises from the discharge of a large quantity of gasoline into the sewers of Conroe, Texas, in January 1994. In 1992, Ahmad purchased the "Spin-N-Market No. 12," a combination convenience store and gas station located at the intersection of Second and Lewis Streets in Conroe. The Spin-N-Market has two gasoline pumps, each of which is fed by an 8000-gallon underground gasoline tank. Some time after Ahmad bought the station, he discovered that one of the tanks, which held high-octane gasoline, was leaking. This did not pose an immediate hazard, because the leak was at the top of the tank; gasoline could not seep out. The leak did, however, allow water to enter into the tank and contaminate the gas. Because water is heavier than gas, the water sank to the bottom of the tank, and because the tank was pumped from the bottom, Ahmad was unable to sell from it.

In October 1993, Ahmad hired CTT Environmental Services ("CTT"), a tank testing company, to examine the tank. CTT determined that it contained approximately 800 gallons of water, and the rest mostly gasoline. Jewel McCoy, a CTT employee, testified that she told Ahmad that the leak could not be repaired until the tank was completely emptied, which CTT offered to do for 65 cents per gallon plus $65 per hour of labor. After McCoy gave Ahmad this estimate, he inquired whether he could empty the tank himself. She replied that it would be dangerous and illegal to do so. On her testimony, he responded, "Well, if I don't get caught, what then?"

On January 25, 1994, Ahmad rented a hand-held motorized water pump from a local hardware store, telling a hardware store employee that he was planning to use it to remove water from his backyard. Victor Fonseca, however, identified Ahmad and the pump and testified that he had seen Ahmad pumping gasoline into the street. Oscar Alvarez stated that he had seen Ahmad and another person discharging gasoline into a manhole. Tereso Uribe testified that he had confronted Ahmad and asked him what was going on, to which Ahmad responded that he was simply removing the water from the tank.

In all, 5,220 gallons of fluid were pumped from the leaky tank, of which approximately 4,690 gallons were gasoline. Some of the gas-water mixture ran down Lewis Street and some into the manhole in front of the store.

The gasoline discharged onto Lewis Street went a few hundred feet along the curb to Third Street, where it entered a storm drain and the storm sewer system and flowed through a pipe that eventually empties into Possum Creek. When city officials discovered the next day that there was gasoline in Possum Creek, several vacuum trucks were required to decontaminate it. Possum Creek feeds into the San Jacinto River, which eventually flows into Lake Houston. * * *

The Conroe fire department determined the gasoline was creating a risk of explosion and ordered that two nearby schools be evacuated. Although no one was injured as a result of the discharge, fire officials testified at trial that Ahmad had created a "tremendous explosion hazard" that could have led to "hundreds, if not thousands, of deaths and injuries" and millions of dollars of property damage.

By 9:00 a.m. on January 26, investigators had traced the source of the gasoline back to the manhole directly in front of the Spin-N-Market. Their suspicions were confirmed when they noticed a strong odor of gasoline and saw signs of corrosion on the asphalt surrounding the manhole. The investigators questioned Ahmad, who at first denied having operated a pump the previous night. Soon, however, his story changed: He admitted to having used a pump but denied having pumped anything from his tanks.

Ahmad was indicted for three violations of the CWA: knowingly discharging a pollutant from a point source into a navigable water of the United States without a permit, in violation of 33 U.S.C. §§ 1311(a) and 1319(c)(2)(A) (count one); knowingly operating a source in violation of a pretreatment standard, in violation of 33 U.S.C. §§ 1317(d) and 1319(c)(2)(A) (count two); and knowingly placing another person in imminent danger of death or serious bodily injury by discharging a pollutant, in violation of 33 U.S.C. § 1319(c)(3) (count three). At trial, Ahmad did not dispute that he had discharged gasoline from the tank or that eventually it had found its way to Possum Creek and the sewage treatment plant. Instead, he contended that his discharge of the gasoline was not "knowing," because he had believed he was discharging water. * * *

> Ahmad argues that the district court improperly instructed the jury on the *mens rea* required for counts one and two. The instruction on count one stated in relevant part:
>
> > For you to find Mr. Ahmad guilty of this crime, you must be convinced that the government has proved each of the following beyond a reasonable doubt:
> >
> > (1) That on or about the date set forth in the indictment,
> >
> > (2) the defendant knowingly discharged
> >
> > (3) a pollutant
> >
> > (4) from a point source
> >
> > (5) into the navigable waters of the United States
> >
> > (6) without a permit to do so. * * *

Ahmad contends that the jury should have been instructed that the statutory *mens rea*—knowledge—was required as to each element of the offenses, rather than only with regard to discharge or the operation of a source. Because Ahmad requested such instruction, we review the refusal to give it for abuse of discretion. * * *

The language of the CWA is less than pellucid. Title 33 U.S.C. § 1319(c)(2)(A) says that "any person who knowingly violates" any of a number of other sections of the CWA commits a felony. . . . The principal issue is to which elements of the offense the modifier "knowingly" applies. The matter is complicated somewhat by the fact that the phrase "knowingly violates" appears in a different section of the CWA from the language defining the elements of the offenses. Ahmad argues that within this context, "knowingly violates" should be read to require him knowingly to have acted with regard to each element of the offenses. The government, in contrast, contends that "knowingly violates" requires it to prove only that Ahmad knew the nature of his acts and that he performed them intentionally. Particularly at issue is whether "knowingly" applies to the element of the discharge's being a pollutant, for Ahmad's main theory at trial was that he thought he was discharging water, not gasoline.

The Supreme Court has spoken to this issue in broad terms. In *United States v. X-Citement Video, Inc.*, 513 U.S. 64 (1994), the Court read "knowingly" to apply to each element of a child pornography offense, notwithstanding its conclusion that under the "most natural grammatical reading" of the statute it should apply only to the element of having transported, shipped, received, distributed, or reproduced the material at issue. The Court also reaffirmed the long-held view that "the presumption in favor of a scienter requirement should apply to each of the statutory elements which criminalize otherwise innocent conduct."

Although *X-Citement Video* is the Court's most recent pronouncement on this subject, it is not the first. In *Staples v. United States*, 511 U.S. 600 (1994), the Court found that the statutes criminalizing knowing possession of a machine gun require that defendants know not only that they possess a firearm but that it actually is a machine gun. Thus, an awareness of the features of the gun—specifically, the features that make it an automatic weapon—is a necessary element of the offense. More generally, the Court also made plain that statutory crimes carrying severe penalties are presumed to require that a defendant know the facts that make his conduct illegal. * * *

Our own precedents are in the same vein. In *United States v. Baytank (Houston), Inc.*, 934 F.2d 599 (5th Cir. 1991), we concluded that a conviction for knowing and improper storage of hazardous wastes under 42 U.S.C. § 6928(d)(2)(A) requires "that the defendant know[ ] factually what he is doing—storing, what is being stored, and that what is being stored factually has the potential for harm to others or the environment, and that he has no permit. . . ." This is directly analogous to the interpretation of the CWA that Ahmad urges upon us. Indeed, we find it eminently sensible that the phrase "knowingly violates" in § 1319(c)(2)(A), when referring to other provisions that define the elements of the offenses § 1319 creates, should uniformly require knowledge as to each of those elements rather than only one or two. To hold otherwise would require an explanation as to why some elements should be treated differently from others, which neither the parties nor the caselaw seems able to provide. * * *

In support of its interpretation of the CWA, the government cites cases from other circuits. . . . In *United States v. Weitzenhoff*, 35 F.3d 1275 (9th Cir. 1994), *cert. denied*, 115 S. Ct. 939 (1995), the court similarly was concerned almost exclusively with whether the language of the CWA creates a mistake-of-law defense. Both cases are easily distinguishable, for neither directly addresses mistake of fact or the statutory construction issues raised by *Ahmad*.

The government also protests that CWA violations fall into the judicially-created exception for "public welfare offenses," under which some regulatory crimes have been held not to require a showing of *mens rea*. On its face, the CWA certainly does appear to implicate public welfare.

As recent cases have emphasized, however, the public welfare offense exception is narrow. The *Staples* Court, for example, held that the statute prohibiting the possession of machine guns fell outside the exception, notwithstanding the fact that "typically, our cases recognizing such offenses involve statutes that regulate potentially harmful or injurious items."

Though gasoline is a "potentially harmful or injurious item," it is certainly no more so than are machine guns. Rather, *Staples* held, the key to the public welfare offense analysis is whether "dispensing with *mens rea* would require the defendant to have knowledge only of traditionally lawful conduct." The CWA offenses of which Ahmad was convicted have precisely this characteristic, for if knowledge is not required as to the nature of the substance discharged, one who honestly and reasonably believes he is discharging water may find himself guilty of a felony if the substance turns out to be something else.

The fact that violations of § 1319(c)(2)(A) are felonies punishable by years in federal prison confirms our view that they do not fall within the public welfare offense exception. As the *Staples* Court noted, public welfare offenses have virtually always been crimes punishable by relatively light penalties such as fines or short jail sentences, rather than substantial terms of imprisonment. Serious felonies, in contrast, should not fall within the exception "absent a clear statement from Congress that *mens rea* is not required. . . ." With the exception of purely jurisdictional elements, the *mens rea* of knowledge applies to each element of the crimes.

Finally, the government argues that the instructions, considered as a whole, adequately conveyed to the jury the message that Ahmad had to have known that what he was discharging was gasoline in order for the jury to find him guilty. We disagree.

At best, the jury charge made it uncertain to which elements "knowingly" applied. At worst, and considerably more likely, it indicated that only the element of discharge need be knowing. The instructions listed each element on a separate line, with the word "knowingly" present only in the line corresponding to the element that something was discharged. That the district court included a one-sentence summary of each count in which "knowingly" was present did not cure the error. * * *

---

## QUESTIONS AND DISCUSSION

**1.** When re-trying the case, what does the judge need to do to avoid having the decision overturned again? What do prosecutors now need to establish in order to convict Ahmad? Is it enough to show Ahmad knew he was discharging gasoline or must it also be established that he knew or should have known that this would specifically violate the Clean Water Act?

**2.** In *Weitzenhoff v. United States,* 35 F.3d 1275 (9th Cir. 1994), *cert. denied*, 115 S. Ct. 939 (1995), a case cited in the *Ahmad* decision, the operator of Honolulu's sewage treatment plant was criminally convicted for discharges from the plant that exceeded their NPDES permits. Most of the discharges occurred at night and were not reported to the state or federal authorities. At trial, the defendants argued that the "knowingly violate" requirement of the Clean Water Act meant they had to know they were violating the discharge terms of their permit. The court, however, held that they only had to know they were discharging the pollutants in question. In other words, the government did not need to prove that the defendants knew their action were unlawful.

*Weitzenhoff* is a "public welfare offense," described in the classic public welfare case as:

> Where . . . dangerous or deleterious devices or products or obnoxious waste materials are involved, the probability of regulation is so great that anyone who is aware that he is in possession of them or dealing with them must be presumed to be aware of the regulation.

*United States v. International Minerals,* 402 U.S. 558, 565 (1971).

In other words, there are certain types of actions that are so obviously unlawful that specific intent to violate the law is unnecessary. Why doesn't the *Ahmad* court regard pumping out a gasoline tank as a public welfare offense?

**3.** What are the downsides to requiring intent for Clean Water Act violations? What are the downsides to treating them as public welfare offenses? In this regard, consider the dissent in *Weitzenhoff.*

> In this case, the defendants, sewage plant operators, had a permit to discharge sewage into the ocean, but exceeded the permit limitations. The legal issue for the panel was what knowledge would turn innocently or negligently violating a permit into "knowingly" violating a permit. Were the plant operators felons if they knew they were discharging sewage, but did not know that

they were violating their permit? Or did they also have to know they were violating their permit? * * *

NPDES permits are often difficult to understand and obey. The EPA had licensed the defendants' plant to discharge 976 pounds of waste per day, or about 409,920 pounds over the fourteen months covered by the indictment, into the ocean. The wrongful conduct was not discharging waste into the ocean. That was socially desirable conduct by which the defendants protected the people of their city from sewage-borne disease and earned their pay. The wrongful conduct was violating the NPDES permit by discharging 26,000 more pounds of waste than the permit authorized during the fourteen months. Whether these defendants were innocent or not, in the sense of knowing that they were exceeding their permit limitation, the panel's holding will make innocence irrelevant in other permit violation cases where the defendants had no idea that they were exceeding permit limits. The only thing they have to know to be guilty is that they were dumping sewage into the ocean, yet that was a lawful activity expressly authorized by their federal permit. * * *

The panel then tries to bolster its construction by categorizing the offense as a "public welfare offense," as though that justified more aggressive criminalization without a plain statutory command. This category is a modernized version of "*malum prohibitum*." Traditionally the criminal law distinguishes between *malum in se*, conduct wrong upon principles of natural moral law, and *malum prohibitum*, conduct not inherently immoral but wrong because prohibited by law. To put this in plain, modern terms, any normal person knows murder, rape and robbery are wrong, and they would be wrong even in a place with no sovereign and no law. Discharging 6% more pollutants than one's permit allows is wrong only because the law says so. Substitution of the modern term "public welfare offense" for the traditional one, *malum prohibitum*, allows for confusion by rhetorical suggestion. The new term suggests that other offenses might merely be private in their impact, and therefore less serious. The older set of terms made it clear that murder was more vile than violating a federal regulation. The category of *malum prohibitum*, or public welfare offenses, makes the rule of lenity especially important, most particularly for felonies, because persons of good conscience may not recognize the wrongfulness of the conduct when they engage in it.

---

## 2. RESPONSIBLE CORPORATE OFFICER DOCTRINE

Many environmental criminal actions are brought against companies and/or company employees. With long chains of command and many people involved at different stages of decisions, the guilty party for a specific action may not be obvious. What if Ahmad, for example, had been told by his boss that bringing in engineers to empty the tanks was too expensive and to "do something about it"? Conversely, what if the boss knew about Ahmad's pumping (or *should* have known) but did nothing to stop it?

Under a theory known as the "Responsible Corporate Officer Doctrine," criminal liability can be imposed on corporate managers or officers who were in a position to know about and prevent a violation, even if they were not the ones who actually committed the illegal act. From the case law, mere knowledge is not enough. A person liable as a responsible corporate officer must also have the ability or authority to influence the corporate conduct causing the violation. The government has successfully used this doctrine to convict high-level corporate officers (even presidents) for environmental violations by lower-level employees.

The Responsible Corporate Officer Doctrine need not lead to criminal sanctions, but the prerequisites of knowledge and failure to act can easily fit the standard for criminal liability in many environmental statutes. Moreover, because knowledge can be inferred, the government may need only to show that a corporate official had both the authority and the capacity to prevent the violation, yet failed to do so. Consider, for example, the following holding in *Waterkeepers N. Cal. v. Ag Indus. Mfg., Inc.*, 2005 WL 2001037 (E.D. Cal. 2005), which summarizes well the state of the law.

> Although it is undisputed that AIM is a corporation, WaterKeepers nonetheless contends that AIM's President, Claude Brown, is subject to personal liability under the CWA pursuant to the "responsible corporate officer" doctrine. It is undisputed that Mr. Brown runs day to day operations at the AIM facility, and is responsible for compliance with environmental laws and regulations, like the CWA.
>
> 33 U.S.C. § 1319(c)(6) provides that in addition to the definition of a "person" subject to enforcement action under the CWA (§ 1362(5) includes a corporation within that definition), any responsible corporate officer may also be held liable. In its motion for summary judgment, AIM argues that Mr. Brown must be dismissed as a defendant because WaterKeepers has failed to demonstrate that Mr. Brown knew that AIM was committing any CWA violations.
>
> In *United States v. Iverson*, 162 F.3d 1015 (9th Cir. 1998), the Ninth Circuit considered the application of the responsible corporate officer doctrine in the context of a CWA case. In that case, the defendant, who was President of a company which manufactured chemical products, including acid cleaners and heavy-duty alkaline compounds, personally ordered the discharge of wastewater residue already refused by the local sewer authority. Because the defendant faced criminal charges under the CWA, the Ninth Circuit considered the scope of the

responsible corporate officer doctrine as it applied to the defendant.

Significantly, the Iverson court determined that the principles of an earlier Supreme Court case, *United States v. Dotterweich*, 320 U.S. 277 (1943), applied under the CWA. 162 F.3d at 1023. *Dotterweich* opined that "[t]he offense (there a violation of the Federal Food, Drug, and Cosmetic Act) is committed . . . by all who do have . . . a responsible share in the furtherance of the transaction which the statute outlaws." *Dotterweich*, 320 U.S. at 284.

A later case also cited approvingly by *Iverson*, *United States v. Park*, 421 U.S. 658, 668 (1975) held that a corporate president cannot escape liability, even if he delegated decision-making control over the activity in question to a subordinate. Park found that the question for the jury is whether the corporate officer had "authority with respect to the conditions that formed the basis of the alleged violations." *Id.* at 674. After considering Park, the Iverson court found that its refinement of the "responsible corporate officer" doctrine applied under the CWA. *Iverson*, 162 F.3d at 1024.

AIM correctly points out that *Iverson* is a criminal case with facts more egregious than those of the case at bar. Nonetheless, the responsible corporate officer doctrine has been applied to both criminal and civil cases. *See, e.g.*, *United States v. Hodges X-Ray, Inc.*, 759 F.2d 557, 561 (6th Cir. 1985).

---

## QUESTIONS AND DISCUSSION

**1.** The government obviously cannot put a corporation in jail, no matter how large the prison. In all but the rarest case, the government is not intentionally looking to put the company out of business, so why does it ever make sense to file criminal charges against a corporation? As noted earlier, part of the reason is rhetorical. Criminal prosecution clearly sends the message that this conduct has gone way beyond the bounds of civil enforcement. Criminal enforcement makes a public statement that something very wrong was done. As a result of the terrible PR generated from a criminal conviction, many companies may be willing to settle for stiff plea bargains and civil penalties. Criminal enforcement actions against a corporation also allows the government to bring people into the Grand Jury to give testimony. This can make it easier to get at the facts and figure out intent.

If there is a plea or criminal conviction, the company is in a harder position than in a civil negotiation. The government, for example, can demand a state of the art compliance plan as part of probation. Finally, a criminal conviction may disqualify the facility or company from government contracts until determination for removal is signed by the Assistant Administrator for Enforcement and Compliance Assurance (after the violator has demonstrated that the conditions giving rise to the violation have been fixed) or until the conviction has been reversed.

**2.** Assume that in *U.S. v. Ahmad* there is another employee working with Ahmad. She is not his boss but does nothing to stop his pumping, either. Could she be charged under the Responsible Corporate Office doctrine? What if she acts as a whistle-blower, informing the EPA about Ahmad's pumping? Section 7622 of the Clean Air Act prohibits employers from discriminating against a whistle blower, but what about enforcement actions? In this regard, consider the legislative history to Section 113 of the Clean Air Act. Could this provide any useful guidance?

> The criminal penalties available under Subsection 113(c) should not be applied in a situation where a person, acting in good faith, promptly reports the results of an audit and promptly acts to correct any deviation. Knowledge gained by an individual solely in conducting an audit report itself should not ordinarily form the basis of the intent which results in criminal penalties.

*Report of the Committee on Legislation and Regulatory Reform*, 12 ENERGY L.J. 153, 157 (1991).

---

## PROBLEM EXERCISE:

## PROSECUTING AN ENVIRONMENTAL CRIME

You are the law clerk for the Chief of the Department of Justice's Environmental Crimes Section. You have just received the following memo from the Seattle regional office.[1]

They wish to bring criminal and civil charges against Carl Fisher for his negligent supervision of a construction project. Write a memo to the Chief, discussing both the legal and policy considerations raised by pursuing criminal sanctions in the case described below.

Carl Fisher was employed by the P & A Company as roadmaster of the Yukon Railroad, which runs between Skagway, Alaska, and Whitehorse, Yukon Territory, Canada. As roadmaster, Fisher was responsible under his contract "for every detail of the safe and efficient maintenance and construction of track, structures and marine facilities of the entire railroad . . . and [was to] assume similar duties with special projects."

One of the special projects under Fisher's supervision was a rock-quarrying project at a site alongside the railroad referred to as "6-mile," located on an embankment 200 feet above the Skagway River. The project was designed to realign a sharp curve in the railroad and to obtain rock for a ship dock in Skagway. The project involved blasting rock

1 The statement of facts is adapted from a Ninth Circuit case.

outcroppings alongside the railroad, working the fractured rock toward railroad cars, and loading the rock onto railroad cars with a backhoe.

At 6-mile, a high-pressure petroleum products pipeline owned by P & A's sister company, P & A Pipeline, Inc., runs parallel to the railroad at or above ground level, within a few feet of the tracks. To protect the pipeline during the project, a work platform of sand and gravel was constructed on which the backhoe operated to load rocks over the pipeline and into railroad cars. The location of the work platform changed as the location of the work progressed along the railroad tracks. In addition, when work initially began in April, 1994, P & A covered an approximately 300-foot section of the pipeline with railroad ties, sand, and ballast material to protect the pipeline from puncture, as was customary. After Fisher took over responsibility for the project in May, 1994, no further sections of the pipeline along the 1000-foot work site were protected.

On the evening of October 1, 1994, Shane Croe, a P & A backhoe operator, used the backhoe on the work platform to load a train with rocks. After the train departed, Croe noticed that some fallen rocks had caught the plow of the train as it departed and were located just off the tracks in the vicinity of the unprotected pipeline. At this location, the site had been graded to finish grade and the pipeline was partially covered with a few inches of soil. Croe moved the backhoe off the work platform and drove it down alongside the tracks between 50 to 100 yards from the work platform. While using the backhoe bucket to sweep the rocks from the tracks, Croe struck the pipeline causing a rupture. The pipeline was carrying heating oil, and an estimated 1,000 to 5,000 gallons of oil were discharged over the course of many days into the adjacent Skagway River, a navigable water of the United States.

Fisher argues that he was simply the roadmaster of the Yukon railroad charged with overseeing a rock-quarrying project and had no idea of the relevant Clean Water Act (CWA) requirements, much less that the CWA even applied to any of his activities. He was at home, off duty, when the incident occurred. He does not dispute, however, that he was aware that a high-pressure petroleum products pipeline owned by P & A's sister company ran close to the surface next to the railroad tracks at 6-mile, and does not argue that he was unaware of the dangers a break or puncture of the pipeline by a piece of heavy machinery would pose to the river below.

CWA Section 1321(b)(3) proscribes the actual discharge of oil in harmful quantities into navigable waters of the United States, adjoining shore lines or waters of a contiguous zone, as well as other specified activity.

CWA Section 1319(c)(1)(A) provides that any person who negligently violates 33 U.S.C. § 1321(b)(3) shall be punished by fine or imprisonment, or both. First-time negligent violators shall be punished by a fine of not less than $2,500 nor more than $25,000 per day of violation, or by imprisonment for not more than one year, or by both. The same statute provides that second-time negligent violators shall be punished by a fine of not more than $50,000 per day of violation, or by imprisonment of not more than two years, or both.

Neither section defines the term "negligently," nor is that term defined elsewhere in the CWA.

---

## PROBLEM EXERCISE:
## PROSECUTORIAL DISCRETION

While the EPA may investigate criminal violations of environmental law, the prosecution is handled by state attorneys, the U.S. Attorney's office, or the Environmental Crimes Section of the Department of Justice.

The following excerpts set out an exchange between the leadership of the Environment and Natural Resources Division of the Department of Justice and Professor Richard Lazarus. Lazarus had written an article criticizing the lack of a clear *mens rea* requirement for many environmental crimes. As you read the exchange, consider who has the better argument over whether DOJ has too much discretion over pursuing environmental crimes.

### Lois J. Schiffer and James Simon, *The Reality of Prosecuting Environmental Criminals: A Response to Professor Lazarus*

83 GEORGETOWN L.J. 2531 (1995).

In his article, *Meeting the Demands of Integration in the Evolution of Environmental Law: Reforming Environmental Criminal Law*, 83 GEO. L.J. 2407 (1995), Richard Lazarus provides a provocative review of federal environmental criminal enforcement. The article contains many interesting points that warrant a longer discussion than is permitted here. However, we fundamentally disagree with significant aspects of the analysis. This response focuses on two weaknesses of Professor Lazarus' analysis: (1) the problems that he identifies are more theoretical than real; and (2) the proposed changes—the consequences of which are largely unconsidered in the article—would seriously undermine legitimate law enforcement. * * *

We disagree with the argument in Professor Lazarus' article that, in the area of environmental law, prosecutions are brought to punish conduct that does not violate "traditional norms of moral culpability" evident in other types of criminal cases. In fact, criminal environmental cases are brought to punish egregious and plainly wrongful conduct. Some examples of the types of conduct recently prosecuted include the following: intentionally discharging pollutants in violation of specific water quality permit requirements; unpermitted discharging of raw sewage into rivers and streams through a bypass pipe without reporting it to the Environmental Protection Agency (EPA); falsifying sample test results required to be reported to the government; surreptitious dumping of chemical wastes on the ground or beside a creek; and failing to follow well-known and easily understood procedures in the removal of asbestos. In all of these cases, the defendants did not need extraordinary expertise in science, engineering, or economics to understand the criminal nature of their conduct.

For environmental crimes, as in other prosecutions, there are incentives and controls—largely overlooked in the article—that guide prosecutors to pursue the most egregious types of violations. For example, federal prosecutors are governed in their exercise of discretion by the Principles of Federal Prosecution, which seek to ensure that all federal laws, regardless of their complexity, are enforced in a fair and reasonable manner. Moreover, in each case, the prosecutor must be prepared to persuade a judge and jury that the defendant committed serious *criminal* conduct. Prosecutors naturally want to be successful in their cases, and thus have an incentive to investigate and prosecute conduct that is illegal for reasons that are clear and evident, rather than cloudy, overly technical, or arcane. * * *

The article argues that certain aspects of environmental law are difficult to "integrate" with criminal law. For example, the article identifies environmental law's "aspirational quality" (the tendency to set ambitious goals for environmental quality) and complexity as characteristics that are problematic for criminal enforcement. In practice, however, prosecutions are not brought for failure to meet aspirations, but rather for specific bad conduct as measured against specific and definite standards. Such conduct includes: failing to comply with permits requiring well-understood treatment systems; stealthy dumping of waste that is known to be noxious; and making knowingly false statements.

Moreover, with respect to complexity, it is important to distinguish the occasionally complex types of proof that are required at trial from the far more straightforward facts confronted by the actors involved in the conduct at issue. For example, the government may require complex laboratory documentation and expert testimony to identify a particular substance and thereby prove that it satisfies the definition of hazardous waste under the Resource Conservation and Recovery Act (RCRA). By contrast, defendants who arrange to dump hazardous waste unlawfully in a ravine may have had no trouble identifying the material, because they may have purchased it, or used it on a day-to-day basis, or routinely disposed of it.

## Richard J. Lazarus, *The Reality of Environmental Law in the Prosecution of Environmental Crimes: A Reply to the Department of Justice*

83 GEORGETOWN L.J. 2539 (1995).

Presumably, the title of the Department of Justice's response to my environmental crimes article—*The Reality of Prosecuting Environmental Criminals: A Response to Professor Lazarus*—is intended to suggest that the article is yet another example of academic commentary divorced from the "real" world of criminal prosecutions. There are, however, *real* problems with the existing program, as defined by Congress, as implemented by the executive branch, and as construed by the courts. . . . The D.C. Circuit's recent ruling in *General Electric Co. v. EPA* [reproduced in Annex 4 of the Problem Exercise at the end of this chapter], suggesting judicially-imposed due process limitations on federal environmental criminal prosecutions, is unlikely to be an aberration. * * *

The Department assumes that it should be the sole judge of what constitutes "legitimate" enforcement. As a practical matter, the Department currently is the sole judge, which is part of the problem. For reasons outlined in my article, the other two branches of government, both legislative and judicial, should be playing a more active role in making those determinations consistent with their constitutionally-assigned functions.

The Department's response never faces this fundamental issue. The Department provides examples to support its view that "criminal environmental cases are brought to punish egregious and plainly wrongful conduct." The Department states that "*[i]n practice* . . . prosecutions are not brought for failure to meet aspirations, but rather for specific bad conduct as measured against specific and definite standards."

What the Department does not acknowledge is that environmental criminal law does not *itself* impose any of those limitations. The scope of felony criminal liability under environmental law is far more sweeping. The issue is not just whether the Department has in fact brought many meritorious cases. Of course it has. The real question is to what extent does environmental criminal law confine potential felony liability to those kinds of cases. The Department is, in effect, saying that the public should simply trust the government to bring the right cases—against truly egregious conduct—as a matter of prosecutorial discretion.

My own view is that it is wrong to rely so heavily and exclusively on the proper exercise of prosecutorial discretion. Prosecutors are not the sole experts in making these kinds of determinations, which ultimately reflect significant policy determinations. Nor are individual prosecutors immune from abusive overreaching, which may never be checked by a jury because of plea bargaining. As described in my article, Congress and the courts have legitimate, albeit different, roles to play in identifying the kinds of conduct warranting the imposition of a felony sanction, particularly the incarceration remedy, against an individual. The same kinds of factors prosecutors have properly taken into account (and should take into account in a more structured way) in exercising their discretion, like environmental law's complexity, are factors that Congress should consider in defining the felony offenses in the first instance and that the courts should consider in their judicial construction. Notwithstanding the Department's claims, there is nothing radical or untoward about my recommendation that the other two branches play a more active role: it is sensible policy.

But even more significant is what the Department fails to acknowledge. What the Department seeks to preserve here is not just the sweeping discretion it currently possesses to decide against whom to seek (or at least threaten to seek) felony conviction. At stake is what the government has to *prove* at trial once it initiates a prosecution. The Department does not want to have to prove facts approximating the kinds of facts traditionally required in felony prosecutions. The government asks, in effect, to be trusted to prosecute only those truly culpable defendants but then wants to be able to secure a conviction at trial against such a defendant without proving the facts that would be required to support a showing of culpability.

For the reasons described in my article, I do not believe that the government should be able to have it both ways. I can certainly understand why the Department of Justice prefers to retain such enormous prosecutorial power. But, absent a showing that the Department would somehow be unable to prove the necessary facts against defendants whose culpability warrants felony incarceration, I see no good reason why the Department should possess that power. As described in my article, there are many ways in which Congress can fashion environmental criminal laws that retain the Department's ability to obtain felony convictions against those individuals deserving such sanctions, while simultaneously safeguarding against possible prosecutorial overreaching and abuse.

---

## QUESTIONS AND DISCUSSION

**1.** How could you restrict this prosecutorial discretion without new statutory authority? Describe what guidelines you might draft for the Environmental Crimes Section.

**2.** What does Lazarus mean by the "aspirational" aspect of environmental laws and why does this make criminal enforcement particularly problematic?

**3.** As a former chief of the Environmental Crimes Section described to one of your authors, despite guidelines, the initial selection process of whether to go civil or criminal can be somewhat arbitrary. If a whistle blower calls, for example, the case is more likely to go criminal. If a site inspector sees something amiss, however, the case is more likely to go civil.

---

## III. CITIZEN SUITS

Up to this point, we have focused on the government's role in enforcement, but nongovernmental organizations have played an equally important role in shaping and strengthening environmental law through litigation. Under the Administrative Procedure Act, private parties can ask the court to hold unlawful and set aside agency actions that are:

> **(A)** arbitrary, capricious, an abuse of discretion, or otherwise not in accordance with law;
>
> **(B)** contrary to constitutional right, power, privilege, or immunity;
>
> **(C)** in excess of statutory jurisdiction, authority, or limitations, or short of statutory right; * * *

5 U.S.C. § 706(2).

The potential to pursue judicial review provides citizens, environmental groups, and industry considerable power in the administrative process—indeed, more so than in any other country. In deciding how to interpret and apply the law, EPA and other federal agencies fully recognize that interested groups will sue if not satisfied with the agency action.

Every major federal environmental law passed since 1970 also has contained a *citizen suit* provision. (The lone exception is the Federal Insecticide, Fungicide, and Rodenticide Act, which the agricultural committees in Congress, rather than the more receptive environmental committees, drafted.) Under the citizen suit provisions, individuals and organizations can pursue two new categories of lawsuits not authorized by the Administrative Procedure Act. First, they can sue anyone or any organization, either public or private, alleged to be in violation of an environmental law, serving in effect as private attorneys general. Environmental groups have actively used this opportunity both to supplement the government's limited enforcement resources and to pursue violations that the government is ignoring. When governmental enforcement efforts declined at the beginning of the Reagan Administration in the early 1980s, groups such as the Natural Resources Defense Council organized enforcement campaigns to take up the slack. Second, individuals or groups can sue the EPA administrator or other relevant governmental officials who are failing to carry out a non-discretionary statutory obligation, such as the promulgation of a required regulation. Environmental organizations used this provision frequently in the 1970s and 1980s to enforce deadlines that Congress had set in the major environmental statutes.

Although deadline lawsuits are less important today given the maturity of most environmental laws, the opportunity to bring private prosecutions remains extremely important. Statutes in other fields, such as antitrust and securities regulation, permit private individuals to sue for damages when injured by violations. In authorizing citizen suits under the federal environmental statutes, however, Congress for the first time explicitly called on private citizens to play a direct public role in using the courts to protect the environment. Importantly, the purpose of citizen suits is not to provide compensation to the plaintiffs for injuries but, rather, to ensure more effective enforcement of environmental laws. Fines collected from citizen suits go to the U.S. Treasury, not to the plaintiffs (though successful plaintiffs can collect legal fees).

## James R. May, *Now More Than Ever: Trends In Environmental Citizen Suits At 30*

10 WIDENER L. SYMP. J. 1–5 (2003).

Environmental citizen suits matter. In 1970, borne in a fulcrum of necessity due to inadequate resources and resolve, and borrowing a bit from common law *qui tam* without the bounty, Congress experimented by providing citizens the remarkable authority to file federal lawsuits as "private attorneys general" to enforce the Clean Air Act (CAA). Unless precluded, forestalled, unconstitutional or otherwise unwise, the archetypal citizen suit provision allows "any person" to "commence a civil action on his own behalf" against either (1) "any person" who violates a legal prohibition or requirement, or (2) the U.S. Environmental Protection Agency (EPA) for failure "to perform any act or duty . . . which is not discretionary."

The experiment worked. Nowadays, most of the dozen and a half bulwarks of federal environmental law, and numerous state and foreign laws, in addition to innumerable legislation designed to promote the interests of consumers, protected classes, investors and other beneficiaries of statutes designed to protect human health and welfare, invite citizen enforcement. * * *

Early on, environmental groups brought nearly all citizen suits. No more. These days, citizen suits are hardly only for democrats and "environmentalists." One in three citizen suits are brought by nontraditional citizens, including companies, landowners, developers, industry, and, ever more frequently, states and faith-based organizations. Citizen suits promote a spectrum of interests, from economic to environmental, and issues far and wide, from sustainability to global climate change. * * *

Citizen suits work; they have transformed the environmental movement, and with it, society. Citizen suits have secured compliance by myriad agencies and thousands of polluting facilities, diminished pounds of pollution produced by the billions, and protected hundreds of rare species and thousands of acres of ecologically important land. The foregone monetary value of citizen enforcement has conserved innumerable agency resources and saved taxpayers billions. * * *

Citizen suits are at the heart of the field of environmental law, and to some extent, all federal law. Three out of every four judicial opinions stemming from the nation's principal environmental enforcement laws involves, at its core, a citizen suit. Citizen suits catalyze environmental enforcement. There are at least 850 citizen suit legal events—judicial opinions, notices of intent to sue, complaints, and consent orders—a year. Citizen suits influence a wide array of federal laws. The five venerable environmental citizen suits the Supreme Court has decided have been cited as authority in the federal judicial system more than 10,000 times. [These cases include *Sierra Club v. Morton*, *Tennessee Valley Authority v. Hill*, *Gwaltney of Smithfield, Ltd. v. Chesapeake Bay Foundation, Inc.*, *Lujan v. Defenders of Wildlife*, and *Friends of the Earth v. Laidlaw Environmental Services*] * * *

From 1995 to 2002, citizens have filed 426, or about one lawsuit a week, and have earned 315 compliance-forcing judicial consent orders, under the CWA and CAA alone. During the same period, under all environmental statutes, citizens have submitted more than 4,500 notices of intent to sue, including more than 500 and 4,000 against agencies and members of the regulated community, respectively. This is an astonishing pace over eight years of about two notices of intent to sue every business day, which easily outpaces EPA referrals for enforcement to the U.S. Department of Justice (DOJ). * * *

*Why Citizen Suits Matter*

There are good reasons for citizen suits. They foster the rule of law, agency accountability, representational democracy, and environmental stewardship. First, citizen suits force rule of law and compliance with national environmental protection objectives. This applies to both federal and state enforcement. Citizen suits are especially vital when noncompliance stands equipoise to nonenforcement: "Citizen resources are an important adjunct to governmental action to assure that these laws are adequately enforced. In a time of limited Government resources, enforcement through court action prompted by citizen suits is a valuable dimension of environmental law." (136 CONG. REC. S3162–04 (1990) (remarks of Sen. Durenberger.)

Second, citizen suits hold unelected governmental agencies accountable: "The [citizen suit] provision is directed at providing citizen enforcement when administrative bureaucracies fail to act." Citizen suits thereby motivate agencies to act: "Authorizing citizens to bring suits for violations of standards should motivate governmental agencies charged with the responsibility to bring enforcement and abatement proceedings." (S. REP. NO. 91–1196, at 36–37 (1970).)

Third, citizen suits help uphold bicameral lawmaking and tripartite governance and help effectuate often inscrutable congressional objectives: "[C]itizens suits authorized in the legislation will guarantee that public officials are making good on our national commitment to provide meaningful environmental protection." (116 CONG. REC. S4358, 33102 (statement of Sen. Scott.) They stem directly from the core of a representation reinforcing democracy: "In a society of Government of and by the people we foreclose participation by citizens at our peril." (*Id.* at 33103.) Foreclosed not, citizen suits help assure laws enacted by Congress, in whom "[a]ll legislative Powers . . . shall be vested" [U.S. Const. art. I, § 1], are "faithfully execute[d]" by the Executive [U.S. Const. art. II, § 1, cl. 8], with "[c]ontroversies" resolved by a Judiciary [U.S. Const. art. III, § 2, cl. 1]. In short, citizen suit authority reflects "a deliberate choice by Congress to widen citizen access to the courts, as a supplemental and effective assurance that [environmental laws] would be implemented and enforced." *Natural Res. Def. Council. v. Train,* 510 F.2d 692, 700 (1974).

Last, citizen suit authority enhances public participation, helps educate law students, shapes public opinion, and encourages responsible environmental stewardship here and elsewhere, regardless of moral reference. The success of citizen suits in the United States has informed the adoption of citizen suit authority by other countries. Citizen suits help to shape international legal norms, including notions of sustainable development. Perhaps most importantly, citizen suit litigators have inspired, and help support, public interest advocacy worldwide.

Environmental citizen suits have left an indelible imprint on modern federal jurisprudence. It is hard to envision modern constitutional, administrative, property and labor law or civil procedure without the body of law environmental citizen suits engender. Try it. Crack open most constitutional or administrative law textbooks, for example, and chances are you will find much of the law taught through citizen suits. * * *

Citizen suit law is also the engine that propels the field of environmental law. The vast majority of the legal opinions issued under the nation's principal environmental statutes that allow citizen suits derive from citizen litigation. . . . In the 30 years from 1973–2002, citizens accounted for more than 1,500 reported federal decisions in civil environmental cases. In the ten years from 1993–2002, federal courts issued opinions in an average of 110 civil environmental cases a year. Of these, eighty-three a year, that is, roughly three in four (75%), are citizen suits.

---

## QUESTIONS AND DISCUSSION

**1.** Each of the five "venerable cases" cited in the excerpt were fundamental cases in the development of environmental law. Who were the plaintiffs in these cases? In the NEPA case, *Sierra Club v. Morton*, Sierra Club, an environmental organization, sued on behalf of its individual members harmed by the proposed development. In the famous snail darter case, *Tennessee Valley Authority v. Hill*, the plaintiffs were a regional association of biological scientists, a Tennessee conservation group, and individuals who are citizens or users of the Little Tennessee Valley area. Hiram Hill, the lead plaintiff, was a law student of Professor Zyg Plater who got interested in the issue while writing a seminar research paper. In the Clean Water Act case, *Gwaltney of Smithfield, Ltd. v. Chesapeake Bay Foundation, Inc.*, the plaintiffs were two environmental groups: the Chesapeake Bay Foundation and the Natural Resources Defense Council. The plaintiff in the Endangered Species Act standing case, *Lujan v. Defenders of Wildlife*, was the environmental group, Defenders of Wildlife, and the plaintiff in the Clean Water Act case, *Friends of the Earth v. Laidlaw Environmental Services*, were the environmental groups Friends of the Earth, Citizens Local Environmental Action Network, Inc., and Sierra Club. Without these concerned citizens and groups making use of their right to file citizen suits, environmental law would look very different today.

**2.** What role should environmental groups and private individuals play in enforcing environmental laws? If the government uses its prosecutorial discretion not to seek an injunction or penalty against a company that has violated the Clean Water Act, should an environmental group be able to sue? Why might this lead to poor environmental policy?

**3.** More fundamentally, should the government encourage citizen suits by allowing courts to award civil penalties to environmental groups or individuals who successfully sue a company for violating an environmental law? Should the government pay rewards to groups or individuals who provide the government with information showing that a company is violating an environmental law and leading to the company's conviction? What are the downsides to creating such incentives for citizen suits?

**4.** To help promote citizen suits, Congress has authorized courts to order defendants to reimburse prevailing plaintiffs for their litigation costs, including "reasonable" attorney fees. Courts calculate fee awards by taking the reasonable time that the plaintiff's attorney has spent on the citizen suit and then multiplying this figure by a reasonable attorney fee rate to get an amount known as the "lodestar." According to the Supreme Court, the reasonable rate for a public interest attorney is the rate that she would bill if in private practice, not the much lower amount that the attorney's environmental organization pays her. Although courts occasionally award more than the lodestar if the lodestar does not fully reflect the quality or competence of council or the case is particularly novel, the Supreme Court has indicated that such "multipliers" should normally not be awarded. Pennsylvania v. Delaware Valley Citizens' Council for Clean Air, 483 U.S. 711, 753 (1987).

**5.** Should Congress add citizen suit provisions to other federal laws (e.g., tax laws, drug laws, or immigration laws)? Are there aspects of environmental law that make citizen suits particularly appropriate in the environmental context?

**6.** The Government Accountability Office issued a report in 2011 examining citizen suits brought against EPA from 1995–2010. The Department of Justice spent an average of $3.3 million per year defending EPA. Which groups do you think accounted for most citizen suits? Industry or environmental groups? Which statute do you think accounted for most citizen suits?

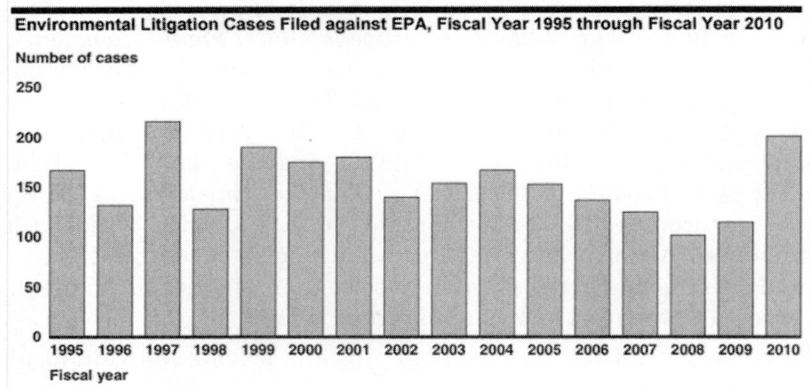


Trade associations (25%) and private companies (23%) accounted for 48% of cases filed. Local environmental groups (16%) and national environmental groups (14%) accounted for just under one-third of the cases. The Clean Air Act dominated citizen suits against EPA, with 1,457 cases. The next closest was the Clean Water Act, with 500, and then RCRA with 151. GAO, ENVIRONMENTAL LITIGATION: CASES AGAINST EPA AND ASSOCIATED COSTS OVER TIME (Aug. 2011).

---

## A. WHEN CAN YOU SUE?

Citizen suit provisions do not permit private plaintiffs to prosecute every violation of an environmental law. First, for largely political reasons, Congress purposefully has excluded some violations from the purview of citizen suits. The Clean Air Act, for example, does not permit lawsuits to enforce many automobile emission standards. Second, the Eleventh Amendment precludes plaintiffs from pursuing citizen suits against states if the suits seek monetary penalties, although purely injunctive actions are still permissible. Finally, most of the citizen suit provisions authorize lawsuits only against persons "alleged to be in violation" of the underlying act. In *Gwaltney of Smithfield, Ltd. v. Chesapeake Bay Foundation*, the Supreme Court addressed whether citizen suits could be brought alleging purely past violations under the Clean Water Act.

## Gwaltney of Smithfield, Ltd. v. Chesapeake Bay Foundation

Supreme Court of the United States, 1987.
484 U.S. 49, 52–67.

■ JUSTICE MARSHALL delivered the opinion of the Court:

In this case, we must decide whether § 505(a) of the Clean Water Act, also known as the Federal Water Pollution Control Act, 33 U.S.C. § 1365(a), confers federal jurisdiction over citizen suits for wholly past violations.

I

The Clean Water Act (Act) was enacted in 1972 "to restore and maintain the chemical, physical, and biological integrity of the Nation's waters." In order to achieve these goals, § 301(a) of the Act makes unlawful the discharge of any pollutant into navigable waters except as authorized by specified sections of the Act.

One of these specified sections is § 402, which establishes the National Pollutant Discharge Elimination System (NPDES). Pursuant to § 402(a), the Administrator of the Environmental Protection Agency (EPA) may issue permits authorizing the discharge of pollutants in accordance with specified conditions. Pursuant to § 402(b), each State may establish and administer its own permit program if the program conforms to federal guidelines and is approved by the Administrator. The Act calls for the Administrator to suspend the issuance of federal permits as to waters subject to an approved state program.

The holder of a federal NPDES permit is subject to enforcement action by the Administrator for failure to comply with the conditions of the permit. The Administrator's enforcement arsenal includes administrative, civil, and criminal sanctions. The holder of a state NPDES permit is subject to both federal and state enforcement action for failure to comply. In the absence of federal or state enforcement, private citizens may commence civil actions against any person "alleged to be in violation of" the conditions of either a federal or state NPDES permit. If the citizen prevails in such an action, the court may order injunctive relief and/or impose civil penalties payable to the United States Treasury.

The Commonwealth of Virginia established a federally approved state NPDES program administered by the Virginia State Water Control Board (Board). In 1974, the Board issued a NPDES permit to ITT-Gwaltney authorizing the discharge of seven pollutants from the company's meatpacking plant on the Pagan River in Smithfield, Virginia. The permit, which was reissued in 1979 and modified in 1980, established effluent limitations, monitoring requirements, and other conditions of discharge. In 1981, petitioner Gwaltney of Smithfield acquired the assets of ITT-Gwaltney and assumed obligations under the permit.

Between 1981 and 1984, petitioner repeatedly violated the conditions of the permit by exceeding effluent limitations on five of the seven pollutants covered. These violations are chronicled in the Discharge Monitoring Reports that the permit required petitioner to maintain. The most substantial of the violations concerned the pollutants fecal coliform, chlorine, and total Kjeldahl nitrogen (TKN). Between October 27, 1981, and August 30, 1984, petitioner violated its TKN limitation 87 times, its chlorine limitation 34 times, and its fecal coliform limitation 31 times. Petitioner installed new equipment to improve its chlorination system in March 1982, and its last reported chlorine violation occurred in October 1982. The new chlorination system also helped to control the discharge of fecal coliform, and the last recorded fecal coliform violation occurred in February 1984. Petitioner installed an upgraded wastewater treatment system in October 1983, and its last reported TKN violation occurred on May 15, 1984.

Respondents Chesapeake Bay Foundation and Natural Resources Defense Council, two nonprofit corporations dedicated to the protection of natural resources, sent notice in February 1984 to Gwaltney, the Administrator of EPA, and the Virginia State Water Control Board, indicating respondents' intention to commence a citizen suit under the Act based on petitioner's violations of its permit conditions. Respondents proceeded to file this suit in June 1984, alleging that petitioner "has violated . . . [and] will continue to violate its NPDES permit." Respondents requested that the District Court provide declaratory and injunctive relief, impose civil penalties, and award attorney's fees and costs. The District Court granted partial summary judgment for respondents in August 1984, declaring Gwaltney "to have violated and to be in violation" of the Act. The District Court then held a trial to determine the appropriate remedy.

Before the District Court reached a decision, Gwaltney moved in May 1985 for dismissal of the action for want of subject-matter jurisdiction under the Act.[1] Gwaltney argued that the language of § 505(a), which permits private citizens to bring suit against any person

---

[1] In its entirety, § 505(a), as codified, 33 U.S.C. § 1365(a), provides:

Except as provided in subsection (b) of this section, any citizen may commence a civil action on his own behalf—

(1) against any person (including (i) the United States, and (ii) any other governmental instrumentality or agency to the extent permitted by the eleventh amendment to the Constitution) who is alleged to be in violation of (A) an effluent standard or limitation under this chapter or (B) an order issued by the Administrator or a State with respect to such a standard or limitation, or

(2) against the Administrator where there is alleged a failure of the Administrator to perform any act or duty under this chapter which is not discretionary with the Administrator.

The district courts shall have jurisdiction, without regard to the amount in controversy or the citizenship of the parties, to enforce such an effluent standard or limitation, or such an order, or to order the Administrator to perform such act or duty, as the case may be, and to apply any appropriate civil penalties under Section 1319(d) of this title.

"alleged to be in violation" of the Act, requires that a defendant be violating the Act at the time of suit. * * *

II. A.

It is well settled that "the starting point for interpreting a statute is the language of the statute itself." The Court of Appeals concluded that the "to be in violation" language of § 505 is ambiguous, whereas petitioner asserts that it plainly precludes the construction adopted below. We must agree with the Court of Appeals that § 505 is not a provision in which Congress' limpid prose puts an end to all dispute. But to acknowledge ambiguity is not to conclude that all interpretations are equally plausible. The most natural reading of "to be in violation" is a requirement that citizen-plaintiffs allege a state of either continuous or intermittent violation—that is, a reasonable likelihood that a past polluter will continue to pollute in the future. Congress could have phrased its requirement in language that looked to the past ("to have violated"), but it did not choose this readily available option. * * *

B.

Our reading of the "to be in violation" language of § 505(a) is bolstered by the language and structure of the rest of the citizen suit provisions in § 505 of the Act. These provisions together make plain that the interest of the citizen-plaintiff is primarily forward-looking.

One of the most striking indicia of the prospective orientation of the citizen suit is the pervasive use of the present tense throughout § 505. A citizen suit may be brought only for violation of a permit limitation "which is in effect" under the Act. 33 U.S.C. § 1365(f). Citizen-plaintiffs must give notice to the alleged violator, the Administrator of EPA, and the State in which the alleged violation "occurs." § 1365(b)(1)(A). A Governor of a State may sue as a citizen when the Administrator fails to enforce an effluent limitation "the violation of which is occurring in another State and is causing an adverse effect on the public health or welfare in his State." § 1365(h). The most telling use of the present tense is in the definition of "citizen" as "a person . . . having an interest which is or may be adversely affected" by the defendant's violations of the Act. § 1365(g). This definition makes plain what the undeviating use of the present tense strongly suggests: the harm sought to be addressed by the citizen suit lies in the present or the future, not in the past.

Any other conclusion would render incomprehensible § 505's notice provision, which requires citizens to give 60 days' notice of their intent to sue to the alleged violator as well as to the Administrator and the State. § 1365(b)(1)(A). If the Administrator or the State commences enforcement action within that 60-day period, the citizen suit is barred, presumably because governmental action has rendered it unnecessary. § 1365(b)(1)(B). It follows logically that the purpose of notice to the alleged violator is to give it an opportunity to bring itself into complete compliance with the Act and thus likewise render unnecessary a citizen suit. If we assume, as respondents urge, that citizen suits may target wholly past violations, the requirement of notice to the alleged violator becomes gratuitous. Indeed, respondents, in propounding their interpretation of the Act, can think of no reason for Congress to require such notice other than that "it seemed right" to inform an alleged violator that it was about to be sued.

Adopting respondents' interpretation of § 505's jurisdictional grant would create a second and even more disturbing anomaly. The bar on citizen suits when governmental enforcement action is under way suggests that the citizen suit is meant to supplement rather than to supplant governmental action. The legislative history of the Act reinforces this view of the role of the citizen suit. The Senate Report noted that "[t]he Committee intends the great volume of enforcement actions [to] be brought by the State," and that citizen suits are proper only "if the Federal, State, and local agencies fail to exercise their enforcement responsibility." S. Rep. No. 92–414, p. 64 (1971), reprinted in 2 A Legislative History of the Water Pollution Control Act Amendments of 1972, p. 1482 (1973) (hereinafter Leg. Hist.). Permitting citizen suits for wholly past violations of the Act could undermine the supplementary role envisioned for the citizen suit. This danger is best illustrated by an example. Suppose that the Administrator identified a violator of the Act and issued a compliance order under § 309(a). Suppose further that the Administrator agreed not to assess or otherwise seek civil penalties on the condition that the violator take some extreme corrective action, such as to install particularly effective but expensive machinery, that it otherwise would not be obliged to take. If citizens could file suit, months or years later, in order to seek the civil penalties that the Administrator chose to forgo, then the Administrator's discretion to enforce the Act in the public interest would be curtailed considerably. The same might be said of the discretion of state enforcement authorities. Respondents' interpretation of the scope of the citizen suit would change the nature of the citizens' role from interstitial to potentially intrusive. We cannot agree that Congress intended such a result. * * *

III.

Our conclusion that § 505 does not permit citizen suits for wholly past violations does not necessarily dispose of this lawsuit, as both lower courts recognized. The District Court found persuasive the fact that "[respondents'] allegation in the complaint, that Gwaltney was continuing to violate its NPDES permit when plaintiffs filed suit[,] appears to have been made fully in good faith." 611 F. Supp., at 1549, n. 8. On this basis, the District Court explicitly held, albeit in a footnote, that "even if Gwaltney were correct that a district court has no jurisdiction over citizen suits based entirely on unlawful conduct that occurred entirely in the past, the Court would still have jurisdiction here." *Ibid.* The Court of Appeals acknowledged, also in a footnote, that "[a] very sound argument can be made that [respondents'] allegations of continuing violations were made in good faith," 791 F. 2d, at 308, n. 9, but expressly declined to rule on this alternative holding. Because we agree that § 505 confers jurisdiction over citizen suits when the citizen-plaintiffs make a good-faith allegation of continuous or intermittent violation, we remand the case to the Court of Appeals for further consideration.

Petitioner argues that citizen-plaintiffs must prove their allegations of ongoing noncompliance before jurisdiction attaches under § 505. We cannot agree. The statute does not require that a defendant "be in violation" of the Act at the commencement of suit; rather, the statute requires that a defendant be "*alleged* to be in violation." Petitioner's construction of the Act reads the word "alleged" out of § 505. As petitioner itself is quick to note in other contexts, there is no reason to believe that Congress' drafting of § 505 was sloppy or haphazard. We agree with the Solicitor General that "Congress's use of the phrase 'alleged to be in violation' reflects a conscious sensitivity to the practical difficulties of detecting and proving chronic episodic violations of environmental standards." Brief for United States as *Amicus Curiae* 18. Our acknowledgment that Congress intended a good-faith allegation to suffice for jurisdictional purpose, however, does not give litigants license to flood the courts with suits premised on baseless allegations. Rule 11 of the Federal Rules of Civil Procedure, which requires pleadings to be based on a good-faith belief, formed after reasonable inquiry, that they are "well grounded in fact," adequately protects defendants from frivolous allegations.

Petitioner contends that failure to require proof of allegations under § 505 would permit plaintiffs whose allegations of ongoing violation are reasonable but untrue to maintain suit in federal court even though they lack constitutional standing. Petitioner reasons that if a defendant is in complete compliance with the Act at the time of suit, plaintiffs have suffered no injury remediable by the citizen suit provisions of the Act. Petitioner, however, fails to recognize that our standing cases uniformly recognize that allegations of injury are sufficient to invoke the jurisdiction of a court. In *Warth* v. *Seldin*, 422 U.S. 490, 501 (1975), for example, we made clear that a suit will not be dismissed for lack of standing if there are sufficient "allegations of fact"—not proof—in the complaint or supporting affidavits. This is not to say, however, that such allegations may not be challenged. In *United States* v. *SCRAP*, 412 U.S. 669, 689 (1973), we noted that if the plaintiffs' "allegations [of standing] were in fact untrue, then the [defendants] should have moved for summary judgment on the standing issue and demonstrated to the District Court that the allegations were sham and raised no genuine issue of fact." If the defendant fails to make such a showing after the plaintiff offers evidence to support the allegation, the case proceeds to trial on the merits, where the plaintiff must prove the allegations in order to prevail. But the Constitution does not require that the plaintiff offer this proof as a threshold matter in order to invoke the District Court's jurisdiction. * * *

Because the court below erroneously concluded that respondents could maintain an action based on wholly past violations of the Act, it declined to decide whether respondents' complaint contained a good-faith allegation of ongoing violation by petitioner. We therefore remand the case for consideration of this question. The judgment of the Court of Appeals is vacated, and the case is remanded for further proceedings consistent with this opinion.

---

## QUESTIONS AND DISCUSSION

**1.** Given *Gwaltney's* holding, what does a plaintiff need to show or allege in order to bring a citizen suit? What can the defendant demonstrate in response to get the suit dismissed? Is there any requirement that the allegation be made in good faith? *See* Sierra Club v. Union Oil of California, 853 F.2d 667 (9th Cir. 1988); Chesapeake Bay Foundation v. Gwaltney of Smithfield, Ltd., 844 F.2d 170 (4th Cir. 1988).

**2.** What happens to the lawsuit if the defendant corrects its activities during litigation? Assume, for example, that after litigation had commenced Gwaltney significantly upgraded its treatment facilities and reduced to almost zero the chance of future wastewater violations. Would the plaintiffs be able to continue their case or should the judge dismiss? The Court's response to this concern is reproduced below.

> Petitioner also worries that our construction of § 505 would permit citizen-plaintiffs, if their allegations of ongoing noncompliance become false at some later point in the litigation because the defendant begins to comply with the Act, to continue nonetheless to press their suit to conclusion. According to petitioner, such a result would contravene both the prospective purpose of the citizen suit provisions and the "case or controversy" requirement of Article III. Longstanding principles of mootness, however, prevent the maintenance of suit when " 'there is no reasonable expectation that the wrong will be repeated.' " *United States* v. *W. T. Grant Co.*, 345 U.S. 629, 633 (1953) (quoting *United States* v. *Aluminum Co. of America*, 148 F.2d 416, 448 (CA2 1945)). In seeking to have a case dismissed as moot, however, the defendant's burden "is a heavy one." 345 U.S., at 633. The defendant must demonstrate that it is "*absolutely clear* that the allegedly wrongful behavior could not reasonably be expected to recur." *United States* v. *Phosphate Export Assn., Inc.*, 393 U.S. 199, 203 (1968) (emphasis added). Mootness doctrine thus protects defendants from the maintenance of suit under the Clean Water Act based solely on violations wholly unconnected to any present or future wrongdoing, while it also protects plaintiffs from defendants who seek to evade sanction by

> predictable "protestations of repentance and reform." United States v. Oregon State Medical Society, 343 U.S. 326, 333 (1952).

*Gwaltney*, 484 U.S. at 66. In response to *Gwaltney*, in 1990 Congress amended the citizen suit provision in the Clean Air Act to permit citizen suits against defendants "alleged to have violated (if there is evidence that the alleged violation has been repeated) or to be in violation." 42 U.S.C. 7604(a)(1). Would the result be any different under the Clean Air Act if the defendant significantly upgraded its pollution control equipment once litigation had commenced?

**3.** Most citizen suit provisions require plaintiffs to provide the government and the defendant at least sixty days' notice prior to filing suit. What happens if the government decides to step in and file suit against the same defendant over the same violation or enters into a consent decree during the notice period? If the goal of citizen suits is to complement and extend the government's enforcement efforts, then presumably the private plaintiffs should be precluded from the suit because the government is now prosecuting the offense.

Can you think of any circumstances in which the public interest might be furthered by maintaining the citizen suit? In this regard, consider the consent decree entered into between the polluting company, Laidlaw, and the South Carolina Department of Health and Environmental Control, described earlier in this chapter. How does the following language in the Clean Air Act address this type of situation?

> (a) [A]ny person may commence a civil action on his own behalf—
>
> (1) against any person (including (i) the United States, and (ii) any other governmental instrumentality or agency to the extent permitted by the Eleventh Amendment to the Constitution) who is alleged to have violated (if there is evidence that the alleged violation has been repeated) or to be in violation of (A) an emission standard or limitation under this chapter or (B) an order issued by the Administrator or a State with respect to such a standard or limitation, * * *
>
> (b) Notice: No action may be commenced—
>
> (1) under subsection (a)(1) of this section—
>
> (A) prior to 60 days after the plaintiff has given notice of the violation
>
> (i) to the Administrator,
>
> (ii) to the State in which the violation occurs, and
>
> (iii) to any alleged violator of the standard, limitation, or order, or
>
> (B) if the Administrator or State has commenced and is diligently prosecuting a civil action in a court of the United States or a State to require compliance with the standard, limitation, or order, but in any such action in a court of the United States any person may intervene as a matter of right.

42 U.S.C. § 7604.

How would you persuade a court that the government is not "diligently prosecuting" an enforcement action?

**4.** *Nature in the Dock.* Section 11 of the Endangered Species Act allows "any person" to file suit to enjoin violations under the statute. In fact, some of the most important ESA cases have featured non-human plaintiffs. In *Palila v. Hawaii Dep't of Land & Natural Resources*, 852 F.2d 1106 (9th Cir. 1988), for example, the judge notes in the very first paragraph that "The Palila (which has earned the right to be capitalized since it is a party to this proceeding) is represented by attorneys for the Sierra Club, Audubon Society, and other environmental parties. . . ." *Id.* at 1107. Nor is this the only example of animal plaintiffs suing (successfully) under the ESA and other environmental statutes.

On its face, naming a bird as the lead plaintiff seems odd, to say the least. The Administrative Procedure Act entitles any person suffering legal wrong because of agency action to judicial review, and defines "person" as an "individual, partnership, corporation, association, or public or private organization other than an agency." 5 U.S.C. § 551(2). Federal Rule of Civil Procedure 17 speaks only of individuals, infants and incompetent persons, and the ESA grants a "person" the right to sue, not "winged creatures." There are, however, quite a few cases on record with non-human plaintiffs, including a Loggerhead turtle, a Bald eagle, a polluted river (the Byram River), a marsh (No Bottom), a brook (the Brown), a beach (Makena), a national monument (Death Valley), and a town commons (Billerica). See, e.g., Loggerhead Turtle v. County of Volusia, 148 F.3d 1231 (11th Cir. 1998); Marbled Murrelet v. Pacific Lumber Co., 880 F. Supp. 1343 (N.D. Cal. 1995); American Bald Eagle v. Bhatti, 9 F.3d 163, 164 (1st Cir. 1993). *See generally* CHRISTOPHER STONE, EARTH AND OTHER ETHICS 6–7 (1987).

Why do plaintiffs do this? One obvious reason is the rhetorical benefit of having an endangered species as a party to the case—"Not only do I speak on behalf of the spotted owl, your Honor, but it was so incensed that it's become a party to the lawsuit!" From the perspective of the plaintiff groups, naming an object or species also has the advantage of avoiding turf wars. If several NGOs are participating in a lawsuit, there is sometimes disagreement over who will get to be the "named" plaintiff, i.e., the first plaintiff on the complaint. By naming an object or species as the lead plaintiff, that issue can be avoided entirely.

Perhaps the more important question, then, is why do defendants allow this? So long as the other named plaintiffs have standing, the Justice Department frequently chooses not to raise the issue of standing for non-humans since the case would go forward with the other plaintiffs, anyway.

The best insight on these issues comes from the description by Professor Denise Antolini, an attorney for the Sierra Club Legal Defense Fund (now EarthJustice) prior to becoming a law professor, of her involvement in *Hawaiian Crow v. Lujan*, 906 F. Supp. 549, 552 (D. Haw. 1991). SCLDF named the endangered crow, known locally as the 'Alala, as the lead plaintiff in a suit for implementation of the bird's recovery plan. As Professor Antolini relates,

> My experience litigating cases with SCLDF in Hawaii (1990–96) was that the federal government attorneys never used to care if we named critters as plaintiffs (and, of course, it makes no practical difference if you have the backup human or organizational plaintiff). Naming critters as plaintiffs in environmental cases is a time-honored tradition. But in our controversial 'Alala ESA case, the humorless private landowner intervenor decided that having the critically endangered crow as the lead plaintiff was just too much (the ranch did not like the adverse publicity, of course, and public image/message was our main reason for having the critter in the lead). The private defendant moved to dismiss the crow. I had a heck of a time writing the opposition brief given that the plain language of the ESA citizen suit provision says "any person may commence a civil suit . . . "We argued "time honored tradition" and "no prejudice to defendant," but in the end, the statute's plain language killed us. Judge Ezra dismissed the crow. (The ranch moved for Rule 11 sanctions too, which the judge graciously brushed aside.) No harm done, of course, because we had Audubon on the pleadings already, and the litigation moved forward without much of a hiccup.

E-mail from Denise Antolini, Feb. 1, 2004, (with reprint permission kindly granted).

Private defendants have successfully objected in other cases, as well. The lawsuit, *Citizens to End Animal Suffering & Exploitation, Inc. v. The New England Aquarium*, 836 F. Supp. 45 (D. Mass. 1993), for example, was originally brought in the name of Kama, a dolphin. The court concluded that Kama did not have standing. *See also,* Coho Salmon v. Pacific Lumber Co., 30 F. Supp. 2d 1231, 1239 n.2 (N.D. Cal. 1998) (observing that, "[w]ithout delving into the vagaries of the term 'entity,' the court notes that, to swim its way into federal court in this action, the coho salmon would have to battle a strong current and leap barriers greater than a waterfall or the occasional fallen tree").

---

## B. STANDING

Whenever an environmental group or individual seeks judicial review or files a citizen suit, one of the first questions that the court will ask is whether the plaintiff has standing to sue. According to the Supreme Court, a party generally must satisfy four elements to establish standing. The first three requirements are constitutionally required by Article III of the United States Constitution and thus cannot be waived. First, the plaintiff must demonstrate that the challenged action has or will cause the plaintiff "injury in fact." Second, the plaintiff must show that this injury can be traced to the challenged action. Third, the plaintiff must show that the court, through some form of available relief, can redress the injury. Thus, for example, a plaintiff might challenge the process used to approve an agency's planned timber sale by demonstrating (1) logging will injure the plaintiff because she regularly hikes through this area, (2) agency approval of the timber sale will lead to the injurious logging, and (3) the court can redress this injury by enjoining the sale until the agency follows proper procedures.

The final requirement for standing is only "prudential," and therefore Congress can eliminate or alter it: the injury must be within the "zone of interests" that the underlying substantive statute is designed to protect. When an organization sues, the organization must show not only that one or more of its members satisfies these standing requirements but also that the goal in seeking judicial relief is "germane to the organization's purposes." Thus, the Minnesota Elk Breeder's Association might have standing problems suing the National Marine Fisheries Service for failure to list a tuna species as endangered.

Are all these standing requirements truly needed? Some academics have argued not. In their view, the question should be whether Congress has authorized individuals or organizations to seek judicial review or other relief in federal court. For example, where Congress has authorized "any person" to pursue environmental violators, as Congress has done in virtually every citizen suit provision, the courts should not erect roadblocks in the way of potential citizen prosecutors. A majority of the current Supreme Court, however, has suggested that the existing standing rules are important for several reasons. First, standing requirements such as "injury in fact" ensure that there is justification for involving the courts in what otherwise might be a largely academic question. If no one has been hurt, judicial intervention is unnecessary. Second, the standing requirements ensure that the plaintiff has sufficient interest in the lawsuit to provide adequate representation of the public interest. Finally, standing is a means of ensuring the separation of powers; absent injury in fact and the other standing findings, courts could be interfering unnecessarily in the discretion of the executive branch. Whether you agree with these arguments, and each has its critics, they have led federal courts to throw a number of citizen suits and other cases out of court. Indeed, environmentalists have worried that the courts have been trying to use standing to roll back decades of environmental activism.

### 1. INJURY IN FACT

Most standing disputes focus on the first requirement of injury in fact. The Supreme Court helped to promote environmental litigation in the early 1970s, and thus usher in stronger environmental protection, by adopting a broad view of what constitutes an injury in the environmental field. In Sierra Club v. Morton, 405 U.S. 727 (1972), the Sierra Club challenged the U.S. Forest Service's approval of Walt Disney Enterprises' plan to develop a ski resort in the Sequoia National Forest. The Supreme Court held that the Sierra Club had not established standing to sue because it had not alleged that any of its members actually used the area of the proposed development and thus would be affected by Disney's plan. But the Court emphasized that standing did not require a showing of *economic* injury, as had traditionally been the case. For standing purposes, injuries can "reflect 'aesthetic, conservational, and recreational' as well as economic values" and can be widely shared among the population. *Id.* All the Sierra Club needed to do therefore was to allege that its members would suffer aesthetic or recreational injury as a result of the proposed development (and that's exactly what the Sierra Club did on remand). Justice William O. Douglas would have gone further and allowed law suits to be filed "in the name of the inanimate object about to be despoiled, defaced, or invaded by roads and bulldozers and where injury is the subject of public outrage." *Id.* In Douglas' view, trees and wildlife, not just people, should have standing in court. *See also,* Christopher Stone, *Should Trees Have Standing,* 59 S. CAL. L. REV. 1 (1985). In all standing cases, however, whether aesthetic harm or more traditional economic or physical injury, the litigant must demonstrate it has suffered a concrete and particularize injury. A generalized, widely-shared injury is insufficient.

For almost two decades after *Sierra Club v. Morton*, the Supreme Court showed no interest in constructing standing barriers to environmental litigation. The so-called *SCRAP* case, decided a year after *Sierra Club v. Morton*, showed how far the Court was willing to go to find standing. United States v. Students Challenging Regulatory Agency Procedures, 412 U.S. 669 (1973). In *SCRAP*, a group of law students challenged an order of the Interstate Commerce Commission approving freight rates that they feared would discourage recycling. The students argued that they had standing because they camped, hiked, and fished in the Washington, D.C., metropolitan area and these activities would become less enjoyable if the freight rates went into effect, resulting in less recycling and therefore more litter and greater natural resource consumption. Although the Supreme Court held that "pleadings must be something more than an ingenious academic exercise in the conceivable" and recognized that the students' line of causation was a bit "attenuated," six members of the Court found that the students had standing. "The basic idea that comes out in numerous cases is that an identifiable trifle is enough for standing to fight out a question of principle; the trifle is the basis for standing and the principle supplies the motivation." *Id.* at 690, n.14

The Court has since been less generous in granting standing. In *Lujan v. Defenders of Wildlife*, 504 U.S. 555 (1992), for example, an environmental organization sought review of the Department of the Interior's decision that the Endangered Species Act does not extend to U.S. agency actions that affect endangered species overseas. Two of the organization's members submitted affidavits stating that they had previously traveled to overseas areas in which species were threatened by U.S. agency actions and that they hoped to go again. The Court concluded that such inchoate plans to return to the areas were inadequate to establish standing; only present and definite plans to return would provide the type of "actual or imminent" injury required for standing. The Court also held that a plaintiff did not have standing simply because he or she had a professional or personal interest in studying or seeing an endangered species.

A critical question in *Lujan* and similar environmental cases is the degree to which Congress can provide standing for parties who would not meet the traditional injury in fact requirement. In *Defenders of Wildlife*, the lower court had held that the plaintiffs had suffered a "procedural injury": the Endangered Species Act required agencies to consult with the Department of the Interior before taking actions that might jeopardize an endangered species, giving all citizens a "procedural right" to insist on a consultation. Four members of the Court concluded that a plaintiff has standing to vindicate such a procedural right only where disregard of that right also impairs "a separate concrete interest." *Id.* at 572. While agreeing that the plaintiffs had not established standing, Justices Kennedy and Souter suggested that "Congress has the power to define injuries and articulate chains of causation" that otherwise would not provide standing, but "Congress must at the very least identify the injury it seek to vindicate and relate the injury to the class of persons entitled to bring suit." *Id.* at 580.

### 2. ZONE OF INTERESTS

The "zone of interests" requirement frequently becomes an issue where an industry group seeks to use environmental laws for economic gain or to thwart governmental actions to improve the environment. In a number of lawsuits, for example, industry groups have tried to block the government from reforming grazing, timber, water, and other resource policies on the ground that the government had not prepared an environmental impact statement under the National Environmental Policy Act (NEPA). Lower federal courts have generally rejected these lawsuits on the ground that NEPA's purpose is to protect the environment, not the economic interest of industry. In other cases, however, courts have concluded that Congress intended to provide standing to industry organizations. In Bennett v. Spear, 520 U.S. 154 (1997), for example, ranchers and irrigation districts, upset by the Department of Interior' decision to reduce their water deliveries because of endangered-species concerns, filed a citizen suit under the Endangered Species Act (ESA) claiming that the department had failed to perform nondiscretionary duties—using the "best scientific data available" and considering the economic impact of designating a particular area as "critical habitat" for a species. Borrowing the logic of the NEPA cases, a lower court held that the ranchers and districts did not have standing because the purpose of the ESA is to protect the environment. The Supreme Court, however, reversed. Noting that the citizen suit provision grants a right to file a citizen suit to "any person," the Court concluded that Congress had not meant to restrict who could bring a citizen suit but contemplated that industry groups might use the provision to avoid "overenforcement" of the law.

### 3. REDRESSABILITY

In authorizing individual citizens and environmental groups to serve as private attorneys general, Congress has been cautious not to make citizen suits into profit-making opportunities. Most of the citizen suit provisions permit citizens and environmental groups to pursue only injunctive relief. A few statutes authorize courts to impose monetary penalties in citizen suits, but the penalties are payable to the United States, not the private prosecutor. In practice, however, plaintiffs often settle their citizen suits on terms that include not only the cessation of violations, but also (1) the payment of monies to the plaintiff or other organizations and (2) agreements to engage in supplemental projects of benefit to the environment.

The requirement that injuries be redressable by judicial action also occasionally trips up environmental plaintiffs. The Supreme Court, for example, has held that a plaintiff does not have standing to bring a citizen suit for environmental violations that have occurred entirely in the past, because neither of the remedies potentially available to the plaintiff (an injunction or a civil penalty payable to the government) could remedy any injury that the plaintiff suffered as a result of the past violation. *Steel Co. v. Citizens for a Better Environment*, 523 U.S. 83 (1998). In a subsequent decision, excerpted below, the Court held that an environmental organization has standing to seek civil penalties in the face of ongoing violations, even though any penalties awarded go to the government, because the penalties will deter future violations.

## Friends of the Earth v. Laidlaw Environmental Services

Supreme Court of the United States, 2000.
528 U.S. 167, 173–210.

■ JUSTICE GINSBURG delivered the opinion of the Court:

. . . In 1972, Congress enacted the Clean Water Act (Act), also known as the Federal Water Pollution Control Act. Section 402 of the Act provides for the issuance, by the Administrator of the Environmental Protection Agency (EPA) or by authorized States, of National Pollutant Discharge Elimination System (NPDES) permits. NPDES permits impose limitations on the discharge of pollutants, and establish related monitoring and reporting requirements, in order to improve the cleanliness and safety of the Nation's waters. Noncompliance with a permit constitutes a violation of the Act.

Under § 505(a) of the Act, a suit to enforce any limitation in an NPDES permit may be brought by any "citizen," defined as "a person or persons having an interest which is or may be adversely affected." Sixty days before initiating a citizen suit, however, the would-be plaintiff must give notice of the alleged violation to the EPA, the State in which the alleged violation occurred, and the alleged violator. § 1365(b)(1)(A). "The purpose of notice to the alleged violator is to give it an opportunity to bring itself into complete compliance with the Act and thus . . . render unnecessary a citizen suit." *Gwaltney of Smithfield, Ltd.* v. *Chesapeake Bay Foundation, Inc.*, 484 U.S. 49, 60 (1987). Accordingly, we have held that citizens lack statutory standing under § 505(a) to sue for violations that have ceased by the time the complaint is filed. The Act also bars a citizen from suing if the EPA or the State has already commenced, and is "diligently prosecuting," an enforcement action. * * *

In 1986, defendant-respondent Laidlaw Environmental Services, Inc., bought a hazardous waste incinerator facility in Roebuck, South Carolina, that included a wastewater treatment plant. Shortly after Laidlaw acquired the facility, the South Carolina Department of Health and Environmental Control (DHEC), granted Laidlaw an NPDES permit authorizing the company to discharge treated water into the North Tyger River. The permit, which became effective on January 1, 1987, placed limits on Laidlaw's discharge of several pollutants into the river, including—of particular relevance to this case—mercury, an extremely toxic pollutant. The permit also regulated the flow, temperature, toxicity, and pH of the effluent from the facility, and imposed monitoring and reporting obligations.

Once it received its permit, Laidlaw began to discharge various pollutants into the waterway; repeatedly, Laidlaw's discharges exceeded the limits set by the permit. In particular, despite experimenting with several technological fixes, Laidlaw consistently failed to meet the permit's stringent 1.3 ppb (parts per billion) daily average limit on mercury discharges. The District Court later found that Laidlaw had violated the mercury limits on 489 occasions between 1987 and 1995.

On April 10, 1992, plaintiff-petitioners Friends of the Earth (FOE) and Citizens Local Environmental Action Network, Inc. took the preliminary step necessary to the institution of litigation. They sent a letter to Laidlaw notifying the company of their intention to file a citizen suit against it under § 505(a) of the Act after the expiration of the requisite 60-day notice period, *i.e.*, on or after June 10, 1992. Laidlaw's lawyer then contacted DHEC to ask whether DHEC would consider filing a lawsuit against Laidlaw. The District Court later found that Laidlaw's reason for requesting that DHEC file a lawsuit against it was to bar FOE's proposed citizen suit through the operation of 33 U.S.C. § 1365(b)(1)(B) [providing that no citizen action may be commenced "if the Administrator or State has commenced and is diligently prosecuting a civil or criminal action"]. DHEC agreed to file a lawsuit against Laidlaw; the company's lawyer then drafted the complaint for DHEC and paid the filing fee. On June 9, 1992, the last day before FOE's 60-day notice period expired, DHEC and Laidlaw reached a settlement requiring Laidlaw to pay $100,000 in civil penalties and to make "every effort" to comply with its permit obligations.

On June 12, 1992, FOE filed this citizen suit against Laidlaw under § 505(a) of the Act, alleging noncompliance with the NPDES permit and seeking declaratory and injunctive relief and an award of civil penalties. Laidlaw moved for summary judgment on the ground that FOE had failed to present evidence demonstrating injury in fact, and therefore lacked Article III standing to bring the lawsuit. * * *

After an extensive analysis of the Laidlaw-DHEC settlement and the circumstances under which it was reached, the District Court held that DHEC's action against Laidlaw had not been "diligently prosecuted"; consequently, the court allowed FOE's citizen suit to proceed.[1] The record indicates that after FOE initiated the suit, but before the District Court rendered judgment, Laidlaw violated the mercury discharge limitation in its permit 13 times. The District Court also found that Laidlaw had committed 13 monitoring and 10 reporting violations during this period. The last recorded mercury discharge violation occurred in January 1995, long after the complaint was filed but about two years before judgment was rendered.

On January 22, 1997, the District Court issued its judgment. It found that Laidlaw had gained a total economic benefit of $1,092,581 as a result of its extended period of noncompliance with the mercury discharge limit in its permit. The court concluded, however, that a civil penalty of $405,800 was adequate in light of the guiding factors listed in 33 U.S.C. § 1319(d). In particular, the District Court stated that the lesser penalty was appropriate taking into account the judgment's "total deterrent effect." In reaching this determination, the court "considered that Laidlaw will be required to reimburse plaintiffs for a significant amount of legal fees." The court declined to grant FOE's request for injunctive relief, stating that an injunction was inappropriate because "Laidlaw has been in substantial compliance with all parameters in its NPDES permit since at least August 1992." * * *

On July 16, 1998, the Court of Appeals for the Fourth Circuit issued its judgment. The Court of Appeals assumed without deciding that FOE initially had standing to bring the action, but went on to hold that the

---

1 The District Court noted that "Laidlaw drafted the state-court complaint and settlement agreement, filed the lawsuit against itself, and paid the filing fee." 890 F. Supp. at 489. Further, "the settlement agreement between DHEC and Laidlaw was entered into with unusual haste, without giving the Plaintiffs the opportunity to intervene." *Ibid.* The court found "most persuasive" the fact that "in imposing the civil penalty of $100,000 against Laidlaw, DHEC failed to recover, or even to calculate, the economic benefit that Laidlaw received by not complying with its permit." 890 F. Supp. at 491.

case had become moot. The appellate court stated, first, that the elements of Article III standing—injury, causation, and redressability—must persist at every stage of review, or else the action becomes moot. Citing our decision in *Steel Co.*, the Court of Appeals reasoned that the case had become moot because "the only remedy currently available to [FOE]—civil penalties payable to the government—would not redress any injury [FOE has] suffered." The court therefore vacated the District Court's order and remanded with instructions to dismiss the action. In a footnote, the Court of Appeals added that FOE's "failure to obtain relief on the merits of [its] claims precludes any recovery of attorneys' fees or other litigation costs because such an award is available only to a 'prevailing or substantially prevailing party.' "

According to Laidlaw, after the Court of Appeals issued its decision but before this Court granted certiorari, the entire incinerator facility in Roebuck was permanently closed, dismantled, and put up for sale, and all discharges from the facility permanently ceased. * * *

Laidlaw argues next that even if FOE had standing to seek injunctive relief, it lacked standing to seek civil penalties. Here the asserted defect is not injury but redressability. Civil penalties offer no redress to private plaintiffs, Laidlaw argues, because they are paid to the government, and therefore a citizen plaintiff can never have standing to seek them.

Laidlaw is right to insist that a plaintiff must demonstrate standing separately for each form of relief sought. ("Standing is not dispensed in gross."). But it is wrong to maintain that citizen plaintiffs facing ongoing violations never have standing to seek civil penalties.

We have recognized on numerous occasions that "all civil penalties have some deterrent effect." More specifically, Congress has found that civil penalties in Clean Water Act cases do more than promote immediate compliance by limiting the defendant's economic incentive to delay its attainment of permit limits; they also deter future violations. This congressional determination warrants judicial attention and respect. "The legislative history of the Act reveals that Congress wanted the district court to consider the need for retribution and deterrence, in addition to restitution, when it imposed civil penalties. . . . [The district court may] seek to deter future violations by basing the penalty on its economic impact."

It can scarcely be doubted that, for a plaintiff who is injured or faces the threat of future injury due to illegal conduct ongoing at the time of suit, a sanction that effectively abates that conduct and prevents its recurrence provides a form of redress. Civil penalties can fit that description. To the extent that they encourage defendants to discontinue current violations and deter them from committing future ones, they afford redress to citizen plaintiffs who are injured or threatened with injury as a consequence of ongoing unlawful conduct.

The dissent argues that it is the availability rather than the imposition of civil penalties that deters any particular polluter from continuing to pollute. This argument misses the mark in two ways. First, it overlooks the interdependence of the availability and the imposition; a threat has no deterrent value unless it is credible that it will be carried out. Second, it is reasonable for Congress to conclude that an actual award of civil penalties does in fact bring with it a significant quantum of deterrence over and above what is achieved by the mere prospect of such penalties. A would-be polluter may or may not be dissuaded by the existence of a remedy on the books, but a defendant once hit in its pocketbook will surely think twice before polluting again.[2]

We recognize that there may be a point at which the deterrent effect of a claim for civil penalties becomes so insubstantial or so remote that it cannot support citizen standing. The fact that this vanishing point is not easy to ascertain does not detract from the deterrent power of such penalties in the ordinary case. Justice Frankfurter's observations for the Court, made in a different context nearly 60 years ago, hold true here as well:

"How to effectuate policy—the adaptation of means to legitimately sought ends—is one of the most intractable of legislative problems. Whether proscribed conduct is to be deterred by *qui tam* action or triple damages or injunction, or by criminal prosecution, or merely by defense to actions in contract, or by some, or all, of these remedies in combination, is a matter within the legislature's range of choice. Judgment on the deterrent effect of the various weapons in the armory of the law can lay little claim to scientific basis." *Tigner v. Texas*, 310 U.S. 141 (1940).

In this case we need not explore the outer limits of the principle that civil penalties provide sufficient deterrence to support redressability. Here, the civil penalties sought by FOE carried with them a deterrent effect that made it likely, as opposed to merely speculative, that the penalties would redress FOE's injuries by abating current violations and preventing future ones—as the District Court reasonably found when it assessed a penalty of $405,800.

Laidlaw contends that the reasoning of our decision in *Steel Co.* directs the conclusion that citizen plaintiffs have no standing to seek civil penalties under the Act. We disagree. *Steel Co.* established that citizen suitors lack standing to seek civil penalties for violations that have abated by the time of suit. We specifically noted in that case that there was no allegation in the complaint of any continuing or imminent

---

2 The dissent suggests that there was little deterrent work for civil penalties to do in this case because the lawsuit brought against Laidlaw by DHEC had already pushed the level of deterrence to "near the top of the graph." *Post*, at 11. This suggestion ignores the District Court's specific finding that the penalty agreed to by Laidlaw and DHEC was far too low to remove Laidlaw's economic benefit from noncompliance, and thus was inadequate to deter future violations. 890 F. Supp. 470, 491–494, 497–498 (SC 1995). And it begins to look especially farfetched when one recalls that Laidlaw itself prompted the DHEC lawsuit, paid the filing fee, and drafted the complaint.

violation, and that no basis for such an allegation appeared to exist. (*Gwaltney*, 484 U.S. at 59) ("the harm sought to be addressed by the citizen suit lies in the present or the future, not in the past"). In short, *Steel Co.* held that private plaintiffs, unlike the Federal Government, may not sue to assess penalties for wholly past violations, but our decision in that case did not reach the issue of standing to seek penalties for violations that are ongoing at the time of the complaint and that could continue into the future if undeterred.

B.

Satisfied that FOE had standing under Article III to bring this action, we turn to the question of mootness. The only conceivable basis for a finding of mootness in this case is Laidlaw's voluntary conduct—either its achievement by August 1992 of substantial compliance with its NPDES permit or its more recent shutdown of the Roebuck facility. It is well settled that "a defendant's voluntary cessation of a challenged practice does not deprive a federal court of its power to determine the legality of the practice." "If it did, the courts would be compelled to leave 'the defendant . . . free to return to his old ways.' " In accordance with this principle, the standard we have announced for determining whether a case has been mooted by the defendant's voluntary conduct is stringent: "A case might become moot if subsequent events made it absolutely clear that the allegedly wrongful behavior could not reasonably be expected to recur." The "heavy burden of persuading" the court that the challenged conduct cannot reasonably be expected to start up again lies with the party asserting mootness.

The Court of Appeals justified its mootness disposition by reference to *Steel Co.*, which held that citizen plaintiffs lack standing to seek civil penalties for wholly past violations. In relying on *Steel Co.*, the Court of Appeals confused mootness with standing. The confusion is understandable, given this Court's repeated statements that the doctrine of mootness can be described as "the doctrine of standing set in a time frame: The requisite personal interest that must exist at the commencement of the litigation (standing) must continue throughout its existence (mootness)."

Careful reflection on the long-recognized exceptions to mootness, however, reveals that the description of mootness as "standing set in a time frame" is not comprehensive. As just noted, a defendant claiming that its voluntary compliance moots a case bears the formidable burden of showing that it is absolutely clear the allegedly wrongful behavior could not reasonably be expected to recur. By contrast, in a lawsuit brought to force compliance, it is the plaintiff's burden to establish standing by demonstrating that, if unchecked by the litigation, the defendant's allegedly wrongful behavior will likely occur or continue, and that the "threatened injury [is] certainly impending." . . . The plain lesson of these cases is that there are circumstances in which the prospect that a defendant will engage in (or resume) harmful conduct may be too speculative to support standing, but not too speculative to overcome mootness.

Furthermore, if mootness were simply "standing set in a time frame," the exception to mootness that arises when the defendant's allegedly unlawful activity is "capable of repetition, yet evading review" could not exist. When, for example, a mentally disabled patient files a lawsuit challenging her confinement in a segregated institution, her postcomplaint transfer to a community-based program will not moot the action, despite the fact that she would have lacked initial standing had she filed the complaint after the transfer. Standing admits of no similar exception; if a plaintiff lacks standing at the time the action commences, the fact that the dispute is capable of repetition yet evading review will not entitle the complainant to a federal judicial forum. See *Steel Co.*, 523 U.S. at 109 (" 'the mootness exception for disputes capable of repetition yet evading review . . . will not revive a dispute which became moot before the action commenced' ")

We acknowledged the distinction between mootness and standing most recently in *Steel Co.*:

> The United States . . . argues that the injunctive relief does constitute remediation because 'there is a presumption of [future] injury when the defendant has voluntarily ceased its illegal activity in response to litigation,' even if that occurs before a complaint is filed . . . ' This makes a sword out of a shield. The 'presumption' the Government refers to has been applied to refute the assertion of mootness by a defendant who, when sued in a complaint that alleges present or threatened injury, ceases the complained-of activity. . . . It is an immense and unacceptable stretch to call the presumption into service as a substitute for the allegation of present or threatened injury upon which initial standing must be based.

Standing doctrine functions to ensure, among other things, that the scarce resources of the federal courts are devoted to those disputes in which the parties have a concrete stake. In contrast, by the time mootness is an issue, the case has been brought and litigated, often (as here) for years. To abandon the case at an advanced stage may prove more wasteful than frugal. This argument from sunk costs does not license courts to retain jurisdiction over cases in which one or both of the parties plainly lacks a continuing interest, as when the parties have settled or a plaintiff pursuing a nonsurviving claim has died. * * *

■ JUSTICE SCALIA, with whom JUSTICE THOMAS joins, dissenting.

. . . The Court's treatment of the redressability requirement—which would have been unnecessary if it resolved the injury-in-fact question correctly—is equally cavalier. As discussed above, petitioners allege ongoing injury consisting of diminished enjoyment of the affected waterways and decreased property values. They allege that these injuries are caused by Laidlaw's continuing permit violations. But the remedy petitioners seek is neither recompense for their injuries nor an injunction against future violations. Instead, the remedy is a statutorily specified "penalty" for past violations, payable entirely to the United States Treasury. Only last Term, we held that such penalties do not redress any injury a citizen plaintiff has suffered from past violations. *Steel Co. v. Citizens for Better Environment*, 523 U.S. 83, 106–107 (1998). The Court nonetheless finds the redressability requirement satisfied here, distinguishing *Steel Co.* on the ground that in this case the petitioners allege ongoing violations; payment of the penalties, it says, will remedy petitioners' injury by deterring future violations by Laidlaw. It holds that a penalty payable to the public "remedies" a threatened private harm, and suffices to sustain a private suit.

That holding has no precedent in our jurisprudence, and takes this Court beyond the "cases and controversies" that Article III of the Constitution has entrusted to its resolution. Even if it were appropriate, moreover, to allow Article III's remediation requirement to be satisfied by the indirect private consequences of a public penalty, those consequences are entirely too speculative in the present case. The new standing law that the Court makes—like all expansions of standing beyond the traditional constitutional limits—has grave implications for democratic governance. * * *

A

The Court's opinion reads as though the only purpose and effect of the redressability requirement is to assure that the plaintiff receive some of the benefit of the relief that a court orders. That is not so. If it were, a federal tort plaintiff fearing repetition of the injury could ask for tort damages to be paid, not only to himself but to other victims as well, on the theory that those damages would have at least some deterrent effect beneficial to him. Such a suit is preposterous because the "remediation" that is the traditional business of Anglo-American courts is relief specifically tailored to the plaintiff 's injury, and not any sort of relief that has some incidental benefit to the plaintiff. Just as a "generalized grievance" that affects the entire citizenry cannot satisfy the injury-in-fact requirement even though it aggrieves the plaintiff along with everyone else, so also a generalized remedy that deters all future unlawful activity against all persons cannot satisfy the remediation requirement, even though it deters (among other things) repetition of this particular unlawful activity against these particular plaintiffs.

Thus, relief against prospective harm is traditionally afforded by way of an injunction, the scope of which is limited by the scope of the threatened injury. In seeking to overturn that tradition by giving an individual plaintiff the power to invoke a public remedy, Congress has done precisely what we have said it cannot do: convert an "undifferentiated public interest" into an "individual right" vindicable in the courts. The sort of scattershot redress approved today makes nonsense of our statement in *Schlesinger v. Reservists Comm. to Stop the War*, 418 U.S. 208, 222 (1974), that the requirement of injury in fact "insures the framing of relief no broader than required by the precise facts." A claim of particularized future injury has today been made the vehicle for pursuing generalized penalties for past violations, and a threshold showing of injury in fact has become a lever that will move the world. * * *

C

Article II of the Constitution commits it to the President to "take Care that the Laws be faithfully executed," Art. II, § 3, and provides specific methods by which all persons exercising significant executive power are to be appointed, Art. II, § 2. * * *

By permitting citizens to pursue civil penalties payable to the Federal Treasury, the Act does not provide a mechanism for individual relief in any traditional sense, but turns over to private citizens the function of enforcing the law. A Clean Water Act plaintiff pursuing civil penalties acts as a self-appointed mini-EPA. Where, as is often the case, the plaintiff is a national association, it has significant discretion in choosing enforcement targets. Once the association is aware of a reported violation, it need not look long for an injured member, at least under the theory of injury the Court applies today. And once the target is chosen, the suit goes forward without meaningful public control. The availability of civil penalties vastly disproportionate to the individual injury gives citizen plaintiffs massive bargaining power—which is often used to achieve settlements requiring the defendant to support environmental projects of the plaintiffs' choosing. Thus is a public fine diverted to a private interest.

To be sure, the EPA may foreclose the citizen suit by itself bringing suit. This allows public authorities to avoid private enforcement only by accepting private direction as to when enforcement should be undertaken—which is no less constitutionally bizarre. Elected officials are entirely deprived of their discretion to decide that a given violation should not be the object of suit at all, or that the enforcement decision should be postponed.

---

## QUESTIONS AND DISCUSSION

**1.** Identify and describe how the majority opinion and the dissent rely on the concepts of specific and general deterrence in supporting their arguments. How might imposing penalties for purely past violations still provide a form of redress?

**2.** The majority and dissent differ sharply over the reach of the holding in *Citizens for a Better Environment*. How would you distinguish the holdings of *Laidlaw* and *Citizens for a Better Environment?*

**3.** Since presumably one can file overdue reports and forms after notice and prior to litigation, does this mean citizen suits cannot be brought for purely paperwork violations, the largest category of enforcement actions? If the government does not bring an action for paperwork violations, does the dissent intend that no citizens can file actions, either? Similarly, what are the implications of the majority and dissent for purely procedural violations?

**4.** What are the incentives created by the *Citizens for a Better Environment* and *Laidlaw* holdings for compliance activities? If you were the Director of Environmental Health & Safety for a company, are you more or less likely to remedy violations prior to receiving a 60-day notice letter? Is there a greater incentive to remedy the violation after receiving a notice letter?

**5.** The dissent uses sweeping language, warning that:

> Elected officials are entirely deprived of their discretion to decide that a given violation should not be the object of suit at all, or that the enforcement decision should be postponed.

Is this not an inevitable, and therefore intended, result of creating citizen suits and empowering citizens to act as private attorneys general? Do you think this rises to a serious separation of powers problem?

Note the Court's statement in *Defenders* that "we have consistently held that a plaintiff raising only a generally available grievance about government . . . does not state an Article III case or controversy." Notwithstanding this claim, however, the Court has been far from consistent. In Sierra Club v. Morton, 405 U.S. 727 (1972), for example, the Court held that "the fact that particular environmental interests are shared by the many rather than the few does not make them less deserving of legal protection. . . ." And in United States v. Students Challenging Regulatory Agency Procedures (SCRAP), 412 U.S. 669 (1973), the Court noted that "standing is not to be denied simply because many people suffer the same injury." *Id.* at 687–88. In a post-*Defenders* case, the Supreme Court again found standing where the plaintiffs' injury was "sufficiently concrete and specific," even though it was "widely shared." Federal Election Commission v. Akins, 524 U.S. 11, 25 (1998). It should come as no surprise that Justice Scalia dissented from this decision. *Id.* at 29.

**6.** Perhaps the most common kind of procedural injury occurs when an agency denies people information which they are entitled to receive by law. The concept of "informational standing" originated with a footnote in an early but important NEPA case. Scientists' Institute for Public Information v. Atomic Energy Commission, 481 F.2d 1079, 1087, n.29 (D.C. Cir. 1973). How should the *Defenders* case be applied in the context of an informational standing claim under NEPA? In City of Olmsted Falls v. Federal Aviation Administration, 292 F.3d 261, 267 (D.C. Cir. 2002), the Court of Appeals for the District of Columbia Circuit held that "a NEPA claim may not be raised by a party with no claimed or apparent environmental interest. It cannot be used as a handy stick by a party with no interest in protecting against an environmental injury to attack a defendant." "Geographic proximity," the Court noted, "might be necessary to show such an injury, but it is not sufficient." *Id.* Is *City of Olmstead Falls* consistent with the *Akins* decision discussed in note 5?

7. Why do you think Congress has made citizen suit provisions the rule for pollution laws but the exception for natural resources laws? Could this be a reflection of the fact that natural resources law is more management and value-based, so we want to leave value decisions to the political and administrative process and not to courts? Or is something else at work?

8. As described in Chapter 8, standing is regarded as a major challenge to climate change litigation. In particular, establishing injury in fact and redressability pose major hurdles to many litigants who must show that particular emissions are likely to harm them, and that a legal remedy is available that will redress their harms. In the Supreme Court case, *Massachusetts v. EPA,* in a close 5–4 vote the majority addressed this issue but narrowed its holding to the special status of standing for sovereign states, holding that, at least in the climate context, sovereign states are owed a "special solicitude" and have a lower threshold for standing than private parties. The Court did not reach the question of standing for private individuals. 549 U.S. 497 (2007). What are the policy justifications for having less stringent standing requirements for states than private parties?

---

## PROBLEM EXERCISE:
## CLEAN AIR ACT VIOLATIONS AND THE WOOD PRODUCTS INDUSTRY*

The year is 2017. Three of the nation's largest wood product companies face the threat of EPA enforcement proceedings. At stake are millions of dollars of fines, tens of millions of dollars for pollution control equipment, and a public relations humiliation. The Office of Corporate Counsel has been requested to provide a briefing to the company's board on the challenges posed to the business. Specifically, the Office staff must prepare a memo reviewing and analyzing the range of options available in response to EPA's threatened enforcement actions: what are their potential advantages and disadvantages, their likelihood of success?

While the Corporate Board will make the final decision, the Chair wants the legal staff's opinion on the best options for the company and how to sell them to the Board. As with all memos to the Board, your memo may be no longer than two pages.** Annexes 1–5 follow this case study.

### The Clean Air Act

The Clean Air Act was passed by Congress in 1970 and regulates emissions from vehicles and stationary sources throughout the country. The part of the Act relevant to this case is Title I: the system of Nationally

---

* This case is based on a real situation, described in a series of articles by Stephen Engelberg in the New York Times (4/26/95, 5/21/95). Some names and details have been changed and the dates moved up to make the case study more current.

** Your professor will tell you which party you represent.

uniform Ambient Air Quality Standards (NAAQS). Under Title I, the EPA has established NAAQS for seven common pollutants. The NAAQS are based on public health data and define the maximum legal concentration of these compounds in the air we breathe (e.g. 1.5 micrograms of lead per cubic meter of air). In essence, the NAAQS establish a quantified legal definition of "clean air." In order to share responsibility between federal and state actors, once the NAAQS are set by EPA, each state is free to meet these standards as it sees fit. The state writes a State Implementation Plan detailing what steps will be taken to ensure the NAAQS will be achieved. Upon EPA approval, the state is then left to implement its plan.

In some parts of the country, because of local geography, concentrated industry, and other factors, the NAAQS are not met (e.g., in Los Angeles they have never been met). These cities and regions with unlawfully high concentrations of air pollutants are called "non-attainment areas" and must meet special requirements restricting new growth and construction.

Similarly, certain areas' air quality is well under the NAAQS limits, such as in low-population rural areas or national parks. To prevent the flight of dirty industries to these clean air regions, the Clean Air Act regulates these areas to ensure the Prevention of Significant Deterioration (PSD) (*see* Chapter 3). In PSD areas, if a major industrial source builds a new plant which emits more than 250 tons annually of VOCs or makes a major modification that will emit more than 40 tons, a permit to operate must be obtained from state and federal authorities (*see* Annex 1). These permits require the new plants or major modifications to employ "Best Available Control Technology" (BACT), informally referred to in the industry as "Most Expensive Control Technology."

The EPA has a wide arsenal of penalties for non-compliance, e.g. operating in a PSD region without a permit (*see* Annex 2). Fines can be levied up to $25,000 per day of non-compliance. While rarely exercised, EPA also retains the authority to shut down a plant's operation through a temporary injunction until it can ensure compliance. Finally, if a company knowingly withholds information from the government that shows it is in non-compliance, the EPA can seek criminal prosecution.

### VOCs and AP–42

In drafting regulations to implement the Clean Air Act, the EPA began investigating the environmental impacts of emissions from the wood products industry. In particular, officials focused on the production of plywood and waferboard. The production processes for both these wood products involve peeling and slicing timber into smaller wood chips which are then dried at high temperatures, glued, and pressed together. The drying of the sap and liquids stored in the wood necessarily releases large emissions of volatile organic compounds (VOCs).

A huge class of organic compounds, VOCs include most everything we can smell (e.g., gas and perfume). In still, warm air, and in the presence of sunlight, VOCs can combine with nitrogen oxides from vehicle emissions and power plants to form lower-level atmospheric ozone (smog). In addition to creating the well-known brown haze of air pollution, smog poses serious health concerns to infants and adults with respiratory ailments.

EPA had originally considered setting emissions limits on all new plywood and waferboard plants but refrained out of concern over technical difficulties in measuring emissions and the industry's weakened finances during a cyclical downturn in business. Because wood mills are often located in PSD areas, close to the sources of timber, they still must measure their emissions at the time of construction or major modification to see if permits are required. To provide guidance to mills in estimating their VOC emissions, EPA issued a technical document in 2002 known as AP–42. AP–42 provides a methodology to calculate VOC emissions from stationary sources' site-specific variables such as each chemical's vapor pressure, specific gravity, concentration, etc. These data are fed into AP–42's formulae and tables to produce an estimated plant-wide emissions total. As with other EPA technical guidance documents, AP–42 contains a disclaimer stating that the document is simply provided as background information for industry estimates and does not represent an agency rule or regulation.

For reasons still unclear, one of the calculations provided in the AP–42 protocol was incorrect. As a result, mills using AP–42 would *underestimate* their actual VOC emissions by 90%, erroneously placing the emissions well below the levels required for a permit under the PSD requirements.

In 2009, the wood industry's research laboratory produced a report, Technical Bulletin 405, pointing out that plywood production emitted far more VOCs than the figures predicted in AP–42. The bulletin was sent to the research departments of the major wood companies and EPA's scientific research department. Neither the industry nor the EPA reacted to the findings of the Technical Bulletin and AP–42 was re-published, with the same mistake, in 2010 and 2013. The mistake was noticed and rectified by EPA in 2015.

There is some debate over the relevance of Technical Bulletin 405. Charles Simon, head of the wood industry research lab at the time of the Technical Bulletin's publication, says it is inconceivable that the companies' top scientists were unaware of the Bulletin's findings. By relying on the underestimates in AP–42, Simon states, "the industry was taking advantage of a regulatory agency's lack of knowledge. That's crystal clear to me." Those in the industry, however, deny they were playing dumb and maintain that the study was filled with so many qualifications and caveats that the EPA, itself, ignored the report's findings.

### The Violations

The fortunes of the wood products market closely track the home building industry. After a period of recession and mill closings in the 1990s, the home building market exploded in the new decade, leading to greatly increased demand for plywood and other wood products. In response, new mills were rapidly built and old ones expanded.

After investigating other industrial sectors for compliance with the Clean Air Act, in 2015 the EPA turned its focus on the compliance record of the wood products industry. As Technical Bulletin 405 had concluded years earlier, the EPA's investigation found that wood mills' VOC emissions were often in excess of the PSD requirements for a permit. Few mills had applied for appropriate permits to operate and even fewer had installed BACT to limit VOC emissions. Apparently, these mills were blatantly in continuing violation of the Clean Air Act. Assume all the plants out of compliance have been operating at least since 2007.

### The Companies

The companies' financial information is set out in Annex 4. Beyond the mills cited in the EPA enforcement proceedings, all three companies have many other operations which pollute, bringing them into regular contact with state and federal environmental officials for air, water and solid waste permits. The strong market for plywood and waferboard is still growing.

### Lincoln Pacific (LP)

EPA first focused its enforcement efforts on LP. Based in Oregon, LP has been fined with some regularity for local pollution violations. Over the last few years, LP had been very successful in the waferboard market where it has gained a large market share. Most of LP's new plants were built without VOC controls, LP contended, because VOC estimates based on AP–42 put the emissions well below 250 tons annually. EPA, however, charged Clean Air Act violations at 14 LP plants and started court proceedings.

In 2016, EPA offered LP a consent decree in which LP would not need to admit any wrongdoing. In exchange, LP accepted an $11 million civil penalty and agreed to install $70 million of pollution control equipment that will incinerate the VOCs before they can escape. The $11 million fine was the largest in the history of the Clean Air Act. LP corporate communication staff was unsuccessful in obtaining EPA's agreement not to publicize the size of the fine and LP has suffered very poor publicity as the "poster child" for EPA's success in cracking down on large polluters.

### Hauser

Based in Olympia, Washington, Hauser is also a major waferboard producer. In 2016, an internal audit at the company's Elkin, North Carolina, plant showed VOC emissions of 1,000 tons a year, ten times what the company had reported to state officials. The tests were confirmed and a review across the company's operations revealed at least 12 other mills with similar emission levels. The EPA inspectors have not yet monitored Hauser's plants.

Hauser regards itself as a company with a progressive environmental record and promotes this image in its PR materials. If the company were to reveal its violations to state authorities, it would be required to pay fines (up to $1.5 million) and install new pollution control equipment at a cost of $20–30 million. This pro-active approach might also stave off federal involvement. Bill Ruckels, former Administrator of the EPA and a member of Hauser's board, has approached EPA informally over such a strategy and EPA has been encouraging. EPA has refused, however, to put anything in writing or commit itself from overfiling a suit for penalties. EPA has a general policy to proceed with enforcement actions in order to recoup the economic benefits a company enjoyed by operating without pollution controls.

**Green Pacific (GP)**

Based in Atlanta, GP has had a mixed record of environmental compliance. To improve the company's environmental performance and reputation, GP hired Lee Roberts, former Administrator of the EPA, as Vice President for environmental affairs. Within 9 months, Roberts had publicly set over 20 environmental targets for the company.

The EPA has given notice that it will start enforcement proceedings against 26 GP plants for PSD permit violations. The senior management of GP has reservations, however, in negotiating a consent decree with EPA. In the 2000s, calculations based on AP–42 showed that the GP plants did not require a PSD permit and GP formally consulted with state and federal officials in deciding whether or not to apply for a permit. Off the record, state officials from Alabama, Virginia and Georgia have told GP they disapprove of EPA's hard line.

GP has a powerful lobbying presence in Washington through its law firm, Wilson & Williams. Wilson & Williams believes it may be able to attach a provision on a bill currently in the Senate Judiciary Committee ("The Comprehensive Regulatory Reform Act"). The provision would prevent federal officials from suing or prosecuting a company whose actions were based upon advice from responsible state or federal officials (see Annex 3). One of the firm's former partners is now the Committee's chief counsel on regulatory issues.

If the bill is amended and goes to the floor of the Senate, it is likely the Justice Department and EPA will try to rally opposition to its passage. While the Clean Air Act, like many other environmental laws, shares implementation and enforcement duties with the states, EPA reserves the independent right to commence legal proceedings against local major polluters. Given the current anti-federal mood in Washington, it is difficult to predict the Administration's influence in opposing the bill. Even if all goes well for GP, it could take eight months or longer before the bill is finally passed into law.

**The Case Law**

The law is mixed concerning retroactive application of agency interpretation and estoppel. In other contexts, the courts have held that the federal government is not bound by misinformed or mistaken officials. For example, if an IRS official gives you the wrong information or a tax form has typographic errors and you underpay your taxes, you are still required at a later date to pay the amount owed. The case, *General Electric v. EPA*, has established a limit to government agencies' enforcement and may be relevant to the current conflict (*see* Annex 5).

**ANNEX 1**

**42 U.S.C. § 7475. Preconstruction Requirements**

(a) Major emitting facilities on which construction is commenced. No major emitting facility on which construction is commenced after the date of the enactment of this part [enacted Aug. 7, 1977], may be constructed in any area to which this part applies unless—

(1) a permit has been issued for such proposed facility in accordance with this part setting forth emission limitations for such facility which conform to the requirements of this part;

(2) the proposed permit has been subject to a review in accordance with this section, the required analysis has been conducted in accordance with regulations promulgated by the Administrator, and a public hearing has been held with opportunity for interested persons including representatives of the Administrator to appear and submit written or oral presentations on the air quality impact of such source, alternatives thereto, control technology requirements, and other appropriate considerations;

(3) the owner or operator of such facility demonstrates, as required pursuant to Section 110(j), that emissions from construction or operation of such facility will not cause, or contribute to, air pollution in excess of any (A) maximum allowable increase or maximum allowable concentration for any pollutant in any area to which this part applies more than one time per year, (B) national ambient air quality standard in any air quality control region, or (C) any other applicable emission standard or standard of performance under this Act;

(4) the proposed facility is subject to the best available control technology for each pollutant subject to regulation under this Act emitted from, or which results from, such facility;

(5) the provisions of subsection (d) with respect to protection of class I areas have been complied with for such facility;

(6) there has been an analysis of any air quality impacts projected for the area as a result of growth associated with such facility;

(7) the person who owns or operates, or proposes to own or operate, a major emitting facility for which a permit is required under this part agrees to conduct such monitoring as may be necessary to determine the effect which emissions from any such facility may have, or is having, on air quality in any area which may be affected by emissions from such source. . . .

## ANNEX 2

### § 7413. Federal enforcement

*(a) In general.*

. . . *(4) Requirements for orders.* An order issued under this subsection (other than an order relating to a violation of Section 112 [42 U.S.C. § 7412]) shall not take effect until the person to whom it is issued has had an opportunity to confer with the Administrator concerning the alleged violation. A copy of any order issued under this subsection shall be sent to the State air pollution control agency of any State in which the violation occurs. Any order issued under this subsection shall state with reasonable specificity the nature of the violation and specify a time for compliance which the Administrator determines is reasonable, taking into account the seriousness of the violation and any good faith efforts to comply with applicable requirements. In any case in which an order under this subsection (or notice to a violator under paragraph (1)) is issued to a corporation, a copy of such order (or notice) shall be issued to appropriate corporate officers. An order issued under this subsection shall require the person to whom it was issued to comply with the requirement as expeditiously as practicable, but in no event longer than one year after the date the order was issued, and shall be nonrenewable. No order issued under this subsection shall prevent the State or the Administrator from assessing any penalties nor otherwise affect or limit the State's or the United States authority to enforce under other provisions of this Act, nor affect any person's obligations to comply with any section of this Act or with a term or condition of any permit or applicable implementation plan promulgated or approved under this Act.

*(5) Failure to comply with new source requirements.* Whenever, on the basis of any available information, the Administrator finds that a State is not acting in compliance with any requirement or prohibition of the Act relating to the construction of new sources or the modification of existing sources, the Administrator may—

(A) issue an order prohibiting the construction or modification of any major stationary source in any area to which such requirement applies;[,]

(B) issue an administrative penalty order in accordance with subsection (d), or

(C) bring a civil action under subsection (b).

Nothing in this subsection shall preclude the United States from commencing a criminal action under Section 113(c) [42 USCS § 7413(c)] at any time for any such violation.

*(b) Civil judicial enforcement.* The Administrator shall, as appropriate, in the case of any person that is the owner or operator of an affected source, a major emitting facility, or a major stationary source, and may, in the case of any other person, commence a civil action for a permanent or temporary injunction, or to assess and recover a civil penalty of not more than $25,000 per day for each violation, or both, in any of the following instances:

(1) Whenever such person has violated, or is in violation of, any requirement or prohibition of an applicable implementation plan or permit. Such an action shall be commenced (A) during any period of federally assumed enforcement, or (B) more than 30 days following the date of the Administrator's notification under subsection (a)(1) that such person has violated, or is in violation of, such requirement or prohibition.

(2) Whenever such person has violated, or is in violation of, any other requirement or prohibition of this title, Section 303 of title III [42 USCS § 7603], title IV, title V [42 USCS §§ 7651 et seq.], or title VI [42 USCS §§ 7671 et seq.], including, but not limited to, a requirement or prohibition of any rule, order, waiver or permit promulgated, issued, or approved under this Act, or for the payment of any fee owed the United States under this Act (other than title II [42 USCS §§ 7521 et seq.]).

(3) Whenever such person attempts to construct or modify a major stationary source in any area with respect to which a finding under subsection (a)(5) has been made.

Any action under this subsection may be brought in the district court of the United States for the district in which the violation is alleged to have occurred, or is occurring, or in which the defendant resides, or where the defendant's principal place of business is located, and such court shall have jurisdiction to restrain such violation, to require compliance, to assess such civil penalty, to collect any fees owed the United States under this Act (other than title II [42 USCS §§ 7521 et seq.]) and any noncompliance assessment and nonpayment penalty owed under Section 120 [42 USCS § 7420], and to award any other appropriate relief. Notice of the commencement of such action shall be given to the appropriate State air pollution control agency. In the case of any action brought by the Administrator under this subsection, the court may award costs of litigation (including reasonable attorney and expert witness fees) to the party or parties against whom such action was brought if the court finds that such action was unreasonable.

(c) *Criminal penalties.*

(1) Any person who knowingly violates any requirement or prohibition of an applicable implementation plan (during any period of federally assumed enforcement or more than 30 days after having been notified under subsection (a)(1) by the Administrator that such person is violating such requirement or prohibition), any order under subsection (a) of this section, requirement or prohibition of Section 111(e) of this title [42 U.S.C. § 7411(e)] (relating to new source performance standards), Section 112 of this title [42 U.S.C. § 7412], Section 114 of this title [42 USCS § 7414] (relating to inspections, etc.), Section 129 of this title [42 U.S.C. § 7429] (relating to solid waste combustion), Section 165(a) of this title [42 USCS § 7475(a)] (relating to preconstruction requirements), an order under Section 167 of this title [42 USCS § 7477] (relating to preconstruction requirements), an order under Section 303 of title III [42 USCS § 7603] (relating to emergency orders), Section 502(a) or 503(c) of title V [42 U.S.C. § 7661a(a) or 7661b(c)] (relating to permits), or any requirement or prohibition of title IV (relating to acid deposition control), or title VI [42 U.S.C. §§ 7671 et seq.] (relating to stratospheric ozone control), including a requirement of any rule, order, waiver, or permit promulgated or approved under such sections or titles, and including any requirement for the payment of any fee owed the United States under this Act (other than title II [42 U.S.C. §§ 7521 et seq.]) shall, upon conviction, be punished by a fine pursuant to title 18 of the United States Code, or by imprisonment for not to exceed 5 years, or both. If a conviction of any person under this paragraph is for a violation committed after a first conviction of such person under this paragraph, the maximum punishment shall be doubled with respect to both the fine and imprisonment.

(2) Any person who knowingly—

(A) makes any false material statement, representation, or certification in, or omits material information from, or knowingly alters, conceals, or fails to file or maintain any notice, application, record, report, plan, or other document required pursuant to this Act to be either filed or maintained (whether with respect to the requirements imposed by the Administrator or by a State);

(B) fails to notify or report as required under this Act; or

(C) falsifies, tampers with, renders inaccurate, or fails to install any monitoring device or method required to be maintained or followed under this Act[,] shall, upon conviction, be punished by a fine pursuant to title 18 of the United States Code, or by imprisonment for not more than 2 years, or both. If a conviction of any person under this paragraph is for a violation committed after a first conviction of such person under this paragraph, the maximum punishment shall be doubled with respect to both the fine and imprisonment.

## ANNEX 3

## Proposed Amendment to Comprehensive Regulatory Reform Act

(A) No civil or criminal penalty shall be imposed by a court, and no civil or administrative penalty shall be imposed by an agency, for the violation of a rule—

(1) if the court or agency, as appropriate, finds that the rule, and other information reasonably (2) available to the defendant, failed to give the defendant fair warning of the conduct that the rule prohibits or requires; or

(2) if the court or agency, as appropriate, finds that the defendant—

(a) engaged in the conduct alleged to violate the rule in reasonable reliance upon a written statement issued by an appropriate agency official, or by an appropriate official of a State authority to which had been delegated responsibility for implementing or ensuring compliance with the rule, after the disclosure of the material stating that the facts, action in compliance with, or that the defendant was exempt from, or otherwise not subject to, the requirements of the rule.

In making its determination of facts under this subsection, the court or agency shall consider all relevant factors, including, if appropriate: that the defendant sought the advice in good faith; and that he acted in accord with the advice he was given.

(B) Except as provided in subsection (C), no civil or criminal penalty shall be imposed by a court and no civil administrative penalty shall be imposed by an agency based upon—

(1) an interpretation of a statute, rule, guidance, agency statement of policy, or license requirement or condition, or

(2) a written determination of fact made by an appropriate agency official, or state official after disclosure of the material facts at the time and appropriate review, if such interpretation or determination is materially different from a prior interpretation or determination made by the agency or the state official and if such person, having taken into account all information that was reasonably available at the time of the original interpretation or determination, reasonably relied in good faith upon the prior interpretation or determination.

(C) Nothing in this section shall be construed to preclude an agency:

(1) from making a new determination of fact, and based upon such determination, prospectively applying a particular legal requirement.

## ANNEX 4

Companies' Financial Information

### LINCOLN-PACIFIC CORPORATION

| | |
|---|---|
| Headquarters | Corvallis, OR |
| 2017 annual sales | $2.2 billion |
| 2017 net income | $177 million |
| Annual sales of waferboard and plywood | 5.5 billion square feet |
| W & P market share | 22% |
| Income from W & P | $18 million |

### HAUSER COMPANY

| | |
|---|---|
| Headquarters | Seattle, WA |
| 2017 annual sales | 9.2 billion |
| 2017 net income | $372 million |
| Annual sales of waferboard and plywood | 3.25 billion square feet |
| W & P market share | 10.8% |
| Income from W & P | $14 million |

### GREEN-PACIFIC CORPORATION

| | |
|---|---|
| Headquarters | Macon, GA |
| 2017 annual sales | $11.8 billion |
| 2017 net loss | ($124 million) |
| Annual sales of waferboard and plywood | 7.5 billion square feet |
| W & P market share | 25.0% |
| Income from W & P | $23 million |

## ANNEX 5

### General Electric v. EPA, 53 F.3d 1324 (D.C. Cir. 1995)

TATEL, CIRCUIT JUDGE

The Environmental Protection Agency fined the General Electric Company $25,000 after concluding that it had processed polychlorinated biphenyls in a manner not authorized under EPA's interpretation of its regulations. We conclude that EPA's interpretation of those regulations is permissible, but because the regulations did not provide GE with fair warning of the agency's interpretation, we vacate the finding of liability and set aside the fine.

I.

GE's Apparatus Service Shop in Chamblee, Georgia decommissioned large electric transformers. Inside these transformers was a "dielectric fluid" that contained high concentrations of polychlorinated biphenyls ("PCBs"), which are good conductors of electricity. PCBs are also dangerous pollutants. "Among the most stable chemicals known," they are extremely persistent in the environment and have both acute and chronic effects on human health. 3 William H. Rodgers, Environmental Law § 6.9, at 461 (1988) (internal quotation marks and citations omitted). Recognizing the dangers of PCBs, Congress has required their regulation under the Toxic Substances Control Act. Pursuant to TSCA, the EPA promulgated detailed regulations governing the manufacture, use, and disposal of PCBs.

Because GE's transformers were contaminated with PCBs, the company had to comply with the disposal requirements of 40 C.F.R. § 761.60. Section 761.60(b)(1) requires the disposal of transformers by either incinerating the transformer, 40 C.F.R. § 761.60(b)(1)(i)(A), or by placing it into a chemical waste landfill after the PCB-laced dielectric fluid has been drained and the transformer rinsed with a PCB solvent. *Id.* GE chose the "drain-and-landfill" option of Section 761.60(b)(1)(i)(B).

The drain-and-landfill alternative required GE to dispose of the liquid drained from the transformer "in accordance with" the terms of Section 761.60(a). Since the dielectric fluid contained extremely high concentrations of PCBs, the relevant provision of Section 761.60(a) was Section (1), a catch-all section applicable to liquids contaminated with more than 500 parts per million ("ppm") of PCBs. This section required those disposing of these particularly dangerous materials to do so solely by incineration in an approved facility. In accord with that requirement, GE incinerated the dielectric fluid after draining it from the transformers. It then soaked the transformers in a PCB solvent—in this case, freon—for 18 hours, drained the contaminated solvent, and immediately incinerated it as well.

In March, 1987, GE changed these procedures, beginning a process that ultimately led to the EPA complaint in this case. While GE continued to incinerate the dielectric fluid, it began a recycling process that recovered a portion of the dirty solvent through distillation. After soaking the transformer, GE poured the dirty solvent into a still that heated the freon, boiling off about 90% of it. The 10% of the liquid that was left, which was highly contaminated with presumably all the PCBs that had been rinsed from the transformer, was immediately incinerated. Meanwhile, the vapor from the still was cooled, recondensing into nearly pure liquid freon that contained less than the regulatory threshold of 50 ppm PCBs and, as an administrative law judge later found, probably less than the detectable level of 2 ppm. GE then used this recycled solvent to rinse other transformers.

GE and EPA agree that the regulations require the incineration of the solvent. They disagree about whether the intervening distillation and recycling process violated the regulations. EPA argues that Section 761.60(b)(1)(i)(B) required GE to dispose of all the dirty solvent "in accordance with the requirements of [Section 761.60(a)(1)]"—i.e., by immediate incineration. GE did not think that section prohibited it from taking intermediate steps like distillation prior to incinerating the PCBs. To GE, distillation was permitted by Section 761.20(c)(2), which allows the processing and distribution of PCBs "for purposes of disposal in accordance with the requirements of § 761.60." GE believed that this section authorized intermediate processing "for purposes of disposal"—processing such as distillation—as long as it complied with the other requirements of the PCB regulations like those relating to the management of spills, storage, and labelling of PCB materials. EPA has not alleged that GE's distillation process failed to comply with those requirements. In fact, as the ALJ later concluded, distillation reduced the amount of contaminated materials, thus producing environmental benefits.

Despite those benefits, EPA charged the company with violating the PCB disposal regulations. After a hearing, an ALJ agreed and assessed a $25,000 fine. On appeal, the Environmental Appeals Board modified the ALJ's reasoning, but agreed with the disposition of the complaint and upheld the $25,000 penalty. In other proceedings, the agency found the company liable for distillation it performed in six other locations, but suspended the fines for those violations pending the outcome of this appeal.

II.

GE argues that EPA's complaint is based on an arbitrary, capricious, and otherwise impermissible interpretation of its regulations. *See* 5 U.S.C. § 706(2)(A) (1988). To prevail on this claim, GE faces an uphill battle. We accord an agency's interpretation of its own regulations a "high level of deference," accepting it "unless it is plainly wrong." Under this standard, we must defer to an agency interpretation so long as it is "logically consistent with the language of the regulations and . . . serves a permissible regulatory function." The policy favoring deference is particularly important where, as here, a technically complex statutory scheme is backed by an even more complex and comprehensive set of regulations. In such circumstances, "the arguments for deference to administrative expertise are at their strongest." * * *

Particularly in the context of this comprehensive and technically complex regulatory scheme, EPA's interpretation of the regulations is permissible. Although GE's interpretation may also be reasonable, at stake here is the proper disposal of a highly toxic substance. We defer to the reasonable judgment of the agency to which Congress has entrusted the development of rules and regulations to ensure its safe disposal.

Had EPA merely required GE to comply with its interpretation, this case would be over. But EPA also found a violation and imposed a fine. Even if EPA's regulatory interpretation is permissible, the company argues, the violation and fine cannot be sustained consistent with fundamental principles of due process because GE was never on notice of the agency interpretation it was fined for violating. It is to this issue that we now turn.

III.

Due process requires that parties receive fair notice before being deprived of property. The due process clause thus "prevents . . . deference from validating the application of a regulation that fails to give fair warning of the conduct it prohibits or requires." In the absence of notice—for example, where the regulation is not sufficiently clear to warn a party about what is expected of it—an agency may not deprive a party of property by imposing civil or criminal liability. Of course, it is in the context of criminal liability that this "no punishment without notice" rule is most commonly applied. But as long ago as 1968, we recognized this "fair notice" requirement in the civil administrative context. In *Radio Athens, Inc. v. FCC,* we held that when sanctions are drastic—in that case, the FCC dismissed the petitioner's application for a radio station license—"elementary fairness compels clarity" in the statements and regulations setting forth the actions with which the agency expects the public to comply. This requirement has now been thoroughly "incorporated into administrative law."

Although the agency must always provide "fair notice" of its regulatory interpretations to the regulated public, in many cases the agency's pre-enforcement efforts to bring about compliance will provide adequate notice. If, for example, an agency informs a regulated party that it must seek a permit for a particular process, but the party begins processing without seeking a permit, the agency's pre-violation contact with the regulated party has provided notice, and we will enforce a finding of liability as long as the agency's interpretation was permissible. In some cases, however, the agency will provide no pre-enforcement warning, effectively deciding "to use a citation [or other punishment] as the initial means for announcing a particular interpretation"—or for making its interpretation clear. This, GE claims, is what happened here. In such cases, we must ask whether the regulated party received, or should have received, notice of the agency's interpretation in the most obvious way of all: by reading the regulations. If, by reviewing the regulations and other public statements issued by the agency, a regulated party acting in good faith would be able to identify, with "ascertainable certainty," the standards with which the agency expects parties to conform, then the agency has fairly notified a petitioner of the agency's interpretation. * * *

In *Rollins Environmental Services, Inc. v. EPA,* as in this case, the EPA accused the petitioner of failing properly to incinerate a solvent that it had used to rinse out containers—in that case, concrete basins—that had once contained PCBs. The relevant rule for rinsing basins stated that "the solvent may be reused for decontamination until it contains 50 ppm PCB. The solvent shall then be disposed of as a PCB in accordance with § 761.60(a)." Rollins reused the solvent several times, but it never reached a concentration of 50 ppm PCBs, and so Rollins disposed of the solvent in a way that was not TSCA-approved. The ALJ found a violation of the regulation, but assessed no financial penalty because he thought the regulations "unclear" and that Rollins' interpretation "had a definite plausibility." On appeal within the agency, the Chief ALJ concluded that the regulation was clear and imposed a $25,000 fine.

Although we held that EPA's interpretation of the regulations was permissible, we agreed with the original ALJ that the language of the regulation was ambiguous and that both interpretations were reasonable. We also pointed out that "significant disagreement" existed among EPA's various offices regarding the proper interpretation of the language. But Rollins had failed to raise the due process issue in his briefs or before the agency, so we allowed the violation to stand. Nonetheless, we concluded that the ambiguity of the regulation justified rescinding the fine against Rollins under TSCA's mitigation provision, which required the agency to take into account the "extent, and gravity of the violation . . . the degree of culpability, and such other matters as justice may require" in setting the amount of the penalty. Dissenting in part, now-Chief Judge Edwards concluded that Rollins had adequately raised the "fair notice" issue and that the regulation clearly did not provide fair notice. He would have vacated the violation altogether, thereby precluding the EPA from using the violation as a basis for increasing fines against the company in later liability proceedings.

Unlike in *Rollins,* GE has clearly raised the due process "notice" issue in this case. Although we defer to EPA's interpretation regarding distillation because it is "logically consistent with the language of the regulations," we must, because the agency imposed a fine, nonetheless determine whether that interpretation is "ascertainably certain" from the regulations. . . . [We] conclude that the interpretation is so far from a reasonable person's understanding of the regulations that they could not have fairly informed GE of the agency's perspective. We therefore reverse the agency's finding of liability and the related fine.

On their face, the regulations reveal no rule or combination of rules providing fair notice that they prohibit pre-disposal processes such as distillation. To begin with, such notice would be provided only if it was "reasonably comprehensible to people of good faith" that distillation is indeed a means of "disposal." While EPA can permissibly conclude, given the sweeping regulatory definition of "disposal," that distillation is a means of disposal, such a characterization nonetheless strays far from the common understanding of the word's meaning. A person "of good faith" would not reasonably expect distillation—a process which did not and was not intended to prevent the ultimate destruction of PCBs—to be barred as an unapproved means of "disposal."

Not only do the regulations fail clearly to bar distillation, they apparently permit it. Section 761.20(c)(2) permits processing and distribution of PCBs "for purposes of disposal." This language would seem to allow parties to conduct certain pre-disposal processes without authorization as long as they facilitate the ultimate disposal of PCBs and are done "in compliance with the requirements of this Part"—i.e., in accordance with other relevant regulations governing the handling, labelling, and transportation of PCBs. EPA argues—permissibly, as we concluded above—that the section allows parties to "use" PCBs in the described manner, but that those uses must still comply with the disposal requirements of Section 761.60, including the requirement that unauthorized methods of disposal receive a disposal permit from the agency. This permissible interpretation, however, is by no means the most obvious interpretation of the regulation, particularly since, under EPA's view, Section 761.20(c)(2) would not need to exist at all. If every process "for purposes of disposal" also requires a disposal permit, Section 761.20(c)(2) does nothing but lull regulated parties into a false sense of security by hinting that their processing "for purposes of disposal" is authorized. While the mere presence of such a regulatory trap does not reflect an irrational agency interpretation, it obscures the agency's interpretation of the regulations sufficiently to convince us that GE did not have fair notice that distillation was prohibited. * * *

Indeed, the agency itself has recognized that its interpretation of Section 761.20(c)(2) is not apparent. It has recently proposed new regulations that would make this implicit waiver for incidental pre-disposal processing explicit by "clarifying" Section 761.20(c)(2). * * *

[It] is unlikely that regulations provide adequate notice when different divisions of the enforcing agency disagree about their meaning. Such is the case here. In 1984, one EPA regional office concluded that companies could distill PCB materials without seeking additional authorization from the EPA. Although GE never proved it, the company asserted in its initial replies to the agency that a second regional office had told it the same thing. While we accept EPA's argument that the regional office interpretation was wrong, confusion at the regional level is yet more evidence that the agency's interpretation of its own regulation could not possibly have provided fair notice. * * *

Notwithstanding the lack of clarity in the regulations themselves, the agency argues that GE was nevertheless on notice of its interpretation. It begins by pointing to a policy statement on PCB "separation activities" issued in 1983, claiming that it provided a sufficiently clear statement of its belief that distillation required agency approval. We disagree. Although some language in that policy statement does appear to address activities like distillation, requiring further approval for "activities that can be construed to be part of, or an initiation of a disposal activity," the statement's primary focus is on preventing parties from using such processes to circumvent the disposal requirements. As the statement notes, "it is possible to physically separate PCBs from liquids . . . without EPA approval as long as these liquids . . . are treated (used, stored, disposed of, etc.) as if they still contain their original PCB concentration." A reasonable interpretation of this language is that a physical separation process that is neither intended to nor actually avoids the disposal requirements for PCBs is permissible "without EPA approval" as long as it is handled in a manner consistent with the PCB regulations. GE's distillation was such a process, since the solvent was at all times handled as if it contained high concentrations of PCBs. EPA's contrary understanding of the policy statement's language is not so obvious that we consider GE to have had fair notice of the agency's reading.

Nor are we persuaded by EPA's argument that GE had actual notice of the regulatory requirements before and during 1987's distillation processing. EPA relies on the fact that in 1986, GE sought and received a permit for an alternative transformer disposal process which included distillation. That permit, however, was for a process that was an alternative to the suggested methods of disposing of *entire* transformers under Section 761.60(b)(1). While GE sought a permit for that alternative, its decision to do so does not mean that it knew EPA required a permit for distillation in itself. Nor did an April, 1987, letter from EPA regarding distillation at GE's Cleveland facility provide GE with notice that it was violating the regulation. That letter merely said that distillation may require a permit. As we have already pointed out, whether permits are required for distillation—let alone authorized under the regulations—is somewhat uncertain, and the EPA has argued here that the permit requirements are irrelevant. . . . Because all the fluids involved were ultimately incinerated, GE reasonably believed that it had complied with the regulations, and the letter did not clearly put the company on notice that the agency believed otherwise.

We thus conclude that EPA did not provide GE with fair warning of its interpretation of the regulations. Where, as here, the regulations and other policy statements are unclear, where the petitioner's interpretation is reasonable, and where the agency itself struggles to provide a definitive reading of the regulatory requirements, a regulated party is not "on notice" of the agency's ultimate interpretation of the regulations, and may not be punished. EPA thus may not hold GE responsible in any way—either financially or in future enforcement proceedings—for the actions charged in this case. Although we conclude that EPA's interpretation of the regulations is permissible, we grant the petition for review, vacate the agency's finding of liability, and remand for further proceedings consistent with this opinion.

---

## IV. CERTIFICATION AND PRIVATE GOVERNANCE

Over the past two decades, increasing partisanship in Washington over environmental policy (and many other issues, as well) has created gridlock for environmental reform. Over twenty major federal environmental laws were passed between 1970 and 1990. Since the Clean Air Act Amendments of 1990 ushering in the Acid Rain Trading Program, however, apart from some minor amendments to the Safe Drinking Water Act and CERCLA, Congress has not been able to pass major environmental laws. Agencies have sought to make up the gap, as with the Clean Power Plan, but environmental advocates have increasingly turned to the marketplace and private agreements to strengthen and expand environmental protection. In the excerpt below, Professor Vandenbergh describes a number of the most significant private initiatives currently underway.

### Michael P. Vandenbergh, *Private Environmental Governance*

99 CORNELL LAW REV. (2013).

*Certification and Labeling Systems.* Ecolabeling systems have grown dramatically in the last two decades, and by now more than 400 have been developed around the world. Many of these labels are awarded to products or services by non-governmental organizations that set standards, certify compliance, and allow certified products or services to display a label. Many of them address the environmental aspects of the goods or services. Some of these certification and labeling systems are designed, implemented, and funded by governments (e.g., the Nordic Swan label), but many have little or no governmental involvement.

Much of the modern certification activity developed soon after, and in some cases is modeled on, the development of the Forest Stewardship Council (FSC), the leading forest certification program. The FSC is an example of private governance emerging to fill a gap after a period of government inaction. Following the failure of efforts to negotiate a binding international agreement on forest protection in the 1980s, environmental and human rights groups turned their attention to creating standards for well-managed forests. They induced a number of leading wood products companies and traders to participate and established the FSC in 1994. The FSC governing body consists of a wide range of private stakeholders, sets standards for well-managed forests, and provides a certification based on private third-party verification. Forest products harvested from certified forests are permitted to display the FSC label. In response to concerns about some aspects of the FSC system, the Sustainable Forestry Initiative (SFI), a competing group with a stronger corporate focus, later emerged. In addition, the Programme for the Endorsement of Forest Certification (PEFC) was formed in 1999 to provide a forest certification program for small forest owners.

Forestry sustainability systems have been widely adopted around the world. Today, more than 14% of all temperate forests (9% of all productive forests) around the world are certified to FSC and PEFC standards. The PEFC certifies 244 million hectares of forest around the world owned by over 750,000 forest owners, and it includes over 9,700 firms in its chain-of-custody program. The U.S. has over 8 million acres (roughly 40% of private U.S. forest land) managed to FSC or PEFC standards.

The Marine Stewardship Council (MSC) is another example of a certification system that emerged as a result of a perceived gap in government action. The MSC was formed by the World Wildlife Fund and Unilever in response to concerns about the sustainability of fisheries supplying fish to consumer markets in Europe, but it is now a global organization. The MSC administers standards for sustainable fisheries, updates the standards periodically with input from a stakeholder advisory group, evaluates fisheries, and allows those that meet certain criteria to label their fish as MSC-certified. As with the FSC, private auditors assess compliance with the MSC standards. The MSC not only enforces its private standards, but it explicitly builds on and adds a private enforcement mechanism to applicable government standards. The MSC is a good example of the complex relationship of public and private environmental governance. The MSC was formed by private organizations and does not operate under government control or with government funding, but one of its requirements for sustainable fisheries is compliance with the non-binding Code of Conduct produced by the United Nations Food and Agriculture Organization. Today the MSC certifies roughly 7% of the seafood caught for human consumption in the world, and roughly 60% of the seafood caught for human consumption from U.S. fisheries. Firms such as Wal-Mart sell only wild-caught fish from MSC-certified fisheries and in 2013 McDonald's announced that it would sell MSC-certified fish at all U.S. locations. A mini-industry has developed in the fisheries area, with for-profit and not-for-profit firms providing technical assistance to fisheries attempting to make improvements to satisfy the demands of large buyers for certified fish. * * *

In addition, many other foods sold in international commerce are subject to private certification and standards systems. For example, in 2010, approximately 20% of all bananas were sold under a certification scheme88 and 8% of global coffee sales were sold as certified, while 17% of global coffee was produced as compliant with these standards. Between 2005 and 2010, global coffee certification grew by 433%. Similarly, in 2010, 7.7% of global tea was sold as certified, and between 2005 and 2010, global tea certification grew by 2,000%.

*Lending Standards.* The Equator Principles are a set of environmental assessment and disclosure requirements that major banks agree to impose on project finance borrowers for projects around the world. In project finance lending, the loaned funds are used for a specific project, and the project is expected to generate the revenues that will enable repayment of the loan. The project also serves as the security for the loan. Some of these projects (e.g., power plants and pipelines) have raised environmental concerns, particularly in the developing world. The Equator Principles emerged after protests by environmental groups and encouragement by the International Finance Corporation (IFC) and World Bank induced several major banks to agree on a common set of standards for environmental impact disclosure and for managing the environmental risks arising from project finance lending. The standards apply to global project finance lending for loans of over $10 million.

The Equator Principles require disclosure that is roughly analogous to the disclosure included in an environmental assessment or environmental impact statement under the National Environmental Policy Act (NEPA). Like NEPA, the implementation of the Equator Principles often does not require any particular environmental outcome, but the system relies on information development and disclosure as a means of influencing which projects receive funding and the design of those projects. Unlike NEPA, however, the Equator Principles also direct lenders to require borrowers to develop and implement plans to reduce environmental impacts. The Equator Principles were initially adopted by a group of banks, not government agencies, although the initial meeting of project finance lenders was convened by the IFC, and the Equator Principles draw on and reference the IFC Performance Standards and the World Bank Group Environmental, Health and Safety Guidelines. The Equator Principles are administered by an unincorporated association of member institutions (the EP Association), and they have been updated twice through a remarkably elaborate public disclosure and comment process that resembles informal notice-and-comment rulemaking.

The Equator Principles have been widely adopted. Roughly 80 of the largest global financial institutions have now agreed to comply. Project finance lending by member banks accounts for more than 70% of global project finance lending in developing countries.

*Commodities Roundtables.* Many goods are sold in commodity markets (e.g., corn, wheat and other grains), and the supply chains are difficult to identify. Consumer or interest group pressure on consumer-facing businesses of the type that contributed to the development of the FSC and MSC certification systems and is unlikely to result in changes in production methods for commodities, since food retailers typically do not buy directly from the producers, and the goods do not have a clear consumer brand identity. Despite the barriers to development of private governance systems for commodities, in the last decade environmental groups, retailers, producers and others have responded by forming commodity roundtables for palm oil, cotton, and other commodities. An example is the Roundtable on Sustainable Palm Oil, which seeks to create an adequate chain of custody and to certify suppliers of palm oil. As with many international private governance initiatives, the private activities in this area in some cases include governmental involvement and in others exist alongside similar government initiatives.

Commodity programs have developed a remarkable degree of flexibility to account for the challenges arising from these goods. For example, GreenPalm is a program started by the World Wildlife Fund that addresses palm oil and that has combined environmental certification with a trading system. Palm oil is an ingredient in nearly half of all supermarket products, and these products often have blends of many different types of palm oil. As a result, certifying only a subset of palm oil producers will not result in large quantities of palm oil that are totally from certified sources, and switching the entire supply chain to sustainable palm oil would be difficult. The GreenPalm plan allows a business to obtain a certificate for every ton of palm oil it can certify as sustainable. Businesses can then trade these certificates to offset non-sustainable production. Although this approach results in products being labeled as certified that have some non-certified palm oil, it led to the production of one million tons of certified palm oil in the first two years. This resulted in $9 million dollars paid to producers to stimulate the development of sustainable palm oil production.

*Green Building Standards.* The private standards established by the U.S. Green Building Council (USGBC), Leadership in Energy and Environmental Design ("LEED"), influence the design and construction of buildings in the U.S. The LEED standards allow builders to certify compliance with efficiency and environmental requirements at several levels of stringency (Platinum, Gold, Silver, and Bronze). The USGBC, a non-governmental organization, establishes, modifies, and administers the LEED standards with input from a stakeholder groups. The LEED process also involves private verification that is financed in part by certification charges.

As of 2012, LEED-certified buildings accounted for 2 billion square feet of occupied space in the U.S. Additionally, the total value of LEED-certified non-residential construction projects in 2010 was $54 billion—35% of the total market. Estimates project that LEED-certified projects will make up 48% of the non-residential construction market by 2015. Advising clients on the LEED standards now is an important aspect of the practice of law for many environmental and land use lawyers.106 Industry groups now lobby the USGBC regarding the content of the LEED standards in ways that might have been directed at Congress or the Environmental Protection Agency two decades ago. * * *

*Supply Chain Contracting*. Not all private governance mechanisms involve collective standard setting. Even though they are not required to do so by any public or private standard, a growing number of corporate buyers impose environmental requirements on their global suppliers. In some cases these requirements simply obligate the buyer to comply with domestic environmental laws, but in many cases the contract terms require the suppliers to exceed public regulatory requirements. . . .

Contracts of this type may require suppliers to adopt an environmental management system, not use certain toxic chemicals, or to reduce energy use or carbon emissions. For instance, Hewlett-Packard imposes toxics use reduction requirements on all of its suppliers. In a recent initiative, several leading footwear and apparel companies have committed to eliminate toxic discharges from their supply chains by 2020. Wal-Mart, meanwhile, imposes energy efficiency requirements on its suppliers. Note that Wal-Mart does not just demand lower prices from suppliers, which any firm can be expected to do in a private market transaction. Instead, it demands less energy use, which typically correlates with lower emissions of greenhouse gases and other air pollutants. The motivations are complex, but the important aspect of the supply chain contracting in this case is that it serves an environmental protection function (e.g., reducing air pollution) that Wal-Mart has no public law obligation to address in its supply chain contracts.

Supply chain contracts that impose environmental requirements on suppliers are surprisingly common. A study published in 2007 concluded that more than half of the firms in eight industrial sectors impose private environmental requirements on their suppliers. A larger recent study of firms in many sectors concluded that roughly 40% of the firms surveyed reported that they impose such requirements. Anecdotal reports suggest that private corporate supply chain requirements imposed by major retailers on product manufacturers are becoming the de facto constraints on the presence of toxics in consumer products.

In addition, the potential influence of supply-chain contracting requirements is huge. At least 65,000 multinational corporations (MNCs) operate roughly 850,000 affiliates around the world, and supply-chain contracting occurs among these affiliates as well as with millions of third-party firms. Wal-Mart alone does $18 billion per year in business with

China, has over 10,000 Chinese suppliers, and would be China's sixth largest trading partner if it were a country. Regardless of one's views of Wal-Mart or its motivations for imposing environmental requirements on suppliers, the potential effects of Wal-Mart's insistence on environmental performance over and above its public legal requirements may be larger than many current international or national regulatory measures. * * *

*Resource Agreements.* In some cases, multiple forms of private governance emerge in response to a resource problem. These responses often involve supply-chain contracting, but they have distinctive features because there is some collective activity among the buyers and because the agreements are directed at a small number of large suppliers, who in turn are expected to regulate the conduct of a large number of small enterprises. For example, deforestation associated with beef production in Brazil is the largest source of carbon emissions in Brazil and a substantial contributor to global emissions totals. The Brazilian national and subnational governments have been unable to combine the standards and enforcement necessary to address deforestation associated with cattle grazing. After a campaign by an environmental advocacy group in Europe, however, McDonald's, Burger King, Adidas, Nike, and other major global buyers of Brazilian beef and leather entered into agreements with many of the major Brazilian slaughterhouses in which the slaughterhouses agreed to phase out purchases of beef from recently-deforested areas. The agreements were negotiated by a group of buyer companies, suppliers, and environmental NGOs, but they yielded a series of bilateral agreements between the companies and the suppliers rather than a common standard among the companies. The enforcement of these agreements remains to be seen, and other buyers with less concern about deforestation may undermine the agreements in the long run, but the agreements include a large share of the Brazilian beef market, so even imperfect implementation may yield substantial emissions reductions.

---

## QUESTIONS AND DISCUSSION

**1.** Why do you think private certification labels and other market-based strategies have become so popular in recent years? If you were working for an environmental group, how would you assess the pros and cons of addressing forest management, fisheries, or green building design through purely private measures rather than the more traditional lobbying for changes to international, federal, state or municipal laws? How can one complement the other?

**2.** Campaigns to change the purchasing policies of Wal-Mart, McDonalds or Home Depot are known as a "leverage" strategy. More people buy groceries from Wal-Mart than any other store in the country. These retailers act as bottlenecks in the supply chain, funneling goods purchased from many wholesale vendors and making them available in stores and restaurants across the country. Do you see why changing the purchasing practice of a bottleneck company can leverage their market position and prove much more effective for an environmental group than trying to change (1) the purchasing behavior of millions of individual consumers or (2) the manufacturing and business practices of thousands of upstream suppliers? *See generally* James Salzman, *Beyond the Smokestack: Environmental Protection in the Service Economy,* UCLA L. REV. 411, 460 (2000).

When do you think a leverage strategy would prove ineffective? What would you want to know about the seafood industry to assess whether to pursue a leverage strategy to promote more sustainable fisheries?

**3.** Do you pay attention to green labels on products? More generally, what are the most important prerequisites for an effective private certification and labeling system? What are the most important prerequisites for an effective private lending standard system? For green-building standards?

Do these private initiatives strike you as complementary to governmental regulation or potentially more effective, displacing agency activity in some areas?

**4.** The main force behind enforcement is sanction—the hammer that keeps the bad apples in line. What do you think the sanctions are for violating private certification systems such as FSC or MSC? What about Wal-Mart or Hewlett-Packard's?

**5.** As the casebook describes in Chapter 6, it turns out that most consumers don't respond to green labeling for most product categories. Patagonia dropped carbon footprint information from its website in 2012. If consumer preferences for green goods are fairly weak, why might companies still seek to green their supply chain because or reputational concerns?

**6.** A key aspect of certification strategies lies in the stringency of the standards. Should consumers be satisfied, or even impressed, with FSC or MSC certification? "Greenwashing" has long been a concern of environmental groups. Nothing prevents timber companies from issuing their own environmental label with much laxer standards than FSC. Faced with a range of products on the market shelf, each sporting its own green label, what is a consumer to do?

The Federal Trade Commission has recognized this concern and issued a series of regulations defining specific environmental terms. Revised in 2012, the *Federal Trade Commission's Guides for the Use of Environmental Marketing Claims,* known as the "Green Guides," forbid the use of deceptive and over-reaching environmental claims lacking adequate proof or qualification. The revised Guides cover claims concerning carbon offsets, renewable energy, non-toxic and free-of claims, among many others. For example, marketers cannot claim a product is "green" or "eco-friendly" without substantiation of specific benefits. The guides discuss appropriate claims for carbon offsets, "free-of" claims, non-toxic claims, made with renewable energy claims, etc. "Sustainable," "natural," and "organic" claims for textiles and agricultural products are regulated by the U.S. Department of Agriculture's National Organic Program.

# CHAPTER 12

# PRIVATE LITIGATION

CHAPTER OUTLINE



---

Before there were comprehensive environmental statutes conferring enforcement powers on federal and state agencies and citizens (*see* Chapter 11), environmental harms were primarily addressed through private litigation. Indeed, private litigation, primarily in two forms—common law claims involving alleged property damages and personal injuries and insurance recovery litigation—has long been and continues to be a major practice focus for many environmental law practitioners. This chapter uses common law claims and insurance recovery claims to explore the nature and nuances of private litigation involving alleged environmental harms.

## I. COMMON LAW CAUSES OF ACTION

### A. THE CASE FOR THE COMMON LAW

Most comprehensive treatments of the evolution of environmental law begin with the common law as the first meaningful stage of development. *See, e.g.*, E. Donald Elliott, et al. *Toward a Theory of Statutory Evolution: The Federalization of Environmental Law*, 1 J. L. ECON. & ORG. 313, 315 (1985). In particular, over time nuisance doctrine developed into a powerful means of regulating the environment, so much so that

> [t]here is no common law doctrine that approaches nuisance in comprehensiveness or detail as a regulator of land use and technological abuse. Nuisance actions reach pollution of all physical media—air, water, land, groundwater—by a wide variety of means. Nuisance actions have challenged virtually every major industrial and municipal activity that today is the subject of comprehensive environmental regulation.

WILLIAM H. RODGERS, ENVIRONMENTAL LAW, § 2.1 at 112–13 (2d ed. 1994). Indeed, from the beginning of the twentieth century courts had enjoined the operation of industries found to cause pollution of agricultural land, Whalen v. Union Bag and Paper Co., 208 N.Y. 1, 101 N.E. 805 (1913); enjoined facilities emitting noxious odors, Costas v. City of Fond du Lac, 24 Wis.2d 409, 129 N.W.2d 217 (1964); Steifer v. Kansas City, 175 Kan. 794, 267 P.2d 474 (1954); and awarded damages against plants found to have polluted waters, Harrisonville v. W.S. Dickey Clay Manufacturing Co., 289 U.S. 334 (1933). By the time Congress turned its attention to air, water, and land pollution in the early 1970s, the common law had established the causal connections between pollution and environmental harm, and between environmental harm and economic injury, and had endorsed the need for and practical availability of remedies. The common law thus provided much-needed legitimacy to the public law agenda for pollution control.

Evidence for this view is found in the earliest days in the history of nuisance law in the pollution control context. A century ago the U.S. Supreme Court decision in Georgia v. Tennessee Copper Co., 206 U.S. 230 (1907), suggested that the common law could play an important and innovative role in pollution control. After private agricultural landowners were unsuccessful in stopping harmful air emissions from copper smelting plants in the eastern reaches of Tennessee, see Madison v. Ducktown Sulphur, Copper & Iron Co., 113 Tenn. 331, 83 S.W. 658 (1904), Georgia's public nuisance claim against the Tennessee companies fell on sympathetic ears at the Supreme Court. The Court was "satisfied by a preponderance of the evidence that the sulphurous fumes cause and threaten damage on so considerable a scale to the forests and vegetable life, if not to health, within the plaintiff State" as to justify an injunction. 206 U.S. at 238–39. Indeed, in a later remedial decree the court, much like a modern administrative agency, required the company to keep daily records of its operations, to submit to court-appointed inspectors, to meet performance standards for emission rates, and to comply with maximum total daily emission loads. *See* 237 U.S. 474 (1915). Although the court later relaxed some of the limits during wartime, ultimately the case had a technology-forcing effect as the fear of liability led the industry to develop a new smelting process that allowed reclamation of the sulfur. If the common law can produce this kind of result, who needs legislation?

But confidence in the capacity of the common law eventually waned. The death knell to this sort of hopeful thinking came in the famous case of Boomer v. Atlantic Cement Co., 26 N.Y.2d 219, 257 N.E.2d 870 (1970), in which New York's highest court declined to enjoin a cement plant's air emissions, ruling instead that a damages remedy, previously not available under New York law, was the more efficient approach. While known mostly for the shift in remedial doctrine, the court's rationale for backing off injunctive relief sent a loud message to legislatures that their help was needed:

> A court performs its essential function when it decides the rights of parties before it. Its decision of private controversies may sometimes greatly affect public issues. Large questions of law are often resolved by the manner in which private litigation is decided. But this is normally an incident to the court's main function to settle controversy. It is a rare exercise of judicial power to use a decision in private litigation as a purposeful mechanism to achieve direct public objectives greatly beyond the rights and interests before the court.
>
> Effective control of air pollution is a problem presently far from solution even with the full public and financial powers of government. In large measure adequate technical procedures are yet to be developed and some that appear possible may be economically impracticable.
>
> It seems apparent that the amelioration of air pollution will depend on technical research in great depth; on a carefully balanced consideration of the economic impact of close regulation; and of the actual effect on public health. It is likely to require massive public expenditure and to demand more than any local community can accomplish and to depend on regional and interstate controls.
>
> A court should not try to do this on its own as a by-product of private litigation and it seems manifest that the judicial establishment is neither equipped in the limited nature of any judgment it can pronounce nor prepared to lay down and implement an effective policy for the elimination of air pollution. This is an area beyond the circumference of one private lawsuit. It is a direct responsibility for government and should not thus be undertaken as an incident to solving a dispute between property owners. . . .

257 N.E.2d at 871. The date of the opinion, not coincidentally, marks the advent of the wave of federal legislation regulating air, water, and land pollution.

Yet it is by no means the case that the common law is dead as far as the environment is concerned. Rather, just as statutes such as CERCLA and the Clean Water Act recognize that pollution of land and water resources poses a threat to human health and environmental quality, the common law recognizes the same, though the manner in which proof of causation and injury are measured is different in many respects from the ways those matters are handled in regulatory enforcement regimes.

Indeed, a number of commentators, many of whom refer to themselves as "free market environmentalists," argue that the genius of the common law provides for more effective and efficient environmental protection than the traditional reliance on government regulation.

## Richard Epstein, *Environmental Law 101*

Speech at the Hoover Institution on October 27, 1998.

To think clearly about property rights and the environment, we must expose the false conflict that is said to separate them. Our initial query should ask how the cause of environmental protection would fare if all we had at our disposal were the traditional principles of property law. How well would the faithful application of these principles protect the environment?

My first point is that every owner of property must worry about the actions of his neighbors. To the extent that one person, as an owner of property rights, insists that he have unlimited rights to use his property just as he pleases, then, under the principle of parity, he must concede to his neighbors the same unlimited use of their property. Stated bluntly, nothing in the theory of property rights says that my property is sacred while everybody else's property is profane. That single constraint of parity among owners should lead every owner to think hard. The more usage rights he claims for himself, the more usage rights he must allow to others. The more he limits the uses of others, the more he must limit his own uses. This system of parallel restrictions on the use of property will rarely lead to the toleration of any and all uses of property. For example, if you woke up in the morning and took a deep breath of a mixture of carbon monoxide and sulfurous acid, you would be prompted to say, "You know, I'm willing to stop that kind of activity even if it follows that I can no longer inflict the same misery on my neighbors."

This recognition of the noxious uses of private property is the source of the common law of nuisance. That law dates from medieval times, certainly by 1215, at the time of the Magna Carta. It is no new socialist or environmentalist creation for the twentieth century. When the common law of nuisance restricts the noxious use of property, it benefits not only immediate neighbors but the larger community. If I enjoin pollution created by my neighbor, others will share in the reduction of pollution. Simply by using private actions, we have built a system for environmental protection that goes a long way toward stopping the worst forms of pollution.

## ENTER THE GOVERNMENT

Yet before we leap for joy, we must recognize that private actions are not universally effective in curbing nuisances. Sometimes pollution is widely diffused—waste can come from many tailpipes, not just one—so that no one can tell exactly whose pollution is causing what damage to which individuals. Under those circumstances, private enforcement of nuisance law can no longer control pollution. Now the task of the lawyer and system builder is to find a coherent way for government action to pick up the slack in environmental protection. The governing principle is simply this: Wherever it's hard to organize private actions against admitted wrongdoers, then it is permissible to resort to direct government regulation, either to stop the pollution before it begins or to fine the perpetrators when and where it occurs. We do not change the substantive standards of right and wrong, but we do use state regulation to fill in the gaps in private enforcement. So, with tailpipe emissions, a believer in property rights should say, "Look, if it is practical to use private actions against all drivers on the Santa Monica freeway, by all means do so. But since we all know that's an administrative impossibility, state regulation of tailpipe emissions is clearly a noncontroversial use of government power." Public enforcement of antipollution norms should take into account the severity of the harm just as private rights of action should.

## WIDE-OPEN SPACES

These simple arguments use a set of common-law property rights to allow for both private and public enforcement of the nuisance law. But often when individuals worry about their local environments, they're not particularly happy to treat the nuisance law, however enforced, as the upper bound of their personal protection. They want (especially as their wealth increases) more by way of aesthetics and open spaces. Fortunately, our legal system has a way to accommodate these newer demands. One of our most important land-use control devices is the system of covenants by which all the holders of neighboring lands agree among themselves and for their successors in title (that is, for anybody who takes their land by sale, gift, or will) that they will abstain from certain kinds of behavior in exchange for imposing parallel restrictions on other owners. So if members of a homeowners' association want to keep, for example, open spaces for the benefit of all subdivision residents, they can use contracts and deeds to make sure that each owner dedicates a portion of his land for open space. Or they could acquire in their common name some open spaces. Or they could form a governance structure that allows for future provision for open spaces. These possibilities for the development of, as it were, a private sort of environmental protection are not simply hypothetical devices. They are routinely used with great success throughout the United States. The richer our population, the greater its willingness to spend resources on environmental protection. Most people want to equalize the benefits that they provide for themselves privately in their houses and publicly in their open and our shared spaces. For many years our legal system has provided them with devices to achieve these results in a perfectly coherent fashion.

## ENTER THE GOVERNMENT (AGAIN)

In addition, it is possible to identify at least one other device to advance the cause of environmental protection: government purchase or, if necessary, condemnation. Let us suppose that some valuable natural landmark is of no particular value to its owner but of great value to the public at large. However unfashionable it may sound to some people, that natural landmark could be purchased in one of two ways. A private nature conservancy group could decide to buy this resource in its natural condition to prevent any rival from doing so. That approach falls squarely within the classical property rights system, for the nature conservancy is just as legitimate a bidder as an industrial plant. In contrast, if no private bidder is available, a strong popular sentiment in favor of acquisition could lead the state to buy or condemn that property for public use, which includes its preservation for environmental ends. Specifically, the state can purchase or condemn at a fair valuation any valuable form of habitat for the benefit of some endangered species. There is both a private consensual means and a public coercive means to preserve the environment. Compensation—but only when it is fully calculated—is the lubricant that prevents government abuse from taking place.

In sum, the system of public and private enforcement of nuisances and public and private purchases of environmentally sensitive sites is the way that sound environmental policy should proceed. Here the state can stop wrongful conduct without compensation but cannot limit the ordinary use of property unless it is prepared to provide compensation. Requiring compensation in the second class of cases has the added benefit of introducing some democratic responsibility into the process of state regulation; it helps makes the costs visible to the public at large. That in turn will require environmentalists to make the benefits visible as well. Once both costs and benefits are on the table, it becomes possible to enter into an intelligent public debate as to whether the anticipated benefits justify their associated costs.

## THE MODERN SYSTEM: FROM SENSE TO NONSENSE

Ironically, the environmental work done today in the United States often takes a very different form. The tension between property rights and the environment invites a titanic struggle because the traditional rules of nuisance, restrictive covenants, and purchase and condemnation are regarded as only minimal first steps for dealing with the problems we face. But what does this alternative legal system look like? What drives it?

To place these issues in perspective, let me mention a couple credos of the modern environmental movement. One holds that any change in the external world involves the commission of some form of environmental harm. The movement thus builds into the calculus an extraordinary preference in favor of the status quo. Sometimes this preference goes beyond the odd to the grotesque. Much environmental litigation has taken place over the question of whether a landowner is entitled to clean up a mess on his property that was left by some industrial plant decades ago in order to facilitate useful development. The system simply doesn't trust private people to behave in a responsible fashion even when they will both incur the costs of the cleanup and derive many of the benefits that it produces.

From this initial point comes the further claim that it is always possible to harm the environment even if one does no harm to one's neighbors. We now have a set of rules that allows us all to become busybodies in the lives of one another whenever there is any alteration of land, be it building or parking pad or removing old vegetation and putting new plants in its place. The threshold for government intervention is sharply lowered. Any alteration in land will do it, even if it is "harm" to your own property. The upshot is that each owner starts to have powerful veto rights over all her neighbors—rights that are sometimes exercised for bad reasons as well as good ones. The law thus encourages perpetual conflict between neighbors over every use or alteration. Ownership no longer provides a zone of freedom. Instead it simply marks out the person who must first obtain a government permit to initiate change. And if one permit can be required, why not a thousand?

### THE POWER SHIFT

The upshot is a massive shift of the political center of gravity from the individual to the state. The traditional view of property allowed an owner to do something on his land until a neighbor could show tangible harm from his activities. That rule has been displaced by one that says no action can take place until approvals have been obtained and that these will not be allowed until you have ruled out all possibility of environmental harm, not only to your neighbors' but to your own land. The government's ability to issue permits, and to issue them on onerous conditions, institutes an odd form of tyranny that will both hamper the cause of environmental protection and give rise to vast antagonistic political struggles that produce much heat but little light.

Ultimately, then, the modern system fails because it does not trust that private incentives will work. In the end, it cannot believe that property owners will act in a rational fashion to protect their own property.

### THE MEN OF 1215

The lesson that we should take away from these examples is that good, rudimentary economic theory gives a clear view of the issue. It may well be that the men of 1215 did not understand the fine points of the common-law system they developed. But they surely built better than they knew. In large measure our job is not to dismantle the structures they put together but to explain why they rest on firm foundations that should be respected and applied to the problems of our time. In a free society we should always use our modern intellectual tools to explain and defend our ancient and honorable institutions. That proposition applies to environmental protection and property rights as much as it does to any other area.

---

## QUESTIONS AND DISCUSSION

**1.** Take a moment to think about what environmental protection would look like in the United States if there were no state or federal environmental protection agencies. What are the arguments that the common law would be up to the task?

**2.** Now consider some of the limitations of the common law. Epstein identifies at least one—the transaction costs of private remedies in a collective action situation (e.g., drivers on the Santa Monica freeway). How does primary reliance on the common law for environmental protection compare to reliance on regulation in terms of:

- Prospective versus retrospective remedies
- Transaction costs
- Evidentiary burdens
- Injured parties being able to seek relief
- Symbolic power

**3.** In which settings might you expect reliance on the common law to be preferable to reliance on regulation? *See* Jason J. Czarnezki and Mark L. Thomsen, *Advancing the Rebirth of Environmental Common Law*, 34 B.C. ENVTL. AFF. L. REV. 1 (2007).

**4.** For a detailed examination of these issues, *see* ROGER MAINERS AND ANDREW P. MORRISS, eds., THE COMMON LAW AND THE ENVIRONMENT: RETHINKING THE BASIS FOR MODERN ENVIRONMENTAL LAW (2000).

**5.** This section continues by exploring the three main contexts in which common law actions involving the environment are framed: (1) allegations of property damages from pollution; (2) allegations of personal injuries resulting from exposure to hazardous substances; and (3) allegations of fraud committed in connection with contracts for sale of assets. The materials then turn to three settings in which the common law addresses environmental harm issues in ways quite different from the manner in which statutory enforcement claims are positioned: (1) claims involving alleged ecological injuries; (2) claims against the government; and (3) expert testimony and the burden of proof. As you work through the materials, consider how close the actual common law doctrine comes to fulfilling the vision of free market environmentalism.

---

## B. PROPERTY DAMAGE LITIGATION

### 1. LIABILITY FOR IMPROPER LAND USE

Pollution does not respect property boundaries. The common law has developed a number of causes of action that can be used when conduct on one parcel of property has led to contamination of resources on another property. Indeed, because long latency periods and incomplete scientific knowledge lead to inherent difficulties of proof in environmental common law cases, "plaintiff's lawyers have worked hard at creating new approaches to proof of causation . . . and novel theories that interweave common and statutory law." Janet Kole et al., *Toxic Tort Litigation: Theories of Liability and Damages*, in ENVIRONMENTAL LITIGATION 108, 109 (Janet Kole et al., eds., 2d ed., 1999). As the following case suggests, therefore, applying the common law doctrines, even to instances in which the source of pollution is obvious, is not always as straightforward and one might imagine.

### Corvello v. New England Gas Co., Inc.

United States District Court for the District of Rhode Island, 2006.
460 F. Supp. 2d 314.

■ TORRES, CHIEF JUDGE:

The plaintiffs in these four cases reside on and/or own property in Tiverton, Rhode Island. They brought these actions against New England Gas Company ("NE Gas"), an unincorporated division of Southern Union Company ("Southern Union"), alleging that, approximately fifty years ago, hazardous substances that were the by-product of a coal gasification process utilized by Fall River Gas Company ("FRGC"), NE Gas's predecessor, were deposited as fill on the plaintiffs' property.

The multi-count complaints assert claims for negligence, gross negligence, violation of the Rhode Island Hazardous Waste Management Act ("HWMA"), R.I. Gen. Laws 23–19.1–22, strict liability, infliction of emotional distress, private nuisance, and public nuisance. The relief sought includes monetary damages for the plaintiffs' loss of use and enjoyment of their properties, for diminution of the properties' value and for emotional distress as well as punitive damages, costs and attorneys' fees. Some of the plaintiffs also are requesting declaratory and/or injunctive relief.

NE Gas and Southern Union have moved, pursuant to Fed.R.Civ.P. 12(b)(6), to dismiss all of the plaintiffs' claims. . . .

#### *Background Facts*

All four complaints allege essentially the same facts and, with one exception, make identical claims. The facts alleged are as follows.

At some unspecified time before it was acquired by Southern Union, FRGC operated an electric power-generating facility near the property now owned by the plaintiffs. The facility produced "coal gasification waste material," some of which allegedly was deposited as fill on or near the plaintiffs' property, apparently by contractors. The Corvello complaint states that the fill was deposited "prior to the construction of homes" in the area.

In August 2002, the Town of Tiverton was installing a sewer interceptor line in an area near the plaintiffs' property. Some of the excavated soil was an unusual blue color and emitted a distinctive odor characteristic of polyaromatic hydrocarbons.

A Rhode Island Department of Environmental Management ("RIDEM") investigator determined that the blue color indicated that the soil was "coal gasification waste material" that contained toxic and hazardous substances and that some of the substances, notably polyaromatic hydrocarbons ("PAH's"), cyanide and naphthalene, exceeded RIDEM's established exposure criteria. Further investigation disclosed the presence of these substances in the soil under the streets in the neighborhood and on some of the surrounding property.

RIDEM issued a "letter of responsibility" to the defendants and the Town of Tiverton placed an emergency moratorium on excavation in an area that encompasses the plaintiffs' properties. The moratorium precludes the issuance of building permits for any construction requiring excavation.

The plaintiffs in *Corvello, Burns,* and *Bigelow* brought actions in the Rhode Island Superior Court which were removed to this Court. The plaintiffs in *Reis* brought an action in the United States District Court for the District of Massachusetts which was transferred to this Court.

All of the complaints contain claims for negligence, strict liability, private nuisance and public nuisance. The *Corvello* and *Reis* complaints also include claims for gross negligence, and the *Corvello* complaint includes claims for infliction of emotional distress, and violation of the HWMA, R.I. Gen. Laws § 23–19.1–22.

### *Analysis*

I. *Negligence*

A. *Breach of Duty*

The defendants argue that the negligence claims should be dismissed because the complaints do not allege any facts that would establish the violation of a duty owed by the defendants to the plaintiffs. More specifically, the defendants argue that they have not breached any duty owed to the plaintiffs because the coal gasification waste material was deposited long before the area in question was developed and, therefore, any alleged harm to the plaintiffs was too remote and speculative to be reasonably foreseeable.

The defendants rely on *Hydro Manufacturing, Inc. v. Kayser-Roth Corp.,* 640 A.2d 950, 955 (R.I.1994) and *Wilson Auto Enters., Inc. v. Mobil Oil Corp.,* 778 F. Supp. 101, 104 (D.R.I.1991), but that reliance is misplaced. Both cases involved negligence claims against prior owners of the plaintiffs' property for activities that allegedly contaminated the soil and/or ground water. In each case, the Court rejected the claim on the ground that the possibility that a property owner's use of his property might cause injury to future owners was too remote to impose a duty to future purchasers to refrain from such use.

In *Wilson,* the contamination allegedly resulted from the defendant's operation of a gas station on the property. The Court found that allegation insufficient to state a claim because the plaintiffs had an opportunity to inspect the property before purchasing it and, under the doctrine of *caveat emptor,* they had a responsibility to do so, especially since the property's use as a gas station made the possibility of contamination fairly predictable. *Wilson,* 778 F. Supp. at 105. However, Judge Lagueux suggested that the result might have been different if a claim of contamination had been asserted by owners of nearby property because, unlike the plaintiff in that case, "Mobil's neighbors in Foster may have had no choice in becoming victims of Mobil's alleged chemical leaks." *Id.*

In *Hydro Manufacturing,* the purchaser of property on which the defendant previously had operated a textile plant sought to recover for contamination allegedly caused by the defendant's negligence in allowing hazardous materials to spill on the ground. The Court affirmed the entry of summary judgment in favor of the defendant holding that prior owners of property do not "owe remote purchasers a duty to maintain the property and to refrain from any activity that may harm the property" because "the duty that sellers owe to subsequent purchasers is established primarily through contracts between the parties who theoretically reach an arm's-length agreement on a sale price that reflects the true value of the land." *Hydro Manufacturing,* 640 A.2d at 955 (citations omitted). The *Hydro Manufacturing* Court pointed out that a prospective buyer can obtain protection by inspecting the property, obtaining representations or warranties from the seller and seeking indemnity or a reduction in the sale price to reflect the land's actual economic value. *Id.* at 955–56.

This case is distinguishable from *Wilson* and *Hydro Manufacturing* because these plaintiffs are not subsequent purchasers of FRGC's property. Accordingly, these plaintiffs presumably, were not alerted to the possibility that waste generated by FRGC had contaminated their property; and, therefore, they would have had no reason to perform environmental tests before buying the property. Nor did these plaintiffs have any opportunity to bargain with or obtain representations and warranties from FRGC. Rather, the plaintiffs are like the neighbors referred to in *Wilson* who had no choice about becoming victims of the alleged contamination.

In short, the limited *caveat emptor* exception that precludes contamination claims by a landowner against a previous owner is not applicable in this case and does not relieve the defendants of their duty to refrain from conduct that contaminates or otherwise harms neighboring properties. *See O'Donnell v. White,* 23 R.I. 318, 50 A. 333 (R.I.1901) (municipality held liable for negligently throwing earth and gravel on owner's property while filling in streets).

III. *Strict Liability*

A defendant who knowingly engages in abnormally dangerous activity or causes an abnormally dangerous condition to exist, may be held liable for any resulting harm to persons or property even if the defendant exercised reasonable care. Restatement (Second) of Torts § 519(1) (1977).

The Rhode Island Supreme Court has said that "whether a defendant should be held strictly liable for ultra-hazardous or abnormally dangerous activities is a question of law." *Splendorio v. Bilray Demolition Co., Inc.,* 682 A.2d 461, 465 (R.I.1996). However, it also has stated that determining whether an activity is ultra-hazardous or abnormally dangerous requires consideration of a variety of factors set forth in the Restatement (Second) of Torts and that "[t]he weight apportioned to each [factor] should be dependent upon the facts in each particular case." *Splendorio,* 682 A.2d at 466. The factors to be considered are:

> "(a) existence of high degree of risk of some harm to the person, land or chattels of others;
>
> "(b) likelihood that the harm that results from it will be great;
>
> "(c) inability to eliminate the risk by the exercise of reasonable care;
>
> "(d) extent to which the activity is not a matter of common usage;
>
> "(e) inappropriateness of the activity to the place where it is carried on; and
>
> "(f) extent to which its value to the community is outweighed by its dangerous attributes."

*Id.* (quoting Restatement (Second) of Torts § 520 (1977)).

Generally, "[a]n activity is not abnormally dangerous if the risks therefrom could be limited by the exercise of reasonable care." *Splendorio,* 682 A.2d at 466 (quoting *G.J. Leasing Co. v. Union Elec. Co.,* 854 F. Supp. 539, 568 (S.D.Ill.1994)). The mere fact that an activity involves an ultra-hazardous or abnormally dangerous substance is not, by itself, sufficient to trigger strict liability. As the *Splendorio* Court stated, "if the rule were otherwise, virtually any commercial activity involving substances which are dangerous in the abstract automatically would be deemed as abnormally dangerous. This result would be intolerable." *Splendorio,* 682 A.2d at 465–66 (quoting *G.J. Leasing Co.,* 854 F. Supp. at 568). Accordingly, the abnormal risk of harm must arise from the manner in which the defendant dealt with a dangerous substance. *Splendorio,* 682 A.2d at 466. Put another way, the substance must be used in a way that creates an unreasonable risk of harm.

In *Splendorio,* the Court upheld the entry of summary judgment in favor of a company hired to develop an abatement plan for any asbestos found in buildings that were being demolished. The plaintiffs claimed that asbestos in the debris removed from the site by the demolition company contaminated their property and that the defendant, as the architect of the plan, was strictly liable. However, the Court found that, even though asbestos may be an abnormally dangerous substance, strict liability did not apply because the task performed by the defendant was not inherently dangerous and its "value to the community . . . far outweighed its dangerous attributes." *Id.* at 466.

In this case, although the determination as to whether the defendants' activities were ultra-hazardous or abnormally dangerous ultimately may be a question of law, that determination cannot be made until evidence is presented with respect to the facts upon which the determination must be based. At this juncture, the relevant facts are unknown. There is no evidence regarding such matters as exactly what substances were deposited on or near the plaintiffs' property, what role the defendants may have played in depositing them, exactly what dangers the substances pose, whether that danger was recognizable at the time of disposition and whether the danger could have been eliminated by the exercise of reasonable care. Therefore, this Court cannot say that the plaintiffs will be unable to prove any facts that may entitle them to relief on their strict liability claims.

IV. *The Nuisance Claim*

A. *Nuisance, in General*

As so aptly stated by the late Professor Prosser, "[t]here is perhaps no more impenetrable jungle in the entire law than that which surrounds the word 'nuisance'" "the application of which too often has demonstrated a tendency "to seize upon a catchword as a substitute for any analysis of a problem." W. Page Keeton et al., Prosser and Keeton on the Law of Torts § 86, at 617 (5th ed.1984) [hereinafter "Prosser"]. The lack of analysis and seeming inconsistency in dealing with nuisance claims stems, partly, from the historical development of nuisance doctrine; partly, from a failure to clearly define what constitutes a nuisance; and, partly, from differences in describing the kinds of conduct required to support a nuisance claim. *Id.* Much of the uncertainty is rooted in the fact that the causes of action for both private and public nuisance developed on a case-by-case basis, along separate tracks and based on different principles.

Historically, claims for private nuisance have been "narrowly restricted to the invasion of interests in the use or enjoyment of land" caused by a defendant's use of his own property. *Id.* at 618. By contrast, claims of public nuisance "extend[ed] to virtually any form of annoyance or inconvenience interfering with common public rights." *Id.* Moreover, until recently, an action for public nuisance, generally, could be maintained only by a duly authorized representative of the public. *See id.* § 90, at 643–46.

A great deal of the confusion surrounding present day nuisance law arises from a failure to recognize that "[n]uisance, either public or private, is a field, or rather two distinct fields, of tort liability." Restatement (Second) of Torts § 822 cmt. a (1979). Fortunately, Rhode Island law generally recognizes the historical distinction between the two types of nuisance claims and also defines "nuisance" as a substantial and unreasonable interference with a plaintiff's protected interests. *Hydro Manufacturing, Inc. v. Kayser-Roth Corp.,* 640 A.2d 950, 957 (R.I.1994).

Under Rhode Island law, "[a] cause of action for private nuisance 'arises from the unreasonable use of one's property that materially interferes with a neighbor's physical comfort or the neighbor's use of his real estate' " and "a public nuisance is an 'unreasonable interference with a right common to the general public.' " *Id.* (quoting *Weida v. Ferry,* 493 A.2d 824, 826 (R.I.1985)). *See* Restatement (Second) of Torts §§ 821B, 821D (1979). As Prosser states, "[t]he interference with the protected interest must not only be substantial, but it must also be unreasonable." Prosser § 87, at 629.

The conduct giving rise to a nuisance claim may consist of "an act; or a failure to act under circumstances in which the actor is under a duty to take positive action to prevent or abate the . . . invasion [of the protected interest]." Restatement (Second) of Torts § 824. Liability also may be predicated on the conduct of servants, agents or independent contractors. *Id.* cmt. c.

The critical inquiry in deciding whether an interference with the protected rights of others is "unreasonable" is whether "the gravity of the harm caused outweighs the utility of the conduct," Prosser § 88A, at 630 (5th ed.1984). *See* Restatement (Second) of Torts § 826 (enumerating the factors to be considered in determining reasonableness). Put another way, a plaintiff must establish that "the harm or risk . . . is greater than he ought to be required to bear under the circumstances." *Citizens for Preservation of Waterman Lake v. Davis,* 420 A.2d 53, 59 (R.I.1980) (citing Restatement (Second) of Torts, § 822 cmt. g at 112).

B. *Private Nuisance*

The plaintiffs allege that the disposal of FRGC's coal gasification waste on their property and on nearby properties has created a private nuisance. The defendants argue that the complaints fail to state a claim for private nuisance because they do not allege that the nuisance resulted from activities conducted on the defendants' property or that the plaintiffs' homes and the defendants' facility are "neighboring" properties.

As already noted, in order to prevail on their private nuisance claims, the plaintiffs must show that the interference resulted from the defendants' unreasonable use of their own property. *Hydro Manufacturing,* 640 A.2d at 957 (quoting *Weida v. Ferry,* 493 A.2d 824, 826 (R.I.1985)); *accord Citizens for the Preservation of Waterman Lake,* 420 A.2d at 59. Here, the complaints do not allege that the contamination was caused by FRGC's use of its property. Rather, they allege that the contamination resulted from transporting hazardous material from FRGC's property and depositing it on or near the plaintiffs' property. Consequently, although it seems clear that the alleged interference with the plaintiffs' property interests is of a magnitude that satisfies the requirement of substantial interference, and while the plaintiffs may have viable claims against the defendants under theories of negligence, intentional tort and/or strict liability, they have failed to state claims for private nuisance.

C. *Public Nuisance*

The plaintiffs allege that the disposal of FRGC's coal gasification waste on their property and on nearby property also has created a public nuisance that harms them. The defendants argue that the complaints fail to state claims upon which relief may be granted because the alleged harm relates only to private properties belonging to the individual plaintiffs and not to any "right common to the general public" as required by *Hydro Manufacturing.* NE Gas Mem. Mot. Dismiss at 14–15.

In order to prevail on a public nuisance claim, a plaintiff must establish that a defendant unreasonably interfered with a "right common to the general public" and that the plaintiff sustained "special damages" as a result of the interference. *Hydro Electric Manufacturing,* 640 A.2d 950, 957–58 (citing *Iafrate v. Ramsden,* 96 R.I. 216, 190 A.2d 473, 476 (R.I.1963); *Clark v. Peckham,* 10 R.I. 35 (1871)).

A right "common to the general public" is a collective right that is shared by everyone in the community. It differs from a right that is possessed only by certain individual members of the public. *See* Restatement (Second) of Torts 821B cmt. g. Thus, a public nuisance has been described as something "that unreasonably interferes with the health, safety, peace, comfort or convenience of the general community." *Citizens for Preservation of Waterman Lake,* 420 A.2d at 59.

A public nuisance may consist of an " 'aggregation of private injuries [that] becomes so great and extensive as to constitute a public annoyance and inconvenience, and wrong against the community.' " *Sullivan v. Amer. Mfg. Co. of Massachusetts,* 33 F.2d 690, 692 (4th Cir. 1929) (quoting *Wesson v. Washburn Iron Co.,* 95 Mass. 95, 13 Allen 95, 90 Am. Dec. 181 (Mass.1866)). However, the fact that a condition interferes with the private rights of a substantial number of individuals does not, by itself, make it a public nuisance. *See Iafrate,* 190 A.2d at 476 (a plaintiff must demonstrate that "the acts complained of interfered with any interest of plaintiffs common to the general public.") (quoting Prosser). The distinction is illustrated by Prosser's example of a polluted stream. The pollution would be a private nuisance if it interferes only with the use and enjoyment of property belonging to a number of riparian owners but it would be a public nuisance if it kills all of the fish, thereby depriving the public of the right to fish in the stream. W. Page Keeton et al., Prosser and Keeton on the Law of Torts § 90, at 645 (5th ed.1984).

An action for public nuisance may be maintained by a private citizen who "suffers special damage, distinct from that common to the public." *Hydro Manufacturing,* at 957 (quoting *Iafrate v. Ramsden,* 96 R.I. 216, 190 A.2d 473, 476 (1963)). Under Rhode Island law, a private citizen also may bring an action "to abate the nuisance and to perpetually enjoin the person or persons maintaining the nuisance." R.I. Gen. Laws § 10–1–1.

In order to satisfy the "special damage" requirement, a private plaintiff must show that he has " 'suffered harm of a kind different than that suffered by other members of the public exercising the right common to the general public that was the subject of interference.' " *Hydro Manufacturing,* 640 A.2d at 958 (quoting Restatement (Second) of Torts § 821C(1)). *See* Prosser § 90, at 646 ("[a] private individual has no action for the invasion of the purely public right, unless his damage is in some way to be distinguished from that sustained by other members of the general public."). Consequently, it is not enough for a private plaintiff to show that he has suffered "the same kind of harm or interference but to a greater extent or degree" as other members of the public. Restatement (Second) of Torts § 821C cmt. b (1979). Rather, the harm shown must be separate and distinct from the harm suffered by the general public. *Hydro Manufacturing,* 640 A.2d at 958.

"Special damages" may include personal injury to the plaintiff, damage to the plaintiff's property or substantial interference with the use and enjoyment of the plaintiff's property; but, in order to be compensable under a public nuisance theory, the damages must have been caused by interference with the public right. *See Hydro Manufacturing,* 640 A.2d at 957–58; Prosser § 90, at 648. Thus, in *Hydro Manufacturing,* the Court rejected a public nuisance claim by a landowner whose property was forfeited under CERCLA as a result of contamination caused by a prior owner that polluted the groundwater. The Court held that the landowner could not maintain a public nuisance action against the prior owner because the public right interfered with was "the right to pure water" and the landowner "did not allege that it suffered special damages stemming from [the defendant's] interference with [the plaintiff's] use and enjoyment of the ground water at the site or of its right to pure water." *Id.* at 958. The Court noted that the landowner's damages flowed from the forfeiture of its property and "not in the exercise of a public right." *Id.*

In this case, although the complaints do not specifically allege that the coal gasification waste poses a threat to public health or otherwise unreasonably interferes with a right common to the general public; it does allege that the waste contains a number of highly toxic substances and that the presence of those substances has prompted the Town to impose a building moratorium in the area. Consequently, this Court cannot say that the plaintiffs will be unable to prove any facts that would entitle them to relief on their public nuisance claims.

V. *The Emotional Distress Claim*

The emotional distress claim set forth in the Corvello complaint does not state whether it is a claim for intentional infliction of emotional distress or negligent infliction of emotional distress. That omission is significant because the elements that must be proven in order to prevail on a claim of intentional infliction of emotional distress differ from the elements that must be proven to prevail on a claim for negligent infliction of emotional distress.

In order to prevail on an *intentional* infliction claim, a plaintiff must prove, among other things, that, (1) the defendant acted with intent to cause emotional distress or with reckless disregard as to whether emotional distress would result and (2) the defendant's conduct was "so outrageous in character, and so extreme in degree, as to go beyond all possible bounds of decency, and to be regarded as atrocious, and utterly intolerable in a civilized community." *Swerdlick v. Koch,* 721 A.2d 849, 863 (R.I.1998) (quoting Restatement (Second) of Torts § 46 cmt. d, at 73). By contrast, a *negligent* infliction claim only requires proof that the defendant acted negligently. *Id.* at 864.

A second distinction is that, in order to prevail on a claim for negligent infliction, a plaintiff must show that (1) he witnessed the incident allegedly causing the distress, and (2) he was threatened with injury by being "in the zone of physical danger" or he is "closely related" to a person who was seriously injured. *Id.* This requirement reflects courts' reluctance " 'to impose potentially unlimited and undeserved liability upon a defendant who is guilty of unintentional conduct.' " *Marchetti v. Parsons,* 638 A.2d 1047, 1050 (R.I.1994) (quoting *Reilly v. U.S.,* 547 A.2d 894, 897–98 (R.I.1988)).

Under either theory, a plaintiff also must establish (1) a causal connection between the defendant's conduct and the emotional distress and (2) physical symptoms manifesting the distress which must be linked to the defendant's conduct by medical evidence. *Marchetti v. Parsons,* 638 A.2d at 1052; *see Jalowy v. The Friendly Home, Inc.,* 818 A.2d 698, 710 (R.I.2003).

At oral argument, counsel stated that the complaint was intended to assert claims for both intentional and negligent infliction of emotional distress. However, in ruling on a motion to dismiss, this Court must base its decision on the complaint as written and not on what counsel, later, may say was intended.

Applying this test, it seems clear that the Corvello complaint asserts a claim for intentional infliction of emotional distress. It describes the defendants' acts and omissions as "outrageous" and "so extreme in degree as to go beyond all possible bounds of decency." It also alleges that the defendant "knew or was reckless in not knowing that its acts and omissions would inflict emotional distress on the plaintiffs." The allegations address elements that are unique to a cause of action for intentional infliction. Furthermore, the Corvello complaint does not allege that the defendants were negligent or that the plaintiffs are within a zone of physical danger, both of which are elements of a claim for negligent infliction.

The defendants argue that the complaint fails to state a claim for intentional infliction because the fact that the plaintiffs did not own or occupy their properties when the coal gasification waste allegedly was deposited precludes a finding that the defendants acted with the requisite intent to cause emotional distress *to the plaintiffs*. This Court finds that argument persuasive.

It is well established that intent to cause emotional distress cannot exist in the abstract and, like any other intentional tort, it requires a victim who is the object of the defendant's intentional act. *Lewis v. General Elec. Co.,* 37 F. Supp. 2d 55, 60 (D.Mass.1999); *Collins v. Olin Corp.,* 418 F. Supp. 2d 34, 56 (D.Conn.2006). In *Lewis,* the Court dismissed an intentional infliction of emotional distress claim brought by homeowners against a corporation that allegedly dumped contaminated soil near their properties because there was no indication that the defendants' actions were directed at the plaintiffs. *Lewis,* 37 F. Supp. 2d at 60. In doing so, the Court observed that "[t]he focus of cases 'dealing with intentional infliction of emotional distress has been on the emotional distress of a person against whom the extreme and outrageous conduct was directed.' ") (quoting *Nancy P. v. D'Amato,* 401 Mass. 516, 517 N.E.2d 824, 827 (Mass.1988). Similarly, in *Collins,* the Court dismissed a claim of intentional infliction of emotional distress brought by neighboring landowners against a municipality for allowing a wetland to be filled with allegedly contaminated soil because "[t]he plaintiffs were not living at the landfill sites at the time of the dumping; indeed, the area was not developed and their residences were not constructed until after the dumping on that property was long completed." *Collins,* 418 F. Supp. 2d at 56. Accordingly, the *Collins* Court stated that, "it cannot be found as a matter of law that [the municipality] knew or should have known that its actions or omissions would inflict emotional distress on the plaintiffs." *Id.*

In this case, since the complaint indicates that the coal gasification waste was deposited before the Corvello plaintiffs acquired their property, the defendants' actions could not have been intended to cause emotional distress to the Corvello plaintiffs; and, therefore, the plaintiffs cannot prevail on their intentional infliction claim.

The absence of any allegation that the plaintiffs have physical symptoms resulting from their emotional distress also is fatal to their intentional infliction claim. As already noted, physical manifestations are a *sine qua non* to recovery for intentional infliction of emotional distress and it would be a waste of time, effort and resources to require the defendants to ferret out, via discovery, the absence of facts that have not been in order to move for summary judgment.

Of course, the plaintiffs' inability to prove claims for the torts of intentional or negligent infliction of emotional distress does not necessarily mean that they are precluded from recovering for any emotional distress that they may have suffered. If the plaintiffs succeed on any of their other surviving claims and can demonstrate some other type of injury, they may be entitled to recover consequential damages for emotional distress suffered in connection with that injury. * * *

VII. *Punitive Damages*

The defendants argue that any claims for punitive damages should be dismissed because the complaints fail to allege that FRGC acted with malice or wickedness.

It is true that, under Rhode Island law, the standard for awarding punitive damages is a very strict one. Thus, a "party seeking punitive damages has the burden of producing 'evidence of such willfulness, recklessness or wickedness, on the part of the party at fault, as amount[s] to criminality, which for the good of society and warning to the individual, ought to be punished.' " *Palmisano v. Toth,* 624 A.2d 314, 318 (R.I.1993) (quoting *Sherman v. McDermott,* 114 R.I. 107, 329 A.2d 195, 196 (R.I.1974)). However, while it may be advisable to use those terms where punitive damages are being claimed, there is nothing magical about the words themselves. All that is required is that the allegations in a pleading, if proven, be sufficient to support a finding of malice, recklessness or wickedness.

Here, the complaints satisfy that requirement. They allege that the "[c]oal gasification waste material contains lead, arsenic, cyanide and other hazardous substances;" that the defendants "knew or should have known that the hazardous substances . . . would cause harm;" and that the defendants "knew or should have known that there was a high degree of risk associated with the handling, disposal and/or release of the hazardous substances." Based on those allegations, it is possible that the plaintiffs might be able to prove the degree of culpability necessary to support an award of punitive damages.

It is true, as the defendants suggest, that whether evidence is sufficient to support an award of punitive damages is a question of law for the Court. *Palmisano,* 624 A.2d at 318 (citing *Davet v. Maccarone,* 973 F.2d 22, 27 (1st Cir. 1992)) (court makes "initial determination whether an award of punitive damages is appropriate in a given case."). However, in most cases, the Court cannot make that determination simply by reading the complaint but, instead, must wait until the evidence is presented. This, clearly, is one of those cases.

***Conclusion***

For all of the foregoing reasons, it is hereby ORDERED that the defendants' motion to dismiss is DENIED with respect to the counts contained in the plaintiffs' complaint that assert claims for negligence, strict liability and public nuisance and with respect to the requests for punitive damages. The motion to dismiss is GRANTED with respect to the counts asserting claims for gross negligence, private nuisance, [and] infliction of emotional distress.

---

## QUESTIONS AND DISCUSSION

**1.** *Corvello* provides a methodical survey of the different common law theories of liability a plaintiff can employ in connection with contamination of property. The opinion is not remarkable in this sense. For example, each year the American Bar Association Section on Environment, Energy, and Resources publishes a *Year in Review* compiling case development in a wide variety of areas, and each year it reports at least a dozen cases like *Corvello*—they march through the theories of liability and reach different outcomes based on variations in state law and the facts.

**2.** *Corvello* illustrates both the limits and the flexibility of the common law. The private nuisance claim, for example, was defeated as a matter of law because the alleged nuisance did not emanate from the defendants' property. By contrast, that fact posed no legal obstacle at all for the public nuisance claim. How does this disparate treatment of essentially the same claims shed light on the free market environmentalism thesis discussed above in Part A of this section?

**3.** A similar theme that runs through most of the cases of this sort is the distinction between claims brought by successors in interest in the contaminated property against prior owners, versus claims brought by neighboring landowners not in the chain of title to the property from which the pollution allegedly emanated. The core theories of liability—nuisance, negligence, and trespass (the last not being raised in *Corvello*)—are usually difficult to establish in suits by one owner against prior owners because of a lack of the proper relationship to establish liability. Consider also the consequences of the common law negligence doctrine, endorsed in *Corvello*, that prior owners of property do not owe remote purchasers a duty to maintain the property and to refrain from any activity that may harm the property because the duty that sellers owe to subsequent purchasers is established primarily through contracts between the parties who theoretically reach an arm's-length agreement on a sale price that reflects the true value of the land. Most state courts bar such claims using similar reasoning. *See* Janet Kole et al., *Toxic Tort Litigation: Theories of Liability and Damages*, in ENVIRONMENTAL LITIGATION 108, 118–20 (Janet Kole et al., eds., 2d ed., 1999). If you were working with a company planning to acquire several industrial facilities that had been in operation for 50 years under different owners, what advice would this doctrine lead you to provide? *See* Chapter 13.

**4.** As explained in Chapter 5, CERCLA creates a right of recovery in such circumstances, though its parameters are subject to nuances of the statutory regime. CERCLA also expressly preserves traditional state tort law claims:

> Nothing in this [Act] shall affect or modify in any way the obligations or liabilities of any person under other Federal or State laws, including common law, with respect to releases of hazardous substances or other pollutants or contaminants.

42 U.S.C. § 9652(d). But preserving state common law claims does not repair the common law doctrines that limit the effectiveness of causes of action such as private nuisance and trespass in dealing with complex circumstances such as those presented in *Corvello*. There is some evidence, though, that CERCLA litigation enforcing its statutory strict liability regime has led courts to be more liberal in finding common law strict liability attaches. *See* Alexandra B. Klass, *From Reservoirs to Remediation: The Impact of CERCLA on Common Law Strict Liability Environmental Claims*, 39 WAKE FOREST L. REV. 903 (2004).

**5.** As discussed in Chapter 8, although it has achieved no success on the merits in court thus far, there has been a recent renewed interest in public nuisance claims as a means of redressing injuries alleged to be associated with pollution, the new twist being a focus on greenhouse gas emissions as the nuisance and global climate change as the agent of injury. If you were the attorney for a state suing major sources of greenhouse gas emissions, how would you satisfy the tort requirements for duty of care, breach of that duty, cognizable injury, and remedy? Do utilities have an absolute duty not to emit greenhouse gases? If that duty is not absolute, how could one determine the "reasonable" level of greenhouse gas emissions? *See* David Hunter and James Salzman, *Negligence in the Air: The Duty of Care in Climate Change Litigation*, 155 U. PA. L. REV. 101 (2007).

---

## 2. PRODUCTS LIABILITY

Plaintiffs in common law claims involving contamination of property often cast their nets wide in search of potential defendants. In many cases, for example, contamination is the result of the misuse, or even proper use, of chemicals or products supplied by manufacturers having no connection to the end user whose acts lead to the contamination. Litigation claiming the manufacturer is responsible in such cases has involved asbestos, fertilizers, pesticides, formaldehyde, drain cleaners, vinyl chloride, plutonium, Agent Orange, ammonia, and other more exotic chemical products. *See* J.D. LEE AND BARRY LINDAHL, 3 MODERN TORT LAW: LIABILITY AND LITIGATION § 28:1 (2d ed. 2006 Supp.). Should the manufacturer be liable along with the end user in such instances?

## United States v. Union Corp.

United States District Court for the Eastern District of Pennsylvania, 2003.
277 F. Supp. 2d 478.

■ GILES, CHIEF JUDGE:

[The United States brought an environmental clean-up and cost-recovery action against potentially responsible parties (PRPs) under the Comprehensive Environmental, Response, Compensation and Liability Act (CERCLA), and sought injunctive relief under Resource Conservation and Recovery Act (RCRA). The PRPs filed a third-party contribution claim against Monsanto, which was the manufacturer of hazardous chemicals found at the contaminated site, and the city that owned the sewer systems that carried the hazardous chemicals to the site. On the third-party defendants' motions for summary judgment, the court held that: (1) CERCLA did not per se exempt the city sewer systems from its definition of "facilities" subject to liability for contribution costs; (2) the court's prior findings that the PRPs who owned and operated the recycling operation were liable under CERCLA for clean-up costs at contaminated site, and that city's sewage system was not significant source of contamination at site, did not necessarily release the city from CERCLA liability or collaterally estop the PRPs from seeking contribution; and (3) a fact question as to whether a hazardous substance was released into the environment at the contaminated site by the city sewer system precluded summary judgment for city on CERCLA claim. The remaining issues focused on Monsanto's common law liabilities as the manufacturer of the hazardous chemicals.]

### *II. FACTUAL BACKGROUND*

The Metal Bank Superfund Site located at 7301 Milnor Street near Cottman Avenue in Philadelphia is contaminated with PCBs and other hazardous substances traceable, at least in part, to Metal Bank's transformer reclamation operations on the Site. The City utilizes a combined sewer system in the neighborhood of the Site and has a municipal combined stormwater/sanitary sewer outfall ("CSO") at the foot of Cottman Avenue.

In the late 1800s through the 1940s, engineers designed combined sewers (sewers which carry sanitary sewage and storm runoff in a single pipe) to convey sewage, horse manure, street and rooftop runoff, and garbage from city streets to the nearest receiving body of water. As of the early 1950s, most sewer systems were constructed as separate systems (sanitary sewage in one pipe; storm water sewage conveyed in another pipe). However, in the late 1950s, treating wastewater became the municipal standard. Interceptors were built to transport all wastewater (from either combined or separate systems) to treatment plants. Nevertheless, during heavy storms, the total volume of the wastewater could become too large for the interceptors to handle. To protect treatment plants and avoid sewer back-ups into homes, businesses, and streets, the overflows were discharged into bodies of water like the Delaware River. The City's CSO is the first overflow for the sewage interceptor/collector serving northeast Philadelphia and empties into the northeastern corner of the embayment adjacent to the Metal Bank property during periods of heavy rainfall. The Metal Bank defendants assert that the City has thereby discharged waste containing hazardous materials into the mudflat area from the CSO.

Prior to implementation of PCB ban regulations in 1977 pursuant to the Toxic Substance Control Act ("TSCA"), Monsanto was the sole manufacturer and seller of PCBs in the United States. PCBs were utilized for various industrial purposes, including as a constituent of insulating fluid used in electrical transformers and capacitors. Although defendants did not receive PCBs or PCB-laden materials directly from Monsanto, some of the transformers and capacitors purchased by the utility companies and ultimately processed at the Site contained PCBs.

## *III. ANALYSIS*

* * *

### Monsanto Is Not Liable Under State Law

The third-party plaintiffs assert contribution and indemnification claims against Monsanto based upon state law theories of strict product liability, abnormally dangerous activity and trespass. Pennsylvania law applies.

#### a. Strict Product Liability

The Pennsylvania Supreme Court has adopted the strict products liability doctrine in Section 402A of the Restatement (Second) of Torts. To prevail under section 402A, a plaintiff must prove the existence of 1) a product; 2) the sale of a product; 3) a user or consumer; 4) a defective condition, unreasonably dangerous; and 5) causation.[2] *Ettinger v. Triangle-Pacific Corp.*, 799 A.2d 95, 102 (Pa.Super. 2002). "If any of these

---

[2] Section 402A of the Restatement (Second) of Torts provides:

(1) One who sells any product in a defective condition unreasonably dangerous to the user or consumer or to his property is subject to liability for physical harm thereby caused to the ultimate user or consumer, or to his property, if

(a) the seller is engaged in the business of selling such a product, and

(b) it is expected to and does reach the user or consumer without substantial change in the condition in which it is sold.

(2) The rule stated in Subsection (1) applies although

(a) the seller has exercised all possible care in the preparation and sale of his product, and

(b) the user or consumer has not bought the product from or entered into any contractual relation with the seller.

requisite elements remains unsatisfied, § 402A has no applicability." *Id.* (citing *Schriner v. Pennsylvania Power & Light Co.,* 348 Pa.Super. 177, 501 A.2d 1128, 1132 (1985)).

"[A] product is defective if it lacks any element necessary to make it safe for its intended use or contains any condition that makes it unsafe for its intended use." *Kalik v. Allis-Chalmers Corp.,* 658 F. Supp. 631, 635 (W.D.Pa.1987). "There are three different types of defective conditions that can give rise to a strict liability claim: design defect, manufacturing defect, and failure-to-warn defect." *Phillips v. A-Best Products, Co.,* 542 Pa. 124, 665 A.2d 1167, 1170 (1995). The defect must have existed at the time that the product left the manufacturer's hands. *Commonwealth v. United States Mineral Products Co.,* 809 A.2d 1000, 1027 (Pa.Cmwlth.2002).

The third-party plaintiffs urge the court to find Monsanto liable on theories of design defect and failure-to-warn defect. Liability for a design defect attaches where there is a discrepancy between the design of a product causing injury and an alternative specification that would have avoided the injury. *Stecher v. Ford Motor Co.,* 779 A.2d 491, 502 (Pa.Super.2001). A product is defective due to a failure-to-warn where the product was "distributed without sufficient warnings to notify the ultimate user of the dangers inherent in the product." *Mackowick v. Westinghouse Electric,* 525 Pa. 52, 575 A.2d 100, 102 (1990). Under either theory, the third-party plaintiffs must show that the alleged defect rendered the product unfit for its intended purpose. This they cannot do.

"The intended use of a product includes any use reasonably foreseeable to the manufacturer." *Kalik,* 658 F. Supp. at 635 (citing *Sheldon v. West Bend Equipment Corp.,* 718 F.2d 603, 608 (3d Cir. 1983)). As a matter of law, "the recycling of a product, after it has been destroyed, is not a *use* of the product reasonably foreseeable to the manufacturer." *Kalik,* 658 F. Supp. at 635 (citing *Johnson v. Murph Metals, Inc.,* 562 F. Supp. 246 (N.D.Tx.1983)) (emphasis added).

In *Kalik,* claims brought by the owners of a site to recover cleanup costs of PCBs were found not to be actionable because the dismantling and processing of junk electrical components was not a reasonably foreseeable use of the manufacturers' products. 658 F. Supp. at 635; *see also Monsanto Co. v. Reed,* 950 S.W.2d 811, 814 (Ky.1997) ("[A]s a matter of law, that the dismantling and processing of junk electrical components was not a reasonably foreseeable use of GE's [electrical transformers]."); *High v. Westinghouse Elec. Corp.,* 559 So.2d 227, 227–230 (Fla. 3d DCA 1989), *decision approved in part, quashed in part,* 610 So.2d 1259 (Fla.1992) (as a matter of law, the unsealing, stripping, and dumping of the PCBs contained in defendant's transformers to salvage junk components were not reasonably foreseeable uses of the product and the employee was not an intended user); *Wingett v. Teledyne Indus., Inc.,* 479 N.E.2d 51, 56 (Ind.1985) (a manufacturer's potential liability for products placed in the stream of commerce does not extend to the demolition of the product); *Johnson,* 562 F. Supp. at 249 (the creation of dangerous gases through the smelting of battery scrap metal is not a foreseeable "use" of a defendant's automotive batteries).

Here, the evidence shows that Monsanto sold PCBs for incorporation into dielectric fluid used in the manufacture of electrical transformers and capacitors. The transformers and capacitors containing the fluid were sold to consumers who used them for 20–30 years. The court finds that the defendants' discharge of PCBs when dielectric fluid was drained from transformers and capacitors to salvage iron casings and copper cores was not an intended or reasonably foreseeable use of Monsanto's product.

**b. Strict Liability for Abnormally Dangerous Activity**

Third-party plaintiffs have asserted a claim against Monsanto for strict liability based upon the manufacture and sale of PCBs and argue that this qualifies as an abnormally dangerous or ultra-hazardous activity, entitling it to invoke strict liability principles. In opposition, Monsanto argues that it cannot be held liable for engaging in an abnormally dangerous activity based upon its manufacture of a non-defective product. The court agrees.

"While the common law doctrine of absolute liability is 'less than fully settled' in Pennsylvania . . . , the Superior Court of Pennsylvania, in several cases, has adopted sections 519 and 520 of the Restatement (Second) of Torts for determining whether an activity is abnormally dangerous." *Banks v. Ashland Oil Co.,* 127 F. Supp. 2d 679, 680 (E.D.Pa.2001) (internal citations omitted).[3]

"Pennsylvania use[s] the six factors of § 520 to balance policy reasons for and against the imposition of absolute liability." *Earp v. Andgrow Fertilizer, Inc.,* 1989 WL 1003890, *4 (Pa.Com.Pl. Oct 12, 1989). "Illustrations [of abnormally dangerous activities] in the Restatement range from blasting to the storage of large quantities of water on hilltops overlooking residential development." *Earp,* 1989 WL 1003890, *4.

However, "[n]o court of th[e] Commonwealth [of Pennsylvania] has ever imposed liability on the manufacturer of a non-defective product for engaging in an abnormally dangerous activity." *Mazzillo ex rel. Estate of Mazzillo v. Banks,* 1987 WL 754879, *4 (Pa.Com.Pl.1987). "To recognize liability of a manufacturer or distributor would virtually make them the insurer for such products as explosives, hazardous chemicals or dangerous drugs even though such products are not negligently made nor contain any defects." *Id.* This interpretation would "give the doctrine of absolute liability an unduly expansive meaning." *Id.* Federal courts must

---

3 Section 519 of the Restatement (Second) of Torts provides:

(1) One who carries on an abnormally dangerous activity is subject to liability for harm to the person, land or chattels of another resulting from the activity, although he has exercised the utmost care to prevent the harm.

(2) This strict liability is limited to the kind of harm, the possibility of which makes the activity abnormally dangerous.

"permit state courts to decide whether and to what extent they will expand state common law." *City of Philadelphia v. Beretta U.S.A. Corp.*, 277 F.3d 415, 421.

Other jurisdictions have made it clear that "ultrahazardousness or abnormal dangerousness is, in the contemplation of the law at least, a property not of substances, but of activities." *See, e.g., Indiana Harbor Belt R. Co. v. American Cyanamid Co.*, 916 F.2d 1174, 1181 (7th Cir. 1990). Thus in *Indiana Harbor,* the seventh circuit explained that the relevant activity was not the manufacture of acrylonitrile, the toxic chemical involved in that case, but "the transportation of acrylonitrile by rail through populated areas." *Id.* The court held that "[w]hatever the situation under products liability law (section 402A of the Restatement), the manufacturer of a product is not considered to be engaged in an abnormally dangerous activity merely because the product becomes dangerous when it is handled or used in some way after it leaves his premises, even if the danger is foreseeable." *Id.*

Similarly, in *Richmond, Fredericksburg and Potomac R. Co. v. Davis Industries, Inc.*, 787 F. Supp. 572, 575 (E.D.Va.1992), where a scrap recycling facility sued PRPs under CERCLA and one of the PRPs impleaded the manufacturer of PCB-containing air conditioners, the court held that liability could not be imposed upon the manufacturer for an abnormally dangerous activity. Explaining that a claim under § 519 could not be "saved by shifting the focus from the toxic substances contained in Carrier's gas air conditioners to Carrier's activity—manufacturing gas air conditioners containing PCBs," the court determined that "[t]o hold otherwise [would] convert[ ] the manufacturer into an insurer." *Id.; see also City of Bloomington, Ind. v. Westinghouse Elec. Corp.*, 891 F.2d 611, 614 (7th Cir. 1989)(affirming dismissal of § 519 claim against Monsanto because "the harm to the City's sewage and landfill was not caused by any abnormally dangerous activity of Monsanto but by the buyer's failure to safeguard its waste.").

The court finds that the Pennsylvania Supreme Court would agree that abnormal dangerousness in the context of sections 519 and 520 of the Restatement (Second) of Torts is a property of *activities* and not of substances. Moreover, this court having found Monsanto not liable under principles of strict product liability, it would be incongruous to hold Monsanto liable under section 519 for manufacturing the same product. It is not the role of federal courts to engage in "judicial activism," but rather to "apply the current law of the jurisdiction, and . . . leave it undisturbed," *Beretta U.S.A. Corp.*, 277 F.3d at 421 (citing *Leo v. Kerr-McGee Chem. Corp.*, 37 F.3d 96, 101 (3d Cir. 1994) (quoting *City of Philadelphia v. Lead Indus. Ass'n,* 994 F.2d 112, 123 (3d Cir. 1993))). The court finds that the manufacture and sale of PCBs is not an abnormally dangerous activity as a matter of Pennsylvania law.

### c. Common Law Trespass

Under Pennsylvania law, "trespass" is defined as unprivileged, *intentional* intrusion upon land in possession of another. *Reynolds v. Rick's Mushroom Service, Inc.*, 246 F. Supp. 2d 449 (E.D.Pa.2003); *Graham Oil Co. v. BP Oil Co.*, 885 F. Supp. 716, 725 (W.D.Pa.1994)(citing *Kopka v. Bell Telephone Co.*, 371 Pa. 444, 91 A.2d 232, 235 (1952)) (emphasis added). . . . [O]ne is subject to liability to another for trespass, irrespective of whether one thereby causes harm to any legally protected interest of another, if one "*intentionally* enters land in the possession of another or causes a thing or a third person to do so, remains on the land, or fails to remove a thing which one is under a duty to remove." Restatement (Second) of Torts, § 158 (emphasis added). However, "one whose presence on the land is not caused by any act of his own or by a failure on his part to perform a duty is not a trespasser." *Id.* at Comment (F).

"Pennsylvania courts have [also] adopted the section[ ] of the Restatement (Second) of Torts that deal[s] with continuing trespass." *Graham Oil Co.*, 885 F. Supp. at 725–726. Pursuant to section 161, "continuing trespass" is "[t]he actor's failure to remove from land in the possession of another a structure, chattel, or other thing which he has tortiously erected or placed on the land." Restatement (Second) of Torts § 161(1). "In order to maintain a claim for continuing trespass, a plaintiff must plead that the defendant committed and continues to commit harm-causing actions, not merely that the harm continues to result from actions which have ceased." *Graham Oil Co.*, 885 F. Supp. at 726.

The precise issue presented here was addressed by the seventh circuit in *City of Bloomington, Ind. v. Westinghouse Elec. Corp.*, 891 F.2d 611, 614 (7th Cir. 1989). In that case, the plaintiff City sued Monsanto as manufacturer and seller of PCBs, for damages resulting from the contamination of city's landfill, sewer system and sewage treatment plant from use of the chemicals in the buyer's manufacturing operations. The court held that there could be no trespass absent the actor's intentional entry and referring to Comment j to § 158, explained that "there is no liability where a defendant has caused entry of a third person (here Westinghouse) unless the actor (here Monsanto) intentionally causes the third person to enter land by command, request, or physical duress." *Id.* at 615. Since at the time of the sale of PCBs to Westinghouse, "Monsanto did not know that Westinghouse would deposit harmful waste on City property," and since "Monsanto certainly did not command, request, or coerce Westinghouse into doing so," the court found the requisite trespassory intent lacking. *Id.* The court emphasized that "in accordance with the Restatement principles, courts do not impose trespass liability on sellers for injuries caused by their product after it has left the ownership and possession of the sellers." *Id.*

The court adopts the seventh circuit's analysis under § 158. Monsanto did not deposit or compel another to deposit PCB wastes at the

Site. Moreover, the court has already found that Monsanto could not reasonably have foreseen that its product would be deposited at the Site. Therefore, Monsanto cannot be liable in trespass.

---

### QUESTIONS AND DISCUSSION

**1.** "Much toxic tort litigation can . . . be viewed as a subset of products liability law." Janet Kole et al., *Toxic Tort Litigation: Theories of Liability and Damages*, in ENVIRONMENTAL LITIGATION 108, 108 (Janet Kole et al., eds., 2d ed., 1999). The theories of liability in Monsanto, of course, were expressly about a product, and the court's rulings are consistent with the way most other courts have come out when a product is misused by an end user. The result is that the common law cuts off liability in ways that might not produce the best result in terms of overall environmental protection, but which do respond to notions of fairness and judicial economy. So, once again, how does this outcome shed light on the free market environmentalism thesis discussed above in Part A of this section?

**2.** Consider what you learned about CERCLA liability in Chapter 5. Could the government have named Monsanto in these circumstances in a unilateral remediation order under section 106 of CERCLA or sought recovery of its response costs from Monsanto in a section 107(a) cost recovery action? What is Monsanto's "potentially responsible party" status under CERCLA?

---

## C. PERSONAL INJURY LITIGATION

Another major battleground of common law claims involving environmental harms are the so-called "toxic tort" suits, made famous by the book and movie, *A Civil Action,* in which the plaintiff alleges liability for personal injuries allegedly caused by exposure to hazardous substances. Toxic tort litigation is a vast field of practice presenting many complex substantive and procedural issues. Causation can be difficult to prove, particularly in the absence of manifested physical illness or injury. Many claims for relief in toxic tort cases, for example, are based on novel theories of injury and causation, such as alleged fear of contracting an illness potentially associated with exposure to a particular substance, and seek relief in nontraditional forms, such as the costs associated with medical monitoring designed to detect onset of the illness at an early stage. Toxic tort cases also are often framed as class actions involving numerous plaintiffs allegedly exposed to the same substance by one or more defendants. In what is one of the most instructive and concise guides to toxic tort practice, practitioners D. Alan Rudlin and Christopher R. Graham describe the field as follows:

> Toxic tort litigation is a unique area of the law, joining questions of fate and transport, exposure, and dose with expert opinions about whether there is a proven causal link to personal injury

> or other damage claims. Strategic and tactical issues abound but are often moving targets. To succeed, counsel must understand how the litigation fits together, make creative suggestions to judges handling the cases' complexities, and try to make wise decisions early on that will ultimately affect the resolution perhaps years later. Because, at least in law firms, the lawyers who are most familiar with the intricacies of environmental laws and regulatory requirements are often not necessarily the lawyers who spend much time litigating before juries, toxic tort cases are ideally suited for a team alliance of regulatory and trial lawyers.

*Toxic Torts: A Primer*, NATURAL RESOURCES & ENV'T, Spring 2003, at 203, 258. The following case demonstrates the complexity of toxic tort suits combining these substantive and procedural features.

## Lockheed Martin Corp. v. Carrillo

California Supreme Court, 2003.
63 P.3d 913.

■ WERDEGAR, J.

In this action for medical monitoring of the residents of a geographic area affected by defendants' toxic chemical discharge, the question before us is whether plaintiffs, in moving for class certification, have met their burden of demonstrating that common issues of law and fact predominate. We conclude they have not. We therefore affirm the judgment of the Court of Appeal.

BACKGROUND

Plaintiffs Roslyn Carrillo et alia allege that defendants Lockheed Martin Corporation et alia, in the course of conducting manufacturing operations in the City of Redlands, beginning in 1954, discharged dangerous chemicals that contaminated the city's drinking water with harmful toxins and that this contaminated water was used by a large portion of the city's residents. In December 1996, on behalf of themselves and persons similarly situated, plaintiffs filed this action in the San Bernardino County Superior Court. Plaintiffs pray that the court order defendants to fund a court-supervised program for the medical monitoring of class members, and for punitive damages.

Plaintiffs moved for certification of a "medical monitoring" class and a "punitive damage" class, defined identically as "People who were exposed to water contaminated with any of the following chemicals: TCE, PCE, TCA, other solvents, Ammonium Perchlorate, Perchlorate, other unknown rocket fuel components and rocket fuel decomposition products, Beryllium, Carbon Tetrachloride, Vinyl Chloride, Hydrazine (and Hydrazine derivatives), Nitrosamines (and Nitrosamine derivatives), Epoxides (and Epoxide derivatives), Triazines (and Triazine derivatives), at levels at or in excess of the dose equivalent of the M.C.L. (Maximum

Contaminant Level), or in excess of the safe dose where there is no MCL, for some part of a day, for greater than 50% of a year, for one or more years from 1955 to the present" within specified geographical limits. Plaintiffs' class definition indicated that review of relevant water quality documents was ongoing and that the definition would be amended if additional chemicals were identified.

One of plaintiffs' attorneys declared that estimating the number of persons in the class was difficult, because the University of Redlands is located within the specified geographic boundaries, and persons residing, working or studying within the defined area may qualify as class members. The attorney's best estimate was that the class includes between 50,000 and 100,000 people.

The trial court certified the classes, finding that plaintiffs had met their burden of proof under Code of Civil Procedure section 382: "The Court finds that the plaintiffs have a realistic chance of success on the merits. Specifically, the Court finds that the plaintiffs have shown that there is a realistic chance that the defendants caused contaminants to be leaked into the water table beneath Redlands and that this contaminated water was served to the members of the proposed class." The court also found that there is an ascertainable class, concluding it was "not necessary to determine the levels of toxins received by each plaintiff at this time and that the geographic limits placed on the class are reasonable and related to the alleged contamination." The court concluded, finally, that members of the class have a well-defined community of interest and that common questions of law and fact predominate in the action.

Parties objecting to certification filed three writ petitions in the Court of Appeal, which that court consolidated. Opining that individual issues raised by plaintiffs' claims "clearly predominate, making class certification inappropriate," the Court of Appeal granted a writ of mandate directing the trial court to vacate its order certifying the classes. We granted plaintiffs' petition for review.

DISCUSSION

### I. Suitability of Medical Monitoring Claims for Class Treatment

We first addressed the availability of medical monitoring as a form of damages in *Potter v. Firestone Tire & Rubber Co.* (1993) 863 P.2d 795 (*Potter*). There, residents of homes located near a landfill at which the dumping of toxic substances was prohibited brought, as individual claimants, an action against a tire manufacturing company that had dumped toxic waste materials, alleging that their water supply had thereby been contaminated. The plaintiffs sought damages for, inter alia, fear of cancer and the costs of medical monitoring. Recognizing that " 'expenditures for prospective medical testing and evaluation, which would be unnecessary if the particular plaintiff had not been wrongfully exposed,'" are "'detriments proximately caused'" by negligent disposal of toxic substances, we held that "the cost of medical monitoring is a compensable item of damages where the proofs demonstrate, through reliable medical expert testimony, that the need for future monitoring is a reasonably certain consequence of a plaintiff's toxic exposure and that the recommended monitoring is reasonable"

"In determining the reasonableness and necessity of monitoring," we stated, "the following factors [(hereafter the *Potter* factors)] are relevant: (1) the significance and extent of the plaintiff's exposure to chemicals; (2) the toxicity of the chemicals; (3) the relative increase in the chance of onset of disease in the exposed plaintiff as a result of the exposure, when compared to (a) the plaintiff's chances of developing the disease had he or she not been exposed, and (b) the chances of the members of the public at large of developing the disease; (4) the seriousness of the disease for which the plaintiff is at risk; and (5) the clinical value of early detection and diagnosis." (*Potter, supra,* 6 Cal.4th at p. 1009, 25 Cal.Rptr.2d 550, 863 P.2d 795.)

We have not previously addressed the prerequisites for class treatment of medical monitoring claims. "Section 382 of the Code of Civil Procedure authorizes class suits in California when 'the question is one of a common or general interest, of many persons, or when the parties are numerous, and it is impracticable to bring them all before the court.' The burden is on the party seeking certification to establish the existence of both an ascertainable class and a well-defined community of interest among the class members." (*Washington Mutual Bank v. Superior Court* (2001) 24 Cal.4th 906, 913, 103 Cal.Rptr.2d 320, 15 P.3d 1071 (*Washington Mutual*).)

Plaintiffs assert that separate litigation of each class member's medical monitoring claim would unnecessarily consume vast judicial resources and time. They also urge us to repudiate the Court of Appeal's suggestion that the presence of individual issues generally precludes class certification in mass toxic exposure cases, arguing any such categorical foreclosure would render our decision in *Potter* meaningless. Defendants, on the other hand, emphasize that *Potter's* proximate cause rationale for recognizing medical monitoring costs as damages logically extends only to such "increased or different monitoring" as a defendant's conduct actually necessitates. In light of their due process right to litigate each individual plaintiff's actual toxic dosage and relevant personal characteristics, defendants argue, individual issues in the case predominate over common ones, such that the community of interest required for class certification is lacking.

The certification question is "essentially a procedural one that does not ask whether an action is legally or factually meritorious." (*Linder v. Thrifty Oil Co.* (2000) 23 Cal.4th 429, 439–440, 97 Cal.Rptr.2d 179, 2 P.3d 27 (*Linder*).) "The community of interest requirement [for class certification] embodies three factors: (1) predominant common questions of law or fact; (2) class representatives with claims or defenses typical of the class; and (3) class representatives who can adequately represent the class." (*Richmond v. Dart Industries, Inc.* (1981) 29 Cal.3d 462, 470, 174 Cal. Rptr. 515, 629 P.2d 23.) Plaintiffs acknowledge it is their burden to establish the requisite community of interest and that "the proponent of certification must show, inter alia, that questions of law or fact common to the class predominate over the questions affecting the individual members." (*Washington Mutual, supra,* 24 Cal.4th at p. 913, 103 Cal.Rptr.2d 320, 15 P.3d 1071.)

"The ultimate question in every case of this type is whether . . . the issues which may be jointly tried, when compared with those requiring separate adjudication, are so numerous or substantial that the maintenance of a class action would be advantageous to the judicial process and to the litigants." (*Collins v. Rocha* (1972) 7 Cal.3d 232, 238, 102 Cal.Rptr. 1, 497 P.2d 225; see also *Linder, supra,* 23 Cal.4th at p. 435, 97 Cal.Rptr.2d 179, 2 P.3d 27.)

In sum, no per se or categorical bar exists to a court's finding medical monitoring claims appropriate for class treatment, so long as any individual issues the claims present are manageable. Accordingly, we shall review the certification ruling before us in light of the established standards for class certification generally.

## II. Plaintiffs Demonstrated Presence of Some Common Issues

As indicated, in granting plaintiffs' certification motion, the trial court expressly found that common questions predominate and determined that any individual issues that might arise at the time of trial are manageable. "Because trial courts are ideally situated to evaluate the efficiencies and practicalities of permitting group action, they are afforded great discretion in granting or denying certification." (*Linder, supra,* 23 Cal.4th at p. 435, 97 Cal.Rptr.2d 179, 2 P.3d 27.) Nevertheless, "we must examine the trial court's reasons for [granting] class certification." (*Id.* at p. 436, 97 Cal.Rptr.2d 179, 2 P.3d 27; see also *Washington Mutual, supra,* 24 Cal.4th at p. 914, 103 Cal.Rptr.2d 320, 15 P.3d 1071.) In particular, we must consider whether the record contains substantial evidence to support the trial court's predominance finding, as a certification ruling not supported by substantial evidence cannot stand. (*Linder, supra,* at pp. 435–436, 97 Cal.Rptr.2d 179, 2 P.3d 27; see also *Richmond v. Dart Industries, Inc., supra,* 29 Cal.3d at p. 470, 174 Cal.Rptr. 515, 629 P.2d 23.)

At the outset, the record reveals that plaintiffs' claims sound generally in negligence, entailing proof of the "well-known elements of any negligence cause of action, viz., duty, breach of duty, proximate cause and damages." (*Artiglio v. Corning Inc.* (1998) 18 Cal.4th 604, 614, 76 Cal.Rptr.2d 479, 957 P.2d 1313.) Addressing whether questions common to the class predominate over questions affecting members individually, therefore, required the trial court to consider these elements.

Whether defendants in disposing of their chemical wastes owed a duty of care to the class members, i.e., to the persons who lived for the specified period within the specified geographical area, is a question of law for the court. (*Parsons v. Crown Disposal Co.* (1997) 15 Cal.4th 456, 472, 63 Cal.Rptr.2d 291, 936 P.2d 70.) Defendants proffer no reason why a court would need to engage in individualized analysis in order to answer that question. The trial court rationally could conclude that the duty element of plaintiffs' claims will be susceptible of common proof.

Additionally, how and when defendants disposed of toxic chemicals and whether defendants' conduct was negligent are, as the Court of Appeal recognized, significant common issues of fact in this case. The parties already have presented extensive evidence (including well sampling and other hydrological data) about the pattern and degree of contamination of Redlands groundwater with various chemicals and the potential health consequences to humans of exposure to those chemicals. Defendants have conceded that common issues are present in the case because defendants' acts allegedly are the same with regard to each plaintiff. Thus, the record also contains substantial evidence supporting the conclusion that the breach of duty element of plaintiffs' claims will be susceptible of common proof.

As noted, when first recognizing the medical monitoring remedy in *Potter,* we focused on the causation and damages elements of such claims, stating that in order to recover plaintiffs must demonstrate, through reliable medical expert testimony, both that the need for future monitoring is a "reasonably certain consequence" of toxic exposure and that the monitoring sought is "reasonable." (*Potter, supra,* 6 Cal.4th at p. 1009, 25 Cal.Rptr.2d 550, 863 P.2d 795.) Defendants take the position that plaintiffs in moving for class certification have failed to demonstrate either that the causation ("reasonably certain consequence") or the damages ("reasonable" monitoring) elements of their medical monitoring claims will be susceptible of common proof.

Plaintiffs clearly are in a position to address some aspects of causation and damages on a class basis. Defendants concede, for example, that "the toxicity of the chemicals" allegedly discharged and "the seriousness of [any] disease for which the plaintiff is at risk"—both factors discussed in *Potter, supra,* 6 Cal.4th at page 1009, 25 Cal.Rptr.2d 550, 863 P.2d 795—would be susceptible of common proof. And as the Court of Appeal noted, "the amount of contaminants that entered the groundwater; and, when, where, and at what levels were contaminants pumped by the city's wells entered into the domestic water system" are significant common issues of fact in this case.

Plaintiffs contend that, on the theory of liability they intend to present, each individual's exact dosage of each discharged chemical will not be relevant. According to expert testimony already in the record, plaintiffs argue, "anyone living or working in the area of contamination for at least six months has a plausible claim for medical monitoring."

Class membership, plaintiffs stress, is restricted by definition to persons who have received a specified "medically significant" minimum dosage "for some part of a day, for greater than 50% of a year, for one or more years from 1955 to the present" within specified geographical boundaries. All who meet that definition, plaintiffs propose to prove, "will require a generalized monitoring program for the diseases caused by such exposure." On such a theory, plaintiffs argue, specific individual dosages above the specified minimum are not relevant and, therefore, "the significance and extent" of toxic exposure (*Potter, supra,* 6 Cal.4th at p. 1009, 25 Cal.Rptr.2d 550, 863 P.2d 795) will involve largely common proof.

The trial court in ruling on the certification motion apparently took plaintiffs' minimum dosage liability theory into account, stating that "proof of the [actual] dosage received [by each plaintiff] is not necessary at this time." Strictly speaking, that is correct, as in ruling on certification a court does not "ask whether [plaintiffs'] action is legally or factually meritorious." (*Linder, supra,* 23 Cal.4th at pp. 439–440, 97 Cal.Rptr.2d 179, 2 P.3d 27.) Moreover, nothing in *Potter* precludes liability premised on a theory that a defendant's negligence has necessitated increased or different monitoring for all, or nearly all, exposed individuals, as long as the need is "a reasonably certain consequence of the exposure." (*Potter, supra,* 6 Cal.4th at p. 1006, 25 Cal.Rptr.2d 550, 863 P.2d 795.) That a class of water consumers could, under particularly egregious circumstances, demonstrate that everyone who drank from a polluted municipal water system over a specified period is at significant risk for having received a dose sufficient to cause serious disease and, therefore, needs special monitoring, is not inconceivable. Thus, on an appropriate theory, even dosage issues may be susceptible of common proof.

**III. Plaintiffs Failed to Demonstrate Common Issues Predominate**

Plaintiffs' burden on moving for class certification, however, is not merely to show that some common issues exist, but, rather, to place substantial evidence in the record that common issues *predominate.* (*Washington Mutual, supra,* 24 Cal.4th at p. 913, 103 Cal.Rptr.2d 320, 15 P.3d 1071.) As we previously have explained, "this means 'each member must not be required to individually litigate numerous and substantial questions to determine his [or her] right to recover following the class judgment; and the issues which may be jointly tried, when compared with those requiring separate adjudication, must be sufficiently numerous and substantial to make the class action advantageous to the judicial process and to the litigants.'" (*Id.* at pp. 913–914, 103 Cal.Rptr.2d 320, 15 P.3d 1071, quoting *City of San Jose v. Superior Court* (1974) 12 Cal.3d 447, 460, 115 Cal.Rptr. 797, 525 P.2d 701.)

While the record on certification undoubtedly contains substantial evidence that many Redlands residents were exposed to toxic chemicals during the class period, evidence of exposure alone cannot support a finding that medical monitoring is a reasonably necessary response. (*Potter, supra,* 6 Cal.4th at p. 1009, 25 Cal.Rptr.2d 550, 863 P.2d 795.) As defendants emphasize, that all plaintiffs exposed to Redlands water received identical *dosages* of any toxic chemicals it contained is unlikely. On the one hand, duration of exposure to polluted water will vary among class members, as the class would include numerous people who lived in Redlands for a relatively short period of time during the more than 40-year class period. On the other hand, as the Court of Appeal observed, severity of exposure among class members may vary according to the amount of water they used.

Examination of the instant record reveals that plaintiffs have not provided substantial evidence that they are in a position to resolve possible dosage issues with common proof. Each class member's actual toxic dosage would remain relevant to some degree even if plaintiffs' "minimum dosage" liability theory ultimately were to prove viable. Membership in the class as plaintiffs have defined it requires, not merely exposure to water contaminated with one or more of the chemicals listed in the definition, but exposure "at levels at or in excess of the dose equivalent of the M.C.L. (Maximum Contaminant Level), or in excess of the safe dose where there is no MCL" for at least the defined minimum period of time. But plaintiffs' experts did not unqualifiedly opine that all who resided in Redlands for the defined period likely received such dosages. Dr. Dahlgren was "asked to *assume* that there [was] a clinically significant exposure to these chemicals among members of a group that is geographically defined as residing within Redlands." (Italics added.) And Dr. Teitelbaum's opinion that "risk of disease due to the toxins is spread over the whole exposed population" was qualified with the observation that "[t]he outcome of the exposure . . . is determined by many factors including the dose, and the genetic makeup of the target individual."

Moreover, regardless of how a particular medical monitoring class might be defined, a plaintiff must demonstrate that "the need for future monitoring is a reasonably certain consequence of [the] toxic exposure" (*Potter, supra,* 6 Cal.4th at p. 1009, 25 Cal.Rptr.2d 550, 863 P.2d 795), i.e., that the plaintiff faces a "significant but not necessarily likely risk of serious disease" (*id.* at pp. 1008–1009, 25 Cal.Rptr.2d 550, 863 P.2d 795). For the following reasons, we conclude plaintiffs have not placed in the record sufficient evidence to warrant the trial court's concluding that they are likely to be able to make that demonstration with common proof.

Taken as a whole, the medical expert testimony plaintiffs presented in support of their motion for class certification is too qualified, tentative and conclusionary to constitute substantial evidence that plaintiffs, by adopting a liability theory that makes actual dosages and variations in individual response irrelevant, will be able to prove causation and damages by common evidence. As the record stands, therefore, the causation and damages issues raised by plaintiffs' claims must be counted among those that would be litigated individually, even if the matter were to proceed on a class basis. Especially when considered in light of the trial court's finding that the class consists of an estimated 50,000 to 100,000 people, that conclusion fatally undermines the trial court's predominance calculation.

In light of the foregoing, we conclude that the trial court's predominance finding is not supported by the record. The questions respecting each individual class member's right to recover that would remain following any class judgment appear so numerous and substantial as to render any efficiencies attainable through joint trial of common issues insufficient, as a matter of law, to make a class action certified on such a basis advantageous to the judicial process and the litigants.

### IV. Conclusion

Although the Court of Appeal erred to the extent it stated or implied that no action in which plaintiffs seek medical monitoring as a remedy may ever appropriately be certified for class treatment, we agree with the court that the trial court abused its discretion in granting the instant certification motion.

---

## QUESTIONS AND DISCUSSION

**1.** As the *Lockheed Martin* court explained, the plaintiffs did not need to prove present or future individual injury to be entitled to the medical monitoring remedy under California law, but rather need only have proven medical monitoring is reasonably necessary as a result of exposure to the toxic chemicals. Moreover, the plaintiffs argued that once exposure to a threshold level of the chemicals is proven, all such exposed plaintiffs are entitled to the same medical monitoring. So in what way was proof of an exact individual amount or exposure or particular risk necessary for each plaintiff? The court noted the testimony of one of the plaintiffs' experts, that "[t]he outcome of the exposure . . . is determined by many factors including the dose, and the genetic makeup of the target individual," but the "outcome of exposure" isn't the reference point for the medical monitoring remedy. What is it, then, that the court believed would have to be litigated individually in connection with the causation and damages issues?

**2.** Assuming the plaintiffs could individually establish the basis for medical monitoring, what public policies would you have argued would have been served by allowing certification of the class in *Lockheed Martin*? Would class treatment be more likely to result in a uniform medical monitoring program for the plaintiffs? Would class treatment provide lower transactions costs not only for the plaintiffs, but for the defendants? Would class treatment have provided a better baseline of health data for purposes of public health agencies? Would class treatment increase the deterrent effects of the medical monitoring remedy? If the answer is yes to any or all of these, are these good reasons to lean in favor of class treatment, or are there countervailing considerations that need to be taken into account? Class treatment also can be difficult to establish in property damage claims, presenting similar questions. *See* Smith v. ConocoPhillips Pipe Line Co., 801 F.3d 921 (8th Cir. 2015) (allegations of fear of contamination did not support certification); Bell v. Cheswick Generating Station, 2015 WL 401443 (W.D. Pa. 2015) (allegation of "similar" property damages insufficient for certification).

**3.** The medical monitoring remedy is a significant departure from the well-established principle of tort law that an individual must manifest some physical injury or illness attributable to the negligent acts of another in order to recover. The mere threat of a harm, in other words, usually is not enough. Yet over twenty state and federal courts have recognized the medical monitoring cause of action. The tide may have turned against the remedy, however, after the United States Supreme Court rejected it as a form of relief under the Federal Employers' Liability Act in Metro-North Commuter R.R. v. Buckley, 521 U.S. 424 (1997). While interpreting a federal statutory cause of action against the government, the policy rationale the Court used—that the medical monitoring remedy would threaten a flood of litigation based on unpredictable liability—has been adopted by a number of state and federal courts in the common law toxic tort context to reject the cause of action. *See, e.g.*, Duncan v. Northwest Airlines, Inc., 203 F.R.D. 601 (W.D. Wash. 2001); Wood v. Wyeth-Ayerst Labs, 82 S.W.3d 849 (Ky. 2002); Hinton v. Monsanto Co., 813 So.2d 827 (Ala. 2001). Before *Lockheed Martin*, moreover, there had been considerable differences among the courts on the question of the appropriateness of class treatment for the medical monitoring action, and *Lockheed Martin* may suggest that even in states that recognize the action, class treatment will be difficult to obtain. For a thorough discussion of these issues and a tally of the cases decided through 2003, see Daniel L. Martens and Ernest J. Getto, *Medical Monitoring and Class Actions*, NATURAL RESOURCES & ENV'T, Spring 2003, at 225.

**4.** The late Professor Jamie Grodsky, in a sweeping survey of the medical monitoring remedy, observed the paradox that results when courts limit medical monitoring remedies to cases where the plaintiff has manifested physical injuries or illnesses—the very point of medical monitoring is to detect the onset of such physical impairments at the earliest possible stage, not after they have already required medical *treatment*. She also argued that the increasing knowledge of genomics and genomic technology will convert the sharp risk-injury bifurcation that has plagued the medical monitoring remedy into more of a continuum of understanding about how chemical exposure leads eventually to manifested illness or injury. In her view, as we come to understand more about how exposure causes genetic alterations, and how genetic alterations in turn lead to what the common law traditionally recognizes as injury, evidence of genetic "injury" ought to be considered sufficient to satisfy even the demands of traditional tort law's physical injury test. *See* Jamie Grodsky, *Genomics and Toxic Torts: Dismantling the Risk-*

*Injury Divide*, 59 STANFORD LAW REV. 1671 (2007). Yet would this approach have led the *Lockheed Martin* court to have favored class certification, or to pull back from it even more than they did?

**5.** What are the toxic tort claims of the future? Will nanotechnology lead to mass personal injury claims? How about global climate change? How well does the free market environmentalism thesis discussed above in Part A of this section support relying on toxic tort claims to manage problems of this nature?

---

## PROBLEM EXERCISE

Do you recall Energena, your long-time energy generation client from the Problems in Chapter 10 that is planning a move into renewable energy sources such as wind generation? It has its eyes on an undeveloped 1500-acre tract owned by AmmoCorp. AmmoCorp has used the site for ammunitions production and testing for the last 75 years. Although AmmoCorp has few records of company operations on the site prior to 1970, it is aware that it and other munitions manufacturers that operated production and manufacturing sites during World War II and the Korean War engaged in significant on-site waste disposals and have faced significant remediation liabilities under CERCLA and related state remediation laws. No one in AmmoCorp knows the full site history, including how prior owners may have used the site. It is known that the site was used for a variety of industrial and agricultural uses.

Energena is concerned that if it acquires the site and begins development, it will uncover waste disposal areas requiring remediation. On the other hand, Energena is eager to acquire the site to begin its first wind farm facility—waiting for AmmoCorp to investigate and remediate the site would add costly delays to the project.

Energena is also concerned that if it does engage in remediation, it will open the door to common law liabilities from adjacent landowners, including several communities, might have for property damages and personal injuries. Some chemicals associated with munitions are known to present significant groundwater contamination problems when not disposed of properly, and several are highly toxic to humans and other species.

Energena wants to know what measures it can take to ensure that remediation, which, as explored in Chapter 5, will undoubtedly be conducted under government oversight and subject to public disclosure to testing results, does not amplify the potential exposure to common law liabilities for property damages and personal injuries. Indeed, how does anyone engaged in government supervised or mandated remediation of contaminated property avoid having the remediation project supply the evidence and template for plaintiffs in common law property damage and personal injury cases? In particular:

- How should negotiations with government agencies administering the remediation program be structured?
- How should the flow of information between your client and the government be controlled to minimize the effect of supplying evidence for common law liability plaintiffs?
- How should the consultants hired to conduct the remediation be prepared in terms of responding to press and attorney contacts, communicating government and other third party representatives, and maintaining the security of information?
- How should remediation investigations on offsite properties be structured?
- Should remediation cleanup levels be enhanced to reduce common law liability risks?

Now consider how you would address these and other concerns if you were representing the government agency administering the remediation program, and then if you were representing members of a residential community that claim their groundwater is contaminated with chemicals of the sort associated with munitions. For insights see Michael Daneker, *When Two Worlds Collide: Interactions between Superfund and Medical Monitoring*, NATURAL RESOURCES & ENV'T, Spring 2003, at 232.

---

## D. FRAUD CLAIMS LITIGATION

Section 525 of the *Second Restatement of Torts* defines the standard for establishing fraudulent misrepresentation as follows:

> One who fraudulently makes a misrepresentation of fact, opinion, intention or law for the purpose of inducing another to act or to refrain from action in reliance upon it, is subject to liability to the other in deceit for pecuniary loss caused to him by his justifiable reliance upon the misrepresentation

This common law theory of liability has proven fertile ground for common law actions when the purchaser of property finds that conditions were not as expected and it is holding the bill for extensive remediation or economic losses from inability to use the property as planned. As the following case (also discussed for different purposes in Chapter 13) shows, however, recovering under a fraud theory of liability in such cases is not as easy as it might appear on the surface.

## Keywell Corp. v. Weinstein

United States Court of Appeals for the Second Circuit, 1994.
33 F.3d 159.

■ JACOBS, CIRCUIT JUDGE:

Keywell Corporation ("Keywell") has incurred costs for environmental cleanup at an industrial facility that it purchased in 1987 from Vac Air Alloys Corporation ("Vac Air"). Defendants-Appellees Daniel C. Weinstein ("Weinstein") and Anthony Boscarino ("Boscarino") were shareholders, officers and directors of Vac Air prior to the purchase and at the time of the transaction, and were signatories to the Purchase Agreement. Keywell has brought suit against Weinstein and Boscarino, (i) alleging that they induced Keywell to buy the property by making misrepresentations bearing upon the environmental risks at the premises, and (ii) alleging that, as owners and operators of Vac Air, they are strictly liable to Keywell for their equitable share of response costs pursuant to §§ 107(a) and 113(f) of the Comprehensive Environmental Response, Compensation, and Liability Act ("CERCLA"). 42 U.S.C. §§ 9607(a) and 9613(f). Following the parties' submission of cross-motions for summary judgment, the district court dismissed Keywell's claims, finding as a matter of law that Keywell could not have reasonably relied on the allegedly fraudulent misrepresentations, and that Keywell had contractually released its right to sue defendants under CERCLA.

BACKGROUND

The facts, drawing all justifiable inferences in favor of the non-movant Keywell, are as follows. Weinstein founded Vac Air in 1966 and, until the time Keywell purchased certain Vac Air assets in December 1987, was a principal shareholder, president, chief executive officer, and member of the board of directors of the company. Boscarino joined Vac Air in 1971 as an assistant to the secretary/treasurer, and by 1978 he had become a stockholder, director, and vice-president of the company. Both Weinstein and Boscarino took an active part in conducting the business of Vac Air, which included the operation of a metals recycling plant located in Frewsburg, New York (the "Frewsburg plant").

From the time Vac Air was founded in 1966 until Keywell's acquisition of assets in December 1987, the Frewsburg plant recycled scrap metal—a process that entailed the use of trichloroethylene ("TCE"), a chemical now categorized as a hazardous substance by the Environmental Protection Agency (the "EPA"). Two by-products of the recycling process are TCE sludge and TCE oil. During the 1970s, workers at the Frewsburg plant placed TCE sludge in ponds or pits on the property. In addition, they sometimes spread the sludge directly on the ground, where it would dry into a more manageable consistency that could then be moved off site. During the same period, TCE oil was occasionally dispersed on the plant's roads to act as a dust-suppressant. Both Weinstein and Boscarino were aware of at least some of these practices, which ceased in the late 1970s after Vac Air hired a firm to dispose of TCE waste off site.

In 1985, during an unrelated excavation on the property, workers unearthed decomposed remnants of storage drums that had apparently once been filled with a TCE-infused waste product and buried. Weinstein and Boscarino were aware of this discovery, and, upon the advice of counsel, sent a fragment of one of the drums to an independent laboratory for a chemical analysis. That analysis suggested that the buried materials did not pose an environmental problem for Vac Air.

Two years later, on November 10, 1987, Keywell entered into an agreement with Vac Air to purchase certain assets, including the Frewsburg plant (the "Purchase Agreement"). Following execution of the Purchase Agreement (but before the closing on December 16, 1987), Keywell retained the environmental consulting firm of Conestoga-Rovers and Associates ("CRA") to conduct a due diligence environmental audit of the Frewsburg plant. As part of the audit, CRA inspected the site and interviewed Vac Air employees, including Boscarino. The trial testimony of CRA representative Alan Van Norman suggests that Boscarino was asked about waste disposal, and responded that there had been no on-site dumping of hazardous materials.

Upon completion of its audit, CRA issued a report to Keywell. CRA warned that, simply by virtue of the metal recycling that took place there, the Frewsburg plant might be identified by the EPA as a possible source of environmental contamination. CRA's report also contained the following relevant findings and warnings. TCE was present in drainage water samples. Although the nature of past off site disposal of TCE sludge was undetermined, Vac Air personnel had assured CRA that no on-site disposal of waste materials had been made. The proximity of the Frewsburg plant to the municipal water supply justified concern about TCE contamination in the groundwater, for while the possibility of contamination was low, the potential cost could be high. CRA therefore recommended that Keywell conduct additional tests of the groundwater.

Keywell decided not to conduct the further testing that CRA recommended and proceeded to close the sale with Vac Air. The Purchase Agreement provided that "[t]he representations and warranties of [Vac Air] and the Management Stockholders [including Weinstein and Boscarino] herein contained shall be true at and as of the Closing Date, shall be made again at and as of the Closing Date, and shall be true as so made again. . . ." Purchase Agreement ¶ 6.1. In the Purchase Agreement, Vac Air and its management made the following representation bearing upon environmental exposures:

> Environmental Matters. There has been no storage, disposal or treatment of solid wastes or hazardous wastes by [Vac Air] at any of the leased or owned property included in the Assets [including the Frewsburg plant] in violation of any applicable law, ordinance, rule, regulation, order, judgment, decree or permit or which would require

remedial action under any applicable law, ordinance, rule, regulation, order, judgment, decree or permit. There has been no material spill, discharge, leak, emission, injection, escape, dumping or release of any kind onto the properties to be purchased under this Agreement, or into the environment surrounding such properties, of any toxic or hazardous substances as defined under any local, state, Federal or foreign regulations, laws or statutes, other than those releases permissible under such regulations, laws or statutes or allowable under applicable permits.

Purchase Agreement ¶ 2.14.

In June 1990, Keywell learned that a grand jury was investigating the possibility that Vac Air had engaged in on-site disposal of hazardous waste at the Frewsburg plant. After further tests revealed the presence of TCE in the municipal water supply, Keywell entered into an agreement with the New York State Department of Environmental Conservation to institute a comprehensive clean-up plan. Weinstein terminated his employment with Keywell on December 28, 1990. Boscarino was fired by Keywell on March 11, 1991.

On March 12, 1991, Keywell filed the present lawsuit in the United States District Court for the District of Maryland, seeking to hold Weinstein and Boscarino strictly liable for clean-up costs under CERCLA, 42 U.S.C. §§ 9607(a)(2), 9613(f), and alleging that their fraudulent misrepresentations induced Keywell to purchase the Frewsburg plant. Keywell sought money damages on its fraud claim rather than recission of the Purchase Agreement. Eventually the case was transferred to the Western District of New York, where the parties cross-moved for summary judgment.

In a decision issued on March 17, 1993, the district court . . . granted summary judgment against Keywell on its state-law fraud claims, finding that Keywell could not have reasonably relied on the alleged fraudulent misrepresentations.

A. Fraud

Keywell claims that the defendants fraudulently misrepresented that there had been no on-site disposal of hazardous substances at the Frewsburg plant, and that waste materials generated by the plant had been disposed of properly. Keywell further states that these misrepresentations induced it to purchase the Frewsburg Plant at a price that did not reflect the environmental risks known to the defendants.

While the parties chose Maryland law to govern their contract, they do not dispute that questions concerning the validity of the contract should be determined by the law of the jurisdiction in which it was made. See Recovery Consultants, Inc. v. Shih-Hsieh, 141 A.D.2d 272, 534 N.Y.S.2d 374, 375 (1988). We agree that New York law applies. In New York, a plaintiff claiming fraudulent misrepresentation must prove that (1) defendant made a material false representation, (2) defendant intended to defraud plaintiff thereby, (3) plaintiff reasonably relied on the representation, and (4) plaintiff suffered damage as a result of such reliance. The district court granted summary judgment in favor of defendants because it found—as a matter of law—that any reliance by Keywell on the defendants' representations regarding TCE disposal would have been unreasonable. Viewing the evidence in the light most favorable to Keywell, as we must in reviewing this grant of summary judgment, we conclude that a reasonable jury could find that Keywell reasonably relied on the defendants' statements.

Keywell claims that it relied on two separate representations when it agreed to purchase the Frewsburg plant. First, Keywell asserts that Boscarino told the CRA investigators that there had been no on-site burial of hazardous waste. Second, Keywell points to the environmental representations made in the Purchase Agreement (which both Weinstein and Boscarino signed) to the effect that no hazardous material had been released or disposed of on the premises of the Frewsburg plant. The district court determined that Keywell could not have reasonably relied on these representations because CRA's environmental audit had put Keywell on notice that the representations may have been false. The court noted that CRA's report alerted Keywell to the possibility of groundwater contamination, the extent of which could only be determined through additional testing, and that Keywell decided not to conduct this recommended testing. The district court also found that any reliance was unreasonable because Keywell was experienced in business matters and had access to files containing information about the discovery of the buried TCE-tainted material.

When a party is aware of circumstances that indicate certain representations may be false, that party cannot reasonably rely on those representations, but must make additional inquiry to determine their accuracy:

> [if plaintiff] has the means of knowing, by the exercise of ordinary intelligence, the truth, or the real quality of the subject of the representation, he must make use of those means, or he will not be heard to complain that he was induced to enter into the transaction by misrepresentations.

Mallis v. Bankers Trust Co., 615 F.2d 68, 80–81 (2d Cir. 1980) (applying New York law). "Decisions holding that reliance on misrepresentations was not justified are generally cases in which plaintiff was placed on guard or practically faced with the facts." Id. at 81; see Ittleson v. Lombardi, 193 A.D.2d 374, 596 N.Y.S.2d 817, 819 (1993). Moreover, "[w]here sophisticated businessmen engaged in major transactions enjoy access to critical information but fail to take advantage of that access, New York courts are particularly disinclined to entertain claims of justifiable reliance." Grumman Allied Industries v. Rohr Industries, Inc., 748 F.2d 729, 737 (2d Cir. 1984).

Obviously, Keywell was aware of CRA's environmental report warning of TCE contamination and advising further testing to determine the actual extent of the problem. However, we do not agree that Keywell was thereby "placed on guard or practically faced with the facts" so that Keywell's reliance on defendants' representations was unreasonable as a matter of law. According to deposition testimony by Keywell's environmental consultants, the contamination revealed in the report was entirely consistent with incidental spillage of solvents that could be expected at any metals recycling plant, and did not contradict the defendants' representations that there had been no dumping or other release of hazardous substances on the Frewsburg property. The environmental audit contained a statement that "[p]lant personnel have informed CRA that on-site disposal of waste materials was not practiced." The audit did not indicate that this assurance was in any way at odds with the results of its investigation. In fact, the defendants' representations that there had been no on-site disposal may have influenced Keywell's decision to reject CRA's recommendation for further testing. A reasonable jury could conclude that Keywell, having conducted environmental due diligence and received a report that was consistent with the defendants' representations, had no obligation to investigate further, and that Keywell would have authorized further testing by CRA at any spot identified by defendants as a place where buried waste had been found. Keywell has raised genuine questions of fact as to whether CRA's environmental findings were consistent with the defendants' representations, and whether Keywell should have undertaken additional testing given the representations made to CRA during its investigation and the defendants' willingness to make these express representations in the Purchase Agreement.

The district court provided an alternative ground for dismissal based on its finding that Keywell, for various reasons, was not entitled to rescind its contract with the defendants. Keywell does not contest this part of the district court's ruling. However, Keywell's fraud claim cannot be dismissed simply because rescission is not an available remedy. In Count I of its complaint, which alleges common law fraud, Keywell seeks money damages. A defrauded party is permitted to affirm a contract and seek relief in damages. See, e.g., Clearview Concrete Products Corp. v. S. Charles Gherardi, Inc., 88 A.D.2d 461, 453 N.Y.S.2d 750, 754 (1982) ("Upon discovering fraud, a purchaser may tender return of the property and seek rescission or he may retain the property and seek recovery of damages deriving from the fraud."). Difficult as it may be, Keywell may be able to show, without inviting speculation, that some definable portion of its environmental costs are attributable to what defendants allegedly misrepresented, rather than to what Keywell did know. However, Keywell's election to affirm the contract rather than seek rescission impacts Keywell's rights to avoid contractual limitations on damages for breach of representations and warranties. These limitations have an important bearing on Keywell's CERCLA claims.

[The court's discussion of the CERCLA claims is reproduced in the edited version of the case appearing in Chapter 13 with the materials on drafting contracts].

---

## QUESTIONS AND DISCUSSION

**1.** Does it strike you as ironic that the diligence Keywell exercised by hiring consultants to investigate site conditions could undermine Keywell's fraud claim against Vac Air's officers? The court observes that it may be difficult for Keywell to show that "some definable portion of its environmental costs are attributable to what defendants allegedly misrepresented, rather than to what Keywell did know" as a result of the site investigation. How could Keywell have protected against that effect—i.e., that the more it knew from the site investigation, the less any misrepresentations by the seller could form the basis of a fraud claim? How could a seller in Vac Air's position avoid having any of its employees statements used against it (or the employees) as the basis of a fraud claim?

**2.** The point of taking into account the information a buyer has obtained through a site investigation is to determine whether the buyer has in fact and justifiably relied on the seller's allegedly false representations. Hence, if the buyer agrees in the contract that it has relied exclusively on the site investigation, no claim in fraud will arise based on alleged false statements by the seller. *See* M & M Realty Co. v. Eberton Terminal Corp., 977 F. Supp. 683, 689–90 (M.D. Pa. 1997). On the other hand, if the seller has conducted a site investigation and, relying exclusively on the investigation, represents that the property is not contaminated, no fraud would be committed if in fact the property was contaminated. *See* Adams v. NVR Homes, Inc., 135 F. Supp. 2d 675, 692 (D. Md. 2001).

---

# E. ECOLOGICAL INJURY LITIGATION

All of the common law cases studied thus far in this section involve claims that *pollution* of some kind caused damage to the value of property or exposures harmful to human health. But what of degradation of natural resources through conversion to some other form of land use, such as agriculture or a resort development—i.e., environmental harms that do not result from the release of pollutants? Does the common law have anything to say about injuries flowing from that form of environmental harm?

## J.B. Ruhl, *Ecosystem Services and the Common Law of "The Fragile Land System"*

20 NATURAL RESOURCES & ENVIRONMENT 3 (Fall 2005).

[There is almost universal support for the proposition that] the source, the very backbone of the wave of federal pollution control laws the federal government enacted in the 1970s, was the common law of nuisance. And many observers also agree that there has been a profound shift of emphasis in environmental policy from controlling smokestacks and discharge pipes to managing ecosystemwide phenomena such as habitat loss, invasive species, and nutrient-laden runoff—what today goes under the umbrella term of ecosystem management.

What is missing from this more recent focus on ecosystems and their sensitivity to human insult, however, is any notion that legislative initiatives might find some guidance in the framework of the common law. How is it that the common law of nuisance is regarded as the genesis of pollution control law, but for the law of ecosystem management it is as if the common law never happened? In fact, the more frequent prognosis is worse than that—it suggests that the common law simply *cannot* be a factor in shaping the law of ecosystem management.

For example, in *Lucas v. South Carolina Coastal Commission*, 505 U.S. 1003 (1992), Justice Scalia announced the majority's ruling that where a new regulation denies all economically beneficial or productive use of land—in that case a blanket prohibition of development in coastal dune areas—it must be treated as a *per se* taking of property for which just compensation is due under the Fifth Amendment. Justice Scalia's caveat was that just compensation would not be due if the regulation does no more than simply "duplicate the result that could have been achieved in the courts—by adjacent landowners (or other uniquely affected persons) under the State's law of private nuisance, or by the State under its complementary power to abate nuisances that affect the public generally." *Id.* at 1029. In his concurring opinion, Justice Kennedy expressed concern with the idea that state regulation could go no further than duplicating the common law of nuisance without exposing itself to the now infamous "categorical taking" problem, for as he put it, "[c]oastal property may present such unique concerns for a fragile land system that the State can go further in regulating its development and use than the common law of nuisance *might otherwise permit*." *Id.* at 1035 (emphasis added). In other words, Justice Kennedy took it as a given, as Justice Scalia and the majority also clearly did, that the common law could not reach the "fragile land system." Indeed, although leaving the final say to state courts, Justice Scalia surmised that "it seems unlikely that common-law principles would have prevented erection of any habitable or productive improvements on petitioner's land." *Id.* at 1031. But why not?

This article explores that question through a posited evolution of the common law that is both radical and mundane. It is radical in the sense that it challenges the deeply rooted idea that the common law has no place in the law and policy of ecosystem management. It is mundane in the sense that the common law doctrine proposed to fill the gap is quite ordinary—the law of nuisance. At bottom, therefore, it is about economic injury, not the environment at large. It is not a charter for courts to police the nation's biodiversity, or to restore what we believe to be some past state of nature, or to devise and enforce broad personal rights in environmental quality. Indeed, being based on the law of nuisance, it is grounded in terms and concepts so familiar in the common law as to appear quite plain vanilla.

*The False Start of Ecosystem Management Legislation*

By contrast [to pollution control laws], the public law agenda for ecosystem management has no common law roots. In 1993, when Vice President Al Gore's National Performance Review called for federal agencies to support a "proactive approach to ensuring a sustainable economy and a sustainable environment through ecosystem management," there was absolutely no foundation from which to begin, common law or otherwise. The case could have been made that the initiative would be an extension of the Endangered Species Act (ESA), which, after all, proclaims that it is intended to "provide a means whereby the ecosystems upon which endangered species and threatened species depend may be conserved." 16 U.S.C. § 1531(b) (2004). But the ESA hardly enjoys broad-based legitimacy—it remains one of the most controversial of environmental laws—and in fact its provisions make for a rather clumsy ecosystem management framework. *See* J.B. Ruhl, *Ecosystem Management, the Endangered Species Act, and the Seven Degrees of Relevance*, 14 NAT. RESOURCES & ENV'T 156 (2000). Ecosystem management, in other words, was left to building itself from the ground up.

At about the same time, our knowledge of ecosystem dynamics and the fragility of some natural resource systems began growing by leaps and bounds, making the case for an ecosystem management initiative quite compelling. The landmark contributions in the field appeared in the mid-1990s, defining the basis and framework for ecosystem-scale management of natural resources. *See* Norman L. Christensen et al., *The Report for the Ecological Society of America Committee on the Scientific Basis for Ecosystem Management,* 6 ECOLOGICAL APPLICATIONS 665 (1996); R. Edward Grumbine, *What Is Ecosystem Management?*, 8 CONSERVATION BIOLOGY 27 (1994). For my purposes, however, the most important development was the emergence of a branch of ecosystem management focused on the economic value humans derive not from natural resource commodities such as timber, or from recreational uses, but from ecosystem functions such as flood control, pollination, thermal regulation, and storm surge mitigation—what ecologists today call ecosystem services. *See* NATURE'S SERVICES: SOCIETAL DEPENDENCE ON NATURAL ECOSYSTEMS (Gretchen Daily ed., 1997). Through enhanced understanding of ecosystem service values associated with natural resources, the case for ecosystem management took on a previously unnoticed economic dimension. And, given the relation between intact ecosystems and the delivery of these economically important services—in essence, the ecosystem resources are the natural capital necessary for production of the services—it seemed to me and a few other lawyers at the time that the law ought to pay attention to whether ecosystems are being properly managed to enhance overall social wealth. *See* James Salzman, *Valuing Ecosystem Services*, 24 ECOLOGY L. Q. 887 (1997); J.B. Ruhl, *Valuing Nature's Services—The Future of Environmental Law?*, 13 NAT. RESOURCES & ENV'T 359 (1998).

Yet public legislation, so effective at combating pollution of air, water, and land, is faltering at the prospect of forming a coherent ecosystem management regime, much less one with any focus on ecosystem service values. In the ten plus years since Vice President Gore began the ecosystem management initiative, not much concrete has happened. Federal agencies, particularly the public land management agencies, scrambled around for several years pronouncing their commitment to the cause, thereby striking fear into the hearts of western land interests. *See* Rebecca W. Thompson, *"Ecosystem Management"—Great Idea, but What Is It, Will It Work, and Who Will Pay for It?*, NAT. RESOURCES & ENV'T, Winter 1995, at 42. Congress managed no more than to introduce a bill, the Ecosystem Management Act of 1995, which did not even define ecosystem management! *See* S. 2189, 104th Cong., 1st Sess. (1995) (requiring an appointed commission to study the question of how to define ecosystem management). Indeed, in a law school casebook, I had to conclude that, at best, "the ESA and a collection of other laws contain elements and programs that can explicitly or impliedly be advanced toward developing ecosystem-level policies designed to conserve biodiversity." JOHN NAGLE & J.B. RUHL, THE LAW OF BIODIVERSITY AND ECOSYSTEM MANAGEMENT 297–98 (2002). For example, EPA has pronounced its adoption of a "watershed approach," but by this the agency means a concerted effort to use watershed-based ecosystem management principles to guide implementation of a broad array of authorities. *See* Memorandum from G. Tracy Meehan, III, Assistant Administrator to Office Directors, Re: Committing EPA's Water Programs to Advancing the Watershed Approach (Dec. 3, 2002). EPA has no true watershed-based statute to administer. In short, ecosystem management law is a cobbled-together body of law, if it can even be called that much.

Ecosystem management finds itself in this fragmented and stalled condition because, unlike the antipollution legislation, it had no common law foundation on which to build its structure and legitimacy. Perhaps out of arrogance, or ignorance, or the failure fully to appreciate the importance of the common law to antipollution legislation, ecosystem management legislation tried to leapfrog its common law formative stage, and it has gained little traction as a result. The question is whether the common law can overcome its reputation as having little meaningful to add to the field and backfill a foundation for the public law of ecosystem management. There is a basis for hope in this regard.

*The Common Law of Ecosystem Services*

Many commentators before me have advanced the case that the common law is profoundly adaptive. *See* J.B. Ruhl, *Complexity Theory as a Paradigm for the Dynamical Law-and-Society System*, 45 DUKE L.J. 849, 916–20 (1996). We know industrialization has harmed our ecosystems, that federal legislation does not hold all the answers, and that the ecological frontier, if anything, is vanishing. And we know much more today than we did thirty years ago about ecosystem services. As Justice Scalia acknowledged in *Lucas*, "changed circumstances *or new knowledge* may make what was previously permissible [under common law] no longer so." 505 U.S. at 1031 (emphasis added). Hence, there is no reason why the common law cannot make an adaptive move to fill some of the gap in ecosystem management which, as discussed in the previous section, federal legislation has left open and is not likely to fill without help.

So, what would be the organizing principles for the evolution of a common law doctrine of ecosystem management? It is too easy to propose that the common law simply reverse direction and place a "green thumb on the scales of justice" in favor of protecting ecosystems in general. Nor will it be as easy as simply pointing out the objectives of ecosystem management and inviting the common law to have at it. There has to be a concrete theme to motivate the interest and action of private litigants and the courts, and that theme must have dimensions fitting within the basic contours of common law doctrine and institutions. This includes articulating a coherent statement of rights and liabilities that are susceptible to analysis through commonly understood and applied principles of proof of breach, injury, and causation, as well as a remedial system that provides efficient and equitable outcomes. In other words, the approach has to be legally practical.

Unfortunately, the discipline of ecosystem management is for the most part brimming with themes that are decidedly impractical for these purposes. Its organizing principles include conserving biodiversity, restoring naturalness, providing safe harbor for native species, and the implementation technique of adaptive management. Impressive sounding as these terms may be, they are square pegs to the common law's round holes.

By contrast, the ecosystem services branch of ecosystem management holds great promise for the common law. Most of ecosystem management is devoted to keeping ecosystem functions healthy for the sake of ecosystems, whereas the study of ecosystem services is devoted to articulating which ecosystem functions provide service values to humans that would be costly, but clearly necessary or desirable, to replace were they to degrade in quantity or quality. Moreover, because ecosystem services are the product of ecosystem functions, and ecosystem functions are the product of ecosystem structure, it follows as a matter of economic theory that the relevant ecosystem structure is no less than the "natural capital" necessary for providing economically valuable services to humans. And this new focus in ecology is producing a rapidly mounting body of research attaching real numbers to ecosystem service values at local and regional scales.

Recently, for example, researchers studying pollination services in Costa Rica demonstrated that the conversion of land from forest to grazing uses reduces the local populations of wild pollinator species enough to diminish productivity of nearby coffee plantations by more than 20 percent, resulting in a loss of $64,000 annually for a typical plantation. *See* T.H. Ricketts, *Tropical Forest Fragments Enhance Pollinator Activity in Nearby Coffee Crops*, 18 CONSERVATION BIOLOGY 1262 (2003). On a larger scale, more than twenty years ago law professor Oliver Houck demonstrated that the loss of coastal wetlands in Louisiana was costing the state billions of dollars in lost service values. *See* Oliver Houck, *Land Loss in Coastal Louisiana: Causes, Consequences, and Remedies*, 58 TULANE L. REV. 3 (1983). The idea took some time to catch on, but Louisiana recently embarked on an "Americas Wetland" campaign to call attention to its vanishing coastal wetlands, including a major push to gain federal assistance by noting the economic consequences of having its "working coastline" of oil rigs, ports, fishing villages, and New Orleans casinos flooded by the combination of rising sea levels and falling coastline levels. *See America's Wetland Campaign*, www.americaswetland.com. Ecosystem services are not about just birds and bees—they are about money, and lots of it.

Armed with that core set of principles, it is remarkable how straightforward an exercise it is to outline a set of common law rights and liabilities that put ecosystem services into play as the essential fabric of a new stage in the development of environmental common law. Every law student learns the black letter doctrine of nuisance: one commits a nuisance when his or her use of land unreasonably interferes with another person's reasonable use and enjoyment of his or her interest in land. Lawyers through the ages have had no problem agreeing that odors from a pigsty, or fumes from a copper smelting plant, or chemical pollution of a lake or stream are within the ballpark of nuisance so defined. Why should matters be any different when one person's use of land severs the flow of economically valuable ecosystem services to another person's use of land?

Nuisance law is quite a thicket on the question of what is unreasonable, but that is both the beauty and the frustration of the common law. It is made for this kind of balancing inquiry, which Justice

Scalia described as an "analysis of, among other things, the degree of harm to public lands and resources, or adjacent private property, posed by the [landowner's] proposed activities, the social value of the [landowner's] activities and their suitability to the locality in question, and the relative ease with which the alleged harm can be avoided through measures taken by the [landowner] and the government (or adjacent landowners) alike." 505 U.S. at 1031 (citations omitted).

To be sure, it is not expected that every loss of natural capital should be or would be branded unreasonable under this test. Some natural capital is more critical than most, in that its degradation or destruction leads to significant economic injury on other lands. But given that we increasingly know where natural capital is located, where the ecosystem services it produces flow, and the value of those services at benefited properties, there is no reason why nuisance law in both its public and private stripes could not sort through questions about whether the destruction of natural capital in discrete cases is reasonable or not.

Not far from where I live and teach in Florida, for example, one can see quite palpable evidence of the importance of coastal dunes to the mitigation of hurricane storm surge damage at inland locations. There is a staggering difference in outcome between inland areas shielded by intact dunes and those inland of coastal development that did not retain dunes. On a far more devastating scale, surely the media coverage of Katrina, which repeatedly made the point that damage in New Orleans would have been mitigated had the coastal wetlands not been so severely degraded, has focused the nation's mind on the economic importance of ecosystem services. Under Justice Scalia's version of the nuisance balancing test, the harm to the public resources and private property resulting from the impaired dune and wetland systems unquestionably was severe, likely far outweighing the social utility of development that destroyed the resources, and the owners of prior intact dune and wetland areas were in the best position to avoid the harm. Were those resources thus critical natural capital, the destruction of which was unreasonable in relation to the expectations of inland property owners whose homes and businesses are now in splinters?

It is my belief that the common law is equipped to answer that question and others like it. The fact that it has not until now attempted to do so does not mean that it cannot, or will not have the opportunity, or simply is against all notion of it. The only missing ingredient until now has been the storehouse of knowledge ecologists and economists are building about the value of ecosystem services. This is precisely the kind of new knowledge Justice Scalia confirmed in *Lucas* can transform the common law and "make what was previously permissible no longer so." 505 U.S. at 1031. As sovereigns and landowners become aware of this new knowledge and begin to appreciate the cost imposed to them when others sever the flow of ecosystem services to their lands, they *will* sue in public and private nuisance actions. Indeed, such a claim recently was initiated with respect to the losses suffered in Katrina, alleging that those responsible for the disruption of wetland processes are also responsible for the economic losses that followed. *See* Barasich v. Columbia Gulf Transmission Co., Civ. A. No. 05–4161 (E.D. La. Complaint filed Sept. 13, 2005). And when lawyers and experts use this new knowledge to demonstrate to courts the cause of the injury and the value of the services lost, the courts *will* award damages, injunctions, and other relief. And it will all seem quite mundane, because there will be nothing about it that is out of the ordinary for the common law.

---

## QUESTIONS AND DISCUSSION

**1.** Going beyond the suggestion that the common law has been overlooked in the development of ecosystem management law is the argument that common law institutions have *deliberately* pursued anti-environmental policies to facilitate other interests such as the protection of property rights and promoting economic uses of land. Evidence for this view was comprehensively assembled by law professor John Sprankling in *The Anti-Wilderness Bias in American Property Law*, 63 U. CHI. L. REV. 519 (1996), in which he systematically surveys property law doctrines such as waste, adverse possession, trespass, and nuisance, and argues that they were and remain "tilted toward wilderness destruction" in order "to encourage the agrarian development" of the nation. *Id.* at 521. He points out, for example, that American law abandoned the British version of the waste doctrine, which banned forest clearing for cultivation, and replaced it with the view that clearing for cultivation was "good husbandry." *Id.* at 534–35. And American trespass law developed in many states so as to tolerate, if not to endorse, open grazing of livestock on the unenclosed lands of another landowner. *Id.* at 548–49. These and other examples of his thesis, Sprankling argued, flowed from the abundance of wilderness America enjoyed relative to England, the need to build an economy, and the exalted position in which Americans generally place private property rights. He concluded that, "all other things being equal, the property law system tends to resolve disputes by preferring wilderness destruction to wilderness preservation." *Id.* at 520.

**2.** Whether you accept Sprankling's thesis or merely that the common law has been benign with respect to ecosystems as it is being leap-frogged by legislative and administrative initiatives, how realistic do you think it is to hope for the evolution of the common law suggested in the article by Ruhl? Is it more likely that judges will pick up the ball than Congress and state legislatures?

**3.** Assuming that property owner A could demonstrate that an adjacent property owner B's destruction of natural capital on B's property has directly impaired the use and enjoyment of A's property, and that A could credibly quantify the injury, what policy reasons would one make for arguing that the common law should *not* recognize that as cognizable in a claim for nuisance or some other form of common law action?

**4.** In Palazzolo v. State, 2005 WL 1645974 (R.I. Super. Ct., 2005), a Rhode Island trial court considered a regulatory takings claim the United States Supreme Court had left dangling in Palazzolo v. Rhode Island, 533 U.S. 606 (2001). The Supreme Court rejected the claim that state agency denial of a permit to fill and develop a marsh area adjacent to a pond constituted a categorical taking of property, on the ground that the agency allowed Palazzolo to develop some of his parcel, leaving it to the state courts initially to decide whether the permit denial was a regulatory taking. The state trial court reasoned that the *Lucas* opinion, discussed in Ruhl's article, makes a finding of public nuisance a preclusive defense to takings claims, and found that "clear and convincing evidence demonstrates that Palazzolo's development would constitute a public nuisance" on the following grounds:

> Palazzolo's proposed development has been shown to have significant and predictable negative effects on Winnapaug Pond and the adjacent salt water marsh. The State has presented evidence as to various effects that the development will have including increasing nitrogen levels in the pond, both by reason of the nitrogen produced by the attendant residential septic systems, and by the reduced marsh area *which actually filters and cleans runoff*. This Court finds that the effects of increased nitrogen levels constitute a predictable (anticipatory) nuisance which would almost certainly result in an ecological disaster to the pond.

*Id.* at *5. *Palazzolo* thus involved the type of transboundary property rights issue that is likely to be ubiquitous for the law and policy of natural capital and ecosystem services, and the case demonstrates the easy time public nuisance law should have for integrating those values into a straightforward analysis: Palazzolo owned the marsh; the marsh filtered and cleaned runoff into the pond; those services were positive externalities flowing off of Palazzolo's property; the public in general enjoyed the economic benefits of that service; Palazzolo therefore had no property right to fill the marsh. It's that simple.

**5.** Or is it? As easily as the *Palazzolo* court integrated ecosystem services into public nuisance doctrine, the decision also illustrates the difficulty of making the same move in private nuisance doctrine or in affirmative claims of public nuisance. The nuisance analysis arises in cases like *Palazzolo* only in connection with the government's assertion of the nuisance exception to the landowner's regulatory taking claim. If the government can establish the exception under the public nuisance branch simply by demonstrating the *qualitative* effect on ecosystem service delivery, it need not establish proof of *quantitative* economic harm to specific property owners. The government's litigation incentives thus are far different from those a private landowner or sovereign might advance through an affirmative nuisance claim against conduct like Palazzolo's filling of the marsh.

In *Palazzolo*, for example, although the court acknowledged the "valuable filtering system" the marsh provided and that the pond and marsh system provided "amenity value to . . . the land owners in the area," 2005 WL 1645974 at *3, the curtailment of ecosystem service values to private landowners did not register in the record or with the court. The court simply noted that "no neighboring landowner has made a private nuisance claim" and that the potential for obstruction of views of the water would not constitute a private nuisance under Rhode Island law. *Id.* at *6. Would it have been likely, however, that any neighboring landowner would advance a private nuisance claim having to do with loss of the marsh filtering function before it was known whether the state would grant the permit for the project in the first place. In short, is the law of ecosystem services in nuisance doctrine is likely to develop significantly in the context of government defense of regulatory takings claims—or is it more likely emerge when private landowners and sovereigns start suing over the adverse effects of natural capital degradation?

---

## F. COMMON LAW CLAIMS AGAINST THE GOVERNMENT

Not all parties in private litigation need be private entities—a private plaintiff might have common law claims against a governmental entity. Suing the government, however, opens up a completely different set of problems for the plaintiff to overcome. For one thing, under the doctrine of sovereign immunity the United States is immune from suit except when Congress has waived the Government's immunity, and the same is true for many states with respect to claims based in state law. Congress has done so for some claims seeking monetary relief. For example, Congress waived immunity for suits against the United States for money damages under the Tucker Act and the Federal Tort Claims Act. And plaintiffs seeking non-monetary relief in the form of judicial review of an action by a federal agency may proceed under the Administrative Procedure Act. The following case describes some of the hurdles plaintiffs face in establishing that either kind of waiver applies.

### San Carlos Apache Tribe v. United States

United States District Court for the District of Arizona, 2003.
272 F. Supp. 2d 860.

■ BURY, DISTRICT JUDGE:

Plaintiffs, the San Carlos Apache Tribe (Apache Tribe) brought this action in 1999. They sought and were denied a Temporary Restraining Order and a Preliminary Injunction against Defendants the United States of America, the Secretary of the United States Department of the Interior, the Bureau of Indian Affairs (BIA) operating the San Carlos Indian Irrigation Project (SCIIP) for the benefit of the San Carlos Irrigation and Drainage District (SCIDD) and the Gila River Indian Community (GRIC). The SCIDD and GRIC are interveners in this action.

Plaintiffs seek to enjoin the release of water from the San Carlos Reservoir ("Reservoir" or "Lake"), except for 10 cubic feet per second, until there is a minimum pool of 75,000 acre-feet of water in the Reservoir. The Reservoir sits on federal land, but lies within the San

Carlos Apache Tribe Reservation. The Apache Tribe runs a concession operation for fishing and camping in and around the Lake that has provided revenues of half a million dollars up to in excess of two million dollars a year. The water in the Reservoir is subject to being drawn down for irrigation purposes every year, which jeopardizes the recreational activities at the Lake, especially when there are drought conditions in Arizona.

The Reservoir was completed in 1928, and the amount of water in it has fluctuated considerably depending on snow-pack, runoff, precipitation, carryover, and agricultural needs. The Reservoir has fallen below 75,000 acre-feet for all or part of 399 of the 720 months between 1937 and 1997. The Reservoir has been completely drained or drained below 1,000 acre-feet on 21 occasions between 1934 and 1995 because of a lack of water. The Reservoir has filled to overflowing 8 times during 5 different years. Since March of 1999, the Reservoir has been below 75,000 acre-feet for all or part of 27 of the 41 months. The Reservoir level was at 25,810 acre-feet October 8 and 9, 2000.

The Plaintiffs allege that the Defendants' release of water from the Reservoir violates the federal common law of public nuisance, the National Historic Preservation Act (NHPA), the Archeological Resources Protection Act (ARPA), the Native American Graves Protection and Repatriation Act (NAGPRA), the National Environmental Policy Act (NEPA), and the Fish and Wildlife Coordination Act (FWCA). . . .

***Background and History of the Case***

The *Akimel O'Odham* (Pima) Indians are an agrarian people who were practicing irrigated agriculture before the Spanish arrived in North America. In the late 1700s, the *Peeposh* (Maricopa) Indians formed an economic and military confederation with the Pima Indians that prospered until the arrival of the EuroAmericans, who diverted the Gila and Salt Rivers away from the Confederation. Robbed of the water it needed to sustain its agriculture, the Pima and Maricopa Indians were reduced to poverty, malnutrition, and starvation.

In 1924, in an effort to rectify the loss of water, the United States Congress enacted the San Carlos Project Act, as follows:

> For the purpose, first of providing water for the irrigation of lands allotted to the Pima Indians on the Gila River Reservation, Arizona, now without an adequate supply of water, and second, for the irrigation of such other lands in public or private ownership, as in the opinion of the Secretary, can be served with water impounded by said dam, without diminishing the supply necessary for said Indian land.

The San Carlos Project Act authorized construction of the Coolidge Dam and creation of the San Carlos Irrigation Project (SCIIP). The federal government purchased the land for the Coolidge Dam site from the Apache Tribe. Consequently, the dam sits on federal property, but lies within the confines of the San Carlos Apache Reservation. Prior to inundation of the Lake in 1928, the lake-bed was the site of the town of "old" San Carlos where the Apache Tribe resided. Additionally, the waters impounded behind Coolidge Dam cover tribal cemeteries, graves, and archaeology sites that contain and protect human remains, private homes, a grain mill, and many other historical sites, many of which have significant spiritual and cultural meaning to the Apache Tribe.

The federal government financed the construction of the Dam by equal reimbursement from the sale of Pima Indian-owned lands (GRIC) and implementation of a repayment plan to cover private lands (SCIDD) that would be served from the waters impounded by the dam. The Coolidge Dam was built near the confluence of the San Carlos and Gila Rivers, approximately 90 miles southeast of Phoenix, Arizona.

Coolidge Dam is operated by BIA to serve as an agricultural water storage facility, with no legislative intent for the facility to serve flood control, recreation, or fish and wildlife functions. The purpose of the dam is to provide irrigation water . . . to approximately 50,000 acres of Pima Indian land . . . and 50,000 acres of private non-Indian land. . . .

***Federal Common Law Claim of Nuisance***

Plaintiffs allege that the drawdowns and draining of the Lake by the Defendants threaten injury and pose health risks to the public at large and to the Apache Tribe and its members. Plaintiffs allege that these threats constitute a public and private nuisance. Plaintiffs seek injunctive relief in the form of an Order from this Court that Defendants abate this nuisance.

Section 1331 of Title 28 provides that "the district courts shall have original jurisdiction over all civil actions arising under the Constitution, laws, or treaties of the United States." Section 1362 also provides subject matter jurisdiction over this case because "the district courts shall have original jurisdiction of all civil actions, brought by any Indian tribe or band . . . , wherein the matter arises under the Constitution, laws or treaties of the United States."

Jurisdiction exists over violations to the federal common law as well as those of statutory origin, *Illinois v. City of Milwaukee,* 406 U.S. 91, 100 (1972), and, therefore, this Court has subject matter jurisdiction over Plaintiffs' common law nuisance claim.

Under the doctrine of sovereign immunity, the United States is, however, immune from suit except when Congress has waived the Government's immunity. *Tucson Airport Authority v. General Dynamics Corp.,* 136 F.3d 641, 644 (9th Cir. 1998). Neither 28 U.S.C. § 1331 nor § 1362 waives sovereign immunity. *See Pit River Home and Agri. Co-op. Ass'n v. United States,* 30 F.3d 1088, 1098 n. 5 (9th Cir. 1994) (explaining that sections 1331 and 1361 do not waive the sovereign immunity of the United States) (*citing Holloman v. Watt,* 708 F.2d 1399, 1401 (9th Cir. 1983) (§ 1331 not a waiver), *cert. denied,* 466 U.S. 958 (1984); *Smith v.*

*Grimm,* 534 F.2d 1346, 1352 n. 9 (9th Cir.) (§ 1361 not a waiver), *cert. denied,* 429 U.S. 980 (1976)); *see also Assiniboine and Sioux Tribes of the Fort Peck Indian Reservation v. Montana Board of Oil and Gas,* 792 F.2d 782 (9th Cir. 1986) (noting that section 1362 does not waive sovereign immunity).

Congress waived immunity for suits against the United States for money damages under the Tucker Act and the Federal Tort Claims Act (FTCA). Contract claims are brought under the Tucker Act. The FTCA is the exclusive remedy for torts committed by Government employees in the scope of their employment. *United States v. Smith,* 499 U.S. 160, 163 (1991). Defendants argue that the FTCA is the only avenue of relief available to the Plaintiffs and that Plaintiffs failed to give notice of their claim to the agency as required by the FTCA. Consequently, Plaintiffs may not proceed under the FTCA. Defendants argument fails, however, because Plaintiffs do not seek monetary damages.

Plaintiffs seeking non-monetary relief in the form of judicial review of an action by a federal agency may proceed under the Administrative Procedures Act (APA). In 1976, Congress amended the APA to specifically waive sovereign immunity in suits brought against the United States seeking relief "other than money damages."

The APA provides as follows:

> A person suffering legal wrong because of agency action, or adversely affected or aggrieved by agency action within the meaning of a relevant statute, is entitled to judicial review thereof. An action in a court of the United States seeking relief other than money damages and stating a claim that an agency or an officer or employee thereof acted or failed to act in an official capacity or under color of legal authority shall not be dismissed nor relief therein be denied on the ground that it is against the United States or that the United States is an indispensable party.

5 U.S.C. § 702.

The APA does not provide an independent basis for jurisdiction, *Assiniboine,* 792 F.2d at 793 (citing *Califano v. Sanders,* 430 U.S. 99 (1977)), but it waives sovereign immunity in non-monetary relief claims brought under federal question statutes 28 U.S.C. §§ 1331 and 1362. *Id.* The APA also provides the frame work for review of Plaintiffs' nuisance claim. 2 Fed. Proc. Law Ed., § 2:266 (APA provides framework for judicial review of agency actions once jurisdiction is otherwise established) (*citing Gallo Cattle Co. v. United States Dept. of Agriculture,* 159 F.3d 1194 (9th Cir. 1998)).

The initial difficulty this Court faces in analyzing its jurisdiction over Plaintiffs' nuisance claim is that Plaintiffs have wholly ignored the APA. They failed to plead the APA as a jurisdictional basis for their claims in the Complaint and refuse to recognize its significance even in the responsive brief to the motions for summary judgment. Consequently, Plaintiffs have failed to identify for the Court the requisites in their claim necessary for proceeding under the APA.

Section 702 of the APA includes important exceptions to administrative review. Section 702 states: "Nothing herein . . . confers authority to grant relief if any other statute that grants consent to suit expressly or impliedly forbids the relief which is sought." Section 704 adds: "Agency action made reviewable by statute and final agency action for which there is no other adequate remedy in a court are subject to judicial review." Judicial review is not available when the "agency action is committed to agency discretion by law." 5 U.S.C. § 701(a)(2).

Additionally, when review is not sought pursuant to specific authorization in a substantive statute, but only under the general review provisions of the APA, 5 U.S.C. § 702, Plaintiffs must satisfy two requirements: 1) they must show that they have been affected by some "agency action" as defined in section 551(13), 5 U.S.C. § 701(b)(2), and the "agency action" must be a "final agency action" pursuant to section 704; 2) they must prove that they have suffered a "legal wrong" or are "adversely affected or aggrieved" by that action "within the meaning of a relevant statute," which requires a showing that the injury complained of falls within the "zone of interests" sought to be protected by the relevant statute. *Lujan v. National Wildlife Federation,* 497 U.S. 871, 882–883 (1990).

As to the second factor, the injury the Plaintiffs complain of must fall within the zone of interests sought to be protected by the statutory provision whose violation forms the legal basis of the complaint. *Id.* As to the first factor, "agency action" for purposes of § 702 is defined in 5 U.S.C. § 551(13), 5 U.S.C. 701(b)(2), as follows: "the whole or a part of an agency rule, order, license, sanction, relief, or the equivalent or denial thereof, or failure to act." *Id.* at 882.

Plaintiffs allege that the ongoing operation of the dam, which includes sometimes releasing water so that the Lake is drawn down to a point that allegedly results in a public nuisance, is not the type of agency action covered by the APA. In *Lujan,* the Supreme Court held that the land withdrawal review program operated by the Bureau of Land Management (BLM) was not agency action, much less final agency action, because the complaint did not refer to a single BLM order or regulation, or even to a completed universe of BLM orders and regulations, but rather referred to continuing and constantly changing BLM operations of reviewing withdrawal revocation applications and its classifications of public lands and its general responsibilities of developing land use plans. *Id.* at 890.

The Court reasoned that the APA did not lay before the courts the wholesale correction of agency programs, *id.* at 893, 110 S. Ct. 3177, but "only provides for intervention in the administration of the laws when, and to the extent that, a specific 'final agency action' has an actual or immediately threatened effect," *id.* at 894, 110 S. Ct. 3177 (*citing Toilet Goods Assn. v. Gardner,* 387 U.S. 158 (1967)).

The day to day operation of the dam is not a final agency action reviewable under the APA. Agency action is "final" and reviewable if a minimum of two conditions are met: 1) the action marks the consummation of the agency's decisionmaking process . . . it must not be of a merely tentative or interlocutory nature, and 2) it must be one by which rights or obligations have been determined, or from which legal consequences will flow. *Nippon Miniature Bearing Corp. v. Weise,* 230 F.3d 1131, 1137 (9th Cir. 2000) (*citing Bennett,* 520 U.S. at 177; *see e.g., Gallo Cattle Company v. United States Department of Agriculture,* 159 F.3d 1194 (1998) (explaining that decision to not allow Gallo to pay its assessments into escrow accounts is not final agency action because obligation to pay assessments arises pursuant to the Dairy Promotion Program not from the agency's decision); *FTC v. Standard Oil Co.,* 449 U.S. 232, 241 (1980) (noting that the action must be a definitive statement of the agency's position with concrete legal consequences); *Ecology Center, Inc. v. United States Forest Service,* 192 F.3d 922, 925 (9th Cir. 199) (explaining that failure to monitor as required by Kootenai National Forest Plan is not final agency action because monitoring is not an action that marks the culmination of a decision making process).

Plaintiffs do not explain how sometimes allowing the Lake to drop to the alleged harmful levels or even draining it marks the culmination of a decision making process by the Federal Defendants, nor are there any legal rights or obligations determined by the practice. *See, Ecology Center, Inc.,* 192 F.3d at 925 (monitoring duty is mandatory under the Plan, but legal consequences do not necessarily flow from that duty, nor do rights or obligations arise from it). The challenged drawdowns merely reflect the rights and obligations of the respective parties to the waters in the Reservoir. . . . Consequently, Plaintiffs' nuisance claim is not reviewable under the APA and must be dismissed.

---

## QUESTIONS AND DISCUSSION

**1.** The message of *San Carlos Apache Tribe* is really nothing more than black letter administrative law: Suing the government under the Administrative Procedure Act requires that the action challenged be a final agency action. After decisions such as *Lujan* this has become difficult even for run of the mill judicial review claims alleging violation of statutory standards or procedures. Why should it be any different for a claim based in common law doctrines?

**2.** On the other hand, the court also made it clear that it would have had subject matter jurisdiction of the federal common law public nuisance claim had the underlying actions been within the scope of APA review. What is "federal common law," and what menu of claims might a plaintiff levy against the federal government for environmental effects of its actions?

---

## G. EXPERT TESTIMONY AND THE BURDEN OF PROOF

Many common law environmental claims involve expert testimony bearing on questions of causation and injury.

> Whether a toxic tort plaintiff seeks compensatory damages for injury to property or for personal physical injury, long latency periods can complicate statutes of limitations analysis as well as create physical problems of proof and evidence gathering. In addition, because of the typically long latency period and imperfect scientific knowledge about disease etiology, toxic tort personal injury claims may raise complex questions of medical or scientific causation. The disciplines of epidemiology and toxicology, which are often brought to bear on the general causation question of whether a substance is capable of causing a disease, do not answer the specific injury question as to which members of an exposed population contracted the disease from the exposure. The identity of the defendant from among several possible sources responsible for a particular toxic release or exposure, often confounds plaintiffs. . . . As a consequence of these vexing causation issues, toxic torts almost always require experts from any number of scientific fields, including medicine, toxicology, epidemiology, and industrial hygiene.

Janet Kole et al., *Toxic Tort Litigation: Theories of Liability and Damages*, in Environmental Litigation 108, 109 (Janet Kole et al., eds., 2d ed., 1999).

Several Supreme Court decisions have had a profound effect on how expert testimony is packaged in such cases. The Court's decision in *Daubert v. Merrell Dow Pharmaceuticals, Inc.*, 509 U.S. 579 (1993), outlined the "gatekeeping" function to be performed by the trial judge in assessing the admissibility of expert scientific testimony, requiring courts to determine whether the expert is proposing to testify to scientific knowledge that will assist the trier of fact in understanding or determining a fact in issue. To perform that function, the trial courts are to ask whether the theory or technique offered can be tested; whether it has been subjected to peer review and publication; what the known or potential rate of error is; and whether it is generally accepted in the relevant scientific community. Yet, according to the Court's later decision in *Kumho Tire Co. v. Carmichael*, 526 U.S. 137 (1999), it is in the trial court's discretion to apply the *Daubert* factors, and the court "should consider the specific factors identified in *Daubert* where they are reasonable measures of the reliability of expert testimony." *Id.* at 152. Not surprisingly, after *Daubert* a substantial focus of private litigation involving common law environmental claims focuses on motions to exclude expert testimony.

The "battle of experts" that is typical of such cases also raises the question of how to trace causation and injury in what are often exceedingly complex circumstances that no expert for either party is likely to unravel definitively. Should the ultimate burden of proof—usually placed on the plaintiff—be reassigned in such cases to avoid unfairness or to serve public policy? If so, under what circumstances and based on what threshold of proof by expert testimony? The following case illustrates the kind of inquiry courts perform to implement *Daubert* and the burden of proof in such cases.

## Martin v. Shell Oil Co.

United States District Court for the District of Connecticut, 2002.
180 F. Supp. 2d 313.

■ HALL, DISTRICT JUDGE:

This case arises out of the discovery of a chemical known as methyl tertiary-butyl ether ("MTBE") in the groundwater near a Shell service station. The plaintiffs, Catherine Martin and Dorinda Frug (collectively "Martin"), allege that the MTBE found in their wells is attributable to the defendants, Shell Oil Company and its successor-in-interest, Motiva Enterprises, LLC (collectively "Shell"). Martin's complaint lists six causes of action: negligence, negligence per se, strict liability, gross negligence, private nuisance, and trespass.

In its motions, Shell argues that Martin's experts on causation should be excluded because their opinions are scientifically invalid, contrary to the evidence, and generally inadmissible. Further, Shell seeks summary judgment on Martin's claims because she lacks proof of causation and damages and based on other grounds specific to each claim. Martin contends that her experts are admissible and that she has sufficient evidence of causation and damages and defends each cause of action. Martin also advocates a different standard for proof of causation and admissibility of expert testimony, which the court addresses in this ruling.

### I. FACTUAL BACKGROUND

On March 25, 1992, the Connecticut Department of Environmental Protection ("CTDEP") issued an order finding that Shell owned and maintained an underground storage tank at its 912 Danbury Road property in Wilton and that groundwater at that site was polluted with components of gasoline. For at least ten years, site-specific hydrogeologic investigations and groundwater monitoring have been conducted in the Shell Station area by the CTDEP and environmental consultants for the service stations and industrial facilities in that area. For the shallow overburden, data from monitoring wells at the Shell station and the

Wilton Shopping Center have consistently demonstrated that groundwater flow is to the north-northwest at the station.

Catherine Martin lives in a home approximately 800 feet east of the Shell Station mentioned in the 1992 Order and has lived at that location since 1975. Dorinda Frugé lives in a home approximately 1400 feet south of the Shell Station and has lived at that location since 1993. The only substance related to gasoline that has ever been detected in the plaintiffs' wells during the plaintiffs' residence is MTBE. While living at these properties, the plaintiffs allege that, based on the contamination, they suffer various health problems, their water has a bad taste or odor, the property is barren, and they fear they may develop cancer.

Gregory Shkuda ("Shkuda") is an environmental consultant with a doctorate degree in organic chemistry from New York University. Shkuda submitted an expert report on behalf of the plaintiffs that expressed his opinion that the MTBE contamination from the Shell Station had traveled south and east to contaminate the plaintiffs' property. He relied heavily on an analysis of the geology and groundwater flow of the Nutmeg River Valley and a distinction between shallow and deep bedrock groundwater flow.

Myron Mehlman ("Mehlman") is a toxicologist with a doctorate in chemistry from the Massachusetts Institute of Technology. Mehlman submitted an expert report on behalf of the plaintiffs that expressed his opinion that the MTBE contamination of the plaintiffs' property caused the plaintiffs' health symptoms. He did not examine the plaintiffs or perform any differential diagnosis.

## II. STANDARD OF REVIEW

For the motion in limine, the court evaluates the experts' reports under Rule 702 of the Federal Rules of Evidence. Fed.R.Evid. 702 (2001). The rule reads:

> If scientific, technical, or other specialized knowledge will assist the trier of fact to understand the evidence or to determine a fact in issue, a witness qualified as an expert by knowledge, skill, experience, training, or education, may testify thereto in the form of an opinion or otherwise, if (1) the testimony is based on sufficient facts or data, (2) the testimony is the product of reliable principles and methods, and (3) the witness has applied the principles and methods reliably to the facts of the case.

*Id.*

The Supreme Court's decision in *Daubert v. Merrell Dow Pharmaceuticals, Inc.*, 509 U.S. 579 (1993), outlined the "gatekeeping" function to be performed by the trial judge in assessing the admissibility of expert scientific testimony under Rule 702. The essence of the trial court's function is to determine whether the expert is proposing to testify to scientific knowledge that will assist the trier of fact in understanding or determining a fact in issue. *Daubert,* 509 U.S. at 592–93. With respect to what constitutes "scientific knowledge," the Supreme Court declined to articulate a "definitive checklist or test." and emphasized that "[t]he inquiry envisioned by Rule 702 is . . . a flexible one." *Id.* at 592, 595.

Nonetheless, the *Daubert* Court identified several factors to be considered by the trial court in determining whether a proposed submission is sufficiently reliable under Rule 702. *Id.* at 592–95. These include whether the theory or technique offered can be tested; whether it has been subjected to peer review and publication; what the known or potential rate of error is; and whether it is generally accepted in the relevant scientific community. *Id.*

In *Kumho Tire Co. v. Carmichael,* 526 U.S. 137 (1999), the Court reemphasized that the gatekeeping inquiry "must be 'tied to the facts of a particular case' " and that *Daubert's* list of factors "was meant to be helpful, not definitive." *Id.* at 151 (quoting *Daubert,* 509 U.S. at 591). Thus, it is in the trial court's discretion to apply the *Daubert* factors, and the court "should consider the specific factors identified in *Daubert* where they are reasonable measures of the reliability of expert testimony."

## III. DISCUSSION

### A. Causation and Damages

#### 1. *Expert Gregory Shkuda*

Shell challenges the relevance and reliability of Shkuda's opinion. As a relevance challenge to Shkuda's report, Shell argues that he has never visited the contamination site in the context of this litigation and uses data from a location seventy-five miles away while ignoring information gathered specifically from the Shell Station. As a reliability challenge, Shell argues that Shkuda did not conduct any hydrogeologic tests to validate his theory, that he extrapolated from a study that does not support his opinion, and that he did not perform a differential analysis to eliminate other possible sources of MTBE contamination.

Shkuda's report provides an explanation of how MTBE from the Shell Station site could have migrated to the plaintiffs' property, and he uses accepted techniques in analysis of chemical migration in groundwater flow. The defendants' relevance challenges focus on the source of Shkuda's data for his opinion. First, Shell claims that the Nutmeg River Valley is not the same river valley within which the contamination site and plaintiffs' property are located. Shkuda argues that the study, conducted by the United States Geological Survey of the Department of the Interior, provides a relevant and reliable basis for comparison because the Nutmeg River Valley has a similar geological setting to the Norwalk River Valley where the properties at issue are located. Second, Shell argues that by focusing only on the Nutmeg study, Shkuda ignored site-specific data on the groundwater flow at the Shell Station. Shkuda, however, claims that he examined the data and formulated an explanation for why the site-specific data does not show a southerly or easterly flow—by distinguishing shallow and deep bedrock groundwater flow.

The court concludes that Shkuda's opinion is relevant to whether the contamination at the Shell Station could have migrated to plaintiffs' property. While Shell's concerns may affect the weight that the fact finder will give Shkuda's opinion, they do not affect its admissibility because accepted scientific principles justify the relevance of the Nutmeg Study given the similarity of the geological setting of the contamination site and the study.

Shell's reliability objections focus on Shkuda's methodology. Shell argues that Shkuda did not test his explanation. Contrary to Shell's characterization that Shkuda failed to perform hydrogeologic surveys because the plaintiffs feared it would produce results contrary to his report, Shkuda explains that the surveys were not performed because they would cost $70,000–100,000 to complete. Shell also challenges the conclusions Shkuda draws from the Nutmeg study. Shell appears to believe that the only conclusions ascertainable from the Nutmeg study would be those made in the study itself. Shkuda, however, draws on the data in the study, his experience, and other published works in the field to explore a possible difference in groundwater flow at varying depths. Finally, Shell claims that Shkuda failed to perform a differential analysis to eliminate other possible sources of MTBE contamination.

The court concludes that Shkuda's opinion is reliable. The *Daubert* factors and scientific methodology require that an opinion be testable, not that it necessarily be tested. While the plaintiffs place themselves at risk of strong cross-examination, the underlying explanation is not flawed for failure to test an explanation, especially at a cost of $70,000–100,000. Further, reliance on published data, as part of scientific methodology, does not require an expert to draw the same generalized conclusions as the publisher, if a more nuanced approach would yield different results. Finally, Shell has not cited any case law for the notion that a differential analysis would be required of Shkuda. As with the relevance objections, Shell's reliability objections merely affect weight, not admissibility. For these reasons and based on the record before it, the court declines to exercise its discretion to preclude Shkuda from testifying at trial.

2. *Expert Myron Mehlman*

Shell challenges the relevance and reliability of Mehlman's opinion. As challenges to Mehlman's report, Shell argues that his opinion lacks sufficient factual foundation, that he did not perform a differential diagnosis and is not qualified to do so, and that his opinion establishes causation based solely on temporal association. Shell also claims that Mehlman is not qualified to give an opinion on medical monitoring.

Mehlman's report provides a basis for concluding that the MTBE contamination on the plaintiffs' property affected the plaintiffs' health and property, and he uses accepted techniques in toxicology. Shell challenges the relevance of Mehlman's report because, in the report and his deposition, he refers to MTBE in conjunction with other gasoline components as causing health problems. Shell points out that no other gasoline components have been found on plaintiffs' property, only MTBE. In his Declaration attached to Martin's response to the motion in limine, Mehlman clarifies that his studies illustrate that MTBE causes "acute adverse effects and illnesses in humans" and that these effects are "exacerbated" by the presence of other gasoline components.

Shell also argues that Mehlman's report is not reliable because he did not perform a differential diagnosis and is not qualified to do so. Shell cites cases that require differential diagnosis; however, those cases often involved an attack on an expert with little expertise in the field or strong opposition from the scientific community to the expert's conclusions. *E.g., Mancuso v. Consol. Edison Co.,* 967 F. Supp. 1437, 1451 (S.D.N.Y.1997); *Rutigliano v. Valley Bus. Forms,* 929 F. Supp. 779, 786 (D.N.J.1996). Also, as Martin points out, specific causation, the question at issue in most differential diagnosis cases, may be established by other theories such as temporal association, which Mehlman invokes. *See generally Bonner v. ISP Tech., Inc.,* 259 F.3d 924, 930–31 (8th Cir. 2001). If Mehlman is not required to complete a differential diagnosis, he need not be qualified to do one.

Shell challenges Mehlman's reliance on temporal association, claiming it is an unreliable basis for causation. Shell argues that Mehlman's opinion rests solely on the notion of temporal connection. Mehlman asserts that he used his expertise and knowledge of toxicology, published materials in the field, and temporal association as the basis for his opinion that MTBE contamination caused plaintiffs' injuries.

The court concludes that Mehlman's opinion is admissible. The cases cited by Shell for the requirement of differential diagnosis and ignoring temporal association are distinguishable and often involved egregious instances of unqualified experts or wildly aberrant theories in a particular field. Mehlman has employed known and accepted toxicology methods to arrive at his opinion, and any arguments by Shell only affect the weight, not admissibility, of his testimony. For these reasons and based on the record before it, the court declines to exercise its discretion to preclude Mehlman from testifying at trial.

Shell also argues that Mehlman is not qualified to testify about medical monitoring, claiming he denied his expertise in that field during his deposition. Martin claims that Mehlman only denied his expertise in conducting medical monitoring, not in determining whether it would be appropriate. Martin cites Third Circuit cases that allowed a toxicologist or other non-medical experts to discuss the propriety of medical monitoring. *See In re Paoli R.R. Yard PCB Litig.,* 916 F.2d 829, 858–59 (3d Cir. 1990); *Merry v. Westinghouse Elec. Corp.,* 684 F. Supp. 847, 851–52 (M.D.Pa.1988). Based on the record before it, the court concludes that

Mehlman has sufficient expertise and admissible opinions on whether medical monitoring would be appropriate.

3. *Martin's Standards for Causation and Experts*

In the context of her response, Martin has raised two issues that the court will clarify before proceeding. First, Martin argues that a burden-shifting analysis for causation should apply in cases where the defendants failed to test their product before putting it on the market or to conduct tests after health hazards became known. The closest case cited by Martin involved a bench trial over gel bleed in breast implants. *Barrow v. Bristol-Myers Squibb,* 1998 WL 812318 (M.D.Fla. Oct. 29, 1998). The *Barrow* court considered an argument that placing the burden on the plaintiff to show causation in toxic tort litigation would be unfair and would create a negative incentive for corporations to test their products because proof of causation would exist. *Id.* at *38. The court laid out an academically proposed alternative, but concluded that "despite this Court's view of the unfairness of placing the burden of proof as to causation on the plaintiff in a case such as this, the Court is bound to apply the law as it is presently constituted and to find that Plaintiff has failed to prove causation."

Other cases cited by the plaintiff for imposing the burden of proof for causation on the defendant refer to common-law theories. Common-law theories of joint causation may be invoked where multiple defendants engage in an activity and it would be unfair for the court to force the plaintiff to prove which defendant actually caused the plaintiff's injury. In these cases, the law has permitted shifting the burden to the multiple defendants. The case of *In re MTBE Products Liability Litigation,* 175 F. Supp. 2d at 619–20 (S.D.N.Y.2001), explores the different bases for joint causation—alternative liability, market share liability, enterprise liability, and concert of action liability—in the context of MTBE litigation against several companies as potential sources of injury.

The plaintiff has presented no case law to support its argument that the burden for proving causation should shift to the defendant. The *Barrow* court recognized a potential policy problem with placing the burden on the plaintiff, but resorted, as must this court, to applying the law as it stands. Moreover, the basis for the common-law burden-shifting theories is inapplicable here. The theories seek to avoid the unfair situation where the plaintiff has no possible means of apportioning liability as to any one defendant in particular, which threatens to deny the plaintiff any recovery because causation as to each defendant is left unproven—even though liability can otherwise be established as to a set of potential defendants. Here the plaintiffs allege only one potential source for the MTBE on their property, which eliminates any problem of apportioning liability and thus any need for the burden-shifting theories. Therefore, Martin should not expect to rely on any theory of burden shifting for causation.

The other issue raised by Martin involved the standard of review for experts. Martin argues that the court should apply a lax interpretation of *Daubert* to plaintiffs' experts, but a stricter interpretation to defendants' experts because they failed to test their product during or after manufacture. The court notes that *Daubert* and Rule 702 do not contemplate any distinction between experts based on party status or conduct. The court serves its gatekeeping function by insuring that expert testimony is relevant and reliable. The two cases cited by Martin involve reasonable inferences that may be drawn and viable causes of action that may be pursued in light of defendant's conduct and public policy, but those decisions do not modify the admissibility of evidence. *See Fernandez v. Chios Shipping Co.,* 542 F.2d 145, 154–55 (2d Cir. 1976); *Enright v. Eli Lilly & Co.,* 570 N.E.2d 198 (1991). Accordingly, the court concludes that both parties should be held to the same standard for the admissibility of expert testimony.

---

## QUESTIONS AND DISCUSSION

**1.** As the *Shell Oil* case illustrates, *Daubert* intensified trial lawyers' practice regarding introduction of expert testimony, with toxic tort cases being a focal point to this day. *See, e.g.*, C.W. v. Textron, Inc., 807 F.3d 827 (7th Cir. 2015) (expert did not adequately draw from reliable sources); Burst v. Shell Oil Co., 2015 WL 4710147 (E.D. La. 2015) (expert opinion relied on studies that left too large a gap between the findings and the expert's testimony). The nature of this practice challenge is described in In re Paoli R.R. Yard PCB Litigation, 35 F.3d 717, 798 (3d Cir. 1994):

> *Daubert* holds that admissibility under Rule 702 is governed by Rule 104(e), which requires the judge to conduct preliminary fact finding, to make a preliminary assessment of whether the reasoning or methodology underlying the testimony is scientific, and thus enable the judge to exclude evidence presented in the plaintiff's prima facie case. . . . [I]t is plain that the proponent must make more than a prima facie showing . . . that a technique is reliable. . . . [N]ovel scientific evidence carries with it concern over trust worthiness and reliability akin to those raised by offers of hearsay. When there is a serious question of reliability of evidence, it is appropriate for the court to exercise to some degree an evidentiary screening function.

**2.** Consider the argument Professor Jamie Grodsky made, discussed above in Section I.C of this chapter following the *Lockheed Martin* case, that emerging knowledge in genomics technology will allow experts to detect genetic injury from chemical exposures. What kinds of expert testimony issues would you anticipate confronting were you representing a plaintiff alleging this kind of injury as the basis for a claim for medical monitoring costs? One commentator, anticipating some of the developments Grodsky outlined, suggests that

> expert testimony relying on this novel methodology will be particularly vulnerable to exclusion under Daubert's reliability standard. At least some experts believe that this will not be a significant hurdle, as such studies are likely to be peer reviewed and published; the methodology has also become widely accepted, particularly in the pharmaceutical industry. But the larger problem will come when experts attempt to draw conclusions on individual cases from the data gleaned from the studies. The combination of hereditary and external factors may create obstacles that cannot be overcome by the ipse dixit of the testifying expert. The fact that this technology is new may mean that courts will be wary of it for some time and lean on the side of exclusion. How the courts treat this new generation of genetic testing will go far in demonstrating just how receptive the Daubert doctrine is to new and emerging techniques.

Jean Macchiaroli Eggen, *Toxic Torts and Causation: The Challenge of Daubert After the First Decade*, NATURAL RESOURCES & ENV'T, Spring 2003, at 213, 260.

**3.** Why would a court ever apply a lower threshold of admissibility for the plaintiff's experts than for the defendant's, or impose the burden of proving no exposure-injury causation to the defendant? Would this reduce the transaction costs of bringing toxic tort claims? Would this provide more deterrent effect to unsafe production and use of chemicals? Would this provide more fairness to plaintiffs concerned about future medical impairment? Even if the answer to all three questions is yes, what objectionable costs and effects could such an approach lead to?

## II. INSURANCE RECOVERY LITIGATION

The statutory programs covered in Part I of this text, as well as the common law claims covered in the previous section of this chapter, can impose massive liabilities and costs on regulated entities in the form of compliance technology expenditures, enforcement penalties, remediation costs, and the demands of injunctive relief. When might such obligations trigger coverage under insurance policies? Many a dollar have been paid to attorneys to wrestle over that question.

Insurance is a means of guarding against an unknown risk of loss, such as costs associated with environmental laws, by paying a known cost in the form of a premium. Based on its understanding of industry practices and the patterns of losses in general, an insurer attempts to calculate a premium that will yield a profit after all claims entitled to coverage are paid. The problem in the context of losses associated with environmental laws was that virtually nobody—not the government, not the regulated industries, and not the insurance industry—had any idea how sky high the costs of environmental compliance would rise by the 1980s, particularly in connection with remediation of contaminated lands under CERCLA and its state counterparts. The result was that, by the mid-1980s, insurers and insureds were engaged in tooth and nail battles around the country over the interpretation of provision in insurance contracts that were executed both before and after the rise of the environmental statute regimes. The siege is by no means over. As it has been described:

> Coverage litigation has spread to every jurisdiction in the country. Literally, thousands of court decisions have addressed one or more coverage issue. This litigation has even spawned a new group of reporting services to keep lawyers abreast of the rapid developments. In addition, coverage litigation has occupied the time of thousands of lawyers. Indeed, some reports have suggested that fifty percent of all money spent on Superfund cleanup is spent on legal fees, including the cost of insurance litigation.

John E. Heintz and Richard D. Milone, *Insurance Coverage Litigation Issues*, in ENVIRONMENTAL LITIGATION, 207, 207 (Janet S. Kole et al., eds., 2d ed., 1999).

Two kinds of insurance policies have been at center stage in this struggle. The first is the standard Comprehensive General Liability (CGL) policy that entered the market in the 1960s—the traditional policy businesses purchased to cover losses like those associated with environmental law liabilities. The approach of the standard CGL is to provide coverage for losses except where excluded, which the insurance industry believed would make the policy attractive in the market. They were right. As environmental liabilities escalated far beyond what had been imagined possible, however, the battlefront for CGL policies focused on what kind of legal claims and obligations were covered and whether the circumstances that gave rise to the costs of compliance fit the scope of the policy, which in practice covered "accidents" or "occurrences" that took place during the period covered by the policy.

As the insurance industry grew wiser to the problem, by the 1980s most CGL policies included a "pollution exclusion" clause that precluded coverage for pollution, but which in some cases retained coverage for costs associated with "accidents" such as one-time spills of chemicals. The second front of litigation bore down on the meaning of these pollution exclusion clauses.

Because many present day environmental liabilities are associated with events that occurred well before the pollution exclusion clauses became a standard provision of the CGL policy, both types of policies continue to be the focus of litigation today. The three cases in this section provide a glimpse at just the tip of this litigation iceberg.

## A. LEGAL CLAIMS AND OBLIGATIONS

### Northern Illinois Gas Co. v. Home Ins. Co.

Illinois Court of Appeals for the 1st District, 2002.
777 N.E.2d 417.

■ JUSTICE MCBRIDE delivered the opinion of the court:

This dispute arises out of a declaratory judgment action filed by plaintiff-appellant, Northern Illinois Gas Company, now known as Nicor Gas (Nicor), against defendant-appellees: The Home Insurance Company (Home); Certain Underwriters at Lloyd's and Certain London Market Insurance Companies (London); Lexington Insurance Company (Lexington); Century Indemnity Company (Century); Northwestern National Insurance Company (Northwestern); Stonewall Insurance Company (Stonewall); and Yasuda Fire and Marine Insurance Company of Europe Limited (Yasuda) (collectively referred to as the Insurers). Nicor filed the declaratory action seeking indemnification from the Insurers to recover the costs of investigating and remediating environmental contamination at six manufactured gas plant (MGP) sites located in Illinois. The Insurers filed various motions for summary judgment. The trial court granted some of those motions on February 10, 2000. Nicor now appeals those rulings.

Two issues are raised on review. First, whether the trial court erred in granting the Insurers' motions for summary judgment on the ground that Nicor should not be indemnified for expenses it voluntarily incurred for investigation and remediation of five MGP sites. Second, whether the trial court erred in granting the Insurers' motions for summary judgment on the ground that the environmental contamination at the various sites did not constitute "occurrences" under the policies at issue. We state the following background facts.

Nicor seeks indemnification for the costs of investigating and remediating property damage at several MGPs located in Aurora, Belvidere, Bloomington, Lockport, Ottawa, and Streator, Illinois. The record reveals that some of these MGPs were in operation as early as the mid 1800s. One of the by-products of the gas manufacturing process was tar, which was either sold or stored in various underground containment structures located on site at the MGPs. In the 1900s, the introduction of natural gas made manufactured gas production obsolete. Thus, by the early 1950s, all six of the facilities in question were no longer operational.

At the time the MGPs were retired, the owners made efforts to extract some of the tar from the underground containers, but some of the tar remained in these structures. The underground tanks were then emptied of usable material and filled with building debris or alternative materials to bring them to ground level.

The record reveals that in the years after the MGPs were sealed, coal tar and coal tar water mixtures were released from the structures into the surrounding soil and groundwater. The release of these substances contaminated the groundwater, soil, and the surrounding environment.

James Janssen, an official with the Illinois Environmental Protection Agency (IEPA), testified that the IEPA became aware of environmental pollution at MGP sites in 1983. From 1983 to the present, the IEPA has been involved with the immediate removal and voluntary cleanup program at MGP sites in Illinois. Although the name of the voluntary cleanup program changed to the "pre-notice program," and then to the "site remediation program" over the years, Janssen said that these programs were one and the same. In 1987, Janssen said that a meeting was held at which Illinois utility companies were informed by the IEPA that "they may want to investigate" potential environmental problems at MGPs under their control. He further testified that the purpose of the voluntary cleanup program was to allow the State to offer its review, comment, and ultimately concurrence on the clean up activities undertaken at sites where contamination was present. According to Janssen, no consent decree or court filing was required for a utility to become involved with the voluntary cleanup program. He further stated that no representation was ever made to a landowner that it was "legally obligated" to enroll a site in the voluntary cleanup program, and that the program was "non-adversarial." In essence, Janssen explained that the property owners were coming to the IEPA and seeking the IEPA's input into the process of handling contamination.

Robert O'Hara, an IEPA project manager for the site remediation program, testified that the site remediation program is voluntary in nature as opposed to action taken by the IEPA under section 4(q) of the Environmental Protection Act (415 ILCS 5/4(q) (West 1998)). Action taken by the IEPA under section 4(q) involves the IEPA providing notice to a utility that it intends to take certain adversarial action in the event the utility fails to adequately respond to a cleanup request. 415 ILCS 5/4(q) (West 1998).

In 1992, the record demonstrates that Nicor began to enroll its sites into the IEPA's voluntary cleanup program. O'Hara testified that, to his knowledge, Nicor had enrolled all six sites at issue into the voluntary cleanup program.

With respect to the Ottawa site, the record reveals that Nicor drafted a review and evaluation services agreement concerning reimbursement of the IEPA's oversight costs incurred in overseeing the cleanup at the Ottawa location. Nicor asked the IEPA to sign this agreement. However, in a letter dated May 12, 1997, the IEPA wrote back in response stating:

> "Please be advised that the Division of Legal Counsel has determined that the draft Review and Evaluation Services Agreement is substantially in conflict with Title XVII of the Environmental Protection Act and contains misstatements of

> law and fact. Specifically, * * * [t]he eighth paragraph beginning 'WHEREAS' states that the Illinois EPA has requested that Northern Illinois Gas and Commonwealth Edison Company perform necessary and appropriate actions at the site. The Illinois EPA has not provided notice to either Northern Illinois Gas or to Commonwealth Edison Company for the conduct of any response actions necessary to eliminate or mitigate significant risks to human health and the environment presented by the release of any hazardous substances at the site."

The record reveals that Nicor then undertook some measures to begin remediation at the sites in question. Nicor argues that in doing so, it has incurred millions of dollars in expenses for investigation and cleanup at the various sites. As a result, Nicor seeks reimbursement from the Insurers for the costs incurred for the remediation and cleanup of the sites at issue.

Nicor claims that for an extended period of time, including but not limited to the period 1955 to 1985, it purchased a series of comprehensive general liability policies from a variety of insurance companies. In addition to the general liability policies, certain excess and umbrella policies were purchased. These policies were issued by the Insurers, specifically Home, Lexington, and Century. There are slight variations in the language of the Insurers' policies, but they are all policies that provide coverage in the event of an "occurrence." For instance, the applicable coverage language in the Home policies states:

"The Company hereby agrees to indemnify the Insured for all sums which the insured shall be obligated to pay by reason of the liability imposed upon the insured by law, or assumed by the Insured under contract or agreement, for damages, direct or consequential, and expenses, all as more fully defined by the term 'ultimate net loss,' on account of personal injuries and property damage caused by or growing out of each occurrence."

Similar language in one of the Lexington policies provides:

> "Underwriters hereby agree to indemnify the Assured for all sums which the Assured shall be obligated to pay by reason of the liability imposed upon by law * * * for damages * * * on account of * * * property damage caused by or growing out of each occurrence."

The policies define the term "occurrence" as follows: "The term 'occurrence,' wherever used herein, shall mean one happening or series of happenings, arising out of or due to one event taking place during the term of this policy" (or "contract" in the case of the Home policies). None of the policies in question was in effect during the time the Nicor MGPs at issue were operational.

On December 20, 1995, Nicor filed a declaratory judgment action against the Insurers. Home (joined by Lexington and Century) moved for summary judgment concerning policies issued between 1955 and 1976 on the ground that no "occurrences" as defined in the policies occurred during those years. The trial court granted the Insurers' motions for summary judgment concluding that there was "only mere speculation that any occurrence, as defined in the policy, took place during the policy period."

Home (joined by Lexington and Century) also moved for summary judgment on the ground that Nicor was not "legally obligated to pay" for the investigation and remediation at the Aurora, Belvidere, Bloomington, Ottawa, and Streator sites. As noted above, the Lockport site was not included in the summary judgment motions made by these insurers because Nicor had been sued by a private party for response costs associated with contamination at that site. The trial court granted the summary judgment motions of these insurers on the grounds that the insurance contracts did not contain a duty to indemnify Nicor's voluntary cleanup actions and that there was no genuine issue of material fact which would preclude summary judgment in favor of the movant insurers.

We first consider whether the trial court erred in granting the Insurers' motions for summary judgment on the basis that Nicor voluntarily incurred expenses in investigating and cleaning the applicable sites. The relevant policy language provides the following:

> "Underwriters hereby agree to indemnify the ASSURED for all sums which the ASSURED shall be obligated to pay by reason of the liability imposed upon the ASSURED by law, or assumed by the ASSURED under contract or agreement, for damages * * * on account of personal injuries and the property damage caused by or growing out of each occurrence."

The parties are in agreement that, while there are slight variations among the policies at issue, the basic wording is substantially the same.

Nicor claims that because it was legally obligated to pay the costs of responding to the contamination by reason of liability imposed by law or alternatively based upon its agreements with the IEPA, the Insurers were obligated to indemnify it for the costs incurred under the above policy language.

As a preliminary matter, our supreme court has held:

> "The construction of an insurance policy and a determination of the rights and obligations thereunder are questions of law for the court which are appropriate subjects for disposition by way of summary judgment. [Citations.] In construing an insurance policy, the primary function of the court is to ascertain and enforce the intentions of the parties as expressed in the agreement.

> [Citations.] To ascertain the intent of the parties and the meaning of the words used in the insurance policy, the court must construe the policy as a whole, taking into account the type of insurance for which the parties have contracted, the risks undertaken and purchased, the subject matter that is insured and the purposes of the entire contract. [Citations.]" *Crum & Forster,* 156 Ill.2d at 391, 189 Ill.Dec. 756, 620 N.E.2d 1073.

In Illinois, the general rule "is that an insurer's duty to defend and its duty to indemnify are separate and distinct, with the duty to defend being broader than the duty to indemnify." *Douglas v. Allied American Insurance,* 727 N.E.2d 376 (2000). Here, the question is whether the Insurers were obligated to indemnify Nicor for remediation expenses under the policies.

This court recently held:

> " '[T]he question of whether the insurer has a duty to indemnify the insured for a particular liability is only ripe for consideration if the insured has already incurred liability in the underlying claim against it.' [Citation.] In other words, the duty to indemnify arises when the insured becomes 'legally obligated' to pay damages in the underlying action that gives rise to a claim under the policy. One does not become legally obligated until a judgment or settlement is reached between the parties. [Citation.]" (Emphasis omitted.) *Guillen v. Potomac Insurance Co. of Illinois,* 751 N.E.2d 104 (2001).

Nicor suggests that *Zurich Insurance Co. v. Carus Corp.,* 689 N.E.2d 130 (1997), decided by this court, is not dispositive of the indemnification issue because the policies in *Carus* involved the duty to defend whereas the policies in this case are only indemnification policies. In *Carus,* the plaintiff-insurer sought a declaratory judgment action against the defendant-insured, Carus Corporation—a chemical manufacturer, under general liability policies issued to Carus by several insurers. The plaintiff sought a declaration as to whether the insurers owed Carus reimbursement for expenses incurred during an investigation of possible contamination in the soil and groundwater.

The policies in *Carus* stated the following:

> " 'The Company will pay on behalf of the insured all sums which the insured shall become legally obligated to pay as damages because of:
>
> Coverage A. bodily injury
>
> Coverage B. property damage to which this insurance applies, caused by an occurrence, and the company shall have the right and duty to defend any suits against the insured seeking damages * * *.' " *Carus,* 689 N.E.2d 130.

In 1991, the IEPA and the United States Environmental Protection Agency (USEPA) made an assessment of the Carus chemical facility. Carus notified its insurers of the results of a site screening inspection (SSI) in 1992. In order to avoid being placed on the USEPA's national priorities list, Carus petitioned the IEPA to proceed under the site remediation program. In 1993, Carus was notified that the IEPA intended to conduct an SSI on certain property adjacent to the Carus chemical facility. Several of Carus' insurers were notified of this investigation and they denied coverage. In 1994, the IEPA notified Carus that hazardous substances had been found on the property. In 1995, the plaintiff filed a declaratory judgment action seeking a determination that it had no duty to defend or to indemnify Carus in the absence of a lawsuit. All parties filed motions for summary judgment and the trial court granted the insurers' motions and denied Carus' motion. The issue in *Carus,* as defined by the court on appeal, was whether the insurers were "required to indemnify Carus for expenses incurred while participating in the IEPA's site remediation program." *Carus,* 689 N.E.2d 130.

Relying on the supreme court decisions in *Outboard Marine Corp. v. Liberty Mutual Insurance Co.,* 607 N.E.2d 1204 (1992), and *Lapham-Hickey Steel Corp. v. Protection Mutual Insurance Co.,* 655 N.E.2d 842 (1995), this court found that the insurers had no duty to defend or to indemnify Carus on the ground that the language in the policies required the environmental agencies to initiate a proceeding in a court of law in order for there to be coverage. *Carus,* 689 N.E.2d 130. Specifically, the court held:

> "The rule coming out of *Outboard Marine* and *Lapham-Hickey* is clear: an insurer's duty to defend and indemnify is triggered by a suit against the insured, and in the absence of a lawsuit, no such duty exists. Since no suit was brought against Carus, the insurers had no duty to defend or indemnify." *Carus,* 689 N.E.2d 130.

In *Lapham-Hickey,* the supreme court concluded that the word "suit" within an all risks liability policy, required an action in a court of law and did not apply to "allegations, accusations or claims which have not been embodied within the context of a complaint." *Lapham-Hickey,* 655 N.E.2d 842.

Nicor claims that the reasoning of *Carus* cannot control indemnity-only policies like the ones in the instant case because such an interpretation would render the policies "illusory" and no obligations would be imposed on the insurers. We disagree, as discussed in detail below, because the issue is whether coverage under the instant policies was properly triggered by the voluntary efforts of remediation initiated by Nicor.

As pointed out above, Nicor contends that the holding in *Carus* is not dispositive because the policies therein contained language that the insurers had a duty to defend "any suits against the insured seeking damages * * * ." *Carus,* 689 N.E.2d 130. Thus, Nicor suggests that *Carus* was limited to policy language requiring that a "suit" be brought against the insured before the insurer had a duty to indemnify. Nicor points out that the indemnity-only policies in this case contain no language requiring that a suit be brought against the insured before the insurer can have any duty to indemnify. However, a reading of *Carus* reveals that the court also based its holding on the fact that Carus never became "legally obligated to pay" its investigation and remediation costs. *Carus,* 689 N.E.2d 130.

We also disagree with Nicor that the *Carus* court's reliance on the "obligated to pay" language was merely *dicta* because the court clearly stated that no document Carus ever received from an environmental agency triggered the obligation. *Carus,* 689 N.E.2d 130. The policy in the instant case reveals similar language, "Underwriters hereby agree to indemnify the ASSURED for all sums which the ASSURED shall be obligated to pay by reason of the liability imposed upon the ASSURED by law, or assumed by the ASSURED under contract or agreement, for damages." Thus, we find *Carus* to be controlling because it did not only rely on the "suit" language, but also considered the "obligated to pay" language, which is similar to the policy language at issue in this case.

We also conclude that the trial court correctly held that no material question of fact existed which would preclude summary judgment on the issue. As Lexington observed in its brief, the record revealed that the IEPA never issued a section 4(q) notice of potential liability to Nicor under the Environmental Protection Act. 415 ILCS 5/4(q) (West 1998). Further, no evidence demonstrated that any court action or administrative proceeding had been brought against Nicor by the IEPA. Instead, the record indicated that Nicor, on its own volition, enrolled the sites at issue into the site remediation program. Because Nicor could not offer any evidence that it was obligated to pay these remediation costs by reason of liability imposed upon it by law, we find that summary judgment was proper.

Because our ruling on the first question is dispositive of this appeal, we need not consider whether the trial court erred in granting the Insurers' motions for summary judgment on the ground that the environmental contamination at the various sites did not constitute "occurrences" under the policies at issue. For the reasons above, we affirm the order of the trial court.

---

## QUESTIONS AND DISCUSSION

**1.** The reasoning the court employed in *Northern Illinois Gas* is consistent with that followed in many states: (1) insurers have no duty to defend or to indemnify in connection with remedial costs unless environmental agencies initiate an administrative or judicial proceeding; (2) the insured does not become legally obligated until a judgment or settlement is reached between the parties to that proceeding; therefore, (3) an insured who engages in voluntary remediation is not "obligated" to pay these remediation costs within the meaning of the CGL policy—i.e., by reason of liability imposed upon it by law. So, no coverage. What incentives does this approach present to owners of insurance policies? How would you have advised a client in Nicor's position to have proceeded?

**2.** On the other hand, many states adopt the contrary view, that if an insured is obligated to remediate contaminated land under applicable environmental laws, the filing of a lawsuit is an unnecessary step for triggering coverage. So long as the insured is working in cooperation with the government to accomplish compliance with applicable remediation requirements and standards, even if purely voluntary or under the terms of a voluntary consent decree, the payment of funds toward the remediation is the functional equivalent of a settlement and thus is covered under the policy in the absence of clear language to the contrary. *See* Weyerhauser Co. v. Commercial Union Ins. Co., 15 P.3d 115, 135–36 (2000). What incentives does this approach present to owners of insurance policies? How would you have advised an insurance company client to write its policies in such a state?

**3.** In some states, had a company in Nicor's position received so much as a letter from the government notifying it that it is potentially liable for remediation, coverage under the traditional CGL policy would be triggered, but in other states it would not. *See* R.T. Vanderbilt Co. v. Continental Casualty Co., No. 17178 (Conn. Apr. 26, 2005) (summarizing different approaches among state courts that have decided the issue). If you were representing an insured client in a state that recognizes such a letter as a coverage trigger, would you advise it to seek such a letter before incurring response costs? If you were representing the government agency receiving such a request, would you advise it to issue such a letter?

---

## B. ACCIDENTS AND OCCURRENCES

### EnergyNorth Natural Gas, Inc. v. Underwriters at Lloyd's

Supreme Court of New Hampshire, 2004.
848 A.2d 715.

■ DUGGAN, J.

The United States District Court for the District of New Hampshire (*McAuliffe*, J.) certified the following question of law, *see Sup.Ct. R.* 34:

> What "trigger-of-coverage" standard should be applied under New Hampshire law to determine the point at which an "accident" or "occurrence" causing "property damage" took place, within the meaning of the accident- and occurrence-based

> insurance policy provisions at issue, where an insured alleges that: hazardous contaminants leaked and spilled onto the site over time, before 1952, and migrated through soil and groundwater, causing continuous injury to the pertinent property, from the time the leaks and spills occurred through the periods of coverage under the policies (1958–1983), which property damage was ordered by governmental agencies to be cleaned up in approximately 1996[?]

We adopt the district court's recitation of the facts. The plaintiff, EnergyNorth Natural Gas, Inc. (EnergyNorth), is the successor to companies that operated manufactured gas plants (MGPs) at sites in Laconia and Nashua. The plants began operating before 1900 and ceased MGP operations in 1952. In 1996, the New Hampshire Department of Environmental Services notified EnergyNorth of the existence of pollution damage at the MGP sites and required it to undertake investigative and remedial action, which resulted in EnergyNorth incurring substantial costs.

Underwriters at Lloyd's, Utica Mutual Insurance Company (Utica), St. Paul Fire and Marine Insurance Company (St. Paul) and Century Indemnity Company (Century Indemnity) issued the various comprehensive general liability (CGL) insurance policies in question. The policies became effective in 1958, and provided coverage until 1983. These policies insured against liabilities associated with property damage resulting from "occurrence(s)" or "accident(s)."

EnergyNorth brought a declaratory judgment action against the defendants in federal district court seeking indemnification for costs associated with investigating the pollution damage at the MGP sites and restoring the property. In its pleadings, EnergyNorth asserted that the pollution damage was predominantly caused by inadvertent leaks and spills during the years of MGP operations, particularly from underground gas holders and associated piping, and from unlined tar pits. EnergyNorth further asserted that the toxic wastes discharged into the environment continuously migrated through soil and groundwater at the sites, causing continuous discrete property damage as they moved. EnergyNorth argues that the continued migration of toxic wastes resulted in property damage due to "accident(s)" or "occurrence(s)" as those terms are used in the policies; therefore the defendants' CGL policies were triggered and provide coverage for the clean-up costs. The defendants argue that their respective CGL policies were not triggered.

The term "trigger" does not appear in the policy language, but rather describes "that which, under the specific terms of an insurance policy must happen in the policy period in order for the potential of coverage to arise. The issue is largely one of timing—what must take place within the policy's effective dates for the potential of coverage to be 'triggered'?" *Montrose Chem. Corp. v. Admiral Ins. Co.,* 913 P.2d 878, 880–81, n. 2 (1995) (emphasis omitted). Determining the type of event that will trigger coverage under the particular language of a policy is the first step in assessing whether the policy provides coverage for the claim made against it. *See* Fischer, *Insurance Coverage for Mass Exposure Tort Claims: The Debate over the Appropriate Trigger Rule*, 45 Drake L.Rev. 625, 631–32 (1997). This determination depends upon the language used in the policy and the relevant state law. *See CPC Intern. v. Northbrook Excess & Surplus Ins.*, 46 F.3d 1211, 1222 (1st Cir. 1995); Andrea, *Exposure, Manifestation of Loss, Injury-in-Fact, Continuous Trigger: The Insurance Coverage Quagmire*, 21 Pepp. L.Rev. 813, 830 (1994).

Other jurisdictions have generally recognized four approaches to determine how coverage under an insurance policy is triggered: (1) manifestation; (2) injury-in-fact or actual damage; (3) exposure; and (4) continuous trigger. 23 E. Holmes, *Appleman on Insurance 2d* § 145.3(B)(1), at 13–14 (2003).

Under a manifestation theory, "the date of loss is assigned to the policy period when property damage or actual damage is discovered, becomes known to the insured or a third party, or should have reasonably been discovered." *Id.* § 145.3(B)(2)(a), at 14. The injury-in-fact theory "implicates all of the policy periods during which the insured proves some injury or damage." *Id.* § 145.3(B)(2)(b), at 15. Under the exposure theory, "all insurance contracts in effect when property was exposed to hazardous waste would be triggered." *Id.* § 145.3(B)(2)(c), at 16. Finally, pursuant to the continuous trigger theory, "any policy on the risk at any time during the continuing loss is triggered[.]" *Id.* § 145.3(B)(2)(d), at 17.

In some situations, there is little practical difference between the particular theories utilized. For instance, "there is little practical difference between 'exposure' and 'injury-in-fact' in instances where contamination occurs almost immediately upon release." *Quaker State Minit-Lube, Inc. v. Fireman's Fund Ins. Co.*, 868 F. Supp. 1278, 1304 (D.Utah 1994), *aff'd*, 52 F.3d 1522 (10th Cir. 1995). Likewise, "[w]here the release or discharge of hazardous waste into the environment is identifiable, or even obvious, 'manifestation' occurs simultaneously with 'exposure' and 'injury.'" *Id.* Under the continuous trigger theory, however, it is assumed "without substantiation, that once property damage begins it always continues and that property damage results when property is first exposed to hazardous materials." Holmes, *supra* § 145.3(B)(2)(d), at 17. Thus, the continuous trigger theory "typically maximizes insurance coverage since all policies on the risk from the date of initial exposure through manifestation are triggered" regardless of proof of actual property damage during the policy period. *Id.*

Because the interpretation of the insurance policies in this case involves an unresolved issue of New Hampshire law, namely, what "trigger of coverage" theory applies, the district court certified the question to this court. In resolving this issue, we must look to the language of the policies in question. *See Quaker State Minit-Lube, Inc.*,

868 F. Supp. at 1303 (adopting a trigger-of-coverage theory that was "consistent with the pertinent policy language").

The interpretation of insurance policy language is a question of law for this court to decide. *Godbout v. Lloyd's Ins. Syndicates,* 834 A.2d 360 (2003). We construe the language of an insurance policy as would a reasonable person in the position of the insured based upon a more than casual reading of the policy as a whole. *Id.* Policy terms are construed objectively, and where the terms of a policy are clear and unambiguous, we accord the language its natural and ordinary meaning. *Id.* We need not examine the parties' reasonable expectations of coverage when a policy is clear and unambiguous; absent ambiguity, our search for the parties' intent is limited to the words of the policy. *Id.* Where, however, the language of the policy reasonably may be interpreted more than one way and one interpretation favors coverage, an ambiguity exists in the policy that will be construed in favor of the insured and against the insurer. *High Country Assocs. v. N.H. Ins. Co.,* 648 A.2d 474 (1994).

As a threshold matter, we must determine whether the policies are ambiguous. The fact that the parties may disagree on the interpretation of a term or clause in an insurance policy does not create an ambiguity. *Oliva v. Vermont Mut. Ins. Co.,* 842 A.2d 92, 95 (2004). In addition, policy provisions are not ambiguous merely because it is difficult to apply the factual situation to the specific policy language. *Id.* We will not create an ambiguity simply to construe the policy against the insurer. *Int'l Surplus Lines Ins. Co. v. Mfgs. & Merchants Mut. Ins. Co.,* 661 A.2d 1192 (1995). We review each of the policies in turn.

*I. St. Paul and Utica Occurrence-Based Policies.*

First, we review three occurrence-based policies. The two policies issued by St. Paul were effective between 1978 and 1982. The policy issued by Utica was effective between 1974 and 1978. The pertinent policy language in one of the St. Paul policies and the Utica policy is as follows:

> The Company will pay on behalf of the Insured all sums which the Insured shall become legally obligated to pay as damages because of:
>
> Coverage A. bodily injury or
>
> Coverage B. property damage
>
> to which this insurance applies, caused by an occurrence. . . .
>
> . . .
>
> "occurrence" means an accident, including continuous or repeated exposure to conditions which results in bodily injury or property damage neither expected nor intended from the standpoint of the Insured.
>
> "property damage" means (1) physical injury to or destruction of tangible property which occurs during the policy period,

> including the loss of use thereof at any time resulting therefrom or (2) loss of use of tangible property which has not been physically injured or destroyed provided such loss of use is caused by an occurrence during the policy period.

The third policy, also issued by St. Paul, provides excess coverage and has slightly different wording. The pertinent policy language is as follows:

> The Company will indemnify the Insured for all sums which the Insured shall become legally obligated to pay as damages . . . on account of:
>
> 1. Personal Injuries,
> 2. Property Damage,
> 3. Advertising Offense,
>
> to which this Policy applies, caused by an occurrence.
>
> . . .
>
> The term "Occurrence" means . . . with respect to property damage, an event, including injurious exposure to conditions, which results during this policy period in such personal injury, or property damage neither expected nor intended from the standpoint of the Insured.

"Property damage" is not defined in the St. Paul excess policy.

Several courts have reviewed policy language identical to that used by St. Paul and Utica. *See, e.g., Cessna Aircraft Co. v. Hartford Acc. & Indem. Co.,* 900 F. Supp. 1489, 1500–04 (D.Kan.1995); *Quaker State Minit-Lube, Inc.,* 868 F. Supp. at 1294. In *Cessna Aircraft*, Cessna sought indemnity from various insurance companies for property damage and associated clean-up costs resulting from groundwater contamination allegedly caused by improper disposal of hazardous materials. *Cessna Aircraft Co.,* 900 F. Supp. at 1493–95. In reviewing the pertinent policy language, the court held that the policies were unambiguous: "[p]roperty damage clearly must occur during the policy period." *Id.* at 1501. Accordingly, "coverage under these policies is 'triggered' by a showing that property damage occurred during the policy period." *Id.* at 1503. In reaching this conclusion, the court rejected the application of a manifestation theory, finding that "application of the 'injury-in-fact' trigger is more consistent with the language of the . . . policies." *Id.*

Similarly, in *Quaker State*, the court adopted the "injury-in-fact" trigger because it was "consistent with the pertinent policy language." *Quaker State Minit-Lube, Inc.,* 868 F. Supp. at 1303. The court noted, however, that when contamination is continuous, "the 'injury-in-fact' theory may also operate to trigger coverage on a continuous basis." *Id.* at 1302, n. 38. Thus, the court concluded that, using an injury-in-fact trigger, an occurrence took place each time property damage was inflicted and that, where alleged contamination and property damage are continuing, " 'injuries-in-fact' triggering coverage are also continuing." *Id.* at 1304.

The holdings in *Cessna Aircraft* and *Quaker State* are supported by the drafting history of the standardized CGL policy language. See *Montrose Chem. Corp.,* 913 P.2d at 890. We review this history because "the presence of standardized industry provisions and the availability of interpretative literature are of considerable assistance in determining coverage issues. Such interpretative materials have been widely cited and relied on in the relevant case law and authorities construing standardized insurance policy language." *Id.* at 891.

Most significant in the drafting history of the standardized insurance policy language is the change in language that was implemented in 1966. *Id.* Prior to 1966, third-party CGL policies covered damages caused by "accidents." *Id.* In 1966, however, the standardized form CGL policy was changed from being "accident-based" to "occurrence-based." *Id.* In making this change, "one of the drafters explained that in some exposure type cases involving cumulative injuries it is possible that more than one policy will afford coverage." *Id.* (emphasis omitted). In addition, the then-secretary of the National Bureau of Casualty Underwriters noted that the new "occurrence-based" policy retained the term "accident" in the definition of "occurrence" in order to "clarify the intent with respect to time of coverage and application of policy limits, particularly in situations involving a related series of events attributable to the same factor. Under such circumstances only one accident or occurrence is intended as far as the application of policy limits is concerned." *Id.* at 892 (quotation omitted).

The drafting history leaves "little doubt that the definition of 'occurrence' in the newly drafted standard form CGL policy was intended to provide coverage when damage or injury resulting from an accident or 'injurious exposure to conditions' occurs during the policy period." *Id.* The drafting history also reveals that:

> The term "accident" was left in the definition of occurrence for the purpose of circumscribing the policy limits applicable to each occurrence. The drafters did not intend to require that an "accident" in the literal sense, e.g., a sudden precipitating event, occur during the policy period in order to trigger potential coverage for ensuing damage or injury. The reference to injurious exposure to conditions resulting in bodily injury or property damage eliminates any requirement that the injury result from a sudden event.

*Id.* (quotation, brackets and ellipses omitted). Moreover, the drafting history demonstrates that "the drafters of the standard occurrence-based CGL policy . . . contemplated that the policy would afford liability coverage for all property damage or injury occurring during the policy period resulting from an accident, or from injurious exposure to conditions." *Id.*

We are persuaded by the drafting history of the standardized insurance policy language and interpretation of the policy language in *Cessna Aircraft* and *Quaker State*. We similarly find no ambiguity in the language in these three policies. They clearly provide that the occurrence of property damage during the policy period is the operative event that triggers coverage. "Occurrence" is defined in the St. Paul and Utica policies as "an accident, *including continuous or repeated exposure to conditions* which results in . . . property damage." (Emphasis added.) The St. Paul and Utica policies define "property damage" as "physical injury . . . which occurs during the policy period." Similarly, the St. Paul excess occurrence policy applies to "property damage . . . caused by an occurrence." The excess policy defines "occurrence" as "an event, *including injurious exposure to conditions*, which results during this policy period in . . . property damage." (Emphasis added.)

The language of these three policies unambiguously distinguishes between the causative event—an accident or continuous or repeated exposure to conditions—and the resulting property damage. It is the property damage that must occur during the policy period, and "which results" from the accident or "continuous or repeated exposure to conditions." Thus, the language of the three policies embodies an "injury-in-fact" trigger, and where the alleged contamination and property damage are continuing, "injuries-in-fact" triggering coverage are also continuing. *Quaker State Minit-Lube, Inc.,* 868 F. Supp. at 1304.

Our adoption of the "injury-in-fact" trigger for the policies at issue is consistent with our holdings in *U.S. Fidelity & Guaranty Co., Inc. v. Johnson Shoes, Inc.,* 461 A.2d 85 (1983), and *Peerless Insurance Co. v. Clough,* 105 N.H. 76, 193 A.2d 444 (1963). While neither *Johnson Shoes* nor *Peerless* expressly adopted a trigger-of-coverage theory, they both involved questions of insurance coverage in occurrence-based policies.

In *Johnson Shoes*, the insurer denied coverage in an environmental contamination case on the ground that the policy only covered "occurrences" taking place during the policy period. *Johnson Shoes, Inc.* 123 N.H. at 153, 461 A.2d 85. Oil had apparently leaked from an underground storage tank and, after the policy period ended, spilled over onto neighboring property. *Id.* 85. We noted that Johnson Shoes proved that the tank was leaking while the insurance policy was in effect. *Id.* We affirmed the trial court's ruling finding coverage without adopting a specific trigger-of-coverage legal theory. *Id.*

In *Peerless*, the insurer denied coverage for fires resulting from the insured's negligent construction of fireplaces on the ground that the negligent act, and not the fires, had to occur within the policy period for coverage to be triggered. *Peerless Insurance Co.,* 193 A.2d at 444. We disagreed and held that "the time of the occurrence resulting in the loss or damage, and not the time of the negligence, determines whether there is coverage under the policy." *Id.*

At most, *Johnson Shoes* and *Peerless* stand for the proposition that coverage can be triggered by the occurrence of property damage while the policy is in effect. Neither *Johnson Shoes* nor *Peerless* held that for coverage to be triggered under an occurrence-based policy, the wrongful act must occur within the policy period; nor did they hold that the injury must be discovered or manifest itself within the policy period. We thus conclude that under New Hampshire law, for these three policies, the trigger of coverage theory is injury-in-fact.

*II. Underwriters at Lloyd's and Century Indemnity Accident-Based Policies.*

We now turn to the two accident-based policies, one issued by Underwriters at Lloyd's and one issued by Century Indemnity. The Underwriters at Lloyd's accident-based policy provides:

> WE THE UNDERWRITERS hereby agree, subject to the terms, conditions and limitations hereinafter mentioned, to indemnify the Assured in respect of accidents occurring during the policy period commencing [policy commencement date] and ending [policy end date] for any and all sums which the Assured shall by law become liable to pay . . . as damages. . . .
>
> (b) for damage to or destruction of property of others (excluding property under the Assured's care, custody or control) caused by accident, hereinafter referred to as "Property Damage", arising out of the hazards covered by and as defined in the underlying policy/ies specified in the Schedule herein and issued by the [Primary Insurers' Names], hereinafter called the "Primary Insurers,"
>
> . . .
>
> 1. ACCIDENT. The word "accident" shall be understood to mean an accident or series of accidents arising out of one event or occurrence.

The Century Indemnity accident-based policy provides:

> Coverage B—Property Damage Liability
>
> To pay on behalf of the *insured* all sums which the *insured* shall become legally obligated to pay as damages because of injury to or destruction of property, including the loss or use thereof, caused by accident.
>
> . . .
>
> This policy applies only to accidents which occur during the policy period. . . .

Again, we find no ambiguity in either policy. The Underwriters at Lloyd's policy unambiguously states that it covers "accidents occurring during the policy period." Similarly, the Century Indemnity policy "applies only to accidents which occur during the policy period." Thus, the accident must occur within the policy period; the resulting damage, however, does not necessarily have to occur during the policy period.

Although we conclude that coverage is triggered under these policies when an "accident" occurs during the policy period, we disagree with Century Indemnity's assertion that the "accident" triggering coverage is limited to a "discrete causative event." Notably, neither policy specifies when an "accident" is deemed to occur.

We have previously interpreted "accident" to mean an undesigned contingency, a happening by chance, something out of the usual course of things, unusual, fortuitous, not anticipated and not naturally to be expected. *Vermont Mut. Ins. Co. v. Malcolm,* 517 A.2d 800 (1986). Because this definition does not incorporate a temporal component, the term "accident" is not as limited as Century Indemnity asserts. *See, e.g., Chemical Leaman Tank Lines v. Aetna Cas. & Sur.,* 817 F. Supp. 1136, 1147–48 (D.N.J.1993) (holding that the term "accident" does not necessarily have a temporal component), *aff'd. in part and remanded on other grounds,* 89 F.3d 976 (3d Cir. 1996), *cert. denied,* 519 U.S. 994 (1996).

Moreover, in *Hudson v. Farm Family Mutual Insurance Co.,* 697 A.2d 501 (1997), we held that injury caused by gradual and continuous exposure to electrical voltage triggered coverage under a policy covering "sudden and accidental damage" because "the term 'sudden and accidental' is . . . reasonably susceptible to an interpretation consistent with 'unexpected and unintended.'" Accordingly, the accident-based policies at issue here are triggered by "accidents" occurring within the policy period, which is not limited to a single, discrete event. We therefore conclude that, under New Hampshire law, the language of the two accident policies clearly embodies an exposure trigger, and where the alleged migration of toxic wastes is continuing, multiple exposures triggering coverage are also continuing. *Cf. Quaker State Minit-Lube, Inc.,* 868 F. Supp. at 1304 (recognizing multiple "injuries-in-fact" triggering coverage where there is continuous contamination).

We therefore conclude that, under New Hampshire law, the language of the policy clearly embodies an exposure trigger, and where the alleged migration of toxic wastes is continuing, multiple exposures triggering coverage are also continuing.

---

## QUESTIONS AND DISCUSSION

**1.** *EnergyNorth* illustrates the importance to insurance coverage questions of defining exactly what happened and when relative to the periods covered under the policy. The *EnergyNorth* court distinguishes between the causative event—an accident or continuous or repeated exposure to conditions—and the resulting property damage. In the court's view, it is the property damage that must occur during the policy period, and "which results" from the accident or "continuous or repeated exposure to conditions," and where the alleged contamination and property damage are continuing, "injuries-in-fact" triggering coverage are also continuing. Several other jurisdictions agree with this interpretation. *See* Quaker State Minit-Lube Inc. v. Fireman's Fund Incs. Co., 868 F. Supp. 1278 (D. Utah 1994), *aff'd*, 52 F.3d 1522 (10th Cir. 2005); Cessna Aircraft Co. v. Hartford Accident & Indemnity Co., 900 F. Supp. 1489 (D. Kan. 1995); Montrose Chem. Corp. v. Admiral Ins. Co., 913 P.2d 878 (Cal. 1995). If this were not the case, most CGL policies issued after, say, 1970, would have had no application to the continuing contamination of resources caused by events occurring in the 1950s or, as in the *Northern Illinois Energy* case from above, the mid-1800s.

**2.** *EnergyNorth* follows the general rule that where the language of the policy reasonably may be interpreted more than one way and one interpretation favors coverage, an ambiguity exists in the policy that will be construed in favor of the insured and against the insurer. How would you have drafted a provision to clearly exclude coverage for the type of "occurrence" that was involved in the case?

---

## C. POLLUTION EXCLUSION CLAUSES

The answer to the previous question was thought to be the "pollution exclusion" clause. As the insurance industry faced the prospect of ever increasing exposure for coverage of remediation costs, insurers inserted pollution exclusion clauses into CGL policies, the idea being that coverage for liabilities associated with pollution would be purchased through separate, specialized "environmental impairment liability" policies. The "standard" pollution exclusion clause provided an exception for the "sudden and accidental" release of pollution, whereas a more aggressive "absolute exclusion" version provided no such exception. The following two cases are examples of the contentious litigation that has ensued over the interpretation of these newer CGL policy provisions.

### Travelers Casualty and Surety Co. v. Ribi Immunochem Research, Inc.

Supreme Court of Montana, 2005.
108 P.3d 469.

■ JUSTICE BRIAN MORRIS delivered the Opinion of the Court.

We must determine whether a comprehensive general liability (CGL) policy provides coverage for environmental damage caused by the intentional disposal of hazardous wastes into a landfill that results in the unintentional migration of the wastes into the groundwater. The Twenty-First Judicial District Court, Ravalli County, found that the policy's pollution exclusion bars coverage for the environmental contamination due to the intentional nature of the dumping. We affirm the District Court's decision to deny coverage to Ribi Immunochen Research, Inc.

(Ribi) under a CGL policy provided by Travelers Casualty and Surety Company (Travelers).

* * *

FACTUAL AND PROCEDURAL BACKGROUND

Ribi, a corporation located in Hamilton, Montana, at all times pertinent to these proceedings, develops biopharmaceutical products. From 1981 to 1985, Ribi used toxic solvents to extract and purify its products. Ribi routinely disposed of its hazardous wastes at Bitterroot Valley Sanitary Landfill (BVSL) for most of this period. Ribi employees transported containers of waste to BVSL each month and poured the liquid contaminants into an open, unlined, earthen pit that measured six feet deep, four feet wide, and eight feet long. Ribi recognized the hazardous nature of its chemical solvents, but hoped that much of the waste would evaporate before migrating through the landfill into the shallow groundwater. Subsequent analysis revealed, however, that the hazardous contaminants migrated into the groundwater approximately 13 to 34 minutes after each disposal.

The Environmental Protection Agency (EPA) discovered groundwater and soil contamination in 1987 resulting from Ribi's waste disposal at BVSL. The National Institute of Health (NIH) later excavated and cleaned the contaminated soil and groundwater. Neighboring property owners sued Ribi in 1993 for personal injury and property damages. The State also sued Ribi in 1997 to recover its response costs arising from contamination in and around the landfill. The next year, 1998, the United States sought contribution from Ribi for NIH's response costs. Ribi eventually settled the claims with all three parties. This litigation arises from the relationship between Ribi and its insurer-Travelers-regarding Ribi's requests for insurance coverage and defense against those three claims.

Travelers issued the CGL policy to Ribi from 1982 through 1985. Ribi filed a claim with Travelers to recover the cost of remediating the damages caused by the contamination. In response, on December 6, 1993, Travelers executed a reservation of rights letter for the neighboring property owners' claims in which it informed Ribi that it owed no indemnity obligation to Ribi and therefore no defense. Travelers also sent Ribi a separate letter on February 10, 1994, regarding its intention to seek reimbursement for defense costs. Travelers and Ribi eventually agreed that Travelers would pay fifty percent of Ribi's defense costs in its suit with the neighboring property owners.

Travelers executed additional reservation of rights letters on January 25, 1996, and March 10, 1999, in response to Ribi's further demand for defense and indemnity of claims brought by the state and federal governments. Travelers again informed Ribi that it owed no indemnity obligations and therefore no defense and also notified Ribi of its intention to seek recoupment of any defense costs in the two government actions. Ribi raised no objections and thereafter, Travelers defended Ribi under its reservation of rights, paying one-hundred percent of the defense costs in the government suits.

Ribi regularly submitted claims to Travelers for defense costs and indemnification under the policies throughout these third-party lawsuits. Travelers denied Ribi's claims and finally brought an action seeking a declaration that it had no duty to provide insurance coverage and defense for these environmental claims. Ribi counterclaimed against Travelers for breach of contract, declaratory relief, breach of the covenant of good faith and fair dealing and violations of the Unfair Claims Settlement Practices Act under § 33–18–201, MCA.

Travelers filed a motion for summary judgment on December 12, 2001, on the declaratory judgment issue and also sought to recoup expenses incurred as part of its defense against the third-party suits. Travelers also refuted Ribi's counterclaim that it had breached the duty of good faith and fair dealing or violated the Unfair Claims Settlement Practices Act in denying Ribi's claims. The District Court granted summary judgment to Travelers on the coverage issue thereby negating all of Ribi's contract-based claims. The court further allowed Travelers to recoup its defense costs in the government suits expended after March 10, 1999. With respect to the neighboring property owners' suits, the District Court initially denied Travelers's recoupment claims, but later amended its order to include those costs expended after February 10, 1994. This appeal followed.

DISCUSSION

Whether the District Court erred in determining that the CGL policy's pollution exclusion provision bars coverage for Ribi's hazardous waste disposal in that the disposal was not "sudden or accidental."

The District Court determined that Ribi's disposal constituted an "occurrence," possibly triggering coverage under the CGL policy, but it found no coverage based upon the fact that Ribi's long-term disposal of hazardous wastes could not be deemed "sudden and accidental" as defined in the CGL policy's pollution exclusion. Ribi argues that the District Court erred in determining that the "sudden and accidental" exception contains a temporal element and instead contends that the term "sudden" should be understood to mean unexpected, and not necessarily quick or abrupt. Ribi maintains, in other words, that even though its disposal may have occurred over a period of years, the CGL policy should provide coverage so long as the ultimate migration of the wastes into the groundwater was unexpected and accidental. Thus, Ribi alleges that the ultimate migration of its waste into the groundwater constituted the relevant event under the CGL policy's pollution exclusion rather than its intentional disposal in the landfill.

General rules of contract law apply to insurance policies and we construe them strictly against the insurer and in favor of the insured.

Erickson v. Dairyland Ins. Co. (1990), 785 P.2d 705, 707–08. Courts give the terms and words used in an insurance contract their usual meaning and construe them using common sense. Hardy v. Progressive Speciality Ins. Co., 67 P.3d 892 (2003). Any ambiguity in an insurance policy must be construed in favor of the insured and in favor of extending coverage. Farmers Alliance Mut. Ins. Co. v. Holeman, 961 P.2d 114 (1998) ¶ 25. An ambiguity exists where the contract, when taken as a whole, reasonably is subject to two different interpretations. Courts should not, however, "seize upon certain and definite covenants expressed in plain English with violent hands, and distort them so as to include a risk clearly excluded by the insurance contract." Johnson v. Equitable Fire & Marine Ins. Co. (1963), 142 Mont. 128, 131, 381 P.2d 778, 779.

A. Definition of "Occurrence"

[The court decided to assume that the unintentional damage caused by Ribi's intentional disposal constituted an "occurrence" as defined in the CGL policy.] This assumption transforms our inquiry into whether the pollution exclusion clause in the CGL policy eliminates coverage for damages arising out of the intentional disposal of hazardous wastes into or upon the land.

B. Pollution Exclusion and its "Sudden and Accidental" Exception

A separate pollution exclusion in the CGL policy restricts the otherwise broad sweep of "occurrence." It provides that the policy does not apply to property damages arising out of the disposal of hazardous wastes into or upon the land. The pollution exclusion clause's general thrust disavows any obligations by Travelers to provide coverage in cases such as this where Ribi's disposal of hazardous wastes caused the damages. The pollution exclusion would proscribe Travelers's coverage if we stopped here because Ribi's hazardous wastes undoubtedly contaminated neighboring soil and groundwater.

In this case, however, the CGL policy's pollution exclusion contains an important exception. This exception states that the exclusion does not apply if the disposal is "sudden and accidental." In other words, the pollution exclusion eliminates claims from coverage unless the claim arises from the disposal of hazardous wastes deemed to be "sudden and accidental." Travelers contends that "sudden" includes a temporal element within the CGL policy's context that must be applied to Ribi's disposal of hazardous wastes.

In Sokoloski v. American West Ins. Co., 980 P.2d 1043 (1999), we discussed the meaning of a similar "sudden and accidental" provision in a homeowner's policy. There we concluded that the gradual accumulation of soot and smoke on the walls, ceiling and floor of the insured's home caused by prolonged burning of candles during the holiday season did not constitute a "sudden" release of pollutants. We focused on the fact that the unambiguous language of the "sudden and accidental" exception in a pollution exclusion clause in a homeowner's policy contains a temporal element. We noted that the very use of the two words "sudden" and "accidental" reveals a clear intent to define them to state two separate requirements. In other words, the word "sudden," even if it includes the concept of unexpectedness, also encompasses a temporal element, because the word "accidental" already expresses "unexpectedness."

Thus, we concluded that in order for the word "sudden" to have significant purpose, and not to be surplusage when used generally in conjunction with the word "accidental," it must have a temporal aspect to its meaning, and not merely a sense of something unexpected. Further, recognizing our duty to interpret the contract as a whole, the failure to show one condition, i.e., suddenness, negates the exception to the pollution exclusion resulting in no coverage under the insurance policy. We now extend Sokoloski's holding to the standard pollution exclusion in a CGL policy.

Ribi suggests that we should consider the drafting history of the "sudden and accidental" pollution exclusion to determine its meaning. Extrinsic evidence may be used as an aid in interpreting contract provisions, however, only when the language contained therein is ambiguous. Section 28–2–905, MCA. We have declared identical policy language in Sokoloski to be unambiguous, and, therefore, we deem it unnecessary to consider Ribi's arguments pertaining to the drafting history of the CGL policy's pollution exclusion clause.

C. Burden of Proof

Now that we have determined that the "sudden and accidental" exception to the pollution exclusion contains a temporal element, we must address an issue of first impression: which party bears the burden of proving that an exception to an exclusion applies, such as the "sudden and accidental" exception at issue here. We agree with Travelers that the insured bears the burden of proof.

Courts generally allocate the respective burdens of proof to the insured and insurer consistent with the basic distinction between coverage clauses and exclusionary clauses. The insured must prove in the first place a loss stemming from an "occurrence" of the type included in the general coverage provision. See, e.g., MacKinnon v. Truck Ins. Exchange (2003), 73 P.3d 1205, 1213. In turn, the insurer has the burden of proving the applicability of an exclusionary clause, such as the pollution exclusion. See, e.g., United States Fidelity & Guaranty (D.Kan.1990), 734 F. Supp. 437, 442; Keggi v. Northbrook Property and Cas. Ins. Co. (App.Ct.2000), 13 P.3d 785, 788. We agree with those courts that have allocated the initial burden to the insured to establish that the claim falls within the basic scope of coverage and shifted to the insurer the burden to establish that the claim specifically is excluded.

We now turn to the third and final step in the process. Although courts remain split on the issue, the majority return the burden of proving an exception to an exclusion to the insured. For example, in St.

Paul Fire & Marine Ins. v. Warwick Dyeing Corp. (1st Cir. 1994), 26 F.3d 1195, 1200, the court held that the insured who disposed of various waste materials at a landfill bore the burden of proving that an exception to the pollution exclusion applied. Likewise the court in Fireman's Fund, 702 F. Supp. at 1328, determined that the insured carries the burden of proving the exception to the pollution exclusion because the insured possess the information pertaining to its activities. This allocation appropriately aligns the burden with the benefit as the party seeking the benefit of a particular policy provision bears the burden of proving its application. See Intel Corp. v. Hartford Accident & Indem. Co. (9th Cir. 1991), 952 F.2d 1551, 1557.

The CGL policy's "sudden and accidental" exception creates coverage for environmental contamination where it otherwise would not exist. Correspondingly, the insured bears the burden of proving that the coverage stems from this exception: "[W]hen a policy contains an exception within an exception, the insurer need not negative the internal exception; rather, the [insured] must show that the exception from the exemption from liability applies." 19 G. Couch, Couch on Insurance 2d § 79.385, 338 (1983). Further, if the burden were on the insurer to disprove the exception, the insured would have no incentive to discover whether its disposed wastes gradually were migrating into neighboring groundwater, because "preservation of ignorance would increase the likelihood of insurance coverage." Aeroquip Corp. v. Aetna Cas. and Sur. Co., Inc. (9th Cir. 1994), 26 F.3d 893, 895.

The District Court relied on Travelers Cas. & Sur. Co. v. The Superior Court of Santa Clara (1998), 63 Cal.App.4th 1440, 75 Cal.Rptr.2d 54, for the proposition that the insurer has the burden of making an affirmative showing in a summary judgment motion that the insured cannot establish that the claims fall within the "sudden and accidental" exception to the pollution exclusion. *Travelers* is not persuasive here. Forcing the insurer to prove a negative—that the discharge was not all sudden and accidental—seems unfair where the insured solely possesses the relevant information pertaining to its activities. *Fireman's Fund*, 702 F. Supp. at 1328. By contrast, it would impose an undue burden on the insurer to require it to discover independently evidence of an insured's sudden and accidental disposal of pollutants. We conclude that Ribi had the burden of proving that its disposal of hazardous wastes into the groundwater of neighboring property owners was "sudden and accidental."

D. Relevant Event Under the "Sudden and Accidental" Exception

Next, we must consider whether the "sudden and accidental" exception of the CGL policy's pollution exclusion focuses on Ribi's initial disposal of the hazardous wastes or on the subsequent migration of these wastes away from the disposal site and the corresponding damage. Ribi maintains that the ultimate migration of its wastes into the groundwater constitutes the relevant event under the CGL policy's pollution exclusion rather than its intentional disposal of them into the landfill.

Other courts have taken the opposite approach. For instance, the court in LaFarge Corp. v. Travelers Indem. Co. (11th Cir. 1997), 118 F.3d 1511, held that under Florida law, it is actual discharge, not resulting damages or contamination, that must be "sudden and accidental" in order to fall within the exception to the pollution exclusion clause in comprehensive general liability policies. As discussed previously, basic coverage under the CGL policy arises from the occurrence of unintended damages. And the CGL policy generally excludes from basic coverage those damages that arise from the disposal of hazardous wastes. An important exception to the pollution exclusion exists, however, for those discharges that are "sudden and accidental."

We determine that the language of the CGL policy's pollution exclusion clearly excludes coverage for "property damage arising out of the discharge "of hazardous wastes "into or upon the land" unless "such discharge . . . is sudden and accidental." The occurrence that must be sudden and accidental then, is the disposal of hazardous wastes "into or upon the land" from which the property damage arose, not the unexpected migration and corresponding damages. See, e.g., Warwick, 26 F.3d at 1203 (under Rhode Island law, initial disposal of waste at landfill site was relevant discharge that had to be sudden and accidental for coverage to exist under exception to pollution exclusion clause in general liability policy; release of pollutants from landfill into surrounding environment was not relevant discharge); Transamerica Ins. Co. v. Duro Bag Mfg. Co. (6th Cir. 1995), 50 F.3d 370, 373 (holding under Kentucky law that coverage barred insured's depositing of drums and fiberboard barrels containing ink and glue at landfill, when the disposal took place on regular basis or in ordinary course of business).

To hold otherwise eliminates the distinction between unintentional and unexpected disposal and unintentional and unexpected migration and corresponding damages. The court in Queen City Farms, Inc. v. Central Nat. Ins. Co. of Omaha (1994), 882 P.2d 703, blurred this distinction when it held that "if the damage results from the dispersal of materials into the groundwater from a place of containment where the insured believed they would remain or from which they would be safely filtered, and that dispersal was unexpected or unintended, then coverage is provided under the policies." Queen City Farms, 882 P.2d at 725. We determine instead, that whether the insured intended the hazardous wastes to migrate into the groundwater and cause damage after the intentional disposal into the land proves irrelevant. The disposal must be sudden and accidental to qualify for coverage, not the migration and corresponding damage. Even were we to apply the "sudden and accidental" exception to the ultimate migration of the wastes, in contradiction to our holding today, the migration was not abrupt or quick, only unintentional. We conclude, therefore, that the initial disposal, rather than the migration and any resulting damages, must be "sudden and accidental" in order to fall within the exception to the CGL policy's pollution exclusion clause.

Here Ribi intentionally disposed of hazardous wastes at the BVSL site over a three-year period. If, as we have held, the term "sudden" constitutes both an "abrupt" and a "quick" discharge, then without question disposing contaminants into or upon the land for a period of three years cannot be construed as "sudden." Indeed, Ribi's employees transported containers of waste to BVSL each month and poured the liquid contaminants into an open, unlined, earthen pit that measured six feet deep, four feet wide, and eight feet long. Ribi's intentional disposal of hazardous wastes represents the relevant event and not the later migration of hazardous wastes from the landfill into the groundwater and neighboring property. Ribi's disposal of hazardous wastes into BVSL cannot be construed either as accidental or unexpected, and, therefore, the District Court correctly concluded that the CGL policy's pollution exclusion barred coverage.

---

## QUESTIONS AND DISCUSSION

**1.** The standard pollution exclusion clause, which actually became common in the 1970s, contained the "sudden and accidental" exception that plays center stage in the *Ribi* case. The key move in the opinion is the court's reasoning that "the very use of the two words 'sudden' and 'accidental' reveals a clear intent to define them to state two separate requirements. In other words, the word 'sudden,' even if it includes the concept of unexpectedness, also encompasses a temporal element, because the word 'accidental' already expresses 'unexpectedness.'" Notice that the court, on the ground that this meaning was unambiguous, rejected Ribi's suggestion that the court should consider the drafting history of the "sudden and accidental" pollution exclusion to determine its meaning. Why would the history of the provision's drafting have mattered to Ribi? Possibly because a plausible argument can be made that the insurance industry, as it considered early versions of the pollution exclusion clause, did have in mind the "unexpectedness" meaning of "sudden." *See* John E. Heintz and Richard D. Milone, *Insurance Coverage Litigation Issues*, in ENVIRONMENTAL LITIGATION, 207, 236–40 (Janet S. Kole et al., eds. 1999).

**2.** Ribi was put in a bit of a pickle given the "temporal" principle adopted by the court, that "the occurrence that must be sudden and accidental then, is the disposal of hazardous wastes 'into or upon the land' from which the property damage arose, not the unexpected migration and corresponding damages." Ribi's disposal may have been sudden, but it clearly was not accidental; whereas the migration of the contaminants was accidental, but it was not sudden. Given the idea behind the pollution exclusion clause, should an insured in Ribi's position be denied coverage?

**3.** To make matters worse for Ribi, consider how the court allocated the burden of proof: (1) the insured must prove in the first place a loss stemming from an "occurrence" of the type included in the general coverage provision (which Ribi satisfied); at which point (2) the insurer bears the burden to establish that the claim specifically is excluded (which Travelers satisfied); at which point (3) the burden returns to the insured of proving any exception to an exclusion to the insured. Ribi thus had the burden of proving that its disposal of hazardous wastes into the groundwater of neighboring property owners was "sudden and accidental." The court reasoned that this shifting burden of proof appropriately aligns the burdens with the corresponding benefits as the party seeking the benefit of a particular policy provision bears the burden of proving its application.

---

## Nav-Its, Inc. v. Selective Insurance Company of America

Supreme Court of New Jersey, 2005.
869 A.2d 929.

■ JUSTICE WALLACE delivered the opinion of the Court.

This case concerns the applicability of a pollution exclusion provision in a commercial general liability insurance policy. The question presented is whether the exclusion for injuries caused by the "discharge, dispersal, release or escape of pollutants" bars coverage for personal injury allegedly caused by the exposure to toxic fumes that emanated from a floor coating/sealant operation performed by the insured. An exception to the pollution exclusion allows coverage where the injury takes place inside a building "within a single 48-hour period and the exposure occurs within the same 48-hour period." . . .

I.

The material facts are relatively simple. Plaintiff NAV-ITS, Inc. (Nav-Its), is a construction contractor specializing in tenant "fit-out" work, including the building of partitions, the laying of concrete, the installation of doors, and the application of finishes, such as paint, sealants, and coatings.

On April 22, 1998, Nav-Its entered into a contract to perform fit-out work at the Parkway Shopping Center (Center) in Allentown, Pennsylvania. Nav-Its obtained Comprehensive General Liability (CGL) insurance coverage for its activities at the Center from defendant Selective Insurance Company of America (Selective). Nav-Its hired T.A. Fanikos Painting (Fanikos) as a subcontractor on the project to perform painting, coating and floor sealing work. Fanikos performed that work from July 27 to August 5, 1998. During that time, Dr. Roy Scalia, a physician with office space in the Center, was allegedly exposed to fumes that were released while Fanikos performed the coating/sealant work. As a result of that exposure, Dr. Scalia suffered from nausea, vomiting, lightheadedness, loss of equilibrium, and headaches. He sought medical treatment in September 1998.

In December 2000, Dr. Scalia filed a complaint against Nav-Its and several others for personal injuries arising out of his exposure to fumes at his office from July 27 through July 31, 1998, and from August 3 through August 5, 1998. Nav-Its forwarded the complaint to Selective, seeking defense and indemnification. Relying on the pollution exclusion in its policy, Selective refused to provide coverage to Nav-Its. Dr. Scalia's case against Nav-Its was subsequently resolved through binding arbitration.

Nav-Its then commenced the present action against Selective, seeking a declaratory judgment that Selective was obligated to defend and indemnify it in connection with the underlying personal injury action. Nav-Its also sought reimbursement for the costs incurred in defending the suit filed by Dr. Scalia.

. . . The trial court concluded that Nav-Its had a reasonable expectation that liability arising out of normal painting operations would be covered under the policy. Selective moved for reconsideration, but once again the trial court denied relief. In a written decision, the trial court expanded its reasoning and concluded that the pollution exclusion clause in the policy applied only to traditional environmental pollution claims. . . . On appeal, in an unpublished opinion, the Appellate Division reversed, finding that pollution exclusion clauses are not necessarily limited to the clean up of traditional environmental damage. . . .

II.

Selective's insurance policy provided CGL coverage for Nav-Its for the period May 7, 1998, through May 7, 1999. The policy provided in the "Coverages" section that it "will pay those sums that the insured becomes legally obligated to pay as damages because of 'bodily injury' or 'property damage' to which this insurance applies." Further, Selective was required to defend any suit seeking those damages. The policy contained a pollution exclusion endorsement that provided in relevant part:

> [Selective] shall have no obligation under this coverage part:
>
> a. to investigate, settle or defend any claim or suit against any insured alleging actual or threatened injury or damage of any nature or kind of persons or property which:
>
> 1. arises out of the 'pollution hazard:' or
>
> 2. would not have occurred but for the 'pollution hazard:' or
>
> b. to pay any damages, judgments, settlements, losses, costs or expenses of any kind or nature that may be awarded or incurred by reason of any such claim or suit or any such actual or threatened injury or damage; or

> c. for any losses, costs or expenses arising out of any obligation, order, direction or request of or upon any insured or others, including but not limited to any governmental obligation, order, direction or request, to test for, monitor, clean up, remove, contain, treat, detoxify, neutralize, in any way respond to, or assess the effects of 'pollutants.'

The policy defined pollutants as "any solid, liquid, gaseous, or thermal irritant or contaminant, including smoke, vapor, soot, fumes, acids, alkalis, chemicals and waste." Under the policy, "[w]aste includes materials to be recycled, reconditioned or reclaimed." It also defined "Pollution Hazard" to mean "an actual exposure or threat of exposure to the corrosive, toxic or other harmful properties of any 'pollutants' arising out of the discharge, dispersal, seepage, migration, release or escape of such 'pollutants.' "

The policy also contained a limited exception to the pollution exclusion. That exception provided that the pollution exclusion does not apply to:

> B. Injury or damage arising from the actual discharge or release of any "pollutants" that takes place entirely inside a building or structure if:
>
> 1. the injury or damage is the result of an exposure which takes place entirely within a building or structure; and
>
> 2. the injury or damage results from an actual discharge or release beginning and ending within a single forty-eight (48) hour period; and
>
> 3. the exposure occurs within the same forty-eight (48) hour period referred to in 2. above; and
>
> 4. within thirty (30) days of the actual discharge or release:
>
> a. the company or its agent is notified of the injury or damage in writing; or
>
> b. in the case of 'bodily injury,' the 'bodily injury' is treated by a physician, or death results, and within ten (10) additional days, written notice of such injury or death is received by the company or its agents.
>
> Strict compliance with the time periods stated above is required for coverage to be provided.

IV.

The central question presented in this case is whether we should limit the applicability of the pollution exclusion clause to traditional environmental pollution claims. We begin our analysis by noting the often-stated principles for interpretation of insurance policy language.

Generally, "[w]hen interpreting an insurance policy, courts should give the policy's words 'their plain, ordinary meaning.'" President v. Jenkins, 853 A.2d 247, 254 (2004) (citation omitted). If the policy language is clear, the policy should be interpreted as written. Ibid. If the policy is ambiguous, the policy will be construed in favor of the insured. Doto v. Russo, 659 A.2d 1371, 1376 (1995). Because of the complex terminology used in the policy and because the policy is in most cases prepared by the insurance company experts, we recognize that an insurance policy is a "contract[ ] of adhesion between parties who are not equally situated." Id. at 555, 659 A.2d at 1376 (quoting Meier v. New Jersey Life Ins. Co., 503 A.2d 862, 869 (1986)). As a result, "courts must assume a particularly vigilant role in ensuring their conformity to public policy and principles of fairness." Voorhees v. Preferred Mut. Ins. Co., 607 A.2d 1255, 1260 (1992). "Consistent with that principle, courts also [ ] endeavor [ ] to interpret insurance contracts to accord with the objectively reasonable expectations of the insured." Doto, supra, 659 A.2d at 1376–77. As we explained in Doto, supra,

> [t]he insured's 'reasonable expectations in the transaction may not justly be frustrated and courts have properly molded their governing interpretative principles with that uppermost in mind.' Allen v. Metropolitan Life Ins. Co., 208 A.2d 638[, 644] (1965). Moreover, we have recognized the importance of construing contracts of insurance to reflect the reasonable expectations of the insured in the face of ambiguous language and phrasing, see State, Dep't of Envtl. Protection v. Signo Trading Int'l, 612 A.2d 932[, 938] (1992), and in exceptional circumstances, when the literal meaning of the policy is plain. See Werner Indus. v. First State Ins. Co., 548 A.2d 188 [, 191] (1988) ('At times, even an unambiguous contract has been interpreted contrary to its plain meaning so as to fulfill the reasonable expectations of the insured. . . .'); Sparks v. St. Paul Ins. Co., 495 A.2d 406[, 414] (1985); Gerhardt v. Continental Ins. Cos., 225 A.2d 328[, 332–33] (1966).

Id. at 1377.

We have applied the reasonable expectations doctrine to all forms of insurance contracts.

V.

[I]n response to much of the litigation surrounding the "sudden and accidental" pollution exclusion for environmentally-related losses, the insurance industry proposed a new pollution exclusion, first appearing in 1985, and commonly known as the absolute exclusion clause. That exclusion is much like the exclusion in the Selective policy in the present case. Two of the obvious differences in the proposed absolute exclusion were the elimination of the reference to an "exception for the 'sudden and accidental' release of pollution, and [ ] the elimination of the requirement that the pollution be discharged 'into or upon land, the atmosphere or any watercourse or body of water.' " Am. States Ins. Co. v. Koloms, 687 N.E.2d 72, 81 (1997) (citations omitted).

[C]ommentators have explained that the absolute pollution exclusion was developed to address the expansion of liability for remediating hazardous waste imposed under the Comprehensive Environmental Response, Compensation & Liability Act (CERCLA, 42 U.S.C. § et. seq.) in 1980. Masters, supra, Envtl. Claims. J. at 457; Jeffrey W. Stempel, Reason and Pollution: Correctly Construing the "Absolute" Exclusion In Context and in Accord with Its Purpose and Party Expectations, 34 Tort & Ins. L.J. 1, 29–32 (1998) ("[T]he available evidence most strongly suggests that the absolute pollution exclusion was designed to serve the twin purposes of eliminating coverage for gradual environmental degradation and government-mandated cleanup such as Superfund response cost reimbursement.").

We have reviewed the development of the pollution exclusion to assist our interpretation of the pollution exclusion in the Selective policy. Based on that review, we are confident that the history of the pollution-exclusion clause in its various forms demonstrates that its purpose was to have a broad exclusion for traditional environmentally related damages.

Notably, we have not been presented with any compelling evidence that the pollution exclusion clause in the present case, when approved by the Department of Insurance, was intended to be read as broadly as Selective urges. See Stempel, supra, 34 Tort & Ins. L.J. at 33. ("If the absolute exclusion was intended to reach as broadly as now contended, one would expect to see conclusive ISO memoranda and similar documents"). To be sure, read literally, the exclusion would require its application to all instances of injury or damage to persons or property caused by "any pollutants arising out of the discharge, dispersal, seepage, migration, release or escape of . . . any solid, liquid, gaseous, or thermal irritant or contaminant, including smoke, vapor, soot, fumes, acids, alkalis, chemicals and waste." If we were to accept Selective's interpretation of its pollution exclusion, we would exclude essentially all pollution hazards except those falling within the limited "exception" for exposure within a structure resulting from a release of pollutants "within a single forty-eight hour period." We reject Selective's interpretation as overly broad, unfair, and contrary to the objectively reasonable expectations of the New Jersey and other state regulatory authorities that were presented with an opportunity to disapprove the clause. . . .

---

## QUESTIONS AND DISCUSSION

**1.** What, precisely, are "traditional environmental pollution claims" as that term is used in *Nav-Its*? Does the *Nav-Its* court provide a definition or benchmark? It appears that even the insurance company defendant accepted that the exposure to fumes from paint being applied in a workplace is not a traditional environmental pollution event. Why isn't it? Must the activity be regulated under environmental laws? Must the activity also not involve application of a chemical product as intended? One view, which appears to have persuaded the *Nav-Its* court, is that early drafts of the pollution exclusion clause defined pollution as "discharges into or upon the land, the atmosphere or any watercourse or body of water," and that this historical version forever defines the scope of the exclusion. *See* Anderson v. Highland House Co., 757 N.E.2d 329 (Ohio 2001). But why would this control the absolute pollution exclusion, which dropped that language and replaced it with a broad exclusion "for discharge, dispersal, seepage, migration, release or escape of . . . any solid, liquid, gaseous, or thermal irritant or contaminant, including smoke, vapor, soot, fumes, acids, alkalis, chemicals and waste"? Indeed, as seems to be the case with virtually every environmental liabilities insurance coverage issue, courts differ on the question addressed in *Nav-Its* as well, with some courts applying the absolute exclusion literally to any kind of chemical dispersals or exposures. *See* Pure Tech Systems, Inc. v. Mt. Hawley Ins. Co., No. 02–3703 (6th Cir. Mar. 26, 2004); Acceptance Ins. Co. v. Powe Timber Co., Inc., 403 F. Supp. 2d 552 (S.D. Miss. 2005) (absolute exclusion barred recovery for personal injuries resulting from inhalation of fumes from treated woodchips sold or given away for mulch); Continental Casualty Co. v. Advance Terrazzo & Tile Co., No. Civ. 03–544MJDSJM, 2005 WL 1923661 (D. Minn. Aug. 11, 2005) (absolute exclusion barred recovery for personal injuries resulting from carbon monoxide poisoning).

**2.** As the use of the absolute pollution exclusion became more common, insurance coverage for "traditional environmental pollution claims" became more specialized, more limited, and more expensive. Nevertheless, policies are being written to cover pollution legal liability, remediation cost overruns, remediation design failures, and other discrete sources of liability under environmental law. *See* Joel S. Moskowitz, *Environmental Liability and Real Property Transactions* § 24.11 (2010–1 Supp.). Indeed, the AIG Insurance Company offers over 15 different environmental liability insurance products ranging from broad pollution liability coverage for industrial plants to coverage for spills caused by third-party vendors of a company's products. *See* AIG Environmental Insurance Products, http://www-153.aig.com/business/products/environmental. Many of these products, however, have limited terms, high deductibles, and cover only claims made during the policy term, not events occurring during the policy term claims over which might be made many years after the policy period terminates. They are, in other words, decidedly more favorable to the insurer than is the CGL policy. Because these insurance products are relatively recent, case law interpreting their terms has not substantially developed. Also, because old policies could provide coverage for problems discovered many years later, the questions addressed in the cases covered in this section remain relevant. For an extensive discussion of these new instruments and issues they raise, see Ann M. Waeger, *Current Insurance Policies for Insuring Against Environmental Risks*, WestLaw: SU035 ALI-ABA 1685 (2013)

---

## PROBLEM EXERCISE

Energena and AmmoCorp remain in deep negotiations about the wind farm site (see the Problem Exercise following the section on personal injury litigation). Notwithstanding its concerns about the AmmoCorp site, Energena is eager to acquire the site to establish its first wind farm. AmmoCorp is reluctant to turn over title to the site without a better understanding of how to avoid liability for contamination should any turn up when Energena begins work. Both companies remain concerned about potential common law and statutory liabilities, and of the difficulties they may have in seeking recovery under insurance policies or contribution from other responsible parties should remediation be required.

The two companies are approached by Liability Risk Solutions (LRS), a company that specializes in environmental liability "buyouts." LRS proposes to accept all environmental liabilities that may ever be associated with the site based on conditions as they exist today, in return for a hefty fee of course, and to provide complete indemnification for all costs associated with such liabilities to Energena and AmmoCorp. To protect itself, LRS plans to conduct some site history investigations and to estimate its upper end liability exposure, then to purchase environmental liability insurance for any remediation cost overruns. Does this sound like a viable proposal for AmmoCorp? For Energena? For LRS? What additional information should each party obtain?

For discussion of the "environmental liability buyout" transaction, see Joshua A. Bloom, *Environmental-Liability Buyouts: How to Know When It's the Real Thing*, NATURAL RESOURCES & ENV'T, Winter 2006, at 37. For a discussion of site investigations and contractual indemnifications, turn the page.

# CHAPTER 13

# BUSINESS TRANSACTIONS

**CHAPTER OUTLINE**



---

Even a quick perusal of the materials in Part I of the text will reveal the breadth and depth of potential liability lurking in the substantive body of environmental laws. Not surprisingly, one of the primary roles of environmental lawyers is to advise their clients about the scope of those liabilities in different settings. An attorney representing a business with ongoing industrial operations must be able to provide current legal advice about how to achieve and maintain compliance with a myriad of environmental regulations (see Chapter 10). An attorney working for a government enforcement agency must be able to identify and assess the potential liability of an alleged violator in order to advise the agency about the merits of prosecuting an administrative or judicial enforcement action (see Chapter 11). But in no setting is the demand for focused advice more acute than in the context of businesses involved in asset and stock transactions.

Businesses large and small engage in numerous transactions with third parties, such as the purchase of real estate and capital assets or the acquisition of stock, in which a principal concern has become how not to "inherit" environmental liabilities from the other party. Moreover, in many cases the parties concerned with these issues extend beyond the principals. For example, a lender financing a company's purchase of capital assets from another company will be keenly interested in the environmental liability "portfolio" that might accompany the assets.

The awareness of businesses in general to these kinds of environmental liability concerns crystallized in the 1980s with the realization that the Comprehensive Environmental Response, Compensation, and Liability Act (CERCLA, also known as Superfund) imposes potentially extensive liability for remediation of contaminated facilities on persons who had nothing to do with the cause of the contamination (see Chapter 5). A company that unknowingly purchased contaminated real estate, or that acquired another company which itself had caused contamination at a site, could in many circumstances find itself jointly and severally liable for the costs of remediation. Although

CERCLA has long provided a so-called "third party defense" for "innocent landowners," the scope of the defense was and remains quite limited and difficult to satisfy. In short, as the case law under CERCLA unfolded during the 1980s, businesses of all sizes and types became increasingly aware of the potential CERCLA liability problems posed by what previously had seemed routine business events, and private law firms responded by substantially boosting the size and breadth of their environmental law practice groups.

Although this chapter will lean primarily on CERCLA to illustrate the importance of environmental issues in business transaction settings, it is important not to overstate the role of CERCLA in raising business awareness to the need to pay close attention to environmental regulation. As the materials in Part I of the text illustrate, at the same time CERCLA case law was developing its broad interpretation of liability, a wide range of other environmental laws were coming of age and presenting substantial compliance difficulties for businesses. Many of these compliance issues, such as satisfying Clean Air Act emission restrictions (see Chapter 3) or developing land in endangered species habitat (see Chapter 2), can pose debilitating costs no business would wish to "inherit" from another. By the late 1980s, therefore, many businesses realized that environmental law *in general* was something to be reckoned with as a ubiquitous source of liability whenever contemplating a transaction or business organization event. Before long, the age-old question in such settings—"What are the tax consequences?"—was amended to include environmental consequences as well.

Generally speaking, these days an attorney representing a business in transactional settings must consider three sources of possible concern under environmental regulation:

> *Contamination*: This source of concern encompasses the familiar CERCLA suite of liabilities plus any similar law, such as state equivalents of CERCLA, imposing liability for remedial and restoration costs associated with contaminated resources. Also to be considered in this regard are potential common law liabilities for property damages and personal injuries caused by contamination.
>
> *Compliance*: This source of concern encompasses laws that impose some form of ongoing compliance responsibility, such as the need to obtain and satisfy pollution control and land use permits, requirements to report spills and emissions of regulated chemicals, and similar performance and paperwork standards. At any given time, a facility may be substantially out of compliance with such regulations and thus face significant costs of retrofitting, as well as fines and penalties for past noncompliance
>
> *Constraints*: This source of concern encompasses laws that impose potential constraints on development of land or

expansion of facility size or capacity. For example, a tract of undeveloped land may present no contamination problems, but may be costly to develop because of the presence of endangered species. Or, an industrial facility may be completely in compliance with applicable environmental standards at its current manufacturing capacity, but present substantial compliance issues were the prospective purchaser's plans to increase capacity.

As is evident from Part I of the text, the laws associated with these "3Cs" of environmental concern for businesses are diverse and complex. In a significant business transaction event—e.g., the acquisition of nine large industrial chemical manufacturing facilities that have been in operation in six different states for many decades—it would not be unusual to expect dozens of isolated sites of contamination, a multitude of ongoing instances of noncompliance under several different federal and state laws, and, depending on the plans of the acquiring company, a host of development and expansion constraints associated with one or more of the sites. The environmental attorneys representing both parties to the transaction thus must be able to provide advice regarding a wide span of environmental law issues. The materials in this chapter illustrate the extent of that challenge and the ways in which environmental attorneys have manage them.

## I. ENVIRONMENTAL DUE DILIGENCE IN BUSINESS TRANSACTIONS

Businesses have been involved in the acquisition of assets and stock for centuries, and attorneys have been there all along to provide advice about a variety of transactional issues. Principal among the roles of attorneys in this context has been providing advice about potential liabilities associated with the acquisition, many of which, such as unfulfilled contracts, tax consequences, and labor relations, were the bread and butter of such representation long before the dawn of modern environmental law. The approach lawyers have used to identify and evaluate such liabilities is known as *due diligence*. It involves the systematic search for and evaluation of potential liabilities associated with the acquisition target, which then allows the lawyer to provide the acquiring or selling party information and advice necessary for effective negotiation of the terms of acquisition. Usually this due diligence step is outlined in the transaction *purchase agreement*, which specifies the conditions precedent to the final transaction, and is concluded before the transaction *closing*, which is the date on which transfer of the stock or assets occurs. In this section we explore environmental due diligence at two levels—the general reasons for conducting due diligence in any business transaction involving transfer of stock or assets, and the specific reasons for conducting due diligence to qualify for liability exemptions under federal state contamination remediation laws.

## A. PROTECTING BUYER AND SELLER IN STOCK AND ASSET ACQUISITIONS

As businesses became increasingly aware of the sources of environmental liability concerns discussed above—contamination, compliance, and constraints—it was natural for transactional attorneys to incorporate environmental liability in the due diligence process. But this was not a straightforward transition. While due diligence practice requires a thorough understanding of the substantive law, it also demands creativity, tenacity, and sound judgment. Knowing the law is not enough; indeed, even knowing how to identify liability problems and apply substantive law in their evaluation is just the beginning of due diligence. For example, if it were learned that a facility that is planned for acquisition has received several notices of violations from various state and federal agencies, what additional information can be obtained from the agencies about the nature of the violations and the agencies' intended enforcement plans, and how should that potential liability be factored into the acquisition transaction? These are not questions for which complete answers appear in the law books—some experience with the agencies and with similar enforcement issues is likely to help the lawyer perform an adequate due diligence investigation and assessment.

The environmental attorney involved in business transactions is also likely to be enlisted in developing the strategy for the negotiation and drafting of the transaction instruments. If the due diligence process has identified a variety of risks associated with contamination, compliance, and constraints at facilities planned for acquisition, how can the parties manage those risks? Should the seller retain them in all respects? Can the buyer assume some or all of them and adjust the purchase price with confidence the price adjustment reflects the risks being assumed. In either case, how should the transaction documents be drafted to reflect the agreement?

When the need for these services materialized in the 1980s, business lawyers had little experience with environmental law, and environmental lawyers had little experience with business transactions. Hence, it took some time for environmental due diligence and transaction negotiation practice to emerge with well-defined protocols and objectives. Indeed, for a good while there was very little in the way of coherent practice guidelines. By the late 1980s, the due diligence side of this practice area had come to be known as *environmental auditing*, but there was no common ground over what that entailed other than a bunch of lawyers and consultants peering into the potential liabilities of target business assets or entities. One of your authors expressed concern at the time that this lack of standards could lead to problems for lawyers in the future, not the least of which was the potential for malpractice claims relating to audits that failed to detect environmental liabilities:

> Those practicing in the environmental auditing field thus have a choice: either they can wait for . . . litigation to develop the content of appropriate auditing, possibly with disastrous retroactive results, or they can take steps now to shape that standard and possibly avoid such a wave of litigation. While the latter approach clearly is the more responsible for consultants, lawyers, and their clients, thus far little has been done toward its fulfillment. * * * Efforts by some local and regional engineering and consulting roundtable groups to formulate auditing standards and auditor certification procedures are still in their infancy. Any national consensus on the standards seems unreachable given the current pace of development. Likewise, lawyers have not addressed the issue in any organized way; they seem to be content to let litigation shape the standards—possibly at their expense—and thus miss the opportunity to provide input at the formative stage.

J.B. Ruhl, *Devising Standards for Property Transfer Environmental Audits*, 4 NATURAL RESOURCES & ENV'T 31 (Summer 1989).

Over time, however, those engaged in environmental due diligence developed a general set of practices which, while not formalized in any legal sense, served to respond to the concern about lack of standards and exposure to liability. Some industry groups developed checklists and other standard practice guidance, such as the American Society for Testing and Materials (ASTM) Standard E1527–97, *Standard Practice for Environmental Site Assessments: Phase 1 Environmental Site Assessment Process*. But the ASTM procedures could not anticipate all variations, and they provided little guidance in the way how to engage in the practice of uncovering relevant facts and no mention whatsoever of how to advise clients based on the findings. Environmental due diligence, while aided by these standard practice guidances, was as much an art form as it was a technique.

The following materials, intended to be read and discussed together, provide an overview of current approaches to environmental due diligence, transaction negotiation practice, and a case study illustrating the potential pitfalls any environmental attorney would want to avoid. The first installment is from a "how to" article by two skilled environmental transactional practitioners. The second item is a court opinion from a case involving allegations of legal malpractice in connection with environmental due diligence and transaction negotiation a law firm performed for its client's acquisition of an industrial facility. As you review the practitioners' advice about environmental due diligence and the terms of the transaction, take note of what they describe as the essential ingredients of effective practice. Then, as you review the opinion from the malpractice case, see if you can "red flag" where the due diligence and transactional advice the lawyers provided may have left gaps in informing and protecting their client. In both instances, consider in particular this roadmap of the seven stages of environmental transaction practice in which lawyers become involved:

1. Understand the nature of the transaction and the parties' motivations
2. Design the environmental due diligence
3. Execute the environmental due diligence
4. Provide appropriate advice based on the due diligence findings
5. Assist in negotiating the transaction terms
6. Assist in drafting the transaction instruments to reflect the negotiated terms
7. Assist in post-transaction representation, including litigation

Of course, the few pages we have here to devote to this topic cannot begin to explore more than the surface of the practice of environmental due diligence, which is as much an "art" as it is about knowing the law. For what are perhaps the two most comprehensive and current sources of legal and practice guidance, see JOEL S. MOSKOWITZ, ENVIRONMENTAL LIABILITY AND REAL PROPERTY TRANSACTIONS (2d ed. 1995) (cumulative supplements published bi-annually), and ENVIRONMENTAL ASPECTS OF REAL ESTATE AND COMMERCIAL TRANSACTIONS (James B. Witkin ed., 4th ed. 2011).

## Sara Beth Watson and Kristina M. Woods, *Environmental Issues in Transactions: Old Swamps and New Bridges*

15 NATURAL RESOURCES & ENVIRONMENT 75 (2000).

Once upon a time industrial facilities and concerns were bought and sold, and the resulting stock or asset purchase agreements signed, with little or no thought of environmental issues. Enactment of various environmental laws—especially the Comprehensive Environmental Response, Compensation and Liability Act of 1980, 42 U.S.C. §§ 9601 *et seq.* (CERCLA or Superfund), with its retroactive liability provisions—changed all that. As the unexpectedly broad reach of CERCLA and its state analogues became apparent and old, musty agreements were suddenly the subject of fierce litigation, lawyers began to include specific language designed to address environmental issues.

For at least the past fifteen years, almost all transaction documents involving commercial or industrial real property or a regulated industry have contained specific provisions addressing environmental issues. Through experience with implementing these provisions, we have learned that what may have seemed brilliant draftsmanship in the rush to closing seems less than inspired in the actual implementation.

Additionally, although the primary focus of many transaction lawyers has been the strict, joint and several liability of owners and operators under CERCLA and analogous state statutes, the term "environmental issues" encompasses many other important issues that also must be addressed in the transaction documents. Compliance and permitting with respect to ongoing business operations, access to records of past operations and plant activity, litigation arising from environmental issues and, in certain states, restrictions and conditions on property transfers can create significant financial and operational issues. Against this backdrop, this article identifies a broad checklist of issues for in-house or outside environmental transactional counsel to consider, provides some ideas for bridging the gap between the buyer and the seller, and points out a few of the pitfalls along the way.

***First Step: Understanding the Deal***

The first step in drafting effective language is to understand the deal. Unfortunately . . . no "magic-bullet" language works for all transactions. Drafting effective language requires an understanding of where the parties want to be at the end of the transaction, the driving forces behind the transaction, the overall structure of the transaction, the client's risk tolerance and, of course, the applicable law. This can be more difficult than it sounds. Others involved with the transaction erroneously may assume that environmental counsel needs to know only information "related to the environmental issues" and frequently in transactions environmental counsel are given only the "environmental" sections of the contract to review.

Environmental counsel seeking to provide effective guidance in a transaction must understand not only the motivations of his or her client, but of the other side as well. This differs from deal to deal. While almost every seller would prefer to walk away from the transaction after closing without further liability, the seller's actual need to do so will vary. For example, an individual who is retiring and selling out is unlikely to accept provisions that require continuing input on remediation after closing. Moreover, even if the buyer's counsel pushes such terms through during negotiations, the buyer is likely to find that implementation of the provisions is very difficult, time consuming and costly. On the other hand, a seller that will continue in business after the closing may agree to accept an apportionment of liability scheme in which it has some role in remediation after closing. How much is each side willing to give to make the deal work?

Examples of other questions environmental counsel should ask include: What role will lenders play in the transactions? Do lenders have certain (and possibly different) requirements in order to obtain favorable financing? Is the deal an asset purchase or a stock deal? To what extent, if at all, is the buyer going to continue the same operations or business that the seller has conducted? What kinds of facilities are included in the deal? Are they owned or leased? Assuming the deal includes intellectual property or assets such as product formulations, are these assets subject to regulations under [other] statutory schemes? Answering these questions is a step in determining what contract language is needed for the specific transaction.

Environmental counsel also needs to understand the extent of due diligence, including an assessment of the potential environmental liabilities, that the parties will conduct. However, regardless of which party he or she represents, environmental counsel must understand the scope and limitations of any environmental investigations that have been or will be performed. In some transactions, such as those involving a hostile takeover, due diligence may be very limited. In others, the seller may be comfortable only with a full-blown records review and . . . investigation (*i.e.*, involving actual field sampling and analysis) of the real property. Often the scope of due diligence is somewhere in between those two extremes. Obviously, the more information available, the easier it may be to draft appropriate transaction language. . . .

***Access to Records***

Often overlooked is inclusion of specific language in the agreement regarding access to records that may be relevant to environmental issues. If the former owner takes operational records with it, the new owner can be significantly handicapped in assessing on-site or off-site contamination discovered after the deal closes or defending against personal injury claims. Typical representations and warranties regarding access to documents and periods of cooperation are frequently of such a short duration as to be meaningless with regard to environmental issues. The easiest solution is for the buyer to retain the originals or copies of records likely to be pertinent. However, in some instances, the seller may not agree to the buyer's retention of copies or originals of all documents due to concerns regarding the confidentiality of the documents. If the seller is continuing in the same or related business, or if the seller is involved in litigation which also may encompass these documents, the seller may be reluctant to provide copies to the buyer.

***Ongoing Operations—Compliance and Permitting***

If the buyer plans to operate the facility after closing, issues relating to operating permits should be addressed in the agreement. In some instances the change in ownership may cause regulatory agencies to review certain permits. Other permits may not be transferable and the new owner will have to acquire new permits. Language that addresses the need for the parties to cooperate in acquiring the new permits is important for continuing operations. Delay in obtaining permits may affect important production schedules. Also, remediation issues associated with permitting can have a significant impact on the financial aspects of the transaction. For example, when the buyer seeks to transfer or obtain new air permits, the regulatory authorities may set new emissions limits that require the installation of new, costly equipment.

In addition, regulatory scrutiny of the operation resulting from the transaction may result in inspections or file reviews and the discovery of previously unnoticed violations, such as facility improvements that triggered permit modifications that the seller did not obtain.

The agreement should address who is responsible for permit or other regulatory violations resulting from conditions existing at the time of closing but for which regulatory action does not arise until after closing. The regulatory agency almost always will issue the citation to the current owner of the facility. Thus, in the absence of an agreement to the contrary, the buyer will have responsibility for any citations and penalty assessments received after closing, even if the incident or condition leading to the citation occurred on the seller's watch. Here the quality of the buyer's due diligence is helpful in evaluating the likely costs associated with compliance issues. However, in some instances the seller may not allow, or there may not be time for, the kind of due diligence that would identify potential compliance issues. The seller may be concerned that such an investigation will uncover issues that will require it to report violations to regulatory agencies. In this situation, the buyer can accept risks associated with limited knowledge or may attempt to negotiate language that requires the seller to indemnify the buyer for violations existing before closing that results in citations issued after closing.

***On-Site Contamination***

A significant focus of concern is liability for on-site contamination, sometimes referred to as "on-site legacy issues." There are a variety of ways to address on-site contamination. The thoroughness of the buyer's due diligence, whether the seller will continue to exist after closing, and the risk tolerance of the parties are all factors to consider. Contractual language stating that the seller retains liability for conditions existing before closing and the buyer takes liability for conditions arising after closing is common, but such language has many pitfalls, especially for the buyer. Unless environmental due diligence has established a "baseline," there may be no objective way to sort out what contamination existed prior to the closing and what occurred after the closing. Further, unless due diligence indicates that only minimal on-site contamination occurred prior to closing, the buyer may be unwilling to take the risk of acquiring the facility. If significant contamination is indicated, the buyer will be concerned that costs associated with acquiring the facility are likely to be greater than anticipated.

[I]f a lender is involved, that lender may have its own concerns regarding the buyer's assumption of liability. The lender may question whether the discount in purchase price is adequate to cover the liabilities assumed by the buyer, especially if the property is to be the collateral for the loan. . . .

[One] way that parties may address on-site contamination is to have the seller be responsible either in whole or in part for the remediation.

While this approach eliminates disputes over remediation costs, it presents its own set of issues. One consideration is if the work will be done before or after closing. In those instances where remediation can be completed before closing, this usually is the best solution. As a practical matter, however, the work rarely can be completed before closing.

In some situations the parties may agree to have the buyer conduct the remediation and the seller pay for all or part of the remediation costs. This has the advantage of having the party in possession of the property conduct the work. When this approach is used, the seller will want to include deadlines for when the work will be completed. If this is left open-ended the buyer may delay the work, and disputes may arise if the contamination spreads during the period of inaction. In addition, the seller will want to include measures to control the overall costs. For example, the seller may want the right to pre-approve expenditures above a set amount, approve the selection of technical consultants, periodically review and approve work plans and participate in all meetings and conference calls with the regulatory authorities that have jurisdiction over the remediation plan.

Regardless of whether it is the buyer or the seller that will be conducting remediation, the agreement should include a standard for when the work is completed. Any applicable regulatory standards should be referenced. As risk-based clean-up standards have expanded, using contractual language that requires remediation "to statutory or regulatory levels" can be problematic. The parties may have different views on what is the appropriate risk-based standard. For example, the seller may be willing to accept certain institutional controls that the buyer would not accept based on its long-term plans. In addition, institutional controls that may be acceptable to the buyer may not be acceptable to the buyer's lender or may cause the lender to change the terms of the financing.

Environmental counsel also must consider the involvement of regulatory agencies in the remediation process. The discovery of contamination may need to be reported to a regulatory agency, and the agency may require periodic progress reports on remediation. The agreement should specifically indicate whether the seller or the buyer will be responsible for submitting reports and for any penalties for reporting failures or delays.

Where on-site problems will require multi-year remediation programs, counsel needs to develop other language and methods. The parties may attempt to allocate the costs through language that creates long-term—and not always pleasant—relationships. One reason these relationships can be difficult is that they do not and cannot meet the mutually exclusive ideal scenarios of the parties. The seller wants to be rid of the asset and wants to avail itself of as much of its value as possible, while the buyer wants a new asset unquestionably worth at least what it paid and without any baggage or surprises. Instead, to get the deal accomplished, the parties may need to make compromises that will require, at the very least, administrative efforts after closing which may go on for years. How smoothly this long-term relationship proceeds depends greatly on how clearly the agreement is drafted.

Regardless of the overall approach they take to allocating liability, the parties may combine their approach with limits on one or the other party's liability. They could place a monetary cap on the seller's liability. Of course, the parties may have a great deal of difficulty agreeing upon how large the cap will be. In addition, the language must clearly identify what costs are included in the cap. Another possibility is for the buyer to take responsibility for any and all documented releases, but with some specified limits. For instance the agreement can provide that if a spill goes over into a previously contaminated area the seller is responsible for, the buyer does not have to "follow the plume" to its end.

A related issue that the parties should address in any liability allocation is whether allocation of the environmental liabilities is any different if the buyer's activities trigger, exacerbate or hasten the cleanup obligations. The language also should state specifically whether the allocations of liabilities and indemnities apply to contamination that has migrated off-site. Moreover, the parties also should specify whether any indemnities the seller is giving are assignable to any third parties if the buyer later wishes to resell the property, or if any restrictions are to be placed on the assignability. The buyer obviously will want the indemnities to be assignable to the point that they almost "run with the land." The seller, on the other hand, will want the buyer to remain on the hook for any mutual indemnities, and certainly will want to exert some control over the future usage and ownership of the property.

Many of the issues discussed above with respect to allocation of liability are relevant even if the buyer will be conducting a completely different business that has no possibility of creating further environmental problems. The agreement still should address the long-term relationship between the parties. In particular, the parties will need to reach agreement on issues of access, future land use, government communications, and assignability.

### *Off-Site Environmental Liabilities and Toxic Torts*

The parties also will be concerned with off-site environmental liabilities. These generally include "generator" and "past owner/successor" liability under Superfund and certain versions of so-called "toxic tort" liabilities, such as property damage or personal injury claims brought by plaintiffs who have been injured by previous operations from the facility itself or from the operations of a disposal facility where a generator has sent hazardous materials. Many of these types of liabilities are entirely contingent, and will be contingent into the long-term future. Some are not even discoverable in the course normal due diligence. The good news is that these issues usually will only be a problem when the transaction is either an outright merger or a *de facto* merger, where the buyer succeeds to the seller's liabilities to third parties. In an asset purchase context where the seller will remain a reasonably substantial company after closing, counsel can address the whole issue through representations and warranties and . . . [an] indemnity clause. In a straight real estate deal, the issue may not be relevant.

In the context of a merger, where the seller may not be a substantial or long-lived indemnitor after the deal closes, the buyer may not—and in many instances should not—feel comfortable with a simple indemnity. How the parties address this issue will depend greatly upon several factors, all of which the buyer will want to explore in due diligence. These include the type of business and whether it handled or generated hazardous materials and waste, where such waste materials have been sent, how long the business has been in operation (how long it has had to build up liabilities off-site), what other properties the seller or its legal predecessors have owned or operated in the past, and whether the areas surrounding the facility are residential or industrial.

For purposes of negotiating a deal, counsel can divide off-site liabilities into three categories: (1) known but perhaps not reduced to exact dollars; (2) potential but not imminently expected to ripen into a claim unknown and unascertainable by any reasonable due diligence; and (3) potential but not imminently expected to ripen into a claim. Due diligence or pre-sale disclosures may reveal that the seller is already identified as a [potentially responsible party] at a Superfund site or is already a defendant in a toxic tort lawsuit. These are the easier matters to deal with, as they are at least somewhat less contingent and probably can be valued within at least an order of magnitude. The parties often will handle the issue with an indemnity agreement, properly funded if necessary. Of course, that approach may not work if the seller will not continue to exist.

This article provides a relatively quick and general overview of the approach an environmental lawyer may want to take and the issues he or she should consider in handling a transaction involving industrial property and/or a business heavily regulated in the environmental health and safety arena. Every deal has its own quirks, and the best part of environmental transactional work is the opportunity it creates for creativity and helping a client reach its business goals. Like the role of any business lawyer, the environmental lawyer's challenge in these transactions is not to eliminate all risk for the client (a lofty but usually unattainable goal), but to identify the potential risks, work with the technical advisors to scope out the magnitude and likelihood of the risks, point out the problems that may arise if issues are left to chance and ambiguous drafting, and ensure the client understands risks and alternatives so that reasonable business decisions are possible.

## Keywell Corporation v. Piper & Marbury, L.L.P.

United States District Court for the Western District of New York, 1999.
1999 WL 66700.

■ ELFVIN, SENIOR DISTRICT JUDGE:

This attorney-malpractice action is properly here by virtue of this Court's diversity jurisdiction. Keywell Corporation ("Keywell") is in the business of recycling steel and Piper & Marbury L.L.P. ("Piper") is the law firm which first represented Keywell in the latter's 1987 purchase from Vac Air Alloys Corporation ("Vac Air") of a steel-recycling facility in Frewsburg, N.Y. Keywell alleges, inter alia, that Piper's failure to facilitate and provide an adequate environmental audit prior to the purchase resulted in Keywell's incurring approximately $6 million in environmental cleanup costs. Piper has moved for summary judgment, principally on the grounds that Keywell has suffered no damages attributable to Piper.

The purchase agreement provided that Keywell would pay approximately $6 million and assume $20 million in liabilities in exchange for three Vac Air sites, that a number of Vac Air's "management-shareholders" would purchase shares in Keywell and become employee-shareholders thereof, that Vac Air had neither disposed of nor stored hazardous wastes on the subject properties in violation of any law or in any such way as to require remedial action under any law and that such warranties and representations would survive the purchase agreement by two years. Such survival provision is consistently referred to by the parties as "the sunset provision."

On or about November 5, 1987, Piper, with Keywell's approval, hired the environmental consulting firm of Conestoga-Rovers & Associates ("CRA") to perform an environmental audit of the Vac Air sites. CRA's assigned job was to "identify potential environmental problems and to quantify the uppermost cost of remedying such problems." Piper was to assist in CRA's investigation and—using CRA's findings in tandem with its own analysis of facts and applicable laws—advise Keywell and to draft the purchase agreement.

During November 1987 CRA's Alan Van Norman made several visits to the facility. His investigation comprised a visual inspection of the property, a review of various documents and a meeting with Vac Air's then-vice president and officer in charge of environmental affairs, Anthony Boscarino. Piper's prescribed role at this point was to arrange for Van Norman's access to documents and to identify a Vac Air official or officials with whom Van Norman could talk about historic environmental practices at the site. Piper chose Boscarino. According to Van Norman, Boscarino was the only person with whom CRA was permitted by Piper to speak.

During conversations between Van Norman and Boscarino, the latter pledged that Vac Air had not engaged in any on-site disposal of toxic wastes. In addition to their conversations, Van Norman requested of Boscarino "all relevant documents not already provided to Keywell." Van Norman purportedly discovered nothing—either in documents furnished by Boscarino or upon his walking tours of the property—to contradict Boscarino's claims that Vac Air had not disposed of any hazardous wastes at the plant.

As it evolved, Boscarino was lying. Any mystery on the point was laid to rest when the United States Court of Appeals for the Second Circuit took note of the finding by another Judge of this Court, in a related case brought by Keywell—represented by Piper—against Boscarino and Vac Air founder Daniel Weinstein, that Boscarino had at least some knowledge of Vac Air's practice during the 1970s of the dumping of hazardous waste into sludge pits on the site. *See Keywell v. Weinstein*, 33 F.3d 159, 161 (2d Cir. 1994). Not unexpectedly, there were several other Vac Air employees, as federal investigators discovered in 1990, who knew of Vac Air's dumping practices. There was also a 1985 file memorandum, which Boscarino had authored but failed to disclose to Van Norman, that clearly points to a "potential problem" involving "decomposed drums, wood chips and logs" discovered at Frewsburg.

Knowing nothing of the dumping or the "potential problem" memo, and having had no opportunity to talk with other Vac Air personnel, CRA relied on Boscarino, Piper's designated point-person. Accordingly, the CRA investigation team, while it conducted surface soil sampling and a test of the drinking water at the Vac Air plant, did not engage in a more probing investigation. As proof of such reliance by CRA, Keywell offers the testimony of CRA President, Frank Rovers, who maintained that, had he known of the 1985 discovery of decomposing drums, he "would have sent [an employee] out with a backhoe" to determine the extent of the contamination.

As is customary in environmental audits such as this one, CRA drafted a report which it submitted to Piper attorneys November 27, 1987 for review. According to Piper, at least two Piper attorneys reviewed the 28-page draft and suggested changes. Keywell neither saw the draft at this time nor were Keywell's comments or questions solicited by Piper or CRA. CRA adopted many of the changes proposed by Piper.

CRA also prepared a summary of the anticipated costs of remedying potential environmental problems at the three Vac Air sites. In that summary, CRA estimated that the remediation costs could reach $4.8 million and that the cost of treating the groundwater contamination at Frewsburg could reach $1 million. CRA sent this summary to Piper on December 4, 1987 with a cover letter from Alan Van Norman. At the request of Keith Watson, the Piper attorney in charge of the Vac Air-Keywell transaction, Van Norman deleted four of the six paragraphs in this cover letter and sent it back to Watson that day.

On December 7, 1987 Piper forwarded to Keywell CRA's final report. Piper maintains that it sent the report under a cover letter and accompanied by a copy of the cost summary. Keywell executives do not recall having received the cover letter and specifically deny receipt of the cost summary.

On December 9, 1987 Keywell's executives and Piper attorneys convened a teleconference call to discuss the CRA report and its implications for the proposed purchase of Vac Air. The details regarding who said what during this call—and even exactly who participated—are disputed, both parties agreeing that attorney Watson proclaimed the report free of "red flags," but Piper contending that Watson also described "potential cost impacts, to the extent they were quantifiable." The three principal Keywell executives—William Botz, Morton Plant and Joel Tauber—recall that Watson stated Keywell's maximum environmental liability at $1 million and not at $4.8 million. For his part, Watson recalls "walking the client through a series of cost numbers," but remembers no specific mention of either the $1 million figure or the $4.8 million figure.

In the summer of 1989, an unrelated dispute arose between Keywell and the Vac Air management-shareholders who had become Keywell employee-shareholders in 1987. To resolve the matter, Keywell executed a release whereby the two-year sunset provision would be accelerated so that, instead of the warranties and representations terminating on December 16, 1989, they would expire on August 11, 1989. At the time, Piper attorney Jonathan Weiner advised Keywell that, as was the case with the 1987 purchase agreement, the release would not extinguish Keywell's claims for contribution under the Comprehensive Environmental Response, Compensation and Liability Act ("CERCLA"). 42 U.S.C. § 9601 et seq.

In June 1990 Keywell learned that a grand jury had commenced an investigation concerning whether Vac Air had engaged in on-site disposal of hazardous waste at the Frewsburg plant. It soon became clear, as stated supra, that Vac Air employees had routinely dumped waste containing trichloroethylene ("TCE")—a byproduct of the steel recycling process and itself a hazardous substance—into ponds or pits in the north end of the Frewsburg site. Such dumping had resulted in groundwater contamination of an entirely different "order of magnitude" than that deemed by CRA to have existed in 1987.

On March 12, 1991 Keywell filed the aforementioned suit in this Court against Boscarino and Weinstein, seeking contribution under CERCLA and alleging common law fraud. In short, Keywell contended that these two former Vac Air executives had failed to disclose the TCE contamination in advance of Keywell's purchase of Vac Air, thereby fraudulently inducing Keywell to purchase the TCE-drenched site. Judge Skretny of this Court granted summary judgment against Keywell on its CERCLA claims, finding that such had been extinguished by the August 1989 release. On August 27, 1993 and upon a motion for reconsideration, Judge Skretny affirmed his dismissal of Keywell's CERCLA claims and granted summary judgment as to the diversity fraud claims. On August

24, 1994 the Second Circuit's Court of Appeals affirmed such dismissal of the CERCLA claims but reversed and remanded as to the fraud claims. Significant for purposes of the present litigation, the Court of Appeals concluded "that the parties unambiguously allocated liability for CERCLA losses in the [1987] Purchase Agreement." *Keywell v. Weinstein*, at 165. On remand, Judge Skretny chose not to exercise jurisdiction over the state law fraud claims. Subsequently, the New York State Supreme Court, Chautauqua County, dismissed Keywell's fraud claim and Keywell chose to settle the case before it was to be heard on appeal.

It is axiomatic that the relationship between an attorney and his or her client is a fiduciary one. *See Cinema 5 Ltd. v. Cinerama, Inc.*, 528 F.2d 1384, 1386 (2d Cir. 1976). As part of his or her fiduciary duty, the attorney must provide the client with all "information material to the client's decision to pursue a given course of action, or to abstain therefrom." *See Spector v. Mermelstein*, 361 F. Supp. 30, 39–40 (S.D.N.Y.1972), aff'd. in relevant part, rev'd in part, 485 F.2d 474 (2d Cir. 1973). Should the attorney negligently or willfully withhold such information—or torture the same—the attorney will be liable for any losses the client suffers by virtue of having been caused to act without the benefit of the undisclosed material facts. *See Ayala v. Fischman*, 1998 WL 726005 (S.D.N.Y. October 15, 1998).

In its Motion for Summary Judgment, Piper has chosen not to focus on whether it committed legal malpractice, arguing instead that Keywell's malpractice, breach of fiduciary duty and breach of contract claims regarding Piper's representation of Keywell during the 1987 acquisition of Vac Air should be dismissed because Keywell cannot adduce sufficient evidence of any resultant damages. Relatedly, Piper asserts that Keywell cannot show that, were it not for Piper's alleged misconduct, Keywell could have avoided or reduced liability for the cleanup of the Frewsburg site. Accordingly, this Court's analysis is confined to whether Keywell has demonstrated sufficient evidence of its damages and their causation to withstand summary judgment.

Applying the appropriate legal standard, Piper asserts that "Keywell must show that, but for the alleged breach, it would have occupied a better position than it does today." In other words, to prevail in its malpractice action, it is incumbent upon Keywell to demonstrate that, had Piper properly facilitated the uncovering of the true extent of environmental liability lurking at Frewsburg, Keywell either would have walked away from the deal or, in the alternative, could have negotiated a deal in which Vac Air would have had to bear some or all of the cleanup costs.

In an attempt to create a genuine issue of material fact, Keywell offers the sworn affidavit of former Vac Air Vice President Richard Odle:

> "Had environmental conditions at the Frewsburg facility giving rise to significant actual or potential liability been discovered and brought to Vac Air's attention prior to closing, Affiant

> believes, based upon his knowledge and understanding of the process by which the sale of Vac Air was initiated, negotiated and consummated, that a majority of Vac Air's voting shareholders, including Weinstein—a self-proclaimed environmentalist and reputable businessman—would have been willing to renegotiate and consummate the transaction in such a way as to insulate Keywell from liability for such environmental conditions. Vac Air would have agreed to anything reasonable and necessary to consummate the transaction had such environmental conditions been discovered."

Piper . . . asserts that Keywell's claims that it could have renegotiated with Vac Air fail the "economic rationality" test propounded in *Matsushita Elec. Indus. Co. v. Zenith Radio Corp.*, 475 U.S. 574 (1987). As Piper accurately points out, Matsushita requires that, when a claim "simply makes no economic sense," the party opposing summary judgment must come forward with "more persuasive evidence to support their claim than would otherwise be necessary." *Id.* at 587. The "economically irrational" claim in this case, according to Piper, is that the Vac Air shareholders would have approved a deal which would have shifted the economics of environmental liability from Keywell to Vac Air at a time when the nickel market and, by extension, Vac Air's own fiscal fortunes were becoming more and more encouraging. Such want of rational motive is not present in the instant case. There are numerous rational explanations why Vac Air's shareholders would have been amenable to renegotiating a deal with Keywell, not the least being that—per Odle—even with a rising nickel market and improved operations throughout 1987, "Vac Air was plagued by significant cash flow problems."

Piper's remaining arguments in support of dismissing Keywell's claims regarding the 1987 representation fall into two categories. First, Piper asserts that additional groundwater monitoring on CRA's part would likely not have uncovered Vac Air's dumping practices. Notwithstanding Keywell's sufficient rebuttal evidence on this score, this line of argument assumes that CRA would not have discovered the truth by talking with employees and/or officers other than Boscarino or by viewing additional records and files during the November 1987 site inspections. Whether Piper impermissibly circumscribed such inspections by limiting CRA's contact to the furtive Boscarino is a factual question at the very heart of this case, although not, by Piper's design, at the heart of the instant motion. The second set of arguments is grounded on Piper's contention that Keywell would have been unable to secure an alternative site to which Keywell could transplant the Vac Air steel-recycling facility housed at Frewsburg. Even if Piper is correct, such plan represented only one of the options Keywell might well have exercised had it been armed with all the relevant information. After weighing the evidence presented by each side, it is clear that Keywell has presented evidence sufficient to create a triable issue of fact as to whether Piper's alleged malpractice proximately caused the damages Keywell claims.

---

## QUESTIONS AND DISCUSSION

**1.** *Understanding the transaction*. Apply some of the questions Watson and Woods suggest are critical to a lawyer's effective representation to the transaction involved in *Keywell*:

- Was the transaction a transfer of assets or stocks? What difference does that make?
- What were the motivations of the parties? Why was Keywell interested in acquiring the Vac Air facility? Why was Vac Air interested in selling it? What do these motivations suggest about how the two parties would have approached due diligence and transaction negotiation?
- How would you describe the level of due diligence the parties anticipated? Did it appear that Keywell expected a comprehensive environmental audit? How involved was Keywell in designing the audit and monitoring its progress?

**2.** *Designing due diligence*. It certainly appears that Keywell's approach to the due diligence step was simply to hire Piper & Marbury (now DLA Piper) to have them handle it and then deliver a report at the end of the process. That was not an unusual arrangement at the time, and still is not. Nor is it unusual, as happened in *Keywell*, for the lawyers to retain environmental consultants to execute the technical aspects of the audit such as visual inspections, water and soil sampling, and so on. But does it strike you as odd that Vac Air's Boscarino was the only person whom Piper & Marbury permitted the environmental consultant to meet to discuss site history and practices? Why do you think they restricted access?

**3.** *Executing due diligence*. Why did Boscarino lie about waste dumping events at the site? In a similar situation, if you suspected an employee of the target site was lying, and assuming you did not limit yourself to meeting with just one representative of the site, how might you go about further investigation through interviews of knowledgeable individuals?

**4.** *Advising based on the results of due diligence*. The *Keywell* court mentioned that Piper & Marbury lawyers suggested that the environmental consultants delete four of six paragraphs from the draft letter the consultants proposed be used to transmit their final report to Keywell. One of the exhibits in the case provided the full text of the draft letter. It reads as follows, with italicized portions being the four paragraphs that Piper & Marbury lawyers requested be *eliminated*:

> Dear Mr. Carter:
>
> We have enclosed a summary table of environmental concerns identified by CRA. The table identifies the environmental concern,

> scope of remedy and order of magnitude cost by facility and where appropriate identifies the level of concern.
>
> *It is generally expected that U.S. EPA will eventually identify metal recycling plants as sources of environmental contamination and require studies and remedies. In fact, the process has already been applied to many conventional "junk yard" type operations. This anticipated policy will affect all three properties either during their operating life, at the time of future sale or title transfer, or at the time of closure.*
>
> *In addition, at the Frewsburg site it is certain that the separator operation must be upgraded by fine tuning or modification to meet oil and grease discharge requirements. Solvent pretreatment will also be required.*
>
> *It is also likely that solvent contamination of groundwater at the Frewsburg plant will be defined. We recommend that groundwater monitoring be implemented to identify any potential problems.*
>
> *At [another site in the transaction], control of mercury emissions and disposal of stockpiled mercury waste are requirements.*
>
> Please contact us with any questions that might arise.

What is your impression of the impression those four paragraphs might have had on a company considering the acquisition of either of the facilities? Why would an attorney advising Keywell have desired those paragraphs be removed from any communication to Keywell? The solvent contamination of groundwater detected at the Frewsburg facility was one of several conditions itemized on the table summary of conditions that was attached to the letter, with an estimated cost of $1 million. Was that sufficient to alert the client to the matter, making the text in the letter superfluous?

**5.** *Negotiating, drafting, and post-transaction representation.* The purpose of environmental due diligence is to assist the parties to the transaction in negotiating and drafting the transaction agreement, as well as to assist each party in post-transaction decisions. The *Keywell* court mentions related litigation between Keywell and Vac Air (and its shareholders) regarding the interpretation of the contract provisions and the effects of a release of liability the parties negotiated after the initial transaction. See *Keywell Corp. v. Weinstein*, 33 F.3d 159 (2d Cir. 1994). Focusing on that litigation, we explore the topics of negotiating and drafting the transaction documents and providing post-transaction representation in Part II of this chapter.

**6.** A jury trial ultimately was held on Keywell's claims, see *Keywell Corp. v. Piper & Marbury, L.L.P.*, 2001 WL 967567 (W.D.N.Y.2001), at which the court provided the jury these instructions:

> This Court . . . instructed the jury that, in order to find that Piper and Marbury had breached its fiduciary duty to Keywell, it had to find that Piper and Marbury had negligently or willfully failed to convey information in its possession that was important to the decisions Keywell was making, thereby causing Keywell to suffer damages. This Court . . . further instructed the jury that, in order

> to find that Piper and Marbury had committed legal malpractice, it had to find that it "failed to exercise that degree of care, skill and diligence reasonably expected to be possessed by a member of the legal community, a lawyer or a law firm," thereby causing plaintiff to suffer damages. Accordingly, were the jury to find that Piper and Marbury had breached its fiduciary duty by failing to turn over important information to Keywell that Keywell needed to make its decision, it would necessarily have had to have also found that Piper and Marbury had committed legal malpractice by failing to turn over such documents because such would certainly fall below that degree of care, skill and diligence reasonably expected to be possessed by a member of the legal community.

How would you have cast your vote as a member of the jury in response to those instructions?

**7.** Are malpractice claims against environmental due diligence attorneys common? Thankfully not! Indeed, *Keywell* is one of the few published opinions addressing malpractice in an environmental law representation context. Most malpractice claims are settled without litigation, however, so perhaps *Keywell* is simply the tip of a vast underwater iceberg of malpractice claims. Indeed, based on a study of the legal malpractice insurance industry one of your authors conducted in the late 1990s, there was significant concern among insurers beginning in the early 1980s, as they saw the law of CERCLA unfolding, that environmental lawyers would face a daunting number of malpractice claims. *See* J.B. Ruhl, *Malpractice and Environmental Law: Should Environmental Law "Specialists" Be Concerned?*, 33 HOUSTON L. REV. 173 (1996). And yet that did not come to pass, with claims involving environmental lawyers being insignificant compared to other fields. For example, the Attorneys' Liability Assurance Society, which insures over 45,000 attorneys in over 340 law firms, does not even list environmental law as one of its claims categories, including it in the "other" category that accounts for a total of under 2 percent of claims. This is not unlike the experience in other fields that involve complex regulations, such as tax law, or that involve attorney use of scientific and technical information, such as patent law. Perhaps attorneys that enter such fields are particularly careful and talented! Incidentally, the jury in *Keywell* decided in favor of the lawyers, finding they had neither committed malpractice in the advice they provided nor breached any fiduciary duty to Keywell by failing to transmit material information. Was that how you voted?

**8.** How would you integrate climate change considerations into transactional due diligence? Should the buyer's due diligence team conduct a climate change model to determine likely conditions on the land or of the structures and then predict future regulatory or liability risk exposures? As more climate adaptation regulations and initiatives are promulgated at state and local levels, must due diligence include an assessment of adaptation risks?

---

## PROBLEM EXERCISE

Remember Energena, your multi-national energy generation client from Chapter 10 that is planning a move into wind energy? Energena contacts you to discuss its plans to acquire Windergy, a small but growing wind energy producing company with several wind farms already up and running in the United States. The voice-mail from Energena's General Counsel provides these sketchy details:

> It's Grayson from Energena. We've got our eyes on Windergy, which we think will be the perfect opening for us into wind energy. Their big selling point is technology—they're at the front of the pack and have a great testing lab in Nevada. They also have four existing wind farms—in California, Florida, Kansas, and Texas—and have options on sites in several other states. We want to make this work, but want to be sure we don't walk into any environmental landmines. You know the drill. Give me a call to discuss what we'll need to do and time frames.

So, what next? You're the expert—come up with a plan of action. Obviously, to do so you need more information. On the other hand, some steps in the environmental due diligence process are routine and don't depend on specific details of the transaction. We suggest following the sequence of steps discussed in this section of the text as a way of organizing your thoughts.

**1.** *Understand the transaction.* If you could ask the Energena General Counsel just ten questions about the transaction the company has in mind, what would they be?

**2.** *Designing due diligence.* Think back to the "3Cs" of contamination, compliance, and constraints. Brainstorm about possible problems Windergy might have in each category, and which Energena might face if it acquires Windergy or any of its assets. Don't limit yourself to waste disposal and contamination—think about water quality, wetlands, endangered species, and other resource issues. If you could ask Windergy personnel just ten questions to help you design the due diligence, who would they be and what would you ask them?

**3.** *Executing due diligence.* Windergy has a testing lab in Nevada, wind farms in four different states, and sites in its sights in several other states. How will you implement your due diligence design over such a scale? Will you need consultants to help investigate details? What kind of consultants? Who will coordinate their work? What kinds of reports will you request of them?

**4.** *Advising based on the results of due diligence.* What do you have in mind as the ultimate deliverable on your part? Will you collect the consultants' reports and draft a cover memorandum summarizing the findings. That may help your client understand the consultants' advice, but what kind of advice are *you* going to provide?

---

## B. SATISFYING LIABILITY EXEMPTION CONDITIONS THROUGH "ALL APPROPRIATE INQUIRY"

Conducting environmental due diligence makes sense in any business transaction in which the transferred company or assets might trigger one or more of the "3Cs" of contamination, compliance, or constraints. In particular, however, the contamination problem is the "quicksand" of liabilities given the aggressive rules of strict, joint and several liability applied under CERCLA and similar state laws (see Chapter 4). Over time, CERCLA's liability rules appeared especially harsh or counterproductive in three contexts: (1) purchasers of land, such as Keywell, who conducted some level of due diligence but did not discover contamination they had no part in causing nonetheless could be held responsible for remediation; (2) owners of land who had no part in mishandling of waste, but whose property was contaminated by the acts of third parties on neighboring parcels, could be held liable for remediation; and (3) prospective purchasers of contaminated urban properties, known as "brownfields," could be deterred from investing in urban redevelopment out of fear of being held liable for remediation.

As originally enacted, CERCLA provided three defenses: (1) act of God; (2) act of war; and (3) act or omission of a third party. 42 U.S.C. § 107(b). The last of these—the so-called "innocent landowner" defense—seems to address the three contexts just mentioned, but CERCLA as enacted and amended, and its early case law, made the matter far more complicated. To begin with, CERCLA requires that the third party not be in a "contractual relationship" with the person claiming the innocent landowner defense. 42 U.S.C. § 107(b)(3). The statute as originally enacted did not define "contractual relationship," and most courts interpreted the term to include asset purchase contracts, meaning an innocent purchaser of contaminated land effectively had no defense. Moreover, the innocent landowner defense also requires that the person establish, among other things, the exercise of "due care," but no definition of due care was provided in the original text.

Congress attempted a fix of these two problems in the 1986 Superfund Amendments and Reauthorization Act (SARA) by adding a definition of "contractual relationship" to the statute. The new definition specified that instruments transferring land are indeed contracts within the meaning of the defense, but not if the purchaser acquires the land after the events causing the contamination and can show that it "did not know and had no reason to know" of the contamination. 42 U.S.C. § 9601(35)(A). The new provision then addressed what "reason to know" means by establishing the concept of "all appropriate inquiries." Congress directed EPA to promulgate regulations establishing the standards and practices that comprise "all appropriate inquiries." 42

U.S.C. § 9601(35)(B). Even with this new provision, however, concern over the ambiguities of CERCLA's treatment of innocent purchasers persisted. *See* Andria Beeler-Norrholm, *I Didn't Do That! The State of the "Innocent Landowner" Defense*, 18 J. NATURAL RESOURCES & ENVTL. L. 209 (2003–04). Moreover, the SARA amendment did not directly address the so-called "innocent neighbor" problem and was of little help to the "brownfield" purchaser who acquires property with knowledge of the contamination.

Congress took the matter a step further in the 2002 Small Business Liability Relief and Brownfields Revitalization Act. This statute specified conditions for all three contexts and directed EPA to promulgate a unified "all appropriate inquiries" rule using ten criteria that matched closely to the environmental due diligence protocols attorneys had had developed by that time. These include such steps as interviews with personnel, reviews of historical sources such as aerial photographs, visual inspections, and reports of environmental professionals. 42 U.S.C. § 9601(35)(B)(iii). In November 2005 EPA issued its "AAI" rule covering what now amount to three defenses, or "protections," under CERCLA—the innocent landowner defense, the contiguous property owner protection, and the bona fide prospective purchaser protection. The following excerpt is from the preamble explanation of EPA's final rule.

## Environmental Protection Agency, Standards and Practices for All Appropriate Inquiries, Final Rule

70 Fed. Reg. 66070 (Nov. 1, 2005) (codified at 40 CFR Part 312).

I. General Information

A. Who Potentially May be Affected by Today's Rule?

This regulation may affect most directly those persons and businesses purchasing commercial property or any property that will be used for commercial or public purposes and who may, after purchasing the property, seek to claim protection from CERCLA liability for releases or threatened releases of hazardous substances. Under section 101(35)(B) of CERCLA, as amended by the Small Business Liability Relief and Brownfields Revitalization Act (Pub. L. 107–118, 115 stat. 2356, "the Brownfields Amendments") such persons and businesses are required to conduct all appropriate inquiries prior to or on the date on which the property is acquired. Prospective landowners who do not conduct all appropriate inquiries prior to or on the date of obtaining ownership of the property may lose their ability to claim protection from CERCLA liability as an innocent landowner, bona fide prospective purchaser, or contiguous property owner.

II. Background

A. What is the Intent of Today's Rule?

On August 26, 2004, EPA published a notice of proposed rulemaking outlining proposed standards and practices for the conduct of "all appropriate inquiries." This regulatory action was initiated in response to legislative amendments to the Comprehensive Environmental Response, Compensation, and Liability Act (CERCLA). On January 11, 2002, President Bush signed the Small Business Liability Relief and Brownfields Revitalization Act (Pub. L. 107–118, 115 Stat. 2356, "the Brownfields Amendments"). The Brownfields Amendments amend CERCLA by providing funds to assess and clean up brownfields sites, clarifying CERCLA liability provisions for certain landowners, and providing funding to enhance state and tribal cleanup programs. The intent of today's rule is to finalize regulations setting federal standards and practices for the conduct of all appropriate inquiries, a key provision of the Brownfields Amendments. Subtitle B of Title II of the Brownfields Amendments revises CERCLA section 101(35), clarifying the requirements necessary to establish the innocent landowner defense. In addition, the Brownfields Amendments add protections from CERCLA liability for bona fide prospective purchasers and contiguous property owners who meet certain statutory requirements.

Each of the CERCLA liability provisions for innocent landowners, bona fide prospective purchasers, and contiguous property owners, requires that, among other requirements, persons claiming the liability protections conduct all appropriate inquiries into prior ownership and use of a property prior to or on the date a person acquires a property. The law requires EPA to develop regulations establishing standards and practices for how to conduct all appropriate inquiries. Congress included in the Brownfields Amendments a list of criteria that the Agency must address in the regulations establishing standards and practices for conducting all appropriate inquiries section 101(35)(2)(B)(ii) and (iii). The Brownfields Amendments also require that parties receiving a federal brownfields grant awarded under CERCLA section 104(k)(2)(B) to conduct site characterizations and assessments must conduct these activities in accordance with the standards and practices for all appropriate inquiries.

The regulations established today only address the all appropriate inquiries provisions of CERCLA sections 101(35)(B)(i)(I) and 101(35)(B)(ii) and (iii). Today's rule does not address the requirements of CERCLA section 101(35)(B)(i)(II) for what constitutes "reasonable steps."

B. What is "All Appropriate Inquiries?"

An essential step in real property transactions may be evaluating a property for potential environmental contamination and assessing potential liability for contamination present at the property. The process for assessing properties for the presence or potential presence of environmental contamination often is referred to as "environmental due diligence," or "environmental site assessment." The Comprehensive Environmental Response Compensation and Liability Act (CERCLA) or Superfund, provides for a similar, but legally distinct, process referred to as "all appropriate inquiries."

Under CERCLA, persons may be held strictly liable for cleaning up hazardous substances at properties that they either currently own or operate or owned or operated at the time of disposal. Strict liability in the context of CERCLA means that a potentially responsible party may be liable for environmental contamination based solely on property ownership and without regard to fault or negligence.

In 1986, the Superfund Amendments and Reauthorization Act (Pub. L. No. 99–499, 100 stat. 1613, "SARA") amended CERCLA by creating an "innocent landowner" defense to CERCLA liability. The new section 101(35)(B) of CERCLA provided a defense to CERCLA liability, for those persons who could demonstrate, among other requirements, that they "did not know and had no reason to know" prior to purchasing a property that any hazardous substance that is the subject of a release or threatened release was disposed of on, in, or at the property. Such persons, to demonstrate that they had "no reason to know" must have undertaken, prior to, or on the date of acquisition of the property, "all appropriate inquiries" into the previous ownership and uses of the property consistent with good commercial or customary standards and practices. The 2002 Brownfields Amendments added potential liability protections for "contiguous property owners" and "bona fide prospective purchasers" who also must demonstrate they conducted all appropriate inquiries, among other requirements, to benefit from the liability protection.

### C. What Were the Previous Standards for All Appropriate Inquiries?

As part of the Brownfields Amendments to CERCLA, Congress established interim standards for the conduct of all appropriate inquiries. The federal interim standards established by Congress became effective on January 11, 2002. In the case of properties purchased after May 31, 1997, the interim standards include the procedures of the ASTM Standard E1527–97 (entitled "Standard Practice for Environmental Site Assessments: Phase 1 Environmental Site Assessment Process"). In the case of persons who purchased property prior to May 31, 1997 and who are seeking to establish an innocent landowner defense or qualify as a contiguous property owner, CERCLA provides that such persons must establish, among other statutory requirements, that at the time they acquired the property, they did not know and had no reason to know of releases or threatened releases to the property. To establish they did not know and had no reason to know of releases or threatened releases, persons who purchased property prior to May 31, 1997 must demonstrate that they carried out all appropriate inquiries into the previous ownership and uses of the property in accordance with generally accepted good commercial and customary standards and practices.

D. What are the Liability Protections Established Under the Brownfields Amendments?

The Brownfields Amendments provide important liability protections for landowners who qualify as contiguous property owners, bona fide prospective purchasers, or innocent landowners. To meet the statutory requirements for any of these landowner liability protections, a landowner must meet certain threshold requirements and satisfy certain continuing obligations. To qualify as a bona fide prospective purchaser, contiguous property owner, or innocent landowner, a person must perform "all appropriate inquiries" on or before the date on which the person acquired the property. Bona fide prospective purchasers and contiguous property owners also must demonstrate that they are not potentially liable or affiliated with any other person that is potentially liable for response costs at the property. In the case of contiguous property owners, the landowner claiming to be a contiguous property owner also must demonstrate that he did not cause, contribute, or consent to any release or threatened release of hazardous substances. To meet the statutory requirements for a bona fide prospective purchaser, a property owner must have acquired a property subsequent to any disposal activities involving hazardous substances at the property.

Continuing obligations required under the statute include complying with land use restrictions and not impeding the effectiveness or integrity of institutional controls; taking "reasonable steps" with respect to hazardous substances affecting a landowner's property to prevent releases; providing cooperation, assistance and access to EPA, a state, or other party conducting response actions or natural resource restoration at the property; complying with CERCLA information requests and administrative subpoenas; and providing legally required notices.

EPA notes that, as explained below, persons conducting all appropriate inquiries in compliance with today's final rule are not entitled to the CERCLA liability protections provided for innocent landowners, bona fide prospective purchasers, and contiguous property owners, unless they also comply with all of the continuing obligations established under the statute. As explained below, compliance with today's final rule is only one requirement necessary for CERCLA liability protection. We also note that the requirements of today's rule apply to prospective property owners who are seeking protection from liability under the federal Superfund Law (CERCLA). Prospective property owners wishing to establish protection from, or a defense to, liability under state superfund or other related laws must comply with the all criteria established under state laws, including any criteria for conducting site assessments or all appropriate inquiries established under applicable state statutes or regulations.

1. Bona Fide Prospective Purchaser

The Brownfields Amendments added a new bona fide prospective purchaser provision at CERCLA section 107(r). The provision provides protection from CERCLA liability, and limits EPA's recourse for unrecovered response costs to a lien on property for the lesser of the unrecovered response costs or increase in fair market value attributable to EPA's response action. To meet the statutory requirements for a bona fide prospective purchaser, a person must meet the requirements set forth in CERCLA sections 101(40) and 107(r). A bona fide prospective purchaser must have bought property after January 11, 2002 (the date of enactment of the Brownfields Amendments). A bona fide prospective purchaser may purchase property with knowledge of contamination after performing all appropriate inquiries, provided the property owner meets or complies with all of the other statutory requirements set forth in CERCLA section 101(40). Conducting all appropriate inquiries alone does not provide a landowner with protection against CERCLA liability. Landowners who want to qualify as bona fide prospective purchasers must comply with all of the statutory requirements. The statutory requirements include, without limitation, that the landowner must:

- Have acquired a property after all disposal of hazardous substances at the property ceased;
- Provide all legally required notices with respect to the discovery or release of any hazardous substances at the property;
- Exercise appropriate care by taking reasonable steps to stop continuing releases, prevent any threatened future release, and prevent or limit human, environmental, or natural resources exposure to any previously released hazardous substance;
- Provide full cooperation, assistance, and access to persons that are authorized to conduct response actions or natural resource restorations;
- Comply with land use restrictions established or relied on in connection with a response action;
- Not impede the effectiveness or integrity of any institutional controls;
- Comply with any CERCLA request for information or administrative subpoena; and
- Not be potentially liable, or affiliated with any other person who is potentially liable for response costs for addressing releases at the property. * * *

2. Contiguous Property Owner

The Brownfields Amendments added a new contiguous property owner provision at CERCLA section 107(q). This provision excludes from the definition of "owner" or "operator" under CERCLA section 107(a)(1) and (2) a person who owns property that is "contiguous to, or otherwise similarly situated with respect to, and that is or may be contaminated by a release or threatened release of a hazardous substance from" property owned by someone else. To qualify as a contiguous property owner, a landowner must have no knowledge or reason to know of contamination at the time of acquisition, have conducted all appropriate inquiries, and meet all of the criteria set forth in CERCLA section 107(q)(1)(A), which include, without limitation:

- Not causing, contributing, or consenting to the release or threatened release;
- Not being potentially liable nor affiliated with any other person who is potentially liable for response costs at the property;
- Taking reasonable steps to stop continuing releases, prevent any threatened release, and prevent or limit human, environmental, or natural resource exposure to any hazardous substances released on or from the landowner's property;
- Providing full cooperation, assistance, and access to persons that are authorized to conduct response actions or natural resource restorations;
- Complying with land use restrictions established or relied on in connection with a response action;
- Not impeding the effectiveness or integrity of any institutional controls;
- Complying with any CERCLA request for information or administrative subpoena;
- Providing all legally required notices with respect to discovery or release of any hazardous substances at the property.

The contiguous property owner liability protection "protects parties that are essentially victims of pollution incidents caused by their neighbor's actions." S. Rep. No. 1072, at 10 (2001). Contiguous property owners must perform all appropriate inquiries prior to purchasing property.

3. Innocent Landowner

The Brownfields Amendments also clarify the innocent landowner defense. To qualify as an innocent landowner, a person must conduct all appropriate inquiries and meet all of the statutory requirements. The requirements include, without limitation:

- Having no knowledge or reason to know that any hazardous substance which is the subject of a release or threatened release was disposed of on, in, or at the facility;
- Providing full cooperation, assistance and access to persons authorized to conduct response actions at the property;
- Complying with any land use restrictions and not impeding the effectiveness or integrity of any institutional controls;
- Taking reasonable steps to stop continuing releases, prevent any threatened release, and prevent or limit human, environmental, or natural resource exposure to any previously released hazardous substances.

To successfully assert an innocent landowner liability defense, a property owner must demonstrate compliance with CERCLA section 107(b)(3) as well. Such persons must establish, by a preponderance of the evidence:

- That the release or threat of release of hazardous substances and the resulting damages were caused by an act or omission of a third party with whom the person does not have employment, agency, or a contractual relationship;
- The person exercised due care with respect to the hazardous substance concerned, taking into consideration the characteristics of such hazardous substance, in light of all relevant facts and circumstances;
- Took precautions against foreseeable acts or omissions of any such third party and the consequences that could foreseeably result from such acts or omissions.

Like contiguous property owners, innocent landowners must perform all appropriate inquiries prior to or on the date of acquisition of a property and cannot know, or have reason to know, of contamination to qualify for this landowner liability protection.

E. What Criteria Did Congress Establish for the All Appropriate Inquiries Standard?

Congress included in the Brownfields Amendments a list of criteria that the Agency must include in the regulations establishing standards and practices for conducting all appropriate inquiries. In addition to providing these criteria in the statute, Congress instructed EPA to develop regulations establishing standards and practices for conducting all appropriate inquiries in accordance with generally accepted good commercial and customary standards and practices. The criteria are set forth in CERCLA section 101(35)(2)(B)(iii) and include:

- The results of an inquiry by an environmental professional.

- Interviews with past and present owners, operators, and occupants of the facility for the purpose of gathering information regarding the potential for contamination at the facility.
- Reviews of historical sources, such as chain of title documents, aerial photographs, building department records, and land use records, to determine previous uses and occupancies of the real property since the property was first developed.
- Searches for recorded environmental cleanup liens against the facility that are filed under federal, state, or local law.
- Reviews of federal, state, and local government records, waste disposal records, underground storage tank records, and hazardous waste handling, generation, treatment, disposal, and spill records, concerning contamination at or near the facility.
- Visual inspections of the facility and of adjoining properties.
- Specialized knowledge or experience on the part of the defendant.
- The relationship of the purchase price to the value of the property, if the property was not contaminated.
- Commonly known or reasonably ascertainable information about the property.
- The degree of obviousness of the presence or likely presence of contamination at the property, and the ability to detect the contamination by appropriate investigation.

---

## QUESTIONS AND DISCUSSION

**1.** In the AAI rule text, EPA places heavy emphasis on "environmental professionals." Section 312.10 defines the term as follows:

> Sec. 312.10 Definitions.
>
> Environmental Professional means:
>
> (1) a person who possesses sufficient specific education, training, and experience necessary to exercise professional judgment to develop opinions and conclusions regarding conditions indicative of releases or threatened releases (see Sec. 312.1(c)) on, at, in, or to a property, sufficient to meet the objectives and performance factors in Sec. 312.20(e) and (f).
>
> (2) Such a person must:
>
> (i) Hold a current Professional Engineer's or Professional Geologist's license or registration from a state, tribe, or U.S.

territory (or the Commonwealth of Puerto Rico) and have the equivalent of three (3) years of full-time relevant experience; or

(ii) Be licensed or certified by the federal government, a state, tribe, or U.S. territory (or the Commonwealth of Puerto Rico) to perform environmental inquiries as defined in Sec. 312.21 and have the equivalent of three (3) years of full-time relevant experience; or

(iii) Have a Baccalaureate or higher degree from an accredited institution of higher education in a discipline of engineering or science and the equivalent of five (5) years of full-time relevant experience; or

(iv) Have the equivalent of ten (10) years of full-time relevant experience.

Relevant experience, as used in the definition of environmental professional in this section, means: participation in the performance of all appropriate inquiries investigations, environmental site assessments, or other site investigations that may include environmental analyses, investigations, and remediation which involve the understanding of surface and subsurface environmental conditions and the processes used to evaluate these conditions and for which professional judgment was used to develop opinions regarding conditions indicative of releases or threatened releases to the subject property.

The rule also recognizes that even the most experienced environmental professional with a healthy budget often cannot provide complete information. Section 312(g) covers this "data gaps" problem:

To the extent there are data gaps . . . in the information developed as part of the inquiries . . . that affect the ability of persons (including the environmental professional) conducting the all appropriate inquiries to identify conditions indicative of releases or threatened releases in each area of inquiry under each standard and practice such persons should identify such data gaps, identify the sources of information consulted to address such data gaps, and comment upon the significance of such data gaps with regard to the ability to identify conditions indicative of releases or threatened releases of hazardous substances . . . on, at, in, or to the subject property. Sampling and analysis may be conducted to develop information to address data gaps.

Finally, section 312.21 of the rule specifies exactly what the environmental professional must do to report the results of the inquiry, including identification of data gaps:

(c) The results of the inquiry by an environmental professional must be documented in a written report that, at a minimum, includes the following:

(1) An opinion as to whether the inquiry has identified conditions indicative of releases or threatened releases of hazardous substances [and in the case of inquiries conducted for

persons identified in Sec. 312.1(b)(2) conditions indicative of releases and threatened releases of pollutants, contaminants, petroleum and petroleum products, and controlled substances (as defined in 21 U.S.C. 802)] on, at, in, or to the subject property;

(2) An identification of data gaps in the information developed as part of the inquiry that affect the ability of the environmental professional to identify conditions indicative of releases or threatened releases of hazardous substances on, at, in, or to the subject property and comments regarding the significance of such data gaps on the environmental professional's ability to provide an opinion as to whether the inquiry has identified conditions indicative of releases or threatened releases on, at, in, or to the subject property. If there are data gaps such that the environmental professional cannot reach an opinion regarding the identification of conditions indicative of releases and threatened releases, such data gaps must be noted in the environmental professional's opinion in paragraph (c)(1) of this section; and

(3) The qualifications of the environmental professional(s).

(d) The environmental professional must place the following statements in the written document identified in paragraph (c) of this section and sign the document:

"[I, We] declare that, to the best of [my, our] professional knowledge and belief, [I, we] meet the definition of Environmental Professional as defined in Sec. 312.10 of this part. [I, We] have the specific qualifications based on education, training, and experience to assess a property of the nature, history, and setting of the subject property. [I, We] have developed and performed the all appropriate inquiries in conformance with the standards and practices set forth in 40 CFR Part 312."

What is your impression of how these provisions, had they been in effect at the time of the Keywell transaction discussed in the previous section, might have altered how the environmental due diligence unfolded in that case?

**2.** As mentioned in the introduction to this chapter, long before EPA promulgated its AAI rule, the American Society for Testing and Materials (ASTM) developed standardized environmental auditing practices through its Standard E1527, *Standard Practice for Environmental Site Assessments: Phase 1 Environmental Site Assessment Process*. As you should have noticed when reviewing the AAI rule, EPA adopted the ASTM standard as compliant with the AAI standard. The ASTM is a non-governmental standard-setting organization. Its standards are not in the public domain—they must be purchased. ASTM periodically revises its standards, the most recent occasion for Standard E1527 being in 2013. *See* ASTM E1527–13, *available at* http://www.astm.org/Standards/E1527.htm.

**3.** Compliance with the AAI rule is only one necessary showing on the trail toward either of the three defenses. Indeed, one commentator has identified eight remaining risks that, in his opinion, demonstrate that Congress and

EPA are still "tinkering at the edges" of the liability problems CERCLA imposes on land markets. These are:

1. State common law creates an exposure that prospective purchasers cannot prepare for due to its unquantifiable nature.
2. There may also be remaining federal legal exposure under other statutes.
3. A diligence war still needs to be waged, on two fronts, federal and state, as it remains to be seen if states will adopt the federal approach.
4. The rule yields unintended, illogical consequences.
5. It is unlikely EPA will affirmatively assist developers in confirming whether and under what circumstances purchasers can attain and maintain a defense.
6. It remains to be seen what developers will need to do in court to overcome their burden to prove they have satisfied the elements of the new defenses.
7. It may be expensive to prove a federal defense, let alone the potential state counterpart defense (if one is available).
8. The risks above can also lead to a Battle of Experts, which is almost always a costly failure.

*See* Brett McGovern, *All Appropriate Inadequacy*, THE ENVIRONMENTAL FORUM, Sept./Oct. 2006, at 25. Do you agree with these observations? If so, how would you advise a client in a land purchase transaction to deal with them?

**4.** The EPA maintains a website with useful fact sheets about the AAI rule. *See* https://www.epa.gov/brownfields/brownfields-all-appropriate-inquiries. For thorough, practical background on the 2002 Brownfields statute, see Flannary P. Collins, *The Small Business Relief and Brownfields Revitalization Act: A Critique*, 13 DUKE ENVTL. L & POL'Y F. 303 (2003), and David J. Freeman and Robert L. Wegman, *Recently Enacted Law Places New Burdens on Property Owners, Developers*, 33 ENV'T REP. 765 (2002), and for the AAI rule see Jenny McClister, CERCLA's Bona Fide Prospective Purchaser Defense: The Good, the Bad, and the Ugly, Natural Resources 7 Env't, Fall 2014, at 13; Jeff Civins and Mary Mendoza, *Transactional Due Diligence; What Diligence Is Due?*, NATURAL RESOURCES & ENV'T, Winter 2006, at 22, and David J. Freeman and Desiree C. Giler, *AAI Rule Will Have Significant Impact on Parties Seeking Liability Protection*, 35 ENV'T REP. 2127 (2004).

## II. DRAFTING ENVIRONMENTAL CONTRACT PROVISIONS

Armed with the results of environmental due diligence, the buyer and seller in an asset or stock transaction then turn to negotiating the terms of the transaction, which in turn must be put to writing in the transaction instruments. In some cases, of course, the due diligence findings lead one or both parties to withdraw from the transaction under any circumstances, but more often the due diligence identifies various risks the parties then attempt to allocate and manage through a variety of techniques. These include:

- *"As is" clauses.* As the name implies, a party accepting transfer of assets under an "as is" agreement is assuming full responsibility for all liabilities and losses associated with the condition of the property, as well as giving up all common law and statutory causes of action for contribution and indemnification against the seller.
- *Release clauses.* A release clause waives rights the releasing party would otherwise have, and often, but neither always nor exclusively, accompanies an "as is" clause.
- *Representations and warranties.* These refer to statements of fact one party is attesting to be true and promises regarding what a party will do in defined circumstances. They can relate, for example, to conditions at the property, past and future acts by the party, compliance with applicable statutes, and the existence of and response to litigation or enforcement actions. They might be limited to the "best knowledge" of the party making them, and they might "survive" for purposes of providing the basis for a claim based on the contract for only a defined period of time.
- *Obligations to indemnify, defend, and hold harmless.* Usually if the contract includes representations and warranties, it will also include an agreement by the party making them to indemnify the other party for losses attributable to breaches of a statement or promise, such as the costs of remediation, and might also include taking over the responsibility of defending private litigation and administrative enforcement actions. If, as with representations and warranties, the obligations are limited in time, a release clause might be used to make clear that the other party gives up the right to enforce after the defined date.
- *Agreements to remediate.* Because the indemnifying party has the most incentive to control costs, in addition to agreeing to indemnify, a party might also agree to assume (or insist upon) the responsibility for financing and managing any necessary remediation that flows from breaches of representations and warranties.
- *Demarcation lines.* Because contamination and compliance problems at a facility might persist for many years before and after a transaction, one way of allocating risk is to simply place all liability for events and conditions

happening prior to the transaction closing date on the seller and all liabilities for events and conditions happening after the closing on the buyer.

- *Disclosures and exceptions.* In many transactions the parties are dealing with two sets of risks, one associated with known but unresolved problems, such as pending enforcement or permit proceeding or the existence of a migrating plume of groundwater contamination, and the other associated with the potential for yet unknown problems to be discovered after the transaction closing, such as the presence of endangered species or buried waste drums. The parties might use a general set of provisions employing some combination of tools discussed above to cover the unknown risks category, then have the buyer disclose the known problems and except them from the general treatment under the contract. Separate sections of the contract, or side contracts, can then be used to address how known problems will be resolved.
- *Escrows, baskets, and caps.* If the parties believe the risks are significant, are attributable to a variety of conditions and events, or a difficult to predict, they can employ a number of more complex risk management tools. An escrow agreement retains part of the sale proceeds in an escrow managed by an independent third party, from which financial obligations to indemnify can be drawn. A basket, or collection of baskets, is a way of categorizing different kinds of risk and assigning different sets of obligations to each. A cap sets an upper dollar limit on the obligations associated with one or all of the baskets.
- *Purchase of insurance.* As discussed in the materials on insurance recovery litigation in Part II of Chapter 12, new forms of environmental liability insurance are available to address many different kinds of liability exposures. One additional liability allocation strategy increasingly is to have the seller agree to purchase such insurance for the benefit of the buyer.

How these different tools are employed is largely a matter of how the parties negotiate the deal. In the early years of environmental due diligence, business lawyers experienced in using these tools in a variety of contexts—e.g., liability for labor law liabilities and tax law liabilities—had some difficulty applying them to the new and emerging universe of environmental liabilities. Over time, however, practitioners became more adept at drafting the "environmental provisions" in transaction contracts, often as free-standing sections designed specifically and specially for the purpose of allocating environmental liability risks. One of the early practice guides for such purposes appeared in a pair of practitioner articles published in an issue of the American Bar Association's *Natural Resources & Environment*, one written from the purchaser's perspective and the other from the seller's. See William A. Anderson, II and Melinda E. Taylor, *Representing Buyers*, 3 NATURAL RESOURCES & ENV'T, Fall 1988, at 3, and Louis S. Zimmerman, *Environmental Issues in Sales Transactions: The Seller's Perspective*, 3 NATURAL RESOURCES & ENV'T, Fall 1988, at 7. For example, Zimmerman reduced his "seller's perspective" guide to several maxims:

1. The seller should represent and warrant as little as possible about the compliance of the facilities with existing laws and regulations and should expressly except all known noncompliances.
2. The seller should represent and warrant as little as possible about the validity and renewability of environmental permits.
3. The seller should represent or disclose existing environmental conditions which may require the buyer to invest additional funds or may impose on the buyer additional liabilities.
4. The seller should try to have its monetary obligations under the indemnity (as well as certain representations) defined in terms of some maximum exposure in dollars.
5. The seller should try to limit the indemnity and representation obligations to a set period of time.
6. The seller should try to obtain change of law provisions which clearly transfer all change of law to the buyer.
7. The seller should avoid providing indemnities for claims or causes of action which can be resolved or avoided by having the buyer modify current operations or equipment.
8. The seller should obtain from the buyer broad indemnification for post-closing incidents caused in whole or in part by the buyer.

As one might expect, the advice Anderson and Taylor gave for the buyer's perspective was a mirror image the advice Zimmerman gave in favor of the buyer. So the negotiation is in large part about which party moves from one of the default positions and by how much. Much of the advice they offered almost 30 years ago is just as applicable today. See Karen J. Nardi, *Allocating Environmental Liabilities: General Principles and Practice Tips*, NATURAL RESOURCES & ENV'T, Fall 2014, at 22.

Of course, if a dispute arises it will be up to a court to decide what the final terms actually mean, and parties have often been surprised by the results of judicial interpretation. To explore one such case we return once again to the now familiar *Keywell* litigation—here having to do with litigation between the buyer and seller over the terms of the deal.

## Keywell Corporation v. Weinstein

United States Court of Appeals for the Second Circuit, 1994.
33 F.3d 159.

■ JACOBS, CIRCUIT JUDGE:

Keywell Corporation ("Keywell") has incurred costs for environmental cleanup at an industrial facility that it purchased in 1987 from Vac Air Alloys Corporation ("Vac Air"). Defendants-Appellees Daniel C. Weinstein ("Weinstein") and Anthony Boscarino ("Boscarino") were shareholders, officers and directors of Vac Air prior to the purchase and at the time of the transaction, and were signatories to the Purchase Agreement. Keywell has brought suit against Weinstein and Boscarino, (i) alleging that they induced Keywell to buy the property by making misrepresentations bearing upon the environmental risks at the premises, and (ii) alleging that, as owners and operators of Vac Air, they are strictly liable to Keywell for their equitable share of response costs pursuant to §§ 107(a) and 113(f) of the Comprehensive Environmental Response, Compensation, and Liability Act ("CERCLA"). 42 U.S.C. §§ 9607(a) and 9613(f). Following the parties' submission of cross-motions for summary judgment, the district court dismissed Keywell's claims, finding as a matter of law that Keywell could not have reasonably relied on the allegedly fraudulent misrepresentations, and that Keywell had contractually released its right to sue defendants under CERCLA.

BACKGROUND

[The court's opening background discussion is reproduced in Chapter 12 in connection with the materials on fraud claims. To summarize: Both Weinstein and Boscarino were stockholders, directors, and officers of Vac Air and took an active part in conducting the business, which included the operation of a metals recycling plant located in Frewsburg, New York (the "Frewsburg plant"). The Frewsburg plant recycled scrap metal—a process that entailed the use of trichloroethylene ("TCE"), a chemical now categorized as a hazardous substance by the Environmental Protection Agency (the "EPA"). During the 1970s, workers at the Frewsburg plant placed TCE sludge in ponds or pits on the property and sometimes spread the sludge directly on the ground, where it would dry into a more manageable consistency that could then be moved off site. Both Weinstein and Boscarino were aware of at least some of these practices, which ceased in the late 1970s after Vac Air hired a firm to dispose of TCE waste off site. In 1985, during an unrelated excavation on the property, workers unearthed decomposed remnants of storage drums that had apparently once been filled with a TCE-infused waste product and buried. Weinstein and Boscarino were aware of this discovery, but independent laboratory analysis suggested that the buried materials did not pose an environmental problem. Two years later, on November 10, 1987, Keywell entered into an agreement with Vac Air to purchase certain assets, including the Frewsburg plant (the "Purchase Agreement"). Keywell retained the environmental consulting firm of

Conestoga-Rovers and Associates ("CRA") to conduct a due diligence environmental audit of the Frewsburg plant. As part of the audit, CRA inspected the site and interviewed Vac Air employees, including Boscarino. Boscarino was asked about waste disposal, and responded that there had been no on-site dumping of hazardous materials. Upon completion of its audit, CRA issued a report to Keywell warning that, simply by virtue of the metal recycling that took place there, the Frewsburg plant might be identified by the EPA as a possible source of environmental contamination. CRA therefore recommended that Keywell conduct additional tests of the groundwater.]

Keywell decided not to conduct the further testing that CRA recommended and proceeded to close the sale with Vac Air. The Purchase Agreement provided that "[t]he representations and warranties of [Vac Air] and the Management Stockholders [including Weinstein and Boscarino] herein contained shall be true at and as of the Closing Date, shall be made again at and as of the Closing Date, and shall be true as so made again * * *." Purchase Agreement ¶ 6.1. In the Purchase Agreement, Vac Air and its management made the following representation bearing upon environmental exposures:

> Environmental Matters. There has been no storage, disposal or treatment of solid wastes or hazardous wastes by [Vac Air] at any of the leased or owned property included in the Assets [including the Frewsburg plant] in violation of any applicable law, ordinance, rule, regulation, order, judgment, decree or permit or which would require remedial action under any applicable law, ordinance, rule, regulation, order, judgment, decree or permit. There has been no material spill, discharge, leak, emission, injection, escape, dumping or release of any kind onto the properties to be purchased under this Agreement, or into the environment surrounding such properties, of any toxic or hazardous substances as defined under any local, state, Federal or foreign regulations, laws or statutes, other than those releases permissible under such regulations, laws or statutes or allowable under applicable permits.

Purchase Agreement ¶ 2.14.

By way of enforcing such representations, the Purchase Agreement provided that Vac Air and its management would

> indemnify and hold harmless [Keywell] from and against any and all damages, losses and expenses caused by or arising out of (a) any breach of warranty or representation by [Vac Air or its management stockholders], or any non-fulfillment of any agreement or covenant on the part of Seller under this agreement, [or] (b) any liabilities or obligations of Seller * * * which are not listed [in the Purchase Agreement].

Purchase Agreement ¶ 8.1. These representations and warranties would survive for two years, "except that the representations, warranties and agreements incorporated in or set forth in the Indemnity Agreement shall survive to the extent provided therein." Purchase Agreement ¶ 8.

Under the separate Indemnity Agreement, Vac Air undertakes for a period of thirty years to "indemnify and hold Keywell harmless from any loss, damage, cost or expense relating to or arising from the Assets or the Business * * * if the occurrence, event or state of facts which led to such loss, damage, cost or expense arose or existed prior to [December 16, 1987]." Indemnity Agreement ¶ 1. These indemnity obligations, however, are solely the undertakings of Vac Air; the Indemnity Agreement explicitly provides that they "shall be non-recourse to the stockholders, directors and officers of Vac Air [including Weinstein and Boscarino], and shall only be recourse to [certain assets of Vac Air]." Indemnity Agreement ¶ 2.

After Keywell's acquisition of the Frewsburg plant, Weinstein and Boscarino stayed on as managers in Keywell's employ. Prior to the date on which the representations and warranties were due to expire under the Purchase Agreement, various disputes (unrelated to this case) arose between Keywell and the former management of Vac Air. These disputes were resolved on August 11, 1989, by an agreement that the parties intended would "preserve harmony among Keywell's stockholders and promote Keywell's continued success." In this agreement (the "Release"), Keywell unconditionally released the members of Vac Air's Management Group—including Weinstein and Boscarino—from "any claims, liabilities, actions and causes of action Keywell may have under the Purchase Agreement* * *." Excluded from this Release were certain tax liabilities not relevant to the present dispute.

In June 1990, . . . almost a year after the Release was executed, Keywell learned that a grand jury was investigating the possibility that Vac Air had engaged in on-site disposal of hazardous waste at the Frewsburg plant. After further tests revealed the presence of TCE in the municipal water supply, Keywell entered into an agreement with the New York State Department of Environmental Conservation to institute a comprehensive clean-up plan. Weinstein terminated his employment with Keywell on December 28, 1990. Boscarino was fired by Keywell on March 11, 1991.

On March 12, 1991, Keywell filed the present lawsuit in the United States District Court for the District of Maryland, seeking to hold Weinstein and Boscarino strictly liable for clean-up costs under CERCLA, 42 U.S.C. §§ 9607(a)(2), 9613(f), and alleging that their fraudulent misrepresentations induced Keywell to purchase the Frewsburg plant. Keywell sought money damages on its fraud claim rather than rescission of the Purchase Agreement. Eventually the case was transferred to the Western District of New York, where the parties cross-moved for summary judgment.

In a decision issued on March 17, 1993, the district court . . . granted summary judgment against Keywell on its CERCLA claims, finding that Keywell, in signing the Release, had given up its statutory right to seek indemnification for CERCLA liability. The court reasoned that the release of Weinstein and Boscarino from any claims "Keywell may have under the Purchase Agreement" was unambiguous and broad language that included statutory liability under CERCLA. On August 27, 1993, in response to Keywell's motion for reconsideration, the district court issued a second decision, reaffirming its dismissal of the CERCLA claims. The court also granted summary judgment against Keywell on its state-law fraud claims, finding that Keywell could not have reasonably relied on the alleged fraudulent misrepresentations.

DISCUSSION

A. Fraud.

[The court's discussion of the fraud claims is reproduced in Part I.D of Chapter 12.]

B. CERCLA.

Keywell asserts that it is entitled under CERCLA to recover from Weinstein and Boscarino the costs of the environmental clean-up at the Frewsburg plant. Defendants respond that, under the Purchase Agreement, Keywell assumed all environmental liability upon the expiration of the two-year indemnity provision. The district court ruled that the indemnification provision of the Purchase Agreement did not include CERCLA liability, but dismissed Keywell's CERCLA claims nevertheless, on the ground that the Release was "sufficiently broad to include CERCLA liability and thus bars plaintiff's claims * * * against Weinstein and Boscarino." We agree that Keywell gave up its right to assert CERCLA claims by signing the Release, because we conclude that the parties unambiguously allocated liability for CERCLA losses in the Purchase Agreement.

Private parties may contractually allocate among themselves any loss they may suffer by the imposition of CERCLA liability. *See Commander Oil Corp. v. Advance Food Service Equipment*, 991 F.2d 49, 51 (2d Cir. 1993); 42 U.S.C. § 9607(e)(1). Courts will enforce such a contract where the provisions evince a clear and unmistakable intent of the parties to do so. *See Purolator Products Corp. v. Allied-Signal, Inc.*, 772 F. Supp. 124, 130–31 (W.D.N.Y.1991). The Purchase Agreement and the contemporaneous Indemnity Agreement unambiguously allocate to Keywell the risk of CERCLA losses after the expiration of the indemnification period.

Weinstein and Boscarino were signatories to the Purchase Agreement, and in that document made explicit environmental representations and warranties to Keywell. In particular, they warranted (a) that hazardous material at the Frewsburg plant had not been stored, treated or disposed of "in violation of any applicable law," or in such a way as to "require remedial action under any applicable law"; and (b) that there had been "no material spill, discharge, leak, emission, injection, escape, dumping or release of any kind onto [the Frewsburg plant], or into the environment surrounding [the Frewsburg plant], of any toxic or hazardous substances as defined under any local, state, Federal or foreign regulations, laws or statutes * * *." These representations unequivocally cover conduct affecting the environment that could give rise to liability under CERCLA, and effectively warrant that there have been no violations of CERCLA at the Frewsburg plant.

The Purchase Agreement spelled out the scope and duration of the parties' obligations in the event of a breach of any warranty or representation (including the representation concerning environmental exposures). First, "representations and warranties . . . survive the Closing for a period of two (2) years." Purchase Agreement ¶ 8. Second, Weinstein and Boscarino indemnify Keywell for any breach of warranty or representation that may come to light within two years after the closing. Purchase Agreement ¶ 8.1. Third, the maximum indemnification by Weinstein and Boscarino was limited to an aggregate of $5 million, each individual to be liable only for the percentage of $5 million equal to his percentage stock interest in Vac Air. Purchase Agreement ¶ 8.3.

The contemporaneously executed Indemnity Agreement does not affect this understanding, but it does reinforce our conclusion that Weinstein and Boscarino were to have no obligation to indemnify Keywell beyond the two-year period specified in the Purchase Agreement. Thus the Indemnity Agreement provides for Vac Air to indemnify Keywell for thirty years from any loss resulting from circumstances existing at the time the Purchase Agreement was signed, but explicitly provides that "[t]he indemnification obligations of Vac Air * * * shall be non-recourse to the stockholders, directors and officers of Vac Air."

These documents demonstrate and confirm that all obligations of Weinstein and Boscarino to indemnify Keywell were (a) capped at a percentage of $5 million, and (b) limited to two years. Weinstein and Boscarino made explicit environmental representations and warranties, and were liable for breach of those representations and warranties in accordance with the indemnity provisions. While Vac Air's thirty-year duty to indemnify Keywell would apply to CERCLA costs, Keywell agreed that it would forgo recourse against Weinstein and Boscarino after the two-year indemnity period expired.

We conclude that the contracts between and among the parties sufficiently demonstrate an intent to allocate responsibility for CERCLA losses. Under the Purchase Agreement, Weinstein and Boscarino shared with Vac Air the risk of such losses for two years, at which time the risk shifted to Keywell (except insofar as it could recover from Vac Air). The indemnity obligation of Weinstein and Boscarino was cut short by a few months with the signing of the Release on August 8, 1989, which discharged Weinstein and Boscarino "from any claims, liabilities, actions and causes of action Keywell may have under the Purchase Agreement." As the district court explained, Keywell cannot selectively and belatedly rescind isolated provisions of the Purchase Agreement. Therefore, Keywell cannot maintain a suit against the defendants under CERCLA that is barred by the allocation of loss in that contract.

---

## QUESTIONS AND DISCUSSION

**1.** The Keywell transaction employed a fairly plain vanilla approach to risk management that was not an uncommon outcome at the time in the struggle between the seller's and purchaser's interests: the seller represented that no problems existed, indemnified the purchaser for any breaches of that representation, and placed a time limit and financial cap on the seller's exposure. Of course, the seller's officers knew the representation was false, but how likely is it that the buyer thought it was true? How many industrial facilities could live up to the standard expressed in the representation provision used in the Keywell transaction?

**2.** As you know from the attorney malpractice claim Keywell brought against the attorneys who represented it in the transaction, reproduced in section I.A of this chapter, the attorneys "advised Keywell that, as was the case with the 1987 purchase agreement, the [1989] release would not extinguish Keywell's claims for contribution under the Comprehensive Environmental Response, Compensation and Liability Act ("CERCLA")." Based on the materials you covered in Chapter 5 on CERCLA liability, what would *you* have advised a client as to the meaning of terms like those used in the Keywell transaction? To be fair to the Piper & Marbury attorneys, as you should be appreciating by now CERCLA liability has been an evolving morass of rules, often with conflicting judicial interpretations around the nation, since the statute was first enacted. Yet, what was ambiguous about the two-year time limit and the unqualified release? Most likely the attorneys concluded that the statutory cause of action for contribution included in CERCLA would, as a matter of public policy, withstand the effects of such risk-shifting provisions. Indeed, at least one court has held that an "as is" clause—perhaps the most unambiguous of risk allocation tools—did not extinguish a contribution claim under a *state* remediation statute. *See Bonnie Blue, Inc. v. Reichenstein*, 127 S.W.3d 366 (Tex.Ct. App. 2004). The court there recognized, however, that its ruling went against the grain of CERCLA cases, which by and large have enforced contractual language consistent with basic rules of contract interpretation, as the court did in the *Keywell* litigation. It is important to note, however, that no indemnification or other contractual allocation of CERCLA liability prevents the government from pursuing statutory liability claims under CERCLA directly against the contractually protected party. Who is liable under CERCLA is not controlled by who is on the hook under the contract.

**3.** Using the tools outlined at the beginning of this section, what other approaches might Keywell and VacAir have taken with respect to allocation of risk? Given our understanding of the parties' respective motivations from the malpractice court's description—VacAir was short on cash flow and would have moved its position considerably to make the deal happen—why didn't Keywell drive a harder bargain? What bargain would you have driven? How secure would you feel representing Keywell in knowing that VacAir was quickly depleting resources. Could an environmental liability insurance instrument have helped solve the problem? *See* Christopher Alviggi and Dennis M. Toft, *Using Environmental Insurance as a Tool to Close Transactions*, NATURAL RESOURCES & ENV'T, Fall 2014, at 25.

**4.** A myriad of additional issues arises in any business negotiation involving risk exposure associated with contamination, compliance, and constraint issues. If the seller has assumed the obligation to remediate, how does the buyer ensure the seller does not interfere with the post-transaction operations of the facility? Can the buyer in such a case send representatives to meetings between the seller and government agencies or private litigants? What kinds of claims and conditions does the indemnification cover? How clean is clean under the contract? What if regulatory criteria are used to fix that standard, but the regulatory criteria change after the closing? These and many other issues are covered in three symposium issues of *Natural Resources & Environment* adding to the body of materials begun in the 1988 symposium issue in which the articles by Anderson & Taylor and by Zimmerman appeared. *See* Symposium, *Business Transactions*, 10 NATURAL RESOURCES & ENV'T, Spring 1996; Symposium, *Transactions*, NATURAL RESOURCES & ENV'T, Fall 2000; and Symposium, *Transactions*, NATURAL RESOURCES & ENV'T, Fall 2014.

---

## PROBLEM EXERCISE

The General Counsel of Energena has just left you another voice-mail. It seems the plan to acquire the wind energy company, Windergy (see the problem at the end of Section I of this chapter), has evolved into an asset purchase transaction in which Energena will acquire the four wind farms Windergy has in operation and the options it has on several other sites. Windergy will retain its testing lab facility, through which it hopes to become the leader in wind energy technology development. Thus far your environmental due diligence has uncovered several problems you plan to report to Energena:

1. The wind farm in California is located in the range of a reptile species that has recently been listed as endangered under the Endangered Species Act. Energena hopes to be able to expand wind generation at this site.
2. The wind farm in Texas is located on land leased from a city and is in part on the site of what was previously the city's municipal small craft airport.
3. One of the sites under option is located on what was previously an ammunitions manufacturer's testing ground.

Energena has informed you that the deal is likely to be closed before there is time to complete investigation of these and other problems that have been identified. How might you advise Energena to use the different risk-allocation tools in such a way as to protect against the risks associated with that course of action?

# INDEX

References are to Pages

**CONGRESS**



**CONSERVATION**